# David Lloyd George
## Welsh Radical, World Statesman

Paul Spackman

BARNTHORN
PUBLISHING

Published by Barnthorn Publishing Limited.
www.barnthornpublishing.co.uk
ISBN: 978-1-917120-54-8

# CONTENTS

In Memory of My Dear Mother, Joyce E. Spackman
(1932-2009).

# FOREWORD

It is now over 100 years since the only Welsh person ever to be Prime Minister left Downing Street for the last time. In the years which have followed thousands of scholarly pages have been devoted to the study of the life and career of David Lloyd George, from the highly specialised to the broad biography.

The question is bound to be asked: is there room for more? This book, I think, demonstrates why the answer has to be yes.

Of course, scholarship itself does not stand still. There are still papers being discovered, sources newly understood or placed in fresh context. But the real answer lies in the astonishing relevance of so much of the ever-fertile, ever-radical mind of Lloyd George himself. So many of the issues with which we continue to grapple today are direct descendants of his own preoccupations.

So many of the solutions which are part of today's policy repertoire can be traced, and reinvigorated, by looking again at the persistence with which he looked for solutions in his own time. All that comes to the surface again in this new study, from the challenge created by automation to employment, or Lloyd George's greatest and most consistent cause, the land. The struggles experienced by the many – whether they be the agricultural worker, or the victim of an urban housing crisis – as the result of monopolistic land ownership formed a central thread in his political life from the Welsh countryside of the 1880s, through the great People's Budget of 1909, to the campaigns to tackle the poverty of the 1930s. Today, as interest rekindles in Land Value Taxation as an economically progressive means of raising the resources necessary to pay for public services, the Land Campaign he led seems more relevant than ever.

This study casts fresh light on the past, of course, but more importantly it illuminates new possibilities for our own time. Even for those who are familiar with the Lloyd George story, there's much to discover and enjoy.

Mark Drakeford
First Minister of Wales, 2018-2024

# INTRODUCTION

David Lloyd George was the last Liberal, and only Welshman to date, to serve as British Prime Minister. Raised, in his own words, as a 'Cottage-bred man', qualified as a solicitor in 1884, earning a reputation for defending the individual against the establishment, elected Liberal MP for Caernarfon in 1890, he rose to immense national and international prominence and popularity, but is today often unjustly neglected. A century after the end of the Great War (1918), the 'Spanish Flu' Pandemic (1918-1920) that nearly killed Lloyd George–and which strikes such resonance in the era of the COVID-19 pandemic, the signing of the Treaty of Versailles (1919) and the end of Lloyd George's premiership (1922), it is a good time to reassess the legacy of this great statesman in the life of the United Kingdom, indeed of Europe and the wider world.

Lloyd George himself was not all that keen on the biography as a form of literature, certainly concerning his own person. In a letter to author Basil Murray, subsequently inserted as a preface to Murray's 1932 biographical sketch, Lloyd George, by now 69-years-old and out of power for over nine years, wrote that he studiously avoided reading biographies of his own life. He continued, not without humour:

> I have reached the point of life at which we retain very few illusions, and as one who has had perhaps more biographies, lampoons and caricatures than almost any living person it would not be surprising if I retain very few about myself… I cannot read books about things which I know better than the writer with any sort of satisfaction… That is probably why I do not wish to read a biography of myself. In fact, the only biographical notices about myself which I should really be amused to read, but owing to circumstances over which I shall have no control I shall have no opportunity of reading, are my obituary notices. For out of sheer decency even critical writers will be more or less bound on that occasion to preserve a slight bias in favour of the subject matter; and that, to my mind, is, on the whole, the most attractive kind of biography–certainly to the victim.[1]

Lloyd George is sadly now long dead, but his values and achievements live on, and the present author personally believes that his legacy should be remembered and remembered accurately. One of the best methods to do this is to carefully study and record the keys to his life and work, and set

[1] B. Murray, *L.G.* 1932 London Sampson Low, Marston, ppv-vi. The letter is dated 9 February 1932.

them out meticulously for public consideration and appraisal… in short, to produce a biography! Hopefully, the present work is one both critically accurate and of the right 'tone', one that Lloyd George himself may have recognised, even approved of.

In this work I set out to explore the specific and distinctively Welsh roots and influences that helped form his unique charisma and radical outlook by:

- highlighting the extraordinarily broad, original and far-reaching nature of his early 'labourite' views and of his social reforms, that laid the bedrock of much of the 1945-51 Attlee Labour Government's Welfare State legislation;

- emphasizing the crucial importance of Lloyd George taking over the helm of government from the floundering Asquith at the height of the Great War, along with the hitherto neglected role played by his radical ally, Dr Christopher Addison, and the subsequent fatal erosion of Liberalism caused by the displaced and unforgiving Asquith;

- analysing Lloyd George's approach to the treatment of defeated, devastated Germany at the Versailles negotiations, how his more merciful and tolerant approach, if adopted, might have changed the course of history for the better;

- re-assessing his role in Irish affairs between 1916-22, and pointing out those largely responsible for much of the undoubted tragedy and its long-drawn out aftermath;

- showing that the period after his resignation as premier were not, from an 'ideas' point of view, the oft-quoted 'wilderness years', but mostly rather a fertile period of creative, practical plans to solve the immense issues of the 1920s and 1930s, unfortunately neglected by the nation;

- re-examining his legacy and hopefully 're-adjusting' popular, entrenched but misplaced views on Lloyd George as a person, showing the inimical sources of these misjudgements;

- lastly, highlighting the huge and lasting support, hitherto largely neglected by scholars, given to Lloyd George by his faithful, broad-shouldered and industrious wife Margaret; 'Behind every great man there's a great woman' indeed.

As far back as 1995, Marvin Rintala wrote: '[Lloyd George] has, perhaps, to be taken more on his own terms than he has been taken so far by most scholars.'[2] This is still true today, for Lloyd George has hitherto not been studied *contextually* nearly enough. He was a man of his time and a man out of his time, ahead of it in many ways. Coming from no position of privilege, he had the originality of approach shared by so many intelligent 'self-taught' people in a world of 'professionals'.

[2] M. Rintala, *Lloyd George And Churchill*, 1990, Lanham, MD Madison Books, p18.

In the process of my own re-assessment, I have closely re-read and often quoted Lloyd George's own words on key issues, in order to accurately give the tone and temper of his times. Almost uniquely in the political world of his era, Lloyd George was self-made, neither a public school nor a university man; he lived on his wits, his words, his charisma, which gave both his opinions and his speeches and writings their own particular 'flavour' that needs to be savoured in order to try to understand his mercurial mind. I also especially sought to obtain the memories and opinions of the last handful of family members who still personally remembered the man, and those who had reliable, first-hand contact with them. In addition, I have closely re-examined early works on Lloyd George, specifically those published before his premiership, and the subsequent so-called 'wilderness years', before fame, post-war disillusion and other 'clouding' emotions and second-hand opinions drifted across and obscured the landscape, much like the acrid smoke of the battles of the Great War itself.

Lloyd George has considerable credentials as a reforming 'radical', and, through his anti-war, anti-Imperialist stance during the Boer War, his life was often threatened with violence. His life also showed a remarkable degree of adaptability, coming from the backwaters of remote, rural Victorian-era North Wales to the victorious leader of the foremost industrial nation of the world as it fought a new kind of highly mechanized, total war.

I make no apology for the fact that, as a biographer, I find much of Lloyd George's life, thought and achievements to be inspirational. As Mary Stocks (1891-1975), suffragist and social activist, once wrote:

> … we live in an age which seems to take a peculiar delight in debunking virtue and hurling accusations of hypocrisy against earlier generations.[3]

What was true in 1970 is even truer now, and I feel Lloyd George has suffered above the average from this lamentable tendency. This book is my attempt to act as a corrective to this sad trend. I have above all aimed at a human portrait, rather than just another purely political biography.

Of existing biographies, Lloyd George's contemporaries Herbert Du Parcq and J. Hugh Edwards' conscientious multiple works, and William W. Davies' single volume have immense, lasting value for his early years, despite the inevitable dating of their literary style. The two volumes produced by Lloyd George's nephew, Dr William R. P. George (20 October 1912– 20 November 2006) covering his family's history and his uncle's early years, also have original and enduring value. Geoffrey Shakespeare's autobiography is insightful for the early 1920s, of Lloyd George's personality, and for the Anglo-Irish Treaty negotiations. Of the biographical work published immediately after Lloyd George's death, Albert J. Sylvester's *Life* and later *Diaries* are irreplaceable as personal insights from someone who was intimately involved with him from the end of his premiership until his death. Thomas Jones' work is useful for his personal insights into his life after becoming Prime Minister, though disappointingly 'unengaged', Malcolm Thomson's 'Official' work adds little and Frank Owen's

[3] M. Stocks, *My Commonplace Book* 1970, London, Peter Davies, p119.

is overly florid.[4] Don Cregier, Donald McCormick, and John Campbell's works are also determinedly 'colourful', but not without impressionistic value in understanding the 'Welsh Wizard's' mercurial character, especially Campbell's, though each only covers certain periods or aspects of Lloyd George's life. Jack Jones' incisive novel can be profitably read to pick up the Welsh 'feel' of Lloyd George's early public life, tinged by the insight of a fellow Welsh politician.

John Grigg, Bentley Gilbert and Kenneth O. Morgan's works are scholarly, but Grigg's only reaches to 1918, and Gilbert's sadly ambivalent one to 1916, while Morgan's impressive *corpus* is unfortunately spread over disparate publications covering a remarkable 62-year period from 1963-2025. Their work also needs to be 'corrected' through the critically reappraising Welsh 'lens' of Emyr Price, particularly in the re-appreciation of the integrity and significance of Lloyd George's radical pursuit of Welsh causes in the pre-1899 years. Unfortunately, much of Price's pioneering work was only published in his native Welsh, and this has limited the dissemination of his 'game-changing' findings, though his crowning work was published in English. Charles Mowat, Martin Pugh, Hugh Purcell, Alan Sharp and Chris Wrigley have all provided very good, readable, concise accounts.

Travis Crosby's volume is dense but useful in shining a light on some lesser-known aspects of Lloyd George's life, while Ian Ivatt has lifted the veil previously obscuring his complex financial affairs. Peter Rowland supplemented his thorough, huge one volume biography with a ground-breaking work on Lloyd George's father. Marvin Rintala's book on *Lloyd George and Churchill* is wide-ranging, thoughtful and thought-provoking. Ffion Hague's volume beautifully and valuably illumines Lloyd George's relations with the women in his life, particularly bringing his indomitable first wife Dame Margaret into sharper relief. Dr J. Graham Jones, formerly Senior Archivist and Head of the Welsh Political Archive at the National Library of Wales, Aberystwyth between 1980-2011, has produced a stream of invaluable and insightful contributions on all aspects of Lloyd George studies.

My own research, combined with a reappraisal of early works and study of recent investigations by others, now, I believe, enables a 'truer', more holistic picture of Lloyd George the man to finally emerge.

---

[4] It is be regretted that Sylvester never completed his full-length biography of Lloyd George that he was engaged in writing in his old age.

# ACKNOWLEDGEMENTS

The author principally thanks the late David 'Bengy' Carey-Evans, for generously sharing his precious, vivid memories of his grandfather; 'Bengy's daughter Davina Carey-Evans, for her pivotal kindness and hospitality; and the late Emrys Williams, Curator of the Lloyd George Museum from 1990 to 2001, for enthusiastically sharing his unrivalled fund of knowledge and anecdotes. Without these people's valuable co-operation, the writing of this work in its present form would not have begun.

To get an impression of Lloyd George's personality in later life, and an idea of his life from an intimate family perspective, I interviewed his grandson David 'Bengy' Carey-Evans, son of Lloyd George and his first wife, Dame Margaret's daughter Olwen Elizabeth, Lady Carey-Evans (3 April 1892–2 March 1990) and her husband Major Sir Thomas J. Carey-Evans (6 June 1884–25 August 1947). 'Bengy' (14 August 1925–11 August 2023), who lived in Anglesey, was lively, engaging, highly articulate and possessed of a fund of memories about his beloved grandfather.

I was also, through the aid of Davina Carey-Evans, able to access the memories of Bengy's elder brother, Robert Rufus Carey-Evans, known as 'Robin', (21 September 1923–3 February 2022), who lived in Sydney, Australia, and those of his younger cousin William Lloyd George, 3rd Viscount Tenby, (7 November 1927–7 June 2023), son of Lloyd George's youngest son Gwilym, who lived at Crondall, Surrey, nine miles north from Lloyd George's old estate at Churt. During my interview with him, Lord Tenby was gracious, expansive and open, clearly still very fond of his charismatic grandfather, a fine portrait of whom, painted by Arthur Knighton-Hammond at Churt in 1933, graced the family dining room. When Lord Tenby retired from the House of Lords on 1 May 2015, it ended 125 years of continuous family service in Parliament. Lord Tenby kindly put me in touch with David Richard Owen Lloyd George, the current, 4th Earl Lloyd-George, who most hospitably answered my questions on his great-grandfather and other ancestors.

Again through Davina Carey-Evans, I secured contact with Professor Margaret MacMillan, author of the seminal work *Peacemakers* (titled *Paris, 1919* in the USA) and herself the first-born great-granddaughter of Lloyd George, through his daughter Olwen, and her daughter Eluned 'Lyn' Jane (21 March 1921–8 August 2015), Professor MacMillan helped me to comprehend and condense the morass of complex issues surrounding the Paris Peace Conference and resultant Treaty of Versailles. I also thank Philip George, great-nephew of Lloyd George, himself a solicitor still working in the same offices in Porthmadog, for kindly confirming some information and for showing me the back rooms with their simple but evocative artefacts of the era–signs, an engraved window, photos, a wooden, leather-topped desk–all of which helps a biographer envision their subject.

Further, I have benefited greatly from contact with Ruth Nixon (née Longford), the granddaughter of Lloyd George by his second wife, Frances (7 October 1888–5 December 1972), who had a daughter, Jennifer (4 October 1929–5 March 2012). Ruth generously answered my questions, supplementing the information in her fine book on her grandmother. Similarly, I am much indebted to Richard Rhys O'Brien, grandson of Reverend J. T. Rhys, private secretary to Margaret Lloyd George from 1917 to 1922, for the kind gift of his published works and sharing information on which he is working, providing valuable new insights into Margaret's mind and her unstinting support for her husband.

I also acknowledge the kindness of Victoria Lloyd Jones, of Walter Lloyd Jones Saleroom in Barmouth, for acquiring some hard-to-find books and searching out rare journal articles for me, and Jonathan P. Hamer, of Ruthin, for interesting details of his family's past connections with the Lloyd George's in Criccieth and a rare DVD-copy of the 1963 BBC TV *At Home* programme. Thanks too to Sylvia Parry, of Criccieth, granddaughter of Elizabeth Davies, cook to the family whilst Lloyd George was Chancellor of the Exchequer, for permission to use material from a previously unreleased taped interview conducted by David Schilling with her 'nain' (grandmother) in Criccieth in 1986, and other information. My gratitude goes to Alwyn Jones, of Fron-goch, for kindly sharing his knowledge of the former camp there and showing me his extensive collection of material on this unjustly neglected site, so important in both Irish and Welsh political history. I am also grateful to Philip Colley, the great-nephew of Gareth Jones, for providing insight into the epic but ill-fated life of Lloyd George's Foreign Policy Adviser in the early 1930s.

My thanks to Sharon Thomas, current owner of Bryn Awelon, Criccieth, formerly the Lloyd George family residence, now a nursing home, for showing me around parts of the house and grounds. Also, my thanks go to Rob Laker for letting me see his groundbreaking MA thesis on Winifred Coombe Tennant, a close political ally of Lloyd George, whose importance is only just being rediscovered, and to Miriam Williams, Venue Manager of Ty Newydd, Llanystumdwy, for showing me around and providing information on Lloyd George's last home, including the room in which he died. I warmly thank Duncan Hill, Secretary of the Lloyd George Society, for generously helping me settle numerous points of detail that help bring a book alive; also Tony O'Connor of the privately-held Lloyd George Archive at Godalming, Surrey–a splendid resource–for similar kind assistance, and Sarah Cunliffe, for most apt and timely social media promotion. Not least, I thank Ashley Barnett and Neil Thornton of Barnthorn Publishing for believing in the project, Fatima Kamal for a splendid book cover design, Rupert Hague-Holmes for sympathetic editing, and Mark Drakeford, First Minister of Wales from 2018 to 2024, for graciously providing a most thoughtful foreword.

The whole project would not have been possible without the support of my dear partner Jane–daughter of North Walian journalist and editor John E. Roberts (1904-1983)–enriched by thought-provoking discussions, rewarding explorations of Bangor, Barmouth, Blaenau Ffestiniog, Caernarfon, Conway, Criccieth, Fron-goch, Llandudno, Llanfrothen, Llanystumdwy, Nefyn, Pencaenewydd, Porthmadog, Pwllheli, Tremadog and the surrounding area that formed the bedrock of Lloyd George's physical, emotional and intellectual life, and encouragement when the going got tough, as it inevitably did at times in an undertaking of this scale, and my love and heartfelt gratitude goes to her.

Paul Spackman,
Corwen, North Wales,
3 July 2025

**In Memory of my Grandparents, the generation of Lloyd George's Premiership:**

Private William Spackman, No. 29975, 51st Battalion Hampshire Regiment, stationed in Wermelskirchen, Germany, 1919, British Army of the Rhine. His wife, Margaret A. J. Spackman (née Webb), Canteen Worker, HM Explosives Factory, Swindon 'Stratton Works', Bramble Lane, Stratton St Margaret.

Driver Stanley A. Daldry, No. 92662, 3A Reserve Brigade, Royal Field Artillery, wounded at Battle of the Somme, Summer 1916. His wife, Lucy Alice Daldry (née Dummer), Munitions Worker, W. E. Blake Munitions Factory, Wood Lane, Shepherd's Bush, London [she well remembered the infamous explosion of 31 October 1918, in which 13 workers–11 women, two men–died].

# 1

## CHILDHOOD, 1863-1879

David Lloyd George, the 'Welsh Wizard', was born on Saturday 17 January 1863 at 5 New York Place, a typical 'two up, two down' terrace house in Robert Street, in Chorlton-on-Medlock, Manchester, to William and Elizabeth George. The proud father wrote to his niece Anne Williams that same evening that his son was "a sturdy healthy little fellow, stronger and much more lively than his sister, and he has fine curly hair."[5] [6] Apparently the Irish midwife in attendance was as impressed as the father. Holding the new-born in her arms, she exclaimed enthusiastically: "A child that has such beautiful waves in his hair will easily make his living in two countries." This dictum made a deep impression on the mother, as she made frequent reference to it afterwards, especially at each stage of young David's progression up the career ladder.[7]

The couple already had one child, their daughter Mary Ellen, who came to be known as 'Pollie' in the family, born in Newchurch, Lancashire, on 8 November 1861. A few days after David's birth, William wrote to his wife's younger brother, Richard Lloyd.[8]

> I am happy–very happy to say that Betsy [Elizabeth] and the young gentleman continue to get on very well. Betsy got up at about 5 this afternoon and she is still up, for which I am scolding her. I tell her she is overdoing it the first time.
>
> Little Mary is not thrown on one side although a son and *heir* (!!) has arrived. The dear little thing is getting more interesting every day. She is certainly a very sharp child… She has taken wonderfully to little David. She calls him *boy*, *boy* and she gives us much amusement by mocking him when we ask her–how does boy cry.
>
> The woman who is here to wait upon Betsy is very kind to Polly–almost the only thing that is in her favour. She is not a good hand at preparing a bit to eat–she used to work in a factory.
>
> I am glad to say that I am better. My throat has not gathered as I feared. I have been poulticing it till it is nearly raw outside, but that is better than being inside.[9]

---

[5] Anne Williams (née James; December 1838-26 May 1928). She married Captain William Williams, a Master Mariner, on 18 January 1863, the day after little David's birth.

[6] J. H. Edwards, *David Lloyd George, The Man And The Statesman*, 1930, London, 2 Vols Waverley Book Co., Vol.I, p12.

[7] J. H. Edwards, *The Life Of David Lloyd George; With A Short History Of The Welsh People*, 1913-1919, London, 4 Vols, Waverley Book Co., 1913, Vol.II, p1.

[8] Richard Lloyd (12 July 1834–28 February 1917).

[9] Quoted in W. R. P. George, *The Making Of Lloyd George*, 1976, London, Faber and Faber, p62.

William's grandfather was also called William George (1747-1839), a well-to-do farmer of Tresinwen, a substantial holding of 320 acres lying to the south of Strumble Head, and just over five miles from Trecoed, north Pembrokeshire. William himself was born in 1821, the son of David (1782-1828), and of Mary George (née Charles, 1783-1860), from the farm of Trefgarn Owen in the parish of Brawdy, six miles from Trecoed. His parents had married by 1803, and he was named after an older brother who had died in 1818. By the time of his birth, William's father David had leased Trecoed, a farm of 306 acres on the Vaughan estate.[10] It has been said, with as yet no provenance to support or reject the idea, that:

> Prior to the battle of Bosworth [22 August 1485]… two brothers (ancestors of Mr William George) joined Henry Tudor's forces at Milford Haven. They fought at the great battle, and received grants of land in Pembrokeshire as a reward for their services.[11]

Originally apprenticed to a doctor in Haverfordwest, probably Dr George Millard, William had no interest in medicine, but instead found an abiding interest in literature, also studying French, German and algebra.[12] Early in 1841, he made the big decision to move to London and enrol in the new Battersea Teachers' Training Institute, the first of its kind, and the initiative of Dr James Kay and Edward C. Tufnell.[13] [14] For the first time he experienced intellectual fulfilment as he finally found the guidance he had been searching for. He described the experience as the most useful year of his life, "the means by which he was brought from a *miserable*, useless life to… a happy one and not altogether destitute of usefulness to others."[15] After qualifying as a teacher, on 31 January 1842 he took up an appointment at Ealing Grove School, established by Lady Byron in 1833.[16] The school, with some 38 boarders and 50 day boys, had a basic academic curriculum of the 'three R's' plus geography, natural history and religious instruction, combined with three hours per day working in the garden on individual allotments. There was no corporal punishment. The school was under the headmastership of Charles Atlee, to whom Lady Byron formally transferred it in 1848. As well as the small staff, there were several volunteers present helping with tuition, one of whom was Ada Lovelace, Lady Byron's daughter.[17]

William clearly performed his duties well enough, but in his diary for 19 June 1842, he recorded his agonising internal debate over what he would do with his life:

---

[10] P. Rowland, *Lloyd George's Tada,* 2014, London and Cardiff Publish Nation, p29.
[11] W. D. Phillips, *Old Haverfordwest,* [A Reprint of Articles which appeared in the *Pembroke County Guardian* 1924-25], 1926, Haverfordwest, J. W. Hammond; *Mr. D. Lloyd George's Associations With The Town*, p22-25, quote on p24.
[12] Rowland, *Tada*, p49.
[13] Sir James Kay-Shuttleworth (1804-1877), born James Kay, Liberal politician, educationist.
[14] Edward Tufnell (1806-1886), civil servant, educationist.
[15] George, *Making Of Lloyd George*, p39.
[16] Lady Anne Isabella Byron (née Milbanke; 1792-1860), nicknamed Annabella, mathematician, wife of poet Lord Byron 1815-1816.
[17] Augusta Ada King, Countess of Lovelace (née Byron; 1815-1852), mathematician, known for her work on Charles Babbage's proposed mechanical general-purpose computer, the Analytical Engine.

> I am still very unsettled in my mind as to my future plans and prospects. I cannot somehow make up my mind to be a schoolmaster for *life*. My present position does not altogether satisfy me. I want to occupy *higher ground* sometime or other. I want to increase the stock of my attainments but hardly know how to set about it.[18]

This 'higher ground' was the restless William's secret desire to try his hand at writing, as he wrote in his diary on 6 June:

> I must *record something*–have something to show myself for the time that is past–so that I can say that I have lived and did something at a particular time past. In looking back upon my past life, I find it is all of such a dreary character.[19]

He was expressing a common human desire to leave some trace of his existence behind him–how he would have marvelled that this would take the form, not of a literary masterpiece, but of a son who would become a great social reformer and the first Welsh Prime Minister of Britain!

But this was for the future. Spurred on by his ambition, he left–or was transferred from–Ealing Grove School on 31 December 1842, next taking up an appointment at the school at Newbold Verdon in Leicestershire, starting work there on 1 April 1843. This school had also been founded by Lady Byron, in 1818, only a couple of miles from her property at Kirkby Hall. For reasons unknown William left this school abruptly on 25 March 1844, leaving behind many of his possessions, including his precious books. Biographer Peter Rowland argues plausibly, though without hard evidence, on the possibility of unwanted romantic interest in William from Ada Lovelace, Lady Byron's daughter, causing him to flee.[20]

There are no further records of his movements, until he arrived in Liverpool in July 1846, where he first took up a post at Manesty's Lane School. William also taught in the Hope Street Church Sunday School, opened in October 1849 and which was administered by the Unitarians, where he met Unitarian minister Dr James Martineau, one of the School Governors, also Professor of Mental and Moral Philosophy and Political Economy in Manchester New College from 1840-1885, and brother of the famous social theorist and Whig writer Harriet. At some point James presented William with a framed and signed portrait of himself.[21]

After some 13 years absence, for reasons of health, William returned to his native county and, on 3 April 1854, he opened an 'English School for Scientific and Commercial Education' in Upper Market Street, Haverfordwest, the fees being one guinea per quarter.[22] He soon trimmed the name of the school to the 'Commercial Academy', to take account of local sensibilities, and the number of his pupils increased. He then met and fell in love with Selina Huntley, whose family owned an engraving

---

[18] Quoted in Rowland, *Tada*, p114.
[19] Ibid., p114-115.
[20] Ibid, p129-133.
[21] George, *Making Of Lloyd George*, p46. James Martineau (1805-1900).
[22] Ibid., p48; Rowland, *Tada*, p162.

and printing business in Bond Street, London. At the time they met, Selina was in Haverfordwest taking in the fresh air for her health, along with a companion, Miss Legge.[23] Selina had been born on 18 August 1819, her parents third child and first daughter, and in her early twenties she had worked as a milliner at St James's Palace, Pall Mall. Later she was a dressmaker, residing at No. 70 Welbeck Street, a northward continuation of Bond Street. Romance must have blossomed quickly between her and William, as the pair soon married in St George's, Hanover Square, London, on 11 April 1855, during the school's Easter holiday. Returning to Haverfordwest, the couple lived in rooms at the school in Upper Market Street.

By the time they were married the first Mrs George was already ailing, having been diagnosed with *phthisis pulmonalis*–otherwise known as consumption or tuberculosis–in 1853. William therefore must have known that his new wife had only a short time to live. His 18-year-old niece, Martha James, came from Trecoed to care for Selina, being with her when Selina sadly died barely eight months later, on 4 December, aged 36, being buried in St. Thomas' Churchyard, Haverfordwest, four days later. In a death notice, inserted in *The Cambrian* on 7 December, William paid tribute to an 'amiable and beloved wife'.[24] Edwin John, son of the town clerk, then a seven-year-old pupil of William's, and the future father of Augustus John, the artist, remembered her as 'a sweet lady whom the boys liked very much'.[25] Edwin had less happy memories of William, recording that he 'was a severe disciplinarian–rather passionate, sometimes having recourse to the old-fashioned punishment of caning.'[26] Had poor Selina George not died, of course, then history would have been very different.

During 1856, William took up an appointment in Wakefield, in the West Riding of Yorkshire, then, in August 1858, taking another scholastic appointment at the newly built British School at Troed-yr-Allt in Pwllheli, Caernarfonshire. By then, he had spent so much time away from his native county that he had all but forgotten its language. He wrote to a Welsh Baptist Minister in Pembrokeshire:

> I wished to say a few words to you in Welsh–but I am sorry that I cannot do so, although Welsh is my mother tongue–and I knew very little English until I was nine years of age–but I have used English almost ever since. The English language has done with me what the English people have done with our country–taken possession of the richest and largest part of it. No sooner do I use two or three Welsh words than their bolder English brethren thrust forward and the poor timid Taffies [sic] shrink back to hide themselves and I cannot, in spite of the utmost effort, find them again in time.[27]

---

[23] W. D. Phillips first drew attention to Selina in his article of 1924, p23 in his subsequent book *Old Haverfordwest.* Lloyd George was himself listed as a subscriber in the book, but her existence does not appear to have become generally known until Peter Rowland's pioneering work of 2014.

[24] Quoted in Rowland, *Tada*, p170.

[25] Edwin John (1847-1938). Rowland, *Tada*, p170; M. Holroyd, *Augustus John. Volume 1: The Years Of Innocence*, 1974, London, William Heinemann, p9. Augustus John completed Lloyd George's portrait in oil on 16 February 1916; it now hangs in Aberdeen Art Gallery. John described Lloyd George as "a fine subject but a bad sitter'.' The author thanks Victoria Lloyd Jones for this lead on the portrait.

[26] Quoted in Rowland, *Tada*, p165.

[27] Quoted in George, *Making Of Lloyd George*, p45.

Much of our meagre knowledge of William George's thought processes appear therefore to foreshadow his famous son's opinions.

Whilst teaching in Pwllheli, he met Elizabeth Lloyd, known as Betsy, who according to family tradition was in domestic service in several local households before her marriage. The couple met at *Capel Berea* in Criccieth and were duly married in St Peter's, Pwllheli, on 16 November 1859. In a letter to his mother, William wrote that he had been 'lucky enough to win one of earth's best and fairest daughters, and one he felt sure his mother would be proud to welcome as a dear daughter.'[28] Elizabeth had been born in Llanystumdwy on 1 October 1828, the second child and daughter of David (1800-1839), a Baptist minister, and Rebecca Lloyd (1804-1868). Elizabeth was:

> A woman of medium height. Her complexion was fair, her hair very dark, her eyes brown, the expression of her thoughtful features one of great charm. The sound judgment and high principles with which her friends rightly credited her made her an ideal companion for the man she now married.[29]

The couple's first child, a boy, was born in the family home at Highgate in Llanystumdwy on 15 September 1860, but sadly only survived for 12 hours. Obviously acting upon a prior decision, his parents had named him 'David' after both William and Betsy's fathers, and 'Lloyd' in honour of his mother's family. The cause of death was entered by the Registrar as 'suffocation,' the tiny body being buried at *Capel Uchaf* in Criccieth. The burial ground no longer exists, and none of the couple's subsequent children ever knew of their sibling's fleeting existence.[30]

More tragedy followed swiftly, as on 24 September, William's mother Mary died. What transpired next was related many years later by William's 'devoted niece' Anne Williams:

> Through some neglect he did not receive the news of his mother's death until it was almost too late for him to arrive for the funeral. He arrived at Trecoed just as the funeral cortege was leaving the house, and, the nearest station being sixteen miles away, the poor fellow had to walk all the way to his old home, after a long tedious journey, because no conveyance had been sent to meet him, although there were plenty of horses on the farm, and a trap as well. As soon as he arrived, he joined the procession, which meant another mile to walk, as the mother's coffin was carried to the cemetery by the tenants and servants at their express wish, to pay her a last token of respect.[31]

Also living at Highgate at the time was David Lloyd Jones, born on 30 January 1847, the eldest son of Betsy's older sister Elin Jones. It was not unusual at the time in large families for grandparents to

---

[28] H. Du Parcq, *The Life Of David Lloyd George*, 1912-1913, 4 Vols, London, Caxton, Vol.I, p10.
[29] Ibid., p8.
[30] Rowland, *Tada,* p198. Highgate had been the family home since about 1835.
[31] Quoted in Du Parcq, Vol.I, p10.

'adopt' a child to help out, and this was clearly the case with Rebecca Lloyd. When, around July 1861, William took up another school appointment in Newchurch-in-Rossendale, Lancashire, he and Betsy took this nephew David with them. William was essentially a kind-hearted man, and something of his outlook on life can be seen in his farewell address to the pupils and staff of Troed-yr-Allt school:

> To do good, to be useful and beneficial to others, to be of a kind and obliging disposition, tender and compassionate, to feel for the wants and miseries of others, so as to be ready to relieve them,–this certainly is the happiest and noblest temper in the world. Narrow-minded and selfish persons think their own happiness the greater because they have it alone to themselves…[32]

It was hoped to train David as a pupil-teacher, and William devoted time to this end, but David was in delicate health, and concern for his health and welfare was the main thread in letters between William and his brother-in-law Richard Lloyd at this time. Soon he was found to be consumptive, and he declined and died on 2 September 1867, being buried in *Capel Uchaf* graveyard in Criccieth.[33]

Meanwhile, in Newchurch in November 1861, Mary Ellen was born, but William's own health began to give way and he found the position uncongenial. However, among his close friends at this time was Dr John D. Morell, a well-known educationalist, who had begun his career as a Congregational minister before being appointed by Lord Lansdowne to be an inspector of schools in 1848, a position he retained until 1876.[34] Morell was a distinguished philosopher and metaphysician who had studied philosophy under Immanuel Fichte at Bonn. It was through Dr Morell's persuasion that William accepted an appointment to take charge of a large school in Manchester, The Mayfield School, for several months pending the return of the Headmaster, Albert Pope, who was away ill.[35]

Consequently, on or about 20 September 1862, the George family moved to Manchester, taking up residence in "a neat little house" at 5 New York Place in Chorlton-on-Medlock.[36] William was much happier at the Mayfield School in Manchester, which had about 170 pupils with four pupil-teachers. On 5 October he wrote to Betsy's brother, Richard:

> You may be sure that we were both very glad to leave Newchurch. The place itself we could do with very well–though cold & rather damp, it is healthy–the air is much purer there than at Manchester, & neither of us could hold out long without pure air. It was the Newchurch *school* & the people connected with it that did not suit me; & I need not say that I did not suit them. Nearly all the 'Directors' are rough working men who had not the means to act liberally even if disposed to do so–and besides, my temper is such that I would rather be the master of workpeople than their servant. I did not lose much in the way of bad debts–about £2, but I lost

32 Quoted in George, *Making Of Lloyd George,* p58.
33 George, *Making Of Lloyd George*, p33, 57, 59; Rowland, *Tada*, p202, 220-224, 252.
34 John D. Morell (1816-1891).
35 Rowland, *Tada*, p218.
36 Ibid., p219.

several pounds more owing to the bad times. I daresay that made a difference of about £15.[37]

In March of the year of Lloyd George's birth, on account of his failing health, William George again returned to his native Pembrokeshire, with his family, though in the more southerly, more English-speaking part of the county, rather than the northern, mostly Welsh-speaking part that he hailed from. Maybe the loss of his childhood Welsh language ability still troubled him. At any rate, he took up farming at Bullford Farm, Johnston, four miles to the south of Haverfordwest. The annual rent was £30, and the smallholding consisted of a farmhouse, outbuildings and 30 acres of arable and pasture land. It became one of the family traditions that although William:

> … relinquished the life of a schoolmaster, the student was in no way lost. His passion for reading continued with unabated force, and each day's tasks alternated between manual toil and mental studies. Within the domain of the little farm, books shared with agricultural implements the distinction of being necessary requisites, and however hard the day's toil, no day ended without seeing the schoolmaster-farmer deep in his books.[38]

Little David "was little more than a year old when he was laid aside with an attack of croup which was so severe that for some days his life was despaired of."[39] The local doctor, Dr George Griffith, hurried through a snowstorm, and saw the child recover, saying years later 'I never dreamt that in saving the life of that little child, as he lay unconscious in the wicker cradle on that farm hearth, I was saving the life of one of our national leaders.'[40] David was spared, but death in the family was not cheated for long. Working in the fields on a damp day in late May, William caught a chill that soon developed into pneumonia. On 2 June, Betsy summoned another local physician, Dr James D. Brown, but there was nothing to be done, and William died less than a week later, on 7 June 1864, aged only 44. He was buried a few days later in the churchyard of St Cwrda in Trefwrdan/Jordanston, some 20 miles distant, close to the graves of his parents. His tombstone bears the heartfelt inscription:

> *Trwm fu'r tro wywo oi wedd–Gwr ydoedd / O gariadus–nodwedd. / Anwyl i'w deulu'n unwed / Colled ei fyned I'w fedd.*[41]

His widow, Betsy, was only 36. She immediately sent a telegram to her brother, Richard, aged 30, simply saying '*Tyrd Richard*' ['Richard, come!']. Despite having never left the area of his village, he straight away set out to see his sister, a journey of 170 miles, which took him two full days of travelling. The decision was obvious: two months later, on 15 August, the lease on the farm was sold, through the good offices of a Liverpool solicitor, Thomas Goffey, who had befriended William when he was

---

37 Quoted in Rowland, *Tada*, p219-220.
38 Edwards, 1913, Vol.II, p4, from information from Anne Williams, William's niece.
39 Ibid., p4. Croup is a serious respiratory complaint, especially dangerous in small children.
40 D. Williamson, *Lloyd George: A Man Of The People*, 1917, New York, George H. Doran, p3-4. Dr George Griffith (1838-1912).
41 Rowland, *Tada*, p250-251: This translates to "Heavy was that which wilted his face. He was a man of loving disposition beloved unanimously by his family. It is a great loss that he has gone to his grave."

a schoolmaster there, as was most of the few items of furniture.[42] [43] Betsy had written Goffey a letter which revealed her grief:

> I am greatly obliged by your kind letter received the 18th inst. Indeed I cannot tell you what a source of consolation it has been to me in my deep affliction–Well I may believe that my dear husband was your 'dearest friend' and that he was highly esteemed by all his friends there, for such he always considered you and his respect for all his friends in Liverpool was very much. It is a comfort to me to think how much he was beloved by all his numerous friends. Oh! What a dear husband I have lost…
>
> I cannot tell you now when I leave the South–We are trying to find a person to take the place that will pay me something for the lease–and to take the crop under valuation…Some months ago my dear husband thought he was going to lose me–When I recovered he said–I was walking about without knowing what to do. If that would be the case I was determined to leave the place at once–I couldn't stop on a day here but it was me that was to stay and how hard it is upon me to be here after him–The little children's health is pretty well, and myself as well as it could be expected. It cannot be very good for some time…[44]

This sad auction of the family's only possessions formed Lloyd George's earliest recollection:

> The possessions of the family were sold up... The little boy and his sister Mary saw the house they loved being broken up, and neighbours carrying off their purchases. The children tried, by putting pebbles against the gate, to keep out the invaders and save the household goods.[45]

60 years later, lifetime Haverfordwest resident William D. Phillips recalled:

> The auctioneer… was the late Mr Henry Davies… and my fellow clerk, the late Mr J.M. Martin, managed and booked the sale. Having business in the neighbourhood, and passing from Tiers Cross to Johnston, I looked in at the sale to see how things were going… I remember him [Mr Martin] remarking to me at the time, "Do you see that little chap swinging on the gate? He's a little terror. There was one lot being taken away just now, for which he evidently had a strong attachment, for he fiercely resisted it being taken away by the purchaser." As I passed out through the lawn gate, the boy referred to (Mr D. Lloyd George) was swinging on it with intense energy and returned my look at him defiantly.[46]

The family's neighbour, one John Phillips, took over the lease of William's fields with effect from 1

---

[42] Thomas Goffey (14 June 1835 - 22 May 1915).
[43] Rowland, *Tada*, p252.
[44] George, *Making Of Lloyd George*, p65.
[45] Du Parcq, Vol.I, p12.
[46] Phillips, p24. William D. Phillips (1846–8 June 1926).

October and added them to his own. 41 years later, on 18 September 1905, Lloyd George returned to Bullford with his own eldest son, Dick. John Phillips, by then a widower aged 79, was there to greet them. The incident with the stones had clearly made a deep impression on Lloyd George's mind, as he wrote to his brother William the same day:

> Drove to Bullford this morning. Dr. Griffith met us at Tiers' Cross, close to the little Congregational Chapel, which I was told my father often attended. He was very friendly with the Minister–a Mr. Thomas.
>
> The farmer who bought the lease from poor mother met us–a Mr. John [Phillips]. Very nice fellow. He brought with him the Assignment of the Lease which he gave me. Very nice little place, with a touch of real style about it. Most untidily kept. Mr. John [Phillips] told me that its present appearance gave no idea of what it looked like. The trees on the drive all cut down. I saw the gate Mary and I carried stones to–not the old gate. That has been taken down and part of it put up elsewhere. Dick took photographs. It all rather saddened me...[47]

Elizabeth was granted letters of administration for her late husband's estate at Carmarthen on 4 September. In adverse circumstances, William had made good provision for his family. The final balance sheet showed that his total estate amounted to almost a thousand pounds–£718 invested in the building societies, £90 due to him as back-rent for the cottage (received from 'Mr L. James'), £64 for his crops and goodwill, £57 for his horses, carriages and farming implements, £34 for personal effects… and cash in the house of £5, making a grand total of £968. From this there needed to be deducted expenses of £122, reducing the net value of his estate to £846 [£137,363 in 2025]–£56 covering probate and administration costs, £34 in respect of rent and wages and, not least, £32 in respect of William's funeral.[48]

Crucially, Elizabeth kept her husband's small library of books, and moved with her two children back to her native Llanystumdwy in Caernarfonshire, where she lived in a cottage known as Highgate. She was actually pregnant, and gave birth to another boy, William, on 23 February 1865. As was so often the case in those days, conditions were cramped. For the first four years of their life there, David's grandmother, Rebecca Lloyd, also lived in the cottage as head of the household until her death on 19 June 1868, aged 65. Elizabeth and Mary Ellen slept with Rebecca in the larger of the upstairs rooms, while Richard shared his quarters with David and William, who slept together in a narrow wainscot bed.[49]

William George's books were treasured by the whole family, being kept in a glass-fronted cabinet in the parlour. Of prime importance among the books, from which David would come to derive so much benefit, was an eight-volume English translation of *The Ancient History of the Egyptians, Carthaginians, Assyrians, Babylonians, Medes and Persians, Macedonians, and Grecians* by Charles Rollin, first

---

[47] Quoted in George, *Making Of Lloyd George*, p66. Lloyd George never returned to Bullford again.

[48] Rowland, *Tada*, p249

[49] F. Hague, *The Pain And The Privilege: The Women In Lloyd George's Life*, 2008, London, HarperPress, p16.

published in 1730-1738, and which he later claimed to have read in its entirety.[50] There were also a couple of bound volumes of *The Examiner*, which contained information about the American Civil War–still only halfway through being fought at the time of his birth–and a Victorian *History of England*, probably Macauley's, being published in 1848. These were the only English books he recalled from his childhood, though there were more, not least a 14-volume set of *The Penny Cyclopaedia*, published by the Society for the Diffusion of Useful Knowledge, presented to William George by 'The Teachers and Conductors of The Children's Service of Hope Street Church Sunday Schools, as a Token of Respect & Esteem' when he left Liverpool at Christmas 1852.[51]

Other prized tomes included Shakespeare's plays, Burnet's *History of the Reformation* in six volumes; Charles Knight's *The Pictorial History of England* in eight volumes; a well-bound *Webster's Dictionary*; *The Journals of George Fox; Arnold's Life and Correspondence* in two volumes; also a large Peter Williams family bible, given to William before he left Trecoed.[52] As well as these works, there were several volumes in the European Library series, such as Hallam's *Constitutional History* in two volumes; Guizot's 'History of the English Revolution', several anthologies of English poetry, plus many English language and other textbooks. There were also books on education, such as *The Philosophy Of Education,* and *The Schoolmaster: Essays On Practical Education* in two volumes, and, last but not least, the *Report Of The Commissioners Of Inquiry Into The State Of Education In Wales* published by HMSO in three volumes in November 1847. This last, because of the colour of their covers, became notoriously known as 'the Blue Books'.[53]

On 10 March 1846, William Williams, the Welsh-born 'radical' MP for Coventry, had introduced a motion that eventually led to an inquiry into the state of education in Wales.[54] It was the British Government's view at that time that the Welsh were becoming an increasingly unruly and riotous population and therefore threatened the foundations of society. Government officials were convinced that seditious events were coordinated and held in the Welsh language. Kay-Shuttleworth, the Secretary of the Council of Education noted that the Commission would hold "an inquiry into the state of education in Wales, especially into the means afforded to the labouring classes of acquiring a knowledge of the English language", that is, the language of commerce, higher education, government and law. Three deputies were appointed as educational investigators; staggeringly, none of them had a knowledge of Welsh, of Nonconformity, or even of elementary education!

Their conclusions were duly published in the Report. With regards to education, many aspects were criticized by all three, including the poor quality of education provided by unqualified teachers, schools' unsuitable locations and lack of facilities. Due to the ignorance and prejudices of the deputies, these faults were highly exaggerated; in fact, the education of the lower classes in England was no better. Their racist comments concerning the "backwardness" and "barbarity" of the Welsh, and the

---

50 Charles Rollin (1661-1741). Lloyd George read the 8th Edition of 1790.

51 To his friend J. Herbert Lewis in 1907.

52 W. R. P. George, *88 Not Out*, p11; George, *Making Of Lloyd George*, p69. Peter Williams (1723-1796), leading Welsh Methodist, whose Welsh language bible of 1770 subsequently ran to many editions.

53https://www.library.wales/discover/digital-gallery/printed-material/the-blue-books-of-1847. Retrieved 31 March 2021.

54 William Williams (1788-1865). In 1863 he chaired the meeting that launched the campaign for a University of Wales.

alleged immorality of Welsh women, were also highly controversial and insulting to the ordinary people of Wales. Although only six pages out of some 1,252 were devoted to these criticisms, they were discussed extensively by the press, particularly the London papers. The Report was also seen as an attack on the Welsh language due to the deputies' comments regarding its inferior status and that its use restricted the masses in terms of their social prospects. Much of the unfavourable information had been submitted by Welsh Anglican clergymen, and so they and their Church were seen by many Welsh as a "treasonous", internal enemy. Over time, the 'Blue Books' came to help foster a more defensive, self-aware nationalism, these responses evolving into organised political action, which culminated at the General Election of 1868, witnessed by young David.

As regards to the village of Llanystumdwy–'the church in the bend of two rivers' (the Dwyfach and Dwyfawr)–it has not changed vastly since Lloyd George's time, and Highgate remains a prominent building in the main street, diagonally opposite the Grade II listed local inn, *Tafarn y Plu* ('The Feathers'), open for over 200 years.

Thomas De Quincey, as a youth of 17, had passed through the village in the autumn of 1802, as he later recorded in *Confessions of an English Opium-Eater*:

> [I] was generally treated with hospitality; and once in particular, near the village of Llan-y-styndw… in a sequestered part of Merionethshire, I was entertained for upwards of three days by a family of young people with an affectionate and fraternal kindness… The family consisted at that time of four sisters and three brothers, all grown up, and all remarkable for elegance and delicacy of manners. So much beauty, and so much native good breeding and refinement, I do not remember to have seen before or since in any cottage, except once or twice in Westmoreland and Devonshire. They spoke English, an accomplishment not often met with in so many members of one family, especially in villages remote from the high road… On the last morning, however… one of the brothers explained to me that their parents had gone, the day before my arrival, to an annual meeting of Methodists… and were that day expected to return; "and if they should not be so civil as they ought to be," he begged… that I would not take it amiss. The parents returned with churlish faces, and *"Dym Sassenach" (no English)* in answer to all my addresses. I saw how matters stood; and so, taking an affectionate leave of my kind and interesting young hosts, I went my way…[55]

In 1870-72, Reverend John Marius Wilson's *Imperial Gazetteer of England and Wales* described Llanystumdwy as:

> A village and a parish in Pwllheli district, Carnarvon. The village stands on the river Dwy, near the coast, 2 miles WNW [sic] of Criccieth r. station, and 8 ENE [sic] of Pwllheli… The parish

[55] Thomas De Quincey (1785-1859); *Confessions of an English Opium-Eater*, 1823, London, 2nd Edition, Taylor and Hessey, p34-37. Strangely, De Quincey had lived from the ages of 6-11 at Greenhay House in Chorlton-on-Medlock, Lloyd George's birthplace!

> comprises 6,522 acres of land, and 258 of water… Pop., [sic] 1,126. Houses, 236. The property is divided among a few… Gwynvryn is the seat of Major Nanney; Trefan is the seat of S.O. Priestley, Esq.; and Plashen belongs to J.E. Nanney, Esq. The living is a rectory in the diocese of Bangor. Value, £485. Patron, the Bishop of Bangor. The church [St John the Baptist] was rebuilt in 1863. There are chapels for Independents and Calvinistic Methodists, and an endowed school with £31 a year.[56]

Elizabeth's brother Richard was a relatively prosperous shoemaker, employing two or three workmen. He was also an unpaid minister, ordained on 18 April 1859–first in the Scotch Baptists, very conservative, and strict Calvinists, and then in the Church of Christ, the Disciples of Christ (Campbell Movement) being committed to restoring what they saw as primitive Christianity–worshipping at *Capel Uchaf* on Ffordd Caernarfon in Criccieth, then *Capel Moreia* in Llanystumdwy itself. In religious terms, this made the family minority outsiders, as most Welsh-speakers were Nonconformists, either Methodists or Baptists, while the English-speakers were generally members of the Church in Wales, then the established Anglican Church in the Principality. Crucially for his young nephew's political development, Richard was also a strong Liberal.

William, David's brother, retained vivid memories of their uncle, writing:

> As I first remember him, he was active and brisk in all his movements, well-built, of medium height, with a clean-shaven upper lip and bright blue eyes… He was throughout his life a man of very deep religious convictions, and his main object in life was to preach and teach the Gospel of Jesus Christ, and above all to make his own life an embodiment of its principles.[57]

Richard had suffered a considerable injury as a child. William asked his uncle:

> Why he was deaf in one ear and was told that in the Llanystumdwy school in 1840 when he was only six he had been overheard by the teacher talking in Welsh to another boy. For this the teacher struck him so hard with a cane on his head that he was deaf in one ear for the rest of his life.[58]

In the early 1950s, an old lady, Mrs E. Jones, was still living in Highgate, aged well in her 80s. She remembered Richard Lloyd, recalling his preaching: "Very, very clever and convincing he was. He always made you believe whatever he said."[59] Mrs Jones had been baptized by him.

Early Lloyd George biographer, Herbert Du Parcq, ably described Highgate, as it was at the time

---

[56] J. M. Wilson, *Imperial Gazetteer of England and Wales,* 1872, 6 Vols, Edinburgh, London and Dublin, A. Fullarton, Vol.IV, p129.
[57] George, *My Brother and I*, p20.
[58] W. R. P. George, *88 Not Out*, p13.
[59] Quoted in Owen, p18.

he wrote, in 1912:[60]

> The house in which Richard Lloyd lived lies on the right-hand side of the village street as you approach it by the coast road from Criccieth. It is a small substantial stone house. In those days a sign hung over the entrance door, with boots, the symbols of its owner's trade, portrayed upon it, indicating in the Welsh language Richard Lloyd's willingness to make or repair the boots and shoes of the villagers. On the left as you enter the house is the living room. It is a comfortable and homely room, much like the well-ordered kitchen of the Welsh farmhouse, but built upon a smaller and less pretentious scale. It has a stone floor, a wooden ceiling with thin wooden beams, and one of those large inviting hearths which are the glory of the old country cottage. On the other side of the small passage is a little parlour, once used as the shoemaker's "cutting room," but diverted to its present use long before Mr. Richard Lloyd had given up his house and business. A narrow wooden staircase leads aloft to the bedroom, and a pleasant garden lies behind the house. Adjoining it is the workshop in which the shoemaker worked. In the thick wall of his room there is, and was, a convenient hole in the wall near the bench at which the shoemaker sat at his work. In this it was his habit to keep the books he was reading at the time, for every moment he could snatch from his work was given to reading. Sometimes, as an idea struck him or an author's sentiment appealed to him, he would take his pencil and add to the note he was preparing for next Sunday's sermon.[61]

The influence of his uncle, Richard Lloyd, was profound, and went much further than just incorporating his surname into his own. David always carried a small pocketbook, jotted down comments he heard, things seen, ideas, plans–some of these still exist. It was his uncle's habit to pause in his work, note down ideas for sermons on scraps of paper and place them in a small niche in the wall of his cobblers' workshop before resuming his work. He told David: "Whenever a thought strikes you, remember to jot it down at once or the chances are that it will be lost for ever."[62] This sound advice obviously impressed itself on the young boy's fertile mind. Also, regarding Lloyd George's much later Parliamentary Speeches, it may be noted in Hansard, that he repeats controversial points in-between points on which all could agree, using an old Welsh Nonconformist preaching system of stating points three times, transferred into the sphere of politics. It is an interesting and effective way of letting a point sink in, making it more palatable and hopefully ending in more understanding and agreement.[63]

Though small at the time, David also retained memories of his redoubtable grandmother Rebecca Lloyd:

---

[60] Herbert Du Parcq (1880-1949), a barrister, was given access to diaries and other papers by William George, and, greatly helped by his wife Lucy, was an assiduous collector of first-hand material on Lloyd George to whom later biographers owe a great debt: see https://www.theislandwiki.org/index.php/Lord_du_Parcq.

[61] Du Parcq, Vol.I, p13-14.

[62] George, *My Brother and I*, p22.

[63] Observation related to the author by Bengy Carey-Evans, Beaumaris, 11 October 2018.

> Long walks, holding his grandmother's hand, from farm to farm, taking orders for new boots or repairs, and receiving payment for past services rendered. The old lady and the child were everywhere received with warm hospitality; and when justice had been done to a good tea, and much conversation had flowed along with it, the farmer's wife would generally come to business with the remark: "By the way, Beca Llwyd, we owe you a trifle." "Please don't bother about that," Rebecca would reply. "Oh, I would far rather settle it now, if you can remember how much it amounts to," the farmer's wife would proceed. Then, diving into an immense pocket concealed in the voluminous folds of her skirt, Rebecca would, after much rummaging, pull out a bill, remarking: "How very odd that I should happen to have this bill with me. But since you insist on paying it, here it is."
>
> Much the same ritual would be gone through at the next farm; but there, perhaps, payment would be made in butter, bacon, or some other form of produce. Nightfall would see Rebecca Lloyd and her grandson, heavily laden with provisions, and with some ready money in her pocket as well, approaching their humble village home.[64]

From their arrival at Highgate, and especially from Rebecca's death, Betsy had taken over many of the chores involved in running the house–tending the fires, cleaning the rooms, baking bread, the family washing. She had to be resourceful. Highgate was rented from the village shopkeeper, David Jones, who charged the family an annual rent of £7 [£1,137 in 2025] but did absolutely nothing towards the upkeep of his property, his modus operandi being "The rent is mine, the house is yours."[65] The fabric of the cottage was crumbling; in particular, the old oven was in such a bad condition that before she could bake the bread every week, Betsy would have:

> … to contrive somehow to cover up the holes in the oven by using brown paper and paste. Sometimes the brown paper went on fire before the loaves were fully baked, but more often than not the baking was concluded when the singed brown paper burst into flames, and she would exclaim as the loaves were extracted from the oven, that her 'widow's devices' had won the day. On these successful occasions the crusted loaves sounded like a drum when she rapped them. The treat for the children was to dip the crust of a well-baked loaf in buttermilk before eating it.[66]

Each child had their assigned tasks in the household. David's principal one was to keep the garden in order, which he did for the whole time that the family lived at Highgate, proudly recalling later that he "wheeled the barrow, did the manuring, planted the garden and pruned the fruit trees."[67] As he grew older, it also became his responsibility to collect all the firewood that was needed. This he gathered in

---

64 W. W. Davies, p5.
65 George, *Making Of Lloyd George*, p71.
66 Ibid., p71.
67 Quoted in W. W. Davies, p20.

the Ty Newydd woods, especially after a storm. He and his smaller brother would also help with gleaning at harvest time. Lloyd George's interest in agriculture, pursued later on his Churt estate, was nurtured, almost literally seeded, at Highgate, and its locale.

When not at school, engaged in chores or at Chapel, David would go out with his friends Bob Jones, William Williams and a slightly younger boy called Evan Elias, invariably ending up in the woods, accompanied by his black dog 'Bismarck', so named because he had been brought home from Hamburg by a sailor.[68] This often involved trespassing on Squire Ellis-Nanney's land, but there were trout to be caught in the Dwyfor river and nuts and sloes to be picked in the woods, running the gauntlet of the keepers. As Rowland relates:

> A careful watch was usually kept, but on one occasion Davy, Bob and a third boy were caught by a young keeper who demanded their names and addresses. Fortunately for them, he was new to the district. Bob Jones announced that he was John Pritchard and that Davy was his cousin. The third boy followed their lead. The keeper, who let them go after noting down their fictitious names and addresses, was later said to have had a none too pleasant interview with Ellis-Nanney. On another occasion, when he took refuge from the law in the chimney of a half-completed house, Davy was less fortunate: a pair of dangling feet gave him away.[69]

David also remembered the 1868 General Election, held from 17 November to 7 December that year, even though he was not yet six-years-old at the time, and especially the terrible scenes following:[70]

> "It is the first election that I remember," to quote his own statement. "I was a boy at school then, and I was in the blackest Tory parish in the land. I believe that my old uncle who brought me up was the only Liberal in the village, though not the only Liberal in the parish. There were three or four in the parish besides him. One or two of them refused to vote for the Tory candidate, and two or three actually went further, and dared to record their votes for the Liberal. All of them received notice to quit. I remember that some lads who were at school with me in the same class, in a year or two had to leave the neighbourhood. I was very young, but young lads do not forget things of that sort. I knew the reason why they left–because the great Squire of the parish had turned their fathers out of their homes purely because they dared to vote for the Liberal candidate. I will quote from a letter that was written by the trustees of the Willoughby de Eresby estate: 'I feel it necessary to explain that Lord Willoughby de Eresby is a Conservative, and gives all his support to Mr. Pennant, and therefore does not consider it right that you should allow yourself to be led by others to vote against the interests of the estate on which you live and against the wishes of his lordship.' Such were the letters that were circulated. After the

---

68 Edwards, 1913, Vol.I, p25-26; Spender, *Prime Minister*, p24.
69 Rowland, *Lloyd George*, p10.
70 In the first election after the Reform Act 1867, which enfranchised many more men, in Caernarvonshire, Liberal Sir Thomas Love Jones-Parry beat Tory George Douglas-Pennant by 1,968 votes to 1,815.

> election, notices to quit were showered upon the tenants. As a result they were turned out by the score on to the roadside, because they dared to vote according to their consciences. It is [he concluded] my first memory of politics." In that harrowing memory of dark and troublous times, one may surely discover the motive power of his later career.[71]

As a bold young boy, intent on making his mark on the world–in this case, literally–in 1871, when he was eight-years-old, David precociously carved his initials deeply but neatly into the stonework of the ancient village bridge, 'D. LL. G', thus showing that he had already incorporated his beloved uncle's surname with his own. In 1890, hearing of his by-election victory on 10 April, Hugh Jones, the blacksmith from the nearby smithy carved, in a visibly lighter hand, 'MP' underneath, in tribute to the popular local boy made good.[72] For many years the initials 'D.LL.G', with the date '16th January 1871', were also visible on a nearby tree.

From 3 September 1866, at the age of three years and seven months, David went to the local National School at Llanystumdwy, established in 1819, where he stayed until July 1878 when he was 15.[73] Emerging from the infants' class, he climbed the school ladder from standard to standard until he reached the pinnacle of Standard 7. The school authorities presumably thought village children would aspire no higher, but the admirable and forward-thinking headmaster, David Evans had improvised a Standard 7x for outstanding pupils like David, followed by his brother William two years later. Evans taught them the elements of algebra and Euclid, as well as the usual curriculum of the 'three R's', geography and history.[74] But even at the village school, politics intruded. The school was an Anglican foundation and when the children were annually invited to recite the 'Creed' before the local landowner, Sir Hugh Ellis-Nanney, and the Rector, Reverend David Edwards, David, then aged 15, organised a 'conspiracy of silence' by the Nonconformist pupils in protest at this 'wrong', his first demonstration against institutional injustice.[75] As his brother William recorded:

> Imagine the scene when the headmaster stood in front of our joint class and on a signal from him we all stood up. After glancing around to see that the inspectors and visitors were ready he called in a quiet voice for a recital of the Creed. Strangely enough there was no response, and the headmaster, looking rather puzzled, repeated his request in a louder and more imperative tone of voice. He was, however, met with a blank stare from the silent class. By this time the inspectors, the Rector and local gentry seemed to sense that something had gone wrong, and the Rector, a whitebearded and venerable-looking old gentleman, came forward and after whispering something in the headmaster's ear, he stood in front of us and explained in a gentle and coaxing tone of voice that all we need do was to recite the Creed, which he was sure we all

---

[71] Quoted in Edwards, 1913, Vol.I, p30-31.
[72] Personal information and observation, 29 August 2018.
[73] Edwards, 1913, Vol.II, p8.
[74] George, *My Brother And I*, p39.
[75] Sir Hugh Ellis-Nanney, 1st Baronet JP (16 February 1845–7 June 1920). His estate was 12,000 acres, while his home, Plas Gwynfryn, was built in 1876 at a cost of £70,000 [£10.32m in 2025]; it was gutted by fire in 1982.

> knew. The class remained unresponsive in their stony silence. By this time the tension in the room had become quite oppressive and the headmaster's face ashen and pitiful to behold. I was moved to such sympathy by this sight that I was unable to restrain myself any longer and I shouted in a firm voice from one of the back rows of the class-room 'I believe'. The rest of the class immediately chimed in to recite the Creed.[76]

Legend grew that William later received a sound thrashing from his elder brother for breaking the unanimous silence, but this was a fable initially concocted by the usually reliable J. Hugh Edwards in 1913 and unfortunately embroidered by W. Watkin Davies in 1939. The story was specifically denied by William George to his son W. R. P. George whenever he was asked about it.[77] In any case, the protest had already achieved its purpose. Realising the strength of 'nonconformist conscience' amongst the pupils, the authorities henceforth abandoned the practice of making them publicly recite the Creed. With no apparent contradiction, on 6 May 1878, David managed to receive the school's First Class Prize in Religious Knowledge, it being William Anderson's *Treasury of History and Biography for the Young*.

Regarding David's achievement in this area, his teacher, David Evans, was highly influential in far-reaching and unforeseen ways, being:

> … invariably at his best in the Scripture lessons, which were given regularly each morning. He had a passionate fondness for the stirring historical incidents in the Old Testament, which he would narrate with such dramatic force and fervour as to hold the children spellbound. Mr. Lloyd George still recalls the thrilling manner in which the old schoolmaster used to describe the sacrifice of Isaac by Abraham. In his outstretched hand he would hold the cane as typifying the sacrificial knife, and this at the crucial moment would suddenly be dropped to the ground with a crash that reverberated throughout the room where his juvenile audience sat in breathless awe. In the light of subsequent years it can readily be understood that to these dramatic narratives of Old Testament scenes there was no more attentive listener than David Lloyd George. They were his first lessons in the histrionic art–the first appeal to that dramatic instinct which is so deeply embedded in his nature.[78]

'Oratorical' and 'rhetorical' might be better words than 'histrionic', but the point is well made, and most importantly Evans had clearly achieved his primary intention of engaging his pupil's interest. In common with the other boys of the village, when not in school, David found plenty to do outdoors, Du Parcq recording:

> … forty years ago there was a greater variety in boys' sports. In the winter months bandy [a

---

[76] George, *My Brother And I*, p42-43.
[77] W. R. P. George, *88 Not Out*, p16.
[78] Edwards, 1913, Vol.II, p13.

> predecessor of ice hockey] was the favourite game, and when the frost came there was plenty of fun to be got out of sliding on the ice. In the summer there were games of ball, and at all times, as the evening came on, "hide and seek" was the favourite amusement.
>
> Sometimes the games became topical. The events of the day would inspire the imagination of the boys to mimicry of the deeds of heroes. When, in 1909, Mr. Lloyd George visited the school to receive from some of his old schoolfellows an address of congratulation, he spoke of such an occasion. He remembered, he said, the Franco-German War of 1870, and how the war was carried on in Llanystumdwy school. "The boys divided themselves into two parties–French and Prussians. The French entrenched themselves in the porch of the school; and there," said the Chancellor, pointing to Mr. Harry Jones, of Pencorth, "is Napoleon."[79]

As well as the legacy of his father's books, on rainy days Davy also had access to the not-inconsiderable library of his uncle. This included, as well as theological works and volumes of Welsh poetry, quite a few standard English literary classics. He worked his way through each volume, reading Charles Reade's *The Cloister and the Hearth* (1861) at least half-a-dozen times in his youth. Reade's best-known work is a stirring and imaginative telling of the parentage and origins of the great Renaissance humanist scholar, Erasmus of Rotterdam, who rose from obscurity to international fame. The romance, revolving around its central characters of Gerhard Eliassoen and Margaret Brandt, interweaves a dense pattern of themes of common folk making a mark in the world, the importance of giving or being given the right help at the right time, the roles of constancy and chance, loyalty and faithfulness, drunkenness and treachery, the law and justice, with the whole being intended, in Reade's words, to be put by the reader to "a wholesome use", namely not to expect "perfect happiness" in this world, and so to think and act accordingly in this life.[80] Its central theme of the struggle between man's obligations to the temporal and spiritual spheres clearly struck a chord in the young Davy's growing personal and social consciousness.[81]

Davy also enjoyed Alexandre Dumas' *The Three Musketeers* and *The Count of Monte Cristo*, and some of Charles Dickens novels. From his reading of the volumes of *The Examiner* he developed a lifelong fascination with the American Civil War, Abraham Lincoln becoming his hero and providing more political 'grist to his mill'. Later he read Robert Louis Stevenson's *Kidnapped.* The boy had a vividly precocious imagination and aged about twelve or thirteen he composed an epic romance concerning his alter ego, a mighty warrior known as Jack of Abyssinia. In later life his brother William recalled 'Jac was an imaginary hero of my brother's creation–a Welshman who, through a series of strange accidents, found himself in the middle of Abyssinia, and by the power of his genius and bravery gained supremacy over man and beast in that strange land.'[82] Lloyd George himself told Herbert Lewis in 1907:

---

[79] Du Parcq, Vol.I, p22-23.

[80] C. Reade, *The Cloister And The Hearth*, 1933, London, Daily Express Publications, p636.

[81] So highly did Lloyd George regard the book that in November 1917 he presented a personally inscribed copy to South African General Jan Smuts: https://antiquarianauctions.com/lots/mn-mn-3. Retrieved 16 July 2021.

[82] William George, *Atgof A Myfyr*, p50 (*Translated from the Welsh*).

> It was a most blood-thirsty production. I slaughtered thousands of people. The hero was a Welshman who went to Abyssinia and raised an army. It culminated in a rebellion in Wales.[83]

This from a boy who would grow up to protest vehemently against the Boer War, lead Britain through the slaughter of the First World War, campaign ardently for Welsh Home Rule and inveigh against the Italian invasion of Abyssinia!

Besides history, literature and theology, there was politics and news. Every evening, Davy had to walk to Criccieth to get a copy of that day's *Liverpool Mercury* for Uncle Lloyd, so that he could study the political questions of the time after his day's work was done. This would include reports of Parliamentary debates:

> …interesting from the present point of view is the fact that when the days lengthened and the light was strong, David Lloyd George was accustomed to saunter over his nightly journey back to Llanystumdwy, absorbed in perusing the vivid descriptions in the columns of the *Mercury* of the war which at that time was raging between Russia and Turkey.[84] He recalls the stirring memories of those days in the seventies when, day after day, he read with eagerness the thrilling story of the incidents and progress of the campaign. Possibly these accounts provided the stimulus to his inborn aptitude for telling phrase and graphic narrative.[85]

Other tales of Davy's sometimes accident-prone boyhood were still in circulation when J. Hugh Edwards wrote in 1913:

> … On one occasion he nearly lost the fingers of his right hand through the mischievous action of one of his companions in suddenly giving a turn to the smithy winch on which his hand was resting. On another occasion, while at play, one of his companions progged him just below the eye with a pitchfork. A very little higher and the sight would have been lost, but fortunately the only permanent effect is the still-remaining scar. Shortly afterwards he led a party of boys in mock battle to a house that was in course of construction, and, feigning an attack upon the enemy's citadel, he took hold of the lintel. Even in those days jerry building seems not to have been unknown, for down came the structure, and he was buried beneath the debris. The yell of his companions brought the neighbours to the scene, but to their amazement and joy the boy emerged unhurt.[86]

On 7 February 1875, when David had just turned 12 years-old–three years earlier than was usual, "so keen was Richard Lloyd to ensure that David was secured within the fold of the Campbellite

---

[83] Herbert Lewis's Diary, 4 December 1907, NLW; quoted in Rowland, *Lloyd George*, p11. If it was ever in fact actually written down, it is sadly now lost.

[84] The Russo-Turkish War of April 1877-March 1878, resulting in victory for the Russian-led coalition.

[85] Edwards, 1913, Vol.II, p35-36.

[86] Ibid., p27.

Baptists"[87]–his uncle baptized him, along with his 14-year-old sister Pollie in the little stream, *Afon Cwrt*, that runs beside *Capel Uchaf*.[88] It was the first Baptist and Nonconformist chapel to be built in Criccieth, dating to around 1796, rebuilt in 1817. Baptism was by total immersion, the stream having been temporarily dammed to create a small pool for the purpose. Afterwards, the new young communicant took first communion inside the chapel, doubtless shivering with cold. It was an important point in his life, not because of its religious significance , but because "he decided from that day onward to adopt the 'Lloyd' in his name as a second surname, in tribute to the man who raised him."[89] He was no longer 'Davy' George, but David Lloyd George.

As regards the religious ceremony, however, in the night that followed, David seemed to have experienced a negative revelation, not at all what his uncle would have intended![90] It suddenly dawned upon him, with great clarity, that everything he had been taught about faith, even the Bible itself, was nothing more that unfounded imaginings.

> He saw an image of his family's deepest-held beliefs collapsing around him like a building falling into ruin. He sat bolt upright in bed and shouted out loud that God and all the things he had been taught were but a dream.[91]

The exact truth of the matter cannot be established, but it is a fact that Lloyd George never returned to his early fervour. As Grigg relates:

> He would gladly attend a chapel service to hear a good preacher and to sing Welsh hymns. He was attracted by the Gospels as by other Bible stories, but to him the founder of Christianity was a prophet of social reform rather than a personal redeemer.[92]

Soon after this joint baptism, Pollie left the Llanystumdwy school and was sent, with Uncle Richard's financial support, to Miss Wheatley's private girls' boarding school in Criccieth. Pollie was expected to stay at the school for two or three years, but she had only been there two terms when her mother's health gave way and Pollie had to return home to help look after her and her two younger brothers.[93] Any ambitions she may have had for better prospects were sacrificed to those of her brothers, especially David's. Pollie herself suffered from bouts of a recurring illness over the next few years, but otherwise she proved to be a good housekeeper. Her oldest nephew, Dick, left a brief pen-portrait of her later in life:

---

87 W. R. P. George, *88 Not Out*, p18.
88 Long since converted into a private residence, the little building is in the Vernacular style, built of local stone.
89 George, *My Brother And I*, p74; Hague, p30-31.
90 Grigg, *Young Lloyd George*, p.33.
91 Hague, p31, referencing D. R. Daniel Memoir, p9, Daniel Papers.
92 Grigg, *Young Lloyd George*, p34.
93 Hague, p27-28.

> My father's only sister, Mary, was a very able woman but very narrow-minded in religious matters. A very strict Baptist... {but] did our aunt spoil us! Everything we wanted her lavish, generous hand gave us. She was a strong character, definitely uncompromising. She ruled her household well, with hospitality unbounded. Even Uncle Lloyd quailed...[94]

Meanwhile, social reform, debate, ideas–in short, politics–was already starting to take a hold on her brother David:

> "Yonder smithy," he declared in 1909, on the occasion of the presentation already spoken of, as he waved his hand in the direction of a building near the bridge, "was my first Parliament where night after night we discussed and decided all the abstruse questions relating to this world and the next in politics, in theology, in philosophy, and in science. There was nothing too wide and comprehensive for us to discuss, and we settled all the problems among ourselves without the slightest misgiving."
>
> This village smithy was quite one of his favourite resorts. The glow of its fire had a special attraction on the cold, winter nights, when all without was dark and dreary, and equally attractive was the entertaining gossip of its habitués. There was always some topic under discussion... The blacksmith was an elderly man of the name of Hugh Jones, and he was as typical a Welshman in the trend of his interests as he was in cast of countenance. A deacon at the Congregational chapel, his zeal for his denomination was intense. No matter how busy he might be, he could not refrain from having a tilt at the other sects. He was always ready to argue that Independency was the Apostolic mode of Church government, and for that reason had a sanction for its polity which no other sect or denomination could claim.[95]

Early on, David acquired considerable dialectical skill, leading the blacksmith to confide in Richard Lloyd: 'If I had not been particularly well grounded in my subject your lad would certainly have succeeded in flooring me!'[96]

Apart from the smithy, the other place where the 'cognoscenti' of the village congregated was Richard Lloyd's own workshop. Here debate ranged beyond narrow denominational concerns, to include politics, social issues, literature and philosophy, with Richard himself as one of the leading contributors. On Monday evenings, the deacons and elders of the neighbouring churches, together with any other intellectually inclined villagers, would gather round Richard's bench. They would first discuss the previous day's sermons, mulling over the theological implications of the phraseology and the illustrations used. From there they would progress on to politics, not too difficult a transition in Wales at that period, where the great political issue was liberty–that of the tenant struggling under the oppressive squirearchy, and that of the Nonconformist against the tyranny of the Established Church.

---

[94] Lloyd George, *Dame Margaret*, p232.
[95] Edwards, 1913, Vol.II, p31-32.
[96] W. W. Davies, p31-32.

Newspapers reported Parliamentary speeches at length, and Richard Lloyd would often read these aloud, informing his listeners of Gladstone's calls for the electors to put conscience before interest. David was present at these gatherings from the age of around twelve, initially just listening, but increasingly as an active participant.[97]

At the time, the 'Little Bethels' of Wales often played an important part in the cultural life of the small and scattered communities. Apart from sermons, there were three instruments of cultural instruction associated with the chapels, namely the Sunday School, the Literary Meeting, and the Society (commonly known as the *Seiet*). At the Sunday School, adults would meet under an elected leader to study and discuss a Biblical passage, or a theological or philosophical point. Between 1780 and 1914, Wales produced generations of preachers of oratorically outstanding sermons, men who could rouse the fervour of audiences of thousands. Lloyd George was profoundly influenced by this powerful religious and cultural phenomenon. He retained a lifelong interest in hearing Welsh preachers, read many biographies of leading preachers, and later had the portrait of John Jones Talysarn hanging above the dining-room mantelpiece, when residing at Downing Street.[98] Further, his own style of platform oratory was moulded on Welsh preaching traditions. W. Watkin Davies recorded that in his style there was "the same modulation of a naturally beautiful voice, the same lavish use of gesture, the same passion, with its intermingling of humour and pathos, the same love of telling illustration, and the same skill in exploiting to the full the dramatic possibilities of the theme."[99] Lloyd George transformed this "tool" from a religious to a political and social one.

By now, the young David was beginning to realise a growing 'sense of self', some sense of his own specialness and possible destiny. Years later, his own eldest son Richard, asked him the question "When did you first suspect you were a genius?":

> It was not intended ironically (not altogether); and my father tapped me solemnly on the shoulder and said, "Suspect? Suspect? I knew. It does not follow that everyone who believes himself to be one is a genius, of course; but no genius fails to know he is one."
>
> "When did you first believe yourself to be one?" I asked him.
>
> "Early. Very early," my father said. 'As a matter of fact, I was a boy at the time. I liked to climb a certain oak tree and sit perched up high in the branches. Now this was not the hallmark of genius, of course. Most boys in the district liked climbing trees. But I was the only one who, when he got up to sit on the top branch, took out a copy of *Euclid* and began to study it. On one occasion when I did this the singular thought struck me, "What a remarkable, fellow am I, to read *Euclid* on top of an oak tree. Why am I doing this?" I asked myself. And, quick as a flash, I answered myself, "I am special. I am astonishing. *Duw* [sic] I believe I am a genius."
>
> "What made you sit on top of an oak tree to read *Euclid*?"

---

[97] Ibid., p32-33.

[98] John Jones, Talysarn (1796-1857), Calvinistic Methodist Minister, one of the greatest preachers in Welsh history. A Caernarfonshire man, having no formal education, he introduced a new style of preaching, one which emphasised practical matters over doctrine–naturally of interest to Lloyd George.

[99] W. W. Davies, p36.

> "The Olympian heights. The detachment that comes from a proper understanding of the spirit of mathematics," my father said, or words to that effect; and then he wandered off into the world of his private thoughts.[100]

In the succinct estimation of fellow Welsh Liberal MP J. Hugh Edwards, who knew him personally:[101]

> Times without number David Lloyd George had heard his mother refer to a Liverpool lawyer as a man whom she and his father had learnt to revere as one of the best and kindest of men, and one who, in the dark days of her bereavement, generously relieved her of the anxiety connected with the realisation of the effects and appurtenances of the little farmstead. In the haze of those grateful memories the man and his profession became merged into an identity, with the result that for the widowed mother there was no calling that had such a halo as that of the law. David Lloyd caught the glow of his mother's admiration until his one ambition was to become a lawyer.[102]

He was also fired by tales of drama in Pwllheli County Court, where Petty Sessions were held on Wednesdays, relayed to him by his friend Bob Jones. In particular, the courtroom exploits of a solicitor named Marcus Louis, from Ruthin, Denbighshire, proved entertaining, especially his habit of vigorously thumping his bulky bundle of law books during his address to the Bench.[103] However, David faced several obstacles. First, the preliminary law examination required proficiency in Latin and French, neither of which had been taught in Llanystumdwy. The village schoolmaster willingly provided the instruction in Latin, and David acquired enough of the language to be able to adequately translate the first volume of Caesar's *Conquest of Gaul*; how the learning of second language was tackled said a lot about the sacrifice, determination and work-ethic that Richard Lloyd possessed and in large measure passed on to his protégé nephew:[104]

> It so happened that just at that time *Cassell's Popular Educator* was being published in parts and circulated throughout the land. Some of the parts found their way into the shoemaker's home at Llanystumdwy, and among their contents were articles setting out in a clear and popular style a full course of instruction in the French language. A cursory perusal of these articles kindled in Mr. Richard Lloyd the desire and determination so to master the subject as to be able to give his nephew the needful help. A French grammar and dictionary were forthwith procured, and uncle and nephew applied themselves to the task with a zeal that knew no weariness, 'sitting,'

---

[100] Richard Lloyd George, *Lloyd George*, p15.

[101] John Hugh Edwards (1869-1945), born in Aberystwyth, supporter of *Cymru Fydd* in the 1890s, Congregationalist Minister, editor, careful, thoughtful author of three highly useful Lloyd George biographies, Liberal MP for Mid-Glamorgan, 1910-1918, Neath, 1918-1922, and Accrington, 1923-1929.

[102] Edwards, 1913, Vol.II, p72.

[103] George, *My Brother And I*, p52. Marcus Louis (1826-1886), three times Mayor of Ruthin.

[104] Ibid., p51.

> as Mr. Lloyd George himself has said, 'for hours together laboriously spelling out the rudiments of a language.' And thus the old man and the lad trod together the steep and toilsome path that led to ultimate triumph.[105]

Towards the end of October 1877, Richard Lloyd accompanied David on the long train journey to Liverpool, and on 24 and 25 October the young man duly sat for his preliminary law examinations in the imposing, neoclassical St George's Hall. In addition to Latin translation and French, the subjects taken were "composition, dictation, history, geography, arithmetic and elementary Latin".[106] David's ultimate success was spelled out by proud schoolmaster David Evans in the school log-book:

> 1877. *December* 8. D. Ll. George, 1st cl. pupil, successful in passing the preliminary examination of the Incorporated Law Society at Liverpool, and received the certificate.[107]

Finding actual employment was the final hurdle. Whilst seeking work that spring and summer of 1878 that would meet Uncle Lloyd's exacting standards, David briefly fulfilled a pupil-teacher role at his village school, on the understanding that it was a temporary arrangement which implied no endorsement on his part of Anglican faith. 20 years later Lloyd George wrote: "After the village school, I went to the University College at Aberystwyth–now a University; then only a school. This was the end of my school education."[108] Whatever he studied there, it can only have been for a few weeks, for a post had been found for him within a short time of him leaving school.

The blacksmith of Llanystumdwy, John Jones, or *Myrddin Fardd* ('the Bard Merlin') as he was known in the village, was also a poet and amateur, if industrious, antiquarian who examined many parish registers and recorded the inscriptions on many tombstones and in churches, tramping hundreds of miles in the process.[109] He was a friend of both Richard Lloyd and Edward Breese, senior partner of Breese, Jones and Casson, solicitors of Porthmadog, established in 1844, a practice in high repute as one of the best firms in North Wales.[110] Breese was also a Fellow of the Society of Antiquaries of London, author in 1873 of *Kalendars of Gwynedd*, a complete record of the high officers (sheriffs, Members of Parliament, etc.) of the counties of Anglesey, Caernarvonshire, and Merionethshire, still regarded as an authoritative work of reference.

At *Myrddin Fardd's* suggestion, in July 1878, Breese agreed to take David into his office for a six-month trial with the promise that, if he proved industrious and enthusiastic, he would be articled to Randal Casson, the junior partner of the firm.[111] Weekday lodgings were found for him with Mr and Mrs David Lloyd Owen, an elderly auctioneer and his wife who lived in the High Street, and Lloyd

---

[105] Edwards, 1913, Vol.II, p73.
[106] Rowland, *Lloyd George*, p20.
[107] Edwards, 1913, Vol.II, p74.
[108] Rowland, *Lloyd George*, p21; quoting Lloyd George in *Mainly About People*, 10 September 1898. Founded in 1872 as 'University College Wales, Aberystwyth', in what is now the Old College building near the sea front, it became a university in 1893.
[109] John Jones (1836-1921). He eventually received a civil list pension for his contribution to Welsh literature.
[110] Edward Breese (13 April 1835–10 March 1881).
[111] Randal Casson (10 February 1850–2 April 1914).

George now began his career in the adult world, starting to test his semi-independence. Because of the young man's youth and inexperience, Breese further agreed to personally keep an eye on his welfare. During this trial period, Breese invited David to call on him often at his home, Morfa Lodge, an invitation David accepted most readily. They also had work-related contact, as one of David's early morning tasks was to bring the office mail to the Breese home. Sometimes he was invited to meals, including at least once to Christmas dinner. Occasionally, he played with the Breese children; he was clearly winning the trust and approval of the family.

Fortune was starting to smile on the young man, blending, as so often in his life, his own achievements with favourable circumstances.

# 2

## YOUTH AND APPRENTICESHIP, 1879-1890

In Porthmadog, young Lloyd George proved his worth, and, on 24 January 1879, Uncle Lloyd called at the firm's premises and paid the required articles fee of £100–then two years' wages for a clerk–and £80 stamp duty, which was met from his life savings. On 28 January, just 11 days after his 16th birthday, David was formally articled to Randal Casson, the junior partner.

The partnership specialised in land law. In fact, they were the solicitors for the Tremadog Estate, consisting of the reclaimed land on which Porthmadog (Portmadoc until 1974) had been built. The firm had been founded by David Williams, uncle of Edward Breese and friend of William Madocks, landowner and Whig MP for Boston in Lincolnshire from 1802-1820, then for Chippenham in Wiltshire from 1820-1826.[112] [113] With his background and connections, Madocks was familiar with, and interested in, the benefits of land reclamation, landscaping and agricultural improvement, both in Lincolnshire and along the former marshes by the River Thames.

In 1798 Madocks had purchased the Tan-yr-Allt estate, on the western bank of Traeth Mawr, an immense expanse of sand and tidal marsh which formed the estuary of the Afon Glaslyn. He first set about reclaiming Penmorfa Marsh, some 1,082 acres of land, enclosing the area with a semi-circular two-mile long embankment of sand covered with turves, completed in 1802. Emboldened by this success, he next proposed constructing a substantial stone-filled, 1,600-yard embankment across the mouth of the Glaslyn–the Cob–enclosing a further 6,000 acres and providing safe passage across the estuary. He also began building the beautifully proportioned model town of Tremadog, which he planned himself. The building of the embankment, a colossal undertaking employing some 200-300 men, was completed in July 1811, breached by a great storm in February 1812, repaired and finally opened in September 1814, having cost some £60,000 [£6.11m in 2025], far more than the initial estimate of £23,500, but leaving a lasting legacy.

Tenants in the houses on the Tremadog Estate were required to insure their properties against fire

---

[112] David Williams (1799-1869), Liberal MP for Merionethshire, 1868-1869.

[113] William A. Madocks (1773-1828). Percy Bysshe Shelley lived at Plas Tan-yr-Allt with his first wife Harriet from September 1812–February 1813; after an alleged assassination attempt, the Shelley's briefly decamped to stay with the nearest gentleman in the area who they trusted, one David Ellis-Nanney (1759-1819), seven miles away: Nanney was Squire of Gwynfryn at Llanystumdwy, and Attorney-General for North Wales. Dying without issue, he bequeathed his estate to his nephew, Owen Jones of Bryn-hir, on condition that he assume the name of Ellis-Nanney. Owen was the father of Sir H. J. Ellis-Nanney, the unsuccessful opponent of Lloyd George in Caernarvon Boroughs in 1890! In 1851 Ellen M. Greaves, the mother of Lloyd George's friend Clough Williams-Ellis, was born at Tan-y-Allt; between 1886-1891 Randal Casson's widowed mother-in-law, Lady Lucy Nisbet, lived there. Current owners Mark White and Howard Mattingley have been most gracious and informative hosts on numerous visits, often partly for local research purposes.

with Breese, Jones and Casson, and the company's most junior employee was naturally delegated to be the one to collect the rents and premiums. The accounts ledgers show that, on 12 November 1878, Lloyd George received 15 shillings from the company's cashier for delivering leases, engrossing mortgages, examining rate appeals and attending court hearings in order to be able to report upon them.[114] His studies were concentrated on land law, Joshua Williams *Principles of the Law of Real Property* being his handbook.[115]

The issue of land was an important one to Lloyd George in many ways, and it seems likely that his experiences at this time coloured his views for the rest of his life. He always made a distinction between the kind of landowner who improved their property and so deserved higher rents, and those who merely exploited increases in value that they had not contributed to. Some 30 years later, when the price of land in the Thames Basin increased from three pounds to £3,000 an acre, solely due to the decision of the Port of London to expand its docks and harbour facilities, Lloyd George compared the undeserving beneficiaries with William Madocks. He had reclaimed Portmadoc from the sea but still charged reasonable rents and sold houses to sitting tenants at affordable prices. It is perhaps not too great a stretch to think that some of his own land improvement schemes on the poor soils of his estate at Churt in his later years were in much the same vein, making land productive for the benefit of all.

His experiences in Porthmadog had a further effect on Lloyd George's developing outlook. The authors of *Porthmadog Ships* make the point that:

> It is as well to remember, when reading his speeches during the debates on the Merchant Navy or considering his crucial role in the matter of convoys in the First World War, that Lloyd George had been a young solicitor who had walked the quays of Porthmadog near to his offices, that he had grown up among the seamen who manned Porthmadog ships, and that his sister had married a master mariner from a nearby village.[116]

The senior partner in Lloyd George's new firm, Edward Breese, was Clerk of the Peace, and Clerk of the Lieutenancy of the County of Merioneth, and in politics, a Liberal, being the Party's agent for Merioneth and South Caernarvonshire. He was thus active in local electioneering. Of the young Lloyd George, Breese said at the time "Mark that lad, some day he will be one of the leading men in the land. I have never known anyone who can master a thing so quickly as he can."[117]

Lloyd George had a broad apprenticeship:

> All the various matters appertaining to county administration that fell within the jurisdiction of the Quarter Sessions previous to the creation of the County Councils–matters dealing with

[114] George, *Making Of Lloyd George*, p29.
[115] First published in 1845, the work ran to 18 editions in the 19th Century.
[116] E. Hughes and A. Eames, *Porthmadog Ships*, 1975, Caernarfon, Gwynedd Archives Service, p52.
[117] Edwards, 1913, Vol.II, p76: W. W. Davies, p45.

> agricultural rating, assessments of land and houses, as well as matters that hinged upon the administration of licensing and criminal law–came almost daily within the sphere of his observation and duty, and as a result his knowledge rapidly increased.[118]

The testimony of a fellow, more senior clerk who worked with Lloyd George at this time throws interesting light on his character. J. Jones Morris, afterwards a solicitor in Porthmadog, recollected:

> I was articled to Robert Jones… and… I remember Mr. David Lloyd George coming to the office and being articled to Mr. Randal Casson… We sat for some time at the same desk. In the first months of his articleship he used to come daily from Llanystumdwy, and he invariably carried a book with him. I well recollect that Hallam's *History of England* was the first book that he brought.[119] I remember riding over to Llanystumdwy to obtain his signature, as well as that of his mother, in connection with his articles; and I particularly remember that, after he had been at the office only a few weeks, he prepared a summons, for some offence or other, to an applicant. I told him then what I myself had been told, that we were to be very careful in the preparation of the summonses, and that on no account were they to go out of the office until they had been approved by one of the principals of the firm. In the particular summons which he had prepared there was a slight informality. I drew his attention to it and urged him not to prepare any summonses in the future without first submitting them to Mr. Casson. To this he replied in Welsh: *'Mae arnaf eisio dysgu'* (I want to learn)–a remark which may well be regarded as an index to his characteristic determination. I think that the first experience he obtained in accounts was when he kept the account of fines and fees of the firm, who at the time acted as Clerks to the Justices for two divisions–the Eifionydd division, in the County of Carnarvon, and the division of Ardudwy-moch-Artro, in the county of Merioneth.[120]

At this time, articled clerks were not paid a salary, and his mother Elizabeth, had to pay for his week-day lodgings, but Lloyd George had a working arrangement with the managing clerk at his office to assist him in the weekly house to house collection of industrial insurance premiums. The small sums he was given for this assistance therefore supplemented his weekly allowance. Porthmadog was rapidly expanding, with a fine harbour that sent large quantities of high-quality roofing slate from the Ffestiniog and Llanfrothen quarries all over the world. A mineral railway ran to Tremadog, and, to the north, there was an industrial area with foundries, timber sawmills, slate works, a flour mill, soda-pop plant and gasworks. Calling at the households to collect premiums from the workers "gave Lloyd George for the first time in his life an insight into the poverty and social deprivation suffered by *Y Werin*, the majority of the people."[121]

---

[118] Edwards, 1913, Vol.II, p75-76.

[119] Henry Hallam (1777-1859), barrister and historian. His conscientious use of sources in his *Constitutional History of England* (1827), covering 1485-1760, made it a standard of Whig constitutionalist history.

[120] Quoted in Edwards, 1913, Vol.II, p76-77.

[121] W. R. P. George, *88 Not Out*, p21.

In Porthmadog Lloyd George occasionally attended a small Baptist Chapel of his own sect, that of the Disciples of Christ. Nearby was a candle-house which used tallow from the local tannery to produce candles for the underground Ffestiniog slate quarries. The candlemaker was one John Roberts, deacon and frequent preacher at the chapel, yet another friend of Uncle Lloyd. Lloyd George was associated with this individual for several years, and the man clearly made an impression on him. In his diary for 24 April 1886, he noted: "J R is a socialist–an out-and-out one. We agree there."[122] Lloyd George's brother, William, remembered Roberts, later writing:

> The candle-house was situated in a by-street just behind the little chapel. It was a popular meeting place for young people who liked to congregate once the day's work was over to discuss topics of popular interest and Dafydd frequently joined them. John Roberts had very little that was good to say of either of the two great parties of those days, the Tory and the Liberal parties. 'A plague on both your houses' would be the phrase to describe his feelings towards them. He would declaim at length on the extravagance of the Royal Family and the corruption of the idle rich. When I think of the seeds scattered around in that dimly-lit tallow-shed I cannot help wondering how many of them found fertile ground in the heart of the young lawyer-to-be.[123]

It was at this point that Uncle Lloyd, handicapped by failing eyesight, gave up bootmaking, and took a lease on a small house, *Morfin*, on Tan-y-Grisiau Terrace, in Criccieth, owned by a leading member of his 'flock', a wealthy ironmonger, Griffith P. Williams of Eifion Stores.[124] The family moved there from Highgate in May 1880. Lloyd George seems to have had absolutely no qualms at leaving his childhood home. In his diary for Sunday 9 May, he recorded simply: "To Llanystumdwy & slept there for the last time, perhaps for ever." The next day he wrote frankly: "Left Llanystumdwy without one feeling of regret, remorse or longing."[125] The young man had rapidly expanding new horizons.

Despite his obviously genuine desire to improve and succeed at his work, there is a more than a hint that he was not perfectly suited to be an articled clerk, as his restless intellect, enthusiasm and imagination reached out for greater stimulation:

> It is an interesting fact that, ambitious as he was to succeed in the law, it was not long before he began to realise that the profession left untouched the main tracts of his chief interests. In those early years he would often complain of the irksome necessity of being tethered to a desk in order to pore over musty parchments with their archaic phraseology, or of attending petty sessions in the matter of petty offences, while great and vital issues, on which depended the health and welfare of the toiling millions, were being fought upon the broad field of battle. Such considerations often made him look with wistful eyes in the direction of the Press with its

---

122 Ibid., p21.
123 George, *My Brother And I*, p110-111.
124 Griffith Williams (1845-1917).
125https://viewer.library.wales/4922647#?c=&m=&s=&cv=44&manifest=https%3A%2F%2Fdamsssl.llgc.org.uk%2Fiiif%2F2.0%2F4922647%2Fmanifest.json&xywh=240%2C681%2C561%2C690&r=90. Retrieved 22 November 2020.

unrestricted opportunities for influencing public opinion.[126]

"I believe," he remarked on one occasion, during conversation, "that I should have made a good journalist." Most assuredly he would. He possessed in the highest degree the instinct of the true-born journalist. His unfailing resourcefulness of arresting phrase, his appreciation of the dramatic, together with his power, amounting to genius, for striking the popular imagination and for galvanising the elemental emotions of the masses into irresistible impulses, would have readily gained for him both place and power within the realm of 'the fourth estate.'"[127]

One cannot but concur with Edwards' shrewd observations, so accurate in summing up the roving energy of the man. And, indeed, it was at the very period that Lloyd George first 'broke into print', as he reached out to make a mark on the wider world, to try and change it for the better with his words:

> … in the autumn of the year 1880 the late Lord Salisbury delivered a speech at Taunton, in the course of which he assailed, with characteristic invective, the Liberal Ministry then in power. Lord Salisbury's gibes had the immediate effect of incensing the young clerk, and instinctively he sought the medium of the Press for the expression of his wounded feelings. Over the nom de plume of "Brutus"–the choice of which marks the trend of his Shakespearian predilections–he contributed an article to the columns of the North Wales Express–a weekly newspaper published at Carnarvon–in which he dealt in vigorous fashion with the offending speech. This was Mr. Lloyd George's first contribution in print, and so highly did the editor appraise its trenchant criticism that he accorded it a prominent place on the "leader" page. Emanating from a youth who was only in his seventeenth year, the article showed a fullness of political information, an intimacy with current politics, and a deftness of phraseology which would have done credit to an experienced politician. Even thus early did Mr. Lloyd George carry an old head upon young shoulders.[128]

His diary entries reveal the anxiety, the eager anticipation and pride which accompany a first appearance in print:

> November 1, 1880. –… Do not relish the idea of that refusal which Editor overwhelmed with a redundance of such trash will have to accord to some of them.
> November 5, 1880. –When I eagerly opened the "North Wales Express" this morning, I found my own contribution on same page as leading article. I had first of all looked up "Notices to Correspondents," expecting to find a refusal of my letter, but disappointed on the right side.[129]

126 Edwards, 1913, Vol.II, p78-79.
127 Ibid., p79.
128 Ibid., p79-80. Robert Gascoyne-Cecil, Marquess of Salisbury, (1830-1903), Tory Prime Minister, 25 June 1895–11 July 1902, the last Prime Minister to head their administration from the Lords. Salisbury delivered his speech on 26 October 1880.
129 Quoted in Du Parcq, Vol.I, p34.

Under the 'Political Shreds' column was printed Lloyd George's astonishingly mature article:

THE MARQUIS OF SALISBURY

He is a relic of what he has been; the ruins of a character which, if not noble, at least seemed to be stable. Office proved to be too much for him. It has shattered his reputation. The prejudice and rancour of his unalloyed Toryism he still retains, but the consistency and integrity of character which whilom graced these propensities have departed. As witness his latest public ebullition–a post-prandial speech at Taunton.

He offered some animadvertent and invidious remarks upon the "reticence" and "frugality of information" of the Government. Let us not doubt his sincerity. He may be congratulated upon his dismissal from office. It appears to have worked in him an incalculable change. He was unscrupulous, he is now squeamish. The practiser of mystery, he denounces reticence. Whereas conclusion of a secret convention (in a manner, be it noted, not altogether characterised by straightforwardness) was regarded as the height of statesmanship and no departure from political virtue, it appears now to his enlightened conscience that not divulging in the most uncompromising manner the minutest detail of the intentions and actions of Executive Government is a public grievance which ought to be resented. It is not for me to determine whether it be that the heinousness of his own offence has aroused him to such an extent to the iniquity of secrecy, or that he is subject to a common failing in humanity–the regarding as a virtue in ourselves what seems to be a vice in others. Anyway, the inconsistency is palpable. He further informed his audience that the Powers which had sent the naval demonstration to the coasts of Albania had met with "what amounts to a refusal" of their demands by the Porte. The premature and inconvenient discovery of secret conventions may be vamped by prevarication; but by what quirk, quibble, or distortion of language can a mind, even though trained with the greatest shuffler of the age, make out the concession of a demand to be its instant refusal? The Powers demanded Dulcigno [Ulcinj] for Montenegro, and the Porte has conceded its surrender. The proposed prosecution of the Irish leaders was declared to be of dubious wisdom. How then justify the futile prosecutions of the late Government? Was it its tendency to "oppression" and its "impossibility" which recommended the course to Lord Salisbury and his colleagues? It is not unlikely. Imperialism had a large share in their counsels, and it is patent, indeed admitted by the noble lord, that he has been a party to certain schemes and proposed transactions which he subsequently did not feel it his "bounden duty" to carry into execution, and he has sometimes scoffed at the possibility of "compelling their performance."

Toryism has not been barren of statesmen–real and not charlatan–statesmen who prized the honour of England above the interests of party–who really hated oppression and demonstrated their detestation of it, not by pleading immunity from condign punishment for the instigation of foul and atrocious crimes, but by the laudable assistance which they rendered in the name of England to weak nationalities in their desperate struggles for Liberty–for freedom from the yoke

> of inhuman despots–for very existence. By so much was the Canning[130] of ancient Toryism superior, nobler than the Salisbury of modern Conservatism.[131]

Du Parcq was the first to pick up on a very important aspect of Lloyd George's style and literary mannerisms at this time. That was the fact that Lloyd George was always a thorough first-language Welsh speaker, his whole train of thought was Welsh, something often glossed over even by Welsh authors too caught up in the issues of his being born in England and giving his great parliamentary speeches in English. Du Parcq–born in Jersey–astutely developed his argument:

> There is one striking feature of Mr. Lloyd George's intellectual development which has been little noticed. Opinions may differ as to the place he deserves among modern masters of English. We have to judge him as a speaker rather than as a writer, and his speeches owe so much of their effect to charm of voice and manner that one is a little doubtful whether these graces do not lend them a distinction which they might not achieve by their literary merit alone. It is safe to say, however, that his speeches, even when they are read in the tame surroundings of the library, bear comparison with those of most speakers of acknowledged distinction of the present day. His periods have not the well-rounded smoothness that characterises one of Lord Rosebery's orations… and he does not deal the short, sharp, smashing strokes which mark the eloquence of Mr. Asquith as they did that of Mr. Joseph Chamberlain.[132] But when the time comes to consider the oratory of his later years it will be found, as I venture to think, that he has forged out of the King's English a weapon at once of use and beauty. What is remarkable is that he has achieved these results with a language which is emphatically not his own.
>
> As an infant he heard some English, but from the day he first set foot in Llanystumdwy Welsh was the language of his early life.
>
> At school he learned English as English boys learn a foreign language. He speaks Welsh to this day whenever his listener can understand it. The accent of that language clings closely to most of those whose allegiance it has once claimed, and years of residence in England, together with the habitual use of the English tongue, are seldom sufficient to shake it off. If any accent is discernible in Mr. Lloyd George's speech, it is so slight as to be inconspicuous to the most sensitive critic. More than this, he has acquired for the purposes of his oratory a simple and easy English style. His early writings show that this end was not reached without constant and unremitting labours. In his youth he got much practice with his pen, and as a rule wrote in English… [H]is tendency was to use words which strike an English ear as pedantic in their archaism or pretentious in their length and rarity. That defect of style, common in those who begin to handle any language, is most general where a writer is embarking upon the partially known regions of an alien tongue…

---

130 George Canning (1770-1827), Secretary of State for Foreign Affairs (1822-1827), Prime Minister from April to August 1827.

131 Quoted in Du Parcq, Vol.I, p34-36.

132 Joseph Chamberlain (1836-1914), Mayor of Birmingham, 1873-1876, Liberal MP for Birmingham, 1876-1885, President of the Board of Trade, 1880-1885, Liberal Unionist MP for Birmingham West, 1886-1914, Secretary of State for the Colonies, 1895-1903.

> ... [His] notes of speeches or addresses [were] written roughly in pencil, with many interlineations and erasures, usually upon... any chance scrap of paper... It... was his habit for some years to write out his more important speeches and learn them by heart, while for slighter efforts he depended upon fairly full notes, unless necessity called for an impromptu effort.[133]

Later in life, Lloyd George gave an interview to Donald McCormick, shedding:

> ... light on his affinity with the River Dwyfor and the mountains of North Wales. When I seek for strength and courage I always say go to the mountains and the little streams for these qualities. That is where the greatest preachers of Wales have found their inspiration. You cannot beat it. 'The Banner of the Dawn', 'The mists of the mountains, which as they begin to rise give promise of a brighter day.' There you have it all...[134]

His revelation of the well-spring for his inspiration, and of his style of delivery, could not be made more clearly.

Randal Casson took his young clerk under his wing and even involved him in local politics, being a Gladstonian Liberal himself. On 25 March 1880, Lloyd George recorded that he "went up to Llanfrothen with Mr Casson with the intention of canvassing."[135] It was the time of the culmination of Gladstone's famous Midlothian campaign, since credited as the first modern political campaign, combining the passion of Gladstone's extraordinary oratory, and the structuring of appearances as media events, with the intention of gaining maximum impact in the morning and evening newspapers. It set the stage both for Gladstone's personal comeback as a politician and for the Liberals decisive return to power in the general election of 31 March–27 April that year. In Caernarvonshire, on 6 April, Liberal challenger Watkin Williams[136] decisively trounced the sitting Tory, George Douglas-Pennant[137]. The youthful Lloyd George was clearly being swept along in the tide, recording optimistically in his diary the next day that the result was "victory beyond the most sanguine expectations... a great blow to landlord terrorism."[138]

A few months after the election, Williams resigned on being appointed a judge of the Queen's Bench Division of the High Court of Justice. William Rathbone[139], a Liverpool merchant and noted philanthropist, was selected to fight the constituency for the Liberals in the by-election of 2 December 1880, the Tory candidate being Hugh Ellis-Nanney. The choice of this opposing candidate unleashed a new antagonistic energy in the young Lloyd George, still only 17. He wrote a long, but incisive, hard-

---

133 Du Parcq, Vol.I, p52-53.
134 McCormick, p20.
135 George, *Making Of Lloyd George*, p93. Of course, he cannot have known how his association with Llanfrothen would make him famous throughout Wales only eight years later.
136 Sir Charles Watkin Williams (1828-1884).
137 George Douglas-Pennant, 2nd Baron Penrhyn (1836-1907), owner of the 72,000 acre Penrhyn Estate, including Bethesda quarry, with 3,000 quarrymen, in good years producing £150,000 [£24.92m in 2025] a year.
138https://viewer.library.wales/4922647#?c=&m=&s=&cv=34&manifest=https%3A%2F%2Fdamsssl.llgc.org.uk%2Fiiif%2F2.0%2F4922647%2Fmanifest.json&xywh=509%2C-119%2C1112%2C1370&r=90. Retrieved 22 November 2020.
139 William Rathbone VI (1819-1902), Liberal MP for Liverpool, 1868-1880, Carnarvonshire, 1881-1885, and Arfon, 1885-1895.

hitting article for the *North Wales Express* of 19 November, again under his pen-name 'Brutus', addressing Ellis-Nanney directly:

> You must be very diffident of the spell the Conservative name has upon the Conservative electorate to exchange it for such an unusual term, and to so plausibly qualify your support–"an *independent* support to the *Constitutional party*."
>
> You refer to an increase of taxation by the Liberal Government. When your ardour is tempered by the contempt of a great constituency you may then agree with me that it requires an unscrupulousness which is rare, even amongst the electioneering desperadoes, to publish such a statement. Did not politicians of the "Constitutional Party" clamour for the abolition of the malt tax? Did not the very same politicians when in office betray their infatuated friends, or more properly supporters–the farmers, by failing to redeem their promises and to justify their clamours? Was it not the abolition of this long-standing and crying grievance that necessitated the imposition of additional taxation? And, moreover, is it not merely temporary and thus in felicitous contrast in duration as well as purpose, to the burdens imposed by the late Government?
>
> You simulate indignation in your address, as elsewhere, at the "support given by the Government to the admission into Parliament" of a "professional opponent of the Christian religion."[140] This care of the interests of the Christian religion is praiseworthy, and you will doubtless be thanked for it by its representatives. But do you remember anything about a Government whose conduct was infinitely meretricious–whose policy made Afghan mothers husbandless, their children fatherless, and both homeless–saturated the Afghan snows with the blood of patriots, and drove hatred of our very name and presence at the point of the sword into the heart of the Afghan nation[141]; whose policy made Zululand moan the loss of thousands of its brave sons, devastated its fertile plains, turned its happy kraals into sombre mortuaries, and sacrificed its nationality upon a pyre erected with the carcases of its defenders?[142] You had better recant the defence of such a policy before you attack the present Government for acts which are infinitesimally less pernicious and more just. You revolt at tolerated scepticism–why not at perpetrated crime?
>
> I think that your reference to the conduct of some members of the Liberal Party with regard to Irish policy is hardly fair. You will admit that one member of a party cannot be held responsible for the extravagancies of another member. But is it not the unbudging and too successful resistance the party you belong to–the Constitutional Party–have accorded to every measure designed for the benefit of Ireland, together with the tyrannical oppressions of Irish landlords–are not these the true incentives of Irish outrages? Have not these goaded the people into crime? These outrages are not the dandlings of Liberal encouragement, as you would have it, but the prodigies of Tory oppression. A famishing nation are tired of catering for pampered

[140] Charles Bradlaugh (1833-1891), atheist, founder of the National Secular Society in 1866, Liberal MP for Northampton, 1880 until his death.

[141] The Second Anglo-Afghan War of November 1878–September 1880, which led to Afghanistan becoming a British Protectorate.

[142] The Anglo-Zulu War of January–July 1879, which led to the annexation of the Zulu Kingdom.

landlords, and we have the sight of a few supercilious and exacting landlords starving a race, and a race in arms against these landlords.

You speak of the "so-called Concert of Europe." Why insert "so-called"? Is it not a generally recognised principle amongst "patriotic Welshmen" that things should be called just what they are? I can answer without presumption for the Liberal and unpatriotic(?) section of Welshmen that such is the case with them. It strikes me that the word is superfluous, if it was not meant to answer your purposes by making up in words what your address lacks in wisdom. How the conduct of the Government in relation to the Concert of Europe imperils the peace of the Continent seems to me obscure. You certainly do not mean to suggest that the expulsion of that quarrel-generator, the Turk, from any part of Europe would imperil the general peace. If it would, then the sooner the better. And how do you make out the conduct of the Government does not tend to the dignity of England? Did the demonstration which the late Government indulged in, for a purpose far more unworthy of England, tend to anyone's dignity? That demonstration which was sent to give England's veto to the enfranchising career of the liberator of enthralled millions, which paraded England's power and registered it in the Bulgarian heart as the mainstay of despotism and the stifler of aspiring liberty.[143]

The complaint as to undue taxation of the agricultural and mining interests comes with bad grace from you.

When, during the unexampled depression of trade which we are now happily surviving, when almost every landlord throughout the kingdom returned a heavy percentage of his rent, did not you increase the rents of your tenants? If you feel that agricultural interests are too heavily burdened, return some of your own exacting tributes, and I have no doubt but that the tenants will feel that it is more an act of justice than generosity on your part; and as to mining interests, it is loudly broached that they have not received the attention which they deserved at your hands.

You vaunt your Welsh origin, and I find mural literature stating your patriotism to be the basis of the claim to the suffrages of the electors. Patriotism does not mean the sacrifice of national weal on the altar of national prejudice.

You profess great interest in the advancement of Higher Education in Wales. Mr. Rathbone has paid £10,000 towards the support of a college in Liverpool, and has given handsome donations to our Welsh University. How much have you paid for a claim to vaunt your interest in Intermediate Education in Wales? Is it true that you have not contributed a single mite towards the maintenance of the Welsh National University?

You profess to "give hearty support to all measures having for their object the promotion of the welfare of all classes in the country." Doth any good come out of Toryism? Are we to expect grapes from thorns or figs from thistles? It is quite as preposterous an idea expecting beneficial measures from Conservatives…

If my information be correct you are just the man whom the electors of Carnarvonshire would delight to reject with contumely.[144]

---

143 British pressure resulted in the newly created Bulgarian State, a product of the Treaty of San Stefano of 3 March 1878, being split again by the Treaty of Berlin on 13 July 1878.

144 Quoted in Edwards, 1913, Vol.II, p81-85.

The forthright, well-informed young man's views clearly 'chimed' with the electors, as they voted in favour of the Liberal candidate by the large majority of 1,029 votes. This election proved important to Lloyd George's political development, as it brought him into personal contact with Members of Parliament for the first time and, through his accompaniment of leading speakers to meetings, gave him some experience of political polemics. His diary records his involvement:

> *November 17th* Attended Mr Rathbone's meeting at Criccieth. Very enthusiastic, considering that it was regarded as the stronghold of Toryism… Rathbone is a very poor orator, but a sensible speaker. Mr W. S. Caine[145], M.P. for Scarboro', present. He is a very good speaker… They dragged Rathbone's carriage… all the way from Tremadoc to Portmadoc. Torch-bearers preceded and surrounded him. Altogether, the reception was most enthusiastic. Walked home to Criccieth, arriving about midnight.
>
> *November 26th* Brutus's address to the electors [his latest article] appears in large characters on the *North Wales Express* posters. Mr Nanney's meeting broke up in confusion.
>
> *November 30th* Starting 6.30 a.m for Dolbenmaen, and acting as Liberal Committeeman. Committee met in a stinted bed-chamber with scarcely enough light at times to strike off the right votes. Left in the evening as one of the Liberal custodians of the ballot box to Caernarvon.[146]

By this time Lloyd George was a handsome young man, but perhaps a little serious and unapproachable. On 24 September 1879, he noted that J. G. Jones, Clerk of the County Council Office, had told him that he was "regarded as independent and reserved". He took this as a criticism and proposed taking action to correct this perceived fault:

> I am not acquainted with the great majority of the people of Portmadoc and therefore cannot make myself familiar with them. However, I feel I cannot continue independent and reserved towards unacquainted people if I really mean to be a success as a lawyer. We should study people as well as their conveniences; besides, instead of making myself more respected I will make myself a perfect fool and a snob in the sight of the people. I would be regarded as a would-be nuisance to society and a plague in everyone's eyes. Let me try to make myself more affable towards everyone–a beggar even is not to be scorned… Clients are not to be gained by a 'hitherto-thou-shalt-come-and-no-further' mien and attitude. Think of it.[147]

Soon after this Edward Breese was accidentally shot in the eye during a pheasant shoot, Lloyd George recording in his diary for 1 October 1880: "a great calamity for him–heartily sorry for him, and the fact that he has lost an eye in pursuit of a cruel and degrading game of pheasant shooting–it will be an

---

145 William S. Caine (1842-1903), temperance advocate, Liberal MP for Scarborough, 1880-1885. His daughter Ruth (1871-1946) married John Herbert Lewis in 1897.
146 Quoted in George, *My Brother And I*, p36-37. Dolbenmaen is five miles north of Criccieth.
147 Ibid., p108.

eyesore to him and a heartburn thro' life."[148] In fact, this calamity severely affected Breese's health, leaving him little life left, as serious complications set in. On 10 March the following year he died in a nursing home in Marylebone, London, aged 45. The whole affair affected Lloyd George deeply, being Breese's protégé, as he recorded in his diary:

> *March 10th 1881*: About 6.30 telegram came that all was over with Mr. Breese. Cannot help crying. It is a great loss for me in many ways. He was a kind master, a thorough man.[149]

He attended the funeral at Holy Trinity in Penrhyndeudraeth five days later, recording:

> *March 15th 1881*: I never attended [a funeral in which] such respect and feeling was so generally manifested by relatives friends and spectators. A man capacitated for great things, obstructed in their attainment by ill-health, and finally altogether cut off by death, and thus prematurely! Cruel fate. He ruled supreme where he reigned by sheer force of character. As his coffin was lowered into the grave, the sun shone on it. Striking coincidence.[150]

On 7 November 1881, Lloyd George arrived in London to take the Law Society's intermediate examination. He was met by a relative who occupied his interest to alleviate pre-examination nerves by taking him to Madame Tussaud's ("horror of horrors. I shall never go again"), Charing Cross Station ("saw electric lighting for the first time"), and the British Museum ("interesting but too much of a good thing").[151] He also went to Covent Garden and heard famous soprano Adelina Patti sing in *Don Giovanni*.[152] On Friday, 10 November, he apprehensively sat the examination, going in at 9.40am: "It seemed ages waiting for the papers. When they came I cast an electric glance over them–sweating in the attempt. However, I found I could answer them pretty fairly–all of them."[153]

The following day, he visited the Palace of Westminster for the first time, and here his ambitions were kindled, noting in his diary:

> Went to the Houses of Parliament–very much disappointed with them. Grand buildings outside, but inside they are crabbed, small and suffocating, especially House of Commons. I will not say but that I eyed the assembly in a spirit similar to that in which William the Conqueror eyed England on his visit to Edward the Confessor, the region of his future domain. Oh, vanity![154]

On the evening following the examination, Lloyd George wrote to Randal Casson confidently assuring

---

148 Ibid., p113.
149 https://viewer.library.wales/4922754#?c=&m=&s=&cv=12&manifest=https%3A%2F%2Fdamsssl.llgc.org.uk%2Fiiif%2F2.0%2F4922754%2Fmanifest.json&xywh=0%2C-859%2C2848%2C3507&r=90. Retrieved 16 November 2020.
150 https://viewer.library.wales/4922754#?c=&m=&s=&cv=13&manifest=https%3A%2F%2Fdamsssl.llgc.org.uk%2Fiiif%2F2.0%2F4922754%2Fmanifest.json&xywh=816%2C394%2C702%2C864&r=90. Retrieved 16 November 2020.
151 George, *Making Of Lloyd George*, p101.
152 Cregier, p16.
153 Quoted in George, *My Brother And I*, p115.
154 George, *Making Of Lloyd George*, p101.

him that he had passed. Casson immediately replied: "I never had the least doubt myself but that you would find it quite easy and I can only congratulate you and wish you all speed in the future." He then made a most generous offer, accompanied by a postal order that would allow its acceptance: "By all means, stay away a week or a little longer if you like. There is plenty to see and do in one's first visit to London, and I hope you will enjoy yourself thoroughly."[155]

On his return from London, Lloyd George also briefly joined 'No 4 Company' of the Portmadoc Volunteer Force[156], which Casson had long and successfully captained, and began drilling on Saturdays. His association with the unit was not always a great success:

> At first I had intended to drill with the recruits but somehow by mistake I joined the battalion. A very awkward predicament. My braces broke just before the drill and my trousers were continually coming down.[157]

He did not tell Uncle Lloyd that he bore arms on a Saturday afternoon, sometimes drank beer with his patron and worked in his garden on a Sunday. A fortnight's camp at Morfa Conway in June 1882 had to somehow be explained as a holiday with friends; the highlight of the camp came when, "with fixed bayonets, they pursued a herd of cattle, which had strayed into the camp grounds off the mountainside."[158]

On 28 November 1881, Lloyd George was elected as a member of the Portmadoc Debating Society, and on 23 January 1882, he spoke for the very first time in a debate, on the motion "That Irish landlords should not be compensated in respect of any reduction of rents consequent on the Irish Land Act." He admitted in his diary that he had been nervous but:

> … when I proceeded to compare the condition of the Irish to the slave's, someone… bawled out 'No, No'. I fired up and turned to him and repeated what I had said previously, adding, as if it had only just struck me, 'the Irish tenants condition is, if anything, worse. The slave was hard worked–the Irish tenant was also ill fed'… This was the argument which was best delivered by me and most clearly expressed. The modulations of my voice was everything that I could desire–pitched in a high tenor voice which I sustained without tremor all through–rather too high, perhaps–all my other arguments were rather failures, i.e. no one seemed to understand–I had rather forgotten them… I did not get through my peroration as intended, nor did I deliver some epigrams to remarks that I had intended to. I sat down rather abruptly and was heartily cheered…[159]

---

155 Quoted in George, *My Brother And I*, p116.

156 The Volunteer Force of 1859-1908 was a precursor to the Territorials. Obituaries of 'Mr R Casson, Portmadoc', *North Wales Chronicle*, 9 April 1914, p5; 'The Late Mr Randal Casson', *Cambrian News*, 10 April 1914, p7. Casson died of pneumonia whilst on holiday in Sicily, being buried at Taormina.

157 George, *Making Of Lloyd George*, p104.

158 George, *My Brother And I*, p119.

159 Quoted in George, *My Brother And I*, p118.

Lloyd George was learning his craft; he had forgotten to include part of his argument, but he had not needed to refer to his notes, and he persisted with his contributions. The *North Wales Express* noted that his "argumentative and nervous speech shook the very foundations of the landlords' claim to compensation."[160]

In March 1882 he opened, on the affirmative side, a discussion on the question "Should the County Franchise be assimilated to the Borough Franchise?" On a division, ten voted for the affirmative, five for the negative. Though he was the Society's youngest member, he gained the reputation of being its ablest debater. In November he seconded a keenly contested motion on a matter of domestic policy, "That ladies be admitted members of this Society without payment of an annual subscription." It is regrettable to observe that this proposal, which must be allowed to have been chivalrous, however unsound in its financial aspect, was defeated by the casting vote of the chairman. He was a regular attender at its debates throughout the year:

> The range of its discussions during this period was wide and catholic. "Fair Trade versus Free Trade" was the subject one week; "Has Portmadoc reached the Climax of its Prosperity?" the next. Mr. [Charles] Bradlaugh and the Channel Tunnel, Trade Unionism and Phonetic Spelling, were discussed with equal vigour and enthusiasm. Mr. William Williams, his old schoolfellow, tells how, driving along the road on a winter's evening, he saw ahead of him the figure of a youth vigorously gesticulating as he tramped towards Portmadoc. Overtaken, the young man turned out to be David Lloyd George, declaiming as he walked the speech that was to be delivered at that night's meeting.[161]

Through all this, the young man was fast extending his range and depth of knowledge, his skills of oratory and critical analysis, and his self-confidence. At this time, he read A. M. Sullivan's *New Ireland* (1877), noting in his diary for 2 November 1882:

> It gives the Irish Question in a new light–of course he is partial to Irishmen, but I think on the whole he is about fair–anyhow it is a very cleverly written & refreshing book. It has had one effect on me–it has made me more Irish than before, even.[162]

He also read US reformer Henry George's best-selling *Progress And Poverty: An Inquiry into the Cause of Industrial Depressions and of Increase of Want with Increase of Wealth: The Remedy* (1879) and was "greatly impressed by it."[163] This reading, and the testing of his ideas and oratorical skills at the Society, was truly a crucible in his development as a public person and professional man.

---

160 *North Wales Express*, 3 February 1882, p8.

161 Du Parcq, Vol.I, p40-41.

162https://viewer.library.wales/4922754#?c=&m=&s=&cv=291&manifest=https%3A%2F%2Fdamsssl.llgc.org.uk%2Fiiif%2F2.0%2F4922754%2Fmanifest.json&xywh=1066%2C448%2C878%2C713. Retrieved 20 November 2020. Alexander Sullivan (1829-1884), Irish Nationalist politician and lawyer.

163 George, *My Brother And I*, p127. Henry George (1839-1897), American political economist and journalist.

Only one of his speeches at the meetings of the Society seems to have been reported in a newspaper. The following is an extract from the *North Wales Express* for November 24, 1882:

> Those persons who were in ignorance respecting the causes which led to the late war in Egypt would have done well to have visited the Portmadoc Debating Society on the 13th inst... Some of the speeches delivered were excellent… especially the speech of Mr. Lloyd George, [who], in a most eloquent harangue, full of clinching arguments, denounced the war as a wicked one. He showed that the Suez Canal was in no danger at the hands of Arabi, and that the Khedive, Tewfik Pasha, was as guilty of revolt as Arabi Pasha was, because the latter was not dismissed by him till he saw that the Army had gone over to Arabi. The foreign control was a great injustice to the Egyptians. The peasants of the country were being driven to the greatest poverty by the shameful taxation imposed by the rotten government of the country upon them. They were glad to get any man to come and deliver them from their pitiful state. Arabi Pasha was a man that had risen from amongst them–a man who knew all about their wants, because he had felt their wants himself.
>
> We read with regret that, in spite of Mr. Lloyd George's eloquence, there was a large majority in favour of the war, two members remaining neutral.
>
> The "*Carnarvon Herald*" was at least equally flattering in its references to this speech:
>
> The speech delivered by Mr. George against the war was very good, and it would probably have gained praise had it been delivered in the House of Commons. The matter, the words, and the style, together with the freedom with which it was delivered, took everybody by surprise, and made a deep impression upon all present.[164]

In August 1882, Lloyd George signed the anti-drinking pledge of the Blue Ribbon Society, a temperance movement. Despite this, he took a little while to catch up with his promise in practice, noting on 12 August concerning a legal trip from Porthmadog to Beddgelert:

> To Beddgelert with 11 o'clock coach… walking, fearfully hot, had my feet and face blistered… bathed them in Llyn Dinas, serving writs. Had a glass of port with police officer, had a glass of beer before starting for Port with J.B., another at Prince Llewelyn Beddgelert and a glass of port with some bread and chop at Thomas's house, so that's keeping the Blue Ribbon pledge grandly![165]

On 22 August 1882, a music festival was held within the walls of Criccieth Castle. Although mostly musical in nature, there were also a few other categories on the programme, including a prize for the best essay on the advantages and disadvantages of the 'Cash and Credit' systems. William George decided to enter this competition. When his brother finding out what he was doing, David said to him "You take Credit and I'll take Cash." Their resulting essay was duly submitted to the Secretary under

---

[164] Du Parcq, Vol.I, p41-42.

[165] Quoted in Price, 2006, p11.

the pseudonym 'Juventus Mundi', a name borrowed from the title of a book by Gladstone. On the day of the Festival, David was present at the adjudication, recording:

> Our Essay came tenth on the programme. A short adjudication during the reading of which my heart beat tumultuously especially towards the end when I saw prognostications of our success. He rather disapproved of the language–too many English words used–but he praised the style. He said that the treatment of the advantages of Credit (written by William) was very thorough but he ran down all those poste haste messages of ours as superficial.
>
> The Reverend John Owen, M.A. (Conductor) called, 'Juventus Mundi', and up I jumped and went on to the stage and told Owen it was myself and my brother, thereupon he cracked some jokes as to a joint concern. I appeared on the stage with my hat on my head and my whole nervousness had disappeared. I received £2 2., and was invested by Miss [M.] Whittington with the 1st Prize Essay I ever wrote. There was some cheering. Before the meeting was quite over I went and told Uncle. He was elated tho' he said that had he known then he would have tried to persuade me not to compete. He does not believe in these meetings.[166]

On 2 June 1883, the *Carnarvon and Denbigh Herald* published some contributions for a "literary stall" at a "Fancy Fair" at Caernarvon. The object of these contributions had been to encapsulate various people well known in Portmadoc and the neighbourhood with suitable quotations. Lloyd George was among them, and the verse attached to his name was a quotation from Dr Samuel Johnson:

> When first the college rolls receive his name,
> The young enthusiast quits his case for fame,
> Resistless burns the fever of renown,
> Caught from the strong contagion of the gown.

Lloyd George duly noted in his diary that day with considerable self-knowledge:

> Tit-bit poetry in 'Carnarvon and Denbigh Herald,' referring to my thirst for renown, etc. Perhaps(?) it will be gratified. I believe it depends entirely on what forces of pluck and *industry* I can muster.[167]

Lloyd George's Articles were due to expire on 25 January 1884. The day before his principal, Randal Casson, wrote to him candidly but warmly, enclosing a gift of £5 and looking back over their five-year association:

> Sometimes… a little apparent friction, but looking at it as I do, that one is under a considerable amount of responsibility in undertaking an articled pupil, I feel it better to err on the side of

166 Quoted in George, *My Brother And I*, p148.
167 Du Parcq, Vol.I, p42.

> apparently requiring too much than the easier and more usual course which is adopted. It is a great satisfaction to me to be able to tell you that I am gratified thoroughly with the industry and capability which you have evinced, and I look forward to a good future for you. You can always count on me as a good friend I hope–and I shall always do what I can for your welfare.[168]

Lloyd George replied gratefully the same day in like manner:

> The sentiments which you are good enough to express concerning my behaviour are to me truly encouraging and I cannot but ever regard it as a triumph to have won such expressions of esteem from a gentleman who I always knew to be sincere as well as discerning. As to the 'apparent frictions' you refer to, it behoves me to obliviate them as much as possible as I invariably found in the end that they were due to some blunders of my own; and I shall always appreciate the honourable motives which prompted you to take the pains you did to assist me to acquire competency in the profession you instructed me in.
>
> Your assurances of friendship and help for the future are necessarily very valuable to me and I trust that my conduct will never be such as to give you cause to retract them…[169]

In fact, there would be some future 'friction', but nothing irreparable. On the evening of 19 April 1884, Lloyd George set off for London to sit his final law examinations. He had been due to sit them in January, but a technicality regarding the dates of the examinations–his 21st birthday fell halfway through the sittings–had enforced a postponement, time he spent in revising hard, realising that this was a 'make-or-break' stage in his life.[170] Nephew W. R. P. George later recorded: "He was in a bad way in London sitting the final: 'bad headache and neuralgia'; 'to bed 11.30, weary and ill–almost crying'; 'nearly fainted in Holborn on my way to the Law Society's Hall in Chancery Lane'."[171] He sat the Finals on 22 and 23 April, along with 204 other candidates from all over the country. 61 of them, including Lloyd George, had also entered for the voluntary Honours Examination, the entries for which would only be considered if the marks obtained in the standard papers were significantly above the ordinary pass level.

After the ordeal was over, Lloyd George decided to stay on in London for a few days, sampling an eclectic mix of what the capital of the Empire had to offer. He visited a phrenologist in Ludgate Circus, who, no doubt ascertaining his subject's main concern, apparently informed him that he would one day be Prime Minister.[172] He also visited various Nonconformist chapels where he listened to some

---

168 Quoted in George, *My Brother And I*, p119.

169 Ibid., p120. See also D. Devlin, *The Casson Family In North Wales*, 2019, Llanrwst, Gwasg Carreg Gwalch, pp267-270. Casson kept Lloyd George's letter for the rest of his life.

170 Rowland, *Lloyd George*, p37.

171 Quoted in George, *88 Not Out*, p26.

172 Rowland, *Lloyd George*, p37. Lloyd George also consulted 'Professor' Joseph M. Severn–President of the British Phrenological Society in 1905–in April 1903 and November 1909. Severn reported that he was "a genius of a very high order" with "an important and great future ahead of him", that he was "naturally very progressive" with a "strong sense of justice", "capable of exerting an extended influence, highly beneficial to his fellow men in the progressive welfare of mankind."; J. M. Severn, "Phrenological Reading Of Mr. Lloyd George", in *The Business Head Of The Future*, 1913, London, International Psychic Gazette, p4-6.

of the best preachers of the day, including Charles Spurgeon at the Metropolitan Tabernacle in the Elephant and Castle, Southwark.[173]

On 28 April, he visited the House of Commons, having the satisfaction of listening to a parliamentary debate for the first time, stoking his political ambitions still higher. The principal business of the House that day was the opening of the Committee Stage of the Government's Reform Bill, the main element of which was the Liberal's desire to extend to country householders the franchise which Disraeli had conferred on borough householders in 1867. Lloyd George was most impressed by Prime Minister William Gladstone, then in his second term of office. He noted in his diary that evening:

> Heard the Grand Old Man. Is really grand–there is no one so outstanding. His voice is indescribable, rather husky at first, but when it clears up it is piercing and silvery. His manner is rather vehement, the way he dressed Raikes[174] brought the House and Gallery down. The scorn and bitterness of his voice was inimitable.[175]

News that he had passed the Final Examinations with Third Class Honours reached him on 9 May. On 8 July, he duly again travelled to London to be formally admitted to the Roll of Solicitors, along with the 157 other successful candidates. There were no First Class awards on this occasion, but three of the 61 Honours candidates had been placed in the Second Class and 19, including Lloyd George, in the Third.[176] Lloyd George was not impressed by the occasion, decrying "the perfectly ludicrous ceremony": "The Master of the Rolls, so far from having anything to do with it, was actually listening to some Q.C. at the time, and some fellow of a clerk swore us to a lawyerly demeanour in our profession at the back of the Court, and off we shambled to the Petty Bag Office to sign the rolls." "It is a shame", he concluded bitterly, "that articled clerks should be dragged all this way to undergo such a ridiculous farce, when money is scarce with them."[177]

In the late autumn of that year, Lloyd George penned three articles for the *North Wales Observer and Express*, under the heading "Nota Benes: by a J pen." The first, published on 5 September 1884, "castigated the local undemocratic nature of the Liberal hierarchy and parliamentary representation, demanding new style, more radical Welsh parliamentary candidates for the future and the need to adopt Chamberlainite policies."[178] The second, published on 17 October, dealt with Joseph Chamberlain, then the darling of the Radicals:

> Mr. Chamberlain is unquestionably the future leader of the people. Anyone who reads his speeches will know the reason why. He does not argue closely, like Sir Charles Dilke, nor does

---

173 Charles Spurgeon (1834-1892), 'Prince of Preachers' in the Reformed Baptist tradition.
174 Henry Raikes (1838-1891), Tory MP for Cambridge University, 1882-1891.
175 Quoted in George, *88 Not Out*, p26.
176 Rowland, *Lloyd George*, p39.
177 Du Parcq, Vol.I, p43; George, *My Brother And I, p120.*
178 Price, 2006, p16.

> he discourse with the polished eloquence of Mr. Trevelyan[179]; and yet his speeches have far greater effect upon public opinion that those of either of the two. The explanation is ready. He understands the sympathies of his countrymen. It is therefore that he speaks intelligibly and straightforwardly, like a man who is proud of the opinions which he holds. He has no dread of Tory misconstruction. He does not hedge round his sentences, lest the viper sting them. He is a Radical, and doesn't care who knows it as long as the people do. He is convinced that the aristocracy stands in the way of the development of the rights of man, and he says so unflinchingly, though he be howled at as an ill-mannered demagogue by the whole kennelry of gorged aristocracy, and of their fawning minions.[180]

Soon, Lloyd George and others would be cruelly disabused of their belief in Chamberlain as he veered to the Right over Irish Home Rule in 1886, but for now he was a reforming hero. Meanwhile, Lloyd George's third article, published on 7 November, was again critical of the local Liberal party, demanding more democracy, as the 1885 general election loomed.

The fact was that, by now, he was more interested in the Portmadoc Debating Society and politics than in the minutiae of the law. Nevertheless, Casson offered him a place as assistant solicitor, at a salary of one pound a week, with commission for any new business he brought in. At first, Lloyd George was put in charge of a small office in Criccieth, but the premises were soon closed down due to lack of business. Next it was proposed that he should become the managing clerk of an office that the firm were considering opening in Dolgellau, some 19 miles away, but on consideration the idea was rejected.[181]

By this time the relations between Casson and Lloyd George had soured, the younger man chafing at his inferior position, as his own ambitions grew. On 28 May 1884 he recorded in his diary:

> Had a sharp tussle with Mr. Casson in early morning. He interfered in what I thought a very supercilious and offensive manner and I naturally resented it. It is now I am beginning to realise what I had all along feared – that he would treat me as the rest of his urchins directly I became one of them. It struck me forcibly upon brooding the matter that I would do far better myself than by hanging on to him.[182]

He determined to set up in privately, in competition with his old mentor, establishing his own practice at the end of the year in the back parlour of his uncle's house, *Morfin*, on Tan-y-Grisiau Terrace in Criccieth. And so, up went a small brass plate on the front door– 'D. Lloyd George, Solicitor'. Satisfying as this was, Lloyd George was nonetheless anxious:

> After an apprenticeship to the law of five and a half years my uncle's small fortune was exhausted, and I had not money enough left even to buy my robes. In Wales a solicitor has to

---

179 Sir George Otto Trevelyan (1838-1928), Liberal MP for Hawick Burghs, 1868-1886.
180 Quoted in Du Parcq, Vol.I, p60.
181 Rowland, *Lloyd George*, p39-40.
182 https://viewer.library.wales/4923077#?xywh=552%2C917%2C1021%2C540&cv=117. Retrieved 5 August 2025.

> appear robed before he gets audience to the County Court. The robes cost about three guineas, and, if I remember rightly, I had to wait till I had got one or two cases before I was able to meet this outlay.[183]

Criccieth was a prosperous, growing town at the time, its population rising from 901 in 1871, to 1,213 in 1881 and 1,507 in 1891. Part of this prosperity was due to the rise in late Victorian seasonal tourism; the Aberystwyth and Welsh Coast Railway having opened its station there on 2 September 1867. In their first years in Criccieth, the Lloyd family needed to supplement their income by taking in visitors in the summer months. With limited space and five adults in the family, this meant some inconvenience and even discomfort, especially when it involved Lloyd George and his brother William having to sleep in the attic. Occasionally, it brought some interest, as was the case for a few weeks in August 1884 when the visitor was the novelist H. Rider Haggard, himself just about to be called to the Bar, who may have related some of his colourful impressions of South Africa to Lloyd George.[184] William later recalled "how thrilled I was that the author of *King Solomon's Mines* was staying in the house with us. This made quite an impression on both Dafydd and myself."[185]

Regarding legal practice, Casson might have had reason to resent his young protégé for abandoning his firm and setting up a rival business. But ultimately, they remained on cordial terms. Lloyd George made his first appearance in court as an advocate on 13 January 1885, on behalf of Owen Price, the County Court bailiff in Porthmadog. He recorded that day's events later:

> At Portmadoc. Whilst getting my dinner at Temperance Price asked me to defend someone for assault. This was about 12.20. Saw parties, rushed down to Police Station. Very much tempted at first to decline to go. Although I felt so very timorous got fellow off to his immense joy… got 14/6 for case.[186]

Gradually, further successes followed, and he quickly became "a familiar figure in the police courts and the county courts of Porthmadog, Ffestiniog, Pwllheli and Dolgellau, where he was generally highly regarded as a quick-witted, sharp-tongued, contentious advocate, fully capable of mastering a brief very quickly and completely."[187]

Uncle Lloyd kept a diary, in which he recorded some of his nephew's doings in this early phase of his legal life:

> 16th. Pentrefelin County Court. D.Ll.G. making his debut.–Allanson against him–victorious on every point–a very complicated case and most unmanageable parties–he can hardly meet more

[183] Quoted in Edwards, 1913, Vol.II, p98.

[184] Grigg, *Young Lloyd George*, p38-39; T. Pocock, *Rider Haggard And The Lost Empire*, 1993, London, Weidenfeld and Nicolson, p60.

[185] George, *My Brother and I*, p85. H. Rider Haggard (1856-1925) published *King Solomon's Mines* in September 1885.

[186] Diary Entry for 30 January 1885. Quoted in George, *My Brother And I*, p136.

[187] Jones, *Lloyd George And The Carnarvon Boroughs*, p28.

> critical circumstances during a long career, if spared, than this, of its kind. Had another case offered him in Court, R.E. Harlech, and succeeded in both.
>
> 8th. Wet again. D. Ll.G. waited until the 11 o'clock train in order to interview J.O. and R.O. He advised the former not to send him on his behalf to Caernarvon with such a case.–Much trouble in persuading him that to give the best advice is a lawyer's duty, not to go to law.
>
> D. Ll.G. off to Ffestiniog–his first day of attendance in his professional capacity–got several cases there and at Penrhyn–name not placed on window a drawback I believe–home by 8 train–several callers–…
>
> 30th. … D.Ll.G. appeared for the first time in Portmadoc Magistrates Court for people from the neighbourhood of Garn. Won with praise, and promised every case from there before long.[188]

Local biographer W. W. Davies noted that:

> For a long time he was the *bête noire* of County Justices, who had always been accustomed to a good deal of deference on the part of solicitors, notwithstanding their manifold bias in favour of all matters pertaining to the gentry and their rights. It was something unpleasantly new for them to be confronted by a young man who cared not a straw for the gentry or their rights, and whose bias was clearly in favour of the under-dog. For some time relations were far from cordial; and what the newspapers call "scenes in court" were of frequent occurrence.[189]

Here can be seen the dovetailing of Lloyd George's legal and political work into the same stream, much as the Dwyfach and Dwyfawr merged at Llanystumdwy, and that together, they created a powerful impetus in favour of ordinary working people, particularly at this time of poor Welsh workers against their gentrified English oppressors. Sometimes, Lloyd George relied upon his ready wit in order to make his point, and then, "as in after years in the House of Commons, it brought him, in the long run, a richer reward than did the fierce invective in which he was, in those early days, too prone to indulge."[190]

One such example comes from the Merionethshire Sessions, then presided over by Samuel Pope, QC.[191] W. W. Davies again:

> It appears that Lloyd George was laying down certain disputable legal propositions with more assurance than befits a young advocate. "No, no," interposed Mr. Pope, "this won't do. Mr. Lloyd George is laying down the law as if he were a Judge in the Court of Appeal. It is necessary for me to point out that we here do not believe in the infallibility of Mr. Lloyd George." Quick as lightning came the reply: "Neither do we in these parts believe in the infallibility of a Pope."

---

188 Quoted in W. W. Davies, p49-50.

189 W. W. Davies, p51.

190 Ibid., p52.

191 Samuel Pope (1826-1901), Liberal, temperance advocate, freemason, a leader of the parliamentary bar.

> The Court dissolved in laughter, in which Mr. Pope himself led the way; and the atmosphere was cleared of the thunderclouds which had previously been gathering so thick and heavy.[192]

He also continued to be influenced by his boyhood hero, 'Honest Abe', Abraham Lincoln. When Lloyd George set up his own practice as a solicitor, he came across a precept of Lincoln's, who had himself been a struggling lawyer, before he became a politician. It ran: "As a peace-maker the lawyer has a superior opportunity of being a good man… Never stir up litigation… There's a vague popular belief that lawyers are necessarily dishonest… Let no young man choosing the law for a calling for a moment yield to the popular belief." Lloyd George copied and framed this statement and kept it on his desk as a reminder.[193]

In June 1885, Lloyd George appeared before a new judge, Mr Brynmor Jones[194], in several actions at the Pwllheli County Court within a fortnight of the latter's appointment, and Lloyd George later confessed that, while the judge was deciding points of law and giving judgment he was quietly taking stock of him. He noted with the keenest gratification his shrewdness and cleverness, his great knowledge of the law, and his unfailing courtesy to solicitors who appeared before him. "If he continues like this," wrote the young advocate in his enthusiasm, "he is just the sort of fellow I'd wish."[195]

Brynmor Jones was also observing the young solicitor, as he later recounted to J. Hugh Edwards:

> It was in June, 1885, that I was appointed judge of the Mid-Wales County Court Circuit… and in due course held a court at Portmadoc. On my first visit there I tried a few defended cases in which solicitors were engaged. In one there appeared a particularly boyish-looking advocate, thin and rather pale. I was attracted by his youthful appearance and his talking voice, as well as by a certain earnest, eager, but yet restrained manner, and remember noticing as the hearing proceeded that his way of handling his case was in strong contrast with the inexperience which might be presumed from his youthfulness. A point of law arose, he was ready with his authorities; he asked no dangerous questions in cross-examination; he stuck to relevant points; he made no attempt at eloquence in his speech. I gave judgment for his client on quite sound but rather technical grounds, and recollect the humorous look (I see the papers call it now the "merry twinkle") in his eyes when he asked for costs and got them.
>
> … When the case was over I said to the Deputy Registrar: "What's the name of that young fellow?" He replied, "David Lloyd George–only just admitted." I said, "Well, he did that case uncommonly well. He'll get on."[196]

---

192 W. W. Davies, p53. Lloyd George's jest was relatively topical, as the doctrine of Papal Infallibility had only been declared in the Dogmatic Constitution *Pastor aeternus* at the First Vatican Council on 18 July 1870.

193 Owen, p29. Lincoln made the notes on 1 July 1850 (?) for a lecture he intended to give, though it is not known whether he ever actually delivered it. *Complete Works of Abraham Lincoln*, Vol.2, 1905, Eds. J. G. Nicolay and J. Hay, New York, Tandy-Thomas: *Notes For Law Lecture,* p142-143.

194 David Brynmor Jones (1851-1921), Liberal MP for Stroud, 1892-1895, Swansea District, 1895-1914, later Chairman of the Welsh Parliamentary Party.

195 Quoted in Edwards, 1913, Vol.II, p126.

196 Ibid., p127-128.

It was in June 1884 that Lloyd George first met the girl who was to become his wife, Margaret (or 'Maggie') Owen, "a sensible girl without fuss or affectation about her" as he recorded at the time.[197] Maggie was over three years younger than Lloyd George, having been born on 4 November 1866, the only child of Richard and Mary Owen of *Mynydd Ednyfed Fawr,* a substantial farmstead of 180 acres on a good site to the north of Criccieth. Richard was a deacon in the Calvinistic Methodist community of *Capel Mawr* in Criccieth–and a supporter of the Liberal Party. He claimed descent from Owain Gwynedd[198], while Maggie herself liked to claim that she was directly descended from Hywel Dda[199] on her mother's side. Maggie was born with '*bys yr Eifion*' (Eifion's finger), a crooked little finger on her right hand that, tradition had it, marked those descended from the 14th Century knight Hywel y Fwyall (Howell of the Battle-axe), whose crooked finger gave him the sure grip which helped make him one of the best axemen in Wales. Howel was one of the Welshmen who fought at the Battle of Poitiers in 1356, and was knighted by the Black Prince, receiving the constableship of Criccieth Castle in 1359. Maggie delighted in bearing the physical mark of her nobility.[200] She had been one of the first boarders at Dr Williams' School in Dolgellau, which opened its doors on 7 February 1878, with 30 pupils, and Miss Emily Armstrong as first Headmistress. Maggie perfected her reading and writing, developed a passion for art and gardening, but a marked distaste for cooking and mundane household chores, as reflected in her report for the third term of 1879.[201]

On 13 July 1885, Lloyd George's sister Pollie organised a day trip on the steamer *Snowdon* from Portmadoc to Bardsey Island, two miles west of the tip of the Llŷn Peninsula. 16 young men and women were in the group, all members of local chapels. For two of them, it would be a momentous day. On arriving at the tiny but beautiful island, the group soon split up into groups of two or three to explore and eat their picnic lunches. David found himself in the company of his sister and one of her friends. He subsequently recorded in his diary for that day: "I was with Miss Owen, Mynydd Ednyfed, mostly. MEG (my sister) with us–Enjoyed myself immensely."[202] From now on, unlike his few previous brief meetings with her, David was taken by Maggie's grace and quiet confidence, and pretty face with lively grey-blue eyes. A mutual attraction had begun to spark between the two young people.

By 1885, Lloyd George had established a reputation as a fiery young orator on Liberal platforms. He took some part in the Merioneth contest in the general election of 24 November–18 December 1885, the first to be held after the Representation of the People Act, 1884–the 'Third Reform Act'–and the Redistribution of Seats Act, 1885. These Acts had considerably expanded the size of the

---

197 George, *Making Of Lloyd George*, p136.

198 Owain ap Gruffudd (c.1100 - 23 or 28 November 1170), King of Gwynedd, North Wales, from 1137 until his death. Called Owain Mawr (*Owain the Great*), the first to be styled "Prince of Wales".

199 Hywel Dda (*Hywel the Good*) (c.880-950), King of Deheubarth who by 942 ruled most of Wales. Esteemed among medieval Welsh rulers, codifier of traditional Welsh law, thenceforth known as the Laws of Hywel Dda.

200 Lloyd George, *Dame Margaret*, p42; Hague, p57. Howel y Fwyall (fl.1356 - died 1381).

201 https://www.peoplescollection.wales/items/387712 . Retrieved 12 December 2018. For the school's early years see W. Gareth Evans *An Oasis In the Wilderness: The Establishment of Dr Williams' School, Dolgellau, Journal of the Merioneth Historical and Record Society*, XII, II, 1995, p155-176.

202 George, *Making Of Lloyd George*, p138.

electorate to around 60% of the adult male population, over 5,500,000. In Merioneth, the electorate expanded from 3,469 in 1880, to 9,333 in 1885.[203] Lloyd George naturally saw this as fertile ground for radical campaigning. In Blaenau Ffestiniog, he joined '*Senedd Bethania'*, the 'Bethania Parliament', another parliamentary debating society, its proceedings and his part in them being given regular publicity in the pages of '*Yr Herald Cymraeg*'.[204]

During 1885, he spoke fierily several times in both Merionethshire and Caernarfonshire, espousing radical Welsh nationalism, and in support of Chamberlain's 'Radical Programme'. Dubbed the 'Unauthorised Programme', it advocated land and housing reform, more direct taxation, free public education, the disestablishment of the Anglican Church, universal male suffrage, and increased protection for trade unions. In the election, Lloyd George backed the quarrymen's choice, Morgan Lloyd[205], against the official Liberal candidate, Henry Robertson.[206] Lloyd came a respectable third, after the Tory candidate and the winner, Robertson. However, Lloyd George had made his mark. In Caernarfon Boroughs, he supported Sir Love Jones-Parry, and in Eifion, J. Bryn Roberts, both moderate Gladstonians.

In the election overall, the Liberals won the most seats (319) but failed to gain an overall majority. As the Irish Nationalists (86) held the balance of power between them and the Tories (247), who sat with an increasing number of allied Unionist MPs, this exacerbated divisions within the Liberals over Irish Home Rule and led to a Liberal split and another general election in 1886.

Meanwhile, Lloyd George made a particular impact in a brilliant performance in front of a crowd of some 1,800 slate quarrymen packed into the imposing, octagonal-fronted Market Hall at Blaenau Ffestiniog[207] on 12 February 1886, when the main speaker was the Irish nationalist and land leaguer Michael Davitt.[208] Lloyd George recorded in his diary with great self-possession:

> I went to meeting having no intention of spouting when M. D. Jones[209] announced… that I was to speak there. I was astounded. Hall packed, many keen men there in good position. However, having listened to Michael Davitt I retired to a room, a sort of lobby, and… I tried to spin out a speech. Got on very well. I had a few ideas upon the question so I determined to set them together with a few extempore ideas. I hit upon a good joke, I think, about Michael wrestling with the devil, and one or two other good hits. As my turn approached and it was getting late I decided not to speak; when egged on I had made up my mind simply to apologise to them on

---

[203] Price, 2006, p21.

[204] Ibid., p22.

[205] Morgan Lloyd (1822-1893), Barrister, Liberal MP for Beaumaris from 1874 until the seat was redistributed, JP for Merioneth, he stood as an Independent Liberal. Like Robertson, an opponent of Irish Home Rule.

[206] Henry Robertson (1816-1888), Scottish mining engineer, railway builder, industrialist and Liberal MP for Shrewsbury, 1862-1865, 1874-1885, then Merioneth, 1885-1886.

[207] By 1881 the population of Blaenau was 11,274. The Market Hall was opened in 1864, extended in the early 1880s. Falling into disuse in 1985, in 2021 it was given Grade II Listed Status.

[208] Michael Davitt (*Mícheál Mac Dáibhéid*; 1846-1906), one-armed Irish republican and agrarian campaigner, founder of the Irish National Land League, 1879, Irish National Federation MP for North-East Cork, 8 February–9 May 1893, South Mayo, 19 July 1895–25 October 1899.

[209] Reverend Michael D. Jones (1822-1898), land reformer, pioneer of the Welsh settlement in Patagonia known as Y Wladfa, a father of modern Welsh nationalism. Principal of Bala Independent Theological College, 1855-1892.

> the ground of the lateness of the hour and the fact of my having not received notice. I thought I would just try on the joke about Michael. I did so and it created a roar of laughter. The audience began to listen and beamed at me. Thus encouraged I went on with cordial and warm plaudits, my extempore bits taking best, evoking two rounds of cheering. I was now on my legs and I spoke with great warmth and vigour both of gesture and of voice. When I sat down there was loud cheering, and I felt I had made my mark at Ffestiniog and what was better there were present men from all the surrounding districts from Garn to Llanrwst and thence to Trawsfynydd. I have made a good thing of a splendid opportunity. Regarding Michael Davitt I am very favourably impressed by his presence–he appears to be very earnest and sincere … he was listened to with unflagging interest & what is still more astonishing the audience caught his points tho' probably not more than ⅓rd understood him … told me that… tho' he could not understand me he knew very well that I was very eloquent.[210]

Early biographer J. Hugh Edwards also noted this landmark occasion:

> At the close of Davitt's address Michael Jones, who was in the chair, turned round to Mr. Lloyd George, who was seated near him on the platform, and requested him to move a vote of thanks to the Irishman. At once he rose and delivered a speech which completely captivated the audience with its scintillations of wit, its flashes of phrase, and still more so by the passion of its appeal. The speech reflected all those inherent characteristics which have since made him one of the most effective of public speakers. "I confess," he declared at the outset, "that when I look at the two Michaels on the platform I am reminded of the fight that the Archangel Michael had with Satan. Though that Michael, being single-handed, was unable to dispose of Old Nick, I trust that two Michaels will be able to bring the cause of the farmers and the working men to a successful issue."
>
> Mindful of the antipathy of a large section of the community in regard to Michael Davitt, the young orator boldly seized the opportunity of delivering a glowing eulogy of the man and his work. "Mr. Michael Davitt," he declared, "is a man who has not only done much for humanity but has also suffered much for humanity. To oppose a man because he does not belong to our nation," he added, with a touch of contempt in both voice and countenance, "is most narrow-minded, and contrary to the principles of our religion."
>
> On that occasion, as so frequently since, his dexterity in calling up at will striking illustrations from the Scriptures came readily to his aid, and with a Welsh audience there is nothing that makes so direct and overpowering an appeal as a Biblical reference skilfully handled. "You remember the parable of the man who fell among thieves," he continued, "and you do not require to be reminded that his neighbour was not the man who belonged to his own nation, but a stranger from Samaria–not the priest and the Levite. The farmers of Wales have fallen among thieves," he added in quick application of the force of the simile; "but the Welsh priests are a great deal worse than the priest referred to in the parable. The priest in the parable merely passed by without taking notice of the man, but the Welsh priests have joined the robbers. Mr.

210 https://www.peoplescollection.wales/items/11418 Diary of DLG for 1886, Images 33, 34. Retrieved 11 December 2019.

Michael Davitt, on the other hand, is the stranger from Samaria–an Irishman–who has come here to bind up our wounds. Let us respect him on that account. The people who have objected to Michael Davitt's visit to Wales are those who on bended knees have begged princes to come into Wales to preside over Eisteddfodau. Why, then, object to the introduction into the district of a man who has done so much for his fellow men?" The appeal was irresistible, and it is said, on the authority of one who was present at that gathering, that its fervour was such that the sullen opposition to Michael Davitt was there and then dissipated amid the sound of a great cheer.

Then, turning from the man to the movement shadowed in him, the youthful orator proceeded: "There is a need for this movement, for there is the greatest misery existing in the country. Working men are starving. The aristocracy are squandering the money earned by the sweat of the working man's brow. Whilst working men are starving, the aristocracy are feeding their game with food that ought to go to the people–'the bread of the children is given to the dogs,'" he exclaimed in another apt quotation from the Scriptures. "What the masses really need is union. They have now the power, but it is astonishing how in an election they will vote against their own interests. They will even vote for a landlord who will go into Parliament to betray their interests. They will vote for Tories without the slightest hesitation–not that they believe in Toryism or that they like their slavery. A philosopher once said that the way to make a man happy was by whipping him until he came to feel that he was happy. The Tory working men do not exactly believe in such a theory as that, but they vote for the Tories because they want something from the Tories–to rent a piece of land which the Tories possess, or they are afraid of being turned out of their homes which are the property of the Tories. Let working men unite, and then all the forces of the enemy cannot overcome the stern sons of Eryri."

"Military strategists declare that a wall of sand is one of the strongest means of resisting attack. What is the reason? A handful of sand can be blown away by a puff of wind, but particles of sand combined in an earthwork is one of the best means of resisting attack. Working men acting separately are only as particles of sand to resist the power of the landlord, but let the working men combine together to give firm expression to their demands, then no opposition, however powerful, will be able to stand before them. Let us in Wales," he concluded, "follow the example of Ireland by establishing in our midst a powerful Land League, and let us all join it."

The tornado of applause which swept the meeting as Mr. Lloyd George resumed his seat demonstrated beyond doubt that, young and comparatively unknown as he then was, he had struck a deeper note in the audience than either of "the two Michaels." The discerning divined that a prophet had arisen in Israel, and for many a long day the quarrymen of Festiniog recalled the magnificent speech of the young attorney.[211]

Lloyd George, at only 23 years of age, was making his first major public speech, and he impressed Davitt. "You must get this fellow into Parliament", Davitt told Rev. Michael D. Jones. "He is saying in Wales what we are saying in Ireland." The *North Wales Chronicle* recorded, without naming him, that

[211] Edwards, 1913, Vol.II, p131-134, following *Cambrian News*, 19 February 1886, p7.

a "young lawyer from Criccieth" had concluded the meeting, noting: "We will do him the credit of saying that he certainly was the most eloquent, and spoke with more telling effect than any of the other speakers. His oratory was worthy [of] a better cause; but he is decidedly a favourite with the people."[212]

1886 saw a major sea change in the nation's politics. On 8 April, Prime Minister Gladstone introduced his Government of Ireland Bill, commonly referred to as the First Home Rule Bill, aiming to create a devolved assembly for Ireland that would have specific areas of responsibility. It was very much Gladstone's own personal project, having–fatefully, as it turned out–excluded both the Irish MPs and his own ministers from the process of drafting the complex legislation. In his famous Home Rule speech on 7 June, he beseeched Parliament to grant Home Rule to Ireland in honour rather than being compelled to one day in humiliation. The next day the vote was taken: 341–including 93 Liberals–voted against the Bill, only 311 for it. Parliament was dissolved on 26 June and a general election called. Of immediate catastrophic effect, the formerly radical Joseph Chamberlain had already resigned from his Cabinet post as President of the Local Government Board on 3 April. Along with the Whig Lord Hartington, Chamberlain engineered the formation of the Liberal Unionist Party, which then formed a political alliance with the Conservatives in opposition to Irish Home Rule.[213] Believing that Home Rule would lead to the independence of Ireland, and thus the dissolution of the United Kingdom of Great Britain and Ireland, and seeing themselves as the defenders of that Union, they adopted the title of 'Liberal Unionists'. Their effective defection from the Liberals kept the latter from power or influence for all but three of the next 20 years.

On his defection, Chamberlain had initially proclaimed the creation of a new organisation, the National Radical Union, whose 'Unauthorised Programme' proposed federalism as the solution to the Irish problem. Lloyd George's imagination was fired, and he decided to attend the Union's inaugural meeting in Birmingham, the centre of Chamberlain's power base, with a view to possibly joining. He duly caught the train to Birmingham, only to discover that he had confused the dates and was almost a week too early. Prior commitments prevented him from returning to the city on 17 June, the correct date, and so he now committed to engaging wholly in Welsh matters.[214] As at several other pivotal moments in Lloyd George's life story, chance here played a key role.

With the advent of the general election of 1-27 July, building on the success and inspiration of his recent experiences, Lloyd George was seriously tempted to stand for the Liberal candidacy in Merioneth, the vacancy being due to the resignation of the sitting MP, Henry Robertson, now aged 70, one of the few Welsh Liberal MPs opposed to the Home Rule Bill. Before making such a large decision, Lloyd George naturally sought advice from those whose opinion he valued. Dr R. D. Evans was one such person, who later told J. Hugh Edwards:

---

212 *North Wales Chronicle*, 20 February 1886, p8.

213 The Conservatives and Liberal Unionists merged into the Conservative and Unionist Party on 9 May 1912.

214 Edwards, 1913, Vol.II, p143.

> He happened to be staying with me at Ffestiniog over the week-end, and he confided in me that he was very anxious to enter the list for the Liberal candidature for Merionethshire. We discussed the matter together on the Sunday, and I strongly advised him to go with the early train on Monday morning to Corwen to consult the Rev. Cernyw Williams[215], the Baptist minister, on the matter. I knew that Mr. Williams would be in a position to give him full information in regard to the probable development of the situation.[216]

Evans duly accompanied Lloyd George to the station the next morning, the latter eagerly discussing his chances, though frustratingly the details of his meeting with Williams seem to have gone unrecorded. In broad terms, the minister most likely advised him to stay his hand. Ultimately, though his name was submitted the following Saturday at a meeting of the Merionethshire Liberal Association in Dolgellau by "a medical man from Harlech", Lloyd George–still only 23–decided to withdraw his name in favour of another man. The "coming man in Wales", as one unnamed delegate in Dolgellau called him, had not yet 'come'.[217]

Lloyd George had gathered in Corwen and in other districts in the county that popular feeling was centring on a Tom Ellis[218], whom he had already met in April at a Temperance Festival at Rhiw Chapel in Blaenau Ffestiniog, also a native of the county, being born in Cynlas just outside Bala, and a man in many ways not unlike himself. Both men had spoken at the event, and Ellis wrote to his uncle on 14 June, impressed with "the vigorous young solicitor of Criccieth who worked for Morgan Lloyd last time."[219] At that first meeting, Ellis had gone over to shake Lloyd George's hand, saying "You are a man after my own heart." The pair immediately began exchanging letters and ideas.

Lloyd George set out his views in another local newspaper column:

> Since Mr. Robertson's resignation I have received numerous communications from different parts of the county favourable to my candidature. Having, however, at the outset, pledged myself to support the candidature of Mr. T. Ellis of Cynlas, I declined to enter the lists as long as he remained in the field... It would appear to me that Mr. Ellis possesses beyond any other candidate named, the qualifications essential to constitute an effective Welsh member. Born of, and brought up amongst, the people, he knows their wants. Of their own race and religion, he thoroughly sympathises with their sentiments. Living as they do, in democratic times, Members of Parliament must now represent their constituents, not only in professed opinions but also in real sympathies. This Mr. Ellis does. He has, moreover, shown that he possesses the ability to express with vigour and effect any opinions he may entertain.[220]

---

215 Reverend Hywel Cernyw Williams (1843-1937), author, poet, Baptist Minister at Corwen, 1868-1918.

216 Quoted in Edwards, 1913, Vol.II, p135-136.

217 Edwards, 1913, Vol.II, p136-137.

218 Tom Ellis (16 February 1859–5 April 1899), hugely influential Liberal MP for Merioneth from July 1886 until his death, and a leader of *Cymru Fydd*.

219 Quoted in Masterman, *Forerunner*, p82-83.

220 Quoted in Edwards, 1913, Vol.II, p137.

Privately, Lloyd George rationalised to himself that he would not stand as, in any case, he would not have sufficient resources to sustain him in Westminster if elected:

> I would not be in nearly as good a position as regards pecuniary, oratorical or intellectual quality to go to Parliament now, as, say, five years hence. Now I would put myself in endless pecuniary difficulties–an object of contempt in a House of Snobs. Besides, I am not yet as thoroughly established in judgement as I ought to be.[221]

Lloyd George then campaigned on behalf of his newfound friend, Tom Ellis–at 27, only four years older than himself, though a graduate in Modern History from New College, Oxford. Ellis proceeded to win the seat with a very handsome majority of 1,267, proving what fertile ground the constituency was for progressive Welsh Liberalism at this time, and indeed holding the seat until his untimely death. In the neighbouring constituency of Caernarfon Boroughs, the incumbent Liberal MP, Sir Thomas Love Jones-Parry–the same man whose campaign Lloyd George remembered from 1868–was unseated by a majority of 136 by his Conservative opponent, Edmund Swetenham–an outcome that was soon to have consequences for Lloyd George himself.

The 1886 election proved to be a turning point, for as well as the old commitments to Gladstonian Liberalism–Irish Home Rule, disestablishment, land reform and educational progress–this was the first time that Welsh Home Rule was seriously advocated, and the first time that the Welsh language was used as an electoral medium.[222] A new political spirit was abroad in the land. In Britain as a whole, the election was a disaster for the Liberals: They won only 192 seats, to the combined Tory and Unionist total of 393, the Irish holding steady at 85, and the Marquess of Salisbury became Prime Minister.

Lloyd George, meanwhile, had indeed earned a formidable reputation as a fiery young orator, and as a possible Liberal parliamentary candidate for one of the divisions in north-west Wales at the next general election. How history would have differed, had he stood for and won the Merioneth seat at such an early juncture in his career is uncertain, but the extra experience he gained before he contested and won Caernarfon Boroughs stood him in very good stead. His local standing was further enhanced by his utterly committed participation in the anti-tithe agitation in south Caernarfonshire in 1886-87, where he was singled out by the local Tory press as the primary instigator of the trouble.[223] He was active in the establishment of the local Anti-Tithe League for Llyn and Eifionydd, and at a packed meeting in the Town Hall in Pwllheli, he was elected as Secretary on 9 February 1887.[224]

Amid all this political ferment, on 22 July 1886, Lloyd George confided in his sister Pollie: "Told my sister M.E.G. to-night about M. She is well-pleased and thinks a lot of her, says I may mention the matter [of marriage] to M. shortly but that it would not do to marry for about five years at least."[225]

---

221 George, *Making Of Lloyd George*, p165. Diary entry for 20 June 1886.
222 Jones, 'Thomas Edward Ellis', p29.
223 *Y Genedl Gymreig*, 5 January 1887; *Gwalia*, 12 January 1887.
224 *Y Genedl Gymreig*, 2 February 1887; *Baner ac Amserau Cymru*, 2 February 1887; Price, 2006, p36.
225 Quoted in Hague, p61.

Lloyd George did not wait five years: in the event he waited one month. Maggie had relatives living at Bodfan in Llanwnda, some three miles south of Caernarfon, and towards the end of August she went to stay with them for a few days. Lloyd George thought that this would be his best chance of seeing her without the presence of her mother, who did not approve of him. On 25 August, he met Maggie at 9.45 pm when she returned from a party. He wrote in his diary:

> M came with me for a long drive in carriage (I had brought from Llanwnda). Here I proposed to her. She wanted time to consider, but admitted her regard for me. Although, when I write this, I have not been formally accepted, I am positive that everything is all right so far as the girl is concerned. I left her about mid-night. M. has some of the "coquette" about her–she did not like to appear to jump at my offer.[226]

Lloyd George was wrong in attributing Maggie's hesitation to 'coquetry', as she was rightly concerned by his reputation as being something of a 'ladies' man', also being reluctant to go against the wishes of her beloved parents. On 1 October, Lloyd George recorded in his diary a most revealing conversation he had with Maggie at Mynydd Ednyfed in her parents' absence:

> I pressed M. to come to a point as to what I had been speaking to her about [his proposal of marriage]. She at last admitted that her hesitation was entirely due to her not being able implicitly to trust me. She then asked me solemnly whether I was really in earnest–I assured her with equal solemnity that I was as there is a God in Heaven. 'Well then,' she said, 'if you will be as true and faithful to me as I am to you, it will be allright.' She said nothing about her Mother's frivolous objection to my being a Baptist nor as to her own objection to my sceptical vagaries [his radical political convictions]–for I told her emphatically the other day that I could not even to win her give them up & I would not pretend I had–they were my firm convictions.[227]

Arguments between the pair continued along these lines for some months. Lloyd George loved Maggie, but he was clear-eyed about where his principal passion lay. In early 1887, he wrote her something of a mixed declaration and confession that is psychologically instructive:

> Now once for ever let us have an end of this long standing wrangle. It comes to this. My supreme idea is to get on. To this ideal shall sacrifice everything–except I trust honesty. I am prepared to thrust even love itself under the wheels of my Juggernaut, if it obstructs the way, that is if love is so much trumpery child's play as your mother deems courtship to be. I have told you over and over that I consider you to be my good angel–my guiding star. Do you not really desire my success? If you do, will you suggest some course least objectionable to you out of our difficulty? I am prepared to do anything reasonable & fair you may require of me. I cannot–earnestly–carry on as present. Believe me–& may Heaven attest the truth of my statement–my love for you is

226 George, *Making Of Lloyd George*, p140.
227 Ibid., p141.

> sincere & strong. In this I never waver. But I must not forget that I have a purpose in life. And however painful the sacrifice I may have to make to attain this ambition I must not flinch–otherwise success will be remote indeed…[228]

As Ffion Hague astutely points out, "It is a lawyer's, not a lover's letter. Love is secondary to business–no suitor ever made that clearer."[229] He needed Maggie's support to 'get on' and achieve his ambitions: she did not yet know that these were national, not merely local ones. He used the methods of an advocate, venting his impatience and self-centredly and high-handedly laying down the law regarding his own needs and desires, with little regard for hers in a way quite remarkable, even when making allowance for the differences in late Victorian social mores to those of the present day. Lloyd George played on Maggie's upright sense of duty and obligation, rather than making a purely emotional appeal.

He would soon write another letter–containing a passage that Ffion Hague calls "the most crucial passage in all the letters of Lloyd George and Maggie's long courtship"–almost more breath-taking in its audacity:

> … my ideas as to the qualifications of a wife do not coincide with yours. You seem to think that the supreme function of a wife is to amuse her husband–to be to him a kind of toy or plaything to enable him to while away with enjoyment his leisure hour. Frankly, that is simply prostituting marriage. My ideas are very different–if not superior–to yours. I am of the opinion that woman's function is to soothe & sympathise & not to amuse. Men's lives are a perpetual conflict. The life I have mapped out will be so especially–as lawyer & politician. Woman's function is to pour oil on the wounds–to heal bruises of spirit received in past conflicts & to stimulate to renewed exertion. Am I not right? If I am then you are pre-eminently the girl for me. I have a thorough belief in your kindliness and affection.

He then disingenuously challenged Maggie to make her decision:

> As to setting you free, that is a matter for your choice & not mine. I have many times impressed upon you that the only bond by which I have any desire to hold you is that of love. If that be lost then I would snap any other bond with my own hand. Hitherto my feelings are those of unflinching love for you & that feeling is a growing one.
>
> You ask me to choose–I have made my choice deliberately & solemnly. I must now ask you to make your choice. I know my slanderers–those whom you allow to poison your mind against me. Choose between them & me–there can be no other alternative.[230]

With this ultimatum presented to her in such stark terms, Maggie capitulated and finally accepted the diamond cluster ring Lloyd George had ordered for her on 26 January 1887 from R. Bonner Thomas,

---

[228] Quoted in Hague, p72. Hague has made a totally compelling case, based on internal evidence, for attributing this undated letter to early 1887, rather than to 1885 or 1886 as in earlier authors.

[229] Hague, p72.

[230] Undated letter, quoted in Hague, p77.

a Porthmadog jeweller at 4 Bank Place.

Meanwhile, Lloyd George's practice was flourishing, and he established branch offices in surrounding towns, taking his brother William into partnership in 1887, the latter having obtained First Class Honours on 5 August. Having occupied an office in a very small house from 1885, in 1889 Lloyd George took the end of the lease, then secured the freehold of a building, formerly a tavern called the *Fox Inn* between 1876-1889, as an office in the high street[231] of the larger, equally flourishing Porthmadog, whose population rose during the same timescale from 4,367 to 5,224. A vivid pen portrait of the rising young solicitor was made about this time by D. R. Daniel, soon to become a friend and Liberal colleague, who met him outside Porthmadog police station in 1887: "A young boyish man in simple clothes and Volunteer's leggings closed with laces on the legs. I remember his attractive smile and the incomparable brilliance of his lively blue eyes. He seemed nimble in mind and bearing, more daring in his views, more heroic in his look (though he smiled most of the time) than any of my other (political) friends."[232]

Before opening his permanent Porthmadog office, Lloyd George had also opened ones in rented rooms in Blaenau Festiniog and Pwllheli, making it necessary for him to journey there once a week on market days on the narrow-gauge railway for the purpose of being consulted by clients, and of appearing in cases in the local courts.[233] His first day at Blaenau Ffestiniog–for which he had paid 3s 6d in rent–was on Saturday 24 January 1885. It was not an encouraging start. It was, typically, "raining heavily", and he recorded in his diary that "Not a soul called to see whether I was alive or dead… I must be patient and things will come round."[234] Things did indeed 'come round', and as the business flourished, the Criccieth 'office' was relocated from Morvin House to a room opposite the *Bryn Hir Arms* on the High Street in Criccieth, managed by Uncle Lloyd.[235] The first clerk that Lloyd George employed, at Porthmadog, was John G. Moelwyn Hughes, "a young man of exceptional ability"[236] from Tanygrisiau, Blaenau Ffestiniog, who later recalled:

> It was a rich privilege to be for a number of years under his care and instruction. His example was to me an inspiration. I love to look back upon the delightful time which I spent at his office. No one ever had a kinder employer than I had in him. It is true that he is a man who is easily offended, but I never saw the sun go down upon his wrath. His cheerful salutation in parting for the night would clearly show that all was well. We upheld the respective roles of the principal

[231] Spender, *Prime Minister*, p49. William George & Son merged with Gamlins Solicitors LLP in September 2013, but still occupy the offices at 103 High Street, on the corner with Chapel Street, great-nephew Philip George being a partner there. Personal communication to the author from Philip George, 13 January 2020.

[232] Quoted in Cliffe, p14.

[233] Personal communication to the author by Philip George, 13 January 2020. In time a "compartment in carriage 16 was converted into an office complete with a desk and blinds to ensure privacy for Lloyd George and his secretary." https://www.festrail.co.uk/content/publish/frnews/Heritage_Factoid_No_12.shtml. Retrieved 11 December 2019. Wednesday was "the Pwllheli day". George, *My Brother and I*, p146.

[234] Quoted in George, *My Brother and I*, p135.

[235] Ibid., p138, and personal communication to the author by Philip George, 13 January 2020.

[236] Ibid., p153.

and his subordinate when anyone was in sight, but when there was no one in the office other than the two of us, this rigid relationship dissolved into that of friends.

One felt at once in his company that he was surrounded with a healthy independence which was as vitalising as the mountain air. Some misinterpreted this quality in him and ascribed it to a feeling of pride. Many a time did I hear him deprecate false modesty. Whenever he took up any case in which he perceived that a real injustice was being perpetrated, his whole nature would become thoroughly roused. The merry twinkle in his eye would die down and become superseded as by a flash of lightning. He gave utterance to his convictions without a hair on his tongue or the quiver of a doubt in the tone of his voice. And his written words were exactly as his utterances. In sealing many a letter which I had written to his dictation, I often realised that I was closing the door upon a legion of spirits, and I used to imagine what would happen when the seal was broken.

Very infrequently did I see him fail in anything, and whenever he had made an error he would immediately acknowledge that he was in the wrong.

From the outset I discerned that Mr. George was a man of an unfailing patience and of an unyielding persistency–one who could concentrate all his varied gifts upon one point. He held firmly to the belief that resoluteness engendered strength, that strength fostered "doggedness" and that "doggedness" paved the way for success. A surprising abandon would sometimes seize him so that I feared in both seeing and hearing him. I know that the whole structure of Mr. George's success has been laid on a moral basis. These strong foundations were laid early in his life by the teaching and example of his old uncle, Richard Lloyd–a stalwart to whom Wales is indebted to a far greater extent than she will ever know…

[An] incident, however, served to lead Mr. Lloyd George… to approach the question of dreams, with the result that he and I found ourselves philosophising on dreams and their value as ingredients in a man's life. We agreed… that none but the dreamers really enter into their inheritance, and that every form of wealth is illusory other than that of the visionary. "Where there is no vision the people perish," he exclaimed, and, he added, "therein lies the secret of all true hope, for vision is life." And here may one not rightly characterise the social changes which are now taking place in the land, as the realisation of the early dreams of that youth who hailed from Criccieth? Unquestionably, great principles had been put to the test in the life of that young solicitor, and he had seen visions…

It is worthy of note that he was a great reader. He read without ceasing. We used to dine together each day. If there was no controversial topic under discussion he would read during the dinner hour–read and eat at the same time. I never knew anyone who could read so quickly as he. In my judgment he used to read much too expeditiously. It would take him no time to rush through a book. The range of his reading was both wide and varied. Among his favourite authors at that period were Froude, Gibbon, Ruskin, Emerson, Mazzini, Robertson of Brighton, Kingsley, Scott, R. Louis Stevenson, Adam Smith, Pascal, Burns, and Morgan Llwyd[237] the famous Welsh prose writer, and Ceiriog[238] the great lyric poet of Wales. With characteristic

---

[237] Morgan Llwyd (1619-1659), Welsh Puritan preacher, poet and prose writer.

[238] John 'Ceiriog' Hughes (1832-1887), Welsh language poet, collector of Welsh folk tunes.

> heartiness he would hand on to me the works of those famous authors in which he so much revelled. It was a delightful task to follow in his footprints through such rich fields in literature, and leisurely pause at those spots where he had reared memorials, with his pencil, along the edge of the path. He would always have it that Shakespeare, Burns, and Ceiriog the sweet singer of Wales, were the finest poets; while I, on the other hand, would put in a plea for Milton, Edgar A. Poe, and Islwyn.[239]
>
> He revelled in controversy. We debated the question of baptism a good deal… Not only was he conversant with every verse appertaining to the question, but he even knew the passages that were cognate to it. However, our discussions always ended in the same way–we agreed to differ…[240]

The so-called 'Tithe War' continued to rage angrily in North Wales during the summer of 1887, and Lloyd George took full advantage of the hiring fairs at Llyn to arrange impromptu meetings to stir up local agitation by making highly eloquent and impassioned speeches. Tithes were the centuries-old traditional payments which entitled the Church to a tenth of the tenant's annual income. The payments were usually made in kind in the form of crops, wool, milk and other produce, to represent a tenth of the yearly production. Payment was demanded whether or not the parishioner attended Church, and in predominantly Nonconformist North Wales this naturally caused hardship and fierce resentment. Often, even the local vicar only received a small stipend from what was collected, most going to the wealthy local gentry or the Oxford and Cambridge colleges.

In 1836, the Tithes Commutation Act had been intended to make the collection easier, by substituting the tithe rent-charge for the payment of tithe in kind. This was calculated on the basis of average prices of wheat, barley and oats over the previous seven years. However, when agriculture became depressed, farmers found themselves paying a fixed rent-charge that actually represented far more than a tenth of the current value of their crops. Many impoverished farmers decided to take direct action and refused to pay their tithes. During the late 1880s–which was a time of a general agricultural depression–enforced sales of land and property were implemented by the authorities in order to collect the taxes owed, leading, unsurprisingly, to large and sometimes violent protests taking place in Llanarmon-yn-Iâl on 10 September 1886, Whitford on 20 December 1886, Llangwm on 27 May 1887, Mochdre on 16 June 1887 and Llanefydd on 17 May 1888.[241]

At Llangwm, the angry crowd were barely persuaded to desist from doing great violence to the hated auctioneer and his appraiser. Following the incident, 31 protesters–the Llangwm 'tithe martyrs'–received summonses, eight eventually being tried before Mr Justice Wills at Ruthin Assizes on 28 February 1888, fortunately getting off relatively lightly by being bound over in the sum of £20 each.[242]

---

239 William Thomas, 'Islwyn' (1832-1878), Welsh language poet, Calvinistic Methodist Minister.

240 Quoted in Edwards, 1913, Vol.II, p113-117. John G. Moelwyn Hughes (1866-1944), who after working for Lloyd George from around 1887 to 1890 went on to become a renowned lyric poet, hymn writer, philosopher and Calvinistic Methodist Minister. He wrote the hymn '*Y Ddinas Gadarn*', sung at Lloyd George's funeral.

241 *South Wales Daily News*, 2 September 1887, p3.

242 *Llangollen Advertiser*, 2 March 1888, p3.

The Mochdre protest, where more than 100 police were reinforced by a company of some 200 soldiers of the Cheshire Regiment from Chester Castle, resulted in injuries to 84 people, including 35 police officers, and the Riot Act being read in English and Welsh before the crowd dispersed.[243] After the incident at Llanefydd, the Chief Constable, Major Leadbetter, asked the magistrates for a troop of cavalry as reinforcements, and a troop of the 9th Queen's Royal Lancers was duly sent to Denbigh, where they stayed a month assisting the police in supervising collections at 223 farms in Llanfair Talhaearn, Llansannan, Llanefydd and Mochdre, without further disturbances of the peace.

It was no coincidence that the unrest was worst in Denbighshire, as Denbigh was the headquarters of the Welsh Land, Labour and Commercial League–modelled on the Irish Land League–that lobbied against tithe payment. Denbighshire farmers were not necessarily any more resentful than those in other parts of the country but the presence of the League's headquarters and the influence of Thomas Gee[244] meant that tensions were particularly high in the area. Gee was the owner of the local Welsh-language newspaper *Baner ac Amserau Cymru* and was active in the anti-Tithe campaign, having first brought attention to the subject in 1880. The protestors' actions were praised by Gee's newspaper as the campaign's momentum reached its peak when troops were deployed to the Denbighshire area in May and June 1888 and August 1890 to control the discontent and protect the tithe collectors in carrying out their unpopular duties. So strong was his feeling on the issue that Gee even named his horse '*Degwm*' ('Tithe') and was photographed with the magnificent animal outside Plas Castell in Denbigh. Until his death on 28 September 1898, Lloyd George was "encouraged personally by Gee as well as supported more publicly through his paper."[245]

After the Mochdre incident, a public enquiry had been set up under the chairmanship of a well-respected London stipendiary magistrate, John Bridge.[246] He recommended that the responsibility for the payment of the tithe be transformed from the tenant to the landlord. The 'Tithe War' effectively came to an end when, on 26 March 1891, the Tithe Act came into law, bringing this proposal into effect. From then on, even if the landlord raised the rent to compensate for his having to pay the tithe, the tenant could not refuse to pay this without also refusing to pay the rent and thus face eviction. The struggle had served to bring Welsh issues to the forefront of the British political agenda however, being linked as it was so intrinsically to the campaign for the disestablishment of the Welsh Church. One of the most significant results of the agitation was the 1896 Royal Commission on Land in Wales, which brought many of the tenant farmers grievances into the open and led to improved landlord-tenant relations.

It was at the very time this 'war' was 'hotting up' that Lloyd George gave the first intimation of his

---

243 *Wrexham Advertiser*, 30 July 1887, p6. Anyone protesting after the Act's reading could receive the death penalty, although by this period this was unlikely.

244 Thomas Gee (1815-1898), influential Welsh Nonconformist preacher and journalist from Denbigh, publisher of the twice-weekly Welsh-language newspaper '*Baner ac Amserau Cymru*' from 1857, regarded as an oracle in Wales, that did much to promote Welsh Home Rule and Church Disestablishment.

245 Greenhalgh, I., *Thomas Gee Printer and Publisher: A Brief Biography*, 2001, Denbigh, Gee & Sons, p9.

246 John Bridge (1824-1900); "In the exercise of his summary jurisdiction he well knew how to temper justice with mercy. Few British magistrates have more happily combined dignity and firmness with judicious and unobtrusive benevolence." *Dictionary of National Biography*, 1901 Supplement, Vol.I, p267.

growing political ambitions, as he began to mentally survey wider horizons, noting in his diary on 4 September 1887:

> Got an invitation this morning. I want to cultivate boroughs as, if the Unionist Govt holds together another 3 years, I may stand a good chance to be nominated as Liberal candidate. There are two or three impressions I must be careful to make in the meantime. 1st & foremost that I am a good speaker. 2ndly that I am a sound & thorough politician. 3rdly that I can afford to attend to parliamentary duties. To succeed in the first I must avail myself of every opportunity to speak in public so as to perfect myself & attain some reputation as a speaker. To succeed in the 2nd point I must put into those speeches good sound matter well arranged so as to catch the year [sic] of the intelligent who always lead & gain the name of sound as well as fluent speaker. I must also write political articles on Welsh politics so as to show my mastery of them. To attain the 3rd reputation I must (1) attend to my business well so as to build up a good practice (2) practise economy so as to accumulate some measure of wealth (3) Get all my cases well advertised (4) subscribe judiciously.[247]

The year 1888 was a landmark one for Lloyd George. At 10.15 am on 24 January, one week after his 25th birthday, he married his sweetheart, Maggie Owen.[248] The wedding took place at the little Calvinistic Methodist Chapel in Pencaenewydd[249], a tiny hamlet seven and a half miles inland from Criccieth, Uncle Lloyd conducting the actual wedding ceremony, the Reverend John Owen, the Calvinistic Methodist minister of Capel Mawr in Criccieth–who had only proposed marriage to Maggie himself the previous summer–reading the lesson and leading the tiny congregation in the prayers.[250] The choice of wedding venue was perhaps unlikely, but in fact offered 'neutral ground' between the claims of the different Nonconformist sects that both parties represented. Lloyd George's mother, brother and sister were absent, though Maggie's mother, Mary, was present. Du Parcq relates how:

> That morning, the bridegroom came by train from Criccieth to Chwilog with his uncle, Mr. Richard Lloyd, and breakfasted there with "Myrddin Fardd." Thence they walked three miles to the chapel at Pencaenwydd, where in the presence of a few friends, Mr. Owen, whose misgivings had long since been removed, gave his daughter in marriage to the young lawyer.[251]

Despite the small congregation, the *Carnarvon and Denbigh Herald* painted a picture of a happy day:

> Mr. George, who is well known in this part of the county, is very popular, and the families of both the young people are held in high esteem. Early in the day flags were to be seen in all

[247] NLW MS 20,443A (Lloyd George Papers 2093), Lloyd George's diary for 1887, entry for 4 September 1887.
[248] See Rowland, *Lloyd George*, p58.
[249] The Chapel was built in 1822, remodelled c.1880 in the Simple Round-Headed style of the gable entry type.
[250] John Owen (1849-1917) graciously wrote to Lloyd George on 27 January, declining payment for performing the ceremony for "a couple of friends", wishing them both "long life and real happiness": Quoted in Du Parcq, Vol.I, p80-81.
[251] Du Parcq, Vol.I, p80.

> directions, and there was also a considerable display of bunting. After luncheon the newly-wedded couple left by the mid-day train for London on their honeymoon. The town was illuminated at night and fireworks were let off.[252]

The paper glossed over the presence of a "drizzling mist", that being a rather unremarkable fact in Wales in January! The pair, staying at Parker's Hotel, made the most of their honeymoon, taking in theatrical performances of *Hamlet* at the Globe Theatre[253], also *Puss in Boots* and *HMS Pinafore*, before arriving back in Criccieth on 3 February.

It seems Lloyd George was universally regarded as being a lucky man who had chosen, and been accepted by, a very special lady. Recognizing her thorough 'Welshness', Edwards paid tribute to:

> … her own sterling qualities. It would, indeed, be difficult to discover among the women of Wales one who may be said to epitomise in a higher degree that charm and dignity, that prudence and sagacity, so inherently ingrained in Welsh womanhood than does Mrs. Lloyd George. Passionately devoted to her race, she regards no service or sacrifice on her part too great if only she can advance the welfare of the principality and the highest interests of the people.[254]

Lloyd George's colleague Ellis Jones Griffith MP was moved to declare later:

> If Mr. Lloyd George had married another person, things might have gone differently with him. To have married a Welshwoman who sympathised with her husband's aims for the people, and who has been faithful in her traditions to her own people, has proved to Mr. Lloyd George a tremendous asset both in his public and private life and in his great position.[255]

This was the general consensus at the time, and it has remained so. Lloyd George himself paid revealing tribute to her as a "brave little woman", confessing himself to be a "troublesome person whom she has stood by through good and evil report… I cannot say less without doing her injustice."[256]

In the same month, on 4 January 1888, Lloyd George founded his first newspaper, the weekly *Yr Udgorn Rhyddid* (The Trumpet of Freedom), in Pwllheli, to campaign for land reform, under the editorship of his friend D. R. Daniel, of Four Crosses.[257] This would run until 1898. Lloyd George's Radical and Nationalist position was clear from the outset, as he wrote to Daniel:

---

252 *Carnarvon and Denbigh Herald*, 27 January 1888, p8.
253 The Globe was a Victorian theatre in Newcastle Street, 1868-1902.
254 Edwards, 1913, Vol. II, p158.
255 Ibid., p160.
256 Ibid.
257 David Robert Daniel (1859-1931), political commentator, close friend of Tom Ellis, Organiser for the North Wales Quarrymen's Union, 1896-1906.

> The project is in a fair way to realisation… Will you join? We propose raising a capital of say £100 and limiting our liabilities to that amount, so as to escape the injurious consequences of libel suits. It is to be thorough, nationalist and socialist–a regenerator in every respect.[258]

Lloyd George was not only concerned with land reform: with his sights set on Caernarfon Boroughs, he was also focused on another radical issue that he had already campaigned on in Merioneth in 1885-86, namely that of the enfranchisement of leaseholders, and one of importance to the many slate and granite quarrymen. The issue was "particularly acute amongst quarrymen and workers at Pwllheli (the Glynllifon estate), Nefyn (the Cefn Amwlch estate), Caernarfon (the Faenol estate) and at Bangor (the Penrhyn estate)."[259]

In one article, published on 18 February 1888, he wrote on the wider issue of the House of Lords in terms that foreshadowed his later speeches when he was Chancellor of the Exchequer:

> This establishment militates against the spirit of the age… The basis of true Government is the voice of the people… the House of Lords has secured a reputation as the arch-enemy of all reform. The weakest intellects and the most unclean characters can sit in this noble House. It is admitted readily, even by *The Times*, that the House of Lords requires reform, but its total annihilation is the only cause worth fighting for… securing the fall of this god of oppression would count as one of the victories of freedom and a cause for celebration for generations yet to be born.[260]

He also wrote articles under the name 'Brutus' for various North Wales newspapers on topics such as disestablishment, education, temperance, and the land question.

In April 1888, the Llanfrothen burial case arose. It was a case of conflict between churchmen and nonconformists over burial rights, a battle to persuade the local rector, Reverend Richard Jones, to comply with the Osborne Morgan[261] Burial Laws Amendment Act 1880. It was also a battle to allow a quarryman named Robert Roberts of Ty'r Capel, Croesor, who had died aged 51 on 23 April, to be interred in a consecrated part of the churchyard next to his daughter, Kate Roberts, who had died aged only 21 on 17 June 1884. This was rather than, in Lloyd George's later words, "a spot bleak and sinister, in which were buried the bodies of the unknown drowned that were washed up from the sea in this region of shipwrecks, or of suicides, or of the few Jews that died in the district."[262]

The community was of a fair size, many of the inhabitants being engaged in working in the lead mines: "LLANFROTHEN… in Ffestiniog district, Merioneth... Pop., 830. Houses, 156… The living

---

258 Letter of 12 December 1887, quoted in Price, 2006, p46.

259 Price, 2006, p51.

260 Article of 18 February 1888, quoted in Price, 2006, p51.

261 George Osborne Morgan (1826-1897), Liberal MP for Denbighshire 1868-1885, East Denbighshire 1885-1897, Judge Advocate General 1880-1885. He introduced his Burials Bill in 1870, re-introducing it for ten successive sessions until it finally received royal assent on 7 September 1880.

262 *North Wales Observer and Express*, 16 September 1898, p6.

is a rectory in the diocese of Bangor… The church is dedicated to St. Brothen."[263] The case itself is key to highlighting so much of what was wrong with the political, social, religious and cultural 'scene' in rural Wales at the time, and to the understanding Lloyd George's characteristic outlook and skills that first brought him to public notice, and so bears close scrutiny. Lloyd George himself acknowledged this, confessing:

> I dare say I should have remained many years longer a country solicitor if my name had not been brought into some public notice by what is known as the 'Llanfrothen Burial Case.' It was one of those peculiar harsh cases which excite passion and attract public attention.[264]

Asked for advice, Lloyd George told the family: "Go on, carry the matter right through now, and I will defend you." On 26 April the lock[265] on the churchyard gate was broken, and a new grave dug. What followed was related by Calvinistic Methodist Minister Hugh Jones of Brynygwin, to whose flock Roberts had belonged:

> A bier was borrowed from the local Baptist Chapel, and in the great concourse of people who had come together from far and near, there were found scores of stalwarts who readily carried the corpse over the distance of three miles which lay between the house of the deceased man and the churchyard at Llanfrothen. By the time the funeral reached the churchyard, the locked gate had been forced open, and the mortal remains of the quarryman were quietly and solemnly laid to rest in the manner which he had so ardently desired.[266]

The Rector promptly sued the old quarryman's brother Morris Roberts and seven others for "wrongfully entering the plaintiff's land, digging a grave therein, burying a corpse and conducting a funeral service."[267] The *North Wales Observer and Express* gave a detailed account of the matter on 18 May, giving the flavour of the issues at stake, popular feeling, and of Lloyd George's skilful handling of the matter:

> Great interest was manifested in the proceedings of the Portmadoc County Court on Wednesday, owing to the trial of an action arising from the burial scandal which has been identified with the quiet parish of Llanfrothen... The circumstances connected with the scandal– which gives another instance of the battle which Nonconformity is fighting against English Churchism in Wales–… are further brought to light in the evidence produced at the hearing of the action, which was tried before his Honour Judge Bishop and a jury, called for by the

---

263 *Imperial Gazetteer of England and Wales*, Vol. IV, pp105-106. Spellings corrected.

264 Quoted in Edwards, 1913, Vol.II, p161-162.

265 On display at the Lloyd George Museum.

266 Quoted in W. W. Davies, *Lloyd George*, p57.

267 The mossy gravestones of Roberts and his daughter Kate can be seen in the graveyard behind the disused but still consecrated church, at the time of visiting–23 February 2019–much overgrown, two tiny primroses adding a touch of beauty. Gwynedd Family History Society, *Memorial Inscriptions of the Church of St Brothen, Llanfrothen, Meirionnydd*, Records Series M 232, is most useful. The simple little Grade 1 listed church, so significant in Welsh history, in the care of 'Friends of Friendless Churches', is remote, unsignposted.

> defendants. Shortly after the sitting of the court, the court-room was crowded with an eager audience… A very large number of the Llanfrothen people watched… and among those present were… Church dignitaries.
>
> The plaintiffs to the action were the Rev Richard Jones, rector of Llanfrothen [and two others]… and the defendants, Morris Roberts [and seven others]. The plaintiffs claimed from the defendants the sum of £20 damages for wrongfully entering their land, digging a grave therein, burying a corpse, and conducting a funeral service there without license or consent of the plaintiffs, and in spite of their warning not to do so, also contrary to the provisions of a certain trust deed dated 18th July, 1881, and made between Catherine Owen… of the one part, and the plaintiffs of the other part; and the plaintiffs further claimed the sum of £10 damages for injury done by the defendants or some of them to their or some of their property. The defendants relied upon the following ground of defence:- That the title under which the plaintiffs claimed was barred by the Statute of Limitations… at the time the indenture mentioned in the particulars of claim was executed, and then the statute began to run on the 23rd of March, 1864. Moreover, the defendants counter-claimed to have the indenture mentioned delivered up to be cancelled or amended so that the plot of land thereof expressed to be thereby conveyed be held on the same trusts as the old parish Church of Llanfrothen was and now is, and to have it declared that the said plot of ground forms part, and is an enlargement of the said old churchyard. They also claimed of the plaintiffs the sum of £5 damages for obstructing a burial lawfully conducted by them… and that the case be tried by a jury.
>
> Messrs Carter and Vincent, Carnarvon, appeared for the plaintiffs, whilst the defendants were represented by Mr D. Lloyd George…
>
> Several witnesses for the defence having been examined, the judge put to the jury the question, was the land given verbally or by deed to the rector and parishioners as an addition to the churchyard in 1864; and, in the second place, had it been occupied adversely ever since? If the jury decided in the affirmative, then the verdict would be for the defendants. He would then listen to arguments of legal points in the case, and reserve judgment.
>
> The jury, after retiring to consider their verdict, replied in the affirmative, the result of which is a verdict for the defendants on the facts.[268]

Before the Portmadoc County Court, sitting on 16 and 24 May, Lloyd George did not deny the fact of trespass but said it was in full exercise of his clients' rights. The case hinged on the status of a conveyance through which the burial ground had become part of the church, and Lloyd George, meticulous in his preparation as usual, used "diagrams of the new plot of land made by a local Liberal architect, O. M. Roberts."[269] The jury backed the Nonconformists, but Judge John Bishop, a well-known Tory and Anglican, reserved judgment. When it was delivered two months later, on 25 July,

---

[268]http://cc.bingj.com/cache.aspx?q=rev+richard+jones+st+brothen+llanfrothen&d=4751429705607701&mkt=en-GB&setlang=en-GB&w=pmywrG18eTNws3OfiLz3LtWlIMcDbd0-. Retrieved 6 February 2019. The *Carnarvon and Denbigh Herald*, *Cambrian News*, *Genedl* and other papers farther afield also gave extensive coverage to the case, devoting much praise to Lloyd George's skilful handling of it.

[269] Price, 2006, p57, quoting Gwynedd Archives Services, MSS 766.

he ignored the jury, expressed his disapproval of the defendants' actions–and entered a verdict for the plaintiffs "for £5 5s, and costs on the highest scale."[270]

An amusing, if probably apocryphal, tale is told of Lloyd George during the case that made his name, one apparently familiar to his friends. He allegedly "brought into Court a huge law book–Daniel's 'Chancery Precedents,' or some such portentous tome. "Surely," said the Judge, "you are not going to read all that book?" "If I did," replied Mr. Lloyd George gravely, "Your Honour would know *some* law when I had done."[271]

Lloyd George was, quite justifiably, outraged at the Judge's ruling, and lodged an appeal, the case also giving him a public platform as the representative of the Nonconformist defendant. It was duly heard in the Divisional Court of the Queen's Bench in London on 15 and 17 December, Lord Chief Justice Coleridge and Mr Justice Manisty ruling unhesitatingly in the appellants' favour and awarding them costs. The *Cambrian News* reported:

> Mr Bompas and Mr L. Scrutton, instructed by Mr Lloyd George, Criccieth, appeared for the appellant; and Mr Jeune[272], instructed by Messrs Vincent and Carter, for the respondent, the Rector of Llanfrothen…
>
> The Lord Chief Justice–… This is an attempt to reserve from the operation of the law, which the Rector dislikes, a small addition to the churchyard of the parish of Llanfrothen. The addition was made in point of fact as far back as 1864… The facts of the case as ascertained by the verdict of the jury are exceedingly simple. There is an old churchyard which either because it got full or for some other reason it was desired to add to; and in the year 1864 Mr and Mrs Owen, Brynygwyn, Dolgelley, concurred in desiring that this addition to the churchyard should be made. They communicated that desire to the Rector and parishioners and thereupon certain persons… acting by the permission given by the persons who at that time had a perfect right to give permission, entered into possession and occupation of the land and soon after built a wall round the new addition to the churchyard so as to make it one tenement with the churchyard. In 1881, after the passing of… Mr Osborne Morgan's Burial Act… the then Rector, and I suppose Mrs Owen, being desirous if they could to prevent the operation of the law upon the additional bit of the churchyard, Mrs Owen made a conveyance, which has been referred to in the action, of this piece of land for certain uses and no other uses, that is, burials were only permitted to take place there with the rights of the Church of England. The gentlemen to whom the conveyance was made in 1881 are the plaintiffs in this action, and they bring an action for trespass for burying in that tenement without their permission. The Rector locked up the churchyard, and the defendants, I suppose, actuated by conscientious motives, or at any rate to assert what they believed to be their rights broke open the gates and buried their dead in this part of the churchyard. That is what the action is for. Those are the whole facts of the case, and it is manifest that the governing question of the case was, had Mrs Owen in 1881 a right to execute the conveyance of that date. The course which was taken was this, which I think ought

[270] *North Wales Observer and Express*, 27 July 1888, p7.
[271] Du Parcq, Vol.I, p62-63.
[272] Francis Jeune, later 1st Baron St Helier (1843-1905).

> not to have been taken. She made a conveyance, she having undoubtedly been out of possession from 1864, that is, when she had lost her title to the land. Possession is a question of fact properly… The simple question of fact is, has Mrs Owen been out of possession since 1864? The jury have found that she has. Every circumstance of the case shows that she has. The jury were perfectly right in finding that she has, and if she has there is an end to plaintiffs' claim, because the plaintiffs claim through her, and if she had nothing to convey they could get nothing. It seems to me, therefore, that the County Court Judge was wrong, and his judgment must be reversed.
>
> Mr Justice Manisty–In concurring said… The main question is as to the title to the land and whether or not it can be used and is legally a churchyard… [The plaintiffs] want to prevent burials taking place there unless according to the rites of the Church of England... Keeping strictly to the law and dealing with the land as property, it is clear to me that the plaintiffs have no title at all and whether the defendant could have justified the trespass if they had is not the question… dealing with this as land, the plaintiffs have no title and therefore they have no right to bring the action for trespass.[273]

On the Saturday evening, between hearings, Lloyd George first made the acquaintance of solicitor Alfred T. Davies[274], and invited him on what he said "should prove rather an interesting expedition. It was nothing less than to visit the scenes of the recent murders by 'Jack the Ripper'." Meeting at Aldgate Underground Station at 9.00 pm, the pair were accompanied by a police superintendent from Caernarfonshire around the almost wholly unlit, poverty-stricken, squalid streets. Davies related the tale to "illustrate what, both then and afterwards, was ever a characteristic of Ll.G. He ever liked to get to the bottom of a case or, at any rate, to see things for himself."[275]

In later years, Lloyd George gave his son, Dick, a memorable account of the evening:

> And did you find any trace of the Ripper? I asked him.
>
> I found something worse. Something that Dante's pen alone could describe. Within a hundred yards of sanity and civilisation, a million people lived in conditions that gave the Ripper's actions a character of mercy killings. The gin houses; the doss houses; the stinking alleys and the gruesome cellars; the rickety tenements; the disorderly houses and the thieves' dens. This was London, the capital of the greatest Empire the world has ever known, the centre of the richest country in the world. I set out to investigate a crime that night; I found evidence of ten thousand.
>
> I think that night's experience completed my father's Radical education.[276]

Back in Wales, it was primarily the publicity he gained from the Llanfrothen burial case that won for

---

273 *The Cambrian News*, 28 December 1888, p7.
274 Sir Alfred T. Davies (1861-1949), first Permanent Secretary of the Welsh Department of the Board of Education, 1907-1925.
275 Davies, *Lloyd George I Knew*, pp20-21. The five so-called 'canonical' Ripper killings took place in and around the Whitechapel area of the East End between 31 August–9 November 1888.
276 Richard Lloyd George, *My Father*, p48-49.

Lloyd George the nomination, from among four nominees, as the Liberal Party candidate in the constituency of Caernarfon Boroughs.[277] By 6 July, he had already been provisionally selected by the Liberal Associations of Pwllheli, Nefyn and Criccieth, which gave him the impetus to continue in his efforts.[278] This was shown in an enthusiastic letter he wrote to D. R. Daniel on 5 July, in which he stated:

> You have heard that the South Caernarfon Boroughs have taken up my candidature. There was a meeting at the Pwllheli Liberal Association to consider the selection of a candidate. This meeting unanimously resolved to invite me out… Nefyn has now followed and lastly Criccieth. In both cases, the utmost unanimity prevailed… If either Bangor or Caernarfon follow suit, I shall be the next *Nationalist Candidate* for the Boroughs.[279]

The first choice of candidate had been Reverend Herber Evans[280], an eloquent Congregationalist minister from Caernarvon, long active in Liberal politics, but he declined to relinquish his pastorate.[281] Other candidates for nomination were London barrister Clement Higgins, QC, Professor Henry H. Johnson[282], of Trinity College, Dublin, and the Reverend Lloyd Jones of Rhyl. On 20 August, Lloyd George spoke at a public meeting in Penryhn Hall, Bangor, alongside the Irish Nationalist MP, T. D. Sullivan.[283] Citing the Irish example, he called for Welsh Liberals to give priority to Welsh demands and aspirations, and not to be mere loyalists to the wider Liberal Party. He was thus again putting himself forward as the Nationalist candidate for Caernarfon Boroughs.[284] In November, Higgins retired from the contest. Reverend Dr John Thomas of Liverpool, one of the most influential Welsh Nonconformist ministers of his day, was an enthusiast concerning Lloyd George's candidacy, having heard him speak at Temperance meetings at Ffestiniog and elsewhere. He wrote to his friend Herber Evans: "You require a candidate for the Carnarvon Boroughs, you have him ready at hand in Mr. Lloyd George. Give him his chance. He is destined to become the leader of Wales in the House of Commons."[285]

It may be seen that these worthy, eminent gentlemen:

> … had little chance against one who had already become a local hero. His fame spread as he extended his conquests to wider territory. In August he had been splendidly received at a crowded meeting at Bangor, where he made a speech in Welsh which roused his audience to

[277] In a letter of sympathy which Lloyd George sent to his widow from the National Liberal Club dated 16 October 1903, he acknowledged that it was John Eiddon Jones (1841-1903), Calvinistic Minister and temperance advocate, who had first asked him to stand for the Caernarfon Boroughs.

[278] Price, 2006, p43, 57.

[279] Quoted in Price, 2006, p58. Emphasis added.

[280] Reverend Evan Herber Evans (1836-1896), Independent Minister of Salem Chapel, Caernarfon, 1865-1892.

[281] Cregier, p31.

[282] See *Carnarvon and Denbigh Herald*, *Liberalism At Carnarvon*, 12 October 1888, p5.

[283] Timothy Sullivan (1827-1914), Lord Mayor of Dublin, 1886-1888, Irish Nationalist MP for Westmeath 1880-1885, Dublin College Green, 1885-1892, West Donegal, 1892-1900. Older brother of Alexander Sullivan.

[284] *Y Celt*, 24 August 1888, p7.

[285] Quoted in Edwards, 1913, Vol.II, p187. Reverend Dr John Thomas (1821-1892).

great enthusiasm. Inspired perhaps by his early introduction to Michael Davitt, he paid a tribute in that speech to the Irish members. "They have," he said, "taken the 'starch' out of the House of Commons, which used to be a kind of club-house."

As it turned out, Bangor rallied to his cause. Writing to his family at Criccieth from Glasgow, where, with his wife, he was visiting the Exhibition[286], on August 24, 1888, Mr. Lloyd George says:

Received a telegram from Morgan Richards this morning that I had been unanimously selected at Bangor last night, He also wrote me that my speech had made a very favourable impression. I could quite see for myself at the Monday evening meeting that I was the popular candidate. Despite all the machinations of my enemies I will succeed. I am now sailing before the wind and they against it.

The selection meeting for the Liberal Association's candidate for Caernarfon Boroughs was held at Caernarfon on 3 January 1889. After much deliberation, they chose Lloyd George, 'the people's attorney.' This naturally gave him great satisfaction, as he recorded in his diary that night: "Selection of candidate last thing on programme so I had to wait for two hours. Had excellent reception. Delegates got up and cheered me. Felt position keenly. Could not speak with much verve.[287]

Lloyd George was increasingly now at the "cutting edge." On 24 January elections for the newly created Caernarfonshire County Council took place, the Liberals taking 32 of the 48 available seats. On 31 January, a meeting of the Liberal members was held at the Carnarvon Reform Club to discuss the question of electing the aldermen.[288] The first meeting of the Council took place on 7 February at the County Hall, Caernarfon, and Lloyd George was one of the sixteen aldermen elected, receiving 30 votes.[289] Being only 26, he was soon dubbed the "Boy Alderman", but he went on to retain the position for his whole life, being always re-elected.[290]

The result of the County Council elections in Wales was a triumph for the progressive cause in general. Du Parcq transcribed a note written in his hand from which he delivered a speech at Hope Hall in Liverpool on 12 February 1889:

I assume that the vast majority of those who compose this great audience are Welshmen, and that the whole are Liberals. Now, whether we regard the results of the County Council elections in Wales as Welshmen or as Liberals, they must constitute to one and all of us a source of intense gratification. Those results are a splendid demonstration of the hold the principles of Liberalism have obtained upon the heart of our little country. Those elections afforded the best possible test of the growth in Wales of the national movement, which, after all, is but a phase of the great Liberal movement. The population of Wales, as you well know, rely more than that of any

[286] The International Exhibition of Science, Art and Industry, held in Glasgow, May–November 1888.
[287] Quoted in Price, 2006, p64.
[288] *North Wales Observer and Express*, 1 February 1889, p7.
[289] Ibid., 8 February 1889, p8.
[290] Ibid., 11 April 1890, p.11; *Carnarvon and Denbigh Herald*, 11 April 1890, p4.

> portion of the United Kingdom for their subsistence upon the resources wielded by the aristocracy. Wales subsists on the resources–mineral and agricultural–of its soil. That soil is vested in the Tory aristocracy.
>
> Now that is the great difficulty Welshmen have experienced in supporting the Liberal party at Parliamentary elections. Were it not for that fact Tories would be as scarce in Wales as they are in this meeting to-night. I know that the preponderating majority of those who vote for Tory candidates loathe and repudiate Tory principles. In Wales the Tory party is pre-eminently the party of the loaves and the fishes or–to add a new feature of Christian charity developed by the Primrose League[291]–it is also the party of the Christmas doles… All these immense pollutive influences were focussed and intensified at the County Council elections. Each squire fought not only for Toryism, but also for his own promotion, and the consequence was that throughout the Principality the squirearchy exerted its influence more desperately than ever. What was the result? Wales defied these polluting influences. Wales, despite every terrorism or intimidation, clung with grand devotion to the principles of freedom. Gallant little Wales![292]

Only three days after Lloyd George's Liverpool speech, on 15 February 1889, Maggie gave birth to their first child, Richard–known as Dick–in the same room where she herself had been born. Maggie's parents were nearly as delighted as the new parents themselves; they loved children and would prove to be loving and engaged grandparents in the years ahead.

"The Boy Alderman," as Postmaster General Henry Raikes derisively called him in his first election campaign[293], was not inactive on the County Council, although his eyes were already on a higher place. He soon made it abundantly clear that, in his opinion, County Councils were not parochial committees, gathered to discuss parochial affairs. His spoke out accordingly: at the first regular Council meeting, on 1 April, he seconded Alderman Arthur Acland's resolution which committed the authority to petition parliament in support of leasehold enfranchisement, saying:

> … the question was not one that effected a party, but the community at large, and men of all shades of politics were favourable to it. The present system as a most oppressive one, and it had been proved before the House of Commons that the county of Carnarvon suffered greatly from the injustice attended to it. As an instance of this he pointed out that nearly the whole of the town of Portmadoc was built on leases of only 60 years, and many of the houses, if not the majority of them, had been built by workmen. The presentation the proposed petition would be a credit to the Carnarvonshire County Council. Some might say that the council had nothing to do with such questions, but the country expected a great deal from the county councils, and if they did not do something beyond the mere duties for which they had been elected, the people of Wales would feel disappointed with the new administrative body.[294]

---

[291] An organisation for spreading Conservative principles in Great Britain, 1883-2004.

[292] Du Parcq, Vol.I, p84.

[293] Speaking in Pwllheli at the opening of the Promenade on 7 April 1890, Raikes had said that "the election of a boy alderman was only paralleled by the mediaeval scandal of child cardinals."

[294] *North Wales Observer and Express*, 5 April 1889, p7.

The motion was duly carried by 36 votes to 7.

On the same day, Lloyd George was elected as one of three conservators on the joint committee for the rivers Dyfi, Glaslyn and Mawddach–although, from a letter sent by an anonymous 'Liberal' to the *Carnarvon and Denbigh Herald* a year later, it seems he was not overly active in this regard.[295] He did, however, successfully move a resolution at a meeting in Pwllheli on 16 April 1890 that the salmon licence be reduced from £5 to £1 1s.[296]

On 2 May 1889, he carried a resolution which insisted that tenders should be invited for the supply of clothing and other necessaries for the police force, on the ground that those who paid rates should have an opportunity of benefiting by the expenditure. He further proposed that a committee should be appointed to collect evidence for the Royal Commission which the Home Secretary had promised should consider and report upon the working of the Sunday Closing Act in Wales. This proposal was passed unanimously, Lloyd George being elected as one of the three members of the resulting committee.[297]

In the same month, on 11 May, four quarrymen were charged before the Carnarvon County magistrates with unlawfully fishing with a net in the Nantlle lower lake.[298] They retained Lloyd George for their defence, and:

> … his conduct of the case is a good example of his determined policy of resistance to a Bench he considered prejudiced…
>
> There was no doubt that the accused had fished with a net: the question was whether the lake in which they had fished came within the definition of the term "river" in the Act of Parliament. The importance of the case was that for many years, as was alleged, the public had fished freely in the lake without their right to do so being questioned. In the course of the case the solicitor for the defence contended that the Bench had no jurisdiction.
>
> The Chairman [Captain J. G. Wynn Griffith][299] said that that would have to be proved in a higher Court.
>
> *Mr. George*: Yes, sir, and in a perfectly just and unbiased Court, too.
>
> *The Chairman*: If that remark of Mr. George's is meant as a reflection upon any magistrate sitting on this Bench, I hope that he will name him. A more insulting and ungentlemanly remark to the Bench I never heard during the course of my experience as a magistrate.
>
> *Mr. George*: But a more true remark was never made in a Court of Justice.
>
> *The Chairman*: Tell me to whom you are referring. I must insist upon you referring to any magistrate or magistrates sitting in this Court.
>
> *Mr. George*: I refer to you in particular, sir.
>
> *The Chairman (rising)*: Then I retire from the Chair. Good-bye, gentlemen. This is the first time I have ever been insulted in a Court of Justice. (*He then left the Court.*)

---

295 *Carnarvon and Denbigh Herald*, 5 April 1889, p.7, and 11 April 1890, p6.

296 Ibid., 18 April 1890, p5.

297 Ibid., 3 May 1889, p8: Du Parcq, Vol.I, p84-85.

298 Llyn Nantlle Isaf no longer exists, being drained from 1893 to protect the nearby quarries from flooding.

299 *North Wales Observer and Express*, 17 May 1889, p4.

*Another Magistrate*: In fairness to the Chairman and other magistrates I must say that Mr. George was not justified in making such remarks.

*A third Magistrate*: I decline to proceed with this case until Mr. George apologises.

*Mr. George*: I am glad to hear it.

A fourth magistrate said that he would not sit any longer to hear the case until Mr. George had withdrawn or apologised.

Mr. George took no notice of this remark, and the magistrate therefore vacated his seat.

One of the few remaining magistrates asked Mr. George to tender an apology to the Bench.

I say this [he answered]: that at least two or three magistrates at this Court are bent upon securing a conviction whether there is a fair case or not. I am sorry the Chairman has left the Court, because I am in a position to prove what I have said. I shall not withdraw anything, because every word I have spoken is true.

The result of this uncompromising declaration was the immediate emptying of the Bench. The sporting quarrymen must have begun to anticipate acquittal for want of a Bench to try them. Then came the anti-climax. Four magistrates came back, and the new chairman announced their unanimous opinion that Mr. Lloyd George's remarks were unjustifiable and should have been withdrawn, and that "under all the circumstances it was better that the case should proceed."

"Mr. George offered no remarks."

One almost pities the indignant magistrates, rising one by one from the seat of justice, to return with a tame admonition to the offender whom they could not quell. In at least two cases they followed up the incident with letters asking for an explanation of the solicitor's remark, and retaining liberty for themselves "to read his reply in Court"–a terrible threat.

The letter one of them… got in reply was to this effect:-

… You were not present at the adjourned hearing of the Court you allude to, but if you invite my opinion as to your demeanour at the previous Court I must honestly say that it was such as led me to believe that you were more intent on protecting the fish in the Nantlle lakes against the inroads of quarrymen than upon doing justice in that particular case according to the evidence. This was also the impression made upon less interested onlookers than myself.

It is notoriously a prevalent opinion amongst the masses that no fair play can be expected in poaching prosecutions at the hands of game and fish preserving magistrates. And I emphatically assert that unless justices tainted by game preservation demean themselves so as to remove this impression, the already waning confidence in this tribunal will completely disappear.

The reading of this letter in Court I leave to your discretion and responsibility entirely…[300]

Lloyd George must have unsettled the magistrates, as they dismissed the case against two of the defendants and fined the other two a shilling each.[301]

On 15 October 1889, Lloyd George had a hard-hitting article published in the *Carnarvon and Denbigh Herald*, in which he powerfully advocated the use of the Welsh language in Caernarfonshire County

[300] Du Parcq, Vol.I, p62-64.

[301] Edwards, 1913, Vol.I, p122; W. W. Davies, p52.

Council, both in the chamber and in official forms. Under the title 'Should the Welsh language be accorded equality in the proceedings of the Caernarfonshire County Council?', he argued forcefully for exactly that, stating: "The Local Government Act of last year certainly does not designate the English tongue as the only one in which the proceedings of the Council should be conducted."

He continued:

> Whether there is some antique and long-forgotten Act[302] of the legislature proscribing the official use of the Welsh language, it is scarcely worth the Council's while to enquire. The Act–if such be extant–was intended to provide for circumstances foreign to those now in being and is so obsolete as the laws against heresy and apostasy and deserves the same respect as those antiquated laws.

Lloyd George then moved to a compelling contemporary argument:

> Apart from any question of sentiment, the efficiency of the Council requires that free permission should be given to such councillors as prefer Welsh to express their views in that language and for the simple reason that the English language would of necessity be confined to a minority of the Council.
>
> Moreover, an unfair advantage in all debates would thus be given to such of the councillors, as are least in sympathy with the masses of the Welsh people.[303]

This was Lloyd George advocating powerfully in favour of "greater social equality and democratic entitlement" and calling "for equality for the language at a time when it was not fashionable to do so".[304] Two days later, on 17 October, the Welsh National Council met at Caernarfon at the Guildhall, addressed by Sir William Harcourt, and under the presidency of Stuart Rendel, and Lloyd George was chosen to second a resolution in favour of disestablishment. Further, Mr R. A. Griffith[305] moved a resolution, amended at the suggestion of Tom Ellis MP and unanimously agreed to: "That this meeting is of opinion that a Central Educational Council for Wales should be formed, with full control over all branches of Welsh National Education." Speaking on this, Lloyd George stated:

> I would not have our opponents believe that a motion of this character indicates any difference of opinion in the Liberal camp on matters of principle. The object of the suggested League would be identical with those of the present organisations. It is simply a question of the means to be adopted in order to ensure the attainment of such objects. And I would not have our friends, on the other hand, run away with the idea that the adoption of Mr. Griffith's scheme involves the eradication of the subsisting Federations. It would simply mean an attempt to spread their roots, so as to lay hold on the Welsh masses which form the subsoil of Liberalism

---

302 Lloyd George alluded to the 'Laws in Wales Acts 1535 and 1542', often termed the 'Acts of Union'.

303 Quoted in Price, 2006, p74.

304 Price, 2006, p75, 77.

305 Robert Griffith (1860-1936), native of Caernarfon, solicitor, poet, known by his bardic name 'Elphin'.

in the land. The proposal contains two distinct suggestions–the welding of the two Federations into one central and national body, and the establishment of branches of that league in every locality. As to the consolidation of the North and South Wales Federations into one national council I cannot help thinking that this would effect a vast improvement on the present system. One of the great historical blunders of our forefathers, which conduced to the loss of our national independence, was the division of Wales into the two provinces of North and South. We should profit by the lessons of Welsh history and avoid rather than follow such a calamitous precedent. And what is the practical outcome of the institution of two independent Federations?… Instead of unity and co-operation we find perpetual bickering's and dissensions. The two Federations wasting their energies in attacking each other instead of concentrating their activity in an attack upon the enemy... Wales is already plentifully supplied with religious and political schisms without creating another. It would be an advantage to fuse the two organisations were it only to impregnate the timid, genteel Liberalism of the Northern committee with the robust, plucky Liberalism of the South… It would be desirable from every point of view to consolidate our power. As to the second suggestion contained in the proposal, I consider its adoption sooner or later essential to the triumph of Liberal principles. At present you have merely an organization of leading politicians in every locality. The masses of the people have not yet been reached by our political associations. If this Council is to be useful as a medium for the expression of the political requirements of Wales it must represent in fact as well as in theory the masses of our countrymen. We purport here to-day to represent the Liberals of Wales, but if we investigate the state of things with candour, is there any real foundation for our pretensions? … Is it not really, under the circumstances, nothing less than a fraud on our part to declare that we represent the Liberals of Wales? But if this resolution is passed and carried into operation the whole mass of Welsh Liberals will be organized into one great council; branches of that council could be established in every district, and the annual meeting in future might well claim to speak in the name of Wales, and not merely on behalf of an infinitesimal section of its inhabitants. Its resolutions will then have greater force and influence, as those to whom they will be directed will recognise in their sounds the voice of a whole country… But there is another reason of far wider and deeper importance why an attempt should be made to organize all the available forces of Liberalism in the Principality. The battle is becoming more and more intense, as the disgraceful record of Tory intimidation which occurred during the last bye-elections will amply prove. Anyone who scans the objects of the Welsh National Council must foresee without much prophetic vision that the fight for the attainment of those objects will be a life and death struggle. What are those objects? Emancipation of the land and its tillers, the disestablishment and disendowment of the Church, local option and an extensive measure of local government for Wales. There is not one of these objects but affects the governing classes in their most vital interests. Do you think that they will tamely surrender profits, interests, and privileges which they hold as dear as life without utilising every available weapon in the arsenals of tyranny?… And how do we propose then to protect workingmen who have been deprived of their means of subsistence because of their adhesion to our programme? At present our Liberal organisations can barely eke out a miserable and half-starved subsistence. Now

> unless we can protect the victims of our opponents' intimidating tactics from destitution, such terror will be struck into the heart of the timid and less eager spirits that Liberalism will come an impossibility in our country. But supposing each and every working-man who happens to be subjected to the persecution of a Tory employer of labour, or his minions, were to realise the fact that there was a league, numbering amongst its members 200,000 of the sturdiest of his countrymen, ready to rescue him from the consequences of his devotion to principle... Liberalism would then be the ruling force in our country, and I cannot help harbouring an earnest conviction that thousands who now temporize in order to save themselves and their families from being turned out upon a world whose resources are distributed by monopolists, would welcome the opportunity which such a league would afford them of emancipating themselves from the grip of a tyranny which they must heartily detest…
>
> [After further debate, t]he motion was then put to the vote and lost, the amendment being carried by a large majority.[306]

Lloyd George continued to speak on the issue of disestablishment, and sometimes there was an opportunity for humour in the otherwise tense atmosphere. The new Bishop of St Asaph, Dr A. G. Edwards[307], himself a Merioneth man, and a very able debater, was giving:

> … the promoters of disestablishment some hard knocks, and it is related of him that he was particularly effective in one of the districts. Accordingly, the Nonconformists there brought down Lloyd George to speak at a public meeting in order to counteract the bishop's influence. Lloyd George himself tells the story of how he was introduced at that meeting by the chairman, a leading deacon of the village. "We have suffered much of late from misrepresentations," he said. "The Bishop of St. Asaph has been speaking against us and we all know that he is a very great liar. Thank God we have a match for him here to-night in Mr. Lloyd George." In later years when Lloyd George and the bishop became good friends in spite of their differences of opinion, it was hard to decide which of them enjoyed this story most.[308]

On 7 November 1889, Lloyd George was again active in Caernarfonshire County Council proceedings:

> Alderman Lloyd George, in pursuance of notice, moved "That this Council do petition the Board of Trade in pursuance of the Sea Fisheries Regulation Act for the formation of an official board for Cardigan Bay." The resolution was passed, with the addition of the words, "in conjunction with Cardiganshire and Merionethshire."[309]

---

306 *Carnarvon and Denbigh Herald*, 18 October 1889, p7.

307 Alfred G. Edwards (1848-1937), Bishop of St Asaph, 1889-1934, a strong defender of the rights of the established Church of England in Wales. From 1920-1934 he was also the first Archbishop of Wales.

308 Dilnot, p43-44. The story is also related by W. Algernon Locker in *Lloyd George By Mr. Punch*, p3.

309 *Carnarvon and Denbigh Herald*, 8 November 1889, p5.

Very soon, however, Lloyd George would himself be 'fishing in bigger seas'.

# 3

## WELSH RADICAL MP, 1890-1905

At around 10 pm on 19 March, the sitting Conservative Member for Carnarvon Boroughs, the wealthy barrister and estate agent, Edmund Swetenham, died unexpectedly aged 67 at his residence, Cam-yr-Alyn, Rossett, near Wrexham, from pneumonia contracted after a heavy fall from his horse whilst out fox hunting a few weeks before. This unforeseen event triggered a by-election, one that would drastically change Lloyd George's life, and that of his family, forever. On 20 March, Maggie had arranged to meet Lloyd George at Criccieth station. He had gone to Portmadoc earlier that morning on business, and the couple planned to spend the rest of the day together in Caernarfon. As Maggie arrived on the platform, she was handed a telegram addressed only to 'Lloyd George'. Naturally assuming that it was intended for her, Maggie opened the envelope and read the simple message: "Swetenham died last night."

Now, both had their lives turned upside-down. In 1940, after her husband had represented the Boroughs for a full half century, Dame Margaret, only months before her own death, reflected:

> I thought I was marrying a Caernarvonshire lawyer. Some people even then said he was sure to get on, but it was success as a lawyer that they had in mind. I am sure neither of us guessed then what lay before us. Even when he accepted nomination as the Liberal candidate for the Caernarvon Boroughs it did not seem to make any particular difference. I comforted myself that the general election was two years distant and that we had those two years in which to enjoy ourselves.[310]

On the day, the couple decided to continue with their original plan and travelled on to Caernarvon, but the day was not a success. As Margaret reflected later in the same interview: "The sunshine seemed to have gone from the day… The shadow of the coming election spoilt everything."[311]

When the by-election was called, the Tories found difficulty finding a candidate. A number of possible local nominees, including the eventual candidate Sir Hugh Ellis-Nanney–the very man who had once carried out the school inspections in Llanystumdwy–declined the chance to contest the seat. It seemed that a South Walian barrister, Thomas Marchant Williams, would be selected, but this possibility came to nothing, as the local Tories would not promise support in the following general

---

310 NLW, E. Morgan Humphreys Papers A/1157(i), Dame Margaret Lloyd George interviewed by Humphreys, April 1940.
311 Ibid.

election. Eventually Ellis-Nanney was persuaded to stand; a popular figure locally, something of a philanthropist by the standards of the time, but his health was poor, he was not a Welsh-speaker, and he was a reluctant candidate.

On 24 March, two days after Swetenham's funeral, Lloyd George issued his address to the electors, in which he supported the standard Gladstonian position on Irish Home Rule but devoted more space to Welsh grievances:

> TO THE FREE AND INDEPENDENT ELECTORS OF THE CARNARVONSHIRE DISTRICT BOROUGHS
> FELLOW COUNTRYMEN,
> Owing to the sad and unexpected circumstance of the death of our late Member, Mr. Edmund Swetenham, Q.C., you are suddenly called upon to elect another representative to Parliament.
> You now have the opportunity of blotting out the stain which has for the last three years tarnished your Parliamentary record, and of restoring the wonted allegiance of these ancient Boroughs to the great principles of Liberalism.
> Recent By-Elections prove that the country is sick and tired of Mr. Balfour's baton-and-bayonet rule in Ireland, and of his desperate attempts to repress by martial law legitimate aspirations of a generous nation. I come before you as a firm believer in and admirer of Mr. Gladstone's noble alternative of Justice to Ireland.
>
> Whilst fully recognising that the wrongs of Ireland must of necessity have the first claim upon the attention of the Liberal party, I am deeply impressed with the fact that Wales has wants and aspirations of her own which have too long been ignored, but which must no longer be neglected. First and foremost amongst these stands the cause of Religious Liberty and Equality in Wales. If returned to Parliament by you, it shall be my earnest endeavour to labour for the triumph of this great cause. Wales has for many a year yearned in her heart for the attainment of that religious equality and freedom which is impossible whilst the English Church as by law established is imposed upon us as the National Religion of Wales, and is maintained by Welsh national endowments, and whilst clerical bigotry dominates over our Churchyards.
>
> The Liberal party has recently placed the Disestablishment and Disendowment of the English Church in Wales in the forefront of its platform, and I earnestly trust that you, the electors of a Nonconformist constituency, will not openly reject this proffered boon by returning a Tory representative. I believe that our land and labour laws work inequality and injustice, and I am in favour of measures for simplifying and cheapening the Transfer of Land; for the Taxation of Ground-rents; the Enfranchisement of Leaseholds; and for improving the condition of the Tenant Farmer and Labourer.
>
> I have always been a consistent advocate of Temperance, and had the privilege of being largely instrumental in bringing about the adoption of the "Direct Veto" by the party at the recent Liberal Conference in Manchester. If returned to Parliament, I shall do all in my power to support measures which have for their object the removal from our midst of the disastrous temptations of strong drink.

I take a keen interest in our river and sea fisheries, and had the honour of being the first member of the Carnarvonshire County Council to propose the application of the Sea Fisheries Regulation Act to the sea-board of this county. I should like to see the powers of that Act amplified and made more practicable.

I believe in a liberal extension of the principle of Decentralisation. There are also such questions as "One Man One Vote," "Graduated Taxation," "A Free Breakfast Table," and many another much-needed Reform; but what availeth it even to enumerate them while there is a Tory Government in power?

The contest will in the ordinary course of things be over in a fortnight or three weeks' time, and I fear I cannot therefore hope to have the pleasure of making the personal acquaintance of each of you; but I venture to think, nevertheless, that you will, at this important juncture in the history of our country, neither "from fear, favour, affection, nor hope of reward," set aside her supreme claim upon your consideration.[312]

On 27 March the *South Wales Daily News* reported:

The contest for the Carnarvon Boroughs has commenced in good earnest. Mr LLOYD GEORGE… has not let the grass grow under his feet. He has already addressed a number of meetings in the constituency, and has everywhere received with an enthusiasm which augurs well for his chances. We… have no hesitation in saying that the Welsh Liberals of the Carnarvon Boroughs could desire no better man to represent them…[313]

Biographer Emyr Price rightly observed:

Contrary to the belief of many historians who have written about his early career, Lloyd George was undoubtedly a radical nationalist, with a labourist slant to his social and economic policies. He was intent on pushing for Welsh Home Rule. More than any other contemporary politician, he was ready to press this case to the limits and especially in the early 1890s. This was not posturing nor tactics… indeed, it was a standpoint held with conviction, and a commitment which was very high-risk, especially in a constituency which was Conservative held and where many Liberals might well scoff at such an extreme policy.[314]

This is a most important and long overdue re-assessment.

On 28 March, the *Carnarvon and Denbigh Herald* reported on Lloyd George's selection meetings, an important glimpse into electoral procedure at the time, the local personalities and tensions, the prevalent local concerns, and, above all, Lloyd George's already considerable oratorial skills– persuasive, humorous, self-assured, issue-focused:

---

[312] Quoted in Du Parcq, Vol.I, p95-96.
[313] *South Wales Daily News*, 27 March 1890, p2.
[314] Price, 2006, p58.

At a meeting of delegates, numerously attended from all the contributory boroughs, held in Carnarvon on Monday afternoon last… a unanimous feeling prevailed in favour of the candidature of Mr. Lloyd George…

Mr. George said he had been very much encouraged by the Liberal offers made to him by several Carnarvon and Bangor solicitors who placed their services as election agents at his disposal… free of charge. When the heavy charges and expenses connected with electioneering was taken into consideration, it would be easily understood that these expenses would practically debar any candidate coming forward from amongst the masses and he was not only for the people but of the people, and as the expense would be a serious consideration and hindrance in his case he could not but thankfully accept the proffered gratuitous assistance… He asked them not to fight for him on personal grounds, but rather fight to the bitter end for liberty and for their principles; he was not going to conduct the contest as if fighting for himself, but rather to secure a triumphant victory for those principles which he believed the vast majority of the electorate held dear. If they won this contest it would be another blow to the shackles of downtrodden Ireland. If he was to fight the contest, he preferred doing so on an honest programme. They all knew his opinions, and he knew the opinions of the boroughs, and would meet them as conscientiously as he could…

… On Monday evening a meeting was held by the Liberals of Carnarvon for the purpose of making the necessary arrangements for the successful prosecution of the town's canvass. The meeting, which was crowded, was characterised by the greatest enthusiasm from beginning to end." Lloyd George made his address, again urging "every Liberal to be up and doing." Towards the close of the meeting, the Rev. Evan Jones, Moriah, Carnarvon, wanted Lloyd George "to make it a condition of his supporting Gladstone in his Home Rule scheme that a measure of disestablishment for Wales should also be passed either concurrently with, or immediately after, the passing of the Home Rule Bill and before the dissolution of Parliament… Several persons protested against this", including the Chairman and Lloyd George himself. Some further remarks [on disestablishment] having been made, a vote of confidence in Mr. George was passed…

"MEETING AT NEVIN. Mr. Lloyd George held a most enthusiastic meeting at Nevin on Tuesday evening... Addresses were delivered by… the Candidate… and others, and a resolution of confidence In Mr. Lloyd George was unanimously passed.

MEETING AT PWLLHELI. On Wednesday evening, a meeting was held in the Town Hall, Pwllheli…

Mr. William Abraham, M.P. for West Limerick… hoped that they would return Mr. Lloyd George in order to give expression to the real needs of their country … Mr. Lloyd George was sound on the Irish question…

Mr. Lloyd George… said that... [t]he great questions in Wales were the disestablishment and disendowment of the Church. Now these questions were put before this constituency, and if they returned a candidate who supported these questions, Parliament would see that Wales wanted the Church disestablished… To return a Liberationist would be in itself an argument for disestablishment. Therefore, the present election was a most important one… As a Dissenter he favoured Disestablishment. The Church received £300,000 annually from the country and did not give any advantage in return. There were the churchyards of the country. They should be in the hands of the people, and not as at present, in the hands of a narrow-minded clergy. He referred to the Llanfrothen burial scandal… He believed that the land laws of the country should be thoroughly reformed. Lands could be improved and made to produce five-fold more than what they produced at present. If this were so, more people would have employment, which, of course, would have beneficial results in the towns, as all lived more or less on the land. The enfranchisement of leaseholds was an important question… If they took the question of ground rents into consideration, they would find how unjust they were… He favoured the veto in the granting of public-house licenses, as moral suasion was not sufficient… [and] roused the audience into great enthusiasm when speaking upon the Irish question. Wales had long waited for her rights, but the time had at last arrived. They all should be unanimous in demanding their rights…

GREAT LIBERAL DEMONSTRATION AT CARNARVON. On Thursday evening last, a most enthusiastic meeting was held in the Guild Hall, Carnarvon, in favour of Mr. Lloyd George's candidature. The spacious hall was crowded in every part, and the utmost unanimity prevailed… [O]n the platform were… The Revs. E. Herber Evans and Owen Davies, Carnarvon;… Messrs. W. Abraham, M.P.; D. Lloyd George, the candidate; T. Gee, Denbigh [the publisher]… David Thomas, Bryngwyn…

Mr. David Thomas, chairman of the local Liberal Association [moved the first resolution]: "That this meeting strongly condemns the policy pursued by the present Government in Ireland, and heartily approves of the programme of the Liberal Party… as embodied in Mr. George's address."…

The Rev. Owen Davies seconded… He believed that every important consideration to be looked for in a candidate was to be found in Mr. Lloyd George … Mr. Lloyd George had, long ago, made up his mind on [disestablishment]; he was not going up to Parliament to learn, he was going there because he had learnt…

The resolution… was carried with acclamation… Mr. Lloyd George... said [that]... after fishing in London and all over the country their opponents had succeeded in persuading the Squire of Gwynfryn to lead them in battle... He was a capital representative of his party, he was one of the aristocracy, a landlord and moneyed gentleman. They now had, on the one hand, a member of the aristocracy, and on the other hand one of the masses, one of the people themselves, bred and born amongst the people. He (Mr. George) had read the report of the previous night's Conservative meeting, from which he saw that one great qualification which Mr. Nanney possessed in order to become the Tory party's candidate was that he was a man of wealth, and that the great disqualification in the speaker's case was that he was not possessed of any wealth… He had once heard a man wildly declaiming against Mr. T. E. Ellis as a Parliamentary representative, but, according to that man, Mr. Ellis' disqualification consisted mainly in the fact that he had been brought up in a cottage. The Tories had not yet realised that the day of the cottage-bred men had at last dawned… the Tories of the present day did not appear able to realise that… the day of the masses had now dawned… It was not necessary for

> him to tell them that he was in favour of disestablishment. It had been the dream of his life, and he hoped to see that dream soon realised. Why should the Church of the aristocracy be imposed upon us as the national religion of Wales and maintained by Welsh national endowments, whilst the Church of the people was placed on such an unequal ground?… And with respect to Welsh matters, before they could expect any measure of justice done for Wales they must clear the board of the Irish matters first–justice must be done to Ireland before the way would be clear for them in Wales to obtain what they so loudly called for. Referring to Mr. Balfour's treatment of the Irish, he said this was the man who also slighted them in Wales, and positively ignored them, and in whose opinion they were not worth mentioning as a people. And yet that was the man whom Sir John Puleston[315] exalted to such an extent in his speech the previous evening… Complaints were sometimes heard that promises were made at election times which were not realised. They must remember that progress walked very slow, but as sure as the Liberal party had promised great and good measures those measures would become actual facts as soon as possible. They (the electors) ought to expedite matters by keeping the way clear of all hindrances and let them all travel towards the dawn of liberty.
>
> The Rev. Dr. Herber Evans moved the following resolution "That having heard the address of Mr. D. Lloyd George… this meeting is of opinion that he is a fit and proper person to represent these boroughs in Parliament…", before proceeding: "Mr. Lloyd George is the selected Liberal candidate of these boroughs… I am at one with Mr. George on every point in his address… [He] is… a young man of energy, intelligence, and unblemished character, a real Welshman, a Nonconformist well versed in our sufferings, and so a brave defender of our right, the disestablishment of the Church of England in Wales…
>
> … The motion was then passed amid cheers.
>
> … Mr. Thomas Gee… was received with tremendous cheering. Speaking in Welsh he observed that he wondered at the thought that there was any necessity for discussing Liberal principles in a town like Carnarvon, where they had five Liberal newspapers, and not a single Tory paper… The business they wanted to settle first was the question of Disestablishment…"
>
> After briefly establishing that the candidate was sound on his proclaimed Liberal principles, Gee concluded: "Well; you will do. I consider the boroughs of Carnarvon have a candidate who is thoroughly healthy in the faith…"[316]

Lloyd George secured funding of about £250 [£41,053 in 2025] from a local Methodist. Candidates were nominated on 2 April. Campaigning, Tory speakers contrasted the local focus of Ellis-Nanney, with the scale of Lloyd George's talents and national interests. A contrast was drawn between the wealthy Tory landowner and the Liberal from a lower social stratum. Lloyd George, in turn, demonstrating his already considerable oratorical skills, ridiculed the Tory arguments. Indeed, his oratory was key to his success, as the more perceptive of his opponents could not help but acknowledge. J. Hugh Edwards noted:

---

[315] Sir John Puleston (1830-1908), Welsh journalist, Tory MP for Devonport 1874-1892, Constable of Caernarvon Castle 1890-1908.

[316] *Carnarvon and Denbigh Herald*, 28 March 1890, p5.

> Just at this juncture the late Mr. Tobit Evans[317]–at that time the chief Liberal Unionist Agent for the Principality–arrived at Carnarvon for the purpose of ascertaining the exact trend of the contest. He interviewed canvassers and pressmen and he entered into conversation with the most prominent and best-informed of the local men. With the evening's post he dispatched to the Unionist headquarters in London a full report of his investigations. He declared that dissension had already crept into the Liberal ranks, that denominational bias was in an active state of fermentation, and that there was a consensus of feeling that the revolt of the Rev. Evan Jones would lead to the defection of a large number of Nonconformists from the Liberal standard. On the strength of these facts he predicted a sure and a substantial victory for the Unionist candidate. Having dispatched his message, Mr. Tobit Evans wended his way to the pavilion at Carnarvon, where Mr. Lloyd George was advertised to speak that evening. The place was crowded, and in due time the youthful candidate made his appearance. The Unionist agent, eager to spy the nakedness of the land, marked with serene satisfaction the presence of a large neutral zone in the meeting where the advent of the candidate had evoked neither applause nor enthusiasm. Mr. Lloyd George devoted his speech to the advocacy of the measures adumbrated in his election address, and the audience was listening with content when suddenly the orator's voice quivered with the note of emotion. "I once heard a man wildly declaiming against Tom Ellis as a Parliamentary representative," he proceeded to say, amid the hush that had fallen upon the great assembly, "for according to that man Mr. Ellis's disqualification consisted mainly in the fact that he had been brought up in 'a cottage.' The Tories have not yet realised," cried Mr. Lloyd George, as his voice rang through the building like the clear note of a great bell, "that the day of the cottage-bred men has at last dawned."
>
> The exclamation, so vivid in its representation and so fervid in its note of appeal, revealed to the audience the dramatic contrast between Mr. Lloyd George and the territorial magnate who was then opposing him, and in an instant the whole assembly sprang frantically to their feet, and the rafters of the hall reverberated again and again with the thunder of their applause… Amid this remarkable demonstration, the Unionist agent hurried forth into the street. As soon as he reached his hotel he penned a fresh message to the party headquarters. "I much regret," he wrote, "that I find myself compelled to reverse my previous opinion of the prospects of the contest. I attended Lloyd George's meeting at Carnarvon this evening, and under the sway of his marvellous oratorical powers the audience was electrified beyond anything I have ever witnessed in the whole course of my life. Strong men broke down with emotion, while those who have hitherto been neutral and even indifferent were swept off their feet with the whirlwind of his eloquence. A man who can make so thrilling and overpowering an appeal to the emotions is absolutely invincible in Wales, and for that reason I feel compelled to warn you that in my opinion the seat is lost to our party."[318]

Lloyd George's observation about the 'cottage-bred man' was later much quoted. It is worth noting that, because of his well-known radical views, even at this early stage in his career, he could not even

---

[317] Henry Tobit Evans (1844-1908).

[318] Edwards, 1913, Vol.II, p221-223.

depend on the support of Liberals in his own constituency. Lloyd George toured the constituency non-stop, speaking in a different part of it each night, no small feat as the constituency was composed of six separate boroughs, scattered over some 25 miles.[319] His energy began to pay off, as some of the remote cottages and farmsteads had never before been approached personally by an electioneering politician. The three smallest boroughs (Criccieth, Nefyn and Pwllheli) were the most agricultural and strongly Liberal parts of the seat. In a close election, this support was to prove decisive for the Criccieth-based candidate–Lloyd George.

One of the few Liberals who aided his campaign was Sir Wilfrid Lawson[320], who recalled:

> During the Easter Recess… I went down to help Lloyd George… a fine time we had, a great feature in the Welsh contests being the singing. There was one song of which, being in Welsh, I did not, of course, understand a word, except the finale which was always "George and Gladstone," sung with tremendous emphasis and which rang in my head for days and days afterwards. Almost the only Liberal Member besides myself who came down to help George was Mr. Acland…[321] [322]

Of the larger communities, Bangor was the most strongly Tory borough in the constituency, having the Anglican cathedral and three Conservative Clubs. Caernarfon had a Conservative Working Men's Club, an Anglican Training College, four Anglican churches, a militia barracks and 45 taverns–not naturally propitious electoral territory for a radical Liberal Nonconformist advocating temperance and Welsh nationalism! Conway also had a substantial body of committed Tory voters, as previous elections had shown. Even in the three smaller, more intensely Welsh boroughs, Lloyd George faced significant difficulties. Both Criccieth and Pwllheli contained a considerable number of Tory voters, while Nefyn contained a Conservative Club and several taverns. The electorate was still largely composed of the affluent middle classes, businessmen and men from the professions, farmers and a few skilled artisans. Lloyd George could not even be sure of Nonconformist support, as it was noted that at his first campaign meeting in Nefyn's Madryn Hall not a single Baptist was present. Fearing that his views might be regarded as too extreme, Lloyd George began to tone down his speeches to appeal to the widest possible audience. This naturally led his opponents to pillory him as back-tracking on his manifesto.

Nefyn was the smallest and least known borough, certainly outside of North Wales, on the remoter northern coast of the Llŷn Peninsula, unlike the others in the constituency. The sea had always played

---

[319] The population of the Boroughs, according to the census of 1881, was 28,391, and in 1890 the electorate numbered 4628, distributed as follows - Carnarvon, 1517; Bangor, 1509; Conway, 580; Pwllheli, 622; Nefyn, 370; and Criccieth, 215. See *Carnarvon and Denbigh Herald*, 11 April 1890, p5.

[320] Sir Wilfrid Lawson (1829-1906), temperance campaigner, agriculturalist, radical, anti-imperialist Liberal MP for Cockermouth, the Commons' leading humourist.

[321] Acland had owned an estate at Clynnog in Caernarvonshire since 1880.

[322] W. Lawson, *A Memoir*, 1909, Ed. G. W. Russell, London, Smith, Elder & Co., p201-202. Lloyd George composed the words himself, setting the words to the tune of 'Marching Through Georgia', a popular Unionist song from the American Civil War in 1865. See Cregier, p35.

an important part in its economy; and fishing, particularly for herring, had been the prime trade for much of the 18th and 19th Centuries, to the extent that the town's coat of arms bears three herrings. Herring were locally referred to as 'Nefyn beef'.[323] By 1910, Nefyn had 40 herring fishing boats, each crewed by three or four men, but herring fishing ceased around 1918. The area had nurtured many ship's captains, and shipbuilding was also an important local industry until the same period, both wilting in the face of increasingly large-scale international competition.

Voting took place on 10 April. The unusual nature of this by-election was noticed, the *Carnarvon and Denbigh Herald* exclaiming:

> Never in the history of the constituency was a keener, more determined struggle witnessed... No stone was left unturned on the Conservative side... One voter was brought all the way from Wolverhampton; and three Carnarvon plasterers, employed at the new houses now being built on the fine Pwllheli beach, were brought by car–a distance of some twenty miles at least–to record their votes for Mr. Ellis Nanney... No election in North Wales has ever drawn so much public attention to itself as the one just decided in the Carnarvon Boroughs. All previous contests were fought from first to last mainly with the help of local men; but such was the importance attached to this last struggle that no fewer than seventeen Members of Parliament, Welsh, English, Scotch and Irish, took part in the conflict.[324]

In the event, the election count was a tense affair, as it was soon apparent that the result would be 'a close-run thing'. In 1886, the Tory Swetenham had taken the seat with a majority of 136. Lloyd George spent polling day with supporters at Pwllheli before meeting up with Uncle Lloyd at Avonwen. The following day, 11 April, he went to the Guildhall in Caernarfon, where the count took place. At first, it seemed Ellis-Nanney would be elected, but then John T. Roberts, Lloyd George's electoral agent, spotted a sheaf of twenty Liberal votes had been put in the Conservative pile. The Tories then demanded a recount themselves, one voting slip being returned to their pile. Eventually, around midday, the Mayor, John Issard Davies, declared that David Lloyd George was elected by 1,963 votes to 1,945, a wafer-thin margin of 18 votes. This was on an 89.5% turnout, the largest the constituency had ever had, and a 2.1% swing to the Liberals. The narrowness of Lloyd George's victory led the local Tory *Y Gwalia* newspaper to spuriously claim that he had only won the seat because a severe storm at sea, which had lasted for two days, had prevented a host of Tory-voting Nefyn fishermen from coming ashore to cast their votes![325]

"The banner of the Red Dragon has been borne aloft in triumph," Lloyd George exclaimed that afternoon, as the great crowd surged around him shouting and cheering in its jubilation.[326] Although Lloyd George would go on to represent the constituency for nearly 55 years through a series of 14 unbroken electoral wins, he did not win a majority of the votes in all six boroughs until 1906, by which

---

[323] J. Ifor Davies, p15.

[324] *Carnarvon and Denbigh Herald*, 11 April 1890, p4.

[325] *Y Gwalia*, 16 April 1890.

[326] Quoted in Edwards, 1913, Vol.II, p223.

time he was very much a national political figure. That day, a more human story played out. After Caernarfon, Lloyd George had to attend more celebrations at Bangor before he could catch the evening train back to his home in Criccieth. Much later, his son, Richard, took up the tale:

> Of course his own townsfolk were wild with joy... At the station almost the entire population jammed together in a cheering mass awaited the return of their conquering hero. On his arrival he was shepherded into the inevitable open carriage, drawn by scores of his followers, and so another triumphal procession began. The sound of their jubilant cries brought my mother and her parents to the door of the farmhouse when the procession was still a mile distant, and far below them.
>
> Now the road that leads from the village green to Mynydd Ednyfed Fawr is steep. Even for the lusty enthusiasts, hauling on the ropes attached to the vehicle in which my father was seated, it must have been heavy going. But obviously the only possible end of the victory parade was their hero's own doorstep. And so they slogged along up the hill with the singing torchbearers ahead and behind.
>
> When they were still a quarter of a mile away my mother issued an order to Sally, my nurse, a very determined and formidable young lady. With satisfaction and alacrity Sally proceeded to obey the command. Down the sweeping road… she ran. Not until she reached the closed gates that barred the way up to the house did she halt. Here… she awaited the arrival of the cavalcade. The flickering flares of the torches revealed her to the leaders of the procession when they were within a few feet of her. She must have presented a formidable appearance, for they stopped their singing in the middle of a bar and came to a dead stop.
>
> "What is all this going on?" she demanded, in Welsh of course. And without waiting for an answer, "You're to stop your noise. Do you want to wake the baby?"
>
> So out of the carriage stepped my father, and alone he made his ignominious way through the gate and up to the house while his subdued followers turned about and retraced their steps down the hill![327]

The forces that had been arrayed against him had been considerable–and not all of them legal. On his way to London a week later to take his seat at Westminster, the new member was met by a great body of his supporters in the constituent borough of Conway, amid scenes of great enthusiasm. Speaking in the Market Hall, he declared:

> Our victory is really great, when we take everything into consideration–the great powers arrayed against us, the influence of the aristocracy and the prestige of the rich, all of which were arrayed on the Tory side. Employers of labour, I have no hesitation in saying, used their influence in intimidating those in their employment to give their votes for the Tory candidate. There were also other forces at work in the contest, such as the lavish distribution of coal. One hears of coal being distributed freely at Christmas, but, on account of the election, it was given even

[327] Lloyd George, *Dame Margaret,* p95-96. The people of Llanfrothen, though not in his constituency, also celebrated their hero, lighting fireworks on the hillsides and cheering "Lloyd George for ever": D. Evans, p101.

> more freely in the Boroughs at Easter time. I am very glad, however, to think that the Carnarvon electors have shown themselves to be fireproof, and are not to be led away by coal from the path of duty. They are actuated by principles rather than by fuel.[328]

When Tom Ellis heard the result, he wrote at once to Lloyd George from Cairo, where he was recuperating from a serious bout of typhoid fever:

> The first news that I received on reaching Cairo was the lamented death of Mr. Swetenham... I wondered, however, a thousand times… how in the world he had been elected to represent my countrymen in the Caernarvon Boroughs. *For it was one of the chief principles of his policy that Wales ought not to expect to obtain any special legislation, and that to merge herself and her national identity in the life of England and Anglicanism was her duty and her only solution.*
>
> *You take a very different view of the future of Wales and national life*, and so I believe do the great majority of my countrymen.
>
> *You believe, as I also do, that Wales may and should live her own life, freely, boldly, honestly, and without cringing to anybody*,–for the reason that this is the surest way of gaining respect and a high character for her commercial men and her working people, and that such is the portion appointed to her by Providence. *By respecting her own history and life*, Wales will gain the respect of her neighbours.
>
> You believe, too, that the most effectual means of enabling Wales to win her proper position in political life is *to form a Welsh Party in the Imperial Parliament*, and that it is one of the privileges of young Welshmen to do what lies in their power to strengthen the arm and facilitate the attainment of the aims of the Welsh party.[329]

The letter shows a deep agreement and understanding between the two young politicians with a genuine, if almost poetic, vision of the future that seemed so close to being within their grasp.

Lloyd George duly became the "Boy MP", taking his seat at Westminster on 17 April 1890, introduced by Stuart Rendel[330] and Arthur Acland.[331] It was Budget Day, and Margaret pasted a newspaper report filed by Mrs [Margaret] Verney into her scrapbook:

> It was a striking sight, the closely packed benches, the Chancellor of the Exchequer [George Goschen][332] with many little volumes of notes, bracing himself up for a grand effort; while immediately below the venerable figure of Lord Cottesloe[333] stood the young M.P. for the Caernarvon Boroughs, nearly seventy years his junior, pale with excitement and the thoughts of the career opening before him, waiting for the last answer to be given before taking his seat …

---

328 Quoted in Edwards, 1913, Vol.II, p224. See also *Carnarvon and Denbigh Herald*, 18 April 1890, p6.
329 Quoted in Hughes Jones, p34-35.
330 Stuart Rendel (1834-1913), Liberal MP for Montgomeryshire, 1880-1894, the leader of the Welsh MPs.
331 Arthur Acland (1847-1926), Liberal MP for Rotherham, 1885-1899. One of the principal sponsors of the 1889 Welsh Intermediate Education Act, making the new County Councils in Wales responsible for education, a reform not introduced in England until 1902.
332 George Goschen (1831-1907), Chancellor of the Exchequer, 1887-1892.
333 Thomas Fremantle, Baron Cottesloe (1798-1890).

> When at last the young member… advanced to the table between Mr. Stuart Rendel and Mr. Arthur Acland the cheers were loud and hearty…[334]

As historian Robert Ensor observed: "On the back benches appeared another man of destiny… Black-haired, blue-eyed, Welsh-speaking, addicted to picture-phrases, using English with great wit and fluency, but with the air of a foreign language, this young man seemed then an incarnation of the Celtic spirit."[335]

His first intervention followed swiftly, when during Questions on 24 April, he asked:

> I beg to ask the First Lord of the Treasury whether the Government intend to introduce any legislation to carry out the unanimous recommendations of the Town Holdings Committee, which reported last year in favour of the exercise by Local Authorities of powers which would facilitate the acquisition by leaseholders, especially of the industrial classes, of the freehold of their dwelling-houses, and to the effect that all Religious Bodies to whom land has been granted on lease for the erection of their places of worship and schools, should be empowered to purchase the fee subject to payment of fair compensation?
>
> Mr. W. H. Smith[336] I am not aware that any recommendations of the Committee were unanimous. But whether that is so or not, I am not able to undertake that legislation on these lines will be proposed by the Government during this Session, especially as the Town Holdings Committee have not completed the whole of their duties.[337]

On 29 May, Lloyd George went with a party of some 1,000 people organised by Engedi Calvinistic Methodist Chapel, Caernarfon, to Hawarden, as did many Liberal groups at that time. The climax of the day was an address by Gladstone from the terrace of his home at Hawarden Castle. After his address:

> … a number of the leading politicians among them were invited into the Castle for a personal chat with the veteran statesman. They soon discerned that there was method in the invitation, for Mr. Gladstone at once evinced great interest in the controversy which was then raging.[338]

He referred to a special meeting of the North Wales Liberal Association, held in Rhyl on 30 April, at which it was resolved to exact, before the next general election, a pledge from every Liberal candidate for a Welsh constituency that he would support a Liberal Government only if Welsh Disestablishment were introduced concurrently with, or immediately after, Home Rule for Ireland.[339]

---

334 Lloyd George, *Dame Margaret*, p98-99; *Caernarvon and Denbigh Herald*, 2 May 1890, p4.

335 R. C. K. Ensor, *England 1870-1914*, 1936, Oxford, Clarendon Press, p223.

336 William H. Smith (1825-1891), bookseller, newsagent, Tory MP for Westminster, 1868-1885, Strand, 1885-1891, First Lord of the Treasury, 1887-1891.

337 https://api.parliament.uk/historic-hansard/commons/1890/apr/24/the-town-holdings-committee#S3V0343P0_18900424_HOC_171. Retrieved 7 August 2019.

338 Edwards, 1913, Vol.III, p13.

339 Ibid., p6-7.

Gladstone:

> … declared that he regarded the haste of that section of the party responsible for the adoption of the Rhyl resolution as "very unwise," and he strongly counselled "prudence, moderation and unanimity." He then proceeded to inform the company that a measure designed to disestablish and disendow the Welsh Church would be "a very complicated one…" "You must not forget," he added, "that the Welsh Church is essentially part of the English Church…"
>
> In that little band of Welsh politicians who were privileged to listen to the eminent statesman as he passed judgment in private upon the situation, there was one–the newly elected Member for the Carnarvon Boroughs–who was unprepared to subordinate his own judgment even to that of so august an authority as Mr. Gladstone. Again and again in the course of the conversation he pressed the veteran leader for definite information… Were the Liberal leaders as ready to espouse the cause of Wales as they were that of Ireland? Were they prepared to enter into a definite undertaking that Welsh Disestablishment would constitute a leading item in the legislative programme of the next Liberal Ministry? Such questions as these, Mr. Lloyd George persisted in pressing upon the leader… but Mr. Gladstone parried them with the easy grace of an old Parliamentary hand…
>
> The new Member, however, was made of too tough a fibre to be thus lightly disposed of… When, therefore, Mr. Lloyd George, after many attempts, harked back to the question as to the good faith of the Liberal leaders, Mr. Gladstone suddenly… demanded: "Since you set yourself up as the champion of Welsh Nonconformity, perhaps you can tell us how many Nonconformist chapels there were in Wales in the year 1742?"[340]

1742 was significant as it was the year the societies established as the result of the great religious revival in Wales had first joined in an association, marking a significant milestone in the history of Welsh Nonconformity and its secession from the established Church. It was the year that saw the birth of Methodism as a force in the nation's spiritual development. In November 1742, the *Glasgow Weekly History* had published a special article giving "some account of religion in the Principality of Wales". According to this, the Nonconformist congregations in Wales in that year numbered 105. The article was afterwards republished in John Gillies' 'Historical Collections', and it was this that Gladstone–an omnivorous reader–had seen and remembered.

When Lloyd George found himself suddenly confronted with Gladstone's question, he was forced to confess to Gladstone that he could not supply the desired information. "But I can," retorted the eminent statesman in a tone of voice in which exultation mingled with disdain. Though on that occasion he was effectively silenced by Gladstone, Lloyd George was quite unsubdued. Humiliating though it was, the experience was not lost on him. Lloyd George left Hawarden that day convinced that Wales would never receive a measure of disestablishment at the hands of Gladstone–a presentiment which was borne out in the following years. The necessity for the Rhyl policy was

[340] Ibid., p13-14.

revealed to him, and he quickly shaped his course accordingly.[341]

Lloyd George was rapidly finding his feet, his voice and his confidence. In a letter to William on 5 June 1890, he almost boastingly reported a feat of oratory at a temperance meeting in the Free Trade Hall in Manchester:

> I scored a splendid success last night… I aroused the immense and dense audience to a wild fury of enthusiasm… The impression was most marked throughout. The people seemed to be beside themselves with delight. During the delivery of my peroration a profound silence prevailed… When I sat down there was a sight never to be forgotten–the whole audience rose in a body… and the greatest possible confusion prevailed…
>
> As regards voice and gesture I never spoke half as well. I had absolute command over myself and my audience from the very start. [W. S.] Caine said, "You have made your reputation in England by that speech"…[342]

His first years in Parliament saw Lloyd George occupied with "Welsh", "local option" matters: his astonishingly self-assured, detailed maiden speech was delivered to the House at 5.23 pm on 13 June 1890 on the government's Local Taxation (Customs And Excise) Duties Bill, to compensate the holders of liquor licenses which were not renewed by the licensing authorities:

> I may say that the Carnarvonshire County Council have passed a resolution condemning the proposals of the Government, and very few of the Conservative members of the Council ventured to oppose it. I have not the slightest hesitation in declaring that were there an election in Wales at the present moment a clean sweep would be made of all the members who registered their vote in favour of this Bill. I object to the Bill in the first place, because it establishes a new principle in the Licensing Laws. It affirms that you cannot extinguish a licence even if the house is not required for the locality. My second objection is that you are giving £350,000 as compensation to the publicans, without providing that they shall only be compensated on the basis of the profits of legitimate trading. There were 166,000 convictions for drunkenness last year, and there were no doubt many thousands of cases of drunkenness in which there were no prosecutions. If you are going to compensate the publicans you should compensate them on the basis of profits on legitimate trade. Every case of drunkenness really represents a breach of the law committed by a publican, and it also represents an increase in the profits of a publican. If this proposal is carried, the House will be capitalising profits made by a gross and wholesale infringement of the law. We have heard a great deal about law and order in Ireland. I think there ought to be a Coercion Act for publicans armed with all the modern appliances, such as Star Chamber inquiries, informers, "shadows," and Removable Magistrates. Why not punish the publican for an infringement of the law, with the same amount of zeal as the Government display in punishing the Irish Members? If there were such an Act, I believe that very few

---

341 Ibid., p15.

342 Quoted in George, *My Brother And I*, p27-28. Lloyd George wrote in similar vein to Margaret: Morgan, *Family Letters*, p27-28.

publicans would survive the inquisition, and the £350,000 would form an ample sum to compensate those who remained. Another objection I have to make to the Government proposal is that the sum of £350,000 is grossly inadequate for the purposes set forth in the Bill. We are all agreed that a reduction in the number of public houses will promote temperance, but this money will not suffice for any appreciable reduction. Take instances in my own constituency. Eifion, a small town, is infested with licences, and if this sum is to be distributed over the whole of Carnarvonshire, it would take more than £1,000,000 to reduce the number of houses to a point at which they would be sufficient for the wants of the inhabitants. We have been told by the hon. Member for Barrow [W. S. Caine] that it will require £250,000,000 to compensate the whole of the publicans of the United Kingdom. We must reduce the number of public houses by 50 per cent, before we attain the object we have in view, and for that, £125,000,000 will be necessary. Yet this £350,000 is offered to do it all. There never was a more puny attempt made to grapple with a great evil since the days of the Lilliputian King who drew his hanger to attack Gulliver. But that is not all. The Chancellor of the Exchequer was very profuse with his sympathy for temperance, and the President of the Local Government Board was equally profuse. What has been the outcome of all this profusion? This Local Option… as far as Wales at least is concerned, will not have the slightest effect on the drinking habits of the people… This Bill will do nothing at all unless it buys out the most pernicious and worst class of public houses. The pernicious and worst class of public houses are the most profitable, and where they exist there is surrounding them the worst misery and desolation. Why should that class of publican sell? He has a good livelihood, and he could only be induced to sell by the offer of an extravagant price. The Government, in order to attain any success for this measure will have to depend upon the chapter of accidents. A very eminent writer has portrayed the world as governed by chance. It is only in such a world that fortuitous statesmanship of this order can ever hope to succeed. If the proposal of the noble Lord the Member for Paddington [Randolph Churchill] to purchase licences compulsorily had been accepted, this objection would not apply. The County Council then would state their case for the suppression of a licence which, in their opinion, did harm to the public. Unfortunately, the temperance ardour of the noble Lord has evaporated… His, at the best, was a kind of mushroom teetotalism, which grew no one knew why, or when, and which has disappeared, how, no one exactly knows. But from the constant communications of the noble Lord with the licensed victuallers, the Temperance Party in this House have good reason to believe now that it was somewhat of an alcoholic fungus. The noble Lord and the right hon. Gentleman the Member for West Birmingham [Joseph Chamberlain] seem now to have joined in the duty of praising compensation. It was only the other day that the right hon. Gentleman entertained a few of the brewers. So strongly was he in favour of the principle of compensation that he expressed great surprise that it was necessary for them to approach him on the subject. He could quite understand his Liberalism being doubted, but on this great question of compensating the publicans he ought to be above suspicion. But we simple people of Wales can hardly understand either the right hon. Gentleman or the noble Lord. They are to us a great mystery. The right hon. Gentleman not so very long ago, I think it was in Wales, promulgated the doctrine of ransom. Now, if we understand that

> great doctrine, it is the exact converse of compensation. Both the right hon. Gentleman and the noble Lord seem to be a kind of political contortionists… and no one knows which way they intend to travel. My last objection to this proposal is that it delays the great work of temperance reform. There are obstacles to every great reform, and there is no necessity for creating fictitious and artificial barriers to combating this great evil. I believe it is in your power to do much to improve the habits and condition of the people by improving their environments. That is why I believe in this great question of temperance reform. It removes inducements to evil and substitutes incitements to good, and it is because the Government Bill delays that great work that I think the proposal is greatly to be deplored…[343]

The House of Commons is traditionally generous in hearing a new member's maiden speech, but even so, Lloyd George evidently began well. Gladstone was present to hear his turbulent young man. An Opposition front-bench member who sat near him told Lloyd George later, "The Old Man was exceedingly delighted". The press gave him good notice, too. *The Times* alluded to the speech in its leading article. The Tory *Daily Graphic* described it as "rather a clever speech", while the *Pall Mall Gazette* declared that "The new Member for Caernarvon made a capital maiden speech, full of promise for his future career". It was noted that he spoke fluently rather than familiarly; English was still a foreign tongue.[344] Lloyd George himself excitedly wrote home:

> Shortly after I wrote my letter of yesterday to you I got up & spoke for the first time in the House of Commons… There is no doubt I scored a success & a great one. The old man & Trevelyan, Morley, Harcourt appeared delighted. I saw Morley afterwards & he said it was a "capital speech–*first rate*" & he said so with marked emphasis. He is such a dry stick that he wouldn't have said anything unless he thoroughly believed it. I have been overwhelmed with congratulations both yesterday & today… Tom Ellis who is genuinely delighted because one of his own men has succeeded–told me that several members had congratulated *Wales* upon my speech. Stuart Rendel said I had displayed "very distinguished powers"… There is hardly a London Liberal or even provincial paper which does not say something commendatory about it.[345]

Although he campaigned from genuine motives on the issue of temperance, Lloyd George was not a teetotaller himself, though he drank sparingly. It was excess that he minded. Later, during the First World War, when many workers had better wages, he saw drunkenness as spoiling the war effort, so legislation was introduced to reduce the strength of beverages, meaning they contained more water. When this took effect, people would ask for a 'Lloyd George'. After the war, he always had a stock of

---

343 https://api.parliament.uk/historic-hansard/commons/1890/jun/13/committee-1#S3V0345P0_18900613_HOC_181. Retrieved 9 February 2019.

344 W. W. Davies, p101; Owen, p61.

345 Morgan, *Family Letters*, p29. The 'old man' was Gladstone, 'Trevelyan' was Sir George O. Trevelyan (1838-1928), 'Morley' was John Morley (1838-1923), author of *The Life of William Ewart Gladstone* (1903, 3 Vols., London, Macmillan), and at the time between tenures as Chief Secretary for Ireland.

fine wines for guests at Bron-y-de, a very good claret. Personally, he would have a long glass of Irish whiskey with water, accompanied by a cigar, which he would produce from his own leather cigar case stamped 'DLG'.[346]

Amid this, his first session in Parliament, his first daughter, Mair Eluned–named in Welsh after his sister Mary Ellen, was safely delivered at home in Criccieth about 1 am on 2 August. Margaret had not had an easy pregnancy and there was relief that all had gone well, without complications. Lloyd George was further delighted that he now had a daughter. He was informed of the birth by a telegram from his brother William, and he caught the mail train to Criccieth. However, it was only a flying visit, as he straight away returned to London: politics was now his full-time occupation and concern in life.

Lloyd George was lonely in his single-room lodgings in Craven Street, near The Strand, and sought company, not always with Margaret's approval. Soon after the birth of their second child, she reprimanded him for spending a Sunday on the river with S. T. Evans[347], instead of attending chapel. He defended himself, writing on 13 August: "There is a great deal of difference between the temptation to leave your work for the pleasure of being cramped up in a suffocating malodorous chapel listening to some superstitions I had heard thousands of times before & on the other hand the temptation to have a pleasant ride on the river in the fresh air with a terminus at one of the loveliest gardens in Europe [Kew Gardens]…"[348]

All in all, this was a most difficult period in Margaret's life, as biographer Ffion Hague highlighted. In the first seven years of their married life together, Margaret was pregnant for a total of 36 months, gave birth four times–Olwen followed on 3 April 1892 and Gwilym on 4 December 1894:

> … and assuming she nursed each child for six months after birth… there were only fourteen months during the years 1888-95 when she was not either pregnant or nursing. After 1895 Maggie's health was not strong, and she miscarried twice before giving birth to the couple's last child, Megan Arvon, [on 22] April 1902. Maggie's life was centred around her children, her family and chapel. In London, she had none of the support systems she needed to make a home. Her social circle was small and scattered across the city, and getting about with small children was not easy. Lloyd George was wholly preoccupied with the intoxicating world of politics, and kept highly irregular hours. Yes, it was her duty to look after her husband, but did she not have an equal duty to look after her children? In the years ahead, this question was to cause increasing tensions between them.[349]

In his second speech to the House, delivered on 13 August, Lloyd George attacked the expensive grandeur of monarchy. It was not, as he well recognised, a speech likely to make him popular in the House, but it represented his true feelings, and though he weighed consequences, he was never one to fear them: "I cannot gain much in this House by my speech [he wrote the day before], on the

[346] Interviews with author: Bengy Carey-Evans, Beaumaris, 29 May 2019, and Bill Tenby, Crondall, 18 June 2019.

[347] Samuel T. Evans (1859-1918), Welsh barrister, Liberal MP for Mid Glamorganshire, 1890-1910.

[348] Morgan, *Family Letters*, p35.

[349] Hague, p120.

contrary I may lose much influence… My audience is the country."[350] On the day, he stated:

> I object to this Vote… on account of the principle involved… With regard to the first payment, namely £439 3s. 4d., fees paid on the Installation of H.R.H. Prince Henry of Prussia as a Knight of the Garter, I wish to point out that that dignity is, as a general rule, granted for some signal service rendered to the country; but what service has Prince Henry of Prussia ever rendered to this country?… When this honour is conferred upon people here, they have to pay their own installation fees, but that is not so in the case of a foreign prince. Although it may be argued that diplomatic considerations should weigh in these cases, I hold that that argument should only be valid in cases where these honours are bestowed upon persons of distinction…
>
> … I think it positively monstrous that we should be paying these sums for what is absolutely worthless to this country, when there is so much suffering, so much absolute penury and want among our working classes. Shortly before this Supplementary Estimate was issued, the Report of the Sweating Committee appeared, and what a ghastly comment are the main features of that Report upon this expenditure. The Report shows that thousands of hard-working, thrifty men are living a life of hopeless, ceaseless toil, and yet we are asked to spend hundreds in decorating a foreign Prince, and thousands in adorning a mere supernumerary. These items represent principles of expenditure which do a vast amount of harm in this country. Others are induced by this extravagance to spend a vast amount of money on what is perfectly superfluous, and the result is this monstrous sweating system that is a blot on our civilisation. I do not believe that all… this ostentation of wealth, is necessary in order to maintain the Constitution. On the contrary, I think it does far more to repress than to promote sentiments of loyalty.[351]

Lloyd George did not forget his constituents back home in Wales. He visited Pwllheli, for the first time following his election, on 22 September, the local paper reporting his enthusiastic welcome, interesting for the light it shines on the opinions, concerns and priorities of the day, of both the new MP and his constituents:

> Mr. Lloyd George… in a very forcible manner described the duties of an Opposition. It was its duty to oppose all bad measures and try to improve others. That duty had been faithfully carried out, and as a result it may be said that no better work had been done since the year 1867, when Mr. Gladstone and the Liberal Party compelled the Tories to bring in a bill to extend the franchise. The Opposition, when dealing with the Tithes Bill, succeeded in preventing the question of Disestablishment from being thrown further by 20 years. In spite of all the influence of the Bishop and the Dean of St. Asaph and other clergy, and their pressure upon Lord Salisbury and other Conservatives, the Tithes Bill was not passed. It was threatened if the bill was not made law the clergy would withdraw their support to the Conservative party. If that support was withdrawn what would the Tories have left? The acrobats referred to would be as important as the parsons. What was the Tithes Bill? It was a measure to screw out of the farmer,

[350] Quoted in Du Parcq, Vol.I, p109.

[351] https://api.parliament.uk/historic-hansard/commons/1890/aug/13/class-vii. Retrieved 22 March 2019.

> by means of the law, what he conscientiously objected to pay… The tithes had been of greater importance in the sight of the parsons than the morality of the People… The Dissenting religious "giants" of Wales were those who had kept the country from spiritual poverty, whilst the parsons kept the tithes… The Tithes Bill simply meant to keep the money in the hands of the Church. But it failed.[352] Mr. Lloyd George then took up the Irish Land Bill, and said what its object was. The very men who had all along been the source of all the trouble in Ireland were the men who would have been benefitted under the bill, and not the struggling tenants. When the Government was asked to advance money towards making harbours of refuge and towards education they could not do so, and yet they would have advanced money to buy out the Irish landowners, the tyrants of their country. That was one reason why the bill was defeated.

Lloyd George repeated the arguments he had made in the Commons against compensation for publicans, before continuing:

> Seeing what Liberalism had done in the past they all should have confidence in it in the future. Liberals were with their faces towards the rising sun of liberty and religious equality. After Home Rule for Ireland will come Disestablishment for Wales. It was only fair the Irish should have Home Rule first, as they had worked better than the Welsh had. Caesar's property will soon be given to Caesar, the country will have the property that belonged to it and that now was claimed by the Church. The Church could not prove its right to the property, which had, from time to time, been in the possession of the Romish Church, Henry VIII.'s Church, the French Church, Edward VI.'s Church, the Presbyterian and Independent Churches. This being so showed that the nation had the right to do what it pleased with the property. If this national property was rightly used, and distributed throughout the country, the country would be benefitted by it. The Liberals intended to do that… Disestablishment… was an appeal for religious equality and liberty… What he was at the last election he was that day,–one of the Democracy. He was one of themselves, and asked them to help him to go and speak for them… upon the strength of the principles he believed in…[353]

A week later, in St Helen's on 29 September, Lloyd George spoke in support of John Morley, and most of his speech was a witty polemic against the Tory Government's Irish policy. However, whether by good fortune or shrewd far-sightedness, he did make one rather prophetic statement worth noting, stating: "The great battles of Europe were fought in Belgium. They were fought, not for the independence and freedom of Belgium, but for the liberty of Europe against some despot or other."[354]

Lloyd George began writing a column in *Y Genedl Gymreig*, first of all reporting from a Liberal meeting in Sheffield and stating that he would press for an independent Welsh party along Irish lines,

352 Pwllheli had a population of 3,231 in 1891, of whom only 523 (16.2%) attended Anglican Services; *South Wales Daily News*, 21 November 1891, p6.

353 *Carnarvon and Denbigh Herald*, 26 September 1890, p5.

354 Quoted in Grigg, *Young Lloyd George*, p106.

if the next Gladstonian government did not actively support Welsh issues.[355] The following week he wrote concerning the Parnell scandal, going on to add that Welsh aspirations should now be given precedence over Irish ones. He also proposed his old radical hero, Michael Davitt, as the new leader of the Irish party, knowing that Davitt supported Welsh Home Rule. Further, he pressed for Welsh disestablishment and a Welsh national council.[356]

Lloyd George quickly demonstrated a professional attitude towards being a politician. One aspect of this was shown in the importance he attached to bringing the electoral registers up to date, and ensuring that all eligible supporters had their names recorded, by contesting any challenges to their eligibility in the specially constituted electoral courts. On 10 August 1891, he wrote to William Anthony, a supporter in Pwllheli:

> Do you think that a meeting could be convened this week of the South C'vonshire delegates to discuss the state of registration in their respective districts? I well know that under your supervision the work will be done thoroughly. The Registration Courts will decide the issue at the General Election so far as our constituency is concerned. We ought therefore to see that no stone is left unturned to secure the best for us on the Register.[357]

Lloyd George knew all too well that many householders who had been enfranchised by the Third Reform Act 1884 and the Redistribution of Seats Act 1885 were yet unaware of their right to be registered as voters. This was particularly true in primarily rural areas such as the Caernarfon Boroughs constituency. He was active on other local issues that were also likely to attract votes. In January, he had fought to defeat a private railway rate bill that would have adversely affected the Nantlle slate quarry. In February he protested against the appointment of an English-speaking judge to Caernarvon, and, in April, he proposed legislation to open private streams to public fishing.[358]

Another local paper, the *North Wales Express*, gives a further illuminating insight into Lloyd George addressing other Liberals in North Wales at this time. Speaking away from the Commons to other North Walian Liberals who were not constituents, he was less constricted, being more personal, more open and individual. What is maybe surprising to modern eyes, is the high public profile and influence of the Anglican Church, the arguments of whose representative Lloyd George proceeded to utterly shred to pieces, almost as if in the courtroom:

"On Friday evening a crowded meeting of Liberals was held in the Drill Hall, Denbigh, to hear a reply of Mr Lloyd George, M.P., to the speech which the Dean of St. Asaph[359] delivered at Rhyl the previous Friday. Mr Alderman Thomas Gee, chairman of the Anti-tithe League, presided…"

Lloyd George explained that he found no worthy argument in the Dean's address which he could reply to:

---

355 *Y Genedl Gymreig*, 26 November 1890, p7.
356 Ibid., 3 December 1890, p5; Price, 2006, p117-118.
357 Quoted in George, *Backbencher*, p65.
358 Parry, *David Lloyd George*, p33-34.
359 John Owen (1854-1926), Dean of St Asaph, 1889-1892, noted for his combative, controversial views.

> In truth, were it not for some glaring misrepresentations of fact which it contains, one would be at a loss to discover any matter in it worthy of criticism. It is only by reading such feeble defences as this of the Dean's that it is possible to fully realise how very indefensible the Church position must be in Wales. Liberationists owe a debt of gratitude to the Dean for exposing so effectively the weakness of his cause ... He is a disputant who is notorious for the habit he has of deprecating personalities and of inculcating the supreme duty of preserving a courteous demeanour and a Christian spirit in controversy, whilst at the same time he never misses an opportunity of falsifying his own precepts.

He then proceeded to expose and demolish in humorous fashion the Dean's lack of "Christian spirit", before continuing:

> Not so very long ago he had the "presumption"–the word is not mine, I am borrowing from a sacerdotal vocabulary–… to instruct the great Nonconformist assemblies of Wales in the principle of morality… what I complain of is that, whilst doctrinating others with such admirable precepts, he should… have himself transgressed most of them. You may take as an instance the way in which he disposes of my argument about Archbishop Peckham's treatment of Wales[360]… not only because of the very interesting character of the historical facts disclosed and of the great store laid upon the transaction by the Archbishop of Canterbury[361] in his speech at Rhyl, but also because I think it a very fair specimen of the manner in which Church Defence lecturers treat facts–how they garble some–suppress, evade, and misrepresent others to suit their own purposes… We charge the English Church in Wales with being an *Alien Institution*. It is one of the grounds upon which we call for her Disestablishment.

He then outlined the Archbishop's selective use of historical material, adding that his own views were "fortified… by Welsh historians, not prejudiced by any means against the Church." Among the material quoted out of context was a letter written by Llywelyn, Prince of Wales.[362] Lloyd George noted that the Welsh had at that time trusted "professions of ecclesiastical disinterestedness", but that their "descendants are not likely to repeat the blunder." After further dissection of this issue, he held forth on his next grievance:

> The *suppressio veri* of which the Dean has been guilty does not end even here. He has practised the same artifice in his remarks on the *Cromwellian Experiment in Wales*… He does not–he cannot–deny that as a result of this experiment free schools were established in every market town throughout Wales, that 13 preachers developed into 150, and that several thousand copies of the Bible were distributed.

---

[360] John Peckham (c.1230-1292), Archbishop of Canterbury, 1279-1292.
[361] Edward White Benson (1829-1896), Archbishop of Canterbury, 1883-1896.
[362] Llywelyn ap Gruffydd (c.1223-1282), Prince of Wales (*Tywysog Cymru*) from 1258 until his death, last sovereign prince of Wales before its conquest by Edward I.

Instead, Lloyd George complained that the Dean brought a spurious, exaggerated charge against "the Commissioners appointed to administer the fund. It appears, that out of a sum of £345,000, they failed to account the auditors for £9,400" in times of great upheaval and adversity. He maintained that:

> When the judiciary was violently partisan, and the very reason for whose existence lay in its exposing the supposed peculations and frauds of its opponents, the marvel is that the commissioners succeeded so well in exonerating themselves that even vehement partisanship failed to detect more than a quarter per cent. of error in their accounts. But what think you of the method of debate which allows an ecclesiastic in the Church to suppress facts in order to be able to vilify the memory of opponents with a charge of embezzlement; Why, a prosecuting attorney would scorn to imitate such tactics with criminals, and yet it is done to traduce men who performed great services for their country by one who presumes to give lessons in "honesty," "fair argument," and the display of "Christian spirit".

After taking the Dean to task for deliberately and misleadingly calling an evidently pro-Tory newspaper the "leading Liberal organ" in North Wales, he continued:

> What strikes one as more remarkable than the Dean's allusions are his omissions. Whilst he is vehement in the denunciation of certain phrases of mine for their supposed deficiency in "Christian spirit," he has not a word to say about the inhuman outrage perpetrated in the Llanfrothen burial ground, to which I pointedly drew his attention… Wales has not ceased since the days of *Peckham to those of Dean Lewis* to protest against those acts of clerical tyranny and bigotry. Evidence is not wanting that her persistent cry is at last being heard and heeded. Dean Owen appeals to Welshmen "not to lose the religion of their fathers." They are not likely to do so in the hour of its victory when they clung to it so devotedly in the dark hours of persecution… There are individuals who have forsaken that faith… Wales is on her guard against them. Verily they have their reward. But so will Wales have hers…[363]

1892 saw a general election being held from 4 July to 26 July. It also saw the Tories and their Liberal Unionist allies, led by Lord Salisbury, again win the greatest number of seats (314), but no longer a majority as Gladstone's Liberals won 80 more seats than in 1886 (272). Despite being split between Parnellite (9) and anti-Parnellite (72) factions, the Irish Nationalist vote held up well. As the Liberals did not have a majority on their own, Salisbury refused to resign and waited to be defeated in a vote of no confidence on 11 August. William Gladstone, now aged 82, duly formed a minority government dependent on Irish Nationalist support, his fourth Ministry. For Lloyd George, it was his first contest as part of a general election. In the event he did well, polling took place on 9 July, with the count on 11 July. There was a repeat of the 'mistake' in the 1890 by-election:

---

[363] *North Wales Express*, 18 December 1891, p6.

> It is alleged that some mistake was made in counting the ballot papers and that Mr J. T. Roberts made a discovery which helped to swell Mr Lloyd-George's majority. Two bundles belonging to Mr George were found amongst Sir John Puleston's papers. How they came there is a mystery which has caused a great deal of talk.[364]

Around midday, it was announced that he had increased his majority to 196 against the experienced and well-liked Tory candidate, who was constable of Caernarvon Castle.

On 22 July, Lloyd George spoke at Conway, nailing his colours to the mast with a bluntly unmistakable message to the new Prime Minister:

> It is very important that Liberal statesmen should understand clearly why Wales is so overwhelmingly Liberal at the present moment. It is not to install one statesman in power. It is not to deprive one party of power in order to put another in power. It has been done because Wales has... demonstrated its determination to secure its own progress... The Welsh Members... must this time get something for our little country, and I do not think that they will support a Liberal Ministry–I do not care how illustrious the Minister may be who leads it–unless it pledges itself to concede to Wales those great measures of reform upon which Wales has set its heart. Wales has lived long on promises. She has in hand a number of political I.O.U.s from the leaders of one or other of these great parties in the State. One of these debtors is at the present time in a position to take up the note, and Wales is in a splendid position, by the exigencies of the electoral results, to insist upon prompt payment.[365]

From 29-31 August, Lloyd George made his first brief trip abroad, when he and Samuel Evans, along with seven other British MPs, attended the Fourth Annual Congress of the Inter-Parliamentary Union (IPU) in Berne, Switzerland, founded 'to promote personal contacts' and 'with a view to strengthening and developing democratic institutions'. The conference itself was held in the Swiss Parliament House, which Lloyd George described as stylistically simpler than "many a Methodist chapel" he knew.[366] 13 nations were represented, the main business of that Congress being the institution of an arbitration court.[367]

On 13 September, Gladstone, braving threatened afternoon rain, stood on a platform on a huge rock in the natural amphitheatre at Cwm Llan, on the southern slopes of Snowdon. Accompanied by Lloyd George, Tom Ellis and J. Bryn Roberts, he addressed a crowd estimated at 2,500 by the *Times*, 2,000 by Lloyd George's brother William, and 1,500 by the *North Wales Observer*, the outcrop the Prime Minister stood on becoming known as 'Gladstone's Rock'. Sir Edward Watkin[368], Gladstone's host on the occasion, the then Liberal Unionist MP for Hythe in Kent, had built a summer chalet on his newly acquired 1,500 acre estate of Hafod-y-Llan in Nant Gwynant. He then financed the building of a path–

---

364 *Carnarvon and Denbigh Herald*, 15 July 1892, p6.
365 Quoted in Grigg, *Young Lloyd George*, p117-118.
366 Ibid., p127.
367 http://archive.ipu.org/conf-f/004.pdf. Retrieved 16 March 2025.
368 Sir Edward Watkin (1819-1901), son of a Manchester cotton manufacturer of Welsh descent.

which continues to bear his name–to allow his family and guests to walk direct from the chalet to the summit of Snowdon. Gladstone's visit was ostensibly to declare the path open and "free for ever for public use." Local historian David E. Jenkins recorded that:

> Shortly after mid-day the hanging clouds began to lift, and it turned out a delightful afternoon… When the sun had come forth from behind the dense clouds, it came to cast its gleams upon the hundred cataracts of Cwmllan, which the morning rains had coloured and quickened. Nature, indeed, seemed to have come to a good understanding with the important occasion, and vied with the two thousand people in the heartiness of its welcome.[369]

Gladstone, "in the best of spirits", congratulated them warmly on the fact that 28 of Wales's 30 MPs were Liberals. He hoped his government could move as far and as fast as possible to meet their wishes. "The question of Welsh disestablishment–and with disestablishment, of course, disendowment goes–does not want any argument in this place... Your minds are very well made up, but I will say one word more… on the subject of the land question...". He spoke of the distinct differences in the English and Welsh situations, remarking on his surprise and pained astonishment on learning that, while agricultural rents had been lowered by some 24 per cent in England, the figure in Wales was only some seven per cent. He referred to the fact that "in Wales there were actually four counties in which during that period of distress the rents… were actually raised, and I regret to say that one of those counties was the county of Carnarvon. That is a serious question, and I only refer to it now for the purpose… of assuring you that such a question as that cannot fail to receive the serious attention and consideration of the Government which has just taken office."[370]

It was not a radical speech, but it struck the right chord for the occasion and was generally well-received. Lloyd George had not intended speaking, but "in response to a request by the gathering, supported the resolution. He observed that after what Mr Bryn Roberts and Mr Ellis had said about the Liberalism of Eifion and Merioneth respectively, desired to say something in praise of the Liberalism of the Carnarvon Boroughs which had accomplished that which the other divisions had no chance of doing, viz., winning a victory for liberty when Liberalism was at a low ebb. At the last election, while Mr Bryn Roberts increased his majority and Mr Ellis doubled his, the majority in the Carnarvon Boroughs was increased eleven times. He therefore thought that the Carnarvon Boroughs had good reason for congratulating the great leader of the Liberal party upon his present visit to Wales…"[371]

Lloyd George's brother William was present, along with their mother. He summed up Gladstone's performance thus: "*He managed to say very little of what we expected him to say*, but he said it very cleverly, gracefully and commandingly."[372] Lloyd George himself later recalled:

---

[369] D.E. Jenkins, *Bedd Gelert: Its Facts, Fairies & Folk-Lore*, 1899, Portmadoc, Llewelyn Jenkins, p251.
[370] *The Times*, 14 September 1892, p4. If Monmouthshire was included, there were 34 MPs.
[371] *North Wales Observer and Express*, 16 September 1892, p8.
[372] George, *Backbencher*, p106.

> I may mention, as the most agreeable incident of my political life, that I spent a couple of days in the society of Mr Gladstone in Sir Edward Watkin's chalet on Snowdon. They were the most delightful and instructive days of my life. I had an opportunity of seeing that wonderful versatility and that extraordinary range of knowledge which was one of that great man's most marked characteristics.[373]

Later still, he elaborated on the incident again, one that clearly held great importance for him, in his *War Memoirs:*

> I was invited by Sir Edward Watkin to meet him at dinner at the Watkin chalet… It was a small party. Apart from the members of the family, the late Tom Ellis and I were the only other guests. Mr. Gladstone did practically all the talking… and the rest of us, only too thrilled to meet and hear this great figure from a past world, were naturally content to listen in silence…
>
> He… launched out into a wonderful panegyric on the people of France. I think it arose out of a reference to the Channel tunnel which Sir Edward Watkin was then promoting. Mr. Gladstone made it quite clear that in his judgment the French were a much more enlightened, broadminded and civilised people than those over whose destinies he was at the moment privileged to preside. The Radicals of that day might not have accepted his perfervid eulogies on the superiority of French intelligence, but apart from that his outburst more or less represented the Radical attitude towards the French Republic and its citizens at the time when I came into active politics…[374]

On 13 February 1893, Gladstone spoke for two and a half hours in the Commons to introduce his Government of Ireland Bill, better known as the Second Home Rule Bill, after his first attempt had been defeated in 1886. In a letter to Margaret the same evening, Lloyd George wrote admiringly of the Prime Minister's speech: "Old man's speech just over. Marvellous performance."[375] At one of his own speeches at a Welsh Nationalist meeting that Spring in support of the Bill, he displayed a famous example of his ready wit:

> 'Home Rule for Ireland! Home Rule for Wales! Home Rule for Scotland! Yes, and Home Rule for England, too!' declaimed the orator.
> 'Home Rule for Hell!' interrupted 'the voice'.
> 'Quite right,' said Lloyd George, 'let every man speak up for his own country.'[376]

Though taking no active part in the parliamentary debates, in his letter to the '*Genedl*' for 18 April 1893, he showed his politically astute impressions of the Home Rule fight:

---

373 *North Wales Observer and Express*, 16 September 1898, p6.
374 Lloyd George, *War Memoirs*, Vol.I, p2-3.
375 Quoted in Grigg, *Young Lloyd George*, p130.
376 Quoted in Owen, p82.

So far as I can judge at present, the Government side has proved by far the stronger in the fight. That I believe to be the prevailing opinion in the House. The speeches in support of Home Rule have been much more solid, eloquent, and convincing than those delivered against it…

… we had a masterly speech from Michael Davitt… This was one of the most remarkable speeches ever delivered in the House of Commons. Mr. Davitt was pleading for a cause for the sake of which he had suffered nine long years of penal servitude. It was a wonderful sight–the Prime Minister on the one side, on the other a former leader of the House of Commons, Mr. Balfour, and many of the foremost politicians of the day, listening in respectful silence to an ex-convict who had worn chains and dragged trucks in Dartmoor prison… He was generally considered to be a hot-headed fanatic, imbued with wild ideas… Not so, however. He speaks in a low tone, in simple words, and the views he expressed were quite moderate. In spite of the cruel persecution he has suffered… he has no malice towards his persecutors. He refers to them without a touch of bitterness. He proclaimed peace–and who has a better right to do so?–between his down-trodden countrymen and their opponents. Michael Davitt is a truly great man…

Another splendid effort was the speech delivered by Mr. John Redmond[377], the Parnellite leader; a man of exceptional ability… At the death of Mr. Parnell he had not yet succeeded in attaining to a position of any prominence; but… he has developed immensely. Just now, I doubt if there is a better speaker within the House of Commons. His speech on Thursday was especially striking… [and[… worthy of a hearing. I cannot at present recollect anything approaching its eloquence since I have been in Parliament. His audience was electrified by its harrowing description of the hopeless condition of Ireland bleeding to death under her deadly wounds.

The third great speech of the debate was that of Mr Asquith.[378] Some time ago… I ventured to prophesy then that he would occupy, with more dignity and usefulness, the position which Mr. Chamberlain held in the Liberal party previous to 1885. This becomes more apparent day after day. His great speech on Friday night was a decided step upwards. He properly roasted Chamberlain and Balfour, whilst, at the same time, he made a strong and clear defence of the Bill. The Liberals are easily holding their own these last days…[379]

Fatally for its ultimate success, however, Gladstone had drafted the Bill entirely himself, in near secret, thus alienating some potential supporters and allowing flaws to enter the final draft. Nevertheless, Lloyd George was a supporter of his leader's well-intentioned initiative. The second reading of the Bill on 21 April in the Commons passed by a majority of 347 to 304. On the third reading, on 1

---

[377] Redmond was Irish Parliamentary Party MP for Waterford City from 1891 until his death on 6 March 1918. Charles Stewart Parnell had died on 6 October 1891, aged 45, his party riven in two by his involvement in the scandalous adultery case involving Katharine O'Shea, whom he subsequently married. In 1890, John Redmond had led 28 pro-Parnellites in forming the Irish National League, while Justin McCarthy led 44 anti-Parnellites in forming the rival Irish National Federation. In 1900 the two factions merged to form a new Irish Parliamentary Party under John Redmond. Now Parnell is seen as a formidable parliamentarian, many believing that Home Rule could have been won without bloodshed, had he not been brought down by personal circumstances.

[378] Herbert Henry Asquith, 1st Earl of Oxford and Asquith (1852-1928), barrister, Liberal MP for East Fife, 1886-1918, Paisley, 1920-1924, Home Secretary, 1892-1895, Chancellor of the Exchequer, 1905-1908, Prime Minister, 1908-1916, Liberal Leader, 1908-1926.

[379] Quoted in Du Parcq, Vol.I, p158-160.

September, the Bill passed by a slimmer majority of 301 to 267 votes. However, in the Tory-dominated House of Lords, on 8 September the Bill failed on a vote of 41 in favour to 419 against. The stakes were being 'stoked' higher for the future.

Lloyd George was closely allied to the cause of 'labourism', the cause of the working man, at this time, as evidenced by his close involvement in the bitter strike at the Llechwedd Quarry at Blaenau Ffestiniog, which lasted from 17 May to 5 September 1893. The strike ultimately failed, as the North Wales Quarrymen's Union ('NWQU') was weak at Llechwedd: out of a total workforce of 486, only 125 were members, and of those, only 75 had paid their subscriptions up to date. The strike, the biggest ever at Blaenau Ffestiniog, got prominent notice in R. Merfyn Jones seminal work on the North Wales Quarrymen, but Lloyd George's part in proceedings failed to get a mention.[380] On Saturday 12 August the workforce gathered at Caernarfon Pavilion under the NWQU's General Secretary, W. J. Williams. The Assembly was addressed by a number of speakers, including Tom Ellis and Lloyd George. In supporting the resolution "That, in face of the general failure to get quarry proprietors to join the men in the establishment of joint boards of arbitration, this meeting begs to the conviction that it is of the utmost importance for the good of the slate industry and in the community at large that such boards in labour matters be established by law, with the necessary compulsory powers, and call upon the party in power to take the matter in hand without delay", Lloyd George, being enthusiastically received, powerfully declaimed:

> … certain phases of this dispute had made it a matter upon which the public ought to express an opinion, for if the men were in the right, there was a danger of their being overpowered unless they received assistance from outside. Even a person apprehended for killing a rabbit was afforded an opportunity of defending himself, but this right was denied to six of the best quarrymen of Festiniog simply because they happened to be the leaders of the men. The men had suggested that the matter in dispute should be referred to arbitration. On the question [of] arbitration he proposed to appeal to Mr [John E.] Greaves himself… In refusing to admit the leaders, he had undoubtedly attacked the principle of union and combination. That being the case, the whole mass of workmen in North Wales should support the men in their manly defence against the attempt made to crush them. Even granting that the Llechwedd men at the outset had not acted properly, they were to be praised for the spirit of contrition displayed by them, and for the humble manner in which they had approached their employers. Messrs Greaves ought to be proud of their men, for had they not materially aided in placing them in position of wealth and comfort? Mr Greaves had three mansions, which had been maintained by the sweat of the quarrymen. The latter worked in the bowels of the earth, in the midst of sufferings and toil, endangering their lives and limbs, and all this went to increase the wealth of the quarry-owners. Against this he said nothing further than that a return for all this wealth the employers ought to treat their men with some consideration. Since this was a battle between the

[380] R. Merfyn Jones, *The North Wales Quarrymen, 1874-1922*, 1981, Cardiff, Univ. of Wales Press, p162-174.

> masses and the capitalists it behoved every Welshman and every quarryman who cherished the principle of union to stand by the Llechwedd men in this conflict.[381]

The resolution was overwhelmingly passed, but it went unheeded by the authorities. In October, eight ordinary quarrymen were accused by the employers of violence against a 'blackleg' who had returned to work on 3 July. After an initial hearing at Penrhyndeudraeth Magistrates' Court, where they were defended by William George, the case was transferred to the Merioneth Quarter Sessions at Bala, on 17 October, where great interest was taken in the case, Lloyd George now acting as defence counsel against Mostyn Roberts, Caernarfon, for the prosecution.[382] The *North Wales Observer* recorded:

> Rowland Edwards, E. R. Edwards, David Thomas Roberts, Ellis Hughes, and W. D. Hughes, were charged with violence to R. D. Hughes, with a view to compel him to cease working at the Llechwedd Quarry. The grand jury returned no true bill against all these men, and also against G. D. Williams and Hugh Jones, for a similar offence on R. Owen Hughes. In connection with the last case, true bills were returned against Humphrey Jones, E. R. Edwards, and Rowland Edwards, but after a protracted hearing, extending till ten o'clock at night, the charges against these men were dismissed. The result was received with considerable cheering…[383]

In Spring 1894, Lloyd George led a revolt of four Welsh members against the Rosebery Government because of its attitude on Welsh disestablishment. A Welsh Church Suspensory Bill had been introduced on 23 February 1893, and, with Irish support, obtained 301 votes to 245 on its first reading, but it had made no further progress in the Commons. After Gladstone retired on 2 March 1894, following the defeat of the Second Home Rule Bill, the Welsh Liberal members chose Lloyd George to serve on a deputation to Chancellor of the Exchequer William Harcourt[384] on 16 March to press for specific assurances on Welsh issues. When those were not provided, they resolved to take independent action, if the government did not bring a bill for disestablishment. When that was not forthcoming, he and several other Welsh Liberals–David A. Thomas, MP for Merthyr Tydfil, and Francis Edwards, MP for Radnorshire–refused the whip on 14 April, J. Herbert Lewis, MP for Flint Boroughs joining them on 5 May, as they became known as 'the Four.'

Lloyd George had to defend his stand to his constituents at an initially hostile meeting at the Reform Club in Caernarvon that evening. Controversially, he claimed that the "English regarded the Welsh as parasites, but he wished to show that they were mistaken. The Cabinet was 'a Cabinet of Churchmen'… The Welsh Members must 'stand on the ground of independency and tell the Government that they would not receive Welsh support to break their pledges to Wales'."[385] It would

---

381 *North Wales Observer and Express*, 18 August 1893, p6. Greaves professed to be a Liberal!

382 Price, 2006, p144-145. Price brought this important case to light, unnoticed by all previous biographers, underlining Lloyd George's "unionism and labourist sympathies… long before 1906.": p145.

383 *North Wales Observer and Express*, 20 October 1893, p5. A much more detailed account is in Supplement to *Cambrian News*, 20 October 1893, p1-2.

384 William Harcourt (1827-1904), Home Secretary 1880-1885, Chancellor of the Exchequer 1886, 1892-1895.

385 Quoted in Grigg, *Young Lloyd George*, p149, from *North Wales Observer and Express*, 20 April 1894.

appear the majority at the meeting were persuaded by his rhetoric. Meanwhile, Lewis even tried to get Tom Ellis to resign his government post and join the revolt, but to no avail. Lloyd George and Lewis were risking their careers for their principles. Ellis was angry with Lloyd George, writing to their mutual friend D. R. Daniel on 30 April: "George is very threatening. He means to be on the warpath. His whole attitude is to upset the apple cart."[386]

Lloyd George made another inflammatory speech in Penrhyn Hall at Bangor on 14 May, this time accompanied by his three cohorts, at which he stated "Our support has fetched nothing in the political market and it is time in the interests of Wales to initiate a new policy."[387] As Emyr Price notes: "That policy, manifested later that month, was the attempt to launch the new Cymru Fydd, Young Wales movement…"[388] On 24 May the *Liverpool Daily Post*, which had wide circulation in North Wales, published an interview with Lloyd George, in which he stated: "There are many who deny our national existence and we can hardly be surprised at that, because our support has been so entirely given to one party, that our separate entity as a nation has become merged into one political party… the ultimate result of this independence will be to form a new Welsh National Party."[389] The very next day, the *North Wales Observer and Express* printed the draft constitution of Cymru Fydd that he had formulated.[390] In this draft, Lloyd George proposed setting up Cymru Fydd branches across Wales, replacing existing Welsh Liberal ones. These would be local and democratic, but accountable to a central executive council. This would elect main officials from lists from the branches. In other words, he aimed at nothing less than "a root-and-branch restructuring of Welsh politics."[391]

The league had revolutionary objectives, including "disestablishment, land reform, local option; the extension of popular education; the vote for men and women over twenty-one; the securing of good working conditions in the coalmining and slate-quarrying industries and the promotion of the Welsh language as an official language of government and public and industrial life in Wales. But, underlying all these issues, was the establishment of Federal Home Rule for Wales, to secure a more just and egalitarian society."[392]

On 23 May, Lord Rosebery had declared at Birmingham that the Government would not go to the country until disestablishment had been passed by the Commons. Two days later, the Welsh Members recorded what was, effectively, a vote of confidence in him, rejecting the 'Four's' demand for more militant action.[393] Reluctantly, the 'Four' accepted this *fait accompli* and re-joined the official Liberals on 29 May, even if, in Lloyd George's case at least, it was "in name only."[394]

Immediately following these events, even a political opponent like the Unionist lawyer, T. Marchant

---

386 Quoted in Price, 2006, p140.
387 Ibid., p140.
388 Ibid., p140.
389 Quoted in Price, 2006, p142.
390 Price, 2006, p142.
391 Ibid., p143.
392 Ibid., p143.
393 Grigg, *Young Lloyd George*, p151-152.
394 Price, 2006, p142.

Williams[395], could see that Lloyd George was already an outstanding debater and parliamentary tactician with a future, writing a perceptive potted biography:

> One of the main elements of Mr Lloyd George's character is push. He is largely endowed, too, with worldly wisdom. A superficial observer of the man may pronounce him rash and indiscreet; all who are thoroughly familiar with his history will, however, unite in saying that his rashness and indiscretion must be more apparent than real, for they always prove advantageous to him as a party politician by strengthening his position in his constituency and in the country generally. Even this little revolt of his, untimely though it may seem to most of us, will tell hereafter, we feel confident, to his advantage. It is distinctly in his favour that he has the courage to revolt at all. If the Government yield to his demands, great will be his reward; if the Government decline to yield to his demands, great will be the disgrace in the sight of the Welsh people, not of Lloyd George, but of the members who have refused to follow his lead... The courageous little rebel has entirely over-shadowed the fallen parliamentary champion of Welsh Disestablishment.
>
> Mr George has a very interesting personality. He is very affable, very frank and outspoken. He has a bright and intelligent face and (in private life) very pleasing manners...
>
> Take him for all in all, he seems by far the best-fitted of the Welsh members for the leadership of the National party in the House of Commons... He is quick-witted; he is eloquent; he is daring; in a word, he is perhaps the truest Celt that Wales has ever sent into the House of Commons.[396]

Lloyd George wrote extensively for Liberal papers, such as the *Manchester Guardian*. In Wales during the same period, he campaigned for the *Cymru Fydd* movement and for the amalgamation of the two Liberal Federations, north and south. Literally 'Wales To Be', more commonly known in English as 'Young Wales', the movement had been founded by Welshmen in London in 1886, modelled on–but not a copy of–the Young Ireland movement. A second branch was founded in Liverpool in 1887, and the first branch in Wales was set up in Barry by W. Llewelyn Williams[397] in 1891. Initially, the focus was almost entirely on cultural and literary matters, but from 1888 Home Rule became the core of its raison d'être. Some even hoped it would oust the Liberal Party in Wales and become an independent national party.

Tom Ellis, MP for Merioneth, both a prominent member of *Cymru Fydd,* and a rising star of the Liberal Party, gave a speech in Bala on 18 September 1890 appealing for a Welsh parliament, as well as a national university, library and museum. However, the movement's impetus was interrupted in mid-August 1892, when Ellis accepted the second whip's office in Gladstone's fourth and final

---

395 Sir Thomas Marchant Williams (1845-1914), Welsh nationalist, lawyer, and author.

396 T. Marchant Williams, *Mr David Lloyd George*, in *The Welsh Members of Parliament*, 1894, Cardiff, Daniel Owen, p26.

397 (William) Llewelyn Williams (1867-1922), journalist, lawyer, radical Liberal MP for Carmarthen Boroughs, 1906-1918. He fell out with Lloyd George over conscription in January 1916, becoming an Asquithian. On his deathbed he wrote to Lloyd George attempting a reconciliation.

ministry, "grasping the Saxon gold" as nationalist J. Arthur Price called it.[398] This move was against the advice of Lloyd George and Herbert Lewis, who now assumed leadership, and branches began to mushroom all over north and mid-Wales and parts of the southern coalfield. On 22-23 August 1894, a national *Cymru Fydd* League was founded at Llandrindod Wells, with Beriah Gwynfe Evans[399] as its national organizer, and with the preservation of the Welsh Language being one of the main aims set out in its new constitution. Lloyd George was highly active in its promotion that year, speaking the length and breadth of Wales on its behalf. In January 1895, a new journal called *Young Wales* was launched, with J. Hugh Edwards as its editor, the very first issue containing a eulogistic article by him on Lloyd George as a 'Leading Young Welshman', suggesting that Lloyd George might fairly describe "the whole of Wales as his constituency", and promoting him as "a man with a *national* policy."[400] At Aberystwyth on 18 April 1895, *Cymru Fydd* merged with the North Wales Liberal Federation to form the Welsh National Federation, under the chairmanship of Thomas Gee.

On 25 February 1895, the government had introduced a revised Welsh Disestablishment Bill, which Lloyd George naturally supported. He now tried to use this measure as a lever for forcing through a kind of Welsh Home Rule. On 26 March he spoke for an hour in the House, insisting that:

> It was on behalf of the Welsh people that 31 out of 34 of the Welsh representatives in the House protested against a State connection, which they maintained was doing damage to the cause of religion in the Principality, and that they entreated the House to apply their [Welsh] national property for better, holier, and more Christian ends, in assuaging suffering, in succouring distress, in relieving and, if possible, redeeming their people, by giving them that training and discipline which would enable them to overcome and compete with those evils which the present system encouraged.[401]

The bill came before the House in committee for the first time on 3 May, and Lloyd George put down an amendment for the appointment of a Welsh National Council, such as had been advocated at Aberystwyth in April.[402] On 20 May, Home Secretary Herbert Asquith opposed Lloyd George's amendment, but on further representations from Lloyd George and Herbert Lewis "promised that the matter could be discussed later on with reference to the ninth clause."[403] Lloyd George then wanted to withdraw his own amendment, but the Tories–who he had somewhat riskily persuaded to back him–now refused to allow its withdrawal, hoping to defeat the weak government. The amendment was defeated by the narrow margin of 198 votes to 188, Lloyd George voting against his own amendment, along with other Welsh members.

---

398 Quoted in Price, 2006, p135.

399 Beriah Gwynfe Evans (1848-1927), journalist, later biographer of Lloyd George.

400 J. Hugh Edwards, *D. Lloyd George, M.P.*, *Young Wales*, 1, 1, January 1895, p12-17; quotes, p16, 17.

401 https://api.parliament.uk/historic-hansard/commons/1895/mar/26/established-church-wales-bill#S4V0032P0_18950326_HOC_171. Retrieved 4 November 2020.

402 George, *Backbencher*, p163-164.

403 Ibid., p167.

In June he, Herbert Lewis and Carvell Williams[404] continued their efforts, though Lewis's involvement was much reduced by the sudden death of his beloved wife Adelaide ('Ada') on 7 June. As Kenneth Morgan put it: "it is testimony to his close relationship with Lewis at this time that he spent much time and trouble interrogating the hapless doctor whom he correctly suspected of giving a wrong diagnosis of Mrs. Lewis's medical condition, and arranging for a *post mortem*… The whole episode casts light on a tender, gentle side of Lloyd George which his critics often miss."[405] In any case, Rosebery's government was floundering. On 20 June, its majority on the Welsh Bill fell to seven; the next day, the government was defeated by seven votes on a motion of censure concerning Secretary for War Henry Campbell-Bannerman's[406] alleged mishandling of cordite supplies to the army. Rosebery chose to treat it as a vote of censure on his government and, on 22 June, he resigned.

In the general election of 13 July–7 August, the Liberals would be heavily defeated, and Lloyd George had a major fight on his hands in his still marginal seat against his old adversary, Ellis-Nanney. At a packed rally in the Guild Hall at Caernarfon on 5 July, he declared:

> That there was a cry in some quarters that the Liberal Government did not carry their measures through even after promising the same. There were two obstacles in the way. The first was the House of Lords, which thwarted and hindered every good measure having for its object the benefit of the masses. They would have to abolish a house which represented nobody but itself. The second obstacle was that the pressure of business on the Imperial Parliament was such, owing to the vast extent of the British Empire, that it could devote but little time, comparatively, to home matters. The only remedy to meet that state of things was to grant Home Rule all round, so as to deal with local matters, leaving imperial questions to be dealt with by the Imperial Parliament. Referring to the questions of old age pensions, Mr George said that he had that day come across a pamphlet which was distributed on the question. The framers of that scheme estimated that £5,000,000 would be required annually to meet the object. He was in favour of old age pensions. But where was the money to come from? He had three or four suggestions. Was Mr Nanney prepared to apply the tithe towards it? In the olden times the tithes were given to the poor. But by now the order of things had been reversed. The poor were in the workhouse, whilst the parsons received the tithe. The tithes of this country were the property of the poor, and the poor had been robbed of them… Sir William Harcourt, in his last Budget, which was one of the best, if not the very best, ever introduced to the House of Commons, imposed a death-duty of 10 percent, on the property of millionaires... It was but right that such property should be heavily taxed for the benefit of the State that had enabled the millionaire to accumulate the property. Suppose that the death duties were increased towards the formation of old age pensions–what would Mr Nanney say–or rather what would his paymaster, the Duke of Westminster, say, who had become possessed of about ten or twenty millions, not through

404 John Carvell Williams (1821-1907), Nonconformist campaigner, Liberal MP for Mansfield, 1892-1900.

405 Morgan, *Lloyd George's Flintshire Loyalist*, p22.

406 Sir Henry Campbell-Bannerman (1836-1908), popularly known as 'CB', Liberal MP for Stirling Burghs, 1868-1908, Chief Secretary for Ireland, 1884-1885, Secretary of State for War, 1886, 1892-1895, Liberal Leader, 1899-1908, Prime Minister, 1905-1908, the first to be officially titled 'Prime Minister', the term coming into official usage five days after he took office.

> his own exertions and energy, but as the result of the labour and the lives of the miners. What could be wrong in charging that property for the benefit of the people, and not to have it squandered on race-horses and hounds. His (Mr George's) principle was–people first, horses after…[407]

Lloyd George's nephew, W. R. P. George, made an astute comment regarding this important speech, in terms that cannot be bettered:

> I believe it is amongst the first of his speeches dealing specifically with the issue of taxing the "haves" to provide for the "have-nots" in society, and singling out the properties of the great landed proprietors and industrial barons as obvious sources for the provision of financial aid for those in need. It was no co-incidence that great landowners, such as Assheton-Smith[408] and Lord Penrhyn in his own constituency, were in the forefront of the campaign to oust Lloyd George from Parliament. They instinctively realized from the commencement of his career the threat his views, if implemented, posed to their vested interests.[409]

Lloyd George pulled no punches, stating forthrightly in his manifesto that Wales would never secure social justice until it had its own parliament of a status "second to none among civilized nations," adding:

> If we today love our country, our foremost desire is to see our country free from unjust laws, from ignorance, from drunkenness and immorality, from every oppression that falters the nation. In a word, I am a Nationalist because I am a Liberal and a Liberal because I am a Nationalist… I believe the future of Wales would be safer in the hands of her own sons and daughters who are attached to their country, than in the hands of those, who for the past 50 years have refused to listen to her appeals and redress her grievances. That is why I would give to Wales the right to manage such affairs as are distinctively her own, leaving the Imperial (London) parliament full control appertaining to the Empire at large…[410]

He further emphasized that such a powerful federal parliament would enable radical social, labourite and Nonconformist reforms such as Westminster had signally failed to provide:

> In my opinion, this parliament is the easier and most effective way to secure Disestablishment for Wales, a measure of land reform to protect Welsh agriculturalists and labourers; a measure dealing with Leasehold Property, which would prevent the landlord depriving businesses and working men of houses they have built at the cost of their own hard won earnings; a measure which would put the control of the liquor traffic in the hands of the people: such adequate

---

407 *Carnarvon and Denbigh Herald*, 12 July 1895, p3.
408 George W. Assheton-Smith (1848-1904), owner of the 30,000 acre Faenol estate and Dinorwig slate quarry.
409 George, *Backbencher*, p180.
410 Quoted in Price, 2006, p154.

> provisions for the old and disabled and amongst the honest and industrial workers as would place them beyond the fear of poverty or want when their physical powers fail either through age or sickness and a number of other measures calculated to elevate the people and for which Wales has long become ripe.[411]

Importantly, he aimed too at inclusivity, declaring that incomers to Wales, whether English, Scots, Irish or those from further afield, were welcome to join his Young Wales movement, the "adopted sons of Cambria" as he called them, referring especially to those who had come seeking work in Wales docks, coal-pits, quarries and manufacturing industries. He concluded idealistically: "I earnestly appeal to you in the name of principle and conscience to put aside all personal and minor considerations and to record your votes in support of all those exalted ideas, which have always distinguished Wales as true to the cause of freedom and justice."[412]

He strongly backed up these manifesto points in his speeches throughout the constituency, particularly concerning old age pensions and on delivering Welsh Home Rule to serve "*the dearest interests of the Welsh common people*".[413] In the midst of the campaign, the Tories suffered the loss of their respected election agent, Carnarvon solicitor George H. Owen, the former secretary of the North Wales Landowners and Property Defence Association, who committed suicide on 9 July, leaving a note stating that "this election has shattered me".[414] In the event, Lloyd George did well to retain his seat, beating Hugh Ellis-Nanney by 194 votes on Polling Day, Saturday 19 July. The votes were counted the following Monday. Carried shoulder-high to Carnarvon Liberal Club at 27 Bangor Street, Lloyd George declared: "The wave of Toryism which swept over England has rushed up in vain against the rocks of Eryri [Snowdonia–the land of the eagles]. These firm, immoveable rocks have struck it back, seething and foaming in its spent energy."[415]

The *Manchester Guardian* opined: "No candidate in this election has had to face a more bitter and desperate opposition than that which has been offered to Lloyd George's return."[416] Despite this, after the election, his activities in May-June 1895 came under fire, and blame for the Liberal defeat was laid at his door. John Bryn Roberts[417], the Liberal MP for neighbouring constituency of Eifion or South Caernarfonshire, who had no sympathy for either Lloyd George or Welsh Home Rule, had already written to Asquith, the Home Secretary, on 18 May, warning him about Lloyd George's freelance nationalist tactics:

> I understand that a deputation of Welsh members propose waiting upon you to press for the adoption by the Govt. of Mr Lloyd George's amendment to substitute a national council for

---

[411] Ibid., p155.
[412] Ibid., p155.
[413] Ibid., p156.
[414] *North Wales Observer and Express*, 12 July 1895, p5.
[415] Quoted in George, *Backbencher*, p182.
[416] *Manchester Guardian*, 22 July 1895.
[417] John Bryn Roberts (1843-1931), lawyer, Liberal MP for Eifion, 1885-1906, afterwards a judge.

the Commissioners to be appointed under the Welsh Church Bill. I think that you ought to be acquainted with the fact that the Welsh members are by no means unanimous on the question…

The object is to help on the question of Welsh Home Rule, a movement that has no hold whatever on the Welsh people at large…

I hope the Government will stick to the Bill on this point & if that is done the support of the amendment will collapse.[418]

Roberts continued his sniping after the election, while Herbert Lewis continued to loyally defend Lloyd George, arguing that Lloyd George was entirely right in trying to push Welsh Liberalism in a more openly nationalist direction. Lloyd George was unrepentant when speaking at the relaunch of the Young Wales League at Llandrindod Wells on 5 September. Tom Ellis was also supportive, publishing a letter in the *Guardian* on 16 November stating "that Asquith had accepted Lloyd George's amendment and that this had been made known to the Welsh members; that he had, as Chief Whip, warned Asquith that the Government would be defeated on the issue if it refused to accept the amendment; that the Government had been defeated on the cordite vote, and that he had informed Lloyd George that several of the Welsh members did not approve of the method he'd employed to get his amendment accepted."[419]

On 30 November, Asquith himself felt compelled to complain to Ellis in response:

I would have preferred to hold aloof from controversy… I read your published letter and substantially agreed with it. It is not, however, strictly accurate to say that we 'accepted' Ll. George's amendment, and I think you shewed rather too great a tendency to whitewash him, after the underhand and disloyal fashion in which he undoubtedly acted. So far as I remember, he had no associate or apologist among the Welsh members except H. Lewis.[420]

Concerning the accusation that Lloyd George had consorted with the Tories, Thomas Gee wrote in *Y Faner*:

Mr. George is blamed for having entered into some form of association with the enemies of the Liberal Government in order to force Mr. Asquith to adopt his amendment. I am not going to defend the course he took, but everyone knows that it is only by a combination of various *forces* that parliamentary battles are won. Mr. George's method of carrying his point was just as honest as those generally adopted in Westminster.[421]

Significantly, the memory of these events was to haunt relations between Asquith and Lloyd George far into the future, with unfortunate and maleficent results. All the evidence down the years points at

---

[418] J. Bryn Roberts, MP, to H. H. Asquith, 18 May 1895, Bodleian Library, Oxford, Asquith Papers.
[419] George, *Backbencher*, p173.
[420] NLW, T. E. Ellis Papers 74, Asquith to Ellis, 30 November 1895.
[421] Quoted in George, *Backbencher*, pp173-174. [*Translated from the Welsh*].

Asquith, and his disingenuous vanity, as being the principal source of the sourness and ill-will that poisoned and eventually all but destroyed traditional Liberalism in Britain.

Acrimony and divisiveness continued to plague Liberal unity of purpose in Wales itself. In the October 1895 edition of the *Young Wales* journal, Lloyd George wrote an article under the heading 'National Self-Government For Wales'.[422] In it, he forcefully reiterated the aims of the Young Wales League, arguing that the only way for Wales to progress was through federal Home Rule for all the nations of the United Kingdom, including Ireland, stating:

> The only practical remedy left for discussion is to be found in some system of Federalism which confers upon each separate nationality the right to manage its own domestic affairs. This has the advantage of going straight to the source of all the trouble. Neither foreign policy, nor the hostility of other nationalities, nor the necessity of dealing with the affairs of a colonial empire… can possibly interfere with the work of a local legislature engaged only with its own domestic concerns.[423]

There could be no more forthright declaration on Lloyd George's part. In the same issue of the journal, D. A. Thomas wrote that he saw "no immediate prospect" of securing Home Rule.[424] W. Llewelyn Williams promptly penned a stout defence of Lloyd George, leading with the statement "Wales has never produced a better fighting man than Lloyd George."[425] The gap between North and South Walian aspirations now became increasingly evident. In late October, William Evans, the secretary of Rhondda Labour and Liberal Association, wrote to Lloyd George, inviting him to address one or two of a series of meetings in the Rhondda Division for the purpose of reorganising the Liberal forces within the district. The invitation, however, was coupled with certain conditions. It was unanimously passed by the executive of the Association that the following suggestions should be given to all speakers invited: (a) To confine themselves to the importance of local organisation and Liberal principles. (b) Not to make reference to any national or federal movement.

Not unnaturally, this was like a 'red rag to a bull' to Lloyd George, who angrily replied on 1 November:

> Your committee can hardly be serious in their invitation to me. They ask me to address political meetings in the Rhondda–a district where the spirit of Welsh patriotism is probably more dominant than in any other equally large industrial centre throughout the whole of Wales. But in speaking to the warm-hearted Nationalist miners of the Rhondda a Welsh member is to be barred every reference to 'any National movement.' What is meant by the 'Federal Movement,' which is coupled with Nationalism in the prohibitive tariff of the Executive Committee of the Rhondda Labour and Liberal Association, I cannot comprehend. But may I ask for a slight

---

[422] D. Lloyd George, *National Self-Government For Wales, Young Wales*, 1, 10, October 1895, p231-235.
[423] Ibid., p233.
[424] *Young Wales*, 1, 10, October 1895, p238.
[425] W. Llewelyn Williams, *O Fon I Fynwy, Young Wales*, 1, 11, November 1895 p251-254; quote, p251.

explanation? I observe that speakers are to be permitted to descant on 'Liberal principles.' Does not Irish Home Rule stand first on the Liberal programme? How can one discuss that without referring to a 'National Movement'? But perhaps it is allusions to the movement of the people in one's own native land that are alone to be treated as heretical in the Index Expurgatorius of the R.L. and L. Ass. Surely, the gentlemen of the executive must be jesting, for if they are in earnest I must treat their suggestions as a gratuitous and rather stupid insult. They know, or at least they ought to know, that any self-respecting Welshman would be ashamed to accept an invitation to any society where the hopes and ideals of his nationality are treated as a prescribed subject.

I am always happy to address meetings in the Rhondda, for the enthusiasm there is an inspiration, and I shall be pleased to come down at any convenient time in the future, but I must be permitted to dwell on the one political subject which my experience of South Wales audiences proves to me to have the warmest corner in their hearts, and that is, the welfare of their native land,–I mean the Welsh National movement.[426]

The AGM of the South Wales Liberal Federation ('SWLF') was held on 16 January 1896 at the Temperance Hall in Newport, Monmouthshire, chaired by the English-born, anti-nationalist MP for Monmouth Boroughs, Albert Spicer.[427] There were indications that the meeting had been packed with anti-Cymru Fydd members, fifty Englishmen from Newport "swamping" the platform.[428] Areas known to be supportive of Lloyd George, East Carmarthen and West Monmouthshire, had been refused tickets, while Pembroke and Cardigan received notices too late to elect delegates.[429] A motion to unite the SWLF with the new Welsh National Federation, moved by the eminent independent preacher Reverend H. Elvet Lewis[430], was heavily defeated by 133 votes to 70, mostly because of the antipathy between delegates from the anglicized parts of Newport, Cardiff, Barry and Swansea, and the rest of Wales. Speaking against the motion, Alderman Robert Bird[431]–another Englishman–declared: "they had in South Wales, from Swansea to Newport, a cosmopolitan population that was not altogether Welsh, and that would not... submit to the domination of Welsh ideas." Alfred Edmunds of Merthyr declared that "Glamorgan and Monmouth were not to be dictated to by the isolated county of Caernarvon."[432]

Many Welsh Liberals had become indifferent to the Welsh national cause, except in religious terms. Lloyd George was howled down and refused permission to speak. The fierce opposition was led by the SWLF President, David A. Thomas[433], the same man who had supported Lloyd George less than two years previously. His ill-will was manifest. After a motion to convene another Welsh National Convention at Swansea to discuss the issue further was acrimoniously dismissed, all the SWLF

426 *South Wales Daily News*, 6 November 1895, p5.
427 Albert Spicer (1847-1934), Liberal MP for Monmouth Boroughs, 1892-1900, Hackney Central, 1906-1918.
428 *Young Wales*, 2, 1, January 1896, p24.
429 J. Herbert Lewis Papers, NLW, 3/19, DLG to Lewis, 16 January 1896.
430 Reverend Howell Elvet Lewis (1860-1953), widely known by his bardic name 'Elfed'.
431 Robert Bird (1839-1909), born in Soundwell, near Bristol, moved to Cardiff in 1872.
432 *South Wales Daily News*, 17 January 1896, p6.
433 David A. Thomas, Viscount Rhondda (1856-1918), Liberal MP for Merthyr Tydfil, 1888-1910, SWLF President 1894-1897.

delegates decamped, en masse, to celebrate their victory over Lloyd George and Young Wales at a sumptuous dinner at nearby Collier's Restaurant–paid for by Thomas.[434] Lloyd George and the Young Wales delegates remained in the hall, naturally bitter. Lloyd George called the SWLF delegates "a small coterie of English capitalists, who had come to Wales and made their fortunes there," adding that "Wales belonged to the Welsh people, and the Welsh people had as good a right to have their policy directed in accordance with Welsh views, as the English people had to have England governed according to English principles, or Ireland controlled according to Irish ideas. This was not a question as between North and South, but for the whole of the people of Wales, whether Welshmen or Englishmen."[435]

Lloyd George wrote to his wife Margaret the same day:

> The meeting of the Federation was a packed one. Associations supposed to be favourable to us were refused representation & men not elected at all received tickets. There were two points of dispute between us. By some oversight they allowed me to speak on one & we carried it–as it turned out not because the majority of the meeting was with us but because they went to the vote immediately after my speech & I can assure you the impression made could be felt. I simply danced upon them. So they refused to allow me to speak on the second point. The majority present were Englishmen from the Newport districts. The next step is that we mean to summon a Conference of South Wales & to fight it out. I am in bellicose form & don't know when I can get home.[436]

Shortly after that fateful meeting, *Cymru Fydd* collapsed,[437] marking "the end, the death knell, of the Young Wales League, to all intents and purposes, and Lloyd George's long-cherished hopes of establishing a powerful, all-Wales movement for Home Rule and establishing an independent Welsh party."[438] From time to time, Lloyd George still tried to introduce Welsh Home Rule and Young Wales ideals into the political agenda until 1899, but it was by now a dead letter. In 1898, at a meeting in Cardiff, it would again be capitalist entrepreneur and coal magnate, D. A. Thomas, assisted by J. Bryn Roberts, who would thwart Lloyd George's attempt to set up a democratic, all-Wales National Liberal Council.[439]

Lloyd George may have been disappointed, but not wholly surprised. On 19 November 1895, he had written to Maggie from Tredegar "Got a capital meeting last night altho' the audience in these semi-English districts are not comparable to those I get in the Welsh districts. Here the people have sunk into a morbid footballism."[440] This moment formed a watershed in his career, the first rebuff he

---

434 *South Wales Daily News*, 17 January 1896, p6; Price, 2006, p174.
435 *South Wales Daily News*, 17 January 1896, p6.
436 Morgan, *Lloyd George*, p94.
437 See W. George, *Cymru Fydd: Hanes Y Mudiad Cenedlaethol Cyntaf*, 1945, Liverpool, Gwasg y Brython; K.I. Jones, *Syr Herbert Lewis 1858-1933,* 1958, Cardiff, University of Wales Press.
438 Price, 2006, p176.
439 Ibid., p178.
440 Morgan, *Family Letters*, p91.

had so far encountered. He realised that, while Welsh Liberals were firm for Church disestablishment, land reform, education and temperance, and for national equality within the British Isles, they did not want separatism. Unlike the Irish, they did not want to be cut off from England or from the imperial system. Apart from Herbert Lewis and William Jones, no other Welsh Liberal MPs would openly support Lloyd George. In South Wales, he had to rely on the support of two preachers, Elvet Lewis and J. Towyn Jones[441], the eminent Welsh-language scholar and poet, John Morris-Jones[442], and especially W. Llewelyn Williams, sub-editor of the *South Wales Daily News*, the main Liberal-supporting daily newspaper in South Wales. Having to depend on such extra-parliamentary public figures and intellectuals gave the unfortunate impression that the movement was "the preserve of a limited clique of the intelligentsia, despite Lloyd George's own radical views."[443]

This was very much a lost opportunity for the growth and development of Welsh cultural and political unity and identity. It was not until 1910 that E. T. John[444] began to campaign again on Federal Home Rule, introducing, under the ten-minute rule, a Welsh Home Rule Bill on 11 March 1914–proposing a 90-member Legislature, with votes for women and proportional representation, well over a century before the coming into existence of a 96-member *Senedd* on 7 May 2026. It was not until 5 August 1925 that the more narrowly political *Plaid Genedlaethol Cymru* (the National Party of Wales, later *Plaid Cymru*, the Party of Wales) was founded, after a meeting of just six men at the National Eisteddfod held at Pwllheli. However, until the 1950s, and after Lloyd George's death, the party had only a marginal role in Welsh politics.[445] It could be said, to a considerable degree, that Plaid Cymru 'stole Lloyd George's clothes' from the 1890s, and that his aims only started to come to fruition in the changed circumstances of later times, when Wales had lost over half a century of potential national development. Wales was not ready for Lloyd George's pioneering, separate, radical national party in the 1890s. By the 1960s, it was ready to try to overcome the previous centuries of apathy and cultural, social and linguistic suppression, and Plaid Cymru really began to take root.[446]

It was this experience that led Lloyd George away from more specifically Welsh concerns to broader, markedly radical action within the Liberal Party in British politics. As Harold Spender wrote "Wales practically gave him to England."[447] Or, as Emyr Price put it, "Lloyd George increasingly became a British politician as he realized that he could serve Wales and secure radical changes in society only through the Westminster Parliament he had criticized so bitterly. He came to this conclusion, however, only after his long pioneering efforts for Welsh Home Rule and an independent

---

441 Josiah Towyn Jones (1858-1925), Congregationalist Minister, Liberal MP for Carmarthenshire East, 1912-1918, Llanelli, 1918-1922.
442 Sir John Morris-Jones (1864-1929), grammarian, academic, Welsh-language poet.
443 Price, 2006, p169.
444 Edward T. John (1857-1931), known as E.T. John, radical Liberal MP for East Denbighshire, 1910-1918, author of *Home Rule for Wales: Addresses to "Young Wales"*, 1912, Bangor, Jarvis & Foster. His Bill did not proceed beyond a First Reading, attracting the support of only nine Welsh members. See *Herald of Wales*, 14 March 1914, p6, where Lloyd George is quoted as saying: "Were self-government conceded to Wales, she would be a model, to the nationalities of the earth, of a people who have driven oppression from their hillsides and initiated the glorious reign of freedom, justice and truth."
445 The Carmarthen by-election of 14 July 1966 was significant in that it resulted in the election of the first ever Plaid Cymru MP, ironically the contest being caused by the death of Megan Lloyd George, the Labour MP.
446 See Emyr Price's masterful, detailed and persuasive analysis, 2006, p178-183.
447 Spender, *Prime Minister*, p114.

party had been rejected by his own people and, particularly, by his own party."[448] Exactly so: the 'failure', if such it was, was on the part of Wales, not on the part of Lloyd George. In January 1895, J. Hugh Edwards wrote that Thomas Gee had recently made a speech in which he had declared that "he not only thanked Heaven for a such a representative such as Mr. Lloyd George, but that he firmly believed that, were Wales to now lose Mr. Lloyd George's services, the loss would be felt for generations."[449] Sadly, this proved to be prophetically true. Lloyd George's attachment to Cymru Fydd and its aims was totally genuine, and he only abandoned it as a vehicle for Welsh radical advancement in the face of both public apathy, political rejection and opposition from the Welsh labouring classes, and the Welsh Liberal establishment themselves.

As W. W. Davies put it insightfully:

> Lloyd George came to the conclusion that the old Liberalism was losing its hold upon the people, and would never have power enough to pass into law the measures long overdue unless it imported fresh strength from some quarter. Promptly and accurately he divined the only quarter from which such accession of strength was to be expected: it would come from the longing of the working classes for drastic social reforms, and for a bold challenging of the forces of privilege and monopoly. In a flash he saw a new vision–the vision of the peasants of Wales united with the working classes of England in a great crusade for their own emancipation. They were, indeed, very different; but out of the common need, unity would spring. Thus the aims of the champion of Wales became merged in the wider aims of the champion of the lower classes of both nations. To say (as many of his critics said then, and as has been said, with much less excuse, more recently) that Lloyd George forgot Wales, is not merely an untruth, it is a gross misreading of the whole situation, arguing a complete inability to interpret the movement of history. He remembered Wales all the time; but his unerring political instinct told him that the interests of Wales could best be served by identifying them with those of the rising English democracy. Undoubtedly he was right. The need for higher wages, shorter hours of work, better houses, old age pensions, insurance against sickness and unemployment, taxation of unearned increment, progressive taxation of large incomes, control of the land by the community–all these, and many similar things, know nothing of national frontiers. It was only slowly that Lloyd George shook himself free from the bonds of a narrow nationalism; but the process of emancipation began in 1895, to the great advantage of Wales as well as England.[450]

Although one of Lloyd George's personal goals may have failed, his personal stock was rising, W. Llewelyn Williams noting:

> Mr Lloyd George has more than justified the high opinions that were entertained of him by his friends… [He] is recognised to-day as the finest Parliamentarian that Wales has yet sent to the

---

448 Price, 2006, p178.

449 *Young Wales*, 1, 1 January 1895, p17.

450 W. W. Davies, p134-135.

> House of Commons, for with infinitely little resources he has 'scored' repeatedly over the 'strongest Government of modern times'. Sir William Harcourt paid the young member for Caernarvon a handsome compliment publicly on the floor of the House for the way in which he has fought the Tory Government; but even stronger expressions of admiration have been used by politicians on both sides of the House in private. Mr Lloyd George not only has shown… a readiness in debate, and a keen perception of the weak points of the Tory case, but he has been able, by this pluck and resolution, to do more than any other man to infuse a new courage into the Liberal ranks, and to discredit the methods and the policy of an overbearing majority… This year he has only been called upon to show 'grit' and cleverness in fighting the enemy; last year he was put to a far more severe test–of standing up for principle against his friends.[451]

Lloyd George continued to be involved in contentious debate, including that surrounding the innocuous-sounding Agricultural Land Rating Bill, introduced on 20 April 1896. The Bill was intended to relieve hard-pressed British agricultural interests–excluding Ireland–which had suffered through the severe agricultural depression of the last decade and a half. It provided for the reduction of up to 50% in the rates for all land under cultivation. The idea was to relieve landlords by providing subsidies, while also encouraging them to keep land in cultivation to provide work for tenants and farm labourers. Lloyd George had a radically different view. He attacked the measure not as a solution to agricultural distress, but as a raid on the public purse by entrenched landed interests. He claimed that the proposed Bill was a shocking example of a conflict of interests, as Tory ministers would themselves benefit materially from it. It would profit them directly, whereas the tenant and labourer would gain nothing. Why should the landlords, already wealthy, benefit at the expense of others? As he stated during the Committee Stage of the Bill, the purpose of the Bill was to allow "one class to benefit at the expense of the rest of the community".[452]

During these extensive debates, Lloyd George demonstrated both extensive knowledge of agricultural practices across the country, and of parliamentary procedure in his attempts to alter the bill. At around 3.30 am on 22 May, his obstructive tactics brought about official censure from the Speaker, William Gully, who 'named' him and six others, Herbert Lewis and five Irish Members, including Michael Davitt and John Dillon[453], suspending them from the House for a week. Despite being ultimately unsuccessful in derailing the bill, these efforts garnered Lloyd George respect and acclaim–sometimes grudging–from across the political spectrum. Privately, Sir William Harcourt said to a friend that "all the Scotch members together are not worth Lloyd George's little finger", and to Lloyd George himself "You are too gifted a man to fritter away your powers in playing the part of a mere free-lance. You are destined for much higher things."[454]

"To the credit of Mr. Lloyd George," observed the *Daily Chronicle*:

---

451 W. Llewelyn Williams, *Through Welsh Spectacles*, *Young Wales*, 2, 20, August 1896, p192.

452 Crosby, *Unknown*, p27.

453 John Dillon (1851-1927), Irish Parliamentary Party MP for East Mayo, 1885-1918, Leader in 1918.

454 Quoted in W. W. Davies, p142, 143.

> … must be put the first beginnings of the fight on the Agricultural Rating Bill. He is a man of great ability, ingenuity, force and readiness of mind, and he has a remarkable eye for weak points in a debate. His keen criticisms have often been caught up later by the Front Opposition Bench and adopted as the main line of attack. This was especially so on the Rating Bill, and many of the points over which Liberal speakers waxed most eloquently were first suggested by Mr. Lloyd George. Of all the men on the Liberal side, he has made the greatest mark this session.

Even more significant, in a sense, was the tribute paid him by journals 'on the other side'. "Mr. Lloyd George," declared the *Daily Mail*:

> … is far and away the most nimble, bold and hard-working young Radical in the House at the present time. He has dropped Wales, and now goes in for harassing the Government all round. He speaks on all manner of questions almost entirely without the aid of notes, and it is very uncommon for the Speaker to rule him out of order.[455]

Lloyd George's mother, Elizabeth, died on 19 June 1896, much weakened by diabetes[456], at the age of 68. Lloyd George was in London and travelled back to Criccieth for the funeral on 23 June. Richard Lloyd recorded the occasion:

> Very few but ourselves there… Maggie unable to leave bed, great loss of her company and help. All of us agreeing D.Ll.G. had better return to London for his own sake; feeling keenly and affecting his health. His going, we thought, would be of help by absorbing himself in London and public business.[457]

Lloyd George wrote to his friend Herbert Lewis "My uncle, brother & sister are very cut up. My poor mother was everything to them. She managed the home up to within a few hours of her death."[458]

On 21 August 1896, Lloyd George escaped from his sorrows and politics, sailing from Southampton on RMS *Clyde* on a two-month journey to the rather unlikely destination of South America, accompanied by Herbert Lewis and Henry Dalziel.[459] It was essentially a business trip, as he and Lewis had been investing time and money in a highly speculative enterprise known as the Welsh Patagonian Gold Fields Syndicate Limited, and they had decided to go and make their own assessment of the probable returns on any potential future investment. Lloyd George had become one of the directors after the company was formed on 11 November 1892 by a mining agent from Harlech, Captain David Richards, with an initial capital of £10,000.[460] Co-signers of that initial Memorandum

455 Quoted in Edwards, 1913, Vol.III, p145.
456 George, *My Brother And I*, p91.
457 Quoted in George, *Backbencher*, p200. Margaret lost the baby she was pregnant with soon after; Hague, p129.
458 NLW, Sir John Herbert Lewis Papers D30/46, DLG to JHL, 30 June 1896.
459 Sir Henry Dalziel (1868-1935), Liberal MP for Kirkcaldy Burghs, 1892-1921, advocate of home rule for Scotland, Ireland and Wales.
460 See Grigg, *Young Lloyd George*, p178-195; J. Lindsay, *'Not Eldorado': W.J. Parry And The Welsh Patagonian Gold Fields Syndicate', Trans. Of the Honourable Society of Cymmrodorion*, 3, 1997, p136-163; George, *Backbencher*, p107-117.

of Association were men of the stature of Tom Ellis MP, Reverend Michael D. Jones and Edwyn C. Roberts.[461] The company's office was in Effingham House, Arundel Street, London, the nominal Chairman being Thomas Lewis, Liberal MP for Anglesey, with Lloyd George as the pro-active Vice-Chairman. The other directors were Major Evan R. Jones, Liberal MP for Carmarthen Boroughs; E. Vincent Evans, Secretary of the Honourable Society of Cymmrodorion; and R. O. Davies, a prosperous London draper who lived at Grasgarth, Acton, and who was a friend of Lloyd George. Half of the initial capital was to be the value of Richards' shares. There was difficulty in raising the rest, but, after abortive negotiations with French financiers in Paris, Lloyd George persuaded Thomas J. Hughes, a prosperous Bethesda chemist, to take 1,100 shares. Lloyd George took 1,000, his brother William took 600, Dr Gavin Brown Clark, Liberal (Crofters) MP for Caithness, 500, Fred Woodman–who became company secretary–380, William J. Parry[462] of Coetmor Hall, Bethesda, 250, and Major Jones, 50.

Parry, the son of a successful quarryman, and a multi-faceted man in his own right, had made two voyages to Patagonia on behalf of the syndicate of investors, from October 1893 to February 1894 and from March to September 1894, in earnest, but ineffectual, efforts to rescue the interests of the inefficient, failing company at the goldfields of Corcovado, Tecka and Mica. Although speculative, the venture was not entirely unfeasible, as initial yields appeared to be good, with 24 grammes being recovered from 14 lb of excavation.[463]

Upon arrival in Montevideo, capital of Uruguay, they found the state telegraph system was run by a Welshman named Jones, and he communicated with various ministers of state, ensuring that the visitors were greatly facilitated in enjoying their visit. They reached Buenos Aires, capital of Argentina, on 12 September, and on 19 September were the guests of honour at a state banquet, attended by two former Presidents, Julio Roca and Carlos Pellegrini–a relative of John Bright and a fluent English-speaker–along with various ministers and representatives of all the English banks and commercial houses. They were also admitted temporarily to membership of the leading '*Progresso*' club. The travellers then "spent several delightful days in the Cordova mountains", the government offering them the services of a gunboat to transport them to the famous Welsh colony at Chubut in Patagonia. Sadly, this was impossible due to time constraints, but they did get to meet a considerable number of their fellow countrymen, including *Y Bonwr* Lewis Jones, the 'father' of the Welsh colony, and the recognised chief of the settlers. Jones, then nearing the end of his life, had been born in Caernarfon and had first sailed to the Argentine to explore Patagonia in 1862. He had explored the area near the mouth of the Chubut River, to which he gave its Welsh name, Camwy.[464]

Lloyd George interviewed Señor Tello[465], the Governor of Chubut, then a national territory. Lloyd

---

461 Edwyn C. Roberts (1837-1893), one of the pioneers of the Welsh settlement in Patagonia. He died in Bethesda on 17 September 1893, a few days before he was due to return to Patagonia.

462 William John Parry (1842-1927), prominent in the creation of the North Wales Quarrymen's Union in 1874, member of the first Caernarvonshire County Council, 1889, and its chairman, 1892-93.

463 L. Jones, *Hanes Y Wladfa Gymreig*, 1898, Caernarfon, Cwmni'r Wasg Genedlaethol Gymreig, p177.

464 Lewis Jones (1837-1904).

465 José Eugenio Tello (1849-1924), Governor of Chubut, 1895-1898.

George was clearly interested to hear that these "Galleuses" in a distant land were also fighting for their language and religion:

> When he [the Governor] heard that I was a Gallensis–as they call the Welsh out there–his first words to me were in the dialect of South Wales, "Shwd mae y machan i?2 ("How are you, my boy?") His stock of Welsh, however, was limited. He… was lost in astonishment over the numerous eisteddfodau held [by the settlers]. A singing race was a novelty, a curiosity to him, and so were their many chapels and strict Sabbatarianism. Lately he had been having a good deal of trouble over the military drills. Everybody in the Argentine has to be drilled, you know. The Welshmen don't object to that, but they object to its being done on a Sunday, so they refused to turn out… The poor Governor could not account for such a state of things… However, the matter is being satisfactorily arranged at last. Another burning question is that of the Welsh language. "If I tell them that they are English," said the Governor, "they get in a fury, and say they are not. If I want them to speak Spanish, they say that they are British subjects. They won't have any one who does not know Welsh in the schools, and they will have their own way. And one young lady (who is now in this country)[466] refuses ever since that bother to salute me in the street."… "Then," he continued, "they… won't keep cattle; they won't make butter and cheese, but they grow corn, corn, corn."
>
> I suggested to him that he must find such a people rather troublesome. "Ah! senor," he answered, "not at all. They are a fine people; they are a brave people, a noble people… Send me more of them–as many as you like of them." I hinted that the land would not bear many more. "More?" he replied; "there is plenty of room for them among the hills. A party of them have already gone up the Andes to Cwm Hyvryd, and there is room for more." So I believe, from what I could gather, that their present condition is good, and their future promises well.[467]

Lastly, Lloyd George and Herbert Lewis visited the Chamber of Deputies, and "could not help being interested in the manner in which the two Chambers work, and how Ministers, for instance, are brought from the Upper to the Lower house to answer a challenge."[468]

Some authors[469] imply something was amiss with their purpose in not actually reaching Patagonia itself, although a site visit had been the ostensible purpose of their journey. However, as there is nothing in surviving records to give any clues, the matter must remain, unless new evidence surfaces, speculative. Their ship docked back in Southampton around 23 October. The investment proved to be an irretrievable disaster. It was planned to form a new syndicate of investors, but no new backers could be found and so its affairs were formally wound up on 6 December 1900–too much trust had

---

[466] Eluned Morgan (1870-1938), Welsh Patagonian author, daughter of Lewis Jones. In Britain from June 1896 to March 1898, she met Lloyd George in London prior to his voyage to Buenos Aires. See Celia Codeseira del Castillo *Algas marinas. Crónica de viaje desde Londres a la Patagonia por Eluned Morgan, Revista Cruz de Sur*, 2013, III, 5, p59-99; particularly p69.

[467] Quoted in Du Parcq, Vol.I, pp195-196, from the *Manchester Guardian* of 26 October 1896. For an excellent photographic record of the land and its Welsh colonisers, see L. Priamo, M. Valledor, Eds,. *Una Frontera Lejana: La Colonización Galesa Del Chubut, 1865-1935*, 2003, Buenos Aires, Fundacion Antoraches [Spanish and English Language].

[468] Quoted in Du Parcq, Vol.I, p196.

[469] For instance, Grigg, *Young Lloyd George*, p192; Rowland, *Lloyd George*, p119.

been placed in Richards, who had failed to organise the mining enterprise properly. The *London Gazette* published a notice of its dissolution on 5 November 1907. Remembering that MPs received no remuneration at this time, Lloyd George was largely reliant on his hard-worked brother William's financial support at this time. In John Grigg's words, it was legitimate that: "Since there was no immediate prospect of office, his thoughts naturally turned to business, and to the type of business in which the maximum profit might be achieved in return for the minimum effort."[470] However, he had allowed his own good name to be used as a 'draw' for others to get involved in a speculative venture of which they might otherwise have been wary: "His motive–to be able to fulfil his destiny in politics without financial anxiety–was perfectly honourable. But the same cannot be said of his methods."[471] He did nothing illegal, but his attitude was perhaps cavalier.

In August 1896, there occurred an incident which could potentially have derailed his whole political career, when the respondent in a divorce case, one Mrs Catherine Edwards, the wife of a well-known doctor, David Edwards, from Cemmaes, Montgomeryshire, claimed that Lloyd George was the father of her child. David Edwards had been a friend of Lloyd George's since early 1894 and an active supporter of the Liberal Party. Catherine Edwards, known as Kitty, was herself a distant relative of Lloyd George's wife Margaret, remembered by her as "a pretty, pert, amiable young woman at the time, with a carefree disposition."[472] In those days, and for many years after, to be cited in divorce proceedings was likely to be catastrophic to one's political career, as had happened recently to Dilke[473] and Parnell[474]. Lloyd George did not appear in court in person, but the case was followed by the public in the press.

Lloyd George had indeed stayed with Dr Edwards on occasion when speaking in that part of the county. This was not in dispute. The Edwards' had been married on 5 May 1887 and had lived together until August 1896, having a daughter Gwen, aged 5 years. They had, however, been estranged and occupied separate bedrooms since May 1894. On 10 August, Catherine signed a statement, one that was made in her husband's handwriting[475]: "I, Catherine Edwards, do solemnly confess [the words "that I am pregnant" struck out] that I have, on the 4th of February 1896, committed adultery with Lloyd George, M.P., and that the said Lloyd George is the father of the child, and that I have on a previous occasion committed adultery with the above Lloyd George."[476] On 13 August, Dr Edwards threw Catherine out of the house, and she duly gave birth to a near full-term, but small and weak,

---

470 Grigg, *Young Lloyd George*, p178.
471 Ibid., p195.
472 Richard Lloyd George, *Lloyd George*, p62. Catherine's maiden name was Owen.
473 Sir Charles W. Dilke (1843-1911), radical Liberal MP for Chelsea, 1868-1886, for Forest of Dean, 1892-1911. Touted as a possible future prime minister, his aspirations to high political office were ruined in February 1886 after a notorious divorce case involving Virginia Crawford (1862-1948), wife of fellow Liberal MP, Donald Crawford. Dilke was almost certainly innocent, "politically annihilated by a woman's false accusations", possibly with the collusion of Joseph Chamberlain or Lord Rosebery in "an elaborate conspiracy" to destroy a perceived rival. R. Jenkins, *Sir Charles Dilke: A Victorian Tragedy*, 1958, Rev. 1965, London, Collins, p11.
474 Charles Stewart Parnell (1846-1891), hugely influential Leader of the Irish Parliamentary Party, brought down by an adultery and divorce scandal in November 1890.
475 George, *Backbencher*, p215.
476 Quoted in Rowland, *Lloyd George*, p120. See also https://papuraunewydd.llyfrgell.cymru/view/3371649/3371658 . Retrieved 13 March 2019.

baby girl, Margaret, on 19 August 1896 at a temperance hotel called 'The Tower' at Penygroes, some six miles south of Caernarvon. The child did not survive to adulthood. Mrs Edwards did not register the birth until 7 October and, when she did, the father was declared to be 'David Edwards–Surgeon.'[477]

With Lloyd George away in South America, his election agent in Caernarfon, R. O. Roberts, a solicitor, first 'tipped off' William George by letter on 9 October, denouncing the way the attack had come while Lloyd George was away and unable to defend himself, and tracing it to "a prominent Conservative and member of the Yacht Club."[478] "Before the end of 1896, William George had endeavoured to sort things out by interviewing Mrs Edwards at the offices of her own solicitor. She told him, on this occasion, that there was no truth whatsoever in the so-called confession and that her husband had forced her to sign it by threatening her with a carving knife. She subsequently confirmed this in writing, but the saga was very far from over."[479]

On 13 January 1897, Catherine Edwards presented a petition for a judicial separation from her husband on the grounds of cruelty. He retaliated by denying the charge and in March submitting a counter-petition for divorce on the grounds that his wife had committed adultery with Edward Wilson, the stationmaster at Cemmaes, and that the child born on 19 August was not his. At the preliminary hearing in the divorce court on 19 July 1897 (Edwards *v.* Edwards and Wilson). Dr Edwards asked for leave to proceed with his petition without citing the person named in his wife's confession–referred to throughout as "A. B."–as the co-respondent. He declared that he had been unable to find any evidence against "A. B.", and that he firmly believed Wilson to be the guilty party.

The President of the Court was Judge Francis Jeune–the same man who had unsuccessfully defended the Rector of Llanfrothen nine years before![480] After the reading the letters from "A. B." to Dr Edwards, he agreed that they were quite in order and that the confession had been withdrawn but suggested that "A. B." should have the opportunity, if he so wished, of being joined to the case so that he might deny the allegation on oath. Lloyd George was partially relieved that an affidavit alone would suffice and, after consulting with William, decided to submit one. He was in a 'cleft stick'–to decline the court's invitation would imply he had something to hide, something he could not do as so many people already knew the identity of "A. B." Equally, to accept this opportunity of clearing his name meant that all the lurid details of Catherine Edwards's confession would have to be made public.

Lloyd George submitted his affidavit. On 12 August, the President stated that the petition could proceed without "A. B." being named as a co-respondent, and the case came up for hearing on 18 November. Lloyd George produced to counsel the record of the Parliamentary division lists to show that, on 4 February, he had been, until early morning, voting in the House of Commons. Counsel on both sides agreed that they were "satisfied that the imputation against Lloyd George was without

---

[477] George, *Backbencher*, p222.

[478] Quoted in George, *Backbencher*, p209-210.

[479] Rowland, *Lloyd George*, p126.

[480] To the author's belief, the first time this connection has been noted. William George mentions Jeune in his chapter *My Brother And I*, '*Agonizing Trials*', p194-204, and W. R. P. George mentions him in his chapter *Backbencher*, '*The Edwards Divorce Affair*', p207-237, but neither notes the previous connection.

foundation" and "an invention to protect a guilty man by naming an innocent one."[481] He was therefore cleared of the charge. In his judgement, Jeune stated:

> It not infrequently happens that a woman makes a confession against a man who is not the real adulterer. There are various reasons to tempt a woman to do so. In these circumstances I have no hesitation in saying that I think no case whatever has been made out against Mr. Lloyd George–I think it was in the interests of Mr. Lloyd George himself that the written confession has been brought forward and dealt with fully.[482]

Dr Edwards was duly granted his *decree nisi* on 18 November 1897. Unfortunately, this was not the end of the matter. Dr Thomas Pugh Beddoes, of Aberystwyth, intervened, filing a plea that the decree be rescinded. He had befriended Catherine Edwards, employing her as his secretary, and was convinced that not all the details of Dr Edwards conduct had been disclosed to the court. The case duly came before Judge Jeune on 16 June 1899, and this time Catherine herself gave evidence. Under cross examination, it transpired that she had written incriminating letters to a man named Gillet who she had long known, asking him to call on her when her husband was not at home. The case collapsed, and the *decree absolute* was granted on 23 June 1899.[483]

In December, the local executive councils of the Caernarvon Boroughs Liberal Association passed unanimous resolutions of sympathy with Lloyd George in his "cruel plight", congratulated him upon the complete vindication of his character and assured him of their unswerving loyalty. Lloyd George had written to the secretary of the Association a long letter in which he said:

> Our slander law is still uncivilised. Here was one of the greatest imputations on a man's honour that could ever be invented... and yet I was helpless in the matter. My accuser I could not bring to justice, as she had not published the charge within the legal meaning of that term; a communication made by a wife to her husband does not constitute 'publication'. The horrible anguish of mind, the impairment to health, the possible loss of reputation counted for nothing in the eyes of our slander law... Surely the law should be placed on a more humane footing?[484]

Margaret remained steadfast in her support for her husband throughout the long-drawn-out affair. In a private, undated note to William George, she wrote: "This world is a very cruel one, don't you think so? The innocent must suffer in order to shield the culprits. There are several persons in this matter who are left out of it altogether, who no doubt are guilty of misbehaving with this woman."[485] Margaret was on the platform with her husband when he spoke at a packed meeting in Caernarfon Pavilion on 30 October 1897, referring to the visiting Asquith as "the coming Liberal Prime Minister", over ten

---

481 McCormick, p45. A long-acknowledged problem here is that the Commons did not sit on the day in question. The documentation must have been the minutes of some other political meeting.
482 Quoted in George, *Backbencher*, p229.
483 *Carnarvon and Denbigh Herald*, 23 June 1899, p2.
484 *The Times*, 29 November 1897, quoted in McCormick, p46.
485 Quoted in George, *Backbencher*, p223.

years before he actually became so. Her presence spoke volumes.[486]

This early case showed an unfortunate pattern in Lloyd George's life. A virile man, by inclination he most certainly enjoyed the company of vivacious, attractive and intelligent women, but political enemies, fame-seekers and scandalmongers could never leave the issue alone, and such innuendo dogged him all his life. Gordon West noted that the "personality and appearance of Lloyd George, combined with the publicity he received" fascinated women: "Many wrote him letters of intense admiration, and made him unqualified offers of their services."[487] His eldest son, Richard, recognised one source of the problem:

> He was considerably sought after as a guest–young, witty, entertaining, personable, highly-publicised always in the districts where he spoke. All his life he was flattered by those who felt themselves encircled in the aura of success which he radiated; and amongst these were women, countless women, bored with their relatively humdrum lives, who seized the opportunity to bask in a little temporary reflected glory through their association with him.[488]

Frank Owen neatly summed up the tenuous nature of these allegations: "Throughout his career he was the victim of charges of this nature. In Wales the gossip related to London. And in London the rumours referred to Wales."[489] 60 years later, Travis Crosby similarly concluded: "Given the substantial number of Lloyd George's purported affairs, amours, flirtations and the like, one may wonder how he had time to do the nation's business… whether or not he was sexually intimate with women must remain an open question. The evidence seems often based upon hearsay."[490] It is entirely plausible that his so-called 'affairs' were merely cases of flirtatious behaviour, with Lloyd George seeking the women's attentions and approval; as Ffion Hague acutely observed, his "self-belief and mental buoyancy needed to be constantly fuelled by the devotion of his women. He had to feel that he came first."[491] He would hardly be the only public figure in history to indulge in such seductive behaviour. It is surely now well past time to move on from often ill-informed, ill-intentioned and prurient contemporary gossip to attempt to understand Lloyd George's actual life and relationships.

Meanwhile, industrial unrest was brewing in North-West Wales. The men at Penrhyn Quarry, near Bethesda, then the world's largest slate quarry, had struck a 'bargain' with their supervisors, to work a particular section of the quarry, usually in crews of four. The quality of the rock varied from one part of the quarry to another, and the 'bargain' system gave the quarrymen a degree of freedom, as they were each employed as a sort of contractor. Emilius Young, manager at the quarry since 1886, a Londoner and chartered accountant with no background in quarrying, was eager to scrap the 'bargaining' system, against the will of the quarrymen. Workers attempted to protect the existing

---

486 *Carnarvon and Denbigh Herald*, 5 November 1897, p3; George, *Backbencher*, p239.
487 West, p48.
488 Richard Lloyd George, *Lloyd George*, p62.
489 Owen, p89.
490 Crosby, *Unknown*, p39, 40.
491 Hague, p327.

system and to ensure a pay rise to 5s. a day, but Young and owner Lord Penrhyn responded by dismissing the 71 men connected with the Quarry Committee, a committee of workers entrusted with protecting the men's rights. Thus began a strike at the quarry on 29 September 1896 which would run for nearly 11 months.

The *Daily Chronicle* took up the men's cause, thanks to Lloyd George's influence with its editor Henry Massingham, its readers ultimately contributing £7,516 6s.[492] On 4 January 1897 the *Daily Chronicle* reported that "Messrs. Lloyd George. M.P., and W. Jones. M.P., have placed their services at the disposal of the quarrymen, to address meetings on their behalf in the large centres of population in England."[493] On 9 January Lloyd George made a speech at a conference of farmers from the counties of Carmarthen, Cardigan and Pembroke in the Shirehall, Carmarthen. Speaking in Welsh and pitching his speech to the land concerns of the 1,200-1,300 farmers thronging the building, he continued:

> Let them consider the case of a man whose name had been unpleasantly prominent of late, Lord Penrhyn… One of his forebears, a Scotchman, came to North Wales, and lived in Bangor. Not far off there dwelt a simple, innocent, honest community of small cotters and farmers and shepherds. They were honest, and he had the best proof of their honesty–they did not steal the common land. The mountain was not enclosed, for they looked upon it as belonging to the community. But the Scotchman thought otherwise. To-day, the mountain has been turned into a vast quarry, and the common land had become the source of one man's overgrown wealth–and for this successful negotiation the Scotch family was ennobled. The free mountain had become Lord Penrhyn's quarry, and 3000 Welshmen, the descendants many of them of the simple people who knew not how to rob in legal fashion, had become his hewers of wood and drawers of water. They had been refused the right of free men, the right of combination. Seven of their lives were sacrificed annually on the altar of Lord Penrhyn's wealth, and to-day, because they had claimed the privilege of union, they were debarred by his lordship from the means of sustaining themselves and their families… He trusted the farmers of South Wales would be united, and would band themselves, not only as farmers, but as Welshmen, to resist the forces of oppression and tyranny.[494]

In debate in the Commons on 28 January, Lloyd George again rose to promote the quarrymen's cause, with Penrhyn himself watching from the Peers' Gallery and his son Edward Douglas-Pennant speaking in his father's defence. Lloyd George said:

> The hon. Member for Macclesfield [William Bromley-Davenport][495] had said that these men were paid on the average 5s. 6d. a day, but every man who knew anything about slate quarries knew that there were days when the men could not be employed at all, and Lord Penrhyn in his

[492] Lindsay, p61; W. J. Parry, *The Penrhyn Lock-Out, 1900-1901: Statement And Appeal*, 1901, London, Co-Operative Printing Society, p168.
[493] *Daily Chronicle*, 4 January 1897, p3.
[494] *Carnarvon and Denbigh Herald*, 15 January 1897, p3.
[495] Brigadier-General William Bromley-Davenport (1862-1949), Tory MP for Macclesfield, 1886-1906.

> computation of averages took no account of the weeks and months when the quarries were stopped owing to weather and other reasons. Times of sickness, too, had to be deducted, and accidents… What the men asked was that as long as they worked hard and skilfully, and did their work honestly, they should be paid, not exactly equally, but in proportion to their skill and industry without regard to considerations of luck… Lord Penrhyn had refused to recognise the right of the committee to speak on behalf of the men, though the committee was elected openly and fairly by the men. How could 3,000 men, except through a committee, make known their grievances?…[496]

The next day Lloyd George wrote to Margaret: "Never made a more effective debating speech in the House of Commons. Spoke for 50 minutes in all & roasted Penrhyn."[497] Despite this, and the efforts of others, the dispute rumbled on. Finally, terms of settlement were signed on 18 August 1897[498] which included the rehiring of the dismissed men, but the underlying issues would continue to fester, only to re-emerge more profoundly in 1900, as would become apparent in due course.

On 21 December 1897, Lloyd George travelled to Italy with Henry Dalziel, Timothy Davies[499] and D. R. Daniel, staying at the Grand Hôtel de Russie in Rome. Having obtained an introduction into Vatican circles from Tim Healy, he attended mass in the Pope's private chapel on Christmas Day, recalling later "We talked quite frankly and freely". He wrote to his brother William:

> We had a wonderful day. Monsignor Kelly[500] met us at the Vatican at 8.20. He took us in but we had great difficulty in proceeding further than the ante-room. The officials all said that no one was allowed to enter the Pope's [Leo XIII][501] private Chapel (visitors only allowed to see him at the Sistine). At last the Pope's private secretary was seen. He saw the Pope, and Tim Davies and I got in as "deputados Inglesia"… We were the only visitors present. There were besides us half a dozen of the Pope's personal attendants… The old chap read out and conducted the whole service himself for over an hour. He is over 88! He blessed us all round. After the service we went to St. Peters. Who should I meet there but Sir George Trevelyan. He was very nice. I go to his hotel one of the next days.[502]

On 29 December, Lloyd George revisited the Vatican with Dalziel "to see the pictures."[503] He returned to the UK on 2 January 1898. His daughter Olwen remembered an incident from her father's trip to Rome, relating that she so liked the nougat sweets that the Pope gave him to bring home, that she ate the lot, including the packet that was meant for John Redmond's children. She added: "I don't

---

496 https://api.parliament.uk/historic-hansard/commons/1897/jan/28/motion-for-adjournment. Retrieved 2 May 2022. See Lindsay, p67-70, and Jack Jones, p62-64.

497 Morgan, *Family Letters*, p109.

498 Lindsay, p83-84.

499 Timothy Davies (1857-1951), Carmarthenshire draper, Liberal MP for Fulham 1906-1910, Louth 1910-1918.

500 Monsignor Michael Kelly (1850-1940), Rector of the Irish College, Rome, 1894-1901.

501 Pope Leo XIII, born 1810, reigned 1878-1903. Leo was 87 when Lloyd George saw him.

502 Quoted in George, *Backbencher*, p245-246.

503 Morgan, *Family Letters*, p113.

remember Father punishing me that time, but I do remember his comment afterwards: "That was why the Irish question was never settled!'"[504] Olwen also remembered her father's presence being like "something electric in the house", being great fun, reading the children stories so that they learnt them from him before they read them themselves, classics like Alexandre Dumas' *The Count of Monte Cristo*, Victor Hugo's *The Hunchback of Notre-Dame*, and Charles Dickens' Tales. The family also went camping in Cwm Stradllyn on the lower, southern slopes of nearby Moel Hebog, six miles to the north-east of Criccieth; Lloyd George and the children loved it, but poor Dame Margaret "hated" it, something evident in photographs by the expression on her face.[505]

In January 1898, Lloyd George delivered a powerful, hard-hitting speech, typical of his approach at this period, at a Leicester meeting of the National Liberal Federation, in support of electoral and Parliamentary reform. The electoral anomaly of plural voting was the particular grievance he fastened upon, declaring:

> The grand old Liberal maxim of 'trust the people' has not yet been fully incorporated in an Act of Parliament, We give one vote to one man, and thirty to another, and I have never been able to discover on what principles we have made this unfair distribution. We give one vote, or probably no vote at all, to the man who handles the plough, whilst we give ten votes to the man who handles the hunting-whip. We give one vote, or no vote at all, to the man who sows the seed, whilst we give ten votes to the man who neither sows nor reaps, but only consumes. One vote to the busy bee, and ten to the devouring locust. It occurs to me that if we are going to deprive anyone of votes, we ought to start with the men who contribute nothing to the creation of the wealth and prosperity of the country. He works not; then neither let him vote. But we must not deprive people who work hard, and risk life, health and comfort in order to contribute to the prosperity of the nation. It is not the soil, but the soul of the country that we want to be represented in the House of Commons. After all, have not the drones got a House all to themselves, which they guard as jealously as if it were a pheasant preserve?[506]

Lloyd George's parliamentary stock continued to rise. Thomas Artemus Jones[507] penned his assessment of him in the *Sunday Chronicle* on 24 April 1898:

> Mr. Lloyd George is still a young man. In the few years he has been in Parliament he has established an uncommonly high reputation. Mr. Lloyd George has not enjoyed Michael Davitt's unique experience of learning in penal servitude the political truths he proclaims on the platform. But he too has trodden the often impassable pathway of self-culture… He is one of the very rare men in politics who is an effective platform orator and a skilful debater in the

---

[504] O. Carey-Evans, p3, and information at Lloyd George Museum. It is intriguing that a man of Lloyd George's views would even be interested in seeing the Pope!

[505] https://www.bbc.co.uk/programmes/p013vs5h . Retrieved 24 May 2019. Lady Olwen speaking to BBC 'Yesterday's Witness' in 1968.

[506] Quoted in W. W. Davies, pp144-145. Plural Voting was not fully abolished in the United Kingdom until the passage of the Representation of the People Act 1948.

[507] Thomas A. Jones (1871-1943), barrister, journalist, nationalist, Liberal, Welsh language campaigner.

> Commons… To indicate his gift in a rough and ready fashion, I can only describe it as the sensitive, essentially Celtic, almost feminine instinct for divining and reading the feelings of his audience. No one is endowed with this particular talent to a higher degree than the leader of Young Wales.[508]

Soon, Lloyd George was to be profoundly affected by the loss of three men: William Gladstone, who died on Ascension Day, 19 May 1898; Thomas Gee, who died on 28 September 1898; and Tom Ellis who died on 5 April 1899. Gladstone's coffin lay in state in Westminster Hall between 26-27 May, and Lloyd George went on the first day to file past the coffin with Margaret and Rev. Elfed Lewis. Thomas Gee, who Lloyd George tended to refer to as 'the Grand Old Man of Wales', had long been a supporter and advocate for Lloyd George, viewing him as a Liberal-Radical protégé and using his newspaper, *Y Faner*, to promote his career and enhance his reputation. In some ways it was an almost an affectionate father-son kind of relationship.[509] Lloyd George's friend and fellow Welsh campaigner Tom Ellis died at the Hotel Metropole at Cannes, at the tragically early age of just 40. Never in the strongest health, over-worked and already suffering from flu, Ellis had taken a short holiday with his devoted wife during the Easter parliamentary recess. One night brain fever took place, and in three days he was dead. Speaking spontaneously, and from the heart the same evening at a Liberal meeting in Conwy, Lloyd George declared:

> Mr. Tom Ellis was to him, not merely a colleague and a friend,–he might almost say a brother… It would be a long time before they even would realise what loss Wales had sustained in the removal of Mr Ellis… one of the most honest Liberals this country ever had… He… possessed depth of thought, and a readiness which the public rarely perceived… And, of course, there must be a great deal of ability in a man who had risen, as he had done, being as he was a son of a tenant farmer to so high position as to which he had filled with such distinction. Not only he was the first Welshman to become chief Whip of any party… Probably, too, there was no man in the House of Commons in whom the leaders had more confidence. Although he had never been in the Cabinet, he was consulted on every Cabinet, he was consulted on every important question. Mr Ellis was a man strong in counsel. His wisdom, his judgment, his common sense, made him a reliable counsellor always; and it was a loss, not only to Wales, but to the whole party of freedom, to lose a man of his stamp… He never for a moment despaired the cause of human freedom and human progress throughout the length and breadth of the land… A man in his physical condition, who still maintained so hopeful a spirit, was a man whose courage was of no common order. It did not depend upon physical strength. Its roots were deeper. They were rooted in the fine convictions of the man himself. He was a fine man–the finest Wales ever sent to the House of Commons. He could not express to them that night the sense of personal loss… It had simply paralysed his thoughts, and all they could do at the moment was to send a message of sympathy to those who were near and dear to (Mr Ellis), to the young wife

[508] Quoted in George, *Backbencher*, p256-257.
[509] George, *Backbencher*, p271-272.

> [Annie] who was so left a widow, and to the aged parents who were so proud of their boy… Wales was proud of him, and the whole Liberal party were proud of him… He himself could not speak of politics that night…[510]

He spoke at the funeral at Capel Tegid in Bala on 11 April in similar terms. At the unveiling of the fine statue to Ellis by John Morley in Bala on 7 October 1903, Lloyd George presided over a large group of North Walian MPs of both parties, plus many other 'worthies' and thousands of ordinary folk, Churchmen and Nonconformists, from all over the Principality. Ellis was a son of Wales who broke such boundaries. Lloyd George briefly introduced Morley, saying that one of the greatest statesmen of the period was about to unveil a monument to "the greatest patriot that Wales had ever produced since the days of Owain Glyndwr." Morley then unveiled the statue, delivering his own address, before Lloyd George, on behalf of the subscribers to the National Memorial Fund, which raised £2,000, formally handed over the care of the statue to Bala Urban District Council, saying:

> … it was exceedingly difficult, even to those who knew Ellis well, to judge of him and of his position as a public character… It was doubtful whether a man's contemporaries were those who saw him most clearly... It was just possible that the Welshman of the next century would be in a better position to arrive at a true estimate of Tom Ellis than those who walked arm-in-arm with him on the streets. His work was only beginning to develop, and it must be generations before it attained its true proportions–his work for education, his work for the emancipation and the elevation of the masses of the people, to whom he was attached, and to whose cause he devoted his life. Before one knew how great Tom Ellis would be, one must also know what Wales would become… In any walk of life Tom Ellis would have been a success… but he chose rather to devote all his exceptional gifts to the service of his country.[511]

The decision to ask John Morley, Gladstone's biographer, to unveil the statue, "clearly indicates the desire to establish continuity between the Liberalism of the 'Grand Old Man' and the 'New Liberalism' of Lloyd George, and, by implication, a rejection of 'Cymru Fydd'."[512]

Later in the same month that Ellis died, April 1899, Lloyd George was delighted to hear that the new Liberal Leader, Scotsman Sir Henry Campbell-Bannerman, had asserted to Alfred Thomas MP, chairman of the Welsh Parliamentary Party, when talking about a vacancy arising among the junior Liberal whips, "I wouldn't dream of offering it to Ll.G. It would close his mouth in the House & he will get something much better."[513] Campbell-Bannerman would later make good on his word. In the meantime, on 1 May 1899, Lloyd George was appointed as one of seventeen members of the Select

---

510 *Carnarvon and Denbigh Herald*, 7 April 1899, p8. Only married the previous year, Annie was pregnant, and later in the year gave birth to a son, classicist Thomas I. Ellis (1899-1970).

511 '*Carnarvon and Denbigh Herald*', 9 October 1903, p8.

512 http://www.walesher1974.org/her/groups/GAT/media/GAT_Reports/GATreport_727_compressed.pdf, p10. Retrieved 3 February 2019.

513 NLW, William George Papers, 764, WG to DLG, 26 April 1899. Campbell-Bannerman, 'C.B.', had become Liberal Leader in the Commons, and Leader of the Opposition, on 6 February 1899.

Committee on the Aged Deserving Poor, under the chairmanship of Henry Chaplin[514], President of the Local Government Board, "to consider and report upon the best means of improving the condition of the Aged Deserving Poor, and of providing for those of them who are helpless and infirm; and to inquire whether any of the bills dealing with old-age pensions, and submitted to Parliament during the present Session, can with advantage be adopted either with or without Amendment."

Little noted, is the fact that the committee sent James S. Davy, an inspector for the Local Government Board, to Denmark to study the functioning of the Danish Old Age Relief Act, the '*Alderdomsunderstøttelsen*', of 1891. Davy duly presented a detailed report, stating that the Danish non-contributory system was working well, and that it was almost universally approved of.[515] On 26 July the committee, incorporating Davy's conclusions, reported in favour of a pension scheme with 65 years as the age limit, to apply to British subjects, of not less than 5s. or more than 7s. per week, at the committee's discretion, according to the cost of living. Criminals, those receiving poor relief, or having an income of more than 10s. per week, were to be excluded from the provisions of the bill. Their favourable report was conditioned, however, by a recommendation for the reform of the poor laws upon which, they believed, the success of their pension scheme rested. A departmental committee on aged deserving poor, 1899-1900, was appointed to consider the financial aspects of the proposed bill. No further progress was made, largely due to the Boer War siphoning funds away from social reform measures, but Lloyd George's work with this committee was a significant precursor to his profound achievements as Chancellor of the Exchequer a decade later.

Lloyd George himself wrote to Margaret on 26 July, concerning the committee's report:

> Old Age Pensions is through… I have added some millions on to this Bill for them. I am sure I put on 2 or 3 millions yesterday & a similar sum today. Never mind, it goes all to the poor who really need it. It has the additional advantage of putting these bandits who are now in power in a nice fix. They can neither carry out these recommendations nor drop them–not without discredit… The curious thing is that the Tory members of the Committee are very pleased with me & the Liberals are equally pleased…[516]

Joseph Chamberlain regarded Lloyd George as the "best of the lot" of the committee, whose zeal and ability had "carried with him the progressive Conservatives" and even the Chairman, 'Squire' Henry Chaplin. In June, Chamberlain even "invited him to his private room to discuss the problem in all its bearings. Mr. Lloyd George accepted the invitation, and it is not without significance that Mr. Chamberlain entrusted him with the draft of a scheme which he had himself carefully prepared, remarking, as he handed it over: "I am giving you my own copy and, indeed, the only one in existence."[517] When they next met privately in the House, Lloyd George asked Chamberlain "Will you

[514] Henry Chaplin (1840-1923), Tory MP for Sleaford. Michael Davitt was another member of the Committee.

[515] D. Levine, *The Danish Connection: A Note On The Making Of British Old Age Pensions*, *Albion* 17, 2, Summer 1985, p181-185.

[516] Quoted in Morgan, *Family Letters*, p118.

[517] Edwards, 1913, Vol.III, p183-184. See also Du Parcq, Vol.II, p214-215.

stand by it?", and Chamberlain answered him directly, "Yes".[518] But it was sadly not to be: the legislation would not be passed, and the two men's relationship would soon be soured irrevocably.

At the close of the parliamentary session in August 1899, Lloyd George accepted an invitation from Clifford Sifton, the Liberal Canadian Minister of the Interior, to visit the country and see the great advantages that it could offer to Welsh emigrants, as part of a delegation along with W. Llewelyn Williams, the barrister journalist from Carmarthenshire, and W. J. Rees JP, a Conservative politician from Swansea. Accompanied by William Griffith, the Canadian Government Agent at Cardiff, the party sailed from Liverpool on the newly launched SS *Bavarian* on 19 August, docking in Quebec on 1 September. Du Parcq records a sidelight on Lloyd George's wit:

> On the journey out, some sensible organiser persuaded Mr. Lloyd George to take the chair at a concert in the saloon of the S.S. Bavarian, at which… a collection was made on behalf of a charity–the "Seamen's Home." The eloquence of the chairman charmed a good deal of money into the plate… As there was a school of very large whales spouting outside, he said that it was perhaps permissible that little Wales should spout inside… Becoming serious, he treated his audience to some very fine passages of oratory. He cited Nevin, Carnarvonshire. In every home in that town there was a sailor member, and every one of those homes mourned the loss of a loved one whose grave was in the mighty deep…[519]

From Quebec the little delegation moved on to Montreal, then Winnipeg, before proceeding to Ottawa, where they interviewed Sifton and met other prominent Canadian statesmen. As ever, Lloyd George was interested in the land and its potential productivity, and he was struck by the vast possibilities that the Dominion offered, telling the *Toronto Globe*:

> I am very much impressed at the vastness of Canada's fertile belt. We all knew by looking at the map that Canada was a huge country, but we had no idea that the cultivated part was so great. Not only the wheat-providing plains of Manitoba and of the North-West have surprised me by their abundance of wealth, but also the rich minerals of British Columbia, which seem to me to be unlimited. My only criticism is that the country has been very much under-advertised. The possibilities of Canada strike me as being immense. Everything that tends to make a country great is present. Wheat, cattle, gold, silver, iron, copper, fish, magnificent streams and inexhaustible water-power are in abundance. There is nothing lacking except enterprise and push. The Canadians have not shouted loud enough for themselves... Canada's voice has been drowned by the shouting of the Americans, who have, in consequence, attracted trade where Canadian trade would have been equally successful.[520]

The three delegates also prepared a report, published in May 1900, in which they stated:

---

518 J. L. Garvin, *The Life Of Joseph Chamberlain*, 1933, London, Macmillan, Vol.II, *1885-1895: Disruption And Combat*, p626-627.
519 Du Parcq, Vol.I, p196, quoting from *Western Mail*, 15 September 1899.
520 Quoted in Edwards, 1913, Vol.III, p183-184.

> The greater portion of our time was spent in Manitoba, the North West provinces and British Columbia…
>
> Before starting on our visit to the prairie we were shown over the Government's experimental farm at Brandon. We were greatly struck by the care and minuteness of its cultivation, its fine appointments, especially the ensilage, and its splendid arrangements generally. The exhibition room, full as it was of samples of the various grasses, grains, bush, fruit, and root crops, grown in Manitoba impressed us with the richness and fertility of the soil. The samples we saw of the "No.1 Manitoba hard" wheat, convinced us that there is no country better adapted for grain growing.
>
> In the districts around Brandon, Rapid City, Whitewood, Cannington Manor, Carlyle, and Regina, there is no room for large colonies of settlers, as a good deal of the land has already been taken up. But in all these districts there are still plenty of quarter and half and whole sections (of 160, 320, and 640 acres respectively) the freehold of which can be acquired at prices varying from $3 to $10 or $15 per acre, and which can be paid for by instalments running over ten years. To the north and west of the Moose Mountain, however, there lies an extensive tract of prairie, which is almost entirely unsettled. Owing to its present remoteness from railways and the hardships which are separable from pioneer life in new districts, we would hesitate to suggest the formation there of a large colony of settlers, as experience has shown that greater success is attained when the new settlers locate among those acquainted with the country, the climate and the style of agriculture.[521]

They also gave interesting details of interviews they conducted with settlers, with supporting facts and figures, the whole report being illustrated with excellent line drawings. They noted potential drawbacks for new settlers, but concluded:

> These Districts Offer Great and Generous Inducements to settlers. The land yields good crops without the necessity of manuring. Taxes are light, laws are equitable, administration is pure, institutions are free and liberal, educational facilities are excellent…, railways are enterprising (in fact, the energy and public spirit of all the railway companies from the Canadian Pacific Railway downwards struck us as being one of the most remarkable features in the development of Canada) and as long as a settler does not go too far ahead of a railway… he is certain of a ready cash market for grain and stock.[522]

The party did not neglect to comment on their host country's other great natural assets, noting:

> During our visit to British Columbia, we were greatly impressed with the immense and seemingly inexhaustible mineral resources of the Province. Coal and iron ore, gold and copper, silver and lead, mica and marble, there seems to be no limit to the marvellous natural mineral wealth of the country. At Fernie, near the Crow's Nest Pass… We found that there were several

521 Lloyd George et al., *Report*, p8.
522 Ibid., p16-17.

> Welsh miners… Though… the officials were [not] favourable to anything like a wholesale emigration of Welsh miners, they said there was plenty of work for expert miners who came out in small batches, and that, indeed, no one who was able and willing to work need be afraid of emigrating to Canada…[523]

Leaving Canada "with most pleasant feelings towards her people and Government", they sailed on 7 October, arriving back in England on 16 October.

Just before Lloyd George docked back in Southampton, on 11 October, a state of war had broken out between the British Empire and the Boer farmers of the South African Republic (the Transvaal) and the Orange Free State, the two Boer states going to war over the Empire's influence in South Africa, specifically the Rand gold mining syndicates, and their desire to be free of restrictive laws and heavy taxation on their growing operations. Still in British Columbia, Lloyd George had immediately been 'on the case' as soon as he heard the news of impending war, cabling his brother from Glacier on 18 September:

> The news from the Transvaal threatens to alter my arrangements. War means the summoning of Parliament; the former now seems inevitable. The prospect oppresses me with a deep sense of horror. If I have the courage, I shall protest with all the vehemence at my command against this blackguardism which is perpetrated in the name of human freedom.[524]

Lloyd George was not found wanting in courage, and indeed he was to become increasingly hated for his stand on the war, which he viewed as imperialist aggression, until the war ended on 31 May 1902. During that period, Britain put 448,435 men into the field, against around 60,000 Boer farmers and volunteers, at a cost of £211.16m and taking over two years and seven months to defeat two tiny republics whose combined white populations, as Lloyd George scathingly put it, "did not exceed that of Flintshire and Denbighshire." In the process, Britain would lose 22,092 men, two-thirds to disease rather than to enemy action, with a further 75,430 wounded or sick and 934 missing, while the Boers death toll would be 32,559, of whom 26,370 were women and children in camps. Up to 20,000 African natives also died in the camps. Such was his identification with the underdogs, Lloyd George originally grew his hair long at this time as a pro-Boer protest, wearing his hair in the style of the Boer farmers.[525]

Biographer Don Cregier gave a very useful encapsulation of Lloyd George's evolving political outlook at this period, in all its complexity:

> Lloyd George's foreign policy views were a Palmerstonian[526] mixture of realpolitik, patriotic nationalism (both British and Welsh), and hatred of injustice. Unlike his uncle, Lloyd George

---

[523] Ibid., p18. See also Lewis H. Thomas *Lloyd George's Visit To The North-West, 1899*, *Saskatchewan History*, III, Winter 1950, p17-22.
[524] Quoted in George, *Backbencher*, p286.
[525] Information from Bengy Carey-Evans, Interview with author, Beaumaris, 11 October 2018.
[526] Henry J. Temple, Viscount Palmerston (1784-1865), Whig then Liberal statesman, three times Foreign Secretary, twice Prime Minister.

> was in no sense a pacifist. While scorning jingoism, which he associated with the Tory aristocracy and the urban mob whose votes it sought, and abhorring war's wastage of lives and capital, Lloyd George admired military genius and heroism and commended the use of armed force in a rightful cause.[527]

As a Radical MP, often referred to by now as the "Coming Man", Lloyd George became a 'hate-figure' throughout Britain for his opposition to the war, just at the point that the nation was transitioning from the Victorian to the Edwardian era, to the point, in October 1900, of being "burned in effigy in his own constituency at Nefyn, Pwllheli and Criccieth. His enemies even stuck upon their bonfire a likeness of his uncle, Richard Lloyd. But in this they succeeded only in bringing odium on themselves, for this man's character was beyond assault."[528] Lloyd George himself "nearly lost his seat in Parliament, his law practice, and his life through his anti-war activities."[529]

His attitude towards the war in South Africa was consistent and courageous from the start. He felt certain that waging war upon two small Boer republics, run by Calvinist farmers much like the Welsh, was politically and morally wrong. It is worth noting that the Liberal *Carnarvon and Denbigh Herald* agreed with him, drawing parallels between Wales and the Boer republics and arguing "it is but natural that Welshmen should sympathise with a small nation of farmers that wishes to maintain its independence, to cherish its mother tongue, and to safeguard its national existence".[530] The cause of the war lay, Lloyd George claimed, in the political ambitions and financial interests of Joseph Chamberlain, the Colonial Secretary. The day he arrived back in England–16 October–Lloyd George wrote to his brother: "In my opinion, the way these poor hunted burghers have been driven in self-defence to forestall us, aggravates our crime. There is something diabolical in its malignity."[531]

As early as 27 October 1899, at the very end of the session before Parliament was prorogued, he delivered a stinging attack upon the great Chamberlain which stunned the Commons, *Daily Express* reporter Charles King noting that "the House seemed to shimmer with alarm as the young Welshman stood up and defied him"[532]:

> MR. LLOYD GEORGE… The Opposition charged the Government with having… blundered seriously, in consequence of which this country and the Transvaal had suffered severely... They had gone to war practically on the question of franchise ... The Transvaal Government offered a seven years franchise. What would have been the position if that had been accepted? There were two Chambers in the Transvaal, and in one Chamber aliens would have the right to vote in two years if the Bill of the Boer Government had been passed, and if it had been allowed to come into operation every resident in the Transvaal could have had a vote for the two Chambers. He asked whether any man who supported going to war realised that every man in

527 Cregier, p64.
528 Owen, p104.
529 Farwell, p314.
530 *Carnarvon and Denbigh Herald*, 8 September 1899, p4.
531 Quoted in George, *My Brother And I*, p177.
532 King, p37.

the Transvaal, whether he were born in that country or not, would have had the right to vote for two Chambers in seven years?...

[He] said he had some experience in registration, and the condition of things in this country was a great deal worse than those contained in the Franchise Bill of the Transvaal, with the result that a whole body of men like Wesleyan ministers were disfranchised. In this country it takes three years before a man can get a vote... We had two Chambers in this country, but a man, although he might be a permanent resident, could not get a vote for one Chamber; while for the other–the House of Lords–if he lived for ever he would never get a vote. The Government denied them educational reform in Wales, where there were two millions of people, many of whom were engaged in fighting the battles of the country; but when the Uitlanders of the Transvaal, including Jews and others, claimed electoral reform, this country did not hesitate to go to war on their account. This was not merely wrong, but a palpable act of hypocrisy. This all came of the new diplomacy. What was this new diplomacy? It is carried out with a view of working up public opinion in this country and turning it upon the question of the moment, and by deliberately misrepresenting the concessions made by the other side, which is a shameless proceeding.

... [E]ither there must have been criminal negligence, a negligence involving the lives of hundreds of our soldiers, or there had been deliberate forgery on the part of someone; and he left it to the Government and the officials of the Colonial Office to choose between those two horns of the dilemma... [S]omeone in South Africa must have done it. Here we were in a state of war on documents which misrepresented, intentionally or unintentionally... the concessions made by the Transvaal Government, and it had involved the loss of hundreds of lives up to the present moment, and heaven only knew what it would yet mean to this country. He believed there would be a reaction against the Government before long when the country came to realise the true state of affairs... It was said that we were fighting for the franchise and a pure and honest administration in the Transvaal. The fact was that the war had been forced on by a Government which had divided three millions of money amongst its own supporters by a measure carried by a Chamber composed of landlords, who benefited to the tune of hundreds of thousands of pounds a year–a Chamber for which no native-born British subject had a right to vote. That was the Government and the Chamber which was spending millions of money in order to enforce a pure and honest administration in the Transvaal.[533]

Lloyd George had nailed the lie, nailed the hypocrisy. He wrote to Maggie later the same day:

I spoke in the House today a *chefais hwyl anarferol* [and was in unusually good form]. Glad I did it... You have no idea what a feeling it is. I pitched into them as they had not been pitched into before... Wish you had been there. I got my chance & used it. The Government had published a false translation of the Transvaal documents!... I bullied the Speaker almost. Joe [Chamberlain] got him to call me to order for saying it was done deliberately. I retorted that if

[533]https://api.parliament.uk/historic-hansard/commons/1899/oct/27/third-reading#S4V0077P0_18991027_HOC_58. Retrieved 2 January 2020.

> it was not done deliberately then the negligence was a criminal one seeing that it had sent hundreds of brave men already to their death. Either criminal negligence or forgery. I leave it to the right honourable gentleman to elect. It doesn't matter to me which. The Radicals cheered. Of course I said Chamberlain personally could not have been guilty of such a thing. But I said someone has & I want to know who. I have never uttered such home truths in that House & no one replied to me.[534]

The *North Wales Chronicle* opined that Lloyd George's actions were "the shame of Carnarvonshire", subsequently declaring that they were "a shock to the feelings of nine out of every ten of his constituents" and that "the overruling majority of his regular supporters are against Mr Lloyd George and his Pro-Boer advocacy."[535] Lloyd George wrote to William on 1 November about the overwhelming anti-Boer feeling among his Pwllheli constituents: "This is a pity. But let them do as they may; *I will oppose [the war] even if it means them throwing me out*."[536] Many years later, Richard Humphreys (under his pen name R. o. Fadog) recalled a visit Lloyd George made to Nefyn for a public meeting in the early part of the war:

> The attitude of Mr Lloyd George on the South African war question alienated many of his principal supporters, such as the late Alderman Wm. Anthony, J.P., Pwllheli.
>
> One dark and wet November evening, Mr Lloyd George was to hold a meeting at Nevin, and he gave me a lift from Pwllheli. Alderman W. Eifl Jones and Mrs George were with us. I anticipated trouble at Nevin, but before our carriage reached the town, just at the top of the steep hill that leads to High-street, we were pelted with sods. When we got to the hall a hostile crowd met us at the entrance, and during the holding of the meeting frequent interruptions took place. Mr Lloyd George, however, braved the opposition smilingly. On our way back we were again attacked at the very same place.
>
> The candidate held another meeting at Nevin, and several at Pwllheli, and by sheer force of his eloquence and personality he captured the majority of the voters at Nevin and Pwllheli. At the last meeting held at Pwllheli, Mr J. A. Spender[537] spoke. The eldest son of Mr Lloyd George was on the platform, and Mr Spender took hold of him, placed him on a table, and made some suitable remarks about the youngster. With the eloquence of Mr Spender and Mr Lloyd George, the meeting boiled over with enthusiasm for the candidate.[538]

Despite the outcome at this meeting, things soon got worse for young Richard, who was bullied and physically attacked at school at Dulwich College for being a 'dirty pro-Boer'. He was immediately removed from the school and sent to live with Uncle Lloyd, William George and Pollie at Garthcelyn,

---

534 Quoted in Morgan, *Family Letters*, p124.

535 *North Wales Chronicle*, 4 November 1899, p5, and 9 December 1899, p4.

536 Quoted in George, *Backbencher*, p292.

537 John Spender (1862-1942), Liberal journalist, editor, older brother of Harold Spender.

538 *North Wales Chronicle*, *Reminiscences of Mr Lloyd George*, 15 December 1916, p5.

attending the new Portmadoc Grammar School, where the bullying ceased.[539] Olwen later remembered "It was an awful period for us children… It felt like being a traitor."[540]

On 27 November, Lloyd George made his first public speech in Wales after the outbreak of hostilities, at the Guildhall, Carmarthen, before an audience which was far from friendly. His logic was clear, timeless, relentless and inescapable:

> We want disestablishment, land reform, temperance reform, and self-government to control the affairs of our own country. And all this work is stopped, all this is at an end; the roar of the cannon has commenced. That is why I object to war–because nothing stops progress like war… I am going to speak fearlessly tonight. This is the first political meeting I have addressed in Wales since the war. I have considered carefully and seriously whether I ought to make any allusion to it, but I would be recreant before God and man if, in addressing my fellow countrymen, I did not utter a protest against what I consider to be an infamy. I will do it tonight even if I leave Carmarthen tomorrow without a friend to bid me goodbye…[541]

Following this, in a disastrous week called 'Black Week', from 10-17 December, the British Army suffered three devastating defeats at the battles of Stormberg, Magersfontein and Colenso, with a total of 2,776 men killed, wounded and captured. These bleak events were an eye-opener for the British, who had underestimated their opponents' tenacity, fighting ability and weaponry. This was followed by the disastrous loss at the Battle of Spion Kop on 23-24 January 1900.[542]

On 6 February, in the Queen's Speech debate, Lloyd George delivered a carefully researched speech "charging that the real reason for the war was that Rand capitalists objected to Transvaal miners having an eight-hour day, Sunday holidays, and wages four times higher than British miners, and to paying the Boer government mine royalties of 50 percent compared to 1.5 percent in Britain."[543] In this speech, which so neatly encapsulates his attitude throughout the whole period of the war–"an unnecessary, a damnable, even worse perhaps, a senseless war" as he wrote to D. R. Daniel[544]–Lloyd George declared:

> I venture to say that in the general opinion of the country the greatest mistakes that have been made are those committed in the diplomacy of the Colonial Secretary [Joseph Chamberlain]… The Colonial Secretary said that if the war was unjust and unrighteous it ought not to be prosecuted. That is the view taken, not by a majority, but by a very strong body of people in the country, and a growing one. Whatever line we take in this House, discussion will go on in the country, in workshops and factories, until that conviction is reached. This bloodshed should be

---

539 Hague, p168. The school was founded in 1894.
540 Carey Evans, p20.
541 Quoted in George *Backbencher*, p299.
542 Winston Churchill was present at the battle, as a courier. So was Mahatma Gandhi, active as a stretcher-bearer in the Natal Indian Ambulance Corps he had organised, being awarded the Queen's South Africa Medal.
543 Cregier, p65; https://api.parliament.uk/historic-hansard/commons/1900/feb/06/sixth-days-debate#S4V0078P0_19000206_HOC_210. Retrieved 3 April 2019.
544 Owen, p98.

> put an end to. I think it was John Bright[545] who said that the people took no interest in diplomacy until it had been made interesting by war. That is perfectly true. I ask hon. Members opposite how many people in this country realise that the Boer Government, in the beginning of September, accepted an offer made by our Government in the beginning of August, and how many realise that we are at war now after they had accepted the proposals we had offered? I venture to put it to any lawyer in this House, whether in any court of equity specific performance would not have been enforced on that state of facts. Then we hear a good deal about the intolerable oppression of the Government of the Transvaal. How many workmen in this country realise that the wages earned by miners in the Transvaal were four times as high as at home? How many miners realise that an eight hours day, which they cannot get their own House of Commons to give attention to, is provided for by an Act passed under this oppressive Transvaal Government? How many people in this country realise, when they hear wild, vague talk about the oppression and despotism of the Transvaal, that whereas in Rhodesia, under our own Government, the gold mining royalties are fifty per cent., under this oppressive and despotic Transvaal Government they are only one-half per cent.? Then, I would like to know how many Members of the House know really what are the grievances in regard to which we are fighting... No grievance has excited more sentimental opposition to the Transvaal than the grievance regarding the natives. Ministers of the gospel of peace go preaching war because they are excited by tales of intolerable oppression of the native blacks. But what is the native grievance?… Native touts are sent round all Western Africa to induce natives to come to Johannesburg, and work in the mines. These touts make false representations to the natives in regard to wages and the hours of labour, and when the natives arrive they say "this is not what was promised us," and there are desertions among them to the number of 5,000 a month. What was it that the Uitlanders said? They complained against the Transvaal Government because it did not pass a law to detain these natives, to imprison them, to fine them beyond their means, and afterwards to send them per force to work in their (the Uitlanders') mines under the contracts of employment which had been entered into by fraud. This is the native grievance which these ministers of religion talk about… That is a grievance of the Uitlanders. It means that at the price of the blood of our brave soldiers we are going to renew slavery in South Africa…

Lloyd George was now well into his stride, emphasising that the war was all about profits, "the £.s.d.", continuing:

> … The next is the grievance of the liquor law, and it is really an extraordinary grievance to be fighting for. I quote here from the report of the Associated Chamber of Mines… that the present liquor law is sound in principle, and that certain amendments, if vigorously enforced, will practically stamp out the illicit traffic. These gentlemen are the prohibitioners. You are practically fighting for prohibition. But what a spectacle it all presents for a Government which floated into power on beer to engage in a sanguinary war to enforce prohibition in the

545 John Bright (1811-1889), Radical and Liberal statesman, one of the greatest orators of his generation.

Transvaal… Now, another matter that is brought into the discussion is that of the railways, and it is most extraordinary. What is it that the Uitlanders demand? They demand that the railways which are now in the hands of the private companies shall henceforth be managed by the State. What, managed by a corrupt and inefficient Government?–a Government which is said to be so corrupt that it cannot manage its own affairs! They contend that the Government should not only take over the railways, but manage them as well. That is an extraordinary view for the Uitlanders to take. The next grievance is as to the franchise… There is a great deal said about equal rights and equal privileges between the two white races; but there is really no distinction in the Transvaal between one race and another. There is only that distinction which you find in every other nation in the civilised world between a man who is born on the soil and a man who comes from another country. In this country we draw exactly the same distinction between an Englishman and a foreigner. President Kruger in the Transvaal fixes a fourteen years residence as the qualification for the franchise. In this country we insist practically on seven years; but hardly any Uitlander in this country could get a vote under six or seven years. Now that, in my opinion, does not amount to intolerable oppression. Is it unreasonable that such a distinction should be drawn in a community like that of the Transvaal, where the foreigner is in the majority? If you think that a foreigner ought to wait six or seven years in your country, where the foreigner is a negligible quantity, surely it is not too much to expect that I should impose a period of fourteen years in my country in order to protect my position against the foreigners. But this is my point: President Kruger, who is all-powerful in the Volksraad, was called upon to practically hand over the country to foreigners, and he was entitled to say: "If that be so, I must insist that the Government is a local one." How could you ask President Kruger to hand over his country to the control of a people whose patriotism was the due of a foreign nation? I think it is unfair… Although there was nothing unreasonable in President Kruger's attitude, I think we would have got the five years franchise. There is good ground for thinking so. The right hon. Gentleman the Member for South Aberdeen [James Bryce][546] pointed out that there was a great reform party in the Transvaal–the Liberal party of the Transvaal–headed by General Joubert, and he came within 500 votes of defeating President Kruger.[547] In the Volksraad there was a proposal to reduce the franchise from fourteen to five years. That was before the raid.[548] It was defeated only by a majority of four in a House of Dutchmen elected by the Boers… In a few years' time we might have hoped to convert the best men in South Africa to our way of thinking… The new diplomacy has converted the best friends we had in Africa into those dangerous foes who have inflicted a more grievous succession of blows upon our Empire than any which it has suffered for over a century. The whole disposition of the Boers was changed by the raid, and I think there was real ground for the suspicion that they undoubtedly entertained. Here we had three or four men who have sworn that the Colonial Office was implicated in the raid… There were four gentlemen, at any rate, who believed the Colonial

[546] James Bryce (1838-1922), academic, jurist, historian, Liberal MP for South Aberdeen, 1885-1907.

[547] In the April 1893 Presidential election, Kruger took 7,911 votes to Joubert's 7,246, with allegations of vote rigging: *Joubert, Petrus Jacobus, Encyclopædia Britannica*, Vol.15 (11th Ed.), 1911, p522.

[548] The Jameson Raid (29 December 1895–2 January 1896), an abortive raid by 600 men against the Republic, led by administrator Dr Leander Jameson, employed by Cecil Rhodes, Prime Minister of the Cape Colony.

> Office was behind them, and… they said so at the time… so how can you blame the Boers for believing it? It is rather extraordinary that we have not had all the correspondence published. That would have thrown more light upon the matter… Then there is another point–the clearing of Mr. Cecil Rhodes, the gentleman who had assured these men who went to die in the raid that they were dying for their Queen. Who was it who induced these men to commit an act which deprived them of their professional rank and ruined their professional career for life? To my mind there is no word in the English language adequate to characterise the moral turpitude of that action. It is a count in the indictment which still remains. Now, Sir, I doubt very much whether the conscience of this country will tolerate the problem of this war. What, after all, is this grievance as to the franchise in the Transvaal? I think the country ought really to be in possession of the facts. The foreigner landing in the Transvaal is in a better position in voting for the magistrates and for the election of President than he is in this country; and yet we proceed to teach them at the point of the bayonet the doctrine of equal rights. When the Conservatives were in office, in 1888-1892… not a word was uttered about these intolerable burdens under which our fellow subjects were suffering in the Transvaal… Only nine years have elapsed since the agitation began for a five years franchise in the Transvaal, and we are now at war with that country, although here it took a whole century to lower the franchise. I do not believe the war has any connection with the franchise. It is a question of 45 per cent. dividends; and yet we hear of the obstinacy of President Kruger. It is said that there was no possibility of concession on the part of President Kruger except through the medium of guns and bayonets. When the war began, we heard a great deal about the obstinate and obdurate conduct of President Kruger, but only in July last the Colonial Secretary spoke of the rapidity with which the modifications made by the South African Republic since the Bloemfontein Conference[549] had followed each other, and said that each new scheme seemed to be an advance and improvement on that which preceded it. The statement that President Kruger was so obstinate that he would not consider anything is untrue, and, seeing that the falsehood has led to this bloodshed, it is a crime perpetrated on the country. I should have thought that the greatest pride of the Uitlanders would have been to take part in this conflict and fight for their supposed rights. But how many have availed themselves of the privilege?… Seven thousand of the Uitlanders [sic] are fighting for their intolerable oppressors… Barely a battalion out of the whole 80,000, and the remainder are living in security… I am sure, Sir, that I shall carry the House with me when I declare that such men and their grievances are not worth a drop of British blood.[550]

Lloyd George did not carry the House, with the 'Ayes' 139, to the 'Noes' 352, but Balfour, a parliamentarian since 1874, called it "the best speech I have ever heard in the House of Commons,"[551] even though he of course disagreed with the sentiments expressed in it. William Harcourt, a

---

[549] Held in the capital of the Orange Free State from 31 May–5 June 1899.

[550]https://api.parliament.uk/historic-hansard/commons/1900/feb/06/sixth-days-debate#S4V0078P0_19000206_HOC_210. Retrieved 9 April 2019.

[551] Quoted in Cregier, p65.

parliamentarian since 1868, passed a note to Lloyd George stating, "You have made a speech which Grattan himself might have envied."[552] Henry Campbell-Bannerman said that a famous London actress "begged her escort to bring her again whenever the Member for Caernarvon was likely to speak."[553] Lloyd George had now stepped firmly onto the national stage.

The war also accelerated the process of bringing Lloyd George into greater familiarity with radicalism outside of Wales. He began to work more closely with Irish Nationalists, naturally mostly pro-Boers in their stand against British imperialism, but he also became acquainted with members of the Independent Labour Party led by Keir Hardie.[554] Lloyd George's first contact with Hardie was through their membership of the Stop the War Committee set up in December 1899 by W. T. Stead.[555] A little later, in October 1900, Lloyd George was invited to become a Vice-President of the National Democratic League, another anti-war organization. His association with the League, whose members included Lib-Lab MPs John Burns[556] and Thomas Burt[557], militant socialist Tom Mann[558], as well as radical elements of the Liberal Party, was a further step in his transition from Welsh radical nationalist to British social reformer. He also participated in the League of Liberals Against Aggression and Militarism, formed in February 1900, which gave him an entrée into radical Liberal intellectual circles, but being neither a university man nor a philosopher, he felt less 'at home' in this group.[559]

Even biographer Donald McCormick, no admirer of Lloyd George, is full of praise for his principled stance at this period:

> As to whether Lloyd George s uncompromising attitude and vehement hostility to the war were justified in the light of history is still a debatable point, but he succeeded in clearing the air of cant, humbug and nonsensical jingoism…
>
> The virtue of Lloyd George at this period was that he showed immense moral courage, that he acted as a highly necessary antidote to the unthinking jingoism of a majority of the British people and that, for the first time since John Bright, he forced them to think about war and not just to accept it blindly as a national necessity.
>
> In the nation-wide campaign… on which he embarked as a one-man crusade during the Boer War, his oratory was forceful and sincere, yet factual and well argued. Not only does it still read well… but it is vital documentary material for any historian of that period.[560]

Lloyd George was relentless, becoming the Government's chief rhetorical opponent, often employing

---

552 Henry Grattan (1746-1820), Member of the Irish House of Commons, who campaigned for legislative freedom for the Irish Parliament in the late 18th Century, known as a superb orator.

553 Owen, p98.

554 (James) Keir Hardie (1856-1915), Scottish trade unionist, Independent Labour MP for West Ham South, 1892-1895, Labour MP for Merthyr Tydfil, 1900-1915, Labour Leader, 1906-1908.

555 William Stead (1849-1912), newspaper editor, pioneer of investigative journalism, died on the RMS *Titanic.*

556 John Burns (1858-1943), trade unionist, Lib-Lab MP for Battersea, 1892-1918, President of the Local Government Board, 1905-1914, President of the Board of Trade, February-August 1914.

557 Thomas Burt (1837-1922), one of the first working-class MPs, being Lib-Lab MP for Morpeth, 1874-1918.

558 Thomas Mann (1856-1941), trade unionist, campaigner and organiser, largely self-taught.

559 Cregier, p65-66.

560 McCormick, p48.

stinging wit in his arsenal.[561] On 27 January 1900, he was invited to Oxford to address the Palmerston Club, one of the lights of Liberalism in that university. Speaking in the Senior Common Room of Balliol College, he stated that: "The country was suffering from an over-dose of Imperialism, and the greatest service the Liberal party could render to it was to inculcate the sound, healthy ideas of Fox, Cobden, Bright, and Gladstone." He again attacked Joseph Chamberlain, referring to a recent speech of Chamberlain's in which he had referred to the Transvaal: "mark the superciliousness of his tone in referring to it as "the country we created." The new imperialists would have to procure a revised version of their scripture–a Birmingham edition, commencing "In the beginning Joseph Chamberlain created heaven and earth". He added: "The most deplorable feature of the situation was the way the Liberals of Europe had given us up. There was a time when they looked to Britain for lead and succour. Now they had turned away in sorrow and sadness of heart from the country who was once for them an exemplar of freedom."[562]

The first of what famously became the 'Lloyd George Nights' was at an anti-war meeting in Glasgow City Hall on 6 March. This had become a battlefield for rival mobs of Tory university students and Socialist dockers, the latter being led by Keir Hardie himself, fighting breaking out long before the meeting had even started. Lloyd George eventually gained a rowdy hearing as he managed to present his prepared address. Though the windows of his cab were broken as he left, he escaped injury. Keir Hardie and three of his womenfolk were set upon by hooligans, and knocked about until rescued by the police.[563] Lloyd George endured the:

> … tumultuous experience–the worst public meeting row I have ever witnessed–10,000 people outside, trying to break in to the meeting–surging, struggling, fighting, yelling–howling like savages–a small Armageddon going on inside, and hundreds of the Foe got into the meeting… I waited patiently for my chance, then I shot out a couple of sentences about the terrible list of casualties in that day's papers. A hush instantly fell on the whole audience. I took advantage of that to pour shot and shell into the rowdies on their want of fair play etc. I spoke for forty minutes, and got a splendid hearing…[564]

Two days later the *Labour Leader*, organ of the recently formed Labour Party, opined that: "The triumph of the evening, however, was the fine oratorical speech of Mr. Lloyd George–tact–arguments–apt quotations and impassioned appeal followed each other in quick succession–completely captivating the audience and betimes rousing it to bursts of wildest enthusiasm."[565] The overwhelmingly majority of the public remained fervently jingoistic at this stage of the war. Lloyd George came under increasing attack, and local Liberals did their best to dissuade him from speaking in Penrhyn Hall, Bangor, in his own constituency. He refused to be put off, and in a letter of 22 March

---

561 See J. W. Auld, *The Liberal Pro-Boers, Journal of British Studies*, 14, 2, May 1975, p78-101.
562 *North Wales Observer and Express*, 2 February 1900, p7.
563 Owen, p99.
564 Quoted in George, *My Brother And I*, p178.
565 Ibid., p178.

to his brother William he gave his cogent reasons:

> *I am going to Bangor.* I mean to insist upon it. I hear the talk of the leading Liberals is strongly opposed to a meeting at this juncture, and they entreat me not to go. But I will not listen. Here are my reasons:
> (a) There may be a General Election soon.
> (b) You may rely upon Chamberlain planning dissolution in the height of the War.
> (c) If the policy of abstaining from meetings to instruct the people in arriving at a sound judgement is pursued–such judgment will go, by default, against us, and we will be hopelessly beaten–and we deserve to.
> (d} If the Association still deprecate meetings I resign my candidature–as I cannot hope to succeed if I am shut up.[566]

Lloyd George got his way, and duly gave his speech at Penrhyn Hall, Bangor on 11 April. It was another very rowdy night, and he was interrupted throughout his speech:

> Outside the Hall, a large mob alternately howled "Pro-Boer!" and rendered (with cornet accompaniment) "Soldiers of the Queen", and steadily flung stones through the windows. ("Another Imperial argument," commented Lloyd George as each shower landed.) A strong body of police had been brought into the town to guard against the doors being rushed and they were thoroughly needed. Inside the Hall, strong-arm squads of stewards eventually ensured some kind of order, though Lloyd George had to fight against continual interruption for more than an hour…[567]

In his speech he appealed:

> … to the chivalry and generosity of Welshmen especially. The population of the Republics was not more than that of Carnarvonshire and Anglesey. Carnarvonshire and Anglesey against the British Empire! It ought to appeal to our sense of shame… They had heard talk about workmen's dwellings and old age pensions. They could have had a pension to every old man in the land, and built 300,000 workmen's cottages with the money spent on this war. This was the record of the Government he was there to protest against… I beg of you, I entreat of you not to commit yourselves as a nation to so desperate an enterprise, an enterprise that will cost millions of money and thousands more of lives. And above all, I do beg Wales to have no part in this. I supplicate my countrymen to have a superstitious horror of it. I fear it for the sake of Wales. I have been asked why should I take this part, and told that my business is to fight for those reforms the Welshmen demand. It is for the sake of those reforms that I beg Wales to have nothing to do with this job… The turn of Wales will come to stand at the bar of the Empire. I do wish that when that time comes that she shall not falter from the consciousness

---

[566] Quoted in Owen, p99.
[567] Owen, p100.

> of any wrong she has done, and that her voice shall not be choked with the blood of the two small nationalities, like herself, that she helped to crush.[568]

The motion "That this meeting emphatically condemns the policy of Mr Chamberlain, which has led to the disastrous war now devastating South Africa" was subsequently carried with "practical unanimity." After the meeting was over, Lloyd George was lucky to escape with his life. On arrival, a clod of earth had been thrown at him as he drove up to the front entrance. As he left by the same door, he became separated from his party, including Margaret, and, as he was entering High Street from Waterloo Street, a zealous patriot struck him a violent blow on the head with a bludgeon. Lloyd George's hat was crushed, and he was temporarily stunned. He managed to make his way into the nearby Central Cafe, where the proprietor slammed the door behind him just in time. Police hurried there, holding off the mob until midnight. While his constituents hooted him, sang loyal songs and hymns and surged and barged against the constabulary, their MP, now re-united with his wife, made his way out by a back door.[569]

The local Liberal paper reported:

> Mr Lloyd George has achieved many oratorical triumphs in the cause of progress and righteousness. But those who had the privilege of listening to him at Bangor will not readily believe that he has ever delivered a speech which, in courage, lucidity, pathos and persuasiveness excelled the eloquent oration of Wednesday… Thick must be the skull that is impervious to the force of the argument; hard must be the heart that does not respond to the pathos of the appeals in favour of peace and conciliation.[570]

It was very likely another closely contemporaneous speech that was referred to in connection with Dr Griffith Evans[571], a pioneering, former army veterinary surgeon who admired the young Lloyd George as a fellow supporter of temperance and anti-imperialism. Lloyd George stayed several times with him at his home, Brynkynallt, in Lon Pobty on the outskirts of Bangor. On one such occasion Evans:

> … accompanied him to a meeting in a Bangor chapel, and sat on the platform with [his wife] Katie as the future Prime Minister tried to make a pro-Boer speech. An angry audience pelted Lloyd George with rotten eggs and tomatoes, and when Katie's bonnet was knocked askew, Griff took her and his guest out of the building by a back door to escape the hostile crowd in the High Street. Accompanied by a policeman, they scrambled up a dark wood and into Brynkynallt garden by a side gate. Next morning, Mair Evans, then in her late teens, asked Ll G

---

568 *Carnarvon and Denbigh Herald*, 13 April 1900, p8.
569 Ibid., p8; George, *Backbencher*, p313; *North Wales Observer and Express*, 13 April 1900, p8.
570 *Holyhead Mail and Anglesey Herald*, 19 April 1900, p1.
571 Griffith Evans (7 August 1835–7 December 1935).

> for his autograph, and he wrote in her book: "Let us march always with our faces towards the dawn–Victor Hugo".[572]

Now the tide of the war, after running heavily in favour of the Boers, began to turn inexorably as hugely superior British numbers and a change of British commanders began to tell, with Lord Roberts[573] having replaced the bungling Sir Redvers Buller[574] on 23 December 1899, accompanied by a large number of reinforcements. On 15 February 1900, Kimberley was relieved, and on 13 March Bloemfontein, the capital of the Orange Free State, fell. On 18 May Mafeking was relieved, on 31 May, Johannesburg fell, and on 5 June, so did Pretoria, the capital of the Transvaal. With the two Boer states formally annexed, it looked as though the war was virtually over, but substantial Boer forces, the 'Bitter-Enders', fought on, fighting a courageous but desperate mobile guerrilla war that dragged on for nearly another two years.

On 5 July, at Liskeard, in the Cornish constituency of the anti-war Liberal Unionist MP, Leonard Courtney[575], Lloyd George attempted to speak under the auspices of the South Africa Conciliation Committee, chaired by Arthur Quiller-Couch[576], with the expectation of "some demonstration of opposition … These expectations proved only too well justified… the platform was stormed by a party of young fellows, many of whom wore miniature Union Jacks, and the meeting was broken up in confusion."[577] Miss Emily Hobhouse[578], secretary of the Committee, rose and tried to remind the rowdy audience that "manners maketh man." This was met with derision, the singing of 'Men of Harlech', and the stamping of feet. Miss Hobhouse gave up her attempt to speak and sat down. Meanwhile:

> Mr. Lloyd George stood smiling at the table, he did not attempt to utter a syllable. It was perfectly evident that the crowd would not hear the Welsh MP at any price… Presently a further demonstration attracted attention to the floor from the hall… At this point the police made their appearance on the platform.[579]

Aided by the police, the would-be speakers left safely.

Lloyd George had come to detest the Chamberlain family, using in his campaign the witty line

---

572 J. Ware and H. Hunt, *The Several Lives of a Victorian Vet*, 1979, London, Bachman and Turner, p192. As an "old friend" Lloyd George sent Evans "heartfelt solicitations" in a telegram from Criccieth on his hundredth birthday, concluding: "It is an added joy to me today to send greetings to one of my constituents who actually had contact with Abraham Lincoln of whom I have always been so great an admirer." It is reproduced on the dust jacket of Ware and Hunt's book.

573 Field Marshal Frederick Roberts, Earl Roberts (1832-1914).

574 General Sir Redvers Buller (1839-1908).

575 Leonard Courtney (1832-1918), radical Liberal Unionist MP for Liskeard, 1876-1885, Bodmin, 1885-1900, advocate of proportional representation in Parliament, de-selected on 16 June for his anti-war views.

576 Arthur Quiller-Couch (1863-1944), Liberal activist, novelist who published under the pseudonym 'Q'.

577 Farwell, p314-315, quoting the *Cornish Times*, 7 July 1900.

578 Emily Hobhouse (1860-1926), welfare campaigner, pacifist, born in nearby St Ive, author of *The Brunt of the War and Where it Fell*, 1902, London, Methuen. Dubbed the "Angel of Love" by grateful Boer women. See J. Fisher, *That Miss Hobhouse: The Life of a Great Feminist*, 1971, London, Secker & Warburg.

579 Farwell, p315, quoting the *Cornish Times*, 7 July 1900.

printed in *The Speaker*, "So true is the doctrine that as the British Empire expands the Chamberlain family contracts", which incensed Joseph Chamberlain.[580] On 25 July, in replying to Chamberlain in the Commons, he said:

> The right hon. Gentleman… is so essentially a political manager that he is always electioneering. He is a kind of political agent, and so permeated is he with that instinct that he has made up his mind that if this war cannot be a military success, at any rate he will make it an electioneering success… That is electioneering; it is not statesmanship; and it is not the way to settle the peace of South Africa.[581]

Lloyd George proved correct in his estimation that Chamberlain would push for an election. With the war formally but wrongly declared ended on 3 September, a general election was called for over the period 26 September–24 October 1900; with Salisbury ill, Chamberlain was its prime mover and campaigner. At Nefyn, on 15 September, Lloyd George staked all, telling his initially unenthusiastic audience:

> Five years ago the electors of the Carnarvon Boroughs handed me a strip of blue paper, the certificate of my election, to hand to the Speaker as their accredited representative. If I never again represent the Carnarvon Boroughs in the House of Commons, I shall at least have the satisfaction of handing back to them that blue paper with no stain of human blood upon it.[582]

This now brought the audience to their feet with "a storm of cheering".

Chamberlain 'played dirty', labelling all Liberals as 'Pro-Boer', campaigning under the slogan 'Every seat lost to the Government is a seat gained by the Boers.' At this first so-called 'khaki election' the Tories, with their Liberal Unionist allies, duly won 402 seats (334 and 68 respectively), crushing the Liberals with 183 seats, the Irish Parliamentary Party with 76, and the nascent Labour Representative Committee–soon to become the Labour Party–with two seats (Merthyr Tydfil and Derby).

John Burns, the radical Liberal MP for Battersea, was keen to see Lloyd George returned to the Commons because of the excellent service he had done in the cause of labour. In a letter penned at the time, he wrote:

> I do hope and believe that Mr Lloyd George's constituents will re-elect him by an even larger majority than last time. He *has rendered great service to* Wales and to Britain. On Labour Questions he has always been keenly sympathetic, useful, practical, and above all, SUCCESSFUL. He has rendered Welsh Miners and *Railway Men*, not to speak of others, *signal service*, which out of loyalty

580 *The Speaker*, 3, 17 November 1900, p166, not *Punch* as so often asserted; J. L. Garvin, *The Life Of Joseph Chamberlain*, 1934, London, Macmillan, Vol.III, *1895-1900: Empire And World Policy*, p613.

581 https://api.parliament.uk/historic-hansard/commons/1900/jul/25/class-ii#S4V0086P0_19000725_HOC_68. Retrieved 1 October 2024.

582 Quoted in Du Parcq, Vol.II, p241.

> for past services ought to command their *unanimous support*. The House of Commons would lose *one of its best and most useful Members* if Mr Lloyd George were not re-elected.[583]

In Caernarvon Boroughs, Lloyd George's constituents clearly agreed with Burns. Polling day was 6 October, and with the result returned shortly after midnight, he retained his seat against his Tory opponent 'Colonel' Henry Platt–a Bangor banker, Anglican, former first mayor of Bangor, Sherriff of Caernarvonshire and of Anglesey, who adopted his Militia rank–with a slightly increased majority, his largest to date, 2,412 to 2,116, a margin of 296 votes.

Of note regarding Lloyd George's life, it was this election that saw Winston Churchill enter the Commons as Tory MP for Oldham. Making his maiden speech on 18 February 1901, he later wrote about first meeting Lloyd George, the start of their long, sometimes turbulent friendship:

> After this debate I first made the acquaintance of Mr. Lloyd George. We were introduced at the Bar of the House of Commons. After compliments, he said 'Judging from your sentiments, you are standing against the Light'. I replied 'You take a singularly detached view of the British Empire'. Thus began an association which has persisted through many vicissitudes.[584]

Lloyd George's record of this event was briefer, writing to his brother William just before he was called upon to speak that:

> Winston Churchill is to reply to me, and as Harcourt said: 'I am going to stay in the House tonight to enjoy the cockfight between you and young Churchill.' He is the new Tory bully. Bydded. [sic: means 'So be it']. Quite prepared.[585]

At this time Lloyd George was still a practising solicitor. The London branch of the firm, Lloyd George, Roberts & Co., that he had set up with Arthur Rhys Roberts[586] at 13 Walbrook, EC1, on 1 July 1897, had prospered. For some years after 1890, he devoted a great deal of his time in the profession, but as politics gradually took up more of his attention, time and effort, it became impossible for him to give the requisite care and attention to legal work. Roberts anticipated that the workload would increasingly devolve on himself and fortunately had a sense of humour about it. Right at the start of their professional relationship, he wrote to Lloyd George concerning the suggestion that he covenant "'to see that the partners… properly enter up their diaries etc.' It's enough to look after my own. Suggestion for PUNCH–D.Ll.G. chased across Palace Yard by A. R. Roberts panting and

---

583 Quoted in *North Wales Observer and Express*, 5 October 1900, p4. The paper noted: "It would be difficult to find stronger testimony than this."

584 W. S. Churchill, *My Early Life: A Roving Commission*, 1930, London, Thornton Butterworth, p378-380. Lloyd George, at a dinner on 17 December 1932, remembered the exchange in almost identical terms; Sylvester, *Life*, p88. He could, of course, have read Churchill's recollections by then.

585 Quoted in George, *Backbencher*, p330.

586 Arthur Roberts (1872-1920), dealt with much of the procedural matters in the Edwards Divorce case from the London end. In June 1900, the pair moved to larger offices in Ormond House at 63 Queen Victoria Street, EC1. Lloyd George formally gave up his partnership in the firm in 1911.

breathless with a solicitor's diary in his outstretched hand!'"[587] It was not, however, until he became President of the Board of Trade, in December 1905, that Lloyd George ceased practising his old profession.

The last case of any importance on which he was engaged was the Penrhyn Quarry dispute of 1900, characteristically on the side of oppressed Welsh workers against an overbearing English owner. For years a long-drawn-out struggle had persisted between the great Caernarvonshire magnate, Lord Penrhyn, and his quarrymen. One of the incidents in the contest was a prosecution, instituted on behalf of Lord Penrhyn on 13 November 1900, against 26 strikers under the Conspiracy and Protection of Property Act, 1875, for alleged "acts of violence and intimidation". The case was tried at the Bangor Police Court, and as the famous London advocate Sir Charles Mathews was to appear for the prosecution, the accused men engaged Lloyd George to conduct their defence.[588] On very slim grounds, 300 dragoons had been summoned by Colonel Arthur Ruck, Chief Constable of Caernarfonshire, to patrol the Bangor area, an act for which his own Standing Joint Police Committee, Caernarfon Town Council, Bangor City Council and Bethesda Urban District Council condemned him and protested to the Home Secretary, Asquith.[589]

The hearing, on 21 November, lasted ten hours. Lloyd George–wearing a white chrysanthemum in his button-hole–alleged that Penrhyn's action in dismissing the 26 men had 'prejudiced the case the Court had to try.' He continued:

> In the case of a riot there exists a feeling that the law should be vindicated and somebody punished. That may be all very well in martial law, where one man had his farm burnt in South Africa because another had broken the railway, but this Court today at Bangor is not a drumhead Court Martial, but a simple Court of Justice where each man has to be tried according to the evidence… The prosecution evidence has been given in the crawling, cringing spirit which is rewarded at the Penrhyn Quarry at the expense of the workmen.[590]

He next made a most telling point:

> One solitary policeman in dead of night alone executed warrants for the arrest of the twenty six defendants without any disturbance. Why had 300 dragoons and 180 police been brought into the city of Bangor to keep such peaceable men in order?[591]

William George then continued with the defence, his brother having to leave for London. Mathews subsequently acknowledged Lloyd George's skill as an advocate, his grasp of the case, and his devastating cross-examination. So successful were his efforts, that 20 of the accused were acquitted,

---

587 Quoted in George, *Backbencher*, p250.
588 See *The Disturbances At The Penrhyn Slate Quarries*, *North Wales Observer*, 17 November 1900, p7.
589 W.J. Parry, *The Penrhyn Lock-Out, p171, 174; R. Merfyn Jones, p211, 246, 253; Lindsay, p112-113.*
590 *Quoted in George, Backbencher,* p407.
591 Ibid., p407-408.

whilst one was fined for assault and five for intimidation. None were imprisoned. "It was a fine and appropriate close to a brief, but brilliant, legal career."[592]

Sadly, this was far from the end of the matter. A strike began on 22 November, all 2,800 men walking out, lasting for three agonising years. Known as the 'Great Strike of Penrhyn', '*Y Streic Fawr*', this was the longest dispute in British industrial history. During the strike, the community was bitterly divided between those who struck and those who crossed the picket line. Many locals put cards saying *'Nid oes bradwr yn y tŷ hwn'* ('There is no traitor in this house') in their front windows.

Penrhyn Quarry and the adjoining community of Bethesda were in the constituency of William Jones, Liberal MP for Arfon. On 5 March 1903, he moved an adjournment of the House for the purpose of discussing a definite matter of urgent public importance–namely, "The severe privation and loss arising from the struggle in the Penrhyn quarry district… and the failure to put into operation the provisions of the Conciliation Act to terminate the dispute." The fatal flaw in the law relating to trade disputes at the time was that, under the Conciliation Act, 1896, both sides had to request the Board of Trade to conciliate before the Board could act. Lord Penrhyn, wishing to crush all opposition, persistently and obstinately refused to join in requesting the Board to intervene. Gerald Balfour[593], President of the Board of Trade, made a feeble defence, leading Lloyd George to weigh in scathingly, stating:

> The dispute had been prolonged for two and a half years, the whole industry of a district had been paralysed; and, in addition, they had the constant risk of infringements of the law on one side or the other. Infringements were not always on the side of the strikers. He had heard of men who were employed in the quarry who were armed with revolvers, and who had threatened other men from time to time. There was also the case of a man who was driven to madness by hunger… Two and a half years of hunger and privation would drive men to madness. What might not happen in that district? And if anything happened, the responsibility, in the first instance, would undoubtedly rest with Lord Penrhyn, whose stubbornness had been unparalleled, and who had declined every offer of arbitration… The men were fighting under very disadvantageous circumstances.
>
> In the correspondence between Lord Penrhyn and the Carnarvon County Council he wrote one day from Penrhyn Castle, the next day from a shooting-box in Conway Bay, another day from Newmarket, and a fourth day from a palace in London. What comparison was there between a man of that kind, and men who had not got a shilling, except as alms from the public? If there was a Report from an impartial conciliator appointed by a Unionist Government, public opinion would back up the men. Was the President of the Board of Trade afraid of that contingency? Was he afraid to give them a weapon which would help them to keep their children from starving?
>
> … Was the President of the Board of Trade afraid of Lord Penrhyn's society friends that he would not put an Act of Parliament into operation to protect these poor men who were striving

592 W. W. Davies, p200.

593 Gerald Balfour (1853-1945), President of the Board of Trade, 1900-1905, younger brother of Arthur Balfour.

> for their rights? If he did so, and there was no result, after all Parliament was the master in this country. What was this quarry? He would not go into the question of Lord Penrhyn's title, but this was common land within the memory of living man. If by prescription Lord Penrhyn had got a legal title, could not the Parliament of Great Britain say: "Here is land which belongs to the people of the district; you are utilising a time title to a property which does not belong to you for the purpose of starving out men."[594]

On 4 April, Lloyd George delivered a speech on 'Trusts and Monopolies' to an audience of some 2,000 Liberals in Newcastle in which he stated, in terms which began with a contemporary-sounding ring:

> [An] illustration of the dangers of uncontrolled power over the resources of the soil is supplied by the Penrhyn case! Originally the whole of the Penrhyn quarry was common land. Great lords came there, and got an Enclosure Act. It is now their property. At the beginning of the last century a family of slave-owners from Jamaica came over and took over the quarry, and founded the new Penrhyn dynasty. And the quarry has been worked on slave-driving principles ever since.[595] I am not going into all the details of the dispute between the workmen and the employer. It is sufficient to say that these men protest in the name of self-respect and manliness against the terms which degraded them. They say: "If we are wrong we will submit to the arbitrament of any honourable body of men, of any creed, of any party in the land."… Although they are Liberals they say, "We will submit our case to the Prime Minister,… to any man nominated by the Board of Trade" nay, they say, "We will submit the settlement of the dispute to Lord Penrhyn's own counsel." What is the answer? "I am the sole judge." Really, there ought to be a limit to this sort of thing.
>
> And to-day you have great distress in that community. I can hardly trust myself to speak of it. Every man who comes tells me one story he is just stricken down by the pinched, hungry look of little children. A school attendance officer finds children in a house. "How is it," he asks, "the children are not at school?" "They are in bed," says the mother. "In bed?" "Yes," she says, "I have not a crust to give them for breakfast." The suffering is intense, all through the cruel arbitrament of this one man. These men have endured hardships that I cannot depict. They have faced it all. There has never been a struggle in the history of Labour where men have shown such tenacity, such unflinching courage. I can understand them. They are mountaineers, and I know the feeling of mountaineers towards the mountains. They are working among mountains… and they say, "We will endure anything rather than desecrate the hills with slavery."…

---

[594] https://api.parliament.uk/historic-hansard/commons/1903/mar/05/the-penrhyn-quarry-dispute#S4V0118P0_19030305_HOC_272. Retrieved 14 November 2020.

[595] The Pennants owned extensive estates in Jamaica from 1665 until 1940. After emancipation, in late 1835 George H. Dawkins-Pennant (1764-1840) received £14,683 17s 2d [£2.38m in 2025] in compensation for the 764 slaves on his four sugar plantations: https://www.ucl.ac.uk/lbs/person/view/22227. Retrieved 25 March 2025. Richard Pennant (1737-1808), a noted anti-abolitionist MP, acquired the Bethesda quarries on his marriage to Anne Warburton in 1765, and began their rapid expansion from the 1770s.

> But what about the interests of the community? Here is a thriving industry. Here is a loyal, industrious, God-fearing community, brought to the verge of starvation. Here are towns in the district whose trade is withering, and I put this to those gentlemen who talk about foreign competition here is the building trade throughout the country suffering, and here are slates coming from America for the first time, and establishing a foothold in British markets from which you cannot dislodge them. We are living in an age of keen competition. There is a great struggle for life, not merely amongst individuals, but amongst nations, for commerce, trade, supremacy. No nation can afford to allow mediaeval notions, to allow either the insatiable greed or the insensate pride of any aristocrat to stand in the way of an industry. I am delighted to find that the Liberal party is a whole, without any division, one mind, one purpose, in putting an end to this tyranny of Lord Penrhyn.[596]

Despite the strength of feeling expressed, it was somewhat late in the day. Lloyd George had often made references to Penrhyn, and on 22 May 1901 he attended a 'crowded meeting' at the Memorial Hall in London in support of the quarrymen, along with D. R. Daniel, fellow Liberal MPs William Abraham ('Mabon') and William Jones, as well as socialists Keir Hardie, George Barnes, Pete Curran and Robert Blatchford, who chaired the meeting.[597] Later, Lloyd George also attended delegations to the Trades Union Congress, (TUC), on the quarrymen's behalf, in 1902 appealing for union support for them so that "while they were fighting their children should be placed beyond the reach of starvation."[598] After addressing the Congress at Holborn Town Hall on 3 September, he wrote to Margaret:

> I've been to the Trades Union Congress to plead for the Bethesda Quarrymen… Gave me a fine reception and passed a resolution unanimously to support them. I think they have been saved. But very severe things were said about (D. R.) Daniel I am sorry to say. Unions that had paid £10 a week regularly refused balance sheets saying how the money was being spent.[599]

It was not until April 1903 that Lloyd George and William Jones, at a meeting in London, "set up a committee to organise a Welsh movement in support of the quarrymen, a movement which does not seem to have grown any further from its inception."[600] The *Daily News*–of London–had already reprimanded the 'Welsh party', and the pair in particular, on 24 November 1902 for its indifference, and other voices increasingly called for labour to be represented by its own people, not the representatives of the middle classes. It was no coincidence that Bethesda got its first branch of the Independent Labour Party, (I.L.P.), in 1908, the year after Lord Penrhyn's death.[601]

---

596 Lloyd George, *Better Times*, p10-12.

597 Lindsay, p132. Peter Curran (1860-1910), a founder of the GFTU and Labour Representation Committee (LRC). Robert Blatchford (1851-1943), socialist campaigner, journalist, ILP member.

598 Wrigley, *David Lloyd George And The British Labour Movement*, p15.

599 Morgan, *Family Letters*, p138.

600 R. Merfyn Jones, p275; *Yr Herald Cymraeg*, 14 April 1903, p4.

601 See R. Merfyn Jones, p278-281.

Meanwhile, on 27 April 1903, Asquith, on behalf of the Liberals proposed a motion of censure on the government "That, in view of the grave social and public interests involved in the continuance of the industrial dispute at Bethesda, this House condemns the inaction of His Majesty's Government, and declares its opinion that prompt intervention on their part is imperative to arrive at a just and effectual settlement." Lloyd George interjected to state: "that this is a matter which goes far beyond the case of Lord Penrhyn. What then becomes of the contention of the Prime Minister that there is only a trivial matter in dispute. This question is important, because the dispute is one which is devastating a whole country side. It is injuring the trade of the country, and it is having the effect of introducing foreign slates which otherwise would never have obtained a footing in our markets."[602]

In fierce debate with William Bromley-Davenport, he strongly defended the position of the quarrymen, citing their conciliatory attitude, before concluding:

> It is perfectly true that this is a matter of considerable importance outside the district itself. It is not merely a question of the distress in Bethesda, or that a once thriving community is withering away. It is all very well to talk about the present prosperity of the quarry. Lord Penrhyn appeared by counsel before the Quarter Sessions to have his assessment lowered because he was not making the money he used to out of the quarry. The slate trade throughout the kingdom is suffering. Slates which had hardly a chance before are pouring in from the Continent and America, and once they get in it will be very difficult to keep them out. It is a matter of the greatest possible importance to the whole of the community. I hope that nothing has been said in this debate to prevent the possibility of conciliation… The men have been perfectly willing, and are still willing, to meet Lord Penrhyn, and I ask… the President of the Board of Trade, to consider whether he cannot see his way even now to suggest to Lord Penrhyn that he should meet his men.[603]

The motion floundered, the government easily surviving by 316 votes to 182. Lord Penrhyn continued to resist all arbitration or conciliation. In late September, the General Federation of Trade Unions stopped its payments to the strikers, and in late October declared that as far as it was concerned "the dispute is over." On 7 November 1903, a meeting in Bethesda voted narrowly by 192 to 161 to return to work[604], and subsequently 1,800 men reluctantly returned in piecemeal fashion, still without union recognition. Another 1,000 would never return, and the Welsh slate industry had begun its slow but inexorable decline.

To return to the time when the strike began, on 10 December 1900, Lloyd George spoke in the Commons on the subject of 'Ministers of the Crown and Members Holding Office (Interest in Contracts)', and delivered a forensic, blistering attack on what he rightly regarded as war-profiteering. As far as he had been able to ascertain, Joseph Chamberlain, Secretary of State for the Colonies, as

---

602 https://api.parliament.uk/historic-hansard/commons/1903/apr/27/bethesda-industrial-dispute-1. Retrieved 5 December 2020.
603 https://api.parliament.uk/historic-hansard/commons/1903/apr/27/bethesda-industrial-dispute-1. Retrieved 5 December 2020.
604 R. Merfyn Jones, p215.

well as his son Austen Chamberlain[605], Financial Secretary to the Treasury, were shareholders in three companies–Hoskins and Sons, Ltd., The Birmingham Trust (holding shares in Tubes, Ltd., and Elliot's Metal Company), and Kynoch Ltd.–which, in the course of the Boer War, had amassed huge profits from Government contracts for armaments by cutting out all other competitors. After detailing the companies close contractual ties to the British Admiralty, the Chamberlain family's extensive shareholding in them[606], and the law concerning MPs dealings with contractors, he proceeded to detail how the companies had fared since the Chamberlains involvement and their considerable increase in profitability since gaining the government contracts.

He noted that Joseph Chamberlain had been what might now be considered to be 'economical with the truth':

> The right hon. Gentleman, in reply to the statement about the Birmingham Trust and the other companies set forth in the Morning Leader[607], stated that he was not aware that he had any interest at all in Tubes. I observe that he did not make any reference at all to his interest in Elliot's, and I think there is a very good reason. This is a company which has large contracts with the Government and supplies large quantities of materials to the naval dockyards…

He noted too just why the contractual issue was so important:

> Most of these companies to which I have referred describe themselves its contractors to the Admiralty. Of course it is not merely the quantity of material supplied by them to the Admiralty; it is the fact that to all their customers and to all whom they solicit for orders this statement is made, and they are able to advertise themselves as firms which have the confidence of Her Majesty's Government. In regard to municipal corporations a £50 contract disqualifies a member; why should Ministers of the Crown be excepted? In referring to the Birmingham Trust the right hon. Gentleman the Colonial Secretary says–I hold a very small portion of the capital of this company. Then he says–I do not know whether it is invested in Tubes or not. And he says–I did not know Tubes were interested in Government business. Then he says–… I have a small portion of Trust shares; they in turn have a small portion of their funds invested in Tubes; Tubes does some business with the Government. Supposing the real facts were put, would not this be the correct way of stating them? The right hon. Gentleman has a considerable holding in the Birmingham Trust; the Birmingham Trust have a substantial holding in Tubes and Elliot's; Elliot's do most of their business with the Government; Tubes do… the whole of their business with the Government. Does the right hon. Gentleman now mean to say that his is a correct version of the case? I am simply contrasting the defence which he made in the answer published as an authorised version… and in so doing I am overlooking the very important fact that

605 Austen Chamberlain (1863-1937), Liberal Unionist MP for East Worcestershire, 1892-1914, Financial Secretary to the Treasury, 1900-1902, Chancellor of the Exchequer, 1903-1905.
606 Including another brother, Arthur Chamberlain (1842-1913), Chairman of Kynoch Ltd. of Lion Works, Wilton, Birmingham, from 1889 until his death.
607 See *The Speaker, More Chamberlain Disclosures*, 3, 6 October 1900, p4-5.

> members of the right hon. Gentleman's own household own over £5,000 worth of shares in Elliot's, let alone the interest held by the Financial Secretary to the Treasury, I presume as trustee...

Lloyd George warmed to his subject, honing in on Kynoch's:

> Kynoch's, when investigated by the House of Commons, were very much worse than anything which had previously been said about them. In this company the shares of the right hon. Gentleman's relations are of the value... of something between £230,000 and £250,000, which is the amount they hold in Kynoch and Co., Limited. The Financial Secretary to the Treasury has an interest–again, I assume, as trustee–amounting at their present value to £15,000. They manufacture cordite and munitions of war. With regard to this company, it has a kind of bearing upon all the other companies, because there has been undoubted favouritism, and it shows the danger of men holding high and influential positions and the Government having an interest in this company, because, for some reason or other, unmistakable favouritism has been shown towards this company...

He continued, showing chapter and verse of the favouritism that Kynoch's had continued to receive, including preferential tendering opportunities concerning the supply of cordite–"a thing which is perfectly unprecedented in the history of this country"–and through which the Chamberlains had so vastly profited, even in the face of complaints from the Director of Army Contracts and a report made upon the quality of the goods provided, essentially saying that Kynoch's provided the worst cordite of the companies examined, also being in arrears with their deliveries.

> The right hon. Gentleman complains... that we have suggested corruption ... All I can say is that I have simply stated the facts... What I do ask is this–What interpretation does the Birmingham Stock Exchange place upon the business? Four-fifths of them are the right hon. Gentleman's friends, and yet their view of the matter was that the change of Government was worth an addition of thirty-three per cent, to the value of the shares of the company in which the right hon. Gentleman's family held the largest interest... Let the House not forget that this is the only case which has been investigated, and the result of the investigation has been to display and expose the most disgraceful condition of favouritism towards one company...
>
> ... All these are published facts,... facts which are necessarily public, for it is information which the law insists upon being open to the public for the information of the public, and for the protection of the public against transactions of this character and others... Those are the facts which we have brought before the House... and I do say that they demand an explanation... It is not that charges of corruption are brought against any Minister of the Crown, for that is not insinuated, but I do say, to use a phrase uttered by the right hon. Gentleman, "it is not treasonable but it is improper." That is exactly the description that can be given to some of these investments. The investments... are certainly improper... [A]lthough there is no charge or suggestion of corruption, still things have been done which would set up a precedent which

could legitimately be used later on to justify corruption itself. Corruption is a question of intention and of motive, but the House of Commons, in framing regulations of this kind, cannot inquire into motives… You are bound to examine the facts, and to judge upon them. These rules are laid down not altogether to prevent corruption or to hit corruption, but to prevent circumstances that might justify corruption in others. They are rigidly, sternly enforced against the officials of the Civil Service…

I know of nothing in regard to which those rules ought to be enforced with greater rigidity than in war contracts… although no pressure is brought to bear on officials to give contracts to favoured firms, there is a knowledge in the minds of those gentlemen who deal with the contracts, when they are distinguishing between two or three different firms, that there is one firm which has at its back most powerful influence in the Government of the day; and who will suggest that that is not an influence which has to be combated with? Anyone who reads the evidence given before the Select Committee will see that officials at the Admiralty are at a loss to explain why Kynochs are preferred… It was not because Kynochs' goods were better worth; for you find that they were worse… It was this unconscious influence which they themselves were unable to appreciate–the constant influence of a powerful personality at the back of the company. The right hon. Gentleman himself manifested this in the House of Commons in regard to Kynochs…

Now there is this danger in regard to these contracts. I do not say it exists with regard to the right hon. Gentleman, but if Ministers of the Crown are allowed to have large interests, direct, or indirect, in firms providing munitions of war to the Government, I know of no greater danger to the peace of the country or to its security. It is not that any Minister you can imagine sitting in this House would ever deliberately, for the sake of promoting his own private interest, engage in war… But there is again the subtle influence of the constant action of a man's permanent interest upon his judgment. It does give him a bias without his knowing it…

… I brought the subject forward on the ground of the importance of ensuring that regulations of this character… should be rigidly enforced… I do not say that the Secretary for the Colonies or the Financial Secretary to the Treasury has done anything to lower the standard of proud pre-eminence which we enjoy as a country in this matter. What I do say is that they have given legitimate ground for uneasiness, and, above all, they have established precedents, which, if they are followed, would lead to something infinitely worse than anything I have spoken of to-day. I beg to move the Amendment standing in my name.[608]

The main purpose of Lloyd George's sweeping attack on the Chamberlain family was to persuade the House to accept a bill prohibiting Cabinet Ministers from holding shares in companies which dealt in Government contracts. The motion was rejected by 269 to 127 votes. In defending themselves against the well-substantiated accusations brought forward by him, the two Chamberlains were only able to retaliate by weak and unconvincing statements. In fact, the case was even worse than Lloyd George knew: "During the Boer War Beckett and Company of Pretoria, the Transvaal agents of Kynoch's,

[608] https://api.parliament.uk/historic-hansard/commons/1900/dec/10/ministers-of-the-crown-and-members#S4V0088P0_19001210_HOC_151. Retrieved 8 March 2019.

sold twelve million rounds of ammunition to the Boer army."[609] Yet an overwhelming majority in the House immediately rallied round the cause of the Chamberlain family. The attack by the Welsh outsider, it was felt, had been directed against the whole caste, and had therefore to be countered by the democratic measure of a majority vote. No such direct attack was made again in the House, by any Party, until the 'cash-for-questions affair' of 1994, the 'life peerages scandal' of 2006-2007 and the 'parliamentary expenses scandal' of 2009. It was this debate in Parliament in 1900 which first exposed the roots of that system from which Britain's ruling classes derive–and have often tried to continue to derive–their power and sustenance.

The Liberal paper, the *Daily News,* supported the war under its editor E. T. Cook. But, in January 1901, Lloyd George played a leading part in helping to organise something of a coup by getting an anti-war syndicate of Liberal businessmen, led by the Quaker George Cadbury and Franklin Thomasson, to buy a controlling interest of the shares, forcing the paper to adopt a pro-Boer approach under new editor R. C. Lehmann, a militant anti-imperialist. At last, they had an outlet for their point of view.

In the Commons on 18 February, Lloyd George decried, with repeated, disgraceful Tory ministerial laughter and cheers in his ears:

> The burning of Boer homes… and the burning of farms… There is no one here who is going to criticise that action if treachery is proved against the occupants of these farms. It may or may not be condign punishment… I am not going to challenge the burning of the houses of men guilty of such treachery; but I do criticise and censure the conduct of men who, for the treachery of others, burn the homes over their heads of people who are perfectly innocent… It is war not against men, but against women and children.[610]

In June, Emily Hobhouse, founder of the Distress Fund for South African Women and Children, newly returned from a five-month fact-finding mission at the British concentration camps of Bloemfontein, Norvalspont, Aliwal North, Springfontein, Kimberley and Orange River, delivered her findings entitled 'Report of a Visit to the Camps of Women and Children in the Cape and Orange River Colonies', to the British Government, where she was generally received with scathing criticism and hostility. On 14 June she had an interview with Liberal Leader of the Opposition, Henry Campbell-Bannerman. Hobhouse recorded that:

> He alone, greatly occupied as he was, seemed to have the leisure and the determination to hear and understand everything. For nearly two hours he listened with rapt attention, now and then putting a question to elucidate a point. He left the impression of a man who spared no time or pains to arrive at truth, and in whom wisdom and humanity were paramount.[611]

---

[609] Rintala, *Made In Birmingham*, p128.

[610] https://api.parliament.uk/historic-hansard/commons/1901/feb/18/address-in-answer-to-his-majestys-most#S4V0089P0_19010218_HOC_324. Retrieved 1 October 2024.

[611] Quoted in Spender, *Campbell-Bannerman*, Vol.I, p335.

The same day Campbell-Bannerman, much moved by her account[612], gave an impassioned speech at a dinner given by the National Reform Union at the Holborn Restaurant, turning on critics and asking:

> What was this policy of unconditional surrender? It was that now we had got the men we had been fighting against down, we should punish them as severely as possible, devastate their country, burn their homes, break up their very instruments of agriculture and destroy the machinery by which food was produced. It is that we should sweep… the women and children into camps in which they were destitute of all the decencies and comforts and many of the necessaries of life, and in some of which the death-rate rose so high as 430 in the 1000. He did not say for a moment… that this was the deliberate and intentional policy of His Majesty's Government, but it was the policy of the writers in the press who supported them, and at all events, it was the thing which was being done at this moment in the name and by the authority of this most humane and Christian nation… A phrase often used was that 'war is war,' but when one came to ask about it one was told that no war was going on, that it was not war. *When was a war not a war? When it was carried on by methods of barbarism in South Africa.*[613]

On 17 June he defended his discriminating use of the phrase in the Commons, before Lloyd George launched into "the condition of the camps of detention in South Africa, and the alarming rate of mortality amongst the women and children detained there", making good use of Hobhouse's findings, stating:

> For the sake of the credit and good name of this country something should be done to put an end to this condition of things, which is going from bad to worse… This lady has made some reports as to what was taking place in the best of these camps–the best equipped and the longest established–and they are sufficiently deplorable. These were camps, not of fighting men, every one of whom would pass a physical test, but of women, many of whom were in a weak condition, and of children. Food, insufficient; such as was supplied, bad; the women herded together, sometimes twelve in a tent; tents leaking; clothes saturated; not much clothing allowed; little children half starved; the food they had, bad; their clothes soaked through with rain and dew. What marvel is it that the right hon. Gentleman has to tell us this tale of hundreds of children dying?… Then she goes on to say–It is in the name of little children who are living in open tents, without fires, and possessing only the scantiest clothing, that I ask for help. An appeal has to be sent by the wife of the Military Governor of Johannesburg to America to provide for the women and children we have taken under our protection.
>
> This, Sir, is the idea of bringing a great war to a successful issue. We are told that war is war, and that, after all, these are the necessary consequences of a state of war. I do not think that is so. We know perfectly well that this is the result of a deliberate policy. I cannot challenge that policy at the present moment… I say that this is the result of a deliberate and settled policy… The military authorities knew perfectly well it was to be done, and they had ample time to

612 O'Connor, p58-59.

613 Quoted in Spender, *Campbell-Bannerman*, Vol.I, p336. Emphasis added.

> provide for it. They started clearing the country about six months ago, and it is disgraceful that five or six months after that children should be dying at the rate of hundreds per month in the different camps… The rate of mortality among children–and I think this is the most disgraceful fact in the whole situation–is higher than that amongst the soldiers who have braved all the risks of the field. The mortality amongst our own troops is something like thirty-six per thousand. When the epidemic was at its height in Bloemfontein the death rate was fifty-two per thousand. Even taking the argument that war is war, and that women and children should not be altogether exempt from its dangers, it is unfair to class the mortality of soldiers in the field with that of women and children… [T]he mortality amongst the women and children in these camps is 450 per thousand, and we have no right to put the women and children in this position. What is the assumption of the right hon. Gentleman? He says that it is by voluntary submission on the part of these women and children that they are refugees, and that they sought our protection. If they are seeking our protection, then we are ill requiting their confidence. They are British subjects, and they are voluntarily British subjects. They came voluntarily to seek the protection of the British flag, and how do we treat them? Why, we half starve them. We give them bad food, no shelter, we clothe them badly, their houses are burned, and their stock taken away. This is how you treat those who have voluntarily submitted to us. This is the first object lesson for them under British rule…[614]

Predictably, Lloyd George lost the vote by 252 to 149, fifty Liberals–including Asquith and Sir Edward Grey[615]–abstaining, but he had made his point forcefully. What made Lloyd George hated by some was exactly what made him admired by others, his friend Harold Spender[616] writing:

> Whatever differences there may exist as to the South African War, no one disputes that Mr Lloyd George has gained great political distinction during the last two years. Hitherto, his fame was mostly confined within the borders of Wales; and, perhaps, some future historian will say that Wales blundered in not asserting a monopoly over Mr George's talents… But Wales' loss has been England's gain, and at a time of great political dearth in political leadership, it has been no small help to English Radicals that they should receive such a timely reinforcement…
>
> He has fought election after election in the Carnarvonshire Boroughs, gradually increasing his majority in the face of most hostile forces… Wisely he remains on his own ground, and knows that every effort spent on his native soil adds to his strength at Westminster. From each election he goes back to Parliament stronger; and never stronger than at the Election of 1900…
>
> For a young man of 37, this is surely a remarkable career. Here is a man without university training, without high birth, without riches, who has already climbed to a high political reputation. What is the secret of his power? I answer–Character. Mr Lloyd George has now plenty of self-acquired culture. He has read many books, and he has travelled much during the

---

614 https://api.parliament.uk/historic-hansard/commons/1901/jun/17/south-african-war-mortality-in-camps-of. Retrieved 13 May 2019.

615 Sir Edward Grey, Viscount Grey of Fallodon (1862-1933), Liberal MP for Berwick-upon-Tweed, 1885-1916, Foreign Secretary 10 December 1905–10 December 1916.

616 (Edward) Harold Spender (1864-1926), Liberal politician, author, journalist and lecturer.

> last ten years. But all these things are but the trappings–the garnishing's of the real man. His root-power lies far beyond anything that is received by training or education. It lies in a certain fund of unexhausted strength, a certain fount of aboriginal power. He is not yet 'sickled o'er with the pale cast of thought'. Take a recent event in his career–the purchase of the Daily News. While all the wise men of the Liberal Party were shrugging shoulders and drawing long faces... the young shepherd went apart, and took his two smooth stones from the brook. It is thus that the giants are killed and the heights conquered–by not believing them to be unconquerable. Thus, action has its root in faith, and hoary wisdom is ashamed. It is said that when a friend protested to Mirabeau[617] that a thing was impossible, he replied angrily,–"Do not utter that foolish word in my presence". In that, at any rate Mr Lloyd George is like Mirabeau. He has cut out the word 'impossible' from his vocabulary.
>
> But the audacity of Mirabeau was the audacity of contempt and pride. It was beaten by the facts. The audacity of Lloyd George has a deeper root. He believes in the goodness of men. He believes that in the worst pass you can always rally the good in man if you call it out in the right way. He can remove mountains because he believes in humanity.[618]

Fenner Brockway[619], then attending the School for the Sons of Missionaries, in Blackheath, London, was so inspired and influenced by Lloyd George that he later recorded in his autobiography:

> The Boer War started my interest in politics. At the beginning I was all patriotic, wearing buttons with generals' portraits–White and Buller–on my chest, but before the end, captivated by Lloyd George, I became pro-Boer, joining the Young Liberals...[620]

Just how much an even wider section of society hated Lloyd George, and his views, was shown on 18 December 1901, when he attempted to address a very hostile crowd in the Town Hall in Birmingham, after being invited by the Birmingham Liberal Association to give a speech against the Boer War and criticising Birmingham's Liberal Unionist MP, Joseph Chamberlain, still Secretary of State for the Colonies. Trouble was inevitable in the heart of Chamberlain's fiefdom, and the local Unionist Press–the *Birmingham Mail* and the *Birmingham Daily Post*–did its utmost to provoke confrontation. Two days before the meeting, the *Mail* wrote in its irresponsible, inflammatory leading article:

> Mr. Lloyd George has studiously acquired the reputation of the most violent pro-Boer in the country... This Welshman has used language respecting the Ministers of his country and the soldiers of the King which, if uttered respecting any Continental Ministry, would have caused him to be arraigned for treason, and sentenced to a very considerable term of imprisonment. A hundred years ago in England he would have stood a very excellent chance of losing his head, a feat which, metaphorically, he performs every time he addresses a public meeting. His

617 Honoré Gabriel Riqueti, Comte de Mirabeau (1749-1791), orator, moderate leader of the early stages of the French Revolution.
618 Harold Spender, *Mr D. Lloyd George, M.P.*, *Young Wales*, 7, 75, March 1901, p67-69.
619 (Archibald) Fenner Brockway (1888-1988), anti-war activist, socialist politician, humanist campaigner.
620 F. Brockway, *Towards Tomorrow*, 1977, London, Hart-Davis, MacGibbon, p15.

> particular antipathy has always been towards the Colonial Secretary, and he has described the member for West Birmingham by every insulting epithet from Judas downwards…
>
> … the mere fact of bringing this "politician" to Birmingham, the city which has given so nobly and so freely of her sons to fight her battles… is an insult to the city, and to every loyal inhabitant. No doubt care will be taken to sedulously select the audience, no one will be admitted without a ticket; we may be sure those pieces of paste-board will only be issued to the chosen worshippers of their brother Boers.[621]

Despite being asked by the Charles Rafter, the new Chief Constable of Birmingham City Police, to cancel the address because the police could not guarantee his safety, Lloyd George refused. He consulted his wife, Margaret, she said he must go, and in so doing he nearly found himself the victim of a riot. Arriving early at a nearly deserted New Street Station soon after 2.00 pm, he had tea with his hosts, William Evans and his wife, in Hagley Road, before taking a hansom cab to the Town Hall. Soon after Lloyd George arrived there at 6.30 pm, some 50,000 rowdy pro-war protesters gathered in Victoria Square, surrounding the Hall, which was guarded by 350 policemen, barricades had been erected and nearby buildings boarded up. Although the "peace meeting" inside was supposed to be attended only by people who had an invitation, many of the 7,000 people jammed inside had entered with forged tickets and began shouting and throwing objects as soon as Lloyd George rose to speak. He was shouted down after delivering his opening line: "This is a rather lively meeting for a peace meeting," and managed to say little else that was audible as the unrest escalated dangerously, except for the acid observation:

> We are told that speeches delivered in this country reach the ears of the Boers. If that be so, the Boers will know when Birmingham Unionists promise them free institutions how to interpret the promise. I have been called an enemy of my country. Why? Because, in common with thousands of others, I have not allowed my judgment to be swept away by the unthinking clamour of the multitude. The real enemies of the country are men who decline to discuss a matter of so much moment to the future of their native land with the calmness and fairness which such an intricate problem demands…
>
> The Union Jack is the pride and property of our common country, and no man who really loves it could do anything but dissent from its being converted into Mr. Chamberlain's pocket-handkerchief. It is enough for me to emphasise the fact that the Press of Birmingham, which used to be the champion of free speech, has for days been stirring up its friends to deny liberty of debate to us solely on the ground that we are an insignificant minority in this town. And in this respect I may also add–because it has a significance of its own–that the Liberal Unionist Press has behaved more disgracefully than the Conservative papers of the town.[622]

Now the situation became intolerable and totally unsafe, as the crowd outside began breaking

621 Quoted in Du Parcq, Vol.II, p281.

622 Ibid., Vol.II, p291.

windows, pelting the walls with bricks and other missiles, and battering in the entrance doors with a telegraph pole brought for the purpose. Rafter then personally escorted Lloyd George from the platform to a secure room behind. To effect his escape, Lloyd George was, with difficulty, persuaded to dress in a policeman's uniform overcoat and helmet. After a brief rehearsal at keeping in step with his new comrades, he then marched out of the Hall in the middle of a small force of Birmingham police, into the dark night with snow falling. One sharp-eyed man called out "There he is–it's the middle chap,"[623] but, fortunately in the commotion, he was ignored, and the small force continued down Paradise Street and Easy Row until the safety of Ladywood Police Station was reached, two miles away.[624] In the subsequent rioting around the Town Hall, the police launched a baton charge: one man, Ernest Curtin, was killed and 27 taken to Birmingham General Hospital with serious injuries. 13 arrests were made. Lloyd George spent the night with William Evans, under guard, before returning to London by train the next morning.

On 21 January 1902, Lloyd George spoke against the amendment "that this House, while prepared to support all proper measures for the effective prosecution of the war in South Africa, is of the opinion that the course pursued by Your Majesty's Ministers, and their attitude with regard to a settlement, have not conduced to the early termination of the war and the establishment of a durable peace", tearing it to shreds, and holding a crowded Commons with mordant criticisms of his leader:[625]

> He regretted very much that he was unable to vote for the Amendment. The Amendment laid down no terms of a settlement; it simply laid down two contradictory propositions, and this had been called a compromise. It was not his idea of a compromise… The first part declared in favour of a prosecution of the war. He could not comprehend the position. In one breath they declared that the war was unjust and then turned to the Government and said, "Unjust though it be, we will support you in prosecuting it." The Boers were said to be fighting for freedom and independence, and then Members were invited to vote for shooting and capturing these Boers. He regretted he could not accept that position. It meant that one set of gentlemen were asked to support what they regarded as a criminal enterprise as an inducement for another set of gentlemen to vote for a proposition they did not believe to be true… That was not his notion of a compromise. He did not think they would ever get any unity, he did not think they would ever get any working basis, on these lines. He sincerely regretted it, because he believed that unity was necessary for peace, and unity was possible on the terms of settlement, and he was sorry that another had not been confined to a declaration of the principles laid down on that point by Lord Rosebery at Chesterfield [on 16 December 1901]… Compromise on the question of terms could be arrived at… but, when they came to deal with the question of origin, and with the question of prosecuting the war, it was a mistake to attempt anything in the nature of a compromise. A party who opposed a war at any time was bound to bring upon itself unpopularity, and he did not deny that opposition to the war had brought unpopularity upon

---

623 Edwards, 1913, Vol.III, p230.

624 The helmet and whistle borrowed from PC William Thomas are in the Lloyd George Museum.

625 Spender, *Campbell-Bannerman*, Vol.II, p23-24.

the liberal party; but, after all, let them face it like men. Let them not try to get out of it by shuffling in this way. There were some who believed the war was wrong and that it would bring disaster to the Empire, but what was the position? They could not vote for an Amendment like this except on the assumption that if they had the opportunity they would put it into action. Every man should vote as if his individual vote would carry the declaration into operation. It was not impossible. The present Government was not immortal. His own opinion was that, though the country at the present moment was stubbornly bent on pursuing the war… and he was not sanguine that it was going to change its mind, he believed the people of the country were as sick and tired of the war as Lord Milner[626] said the people of the Cape were; but they were still bent on prosecuting the war to what they regarded as the only issue ... He did not think, however, that the people were confident that the Ministry had done their best to carry out the purpose they had set themselves; and if the people saw that all their great efforts resulted in something tantamount to failure… the national pride would impel them first of all to say there was some defect in their Ministers, rather than lack of strength in the Empire.

… [T]he penalty of failure must be paid by Ministers. That did not mean the abandonment of the war, but it might mean that the "alternative Government" might have its chance; and he asked Members who voted for the Amendment if their party came into power would they vote for the prosecution of an unrighteous war–for that was the policy of the Amendment–a war which they regarded as a disaster to the Empire? Would they go on with such a war? If not, then what was the meaning of this Amendment? If they were prepared to go on with it, what did the denunciations of the war in the past mean? No, there was only one party in the country who could prosecute the war effectively… and that was the party who believed in it. They could not prosecute a war with a halting conscience. They must put their whole heart, their whole strength, and their whole might into it, and he was proud to believe that the right hon. Gentlemen on the front Opposition Bench could not do that. Their position was a clear one–or at least it ought to be. It was to say, "This is not a war of ours. It was started by hon. Members opposite… It is in pursuance of their policy. They accept responsibility for it." The policy of the right hon. Gentlemen on the Opposition Bench was perfectly clear. It was to say: "The war is your business. We can have nothing whatever to do with it." He appealed earnestly to right hon. Gentlemen now, not by voting for this Amendment, to accept any share of the responsibility for the war. It was a mistake, even if it brought temporary popularity on the party, to pawn, as it were, the heirlooms of that party in order to buy off unpopularity. At any rate, as long as they faced it they would have the respect of the country. But, on the other hand, if they did adopt that course, they would simply substitute for an unpopularity, which was undeserved as long as it came from the adhesion to a definite principle, a contempt which was thoroughly well merited.[627]

---

626 Alfred Milner (1854-1925), Governor of Cape Colony and High Commissioner for Southern Africa, May 1897–March 1901, Administrator of Transvaal and Orange River Colony, January 1901 - June 1902, then 1st Governor to April 1905, Minister without Portfolio, 10 December 1916–18 April 1918, Secretary of State for War, 18 April 1918–10 January 1919, Secretary of State for the Colonies, 10 January 1919–13 February 1921.

627 https://api.parliament.uk/historic-hansard/commons/1902/jan/21/south-africa-couduct-of-the-war#S4V0101P0_19020121_HOC_286. Retrieved 13 May 2019.

The amendment was lost by 333 to 123. "It was related that Campbell-Bannerman met Mr. Lloyd George in the Lobby the same evening and said cheerily, 'Well, are you feeling cooler now?'"[628]

Towards the end of the war, British tactics of containment, denial, and harassment began to yield results against the guerrillas. The sourcing and co-ordination of intelligence became increasingly efficient with regular reporting from observers in the blockhouses, from units patrolling the fences and conducting "sweeper" operations, and from native Africans in rural areas who increasingly supplied intelligence, as the 'scorched earth' policy took effect and they found themselves competing with the Boers for food supplies. Kitchener's[629] forces at last began to seriously affect the Boers' fighting strength and freedom of manoeuvre and made it harder for the Boers and their families to survive. Despite this success, almost half the Boer fighting strength, 15,000 men were still in the field fighting. Kitchener's tactics were very costly: Britain was running out of time and money and needed to change tack. They offered terms of peace on various occasions, notably in March 1901, but were rejected by Botha and the "Bitter-enders" among the commandos. They pledged to fight until the bitter end and rejected the demand for compromise made by the "Hands-uppers". Their reasons included hatred of the British, loyalty to their dead comrades, solidarity with fellow commandos, an intense desire for independence, religious arguments, and fear of captivity or punishment. On the other hand, their women and children were dying every day and independence seemed impossible.

On 20 March 1902, there was a heated debate in the Commons regarding the general war situation in South Africa. It was opened by Campbell-Bannerman, who berated the Government on their refusal to provide accurate information on the progress of the war, stating "This is a Government, not of "I do not remember," but of "I do not know." This is claimed on all occasions." Joseph Chamberlain's reply was interrupted by Irish member John Dillon, who called him "a damned liar." Dillon refused to retract his statement at the request of the Speaker. Immediately Balfour, as Leader of the House, proposed Dillon's suspension, the motion being carried by 248 votes to 48. Lloyd George was one of the 48 'Noes', voting with the Irish Nationalists, the only Welsh member to do so.[630] In the resumed debate, Lloyd George again spoke out in favour of making peace, whilst vigorously attacking the Government's selective presentation of information to the Commons:

> We are really not getting the facts. I have called attention to all those estimates as to the duration of the war. I do not pretend to any military knowledge at all. I simply criticise from the facts which appear in the newspapers, and it always seems to me that the Government will not take into account the real difficulties. I recollect the Colonial Secretary getting up in July last and saying that after consultation with his military advisers in the Transvaal he had come to the conclusion that a considerable number of troops would return to this country in September last. By the way, that was the Second estimate for that financial year. Some of us got up and pointed out and gave reasons why we thought that estimate was too sanguine, and we were laughed at…

---

628 Spender, *Campbell-Bannerman*, Vol.II, Note, p24.

629 General Herbert Kitchener (1850-1916) took over as C-in-C from Roberts on 12 December 1900.

630 https://api.parliament.uk/historic-hansard/commons/1902/mar/20/south-african-war-general-observations#S4V0105P0_19020320_HOC_248. Retrieved 3 January 2020.

> Then we come to the estimate of this year. A fortnight ago we had a discussion, and the right hon. Gentleman met all our suggestions with scorn. He said–In a very few months we think we can reduce the number of troops… I wonder whether the Secretary of State for War thinks so, because immediately after that statement came the news of a great disaster… The estimates of the Government have failed times without number, and unless I am mistaken–and nobody abhors this horrible bloodshed more than I do–they will break down again… but this year–the third year of the war–the estimate is for a period of nine months, which runs into the fourth year of the war. The truth of the situation is at last dawning upon the Government…
>
> … We are told that the terms we favour are absolute surrender to the Boers; that is nonsense. Taking the very outside, we have gone to war to establish equal rights. Does anybody doubt that we could get them at the present moment? Is it an absolute surrender to get what you went to war for? It is evident we could have control of the foreign relations. The Boers are willing to give us the control of foreign relations, an equal franchise, and an indemnity… The terms we propose to the Boers are unconditional surrender, and the terms they offer us are unparalleled in their generosity. What are the terms we offer to the Boers? A British Government, a British Executive, and the British language to be the official language, the Boer language to be tolerated… Where is the suzerainty of the Orange Free State? That State was as independent as Great Britain is at the present moment. The only difference is that we are a great Power and they are a small one. Does that make any difference at all in the inherent justice of the war? Have you the right to be unjust to a man because he is poor and weak and insignificant? Every honest man would say you should treat him with more generosity…[631]

Lloyd George's comments struck a raw nerve in his parliamentary opponents and drew admiration from his supporters. However, he was being outpaced by events. Faced by the intolerable conditions being suffered by their families, the last of the Boers surrendered in May. Boer delegates agreed to the subsequent British terms by 54-6, and the war ended with the signing of the Treaty of Vereeniging in Pretoria on 31 May. The British had finally won and offered generous terms in order to regain Boer support. The Boers were given £3 million for reconstruction and were promised eventual limited self-government, which was granted in December 1906 and November 1907 by the Liberal Government. The treaty ended the existence of the South African Republic and the Orange Free State as independent Boer republics, the Union of South Africa being established as a dominion of the British Empire on 31 May 1910.

Lloyd George, as the spokesman for the Nonconformists, next made a major issue out of the Tory government's Education Act, introduced by Balfour on 24 March and passed under guillotine closure, after much heated controversy on 18 December 1902. It provided local funding for Church of England and Roman Catholic schools, which for Lloyd George represented the religious enemy, and established new Local Education Authorities (LEAs). The bill passed but opposition to it helped reunite the Liberals, contributing to their landslide electoral victory in 1906.

---

[631] https://api.parliament.uk/historic-hansard/commons/1902/mar/20/south-african-war-general-observations#S4V0105P0_19020320_HOC_297. Retrieved 3 January 2020.

On 12 November 1902, Balfour accepted an amendment put forward by Alfred Thomas, the Chairman of the Welsh Parliamentary Party, but instigated by Lloyd George, that 'Any scheme for establishing an education committee of the council of any county or county borough in Wales or of the county of Monmouth or county borough of Newport, shall provide that the county governing body constituted under The Welsh Intermediate Education Act, 1889 for any such county or county borough shall cease to exist, and shall make such provision as appears necessary or expedient for the transfer of the powers, duties, property and liabilities of any such body to the local education authority under this Act, and for making the provisions of this section applicable to the exercise by the local education authority of the powers so transferred.'[632] Lloyd George's successful amendment that the county need only fund those schools where the buildings were in good repair served to make the act a dead letter in Wales, where the counties were able to show that most Church of England schools were in poor repair. Having already gained national recognition for his anti-Boer War campaigns, his leadership of the attacks on the Education Act gave him a strong parliamentary reputation and marked him as a likely future Cabinet member.

On 3 December 1902, Balfour himself paid a great, if slightly qualified, tribute to the quality of Lloyd George's relentless opposition to his bill:

> There is the hon. Member for the Carnarvon Boroughs, who through these debates has played, in my judgment, a most distinguished part, though I confess I wish he had left unsaid, even from his own point of view, a great many things which he sometimes said… I believe that in the opinion of both sides of the House and of the country that the hon. Gentleman has shown himself to be an eminent Parliamentarian…[633]

William George made an illuminating entry in his diary on 30 December:

> D. has made good progress this year. At its beginning probably no man was more unpopular than he owing to the Boer War. Now no name is more respected than his–owing to his fight on the Education Bill. Such is public opinion. D. is the same now as then, but the fickle-minded creatures nearly killed him in Birmingham. Never again do I wish to hear such risks being run by him.[634]

On 17 January 1903, his fortieth birthday, Lloyd George gave his opinion of the government's tactics, published in his 'Address To The People Of Wales':

> In the great majority of cases there is no greater tactical mistake possible than to prosecute an agitation against an injustice in such a way as to alienate a large number of men who, whilst they

---

632 https://api.parliament.uk/historic-hansard/commons/1902/nov/12/education-england-and-wales-bill-2. Retrieved 13 November 2020.

633 https://api.parliament.uk/historic-hansard/commons/1902/dec/03/education-england-and-wales-bill-1#S4V0115P0_19021203_HOC_194. Retrieved 13 November 2020.

634 Quoted in George, *Backbencher*, p355.

> resent that injustice as keenly as anyone, either from tradition or timidity to be associated with anything savouring of revolutionary action. Such action should always be the last desperate resort of reformers… The interests of a whole generation of children will be sacrificed. It is not too big a price to pay for freedom, if this is the only resource available to us. But is it? I think not. My advice is, let us capture the enemy's artillery and turn his guns against him.[635]

As for 'popular opinion', it was indeed divided, as Lloyd George's brother William had noted. Many feared that he may lose his Caernarvon Boroughs seat at the next election due to his stance against the Boer War. In 1903 'feelers' were put out to persuade him to accept the Liberal candidacy for Manchester East, the city of his birth, against no less a person than Prime Minister Balfour, a mark of the growing standing that he held amongst sections of the broader Liberal Party. On 8 October, C. P. Scott, MP for the neighbouring Leigh division of Manchester and editor of the *Manchester Guardian*, wrote at length to Lloyd George urging him to accept, saying "Balfour must be fought & fought seriously." The following day, L. W. Zimmerman of Rusholme, chairman of the Manchester East Liberal Association, did the same, saying the move would result in "a glorious fight, and would, I think, be welcomed by the whole country." On 13 October, Robert Lewis, another local Liberal official, also weighed in strongly in trying to convince Lloyd George to stand in Manchester East as well as Caernarvon Boroughs, stating that the notion of his proposed candidature had "met with the warmest approval among our most influential men."[636]

The chorus swelled. On 22 October, Fred H. Smith of Swinton Park, Manchester, wrote expressing his wish that Lloyd George should stand in Manchester East to "face the Premier of England on the burning questions of the day."[637] Lloyd George was flattered to be asked, and seriously considered the matter, canvassing his brother's opinion and others. On 30 October, Jesse Herbert wrote saying the East Manchester Liberal Association declined to consider any other name until it had received a negative reply from him.[638] Ultimately, Lloyd George took the advice of his Welsh advisors, including Evan Davies of Caernarfon, who on 15 October speculated whether he thought "Wales would willingly allow you to sever your connection?", and J. Bryn Roberts, MP for the Eifion division of Caernarfonshire, who, writing the next day, believed that it would be inadvisable, stating "Our Boroughs are safe as long as you fight their battle but I do not feel so sure of the result if you, though the candidate, were not personally conducting the campaign … Further your success in Manchester (which is quite possible) would be disastrous to our boroughs for I doubt very much whether any other candidate would carry them for Liberalism." Lloyd George therefore refused the invitation and stayed loyal to his existing constituency, channelling his energies there rather than divide them in two.[639]

---

635 Du Parcq, Vol.II, Appendix III, pp412-416, quote on pp412, 413.
636 Jones, *David Lloyd George*, p59-61.
637 NLW, William George Papers, 4494, F. H. Smith to DLG, 22 October 1903.
638 Ibid., 4495, J. Herbert to DLG, 30 October 1903.
639 Jones, *David Lloyd George*, p61. That the seat of Manchester East *was* winnable was proven at the 1906 election, when a relatively unknown Liberal unseated Balfour on a 22.5% swing of the ballot.

Also in 1903, Lloyd George got to know the Zionists intimately. Theodor Herzl[640], founder of the Zionist Organization in August 1897, had authorized the preparation of a draft scheme for a Jewish settlement in East Africa, which became known as the 'Uganda Scheme'. This was prepared by the legal firm of Lloyd George, Roberts and Company, on the instructions of Herzl's go-between with the British Government, Leopold Greenberg.[641] Joseph Chamberlain was aware of the ambitions of the Zionist Organization, having been introduced to Herzl by Israel Zangwill[642] on 23 October 1902 and again on 24 April 1903, a few weeks after the outbreak of the pogroms of 6–9 April in Kishinev, (modern Chişinău, Moldova), then the capital of the Bessarabia Governorate in the Russian Empire, during which 49 Jews were killed, 92 severely injured and 1,500 properties were damaged.

Making a trip to East Africa earlier in the year, Chamberlain noted in his official report that, "If Dr Herzl were at all inclined to transfer his efforts to East Africa there would be no difficulty in finding land suitable for Jewish settlers."[643] Chamberlain duly offered 13,000 square kilometres (5,000 square miles) at Uasin Gishu (also 'Gwas Ngishu'), an isolated area atop the Mau Escarpment. The land was thought suitable because of its temperate hill station-like climate and its relative isolation, being surrounded by the Mau Forest. Given that the offer was in response to pogroms against the Jews in Russia, it was hoped the area could be a refuge from persecution for the Jewish people. Chamberlain saw the land as he was travelling extensively on the Uganda railway, although the land was not in fact in Uganda but in the East Africa Protectorate (modern Kenya), having recently been transferred from the Uganda Protectorate in 1902, as part of the Uganda railway development plan.

Lloyd George drafted a charter for the Jewish Settlement, to be called 'New Palestine', which was submitted to the Foreign Office for approval on 13 July. According to David Fromkin:

> In the summer of 1903 the Foreign Office replied in a guarded but affirmative way that if studies and talks over the course of the next year were successful, His Majesty's Government would consider favourably proposals for the creation of a Jewish colony. It was the first official declaration by a government to the Zionist movement and the first official statement implying national status for the Jewish people. It was the first Balfour Declaration.[644]

The charter that Lloyd George had negotiated included "the appointment of a Jewish official as the chief of the local administration", with permission to have a free hand in municipal legislation and management of "religious and domestic matters". According to Victor Kattan:

> The British Government's legal expert C. J. B. Hurst[645] subsequently examined the document drafted by Lloyd George. The memorandum Lloyd George prepared was far more elaborate

---

640 Theodor Herzl (1860-1904), Austro-Hungarian activist, the father of modern political Zionism, author of *Der Judenstaat*, 1896.
641 Leopold Greenberg (1861-1931), Zionist editor of the *Jewish Chronicle*, 1907-1931.
642 Israel Zangwill (1864-1926), British author at the forefront of cultural Zionism.
643 A. Rovner, *In the Shadow of Zion: Promised Lands Before Israel*, 2014, New York, NYU Press, p52a.
644 D. Fromkin, *A Peace to End All Peace: The Fall of the Ottoman Empire and the Creation of the Modern Middle East*, 2001, New York, Owl Books, p274.
645 Sir Cecil Hurst (1870-1963), Assistant Legal Adviser to the FO from 1902-1918.

than Herzl's original draft for a Jewish-Ottoman Land Company, which was akin to a treaty with an elaborate preamble, articles and clauses. It also provided for arbitration in case of any disagreement between the concessionaires and the Government. Article 1 provided:

1. That the Jewish Colonial Trust (Juedische Colonialbank) (hereinafter called 'the Concessionaires') may and are hereby authorised to enter into and upon the lands comprised in His Majesty's dominions in British East Africa for the purpose of inspecting and examining the same and of ascertaining the condition thereof and the suitability of the same or any part thereof for the establishment of Jewish Settlement or Colony… with full power… to plot out and survey the same to the intent that a portion thereof… if and when found suitable may be identified and with the boundaries and abuttals thereof duly determined by the Concessionaires may be submitted to His Majesty's Secretary of State for the approval of His Majesty's Government.

More controversially, Article 5 included the following provisions:

5. THAT at any time subsequent to the approval of the said lands and before the said 31st December 1909 the Concessionaires may submit to His Majesty's Government for approval by the said Government the terms of a Constitution for the regulations administration and good government of the Settlement whereby provision shall be made inter alia for the following matters and things:-

(a) FOR the introduction and establishment of a form of popular government in the territory which shall be Jewish in character and with a Jewish Governor to be appointed by His Majesty in Council. (b) FOR the granting to the settlement all necessary and proper powers to make ordinances and regulations for the internal administration and all matters necessary for the welfare and good government of the Jewish community and other persons in the said settlement. (c) FOR the levying in and upon the said territory all such tax or taxes and assessments as the settlement may decide for the said purposes of administration and good government… (d) FOR defining the relationship and status of the settlement and all persons therein with any other part or parts of His Majesty's dominions beyond the seas and with any Foreign State… (h) FOR granting to the settlement power to exclude from the said territory any person or persons proposing to enter or settle in the same who shall or may be deemed to be opposed to the interests of the settlement or the governments thereof… and the power… to expel from the territory without being liable for compensation or otherwise any person not fully and completely abiding by the ordinance rules and regulations for the time being in force in the territory or committing or conniving at a breach of the Constitution of the settlement… (k) FOR the preservation of the customs and laws of the native people of the territory with respect to the holding possession transfer and disposition of interests in lands and goods and the succession thereto… (l) FOR the non-interference by the Settlement (except insofar as may be necessary in the interests of humanity and for the preservation of peace) with the religion of any class or tribe of the native peoples of the territory and all forms of religious worship and ordinances as heretofore exercised and practised in the territory…

… [T]here is continuity between Herzl's initial draft for a JOLC, Lloyd George's draft for a Jewish colonisation scheme in East Africa, and the mandate for Palestine that would eventually be drafted by the Zionists in collusion with the British Foreign and Colonial Office. And each

> time, the draft drawn up by the Zionists was 'watered down' by officials at the Foreign and Colonial Office, but their essential objective remained the same throughout: they wanted ultimately to create a Jewish state in Palestine where they would encourage Jews from all over the world to settle so as to solve the Jewish Question and alleviate Britain's 'immigration problem'. In short, Britain was using the Zionists. There is no other way they could have had such intimate and close access to British officials high up in the Foreign and Colonial Office unless the British Government saw some benefit to be gained from it.
>
> According to Lloyd George's draft the main colonisation vehicle was the Jewish Colonial Trust, which then had a capital of £2,000,000. Its principal object was 'the settling of Jews under conditions favourable to their retention and encouragement of the Jewish national idea'. The preamble stipulated that Great Britain's dominions in East Africa 'would be greatly enhanced in value by the foundation there of a Jewish settlement and the creation and direction of public works and the promotion therein of commercial enterprises and the establishment of commercial relationships with neighbouring districts'. It was envisaged that the Jewish Colonial Trust would be the vehicle through which an investigation of East Africa would be financed to inspect the land to ascertain whether it was adequate for Jewish colonisation.
>
> In commenting on the preamble, the Foreign Secretary, Lord Lansdowne[646] noted in the margin that it was 'superfluous, and it contains some objectionable passages'. The Government lawyer C. J. B. Hurst... objected to the proposal to create a constitution for the Jewish settlement that would give it the right to define its relationship and status with other parts of the British Empire, with any other foreign state or with the chiefs of independent tribes in British East Africa. 'Any such provision quite impossible', he noted in the margin. He added, 'foreign relations must remain entirely in the hands of the Crown and without any fetters imposed by previous definition'. It is noteworthy that one of the conditions for statehood in modern international law is the capacity to enter into relations with other states. Evidently, the British Government did not agree to allow the Zionists to create a state in East Africa; they were to remain subject to the laws and regulations of the British Crown at all times.[647]

Herzl tabled the British offer before the sixth Zionist Congress gathered at Basel, on 26 August 1903. He carried the majority vote by 295 to 178, with 98 abstentions, on the question of investigating this offer, after the Russian delegation stormed out. However, Herzl himself died on 3 July 1904, and the 'Uganda Scheme' died with him.

Lloyd George remained connected to his Welsh roots, supporting the idea of pan-Celtic unity and attending the second Pan-Celtic Congress, a gathering of over 400 participants held at Caernarfon Castle from 30 August to 3 September 1904 to promote cultural kinship and mutual understanding between Wales, Brittany, Cornwall, Ireland, Scotland and the Isle of Man.[648] The *Carnarvon and Denbigh*

---

[646] Henry Petty-Fitzmaurice, Marquess of Lansdowne (1845-1927), Secretary of State for War, 1895-1900, Secretary of State for Foreign Affairs, 1900-1905.

[647] V. Kattan, *From Coexistence to Conquest: International Law and the Origins of the Arab-Israeli Conflict, 1891-1949*, 2009, London, Pluto Press, p31-33.

[648] See Marion Löffler, *A Book Of Mad Celts: John Wickens and the Celtic Congress of Caernarfon 1904*, 2000, Llandysul, Gwasg Gomer [Bilingual].

*Herald* reported on the evening concert of Thursday, 1 September:

> During the concert Mr Lloyd George, M.P., whom the Celts call with truth "the great Welsh orator," was espied sitting quietly in the reserved seats with Mrs Lloyd George. Somebody whispered "Lloyd George," a murmur arose, which swelled by and bye into a mighty shout. No artist would have dared face the audience, who for the moment were mad with delight, demanding a speech. Such a scene has never before been witnessed in the Pavilion, and when at last Lord Castletown[649] descended the platform and led the hon. member for the Carnarvon boroughs to the stage, the enthusiasm of the audience knew no bounds. "David of the silver tongue," however, declined to make a speech, but simply addressed a few words of thanks and of congratulation at the success of the union of the Celts…[650]

On 18 October, Lloyd George was back in Caernarfon with Winston Churchill[651], and both addressed an 8,000 strong capacity audience at what had been billed as a 'Free Trade Meeting' from the Pavilion platform and received the warmest of welcomes. Despite the billing, the audience "were treated instead to addresses on Home Rule All Round. Some called it "Devolution," and others baptised it as Local Self-Government; but all the same it spelt "Home Rule." It was a Home Rule meeting, in spite of the fact that every speaker agreed that Home Rule was as dead as a door nail." The Chairman, the Lord Lieutenant of the County Mr J. E. Greaves, then "commenced by putting himself on good terms with the people by calling Mr Lloyd George the best fighting general in the Liberal army–A compliment as neat as it was original–and it greatly pleased the audience. They went mad…"

Speaking in Welsh to the warmed-up crowd after Churchill, Lloyd George stated:

> The most significant thing in connection with the defection in the Unionist ranks was that it was not merely that it was the older and most experienced… that were leaving the party, but the strong, bold, young men, who saw visions, and who would certainly follow a new policy, and would not be frightened by mere newness if they saw any good in it for the country. Experienced men like the Duke of Devonshire and Lord Goschen, and brilliant young men of unquestionable courage and daring like Mr Winston Churchill, both alike, said:- "We see nothing but disaster to our country in this policy, and we will turn our backs even on our party if that is necessary to save our country"… Speaking quite candidly, he saw no chance whatever for the re-introduction of Gladstonian Home Rule. It would not be possible to promote Home Rule for one section only of the United Kingdom… Wales for generations had been yearning for measures in regard to temperance, land, and disestablishment, but they had not obtained them. Why? One reason was that Parliament had too much to do… While they were discussing… [trivial] matters, affairs of the most vital importance to the Empire were neglected… They, as Welshmen, were gradually impressing the leaders of English opinion with the conviction that

---

649 Bernard FitzPatrick, Baron Castletown (1848-1937), Anglo-Irish President of the Celtic Association.

650 *Carnarvon and Denbigh Herald*, 2 September 1904, p8.

651 Churchill had defected from the Tories to the Liberals on 31 May 1904.

> the Cymry were a nation capable of understanding and managing their own concerns. The battle against the Education Act had... demonstrated that Wales had a backbone, that she was determined not to be turned back, that she had interests which she meant to conserve, and principles for which she was prepared to make sacrifices...[652]

Lloyd George was always connected to North Wales in another important way, too, and that was through his life-long partiality for traditional Welsh food. In her retirement, Mrs Blodwen Evans, who worked for the family for 25 years in Criccieth, "recaptured vivid memories of the great statesman's enthusiasm for simple, homely Welsh food. 'How he loved a cacen gri!'"[653] she said. But only Dame Margaret could make it just the way he liked it! Mrs Evans described how he would take a long walk in the afternoon, nearly always along the top road to Llanystumdwy, often coming home soaked to the skin. He would change into dry clothes, then come in to the fire. After a few minutes, he would look at Dame Margaret and say, coaxingly: "Make me a cacen gri...!" And of course, she always would.

> As she made them she used to plaster each one with plenty of butter and pile them on a plate, until they were absolutely soaking with the lovely Welsh farm butter–oh, how he used to enjoy that! Nobody could make a cacen gri like Dame Margaret!

Lloyd George was also fond of pig's head brawn. Though there was a cook as well, he always insisted that Sarah, the housekeeper, made the brawn: "he simply couldn't bear anyone else to make that":

> And with the mutton broth he loved would come a plate of oatcakes–the big, flat Welsh oatcakes curling up at the edges. A pile of them would be placed on the table–nobody else but he would be allowed to cut them–and on the rare occasions when the family dined alone he loved to crumble these into his mutton broth in the old, Welsh country way: "How he enjoyed that!"
> Lloyd George always retained his love of simple Welsh country food. Even when they entertained, which was often... he would often have an omelette or just bacon and egg. On the other hand, Lloyd George liked his guests to have whatever they liked, and so it was usual for many dishes to be prepared... The fish he was fond of was salmon, and he had that often. He liked Welsh lamb, of course, and the local butcher kept Downing Street supplied.[654]

On 20 April 1905, Lloyd George made his first trip to Ireland, routinely overlooked by biographers, accepting the invitation of former Liberal MP, Martin White[655], an early motorist, to accompany him. That day, he informed his brother William that he had just arrived at the Shelbourne Hotel in Dublin. From Dublin, the pair drove to the Imperial Hotel, Cork, Co. Cork; the coastal village of Glengarriff, Co. Cork; to the Royal Victoria Hotel, Killarney, Co. Kerry, through Connemara, before driving to

---

[652] *Carnarvon and Denbigh Herald*, 21 October 1904, p3. The Foundation Stone of the Pavilion (1877-1961), dated '1877', was set in the boundary wall of Bryn Awelon when the property was owned by Megan.

[653] A large Welsh griddle cake baked on a traditional Welsh griddle or bakestone (*planc*).

[654] Mrs Bobby Freeman in Jones, *Lloyd George's Favourite Recipes*, p6.

[655] Martin White (1858-1928), Liberal MP for Forfarshire, 1895-1896.

Westport, Co. Mayo, then returning to Dublin to sail to Holyhead on 26 April.[656] On 25 April, he dined with William O'Brien[657], the Irish Nationalist MP, then at the height of his agitation for land reform. While not of high political importance, Lloyd George's extensive motor trip gave him some background impressions of the Irish heartland, including the poverty of its tenants.

Following on from his brief attendance at the Pan-Celtic Congress the previous year, in June, Lloyd George was interviewed by Herbert Vivian for the *Pall Mall Magazine*, saying: "As for Home Rule, I want local self-government not only for Ireland, but for Scotland, Wales." When questioned on the issue of Home Rule for Cornwall, which was 'inhabited by a separate race', Lloyd George replied "Then let us say local self-government for the West of England, which is largely Celtic." He concluded by stating that "My ideal is the heptarchy", a reference to the Anglo-Saxon division of the present United Kingdom into seven separate kingdoms.[658]

On 1 November, Lloyd George went to Glasgow to speak at St. Andrew's Hall in support of Asquith's successful bid to become the Rector of Glasgow University, stating that the history of the next Parliament would be the greatest in memory, and that it would be associated more with the name of Asquith than with that of any living statesman.[659] He added that the present government "would die with their drawn salaries in their hands."[660] It was his last speech as a backbencher.

Just before this, Lloyd George had been struck by the constriction of the throat that had begun to trouble him for a number of years. He had his tonsils removed, but during his convalescence he suffered a severe throat haemorrhage that, and but for the timely intervention of Elizabeth, 'Mrs Tim', the wife of his friend Timothy Davies–and with whom he had been having a mild flirtation since 1897–might have died.[661] The young Welsh doctor, Dr William Lloyd, summoned by her, ordered complete rest for two months. Lloyd George set off from Southampton with his brother William, bound for Genoa, on 13 November. They moved on to Florence and thence to the Grand Hotel Verdi in Rapallo. There they met an elderly Liberal gentleman fresh from England, who told them that the London newspapers were predicting the government was about to fall. William returned home on 1 December, and, the next day, on finding the *Times* and *Daily Telegraph* announcing the forthcoming resignation of the government, he telegraphed his brother. Lloyd George was back in London on the night of 3 December. Balfour resigned the next day.

On 5 December, Campbell-Bannerman was invited by Edward VII to form a Liberal administration. Would Lloyd George be offered a post? In the event, he was offered a choice between the Post Office or the Board of Trade, and he chose the latter, even though the salary was £500 lower

---

656 https://www.llyfrgell.cymru/fileadmin/docs_gwefan/arddangosfeydd_digidol/david_lloyd_george/llythyron_dllg/William%20George%20Schedule.pdf. Retrieved 1 August 2025. Letters 1585–1589. George, 'Backbencher', p424.

657 William O'Brien (1852-1928), Irish Nationalist MP for Cork constituencies, 1883-1918, United Irish League (UIL) co-founder with Michael Davitt, 1898, All-for-Ireland League (AFIL) founder and leader, 1909-1918.

658 H. Vivian, *Studies In Personality, No.V: Mr. Lloyd George, M.P. Pall Mall Magazine* 35, 14 June 1905, p684-691; quotes, p686.

659 Du Parcq, Vol.III, p446. Asquith won the Rectorship by a majority of 211.

660 Crosby, *Unknown*, p63.

661 George, *My Brother And I*, p87-89. 'Lizzie' (1872-1953), married Davies in 1893.

than the less demanding Post Office position.[662] On 8 December he wrote to William from the National Liberal Club with the good news:

> Board of Trade with a seat in the Cabinet. They want me there as that is the Department most directly associated with the Free Trade fight to defend Free Trade in the House & in the country against Joe's attacks.
>
> I am delighted. I shall have the Labour Department–supervision of railways–Harbours–Bankruptcy–foreshore & above all that grand new building by the House of Commons. Winston and McKenna[663] think I have the most important post in the Ministry at this juncture.
>
> I asked for pledge about Education & the extension of self-Government for Wales–I got both.
>
> Of one thing I am glad. I have a first-rate chief of the permanent staff–Sir Francis Hopwood[664], a very able man, & an excellent Radical.[665]

---

662 Ivatt, *Lloyd George's Presidency*, p24.

663 Reginald McKenna (1863-1943), Liberal MP for North Monmouthshire 1895-1918, First Lord of the Admiralty 12 April 1908–23 October 1911, Home Secretary 23 October 1911–27 May 1915, afterwards Chancellor of the Exchequer to 10 December 1916.

664 Francis Hopwood (1860-1947), Permanent Secretary to the Board of Trade, June 1901–January 1907.

665 NLW, William George Papers, 1718, DLG to WG, 8 December 1905.

# 4

## CABINET MINISTER, 1905-1916

When sworn in as the President of the Board of Trade and a privy counsellor on 11 December 1905, aged 42, Lloyd George was the youngest member of Sir Henry Campbell-Bannerman's new Cabinet, and now in possession of an annual salary of £2,000 per year.[666] He showed exceptional administrative ability with constructive talent and a gift for mediation in industrial disputes, being an efficient, energetic and enthusiastic facilitator and mobiliser, if not always an originator. He recorded his impressions of his first Cabinet meeting on 14 December, writing to his brother:

> Attended my first Cabinet today. Very interesting. Education first.
>
> Today had to decide questions arising over Portmadoc Railway & Criccieth foreshore. Send a word about the first. What is the position of things? It is within my power absolutely to stop the enterprise or to let it proceed...
>
> Tomorrow morning I hold a levee of all my chiefs.
>
> Been busy with educational position in Wales. Macnamara has refused a post under Birrell[667] in the Board of Education. Delighted he has. Would not have trusted him there.[668]

Lloyd George quickly impressed those who met him. The new President, with a staff of 750 and an annual budget of £270,000 per annum[669], was found to be:

> Punctual and industrious, immensely quick to grasp the complicated details of any question. Moreover... he was patient, courteous, considerate, and conciliatory ... "During thirty years," declared an old servant of the House of Commons, "I have only known one member whose manner and way of speaking did not change after he had become a Cabinet Minister. That one is Lloyd George." He has never undervalued himself, nor made pretence to a false modesty; but his entire self-possession, complete absence of affectation, and uniform courtesy to high and low, have preserved him from ever acquiring the sort of stiff pompousness which is far too often the characteristic of the highest servants of the State.[670]

---

666 As the post was not a Secretary of State, he did not get the £5,000 per year that most Ministers received.
667 Augustine Birrell (1850-1933), President of the Board of Education, 1905-1907, Chief Secretary for Ireland, 1907-1916.
668 NLW, William George Papers, 1722, DLG to WG, 14 December 1905.
669 Pugh, *Lloyd George*, p32-33.
670 W. W. Davies, p250-251.

Befitting his new status, Lloyd George also acquired his first private secretary, Cardiganshire-born John Rowland[671], who served him well from 1905 to 1912, being efficient, discreet, and well-versed in the complexities of Welsh political, cultural and religious life.

In the new year of 1906, at the general election held between 12 January-8 February, the Liberals, led by Campbell-Bannerman, won a landslide majority, winning 397 seats. The Tories, led by Balfour, lost more than half theirs, including Balfour's own in Manchester East, crashing to 156, their lowest ever. Labour greatly increased its representation to 29, whilst the Irish Nationalists increased theirs slightly to 82. The Liberals' landslide victory of 125 seats over all other parties cleared the way for passing the remarkable crop of interventionist social legislation known as the Liberal welfare reforms. In Wales, they won every seat. In Caernarfon Boroughs, polled on 20 January, Lloyd George won by 3,221 to 1,997, a majority of 1,224 over his Tory opponent, English timber-importer and temperance campaigner, Robert Naylor, on an 8.4% swing, greater than the 5.4% national average.

Amongst the important measures for which he was now responsible at the Board of Trade was the Merchant Shipping Act, which received royal assent on 21 December 1906, revising load levels and safety requirements, significantly including foreign ships in British ports; confining pilot's certificates to British subjects; and establishing regulations covering the standards of sailors food, medical treatment and accommodation on British registered ships, making it become known as the 'Seaman's Charter'. On the same day, 21 December, Lloyd George pushed through the Census of Production Act, the first of its kind in Britain. Although it even had opposition support from Joseph Chamberlain–at least until his incapacitating stroke on 13 July–it was met with considerable suspicion by manufacturers, and several MPs expressed concerns, namely that manufacturers' trade secrets might be compromised. Nonetheless, the first census was carried out in 1907.

Another significant measure was the Patents and Designs Act, which received royal assent on 28 August 1907, designed to consolidate the enactments relating to patents for inventions and the registration of designs and certain enactments relating to trademarks. Specifically, it compelled patentees to work their patents within the United Kingdom, Part 1.27.(1) stating:

> At any time not less than four years after the date of a patent, and not less than one year after the passing of this Act, any person may apply to the comptroller for the revocation of the patent on the ground that the patented article or process is manufactured or carried on exclusively or mainly outside the United Kingdom.[672]

The Act had much wider implications than just technical innovation, Lloyd George having noted on 20 March: "Deputations today. One most interesting, headed by Alma Tadema, about copyright in pictures and artistic designs."[673]

The path to social reform was by no means clear, however, as Lloyd George and other like-minded

---

671 Sir John Rowland (1877-1941), knighted in 1938.

672 https://www.legislation.gov.uk/ukpga/Edw7/7/29/part/I/enacted. Retrieved 19 January 2020.

673 Quoted in George, *My Brother And I*, p209. Sir Lawrence Alma-Tadema (1836-1912).

radicals were repeatedly blocked by the hostile, reactionary House of Lords. The Education Bill of 1906, which aimed to abolish the financing of religious instruction in Church schools from local rates, was carried by a majority of 192 in the Commons on 27 July but was sent back by the Lords amended to the point of emasculation, being withdrawn from the order book on 20 December. The Education (Provision of Meals) Act did make it through, receiving royal assent on 21 December, providing for free meals for children attending public elementary schools in England and Wales. The Licensing Bill of 1908, which aimed to reduce the number of licences in England and Wales by about 30,000 from 96,000 over a fourteen-year period, with compensation to dispossessed owners to cease at the end of that time, also reducing Sunday opening hours, was rejected outright. In the Commons, it was carried by a majority of 350-113 on 20 November but rejected by an unusually large turnout of peers by a majority of 272-96 on 27 November. Clearly the Lords were not just performing their role of keeping a constitutional watch on the Commons, they were negatively controlling legislation, blocking the majority will of the people–as then constituted–through their elected representatives.

Speaking at the Palmerston Club in Oxford on 1 December 1906, from both his own conviction and from his reading of the growing mood of the country, Lloyd George declared:

> That it was essential to the good government of the country that the road from the people to the throne should be cleared. It was intolerable that every petition of right that came from the people to their sovereign should be waylaid and mutilated in this fashion… If the House of Lords persisted in its present policy, it would be a much larger measure than the Education Bill that would come up for consideration. It would come upon this issue, whether the country was to be governed by the King and the Peers or by the King and the people.[674]

The King took exception to Lloyd George alluding to the throne in his attack on the Lords, and instructed his Private Secretary, Lord Knollys, to write to the Prime Minister on 3 December, protesting that:

> His Majesty has the right, and it is one on which he intends to insist, that Mr. Lloyd George shall not introduce the Sovereign's name into these violent tirades of his, and he asks you, as Prime Minister, to be so good as to take the necessary steps to prevent a repetition of this violation of constitutional practice and of good taste.[675]

In modern parlance, it was the King who was attempting to interfere in the democratic process in an unconstitutional manner and get the elected Prime Minister to 'lean on' a member of his own Cabinet. Campbell-Bannerman replied the following day in conciliatory tones that were still highly supportive of his junior colleague in his frustrated defence of the Education Bill:

---

[674] Quoted in Spender, *Campbell-Bannerman*, Vol.II, p313.
[675] Ibid., p314.

> I venture to submit that, whether his language be thought exaggerated or not, he had at least some excuse for fault-finding, when we have seen the Bill–in Committee, and even more in Report–not only seriously amended but turned upside down… compromise is almost, if not quite, impossible, and indeed is not intended by the Opposition in the House of Lords.
>
> If this be so, I fear that we must be prepared for forcible language being employed generally, and even by Ministers; for it will be hard to restrain the feelings certain to be legitimately roused when a Bill so largely supported in the country, and passed in the Lower House by such a majority, is deliberately converted by the House of Lords into a measure whose purpose is the exact reverse.[676]

Campbell-Bannerman concluded his reply by referencing Lloyd George's defence of his statement, along with his expression of "profound regret" at inadvertently causing offence, giving his explanation that "he would have considered it would be disrespectful to speak of 'the Peers' and 'the people' alone, omitting the reference to the supreme Head of the State; and he therefore used the phrase reported out of respect without the slightest idea of implying any connivance or co-operation; and that it was so understood."[677] The King was only partly appeased, but the matter went no further.

In February 1907, Lloyd George made his second trip to Ireland, visiting Belfast in his capacity as President of the Board of Trade, dutifully following the 'step-by-step' line on Home Rule and warning of the dangers of Irish separatism. In a speech at Ulster Hall under the auspices of the Ulster Liberal Association on 8 February, he insisted that Ireland's schism from the Empire was "unthinkable", and–to 'ringing Protestant cheers'–he declared that "the supremacy of the Imperial Parliament must be maintained. They might depend upon it no scheme would be introduced by this Parliament which would impair in the slightest degree the true predominance and supremacy of the Imperial Parliament."[678] It was not one of Lloyd George's finer moments. He did have something of an ingrained aversion to Roman Catholicism, and this was to fatally skew his approach to Irish affairs. Lucy Masterman wrote of Lloyd George in her diary that he was "not a very keen Home Ruler. He admits it as an abstract proposition but he has a good deal of the Protestant in him."[679]

Liberal MP and friend at this time W. Llewelyn Williams recorded a conversation he had with Lloyd George on 10 February, in his diary:

> … as to his visit to Belfast–the first made by a Liberal Minister for over twenty years. The Whips, it seems, had asked him to go, and he had reluctantly consented. Then [William] Moore KC, the new Ulster member, had publicly threatened to 'Birmingham' George if he went. The Whips and the Cabinet became alarmed. They feared a riot, ending in bloodshed, would result. Pressure was brought to bear on George to cancel the engagement. He refused. Birrell, in quite a friendly way, brought the subject up in the Cabinet. At first, everybody urged him not to go.

---

676 Ibid., p315.
677 Ibid., p315.
678 Quoted in A. O'Day, *Irish Home Rule, 1867-1921*, 1998, Manchester, Manchester University Press, p213. See Du Parcq, Vol.III, p474-477, for more detail.
679 L. Masterman, *C.F.G. Masterman: A Biography*, 1939, London, Nicholson and Watson, p242.

> But on his remaining resolute, they gave way, and George was jubilant over the result. The whole thing passed off peaceably, and the meetings were a triumphant success. This, George thought, would greatly strengthen his position in the Government. 'I was not going to be warned off after promising to go', he said…[680]

In a heated debate in the Commons, on 26 June 1907, a frustrated Lloyd George spoke for all Liberals when he made his famous comment on the Lords in effect being Balfour's 'lapdog':

> We did what we promised at the last election. A mastiff? It is the right hon. Gentleman's poodle. It fetches and carries for him. It barks for him. It bites anybody that he sets it on to. And we are told that this is a great revising Chamber, the safeguard of liberty in the country. Talk about mockeries and shams. Was there ever such a sham as that?… The House of Lords, it seems, defends capital. Of a kind, yes. But generally against whom does it defend capital? Against the House of Commons? Why should this House destroy capital?[681]

During mid-October–early November 1907, he succeeded in averting a major stoppage on the railways, that is in stopping a proposed national strike of the railway unions, the National Union of Railwaymen and the Amalgamated Society of Railway Servants. Trouble had been simmering since the previous November, and the huge task he faced was that of brokering an agreement between the unions and the 29 railway companies. On 21 October 1907 he wrote:

> The Railway strike is demanding all my attention. Things are going well so far. Whatever happens I am coming out on top of this business. I can see my way clear right to the station. Conciliation at first but, failing that, the steam roller. The Companies must give way on that point I am definite.[682]

He knew it would be a "tough job", but by 25 October he felt he had made an "excellent beginning", especially in bringing Lord Claud Hamilton, powerful Chairman of the Great Eastern Railway, to consider his proposals to appoint six of their number to meet with him. He was "sanguine of good results."

Lloyd George acted as mediator between the two groups who never actually met–going back and forth between separate rooms with statements, offers, counteroffers, until agreement was reached. On 31 October he noted: "All day with the Directors. In the morning I had to threaten them. Told them that there must not be a strike on any account." It did the trick, as on 1 November he could note: "Believe I have settled the strike."[683] On 4 November, he presented a delighted Campbell-Bannerman

---

680 https://www.library.wales/fileadmin/fileadmin/docs_gwefan/amdanom_ni/cylchgrawn_llgc/cgr_erth_XXXIVrh3_2008_3.pdf. Retrieved 23 May 2020.
681 https://api.parliament.uk/historic-hansard/commons/1907/jun/26/house-of-lords#S4V0176P0_19070626_HOC_294. Retrieved 26 January 2019.
682 Quoted in George, *My Brother And I*, p212.
683 Ibid., p212.

the terms of settlement, which were signed by all parties on 6 November. While most of the companies refused to recognise the unions–the North-Eastern Railway Company being the exception–Lloyd George persuaded the companies to recognise elected representatives of the workers who were to sit with the company representatives on Sectional Conciliation Boards, one for each company. If those boards failed to agree within two months, then there was to be a Central Board. Should this fail to reach agreement, then either party could request arbitration via a jointly agreed arbitrator.[684] The Railway Conciliation Scheme, 1907, though flawed, was remarkably good considering its rapid genesis, and was in effect a forerunner of the Advisory, Conciliation and Arbitration Service (ACAS), made a statutory body in 1976.

Lloyd George's skill and adroitness in this matter was deeply appreciated by Campbell-Bannerman, who wrote a warm eulogy on his young colleague to King Edward VII on 8 November:

> I have the honour… to enclose for Your Majesty's information a memorandum just received from Mr. Lloyd George intimating the happy results of the negotiations he has been conducting between the Railway Directors and the Railwaymen. He describes in a summary way the nature of the arrangement, embodied in a document signed by both parties; but, apart from the particular merits of the plan, it is a matter of sincere rejoicing that a solution has been found…
>
> I would further venture to say that the country is largely indebted for so blessed a conclusion of a time of great anxiety and danger to the knowledge, skill, astuteness, and tact of the President of the Board of Trade and those around him in his Department.[685]

Shortly after he gave Lloyd George this generous and glowing endorsement, on 13 November, Campbell-Bannerman had a heart attack, and his health declined rapidly. He resigned on 3 April 1908, and died on 22 April, the only Prime Minister to date to die in No.10.

Lloyd George spoke from the heart when he said of the man who had first entrusted him with Cabinet rank:

> I think it will be felt by the community as a whole as if they had lost a relative. Certainly those who have been associated with him closely for years will feel a deep sense of personal bereavement. I have never met a great public figure since I have been in politics who so completely won the attachment and affection of the men who came into contact with him. He was not merely admired and respected; he was absolutely loved by us all… The masses of the people of this country, especially the more unfortunate of them, have lost the best friend they ever had in the high places of the land. His sympathy in all suffering was real, deep, and unaffected. He was truly a great man–a great head and a great heart. He was absolutely the bravest man I ever met in politics. He was entirely free from fear. He was a man of supreme courage. Ireland has certainly lost one of her truest friends, and what is true of Ireland is true of

---

684 See W. Tetley Stephenson, *The Railway Conciliation Scheme, 1907*, *Economic Journal*, 21, 84, December 1911, p503-512.

685 Quoted in Spender, *Campbell-Bannerman*, Vol.II, p370.

> every section of the community of this Empire which has a fight to maintain against powerful foes.[686]

Before the Prime Minister's death, on 11 November 1907, Kaiser Wilhelm II arrived on his yacht at Portsmouth to begin a week long state visit to Britain, heading to Windsor to be hosted by his cousin, King Edward VII. The next evening, Lloyd George attended a function at the Castle, recording his impressions of the man who he would later lead a war against–and some comments regarding his own monarch:

> I got more than my share [of attention] from the Emperor downwards. The Prime Minister and I were sent for *first.* The Duchess of Argyll pounced on me, then the Prince of Wales, but before I said two words in answer to his congratulations, the Emperor left the P.M., held out his hand to me and congratulated me on my settlement of the Railway Strike. He then talked to me so long that it became quite painful. He was with me three times as long as he was with the P.M. He said he had heard of me from Herr Balchin[687], the great German Shipowner, the greatest in the world. Balchin, he told me, had a tremendous opinion of me. He said that whenever I came to Germany, I would receive a great reception. He then went on discussing the load-line on ships, State Railways and what he was doing about State Theatres. He laughed and talked at such length that the King came up and fetched me away…
>
> … The King was against the working man in the matter of the Railway Strike. Thought it was madness on their part to threaten a strike–didn't know what they wanted to strike about–might lose their pensions etc. Tory ydi o yn y bon (He is a Tory at heart). Duw a helpo'r bobol gyda'r penaethiaid yma (God help the people with such overlords). The Emperor was just as bad. I came away hating all Kings.[688]

Shortly afterwards, a huge personal tragedy struck Lloyd George and Margaret, then living at 3 Routh Road, Wandsworth Common in London. Their beloved eldest daughter, Mair, was studying hard for her matriculation exams. She began to suffer a pain in her side, but not wishing to worry her mother, she said nothing until the pain had become agonising and she fell ill at school. On 25 November, the Headmistress, Mrs E. Woodhouse, telephoned Margaret and sent Mair home in a cab that afternoon. Seeing that her daughter was obviously seriously ill, Margaret immediately summoned the family doctor, Dr Pollard, and then asked for a specialist too. Lloyd George was handed a note by a civil servant whilst chairing a routine Board of Trade meeting, telling him of this alarming development and he rushed home. Normally he would have sent for his sister Pollie to help, but she was already ill herself with the cancer that would soon kill her. He decided to engage a nurse, and secured the services

---

686 *The Times*, 23 April 1908, p5. Though little remembered today, Campbell-Bannerman was highly regarded at the time, across party lines, the last of the great Liberal Ministers in the Gladstonian mould.

687 Actually, Albert Ballin (1857-1918), shipowner, general manager of the Hamburg America Line from 1899. Facing the loss of his ships, he committed suicide two days before the end of the Great War.

688 Quoted in George, *My Brother And I*, p213. Lloyd George sometimes reverted to Welsh in private letters when he had something more private or contentious to convey.

of his cousin, Anita Williams, from Fishguard in Pembrokeshire, who was a nursing sister at the Royal Northern Hospital in London.[689]

On the morning of 29 November, the specialist, Henry Fenwick, at last arrived. He diagnosed a burst appendix and recommended an immediate operation which, according to the standards of the day, was to be carried out at home. Margaret set about converting Lloyd George's study into an operating theatre ready for the afternoon ordeal. Poor Mair duly underwent the operation, coming round from the anaesthetic afterwards, but it had been carried out too late. Fully sensible, she asked if she was going to die. Anita, a wise and experienced nurse, mercifully refused to give her false assurances. Mair's last words were "He is just and merciful", before passing away in the early hours of Saturday, 30 November. Margaret and Lloyd George, waiting in the drawing room downstairs, were naturally devastated. Mair was a beautiful and talented girl, especially so in music; she used to entertain her parents by playing the piano and her father could not be reconciled to the fact that 'the white hand was under a crust of earth'.

Mair's burial took place quietly in Criccieth on Tuesday, 3 December, attended by the men of the family only, as was then common. W. Llewelyn Williams recorded:

> I came back last night from poor little Mair's funeral at Criccieth. We were very few present– only the family, Clark (Lloyd George's private secretary), Alfred Thomas, William Jones, and the two Herberts. George bore up very well on the whole, though he broke down badly occasionally. I spent Sunday with him ... Between his sobs, he said once, 'I never wanted to go to heaven before!' I could not help laughing, and he joined in, hysterically.[690]

A beautiful marble relief of her by W. Goscombe John[691] was placed over her grave and family vault. Mair's death impelled Lloyd George to totally immerse himself in his great programme of social reform, driving it on tirelessly.

This was evidenced by what he wrote to Margaret from Manchester the day after the funeral:

> It was the decree of fate which millions besides ourselves are now enduring. What right have we to grumble? More than that I have a profound conviction that cruel as the blow may appear & purposeless as it may now seem it will prove to be the greatest blessing that has befallen us & through us *multitudes whom God has sent me to give a helping hand out of misery and worry a myriad worse than ours*. I can see through the darkness a ray of hope. I am not sure yet what it will reveal but I am certain of its presence & promise.[692]

---

689 Anita (1872–6 June 1943), later nursed Pollie through her last illness, and, to the family's delight, married William George at Hermon Chapel in Fishguard on 23 July 1910.

690 https://www.llyfrgell.cymru/fileadmin/fileadmin/docs_gwefan/amdanom_ni/cylchgrawn_llgc/cgr_erth_XXXIVrh3_2008_3.pdf. Retrieved 1 November 2019. Diary Entry, 5 December 1907. William H. Clark (1876-1952), private secretary to Lloyd George as President of the Board of Trade, 1906-1908, and as Chancellor of the Exchequer, 1908-1910. Alfred Thomas (1840-1927), Liberal MP for East Glamorganshire, 1885-1910. William Jones (1860-1915), Liberal MP for Caernarvonshire North (Arfon constituency), 1895 until his death. 'The two Herberts' were J. Herbert Lewis (1858-1933), Liberal MP for Flint Boroughs, 1906-1922, and John Herbert Roberts (1863-1955), Liberal MP for Denbighshire West, 1892-1918.

691 Sir William Goscombe John (1860-1952), prolific Welsh sculptor known for his many public memorials.

692 Morgan, *Family Letters*, p149. Emphasis added.

When, on 21 June 1914, his brother lost one of his twin sons, David, aged 20 months, he wrote to William:

> I know now what it is for. It gave me a keener appreciation of the sufferings of others. It deepened my sympathy. *Little Mair's death has been the inspiration of all my work to relieve human misery during recent years…* I am never sorry for the dead. My grief is all for the living…[693]

Tragically, Mair's death also drove a wedge between Lloyd George and Margaret: he later spoke of how "after Mair's death they had drifted apart", as they "each had their poignant grief but could not go to each other for sympathy and understanding–there was no sharing of the trouble."[694] Such was Lloyd George's grief at losing Mair that he refused to continue living at Routh Road, and in December the family moved to 5 Cheyne Walk, Chelsea.

Lloyd George was in Manchester immediately after the funeral because he was engaged in trying to arbitrate another industrial dispute, this time involving the Oldham cotton spinning unions, whose fine spinners claimed that their wages were falling behind others in the industry. In late November, accompanied by Hubert Llewellyn Smith[695], Lloyd George went to Manchester to intervene personally. "Within a fortnight, Lloyd George had managed to soothe tempers between the Master Cotton Spinners Federation and the operative spinners, winning a 9 per cent wage increase for the latter."[696] Here again he used his tactic of speaking to both sides separately, acting as the essential lynchpin rather than as a moderator at confrontational joint meetings. This would not have worked for everyone, but it suited Lloyd George's particular and persuasive skills.

That same November, some of Lloyd George's political associates suggested that they might pool together to buy the freehold of the Lloyd George family's new home. His wife Margaret wrote to him on Christmas Eve that some 'good friends' of theirs were anxious to contribute the £3,000 [£461, 195 in 2025] necessary for the purchase. She was keen to accept the offer on the grounds that "People gave Tom Ellis his lease & he had not done one-third what you have done for Wales". On 10 January 1908, Lloyd George wrote to his wife from Nice:

> I am not going to accept the charity of the party, come what may… Tom Ellis did it and was their doormat. I mean to fight my way myself. This is an offer made to me because they find the jealousies and rivalries are so great that they cannot raise the status of my office & CB wants to do something for me. It is very kind of him but I won't have it. I'll take my chance & I know I can rely on your help.[697]

Another interesting light on this time in Lloyd George's life is shed by a family story from Jonathan

---

693 Quoted in George, *My Brother And I*, p.218. Emphasis added.

694 F. Lloyd George, *The Years That Are Past*, p49.

695 Hubert Llewellyn Smith (1864-1945), Permanent Secretary to the Board of Trade, 1907-1919.

696 Crosby, *Unknown*, p73-74.

697 NLW, MS 20,429C, no.1290, DLG to MLG, 10 January 1908. This little-known incident goes some way to counteracting the false view of Lloyd George accumulating money to himself.

Hamer:

> My family's connection goes back to 1907 when John Sharp Higham[698] (on my mother's side) was Liberal MP for Sowerby… John Sharp's son John was just 4 when he fell out of the unlocked door of a speeding railway carriage near Lichfield. He was found at the side of the track and taken to hospital. The doctors recommended finally that he would benefit from quiet recuperation, and so it is believed that David Lloyd George, who had a family residence in Criccieth, recommended that quiet seaside fishing town on the coast "for the good sea air and iron in the water." John Higham's wife Pollie (née Hartley, of the jam firm) finally fell in love with the town and had a house built in Criccieth in c.1912, called Hafod y Bryn, below the Lloyd George residence, on the road up to the [now defunct] golf course. She also donated the final tranche of money necessary to build the Memorial Hall in the town.[699]

In late 1890 Richard Owen, Lloyd George's father-in-law, had built a fine pair of semi-detached houses on Porthmadog Road, Criccieth, with fine, sweeping views of the beautiful Cardigan Bay (*Bae Ceredigion*). One called 'Llys Owen' was for himself and his wife, and the other called 'Bryn Awel' was for David and Margaret.[700]

Now, with Lloyd George 'going up in the world', the 'family residence' was to be 'Bryn Awelon' ('*Hill of Breezes*'), Margaret's choice of name, built between 1908-1909 in the arts & crafts style, incorporating partly half-timbered construction to the main entry façade. The architect was Rowland Lloyd Jones of Caernarfon.[701] As originally built, the house was:

> … unpretentious–a square, two-storied, black-and-white structure, containing two good living-rooms, and half a dozen bedrooms. A small lawn stretched below the veranda, and a good kitchen garden lay behind. At the entrance to the short path leading from the public road to the front door stood two fine iron gates; but these had soon to make way for a solid wooden door, flanked by a tall hedge, to keep out the prying glances of the hundreds of visitors who used to throng there in order to watch the Chancellor sitting reading or chatting on the veranda. The excluded public took their revenge by carving their initials on every square inch of the new door! Bryn Awelon was well planned and comfortable, but in no wise different from the houses which successful village grocers and drapers build for themselves when they retire. Later it was found to be too small. Guests began to come to Criccieth more frequently; and secretaries were always there when the Chancellor was in residence. Mrs. Lloyd George complained that her only drawing-room was turned into an office; and that the whole family and guests had to make the most of the dining-room, which was the only other room in the house. Consequently a third living room was added, and a couple of new bedrooms. An adjoining field was also purchased;

[698] John Sharp Higham (1857-1932), cotton manufacturer, radical Liberal MP for Sowerby, 1904-1918. Pollie Higham (1870-1945), benefactress, died the same day as Lloyd George.
[699] Personal Communication with the author, 23 May 2019. The Foundation Stone of the Memorial Hall was laid by Lloyd George on 3 June 1922, the Hall being formally dedicated on 20 July 1924.
[700] These houses appear on the 25-inch maps (1900, 2nd edition). 'Bryn Awel' is now called 'Pengolwg'.
[701] Rowland Lloyd Jones, elected MSA 1903, County Architect, died on 24 July 1925 aged 66.

> for Dame Margaret, like her husband, is an expert and enthusiastic gardener; and the garden at Bryn Awelon is her own special hobby.[702]

Selwyn Lloyd[703], then an ardent young Liberal, later a Tory MP and Speaker of the House, holidayed each year in Criccieth and in the 1920s became on visiting terms with the Lloyd Georges. He later remembered:

> Brynawelon [sic] was an enchanting house to visit. Dame Margaret was a delightful personality, full of humour and common-sense. We all loved her. Lloyd George himself was more formidable, charming, scintillating, but dominating.[704]

Bryn Awelon increasingly became Margaret's preferred abode, while her husband spent more time in London or later at Churt. It became increasingly Margaret's home alone: by the 1930s, grandson Bill would recall mostly:

> 'Gang activities' with Bengy Carey-Evans and certain boys from Arfonia Terrace, the row of houses leading to the House! Enduring it all with characteristic warmth and a very sure touch was my Nain, Dame Margaret!… My memories of Taid… were principally of him at Churt. We only used to go to Criccieth about once or twice a year–usually in the Summer holidays–and, so far as I can recall, he was seldom there then.[705]

William George has perhaps most sympathetically and accurately of all commentators summarised the situation as it developed between his brother and sister-in-law:

> My brother's philosophy of life differed fundamentally from that of his wife Margaret. To Dafydd life was a battle, and he was never happy unless he had somebody or something to fight. On the other hand, 'Peace and plenty' were Maggie's ideals, and she was never happier than when settled down in her comfortable home in Criccieth with her gardens and grounds in front of her and her children and grandchildren bustling around her.
>
> Not long after the post-war period it appeared to be accepted as a matter of course that the heads of the family should have their separate headquarters… This does not mean, of course, that there had been anything in the nature of a separation between them. On the contrary, it was well understood between them that either would at all times be welcome at the other's place of abode–a privilege not infrequently exercised by both. But generally speaking, each one had enough of their own particular concerns to keep them fully occupied…[706]

---

702 W. W. Davies, p436-437.

703 Selwyn Lloyd, (1904-1978), Speaker of the House of Commons, 1971-1976.

704 Quoted in D. R. Thorpe, *Selwyn Lloyd*, 1989, London, Jonathan Cape, p19.

705 Personal Communication with the author, 23 October 2019.

706 George, *My Brother And I*, p289.

Meanwhile, Lloyd George's 'battles' continued. From January 1908 he followed up his success with the railways by settling a strike of 5,000 shipyard engineers on the north-east and north-west coasts, who, in a time when shipbuilding was going through a severe depression, struck over the immediate reduction of a shilling a week in time rates, and a further reduction of sixpence, to take effect in March. In late April, the men balloted for arbitration and the setting up of conciliation boards, but the employers objected, and lockouts began of a further 22,000 men. Trouble rumbled on:

> Meetings between the President of the Board of Trade and the contesting parties finally achieved agreement. The strikers were to accept the reduction and a conference was to be called to consider setting up a permanent procedure for settling disputes. The stoppage had lost 1,700,000 working days.
>
> The new procedure was ratified in March, 1909. It established that general wage movements were to be negotiated nationally by the [Shipbuilding Employers] Federation and the unions. A minimum period of six months must elapse between wage changes which must not exceed at any one time five per cent for piece-work rates and one shilling a week for time rates.[707]

Lloyd George was also instrumental in the passing of the Port of London Act, which received royal assent on 21 December 1908, this being as the result of him hearing about the bitter rivalry between Tilbury and London docks. The amalgamation of the chaotic and antiquated system of private companies and wharfingers had first been proposed by a Royal Commission in 1902, but the immense task of negotiating between the diverse parties had deterred the Tory government. Now, Lloyd George used his rare talents to clear the 'Augean stable' and provide London with a streamlined port system. To see for himself the opportunities of modernisation, he paid brief visits to Antwerp and Hamburg in May 1907, accompanied by Hudson Kearley.[708] On 22 May, he lunched with shipowner Albert Ballin at Hamburg, before leaving for London.[709] Upon his return, he told *The Times*:

> Both Hamburg and Antwerp are immensely superior to us in their facilities for loading and discharging cargoes, especially in the matter of distribution. The bringing of the State railway lines alongside the quays enables ships to load or unload directly from and to the trucks… with an obvious saving of time, labour and expense… One thing is clear–that London will have to wake up at once, or else… it will be left behind in the competition. At places like Antwerp and Hamburg… the needs of future generations seem to be anticipated in the same way that immediate requirements are met. In London, however, a hand-to-mouth policy seems to prevail.[710]

---

[707] Dougan, D.J., *A history of north east shipbuilding: being an attempt to describe and analyse the development of shipbuilding in the North East of England from earliest times to the end of 1967*, Unpublished MA Thesis, 1968, Durham University, pp144-145: http://etheses.dur.ac.uk/9906/. Retrieved 21 November 2020.

[708] Hudson Kearley, (1856-1934), Parliamentary Secretary to the Board of Trade, 1905-1909, created Lord Devonport, 1910, Chairman of the Port of London Authority, 1909-1925.

[709] *The Times*, 23 May 1907, p3.

[710] *The Times*, 25 May 1907, p14.

The bill did not actually pass into law until Lloyd George had moved on to the Exchequer, but it was very largely his work. The Authority commenced its duties on 31 March 1909, charged with "making good any deficiencies in the Port's accommodation, equipment and service both for ships and goods; to carry out all conservancy duties over sixty-nine miles of the tidal Thames and exercise the powers hitherto vested in the Watermen's Company relative to the registration and licensing of craft and boats as well as lightermen and watermen."[711] It functioned well and soon proved its worth.

Whilst living in London, his wife Margaret preferred to stay living quietly in the family home in Criccieth. Bengy Carey-Evans related that Margaret told Lloyd George in London to be very careful about flirting with society ladies in the city… he was defensive, replying in his letters that he needed his shirts ironing and so on, using the age-old tactic of avoiding the issue by changing the topic. However, the origin of the phrase the 'Welsh Goat', had nothing to do with his alleged sexual infidelities. Each evening ministers were given a box of papers to study, comment on, sign. Each morning, Lloyd George had dealt with all his papers, no matter how much was given him. Sometimes he rose at 4.00 am to work on them. So, eventually, it was said that as he was 'eating' all the paper, like a goat. It was actually the Permanent Secretary to the Board of Trade, Sir Francis Hopwood, who gave his new chief the nickname for "swallowing and digesting–with impressive speed–all the information with which he was fed."[712] The nickname stuck and only later did implacable enemies like Stanley Baldwin use it to malign other alleged aspects of his character.[713]

A couple of days after Asquith became prime minister on 5 April 1908, he wrote to Lloyd George to offer him the post of Chancellor of the Exchequer. Asquith took a gamble in offering Lloyd George such a senior position as he was seen as a left-wing extremist in some quarters. He reasoned that a disgruntled Lloyd George would be less of a problem inside the government than out. Asquith was also aware that Lloyd George was very popular with the general public:

> The offer, which I am privileged to make, is a well-deserved tribute to your long & eminent services to our Party, and to the splendid capacity which you have shown in the administration of the Board of Trade. I know, from experience, both the attractions & the difficulties of the Exchequer. It is at once the most thankless, & the most full of opportunities, in the whole Government.[714]

Lloyd George accepted, becoming Chancellor on 12 April, really being the founding father of the modern Welfare State, introducing radical reform across a broad front. The first Chancellor who had not been to a private school, he was considered to be a "man of the people". In one earlier speech, he had perceptively warned that, if the Liberals did not pass radical legislation, after the next election, the working-class would vote for the Labour Party:

---

711 http://www.pla.co.uk/Port-Trade/History-of-the-Port-of-London-pre-1908. Retrieved 23 June 2020.
712 Hattersley, p187. Grandson Bengy was convinced of this, as is his daughter, Davina.
713 Campbell, *Lloyd George*, p242.
714 NLW, MS 20462C, no.2285, Asquith to DLG, 8 April 1908 ('Secret').

If at the end of our term of office it were found that the present Parliament had done nothing to cope seriously with the social condition of the people, to remove the national degradation of slums and widespread poverty and destitution in a land glittering with wealth, if they do not provide an honourable sustenance for deserving old age, if they tamely allow the House of Lords to extract all virtue out of their bills, so that when the Liberal statute book is produced it is simply a bundle of sapless legislative faggots fit only for the fire–then a new cry will arise for a land with a new party, and many of us will join in that cry.[715]

In introducing the second reading of the Old Age Pensions Bill on 15 June 1908, Lloyd George pointed out:

You have never had a scheme of this kind tried in a great country like ours, with its thronging millions, with its rooted complexities… This is, therefore, a great experiment… We do not say that it deals with all the problems of unmerited destitution in this country. We do not even contend that it deals with the worst part of that problem. It might be held that many an old man dependent on the charity of the parish was better off than many a young man, broken down in health, or who cannot find a market for his labour. The provision which is made for the sick and unemployed is grossly inadequate in this country… These… are problems with which it is the business of the State to deal; they are problems which the State has neglected too long … [W]e are anxious to utilise the resources of the State to make provision for undeserved poverty and destitution in all is branches.[716]

Despite predictable opposition from a small core of right-wing Tories, his approach worked because it was both radical, popular, *and* practical: how was all the Liberal social legislation to be paid for? "With Lloyd George at the Exchequer, the answer was differential direct taxation: for better or worse an infinitely expansive instrument of progressive social reform."[717]

In August, soon after becoming Chancellor, Lloyd George visited Germany. This trip has received far less subsequent publicity than his one in 1936, but in fact it was of much greater significance. On 14 July Lloyd George had met the German Ambassador to London, Count Paul Metternich[718], the meeting arranged by Grey. Here, and again on 28 July, he proposed a reduction in the tempo of German shipbuilding to cool the naval race, suggesting a 3:2 ratio between the British and German fleets. Lloyd George later wrote:

Metternich, reporting this to Berlin, had urged that the British Chancellor of the Exchequer, whom he described as "one of the most outstanding personalities in England, and one who most probably would be called upon one day to stand at the head of a Liberal Government," should be treated with the utmost consideration. The Kaiser accordingly arranged that I should

[715] Speech at Penrhyndeudraeth, 25 September 1906.
[716] Hansard, 4th Series, House of Commons, CXC, cc.584-6, 612, 15 June 1908.
[717] Stocks, p53.
[718] Paul Graf Metternich zur Gracht (1853-1934), Prussian and German Ambassador to London, 1901-1912.

> be invited to pay him a visit. But in the meantime Metternich came over hurriedly to talk to the German Imperial Chancellor, von Buelow[719], who had reprimanded him for his incautious conversation with me. I understand that von Buelow was warned that I should certainly discuss the Navy with His Imperial Majesty, and that if Wilhelm used to my face the sort of remark he had noted on Metternich's report, a grave instance of *lèse-majesté* would be liable to ensue. A hasty warning was sent to Court and I never received the Kaiser's suggested invitation.[720]

The use of the newish invention of the motor car made the journey throughout Germany the more comprehensive.

> As chancellor, Lloyd George was already working on schemes to make the treasury the agent of a new far-reaching programme of social welfare. In Germany, he sought to crystallize his views with first-hand investigation of Bismarckian schemes for social insurance, especially invalidity pensions, broadening into health education and taking in en route German labour exchanges created to cope with the problem of unemployment. He began in Bavaria at Nuremburg, went briefly into Austria, and took the spa waters at Carlsbad, travelled up through the southwest via Stuttgart, Karlsruhe and Frankfurt, ending up in Hamburg, Bremen and the North Sea Coast. In Hamburg, the chancellor was much impressed by the seafaring connections with Britain treasured by the mercantile community there, dating from the days of the Hanseatic League.[721]

Lloyd George was hosted by Charles Henry[722] and his wife Julia[723], and accompanied by Harold Spender, who left an account of the trip. It was an eventful one, not only in political terms. Lloyd George later recorded:

> I was… deeply impressed by a scene I witnessed at Stuttgart… On our arrival there we learnt that a 'Zeppelin' was about to make an exhibition flight. We went along to the field where the giant airship was moored, to find that by a last-minute accident it had crashed and been wrecked. Of course we were deeply disappointed, but disappointment was a totally inadequate word for the agony of grief and dismay which swept over the massed Germans who witnessed the catastrophe. There was no loss of life to account for it. Hopes and ambitions far wider than those concerned with a scientific and mechanical success appeared to have shared the wreck of the dirigible. Then the crowd swung into the chanting of 'Deutschland über Alles' with a fanatic fervour of patriotism. What spearpoint of Imperial advance did this airship portend? These

---

719 Bernhard Martin, Prince of Bülow (1849-1929), Chancellor of the German Empire, 1900-1909.

720 Lloyd George, *War Memoirs*, Vol.I, p8-17, quote on p17; E.L. Woodward, *Great Britain And The German Navy*, 1935, London, Oxford University Press, p171-174.

721 Morgan, *Lloyd George and Germany*, p757. Closer to home, slate from Porthmadog had been used to help reroof Hamburg after its catastrophic fire of 5-8 May 1842, and the trade had quickly become a hugely important business; Hughes and Eames, p31. Sadly, of course, this would end in 1914.

722 Sir Charles Henry (1860-1919), Jewish Australian-born businessman and friend, Liberal MP for Wellington (Shropshire), 1906-1918, then The Wrekin from 1918 to his death.

723 Lady Julia Henry (née Lewisohn, 1872-1927), German-American heiress, married in 1892.

incidents were cracks in the cold surface, through which the hot, seething lava of unrest could be seen stirring uneasily underneath.[724]

Spender recorded another, ominous–with hindsight–incident in Stuttgart:

Parallels from history are dangerous; but they always haunt the mind of a well-read imaginative man. Mr. Lloyd George is very fond of them... when we were sitting in the Orangerie at Stuttgart... the conversation began to turn on the possibilities of a war between Britain and Germany. The parallel of Rome and Carthage came like a flash from Mr. Lloyd George; it brought from him one of those far-reaching forecasts which, in other days, would have earned him the mantle of a prophet. "There is the same commercial rivalry," he said, "the same sea-jealousy, the same abiding quarrel between the soldier and the merchant, the warrior and the shopkeeper, the civilization that has arrived and the civilization that is still struggling to arrive." He paused, and then he added: "I wonder if we shall be as unprepared as Carthage; I wonder if we shall be as torn by faction?"[725]

In Carlsbad on 10 August, Lloyd George was interviewed by the Viennese *Neue Freie Presse*, published on the front page of the morning edition of 12 August. Biographer W. W. Davies summarised:

[He said] that, although he did not suppose that an *entente* between England and Germany was possible at the moment, or even in the near future, yet it was his belief that the tension which was afflicting Europe so grievously could only be effectually ended by a cordial understanding between the two nations. "I believe", he declared, "that we must work for the conclusion of an *entente* between England and Germany in order that we may be able to devote ourselves wholly to the tasks of peace, of progress, and of social reform." Nevertheless, he made it plain that there could be no hope whatsoever of such an *entente*, nor even of the checking of the growing feeling of mutual hostility, unless naval rivalry could be laid aside; for he was as perfectly aware as any Germano-phobe in the British Parliament that England would never tolerate the greatest land power in Europe making itself the greatest sea power as well. Indeed... England was fully determined to maintain the two-power standard. Both countries, he pointed out, were devoting millions of pounds every year to this futile and dangerous rivalry. Would it not be better (and here we see what was nearest his heart all the time) that the money, or at least a good part of it, should be directed to the purpose of enriching the lives of the people? Most emphatically did he repudiate the suggestion that King Edward was bent upon the encirclement of Germany. The King had gone to Réval, he declared, simply and solely to set a seal upon the liquidating of ancient differences between England and Russia which had been accomplished in the previous year.[726] "There must be an end", he said, "to the evil game of setting England and Germany

[724] Lloyd George, *War Memoirs*, Vol.I, p19. The 136m long Zeppelin *LZ4* was completely destroyed when crashing at Flugfeld Stuttgart-Echterdingen on 5 August 1908. The three crew escaped serious injury.
[725] Spender, *Prime Minister*, p348-49.
[726] King Edward VII and Czar Nicholas II met on their yachts on 9 June off Réval (from 1918 Tallinn, Estonia).

> upon each other like two dogs." Finally, he castigated those newspapers in both countries which were for ever trying to excite suspicion and animosity, instead of trying to promote a friendly understanding.
>
> This interview caused considerable stir in many quarters. In France it created much uneasiness; for French policy at the time was directed almost wholly to the detaching of England from Germany, and forcing her into an alliance with herself and Russia. Much excitement was also aroused in Germany and Austria; and while some maintained that England was again holding out the olive branch… others argued that this was but one more Machiavellian device intended to arrest the progress of Germany's new navy. At home in England the interview was praised or blamed according to whether its readers desired to see friendship established with Germany, or regarded such a consummation as already impossible.[727]

On 21 August Lloyd George toured the large plant of the Allgemeine Electricitäts Gesellschaft (AEG) in Berlin[728], then met the Imperial Secretary for the Interior, Dr Bethmann-Hollweg[729], conferring privately for an hour and a half. Lloyd George was on a fact-finding mission; upon his arrival in Berlin he called immediately upon the Secretary:

> Who suggested the best method of getting a grasp on the invalid and old-age pension system, and after several hours spent in visiting the imperial insurance department and examining a number of workmen's dwellings, dined with the Minister of the Interior under the trees in the Zoological Garden restaurant. Most of the Ministers are absent on vacation, but a number of Under Secretaries of State participated in the dinner.[730]

Of Bethmann-Hollweg himself, Lloyd George later wrote: "[He] was an attractive but not an arresting personality. He gave me the idea of an intelligent, industrious and eminently sensible bureaucrat, but he did not leave on my mind an impression of having met a man of power who might one day shake destiny."[731] Their conversation was said to be "confined entirely to old-age insurance." The Germans had had such a scheme in place since 1883, and Lloyd George wanted to know more. Harold Spender said:

> We visited most of the largest towns of the German Empire, and had conversations with employers and workmen–Socialists and trade unionists–as well as with officials. Never was a

---

727 W. W. Davies, p301-302. For the original German, see http://anno.onb.ac.at/cgi-content/anno?aid=nfp&datum=19080812&seite=1&zoom=33; http://anno.onb.ac.at/cgi-content/anno?aid=nfp&datum=19080812&seite=2&zoom=33. Retrieved 4 October 2020.

728 Grigg, *People's Champion*, p163.

729 Theobald von Bethmann Hollweg (1856-1921), Independent, Vice-Chancellor and Secretary of State for the Interior, 24 June 1907–10/14 July 1909, Chancellor, 14 July 1909–13 July 1917.

730 https://timesmachine.nytimes.com/timesmachine/1908/08/22/104749271.pdf. Retrieved 17 January 2019.

731 Lloyd George, *War Memoirs*, Vol.I, p18.

> statesman's holiday spent in a more thorough investigation of a great problem of the lives of the people.[732]
>
> Bethmann-Hollweg did not talk politics until towards the end of dinner. The conversation drifted to King Edward's visit to the Russian Czar at Réval. That visit had caused a great ferment in Germany, and grave suspicions of British intentions. Bethmann-Hollweg voiced those suspicions in the frankest manner. "You are trying to encircle us!" he cried to Mr. Lloyd George. "You and France and Russia are attempting to strangle us!"
>
> Mr. Lloyd George assured him of the friendliness of Great Britain towards all the great Powers; but for the moment he refused to be appeased. He thumped the table with his hand. "The Prussian Government has only to lift a finger," he cried, "and every living Prussian will die for the Fatherland!"
>
> Mr. Lloyd George listened to all this with his characteristic calmness and good-humour. "But what about the other Germans?" he put in at this point.
>
> A shadow passed over the face of the Prussian Minister.
>
> "Oh! they?" he said with a gesture. "They, too, will come along!"
>
> But this was only a flash. On the whole, Bethmann-Hollweg was very friendly; and the facts of his family life showed him Anglophile. He had sent his son to an English University; and admiration for English education was, curiously enough, just at that moment almost as much a fashion in Germany as admiration for German education in England. When we were lunching with a judge at Frankfort Mr. Lloyd George discovered that the daughter of the house had actually been at school along with his own daughter [Olwen] at the famous English girls' school near Brighton–Roedean.[733]

Not intending to hear only the government's view of matters, in Berlin Lloyd George also talked for three hours with Eduard Bernstein, leader of the 'Revisionist' wing of the Social Democratic Party (SPD). In Frankfurt he had already interviewed the general secretary of the Social Democratic trade unions' executive.[734] Hamburg was a great success. On 24 August he spoke at length with Richard Krogmann, the president of the new *Seekasse* (Seamen's Insurance Organization) there, whom he had already met in May 1906.[735] Spender noted:

> The people of Hamburg were remarkably friendly to us. The merchants trading with England gave us an especially enthusiastic reception. They feasted us at a banquet at which sat the Hamburg Prussian Minister–for Berlin keeps a Ministry in the "Free Towns" as a last relic of their former independence.[736]

The *North Wales Express* noted, under the title 'Mr Lloyd George On Peace':

---

732 Spender, *Prime Minister*, p151.
733 Ibid., p154-155. Of course, Spender was writing in 1920, his memory coloured by the war.
734 Grigg, *People's Champion*, p163. Eduard Bernstein (1850-1932).
735 H. Pohlmann, *Richard C. Krogmann 1859-1932: Leben Und Leisbung Eines Hamburgischen Kaufmanns Und Reeders*, 1986, Hamburg, Verein Fur Hamburgische Geschichte, p206.
736 Spender, *Prime Minister*, p156. See also Pohlmann, p206-208.

> Herr Krogmann… delivered a speech of welcome in English. He referred to the negotiations which took place last year regarding the deep load line, and said that with no country did Hamburg have such cordial trade relations as with Great Britain. There had always been competition, and progress governed the world. If England and Germany were not rivals, other nations would step in and thrust them out. In conclusion, Herr Krogmann said Germany knew how to appreciate Mr Lloyd George's efforts to bring about peace and a good understanding between the two countries.
>
> Mr Lloyd George, in reply, said he had come back to Hamburg because he had such pleasant and happy memories of his last visit, when he had learned to love the people of Hamburg so much. On his last visit he had settled the question of the loadline. It was a question full of complications and difficulties, and if we had wanted to quarrel, two nations could have quarrelled over the loadline as well as over anything else. "Instead of that, we came to an arrangement. Instead of sending battleships to drive our arguments into one another's heads with 12-inch guns, we sent Captain Chalmers and you sent Herr Krogmann with good sound arguments instead of 12-inch guns. Helped by the tact and skill of Hamburg, they had settled the matter. Why not settle the loadline of nations, so that ships of State should not be sunk by the burden of armament. England and Germany needed one another; they could help each other; and he proposed the toast, 'Enduring friendship between Great Britain and Germany. May God watch over them and prosper them both.'"[737]

Spender added:

> The authorities of Hamburg provided a launch to take us into every corner of their famous port, so as to show us all the power and pride of their new creation–with all its marvellous up-to-date devices for handling ships and cargoes, its wonderful new docks and elevators, its ingenious and multifarious resources for expediting sea-traffic. It was good to see that port; if only to realise the wisdom of the King's advice to us at home–"Wake up, Britain!"[738]

If Lloyd George was impressed by the Germans, they were impressed by him, Spender recording:

> The German officials told me that they had never had a visitor with a quicker mind than Mr. Lloyd George. After a long day spent in the Central Insurance Office at Berlin, the men who went round with us were very enthusiastic. "He grasps the system more rapidly than any student we have ever had." Mr. Lloyd George, indeed, made a very exhaustive study of the German system. But in his Act he improved upon it and added to it in many important respects.[739]

Returning to England on the SS *Kronprinz Wilhelm*, the party docked in Southampton on 26 August.

---

737 *North Wales Express*, 28 August 1908, p5. In November 1911 Krogmann again met Lloyd George while on a business trip to London: Pohlmann, p208-209.

738 Spender, *Prime Minister*, p156.

739 Ibid., p158-159. The improvements, he footnoted, were "He raised the level of the sick benefit; he added several new benefits; and he paid the doctors better."

On the train to London, Lloyd George gave the Press Association his first reaction to the German social insurance system, saying he was "tremendously impressed with the finished character and perfection of the whole machine." But he was of the opinion that the non-contributory pension was best for old people, and had yet to decide whether or not it would be possible to graft onto the non-contributory system for old age pensions, a contributory system for invalidity and sickness.[740] Apart from ideas and impressions, one thing Lloyd George brought back with him was a splendid dark green Tyrolean cloak, that became almost an inseparable trademark of his, as seen in many photographs taken after this date.[741]

Characteristically, Lloyd George was no sooner back in the country, than he returned to Wales for the National Eisteddfod, held that year on 1-5 September in Llangollen, Denbighshire. The Gorsedd ceremony was held on the Hermitage Field, next to Plas Newydd. The Eisteddfod itself took place on the old Vicarage Field opposite Fronhyfryd. The *Welsh Coast Pioneer* recorded Lloyd George's attendance on the Thursday:

> Mr Lloyd George, with Mrs Lloyd George, entered, and as the popular Chancellor took the chair his fellow-countrymen again leaped to their feet frantically waving their hats and umbrellas, and shouting themselves hoarse in welcome. His presidential address... was brief, and contained... the anticipation that when English civilisation reaches the high level of that of Wales, a British Eisteddfod would be held on the Epsom Race-course. The mountains of Wales had fostered her nationalism, and bred in them a spirit of independence which had enabled them to withstand the assault and oppression of their enemies for so many centuries... Wales was at length beginning to climb upwards... and his faith was firm in his country's future.[742]

His popularity is evident, but the brevity of his address perhaps indicated the Chancellor's tiredness from his recent hectic trip abroad and the pressure of the connected urgent business in hand.

An unlikely seeming figure to accompany Lloyd George to this very Welsh event was Winston Churchill, the quintessential Englishman. In fact, Lloyd George and Churchill were such close friends and allies, that, at least up until the start of the Great War, they were derisively called by their many political enemies 'the Heavenly Twins', as they were held to be as gifted, inseparable but irresponsible children.[743] Churchill, over eleven years younger than Lloyd George, was still the 'junior' partner in the relationship, still not addressing the senior man by his first name in correspondence. When they were out walking at Llangollen, with Lloyd George's friend D. R. Daniel, Churchill suddenly exclaimed:

---

740 *The Times*, 27 August 1908; Grigg, *People's Champion*, p163.

741 W. W. Davies, p306.

742 *Welsh Coast Pioneer*, 10 September 1908, p5. The reporter was Beriah Gwynfe Evans. The Gorsedd stone circle was later moved into the grounds of Plas Newydd.

743 W. T. Stead, *Coming Men On Coming Questions*, No.1, 13 April 1905, p3; Toye, p73, quoting John Burns Diary for 6 February 1912. The term was derived from two novels by Sarah Grand, *The Heavenly Twins* (1893) and *The Beth Book* (1897); see Rintala, *Lloyd George And Churchill*, pix-x.

> You are much stronger than I am. I have noticed that you go about things quietly and calmly, you do not excite yourself, but what you wish happens as you desire it. I am too excitable, I tear about, and make too much noise.[744]

Churchill was given a tour of the proceedings by Lloyd George and daughter Megan, aged five. It was on this occasion that he was introduced to A. G. Edwards, the Bishop of St Asaph, who was to officiate at his forthcoming marriage to Clementine Hozier. Edwards would seem an obscure choice for such a society event, but he was "an old and close friend of Lloyd George and the evidence suggests that it was he who chose the bishop on Churchill's behalf."[745] This was at short notice, as Winston had only proposed to Clementine in August. In his letter of congratulations to Churchill, Lloyd George wrote: "Your luck has followed you into the most important transaction of your life."[746] So, when, on 12 September, Winston and Clementine were married in St. Margaret's, Westminster, Lloyd George was one of the principal guests in attendance. Lloyd George was also the only Cabinet colleague of Churchill's to attend, and the only non-family friend invited to sign the register.[747] The politically obsessed Churchill started talking politics to Lloyd George "in the vestry and was quite oblivious of the fact that he had to take out the bride."[748]

The Old Age Pensions Act 1908 was originally introduced by Lloyd George on 28 May:

> … after the Budget Speech, and reached its Second Reading stage on the 15th June 1908. On moving that the Bill be read a second time, the Chancellor… explained the principles on which the Government had proceeded in framing the measure, and his speech contains practically all the arguments for and against the various schemes that have been propounded, including that which is embodied in the Bill. The Chancellor… said that a contributory scheme was impossible in this country, because it would practically exclude women from its benefits, and because "the majority of working men are unable to deflect from their weekly earnings a sufficient sum of money to make adequate provision for old age, in addition to that which they are now making for sickness, infirmity, and unemployment." In this speech the Chancellor… foreshadowed the changes which ultimately were made in the Bill by the introduction of a sliding scale, and he stated that the Government would not offer any strenuous resistance to the amendment of the Bill in that direction, and that he was quite prepared to give due weight to the considerations in favour of such a scale.[749]

The Act received royal assent on 1 August, providing the first state pension for those over 70, an issue championed by Lloyd George since 1892. It "helped to lift the shadow of fear of the workhouse from

---

744 Quoted in Robert Lloyd George, *David and Winston*, p38.
745 Robert Lloyd George, *David and Winston*, p49.
746 Quoted in Robert Lloyd George, *David and Winston*, p49.
747 Robert *Lloyd George*, David and Winston, p49.
748 Riddell, *Diaries*, 1986, p20. The first entry in Riddell's Diary, dated 17 October 1908. George Riddell (1865-1934), knighted on 28 July 1909 on Asquith's recommendation.
749https://archive.org/stream/oldagepensionsa00britgoog/oldagepensionsa00britgoog_djvu.txt , quoting Hansard, 4th Series, House of Commons, CXC, c.569. Retrieved 26 January 2019.

the lives of countless elderly people".[750] The Labour Party and the Trades Union Congress were disappointed by the proposals, though they were broadly popular with ordinary people. Recipients of the pension generally felt grateful; for decades after, health and old age benefit payments received under the scheme were popularly known as "the Lloyd George benefit" or simply "the Lloyd George".[751]

The Act provided for a non-contributory old age pension for people over the age of 70, with the cost being borne by younger generations[752], set at a weekly pension of 5s a week to single people and 7s 6d for married couples. The level of benefit was deliberately set low to encourage workers to also make their own provision for retirement. To be eligible, they had to be earning less than £31. 10s. per year and had to pass a 'character test'; only those with a 'good character' could receive the pensions. One also had to have been a UK resident for at least 20 years to qualify and people who hadn't worked their whole life were not eligible.[753] Also excluded were those in receipt of poor relief, people being held in 'lunatics asylums', ex-prisoners for ten years after their release, persons convicted of drunkenness (at the discretion of the court), and any person who was guilty of 'habitual failure to work' according to one's ability. The pension was due to be paid from 1 January 1909 and those eligible had to apply to a local pension committee starting in October 1908 set up by the county councils. Forms for applicants were available from the end of September 1908 and had to be returned to the postmaster of the post office that would pay the individual's benefit. The claims were assessed by the pension officers and then sent to the local pension committee for approval.[754] By 31 December 1908 a total of 596,038 pensions had been granted: 338,948 in England (excluding Monmouthshire), 21,956 in Wales (including Monmouthshire), 64,769 in Scotland and 170,365 in Ireland.

Initially, most of the recipients of the pension benefit were women. To remove any stigma in receiving the benefit, the scheme was administered by the Post Office rather than the existing social welfare agencies such as the parish or the workhouses established by the Poor Law Amendment Act of 1834. In Wales, the pension was called *'Coron Lloyd George'* ('Lloyd George's Crown'), where the first person said to receive it was Mr Thomas Thomas, a blacksmith of Gwyddelwern, Merionethshire. The new pensioner had waited outside the Post Office since 6.00 am to collect his coin, which he then promptly handed back to the Postmaster, Mr Lloyd, for safekeeping![755]

On 1 October 1908, Lloyd George had been the principal speaker at the Welsh National Liberal Convention held in the Albert Hall, Swansea, where he had re-stated the old Liberal commitment to freedom and equality, to steady and sure reform. Beyond that, he had underlined his firm commitment to the social element of 'New Liberalism', to "ameliorating the conditions of life for the multitude", declaring:

---

[750] Price, 2006, p191.

[751] Thomson, p179; Rintala, *Lloyd George And Churchill*, p102.

[752] In 1911 the average life expectancy at birth in England and Wales was 51.5 years for males, 55.4 years for females.

[753]https://archive.org/stream/oldagepensionsa00britgoog/oldagepensionsa00britgoog_djvu.txt. Retrieved 26 January 2019.

[754]http://researchbriefings.files.parliament.uk/documents/SN04817/SN04817.pdf. Retrieved 26 January 2019.

[755] On display at the Lloyd George Museum, oddly misdated 1911. Thomas Thomas (c.1826–5 March 1914).

> The new Liberalism, while pursuing this great political ideal with unflinching energy, devotes a part of its endeavour also to the removing of the immediate causes of discontent. It is true that men cannot live by bread alone. It is equally true that a man cannot live without bread… It is a recognition of that elemental fact that has promoted legislation like the Old Age Pensions Act. It is but the beginning of things… In so far as poverty is due to circumstances over which the man has no control, then the State should step in to the very utmost limit of its resources, and save the man from the physical and mental torture involved in extreme penury… The aged we have dealt with during the present Session. We are still confronted with the more gigantic task of dealing with the rest–the sick, the infirm, the unemployed, the widows, and the orphans. No country can lay any real claim to civilisation that allows them to starve. Starvation is a punishment that society has ceased to inflict for centuries on its worst criminals, and at its most barbarous stage humanity never starved the children of the criminal… Is it just, is it fair, is it humane to let them suffer privation? I do not think the better-off classes, whose comfort is assured, realise the sufferings of the unemployed workmen. What is poverty? Have you felt it yourselves? If not, you ought to thank God for having been spared its sufferings and its temptations… By poverty I mean real poverty, not the cutting down of your establishment, not the limitation of your luxuries. I mean the poverty of the man who does not know how long he can keep a roof over his head, and where he will turn to find a meal for the pinched and hungry little children who look to him for sustenance and protection. That is what unemployment means.[756]

On 3 January 1909 the *People*, a Tory-leaning Sunday paper, published an article implying that a senior politician was to be cited as a co-respondent in a forthcoming divorce case which would cause his "social and political ruin and degradation."[757] A subsequent article entitled 'The Price of Peace' claimed that the wronged husband had been bought off with the colossal sum of £20,000 [£3,042,266 in 2025]. The articles were couched in deliberately vague terms but were undoubtedly aimed at Lloyd George with the express purpose of destroying him. He was left with no choice but to fight the allegations, and he assembled his defence team, comprising Rufus Isaacs, F. E. Smith and Raymond Asquith.[758]

They advised him to sue for libel, and the case was heard on 12 March 1909 in the King's Bench Division, before Mr Justice Lawrence, with Sir Edward Carson and Edward Duke acting for the newspaper. Perhaps crucially, Margaret very loyally and bravely turned up at the court to give her full moral and public support to her husband. From the witness box, a pale and agitated Lloyd George stated that "The paragraphs are an absolute invention, every line of them."[759] The unsupported allegations were indeed wafer thin, and the proceedings took little more than half an hour to conclude: the proprietors of the *People* admitted the libel and expressed their profound and unqualified regret

[756] *The Cardiff Times*, 3 October 1908, p7.
[757] Quoted in Hague, p237.
[758] A weekly tabloid, *The Bystander*, had already published a similar story under the heading *Mr Chancellor's Troubles* on 29 July 1908. The proprietor immediately admitted the libel and offered to make reparation out of court. On 16 September the paper published a full apology and paid £315 to Lloyd George's designated charity, the Caernarvon Cottage Hospital. See Owen, p162-163.
[759] *People*, 14 March 1909.

for the publication of the paragraph concerned. To Lloyd George himself they "wished to offer the most sincere and frank apology, without reserve of any kind and to say that the statements were unfounded and absolutely without justification."[760] They further agreed to pay damages of £1,000, the judge remarking that he considered Lloyd George had acted with "extreme moderation" in accepting so little.[761] The judge explained that he had taken the unusual course of allowing the case to be heard at once, though the pleadings had only been completed the day before. The Chancellor was actually framing his Budget, and he could not do his duty to his office or his country with such a charge hanging over his head. A relieved Lloyd George decided to use the money to build a village institute in Llanystumdwy on land donated by William George, observing that it was "Not due to the greatness of my own benevolence, but the hatred of my enemies."[762]

It was at this time that the *Carnarvon and Denbigh Herald* published an insight into Lloyd George's life at No. 11 Downing Street, penned by T. P. O'Connor:[763]

> "It is," he says, "a simple home, even though it finds itself in the splendid opulence of 11, Downing Street. A couple of young Welsh girls attend to the small wants of the little household…
>
> And of that home the brightest, the prettiest, most fascinating figure is Megan. Who is Megan? It is a question which Megan herself would find it hard to answer. To the world she is Lloyd George's youngest daughter… But this is only the obvious.
>
> Megan… has childhood's extraordinary power of creating a world of dreams which is as real to her as the world of reality…
>
> You will see her in the photograph taken of Lloyd George the other day, when he was so cordially greeted by the German working-men leaders in St. James's Park…[764]

This is interesting as it emphasizes the 'Celtic' nature of the household, its focus on Megan with no mention of Dame Margaret, but the respect accorded Lloyd George by the German workers after his visit to their home country. Everyone liked Megan–even Violet Asquith, who shared the same ingrained dislike of Lloyd George and all his works that prejudiced the political judgement of all her family, found Megan "delightful."[765]

Regarding the Welsh nature of the household, the virtual core of it was Sarah Jones, the shrewd and capable housekeeper brought with them from Criccieth. Born in 1871, she had entered the family employ in 1902 and she became a dominant fixture, staying with the family as housekeeper until just a couple of years before her death in 1958.[766] She was invariably addressed as 'Lallie', which may have

---

760 George, *My Brother And I*, p202.
761 For more detail, see *Evening Express*, 12 March 1909, p3.
762 Quoted in Owen, p164.
763 Thomas P. O'Connor (1848-1929), Irish Nationalist MP for Liverpool Scotland from 1885 until his death.
764 *Carnarvon and Denbigh Herald*, 7 May 1909, p5.
765 Bonham Carter and Pottle, *Lantern Slides*, p203. Diary entry for 18 April 1909.
766 The author thanks Robert D. Cadwalader, historian of Criccieth, for this information.

been tiny Megan's infantile attempts to pronounce 'Sarah' or, more likely, 'Sally'.[767] Grandson Owen later recorded:

> Although she came originally as nurse to Megan, her duties expanded to all departments, including helping my grandfather to dress. He was always quite hopeless with his fingers and incapable even of tying his shoelaces… Lallie remained with the family for over fifty years and was always the first person we grandchildren sought out on arrival at Criccieth.[768]

It was around this time–1909–that Lizzie Jones arrived, aged about 12, as a junior parlour maid. She also came from the Criccieth area, completing a domestic staff of seven, and was soon sent to school to learn to cook a variety of dishes that would suit the increasing number of foreign guests at No. 11. On 2 March 1916, she was married from the house, becoming the wife of Corporal Griffith Davies, twice wounded at Gallipoli and a King's Messenger. In old age, she remembered the kindness of Margaret, Lloyd George liking his milk puddings, and the dining room being locked, the diners helping themselves to a buffet, so that they could have undisturbed confidential conversations.[769]

Even in London, Lloyd George remained interested in Wales and Welsh concerns. Liberals had long been prominent in the campaign to establish a National Library of Wales, part of the social and political movement towards increasing Welsh consciousness and the desire to create institutions to embody it. A national library was first seriously proposed at the National Eisteddfod in Mold in 1873. In July 1891, Tom Ellis revived the campaign at a conference of Welsh local authorities in Shrewsbury. Stuart Rendel also fought for the library, in 1897 donating the site for a library building at Grogytha, Aberystwyth. Perhaps the most influential figure, however, was J. Herbert Lewis. He used every opportunity in debates in the Commons to advocate the establishment of a national library and later–in 1909–became the charter Vice President of the Library.[770] In June 1905, the Tory government relented and finally granted Wales its wish, leading to stiff competition between Cardiff and Aberystwyth for the location of the Library and its sister institution, the National Museum.

Lloyd George was in favour of Aberystwyth as the location of the Library. He was also, in his position as Chancellor of the Exchequer, in a position to give the nascent Library a crucial government grant. "What's the use of being a Welsh Chancellor of the Exchequer", he said to Herbert Lewis on 26 February 1909, "if one can do nothing for Wales?"[771] The Library was granted £2,500 per annum, and £500 a year for two years to catalogue manuscripts. The following year he granted £4,000. "Herbert Lewis was of the opinion that the National Library of Wales owed more to Lloyd George

---

[767] Jones, *Radical Life*, p16; Carey-Evans, p24.

[768] Lloyd George, *Two Grandfathers*, p17.

[769] The author thanks Sylvia Parry, granddaughter of Elizabeth Davies, for her kind permission to use information contained in an interview recorded with her Nain in 1986, plus copies of her Nain's Marriage Certificate and a notice from an unnamed contemporary newspaper.

[770] In early June 1925, walking in Cwm Woods above Aberystwyth before a meeting of the Library's council, Lewis fell 30-40 feet down a disused quarry, injuring his spine and leaving him permanently paralyzed. Elected President of the Library in 1926, it was an honorific appointment.

[771] Herbert Lewis Diary, 26 Feb., 11 Mar. 1909. NLW, Penucha MSS.

than to any other person."[772] Lewis later wrote to Lloyd George to thank him for this "courageous act", adding "The Library will be, at, I hope, a very distant date your literary mausoleum."[773] Lloyd George also granted £500 for the National Museum at Cardiff, and £1,500 the following year, and £15,000 for the Welsh Colleges. No government funds, however, were forthcoming for the building of the Library, which had to rely on donations: construction started in 1911 and was not completed until 1937.

Funding was further tightened by the ratchetting up of the Anglo-German naval arms race. After the German Naval Law of 27 March 1908, the Admiralty abandoned its plan for reduced construction and, in December 1908, proposed building at least six more dreadnought battleships.[774] Opposition in the Cabinet centred on the cost, led by Lloyd George and Churchill, who both saw such military expenditures as threats to the welfare reforms promised by the Liberals. Lloyd George warned Asquith that Liberal MPs would revolt at a proposal adding an estimated £38 million in naval expenditures to the budget. However, the Conservative opposition, the Navy League, and British arms industry advocated for the spending. In popular sentiment, they were joined by King Edward VII, who supported the construction of eight more dreadnoughts. George Wyndham[775], former Under-Secretary of State for War from 1898-1900, coined the popular slogan 'We want eight and we won't wait!'

Within the Cabinet itself, Lloyd George faced opposition from probably three-quarters of its members, leading to there being 14 meetings devoted to his budgetary proposals.[776] Despite being associated in the same 'Radical' camp as him, many of those attacking Lloyd George were men like Reginald McKenna, John Morley, Lord Loreburn[777], Lewis Harcourt[778] and John Burns, who despite having been anti-imperialists during the Boer War, were against rising expenditure, especially if some of it was going towards armaments. Indeed, Harcourt was amongst the Budget's foremost critics, Lloyd George's biographer Malcolm Thomson stating that he was "the most inveterate in obstructing his proposals, while posing all the time as an ardent Radical".[779]

Thus, in a position of supreme irony, Lloyd George had to rely on Liberal imperialists like Carrington[780], Churchill, Haldane[781] and Asquith to force his Budget through, those who accepted the

---

[772] D. Jenkins, *A Refuge in Peace and War: The National Library of Wales to 1952*, 2002, Cardiff, University of Wales Press, p138.

[773] Letter of 23 February 1910, quoted in Grigg, *Lloyd George And Wales*, p9. In a sense the NLW is indeed Lloyd George's literary mausoleum, being one of the main centres for Lloyd George documentation, holding seven important archives. Only the Parliamentary Archive of the House of Lords surpasses it.

[774] When commissioned on 2 December 1906 HMS *Dreadnought* revolutionised naval technology, being the most heavily gunned and fastest battleship in the world. She cost £1,785,683 [£277.47m in 2025] to build. Such was the pace of the technological arms race she unleashed that by 1914 she was already obsolete.

[775] George Wyndham (1863-1913), Tory MP for Dover from 1889. He died just before the outbreak of war, thus not seeing the tragic consequences of his militant brand of jingoistic imperialism.

[776] Packer, p14.

[777] Robert Reid, Earl Loreburn, (1846-1923), judge, radical Liberal MP, Lord High Chancellor, 1905-1912.

[778] Lewis Harcourt (1863-1922), son of Sir William Harcourt. First Commissioner of Works, 1905-1910.

[779] Thomson, p183.

[780] Charles Wynn-Carington (1843-1928), known as Earl Carrington, 1895-1912, President of the Board of Agriculture, 1905-1911.

[781] Richard Haldane (1856-1928), lawyer, philosopher, Liberal MP for Haddingtonshire, 1885-1911, Secretary of State for War, 1905-1912, responsible for the vital 'Haldane Reforms' of the Army, created Viscount Haldane, 27 March 1911, Lord Chancellor, 1912-1915, 1924. Labour from 1923.

need for new taxes for the Royal Navy and were less hostile to a greater role for the state in social reform. Carrington, a noted land reformer, was a particular supporter of Lloyd George's redistributive Budget, which he regarded as "bold, Liberal and humane".[782] This new configuration was of great significance. Previously, the main division in Liberalism had been between Radicals and Imperialists. After 1909 a new one appeared, cutting across old battle lines, between those who supported or opposed higher taxation and social reform.

Despite his support, Asquith wrote a few pathetic lines to amuse John Morley, which aptly demonstrate his real, cynical feelings about Lloyd George even as early as 1909:

George moves in a mysterious way,
His little sums to make:
Loose logic, lax arithmetic,
Contribute to the fake…[783]

In response to the broad support for increased naval strength, on 23 February 1909 Asquith arranged a compromise to start the construction of four dreadnoughts in the next financial year, with an additional four more by spring 1910, if they were needed. On 29 March the government defeated a Tory motion of no confidence by 353-135 votes. As Churchill wittily put it: "In the end a curious and characteristic solution was reached. The Admiralty had demanded six ships: the economists offered four: and we finally compromised on eight."[784] In turn, John Morley remarked of the bellicose Churchill: "If he ever goes to the Admiralty it will be sixteen we'll need, not eight." Lord Fisher made a jocular threat, "which was repeated in select circles, to call the four extra Dreadnoughts, Lloyd, George, Winston, and Churchill, in memory of the fight which had taken place in the Cabinet."[785]

The 'People's Budget' was introduced in Parliament by Lloyd George on 29 April 1909, with the House packed to capacity. He began his speech at 3.06 pm giving a poorly delivered five-hour oration with only a half hour adjournment when he was provided with a cup of beef tea to alleviate his fatigue, as he was suffering from a throat infection. He argued that the 'People's Budget' would eliminate poverty, and commended it in stark terms:

> This is a war Budget. It is for raising money to wage implacable warfare against poverty and squalidness. I cannot help hoping and believing that before this generation has passed away, we shall have advanced a great step towards that good time, when poverty, and the wretchedness and human degradation which always follows in its camp, will be as remote to the people of this country as the wolves which once infested its forests.[786]

---

782 Crosby*, Unknown*, p411.

783 Asquith to Venetia Stanley, 13 January 1915, in M. and E. Brock, Eds., *H. H. Asquith: Letters To Venetia Stanley*, 1985, Oxford, OUP, p378. His patronising, undermining antipathy to Lloyd George is already clear here, long before the latter supplanted him as Prime Minister, the oft-alleged cause of his dislike.

784 Churchill, *World Crisis*, Vol.I, p27.

785 Roch, p31.

786 For full text, see Du Parcq, Vol.IV, pp649-677. Concluding quote, p677.

From the press gallery, witnessing the Chancellor's radical proposals, Charles King speculated:

> It seemed like the sudden swinging back of the door now open to a new era, shall we say to the Liberal Party? Or shall we say in the closing of the career of the Liberal Party as we have known it? Who shall say whether in the future a few years hence there will be a Liberal Party in existence, or whether the advancing tide of Socialism shall have swept its most advanced remnants into the Socialistic ranks?[787]

Lloyd George's proposals met much opposition, both in Parliament and in the press, the Northcliffe Press (who published both *The Times* and the *Daily Mail*) strongly urging rejection of the budget. Lloyd George derided Lord Rothschild over his opposition, stating at a luncheon given by the Land and Housing Reform Joint Committee at the Holborn Restaurant on 24 June:

> I really think we are having too much Lord Rothschild. Are we to have all ways of reform, financial and social, blocked, simply by a notice-board; 'No Thoroughfare. By Order of Nathaniel Rothschild'?[788]

Then, fulfilling a promise made a month earlier, he made a fiery, eloquent speech before 4,000 people at the Edinburgh Castle music hall in Limehouse, one of the poorest areas of East London, on the evening of 30 July, one of the most famous, important and effective speeches of his life. To the expectant crowd, he vindicated his proposals as much as attacking his detractors, declaring passionately:

> A few months ago, a meeting was held not far from this hall in the heart of the City of London, demanding that the Government should launch into enormous expenditure on the Navy. That meeting ended up with a resolution promising that those who passed the resolution would give financial support to the Government in their undertaking. There have been two or three meetings held in the City of London since… but not ending up with a resolution promising to pay… What has happened since to alter their tone? Simply that we have sent in the bill. We started our four Dreadnoughts. They cost eight millions of money. We promised them four more. They cost another eight millions.
>
> Somebody has got to pay; and then these gentlemen say: Perfectly true; somebody has got to pay but we would rather that somebody were somebody else. We started building; we wanted money to pay for the building; so, we sent the hat round… and there has been such a howl ever since that it has completely deafened us…
>
> But they say, 'It is not so much the Dreadnoughts we object to; it is Pensions'… The Budget… is introduced not merely for the purpose of raising barren taxes, but taxes that are

[787] King, p307.

[788] C. Roth, *The Magnificent Rothschilds*, 1939, London, Robert Hale, p130. Nathaniel Rothschild, 1st Baron Rothschild (1840-1915), banker and Liberal Unionist politician.

fertile, taxes that will bring forth fruit–the security of the country, which is paramount in the minds of all. The provision for the aged and deserving poor–it was time it was done. It is rather a shame for a rich country like ours… that it should allow those who have toiled all their days to end in penury and possibly starvation. It is rather hard that an old workman should have to find his way to the gates of the tomb… through the brambles and thorns of poverty. We cut a new path for him… through fields of waving corn. We are raising money… so that 200,000 paupers shall be able to join in the march. There are so many in the country… with great wealth, and if there are amongst them men who grudge out of their riches a fair contribution towards the less fortunate of their fellow-countrymen they are very shabby rich men. We propose to do more by means of the Budget. We are raising money to provide against the evils and the sufferings that follow from unemployment. We are raising money for the purpose of assisting our great friendly societies to provide for the sick and the widows and orphans. We are providing money to enable us to develop the resources of our own land. I do not believe any fair-minded man would challenge the justice and the fairness of the objects which we have in view in raising this money.

But there are some of them who say, 'The taxes themselves are unjust, unfair, unequal, oppressive notably so the land taxes.' They are engaged… in assailing these taxes with a concentrated and sustained ferocity… Now, are these taxes really so wicked? Let us examine them; because it is perfectly clear that the one part of the Budget that attracts all the hostility and animosity is that part which deals with the taxation of land…

Lloyd George said he did not want his listeners to consider merely "abstract principles", but to consider "concrete illustrations" of how his Budget proposals would work. The first was "the tax on undeveloped land and on increment," shown through the example of his experiences with the Port of London and what he called "the fraud of the few and the folly of the many." He moved onto an example nearer to home:

I am a member of a Welsh County Council… The police committee the other day wanted a site for a police station. Well, you might have imagined that if a landlord sold land cheaply for anything it would have been for a police station. The housing of the working classes that is a different matter. But a police station means security for property.

Not at all. The total population of Caernarvonshire is not as much… as the population of Limehouse alone… And yet they demanded for a piece of land which was contributing 2s. a year to the rates, £2,500 an acre! All we say is, if their land is as valuable as all that, let it have the same value in the assessment book as it seems to possess in the auction-room. There are no end of these cases…

Now I come to the reversion tax… You have got a system in the country which is not tolerated in any other country of the world, except, I believe, Turkey; the system whereby landlords take advantage of the fact that they have got complete control over the land to let it for a term of years, spend money upon it in building, in developing it. You improve the building, and year by year the value passes into the pockets of the landlord, and at the end of sixty, seventy, eighty or ninety years the whole of it passes away to the pockets of a man who never spent a penny upon it… I know… quarry districts in Wales where a little bit of barren rock where you could not feed a goat, where the landlord could not get a shilling an acre for agricultural rent, is let to quarrymen for the purpose of building houses, where 30s or £2 a house is charged for ground rent. The quarryman builds his house. He goes to a building society to borrow money. He pays out of his hard-earned weekly wage contributions to the building society for ten, twenty or thirty years. By the time he becomes an old man he has cleared off the mortgage, and more than half the value of the house has passed into the pockets of the landlord…

These are the cases we have got to deal with. Look at all this leasehold system. This system… is not business, it is blackmail…

There is a limit even to the wrath of outraged landlords. We must really appease them; we must offer up some sacrifice to them. Suppose we offer the House of Lords to them? Well, you seem rather to agree with that. I will make the suggestion to them.

… I have just one other land tax, and that is a tax on royalties. The landlords are receiving eight millions a year by way of royalties.

What for? They never deposited the coal there. It was not they who planted these great granite rocks in Wales, who laid the foundations of the mountains.

Was it the landlord? And yet he, by some divine right, demands as his toll–for merely the right for men to risk their lives in hewing these rocks–eight millions a year… I went down to a coalfield the other day, and they pointed out to me many collieries there. They said: 'You see that colliery there. The first man who went there spent a quarter of a million in sinking shafts, in driving mains and levels. He never got coal, and he lost his quarter of a million. The second man who came spent 100,000–and he failed. The third man came along, and he got the coal'. What was the landlord doing in the meantime? The first man failed; but the landlord got his royalty, the landlord got his dead-rent … The second man failed, but the landlord got his royalty.

These capitalists put their money in, and I said: "When the cash failed what did the landlord put in?" He simply put in the bailiffs. The capitalist risks, at any rate, the whole of his money; the engineer puts his brains in; the miner risks his life.

I was telling you I went down a coalmine the other day. We sank into a pit half a mile deep. We then walked underneath the mountain, and we did about three-quarters of a mile with rock and shale above us. The earth seemed to be straining–around us and above us–to crush us in.

You could see the pit-props bent and twisted and sundered until you saw their fibres split in resisting the pressure. Sometimes they give way, and then there is mutilation and death. Often a spark ignites, the whole pit is deluged in fire, and the breath of life is scorched out of hundreds of breasts by the consuming flame. In the very next colliery to the one I descended just a few years ago three hundred people lost their lives in that way. And yet when the Prime Minister and I knock at the door of these great landlords, and say to them: "Here, you know these poor fellows who have been digging up royalties at the risk of their lives, some of them are old, they have survived the perils of their trade, they are broken, they can earn no more. Won't you give them something towards keeping them out of the workhouse?" … They say: "You thieves!" and they turn their dogs on to us, and you can hear their bark every morning. If this is an indication of the view taken by these great landlords of their responsibility to the people who at the risk of life create their wealth, then I say their day of reckoning is at hand.

The other day at the great Tory meeting held at the Cannon Street Hotel they had blazoned on the walls, "We protest against the Budget in the name of democracy, liberty and justice." Where does the democracy come in in this landed system? Where is the liberty in our leasehold system? Where is the seat of justice in all these transactions?…

I claim that the tax we impose on land is fair, is just and is moderate. They go on threatening that if we proceed, they will cut down their benefactions and discharge labour. What kind of labour?…

… They are going to cut down productive labour–their builders and their gardeners–and they are going to ruin their property so that it shall not be taxed.

All I can say is this–the ownership of land is not merely an enjoyment, it is a stewardship. It has been reckoned as such in the past; and if they cease to discharge their functions, the security and defence of the country, looking after the broken in their villages and in their neighbourhoods then these functions which are part of the traditional duties attached to the ownership of land, and which have given to it its title–if they cease to discharge those functions, the time will come to reconsider the conditions under which the land is held in this country.

No country, however rich, can permanently afford to have quartered upon its revenue a class which declines to do the duty which it was called upon to perform since the beginning. And, therefore, it is one of the prime duties of statesmanship to investigate those conditions…

We are placing burdens on the broadest shoulders. Why should I put burdens on the people? I am one of the children of the people. I was brought up amongst them. I know their trials; and God forbid that I should add one grain of trouble to the anxieties which they bear with such patience and fortitude. When the Prime Minister did me the honour of inviting me to take charge of the National Exchequer at a time of great difficulty, I made up my mind, in framing the Budget which was in front of me, that at any rate no cupboard should be barer, no lot would be harder. By that test I challenge them to judge the Budget.[789]

It was unheard of for a Cabinet member to make such an appeal in this period, and it heralded a new era of populist politics. Despite the speech sounding mild to modern ears, the Tory press reacted in a predictably rabid manner, cartoonists depicting the Chancellor as a highwayman, poacher, pirate, French Revolutionary, and bomb-throwing anarchist. A doggerel verse began circulating around Mayfair and Belgravia:

Lloyd George, no doubt, when life ebbs out
Will ride in a blazing chariot.
He'll ride in state on a red-hot plate
'Twixt the Devil and Judas Iscariot.
Ananias that day to the Devil will say–

789 https://www.parliament.uk/about/living-heritage/evolutionofparliament/houseoflords/parliamentacts/collections/limehouse/. Retrieved 25 January 2019.

"My right to precedent fails,
Move up a bit higher away from the fire,
Make room for this bounder from Wales."[790]

In the middle of this political turmoil, Lloyd George suffered another personal loss, that of his only sister, Pollie, his good friend, supporter and companion. She died of cancer in Criccieth on 9 August aged 47, having been ill for several years. Having had no career, she had become highly devout, channelling her energies into chapel life and the local community, living in Morvin House and then at Garthcelyn until her death. Her devotion to her family was such that she did not leave even after she married in 1897. Her husband, Philip Davies[791], was a sea captain from Pwllheli, often away for months at a time, and during those periods she acted as housekeeper and hostess for aging Betsy, Uncle Lloyd and bachelor William. Pollie had been thirty-five when she had married, and never had children. Thus, she took an active interest in her nieces and nephews. She was strict with them, a rigorous keeper of the Sabbath, but she also liked taking them on outings to Tripp Farm overlooking the sea, with games on the beach and a large picnic afterwards, or to Beddgelert, a beauty spot only some eleven miles distant.[792] Her premature loss was keenly felt. Lloyd George received the news as he was preparing his Budget. Later, sitting on the front benches in the Commons, he said to Charles Masterman: "How death alters things! All this seems to me like the chattering of apes!"[793]

He remained interested in the world and new things, however, viewing the opening day of the eight-day Grande Semaine d'Aviation de la Champagne on 22 August, held on the Bétheny Plain 5 km north of Reims, now celebrated as the first international public flying event, confirming the viability of heavier-than-air flight. Lloyd George, and fellow Liberal MP Sir Henry Norman, had motored from Boulogne, stopping the previous night at Compiegne. The Chancellor was much impressed and did not hesitate to express a wish that such a meeting could be held on Salisbury Plain or some other convenient spot in the British Isles.[794] Lloyd George, as usual, was thinking ahead. Only one of the 22 aviators was British, and Lloyd George told the *Daily Mail* "how hopelessly behind we are in these great and historic developments. I really felt, as a Britisher, rather ashamed that we were so completely out of it."[795]

Nonetheless, it was his absorption in the Budget that, in a sense, helped him through the loss of his sister. That, and the fact that he was still emotionally numbed after the loss of his dearly beloved daughter, Mair, only 20 months before. So, undeterred, Lloyd George followed up his earlier address with another to a capacity audience of over 4,000 in the Palace Theatre, Haymarket, Newcastle upon

790 Cregier, p128-129, quoting A. E. Gibby, Letter, *Manchester Guardian Weekly*, 6 April 1967.
791 Philip Davies (1863-1935). In the late 1880s he commanded the *Cambrian Prince*, a large square-rigger, on a voyage around Cape Horn to Batavia and Java: Hughes and Eames, p124. By the time of his wife's death, he was captain of the steamship *Suffolk*: see *North Wales Express*, *Mr Lloyd George's Bereavement: The Death Of Mrs Philip Davies*, 13 August 1909, p5. Philip was the uncle of Professor Seaborne Davies (1904-1984), briefly Liberal MP for Caernarvon Boroughs after Lloyd George, 26 April–5 July 1945.
792 Hague, p146.
793 L. Masterman. *C. F. G. Masterman*, p138-139.
794 https://www.gracesguide.co.uk/1909_Rheims_Aviation_Week;
https://en.wikipedia.org/wiki/Grande_Semaine_d%27Aviation_de_la_Champagne. Retrieved 18 August 2022.
795 Thompson, *Northcliffe*, p177.

Tyne, delivered on 9 October, making famously witty, trenchant observations regarding his obstructive opponents in the Lords. Its rhetoric was little short of revolutionary, and he delivered his "plain, straight talk" despite Asquith having written to him two days before asking him not to do anything that might compromise an attempt by the King to mediate with Balfour and Lansdowne.[796] However, the tide of history was with Lloyd George, who said:

> The Budget… has emerged out of its forty days and forty nights in the wilderness rather strengthened and improved… We have done our best to meet every hard case that was presented to us… and done it amidst the taunts of the very people who pressed them upon us whenever we listened to them, as I have had to do for five months. I have done five months' hard labour.
>
> Although we have made alterations and modifications, the Bill in its main structure remains. All the taxes are there. The land taxes are there. The super-tax is there. The poor fellows who are receiving only £5,000 a year and £10,000 and £20,000 a year will have to contribute just a little towards the expenses of the country. And then there is the man to whom somebody has left a fortune. He will have to contribute a little more. All these taxes remain… because, after all, when you order "Dreadnoughts," a respectable country like this must pay for them…
>
> … What is the chief charge against the Budget by its opponents? That it is an attack on industry and an attack on property! … it is neither. It is very remarkable that since this attack on industry was first promulgated in the House of Commons trade has improved… Industries which were making losses last year are beginning to make profits this year. The imports and the exports have gone up during the last few months by millions. Industrial investments have been steady… Only one stock has gone down badly; there has been a great slump in dukes. They used to stand rather high in the market, especially in the Tory market, but the Tory Press has discovered that they are of no value.
>
> The dukes have been making speeches recently. One especially expensive duke made a speech, and all the Tory Press said, "Well, now, really, is that the sort of thing we are spending £250,000 a year upon?" Because a fully-equipped duke costs as much to keep up as two "Dreadnoughts," and they are just as great a terror, and they last longer…
>
> Well, now, why should Liberalism be supposed to be ready to attack property? After all, they forget this: I lay down as a proposition that most of the people who work hard for a living in the country belong to the Liberal party. I would say… that most of the people who never worked for a living at all belong to the Tory party. And whenever you go across country you see men building up trade and business… by their enterprise not merely maintaining themselves and their families, but putting something by for evil days, hundreds of thousands… of them belong to the Liberal party.
>
> If you came to the House of Commons you might imagine that all the men who had anything to lose were on the Tory side of the House, and that the men who had nothing to lose all sit on the Liberal side, whereas, as a matter of fact, the richest men in the House of Commons… sit

[796] Gilbert, *Architect Of Change*, p384-96.

on the Liberal side… and yet we are told they are all engaged at the present moment in destroying property and industry and riches. Why are they engaged in the operation?… To pass a measure which taxes them to the extent of hundreds, maybe thousands, of pounds a year… That is the kind of rich men one honours, who are prepared to make sacrifices. Therefore, you may take it from me that the Liberal party is not a party that is likely to engage in a mere wanton war upon industry and upon property in this country. All we ask for is that wealth shall pay its fair share. We are simply seeking to establish in an Act of Parliament a very old friend and honoured fiscal principle that men should contribute to the needs of the State as God has prospered them.

… There are two classes who really object to the Budget. The first are those who are seeking to establish a complete change in the fiscal system of this country to tax food and they know that once this Budget is through there is an end to their desired opportunity. The tax will be on the right shoulders, and they cannot shift it. There is a second, and I think a most powerful class, who are the great landlords of this country… Why are they angrier about the land taxes than about any part of the Budget? We are raising this year eleven or twelve millions of money out of new taxation. We shall probably raise next year something approaching twenty millions by the same taxation. And yet the land taxes this year only produce £650,000.

Why, then, all this anger about these taxes?… The first reason is they are taxes that will grow. They only start at £650,000, and a good start, too. But, year by year, they are bound to grow. The increment duty will grow; the reversion duty will grow; the mineral duties will grow. The increment duty is bound to grow with the growth of the prosperity of this country, and that is a certainty. As you get an advance in science and advance in education it strengthens and develops the intelligence of the people, and directs it; as you get an advance in international ideas about peace, so that the wealth which is produced by the industry of the people is allowed to accumulate and the harvest is not trampled down by the ravages of war, the prosperity of Britain is assured, and the growth of prosperity is assured. As it grows, the value of land taxes will grow.

Not merely are the riches in this country growing, but there are more rich people. Year by year wealth is getting better distributed, and when a man acquires wealth, he wants not merely better housing accommodation, but… more land for recreation purposes, as well as for adornment… the working classes are demanding better homes, too. They are not satisfied with the dull, grey street of the past… They are asking for more air, more light, more room, more verdure, more sunshine, to recruit energies exhausted in toil, and… I believe this Budget will help them to get it. As… these new fruitful ideas develop more land will be required, and the more land you require the more taxes will come from the Budget, and therefore these are taxes that will grow.

… The chief objection of great landlords to this Budget lies in the fact that it has great valuation proposals. Why do they object to valuation?… It goes to the very root of all things in the land question. There has never been a public undertaking in this country, municipal, State, or industrial, there has never been an enterprise but that the landlord has generally secured anything from four to forty times as much for the value of the land as its agricultural price.

When I was at the Board of Trade I saw a good deal of it. I recollect a number of cases that were brought before me of complaints from the trading community as to the oppressive character of railway rates. From every part of the country, from every kind of business and undertaking, there was complaint that the heavy character of the railway rates was interfering with the successes and prosperity of that particular business… I went into it very carefully in hundreds of these cases, and I found in the end that it was not the railway companies that were to blame. They had had to pay for every yard of land they had used and often fifty times its real value.

You may get a railway passing through a barren stretch of country, passing on its way between one great hive of industry and another, where the land is well-nigh worthless… But the railway company comes along and says: 'We want to drive a railway through this wilderness!' What happens? The moment they ask for that land its value goes up enormously. Every trick and chicanery of the law… is exhausted in order to prove that this worthless land has enormous hidden value…

… There is not a railway train goods, luggage, or passenger in which there is not one truck carrying interest on the excessive prices paid to the landlords.

All this is a heavy burden upon industry at the present moment in this country. Now you see where valuation comes in. Take municipalities… You cannot go to a single locality where you do not get cases: schools where the future citizens of the Empire are being trained, waterworks, gas, electricity, anything you want land for, alive or dead, you have got to pay for it four times as much as its agricultural value to these great landlords. Start analysing the rates of any great city, and you will be surprised how much is attributable directly to the excessive prices paid by municipalities for land for purposes which are essential to the very life of the city, to the very life of a civilised community.

Then, to come to business… If you want to found a new business or to extend an old one, the charges for land are extravagant, especially if you want to extend, because you are there. A trader who has been building up a business in a particular locality… cannot carry his trade away as if it were a coster's barrow and plant it in the next street; he has to get his extension where he is. Then comes the landlord, who has done nothing, and demands the highest price he can possibly extort…

Hence the need for State valuation. The State valuer for the first time places a perfectly impartial valuation upon all the land of the kingdom. He separates the value of the land intrinsically from the value which is attributable to the expenditure by its owner. He thus for the first time forces the landlords to look at the value of land not merely from the point of view of a receiver, but of a payer. There is nothing like compelling a man to look at both sides of a question. That is really why they object to valuation. Whenever a great industry in the future requires land it can always quote the State valuation in answer to any extortionate and extravagant demands put forward on behalf of the landlords, and therefore they object, and object to it very strongly.

I should like to give you a few illustrations by way of showing to you how the new Budget taxes will work… Some of you may know the South Wales coalfield. It is not long ago since it was a very wild, unproductive country, most of it common land. Landlord Parliaments soon handed over the property to the great landlords when they discovered there was mineral value in it. At the present moment the South Wales coalfield pays a million and a half per annum in royalties to a few landlords, and in ground rents hundreds of thousands of pounds.

Let me give you just one or two figures which will show what is done there. You get first of all… poor agricultural land, where coal is discovered. The landlord leases the property to somebody who has the necessary enterprise and capital for purposes of development. The landlord himself does not sink any capital in these properties, except in rare instances. Somebody else does that, somebody else faces the risk of a loss, and the landlord takes sixpence a ton in the way of royalties.

What happens when you come to the surface? You must employ workmen for the purpose of carrying on your mining operations, and the workmen must have homes. So they start building, and the landlord then says: "Yes, certainly; by all means you may build, but you must pay a ground rent." There is land now leased in these valleys in South Wales which, within living memory… produced only a shilling an acre, where the landlord is now getting £30 and £40 per acre per annum, simply for the permission to build a few cottages upon it. They are able to build on lease, and in about sixty years the whole of this land will fall into the landlords' hands.

Take the Rhondda Valley… In the year 1851 the total population of the Valley was only a thousand. Today the population is 132,000. The landlords receive annually £200,000 in royalties. They receive £30,000 a year in ground rents. The colliery proprietors there pay in rates £54,000 a year. The landlords do not pay a penny… They charge for the minerals; they charge for the surface; whenever land is wanted for waterworks they charge heavy prices for it, railways have to pay, and between all these charges industry is burdened and the landlords do not contribute a penny towards the heavy and growing rates of the district…

And when I come along and say, "Here, gentlemen, you have escaped long enough, it is your turn now; I want you to pay just 5 per cent, on the £10,000 odd." "Five per cent?", they say to me. "You are a thief; you are worse, you are an attorney; worst of all, you are a Welshman." That always is the crowning epithet. Well, gentlemen, I do not apologise… I am proud of the little land among the hills… Whenever they hurl my nationality at my head, I say to them, "You Unionists! You hypocrites! Pharisees! You are the people who in every peroration… always talk about our being one kith and kin throughout the Empire…" … Well, they have got to stand the Welshman this time!…

I defy any reasonable man anywhere to say that there is any injustice in taxing men under these conditions, when the State needs the money. We want money for the defence of the country; to provide the pensions of the old people who have been spending their lives in tilling the soil at a very poor pittance, in sinking those mines, risking their lives. And when they are old we do not want to starve them or to humiliate them; and we say what better use can you make of wealth than to use it for the purpose of picking up the broken, healing the wounded, curing the sick, bringing a little more light, comfort, and happiness to the aged? These men ought to feel honoured that Providence has given them the chance to put a little into the poor-box, and since they won't do it themselves we have got to do it for them…

Well, now, we are going to send the Bill up all the taxes or none. What will the Lords do?... The more irresponsible and feather-headed amongst them want to throw it out. But what will the rest do? It will depend on the weather. There are some who are not fair-weather sailors, and they will go on. But poor Lord Lansdowne[797] with his creaking old ship and his mutinous crew there he is, he has got to sail through the narrows with one eye on the weather-glass and the other on the forecastle.

But it does not depend on him. It will depend, in the first place, probably on the reports from the country... The real sailing master is Sir Alexander Acland-Hood[798], the chief Whip of the Tory party... But still this is the great Constitutional party, and if there is one thing more than another better established about the British Constitution it is this, that the Commons, and the Commons alone, have the complete control of supply and ways and means; and what our fathers established through centuries of struggle and of strife even of bloodshed we are not going to be traitors to.

Who talks about altering... the Constitution? The... great Constitutional party. As long as the Constitution gave rank and possession and power to the Lords it was not to be interfered with...; as long as the Constitution enforced royalties and ground rents and fees and premiums and fines, and all the black retinue of exaction..., then the Constitution was inviolate... It was something that was put in the same category as religion, that no man should with rude hands touch... But the moment the Constitution looks round; the moment the Constitution begins to discover that there are millions of people outside park gates who need attention, then the Constitution is to be torn to pieces.

Let them realise what they are doing. They are forcing a revolution, and they will get it. The Lords may decree a revolution, but the people will direct it. If they begin, issues will be raised that they little dream of. Questions will be asked which are now whispered in humble voices, and answers will be demanded then with authority. *The question will be asked whether five hundred men, ordinary men chosen accidentally from among the unemployed, should override the judgment, the deliberate judgment of millions of people who are engaged in the industry which makes the wealth of the country.*

... Who ordained that a few should have the land of Britain as a perquisite? Who made ten thousand people owners of the soil, and the rest of us trespassers in the land of our birth? Who is it who is responsible for the scheme of things whereby one man is engaged through life in grinding labour to win a bare and precarious subsistence for himself, and when, at the end of his days, he claims at the hands of the community he served a poor pension of eightpence a day, he can only get it through a revolution, and another man who does not toil receives every hour of the day, every hour of the night, whilst he slumbers, more than his poor neighbour receives in a whole year of toil?... These are the questions that will be asked. The answers are charged with peril for the order of things the Peers represent; but they are fraught with rare and refreshing fruit for the parched lips of the multitude who have been treading the dusty road

797 Leader of the Unionist opposition in the House of Lords, 1905-1915.

798 Sir Alexander Fuller-Acland-Hood (1853-1917), Tory MP for Wellington (Somerset), 1892-1911.

along which the people have marched through the dark ages which are now merging into the light.[799]

So controversial were Lloyd George's methods and measures considered to be that the civil servants of the Exchequer refused to cooperate with him.[800] Lord Rosebery, the former Liberal prime minister, stated that the Budget "was not a Budget, but a revolution: a social and political revolution of the first magnitude… To say this is not to judge it, still less to condemn it, for there have been several beneficent revolutions." However, he opposed the Budget because "Socialism is the end of all, the negation of faith, of family, of property, of Monarchy, of Empire."[801] It was not socialism, but it did mark a most significant break with the previous generations vision of Liberalism, and it created a fierce adverse reaction among rich landowners, in the City of London and in the Lords.

The tone of Lloyd George's speeches at Limehouse and Newcastle may sometimes have been considered 'harsh'[802], but so were the conditions in which the poor were *still* living, and so his words were deliberately uncompromising. Apart from wishing to be plain-speaking, away from the sometimes rather unreal, codified pleasantries of the Commons, his delivery had further, allied purposes. These were to provoke the Lords to reject the Finance Bill, thus forcing the desired–and much-needed–parliamentary showdown that would at last lead to some real, long-overdue radical reform. He further calculated that it would generally demoralize the Tory opposition, whilst positively energizing the Liberals and their supporters and firing them up with a more radical zeal. In all this he proved to be successful.

Lloyd George also had to fight his own party, facing "an appallingly difficult political task in guiding his proposals through Cabinet and in converting his colleagues to his ideas."[803] Sir Robert Chalmers, Chairman of the Inland Revenue, whom Lloyd George regularly consulted on financial matters, commented as the Chancellor entered the Cabinet room in March 1909 "I am sorry for that little man, he is going to fight alone. He has hardly a friend inside there."[804] Dissension and acrimony were the order of the day during the fourteen Cabinet meetings held to discuss and amend the Budget proposals. Lloyd George admitted that he would never have got his proposals through the Cabinet without the strong support of Asquith. On 6 April he told his brother: "Budget-making all day. Got on extremely well. On one business where Cabinet very divided but on which I was very keen P.M. decided in my favour much to my delight."[805] He told a friend: "The Prime Minister has backed me up through thick and thin with splendid loyalty. I have the deepest respect for him and he has real sympathy for the ordinary and the poor."[806]

It subsequently took 72 parliamentary days to discuss the measure in the Commons, there were

---

799 Du Parcq, Vol.IV, p685-696. Emphasis added.
800 Cregier, p120; Jones, *David Lloyd George*, p128.
801 Lord Rosebery, Speech in Glasgow, 10 September 1909; *The Times*, 11 September 1909, p7-8.
802 Crosby, *Unknown*, p95.
803 Jones, *David Lloyd George*, p132.
804 NLW, D. R. Daniel Papers, 2912, 109, diary entry for 29 May 1909.
805 Quoted in Jones, *David Lloyd George*, p140.
806 Owen, p174.

554 divisions and the summer recess was cancelled. Lloyd George was indignantly clear about the issues at stake, never forgetting the futility of armament expenditure, as he wrote in an article of 30 October in *The Nation*: "How futile that expenditure was the African war demonstrated to the world." The money thus "frittered away" could be put to better use, for "schemes sanctioned by the Government for social reform and national development." This the Tories well knew, and:

> For that reason, even if the Budget goes through, I predict that another concerted effort will be made to rouse a fresh naval or military panic, so as to rush the Government into the criminal extravagance of unnecessary armaments on land and sea… So there will be the usual crop of rumours about German plans and preparations. We know now how little foundation existed for the last scare.[807]

Following bitter exchanges, the Budget passed its third reading in the Commons on 25 November by 379 votes to 149. Five days later it was decisively rejected by the Lords by 350 votes to 75, its first rejection of a budget since Commons pre-eminence in financial matters was established by the passing of resolutions in 1671 and 1678 after attempts by the Lords to breach the convention. Lloyd George knew all too well which way matters were trending, but was confident now of the eventual outcome, having written to Margaret on 16 November: "Well the Lords have made up their minds. The Lord hath delivered them unto our hands."[808] Although the Lords were entitled to amend money bills, defeating a Budget went against parliamentary precedent, and on 2 December Asquith moved "That the action of the House of Lords in refusing to pass into law the financial provision made by this House for the Service of the year is a breach of the Constitution and a usurpation of the rights of the Commons." After debate, the motion passed by 349 votes to 134.[809]

The next day Parliament was prorogued in readiness for a general election, to be held from 15 January to 10 February 1910. The real issue was the constitutional power of the upper house, and in the ensuing days Asquith, Churchill and Lloyd George all publicly declared that they would not again hold public office in circumstances where the peers could overrule the people. Speaking at the National Liberal Club in Whitehall Place on 3 December, Lloyd George fervently declared:

> You must handle [the House of Lords] a little more firmly, and the time has come for unflinching and resolute action. For my part, I would not remain a member of a Liberal Cabinet one hour unless I knew that the Cabinet had determined not to hold office after the next General Election unless full powers are accorded to it which would enable it to place on the Statute Book of the realm a measure which will ensure that the House of Commons in future can carry,

---

[807] Lloyd George, *The Issues Of The Budget*, p181.
[808] Morgan, *Family Letters*, p151.
[809] https://api.parliament.uk/historic-hansard/commons/1909/dec/02/house-of-lords-refusal-to-pass-finance. Retrieved 1 August 2019.

> not merely Tory Bills, as it does now, but Liberal and progressive measures in the course of a single Parliament either with or without the sanction of the House of Lords.[810]

To Lloyd George's astonishment, the Liberals came close to losing the election. They were hugely reduced to 274 seats, only two more than the Conservatives on 272.[811] The Labour Party increased their number of seats to 40, while the Irish nationalists dropped to 71 seats. The Liberals remained in power, but only with the support of Labour and the Irish. Lloyd George's vote dropped very slightly in Caernarfon Boroughs, though he still comfortably beat Tory candidate Hugh Vincent, Caernarfon solicitor, serving Mayor of Bangor and an old opponent from the days of the Llanfrothen burial case. John Grigg argued cogently that the reason why the "people failed to give a sweeping, massive endorsement to the People's Budget" was that the electorate in 1910 was "by no means representative of the whole British nation". He pointed out that "only 58 per cent of adult males had the vote, and it is a fair assumption that the remaining 42 per cent would, if enfranchised, have voted in very large numbers for Liberal or Labour candidates. In what was still a disproportionately middle-class electorate the fear of Socialism was strong, and many voters were susceptible to the argument that the Budget was a first instalment of Socialism."[812]

At least it meant that the Budget of 1909 could be relaunched, being reintroduced in the Commons on 19 April and finally passed on its third reading on 27 April. On 28 April, the Lords passed it through all its stages in a single sitting, and on 29 April 1910 the Budget received royal assent. Exactly one year after Lloyd George had introduced his proposals in the Commons, the 'People's Budget' had finally become law. Lloyd George sent his Uncle Lloyd the first copy of the Budget, with a revealing inscription on the flyleaf: "To Uncle Lloyd the real author of this Budget with his pupil's affectionate gratitude. May 31st 1910. D. Lloyd George."[813]

Lloyd George needed to raise at least £16 million in revenue to meet his commitments, an unprecedented amount in peacetime. The Budget itself imposed a 20% tax on the unearned increase in value of land, payable at death of the owner or sale of the land, and ½d on undeveloped land and minerals, increased death duties, a rise in income tax from 1s to 1s 2d in the pound, and the introduction of a 'supertax' of 6d in the pound on the amount by which incomes of £5,000 or more exceeded £3,000. There were taxes also on luxuries, alcohol, tobacco and petrol, so that money could be made available for the new welfare programmes as well as new battleships. Lloyd George pounced on the Lords opposition as an "opportunity to embark on further widespread social and constitutional reform".[814] Essentially, he had to find finance for both 'butter and guns', his two major items of new expenditure being old age pensions at £8.75 million, considerably higher than Asquith's original estimate of £6 million, and nearly £3 million for new naval construction. He "determined that his

810 Quoted in Lloyd George, *Better Times*, p179-180.
811 Bucking the general trend was Christopher Addison (1869-1951), soon to be a great ally of Lloyd George, ousting the sitting Tory and winning Hoxton on a swing of 8.3%.
812 Grigg, *People's Champion*, p240-241.
813 On display at the Lloyd George Museum.
814 Price, 2006, p192.

Budget, far from being a makeshift response to an immediate deficit, would prove once and for all the resources of free trade finance and give free trade a new popularity as against tariff reform. It would provide the fiscal underpinnings for the ongoing programme of social reform that he and Winston Churchill were preparing, and it would offer a way around the veto of the Lords on land valuation and, following the rejection of the Licensing Bill, on licensing as well."[815]

The jubilant and relieved Chancellor was largely successful–"Despite considerable increases in expenditure, including the state's contribution to national health and unemployment insurance, introduced in 1911, Lloyd George realised a succession of surpluses, and no new taxation was required until 1914."[816] Considerably more money than revenue estimates had predicted was actually raised, giving a realised surplus of £5,607,000 in 1910-11 [£844.01m in 2025] and £6,545,000 in 1911-12 [£955.36m in 2025].[817] The exception to this record of success in raising new revenue were the land value taxes. In August 1910 the Inland Revenue sent out ten and a half million 'Form 4s' as part of Lloyd George's 'Domesday Survey', and, by the end of the financial year, 9.6 million had been returned. Though by May 1915 some 78% of the land had been mapped, the outbreak of war effectively killed the measure. The Tories, coming into coalition, also insisted that there should be no return to the campaign. What taxes had been raised had cost more to implement, and the measure–excepting the mineral rights duty–was repealed under the Finance Act of 4 August 1920 by Lloyd George's coalition government, the revenue collected being returned to the contributors.[818]

Around this time, a curious incident occurred on one of his visits home to North Wales. Lloyd George was due to give a speech one Saturday evening at the Pavilion (then newly erected in 1911) in Corwen, a market town then in Merionethshire, and duly arrived by train. Whilst walking from the station towards the venue, the new Conservative Club, then nearing completion, collapsed into the main road, naturally causing some hilarity and comment in the community.[819]

Meanwhile, some of his critics on the left of the party felt that Asquith had not mounted a more aggressive campaign against the Lords. It was argued that, instead of threatening its power to veto legislation, he should have advocated making it a directly elected second chamber. Asquith felt this was a step too far and was more interested in a negotiated settlement. To some, this made him look vacillating. In a speech on 21 February 1910, Asquith outlined his plans for reform:

> Recent experience has disclosed serious difficulties due to recurring differences of strong opinion between the two branches of the Legislature. Proposals will be laid before you… to define the relations between the Houses of Parliament, so as to secure the undivided authority of the House of Commons over finance and its predominance in legislation.[820]

---

815 Murray, *The 'People's Budget' A Century On*, p7.
816 Ibid., p12.
817 https://liberalhistory.org.uk/history/1909-peoples-budget/. Retrieved 6 October 2021.
818 Douglas, p13. Between 1910-1914 it cost just over £2m to collect a little over £600,000.
819 My thanks to Corwen historian Geraint Jones for this story, phone conversation of 21 January 2019.
820 C. Clifford, *The Asquiths*, 2002, London, John Murray, p166.

On 13 April, Asquith sought a guarantee from Edward VII that he would exercise his royal prerogative and create enough peers to overturn the Tory majority in the Lords on the pending Finance Bill, and the next day introduced the Parliament Bill:

> Any measure passed three times by the House of Commons would be treated as if it had been passed by both Houses, and would receive the Royal Assent… The House of Lords was to be shorn absolutely of power to delay the passage of any measure certified by the Speaker of the House of Commons as a money bill, but was to retain the power to delay any other measure for a period of not less than two years.[821]

At this critical juncture, King Edward VII died on 6 May. His son, George V, of a more Unionist persuasion, now had the responsibility of dealing with this difficult constitutional question. Lloyd George had an audience with the new King on 9 May and had an "exceedingly frank and satisfactory talk about the political crisis." He told Margaret that he was not very intelligent as "there's not much in his head." However, he "expressed the desire to try his hand at conciliation… whether he will succeed is somewhat doubtful."[822] A Constitutional Conference was established with eight members; the government was represented by Asquith, the Earl of Crewe[823], Lloyd George and Augustine Birrell, while Balfour, Lord Lansdowne, Lord Cawdor[824] and Austen Chamberlain stood for the opposition. Between 17 June–28 July and 11 October–10 November, the members met on 22 occasions but never came close to an agreement, the issue of Ireland being the main sticking point. Lloyd George himself, backed by Birrell, came near to breaking up the Conference on 28 July by presenting his views as an ultimatum.[825]

Labour leader George Barnes had "called for an immediate creation of peers instead of an election."[826] Tory MP, F. E. Smith, gave public expression to his ideas in a letter written to *The Times* on 15 June, and in a Liverpool speech on 2 July, urging that there should be a "real and honest truce" while the party leaders were conferring on the Lords' veto. More realistically–and more creatively, given subsequent history–in a confidential memorandum dated 17 August, Lloyd George advocated the formation of a coalition government to break the deadlock. By this means he hoped that the statesmen, freed from dependence on their respective parties' extremists, could deal conjointly with the worsening national and international situations.

Lloyd George's so-called 'Criccieth Memorandum', written in London while the Conference was in recess, was a detailed, cogently argued and highly perceptive manifesto for a proactive 'Government of National Unity', a most relevant document for governing the country in a period of crisis, ahead of its time. It was not revolutionary in what it stated, but by its proposals what it could have enabled:

---

821 Grigg, *People's Champion*, p252.
822 Morgan, *Family Letters*, p153.
823 Robert Crewe-Milnes, Marquess of Crewe (1858-1945), Leader of the House of Lords, 1908-1916.
824 Frederick Campbell, Earl Cawdor (1847-1911).
825 C. C. Weston, *The Liberal Leadership And The Lords' Veto, 1907-1910 Historical Journal*, 11, 3, 1968, p508-537; see p527-528.
826 Grigg, *People's Champion*, p278. George Barnes (1859-1940), Labour MP for Glasgow Gorbals, 1906-1922, Labour Leader, 14 February 1910–6 February 1911.

sadly, others did not share Lloyd George's visionary foresight. His idea of collaborative, consensus-based government was a good one, stemming from his habitual non-ideological approach and disregard for convention, and his energetic pragmatism.[827] He would have a lifelong interest in coalition, which sometimes aroused suspicions in others concerning his consistency and integrity, but which in reality reflected his desire for flexibility and getting things done. The document itself, formally entitled 'Coalition against Party Government for dealing with social reforms', is undeservedly relatively unknown. In it, Lloyd George got straight to the point:

> Some of the most urgent problems awaiting settlement, problems which concern intimately the happiness and the efficiency of the inhabitants of these Islands, their strength and influence can only be successfully coped with by the active co-operation of both the great Parties in the State. Parties will always disagree on certain vital issues affecting the government of this country:... but it is rather fortunate at the present moment the questions which are of the most vital importance to the well-being of the great community are all questions which are not only capable of being settled by the joint action of the two great Parties without involving any sacrifice of principle on the part of either but which can be better settled by such cooperation than by the normal working of Party machinery. This country has gained a good deal from the conflict and rivalry of Parties, and it will gain a good deal more in the future from the same cause; but... the time has arrived for a truce, for bringing the resources of the two Parties into joint stock in order to liquidate arrears which, if much longer neglected, may end in national impoverishment, if not insolvency. It must be quite clear to any observer that the rapid rise of great foreign competitors has put us in a position where no time ought to be lost in repairing the deficiencies of our national system and putting our machinery in better order, in order to equip us for a state of things with which we have never before been confronted. For the first time in hundreds of years the Continent has enjoyed a long period of peace and repose and foreign nations have employed the immunity from internal and external conflicts in developing their industrial and commercial equipment to an extent which menaces our supremacy. Under these circumstances, it becomes us to sink our differences and to unite in combined and sustained effort to re-organise the national life of our country in all its branches, so as to put us in a position where we need have no apprehension as to the future of the British Empire whatever the strain may be that shall be put upon its resources. I would summarize the advantages which in my judgment will be gained by attempting a non-Party solution of the great Imperial and National problems to which I have alluded:
>
> (1) None of these great problems can be effectively dealt with without incurring temporary unpopularity.
>
> There is always some essential part of a scheme, sometimes the most useful and far-reaching in its beneficial results, which for the moment has to face a good deal of misapprehension. A large number of people misunderstand it, and it causes an amount of apprehension which experience

[827] Sharp, *Lloyd George*, p19.

alone can dispel. If you have a hostile Party with nearly half the nation amongst its organised supporters waiting to take advantage of every slip, no Ministry will be disposed to take unnecessary risks, and often the unpopular section of a project has to be ruthlessly cut out, in order to save the remnant, although that section may be essential to a complete and successful treatment of the subject.

(2) When you come to subjects of this kind, the equality of the Parties in numbers is in itself a source of weakness, for it means that a Government has only to alienate a comparatively small number of the Electorate of the country in order to incur defeat, and an Opposition has only to win the support of the same number in order to oust their opponents from power. Thus, often the least-responsible, the least well-informed and the most selfish amongst the Electorate may have a decisive voice in determining the issues upon which the whole future of the British Empire may depend. If joint action between the Parties could be negotiated, these undesirable elements would sink to their proper insignificance as factors.

(3) This is a corollary of the two preceding propositions. No settlement is possible without exciting a good many ill-informed prejudices, some of them with an historical basis. They cannot be argued with, they cannot always be voted down; but they are extremely pernicious in their influence upon the settlement of a difficult and complex problem. Separate action means that a Party in opposition is driven into enlisting the support of these prejudices, whether it wishes to do so or not: the more extreme men amongst their own supporters on the platform and in the Press always take advantage of these elements, however enlightened a view the Party leaders may take. Joint action will enable a Government based on the best of the strength of the two Parties to ignore these prejudices.

(4) Parties are now committed through a long course of controversy to particular methods of dealing with problems, and however much the more instructed amongst them may feel that there are other and better alternatives which have not yet been put forward, no Party can afford to abandon the position which it has deliberately taken up and long defended in the presence of the enemy. Governments are therefore driven to the second best method of settling a question, because their Party programme and Party pledges make it impossible for them to take the best course.

(5) Extreme partisans supporting the Government often drive it against its better judgment to attempting legislation on lines which are the least useful in dealing with a question. As a rule the advanced sections of a Party, being propagandist, are the most active, the best organised, the most resolute and therefore the most irresistible. Joint action would make it possible to settle these urgent questions without paying undue regard to the formulae and projects of rival faddists.

(6) No Party has a monopoly of able and efficient men… and it has to depend for the filling up of all the other posts in the Government upon the services of men of second, and even third-rate capacity. Inasmuch as some of these posts are of great importance when you come to questions of national organization, under the present system their presence as the heads of these

Departments presents an effective barrier to reform. The head of a Department is supreme in that Department… It is therefore vital to any scheme of National reorganisation that the best men that the nation provides should be secured as heads during the period of reconstruction. This can only be achieved by drawing upon the resources of both Parties in the State.

What are the questions which call for immediate attention and which could properly and effectively be dealt with by some combined effort as I indicate? There are first of all the questions which come under the category of Social Reform: they affect the health, the vitality, the efficiency and the happiness of the individuals who constitute the races that dwell in these islands.

Housing

The putting an end to a system which houses millions of the people under conditions which devitalize their strength, depress their energies and deprives them of all motive power for putting forth their best.

Drink

The problem of excessive drinking has a most intimate relation to other questions of Social Reform. There is no doubt that a vast number of people in this country destroy their physical, mental, and moral powers owing to their addiction to alcohol… If both Parties put their heads together, they could discover some idea which… would advance the cause of national sobriety.

Insurance

Provision against the accidents of life which bring so much undeserved poverty to hundreds of thousands of homes, accidents which are quite inevitable, such as the death of the bread-winner or his premature breakdown in health. I have always thought that the poverty which was brought upon families owing to these causes presents a much more urgent demand upon the practical sympathy of the community than even Old Age Pensions. With old age, the suffering is confined to the individual alone; but, in these other cases, it extends to the whole family of the victim of circumstances.

Unemployment

… Whatever is done towards improving the trade conditions, we shall at any rate for some time to come have to face a percentage of unemployment, especially in certain precarious trades. No country has been able to avoid it, and, with fluctuations in trade, the constant improvements in machinery, the variations in public demands for commodities and many other reasons, men will be thrown out of employment temporarily, and great difficulty will be found in absorbing this surplus labour. Much misery will thereby be caused, misery often culminating in hunger and starvation…

This question of Insurance illustrates one of the difficulties that must necessarily be encountered by every Government that attempts to grapple with it without first of all securing the co-operation of its opponents. The hardest case of all is that of the man who dies in the prime of life leaving a widow and young children... In Germany they contemplate adding provision for widows under these conditions to their ordinary invalidity insurance... [H]ere one would have to encounter the bitter hostility of powerful organisations... with an army... of [80,000] agents and collectors who make a living out of collecting a few pence a week from millions of households in this country for the purpose of providing death allowances. The expenses of collection and administration come to something like 50 per cent of the total receipts, and these poor widows and children are by this extravagant system robbed of one-half of the benefits... This system ought to be terminated at the earliest possible moment. The benefits are small, costly, and precarious... State insurance costs 10 per cent to administer, and, inasmuch as the State and the employer both contribute, either the premium is considerably less, or the benefits are substantially greater than with the Insurance Companies. But, however desirable it may be to substitute State insurance, which does not involve collection and therefore is more economical, any Party that attempted it would instantly incur the relentless hostility of all these agents and collectors... and a Government which attempted to take over their work without first of all securing the co-operation of the other Party would inevitably fail in its undertaking; so that, if a scheme of national insurance is taken in hand by any Party Government, it must be confined to Invalidity, and the most urgent and pitiable case of all must be left out...

The Poor Law

This requires overhauling and recasting, and I can see nothing in the principles of either Party which are irreconcilable in this matter.

National Re-organisation

There are several questions coming under this head which could be much better dealt with by a Coalition...

There is Education. Not merely could the denominational question be thus much more satisfactorily disposed of,... but there are questions like the raising of the age limit, which is quite essential if the youth of the country are to receive a training which will enable them to cope with the workmen of Germany and the United States of America.

The same observation applies to the development of Technical Instruction in this country. The raising of the age limit would excite a good deal of opposition in many quarters and might gain for a Government great unpopularity even amongst sections of its own supporters who benefit now largely by Boy labour... it is only a Coalition that could... have the strength to face the ignorant and selfish prejudices that will be aroused by any effort to keep the children at School instead of turning them [out] to make money for their parents.

National Defence

... There are undoubtedly directions in which money can be saved: there are others in which it is imperative that more money should be spent. The whole question of National Defence ought to be boldly faced... I am strongly of opinion that even the question of compulsory training should not be shirked. No Party dare touch it, because of the violent prejudices which would be excited… The Swiss Militia system might be considered and those liable to service might be chosen by ballot. We have no such need as continental countries labour under of organising an Army of 3 or 4,000,000 for defence but we might aim at raising 500,000 armed militia to supplement our regular army to provide against contingencies.

Local Government

Our whole system of Local Government is on a very unsatisfactory basis. There are too many Boards & there is no system of intelligent direction, such as is provided by the Burgomasters on the Continent. Whilst there are too many small Boards and Councils, there are too few large ones, and a good deal of work is cast upon the Imperial Parliament which could be much more efficiently discharged by Local bodies on a large scale.

Trade

The various problems connected with State assistance to Trade and Commerce could be enquired into with some approach to intelligent and judicial impartiality if Party rivalries were eliminated. We have, not merely problems connected with Tariffs, but we have the question of inland transport that ought to be thoroughly overhauled. In Germany the Railway is one of the most important weapons of the State for the purpose of promoting the Foreign trade of that country.

The Land

There is no question which would gain more by the elimination of Party strife and bitterness than that of the Land. It is admitted on all hands that the land of this country is capable of much more profitable uses than is now given to it. Both Parties seem to imagine… that the real solution lies in the direction of establishing a system of Small Holdings. I think they have been rather too readily rushed by small but well organised groups of their own supporters into an acceptance of this doctrine. These groups are inspired by men… with little knowledge of land cultivation. The Small holdings craze is of a very doubtful utility… After all, farming is a business and it requires just as much capacity to run successfully a 50-acre farm as it would to manage a 500-acre holding. There ought to be the same knowledge of the qualities of the soil, the same gift of buying and selling, the same skill in making the best of the soil in both cases. It is very rarely that men enjoy a combination of all these gifts, and it is far better that the majority of men should work under competent guidance, direction and command, than that they should undertake the responsibilities of management… The alternatives are worthy of much more careful and thorough consideration than has hitherto been given to them. If a mistake is made it will be irreparable for generations…

Imperial Problems

Schemes for uniting together the Empire and utilising and concentrating its resources… might also to much better advantage be undertaken and put through by a Coalition. They are the most

> delicate and difficult questions that have to be settled by modern statesmanship. In many respects they are the most urgent. Now is undoubtedly the best time to approach them. After all, there are Parties in the Colonies as well as here: there are Parties in our Colonies whose sympathies are more naturally attracted to the Liberals, and some whose views perhaps bear an affinity to the Conservatives… a Govt that represented both Parties would appeal to all sections and would carry infinitely greater weight. In this connection the settlement of the Irish Question would come up for consideration. The advantages of a non-party treatment of this vexed problem are obvious. Parties might deal with it without being subject to the embarrassing dictation of extreme partisans whether from Nationalist or Orangeman.
>
> Foreign Policy
>
> Such a Govt representing as it would not a fragment but the whole nation would undoubtedly enhance the prestige of this country abroad.[828]

The memorandum was shown to the Liberal and Tory leaders. Most Liberals were naturally interested, with the sceptical Asquith being the least favourable.[829] More surprising was the favourable response from the Tory side, from such figures as F. E. Smith and Austen Chamberlain. Asquith showed the memorandum to Balfour, but after consultation with his inner Cabinet, Balfour–himself uneasy about the whole matter–was forced to refuse, the clincher being the adamant opposition of Akers-Douglas, the former Tory Chief Whip, to whom Lloyd George represented all that was to be abhorred in politics.[830] To a large degree, the proposals foundered on Tory opposition to any form of Home Rule or devolution for Ireland.[831]

A second, much shorter 'Supplementary Memorandum' dated 29 October, aimed at fellow Liberals, set out to clarify and develop certain issues.[832] Among the sixteen points, Lloyd George promoted:

> (3) Every effort to be made by Diplomatic means to secure an international understanding which will, if not effect a reduction in the cost of Armaments, at least arrest the alarming growth in expenditure in preparation for war.
>
> (4) A settlement of the Irish Question… to be attempted on some such lines as were sketched by Mr. [Joseph] Chamberlain in his speech on the First Reading of the Home Rule Bill of 1886.[833] Ireland to be treated as a unit for the purpose of any measure of self-government. This settlement should be of a kind which might form a nucleus for the Federation of the Empire at some future date…

---

828 Quoted in Scally, p375-383.
829 Jenkins, *Asquith*, p216-217; Scally, p197.
830 W. W. Davies, p356-357. Aretas Akers-Douglas (1851-1926).
831 Crosby, *Unknown*, p104-106.
832 Quoted in full in Scally, p384-386.
833 https://hansard.parliament.uk/Commons/1886-04-09/debates/824f4824-e7a4-4aa2-ac50-a484dd985da8/GovernmentOfIrelandBill. Retrieved 2 April 2025.

(5) A full and impartial Enquiry to be instituted into the working and results of our Fiscal System and also of the Systems of our Trade rivals.

(7) The Welsh Church Question to be settled on the terms, not of the Welsh Church Bill now before the House, but on the more liberal terms of the Irish Disestablishment Act of 1869, but no factitious vested interests to be created. If, as a preliminary to such a Measure, it is desired to test the opinions of the Welsh people on the Question, a Referendum to be taken in the Principality.

Unfortunately, this further attempt by Lloyd George to reach a constructive, working consensus did nothing to resolve the issue. On 8 November, Balfour formally rejected the plan in an interview with him at 11 Downing Street, leaving the proposals dead in the water.[834] Lloyd George later wrote, with hindsight:

> In the year 1910 we were beset by an accumulation of grave issues–rapidly becoming graver… It was becoming evident to discerning eyes that the Party and Parliamentary system was unequal to coping with them. There was a jam at the legislative dock gates and there was no prospect of the growing traffic being able to get through. The shadow of unemployment was rising ominously above the horizon. Our international rivals were forging ahead at a great rate and jeopardising our hold on the markets of the world. There was an arrest in that expansion of our foreign trade which had contributed to the phenomenal prosperity of the previous half-century, and of which we had made such a muddled and selfish use. Our working population, crushed into dingy and mean streets, with no assurance that they would not be deprived of their daily bread by ill-health or trade fluctuations, were becoming sullen with discontent. Whilst we were growing more dependent on overseas supplies for our food, our soil was gradually going out of cultivation. The life of the countryside was wilting away and we were becoming dangerously over-industrialised. Excessive indulgence in alcoholic drinks was undermining the health and efficiency of a considerable section of the population. The Irish controversy was poisoning our relations with the United States of America. A great Constitutional struggle over the House of Lords threatened revolution at home, another threatened civil war at our doors in Ireland. Great nations were arming feverishly for an apprehended struggle into which we might be drawn by some visible or invisible ties, interests, or sympathies. Were we prepared for all the terrifying contingencies?[835]

There was considerable substance to his conviction that, had his proposal been acted upon, there would have been no revolution in Ireland and, perhaps, no war with Germany. To the end of his life Lloyd George rightly regretted the "'Great Refusal' of 1910", as he put it, adding:

---

[834] Scally, p209.

[835] Lloyd George, *War Memoirs*, Vol.I, p21.

> There is much to be said in favour of the Party system. The open conflict of Parties is better for a country than the squalid intrigues of personal ambitions or of rival interests conducted in the dark. But there are times when it stands seriously in the way of the highest national interests. On these occasions it hinders, delays and thwarts real progress, and in the event the nation suffers heavily. I shall always regard the rejection of the proposals for co-operation in 1910 as a supreme instance of this kind of damage. On the other hand, the ground for co-operation must be one of genuine national well-being.[836]

To varying degrees most modern historians generally concur that Lloyd George was sincere and consistent in his concerted attempt at introducing the fruitful cross-party collaboration of all 'men of good will' for the greater national good.[837] Meanwhile, party politics as usual continued to be paramount, and when a ministerial by-election at Walthamstow on 1 November produced a 1.2% swing to incumbent Liberal John Simon, Asquith decided to call a general election.[838] On 14 November he got a highly reluctant King George V to commit to creating an adequate number of Liberal peers to pass the Parliament Bill, threatening that he and his Cabinet would otherwise resign. Speaking to an audience of 5,000 at the Paragon Theatre, Mile End Road, on 21 November, Lloyd George called on the people to vote for a change in the parliamentary system:

> How can anyone defend the Constitution in its present form? No country in the world would look at our system–no free country, I mean… France has a Senate. The United States has a Senate. The Colonies have Senates. But they are all chosen either directly or indirectly by the people.

Lloyd George was adept at appealing to the level of his audience, and he famously likened the aristocracy to cheese: "The older it is the higher it becomes."[839] According to *The Times* the next morning, his oratory was "greatly to the liking of the 'East Enders.'"[840]

The general election between 3-19 December 1910–the last to be held over several days–produced a Commons which was almost identical to the one elected the preceding January. The Liberals won 272 seats and the Tories 271, but the Labour Party, with 42 seats. and the Irish, with a combined total of 84, ensured the government's survival as long as it proceeded with constitutional reform and Home Rule.[841] In Caernarfon Boroughs, Lloyd George's personal vote increased slightly against the Tory candidate, Anglican barrister Austin Lloyd Jones.

There was still a mood amongst some for cross-party discussion, even if informal. On 18 May

---

836 Ibid., p24.

837 Gilbert, *Architect Of Change*, p413-414, 416; Rowland, *Last Liberal Governments: 1905-1910*, p308; Morgan, *Lloyd George*, p71-72; P. Addison, *Churchill On The Home Front, 1900-55*, 1992, London, Jonathan Cape, p100; Grigg, *People's Champion*, pp272-274; Crosby, *Unknown*, p102-106. Scally, p199, 206, and Searle *Balfour's Secret Coalition*, *passim*, disagree.

838 Grigg, *People's Champion*, p277-278.

839 Ibid., p280-281.

840 Bonham Carter and Pottle, *Lantern Slides*, p228.

841 Owen, p201.

1911, 'The Other Club' was founded by Churchill and F. E. Smith, with the help of Lloyd George, the inaugural dinner in the Pinafore Room at the Savoy Hotel comprising 27 of the original 40 charter members (to include a maximum of 24 MPs). Churchill, then Liberal Home Secretary, and Conservative MP F. E. Smith had not been invited to join the venerable political dining club known simply as 'The Club'. Although both had friends in it, it was alleged that the members thought Churchill and Smith too controversial. They thus established their own, to be called by contrast 'The Other Club'. Lloyd George was also not a member of 'The Club'. The Chief Whips of the two parties were co-secretaries, so that pairs could be arranged, meaning members' dinner would not be interrupted by divisions in Parliament, the club meeting at 8.15pm sharp on alternate Thursdays whilst Parliament was in session. Their express purpose was the bringing together on friendly neutral territory men who respected one another though they belonged to different political parties. In addition to Smith, Churchill and Lloyd George[842], other prominent men in 'The Other Club' included Liberals Freddie Guest[843], Charles Masterman and Neil Primrose (son of Lord Rosebery); Tories including Bonar Law and Admiral Charles Beresford; Irish Nationalist T. P. O'Connor; Sir Francis Hopwood and Sir Arthur Bigge from the judiciary; Sir George Riddell, *Observer* editor J. L. Garvin, and *The Nation* editor H. W. Massingham from Fleet Street: from the Army, Lord Kitchener and Sir John French; also, the former Portuguese Ambassador Marquês de Soveral and actor Sir Herbert Beerbohm Tree.

Election to the club depended on Smith and Churchill believing members to be "men with whom it was agreeable to dine." However, the club was soon seen as suspect by Bonar Law, who resigned from it on becoming Tory leader on 13 November 1911. "I think the club will have to be disbanded," he remarked to Riddell. "I don't think it wise to continue it." "Personally," he declared on another occasion, "on the whole, I think these political friendships have been carried too far… I like Lloyd George. He is a nice man, but the most dangerous little man that ever lived."[844] Bonar Law was ignored, and the club continued. Indeed, it was to remain an important point of social contact for Lloyd George and Churchill as late as the 1930s.[845]

The Parliament Bill, removing the peers' right to amend or defeat finance bills and reducing their powers from the defeat to the delay of other legislation, was introduced by Asquith in the Commons on 21 February 1911, completing its passage through there on 15 May, passing by 362 votes to 241. Completely failing to learn the lesson or heed the warning, a committee of the Lords then amended the bill out of all recognition. According to Lucy Masterman, the wife of Liberal MP Charles Masterman, Lloyd George had a secret meeting with Tory leader Balfour, bluffing Balfour into believing that King George V had agreed to create enough Liberal supporting peers to pass a new Parliament Bill.[846] Although a list of 249 candidates, including Thomas Hardy, Bertrand Russell,

---

842 Lloyd George was Chairman of the Wine and Cigars Committee! J. Nicolson, *Perfect Summer*, p47.
843 Frederick 'Freddie' Guest (1875-1937), Coalition Liberals Chief Whip, 1917-1921, Secretary of State for Air, 1921-1922, first cousin of Winston Churchill.
844 W. W. Davies, p396.
845 Toye, p85.
846 L. Masterman, *C.F.G. Masterman*, p199. Charles Masterman (1873-1927), Liberal MP for West Ham North, 1906-1911. Neville, biographer of Tom Ellis, was their son.

Gilbert Murray, J. M. Barrie, Joseph Rowntree, Lieutenant General Robert Baden-Powell and Sir Thomas Lipton had been drawn up, they had not yet been presented to the King. After the meeting Balfour told Tory peers that, to prevent the Liberals having a permanent majority in the Lords, they must pass the bill. On 10 August 1911, the Parliament Act was passed by 131 votes to 114 in the Lords, and given royal assent on 18 August, meaning that the Lords could no longer prevent the passage of fiscal bills, and could only veto other bills for two years. Lloyd George had "undermined the greatest obstacle to radical legislation and achieved one of his earliest aspirations."[847]

It was with this as the political 'backdrop' that the Investiture of the Prince of Wales took place at Caernarfon Castle on the 13 July 1911. When the Bishop of St Asaph, A. G. Edwards, had suggested the idea of an investiture at the castle, he found his old friend and political adversary Lloyd George responsive:

> It seemed a wild venture. I had never asked him a personal favour. But I knew his character well and could trust him. He has the gift of chivalry… and in victory is a generous opponent. Above all else for my purpose, he has imagination, which the slow-witted interpret as want of principle. The interview brought instant approval and action.[848]

This appealed to Lloyd George's political sense as well, as it would enable him to gratify Welsh national pride and reassure traditionalists across the kingdom unsettled by his radical reforms of the social structure. King George V was also happy to cooperate for similar reasons, in that the ceremony would be a gesture to his Welsh subjects which might also facilitate "his dealings with the difficult Mr Lloyd George."[849]

Lloyd George, the Constable of Caernarvon Castle since 1908, was instrumental in inventing a rather elaborate ceremony in the style of a Welsh pageant. Accompanied by the Lord Lieutenant of Caernarvonshire, the High Sheriff, the Archdruid and the Mayor, with heralds and officers of the Welsh regiments, Lloyd George, himself resplendent in an embroidered uniform, received the royal party at the Water Gate of the immense stronghold. Then he stood silently by the side of the three thrones while Churchill, as Home Secretary, proclaimed the new King's eldest son Edward's styles and titles as Prince of Wales,[850] while Edward was bestowed with the Honours of the Principality of Wales. The assembly sang both 'God Save The King' and 'Land of My Fathers', the Red Dragon flag flying from the Eagle Tower, before the young Edward, then just turned 17, delivered a few sentences in Welsh at Queen Eleanor's Gate, as he had been coached to do by Lloyd George for two or three evenings a week at 11 Downing Street during May and June, including the words "*Mor o gan yw Cymru I gyd*"–"All Wales is a sea of song."[851] What Lloyd George, the 'People's Champion', privately thought

[847] Price, 2006, p193-194.
[848] A. G. Edwards, *Memories*, 1927, London, John Murray, p245.
[849] Duke of Windsor, *A King's Story*, 1951, London, Cassell & Co., p81.
[850] Edward VIII (1894-1972), became King 20 January 1936, abdicated 11 December the same year, afterwards titled Duke of Windsor.
[851] Nicolson, p206; Owen, p210; Cregier, p169. So closely was Lloyd George connected to the ceremony that it has often been wrongly claimed that he not only originated the idea for the investiture's revival, but that he created and stage-managed every detail. In fact, he was simply the most visible member of a committee.

of these monarchical proceedings is a moot point.

Biographer W. W. Davies was a 16-year-old eyewitness to the events–a testimony to the high regard with which Lloyd George was held in by North Walians as much as anything else–recording:

> The little town was full to overflowing. [Within]... the ancient grey walls of the castle... there had assembled all that was brilliant and representative of Welsh life; while accompanying the Royal Family came a crowd of their most distinguished servants–Mr. Asquith... Mr. Churchill... Mr. Balfour... and, of course, the Constable of the Castle. Lloyd George was then at the summit of his marvellous popularity in Wales. A rumour that he would pass through a place in his car was always sufficient to line the roads with eager and enthusiastic crowds... He knew perfectly well that, were he to appear in one hall, and the Royal Family in another, the vast majority of the people would be with him. And for that reason, in order that the King, the Queen, and the Prince might have the whole stage to themselves on that day, he was careful to keep himself well in the background. He performed the Constable's duty of receiving the King at the gate, and of handing to him the key of the castle; but beyond that, he played no part in the ceremony, and gave no opportunity to the crowds to acclaim him...[852]

Edward had actually been created Prince of Wales on his sixteenth birthday, 23 June 1910. But the Investiture, with all its gaudy ceremonial in front of 10,000 Welsh people, was promoted by Lloyd George to play upon the then undoubted popularity of the new King and young Prince. It also helped that Caernarfon of course was both in Lloyd George's constituency and the place where Edward I had originally invented and first bestowed the title of Prince of Wales as currently known on 7 February 1301, the recipient being his son who was born in the castle, the future Edward II.

Despite the success of this event in Wales, it was something of a sideshow in the UK as a whole, the summer of 1911 being marked by very considerable social unrest and public disruption. In this period there were some 864 strikes and lock-outs, involving nearly a million workers and resulting in the loss of ten and a quarter million working days, especially amongst dock workers and railwaymen. This industrial unrest was fuelled principally by economic factors. For much of the nineteenth century, Britain had been the 'Workshop of the World' but, by the turn of the century, Britain's dominance was being threatened, as she was gradually but surely economically overtaken by the USA and Germany. As Britain's share of world trade fell, living standards dropped. In the period 1896-1914, real wages fell by around ten per cent, while from 1909-1912 the cost of living rose twice as quickly as it had done between 1902-1908. Naturally, a new generation of trade union leaders were determined not only to gain higher wages for their members but also to use their power to radically transform the country as a whole.

By 11 August arbitrator Sir George Askwith[853] had come up with an offer that seemed acceptable to most of the striking dockers, and wages were finally raised and some guarantees given by reluctant

[852] W. W. Davies, p381-382. William Watkin Davies (1895-1973), born in Criccieth, raised in Barmouth, son of the Reverend John Gwynoro Davies.

[853] Sir George Askwith (1861-1942), Comptroller-General of the Labour Department at the Board of Trade.

owners, but a mood of profound distrust persisted. One of the most serious strikes was the first national railway strike of 17-19 August. The railway workers leader, Jimmy Thomas[854], had refused to accept the decisions of the Conciliation Board. Meetings were held in Hull, Cardiff, Salford, Bristol, Glasgow, Swansea, and in Liverpool, where striking dockers, sailors and railway workers were led by Tom Mann, on 15 August soldiers of the 18th Hussars had fired on a crowd on Vauxhall Road, injuring 15, two fatally. Despite its short duration, the strike caused deep apprehension in official circles, who feared revolution: a Guards Brigade and the whole of Aldershot garrison–25,000 troops–were transferred to London, Parliament was summoned, and special constables were enrolled.

Lloyd George, although now Chancellor of the Exchequer, took the initiative and intervened. Asquith had merely promised to hold an investigation, meanwhile hoping to keep the railways running, and maintaining the inflammatory military presence in Liverpool and London. Now, at Lloyd George's instigation, Asquith called a Cabinet meeting, at which Lloyd George explained that he did not think that the strike could possibly be settled by force, rather advising a return to mediation. He also "believed it possible that an appeal to patriotism and a reminder of the danger posed to every Englishman's liberty by the German activity in Morocco might prove persuasive. Patriotism was, he believed, the key to unification."[855]

With his personal magnetism and ingenuity, Lloyd George managed to persuade Thomas to call the strike off almost as soon as it had begun. Haldane described how Lloyd George suddenly burst into his room in the War Office, exclaiming:

> A bottle of champagne! I've done it! Don't ask me how, but I've done it. The strike is settled.[856]

He had evidently played his patriotic hand well. Not pleased was the Home Secretary, Churchill, *whose prime responsibility the matter should have been.* He telephoned Lloyd George, saying to the 'triumphant mediator': "I am very sorry to hear it. It would have been better to have gone on and given these men a good thrashing."[857] Have expressed himself thus–in very public school terminology–he left London to play golf. Such threats were not idle. On 19 August, picketing action by 500 railway workers at Llanelli station, during which a train containing strikebreaking workers was held up, was brutally suppressed by the police and army. The troops' commander, Major Brownlow Stuart of the Worcestershire Regiment, ordered his 80 men to bayonet charge the picketers, then had magistrate Henry Wilkins read the Riot Act and ordered his men to open fire, resulting in the deaths of two men, innocent bystanders. Rioting followed and magistrates' homes were attacked and railway trucks set on fire: one wagon contained explosive detonators, resulting in an explosion which killed a further four people, including an innocent woman bystander, and more wounded.[858]

King George V was profoundly relieved at the largely peaceful national solution engineered by

---

[854] James Thomas (1874-1949), Secretary of the Amalgamated Society of Railway Servants (ASRS), Labour MP for Derby, 1910-1936.
[855] J. Nicolson, *Perfect Summer*, p194. Churchill also sent the armoured cruiser HMS *Antrim* to the Mersey.
[856] A. Chamberlain, *Politics From Inside: An Epistolary Chronicle 1906-1914*, 1936, London, Cassell, p437.
[857] Quoted in J. Nicolson, *Perfect Summer*, p195. Lucy Masterman, Diary Entry for 11 September 1911.
[858] See J. Edwards, *Remembrance of a Riot: The Story of the Llanelli Railway Strike Riots of 1911*, 1988. 2010 Llanelli 2nd Ed. BPR Publishers.

Lloyd George, and thankfully telegraphed him on 20 August: "Very glad to hear that it was largely due to your energy and skill that a settlement with regard to this very serious strike has been brought about. I heartily congratulate you and feel that the whole country will be most grateful to you for averting a most disastrous calamity. It has caused me the greatest possible anxiety."[859] Others concurred. Asquith's Principal Private Secretary, Maurice Bonham Carter[860], wrote to his future wife Violet Asquith on 21 August from 10 Downing Street: "I had been down here waiting for the finish of the strike negotiations. The settlement has been a triumph for L.G [sic] who really ran the whole thing. He induced the managers to meet the men and both sides to accept the Government's proposals."[861]

On 14 October, Lloyd George made a speech at Whitefield's Tabernacle on Tottenham Court Road, London, in defence of his National Insurance Bill, which had first been introduced into Parliament on 4 May. He was riding high, and his speech was stirring, lasting two and a quarter hours amid loud and enthusiastic cheering from the packed audience. He began: "I have come here this afternoon to plead for fair treatment for a measure which, in my judgement, will do more to hinder or to assuage human misery than any Bill carried by the Legislature since the abolition of the Corn Laws."[862] He went on to say, "I will fight it through or I will fall." One among the audience was the young Hugh Dalton, himself a future Labour Chancellor of the Exchequer, who later recorded that, despite his rather poor opinion of the Liberal Party:

> I went to Whitefield's Tabernacle to hear Lloyd George speak on his Insurance Bill, and I was deeply moved. The climax came when he declared, in a ringing voice: "I will fight this through or I will fall." And men sprang to their feet, with tears streaming down their cheeks, crying: "Thank God for Lloyd George!" And I confess that I wept too, my Welsh blood stirred within me.[863]

Under the National Insurance Act, 1911, given royal assent on 16 December, Lloyd George followed the example of Germany, which under conservative Chancellor Otto von Bismarck had provided compulsory national insurance against sickness from 1884. Coming into effect on 15 July 1912, it meant male workers who earned under £160 per annum paid a weekly stamp of 4d, female workers 3d, while employers 3d and the state 2d, Lloyd George's "ninepence for fourpence".[864] Under the Act, workers could take sick leave and be paid ten shillings a week for the first 13 weeks, and five shillings a week for the next 13 weeks. Unsurprisingly, it attracted much opposition from those with vested interests, from some on the socialist left, but especially from the conservative right. One aspect of the protest was an anti-stamp licking campaign which reached its climax with a 'Mistresses and Maids

---

859 Quoted in Nicolson, *King George V*, p219-220.

860 Sir Maurice Bonham-Carter (1880-1960), Asquith's Principal Private Secretary, 1910-1916. Married Violet (1887-1969), only daughter of Asquith and his first wife, on 30 November 1915.

861 Bonham Carter and Pottle, *Lantern Slides*, p281.

862 The restrictive, unpopular Corn Laws were repealed on 26 June 1846.

863 Hugh Dalton, *Call Back Yesterday: Memoirs 1887-1931*, 1953, London, Frederick Muller, p70. Dalton, (1887-1962), born in Neath, Chancellor of the Exchequer, 1945-1947.

864 Surely inherent in this was the implication that lower paid women could not afford to pay as much as men.

Rally' at the Albert Hall on 29 November. After shouting "We won't pay!" and racist "Taffy is a Welshman, Taffy is a thief!", the rally culminated in a speech by Lady Desart[865] where she attacked Lloyd George violently and finished with her rallying cry, "England... never did nor never shall lie at the proud foot of a conqueror." The Tory press rabidly denounced the bill as "the malingerer's millennium" and "the cheat's charter."[866]

The successful passage of the bill was materially helped by the strong intervention of Christopher Addison, himself a prominent anatomist, Hunterian Professor with the Royal College of Surgeons, perhaps the most eminent doctor ever to enter the Commons. The bill had been introduced by Lloyd George on 4 May. Addison warmly supported it, but felt that as it stood the bill did not provide doctors with adequate security, and proposed some major amendments to improve it. Lloyd George asked to see Addison, through the mediation of Charles Masterman, and met him with a smile in a room behind the Speaker's chair in the Commons. Addison later recorded of this first meeting:

> [Lloyd George said] 'Masterman has told me a horrible tale of what you say about the Insurance Bill. Let me hear it again.' Addison replied at length, with much force, that under the existing provisions of the Bill, the medical attendance of eight to ten million people would be worked merely as an extension of the existing club system, 'It simply stank in the nostrils of the whole medical profession and if he tried to impose it on them he would find them solid to a man against it. I should do everything I could to back them up, for we would never get a proper health system established in the country on these lines.' Addison had meanwhile canvassed nearly every member of the Commons against the proposals.[867]

At Lloyd George's behest, he spoke in favour of the bill with the British Medical Association (BMA). On 1 August 1911 he spoke in the Commons, passionately defending his proposed amendment to Clause 13 of the bill–afterwards known as 'Addison's Amendment'–overcoming much of the medical fraternity's objections: "Why is it that nowadays we propose an Insurance Bill of this kind? I think it really is due to the fact that we are convinced by sufficient evidence that it is possible, by united efforts, to prevent a great amount of disease."[868] His amendment passed by an overwhelming majority, 387 to 15. The courage with which Addison had backed his convictions won him Lloyd George's respect and admiration, this moment marking "the beginning of a long period of close and intimate work that they were to do together."[869]

As Philip Snowden, then Labour MP for Blackburn, later wrote:

---

865 Ellen Odette Cuffe, Countess of Desart (née Bischoffsheim; 1857-1933). Her cry of 'England' rang hollow, as she was the daughter of a banker of German origin, living in Ireland and becoming a Senator in the Irish Free State in December 1922.

866 W. W. Davies, p377.

867 Morgan, *Portrait Of A Progressive*, p13; Addison, *Politics From Within*, Vol.I, p20.

868 https://api.parliament.uk/historic-hansard/commons/1911/aug/01/clause-13-benefits-to-be-administered-by. Retrieved 13 July 2020.

869 Minney, p125.

> The National Health Insurance Bill was at the time the most unpopular measure ever introduced into Parliament. No man with less energy, tenacity and determination than Mr. Lloyd George could have carried the Bill through in the teeth of the opposition of many powerful vested interests. He had to make many concessions. The influential Friendly Societies had to be conciliated; the great opposition of Insurance Companies had to be bought off by bringing them into the scheme as administrators. The doctors were up in arms and threatened to go on strike. Mayfair demonstrated in the Albert Hall and registered a vow that they would never "lick stamps for Lloyd George".[870]

With 'gallows humour', Lloyd George apparently "used to tell a story in those days of his unpopularity over the Insurance Act. A body was recovered from the Thames. The rescuers, before trying to revive it, turned it over to make sure it was not Lloyd George!"[871]

Despite all this, the measure passed in the Commons on 6 December by 324 votes to 21. It was estimated that some 2,250,000 workers–within a limited number of trades such as building, engineering and shipbuilding–would come within the scope of the unemployment measures, whilst some 15,000,000 would be covered by the sickness and invalidity sections, an enormous leap forward. The Act had profound psychological implications, as it removed the need for unemployed workers to rely on the stigmatised social welfare provisions of the Poor Law. This hastened the end of the Poor Law as a social welfare provider: the Poor Law Unions were abolished in 1929, with the administration of poor relief being transferred to the counties and county boroughs. The Act provided free access to a panel doctor. Acutely aware of the prevalence of the scourge of TB, *y dicau*, particularly in rural Wales, Lloyd George ensured there were funds for research into the disease and provision for free healthcare and sanatoria throughout Wales to treat victims of the white plague.[872] Another major step forward, after pressure from the Co-operative Women's Guild, was the provision for: "Payment in the case of the confinement of the wife or, where the child is a posthumous child, of the widow of an insured person, or of any other woman who is an insured person, of a sum of thirty shillings (in this Act called 'maternity benefit')."

The leading part that Addison had played throughout the tortuous passage of the National Insurance Act was recognised by Lloyd George at a speech he gave at a complimentary dinner given in his honour on 6 February 1914:

> During the few years Dr Addison has been in the House of Commons, I have depended upon him as much as any man… and he has never let me down. During the Insurance Act… I found his advice invaluable… He was loyal to the Government and to the medical profession at the

---

870 P. Snowden, *An Autobiography: Volume One, 1864-1919*, 1934, London, Ivor Nicholson and Watson, p228. Snowden rated "the National Health Insurance Act and the Unemployed Insurance Act… with the amendments… [as] the two greatest measures of social reform ever placed upon the Statute Book." Snowden, p230. Philip Snowden (1864-1937), Labour MP who opposed conscription during the War, Chancellor of the Exchequer, 1924, 1929-1931, expelled from the Party for supporting the National Government.

871 Snowden, p229-230. See also W. W. Davies, p376.

872 Price, 2006, p195.

> same time. He is a first-rate fighter… I have been hunting tigers with him and we both got out of the jungle.[873]

Addison would have frequent working breakfast meetings with Lloyd George from this period until the outbreak of war, providing him with factual memoranda, later recording:

> He is a good talker and a good listener, but you have to know him well before you are sure that he is really listening, for his mind, when he seems to be listening, may often be occupied on some collateral or altogether different issue, as you will find from the sudden interjection of a new question. When he has made up his mind, no one can be prompter, but I have often known him fence with a subject for weeks.
>
> In those days he was a left-wing Radical, as I was, and grasped at any practical proposal likely to be useful to humble folk. I used to think that his mind was at its very best after breakfast, when we went for a quarter of an hour's walk round the Park, to separate afterwards on some agreed understanding at the Foreign Office steps. For several years I think I shared his project as closely as any man, though I very often knew that I had not divined the intention–if there was one formed at all–that was behind his eyes.[874]

Working breakfast meetings were an activity that was something largely of Lloyd George's own devising.[875] He would declare that he could "do three times as much work at breakfast time as at any other time of the day. 'If you find me tired at breakfast time, you can write me off as a political force,'" he would say.[876]

A new force now entered his private life, in the person of Frances Louise Stevenson, a fifth-form acquaintance of his daughter Mair from her time at Clapham High School. Mair had been hoping to read Mathematics at Cambridge and had been in demand at school to help coach less able pupils, including young Frances, who recalled that Mair was "a gentle and charming personality and I had particular reason to like her and be grateful to her, as she would often come to my help in my mathematical difficulties. She was good at mathematics: I was not, and she was always ready to explain away my problems. I liked her very much."[877] Born in London on 7 October 1888 to a Lowland Scottish father and a mother of mixed French and Italian extraction, after Clapham, which she entered on a scholarship, Frances, greatly inspired by her Latin and Greek teacher Miss Trenerry, had read Classics at Royal Holloway College, Egham, then an all-female institution. By her own admission, a less than diligent student, she nonetheless graduated with a third in 1910, being 'capped' by Lord Rosebery. She then took up a residential teaching position at Allenswood, a progressive girl's boarding academy in Wimbledon. Here she acquired the affectionate nickname 'Pussy', which remained with

---

873 Quoted in Morgan, *Portrait Of A Progressive*, p22.
874 Quoted in Minney, p135, from *Politics From Within.*
875 G. Shakespeare, p41. Shakespeare called it "a most horrible innovation".
876 [Stevenson], *Makers*, p17.
877 F. Lloyd George, *Years That Are Past*, p27.

her afterwards.[878]

Fate then took a hand. One day, at the end of July 1911, Lloyd George, acting on the recommendation of Mair's former headmistress, hired the rather shy 22-year-old Frances, 26 years his junior, as a tutor to his youngest daughter Megan, who also subsequently went to Allenswood. Frances later recorded her impressions from her interview at 11 Downing Street:

> I recall… the sensitive face, with deep furrows between the eyes: the eyes themselves, in which was all knowledge of human nature, grave and gay almost simultaneously; eyes which, when they scrutinized yours, convinced you that they understood all the workings of your heart and mind, sympathized with all your difficulties, set you in a place apart. The broad brow; the beautiful profile–straight nose, neat insolent chin. And a complexion as fresh and young as a child's. But there was something more even than this which distinguished him from all other men I had ever met–from all men whom I ever did meet thereafter–a magnetism which made my heart leap and swept aside my judgment.[879]

Frances went to Criccieth for the summer, becoming almost one of the family. The coaching continued throughout the winter, and in summer 1912 Frances went to Criccieth again. During 1912, she and Lloyd George fell in love, and at the end of the year he asked Frances to become both his private secretary and his mistress. He told her that, if he was ever free to marry her, he would do so, but in the meantime he gave her a copy of a book[880] on Parnell in order to make his position clear: "by marrying Kitty O'Shea, Parnell had destroyed his own career and destroyed the Irish Party: and he held that no man has a right to imperil his political party and its objective for the sake of a woman."[881]

Frances hesitated about becoming the mistress of a married man, as she wanted a conventional marriage and many children, but agreed to become his personal secretary on his terms. According to Bengy Carey-Evans, at the start of their relationship, Lloyd George had said to Frances to think about it, to go home and speak with her family about becoming his mistress, a relatively 'advanced' and open-minded attitude for the times. Frances duly did this, going to Scotland at Christmas, her family saying that it was not what they would have wished for her, but that if it was what she really wanted, they would support her. Frances left Allenswood, and on 21 January 1913 they evidently began a sexual relationship together, Frances later recording that they were "married" on that day.[882] Long-suffering Margaret Lloyd George was very soon aware of the situation and increasingly chose to spend her time in North Wales.

Meanwhile, a new international 'situation' arose that served to further increase Lloyd George's

---

878 Ibid., p39.
879 Quoted in Owen, p217.
880 Probably R. Barry O'Brien, *The Life of Charles Stewart Parnell 1846-1891*, 1898, 2 Vols., London, Smith, Elder & Co. In her *The Years That Are Past*, p52, Frances says that Lloyd George gave her Katharine O'Shea's own biography, *Charles Stewart Parnell: His Love Story And Political Life*, but this was not published until 1914, by Cassell in two volumes.
881 Longford, p11.
882 Taylor, *My Darling Pussy*, p2.

profile. He was considered an opponent of war until the Agadir Crisis of April 1911, during which he signalled his change of mood by giving a stirring and patriotic speech at the Mansion House in London on 21 July. The background was complex, as with so much of pre-First World War European diplomacy.[883] France's pre-eminence in Morocco had been upheld by the 1906 Algeciras Conference, following the First Moroccan Crisis of 1905-06. Anglo-German tensions were high at this time, partly due to an arms race between Germany and Great Britain, including German efforts to build a fleet two thirds the size of Britain's. Germany's move was aimed at testing the relationship between Britain and France.

In 1911, a rebellion broke out in Morocco against the despotic Sultan Abdelhafid. By early April, the Sultan was besieged in his palace in Fez. The French prepared to send troops to help put down the rebellion, under the pretext of protecting European lives and property, dispatching a flying column of 20,000 troops at the end of April. On 8 June, the Spanish army occupied Larache, and three days later Alcazarquivir. On 1 July, the German gunboat SMS *Panther* arrived at the port of Agadir, under the pretext of protecting German trade interests. The larger light cruiser SMS *Berlin* then arrived on 5 July, replacing the gunboat.[884] There was an immediate reaction from France and Britain. The British government attempted to restrain France from adopting hasty measures and to dissuade her from sending troops to Fez but failed. In April, Foreign Secretary Edward Grey wrote: "what the French contemplate doing is not wise, but we cannot under our agreement interfere." He felt that his hands were tied and that he had to support France. Britain was worried by *Panther's* arrival in Morocco: the Royal Navy had a base in Gibraltar, and it was thought Germany meant to turn Agadir into a naval base on the Atlantic. In case of war, Britain sent elements of the Mediterranean Fleet to Gibraltar. As in the First Moroccan Crisis, British support of France showed the strength of the 'Entente Cordiale'.

In early September, Germany was hit by financial turmoil. The Berlin stock market plunged by 30 percent in a single day, the public started cashing in currency notes for gold, and there was a run on the banks. The Reichsbank lost a fifth of its gold reserves in one month. It was rumoured that the French finance minister had orchestrated this crisis. Faced with the possibility of being driven off the gold standard, the Kaiser backed down and let the French take over most of Morocco. On 7 July, the German ambassador in Paris informed the French government that Germany had no territorial aspirations in Morocco and would negotiate for a French protectorate on the basis of "compensation" for Germany in the French Congo region and the safeguarding of her economic interests in Morocco. The German terms, as presented on 15 July, while containing an offer to cede the northern part of Kamerun and Togoland, demanded from France the whole of the French Congo from the Sangha River to the sea, to which was later added the transfer of France's right to the pre-emption of the Belgian Congo.

On the evening of 21 July, having conferred with Grey, which made the usually punctual Lloyd George nearly half-an-hour late, he delivered a speech before the Lord Mayor and the Bankers Association at the Mansion House in which he declaimed on the value of national honour:

883 See Clark, *The Sleepwalkers*, p204-213.
884 MacMillan, *The War that Ended Peace*, p439.

> Personally I am a sincere advocate of all means which would lead to the settlement of international disputes by methods such as those which civilisation has so successfully set up for the adjustment of differences between individuals… by some more merciful, more rational, and by a more just arbitrament than that of the sword.
>
> But I am also bound to say this that I believe it is essential in the highest interests, not merely of this country, but of the world, that Britain should at all hazards maintain her place and her prestige amongst the Great Powers of the world. Her potent influence has many a time been in the past, and may yet be in the future, invaluable to the cause of human liberty. It has more than once in the past redeemed Continental nations, who are sometimes too apt to forget that service, from overwhelming disaster and even from national extinction. I would make great sacrifices to preserve peace. I conceive that nothing would justify a disturbance of international goodwill except questions of the gravest national moment. But if a situation were to be forced upon us in which peace could only be preserved by the surrender of the great and beneficent position Britain has won by centuries of heroism and achievement, by allowing Britain to be treated where her interests were vitally affected as if she were of no account in the Cabinet of nations, then I say emphatically that peace at that price would be a humiliation intolerable for a great country like ours to endure. National honour is no party question. The security of our great international trade is no party question; the peace of the world is much more likely to be secured if all nations realise fairly what the conditions of peace must be…[885]

The speech was interpreted by Germany as a warning that she could not impose an unreasonable settlement on France.[886] On 4 November, Franco-German negotiations led to a convention referred to as the Franco-German Accord, under which Germany accepted France's position in Morocco in return for territory in the French Equatorial African colony of Middle Congo (now Republic of the Congo). This 277,130 km² territory, known as Neukamerun, became part of the German colony of Kamerun. The area is partly marshland but gave Germany an outlet on the Congo River. Germany ceded to France 16,705 km² of territory to the southeast of Fort Lamy (now part of Chad).

Edward Grey recorded:

> The speech was entirely Lloyd George's own idea. I did nothing to instigate it, but I welcomed it. The effect was much greater than any words of mine could have been. There was a section, and a considerable section, of opinion in this country that looked upon the Foreign Office in general, and myself in particular, as being unduly anti-German… Anything that I said was therefore liable to produce a certain reaction of antipathy in this section. The Germans knew this well enough, and no doubt prepared to make some discount of what I said. But Lloyd George was closely associated with what was supposed to be a pro-German element in the Liberal Government and in the House of Commons. Therefore, when he spoke out, the Germans knew that the whole of the Government and House of Commons had to be reckoned

---

885 Quoted in Du Parcq, Vol.IV, p791.

886 See K. Wilson, *The Agadir Crisis, the Mansion House Speech, and the Double-Edgedness of Agreements*, *Historical Journal*, 15, 3, 1972, p513-532.

with. It was my opinion then, and it is so still, that the speech had much to do with preserving the peace in 1911. It created a great explosion of words in Germany, but it made Chauvinists there doubt whether it would be wise to fire the guns. The speech certainly had the effect of making the German Government keep in touch with their Ambassador in London and send him instructions…[887]

On 1 August Sir William Tyrell, Grey's private secretary, wrote a remarkable letter to Sir Cecil Spring Rice, British Ambassador to Sweden, stating:

Don't ever forget to teach your children to keep alive the memory of Lloyd George who by his timely speech has saved the peace of Europe and our good name.

I shall never forget the service rendered by him. His courage was great, as he risked his position with the people who have mainly made him…[888]

Haldane and Lloyd George were among the minority in the Cabinet who were usually pro-German, on grounds of a shared religion, philosophy, artistic culture and scientific enquiry. Lloyd George had cleared his speech only with Asquith and Grey, not with the whole Cabinet. Arthur Zimmermann[889], German Under-Secretary of State for Foreign Affairs, indignantly asked the British Ambassador in Berlin, Sir Edward Goschen[890] "Who is Lloyd George to lay down the law to Germany and to stop a quick Franco-German settlement?"[891], and blamed Lloyd George for doing "untold harm both with regard to German public opinion and the negotiations". Count Paul Metternich, the German Ambassador in London, stated: "Well, at all events, we had no idea that public opinion would feel so strongly about it, and Mr. Lloyd George's speech came upon us like a thunderbolt."[892] He "was instructed to protest formally against a speech which had 'a tone of provocation towards Germany.' A hint was even conveyed that the Kaiser considered it to be his due that the offending Minister should be dismissed!"[893]

At this time, Lloyd George seemed to exist almost in the middle of a whirlwind of debate and controversy on all sides, such were his attitudes and the nature of his political reforms. On his second visit to Balmoral in September 1911, he revealed his perceptive observations and inner feelings to his wife Margaret:

I am not cut out for Court life. I can see some of them revel in it. I detest it. The whole atmosphere reeks with Toryism. I can breathe it and it depresses and sickens me. Everybody

---

887 Viscount Grey, *Twenty-Five Years 1892-1916*, 1925, London, 2 Vols., Hodder & Stoughton; Vol.I, p217.
888 Quoted in Cosgrove, p699, quoting Spring Rice MSS. F.O. 800/241.
889 Arthur Zimmermann (1864-1940), German Under-Secretary for Foreign Affairs, 1911-1916, author of the famous Zimmermann Telegram, sent on 16 January 1917, which prompted US entry into the FWW on 6 April.
890 Sir Edward Goschen (1847-1924), Ambassador to Berlin, 1908-1914.
891 Clark, *The Sleepwalkers*, p210.
892 Viscount Grey, *Twenty-Five Years*, Vol.I, p228.
893 W. W. Davies, p385.

> very civil to me as they would be to a dangerous wild animal whom they fear and perhaps just a little admire for its suppleness and strength. The King is hostile to the bone to all who are working to lift the workmen out of the mire. So is the Queen. They talk exactly as the late King and the Kaiser talked to me if you remember about the old Railway strike. 'What do they want striking?' 'They are very well paid', etc.[894]

Meanwhile, Lloyd George was involved in another important, complex issue that was growing in its vociferousness–the campaign for women's suffrage! Public attitudes towards the suffragette movement were adversely affected by militant actions led mostly by members of the Women's Social and Political Union (WSPU), founded on 10 October 1903. On 28 August 1907 the Qualification of Women (County and Borough Councils) Act was passed, clarifying the right of certain women ratepayers to be elected to borough and county councils in England and Wales. On 21 July 1908, the Women's National Anti-Suffrage League (WNASL) was inaugurated. Undeterred, the pro-suffrage groups continued to take direct action. In Bristol, on 13 November 1909, Winston Churchill was attacked with a dogwhip by WSPU member Theresa Garnett, causing widespread anger.

Despite being avowedly pro-women's suffrage and a leading Liberal, Lloyd George was often a target of suffragette activity. On 21 November 1907, he received a deputation from the Glasgow and West of Scotland Association for Women's Suffrage at the North British Station Hotel in Glasgow, Honorary Secretary Nellie Hunter asking him "for a pledge that the Government would bring in a women's suffrage Bill before this Parliament came to the end of its career."[895] Upon the merits of the question, he himself felt no doubts, telling them: "It is such an obviously reasonable thing that I cannot conceive the right of man to deny it."[896]

Although he continued to state his support of the suffrage movement in public speeches, the failure of the Liberal Government to make any progress on implementing change led Christabel Pankhurst to wrongly believe him to be a secret anti-suffragist. Three so-called 'conciliation bills' to provide some enfranchisement to women were put before the Commons, one each year in 1910, 1911 and in 1912, which would have extended the right of women to vote in the United Kingdom of Great Britain and Ireland to around 1,000,500 wealthy, property-owning women. While Asquith's Liberal government mostly supported this, he himself was an intransigent anti-suffragist, and a significant number of backbenchers, both Tory and Liberal, did not support the bills for fear that it would damage their parties' success in general elections. Some pro-suffrage groups rejected the bills because they only gave the vote to propertied women; some MPs rejected them because they did not want any women to have the vote. Liberals also opposed the bills because they believed that the moneyed women whom the bills would enfranchise were more likely to vote Tory than Liberal.

In February 1910 the re-elected Liberal government set up an all-party Parliamentary 'Conciliation Committee' composed of 54 Members (25 Liberals, 17 Tories, 6 Labour and 6 Irish Nationalists)

[894] Morgan, *Family Letters*, 16 September 1911, p158-159

[895] *Shields Daily News*, 22 November 1907.

[896] Quoted in Du Parcq, Vol.III, p596. On 6 October 1913, Lloyd George told his friend Riddell that "Ibsen was a great man. He converted me to women's suffrage. He had wonderful foresight and intuition." Quoted in Riddell, *More Pages*, p179.

charged to draft suffrage legislation. The outcome was the first 'Conciliation Bill', the 'Parliamentary Franchise (Women) Bill: A Bill to Extend the Parliamentary Franchise to Women Occupiers', introduced on 14 June by David Shackleton, Labour MP for Clitheroe, as a private members bill, which proposed that the vote should be given to women who were £10 householders, with the further stipulation that married women could not qualify in respect of the same property as their husbands. The measure received the cautious endorsement of the suffrage societies on the 'half-a-loaf' principle, and of Tories who depicted it as a means of strengthening the anti-radical vote in the country. Both Lloyd George and Churchill opposed it for the very same reason, the former writing to his brother William during the debate on the second reading in July, "Women's Debate going strong. F. E. Smith delivered a crushing speech against. I am dead against this Bill & mean to vote against it."[897] Publicly, he opposed the measure as being insufficiently broad and incapable of amendment. Both Lloyd George and Churchill voted against, but the bill was carried by a majority of 299 to 189 in the Commons, thereafter being referred to a Committee of the Whole House, effectively blocking its progress. Lloyd George wrote again to William "Women Suffrage killed for this year–killed altogether as far as yesterday's Bill is concerned. The suffragettes are for the moment concentrating their hate on Winston, although annoyed with me also."[898] On several occasions violent scenes ensued, including the notorious 'Black Friday' of 18 November in London.

A revised bill, the 'Women's Enfranchisement Bill: A Bill to Confer the Parliamentary Franchise on Women', was introduced by Sir George Kemp, Liberal MP for Manchester North West, as a private members bill on 9 February 1911, a measure which omitted the £10 householder qualification of the previous bill. The bill was promised a week of government time. On its second reading on 5 May, it won a majority of 255 votes to 88, Lloyd George this time voting in favour, due to the bill's broader definition than its predecessor–and to a visit on 28 April from many of Margaret's North Wales female Welsh Liberal friends[899], while Churchill abstained. Indeed, Lloyd George seemed to endorse the revived clamour in favour of 'Votes for Women' at a time when he was fully preoccupied with his National Health Insurance commitments. By the end of the summer, he had come to endorse a comprehensive reform of the franchise on lines which he expounded insistently to the Liberal Chief Whip, the Master of Elibank:

> I am very concerned about our pledges on the Female Suffrage question. We seem to be playing straight into the hands of the enemy. The Conciliation Bill could, on balance, add hundreds of thousands of votes throughout the country to the strength of the Tory Party. We would thus lose more than we could possibly gain out of the Registration Bill. We have never really faced the situation manfully and courageously. I think the Liberal Party ought to make up its mind as a whole that it will either have an extended franchise which would put working men's wives on the Register, as well as spinsters and widows, or that it will have no female franchise at all... We are likely to find ourselves in the position of putting this wretched Conciliation Bill through the

[897] NLW, William George Papers 2403, D. Lloyd George to William George, 11 July 1910.
[898] Ibid. 2404, D. Lloyd George to William George, 13 July 1910.
[899] *The Times*, 28 April 1911, p8.

House of Commons, sending it to the Lords, and eventually getting it through. Say what you will, that spells disaster for Liberalism.[900]

On 7 November Asquith unexpectedly announced that, during the next parliamentary session, he intended to introduce a manhood suffrage bill to include all *bona fide* residents, the bill being capable of amendment, at the discretion of the Commons, to include the enfranchisement of women. Lloyd George wrote to William the next day: "Asquith's declaration on manhood suffrage has taken everyone by surprise. It is entirely my doing. But I am amazed at the readiness & the proflitude [sic] with which he took the fence. I anticipated much more trouble. The Pankhursts are furious."[901]

Indeed, they were. Christabel Pankhurst told an audience at the Pavilion Theatre:

> Mr Lloyd George had done his best to sow dissension and imperil the prospects of woman suffrage... 'Lloyd Georgitis' seemed to be a disease which afflicted men to-day with very few exceptions. But women saw through him. They had always known him as an anti-suffragist, and they must fight him here and now...[902]

The bill was consequently dropped.

As yet another bill–the 'Parliamentary Franchise (Women) Bill: A Bill to confer the Parliamentary Franchise on Women', introduced, once again, as a private member's bill on 19 February by James Agg-Gardner, Tory MP for Cheltenham–was debated in the Commons chamber during March 1912, the suffragettes ramped up their campaign with 'direct action', mostly consisting of breaking windows, leading an exasperated Lloyd George, still one of the ministers more sympathetic to the suffragette cause, to write dejectedly to his brother William:

> 1 March 1912. Suffragettes broken out once more. Smashed PM's windows–shop windows in Oxford St & Charing X. Lunatics.[903]
>
> 4 March 1912. Suffragettes raving mad. Another outbreak of window smashing in West End today. They are destroying the last chance of carrying their Bill.[904]
>
> 5 March 1912. *Newydd. Bydd y Pankhursts a'r Pethicks i gyd yn y gaol cyn y boreu–os y delir hwy.* [News. The Pankhursts and the Pethicks will all be in the gaol before morning–if they are caught.][905]

It was rumoured in political circles that the third bill–this time closely defeated on its second reading on 28 March, by 208 to 222, Lloyd George voting for the measure, Churchill against–had been 'torpedoed' by a whispering campaign initiated by Lloyd George and Churchill that Asquith would

---

900 National Library of Scotland, Murray of Elibank MSS 8802, f.308, DLG to Elibank, 5 September 1910.
901 NLW, William George Papers 2524, DLG to WG, 8 November 1911.
902 *The Times*, 14 November 1911, p8c.
903 NLW, William George Papers 2561, DLG to WG, 1 March 1912.
904 Ibid. 2562, DLG to WG, 4 March 1912.
905 Ibid. 2564, DLG to WG, 5 March 1912. Emmeline Pethick-Lawrence (1867-1954), WSPU Treasurer and founder of the newspaper *Votes For Women*.

resign following the introduction of a private member's women's suffrage bill.

> This heartfelt fear, it was said, led to the loss of Irish Nationalist supporters of the suffragette cause, who looked suspiciously at any factor which might impede or delay the progress of their measure. The fury of the more militant suffragettes knew no bounds; Lloyd George had become their especial bête noir. Every public function which he attended saw the Chancellor harried and threatened by the 'female lunatics'.[906]

At the end of June, he was to address a political meeting at Walthamstow in Essex, a parliamentary division represented by Sir John Simon:

> I am off with Llwydyn [his daughter Olwen] to a meeting at Walthamstow in the Solicitor General's constituency. I shall probably be harried by the female lunatics. I am the only man in the Cabinet who could render them effective help & yet they have pursued me with unexampled malignity. Poor old PM, he has been worried by them these past weeks–& he minds them much more than I do.[907]
>
> On 13 July, about to deliver a speech at Kennington Theatre, Lloyd George was attacked by a member of the Men's Political Union for Women's Enfranchisement (MPU), Charles Gray, who came close to striking him on the head, provoking a scuffle which resulted in the Chancellor being pulled to the ground.[908] Such tactics caused something of a rift in the ranks of the suffragette sympathisers; at the end of August Mrs Fawcett[909] asserted that the militant faction had a 'large share' in causing the defeat of the third Conciliation Bill in March and had become 'the chief obstacles in the way of the success of the suffrage movement in the House of Commons, and far more formidable opponents of it than Mr. Asquith or Mr. Harcourt'.[910]

The year 1912 saw a marked increase in militant action in Wales in particular. Anger at the defeat of the conciliation bills saw the WPSU disrupt a speech by Lloyd George at the Pavilion in Caernarfon on 18 May. The protesters, male and female, interrupted him constantly with shouts of "You are a traitor, Mr Lloyd George", and they suffered 'a severe handling' with clothes torn and hair ripped out and were beaten with sticks and umbrellas. Further violent outbursts inevitably ensued. Upon his return from a late summer vacation at Marienbad, which he had at least ostensibly taken for the sake of his health[911], Lloyd George was again heckled by suffragettes whilst speaking before a crowd of over 13,000 at the National Eisteddfod at Bellevue Park in Wrexham on 5 September. His speech was "interrupted by persistent heckling–'When are you going to give votes for women?' He responded, 'I do not know what these foolish people gain for their cause… I fail

---

906 Jones, *Lloyd George And The Suffragettes*, 2003, p19.
907 NLW, William George Papers 2615, DLG to WG, 29 June 1912.
908 Riddell, *More Pages*, pp81-82, entry for 14 July 1912; *Sheffield Daily Telegraph*, 16 July 1912, p8.
909 Dame Millicent Garrett Fawcett (1847-1929), political activist, feminist, campaigner for women's suffrage.
910 *Evening Standard*, 22 August 1912.
911 See NLW MS 20,431C, DLG to Margaret Lloyd George, 17 and 28 August 1912.

to see what they think they gain by insulting a whole nation in the national festival of its democracy…"[912]

Violent scenes ensued outside the Eisteddfod Pavilion as the suffragette sympathisers were mobbed by the crowd:

> An auburn-haired lady [Kitty Marion][913] had several of her tresses torn out by the roots. In spite of the protection afforded by the police the terror-stricken suffragettes were hustled and knocked about… One of the constables remonstrated with the crowd and a suffragette, whose blouse was in tatters, and whose hair hung across her shoulders replied, "We will go on doing it until we get the vote!"[914]

Just two weeks later, on 21 September, one of the most notorious events in the history of suffrage in Wales took place, when Lloyd George returned to his home village of Llanystumdwy to open the Village Institute, the building financed and presented to the community by the Chancellor himself, using the money awarded him in his 1909 libel action. The opening of the institute was a notably high-profile occasion. The outer gates of the grounds were to be unlocked by Winston Churchill, the First Lord of the Admiralty, and the door of the institute by Sir Rufus Isaacs, the Attorney General.[915] Both ministers were then to deliver short speeches, followed by Lloyd George and his close political associate Charles Masterman. The Chancellor and his wife were then to give tea to the village schoolchildren and old age pensioners, while the new institute was to be the venue of an evening concert with Isaacs presiding and Masterman conducting.[916]

Crucially, a week before the occasion, fully aware that suffragette interruptions were almost certain, the officials of the Criccieth branch of the National Union for Women's Suffrage had communicated with the WSPU:

> The suffrage cause is progressing steadily here under the auspices of the NUWSS [National Union of Women's Suffrage Societies]. Militant methods will only injure the cause which both societies have at heart. Personal attacks on and abuse of Mr Lloyd George on the part of strangers in his native village will naturally not be tolerated, especially on an occasion such as this, which is not even political. Serious damage will be done to the Suffrage cause if any attempt is made to prevent Mr Lloyd George and his guests from speaking.[917]

---

912 *North Wales Weekly News*, 13 September 1912.

913 German-born actress and suffragette Katherina Maria Schäfer, 'Kitty Marion' (1871-1944), shouted "How dare you have political prisoners fed by force!" and tried to rush the platform as the audience sang 'Land of My Fathers', having been force-fed 232 times while on hunger strike in prison. See F. Riddell *Death In Ten Minutes: The Forgotten Life Of Radical Suffragette Kitty Marion* 2018, London, Hodder & Stoughton, p10, 114. A startling photograph exists of Kitty's arrest, her hair wild, being harangued by the crowd.

914 *Carnarvon and Denbigh Herald*, 6 September 1912; *North Wales Chronicle*, 6 September 1912.

915 Rufus Isaacs (1860-1935), Liberal MP for Reading, 1904-1913, Attorney General, 1910-1913, Lord Chief Justice, 1913-1921, Ambassador to the US, 1918-1919, Viceroy and Governor-General of India, 1921-1926.

916 Jones, *Lloyd George and the Suffragettes at Llanystumdwy*, p6.

917 *The Times*, 20 September 1912, p5e.

Significantly, the reply was evasive: "We beg to acknowledge the receipt of your letter. Speculation as to possible antics of ladies to-day is now all the more intense, as the reply is a polite intimation to wait and see." Mrs Pankhurst, it was reported, was unwilling to comment.

For the opening ceremony Lloyd George was accompanied by his wife, children and brother William, together with political associates like Ellis W. Davies (Caernarfonshire Eifion), J. Herbert Lewis (Flintshire), Ellis Jones Griffith (Anglesey) and even Sir H. J. Ellis-Nanney. Masterman delivered the only English language speech, stating:

> As I am the only Englishman speaking this afternoon, perhaps I might be allowed to say in the name of a few hundred thousand Englishmen I am very glad to join in the demonstration. We are grateful to you for having brought him up and taught him the way he should go–with some difficulties perhaps–and given him to us–(cries of 'Oh, no')–for the comfort of some, for the disturbance of others, and for the interest and excitement of all. I think you will all agree with me… when I say that Mr Lloyd George is one of the few men given to us during a century of whom it may be said that his life has changed the world a little.

Lloyd George's opening sentences were immediately drowned by a cry of 'Votes for Women' from a woman near the platform. 'Put her in the river', retorted the crowd as she was escorted away by a police constable and buffeted by the bystanders. As the Chancellor urged his listeners not to harm the suffragette sympathisers who were disrupting the meeting, a succession of interruptions followed. In the words of one of the press correspondents, "Their treatment on the outskirts of the crowd was, however, the reverse of mild. Each was assaulted in turn, and it was only through the intervention of a police constable and the congestion at that particular spot that one woman was saved being placed under the village pump."

Lloyd George spoke as follows: "… I am very anxious that this institute should provide at least one meeting place in the village where the villagers, without distinctions of creed, can come together to promote common objects and find joy in the same common entertainments."[918]

It was noted in the local press that the protestors had been stripped naked by a gang of local rowdies.[919] The London papers, too, reported these alleged incidents graphically and in detail. One of the women present described the events as a "revelation of the latent beast in man", while, in the words of Sylvia Pankhurst, "Men and women were beaten, kicked and stripped almost naked. The hair of the women was torn out in handfuls." It was further reported that the shirts of the protesting women were mercilessly cut up and distributed among the crowd as souvenirs of the momentous occasion.[920] Lurid press publicity inevitably ensued; a large picture of the women being assaulted and mauled dominated the front page of the *Daily Mirror*, and similar photographs occupied a full page in the *Illustrated London News.*

---

918 *North Wales Weekly News*, 27 September 1912.

919 *North Wales Observer and Express*, 27 September 1912.

920 See *Daily Telegraph*, 23 September 1912, and *Daily Mirror*, 23 September 1912.

Ellis W. Davies described the events which he had witnessed:

> When the Chancellor got up to speak he had a great ovation but no sooner had he appealed to the crowd in Welsh to be gentle with any suffragettes present than one of the women quite near the stage shouted "Votes for Women" & in the attempt to lead her out–she herself fighting & kicking those who tried to protect her–the crowd pressed down & [an] ugly rush was made for the platform. No sooner was one disposed of than other women cried in other parts of the field & whilst no doubt in the crush–at times dangerous–feeling got the better of some men, the accounts in the paper were untrue & on the whole the women came well out of a row into which they deliberately entered with a view of breaking up a social gathering & judging by their appearance no one would conclude that they were other than paid rowdies of a low class who did their work merely because they were paid. In time peace was restored but the excitement made it impossible for the Chancellor to speak effectively.[921]

His words were confirmed by a letter sent to Lloyd George a month later, only discovered in Lloyd George's papers in 1987. From Evan William Evans (1860-1925), a native of Dolgellau, a prominent journalist, editor, publisher and avid local historian, it read:

> I find in to-day's paper that questions are to be asked in the House of Commons on Monday about the treatment of the Suffragists at Llanystumdwy. I was present at the meeting and was quite close to two of the women who disturbed the proceedings, and who were ejected.
>
> The reports published in many of the newspapers were greatly exaggerated. It has been repeatedly asserted that the hair of one of the disturbers was actually pulled off in handfulls by the crowd. I was close by at the time and saw what did take place. The hat of the woman was taken off, and handfulls of hair did come off with it. A friend of mine picked up the hat, and I have it now in my possession as well as a considerable quantity of the 'hair' said to have been plucked off. But will you allow me to assure you that this woman did not on that occasion suffer the loss of any of her own hair! It was false hair that was artfully inserted inside the hat in such a way that it looked like natural hair, and of course 'it came off in handfulls'. I have been endeavouring to find out the name and address of the rightful owner of the hat and false hair, but so far I have failed. It was I think a very clever bit of stage acting and it came off well!...[922]

Herbert Du Parcq, who wrote his detailed biography close to the events which he was describing, made exactly the same point:

> They got some rough handling, which Mr Lloyd George did all in his power to restrain. There is, however, fortunately, no doubt that the attack which they provoked was very far from being as savage or as effective as many accounts in the newspapers led the public to believe. The

[921] NLW, Ellis W. Davies Papers 7, diary entry for 21 September 1912.
[922] NLW MS 21,790E, f.352, E.W. Evans to D. Lloyd George, 19 October 1912.

> ladies, expecting, as they were bound to expect, a summary retribution, had been prudent enough to put on old clothes, and these were badly torn; but the personal injuries which they suffered were happily slight.[923]

These more moderate, dispassionate accounts give a more balanced version of the events at Llanystumdwy. At the time, however, the exaggerated language of those involved inevitably received widespread currency in both the local and national press. The *London Evening News* published a lengthy interview with a 'Mrs S. Watson', one of the agitators attacked by the crowd, who claimed:

> I am bruised all down my side and arms and have had the skin kicked off my ankles… I received a violent blow from behind, and my hat was torn off… At that I became half unconscious, but I realised that I was being attacked from all sides… Once I was beaten down to the ground, but two constables and two other men succeeded in getting me up and out from among the hooligans. I was taken to a cottage, but the woman refused to give me admittance… Nearly all my clothing was torn to pieces.[924]

The Conservative *Western Mail* also published detailed accounts of the proceedings, concluding:

> The Welshmen behaved like fiends, and but for the heroic action of the Welsh policemen they would undoubtedly have been killed. One of them informed me that, though the men were bad, she had most to fear from the Welsh women, who took their hatpins out of their hats and made every attempt to use them. Neither would the Welsh women allow the suffragettes to take refuge in their cottages. Wales just now is in the very bad books of those suffragettes who seek relaxation from their domestic duties to cry "Votes for Women", on any and every occasion.[925]

It was a sad irony that the Llanystumdwy Institute, like many other such foundations in England and Wales, had been hailed in the North Wales press as a focal point of the village designed 'to break the monotony of rural life. The Llanystumdwy Institute will do a great deal to supply recreation for the folk of that parish, and make country life there more genial to the young people.'[926]

The opening sentence of the letter sent by E. W. Evans to Lloyd George also referred to the questions about to be asked in the Commons concerning the Llanystumdwy disturbances. Lord Robert Cecil[927] had in fact already asked the Home Secretary for his reaction to the 'serious assaults' which had occurred on 21 September, only to be told that 'the police were unable to identify any of the assailants… Many of the persons at the meeting came from outside the county, and were strangers

---

923 Du Parcq, Vol. III, p607.

924 Quoted in the *South Wales Daily News*, 24 September 1912. Actually, Miss Anna Karlina Watson (of Streatham), alias Mrs Annie Carmichael. Her alleged attacker, Benjamin Evans, a solicitor's clerk, was acquitted in November 1912 due to conflicting testimonies, lack of evidence and alleged provocation.

925 *Western Mail*, 24 September 1912.

926 *Carnarvon and Denbigh Herald*, 27 September 1912.

927 Robert Gascoyne-Cecil (1864-1958), Independent Tory MP for Hitchin, 1911-1923.

to the police who were there on duty, and who were fully occupied in affording protection to the women.'

Cecil persisted, referring to the photographs published in the newspapers, but was given an evasive reply[928]. The matter was again raised the following day[929], and again more forcefully on 21 October by Cecil and Harold Smith[930] who demanded to know whether 'as a result of investigations into the recent disturbances at Wrexham and Llanystumdwy, any information [had] been obtained as to the pulling out of women's hair; and, if so, whether any action [was] to be taken'. The Home Secretary, Reginald McKenna, replied that evidence of two cases of assault had been gathered by the Chief Constable, but he refused to elucidate further as criminal proceedings were likely. A further pertinent question on 'the pulling out of the women's hair' provoked no response. Finally, Smith asked pointedly, 'May I ask if this is an attempt to whitewash the Chancellor of the Exchequer?' 'There is not the slightest ground for any suggestion of that sort', retorted McKenna.[931]

By this time the cause of 'Votes for Women' had been effectively blocked within Parliament. The Liberal government was really in no position to push through any such measure; it was far from united on the matter, and Asquith was firmly in the anti-suffragist camp. The subject largely vanished from Parliamentary debate during what remained of the pre-war period. It re-surfaced briefly in January 1913 during the debate on the government's Franchise and Registration Bill. "Insurance & Women's Suffrage engaging my attention today", wrote Lloyd George to his brother, "Although I hate the militants one must not allow that to deflect his judgement on a great question of principle."[932] "Have no idea what will happen in the voting", he went on a week later, "except that I think we shall be beaten by a small majority. It is entirely the fault of the militant section."[933] In the event, the Speaker, James Lowther[934], ruled that the measure could not be amended to include women's suffrage clauses. Claiming betrayal, the WSPU immediately embarked upon another campaign of destruction. Christabel Pankhurst allegedly designed a strategy which included the "pouring of acids into pillar boxes, the cutting of telegraph wires, and the slashing of pictures in public galleries … [suffragettes] set fire to empty houses, they destroyed golf courses, they threw bombs at churches."[935]

On 19 February an attempt was made to blow up the house, then known as Cliftondown, which was being built for Lloyd George near the golf course at Walton Heath. One device had exploded at 6.10 am, causing about £500 worth of damage[936], while another had failed to ignite. That evening, in

---

928 https://api.parliament.uk/historic-hansard/commons/1912/oct/15/alleged-assaults-upon-women-llanystumdwy#S5CV0042P0_19121015_HOC_223. Retrieved 25 January 2025.

929 https://api.parliament.uk/historic-hansard/written-answers/1912/oct/16/alleged-assaults-on-women-llanystumdwy. Retrieved 25 January 2025.

930 Harold Smith (1876-1924), Tory MP for Warrington, 1910-1922, younger brother of F. E. Smith.

931 https://api.parliament.uk/historic-hansard/commons/1912/oct/21/alleged-assault-on-women-llanystumdwy#S5CV0042P0_19121021_HOC_257. Retrieved 25 January 2025.

932 NLW, William George Papers 2674, DLG to William George, 16 January 1913.

933 Ibid., 2680, DLG to WG, 23 January 1913.

934 James Lowther (1855-1949), Tory MP for Penrith, 1886-1921, Speaker, 1905-1921.

935 S. Kingsley Kent, *Sex and Suffrage in Britain, 1860-1914*, 1990, London, Routledge, p202.

936 The bomb, consisting of 5lbs of gunpowder, was in the first-floor bedroom. It caused a severe amount of damage, and a crack is still visible in the Grade 2 listed Pinfold Manor.

a meeting at Cory Hall, Cardiff, Emmeline Pankhurst, one of the leaders of the militant WSPU, declared "we have blown up the Chancellor of the Exchequer's house… We have tried blowing him up to wake up his conscience … We have tried everything else… I say that for all that has been done in the past I accept responsibility. That I have advised, I have incited, I have conspired."[937]

The WSPU had always insisted that their actions would never physically harm individuals and, like the many other properties they had attacked, the house was uninhabited; but even a minor miscalculation might have led to a different and tragic outcome. Lloyd George was not present, but workmen had been due to arrive at the house soon after 6.00 am, and the primitive fuses used could easily have resulted in the bombs exploding after their arrival. Indeed, after visiting the house with the Lloyd Georges to see the bomb's impact, George Riddell, the owner of the *News of the World,* who had commissioned the house, wrote on 4 March in his diary: "LG [sic] much interested. Said the facts had not been brought out and that no proper point had been made of the fact that the bombs had been concealed in cupboards, which must have resulted in the death of 12 men had not the bomb which first exploded blown out the candle attached to the second bomb, which had been discovered, hidden away as it was. He was very indignant…'"

Shortly after the bombing, Christabel Pankhurst was interviewed by the *Daily Chronicle* in Paris, where she had gone to escape prosecution. In response to the reporter's question, "Aren't you afraid of being called Anarchists?", Christabel made the WSPU position quite clear: "We do not mind at all… we are fighting a revolution". She explained that Lloyd George was a prime target because, while often professing himself in favour of women's suffrage, "he is always betraying us". This was a reference to the repeated collapse of attempts by Lloyd George to effect a reconciliation between the Liberal Government and the suffrage movement: something that militants wrongly attributed to insincerity on his part.

On the centenary of the events, historian Elizabeth Crawford gave the context of them in a nutshell:

> It was no secret that the house being built at Walton-on-the-Hill was intended for Lloyd George. However, he had not yet signed the lease and, when the explosion occurred, had already set out on a motoring holiday in the south of France with Sir Rufus Isaacs… Like Lloyd George and other Liberal luminaries, such as Reginald McKenna and Charles Masterman, Rufus Isaacs was a member of the Walton Heath Golf Club, of which Sir George Riddell was a director. Sir George was an intimate friend of Lloyd George and the club was his power base. Over a round of golf newspaperman and politicians could discuss the issues of the day, retiring later to their country houses nearby. The masculine exclusivity of this circle was a goad to militant suffragettes debarred from the world of parliamentary politics. Although police suspected two WSPU members, Olive Hockin and Norah Smyth, the perpetrators were never caught.
>
> By claiming responsibility for the bombing, Mrs Pankhurst reduced pressure on the Home Office to bring the real culprits to trial. Her Cardiff meeting was attended by a large force of

[937] Quoted in J. Purvis, *Emmeline Pankhurst: A Biography*, 2003, London, Routledge, p210.

> police and her speech transcribed by a reporter of the *Western Mail*, the proprietor of which was none other than George Riddell. The *Mail's* editor assured the chief constable that the shorthand taker had kept his original notes and would be available to give evidence. At a meeting on 21 February in the office of the Home Secretary, Reginald McKenna, the decision was taken to prosecute Mrs Pankhurst for procuring and inciting women to commit offences contrary to the Malicious Injuries to Property Act, 1861. She was arrested on 25 February, sentenced on 3 April to three years' penal servitude and immediately went on hunger strike. No attempt was made to feed her forcibly and the Prisoners' (Temporary Discharge for Ill Health) Bill, which allowed hunger-striking prisoners to be released to recover their health before being reimprisoned, was rushed through to ensure that she did not die in prison. Notorious as the 'Cat and Mouse' Act, it received Royal Assent on 25 April.[938]

The Chancellor was also the recipient of regular assassination threats, and Scotland Yard detectives were assigned to shadow him, which irked him somewhat when he took a late summer holiday at Marienbad, together with Sir Rufus Isaacs and T. P. O'Connor. He continued to be a major target for suffragette violence through until the outbreak of war, when the WSPU suspended their campaign.

One writer argues that the women's suffrage cause during the immediate pre-war years fell victim to the Chancellor's loss of influence which, in turn, he attributes to the impact of the Marconi scandal:

> At a time when the Government was pressing a Franchise Bill and was split on suffrage, the only man with political force enough to secure the inclusion of suffrage, and prevent the break-up of the Government, was being embarrassed by charges of corruption… At the very time when his political instincts told him that the Liberals must break out of the sterility of coercion on suffrage, he was a captive of the chief architect of that policy–the Prime Minister… The Marconi affair is the crucial backcloth to the struggle that, at least in public, went on to amend the Government's Franchise Bill."[939]

It should also be noted that Lloyd George's freedom of manoeuvre was severely restricted, too, by Asquith's implacable opposition to the cause, and by the fact that his fellow Radical 'par excellence' within the Cabinet, Winston Churchill, was at best equivocal on women's suffrage. Whatever the reasons, it is difficult to resist the conclusion that the failure of the pre-war Liberal governments to enfranchise women was one of the worst blots on their record.

On 26 February 1912, a coal strike began at Alfreton, Derbyshire, and soon spread nationwide until around 1,000,000 miners were out. The dispute centred upon the attempt by the Miners Federation of Great Britain, the major trade union representing coal miners, to secure a minimum wage for miners in their district and replace the existing, complex wage structure which made it difficult for a miner to earn a fair day's wage. They wanted 5s. for an eight-hour day for men, and 2s. a day for boys, the 'five and two'. The Cabinet was divided on this. On 18 March Lloyd George met

---

[938]https://history.blog.gov.uk/2013/07/04/mrs-pankhurst-lloyd-george-suffragette-militancy/ . Retrieved 29 April 2019.

[939] D. Morgan, *Suffragists and Liberals: The Politics of Women's Suffrage in England,* 1975, Oxford, Blackwell, p108-09.

Vernon Hartshorn[940], one of the South Wales Miners' Federation leaders, at Riddell's house in London and had a long, frank discussion.[941] By 23 March, Lloyd George told Riddell that "under the circumstances, and to avoid more trouble, he had strongly supported the inclusion of the 5s. and 2s…"[942] The strike caused considerable disruption to train and shipping schedules before the government intervened and effectively ended the strike by passing the Coal Mines (Minimum Wage) Act on 29 March. The Act was flawed, failing to include the 'five and two', but for the first time establishing regional Boards of Trade responsible for deciding minimum wages for underground workers in their area. Employers would then be bound by law to pay this. The strike itself collapsed on 6 April.[943]

During April 1912–June 1913 the so-called 'Marconi Scandal' threatened to disrupt, or even prematurely, terminate Lloyd George's career. Allegations were made that highly placed members of the Liberal government had profited by improper use of information about the government's intentions with respect to the British Marconi Company. They had known that the government, after urging from senior military men, was about to issue a lucrative contract to the Marconi Company for the Imperial Wireless Chain[944] and had bought shares in an American subsidiary. The ministers included in the allegations and rumours about insider trading in Marconi shares were Lloyd George; Sir Rufus Isaacs, the Attorney General; Herbert Samuel[945], the Postmaster General; and Alexander Murray, the Parliamentary Secretary to the Treasury. The allegations included the fact that Isaacs' younger brother, Godfrey Isaacs, was managing director of Marconi.

Lloyd George had indeed acquired 1,000 shares on 17 April from Rufus Isaacs:

> No money changed hands at this point, nor did the shares get transferred, so technically, they did not exist, as it was only on 19 April, two days on, that these American Marconi shares were actually placed on the stock market, at a special price of £3 5s 0d per share, to rise to £4 exactly by the end of that day's stock market trading. Following further share transfer arrangements between two Isaacs brothers and Lloyd George, the latter's share total increased to 1,286 ordinary shares. Lloyd George, sensing some profit, sold out on 20 April… receiving £3 6s 6d per share, thus achieving a capital gain of £743 on the original but unpaid share price of £1 1s 3d. In brief, Lloyd George and his colleagues had acquired American shares at a discount, totally owing to privileged information and pre-launch availability.[946]

It is worth noting that "Godfrey Isaacs had given assurances that the British and American Marconi companies were quite separate entities, regrettably failing to add that they shared the same patents and

---

940 Vernon Hartshorn (1872-1931), Welsh trade unionist, Labour MP for Ogmore, 1918 until his death.

941 Riddell, *More Pages*, p45-46.

942 Ibid., p47.

943 See D. H. Robertson, *A Narrative of the Coal Strike*, *Economic Journal* 22, 87, September 1912, p365-387.

944 The Imperial Wireless Chain was a strategic network of powerful long range radiotelegraphy stations, finally constructed by the government between 1922-1928 to link the Empire.

945 Herbert Samuel (1870-1963), High Commissioner for Palestine, 1 July 1920–30 June 1925, the first Jew to govern the historic land of Israel in over 1900 years, Liberal Leader, 4 November 1931–26 November 1935.

946 Ivatt, p62.

many other common interests."[947]

On 19 July 1912, Herbert Samuel announced that a contract had been agreed between the government and the English Marconi Company. On 25 July, W. R. Lawson, wrote in the weekly, Tory-leaning *Outlook Magazine*: "The Marconi Company has from its birth been a child of darkness… Its relations with certain Ministers have not always been purely official or political." On 8 August Hilaire Belloc's short-lived weekly *The Eye-Witness* also claimed that Lloyd George, Godfrey Isaacs, Murray and Samuel had profited by buying shares, based on knowledge of the government contract. It has often been noted that there was a significant strand of anti-Semitism in the coverage of the 'scandal', with the Isaacs' brothers and Samuel being Jewish, and Lloyd George's Welshness not endearing him to elements of the English establishment itching to find a stick to beat him with over his attacks on them and their unearned privileges.[948] Murray was, of course, another Celt, a Scot. Notably, the affair gained little traction in the mainstream press of any political persuasion.

On 11 October, there was an intense debate in the Commons on the motion "That a Select Committee be appointed to investigate the circumstances connected with the negotiation and completion of the Agreement between Marconi's Wireless Telegraph Company, Limited, Commendatore Guglielmo Marconi, and the Postmaster-General, with regard to the establishment of a chain of Imperial Wireless Stations, and to report thereupon, and whether the agreement is desirable and should be approved…"[949] George Lansbury, Labour MP for Bow and Bromley, rose to state:

> … the Committee I desire to be appointed should be one that will have power… to go into the matter through and through. My object in that has been from a practical point of view–from the point of view of whether this is a business agreement and one that the Government of our country should have entered into with a company like the Marconi Company… the other side of the matter in connection with the gambling in the Marconi shares is one which I think is of sufficient importance and grave enough in respect to the reputation, not merely of the Government, but the House itself, that I should have thought that long ago the Government themselves would have wanted an investigation. The statement has been spread, broadcast publicly, that considerable sums of money have been made out of the sale of these shares, and that they have been made by people who had information in connection with this matter previous to other people…
>
> … I certainly think that no one in any sort of way connected with one side or the other, should have any part or lot in the making of these agreements…

[947] Ibid., p63.

[948] See K. Lunn, *The Marconi Scandal And Related Aspects Of British Anti-Semitism, 1911-1914*, unpublished D. Phil Thesis, 1978, University of Sheffield.

[949] https://api.parliament.uk/historic-hansard/commons/1912/oct/11/marconi-wireless-telegraph-company#S5CV0042P0_19121011_HOC_99. Retrieved 31 July 2019.

> I think it does, at any rate, give rise to at least criticism, and for statements such as have been appearing to appear. I hope there will be no kind of shrinking on the Committee with regard to this matter.[950]

At the end of the debate the motion was agreed to, the resulting committee being composed of six Liberals–including the chairman, Sir Albert Spicer, two Irish Nationalists and one Labour MP, which provided a majority over six Tories. The committee took evidence from witnesses for the next six months and caused the government a great deal of political embarrassment.

On 14 February 1913, the French newspaper *Le Matin* alleged, in an article headed *'Un Scandale Financier en Angleterre'*, that Isaacs and Samuel had abused their position to buy shares in the English Marconi company, subsequently selling them on at four times the amount. Despite printing a retraction and an apology on 18 February, on the advice of Churchill, both men sued the paper for gross libel the next day. Churchill argued that this would provide an opportunity to shape the consciousness of the general public. He suggested that they should employ two barristers, F. E. Smith and Sir Edward Carson, both Tories: "The public was bound to notice that the integrity of two Liberal ministers was being defended by normally partisan members of the Conservative Party, and their appearance on behalf of Isaacs and Samuel would make it impossible for them to attack either man in the House of Commons debate which would surely follow." During the case, Isaacs testified that he had bought shares in American Marconi and sold some on to Lloyd George and Lord Murray.[951] It was not made public during the trial that these shares had been made available through Isaacs's brother at a favourable price. *Le Matin's* apologies were finally accepted on 19 March, and the paper was ordered to pay legal costs. Lloyd George had already testified to the select committee on 28 March. In conclusion, he had said "This is my great fortune", and flourished his dispatch case to exhibit, if required, the contents of his own and his wife's passbooks, furthering offering scrutiny of his brother's investment details.[952]

There was a further tense debate in the Commons on 18 and 19 June, under the motion "That this House regrets the transactions of certain of His Majesty's Ministers in the shares of the Marconi Company of America, and the want of frankness displayed by Ministers in their communications on the subject to the House." Speaking after Isaacs, Lloyd George, as could be expected, spoke spiritedly in his own defence:

> I have spent most of my active life in the service of the House, and I should be deeply grieved indeed if the House of Commons thought that I had been lacking in any respect to it or to its great institutions, and, above all, should I regret it if they thought that I had been lacking in frankness and openness in my dealings…

---

[950]https://api.parliament.uk/historic-hansard/commons/1912/oct/11/marconi-wireless-telegraph-company#S5CV0042P0_19121011_HOC_99. Retrieved 31 July 2019.

[951] Alexander Murray, Baron Murray of Elibank (1870-1920). Forced to resign on 7 August 1912, he was raised to the peerage six days later.

[952] Owen, p232; Ivatt, p65-66.

... The first charge brought against us was the charge of wholesale corruption. These were charges which were circulated for months... They were circulated in a journal owned by a Member of this House, and... the Committee would never have been appointed but for those charges. Still more, although they have been disposed of now, we are discussing this question in the atmosphere created by them... Therefore, I cannot treat charges of corruption brought against us as if they are to be dismissed merely in a sentence. These were the charges that mattered... What I should like to call the attention of the House to is this: The absolute recklessness with which charges of this kind were brought...

... Although it is indiscretion on paper and impropriety on paper, in the background it is corruption, which you will hear for months when it cannot be refuted. The charge has been exploded, but the deadly after-damp remains, and the noxious fumes of these slanders are at this very moment poisoning the blood of people who are considering even minor charges which are brought against us...

... I am entitled to fair play and justice from every Member here–I am asking that the other charges should be considered fairly and as remotely as possible from that atmosphere. I am not going to qualify any statement I will make as to whether it was judicious. I do not mind whether you use the word "judicious," or "wise," or "discreet". I say that looking at all the circumstances it was neither... I accept any of them. It was not... I am not asking any of my Friends or any hon. Member when he gives his vote to sanction anything I have done from the point of view of wisdom or discretion. I certainly ought not to have done it. But there is a vast difference between indiscretion which may be acknowledged and which may be rebuked, and an indiscretion in a private investment which warrants a solemn Vote of Censure from the House of Commons. What I did, I did bona fide. I did it in my own name... At any rate, if I did wrong, and it was a mistake, I had not a notion at the time... that I was transgressing any rule, implicit or otherwise. It was done quite openly... There was no controversy about the agreement... Everybody treated that contract as an accomplished fact. For four months there was not a murmur about it, after it had been blazoned forth and the market had been operating. What happened? I therefore thought the contract was definite... I had absolutely nothing whatever to do with the negotiations. The papers never came before me, and those who had seen the papers know that perfectly well. At the time when they might have come before me I was engaged upon the coal strike, and I could not give a moment's attention to them... That accounts for the fact that I perhaps overlooked the question of ratification and the formal contract.

Let me give... the three cardinal factors that entered into my mind when I entered into the transaction. The company in which I was investing had no contractual relations of any sort or kind with the Government–none, not one penny. Those are the facts which were presented to me at the time. The American company would not profit by a single sixpence, however profitable the contract might be... The second factor was this–I remember the impression–it was a purely and absolutely separate company. The third was, that I was assured that we were purchasing at the market price on that date. Those are the three factors that entered into my mind at that moment. I did not know all the details. I did not examine the charters of incorporation… Perhaps I ought to have done so; I am not challenging that for a moment, but I did not… I ought to have scrutinised all these documents before I entered upon this transaction. I realise frankly all the misconstruction that can be placed upon it–the same name, Marconi, an honoured name…

… I was perfectly frank with the Committee… I want to be equally frank with the House… I do not think any Member of the House would care much to go through the ordeal my right hon. Friend and I have gone through in the last few months, some of it deserved, most of it, and the worst of it, undeserved–calumnies, slanders, insults… What has given me most pain has been the anxiety which a heedless action of mine has given to thousands, inside and outside the House, of those who have been comrades of mine in great struggles. Nothing… has grieved me more deeply than the apprehension lest some thoughtless act should have put in jeopardy, even for an hour, causes in which I have been brought up to believe as a religious faith. I am conscious of having done nothing which brings a stain upon the honour of a Minister of the Crown. If you will, I acted thoughtlessly, I acted carelessly, I acted mistakenly, but I acted innocently, I acted openly, and I acted honestly…[953]

The next day, the debate continued, before the motion was put to the vote, being rejected by 346 votes to 268, it being thereby resolved: "That this House, after hearing the statements of the Attorney-General and the Chancellor of the Exchequer in reference to their purchases of shares in the Marconi company in America, accepts their expressions of regret that such purchases were made, and that they were not mentioned in the Debate of 11th October last, acquits them of acting otherwise than in good faith, and reprobates the charges of corruption brought against Ministers which have been proved to be wholly false."[954] Even Violet Asquith, no fan of Lloyd George, was moved to write in an unusually sympathetic way to a friend on 20 June: "as to Marconi… I think you forget that Rufus [Isaacs] & Lloyd George are my *friends*–that I care for them–that it is a pain to me to see them unjustly pilloried & and going through the fire for an error of judgement. Of course I am biased in so far as I care for them."[955]

The factual matters were at least partly resolved by the findings of the select committee's investigation, which issued three reports on 30 June: all found that ministers had purchased shares in the American Marconi company. The majority (government) report claimed that no minister had been influenced in the discharge of his public duties by any interest he might have had in any of the Marconi or other undertakings, or had utilized information coming to him from official sources for private investment or speculation. The minority (opposition) report, meanwhile, criticised the whole handling of the share issue and found "grave impropriety" in the conduct of Lloyd George, Rufus Isaacs and Murray, both in acquiring the shares at the advantageous price and in subsequent dealings in them. It also censored them for their lack of candour, especially Murray. Although the chairman on the enquiry,

953 https://api.parliament.uk/historic-hansard/commons/1913/jun/18/marconis-wireless-telegraph-company. Retrieved 29 July 2019.
954 https://api.parliament.uk/historic-hansard/commons/1913/jun/19/marconis-wireless-telegraph-company. Retrieved 29 July 2019.
955 Bonham Carter and Pottle, *Lantern Slides*, p387. Letter to Hugh Godley, 20 June 1913. Her brother Raymond had been engaged as a junior counsel in the successful libel case against *Le Matin* on 19 March 1913.

Albert Spicer, signed the majority report, he also published his own report where he heavily criticised Rufus Isaacs for not disclosing at the beginning that he had bought shares in the American Marconi Company. Spicer claimed that it was this lack of candour that resulted in the large number of rumours about the corrupt actions of the government ministers.[956]

If anything, the damage was that done to Lloyd George's influence and the resultant detriment of the radical causes they all sought to promote. Asquith, however, with his caustic eye probably already viewing Lloyd George as a potential future Liberal leadership rival, observed *sotto voce* soon afterwards to Charles Masterman next to him on the front benches "I think the idol's wings are a bit clipped."[957] Lloyd George voiced his own opinion at the National Liberal Club on 1 July:

> There is one martyrdom which I always thought was the least endurable of all. That was where the victim had his hands tied and arrows were shot into his body; and he could neither protect himself and tear them out nor sling them back. I can understand something of that now. For months every dastardly and cowardly journalist in the Tory Press shot his poisoned darts, knowing that the hands were tied behind the back by the principles of honour... My hands are free now free to shield, free to smite, not for myself, but for the cause I believe in, which I have devoted my life to, and which I am going on with…
>
> I should like to say one word about politicians generally. I think that they are a much-maligned race. Those who think that politicians are moved by sordid, pecuniary considerations know nothing of either politics or politicians. These are not the things that move us… In politics there is no cash, and if this campaign of calumny goes on there will be very little credit, either. There is no politician I know of who has attained a high position on either side… by capacity and strength of character–who would not in a business or profession make ten times as much as he makes in politics… The men who go into politics to make money are not politicians. Men go in… for fame. Men go in… for ambition. Men go in from a sense of duty. But for mere cupidity, never!
>
> We all have ambitions… I have an ambition. I should like to be remembered amongst those who, in their day and generation, had at least done something to lift the poor out of the mire...
>
> The real peril in politics is not that individual politicians of high rank will attempt to make a packet for themselves… The real peril is that powerful interests will dominate the Legislature, will dominate the Executive, in order to carry through proposals which will prey upon the community. That is where tariffs–the landlord endowment–will come in.

On 8 August 1913, Masterman, as Financial Secretary to the Treasury, moved, "That the Agreement between Marconi's Wireless Telegraph Company, Limited, Commendatore Guglielmo Marconi, and the Postmaster-General, with regard to the establishment of a chain of Imperial Wireless Stations (Parliamentary Paper, No.217, of Session 1913) be approved." After debate, it was approved by 210

956 Owen, p236.

957 Pugh, *Lloyd George*, p60.

votes to 138. The issue was over, except in the mind of Lord Wolmer[958], who in the first week of September continued to attack Lloyd George in *The Times* letters columns. Wolmer had denounced Lloyd George in a public speech, and, although he later admitted to some small inaccuracy, in his letters he repeated his allegations that Lloyd George had acted improperly. Lloyd George reacted angrily and personally, for which he has been criticised, but it would seem not unreasonable that he would be frustrated at the issue being dragged on for party-political reasons.[959]

Fortunately–in the grand scheme of things–the 'scandal' largely blew itself out as greater issues pressed in on Europe's attention. Herbert Samuel himself later rightly observed:

> A serious outcome of the whole affair was that the public controversy, and the protracted proceedings in the House and in its Committee, caused a year's delay in the ratification of the contract. The consequence was that, when the war came in 1914, the wireless stations in England and Egypt, although begun, had not been completed, and the projected stations in Aden and India had not even been decided upon. But for that delay our scheme would have been in operation, and would have provided the British Empire in its hour of greatest need with an additional means of instantaneous communication, free from danger of interruption, and of the greatest strategic value.[960]

Lloyd George and the others cannot be excused from a charge of a certain moral culpability and naivete, but some context needs to be borne in mind. The rules governing Parliamentary behaviour and of business dealings were considerably laxer then. Another consideration is the fact that MPs did not earn a salary until 10 August 1911, when a payment of £400 per annum [£60,211 in 2025] was introduced by Lloyd George. At the time it was seen as a radical, reforming move, opening a closed, patrician political system to people of all backgrounds, and ultimately creating a House of Commons grounded in the values of social mobility and inclusion.

Crucially, Lloyd George had no intention of creating a class of 'professional politicians'. He made this clear when defending his motion on 'Payment of Members' in the Commons on 10 August 1911:

> The only principle of payment in the public service is that you should make an allowance to a man to enable him to maintain himself comfortably and honourably, but not luxuriously, during the time he is rendering service to the State. That is the only principle, and it is the principle on which we have proceeded… When we offer £400 a year as payment of Members of Parliament it is not a recognition of the magnitude of the service, it is not a remuneration, it is not a recompense, it is not even a salary. It is just an allowance, and I think the minimum allowance, to enable men to come here, men who would render incalculable service to the State… but who

---

958 Roundell Cecil Palmer, Viscount Wolmer (1887-1971), Tory MP for Newton, Lancashire, 1910-1918.

959 M. Bonham Carter, and M. Pottle, Eds. *Lantern Slides: The Diaries And Letters Of Violet Bonham Carter 1904-1914,* 1996, London, Weidenfeld and Nicolson, p389.

960 Samuel, p77.

> cannot be here because their means do not allow it. It is purely an allowance to enable us to open the door to great and honourable public service to these men…[961]

The motion passed by 256 votes to 158.

Lloyd George came from a poor background unlike virtually all the existing Liberal and especially Tory members, and had four surviving children to support. His interest in obtaining more income can thus be seen to be quite natural. As John Grigg argued, unlike most MPs, Lloyd George:

> … had no capital resources, whether self-made or derived from the money-making activities of ancestors (such as those who had done well out of the Reformation). As a young M.P. he had to live off a share, perhaps unduly large, of the profits from the solicitors' firm in which he and his brother William were the founder-partners, supplemented by whatever fees he could earn from casual journalism and lecturing. From the very first his lack of financial independence was intensely irksome to him, not because he cared about money for its own sake, but because he could see that private wealth was a key to political independence.[962]

His measure also greatly facilitated the rise of the nascent Labour Party with its exclusively working-class membership of 42 MPs in the House. The growth of Labour after the 1910 elections was becoming a major determinant in subsequent by-elections up to the outbreak of war. Between 1911-1914 the Liberal Party lost fifteen by-elections to the Unionists, and in six cases this was attributable to the influence of Labour.[963] In these constituencies, the Liberals had won each election since 1906, and in four there had not previously been a Labour candidate. Labour's intervention gave voters an anti-Unionist alternative, leading to the classic British electoral situation of making a Tory victory more likely by splitting the opposing 'progressive' vote. Violet Asquith would call it "that damned split vote".[964]

There was another important issue progressing at this time, which the 'Marconi Scandal' has subsequently rather overshadowed. This was Lloyd George's 'Land Campaign' of 1913-1914. In late June 1912, he had instituted the Land Enquiry Committee, to investigate the condition of workers housing in Great Britain and make recommendations for its improvement. The committee was chaired by Sir Arthur Acland and included five Liberal MPs and the poverty campaigner, Benjamin Seebohm Rowntree, whom Lloyd George had first met in 1907 whilst the President of the Board of Trade. On 14 October 1913, Rowntree published the first volume of his report, 'The Land', dealing with the rural situation, followed by the larger urban volume on 2 April 1914. In it, Rowntree argued that an increase in small landholdings would make agriculture more efficient and productive.

Lloyd George wanted to make this issue the next great Liberal enterprise and began to make

---

961 https://api.parliament.uk/historic-hansard/commons/1911/aug/10/payment-of-members-1. Retrieved 18 October 2021. By comparison, in 2025 MPs basic annual salaries stood at £91,346.

962 J. Grigg, *Lloyd George: From Peace To War 1912-1916*, 1985, London, Eyre Methuen, p44.

963 These were: Oldham (November 1911); Crewe (July 1912); Midlothian (September 1912); South Lanarkshire (December 1913); Bethnal Green South West, Leith (February 1914).

964 Bonham Carter and Pottle, *Lantern Slides*, p289.

speeches based on the information gleaned from these studies, starting with his speech on 'The Rural Land Problem: What It Is' in Bedford on 11 October 1913. He claimed that labourers' income now stood lower in real terms than in the reign of Henry VIII [1509-1547]. He demanded a living wage for them, allotments to be available for those who wanted them, the demolition of rural slums, an end to 'capricious eviction', protection against rent increases arising from improvements carried out by tenants, and defence against the destruction of crops by game kept purely for the sporting pleasure of landlords. He believed that a new, uniform system of land valuation would considerably increase the rate revenue of local authorities, and that this, in turn, could help provide funding for the introduction of social provision in other areas such as education and housing. Land courts could fix higher wages for labourers and lower rents for tenant farmers, both benefits at the expense of landowners.

Lloyd George expanded his points in Swindon in his speech 'The Rural Land Problem: The Remedy', given on the afternoon of 22 October to an enthusiastic audience of 3,000 Liberal delegates from the counties of Gloucester, Dorset, Somerset and Wilts at the GWR Medical Fund Society's huge swimming baths on Faringdon Road.[965] His two-hour peroration was classic Lloyd George, his perennial concerns spelled out in his signature vividly allusive manner:

> Security for the landowner meant immunity from taxation. They are to order "Dreadnoughts"; other people are to pay. They are to increase the Army; and tradesmen, professional men, farmers, labourers, workmen, are to pay. The landowner must be secure from the tax-collectors and, above all, from the Chancellor of the Exchequer… You must give him security. I should like to ask these gentlemen in what respect does the landowner lack security? He has his freehold, and he cannot be deprived of it without the fullest compensation. Is that true of the farmer? If the landowner spends money on drainage, if he spends it in improving the land, if he spends it on building, it is his–nobody can turn him out without paying for it. Is that true of the farmer? It is not security for the landowner that we need–he has it–it is security for the tiller of the soil, and that is the first essential condition of the revival of agriculture…
>
> … We propose, first of all, that we should set up in this country a Ministry of Lands, which will have the control and supervision of all questions dealing with use of land in town and country.[966] To this new Ministry will be transferred the Board of Agriculture and all its existing functions. To these functions will be added new ones–questions of registration of title, land transfer. These will be handed over to the new Ministry with a view to simplifying these things. With all respect to my profession… we would rather like to get the land out of the hands of the lawyers…
>
> I come to a more important function. You recollect in a little Bill which I introduced in 1909… I set up a machinery for valuing the whole land of the Kingdom so that we should see exactly where we were, and the nation should have a sort of Domesday Book with a full record of its most valuable asset. And it is going on. We have valued about two-thirds of the land of

[965] See *Mr. Lloyd George At Swindon*, *North Wilts Herald*, 24 October 1913, p6-7. The present author thanks Duncan Hill for this reference.
[966] On 19 October 1964 the new Labour Government appointed a Minister of Land and Natural Resources. As in other fields of social provision, Lloyd George had arrived at these ideas over fifty years ahead of them.

the Kingdom, and the remaining third will be all valued by about March, 1915, so that we shall have what practically every civilised country in the world except ours has: a valuation of the land of the Kingdom… We propose to hand over the whole of that machinery for valuation to the new Ministry of Lands, and you will see by-and-by why we are doing that. So long as it is a revenue proposition it is always open to them to suggest that we are valuing too low for the sake of increment or that we are valuing too high for the sake of undeveloped tax. Whether you hit them high or hit them low they always complain, and we are going to hand it over to a department which will be perfectly impartial, which will have no revenue designs, and which will have no object on earth except to know what the real value is…

… We are going to hand over to the new Ministry great powers, of the control and supervision over land generally, small holdings, land purchase, disputes between landlord and tenant–which interfere with the proper development of the resources of the land–powers of reclamation, afforestation, and development of uncultivated land. This new power will operate through the Commissioners who will be appointed–Commissioners of a judicial character, who will act judicially, not Courts. There again we are going to keep the lawyer outside. The Commissioners will be men, who all the same will act judicially, not by means of litigation, but by means of seeing for themselves what is going on. I will show you how these Commissioners will proceed in the very first point to which I called your attention, and that is security for the cultivator. When a farmer or a small holder gets notice to quit he sends up at once to the Ministry of Lands, and says the landlord is trying to turn him out of house and home. The Ministry of Lands will send down one of their officers to find out why he is turned out, what offence he has committed, and if the answer… [is connected with politics, the interests of game, or with religious allegiance, then the officer will say]… "Have you no better reason than that? Here is your notice to quit." And he will tear it up and fling it down. Were the landlord to say, "He is a bad farmer," then the officer would say, "Now you are talking." If he is a bad farmer it is not merely in the interests of the country, it is in the interests of the community that a man should do that…

… No individual landowner can be expected to afforest on a great scale, when perhaps it is only his grandchildren who will get the benefit. But… fifty years in the life of a nation, is but a season in the life of man. A nation that is going to be great must have the foresight to look ahead for generations…

It is a great undertaking, it is a gigantic one, but we mean to put it through. It is one that may take time, it is one that may involve us in a struggle with great interests; we are accustomed to that. We have beaten interests before, and we will do it again. But it is a task, which, when it is accomplished, will bring Britain in our judgment a long march nearer the dawn. I believe it will have the effect not merely of filling the countryside with a happy, prosperous, contented peasantry, but it will do more than that–it will free the towns from the nightmares of unemployment and sweating and slums. Then we shall have a Motherland that its children can rejoice in…[967]

[967] D. Lloyd George, *The Rural Land Problem: The Remedy*, 1913, London, Liberal Publication Department. https://babel.hathitrust.org/cgi/pt?id=wu.89101141695&view=plaintext&seq=1. Retrieved 22 January 2020.

In the evening, Lloyd George spoke again, this time as one of a number of MPs addressing an audience of over 5,000 members of the general public at the Drill Hall, New Swindon, at which he naturally reiterated the points he had made earlier. His message found a most receptive audience. He wrote to Percy Illingworth[968], the new Liberal Chief Whip: "Swindon was electric. I have rarely addressed such an enthusiastic meeting. They were the picked Liberals of the West and they were as keen as mustard. The land caught on."[969] The Tories struggled to find an effective counter. Using a typically sporting simile, an internal party memo noted how "our own men are already going in all directions like foxes in a cornfield".[970]

On 1 January 1914, the *Daily Chronicle* reported an interview with Lloyd George at Criccieth, in which he returned to his previously expressed theme that military expenditure impeded social progress. He stated that the lightening of the burden of rates must be an essential part in the programmes of both political parties. He would despise success unless there was a real effort to reduce the overwhelming extravagance in expenditure on armaments. If a saving could be effected it would be possible to sweep away tea, sugar, coffee and cocoa taxes and reduce the income tax from ½d to 2d in the £1.

> The present is a favourable time to overhaul expenditure on armaments, as the strain has become relaxed owing to Sir Edward Grey's diplomacy as Continental nations are directing their energies to the strengthening of their land forces. Germany cannot take chances with her army, and Great Britain can afford to quietly maintain her present superiority at sea without making feverish efforts to increase it. Finally, there is a revolt against armaments throughout Western Europe, and Liberalism must act upon the new temper.

Morally, he was right, but sadly the year would prove his timing to be unfortunate. Lloyd George remarked that his land campaign had trebled the attendance at many Liberal meetings and must dominate political thought until it was settled. A new second chamber, devolution by which the Imperial Parliament would be relieved of provincial affairs, reform in education, and prevention of poverty were other problems with which the Asquith ministry was pledged to deal.[971]

The Land Enquiry Committee published its urban report on 2 April. It dealt with such matters as urban housing, land acquisition and urban tenures. It proposed a system of local rating which would allow considerable discretion to local authorities as to how far they applied Site Value Rating (SVR). It was also argued that increased prosperity in the countryside would drive up demand for goods manufactured in the towns. However, reactions were notably less enthusiastic than those the rural report had garnered, an important factor now that the working-class urban population was fast outstripping the rural agricultural one.[972]

---

[968] Percy Illingworth (1869-1915), Liberal MP for Shipley, 1906 until his death.
[969] Lloyd George to Illingworth, 24 October 1913, Lloyd George Papers (HL) C/5/4/7.
[970] Ridgewell, p26.
[971] *Arms and the Nations: Mr. Lloyd George's Bold Indictment*, *Daily Chronicle*, 1 January 1914, p1.
[972] Douglas, p12.

Nonetheless, progress was being made, with even significant sections of the Labour movement being generally in favour. During 1912-1913 the Fabian Society had conducted its own independent enquiry into 'Land Problems and Rural Development', launched in June 1912, with a draft report appearing as a special supplement to the *New Statesman* on 2 August 1913.[973] Its conclusions were broadly similar to those of the Liberal Land Report. In fact, it lent further support to it, rather than providing Labour with new, alternative ideas. In the *Daily Chronicle* of 16 October 1913, Ramsay MacDonald described the Liberal Land Report as being "masterly" and noted the "striking harmony" between the Liberal and Labour Reports. In a speech at Middleton on 20 October, Arthur Henderson[974] stated that if the government carried out its land programme, "they would have no more loyal supporters than those in the ranks of the Labour Party,"[975] a quite extraordinary endorsement. With this dovetailing of opinions, in early 1914, Lloyd George made a bid for an electoral accommodation with Labour, sending a memo to MacDonald to that effect on 3 March, stating that he had the support of Asquith and the 'inner Cabinet', holding out the prospect of increased Labour representation in the Commons, and in the Cabinet too, if they wished it. In return, Labour would support the government at the next election that was due to be called, to finally solve the Irish issue, and to fight on an agreed programme with three-way contests being avoided by the withdrawal of candidates of both parties. Sadly, neither side would commit, and the initiative was scuppered when Henderson brought the matter before the Labour NEC on 21 April.[976] This was due to 'rank-and-file' distrust, and to both Henderson and MacDonald's scepticism of the Liberal's chances of success at the next election.

Events then overtook everyone and everything. By this time, Europe was brimming with a lethal cocktail of paranoid imperialism, militarism and nationalism. Modern scholarship finds that no nation intended to wage full-scale war, but that the diplomatic web of alliances was so intricate, inherently unstable and interlocked, especially in the Balkans, that as the dominos started to tumble faster, each nation was dragged into war like a sleepwalker. In such tragic fashion, the full horror of the First World War broke upon Britain and her Empire on 4 August 1914. Late in the evening of 3 August, Foreign Secretary Edward Grey had famously said to his friend John Spender, editor of the *Westminster Gazette*, as they looked out of the window in his Foreign Office room overlooking the Mall: "The lamps are going out all over Europe; we shall not see them lit again in our life-time."[977] The British ultimatum to the Germans on Belgian neutrality expired at 11.00 pm, King George V duly declaring war.

Lloyd George was as surprised as virtually everyone else by the outbreak of the war. At 10.50 am on Sunday, 28 June 1914 Archduke Franz Ferdinand, heir to the Austrian throne, and his beautiful

[973] Packer, *Lloyd George, Liberalism and the Land*, p167.

[974] Arthur Henderson (1863-1935), Labour Leader, 5 August 1914–24 October 1917, Minister without Portfolio, 9 December 1916–11 August 1917.

[975] *Manchester Guardian*, 21 October 1913; Quoted in Packer, *Lloyd George, Liberalism and the Land*, p169.

[976] C. Howard, *Macdonald, Henderson, and the Outbreak of War, 1914*, *Historical Journal* 20, 4, December 1977, p871-891; information cited on p872-73.

[977] Grey, *Twenty-Five Years*, Vol.II, p20.

wife Sophie, Duchess of Hohenberg, were assassinated in Sarajevo, the capital of the Austro-Hungarian province of Bosnia and Herzegovina. The perpetrator was 19-year-old Bosnian Serb, Gavrilo Princip, a member of *Young Bosnia,* and one of a group of six assassins organized and armed by the irredentist *Black Hand* secret society. His 'shot that was heard around the world' triggered the 'July Crisis', a series of interrelated diplomatic and military escalations among the major powers of Europe. This was coupled with miscalculations by many leaders that war was in their best interests, or that a general war would not occur, which ultimately resulted in a general outbreak of hostilities.

At this time, Rosika Schwimmer[978] was living in London, serving as International Press Secretary of the International Woman Suffrage Alliance and correspondent of important European newspapers. Her wide knowledge of international affairs gave her an understanding of the imminence of war; on 9 July, she met with Lloyd George at a working breakfast in 11 Downing Street to share her premonitions, but sadly at this stage he dismissed her concerns. Later he wrote:

> An influential Hungarian lady… told me that we were taking the assassination of the Archduke much too quietly; that it had provoked such a storm throughout the Austrian Empire as she had never witnessed, and that unless something were done immediately to satisfy and appease resentment, it would certainly result in war with Serbia, with the incalculable consequences which such an operation might precipitate in Europe. However, such official reports as came to hand did not seem to justify the alarmist view she took of the situation.[979]

On 23 July, nearly four weeks after the assassination, the very day of the Austro-Hungarian démarche to Serbia, with its 48-hour deadline for compliance, Lloyd George made an optimistic speech advocating "substantial economy" in the Commons, saying that Britain's relations with Germany, Austria-Hungary's ally, were "very much better than they were a few years ago… [These two great Empires]… begin to realise they can co-operate for common ends, and that the points of co-operation are greater and more numerous and more important than the points of possible controversy."[980] On 27 July he told C. P. Scott of the *Manchester Guardian* that as "to the European situation there could be no question of our taking part in any war in the first instance. Knew of no Minister who would be in favour of it…"[981] At 11.00 am on 28 July, Austria-Hungary, considering itself to have not received a satisfactory reply, declared war on Serbia and the dominos began to fall. With the Cabinet divided, and most ministers highly reluctant for Britain to get involved, Lloyd George struck Asquith as "more sensible and statesmanlike" at the Cabinet meeting on 1 August, favouring keeping Britain's options open[982]. During it, Lloyd George passed a note to the bellicose Churchill stating, "if patience prevails

---

978 Rosika Schwimmer (1877-1948), Hungarian pacifist, feminist and world federalist. Lloyd George's visitors were always more eclectic than most senior politicians, even if he did not always agree with their views.

979 Lloyd George, *War Memoirs*, Vol.I, p32-33.

980 https://api.parliament.uk/historic-hansard/commons/1914/jul/23/finance-bill#S5CV0065P0_19140723_HOC_359. Retrieved 31 January 2019.

981 Scott, p91.

982 H. H. Asquith, *Memoirs and Reflections 1852-1927*, 1928, London, Cassell, p7.

and you do not press us too hard we might come together."[983]

The next day–as the Germans occupied Luxembourg–through a working breakfast of six ministers at No. 11, an unprecedented Sunday full Cabinet meeting at No. 10, a working lunch of eight ministers at Halkyn House, the Belgrave Square mansion of Lord Beauchamp[984], and a final, evening Cabinet meeting at No. 10, he seemed highly likely to resign if Britain intervened, to "retire for the time being to Criccieth." According to Don Cregier "By arguing on behalf of British action only if there was "substantial violation" of Belgian territory and "interference with Belgian independence," and threatening to resign if anything less was made a 'casus belli', Lloyd George was able to postpone a decision on intervention until more was known of German–and Belgian–intentions."[985] That very evening, the German ambassador to Belgium delivered an ultimatum to the government in Brussels demanding the unimpeded passage of German troops through Belgian territory.

In the early hours of Monday, 3 August, Asquith, as acting war minister, wrote out an order for the mobilization of the army. By the time the Cabinet met at 11.00 am, it was known that the Belgians had rejected the Germans demands. Shortly after noon the Cabinet had before them King Albert I's moving telegram appeal for British "intervention… to safeguard the integrity of Belgium." This was what caused Lloyd George to make up his mind to stay on and fight: "I stay. Its Belgium" he declared to Morley.[986] After lunch at No. 11, Herbert Samuel drove with Lloyd George to the House of Commons, recording: "He [Lloyd George] was warmly cheered by the excited people, waving little Union Jacks. 'This is not my crowd', he said. 'I never want to be cheered by a war crowd.'"[987] As Lloyd George wrote to Margaret after the meeting, which sanctioned British mobilization:

> I am moving through a nightmare world these days. I have fought hard for peace & succeeded so far in keeping the Cabinet out of it but I am driven to the conclusion that if the small nationality of Belgium is attacked by Germany all my traditions & even prejudices will be engaged on the side of war. I am filled with horror at the prospect. I am even more horrified that that I should ever appear to have a share in it but I must bear my share of the ghastly burden though it scorches my flesh to do so.[988]

On 4 September C. P. Scott recorded details of a meeting he had with Lloyd George:

> He and Lord Beauchamp and Morley and Burns had all resigned together on the Saturday before the declaration of war (August 1) on the ground that they could not agree to Grey's giving pledge

---

[983] C. Ponting, *Thirteen Days: The Road To The First World War*, 2002, London, Chatto & Windus, p255.
[984] William Lygon, 7th Earl Beauchamp (1872-1938), First Commissioner of Works, 1910 -1914.
[985] Cregier, p251.
[986] Cregier, p252. The Treaty of London, (19 April 1839), Article VII, required Belgium to "form an Independent and perpetually Neutral State", by implication committing signatory powers to guard that neutrality in the event of invasion. Informed by the British ambassador that Britain would go to war with Germany over the latter's violation of Belgian neutrality, German Chancellor Bethmann-Hollweg famously exclaimed that he could not believe that Britain would do so over a mere "scrap of paper", "*ein Fetzen Papier*".
[987] Quoted in Wasserstein, p164.
[988] Morgan, *Family Letters*, p167.

> to Cambon[989] to protect North coast of France against Germans, regarding this as equivalent to war with Germany. Grey intensely anti-German. Asquith greatly influenced by him. Lloyd George then, as more than once before[,] failed at the pinch. "That old windbag" Haldane counted for nothing. Churchill reckless. On urgent representations of Asquith he [Lloyd George] and Beauchamp agreed on Monday evening to remain in the Cabinet without in the smallest degree, so far as he was concerned, withdrawing his objection to the policy but solely in order to prevent the appearance of disruption in face of a grave national danger. That remains his position. He is, as it were, an unattached member of the Cabinet and sits very lightly.[990]

At 11.00 pm on Tuesday, 4 August, the British ultimatum to Germany to "respect the neutrality of Belgium" expired, and a state of war existed between the two nations. Lloyd George later recalled: "We sat waiting for Big Ben to strike the hour when the ultimatum expired. We all fell quite silent. As the great blows of the hammer sounded on the bell we seemed to be passing into another world."[991] Leaving No. 10 at 11.30 pm he "felt like a man standing on a planet that had been suddenly wrenched from its orbit by a demoniac hand and that was spinning wildly into the unknown."[992] Lloyd George was clearly seen as a key figure whose stance helped to persuade almost the entire Cabinet to support British intervention. He was able to give the more pacifist members of the Cabinet and the Liberal Party a principle–the rights of small nations–which meant they could support the war and maintain united political and popular support.[993]

On 5 August, the Commons voted to approve a credit of £100m [£14,745,679,189 in 2025] for the war effort. By and large, men rushed to volunteer to serve their country, believing the old, pernicious lie that 'it would all be over by Christmas'. On 7 August, the Commons was told that an additional 500,000 men were needed for the army, 67,000 for the navy. The same day Kitchener, the new Secretary of State for War, issued his first appeal for 100,000 volunteers. He got an immediate response with 175,000 men volunteering in a week. There soon appeared Alfred Leete's iconic war poster featuring a pointing Kitchener, and the words: "Britons: [Kitchener] Wants You! Join Your Country's Army!", first issued as the cover of *London Opinion* on 5 September: by the end of the month over 750,000 men had enlisted.

Lloyd George's own priority from 2 August was at the Treasury, where he "reacted with vigour and confidence"[994] in dealing with the immediate monetary crisis, the London Stock Exchange–then the largest securities market in the world–having closed on 31 July for the first time in its 117-year history, not to re-open until 4 January 1915. On 3 August the Postponements of Payments Act, 1914, was passed, establishing a month's moratorium on the payment of outstanding bills. To buy time, Lloyd George got an Order in Council, extending the national bank holiday on Monday 3 August up to and including Thursday 6 August, the longest bank holiday in British history. The extended bank

---

989 Paul Cambon (1843-1924), Ambassador in London, 1898-1920.

990 Scott, p103.

991 Quoted in Spender, *Prime Minister*, p180.

992 Lloyd George, *War Memoirs*, Vol.I, p48.

993 Gilbert, *Organizer Of Victory*, p110-113.

994 Morgan, *Lloyd George*, p82.

holiday gave him a chance to negotiate with all the relevant parties and pass emergency legislation to cope with war conditions. He worked with Walter Cunliffe[995], the Governor of the Bank of England, and others from finance and industry, calming the 'flapping penguins' of the city money markets by preventing the suspension of gold payments and preventing the removal of foreign securities. The Currency and Banknotes Act 1914, passed on 6 August, authorised the issuing of one pound and ten shilling notes. Bearing the signature of John Bradbury[996], the Permanent Secretary to the Treasury, they became popularly known as 'Bradburys'.

On 4 August Lloyd George made a proposal in the Commons for a state insurance scheme against the risks of wartime shipping. The scheme had been long in the making, but only his intervention brought it to fruition.[997] It was designed to safeguard Britain's commerce in general, but its essential flow of foodstuffs in particular. Importantly, the state would reinsure 80 per cent of all war risks on ships leaving port after the outbreak of war, a significant change in government policy.[998] Indeed, Christopher Addison noted approvingly the same day that it was "probably the most Socialistic measure, after [National] Insurance, to which this Government has ever been committed."[999] By 10 August the financial emergency was over, and the bank 'moratorium' ended. In debate in the Commons on 22 August, Lloyd George could declare:

> I think we have done for the banks as much as ever they could have expected of us. We did not do it in order to strengthen their position or to increase their dividends. We did it in order to enable them to finance the trade of the country during a difficult period. If the Government and the country are prepared to take risks, they must take risks as well…[1000]

Lloyd George had not forgotten his native land, his powerful 'An Appeal to Wales" being published bilingually in the *Western Mail* on 8 August. He promoted "three plain duties", all important issues in the highly uncertain first days of the war, by which "the keenest edge of suffering will be tempered to our weaker citizens":

> No one must foolishly obstruct the efforts of the Government, to keep stable the finances of the country. The wealth of Saturday is untouched; no man is poorer… today we are merely asked to forego the privilege of handling gold, and to pay and be paid in notes and silver.
> Men are to be furnished with banknotes, to do the work of gold, and the gold so left free will be fighting equally with our brave soldiers the battle of our liberties. Men and treasure are the

995 Walter Cunliffe (1855-1920), Governor of the Bank of England, 1913-1918.

996 Sir John Bradbury (1872-1950), Permanent Secretary to the Treasury, 1913-1919, the government's Chief Financial Adviser during the war, Principal British Delegate to the Reparations Commission in Paris, 1919-1925.

997 https://hansard.parliament.uk/commons/1914-08-04/debates/e272cde2-7879-4685-97d2-a5b41fd1cd68/WarRisks. Retrieved 29 August 2021.

998 Hazlehurst, p173.

999 Addison, *Four And A Half Years*, Vol.I, p33.

1000 https://hansard.parliament.uk/Commons/1914-08-26/debates/7ed3aa8f-9138-460d-912c-bde6cf6294d6/CurrencyAndBankLoan(Amendment)Bill. Retrieved 13 January 2021. See R. Roberts, *Saving The City: The Great Financial Crisis Of 1914*, 2013, Oxford, Oxford University Press.

> imperative needs of the moment… Will all good men and women, therefore, use the new money, and thus help it into circulation?
>
> … No one should buy more food than is absolutely necessary at any one time. Large buying raises, by the force of sudden demand, prices far beyond their normal level; thus are the poor doubly crushed by diminishing wages and inflated prices. Will all Christians solemnly resolve… to take from the national resources only their needs from day to day?
>
> … All employers of labour should strive to their utmost to keep their men and women employed. Starvation will follow unemployment, and untold misery and suffering will come upon the children… Short time for all is better than no work for many. With some wages our people may secure bare necessities; with no wages, social degradation and ruin are upon them.[1001]

As for risks, Lloyd George was reluctant for his own 20-year old son, Gwilym, to enlist at this stage. He wrote to Margaret on 11 August explaining his position:

> They are pressing the Territorials to volunteer for the war. We mustn't do that just yet. We are keeping the sea for France–that ought to suffice here for the moment especially as we are sending 100,000 men to help her to bear the first brunt of the attack. That is all that counts for Russia will come in soon. I am dead against carrying on a war of conquest to crush Germany for the benefit of Russia. Beat the German Junker but no war on the German people &c. I am not going to sacrifice my nice boy for that purpose. You must write Wil telling him on no account to be bullied into volunteering abroad.[1002]

This statement has sometimes been held against him as an act of hypocrisy, but he was merely expressing a private opinion within a wider context. He did nothing to hinder any of his offspring from serving in France, as the record would soon show. On 25 August he wrote to his brother William, summing up his thoughts at this pivotal time:

> The French have made a bad start. For the moment it looks as if they were outclassed in sheer brain power… I entered into it most reluctantly. Nothing but Belgium would have induced me to throw in my lot with the war party–but now we are in it we must go through with it whatever the cost to us all'.[1003]

At 3.00 pm on 19 September, at the Queen's Hall in Langham Place, Lloyd George duly delivered a passionate call to arms and committed himself to a fight to the finish. In this landmark, prophetic speech, delivered before 3,500 largely London Welsh, with 10,000 more outside, he spoke in terms that may well have inspired Churchill's wartime rallying call to the nation a generation later. A main purpose of the speech was recruitment, Lloyd George playing on his own Welsh roots. He was in the

---

1001 *Western Mail*, 8 August 1914, p4; *Llangollen Advertiser*, 14 August 1914, p7.
1002 Morgan, *Family Letters*, p169.
1003 NLW, William George Papers 2870(4), 25 August 1914.

midst of a battle to persuade Kitchener to allow the creation of a specifically Welsh Army Corps: 'A strong response to his call for men would be proof that an appeal for Welsh recruits could be made on a national basis.'[1004] When Lloyd George rose, journalist Frank Dilnot recorded "His mobile face was touched with gravity, his eyes were thoughtful, not provocative… Responsibility lay on him, and everyone could see it."[1005] Speaking slowly, he began:

> There is no man in this room who has always regarded the prospects of engaging in a great war with greater reluctance, with greater repugnance, than I have done throughout the whole of my political life. There is no man… more convinced that we could not have avoided it without national dishonour. I am fully alive to the fact that whenever a nation has been engaged in any war she has always invoked the sacred name of honour. Many a crime has been committed in its name… But, all the same, national honour is a reality, and any nation that disregards it is doomed.
>
> Why is our honour as a country involved in this war? Because, in the first place, we are bound in an honourable obligation to defend the independence, the liberty, the integrity of a small neighbour that has lived peaceably… We entered into this treaty… to defend Belgium and her integrity… Our signatures do not stand alone there. This was not the only country to defend the integrity of Belgium. Russia, France, Austria, and Prussia–they are all there… It is suggested that if we quote this treaty it is purely an excuse on our part. It is our low craft and cunning, just to cloak our jealousy of a superior civilization we are attempting to destroy…
>
> … It is now the interest of Prussia to break the treaty, and she has done it … She says treaties only bind you when it is to your interest to keep them. 'What is a treaty?' says the German Chancellor. 'A scrap of paper.' …
>
> Treaties are the currency of international statesmanship… This doctrine of the scrap of paper, this doctrine which is superscribed by Bernhardi[1006], that treaties only bind a nation as long as it is to its interest, goes to the root of public law. It is the straight road to barbarism… and the whole machinery of civilization will break down if this doctrine wins in this war.
>
> We are fighting against barbarism. But there is only one way of putting it right. If there are nations that say they will only respect treaties when it is to their interest to do so, we must make it to their interest to do so for the future. What is their defence?… They said: 'We cannot help that.' Rapidity of action was the great German asset. There is a greater asset for a nation than rapidity of action, and that is–honest dealing.
>
> … All these tales about conspiracy have been fanned up since. The great nation ought to be ashamed … She has deliberately broken this treaty, and we were in honour bound to stand by it.
>
> Belgium has been treated brutally… What has she done?… She was one of the most unoffending little countries in Europe. She was peaceable, industrious, thrifty, hard-working,

---

[1004] Gilbert, *Organizer of Victory*, p117.

[1005] Dilnot, p120. Frank Dilnot (1875-1946), editor of the Labour-supporting *Daily Citizen*, 1912-1915.

[1006] Friedrich von Bernhardi (1849-1930), Prussian general, military historian, best known for his bellicose book *Deutschland und der Nächste Krieg* (Germany and the Next War), 1911, advocating a militarist policy of ruthless aggression and of complete disregard of treaties.

> giving offence to no one; and her cornfields have been trampled down, her villages have been burned to the ground, her art treasures have been destroyed, her men have been slaughtered, yea, and her women and children, too… Hundreds of thousands of her people… are wandering homeless in their own land. What is their crime? Their crime was that they trusted to the word of a Prussian King. I don't know what the Kaiser hopes to achieve by this war. I have a shrewd idea of what he will get…
>
> I am not going to enter into these tales. Many of them are untrue; war is a grim, ghastly business at best, and I am not going to say that all that has been said in the way of tales of outrage is true… It is enough for me to have the story which the Germans themselves avow, admit, defend, proclaim. The burning and massacring, the shooting down of harmless people–why? Because, according to the Germans, they fired on German soldiers. What business had German soldiers there at all? Belgium was acting in pursuance of a most sacred right, the right to defend your own home.[1007]
>
> … But their perfidy has already failed. They entered Belgium to save time. The time has gone. They have not gained time, but they have lost their good name…

Lloyd George then made a similar case for the other 'little nation' involved, namely Serbia, and the declaration of war against it by its mighty neighbour Austria, despite its attempts to meet Austrian demands, before continuing:

> That is the story of the little nations. The world owes much to little nations–and to little men... Frederick the Great chose his warriors for their height, and that tradition has become a policy in Germany. Germany applies that ideal to nations; she will only allow six-feet-two nations to stand in the ranks. But all the world owes much to the little five feet high nations… The heroic deeds that thrill humanity through generations were the deeds of little nations fighting for their freedom… if we had stood by when two little nations were being crushed and broken by the brutal hands of barbarism our shame would have rung down the everlasting ages…[1008]
>
> What about England? You go to Greece, the Netherlands, Italy, Germany, and France, and all these lands, gentlemen, could point out to you places where the sons of Britain have died for the freedom of these countries... The test of our faith, the highest standard of civilization is the readiness to sacrifice for others.
>
> I would not say a word about the German people to disparage them. They are a great people; they have great qualities of head, of hand, and of heart. I believe, in spite of recent events, there is as great a store of kindness in the German peasant as in any peasant in the world. But he has been drilled into a false idea of civilization,–efficiency, capability. It is a hard civilization; it is a selfish civilization; it is a material civilization. They could not comprehend the action of Britain at the present moment… a great Empire pledging its resources, pledging its might, pledging the

[1007] Over 6,400 Belgian and French civilians were killed by the Imperial German Army between August-October 1914 in violation of the Hague Conventions of 1899 and 1907. See J. Horne and A. Kramer, *German Atrocities, 1914: A History Of Denial*, 2001, New Haven, Conn., Yale University Press.

[1008] Lloyd George would return to this theme of 'little nations' in Cardiff on 27 October 1916 when he was admitted to the Freedom of the City; See Lloyd George, *Great Crusade*, p59-60.

lives of its children, pledging its very existence, to protect a little nation that seeks for its defence. God made man in His own image–high of purpose, in the region of the spirit. German civilization would re-create him in the image of a Diesler machine–precise, accurate, powerful, with no room for the soul to operate. That is the 'higher' civilization.

What is their demand? Have you read the Kaiser's speeches?... They are full of the clatter and bluster of German militarists... the same swagger and boastfulness...

... I do not believe he meant all these speeches... but there were men around him who meant every word of it. This was their religion. Treaties?... Treaties have gone; the honour of nations gone; liberty gone. What is left? Germany–Germany is left–Deutschland uber Alles...

That is what we are fighting, that claim to predominancy of a civilization, a material one, a hard one, a civilization which if once it rules and sways the world, liberty goes, democracy vanishes, and unless Britain comes to the rescue, and her sons, it will be a dark day for humanity. We are not fighting the German people. The German people are just as much under the heel of this Prussian military caste, and more so, thank God, than any other nation in Europe. It will be a day of rejoicing for the German peasant and artisan and trader when the military caste is broken. You know his pretensions. He gives himself the airs of a demi-god. Walking the pavements–civilians and their wives swept into the gutter; they have no right to stand in the way of the great Prussian Junker...

You know the type of motorist, the terror of the roads, with a 60-h.p. car. He thinks the roads are made for him, and anybody who impedes the action of his car by a single mile is knocked down. The Prussian Junker is the road-hog of Europe. Small nationalities in his way hurled to the roadside, bleeding and broken... Britain ordered out of his road. All I can say is this: if the old British spirit is alive in British hearts, that bully will be torn from his seat. Were he to win it would be the greatest catastrophe that has befallen democracy since the days of the Holy Alliance and its ascendancy. *They think we cannot beat them. It will not be easy. It will be a long job. It will be a terrible war. But in the end we shall march through terror to triumph.* We shall need all our qualities, every quality that Britain and its people possess. Prudence in council, daring in action, tenacity in purpose, courage in defeat, *moderation in victory*, in all things faith, and we shall win.

It has pleased them to believe and to preach the belief that we are a decadent nation... 'a timorous, craven nation, trusting to its fleet.' I think they are beginning to find their mistake out already. And there are half a million of young men of Britain who have already registered their vow to their King that they will cross the seas and hurl that insult against British courage against its perpetrators on the battlefields of France and of Germany. And we want half a million more. And we shall get them.

But Wales must continue doing her duty... I should like to see a Welsh army in the field. I should like to see the race who faced the Normans for hundreds of years in their struggle for freedom, the race that helped to win the battle of Crecy, the race that fought for a generation under Glendower, against the greatest captain in Europe–I should like to see that race give a good taste of its quality in this struggle in Europe; and they are going to do it.

... It is a great opportunity... it has come to-day to us all, in the form of the glory and thrill of a great movement for liberty, that impels millions throughout Europe to the same end. It is

> a great war for the emancipation of Europe from the thraldom of a military caste, which has cast its shadow upon two generations of men, and which has now plunged the world into a welter of bloodshed. Some have already given their lives. There are some who have given more than their own lives. They have given the lives of those who are dear to them. I honour their courage, and may God be their comfort and their strength.
>
> But their reward is at hand. Those who have fallen have consecrated deaths. They have taken their part in the making of a new Europe, a new world… The people will gain more by this struggle in all lands than they comprehend at the present moment. It is true they will be rid of the menace to their freedom. But that is not all. There is something infinitely greater and more enduring which is emerging already out of this great conflict; a new patriotism… I see a new recognition amongst all classes… that the honour of a country does not depend merely on the maintenance of its glory in the stricken field, but in protecting its homes from distress as well. It… is bringing a new outlook for all classes… a new Britain is appearing. We can see for the first time the fundamental things that matter in life and that have been obscured from our vision by the tropical growth of prosperity…[1009]

The meeting was a success, as there was a "big rush of men to the recruiting room immediately after the speech"[1010], but its impact was felt far more widely than just his audience in the Hall:

> The following day, a Sunday, the newspapers carried full reports, and in Monday's papers the editorials vied with each other in effusiveness. Soon letters and messages were pouring in, and it was clear that the speech had created a more profound sensation among people at large than any speech of Lloyd George's since Limehouse, though this time the effect was unifying rather than divisive. Praise came from all sides. Liberal politicians and journalists were on the whole rapturous. Asquith congratulated Lloyd George 'with tears in his eyes', Grey said that 'he wept when he read the peroration', and Masterman called the speech the finest in the history of England… William Brace[1011], a Labour MP and president of the South Wales Miners' Federation, told Lloyd George that Wales was 'proud of her most brilliant son'.[1012]

Even many Tories approved:

> Lloyd George was ideally suited to be the agent of catharsis. Rank-and-file Conservatives, who had hitherto been blinded to his true nature by their own prejudices and his colourful polemics, suddenly saw him for what he was: as robust a patriot as any of their own leaders, but with a grander vision and a more inspiring eloquence. The Northcliffe Press, in its fulsome praise… merely reflected the feelings of its readers.[1013]

---

1009 http://www.gwpda.org/1914/lloydgeorge_honour_1914.html. Retrieved 15 February 2019. Italics added.
1010 Grigg, *From Peace to War*, p167.
1011 William Brace (1865-1947), Liberal-Labour MP for South Glamorganshire, 1906-1918.
1012 Grigg, *From Peace to War*, p167.
1013 Ibid., p168.

Lloyd George's own immediate reaction to this, his first public declaration in favour of the war, was interesting. At heart a man against war, he was "very depressed" at the enthusiasm for it! "He said the audience made him sick–they were far too stodgy and 'comfortable'–'you had to talk your way through layers of fat'."[1014]

Lloyd George remained as Chancellor for the first ten months of the war. His budget of 17 November had to allow for lower taxation receipts because of the reduction in world trade. Estimates showed a deficit of £339,571,000 on the assumption that the war would last until 31 March 1915. Noting that previous wars had been paid for as far as possible out of taxation, he followed suit, doubling the rates of supertax and income tax and increasing duties on beer and tea, expected to produce a yield of £65 million in a full year. To cover the immediate deficit, he announced the issue by the government of bonds under the 1914War Loan, for £350m, which amount calculated to be sufficient until July 1915. The bonds were to be issued at 95–sold for 95% of their face value (par value)–were redeemable between 1925-1928, and were to bear interest of 3.5% per annum. His budget was generally well received, and the measures went through in record time, passing into law on 27 November as the Finance Act, 1914 (Session 2). The 1914 War Loan was a great success and was soon oversubscribed.[1015]

In the midst of the grimness of war, during that first winter, there were still occurrences that showed human touches, even humour, certainly one that son Richard remembered all his life:

> At that time my father was still Chancellor of the Exchequer, but we had taken a house at Walton Heath which my mother preferred to No.11. On the night in question my father had to go up to Town to be present at some big gathering at the Guildhall. The occasion was sufficiently important to make it necessary for him to attend in his uniform as a Member of the Privy Council. So into the knee-breeches and long stockings and silver-buckled pumps he had to get. After an early snack, prior to his leaving the house, he draped himself in the long, voluminous cloak that completed his costume… and made his way to the waiting motor-car…
>
> The speeches over, he started homeward–armed only with his silver-hiked sword. Now even our Napier was not equipped with an electric-light system in those far-off days. The headlights were of the then prevailing acetylene type. It was a moonless, pitch-dark night, visibility nil. Somewhere along the way from Town those lights went out! Mostyn[1016], our Welsh chauffeur, brought the car to a stop, and got out to try to discover the cause of the trouble.
>
> After a moment or two–sitting alone on the back seat in all the glory of his robes, and being for ever impatient–my father decided to get out and stretch his legs… Although in that Stygian blackness he could not see the chauffeur, he could hear him tinkering with the machinery under the lifted bonnet.

---

1014 Stevenson, *Diary,* p2. Entry for 21 September 1914.

1015 See Grigg, *From Peace To War,* p187-190.

1016 Robert Mostyn, Lloyd George's chauffeur, 1910-1915.

> Suddenly the headlights came on full force. The chauffeur jumped into the car and started the engine. Before my father, behind the car and some distance from it, could find his voice, off it rolled.
>
> So it was, when Mostyn pulled up at the entrance to our home at Walton Heath and jumped down and opened the car door, standing smartly at attention–nothing happened. Nobody alighted, because there was nobody inside. Terrified, convinced his master had been kidnapped by German agents, Mostyn had sense enough to get back behind the wheel and start at top speed back along the way he had come. And finally, far off in the desolate countryside, his headlights picked up a dejected figure, trudging along the highway, the red-lined cloak hung over his arm!
>
> *That* story remained for years the surest laugh-provoker in all my mother's extensive repertoire.
>
> It was a good enough story, but to my mother's lively imagination it had to have a happy ending, so this is her version.
>
> The stoppage actually took place on Banstead Downs, a desolate heath bearing no edifice of any description except the grim and extensive L. C. C. lunatic asylum. My poor father was trudging along past the gloomy portals, in his befeathered fore-and-aft hat, and clutching his Georgian sword, when out of the murky shadows steps a policeman:
>
> "Oi!, just a minute, *just* a minute, where do you think you're going at this time of night in that get-up?" My father, tired, but with quiet dignity: "I am the Chancellor of the Exchequer." The policeman, gently and sympathetically taking his arm, "Oh, you are, are you? Well, come in here and have a nice cup of tea and a quiet chat with the Archbishop of Canterbury!"[1017]

Lloyd George's last budget, on 4 May 1915, showed a growing concern for the effects of alcohol on the war effort, with large increases in duties, and a scheme of state control of alcohol sales in specified areas. The excise proposals were opposed by the Irish Nationalists and the Tories and were abandoned. Attempts to reduce alcohol consumption were also being made in most of the belligerent countries on both sides. In Britain, it was Lloyd George who led the campaign against alcohol. He had been told by shipbuilders and heads of war factories, that men's wages had gone up so much that they could earn in two or three days what would keep them in drink for a week. A Newcastle shipbuilder complained that double overtime on Sunday "meant no attendance on Monday." At Bangor on Sunday, 28 February 1915, a sombre Lloyd George gave the first indication that there was a problem with munitions supply:

> We are conducting a war as if there was no war… We stand more in need of equipment than we do of men. This is an engineers' war, and it will be won or lost owing to the efforts or shortcomings of engineers. Unless we are able to equip our armies our predominance in men

[1017] Richard Lloyd George, *Dame Margaret*, p138-139. Lloyd George himself enjoyed telling the story; an alternative ending has him knocking on the door of a great house which turns out to be an asylum. Dressed as he was, and identifying himself as the Chancellor, the man who answers his knock replies "Certainly. Do come in. The rest of the cabinet have been expecting you.": Woodward, *Lloyd George And The Generals*, p34.

> will avail us nothing. We need men, but we need arms more than men, and delay in producing them is full of peril for this country… Output is everything in this war. It is not going to be fought mainly on the battlefields of Belgium and Poland. It is going to be fought in the workshops of France and Great Britain; and it must be fought there under war conditions.

He continued by giving one reason for this dire situation, declaring:

> Most of our workmen are putting every ounce of strength into this urgent work for their country, loyally, and patriotically. But that is not true of all. There are some… who shirk their duty in this great emergency… It is mostly the lure of the drink. These men refuse to work full time, and when they return their strength and efficiency are impaired by the way in which they have spent their leisure. Drink is doing us more damage in the war than all the German submarines put together.[1018]

Interestingly, he also highlighted a distinction between "the best Germany, the Germany of sweet songs and inspiring, noble thought… the Germany of a virile philosophy that helped to break the shackles of superstition in Europe", the humane land of Kant, Schiller and Goethe, and "a Germany that talked through the raucous voice of Krupp's artillery, a Germany that harnessed science to the chariot of destruction and death." Against the latter, he said he preached "a holy war."[1019]

On 29 March, Lloyd George told a deputation from the Shipbuilding Employers Federation:

> I must say that I have a growing conviction based upon accumulating evidence that nothing but root and branch methods will be of the slightest avail in dealing with the evil. There is a feeling that if we are to settle German militarism we must first of all settle with the drink. We are fighting Germans, Austrians and Drink, and so far as I can see the greatest of these deadly foes is Drink.[1020]

Lloyd George started a campaign to persuade national figures to make a pledge that they would not drink alcohol during the war. In April King George V supported the campaign when he issued a statement that "no wines spirits or beer will be consumed in any of His Majesty's houses after today, Tuesday April 6th, 1915." Kitchener and Haldane, the Lord Chancellor, followed the King's example, but Asquith, who was a heavy drinker–having the nickname 'Squiff', refused to take the pledge. The *National Review* commented: "The failure of the Prime Minister to take the King's Pledge has naturally aroused comment." Asquith retorted angrily that Lloyd George had "completely lost his head on drink". In the event, the King's stand carried little weight in the country, and even in the Royal Household the restriction was sometimes interpreted 'liberally'–cider, for some reason, was deemed

1018 Lloyd George, *Through Terror To Triumph*, p76, 81, 84.
1019 Ibid., p88.
1020 Quoted in Rowland, *Lloyd George*, p301.

to be non-alcoholic![1021]

The government was particularly concerned about the amount of alcohol being consumed by female munition workers. Public house opening times in cities and industrial areas were also reduced to 12.00 noon to 2.30 pm and 6.30 to 9.30 pm–these restrictions remained in place until the Licensing Act of 19 May 1988! Before the law was changed, public houses could open from 5.00am in the morning to 12.30 pm at night. Opening hours in public houses near munitions factories had already been restricted in August 1914, and the Defence of the Realm Act 1914 and subsequent modifications banned drinking on trains and the buying of drinks for others, so-called "treating". The strength of beer was progressively reduced. The Central Control Board (Liquor Traffic), set up on 19 May 1915, had considerable powers to control drink production and take over public houses and breweries in naval, military munitions or transport areas. The level of tax on alcohol was also increased. In 1918, a bottle of whisky cost £1, five times what it had cost before the outbreak of war. This helped to reduce alcoholic consumption from 89 million gallons in 1914 to 37 million in 1918. Convictions for drunkenness also fell dramatically. In London in 1914, 67,103 people were found guilty of being drunk. By 1917, this had fallen to 16,567, when there was public discussion of complete nationalisation of the drink industry, or indeed complete prohibition. However, with a keen political sense, Lloyd George's government did not go to these lengths, the measures being presented as an "experiment", rather than a first step.

On 9 March Lloyd George surprised the Commons, moving 'That leave be given to introduce a Bill to amend the Defence of the Realm Consolidation Act, 1914':

> The House will agree that it is vitally important to this country that we should increase the output and every facility for the output of munitions of war. The duration of the War depends upon it, and I think the success of the War depends upon it. We took powers in the Defence of the Realm Act, 1914, to take over and exercise control over any works where war material was being actually produced. We now seek to take powers in respect of works where war material is not being produced at the present time, but which are capable of being used for that purpose… of extending and enlarging our output of munitions." In stating that the Government sought the cooperation of industrialists, Lloyd George added "We are on the look out for a good, strong business man with some go in him who will be able to push the thing through and be at the head of a Central Committee.[1022]

This was the origin of the phenomenon of his famously being said to employ vigorous men of 'push and go'.

The following day, *Observer* editor James Garvin wrote to his son Ged, serving on the Western Front, revealing how Lloyd George was seen by an informed, perceptive man at the time:

---

[1021] Rose, p178-179.

[1022] https://hansard.parliament.uk/Commons/1915-03-09/debates/a3409bcb-82a8-47a6-a058-26a50bbcb1d8/OrdersOfTheDay. Retrieved 1 April 2021. The Act received royal assent on 16 March 1915.

> I breakfasted with Lloyd George at 11 Downing Street on Tuesday morning… We were alone. He was excellent–full of pluck, vision and common sense. His unkempt hair, now that it has rapidly turned to grey, looks almost bard-like. We have always been sympathetic towards each other (except for the Marconi interval) since 1910, and *the talk was worth all the other talks I have had with people of importance since the beginning of the war…* He is worried about the slowness in turning the whole industrial organisation of the Country on to the manufacture of munitions of war, just as the French have done… He told me about the Bill brought in yesterday for enabling the Government to order any manufactory whatever to stop its present business and make war materials: an extraordinary measure for a free Country, a tremendous measure, and it ought to have been brought forward months ago, but better late than never.[1023]

Soon after the 1915 budget, Cynthia Asquith[1024], the Prime Minister's daughter-in-law, lunched with Arthur Balfour, on 22 May, and recorded his comments in her diary:

> He said it was curious how very much more popular Lloyd George–whom one would expect to be such a rock of offence–was with both sides of the House than McKenna. Lloyd George appears to have a kind of licensed irresponsibility and people forgive what they, at the time, considered the most heinous crimes. Of course, he had personal charm ... Lloyd George appears to have gained the appreciative confidence of the City by asking, and taking, the best expert advice in the financial crises of the war.[1025]

Away from polite London table-talk, on the Western Front, by early in 1915 the indiscriminately murderous, brutal, mechanised nature of the new way of mass warfare, of mass slaughter, was becoming all-too-vividly apparent. Later, in his *War Memoirs*, Lloyd George–always concerned with the 'human element'–quoted from the 'Official History of the War': "Munitions and the technique of their use improved, but never again was the spirit or the quality of the officers and men so high, nor the general state of the training, leading and, above all, discipline of the new British armies in France so good. The losses sustained were not only heavy but irreplaceable."[1026] Later, military historian John Keegan agreed, writing that:

> It is true that the Great War, by comparison with that of 1939-45, did little material damage… Yet it damaged civilisation, the rational and liberal civilisation of the European enlightenment, permanently for the worse and, through the damage done, world civilisation also. Pre-war Europe, imperial though it was in its relations with most of the world beyond the continent, offered respect to the principles of constitutionalism, the rule of law and representative government. Post-war Europe rapidly relinquished confidence in such principles… [the Battle

---

1023 Pottle and Ledingham, p16. Emphasis added.
1024 Lady Cynthia Asquith (née Charteris; 1887-1960), married Asquith's son Herbert in 1910.
1025 Asquith, p28. Why Lloyd George should be "a rock of offence" is not explained.
1026 Quoted in Lloyd George, *War Memoirs*, Vol.I, p321.

of the Somme marked] the end of an age of vital optimism in British life that has never been recovered.[1027]

The men lost in the war were not, for the most part, professional soldiers, most being wartime volunteers and enlisted men rather than regulars. The men irreplaceably lost were, in fact, the would-be next generation of husbands and fathers, teachers, doctors, agricultural and industrial workers, engineers and artists.

On 25 May 1915, Asquith was forced to form a wartime coalition, the change of ministry resulting from sustained, intense and not ill-founded attacks on the Liberal government claiming it had badly mishandled the war effort, particularly regarding the Gallipoli Campaign and the 'Shell Crisis'. On 15 May the First Sea Lord, renowned Admiral 'Jackie' Fisher [1028], had resigned amidst bitter arguments with the First Lord of the Admiralty, Winston Churchill, over Gallipoli, causing Churchill's demotion to the Chancellorship of the Duchy of Lancaster on 25 May. Gallipoli was "one of Winston Churchill's biggest mistakes… a military failure, a national humiliation… a tragedy… [which] should never have taken place."[1029] On the morning of 17 May, Asquith, Lloyd George and Bonar Law had a discussion lasting less than 15 minutes in the Cabinet Room, agreeing that to avoid serious, damaging political conflict, the Liberal administration must be replaced by a coalition government.[1030] It was a question of public morale at home, a united front before the enemy, and a show of unanimity, as Italy prepared to enter the war on the Allied side.

Asquith bears full responsibility for the "downfall and ruin" of the last ever Liberal Government, "one of the great Ministries of recent British history."[1031] He called for his colleagues' resignation without consulting them, and without resigning himself. Even King George V only heard of this action after the event.[1032] Many Liberal MPs were naturally surprised and angered at Asquith's high-handedness, especially as he gave them no opportunity to debate the issue in the Commons before declaring a recess on 19 May, merely stating "that steps are in contemplation which involve the reconstruction of the Government on a broader, personal and political basis."[1033]

The new Cabinet included 12 Liberals, nine Tories, one Labour and one non-party (Kitchener), but the Liberals retained the majority of important posts. The Tories failed to gain the seats they had demanded, receiving lesser positions. Dissatisfied, Tory leader Bonar Law continued his attacks. The biggest loss to the Liberals was the multi-faceted, highly capable Haldane, creator of the British

---

[1027] J. Keegan, *The First World War*, 1998, London, Hutchinson, pp8, 321.

[1028] John Fisher (1841-1920), Admiral of the Fleet regarded for his naval reforms. In 1908, he had predicted that war between Britain and Germany would occur in October 1914.

[1029] Wynn, p24. The Allies incurred over 190,000 casualties, including 56,000 dead. Churchill was unrepentant, saying no one but himself could bring the Dardanelles operations to a successful conclusion. Lloyd George said "When any man talks like that he is on the way to a lunatic asylum.": Riddell, *Diaries*, 1986, p118.

[1030] Lloyd George, *War Memoirs*, Vol.I, p136.

[1031] Gollin, A., *Freedom or Control in the First World War: (The Great Crisis of May 1915), Historical Reflections* 2, 2 Winter 1976 pp135-155; quote on p135.

[1032] Fraser, p1, 21.

[1033] Addison, *Four And A Half Years*, Vol.I, p80: See also M. Pugh, *Asquith, Bonar Law And The First Coalition, Historical Journal* 17, 4, December 1974, p813-836.

Expeditionary Force (BEF) serving so well in France, the Territorial Force, the Imperial General Staff and the Officer's Training Corps. Historians generally regard his dismissal as unjust.[1034] It owed much to the *Daily Express*'s campaign relating to his alleged pro-German sympathies, the philosophically-minded Haldane being alleged to have said that Germany was his "spiritual home". In fact, he had said that concerning Professor Hermann Lotze's classroom at Göttingen University, where he had studied for a term in 1874.[1035] Disgracefully, neither Balfour, Haldane's closest Tory friend, nor Asquith, his closest political ally and friend since 1881, did anything to resist Bonar Law's demands.

On 20 May, the *Manchester Guardian* declared unequivocally:

> No Ministry now formed can hope to render its full service to the nation which does not give full and free scope to the contriving genius and powerful initiative to Mr Lloyd George… For the particular work which now above all needs to be done–the organisation of the whole industrial resources of the nation for the purposes of war–there is no one in or out of office who can approach him in capacity.[1036]

On 25 May he was made Minister of Munitions, in response to the 'Shell Crisis', taking on a newly created position in the first coalition ministry. *At the time*, Asquith was most grateful to Lloyd George, writing to him effusively:

> I cannot let this troubled and tumultuous chapter in our history pass without letting you know what incalculable help and support I have found in you all through. I shall never forget your devotion, your unselfishness, your powers of resource, and what is (after all) the best of things, your self-forgetfulness.
>
> These are the rare things which make the squalor and drudgery of politics, with its constant revelations of the large part played by petty and personal motives, endurable, and give to this drabness the lightning streak of nobility.
>
> I thank you with all my heart…[1037]

The 'Shell Crisis' was an acute shortage of artillery shells on the front lines that led to a political uproar. At the start of the war, there was a revolution in doctrine: instead of artillery being considered a useful support for infantry attacks, the new doctrine held that heavy guns alone would control the battlefield. Because of the stable lines on the Western Front, it was easy to build rail lines that delivered all the shells the factories could produce. The "Shell Crisis" emerged in May 1915 because the high rate of fire over a long period was not anticipated and the stock of shells became depleted. The shortage was

---

1034 As did Lloyd George. See *War Memoirs*, Vol.I, p137-138.

1035 Campbell, *Haldane*, p74-75.

1036 Quoted in De Courcy, p279.

1037 Quoted in Lloyd George, *War Memoirs*, Vol.I, p144-145, in Facsimile pp140-141. Lloyd George noted: "This letter… gave me great delight. The black squad of envy had not yet succeeded in poisoning the wells of confidence between captain and second officer."; p145. Lloyd George was the first British 'Minister', rather than secretary of state, etc. The new style echoed French practice; Taylor, *English History*, p31, n.1.

widely publicized in the press, specifically *The Times* and the *Daily Mail*, owned by Lord Northcliffe, the initial trigger being a letter from war correspondent Lieutenant Colonel Charles Repington[1038], titled 'Need For Shells' and published, after censorship, on 14 May in *The Times,* expounding the view of Field Marshal John French that "the want of an unlimited supply of high explosive shells was a fatal bar to our success"[1039] at Aubers Ridge. Early on 17 May Repington met Lloyd George to discuss the tactical consequences of this dire state of affairs.[1040]

Already, on 21 April, while still Chancellor, Lloyd George had stated in the Commons:

> In this War more ammunition has been expended than any army ever anticipated. That is not a miscalculation confined to us… it is perfectly clear that the Germans also were taken by surprise. They had to change their tactics. At first they were firing night and day, but afterwards, when I was there, they were firing at eleven and four o'clock… During the fortnight of fighting in and around Neuve Chapelle almost as much ammunition was spent by our Artillery as during the whole of the two and three-quarter years of the Boer War.[1041]

On his appointment as minister, on 29 May Northcliffe wrote to Lloyd George thanking him for his "great self-sacrifice" in accepting the "weightiest burden of them all", the "heaviest responsibility that has fallen on any Briton for a hundred years."[1042] On 16 June he wrote admiringly to Sir William Robertson Nicoll, editor of *The British Weekly*, that Lloyd George "has risked everything, including health, in an endeavour to save the armies of Flanders and the Dardanelles."[1043] When Lloyd George took charge, the ministry was chaotic: on his first arrival at the office at 6 Whitehall Gardens, he found only two tables and a chair, that were in fact about to be removed![1044] Indeed, it continued on a rather ad hoc basis. He asked for, and got, Christopher Addison as his Parliamentary Secretary, who was therefore closely involved with organising the nascent ministry. Addison fought hard in his new post, beating down the high prices demanded by profiteering big engineering firms, ultimately saving the country some £440 million.[1045]

Lloyd George saw an opportunity to improve terrible factory working conditions, using the precedent of regulating conditions for women, later stating: "A singularly favourable opportunity thus presented itself for introducing into industry a great forward movement for improving the general conditions of the welfare of the workers–an opportunity of which as Minister of Munitions I proceeded forthwith to take full advantage."[1046] In September, Lloyd George empowered Addison to

---

1038 Charles à Court Repington (1858-1925), credited with coining the term 'First World War' on 10 September 1918 and being one of the first to use the term 'world war' in general. C. Repington, *The First World War, 1914-1918*, 1920, London, Constable, Vol.II, p391.

1039 Repington, Vol.I, p36.

1040 Ibid., p39; Fraser, p15-16.

1041 https://api.parliament.uk/historic-hansard/commons/1915/apr/21/unified-administration-of-supply#S5CV0071P0_19150421_HOC_200. Retrieved 17 February 2020.

1042 Northcliffe to DLG, 29 May 1915, Lloyd George Papers, D/18/1/4, House of Lords Record Office.

1043 Quoted in R. Pound and G. Harmsworth, *Northcliffe*, 1959, London, Cassell, p481.

1044 Lloyd George, *War Memoirs*, Vol.I, p146.

1045 Minney, p147.

1046 Lloyd George, *War Memoirs*, Vol.I, p205-206.

look into the health of munitions workers, and as a result of the work of his Health of Munitions Workers Committee–one of the first investigations into occupational safety and health–it was stipulated that workers should have a compulsory day off each week, and that on average workers should not work more than 65 hours a week. By the end of the war more than 700 workplace canteens had also been provided.[1047]

A man of 'push and go', Eric Geddes[1048], Deputy General Manager of the North-Eastern Railway Co. at York, earning the highest salary of any senior executive of a British railway company[1049], sought a post in the new ministry. He was interviewed by Addison, who thought him "first rate", then met Lloyd George, his brother Auckland Geddes later recounting:

> Eric was amazed at the demonstration then afforded of the manner in which he built his Ministry. Although Eric admitted he knew nothing about munitions, his confidence in his ability to get things done so impressed Ll.G. that, without further reference to anyone, he told Eric he intended to 'make him head of a department.'
>
> Eric–no believer in red tape–was nevertheless staggered by the general shape of the new Ministry… in later years [he] declared its successful functioning a miracle. In it he found men, competent in general trade and business, handling technical problems of munitions production with nothing more than native acumen and drive to see them through. Only one among all the heads of departments… had any previous experience of the problems involved.[1050]

Lloyd George was clearly a man in a hurry, relying on his own intuition and instincts to tackle an urgent problem in an unconventional manner. In this venture, he and the people he appointed were, in the event, astonishingly successful and effective. Auckland Geddes–Director of Recruiting at the War Office from May 1916 to August 1917–sketches an illuminating portrait of Lloyd George at this period: "Lloyd George had great charm, great mental quickness and subtlety, but seemed to have less breadth and depth in his thought… brilliant, erratic, always ambitious, sometimes mischievous, he took an impish delight in stamping on the corns of his military colleagues on the Army Council–and at times, it seemed, in exploiting the foibles of his Cabinet colleagues."[1051]

One of these colleagues, Edward Grey, painted a glowing picture of Lloyd George and his prodigious efforts to get things moving:

> His fertility and resource were wonderful; his energy was never depressed by difficulties or daunted by adversity; his spirit was always high. His activity sought any point of importance, where he thought something was not being done that needed to be, or where he saw his way to

---

1047 Morgan, *Portrait Of A Progressive*, p46; Adams, *Arms And The Wizard*, p129.

1048 Eric Geddes (1875-1937), Deputy Director General of Munitions Supply, May 1915-August 1916, Director General of Military Railways and Inspector-General of Transportation with the rank of Major General, August 1916-February 1917, Civilian First Lord of the Admiralty with the rank of Vice-Admiral, July 1917-January 1919, first Minister of Transport, May 1919-November 1921.

1049 Houses of Parliament, Lloyd George Papers, LG/D/1/2/2, Bell to Lloyd George, 30 May 1915.

1050 Geddes, p223.

1051 Ibid., p307.

> set right what was wrong or to give a new impulse. When munitions ran short and he had realized what the needs were and how they would grow, he made the question his own, though it then belonged entirely to the War Office. Kitchener's principle and practice was to leave the work of other people alone, and to tolerate no interference from others with what he regarded as his job. When he found the activity of Lloyd George entering his department he barred the way. The torrent of Lloyd George's activity foamed against the obstruction, and for a time was delayed; but it ended by sweeping before it that part of the War Office that dealt with munitions and depositing it elsewhere. In short, a separate Department of Munitions was formed, and Lloyd George's method was to get things done by searching out the ablest men for his purpose, wherever they could be found, and throwing them into the work. Critics said that he made chaos, but out of it came a department and the Munitions, and but for Lloyd George the country would not have been organized as soon as it was for the work of making munitions.[1052]

Lloyd George also made use of 'extra-governmental' contacts. This included the rather shadowy Basil Zaharoff[1053], then at the height of his powers, who worked for Vickers Ltd. from 1897 to 1927. By 1915, Zaharoff had close ties with Lloyd George and Aristide Briand[1054], and was effectively the "unofficial chief inter-Allied munitions agent." Lloyd George made a bargain with him, namely that "Zaharoff should co-operate in reducing costs on the understanding that he was personally allowed to make larger profits by selling more shells and guns. Thus… Lloyd George was able to claim that he had reduced the cost of eighteen-pounder shells from 22s. 6d. each to 12s. and of Lewis guns from £165 to £35 each…, a considerable achievement."[1055] It may have been one of the 'unholy alliances' of the war, but it was, in the dire circumstances, arguably a necessary evil.

An impression of Lloyd George's immediate, personal involvement and effect is given by the history of the Stokes mortar. On 30 January 1915, Wilfred Stokes trialled his trench mortar of simple design before the Ordinance Board. It consisted of an unrifled 3-inch calibre steel tube into which a bomb could be dropped with a cartridge fitted to its base, which would explode on hitting a striker at the base of the tube and propel the bomb. The War Office did not approve of the type of fuse fitted to the bomb, turning down the invention. Though modified, it was again rejected on 24 March. On 30 June, Lloyd George, accompanied by Major-General Ivor Philipps[1056], witnessed a demonstration at RNAS Wormwood Scrubs and both were impressed with its performance. Despite the weapon's rejection by the War Office, Lloyd George, with a donation of £20,000 from an Indian Maharajah, gave instructions for 1,000 of them to be made. After a successful demonstration in the second week

---

1052 Viscount Grey, *Twenty-Five Years*, Vol.II, pp.248-249. Lloyd George had already pushed hard, with some success, on the need for more and better quality 18-pounder shells since being made a member–along with Kitchener, Haldane and Churchill–of the 'Shells Committee' on 11 October 1914: Adams, *Arms And The Wizard*, p19.

1053 Basil Zaharoff (1849-1936), Greek multi-millionaire arms dealer and industrialist. On 18 July 1917, at Lloyd George's behest, he initiated a series of secret peace negotiations with the Ottomans. See A. J. Maiolo and T. Insall, *Sir Basil Zaharoff and Sir Vincent Caillard as Instruments of British Policy towards Greece and the Ottoman Empire during the Asquith and Lloyd George Administrations, 1915-8*, *International History Review*, 34, 4, 2012 p819-839.

1054 Aristide Briand (1862-1932), Prime Minister, 29 October 1915–20 March 1917.

1055 McCormick, p102.

1056 Major-General Ivor Philipps (1861-1940), Liberal MP for Southampton, 1906-1922, Lloyd George's Principal Private Secretary (Military) to the Ministry of Munitions in 1915.

of August at Shoeburyness Ranges with a new fuse based on that used on the Mills hand-grenade, on 12 August he ordered 100,000 bombs, formally approved on 28 August. The Battle of Loos between 25 September-8 October, saw the mortar's first use in action, and by the end of the war 11,331 had been produced.[1057]

On 19-20 June, Lloyd George travelled to Boulogne, meeting a group of British and French artillery officers to discuss what calibres and numbers of guns and what types and quantity of shells were needed at the Western Front "with men who had first-hand knowledge of the actualities and requirements of the present War." Major General John Du Cane[1058], artillery advisor to GHQ, was present, as was Albert Thomas[1059], the energetic new French Under-Secretary of State for Armaments. Thomas and Lloyd George got along well, and quickly reached an accord, Thomas later stating that "I do not consider the Ministry of Munitions in London or my own office in Paris to be two separate institutions. I consider there is one Munitions Ministry for both countries." Both Lloyd George and Du Cane came away from the conference fully persuaded of the urgent need for many more heavy guns and for more high explosive (HE) shells, rather than the mostly ineffective shrapnel used thus far. Largely bypassing Kitchener at the War Office, on 27 August Lloyd George placed greatly increased production orders, enough to fully equip 100 divisions, far above previous estimates.[1060]

In passing the Munitions of War Act on 2 July, Lloyd George greatly increased the quantity and quality of output, helping to boost national morale. The policy was that:

> No private interest was to be permitted to obstruct the service, or imperil the safety, of the State. Trade Union regulations must be suspended; employers' profits must be limited, skilled men must fight, if not in the trenches, in the factories; man-power must be economized by the dilution of labour and the employment of women; private factories must pass under the control of the State, and new national factories be set up. Results justified the new policy: the output was prodigious; the goods were at last delivered.[1061]

Lloyd George's determination bore fruit: by the end of 1915, 60 national shells and explosives factories had been established with state finance, others privately built with government aid, and the four Royal Ordinance Factories taken over. The monthly output of shells rose from 70,000 in May 1915 to over one million by July 1916. Machine gun production rose from 274 in 1914, to 6,064 in 1915, 33,200 in 1916, 79,438 in 1917 and 120,864 in 1918.

Lloyd George had also already persuaded Kitchener, then Secretary of State for War, to raise a Welsh division, the 43rd Division being renamed the 38th (Welsh) Division on 29 April 1915 and

---

1057 Lloyd George, *War Memoirs*, Vol.I, p369; Adams, *Arms And The Wizard*, p151-154.

1058 Major General John Du Cane (1865-1947), seconded to the Ministry of Munitions during 1916.

1059 Albert Thomas (1878-1932), Socialist, Under-Secretary of State for Armaments, May 1915–December 1916, first Minister of Armaments, December 1916 - September 1917, working closely with Lloyd George. He was the first Director General of the International Labour Organization, from 1919 until his death.

1060 See Lloyd George, *War Memoirs*, Vol.I, pp328-331; Adams, *Arms And The Wizard*, p165-168.

1061 J.A.R. Marriott, *Modern England: 1885-1945*, 1948, 4th Ed., London, Methuen, p376. The Restoration of Pre-War Practices Act 1919, passed on 2 June, repealed, as promised, most of the main measures.

deployed to France between 21 November–6 December that year. Both of his sons, Richard and Gwilym, were commissioned into the Royal Welsh Fusiliers on 19 September 1914 as second lieutenants in the 6th (Carnarvonshire & Anglesey) Battalion[1062], Richard returning from his work in New York to enlist. He soon became a captain on the staff of Brigadier General Owen Thomas[1063], in command of the North Wales Brigade based at Llandudno. He was then seconded to 19th (Service) Battalion (Glamorgan Pioneers), transferred to the Royal Engineers in September 1916, having trained as a civil engineer at Christ's College, Cambridge[1064] before the war, rising to the rank of acting major. With the Glamorgan Pioneers he was involved in "mining and wiring duties" primarily at Mametz Wood [7-12 July 1916] where he was buried alive on two occasions[1065], which led him to suffer from trauma. This, together with trench fever, caused him to need convalescence at the Red Cross Hospital in Bath. It was here that he met Roberta McAlpine: the pair soon fell in love and were married in Bath Abbey on 7 April.[1066] Soon after, Richard returned to duty and was stationed at St Valéry when his daughter Valerie–Lloyd George and Margaret's first grandchild–was born on St Valentine's Day, 1918.[1067] Gwilym, as a temporary lieutenant seconded to 15th (Service) Battalion (1st London Welsh), became Aide-de-Camp to Major General Ivor Phillips, commander of the division, being posted to France on 3 December 1915, mentioned in dispatches[1068], before transferring to the anti-aircraft branch of the Royal Garrison Artillery (RGA) in July 1916, being promoted to Captain on 26 January 1917 and Acting Major on 3 February of that year.[1069]

Lloyd George's eldest daughter Olwen also 'did her bit'. Aged 22, Olwen became a VAD (Voluntary Aid Detachment) nurse, working in an emergency hospital set up at Wern Manor near Porthmadog. 'Llys Owen,' the house in Criccieth where her grandparents had lived and which her mother still owned was empty, so it was let to three Belgian refugee families. One of the men, Emile De Vynck, was a gifted woodcarver. After the war he remained in the district and one of his works, a fine portrait in plaster relief of Lloyd George–which won a medal at the Caernarfon National

1062 https://www.thegazette.co.uk/London/issue/28906/page/7406/data.pdf. Retrieved 18 January 2020.

1063 Owen Thomas (1858-1923), gazetted Brigadier General 31 October 1914, a prolific recruiter, Independent Labour MP for Anglesey, 1918 until his death.

1064 Dick went to Christ's College, Cambridge in 1908, taking the Tripos exams in scientific engineering with honours, graduating B.A. in 1910. He then became an Associate Member of the Institution of Civil Engineers. See Lloyd George, *Tale of Two Grandfathers*, p4.

1065 Lloyd George, *Tale of Two Grandfathers*, p6. Christopher Williams's uncompromising depiction of close-quarter combat 'The Charge of the Welsh Division at Mametz Wood on 11 July 1916' was commissioned by Lloyd George in November 1916. The completed work, full of Williams' despair at the suffering brought on by the war, hung until 1920 in the drawing room at 10 Downing Street, and on his death, Lloyd George called Williams "one of the most gifted artists Wales has produced." In 1904 Williams (1873-1934) had visited the Pan-Celtic Congress in Caernarfon, which prompted him to express his 'Welshness'. He painted five fine portraits of Lloyd George (three in 1912 as Chancellor, two in 1917 as Prime Minister), two of Dame Margaret (1921, 1923) and two of Richard Lloyd (both 1911). See R. Meyrick *Christopher Williams: … An Artist And Nothing Else*, 2012, Aberystwyth, NLW, on this undeservedly neglected Welsh artist.

1066 Hague, p324.

1067 Lloyd George, *Tale of Two Grandfathers*, p3. Lady Valerie Davidia Lloyd George (1918-2000).

1068 *London Gazette*, 4 July 1919, Supplement 31437, p8,537, see https://www.thegazette.co.uk/London/issue/31437/supplement/8537. Retrieved 1 February 2020.

1069 Personal communication from 4th Earl Lloyd-George of Dwyfor on 3 February 2020. Riley, p41, 42, 213. On 23 September 1918 Lieutenant George Mallory (1886-1924), the future Himalayan mountaineer, joined 515 Siege Battery RGA near Arras. His commanding officer was Major Gwilym Lloyd George. He was with the company when the Armistice was declared: D. Robertson, *George Mallory*, 1969. 1999 London Faber and Faber, p122.

Eisteddfod in 1921–was presented by him in 1924 to the Criccieth Memorial Hall in grateful remembrance.[1070] Olwen moved to 11 Downing Street when her mother started the Welsh Troops Comforts Fund. Olwen recalled:

> She had a very good committee, and all over Wales women were knitting scarves, socks and balaclava helmets, and raising money to send chocolate, cigarettes and other comforts to the Welsh troops. Parcels arrived by the score daily… the contents were to be sorted out and re-packed in parcels of identical size and shape before being sent on… to France once a week.[1071]

Enrolling as a Red Cross Volunteer with her friend Dorothy Hudson, daughter of Sir Robert Hudson, head of the British Red Cross Society, Olwen worked as a nurse from her engagement on 31 May to 27 September 1915 at the Red Cross rest station at Boulogne, and from 28 September to 2 November in Hesdigneul. She then worked at Central VAD Headquarters at Devonshire House in Piccadilly, London until June 1916. It was a hive of industry, its palatial rooms having become converted into a myriad of offices handling recruiting, training and managing the staff of hundreds of auxiliary hospitals at home, and sending staff to hospitals overseas.

Little sister Megan, only twelve when war broke out, made her contribution to the war effort by selling flags in London. She had to grow up fast. She later recalled: "One day in 1915 seems to mark the end of my childhood." Her father fetched her from school and took her to a tea shop in Putney. Clearly she was becoming something of the confidante that Mair had once been.

> He told me how the German artillery were pounding our troops, and how we were so short of shells that our gunners were down to one round a day, and he said that the Prime Minister had asked him to take on the job of providing munitions… Should he take it on? Could he do the job?… We sat in that tea-shop for over an hour talking it over, and then he took me back to my school. Next day I heard that he had become Minister of Munitions, and I felt that I had put away some of my childish things.[1072]

Her father's work continued apace. On 19 July 1915, Lloyd George went to Cardiff, accompanied by Arthur Henderson and Walter Runciman[1073], on the next evening reaching settlement with the leaders of 200,000 South Walian coalminers who had been striking since 15 July, effectively meeting all their demands, granting minimum wages of 33s per week for a labourer and 42s for a 'ripper'.[1074] On 21 July, before returning to London, he addressed a meeting in Cory Hall, praising the miners for their

---

1070 https://www.peoplescollection.wales/items/819546. Retrieved 23 January 2020. By June 1915, De Vynck and his family had settled in Pentrefelin. He made many items for local buildings, including the Renaissance-style altar and reredos of St Mary's Church, Tremadog, commissioned in memory of Randal Casson, Lloyd George's old employer, agent to the Tremadog estate, 1896-1911, installed in June 1917. The church closed in 1995.

1071 Carey Evans, p73, 75.

1072 Megan Lloyd George, Radio Talk, 18 June 1950: Quoted in Jones, 'Radical Life', p28-29.

1073 Walter Runciman (1870-1949), President of the Board of Trade, 5 August 1914–5 December 1916.

1074 A 'ripper' was a specialised worker responsible for maintaining and enlarging underground roadways leading to the coal face, considered one of the hardest, most dangerous, and highly skilled jobs underground.

vital efforts in the successful prosecution of the war, also urging them "to make up for lost time".[1075] At the National Conference of Representatives of the Mining Industry at the London Opera House on 29 July, he made an appeal for a spirit of patriotic self-sacrifice. The war had created a greater demand for coal, whilst the labour force had been reduced, 250,000 miners away fighting at the front. He emphasised: "Victory means life for our country. Are we doing enough to secure it? It means the fate of freedom for ages to come. There is no price that is within our power which is too great for us to pay…" and he poured righteous scorn upon those who thought that "Freedom implies the right to shirk. Freedom implies the right for you to enjoy and for others to defend. Is that freedom?"[1076] In a comment written 16 months before Lloyd George became Prime Minister, James Garvin wrote to his son the same day: "What a magnificent speech Lloyd George made to the miners today. He has faults, but he has a trumpet voice and a winged spirit and *he is our real national leader in the war*."[1077]

Despite Kitchener's threat of resignation, Lloyd George persuaded him to recognise Nonconformist chaplains in the army. There had already been an acrimonious Cabinet meeting on 28 September 1914. Kitchener felt that not all minority denominations could be catered for in the army, Lloyd George knew that recruitment into a Welsh Army Corps would rely heavily on Nonconformist support, so he countered that they should be accorded the same rights as native Indian troops, the Sikhs and the Gurkhas, who were accompanied by priests of their own faith. He told Kitchener, "If you intend to send a Church of England Army to the front, say so, but you cannot fight with half a nation."[1078] Kitchener grudgingly backed down, after further clashes on 10, 28 and 30 October, finally also rescinding orders that the troops be forbidden to speak Welsh in barracks or on parade.[1079]

As Minister for Munitions, Lloyd George at last had the power to demand those changes that were necessary to fight the war successfully. He was always conscious of the workers' conditions and part of his reform was an increased role for trade unions, an improvement in health and safety at factories and in workers' housing. He also realised the crucial potential of women–who became known as 'Munitionettes'–in the workforce. On 17 July 1915, over 30,000 women, organized at Lloyd George's request by Emmeline Pankhurst with a £3,500 grant from the Ministry[1080], marched through London for their 'right to serve', at the same wages as men. At the Ministry of Munitions in Whitehall Gardens, Lloyd George told them:

> The women of this country can help, and help enormously. I believe they can help us through to victory. Without them victory will tarry, and victory which tarries means victory whose footprints are the footprints of blood. We want to shorten the war because it means life, and with life it means curtailing in many cases the burden of sorrow which the war brings. That is the great function of women in life, and I believe they are discharging that in coming forward

---

1075 Quoted in *Daily Telegraph*, 22 July 1915, p9.
1076 Lloyd George, *Through Terror To Triumph*, p181, 182.
1077 Pottle and Ledingham, p44. Emphasis added.
1078 Stevenson, *Diary*, p3. Entry for 28 September 1914.
1079 Pretty, p89; Rowland, *Lloyd George*, p289-290.
1080 Adams, *Arms And The Wizard*, p116, 206 n.18.

> at the present moment and saying, 'The brave men fighting for us in the trenches are in peril because they have not sufficient war material, and we can help you.'[1081]

To the *Daily Chronicle*, Lloyd George emphasised "an effectively organised nation for a war such as that which they had embarked upon was [not] possible until they had organised the women of this country as well as the men… It was not merely the question of utilising the services of women for munitions. It was a question of utilising the energies of women for the purpose of discharging the duties and functions of commercial and industrial life which they were capable of doing as well as men."[1082] In this vein, on becoming Minister of Munitions, Lloyd George had made an interesting political statement by taking on the redoubtable Charlotte Marsh as his chauffeuse and motor mechanic. Marsh had been a prominent campaigner for the female vote since 1907, when she joined the WSPU. She had been imprisoned in 1908, 1909 and 1912, going on hunger strike and being force fed. Lloyd George offered the role to Marsh, who accepted "his suggestion that the relationship would promote the victory of the cause of women's enfranchisement."[1083]

Within a year, the Ministry of Munitions had become the largest buyer, seller, and employer in Britain, but despite the energy and commitment of Lloyd George and his staff it took a while for matters to improve, sometimes through conditions beyond their control. Geddes again:

> Vagueness with regard to manufacturing requirements was not the only difficulty with which the new Ministry had to contend. The War Office tended to ignore the Ministry and this aloofness is well indicated by the following letter which Eric received from Mr. Lloyd George– apparently seven days before the Battle of Loos (21st September 1915):…
>
> … I have just heard that there is going to be a great move in France in the course of the next few days. Every available shell, especially high explosive, must be hurried to the front.
>
> Will you please proceed to Woolwich at once, and take every step to send an appreciable proportion of the stock of H. E. shell (concentrate on that) ready to be used. The issue itself is for the War Office. There are quantities of 4.5 shell in stock that would be invaluable. As the move is an offensive one, H. E. is particularly required.
>
> Please wire me a word or two this evening, just to tell me whether anything can be done…[1084]

By June 1917, making around 80% of the weaponry and ammunition used by the British forces, the 950,000 Munitionettes work in the arms' factories revolutionised their position in public life and to all intents and purposes helped to win them the franchise following the war. However, they worked with hazardous chemicals on a daily basis, without adequate protection. Many worked with trinitrotoluene (TNT), prolonged exposure to the nitric acid turning their skin yellow, leading them to be popularly called 'canary girls.' It could also cause severe harm to their immune systems, leading to liver failure,

---

1081 *How We Marched*, *The Times*, 19 July 1915, p15.

1082 See *The Interview with Mr. Lloyd George* and *Mr. Lloyd George's Reply*, *Daily Chronicle*, 19 July 1915.

1083 Charlotte 'Charlie' Marsh (1887-1961).
https://spartacus-educational.com/WmarshCH.htm. Retrieved 5 – November 2024.

1084 Geddes, p225.

anaemia, spleen enlargement, fertility problems and sometimes death.

Lloyd George did not forget Wales and its cultural life, despite his new and pressing responsibilities. Just before becoming Minister of Munitions, accompanied by Margaret, he attended a military Eisteddfod in Llandudno Pavilion on St David's Day, 1 March 1915, stating:

> I came here to see the first-fruits of the efforts which had been made to raise a distinctive Welsh army. I remember… the beginning of that Welsh army. We met, just four of us, in the board-room of the Treasury… the four have become twenty thousand…
>
> … [Looking at the 5,500 Royal Welch Fusiliers marching past today]… I feel prouder of my country than ever. And I have a great pride in Wales. I am proud of its history, proud of its literature, proud of its songs, proud of its language, proud of its bards, proud of its great preachers, and after reading the story of what the Welsh regiments have done at the front I am proud of its soldiers.
>
> … What has been done in Wales in the way of raising an army baffles the thought of everyone… we have contributed more in proportion to our population than any other part of the United Kingdom, and they are still coming in… there are 650 that have come from Carnarvon…
>
> The Chancellor [then spoke in Welsh]:… "I am glad… that Wales has done so well towards raising an army. I believe the position of Wales at the end of this war will depend on what Wales does during the war. There is not a soldier on the battlefield more brave than a Welsh soldier, and I am glad to think that every regiment from Wales has been mentioned by our Commander-in-Chief… I am confident that these boys now in training will go and do likewise…"[1085]

His rousing address, as well as being widely publicised in the press, was listened to by an audience of 4,000 men and women, soldiers and civilians, and, along with other similar ones delivered by him around this time, together with his "messianic aura"[1086], it played no small part in deepening Welsh Nonconformist commitment to the war effort.

Lloyd George was back again in North Wales a few months later, addressing the National Eisteddfod in Bangor–postponed by the outbreak of war the previous year–on Thursday, 5 August 1915. There had been opposition to the Eisteddfod being held, even in 1915. Lloyd George's old 'sparring partner,' the Bishop of St Asaph, A. G. Edwards, had written acerbically to the *Manchester Guardian* on 24 June: "The spectacle of Sir Henry Lewis and the Eisteddfod fiddling, while the Empire is on fire is not edifying."[1087] Edwards failed to grasp the cultural and inspirational importance of the event to the Welsh. As Henry Lewis stated, "the Eisteddfod is no mere holiday gathering, but the meeting of the university of the common people of Wales, and therefore should be held in days of stress and tumult, even as the university capping ceremony was to be held."[1088] Ultimately, it did take

---

1085 *North Wales Chronicle*, 5 March 1915, p7.
1086 Griffiths, p104.
1087 Quoted in Griffiths, p135. The bishop had just lost his own son, Lieutenant Henry L. G. Edwards, killed in action in France on 16 May 1915.
1088 Ibid., p136.

place because it had the crucial backing of 'him', Lloyd George, who saw sound reasons for it to go ahead.

Accompanied by Margaret and Megan, Lloyd George got a magnificent reception as he passed from the station to the Eisteddfod building along a route lined by 4,000 people. Inside, he was introduced by the conductor Lewis D. Jones, 'Llew Tegid,' with some humour, as he remarked "that the Bangor Eisteddfod Committee owed a debt to Mr Lloyd George that they would never realise fully, nor be able to repay. His faithfulness to Wales in the present circumstances would be of everlasting credit to him. 'I am not going to say anything,' he added, 'of his value this moment to Britain, to Europe, to civilization; he will tell you all that himself.'"[1089] Lloyd George duly made a stirring speech, many of his audience standing to hear him, in awe, his speech being widely reported in newspapers of all the home nations and abroad. Naturally speaking in Welsh, Lloyd George exhorted them to 'fight on!':

> No Eisteddfod was ever before held under such a cloud… I am frankly glad that you are holding the Eisteddfod this year. I did not relish the idea of the Welsh Muse being placed in an internment camp with barbed wire to keep her from getting out till the end of the war. She is not an alien enemy, but a native of the hills… and I am delighted that you have set her free once more…
>
> I observe that you have omitted to ask the old-established question, "Is it peace?" Everywhere… the land of Britain trembles with the myriads preparing for war… I know with horror the work that is going on…
>
> "Is it peace?" No! Why not? Because an unclean spirit has possessed the rulers of a great nation. Now and again in the history of the world its peoples have had to fight in order to win… Justice, Liberty, Righteousness. If Right is worsted in this conflict, civilisation will be put back for generations. If Right triumphs, mankind takes a long leap onward on the road to progress…
>
> I am proud to know Wales has flung its whole strength into the struggle for humanity. We have a great Army already in the battlefield. We have a still greater Army ready and eager to support their comrades in the field…
>
> … When the charter of European liberty is drawn up after this war… it will be a source of pride to us that our little country contributed such a large and efficient contingent to the Army that established a new charter for human liberty…
>
> … Britain has another task… It is to see that the suffering and the loss shall not be in vain. The fields of Europe are being rent by the ploughshares of war. The verdure of the old civilisation is vanishing in the desolating upheaval of the conflict. Let us see to it that wheat and not tares are sown in the bleeding soil, and "in due season we shall reap if we faint not."[1090]

Llew Tegid's words concerning Lloyd George's faithfulness to Wales and the unknowing debt it owed him were not empty rhetorical ones. The next day, the *North Wales Chronicle* published an article entitled

[1089] Ibid., p142. Lewis D. Jones (1851-1928).

[1090] Lloyd George, *Through Terror To Triumph*, Chapter XIX, pp184-187. 'Tares' are vetch, weeds.

*The Eisteddfod Then And Now* by 'Our Special Correspondent', who clearly had inside knowledge, which gave a glimpse of his work 'behind the scenes.' At the annual Meeting of the Gorsedd Association and the National Eisteddfod Association on that evening, Lloyd George "made an eloquent appeal to Aberystwyth to emulate the courage displayed by Bangor and not to let another year pass without holding the National Festival. It was necessary if only to maintain the national spirit and confidence... But if the Eisteddfod were kept alive during the troublous period of war it would come out at the declaration of peace like gold purified by fire."[1091]

An interesting 'snapshot' of Lloyd George is given in a letter from *Observer* editor James Garvin to his son, written on Sunday, 19 September 1915:

> I had a good talk with Lloyd George on Friday–found him at half past five at the Ministry lying on his back on a couch. Whatever else he is, he has the large imagination and the temperament of vigour and promptitude. We must get bigger things done, and all things done sooner. There I am entirely with him, as you will see in the *Observer* this week.[1092]

At the Ministry of Munitions, Arthur Lee[1093], the Parliamentary Under-Secretary, pinpointed one of the major remaining problems, namely the lack of balance between shell filling and cartridge production. On 28 December Eric Geddes took over responsibility for this and matters swiftly improved here also. Within six months, production of shells of all calibres had increased from 200,000 per week to 2,000,000 per week, with a disproportionate increase in the number of the much-needed heavy calibres.

Lloyd George radiated confidence. As the "man of the moment", he was interviewed by Dr Mario Borsa, long-time London correspondent and editor-in-chief of *Il Secolo* of Milan, which published the interview on 29 January 1916 under the title '*An Interview with Lloyd George. Why He Has Faith in Victory*'. Asked about the progress regarding munitions, Lloyd George stated:

> We have now 2,500 factories, employing one and a half million men, and half a million women. We have adapted old plants and established new ones on modern lines. We are not only satisfying the requirements of our own army, but we are also supplying our Allies, particularly Russia.[1094]

He was confident in an eventual Allied victory, he said, because:

---

1091 *North Wales Chronicle*, 6 August 1915, p5.
1092 Pottle and Ledingham, p67. Captain 'Ged' Garvin, Killed in Action in France, 23 July 1916.
1093 Arthur Lee, (1868-1947), Tory MP for Fareham, 1900-1918, created Viscount Lee of Fareham, 9 July 1918.
1094 Lloyd George, *Why The Allies Will Win*, p5-6. Lloyd George gives the figure as "half a million women" in the original Italian, not "quarter of a million" as in the English translation. Mario Borsa (1870-1952).

> By next spring we shall have turned out an immense amount of munitions. We shall have for the first time in the war more than the enemy. Our superiority in men and materials will be unquestioned, and I think the war for us is beginning only now.[1095]

Prefiguring his much more famous "knockout" statement to United Press International (UPI) eight months later, he decried the war ending in military "deadlock", declaring "That would not be the end, the victory must be a real and a final victory… This is a war of Democracy… It is a final test between military autocracy and political liberty. It is a grim struggle, but we are going to win; of that I am quite confident… Make no mistake about it. Great Britain is determined to fight this war to a finish."[1096]

On 2 February, 'Mother', the prototype of the new Mark I tanks, was put through its paces around a course at Hatfield Park, simulating the front including trenches, parapets, craters and barbed wire obstacles before Kitchener, Lloyd George, McKenna, Balfour and senior army and naval officers. Kitchener was sceptical, describing the tank as a "pretty mechanical toy", asserting that "the War would never be won by such machines, which would be knocked out by the enemy's artillery", but the others were enthusiastic, an order for 100 vehicles being placed on 12 February, increased to 150 on 21 April. Lloyd George later recorded:

> The experiment was a complete success, the tank achieving even more than it was asked to accomplish. And I can recall the feeling of delighted amazement with which I saw for the first time the ungainly monster… plough through thick entanglements, wallow through deep mud, and heave its huge bulk over parapets and across trenches. At last, I thought, we have the answer to the German machine-guns and wire.[1097]

He duly arranged for his ministry to be responsible for production through its new Tank Supply Department.

Lloyd George also visited the Welsh troops at the front, accompanied by Colonial Secretary Bonar Law, as recorded in the *North Wales Chronicle* for 4 February, with all the expected propagandist overtones. After being received at Divisional HQ by Major General Ivor Philipps:

> The party went to see one of the brigades. The men were delighted at the visit of their distinguished fellow-countryman, and Mr Lloyd George came in for a most cordial reception. Perhaps the most interesting feature of the visit was Mr Lloyd George's meeting with his two sons, Major Richard Lloyd George and Captain Gwilym Lloyd George, the latter of whom is on the headquarters staff. Both looked in the fittest condition, and told their father that they liked the experience immensely.[1098]

---

1095 Ibid., p9.
1096 Ibid., p10, 11, 12.
1097 Lloyd George, *War Memoirs*, Vol.I, pp383-384. Addison was also present and was equally impressed. See Minney, p150. He became Minister of Munitions himself on 10 December 1916.
1098 *North Wales Chronicle*, 4 February 1916, p5.

Interestingly, the same issue of the paper shows how far the nation still was from the 'total war' approach that became the norm when the world next became embroiled in conflagration a few decades later:

> In a circular to munition manufacturers, Mr Lloyd George has made the suggestion, which is practically a command, that all Sunday labour should be abolished in all "controlled establishments." The Minister of Munitions refers to the committee appointed some time ago to study the question of the effect upon the production of munitions of war by continuous labour involving Sunday work. Mr Lloyd George now suggests... that all munition workers should receive one day's rest per week, preferably Sunday.[1099]

Amid his labours, Lloyd George found time to write a skilfully crafted message entitled 'A Lincoln Day Message' to the American people on the anniversary of his hero President Lincoln's birthday, 12 February 1916, comparing the American Civil War with the European conflict, published in the *New York Times*:

> [T]o my mind Abraham Lincoln has always been one of the very first of the world's statesmen, because I believe that the battle which we have been fighting is at bottom the same battle which your countrymen fought under Lincoln's leadership... and... because I desire to say how much I welcome the proof... that the American people are coming to realize this, too.
>
> Lincoln's life was devoted to the cause of human freedom... after years of patient effort he was driven to realize that it was not a mere question of abolishing slavery in the Southern States, but that bound up with it was a larger issue: That unless the Union abolished slavery, slavery would break up the Union.
>
> Faced by this alternative, he did not shrink... from vindicating both Union and freedom by the terrible instrument of war. Nor after the die for war had been cast did he hesitate to call upon his countrymen to make sacrifice upon sacrifice... until, in his own words, there was a new birth of freedom in your land.
>
> Is there not a strange similarity between this battle, which we are fighting here in Europe, and that which Lincoln fought? Has there not grown up in this continent a new form of slavery, a militarist slavery, which has not only been crushing out the freedom of the people under its control, but which in recent years has also been moving toward crushing out freedom and fraternity in all Europe as well?...
>
> We were reluctant, and many of us refused to believe that any sane rulers would deliberately drench Europe in its own blood, so we did not face the facts until it was almost too late. It was not until August, 1914, that it became clear to us, as it became clear to Lincoln in 1861, that the issue was not to be settled by pacific means, and that either the machine which controlled the destinies of Germany would destroy the liberty of Europe or the people of Europe must defeat its purpose and its prestige by the supreme sacrifice of war. It was the ultimatum to Serbia and

[1099] Ibid., p5.

the ruthless attack upon Belgium and France which followed because the nations of Europe would not tolerate the obliteration of the independence of a free people without conference and by the sword, which revealed to us all the implacable nature of the struggle which lay before us.

It has been difficult for a nation separated from Europe by three thousand miles of sea and without political connections with its peoples, to appreciate fully what was at stake in the war. In your Civil War many of our ancestors were blind… It was left for John Bright, that man of all others who most loved peace and hated war, to testify that when our statesmen "were hostile or coldly neutral the British people clung to freedom with an unfaltering trust." But I think that America now sees that it is human unity and freedom which are again being fought for in this war.

The American people under Lincoln fought not a war of conquest, but a war of liberation. We to-day are fighting not a war of conquest, but a war of liberation–a liberation not of ourselves alone, but of all the world, from that body of barbarous doctrine and inhuman practice which has estranged nations, has held back the unity and progress of the world, and which has stood revealed in all its deadly iniquity in the course of this war.

In such wars for liberty there can be no compromise. They are either won or lost… Therefore, we believe that the war must be fought out to a finish…

In holding this conviction, we have been inspired and strengthened beyond measure by the example and the words of your great President. Once the conflict had been joined, he did not shrink from bloodshed…

Despite his abhorrence of all that was entailed, he persisted in it because he knew that he was sparing life by losing it, that if he agreed to compromise, the blood that had been shed on a hundred fields would have been shed in vain, that the task of creating a united nation of free men would only have to be undertaken at even greater cost at some later day. It would, indeed, be impossible to state our faith more clearly than Lincoln stated it himself at the end of 1864.

"On careful consideration," he said, "of all the evidence it seems to me that no attempt at negotiation with the insurgent leader could result in any good… between him and us the issue is distinct, simple, and inflexible. It is an issue which can only be tried by war and decided by victory."

That was the judgment of the greatest statesman of the nineteenth century during the last great war for human liberty. It is the judgment of this nation and of its fellow-nations overseas to-day.

"Our armies," said Lincoln, "are ministers of good, not evil." So do we believe. And through all the carnage and suffering and conflicting motives of the Civil War, Lincoln held steadfastly to the belief that it was the freedom of the people to govern themselves which was the fundamental issue at stake. So do we to-day. For when the people of central Europe accept the peace which is offered them by the Allies, not only will the allied peoples be free, as they have never been free before, but the German people, too, will find that in losing their dream of an empire over others, they have found self-government for themselves.[1100]

[1100] Dilnot, Appendix: *Mr. Lloyd George On America And The European War*, p215-219.

This 'open letter,' rarely noted by Lloyd George biographers, was clearly designed to engage the hearts and minds of the American people in the justice of the Allied cause, whilst also revealing something of Lloyd George's ideals and outlook at this crucial period, just before he himself became a leader in war.

With his success as the Minister of Munitions, Lloyd George very often found himself impatient with the slow and ineffectual way the government conducted the war. He strongly disagreed with Asquith over the question of military conscription. Along with Kitchener, who was pressing hard to put 70 divisions into the field during 1916 to force the Germans to sue for peace that same year[1101], Lloyd George publicly and forcefully supported it and his position within the Cabinet was greatly strengthened when, on 5 January 1916, Asquith had to present a conscription measure, the Military Services Bill, which received royal assent on 27 January, coming into effect on 2 March.[1102] The Act specified that men from 18 to 41 years old were liable to be called up for service in the army unless they were married, widowed with children, serving in the Royal Navy, a minister of religion, or working in one of a number of reserved occupations. A second Act on 25 May 1916 extended liability for military service to married men, and a third Act on 23 April 1918 extended the upper age limit to 51.[1103] The conscription issue divided the Liberals, including the Cabinet. John Simon resigned as the Home Secretary, attacking the government in his resignation speech on 12 January in the Commons, when 35 Liberals voted against the bill, alongside 13 Labour MPs and 59 Irish Nationalists.

In early May, Christopher Addison, David Davies[1104] and Frederick Kellaway[1105] drew up a list of Liberal MPs who would be willing to back Lloyd George in any confrontation with Asquith, who "might be relied upon to support an active policy". As the summer wore disastrously on, Addison and Davies became increasingly convinced that Lloyd George was "the sole acceptable leader capable of winning the war."[1106] On 2 August, Addison wrote to his wife that Asquith might have to resign and that he hoped for "a reconstruction with L.G. [sic] as Prime Minister."[1107]

Asquith's position was weakened further by the government's reaction to the Easter Rising of 24-29 April, mostly centred in Dublin, by some 1,250 poorly armed Irish nationalists of the Irish Volunteers, Irish Republican Brotherhood, Irish Citizen's Army, the Hibernian Rifles and including over 200 women of *Cumann na mBan*. The reading of the Proclamation of the Irish Republic by Patrick Pearse[1108] outside the General Post Office on Sackville Street–now O'Connell Street– Dublin's main

1101 P. Magnus, *Kitchener: Portrait Of An Imperialist*, 1958, London, John Murray, p373.

1102 According to *Observer* editor James Garvin, writing to his son on 30 December 1915, Lloyd George had been prepared to resign if this measure had not been adopted. He added: "He is not perfect any more than the rest of them, but he is a stirring vital creature with a real touch of the man of genius and ready to do anything to get on with the war." Pottle and Ledingham, p127, 128.

1103 Some 4.9 million men were enlisted in the British army between 1914-1918, of whom 2.4 million enlisted prior to the introduction of conscription, 2.5 million after it. Only 1.3 million were actually conscripted. 272,924 Welshmen enlisted, of whom 122, 995 (45%) volunteered.

1104 David Davies (1880-1944), Welsh Liberal MP for Montgomeryshire, 1906-1929, Parliamentary Private Secretary to Lloyd George, June 1916-June 1917.

1105 Frederick Kellaway (1870-1933), Liberal MP for Bedford, 1910-1922, Parliamentary Secretary to the Ministry of Munitions, December 1916-April 1921.

1106 Morgan, *Portrait Of A Progressive*, p50-51.

1107 Ibid., p51.

1108 Patrick Pearse (1879-1916), Commander-in-Chief, Irish Republican Brotherhood.

thoroughfare, marked the beginning of the Rising. However, it was brutally crushed using overwhelming numbers, some 16,000 British troops and 1,000 armed Royal Irish Constabulary by the end, the gunboat HMY *Helga* and heavy field artillery. At least 485 people were killed, including 82 rebels, 260 civilians, 126 British military and 17 policemen, with more than 2,600 wounded all told. 3,430 men and 79 women were arrested, although more than 2,700 had been released by August.

Asquith's Government then committed a cardinal error. As historian Constantine FitzGibbon tellingly encapsulated it:

> When, on Sunday, the Irishmen who had surrendered were marched across Dublin from one prison compound to another, they were at times jeered at and booed by the crowds, particularly in the slum areas. In the countryside the Rising had received only minimal support. Public opinion had been against the Rising before it began, throughout Easter Week, and remained so after its defeat, until the reprisals began.[1109]

The Easter Rising was "the only national rebellion in any European country during the First World War–an ironical comment on the British claim to be fighting for freedom."[1110] Unheeding, the government was widely and bitterly criticised for, under the command of newly appointed Lieutenant General John Maxwell, acting with "plenary powers under martial law over the whole country"[1111], swiftly trying prisoners in illegal secret court martials and executing 15 of the leaders by firing squad in Kilmainham Gaol over a prolonged period between 3-12 May.[1112] A wave of deep revulsion swept across Ireland.

The number could have been higher. Professor Eóin MacNéill[1113], founder of the Irish Volunteers, was also under threat of execution. Despite having tried to call off the Rising, and taking no part in the events themselves, he declared himself to be co-responsible with the executed leaders. John Redmond, Leader of the Irish Parliamentary Party, pleaded for his life as Ireland's greatest living Gaelic scholar. On hearing this, Lloyd George said to Asquith "Good God! We mustn't kill a Gaelic scholar!" and that settled it. MacNéill was tried on 22 May by court martial in Dublin, sentenced to penal servitude for life at Dartmoor Prison, but released in June 1917. Afterwards, Lloyd George rightly took some credit for saving MacNéill's life, saying to Thomas Jones that executing MacNéill would have been like executing T. Gwynn Jones[1114], the famous Welsh poet and Gaelic scholar.[1115]

After making a six-day visit to Dublin from 12 May, and following prolonged discussions, on 21 May, Asquith assigned Lloyd George the task of resolving the Irish problem by undertaking

---

1109 FitzGibbon, p83.
1110 Taylor, *English History*, p56.
1111 P.M.'s report to King George V of Cabinet meeting of 27 April 1916; Quoted in Younger, p36.
1112 A 16th, Sir Roger Casement (1864-1916), was tried in London under the Treason Act 1351, for attempting to obtain German military aid for the Rising and hanged at Pentonville Prison on 3 August.
1113 Eóin MacNéill (1867-1945), Gaelic scholar and nationalist, was released from prison in June 1917, going on to become a Sinn Féin politician and important Irish historian, dying just over six months after Lloyd George.
1114 Professor Thomas Gwynn Jones (1871-1949), leading Welsh literary figure.
1115 Ebenezer, p25.

negotiations between the Unionist and Nationalist factions, on 25 May announcing in the Commons:

> What is now… of paramount importance is… that an agreement such as we sought, and sought in vain, before the War should be arrived at between those representing different interests and parties in Ireland. I believe… that in Ireland itself there is a deep and genuine desire to obtain such an agreement. The Government… are… more than anxious to do everything in their power to facilitate such a happy result. At the unanimous request of his colleagues… (Mr. Lloyd George), has undertaken to devote his time and his energies and his power to the promotion of that result. He has already put himself in communication with the authorised representatives and exponents of the views of the different Irish parties… I believe there is… among Irishmen, no less than among the people of Great Britain, an honest and resolute desire to take advantage of this opportunity for the obtainment of that which, to us as a nation and an Empire… is the greatest boon that could possibly be achieved…[1116]

This statement was tantamount to acknowledging that the Rising had justifiable grievances and that the execution of its leaders had been in largely wrong. Lloyd George then sent to Dublin making this offer to the leaders of the Irish Parliamentary Party, John Redmond and John Dillon. The scheme revolved around partition, officially a temporary arrangement, as understood by Redmond. Lloyd George however gave the Ulster leader Edward Carson a written guarantee stating, "we must make it clear that at the end of the provisional period Ulster does not, whether she wills it or not, merge in the rest of Ireland."[1117] Lloyd George conducted talks with both sides separately, keeping the rival parties 'in play' in the hope that a compromise settlement could eventually be implemented. The country north and south, as well as the Cabinet, were divided on the issue. Ulster Nationalist leader Joseph Devlin[1118] had won support in Belfast on 4 July for temporary exclusion of the six counties of Antrim, Armagh, Down, Fermanagh, Londonderry and Tyrone. Unlike previous attempts at settlement, the Lloyd George proposals had not been submitted to the British Cabinet for agreement prior to being presented to the Nationalist and Unionist delegations.

A modified Act of 1914 as "Headings of a Settlement as to the Government of Ireland" had been drawn up by the Cabinet on 17 June 1916.[1119] The formula then had two amendments enforced on 19 July by Unionists–permanent exclusion and a reduction of Ireland's representation in the Commons. Lloyd George informed John Redmond of this on 22 July, who accused the government of treachery. The government bowed to the combined opposition of Unionists who had never favoured partition, and the Irish Party. Lord Selborne[1120] resigned, while serious opposition came from Lord Lansdowne, Lord Robert Cecil and Walter Long[1121], alarming given the European situation. It was under the pressure of this Unionist opposition that the negotiations eventually collapsed on 27 July. This was

1116 https://api.parliament.uk/historic-hansard/commons/1916/may/25/prime-ministers-statement. Retrieved 15 October 2019.
1117 D. G. Boyce, *British Opinion, Ireland, And The War, 1916-1918*, *Historical Journal*, xvii, 3, 1974, p580.
1118 Joseph Devlin (1871-1934), MP for Belfast Falls, Leader of the IPP, 1918-1921.
1119 *Headings of Settlement as to the Government of Ireland* (Lloyd George Papers, Parliamentary Archive, London, LG/D/15/1/7); [Cd.8310].
1120 William Palmer, Earl of Selborne (1859-1942), President of the Board of Agriculture, 1915-1916.
1121 Walter Long (1854-1924), Irish Unionist, Secretary of State for the Colonies, 1916-1919.

decisive to the future fortunes of the Home Rule movement, the Lloyd George debacle of 22 July finished the constitutional party, sapped Redmond's power and left him demoralised. It simultaneously discredited the politics of consent and created the space for radical alternatives, facilitating the rise of Sinn Féin.

The issue further undermined relations between Asquith and Lloyd George. On 22 May Asquith had written to Lloyd George imploring him to take on the problem, assuring him that his touch was vital and that he would earn the eternal gratitude of the empire if he brought about a settlement. The considerable Unionist opposition and criticism that Lloyd George then faced, coupled with the negotiations lack of success, naturally made him feel that Asquith had been "less than supportive", provoking "further disillusionment and doubts about the prime minister's nerve and constancy".[1122] The confused position was debated at length in the Commons on 31 July. Nationalists continued to demand that the Home Rule Act be implemented and called for senior officials in Dublin to be replaced by Home Rule supporters, who would be in government anyway after the war ended. Unionists countered that, if the Act were to be implemented during the war, six Ulster counties would be excluded and would never submit to coercion; Irish unity could only come about with their consent. Asquith wrote a private letter to Redmond on 28 July, stating "I think it is of great importance (if possible) to keep the *negotiating* spirit alive". But the breakdown of negotiations was inevitable and had irreparably damaged Redmond and the Irish Party.

After the suppression of the Rising, the British authorities in Ireland were left with a large number of rebel prisoners, the round-up that followed the revolt adding to their ranks. These were removed from Ireland and, under Regulation 14B of the Defence of the Realm Act 1914, from 9 June they were interned in a disused whisky distillery that had formerly held German prisoners of war in Fron-goch, a tiny village 2.5 miles north of Bala in Merionethshire, North Wales.[1123] The British government were unsure what to do with these 1,863 internees, among them such notables as Michael Collins[1124], W. T. Cosgrave[1125], Tomás MacCurtain[1126], Terence MacSwiney[1127] and Dick Mulcahy[1128]. Collins, from County Cork, still only 26 years-old, first began to emerge as a major figure in the vacuum created by the executions of the pre-Rising leadership. At Fron-goch he was one of the organisers of a program of protest and non-cooperation with authorities, also giving impromptu lessons in guerrilla tactics, making plans for the 'next time.'

---

1122 Fry, *Political Change In Britain*, p615.

1123 A large commemorative marker stone, erected in 2002 and bearing two plaques stands nearby, with inscriptions in Irish, Welsh and English, at the side of the A4212 Bala to Trawsfynydd road. The buildings were demolished in 1934, the suitably rather bleak site being visited by the author on 1 October 2019.

1124 Michael Collins (1890-1922), revolutionary, soldier, Chairman of the Provisional Government of the Irish Free State from 16 January 1922 until his assassination on 22 August 1922.

1125 William T. Cosgrave (1880-1965); though never officially *Taoiseach* (Ireland's head of government, created in 1937), as the first elected head of government in the Irish Free State, he is recognised as the first such.

1126 Tomás MacCurtain (1884-1920), Sinn Féin Lord Mayor of Cork.

1127 Terence MacSwiney (1879-1920), playwright, author, Sinn Féin Lord Mayor of Cork, who died in Brixton Prison after 74 days on hunger strike.

1128 Richard Mulcahy (1886-1971), army general and commander-in-chief of the Irish Republican Army, Minister for Defence, January–April 1919, 1922-1924.

Conditions in the impromptu Internment Camp were grim, insanitary, overcrowded, rat-infested[1129] and cold, the discipline strict. The camp was divided into two–the north camp with its 35 wooden barracks, the south camp in what had been the stone distillery building–the inmates derisively naming them 'Purgatory' and 'Siberia'. Fortunately, no prisoners died there, although one attempted suicide, but holding all these men together had unintended consequences, the inmates becoming increasingly unruly and uncooperative with their captors. The round-up had hauled in many men of relatively mild nationalist views but throwing them together with more committed rebels had led to their radicalisation. Now they started to plan the next steps in the struggle to separate Ireland from the United Kingdom. Belatedly the authorities realised that they had effectively created *ollscoil na réabhlóide*, the "University of Revolution".[1130] Despite this, requests by Irish MPs in the Commons for their release were refused by both Asquith and Home Secretary Herbert Samuel on 18 October and 14 November respectively.

To step ahead of events a little, after Lloyd George's very first speech in the Commons as Prime Minister, 19 December 1916, he was pressed by John Redmond to release the men:

> You are holding in English prisons… between 500 and 600 untried prisoners… Those men are imprisoned under… the Defence of the Realm Act which gives power to keep interned men who are proved to be of enemy association. If they are not men of enemy association they are illegally detained… You may say they are dangerous men and you do not want to let them loose because they have extreme opinions. Surely that is going back to the old evil English rule in Ireland. These men are dangerous so long as they are where they are… if the right hon. Gentleman wants to create a better atmosphere in Ireland and a better feeling, let him instantly release these men… *Let him do it as a Christmas gift to the Irish people, and let him withdraw the Proclamation of martial law…*[1131]

On 21 December Lloyd George, barely two weeks into his premiership, decided to permanently close Fron-goch, the Chief Secretary for Ireland, Henry Duke, announcing "the time had come when the risk of liberating the internees would be less than the risk which might follow detaining them longer."[1132] The remaining 628 prisoners–including some from Reading Gaol and two women from Aylesbury Female Prison, Winifred Carney and Helena Molony–were sent home before Christmas, released back to Ireland in batches in a futile attempt to minimise the likelihood of their being greeted by anti-British demonstrations. It has often been stated that this was a purely cynical move, motivated to quell Irish-American anger and to persuade the USA to enter the war on the Allied side. There was naturally a strong element of this, but it is also likely that Lloyd George, as a man of Pan-Celtic interests

---

1129 A bitter joke among the prisoners was the similarity of the place name to the Irish word for rat, *francach*.

1130 30 men held at Fron-goch went on to become MPs (TDs) in the new Irish parliament in Dublin, while 19 achieved senior rank in the Free State Army: O'Mahony, p219-221.

1131 https://api.parliament.uk/historic-hansard/commons/1916/dec/19/prime-ministers-statement#S5CV0088P0_19161219_HOC_374. Retrieved 1 October 2019. Emphasis added. Some 1,200 had already been released by August. Lloyd George had been ill for several days before making his appearance.

1132 O'Mahony, p163. Henry Duke (1855-1939), Tory Chief Secretary for Ireland, 31 July 1916–5 May 1918.

and a record of anti-Imperialism, had at least some sympathy with the frustrated, captive Irish, and that the move was partly motivated by an attempt at reconciliation.[1133]

On 7 July 1916 Lloyd George was made Secretary of State for War, succeeding Kitchener who died on 5 June when en route from Scapa Flow to the port of Archangel in northern Russia to attend secret diplomatic and military negotiations with the Tsar and his *Stavka* (military high command), designed to explain the Allies policy and encourage more active support for the war effort on Russia's part. Kitchener had put himself forward to head the mission in a Cabinet meeting on 28 April[1134], a proposal taken up by Asquith and encouraged by the Tsar, demonstrating the universal prestige in which he was held. With him were 13 officials from the Foreign Office and Ministry of Munitions. However, at 7.40 pm, the armoured cruiser on which Kitchener was travelling, HMS *Hampshire*, struck a mine. The ship quickly sank in the heavy seas of a Force 9 gale one and a half miles north west of the Orkney Islands, killing 737 of those on board, including Kitchener, with only 12 crew surviving.

News of Kitchener's death stunned the British public, as he was regarded as integral to the war effort. However, few knew that it had been Lloyd George's intention to accompany Kitchener on the fated visit, in his capacity as the Minister of Munitions. Because the Easter Rising had only recently taken place in Ireland, Asquith had asked Lloyd George to remain behind in London… and there hangs another pregnant 'What if?' question of history. On 22 May Asquith had written in a secret memo: "I hope you may see your way to take up Ireland; at any rate for a short time. It is a *unique* opportunity and there is no one else who could do so much to bring about a permanent solution."[1135] As Lloyd George himself noted: "For me at least this letter has a peculiar interest, for it saved my life!… But for this letter, I should have been with him and have shared his fate. This escape, at least, I owe to Ireland."[1136] He found out about Kitchener's death on the morning of 6 June when arriving to attend a meeting of the War Council at 10 Downing Street: "When I entered the Cabinet Room I found the Prime Minister, Sir Edward Grey, Mr. Balfour and Sir Maurice Hankey sitting at the table, all looking stunned by the tragedy… Maurice Hankey and I quite forgot for the moment that had it not been for the Irish negotiations we also would have shared the same fate."[1137]

Lloyd George was the natural successor appointee, despite the opposition of the King, most of the Tories in the Coalition and almost all of the War Office staff, having been an energetic, efficient and imaginative Minister of Munitions for the past year.[1138] On his appointment, however, he found he

---

1133 O'Mahony, p163. There is a bizarre footnote to Lloyd George's involvement with Fron-goch. On 17 April 1920 a coroner's jury in Cork returned a verdict of wilful murder against Lloyd George following the killing on 20 March 1920 of Tomás MacCurtain, a former Fron-goch internee, now Lord Mayor of Cork and Commandant of Cork Number One Brigade of the IRA. The unanimous verdict read: "We find that Alderman Tomás MacCurtain… died… under circumstances of the most callous brutality; and that the murder was organised and carried out by the RIC officially directed by the British Government. We return a verdict of wilful murder against David Lloyd George… D.I. Swanzy [of the RIC]…" The actual killer, Oswald Swanzy, was assassinated by the IRA, using MacCurtain's own revolver, in Lisburn on 22 August 1920 on the orders of Michael Collins.

1134 Cassar, *Kitchener*, p472.

1135 Quoted in Lloyd George, *War Memoirs*, Vol.I, p420.

1136 Ibid., p420.

1137 Ibid., p456.

1138 Rose, p195-196.

had little control over strategy, as General William Robertson[1139], Chief of the Imperial General Staff, had previously been given direct right of access to the Cabinet so as to bypass Kitchener. Lloyd George found himself unable to prevent the generals from their "unintelligent hammering against the impenetrable barrier".[1140] He did, however, succeed in persuading Douglas Haig, Commander of the British Expeditionary Force, to invite Eric Geddes and his three man team over to France for two days in August to advise on transportation. Haig was so impressed that the visit was extended to a month and then Geddes was appointed Director General of Military Railways and Inspector-General of Transportation, with the honorary rank of Major General. Geddes established his GHQ (Transport) at Monthouis–soon renamed 'Geddesburg' by the troops–and together, they got the ports, railways, roads and canals working efficiently in a coordinated manner and built a 1,000 km light railway network to bring materials to the front lines.

Lloyd George was resolute and clear-eyed in his prosecution of the war effort, rejecting popular talk of peace mediation by President Wilson. In his first statement to American papers as the Secretary of State for War, on 28 September he told UPI war correspondent Roy W. Howard, who was en route to Germany:

> Britain has only begun to fight; the British empire has invested thousands of its best lives to purchase future immunity for civilization; this investment is too great to be thrown away…
>
> … Germany elected to make it a finish fight with England. Now we intend to see that Germany has her way. *The fight must be to the finish–to a knockout.*
>
> The whole world, including neutrals of the highest purposes and humanitarians with the best motives, must know that there can be no outside interference at this stage…
>
> The inhumanity, the pitilessness of the fighting that must come before a lasting peace is possible, is not comparable with the cruelty that would be involved in stopping the war while there remains a possibility of civilization again being menaced from the same quarter. Peace now, or at any time before the final complete elimination of this menace, is unthinkable…
>
> … 'Never again!' has become our battle cry.
>
> This ghastliness must never be re-enacted on this earth, and one method at least of answering that end is the infliction of such punishment upon the perpetrators of the outrage against humanity that the temptation to emulate their exploits will be eliminated from the hearts of the evil-minded amongst the rulers of men.[1141]

His bold statement bolstered home and Allied morale and sent a clear signal to both the Americans and the Germans. In the midst of all this, Lloyd George returned home to his beloved Wales for the National Eisteddfod, held in Aberystwyth, knowing the importance to the Welsh psyche that this would have. Again, his views had been sought in advance, and on 22 November 1915 he had replied

[1139] Sir William Robertson (1860-1933), the only British Army soldier to rise from private to field marshal.

[1140] Jones, *David Lloyd George*, p75.

[1141]https://www.upi.com/Archives/1916/09/29/Lloyd-George-says-We-will-fight-Germany-to-a-knockout/3583010911547/. Retrieved 23 April 2019. Emphasis added.

emphatically:

> I am firmly convinced that our great national musical festival should not be put into a condition of suspended animation during the war… An eisteddfod… is a serious contribution to the best side of a nation's life… Let Aberystwyth give us a sample of what a real Welsh eisteddfod used to be… if it is decided to eliminate some of the big choral contests and to reduce the time to (say) two days, I cannot help thinking that the Eisteddfod will turn out to be a success.[1142]

Even with Lloyd George's strong support, voting on the desirability of going ahead was close, coming down to a vote of 16-14 in favour, with the proviso that it should be curtailed to be of just two days duration with three evening concerts. Evidence of his personal, innovative input appeared on 2 June 1916 when an article, entitled 'National Eisteddfod: A Patriotic Opportunity', appeared in the *Cambrian News*: "The third day will be devoted to a unique feature in connection with the Eisteddfod, namely, a national singing festival which has been arranged on the suggestion of the Minister of Munitions… It is really through the initiative of Mr. Lloyd George that the Eisteddfod is being held this year instead of being further postponed."[1143]

And so, the Eisteddfod duly took place. Lloyd George vigorously defended it's holding in his impassioned speech, delivered on Thursday 17 August, before over 7,000 listeners:

> I have come here at some inconvenience to attend, and if necessary to defend, this Eisteddfod. I have been a strong advocate of its being held. I was anxious there should be no interruption on account of the war in the continuity of the Welsh National Eisteddfod. It is too valuable an institution, it has rendered too great services to our country to risk its life by placing it into a state of suspended animation for an indefinite period …
>
> Let any man look through this programme and see for himself what the Eisteddfod means– prizes for odes, sonnets, translations from Latin and Greek literature, essays on subjects philosophical, historical, sociological. An adequate treatment of some of these subjects necessarily involves a good deal of original research. Art is encouraged; even agriculture is not forgotten. Forsooth, all this effort should be dropped on account of the war?… Hush! No music, please; there is a war on!
>
> Why should we not sing during this war? Why, especially, should we not sing at this stage of the war? The blinds of Britain are not down yet[1144], nor are they likely to be. The honour of Britain is not dead, her might is not broken, her destiny is not fulfilled, her ideals are not shattered by her enemies; she is more than alive, she is more potent, she is greater than she ever was… Why should her children not sing?…
>
> Our soldiers sing the songs of Wales in the trenches …

1142 *Cambrian News and Merionethshire Standard*, 17 December 1915, p6.

1143 Ibid., 2 June 1916, p3.

1144 Witness and historian Bob Owen Croesor (1885-1962), never forget this ringing phrase: D. Evans, p106.

> … They don't ask us to stop singing… They want to feel that while they are upholding the honour of Wales on the battlefields… we are doing our best to keep alive all the institutions, educational, literary, musical, and religious, which have made Wales what it is to them… That is why I am in favour of holding this festival of Welsh literature and of song even in the middle of Armageddon.
>
> But I have another and even more urgent reason… When this terrible conflict is over a wave of materialism will sweep over the land. Nothing will count but machinery and output. Well, I am all for output, and I have done my best to improve machinery and increase output but that is not all. There is nothing more fatal to a people than that it should narrow its vision to the material needs of the hour. National ideals without imagination are but as the thistles of the wilderness, fit neither for food nor fuel… We shall need at the end of the war better workshops, but we shall also need more than ever every institution that will exalt the vision of the people above the workshop and the counting-house. We shall need every national tradition that will remind them that man cannot live by bread alone.
>
> … It is true there are thousands of gallant men falling in the fight, but let us sing of their heroism… Let us sing to the land that gave birth to so many heroes.[1145]

Not without reason, from these years on the Thursdays of the National Eisteddfod came to be known colloquially as '*ddiwrnod Lloyd George*'–'Lloyd George Day'. Unlike Bangor, which made a loss of £986, Aberystwyth ended with a healthy surplus of £823 18s 2d for the various war funds.[1146] The *Cambrian News* glowingly reported:

> From the higher standpoint of national interest, the gathering proved the wisdom of the promoters and confirmed the foresight and intelligence with which Mr. Lloyd George's appeal was made and adopted… there can be no doubt that the best feeling of Wales was represented …
>
> … *in many respects Friday was the most notable because of the unique appropriateness which characterised the holding of a Gymanfa Ganu Genedlaethol (national singing festival). The success of the Gymanfa, financially and morally, contributed largely to the success and eminence of the Eisteddfod, which exceeded the expectations of its most sanguine supporters.*
>
> *The idea of adding the Gymanfa originated in a suggestion by Mr. Lloyd George, who… was keenly sensitive of the advantages of a great national gathering assembled in solemn mood… So successfully was the idea carried out… that the precedent set at Aberystwyth in modifying the scope of the Eisteddfod and in adding the Gymanfa… is certain to be followed in future years.*[1147]

Lloyd George's words about post-war materialism would prove accurate, but in the meantime, back in London, he became increasingly frustrated at the limited gains of the Somme Offensive, which had

---

1145 Lloyd George, *Great Crusade*, p41-46; Quoted in Griffiths, p165-169.

1146 Griffiths, p176.

1147 *Cambrian News and Merionethshire Standard*, 25 August 1916, p3. Emphasis added.

begun disastrously on 1 July, the Fourth Army under Lieutenant General Sir Henry Rawlinson[1148] taking an unprecedented 57,470 casualties, of which 19,240 men were killed, on the first day alone[1149]. Lloyd George criticised General Haig[1150], Commander-in-Chief British Expeditionary Force, to General Foch[1151], commander of the Northern Army Group, on a visit to the Western Front on 12 September–British casualty rates were significantly worse than those of the French, who were more experienced and had more artillery. Lloyd George proposed sending General William Robertson on a mission to Russia–but, with royal backing, he refused to go–, and demanded that eight British divisions be sent to Salonika to help Romania. Having been neutral for the first two years of the war, Romania had entered on the side of the Allied Powers on 27 August 1916, despite its 1883 secret treaty with the Triple Alliance, not accepting that Austria-Hungary had suffered an 'unprovoked attack'.[1152] On 9 October, Robertson threatened to resign, though he was dissuaded by Lord Derby[1153] from doing so.

During this time, as Secretary of State for War, Lloyd George was involved in a pioneering war effort, in the shape of '*The Battle of the Somme*', a documentary and propaganda film, shot by official cinematographers Geoffrey Malins and John McDowell between 26 June and 9 July. The film depicts the British Expeditionary Force in the preliminaries before, and early days of the battle, showing trench warfare, marching infantry, military horses, artillery firing on German positions, British troops waiting to attack on 1 July, treatment of wounded British and German soldiers, British and German dead and captured German equipment and positions. Much of the footage was censored from the public version, as the War Office required the film to contain images that would support the war effort and raise morale. A 77 minute long version was ready by 31 July, and a rough cut was screened at the BEF GHQ at Montreuil, Pas-de-Calais and at the Fourth Army HQ. General Rawlinson commented "some of it is very good but it cut out many of the horrors in dead and wounded."[1154] The film was shown to Lloyd George on 2 August, Frances Stevenson recording: "We went on Wednesday night to a private view of the 'Somme films'… To say that one enjoyed them would be untrue; but… I am glad I have seen the sort of thing our men have to go through."[1155]

The film received final approval for release on 7 August, premièring at the Scala Motion Picture Theatre, London on 10 August, to an audience of journalists, Foreign Office officials, cinema trade figures and officers of the Imperial General Staff. The screening was preceded by the reading of a letter from Lloyd George, exhorting the audience to "See that this picture, which is in itself an epic of

---

1148 Lieutenant General Henry Rawlinson (1864-1925).

1149 Ultimately, more than three million men fought in the battle, which ground on until 18 November 1916, with over one million men wounded or killed–420,000 British, 200,000 French, 450,000 German–making it one of the deadliest in history. For this carnage, the Allies advanced a mere seven miles (12 Km).

1150 General Douglas Haig, Earl Haig (1861-1928), promoted Field Marshal on 1 January 1917.

1151 Marshal Ferdinand Foch (1851-1929).

1152 The author thanks Professor Medina Birau for stimulating his interest in Romanian history and culture.

1153 Edward Stanley, Earl of Derby (1865-1948), Tory, Under-Secretary of State for War from July 1916, Secretary of State for War from 10 December 1916, named as Ambassador to France on 18 April 1918.

1154 Quoted in Philpott, W. *Bloody Victory: The Sacrifice On The Somme And The Making Of The Twentieth Century*, 2009, London, Little, Brown, p302.

1155 Stevenson, *Diary*, p112. Entry for 4 August 1916. Lloyd George did not mention the film in his *War Memoirs*, but of course he had witnessed some of the horrors almost at first hand.

self-sacrifice and gallantry, reaches everyone. Herald the deeds of our brave men to the ends of the earth. This is *your* duty."[1156] On its general release from 21 August, the film was a great success, watched by some 20 million people in Britain in the first six weeks of showing and distributed in 18 other countries. On 28 August, the *Yorkshire Evening Post* printed the comment, attributed to Lloyd George, "If the exhibition of this Picture all over the world does not end War, God help civilisation."[1157] The film was shown to British troops in France from 5 September, and its images–such as the mining of Hawthorn Ridge Redoubt, and a soldier rescuing a mortally wounded comrade from no man's land–remain deservedly iconic to perhaps inspire succeeding generations to abjure war as a solution to human disputes, as Lloyd George suggested.

Meanwhile, a small number of the brand-new Mark I tanks took part in the Somme Offensive at the Battle of Flers-Courcelette on 15 September. They were used to cut through barbed wire to clear the way for infantry and were even driven through buildings to destroy machine gun emplacements. However, these new weapons were used in piecemeal fashion: only 49 were ready in time, and many broke down or became stuck, only 18 contributing to the battle. The tank crews were not fully trained, no training had taken place with supporting infantry, the existing machines themselves were already in need of maintenance, partially obsolescent due to the developments in trench construction, and Haig had been informed that "as many as five hundred tanks might be available if he could wait till January."[1158]

Lloyd George, Churchill, Lloyd George's successor as Minister of Munitions Edwin Montagu, and even the French, pleaded with Asquith to prevent the stubborn Haig from prematurely using the new weapon, as had been agreed in a paper *'Notes on the Employment of "Tanks"'* circulated as far back as late February 1916 by Lieutenant Colonel Ernest Swinton. Swinton had emphasised: "Since the chance of success of an attack by Tanks lies almost entirely in its novelty and in the element of surprise… these machines *should not be used in driblets*… [and] the fact of their existence should be kept as secret as possible until the whole are ready to be launched."[1159] Tragically, all to no avail. Unable to adapt to the ever-changing circumstances, Haig pressed ahead. As Lloyd George commented: "So the great secret was sold for the battered ruin of a little hamlet on the Somme, which was not worth capturing."[1160] Despite this, their effect on enemy morale was noted, leading to a request by the Army Council for 1,000 more on 26 September.

When the news of the first use of these tanks emerged, Lloyd George commented publicly with a positive gloss:

> Well, we must not expect too much from them but so far they have done very well, and don't you think that they reflect some credit on those responsible for them? It is really to Mr Winston

---

[1156] Quoted in S. D. Badsey, *Battle of the Somme: British War-Propaganda, Historical Journal of Film, Radio and Television* 3, 2 1983, p99-115; Quote, p99.

[1157] Quoted in Philpott, p303.

[1158] Gardner, p226.

[1159] E. D. Swinton, *Eyewitness: Being Personal Reminiscences Of Certain Phases Of The Great War, Including The Genesis Of The Tank*, 1932, London, Hodder and Stoughton: 'Notes', p198-214; para.11, p203-204.

[1160] Lloyd George, *War Memoirs*, Vol.I, p385. Swinton agreed, *Eyewitness*, p251.

> Churchill that the credit is due more than to anyone else. He took up with enthusiasm the idea of making them a long time ago, and he met with many difficulties. He converted me, and at the Ministry of Munitions he went ahead and made them… Major [Albert] Stern, a business man at the Ministry of Munitions had charge of the work of getting them built, and he did the task very well. Col [Ernest] Swinton and others also did valuable work.[1161]

Much of the press still argued that the professional leadership of Haig and Robertson was preferable to civilian interference which had led to disasters like Gallipoli and Kut.[1162] On 10 October, a piqued Lord Northcliffe, owner of *The Times,* stormed into Lloyd George's office and, finding him unavailable, allegedly told his secretary J. Davies[1163] "You can tell him that I hear he has been interfering with strategy, and that if he goes on, I will break him"[1164], and the next day, 11 October, Lloyd George also received a warning letter from Howell Gwynne, the Welsh editor of the *Morning Post*:

> You and I are not seeing eye to eye just now. It is a great pity because you are the only man in the Cabinet who sees clearly that we have to beat the Germans thoroughly or go under. The rest of your colleagues are already whispering the words "armistice" and "peace". But why on earth can't you let the Army alone? With it enthusiastically on your side victory over Germany becomes easier while if you quarrel with its leaders you will jeopardise the issue and lose influence in the country… You put those who are anxious to help you in that task in an awkward dilemma.[1165]

Lloyd George was obliged to give his "word of honour" to Asquith that he had complete confidence in Haig and Robertson and thought them irreplaceable, but he wrote to Robertson wanting to know how their differences had been leaked to the press, affecting to believe that Robertson had not personally "authorised such a breach of confidence & discipline". By the end of October, Lloyd George was deeply frustrated by his emasculated position at the War Office, saying bitterly to Sir Max Aitken: "I am the butcher's boy who leads in the animals to be slaughtered–when I have delivered the men my task in the war is over."[1166] On 9 November, he met with Maurice Hankey, observing, "We are going to lose this war"–surely with the implication, *unless* radical steps were taken. He asserted his right to express his opinions about strategy in November, by which time ministers had taken to holding meetings to which Robertson was not invited.

The weakness of Asquith as a planner and organiser was increasingly apparent to senior officials, as well as to himself: he "knew that he had no effective control over the conduct of the war, and was

1161 *The New Armoured Cars*, *The Motor Cycle*, 21 September 1916, p254.

1162 The siege of 8,000 British garrison troops at Kut Al Amara, 7 December 1915–29 April 1916, 160 km south of Baghdad, by the Ottomans. Their ultimate surrender was arguably the worst British defeat of the war.

1163 Sir Joseph Davies (1866-1954), Welsh statistician, Secretary to the prime minister's secretariat, 1917-1920, Knighted in January 1918, Liberal MP for Crewe, 1918-1922.

1164 Beaverbrook, *Politicians And The War*, p323. For Northcliffe's view, see Thompson, *Northcliffe*, p258.

1165 Quoted in Mitchell, p115.

1166 Beaverbrook, *Politicians And The War*, p320.

aware that others knew it."[1167] Although a married man with ten children, since January 1912 he had become obsessed with Lady Venetia Stanley[1168], 35 years younger than himself, by 1915, writing her up to three letters a day, some very passionate, some written during Cabinet meetings or during Commons debates! It has been related:

> A messenger would come into the Cabinet room with a letter from Venetia and he [Asquith] would read it with great concentration and then settle down to reply at length, ringing for the messenger, who would then take the reply for dispatch. Other members of the Cabinet, particularly Lloyd George, were dismayed at the time he spent on his personal correspondence, during meetings over which he should have been presiding, lost in his private thoughts, while grave wartime matters were being discussed.[1169]

It was not just an emotional dependence, as Asquith also sought her advice on how to deal with his political colleagues and even on questions of military strategy, wholly inappropriate and irresponsible behaviour, especially in wartime. He also forwarded other people's confidential letters to Venetia, including those of Lloyd George and Kitchener.[1170] Whether their relationship was sexual is still debated, but distinguished former High Court Judge, Sir Oliver Popplewell, concluded: "from the evidence–both individually and cumulatively–one is driven to the inexorable conclusion that the relationship between Asquith and Venetia was indeed sexual. No judge or jury looking at all the evidence could reasonably reach any other verdict."[1171] Ultimately, Venetia felt overwhelmed by the intensity of Asquith's demands. As a result, she finally accepted rising Liberal MP Edwin Montagu's proposal on 28 April, marrying him on 26 July 1915.[1172] This did not prevent her from having affairs with others, including Lord Beaverbrook, while Asquith immediately began a similar passionate 'correspondence' with Venetia's older married sister, Sylvia Henley.[1173]

In her diary for 12 October 1915, Frances Stevenson recorded that Lloyd George had told her: "that the P.M. has followed the 'wait and see' policy so long that in wartime he cannot be got to understand that it is disastrous… He says it is impossible to get the P.M. to do anything… He just sits there and uses the whole of his crafty brain to squash any plan for action that is put forward."[1174] After the blow of 'losing' his beloved Venetia, Asquith suffered further when his eldest son, Raymond, a lieutenant with the Grenadier Guards, was killed in action at the Somme on 15 September 1916. He was now drinking regularly and heavily enough to be earning his nickname of 'Old Squiffy', already

---

1167 Jones, *Radical Life*, p30.
1168 Venetia Stanley Montagu (1887-1948), aristocrat and socialite.
1169 T. Morgan, *Churchill: Young Man In A Hurry, 1874-1915*, 1982, New York, Simon & Schuster, p519. Robert Harris, in his factually based novel *Precipice*, 2024, London, Hutchinson Heinemann, highlights this disquieting episode using some of Asquith's 560 surviving letters and other official documents. Asquith burned Venetia's correspondence during his last day in office.
1170 Popplewell, p111, 115.
1171 Ibid., p136. Harris concludes "it strains credulity to breaking point, given the characters of Asquith and of Venetia, to suggest… that the affair was not, at least in some sense, physical": Acknowledgements, p448.
1172 Edwin Montagu (1879-1924), Liberal MP for Chesterton, 1906-1918, Cambridgeshire, 1918-1922, Parliamentary Private Secretary to Asquith, 1906-1910, Secretary of State for India, 1917-1922.
1173 See Walker, Part III, *Sylvia Henley*, p129-182, *passim.*
1174 Stevenson, *Diary*, p67, 68.

having once–on 2 April 1911–nearly collapsed, his doctor warning him to substantially reduce his alcohol intake. Lord Crawford, appointed as President of the Board of Agriculture on 11 July 1916, wrote after his first Cabinet meeting the next day: "Asquith somnolent–hands shaky and cheeks pendulous. He exercised little control over debate, seemed rather bored, but good-humoured throughout."[1175] Subsequent meetings did little to improve this initial impression, and two other instances, related by Douglas Haig and old friend Constance Flower, Lady Battersea, also allude to Asquith's wartime drinking. Even Lloyd George's daughter Olwen was once reprimanded by her mother for remarking about Asquith "not knowing what was going on, because he had drunk too much and had fallen asleep."[1176] David Owen, himself medically trained, concludes "By modern diagnostic standards, Asquith became an alcoholic while Prime Minister."[1177]

By now Asquith was arguably unfit to be Prime Minister. Asquith's daughter-in-law Cynthia picked up on the political gossip circulating in the capital, noting on 15 November 1916, in terms coloured by partisan family feeling:

> London appears to be seething with intrigue and politicians behaving like 'politicians'. Lloyd George is hand in glove with Carson and Winston, and they are doing their best to unseat the P.M. and throw out the Government… Lloyd George is to be Prime Minister and Winston is to go to the War Office. They are credited with having 'got at' Bonar Law, and their boast is that they will be in office in a month. Bluetooth[1178] thought it just on the cards that they might succeed… I asked him if he diagnosed Lloyd George as pure knave, but he gives him credit for sincerity in as much that he really thinks himself a Chatham[1179] with a divine mission to save the country, therefore holding any means that will put him in power justifiable.[1180]

In fact, all sides were manoeuvring. Cynthia, by her own admission "not quick about politics", very quickly did a 'volte-face' concerning Lloyd George–having accused him of an insatiable desire for power, by 5 December she was confiding to her diary that he "would greatly prefer Bonar [Law] to be Prime Minister, in order himself to avoid incurring the odium of responsibility."[1181] Both the irony of this, and the general inaccuracy of her 'information', seems to have escaped her.

The incoherent situation could not be allowed to continue, with 20 Cabinet members deliberating without an organised agenda, secretary or minutes. Leadership needed to be taken by a smaller, more streamlined and resolute body with an agreed plan of action and executive powers. On 20 November 1916, Lloyd George, Edward Carson[1182] and Bonar Law, who had become increasingly worried about his own political position since the 'Nigeria Debate'–on the sale of former German assets–in the

---

1175 Quoted in Grigg, *From Peace To War*, p438.
1176 Carey Evans, p87.
1177 D. Owen, *The Hidden Perspective: The Military Conversations 1906-1914*, 2014, London, Haus, p115-116.
1178 Harold Baker (1877-1960), Liberal MP for Accrington, 1910-1918.
1179 William Pitt, Earl of Chatham (1708-1778), Whig political leader of Britain in the Seven Years' War.
1180 Asquith, p234-235.
1181 Ibid., p242.
1182 Sir Edward Carson (1854-1935), Irish Unionist, leader of the 'Unionist War Committee' ginger group.

House on 8 November, met at the Hyde Park Hotel. The meeting was organised by Max Aitken[1183], a Canadian adventurer, millionaire, and close friend of Bonar Law. The trio agreed on the necessity of overhauling the government and further agreed on the mechanism for doing so; the establishment of a small War Committee, chaired by Lloyd George, with no more than five members and with full executive authority for the conduct of the war.

There is an extremely important point here, as it effectively coloured the rest of Lloyd George's life and led to the downfall of the Liberal Party. The demand for the increasingly ineffectual Asquith to be replaced was virtually unanimous amongst those at the centre of British politics not bound to him by personal ties. In 1977, John Campbell wrote, optimistically, that the "myth that Lloyd George plotted ambitiously to oust his leader has been exploded."[1184] And yet it *still* persists, half a century later. It is one of the most pernicious myths in British political history, and needs permanently burying, as it creates a profound misunderstanding of the subsequent history.

Cameron Hazlehurst first demolished this absurdity as far back as 1968, commenting: "The notion that Lloyd George *compelled* men like Bonar Law, Curzon[1185], Austen Chamberlain or Walter Long to do *anything* is fantastic."[1186] Later, Churchill pointed out that Asquith did not summarily dismiss the proposals made, and that if the arrangements were studied with attention:

> It will appear to have contained many features of great advantage to him (Asquith). Viewing the issue from a detached standpoint, as did Sir Edward Carson, that the position of the Secretary of State for War under it would become one both of difficulty and weakness. On him would fall all the brunt of battling with the naval and military Chiefs… Acute differences were certain to develop in both directions between the political and the professional views. The appeal in all cases would have been to the Prime Minister who, free from the friction of the discussions of the War Committee, yet fully informed on every point, would have been able to decide with final authority. On the other hand, Mr. Lloyd George, publicly appointed to preside over the Committee actually directing the conduct of the war, would have been held responsible for every misfortune that occurred, and they were bound to be many. I warned the Secretary of State for War, when he told me what was passing, of these obvious dangers, but he was determined to persist in his course.[1187]

Asquith was to continue as prime minister, and be given honorific oversight of the War Committee, but day to day operations would be directed by Lloyd George. This scheme, although often reworked, remained the basis of all proposals to reform the government until Asquith's fall on 5 December. Until almost the end, both Bonar Law and Lloyd George wished to retain Asquith as premier. But

---

1183 William Maxwell Aitken (1879-1964), Canadian-British newspaper publisher, Tory MP for Ashton-under-Lyne, 1910-1916, created 1st Baron Beaverbrook on 2 January 1917.

1184 Campbell, *Lloyd George*, p13.

1185 George Curzon, Marquess Curzon of Kedleston (1859-1925), Tory, Viceroy and Governor-General of India, 1899-1905, Secretary of State for Foreign Affairs, 1919-1924.

1186 C. Hazlehurst, *The Conspiracy Myth*, in Gilbert, *Lloyd George*, p150.

1187 W.S. Churchill, *The World Crisis: Volume III, 1916-1918, Part 1*, 1927, London, Thornton Butterworth, p249-250.

Aitken, Carson and Northcliffe emphatically did not.[1188]

Crucially, Asquith mistrusted Lloyd George. Writing to Bonar Law–"for your eyes alone"–on 26 November, he rejected the proposals:

> As for Mr Lloyd George, you know as well as I do both his qualities and his defects. He has many qualities that would fit him for the first place, but he lacks the one thing needful–he does not inspire trust… Here again, there is one construction, and one only, that could be put on the new arrangement–that it has been engineered by him with the purpose, not perhaps at the moment, but as soon as a fitting pretext could be found, of his displacing me.[1189]

An extraordinary message to send to a political opponent about a close colleague who had long given loyal, productive service to common causes!

Unknowingly, Lloyd George sent a detailed memo to Asquith on Friday, 1 December, stating:

> 1. That the War Committee consist of three members–two of whom must be the First Lord of the Admiralty and the Secretary of State for War, who should have in their offices deputies capable of attending to and deciding all departmental business–and a third Minister without portfolio. One of the three to be chairman.
>
> 2. That the War Committee shall have full powers, subject to the supreme control of the Prime Minister, to direct all questions connected with the war.
>
> 3. The Prime Minister, in his discretion, to have the power to refer any question to the Cabinet.
>
> 4. Unless the Cabinet, on reference by the Prime Minister, reverses decision of the War Committee, that decision to be carried out by the department concerned.
>
> 5. The War Committee to have the power to invite any Minister and to summon the expert advisers and officers of any department to its meetings.[1190]

Asquith replied to these proposals in detail the same day:

> Though I do not altogether share your dark estimate and forecast of the situation, actual and perspective, I am in complete agreement that we have reached a critical situation in the war, and that our own methods of procedure, with the experience which we have gained during the last few months, call for reconsideration and revision.
>
> The two main defects of the War Committee, which has done excellent work, are (1) that its numbers are too large; (2) that there is delay, evasion, and often obstruction, on the part of the departments in giving effect to its decisions. I might, with good reason, add (3) that it is often

1188 Thompson, *Northcliffe*, p259.
1189 Quoted in De Courcy, p331.
1190 Quoted in Roch, p172-173.

kept in ignorance by the departments of information, essential and even vital, of a technical kind, upon the problems that come before it; and (4) that it is overcharged with duties, many of which might well be delegated to subordinate bodies.

The result is, that I am clearly of opinion that the War Committee should be reconstituted, and its relations to and authority over the departments, etc., more clearly defined and more effectively asserted.

I come now to your specific proposals. In my opinion, whatever changes are made in the composition or functions of the War Committee, the Prime Minister must be its Chairman. He cannot be relegated to the position of an arbiter in the background or a referee to the Cabinet.

In regard to its composition, I agree that the War Secretary and the First Lord of the Admiralty are necessary members. I am inclined to add to the same category the Minister of Munitions. There should be another member, with or without portfolio, or charged only with comparatively light departmental duties. One of the members should be appointed Vice-Chairman.

I purposely do not in this letter discuss the delicate and difficult question of personnel.

The Committee should, as far as possible, sit de die in diem, and have full power to see that its decisions (subject to appeal to the Cabinet) are carried out promptly and effectively by the departments.

The reconstruction of the War Committee should be accompanied by the setting up of a Committee of National Organisation to deal with the purely domestic side of war problems. It should have executive powers within its own domain.

The Cabinet would in all cases have ultimate authority.[1191]

Lloyd George saw a string of visitors at Walton Heath on Saturday 2 December, including Northcliffe, C. P. Scott and Max Aitken. He also saw Henry Dalziel, his old Radical friend and the owner of *Reynolds's Weekly* newspaper. Lloyd George drafted, but crucially withheld from sending, a letter of resignation to Asquith, stating that it was his duty "to leave the Government in order to inform the people of the real condition of affairs."[1192] He did write to Bonar Law stating, "The life of the country depends on resolute action by you now." He also dashed off a hasty note to his brother: "Crisis. We are muddling the War & I have given notice that I shall stand it no longer & unless Asquith puts things right *I go.* Go to tell the public all about it…"[1193] As J. Graham Jones notes "There is no suggestion of an ambition or a conspiracy to oust Asquith from the premiership."[1194] Alone of the Sunday papers, *Reynolds's* led the next day with the sensational headline 'Grave Cabinet Crisis. Lloyd George to Resign. Campaign in the Country to Follow', also implying that Bonar Law would probably accompany him.[1195]

By the late afternoon of Sunday, 3 December, a compromise agreement seemed to have been

1191 Ibid., p173-174.
1192 Quoted in Fair, pD1332.
1193 Quoted in Jones, *David Lloyd George*, p230. Emphasis added.
1194 Jones, *David Lloyd George*, p226.
1195 McEwen, p142; Mitchell, p123.

reached, and Lloyd George and Bonar Law both left Downing Street having had what they believed had been friendly and constructive conversations with the Prime Minister, convinced that the crisis was over, though Lloyd George may have been over-optimistic regarding Asquith's acquiescence.[1196] At 11.45 pm Asquith released a statement to the press, stating: "The Prime Minister, with a view to the most effective prosecution of the war, has decided to advise His Majesty the King to consent to a reconstruction of the Government."[1197] On 4 December, Asquith still appeared to agree to the Lloyd George's demands, accepting the need for an authoritative War Committee with Lloyd George as chairman. However, that morning a leader in *The Times,* written by editor Geoffrey Dawson, using information leaked by Carson[1198], and entitled 'Towards Reconstruction', obliquely stated:

> On Friday… Mr. Lloyd George's decision took shape in the form of written representations to the Prime Minister, and these have since been followed by personal discussion between them. The gist of his proposal is understood to be the establishment forthwith of a small War Council, fully charged with the supreme direction of the war. Of this Council Mr. Asquith himself is not to be a member–the assumption being that the Prime Minister has sufficient cares of a more general character without devoting himself wholly, as the new Council must be devoted, if it is to be effective, to the daily task of organising victory.
>
> Certain of Mr. Asquith's colleagues are also excluded on the ground of temperament from a body which can only succeed if it is harmonious and decisive. On the other hand, the inclusion of Sir Edward Carson is believed to form an essential part of Mr. Lloyd George's scheme, and it is one which will be thoroughly understood.[1199]

This effectively described the compromise as a humiliating surrender imposed upon an ineffective war leader. Infuriated, Asquith promptly wrote to Lloyd George cancelling their pact:

> Such productions as the first leading article in to-day's "Times," showing the infinite possibilities for misunderstanding and misrepresentation of such an arrangement as we considered yesterday, make me at least doubtful as to its feasibility. Unless the impression is at once corrected that I am being relegated to the position of an irresponsible spectator of the war, I cannot possibly go on.
>
> The suggested arrangement was to the following effect: The Prime Minister to have supreme and effective control of War Policy.
>
> The agenda of the War Committee will be submitted to him: its Chairman will report to him daily: he can direct it to consider particular topics or proposals; and all its conclusions will be

[1196] McEwen, p145.
[1197] Quoted in McEwen, p153.
[1198] J. Campbell, *Pistols At Dawn: Two Hundred Years of Political Rivalry from Pitt and Fox to Blair and Brown*, 2009, London, Jonathan Cape, p169. [*H. H. Asquith and David Lloyd George*, p141-194].
[1199] Quoted in Roch, p176-177.

> subject to his approval or veto. He can, of course, at his own discretion attend meetings of the Committee.[1200]

Lloyd George responded immediately:

> I have not seen the "Times" article, but I hope you will not attach undue importance to these effusions. I have had these misrepresentations to put up with for months. Northcliffe frankly wants a smash. Derby and I do not. Northcliffe would like to make this and any other rearrangement under your Premiership impossible. *Derby and I attach great importance to your retaining your present position–effectively.* I cannot restrain, or, I fear, influence Northcliffe. I fully accept in letter and in spirit your summary of the suggested arrangement–subject, of course, to personnel.[1201]

The same day Addison and Kellaway, on their own account, began to canvass the Liberal MPs to discover how many would support Lloyd George. By 6 December, they found that 49 were 'out and out' supporters, while a further 126 would back a Lloyd George government, if it were formed.[1202] This showed that Lloyd George was assured of the support of well over half the number of Liberals in the House, as well as among Unionists. "It was a vital stage in securing broad-based, all-party support for Lloyd George, and was largely Addison's work."[1203] It was what led A. J. P. Taylor to write that, "By this canvass, Addison became the real maker of the Lloyd George government."[1204]

Meanwhile, Asquith continued to consult Reginald McKenna and others hostile to Lloyd George in a stubborn attempt to reconstruct his failing government. Edwin Montagu tried to persuade him to continue in office, on 5 December writing:

> I do not want you to cease to be Prime Minister because I am certain that any other Prime Minister cannot succeed. At the same time… I cannot think of a Government conducting the war without Lloyd George. Whatever office he has held, despite his obvious defects, during the war he has rendered services to the country which cannot be minimised.

He listed his reasons and concluded with his opinion of where the real source of blame for the crisis lay, namely Northcliffe:

> It is lamentable to think that you should let him achieve the victory that he has long sought. He wanted to drive you out; he alone is fool enough not to believe in you. His effects were resisted by Lloyd George, by Bonar Law, by Derby, by Carson, by Robertson. Using information that

1200 Ibid., p177-178.
1201 Ibid., p178. Emphasis added.
1202 Addison, *Four And A Half Years*, Vol.I, p274.
1203 Morgan, *Portrait Of A Progressive*, p54.
1204 A. J. P. Taylor, *Politics In The First World War*, p84.

he had no right to obtain… He published that article to wreck the arrangement… this matter is a matter of the deepest possible chagrin to me…

Concerning Lloyd George, he concluded:

Lloyd George sent for me this afternoon and I spent some time with him. I found him in almost as great a condition of misery and unhappiness as I am myself. Believe me or not as you will, he wanted to work with you. He did not want a victory for Northcliffe. He was completely satisfied with the arrangements you had come to and meant to work them loyally. He does not want, I am confident, to be Prime Minister…[1205]

Ignoring such sound advice, Asquith persisted, and on 5 December sent a challenging letter to Lloyd George, this time marked 'Secret':

The King gave me to-day authority to ask and accept the resignation of all my colleagues, and to form a new Government on such lines as I should submit to him. I start, therefore, with a clean slate.

The first question which I have to consider is the constitution of the new War Committee.

… I have come decidedly to the conclusion that it is not possible that such a Committee could be made workable and effective without the Prime Minister as its Chairman. I quite agree that it will be necessary for him… to delegate from time to time the Chairmanship to another Minister as his representative and locum tenens; but… he must continue to be, as he always has been, its permanent President. I am satisfied, on reflection, that any other arrangement (such, for instance, as the one which I indicated to you in my letter of to-day) would be found in experience impracticable, and incompatible with the retention of the Prime Minister's final and supreme control.

The other question, which you have raised, relates to the personnel of the Committee. Here again, after deliberate consideration, I find myself unable to agree with some of your suggestions. I think we both agree that the First Lord of the Admiralty must, of necessity, be a member of the Committee. I cannot… be a party to any suggestion that Mr. Balfour should be displaced… I believe Mr. Balfour to be, under existing conditions, the necessary head of the Board. I must add that Sir Edward Carson… is not, from the only point of view which is significant to me (namely, the most effective prosecution of the war), the man best qualified among my colleagues, present or past, to be a member of the War Committee.

I have only to say, in conclusion, that I am strongly of opinion that the War Committee… ought to be reduced in number: so that it can sit more frequently, and overtake more easily the daily problems with which it has to deal. But, in any reconstruction of the Committee… the governing consideration to my mind is the special capacity of the men who are to sit on it for the work which it has to do.

---

[1205] Quoted in S. D. Waley, *Edwin Montagu: A Memoir And An Account Of His Visits To India*, 1964, Bombay, Asia Publishing House, Letter quoted in full p107-110; Asquith MS.27, f.186, Bodleian Library.

That is a question which I must reserve for myself to decide.[1206]

His response left Lloyd George with but one choice, and he duly tendered his resignation:

I have received your letter with some surprise. On Friday I made proposals which involved not merely your retention of the Premiership, but the supreme control of the War, whilst the executive functions, subject to that supreme control, were left to others. I thought you then received these suggestions favourably. In fact, you yourself proposed that I should be the chairman of this Executive Committee, although, as you know, I never put forward that demand. On Saturday you wrote me a letter in which you completely went back on that proposition. You sent for me on Sunday and put before me other proposals; these proposals you embodied in a letter to me written on Monday:

The Prime Minister to have supreme and effective control of war policy;

The Agenda of the War Committee will be submitted to him; its chairman will report to him daily; he can direct it to consider particular topics or proposals and all its conclusions will be subject to his approval or veto. He can, of course, at his own discretion attend meetings of the Committee.

These proposals safeguarded your position and power as Prime Minister in every particular. I immediately wrote you accepting them in letter and in spirit. It is true that on Sunday I expressed views as to the constitution of the Committee, but these were for discussion. To-day you have gone back on your own proposals.

I have striven my utmost to cure the obvious defects of the War Committee without overthrowing the Government. As you are aware, on several occasions during the last two years I have deemed it my duty to express profound dissatisfaction with the Government's method of conducting the War. Many a time, with the road to victory open in front of us, we have delayed and hesitated whilst the enemy were erecting barriers that finally checked the approach. There has been delay, hesitation, lack of forethought and vision. I have endeavoured repeatedly to warn the Government of the dangers, both verbally and in written memoranda and letters, which I crave your leave now to publish if my action is challenged; but I have either failed to secure decisions or I have secured them when it was too late to avert the evils. The latest illustration is our lamentable failure to give timely support to Roumania [sic].

I have more than once asked to be released from my responsibility for a policy with which I was in thorough disagreement, but at your urgent personal request I remained in the Government. I realise that when the country is in peril of a great war, Ministers have not the same freedom to resign on disagreement. At the same time I have always felt and felt deeply that I was in a false position inasmuch as I could never defend in a whole-hearted manner the action of a Government of which I was a member. We have thrown away opportunity after opportunity, and I am convinced, after deep and anxious reflection, that it is my duty to leave the Government in order to inform the people of the real condition of affairs, and to give them an opportunity, before it is too late, to save their native land from a disaster which is inevitable

[1206] Quoted in Roch, p178-179.

> if the present methods are longer persisted in. As all delay is fatal in war, I place my office without further parley at your disposal.
>
> It is with great personal regret that I have come to this conclusion. In spite of mean and unworthy insinuations to the contrary… I have felt a strong personal attachment to you as my Chief. As you yourself said on Sunday, we have acted together for ten years and never had a quarrel, although we have had many a grave difference on questions of policy. You have treated me with great courtesy and kindness; for all that I thank you. Nothing would have induced me to part now except an overwhelming sense that the course of action which has been pursued has put the country and not merely the country, but throughout the world, the principles for which you and I have always stood throughout our political lives in the greatest peril that has ever overtaken them.
>
> As I am fully conscious of the importance of preserving national unity, I propose to give your Government complete support in the vigorous prosecution of the War; but unity without action is nothing but futile carnage, and I cannot be responsible for that. Vigour and vision are the supreme need at this hour.[1207]

In effect, Lloyd George had called Asquith's bluff, as the latter was in no realistic position to continue without him, such was his importance in the Cabinet and to the war effort itself. What's more, within hours Balfour, who was ill, had written resigning as First Lord of the Admiralty and signalling his intention of backing Lloyd George, while at a meeting of all the Liberal Cabinet members–except Lloyd George, but including Arthur Henderson–at 5.00 pm, Asquith informed them that Curzon, Austen Chamberlain and Cecil had informed him that they would not remain in a ministry from which Lloyd George and Bonar Law had withdrawn, and that they would support Lloyd George, if he could form a stable government. During the meeting, a letter from Bonar Law was delivered by Carson, stating that all the Unionist ministers desired their resignations to become effective.[1208] The meeting thus concluded that they "could not in any case carry on without Ll.G. [sic] and without the Unionists, and ought not to give the appearance of wishing to do so. The resignation should take effect to-night."[1209] Asquith duly drove to Buckingham Palace and resigned at 7.00 pm. His grasp on reality remained shaky: he told J. H. Thomas, General Secretary of the National Union of Railwaymen, that on "the advice of close friends that it was impossible for Lloyd George to form a Cabinet" he believed that "the King would send for him before the day was out." Thomas replied "I, wanting him to continue, pointed out that this advice was sheer madness."[1210] Liberal backbencher Walter Roch also held that: "It is probable that when Mr. Asquith resigned he felt that he would nevertheless be recalled to power, and asked to form an Administration."[1211] A. J. P. Taylor colourfully essayed that "Asquith was not manoeuvred out of office. He deliberately resigned office as a manoeuvre to rout his critics.

---

1207 Lloyd George, *War Memoirs*, Vol.I, p593-595.
1208 McEwen, p154.
1209 Samuel, p122.
1210 J. H. Thomas, *My Story*, 1937, London, Hutchinson, p43.
1211 Roch, p183. Walter Roch (1880-1965), Liberal MP for Pembrokeshire, 1908-1918. Later author of *Mr. Lloyd George and the War*, his support of Asquith over Lloyd George effectively ended his political career.

His complaints, when this manoeuvre failed, were those of an ageing heavyweight, who has been knocked out by a younger, more agile opponent."[1212]

To Asquith's family, it was Lloyd George who irked them, Cynthia referring to him that day as "a very wily, foxy cad".[1213] Grey was among leading 'Asquithians' who claimed to have identified Lloyd George's intentions earlier, noting "A friend has reminded me that one day, as we came away from a War Council, late in November or early in December 1916, I said to him, commenting on what had passed there, "Lloyd George means to break up the Government." This happened in no long time."[1214] The point was, it needed breaking up, or at least, radically re-invigorating. But Lloyd George had made no attempt to mobilize the Liberal backbenches against Asquith, where he could probably have secured majority support, and this is one of the major pieces of evidence against the calumny that Lloyd George ever intended a 'plot' against his Leader.[1215]

The next day, 6 December, King George summoned a conference at Buckingham Palace, attended by Asquith, Lloyd George, Bonar Law, Balfour and Arthur Henderson, representing Labour. Each tried to persuade Asquith to serve under Bonar Law, on the patriotic grounds of preserving the appearance of national unity. Asquith refused, bitterly, observing "that throughout his alleged mismanagement of the war he could not recall any issue on which a decision had been reached without the concurrence of Lloyd George."[1216] He was asked to consider whether he would be prepared to serve under Bonar Law, and that if he could not, Lloyd George would be asked to try to form a government. Asquith asked indignantly "What is the proposal? That I who have held first place for eight years should be asked to take a secondary position."[1217] The conference broke up at 4.30 pm. On consulting his Liberal colleagues, Asquith remained firm in his earlier decision, full of overweening pride. Rather than join any administration of which he was not the head, he would lead "a sober and responsible Opposition, steadily supporting the Government in the conduct of the War."[1218] This left David Lloyd George as the only man still standing.

---

1212 Taylor, *English History*, p69.

1213 Asquith, p242.

1214 Grey, *Twenty-Five Years*, Vol.II, p255.

1215 C. Hazlehurst, *The Conspiracy Myth*, in Gilbert, *Lloyd George*, p157. Hazlehurst wrote: "What is even more disturbing to the historian is that, although he lost the parliamentary struggle, Asquith so triumphantly captured the history books of a generation." Well, 'There is a Tide in the Affairs of Men', and it is turning.

1216 Rose, p198.

1217 Lloyd George, *War Memoirs*, Vol.I, p596. Riddell also recorded that Asquith had said that "after being Premier he could not accept a subordinate position", *Diaries*, 1986, p175. Asquith's attitude contrasted strongly with that of Balfour, also a former Prime Minister, who accepted the office of Foreign Secretary. It was a crucial decision, Balfour's stature bringing greater credibility to the efforts to form a new administration.

1218 Stamfordham, 'Memorandum'. Quoted in Nicolson, *King George V*, p292.

David Lloyd George, 1906, President of the Board of Trade.

Autographed photo of David Lloyd George, in the author's possession.

Lloyd George's birthplace, 5 New York Place, Chorlton-on-Medlock, Manchester.

Highgate, Llanystumdwy, Lloyd George's home, 1864-1880, seen here c.1920.

Lloyd George launches his Land Campaign, Swindon, October 1913.

Lloyd George, 1915, Minister of Munitions.

Margaret Lloyd George, 1914.

Dame Margaret, 1935.

Lloyd George at the Western Front, September 1916, as Secretary of State for War.

A PRIVATE SECRETARY TO MR. LLOYD GEORGE: MISS F. L. STEVENSON.

Among the unconventional innovations which the Right Hon. David Lloyd George has instituted is the encouragement of the woman worker, upon a scale hitherto unparalleled. Mr. Lloyd George, knowing how ably and loyally the Empire is being served by women, has taken Miss F. L. Stevenson, of whose capability and zeal he has been able to judge while she was serving under him when he was Minister of Munitions, to act as one of his principal private secretaries at the War Office—a compliment to women which they will be slow to forget.—[*Photo. by L.N.A.*]

Frances Stevenson, as Lloyd George's secretary, in 1916.

*Lloyd's News* announces the signing of the Versailles Treaty, June 1919.

Lloyd George making a speech, in characteristic pose.

Lloyd George, still the same years later, in 1925.

Dr Christopher Addison MP, c.1918, a key radical ally of Lloyd George.

Winifred Coombe Tennant, ally, first British female delegate to the League of Nations, August 1922.

TREADING UPON SACRED SOIL: LLOYD GEORGE at the Door of the Log Cabin Inside the Lincoln Memorial at Hodgeville, Ky., Erected on the Spot Where Stood the Original Cabin in Which Lincoln Was Born.

*(Times Wide World Photos.)*

Lloyd George the agriculturalist, at home at Churt in 1940.

Lloyd George at Criccieth, New Year's Day 1945.

Lloyd George's funeral by the River Dwyfor, Llanystumdwy, March 1945.

The author at Ty Newydd, Llanystumdwy, where Lloyd George died, August 2018.

# 5

## PRIME MINISTER AND WORLD STATESMAN, 1916-1922

Lloyd George now took on the task of coalition-building, being invited to form a government at 7.00 pm on Wednesday 6 December. Frank Dilnot–by now with the Radical Liberal-supporting *Daily Chronicle*–was an eyewitness to Lloyd George's summoning:

> At seven o'clock I was at the entrance of the War Office at Whitehall. Through the dark street an automobile dashed up… Three minutes later the War Office doors swung open and two men came hurrying out. The first was the King's messenger, the second was Lloyd George. The latter's shoulders were hunched with haste, his hat was pressed deep and irregularly over his forehead, his face, set hard, was canted forward. He almost scrambled into the conveyance, and three seconds later the automobile was going at top speed for Buckingham Palace. The King had sent for Lloyd George to ask him to become his Prime Minister.[1219]

In just over 24 hours Lloyd George had put together his administration, forming a small War Cabinet instead of the mooted War Council. At 7.30 pm on Thursday 7 December, he kissed the hands of King George V in Buckingham Palace as Prime Minister.[1220] The King recorded in his diary: "Mr Lloyd George came at 7.30 & informed me that he is able to form an administration & told me the proposed names of his colleagues. He will have a strong Government."[1221] Significantly, Christopher Addison was the first MP to shake Lloyd George's hand after he became Prime Minister, the pair also dining together at Lloyd George's first dinner as premier, though the meal was "a frugal, cheerless affair of cold meat and soup."[1222] In Criccieth, Uncle Lloyd, nearing the end of his life, took the news stoically, merely saying "The man is greater than his office."[1223]

Lloyd George's achievement in creating a government was considerable, given that almost all of the senior Liberals sided with Asquith, but the nation was demanding he take vigorous charge of the war. A *Punch* cartoon by Leonard Raven-Hill published on 20 December showed him as "The New Conductor" conducting the orchestra in the "Opening of the 1917 Overture". Lloyd George himself later described what he felt to be the difference between himself and Asquith:

---

1219 Dilnot, p9.
1220 Grigg, *From Peace to War*, p481.
1221 Quoted in Nicolson, p384.
1222 Addison, *Four And A Half Years*, Vol.I, p276-277.
1223 George, *My Brother And I*, p37.

> There are certain indispensable qualities essential to the Chief Minister of the Crown in a great war… such a minister must have courage, composure, and judgment. All this Mr. Asquith possessed in a superlative degree. He gave dignified but not rousing and vigorous leadership to the nation. But a war minister must also have vision, imagination and initiative–he must show untiring assiduity, must exercise constant oversight and supervision of every sphere of war activity, must possess driving force to energize this activity, must be in continuous consultation with experts, official and unofficial, as to the best means of utilising the resources of the country in conjunction with the Allies for the achievement of victory. If to this can be added a flair for conducting a great fight, then you have an ideal War Minister.[1224]

Although during the political crisis General Robertson had advised Lloyd George "Stick to it, you are all right!"[1225] and to form a small War Council, Lloyd George had planned, if necessary, to appeal to the country, his Military Secretary, Colonel Arthur Lee, having prepared a memo blaming Robertson and the General Staff for the loss of Serbia and Romania. Lloyd George was restricted by his promise to the Unionists to keep Haig as Commander-in-Chief and the press support for the generals, although Milner and Curzon were also sympathetic to campaigns to increase British influence in the Middle East.

On Lloyd George being appointed Prime Minister, after months of failure and discontent with the Asquith Government, Unionists, Labour members and the majority of Liberals came together to support a government with him as its leader. But because he did not have the strong support of one single party, his position was always potentially unstable, depending on his personal success in the War campaigns. At not inconsiderable risk, he put his own personal stamp on everything the Government did. When appointed, he formed a small War Cabinet, under his chairmanship, to take control of war policy. At its first meeting, on 9 December, he found it "embarrassing to be addressed as Prime Minister by all the members."[1226] Besides himself, the five-member War Cabinet contained three Tories–Leader of the House of Lords Lord Curzon, Chancellor of the Exchequer and Leader of the House of Commons Bonar Law, and Minister without Portfolio Lord Milner–and Arthur Henderson, unofficially representing Labour. In this way, he managed to avoid the long drawn out and unhelpful discussions that had hindered the work of the Asquith Cabinet. When peace eventually came, Lloyd George's personal stamp on the whole enterprise ensured for him the epithet 'The Man Who Won the War'.

Even the limited amount of Labour Party commitment had been hard to obtain, as it was split on its response to the war and consequent support or opposition regarding the new Government. To a delegation from the Parliamentary Labour Party and the National Labour Executive at the War Office on the day he took office, he said:

---

1224 Lloyd George, *War Memoirs*, Vol.I, p602.
1225 Robertson to Lloyd George, 6 December 1916, Lloyd George MSS E/1/5/5.
1226 Quoted in George, *My Brother And I*, p257.

> The War for the moment is going badly; the country and all the nations which hang upon the triumph of Great Britain are in great peril… we are face to face with the grimmest and most perilous struggle in which this country has ever been engaged… *I hate war; I abominate it.* I sometimes think 'Am I dreaming? Is it a nightmare? It cannot be fact.' But these are questions to ask and answer before you go into a war; once you are in it, you have to go grimly through it, otherwise the causes which hang upon a successful issue will all perish. Delay in war is as fatal as in an illness… I thought, rightly or wrongly, that there was delay, hesitation and vacillation, and that we were not waging this war with the determination, promptitude and relentlessness… with which it must be waged. We cannot send men to carnage without seeing that at any rate everything is being done to give them a fair chance to win through to victory… I do not believe any Prime Minister… can possibly undertake the task of running Parliament and running the War… Whoever undertakes to run the War must put his whole strength into it and he must make other arrangements with regard to Parliament. The King having failed to secure the adhesion of all parties–*I wish myself there were no parties during the War*–to the plan of forming a comprehensive national Government, invited me to form an Administration… You must have an Administration to prosecute the War, and… politicians make one fundamental mistake when they have been in office. They think that the people who are in office, or who have been in office, are absolutely essential to the Government of the country… Well, we are a people of 45,000,000 and really, if we cannot produce at least two or three alternative Cabinets, we must be what Carlyle once called us–'a nation of fools.'… [T]he country is… looking out for a Government that will prosecute the War efficiently… and therefore I am hoping to get the adhesion of men of that character and calibre to form an Administration.[1227]

Only after "very heated discussion", and by a majority of one vote–that of J. H. Thomas–was Labour co-operation obtained.[1228]

Very few Liberal frontbenchers supported Lloyd George. As already noted, the most prominent of those who did was Addison, Frank Owen opining: "The best Liberal capture that Lloyd George could secure was of Dr. Christopher Addison, who had been his Parliamentary Secretary at the Ministry of Munitions, and now took over that office himself [on 10 December]. Dr. Addison was a worthwhile prize, for besides proving himself to be a capable Minister, both in his department and on the Front Bench, he was still a more skilful operator in the lobbies."[1229] There was also H. A. L. Fisher[1230], who became President of the Board of Education; Lord Rhondda[1231], who became President of the Local Government Board and then Minister of Food Control, and Sir Albert Stanley[1232], who became President of the Board of Trade.

George Riddell, a London-born solicitor and newspaper proprietor who often liaised between

1227 Lloyd George, *War Memoirs*, Vol. I, p625-627. Emphasis added.
1228 Ibid., p632.
1229 Owen, p347. His ally Kellaway became the new secretary at Munitions.
1230 Herbert Fisher (1865-1940), prominent historian and educator.
1231 The same man who had opposed the integration of *Cymru Fydd* with the South Wales Liberal Federation in 1896, being much responsible for the movement's demise, earning Lloyd George's enmity.
1232 Albert Stanley (1874-1948), Tory, President of the Board of Trade until 1919.

government and the press, was a close confidant and financial supporter of Lloyd George from 1908 to 1922. His perceptive diary led John Grigg to describe him as "the nearest equivalent to a Boswell in Lloyd George's life".[1233] On 13 August 1917, during Lloyd George's first year as premier, Riddell assessed his character in his diary in mostly glowing terms:

> He is a remarkable combination of forces: a poet, an orator and a man of action. His energy, power of work, and power of recuperation are remarkable. He has an extraordinary memory, imagination, and the art of getting at the root of a matter. What the military call the *coup d'oeil.* He possesses every sort of courage, daring, patience, bravery in the face of personal danger and in the face of responsibility–*courage d'esprit* as the French say. He has no respect for tradition or convention. He is always ready to examine, scrap or revise established theories and practices. These qualities give him unlimited confidence in himself. He has a remarkably quick, alert and logical mind, which makes him very effective in debate. He is one of the craftiest of men, and his extraordinary charm of manner not only wins him friends, but does much to soften the asperities of his opponents and enemies. He is full of humour and a born actor. His oratory has a wide range. On the whole he is a good judge of men. He has an instinctive knowledge of character, often quite uncanny, coupled with a remarkable power of divining the thoughts and intentions of people with whom he is conversing. His chief defects are: (1) Lack of appreciation of existing institutions, organisations, and stolid, dull people, who often achieve good results by persistency, experience, and slow, but sound judgement. It is not that he fails to understand them. The point is that their ways are not his ways and their methods are not his methods. (2) Fondness for a grandiose scheme in preference to an attempt to improve existing machinery. (3) Disregard of difficulties in carrying out big projects. This is due to the fact that he is not a man of detail.[1234]

On his appointment, Lloyd George set about making changes at 10 Downing Street. Margaret found it cold and inconvenient, although the introduction of a new bathroom by Margot Asquith in 1908 had made it more bearable. One of the few concessions to luxury was the German Ibach baby grand piano. It became the centre of musical evenings, which Lloyd George enjoyed, to which he invited Welsh mezzo-soprano Leila Megàne, members of the London Welsh Society and Polish pianist and Prime Minister Paderewski, who actually played it.[1235] The household itself was run by his formidable Welsh housekeeper, Sarah Jones.

From the outset, Lloyd George assumed total control in a way unknown to Asquith or any of his predecessors. Incredibly, until Lloyd George's premiership, there was no secretariat to keep accurate records of the daily agenda or minutes of meetings; this was another of his unsung efficiency reforms, more important than it may at first appear. Before him, the Prime Minister merely sent a summary of each day's Cabinet business to the sovereign. This now became redundant. To support his War

---

1233 Grigg, *War Leader*, p216.

1234 Riddell, *Diaries*, 1986, p194-195. A later assessment, inserted in the diary subsequently. Riddell was not impressed by Lloyd George's contemporary, Churchill.

1235 The beautiful instrument, manufactured in 1896, is at the Lloyd George Museum.

Cabinet, on 2 January 1917, Lloyd George:

> Created a new Cabinet Secretariat based in nearby Whitehall Gardens, headed by Sir Maurice Hankey and his Welsh deputy Thomas Jones, to act as a central organising machine and keep the minutes: the beginnings of today's Cabinet Office. And, impinging directly on Number 10, Lloyd George chose his own secretariat, a novel group of special advisers, initially housed in temporary huts in the gardens of Number 10. This 'Garden Suburb' consisted of five characteristic advisers: Philip Kerr (later Lord Lothian)[1236] who focussed on foreign policy, Professor [W. G. S.] Adams[1237], a Professor of All Souls, Oxford, a Welsh shipping statistician, Joseph T. Davies, and two millionaires: Waldorf Astor, the American owner of *The Observer*, and David Davies, a Welsh industrial baron. Cecil Harmsworth, younger brother of the press baron Lord Northcliffe, later replaced David Davies. The precise role of the Garden Suburb was never defined, but it was a powerful symbol of the new centralisation of government. It had an impact at first in foreign affairs, through Kerr, Irish policy through Adams, and food production, through Astor. It continued until… December 1918 but its influence on the role of Number 10 was lasting.[1238]

Indeed, Harmsworth would later note in his diary for 22 May 1918:

> Those anxious radicals who have imagined Ll.-G. as dominated in Cabinet by the reactionary Tories–Curzon, Milner & Bonar–have been strangely mistaken. On the few occasions that I have been present at Cabinet the Wizard has ruled the roost with no appearance of challenge from any quarter. When, too, he has been absent in France or elsewhere it has been interesting to observe from the Cabinet ministers how many decisions have been deferred "until the Prime Minister returns". He is in truth the life & soul of the party in no merely conventional meaning of the expression. His vivid personality prevails in the Cabinet room as in the world outside. […] An easier chief to work with in some respects it would be difficult to find. He is wholly unaffected & unspoilt by enormous success. I knew him slightly in the dark days of the Boer War when he was certainly the most unpopular man in England. I see no change in his manner now when he is, I suppose, the most popular man in the whole great Alliance. I have often spoken to him more directly than I dare to my brother N[orthcliffe] &, whether he has agreed with me or not, he has never resented anything I have said. The experience… of the other members of the Secretariat has been the same.[1239]

The Prime Minister soon came to find the services of Philip Kerr to be indispensable–he was very

---

1236 Philip Kerr, from 16 March 1930 11th Marquess of Lothian (1882-1940).

1237 George Adams (1874-1966), political scientist. As Principal Secretary, he was responsible for covering Treasury, Home Office, Local Government, Education, Food, Agriculture and Labour Affairs. From early 1917 he worked on the Irish Question and played a key role in arranging the Irish Convention.

1238 https://history.blog.gov.uk/2012/05/01/number-10-under-lloyd-george-1916-1922/. By K. O. Morgan. Retrieved 5 March 2019. Harmsworth replaced David Davies in June 1917, Astor left in July 1917.

1239 Cecil Harmsworth (1869-1948), Diary, 22 May 1918, University of Exeter Special Collections, Cecil Harmsworth Papers.

hard-working, uncomplaining, non-judgemental and, it has been said, "one of the few outstanding men in British public life who worked with Lloyd George and never quarrelled with him right up to the end."[1240] He worked at No. 10 until May 1921, specialising in foreign affairs, remaining a lifelong friend and confidante.

On 12 December, German Chancellor Bethmann-Hollweg read to the Reichstag the text of a peace proposal to be transmitted to the Allied Governments through the channel of the still-neutral United States:

> The most formidable war known to history has been ravaging for two and a half years a great part of the world. That catastrophe... threatens to bury under its ruins the moral and physical progress on which Europe prided itself at the dawn of the twentieth century. In that strife Germany and her allies... have given proof of their indestructible strength... The latest events have demonstrated that a continuation of the war cannot break their resisting power... It was for the defence of their existence and freedom of their national development that the four allied Powers were constrained to take up arms... Conscious of their military and economic strength and ready to carry on to the end, if they must, the struggle that is forced upon them, but animated at the same time by the desire to... bring the horrors of war to an end, the four allied Powers propose to enter even now into peace negotiations. They feel sure that the propositions which they would bring forward and which would aim to assure the existence, honour, and free development of their peoples, would be such as to serve as a basis for the restoration of a lasting peace.
>
> If notwithstanding this offer of peace and conciliation the struggle should continue, the four allied Powers are resolved to carry it on to a victorious end, while solemnly disclaiming any responsibility before mankind and history.[1241]

Coming on the back of Austro-Hungarian victories in Romania, and couched in such vague and overbearing terms, it was everywhere met with distrust and scepticism. Lloyd George made his position clear from the outset.[1242] Rising to give his first speech in the Commons as Prime Minister at 4.10 pm on 19 December, he stated: "I appear before the House of Commons today, with the most terrible responsibility that can fall upon the shoulders of any living man, as the chief adviser of the Crown, in the most gigantic War in which the country has ever been engaged–a war upon the event of which its destiny depends... and the issues which hang on to it are the gravest that have been attached to any conflict in which humanity has ever been involved..."

He proceeded to the crucial point, stating that the "responsibilities of the new Government have been suddenly accentuated by a declaration made by the German Chancellor", making it clear that only a peace that offered "complete restitution, full reparation, effectual guarantees" against repetition

---

1240 Butler, p65.

1241 See E. Caukin Brunauer, *The Peace Proposals of December, 1916–January, 1917*, *Journal of Modern History* 4, 4, Dec. 1932, pp544-571: Quote, p562-563.

1242 Views he reasserted and elaborated upon in his *War Memoirs*, Vol.I, p653-654.

would be entertained by Great Britain. He called for the mobilization of all the national resources, painting not a "gloomy" but a "stern" picture of the military situation, continuing:

> The House has realised that there has been a separation between the functions of the Prime Minister and the Leader of the House. That was because we came to the conclusion that it was more than any one man… could do to undertake both functions in the middle of a great war… Now there are three characteristics in the present Administration in which it may be said it has departed, perhaps, from precedent. First of all, there is the concentration of the Executive in a very few hands; the second is the choosing of men of administrative and business capacity rather than men of Parliamentary experience… for the headship of a great Department; and the third is a franker and fuller recognition of the partnership of Labour in the Government of this country… We realised that it is impossible to conduct war without getting the complete and unqualified support of Labour.

Regarding the special conditions that a state of war placed upon the normal checks and balances of parliamentary procedure, Lloyd George continued by re-stating a fundamental principle, and offering an opinion, that:

> The Government as a whole are accountable to Parliament. The control of Parliament as a whole must, and always must, be supreme because it represents the nation. There is not the slightest attempt here to derogate in any particular from the complete control of Parliament. I do not think the present methods of Parliamentary control are efficient, but that is not a change which has come about through the new Administration.

Moving on to the core issue of food production and distribution, he stated:

> We must call upon the people of this country to make real sacrifices, but it is essential… that the sacrifices should be equal. The over-consumption by the affluent must not be allowed to create a shortage for the less well-to-do…

The Prime Minister continued by touching on profiteering, an apparently inescapable extra curse on wartime populations:

> While the nation is making such enormous sacrifices… it is intolerable that any section should be permitted to make exceptional profits out of those sacrifices and by that means actually increase the burdens borne by others. A good deal has already been done by the late Administration to arrest unfair private profiteering out of the War. The Government have come to the conclusion that they cannot ask the nation for more sacrifices without even more drastic steps yet being taken. There are several ways of dealing with this problem. One is the annexation of all war profits; another is the cutting down of prices so as to make excessive profits impossible. The Munitions Act adopted both of those expedients…

Lastly, Lloyd George spoke about Ireland:

> I wish it were possible to remove the misunderstanding between Britain and Ireland which has for centuries been such a source of misery to the one and of embarrassment and weakness to the other… I should consider that a war measure of the first importance. I should consider it… something that would give strength to the Armies of the Allies. I am convinced now that it is a misunderstanding, partly racial and partly religious. It is to the interest of both to have this misunderstanding removed… I tried once. I did not succeed.[1243]

At this, Labour MP William Thorne called out "Try again!" As already detailed, two days later Lloyd George did try again, ordering the release of the Irish Frongoch internees.

Regarding the German peace proposal, the reply of the Allied Powers was given to the US Ambassador in Paris, William Sharp, on 30 December, rebutting assertions of Allied responsibility for causing the war, stating their devotion to peace and claiming the German proposal was in fact "a war manoeuvre". Significantly, it concluded no peace was possible until "legitimate reparation, guarantees and safeguards for the future" could be assured. On 2 January 1917, Lloyd George rebuffed President Wilson's subsequent request for the belligerents to state their war aims by demanding terms tantamount to German defeat.[1244] Lloyd George also wanted to make the destruction of the Ottoman Empire a major British war aim, and two days after taking office told Robertson that he wanted a major victory, preferably the capture of Jerusalem, to impress British public opinion.

At the Rome Conference of 5-7 January 1917, Lloyd George was discreetly quiet about plans to take Jerusalem, an objective which advanced British interests rather than bringing the war as a whole to a victorious conclusion. Keen to take pressure off the stalemated Western Front, on 6 January, he proposed that the Allies should give major assistance, up to 400 heavy guns, for another Italian offensive from the Isonzo. With such a weight of artillery, the Italians could break through the Austrian lines, push on to Trieste and Ljubljana, and possibly force beleaguered Austria-Hungary out of the war. The capturing of Austrian ports would also neutralise much of the German U-boat threat in the Mediterranean. The French Prime Minister, Aristide Briand, and his Minister of War, General Hubert Lyautey, who had not been consulted and who had staked everything on General Nivelle's upcoming offensive, were not keen on the idea. They agreed in principle but would only lend the guns until May.

General Luigi Cadorna[1245], the Italian Chief of Staff, was keen to accept Allied aid, but thought Lloyd George's offer insufficient. He wanted at least eight divisions to assist in the attack and rejected the offer of guns that would only have to be returned too soon. Lloyd George offered British guns on a longer basis, but Cadorna refused this as well. This infuriated Lloyd George, who would later write

---

1243 https://api.parliament.uk/historic-hansard/commons/1916/dec/19/prime-ministers-statement#S5CV0088P0_19161219_HOC_366. Retrieved 7 April 2019.

1244 See S. Kernek *The British Government's Reactions to President Wilson's 'Peace' Note of December 1916*, *Historical Journal*, 13, 4, Dec. 1970, pp721-766; especially p734, 761, 764.

1245 General Luigi Cadorna (1850-1928), Chief of Staff of the Italian Army, 27 July 1914–9 November 1917.

that Cadorna threw away "the most promising chance afforded to him to win a great triumph for his country."[1246] British generals, however, were pleased; General William Robertson had been disloyally undermining his government's position with the other Allies behind the scenes to prevent Lloyd George's scheme from gaining acceptance.

The second major topic was the Salonika front. The Italians, fearing a resurgent Serbia, were opposed to any major offensive here, and even proposed an evacuation of Monastir, their one gain in the region. The French government wanted Italian and British reinforcements to be sent, which their militaries were not keen to part with. General Maurice Sarrail[1247] had a more drastic proposal, asking "the British and French Governments to shut their eyes or turn their heads for a fortnight" while he moved against the Greek armies loyal to King Constantine I[1248]. Lloyd George, fearing the reaction of other neutrals to what would be a sudden attack on a neutral country, convinced Sarrail to back down. The Greeks would be convinced by diplomatic means to withdraw their forces south of Athens–far from the Allied lines north of Salonika–and Sarrail would have a major advocate in the West in Lloyd George. Sarrail himself was confirmed as 'Commander-in-Chief of the Allied Army of the Orient,' giving him command over all Allied forces in the area.

Returning from Rome, on 11 January, Lloyd George spoke at the Guildhall, London, primarily to help promote the Third 'Victory' War Loan, stating:

> The German Kaiser a few days ago sent a message to his people that the Allies had rejected his peace offer. He did so in order to drug those whom he can no longer dragoon… We were not offered terms; we were offered a trap baited with fair words. They tempted us once, but the lion has his eyes open now. We have rejected no terms that we have ever seen... We all want peace; but when we get it, it must be a real peace… Before we attempt to rebuild the temple of peace we must see now that the foundations are solid. They were built before upon the shifting sands of Prussian faith; henceforth, when the time for rebuilding comes, it must be on the rock of vindicated justice.
>
> I have just returned from a council of war of the four great allied countries upon whose shoulders most of the burden of this terrible war falls... It was one of the most business-like conferences that I ever attended. We faced the whole situation… and we separated more confident than ever. All felt that if victory were difficult, defeat was impossible…
>
> I passed through hundreds of miles of the beautiful lands of France and of Italy, and as I did so I asked myself this question, Why did the peasants leave by the million… in order to face the dreary and wild horrors of the battlefield?… These are great democratic countries… Of their own free will they embarked upon it, because they knew a fundamental issue had been raised which no country could have shirked without imperilling all that has been won in the centuries of the past and all that remains to be won in the ages of the future.[1249]

---

1246 Lloyd George, *War Memoirs*, Vol.I, p859.

1247 General Maurice Sarrail (1856-1929). Of limited competence, he was dismissed on 10 December 1917.

1248 Constantine I (1868-1923), King of Greece, 1913-1917 and 1920-1922.

1249 Lloyd George, *Great Crusade*, p88-91.

Beyond the high-flown rhetoric, Lloyd George left nothing to chance. He instructed the Ambassador to Italy, Sir Rennell Rodd[1250], to increase propaganda efforts in Italy to strengthen Italian public opinion in favour of putting their trust in their Allies and in the Coalition's war aims, emphasising Britain's commitment to a 'just' peace and shared Anglo-Italian liberal values. Rodd began this ambitious campaign in March, largely utilising native Italians in the interests of authenticity, though the work, by its nature, was something of a 'slow burn'.[1251]

Meanwhile, a meeting was arranged on 3 February in the Pavilion at Caernarfon to welcome the local MP who was now Prime Minister, 5,000 enthusiastic well-wishers hearing him declaim with picturesque eloquence: "Time is a hesitating and perplexed neutral... He has not yet decided on which side he is going to swing his terrible scythe... Time is the deadliest of all the neutral powers. Let us see that we enlist him among our Allies." With slow and impressive enunciation, he concluded:

> There are rare epochs in the history of the world when in a few raging years the character, the destiny, of the whole race is determined for unknown ages. This is one. The winter wheat is being sown. It is better, it is surer, it is more bountiful in its harvest than when it is sown in the soft spring time. There are many storms to pass through, there are many frosts to endure, before the land brings forth its green promise. But let us not be weary in well-doing, for in due season we shall reap if we faint not.[1252]

Within weeks of this triumphant speech, Lloyd George had to return home again, as he suffered another close personal loss, that of his uncle Richard Lloyd, who died aged 82 at Criccieth on 28 February. The Prime Minister attended the funeral at the public cemetery there on 3 March. Margaret, who was with Lloyd at the end, wrote, in a letter cancelling an engagement: "He has been more than a father, and Mr. Lloyd George owes everything to him." Richard Lloyd had indeed been a wise and inspiring counsellor, a man of great intellect and character, and Lloyd George always acknowledged his profound debt to him. His death marked the end of an era.

In Britian, the grinding, relentless viciousness of the seemingly endless war was naturally breeding ever-growing political opposition, social unrest and conscientious objection, and this potentially posed a threat to the very life of the new Prime Minister.. One shadowy, little-known episode shows the temper of the times. At 12 Pear Tree Road in Derby lived Alice Wheeldon, suffragist, anti-war campaigner, member of the Socialist Labour Party and the No-Conscription Fellowship. In 1916 her son, William, had his application for exemption from military service as a conscientious objector rejected by a tribunal, had served a prison term, and was in hiding. It was known that Alice and her daughter, Hettie, were sheltering other young men 'on the run' from conscription. On 27 December P.M.S.2[1253] spy 'Alex Gordon' introduced himself to Alice as one such, returning to the house two

---

1250 Sir J. Rennell Rodd (1858-1941), Ambassador to Italy, December 1908–September 1919.

1251 Marcuzzi, p174-175; Rodd, *Social And Diplomatic Memories (Third Series) 1902-1919*, 1925, London, Edward Arnold, p289-291, 307-311, 315.

1252 Quoted in Williamson, p30-31.

1253 Parliamentary Military Secretary Department, No.2 Section, connected with the Ministry of Munitions.

days later with Herbert Booth, 'Comrade Bert', another man who he said was a member of the anti-war movement, but was in fact his recruiter. In a classic entrapment, 'Gordon' persuaded Alice to ask her daughter, Winnie, who lived in Southampton, to post her some poison, the latter obtained from her husband, Alfred Mason, a qualified pharmacist who was a lecturer at Hartley University College, Southampton. 'Gordon' claimed it was to be used to poison guard dogs to aid an escape attempt at a detention camp for conscientious objectors near Liverpool [no such dogs existed]. The package addressed to Alice, containing two vials of curare and two of strychnine, was intercepted on 4 January 1917. Arrested on 30 January, the Wheeldons were charged under the Offences Against the Person Act (1861), Section 4, with 'conspiring to assassinate the prime minister [sic], David Lloyd George, together with the prominent Labour Party war supporter Arthur Henderson and other unspecified persons'.

Unusually, the anti-suffragist Attorney-General, F. E. Smith, himself led the prosecution[1254], the trial opening on 6 March at the Old Bailey before Mr Justice Low[1255]; crucially, Smith refused to call the spy involved as a witness or divulge his name or whereabouts, thus preventing his being cross-examined. In court, Booth claimed that, speaking about Lloyd George and Henderson, Alice remarked:

> "I hope the buggers will soon be dead." Booth claimed that Alice had declared that Lloyd George had been "the cause of millions of innocent lives being sacrificed, the bugger shall be killed to stop it. And as for that other bugger Henderson, he is a traitor to his people but Asquith is the bloody brains of the business. He has not gone as far as Lloyd George, he [Lloyd George] is neither fit for heaven nor bloody hell.[1256]

At this point, Booth stated he had asked Alice what was the best method to poison Lloyd George, and that she had told him of a plan the Suffragettes had formulated to kill him; "We had a plan before… to get a position in a hotel where he stayed and to drive a nail through his boot that had been dipped in the poison, but he went to France, the bugger."[1257]

This was most unlikely and was denied by Alice in her testimony.[1258]

The Wheeldons' case was not helped by the fact that their Persian defence lawyer, Dr Saiyid Riza, failed to highlight key evidence that supported their case, namely a reference to 'the bloke who owns it' in one of the intercepted communications, which clearly indicated that the poison was intended for a dog rather than a human being. Alice herself stated in court: "Being a businesswoman I made a bargain with him [Gordon] that if I could assist him in getting his friends from a concentration camp by getting rid of the dogs, he would, in his turn, see to the three boys, my son, Mason and a young

---

[1254] Smith gave his own account in his *Famous Trials Of History* 1926, London, Hutchinson; *The Plot To Murder Mr. Lloyd George*, p223-230. It has nothing material to add to an understanding of the matter.

[1255] Sir Frederick Low (1856-1917), former Liberal MP for Norwich. He died on 4 September the same year.

[1256] S. Rowbotham, *Friends Of Alice Wheeldon: The Anti-War Activist Accused Of Plotting To Kill Lloyd George*, 1986; 2nd Ed. 2015 London Pluto Press, p55.

[1257] Rippon, p70-71.

[1258] Rowbotham, p55.

man named [Alexander} MacDonald, whom I have kept, get away."[1259] The result of the farcical trial was a foregone conclusion. Found guilty by the jury after 30 minutes retirement, on 10 March, Alice was sentenced to ten years penal servitude, Alfred to seven years and Winnie to five years. Hettie was acquitted. In a curious footnote, Emmeline Pankhurst was allowed to make a statement defending the WSPU, telling the court: "We declare that there is no life more valuable to the nation than that of Mr Lloyd George. We would endanger our own lives rather than his should suffer."[1260]

Sent to Aylesbury Prison, Alice went on intermittent hunger strike, before being moved to Holloway, and released on licence on 31 December 1917 at the personal intervention of Lloyd George, who thought "it was very undesirable that she should die in prison."[1261] On being informed of this by the Governor, Dr Selina Fox, Alice was moved to remark: "It was very magnanimous of him… he has proven himself to be a man."[1262] However, her health was permanently weakened, and she died of influenza during the pandemic just over a year later on 21 February 1919, aged 53, protesting her innocence to the end. The case against the Wheeldons and Masons was at best extremely dubious, symptomatic of the fact that, during the war, the Intelligence Services had become fixated on political opposition at home, and the family's activism and beliefs marked them out. Agent 'Alex Gordon'–real name William Rickard–was an unbalanced and unreliable character: a convicted blackmailer, he had twice been declared criminally insane and was released from the high-security psychiatric Broadmoor Hospital only two years before being employed by P.M.S.2. The Section itself was shut down in June 1917 for its lack of results, questionable methods and use of agent provocateurs, its functions taken over by the War Office and Scotland Yard.[1263]

How much the alleged would-be victim, Lloyd George, knew of the behind-the-scenes machinations is unknown, but with his being newly installed as Prime Minister, and with the war raging in full spate, his personal interest and involvement were probably minimal, if not non-existent. Reports of the alleged plot had appeared in the papers on 1 February 1917, but Lloyd George seemed more concerned that the news would distract the public from a speech he had made in Caernarfon on 3 February on the maritime threat from German submarines, rather than the threat to himself. He told Herbert Lewis that people seemed to be "very much more interested in preparations for my death than in my speech, which was what I wanted them to read."[1264] Concerning his securing Alice's release, it has been suggested that he intervened because he did not want a Suffragette 'martyr' as an embarrassment to the Government[1265]: it is equally likely that as he was at that time working towards enacting votes for women the following year, he did not personally want the blood of an innocent woman on his hands, as he also secured the early release of Alfred and Winnie Mason on 26 January

---

1259 Quoted in Rippon, p85.
1260 Ibid., p118.
1261 Rippon, p139.
1262 Quoted in Rippon, p140.
1263 See N. Hiley, *Internal Security In Wartime: The Rise And Fall Of P.M.S.2, 1915-1917*, *Intelligence And National Security* 1, 3 1986 p395-415; N. Hiley and J. Putkowski, *A Postscript On P.M.S.2*, *Intelligence And National Security* 3, 2 1988 p326-331.
1264 Quoted in Grigg, *War Leader*, p40, from Herbert Lewis Diary, Entry for 6 February 1917, NLW.
1265 Rowbotham, p86.

1919.[1266] Nonetheless, the sentiments swirling around were real enough, and Alice Wheeldon is now rightly regarded as much another 'casualty of war' as anything else.

Getting into his stride as Prime Minister, Lloyd George soon became engaged in frequent attempts to reduce the power of the generals, including trying to subordinate British forces in France to the French General Robert Nivelle.[1267] He backed Nivelle, a seasoned artillery officer, because he felt he had 'proved himself to be a Man' by his successful counterattacks at Verdun as commander of the French Second Army, and because of his promises that he could break the German lines in 48 hours. Nivelle increasingly complained of Haig's dragging his feet rather than co-operating with their plans for the offensive.[1268]

The plan was to put British forces under Nivelle's direct command for the great 1917 offensive. The British would attack first, tying down the German reserves, before the French struck, scoring a decisive victory in two days. It was announced at a War Cabinet meeting on 24 February, to which neither Robertson nor Lord Derby, Lloyd George's successor as Secretary of State for War, had been invited. Ministers felt that the French generals and staff had shown themselves more skilful than the British in 1916, whilst politically Britain had to give wholehearted support to what would probably be the last major French effort of the war. The Nivelle proposal was then given to Robertson and Haig without warning on 26-27 February. The minutes from the War Cabinet meeting were not sent to the King until 28 February, so that he did not have a prior chance to object. Robertson in particular protested vehemently. Finally a compromise was reached whereby Haig would be under Nivelle's orders but would retain operational control of British forces and keep a right of appeal to London "if he saw good reason". After further argument the status quo, that Haig was an ally of the French but was expected to defer to their wishes, was largely restored in mid-March.[1269]

In the event the initial British attack at the Battle of Arras on 9-14 April 1917 was partly successful in attaining its objectives, but at the cost of 158,000 casualties to the Germans 125,000. There had been many delays and the Germans, suspecting an attack, had rationalised their lines 25 miles back to the strongly defended Hindenburg Line. The French attack on the Aisne River on 16-25 April gained some tactically important high ground at the cost of 187,000 casualties, but failed to achieve the promised decisive breakthrough, pushing thousands of demoralised men to desert and some 35,000 in 129 Infantry and 7 Artillery Regiments to mutiny between 17 April–30 June, many of the suffering, mostly peasant soldiers, feeling betrayed by their commanders, specifically refusing orders to attack and be used as cannon fodder.[1270] Nivelle was sacked and replaced by General Philippe Pétain[1271], and while Haig gained prestige, Lloyd George lost credibility, the affair further poisoning relations between himself and the 'Brasshats'.[1272]

---

1266 Rippon, p141.
1267 Robert Nivelle (1856-1924), Commander-in-Chief of the French Armies, 14 December 1916–30 April 1917.
1268 Woodward, *Robertson*, p88-90.
1269 Ibid., pp90-93; Grigg, *War Leader*, p35-44, 82-98.
1270 A. Clayton, *Paths Of Glory: The French Army 1914-18*, 2003, London, Cassell, p140-147.
1271 Philippe Pétain (1856-1951), the 'Lion of Verdun', Commander-in-Chief, 15 May 1917–19 November 1918, promoted Marshal of France.
1272 Taylor, *Politics In The First World War*, p80-81, 86.

On 1 February 1917, the Germans resumed unrestricted submarine warfare in a bid to achieve victory on the Western Approaches, the area of the Atlantic lying to the immediate west of Ireland and parts of Great Britain. Lloyd George had already created the Ministry of Shipping under Sir Joseph Maclay[1273], a Glasgow shipowner who was not, until after he left office, a member of either House of Parliament. The Junior Minister and Commons spokesman was the Italian-born Leo Chiozza Money[1274], Lloyd George's parliamentary private secretary (PPS) since May 1915, with whom Maclay did not get on, but on whose appointment Lloyd George insisted, feeling that their qualities would complement one another. In time, the two did reach a productive working relationship.

The Civil Service secretariat was headed by the youthful but highly able John Anderson[1275], and included Arthur Salter[1276] as director of ship requisitioning. A number of shipping magnates were persuaded, like Maclay himself, to work unpaid for the ministry–as had a number of industrialists for the Ministry of Munitions–, who were also able to obtain ideas privately from junior naval officers who were reluctant to argue with their superiors in meetings. The ministers heading the Board of Trade, for Munitions (Addison) and for Agriculture and Food (Lord Rhondda), were also expected to co-operate with Maclay.

In accordance with the pledge Lloyd George had given in his first speech to the Commons as Prime Minister, from February 1917 nearly 90% of Britain's merchant shipping tonnage was brought under state control–previously around 37% had been under Admiralty control, whilst remaining privately owned, similar measures being in force on the railways. Merchant shipping was concentrated, substantially on Chiozza Money's initiative, on the transatlantic route where it could more easily be protected, instead of being spread out all over the globe, this relying on imports coming first into North America. Maclay began the process of increasing ship construction, although hampered by shortages of steel and labour, and ships under construction in the United States were confiscated by the Americans when she entered the war. In May 1917 Eric Geddes, based at the Admiralty, was put in charge of shipbuilding, with the rank of vice-admiral, and on 17 July he became First Lord of the Admiralty. He shortly came to perform the same excellent job in this as he had done in France. Lloyd George later paid tribute to Geddes, saying he was "a man of exceptional force and capacity… one of the most remarkable men which the State called to its aid."[1277]

As one of his last acts before becoming Prime Minister, Lloyd George had raised the matter of convoys at the War Committee on 2 November 1916, only to be told by the admirals present, including Admiral Jellicoe[1278], that convoys "offered too big a target", and that merchant ship masters lacked the discipline to keep station in a convoy–a judgement of nautical snobbery that was quickly proved to be demonstrably untrue.[1279] In resuming unrestricted submarine warfare, the Germans had the objective

1273 Joseph Maclay (1857-1951), Minister of Shipping, 16 December 1916–31 March 1921.
1274 Leo Chiozza Money (1870-1944), PS to Ministry of Shipping, 22 December 1916–10 January 1919.
1275 John Anderson (1882-1958), later responsible for the development of the WW2 Anderson Shelter.
1276 Arthur Salter (1881-1975), later proponent of a 'United States of Europe'.
1277 Lloyd George, *War Memoirs*, Vol.I, p150.
1278 Admiral of the Fleet John Jellicoe (1859-1935), First Sea Lord, 30 November 1916–10 January 1918.
1279 Lloyd George, *War Memoirs*, Vol.I, p678.

of sinking 600,000 tons of Allied shipping per month. In response, in February the highly capable Maurice Hankey[1280], the secretary of the War Cabinet, wrote a memorandum for Lloyd George calling for the introduction of "scientifically organised convoys", almost certainly after being persuaded by Commander Reginald Henderson[1281] and the Shipping Ministry officials with whom he was in contact. After a breakfast meeting on 13 February with Lloyd George, Edward Carson, the First Lord of the Admiralty, and Admirals Jellicoe and Duff[1282] agreed to "conduct experiments". However, convoys were not in general use until August, by which time the rate of Allied shipping losses was already in decline, after peaking at 874,140 tons in April.

Lloyd George later claimed in his memoirs that the delay in introducing convoys was because the Admiralty mishandled an experimental convoy between Britain and Norway, and because Jellicoe obtained, behind Maclay's back, an unrepresentative sample of merchant skippers claiming that they lacked the skill to "keep station" in convoy. In fact, Hankey's diary shows that Lloyd George's interest in the matter was intermittent. He may well have been reluctant, especially at a time when his relations with the generals were so poor, for a showdown with Carson, a weak administrator who was as much the mouthpiece of the admirals as Derby was of the generals, but who had played a key role in the fall of Asquith and led a significant bloc of Tory and Irish Unionist MPs.

The new Commander of the Grand Fleet, Admiral Beatty[1283], whom Lloyd George visited at Invergordon on 15 April, was a supporter of convoys, as was the new US Naval Liaison, Canadian-born Rear Admiral Sims[1284], the USA having just entered the war. On 25 April the War Cabinet authorised Lloyd George to look into the anti-submarine campaign, and on 30 April he visited the Admiralty. Duff had already recommended to Jellicoe that the Admiralty adopt convoys after a recent successful convoy from Gibraltar.[1285] It is worth noting here that most of the organisations that Lloyd George created during the First World War were so successful that they were replicated at the outbreak of the Second. As Lord Beaverbrook wrote, "Lloyd George… faced a terrible task when full command of the nation came to him. He had special difficulties. There were no road signs on the journey he had to undertake."[1286] The latter's personal efforts to promote convoys were less consistent than he–and Churchill in *The World Crisis* and Beaverbrook in *Men and Power*–later claimed; the idea that he, after a hard struggle, sat in the First Lord's chair on his visit to the Admiralty on 30 April and imposed convoys on a hostile Board is a myth. However, in Grigg's view, the credit goes largely to men and institutions which he set in place, and with a freer hand, and making fewer mistakes, than in his dealings with the generals, he and his appointees took decisions which can reasonably be said to have saved the country. "It was a close-run thing… failure would have been catastrophic."[1287]

Lloyd George initially welcomed the abdication of Tsar Nicholas II of Russia, which took place on

---

1280 Maurice Hankey (1877-1963), Cabinet Secretary, December 1916–August 1938.

1281 Grigg, *War Leader*, p50-51. Commander, later Admiral, Reginald Henderson (1881-1939).

1282 Admiral Alexander Duff (1862-1933), Director, Anti-Submarine Division, December 1916–May 1917.

1283 Admiral David Beatty (1871-1936), Commander-in-Chief, Grand Fleet, November 1916–April 1919.

1284 Admiral William Sims (1858-1936), author of *The Victory At Sea*, 1920, New York, Doubleday, Page & Co.

1285 Grigg, *War Leader*, p52-53.

1286 Beaverbrook, *Decline And Fall*, p301.

1287 Grigg, *War Leader*, p45, 49, 52-53.

2 March, both in a private letter to his brother[1288] and in a telegram of 21 March to the new Russian Prime Minister, Prince Lvov[1289], not least as the war could now be portrayed as a clash between liberal governments and the autocratic Central Powers:

> It is with sentiments of the most profound satisfaction that the people of Great Britain and of the British Dominions across the seas, have learned that their great Ally Russia now stands with the nations which base their institutions upon responsible Government. Much as we appreciate the loyalty and steadfast co-operation which we have received from the late Emperor and the Armies of Russia during the last two and a half years, yet we believe that the Revolution whereby the Russian people have placed their destinies on the sure foundation of freedom, is the greatest service which they have yet made to the cause for which the Allied peoples have been fighting since August, 1914. It reveals the fundamental truth that this War is at bottom a struggle for popular Government as well as for liberty… Freedom is the only warranty of Peace, and I do not doubt that as a result of the establishment of a stable Constitutional Government within their borders the Russian people will be strengthened in their resolve to prosecute this War until the last stronghold of tyranny on the Continent of Europe is destroyed and the free peoples of all lands can unite to secure for themselves and their children the blessings of fraternity and of Peace.[1290]

King George V's biographer, Kenneth Rose, recorded that:

> The King was displeased by the tone of the message, which he found 'a little strong'. Stamfordham complained to Lloyd George that the word revolution had a disagreeable sound coming from a monarchical Government. But as usual the Prime Minister had the last word. He good humouredly replied that the present British monarchy was founded upon a revolution, which Stamfordham could not deny.[1291]

In fact, Lloyd George's telegram had been drafted with the assent of the Russian chargé d'affaires in London, Konstantin Nabokov.[1292] In his *War Memoirs* Lloyd George wrote: "A virtuous and well-meaning Sovereign became directly responsible for a regime drenched in corruption, indolence, debauchery, favouritism, jealousy, sycophancy, idolatry, incompetence and treachery–an accumulation of all those vices that make for utter misgovernment and inevitably end in anarchy."[1293]

Like many, he had been taken by surprise by the timing of the revolution. This was not entirely his fault. Britain had dispatched a delegation as part of an Allied Mission to Petrograd[1294] on 20 January,

---

1288 William George Papers, NLW, Letter 3222 (2), 16 March 1917: "Russia is triumphant. Worth the whole war & its terrible sacrifices".
1289 Prince Georgy Lvov (1861-1925), first post-imperial Prime Minister, 15 March–21 July 1917.
1290 Lloyd George, *War Memoirs*, Vol.I, p970-971. In his Memoirs Lloyd George added: "I stand by every word of that declaration to-day."
1291 Rose, p210. Stamfordham, Memorandum on talk with Prime Minister, 22 March 1917, Royal Archives.
1292 K.D. Nabokov, *The Ordeal Of A Diplomat*, 1921, London, Duckworth, p78-80.
1293 Lloyd George, *War Memoirs*, Vol.I, p954-955.
1294 On 1 September 1914, the name of the capital was changed from Saint Petersburg to Petrograd.

with the object of co-ordinating the following summer's offensives and finalising agreement on the supply of munitions to Russia. It was headed[1295] by Lord Milner, Minister without Portfolio, with John Baring[1296], as Minister Plenipotentiary to act as financial representative, General Sir Henry Wilson[1297] as senior Military Representative, and Walter Layton[1298], a young economist with the Ministry of Munitions, and naturally liaising with the highly experienced Ambassador to Russia, Sir George Buchanan[1299], and Robert Bruce Lockhart[1300], the young Consul-General in Moscow. Lockhart formed a high regard for Milner, for whom he sometimes acted as interpreter.[1301]

The delegation, 51-strong including French and Italians, did not leave Russia until 22 February, but incredibly seemed to pick up little real indication of the seething unrest, anger and despair in the country, despite visiting Moscow, Tsarskoe Selo, Petrograd and the Northern Front army group. They noted the hugely corrupt and inefficient bureaucracy, the lack of munitions, the low morale and high casualty rates in the Imperial Army, but not the underlying political fragility and explosiveness of Russian society. Milner's report stated that:

> There is a great deal of exaggeration in the talk about revolution, and especially about the alleged disloyalty of the army. That the army should be very dissatisfied with the way in which the War has been conducted is only natural. But there is a long distance separating dissatisfaction in the army and the nation, and even the loud public expression of it…, from a genuine revolutionary movement. And, assuming for a moment that a revolution were successful, I should regard with great apprehension its effect on the conduct of the War.[1302]

Milner advanced the generally held opinion by both Russians and Allies in Russia that there would be no revolution till after the war. That he spoke no Russian and never ventured to meet ordinary people in the streets, certainly did not help. The least that can be said is that the French and Italian delegations, the Germans, revolutionaries on the ground and the Bolshevik leader Lenin himself, exiled in Zurich, equally had no awareness of the desperately unstable situation.[1303]

Back in London, Lloyd George hoped–albeit with some concerns–that Russia's war effort would be invigorated like that of Revolutionary France in 1792 in its war against the Coalition. Not unnaturally, he felt somewhat let down by Milner's delegation's lack of perspicacity regarding the extreme seriousness of the situation. Much later, he wrote: "Having regard to the warnings which were blaring at them in every direction, it is incomprehensible that they should have been so deaf and

---

1295 Foreign Secretary Arthur Balfour had already refused the post.

1296 John Baring, Lord Revelstoke (1863-1929), senior partner of Barings Bank.

1297 Field Marshal Sir Henry H. Wilson (1864-1922), Chief of the Imperial General Staff, 19 February 1918–19 February 1922, Ulster Unionist MP for North Down, 21 February 1922 until his death, assassinated in London by IRA gunmen on 22 June 1922.

1298 Walter Layton (1884-1966), editor of *The Economist*, 1922-1938.

1299 Sir George Buchanan (1854-1924), Ambassador to the Russian Empire, 1910-1917.

1300 Robert Bruce Lockhart (1887-1970), Consul-General in Moscow, 1915-1917.

1301 R. H. Bruce Lockhart, *Memoirs Of A British Agent*, 1932, London, Putnam, p163, 207-208.

1302 Quoted in Lloyd George, *War Memoirs*, Vol.I, p942-943.

1303 See Gollin, *Milner*, pp401-406, 528-530: O'Brien, *Milner*, p274-277: Marcuzzi, p157-159.

blind."[1304] However, at the time, he was less critical.

Milner had also written:

> It might be good policy to sacrifice some addition of strength on the Western Front for the purpose of supplying Russia's urgent needs. For it is at least possible that an amount of material which would not make any vital difference to the result of the clash of enormous armaments on the Western Front might make the whole difference between success and failure on the Eastern Front.[1305]

Lloyd George seized on this as support for his frequently stated view that "if a share of the ammunition blazed away in France on senseless and sanguinary attacks, and of the transport material rendered necessary by these tremendous offensives, had been given to the Russians, Serbians and Roumanians [sic], it would have enabled them to roll back the foe and produce decisions."[1306]

In the general misreading of the dire, chaotic conditions in Russia lay one of the roots of the persistent myth, often repeated, that King George V strove to rescue his cousin from the perils of the Russian revolution, only to be thwarted in the attempt by his callous Prime Minister. However, correspondence between the King and his ministers in March and April 1917 tells a wholly different story, one that only explicitly came to light in 1983 through the diligent research of Kenneth Rose, and only ending when the entire, hapless Imperial family were executed in the basement of the Ipatiev House in Yekaterinburg in the early hours of 17 July 1918.[1307]

Lloyd George gave a cautious welcome to the suggestion of the Russian Foreign Minister Pavel Milyukov[1308], made on 19 March and relayed through Buchanan to the Foreign Office in London, that the deposed Tsar and his family be given sanctuary in Britain, although Lloyd George would naturally have preferred that they go to a neutral country like Denmark or Switzerland.[1309] This response provoked a more urgent message from Petrograd, Buchanan reporting that:

> Milyukov was 'most anxious to get the Emperor out of Russia as soon as possible, the extremists having excited opinion against His Majesty'. The ambassador concluded: 'I earnestly trust that, in spite of the obvious objections, I may be authorized without delay to offer His Majesty asylum in England and at the same time assure the Russian Government that he will remain there during the war.'[1310]

---

1304 Lloyd George, *War Memoirs*, Vol.I, p943.

1305 Quoted in Lloyd George, *War Memoirs*, Vol.I, p934.

1306 Lloyd George, *War Memoirs*, Vol.I, p934.

1307 Rose, p209-218. The chief 'populariser' of the original calumnious version of events was Louis, Earl Mountbatten of Burma (1900-1979). See R. Hough, *Mountbatten: Hero Of Our Time*, 1980, London, Weidenfeld & Nicolson, p40. He was a not unbiased source; as a boy he had visited the Imperial Court at St Petersburg, become intimate with the Imperial Family, and developed romantic feelings towards his maternal first cousin Grand Duchess Maria Nikolaevna (1899-1918), whom he had hoped to marry.

1308 Pavel Nikolayevich Miliukov (1859-1943), Foreign Minister, 2 March–2 May 1917.

1309 Foreign Office to Buchanan, 20 March 1917, FO 371/2998, PRO; Rose, p210.

1310 Buchanan to Foreign Office, 21 March 1917; Rose, p210.

Unbeknownst to Lloyd George and the Government, on 20 March King George V had sent a private and personal telegram to Nicholas, as Tsar and Emperor, stating that he would "always remain your true and devoted friend."[1311] On 22 March, Lloyd George invited the King's influential Private Secretary Lord Stamfordham[1312] to Downing Street to discuss matters, joined later by Bonar Law and Charles Hardinge[1313], Permanent Under-Secretary at the Foreign Office. Stamfordham minuted: "It was generally agreed that the proposal that we should receive the Emperor in this country (having come from the Russian Government which we are endeavouring with all our powers to support) could not be refused." The meeting concluded that Buchanan, in formally offering the Tsar asylum, should ask the Russian Government to provide sufficient funds for him to live in suitable dignity.[1314] The next day Buchanan put this to Milyukov, specifying that any announcement must make it clear that the offer had been made at the request of the Russians.[1315] However, Milyukov, despite having requested exactly this, fatally hesitated, neither rejecting nor accepting the British offer he had so urgently sought only two days before, fearing the anger of the increasingly vengeful mob and Soviet agitators if their 'prey' were to be suddenly spirited away out of their grasp. Indeed, while Milyukov delayed, those Russians wishing to revenge themselves on the Tsar increased in strength within the volatile flux of their society.

King George V also began to have second thoughts, as reflected in a letter from Stamfordham to Foreign Secretary Balfour on 30 March, eight days after the Downing Street meeting:

> The King has been thinking much about the Government's proposal that the Emperor Nicholas and his family should come to England. As you are doubtless aware, the King has a strong personal friendship for the Emperor and therefore would be glad to do anything to help him in this crisis. But His Majesty cannot help doubting not only on account of the dangers of the voyage, but on general grounds of expediency, whether it is advisable that the Imperial Family should take up their residence in this country. The King would be glad if you would consult the Prime Minister, as His Majesty understands that no definite decision has yet been come to on the subject by the Russian Government.[1316]

In other words, the King was prepared to do anything to help, except actually help. This put Lloyd George in a difficult position, and Balfour replied, on 2 April, that the Government did not think, "unless the position changes, that it is now possible to withdraw the invitation which has been sent, and they therefore trust that the King will consent to adhere to the original invitation, which was sent on the advice of His Majesty's Ministers".[1317] The King then instructed Stamfordham to write to

1311 Quoted in H. Rappaport, *The Race To Save The Romanovs*, 2018, London, Hutchinson, p58.
1312 Lieutenant Colonel Arthur Bigge, Baron Stamfordham from 1911, (1849-1931), Private Secretary to Queen Victoria, 1895-1901, and to King George V, 1910-1931.
1313 Charles Hardinge (1858-1944), Viceroy and Governor-General of India, 1910-1916, Permanent Under-Secretary at the Foreign Office, 1916-1920, Ambassador to France, 1920-1923.
1314 Stamfordham, Minute of talk with Prime Minister, 22 March 1917, Royal Archives; Rose, p211.
1315 Rappaport, p63.
1316 Stamfordham to Balfour, 30 March 1917; Nicolson, p301; Rose, p211.
1317 Balfour to Stamfordham, 2 April 1917; Nicolson, p301; Rose, p211.

Balfour, outlining his growing concerns surrounding the potential arrival of the Tsar in Britain. The letter, sent on 6 April, stated:

> Every day the King is becoming more concerned about the question of the Emperor and Empress of Russia coming to this country.
>
> His Majesty receives letters from people in all classes of life… saying how much the matter is being discussed, not only in clubs, but by working men, and that Labour Members in the House of Commons are expressing adverse opinions to the proposal.
>
> As you know, from the first the King has thought the presence of the Imperial Family (especially of the Empress) in this country would raise all sorts of difficulties, and I feel sure that you appreciate how awkward it will be for our Royal Family who are closely connected both with the Emperor and the Empress.
>
> You probably also are aware that the subject has become more or less public property, and that people are either assuming that it has been initiated by the King, or deprecating the very unfair position in which His Majesty will be placed if the arrangement is carried out.
>
> The King desires me to ask you whether after consulting the Prime Minister, Sir George Buchanan should not be communicated with, with a view to approaching the Russian Government to make some other plan for the future residence of their Imperial Majesties?[1318]

That same evening, Stamfordham was instructed by the King to write to Balfour again in more peremptory terms:

> He must beg you to represent to the Prime Minister that from all he hears and reads in the press, the residence in this country of the ex-Emperor and Empress would be strongly resented by the public, and would undoubtedly compromise the position of the King and Queen…
>
> Buchanan ought to be instructed to tell Milyukov that the opposition to the Emperor and Empress coming here is so strong that we must be allowed to withdraw from the consent previously given to the Russian government's proposal.[1319]

King George V was a constitutional monarch who was supposed to heed the advice of his ministers. Instead, his language showed him pressuring his ministers to withdraw a firm offer of asylum to the Tsar and his family in a most unconstitutional–and, it must be said, unseemly–manner. The King's close cousin and 'friend' was now an embarrassing 'ex-Emperor' to be shuffled off elsewhere in the cause of self-preservation. Balfour, under this sustained barrage, capitulated, sending a minute to Lloyd George that same night, advising:

> I think the King *is* placed in an awkward position.

[1318] Stamfordham to Balfour, 6 April 1917, Lloyd George Papers, Record Office, House of Lords F/3/2/19; Rose, p212.
[1319] Stamfordham to Balfour, 6 April 1917, Ibid., Letter No.2; Rose, p212-213.

> If the Czar is to come here we are bound publicly to state that *we* (the Government) have invited him–and to add (for our own protection) that we did so on the initiative of the Russian Government (who will not like it).
>
> I still think that we may have to suggest Spain or the south of France as a more suitable residence than England for the Czar.[1320]

Only on 8 April did the Cabinet learn of the King's telegram of 20 March, and then Lloyd George refused to divulge its contents, a most extraordinary situation![1321] On 10 April, Stamfordham went to Downing Street to confront the Prime Minister. Restating by now familiar arguments, he continued that, even if the Government accepted responsibility, the people would believe that this had been done to cover up the role of the King. Lloyd George "admitted the force of these arguments and promised to consult the French Government in the hope that the Tsar might be invited to make his home in France."[1322] Stamfordham then intervened again with Balfour, telling him that His Majesty expected that Buchanan would by now have been informed that the previous agreement to admit the Tsar could no longer be held as binding. Balfour duly sent a telegram on 13 April, which concluded by instructing Buchanan to "say nothing further to the Russian Government on the subject unless they themselves raise the question."[1323] Buchanan concurred, and the original offer of asylum became a dead letter. King George's "*volte-face* was complete."[1324] In June, Lloyd George noted privately to Hardinge that he was glad that the "idea of asylum was dropped as it would have been used by the Germans", which in all probability would have been true.[1325]

The secret of the King's self-preserving involvement in the negotiations was well kept: "Lloyd George honourably refused to justify his apparent abandonment of the Tsar by revealing the pressures which the King's private secretary had brought to bear on the Government."[1326] On 5 July 1932, Laurence Collier, a senior Foreign Office official, noted "I understand Mr Lloyd George was not responsible for the decision, but that it is not expedient to say who was."[1327] However, in 1934, three years after Stamfordham's death, when it became known that Lloyd George was writing his *War Memoirs*, the Government, according to custom, appointed the Cabinet Secretary, Hankey, to decide on the extent to which the former Prime Minister could be permitted to quote from official documents. Hankey recommended that the seven-page chapter dealing with the issue of the deposed Tsar should be suppressed entirely. Naturally, this irked Lloyd George considerably. Two months later, though, he quietly scrapped the original chapter and wrote a new one containing no reference to the King or Stamfordham.[1328] The key passage read: "An agitation had also started in this country,

---

1320 Balfour to Lloyd George, 6 April 1917, Ibid.; Rose, p213.
1321 Rappaport, p59.
1322 Stamfordham, Minute of talk with Prime Minister and Foreign Secretary, 10 April 1917, Royal Archives; Rose, p213.
1323 Quoted in Rappaport, p83.
1324 Rose, p214.
1325 Quoted in Rappaport, p109.
1326 Rose, p217.
1327 Quoted in Rappaport, p275.
1328 Sylvester, *Life*, 9 April 1934, p106-107, 26 June 1934, p110.

which indicated that there was a strong feeling in extensive working-class circles, hostile to the Czar [sic] coming to Great Britain. However, the invitation was not withdrawn. The ultimate issue in the matter was decided by the Russian Government, which continued to place obstacles in the way of the Czar's departure."[1329] This was a diplomatically slanted, sanitised version of events, but it did save the King's honour.[1330]

On 5 April 1917, Lloyd George's friend Lord Riddell called at No.10, and in his diary he left a picture of what the Prime Minister's family life was like at this time:

> L.G. [sic] invited me to go upstairs to dinner. It was served in the great dining-room. So far as the food, service, and appointments were concerned, it looked as if a small suburban household were picnicking in Downing Street–the same simple food, the same little domestic servant, the same mixture of tea and dinner. And yet with all that an air of simple dignity and distinction pervaded the room–no affectation, no pretension, nothing mean, nothing ignoble. Mrs. L.G. is a quiet, dignified woman and brave as a lion.
>
> L.G. spoke in high terms of Wilson's speech.
>
> ... L.G. says that David Davies, M.P., who went with Milner to Russia, sent home more useful and accurate information than any other member of the party. He foreshadowed the revolution, whereas Milner and the others were of opinion that nothing was likely to happen. The conversation turned on personal qualities. L.G. remarked, "I have one quality which I never get credit for. I am one of the most patient men in the world." The whole family agreed he was patient in big things, but strongly protested that he was often impatient in small ones. To which he laughingly assented.[1331]

Peace was increasingly in the air, though sadly not to be realised for some time. On 24 March, Emperor Karl I[1332] of Austria-Hungary signed a letter, handed to the brother of Empress Zita[1333], Prince Sixtus[1334], for transmission to the French President, Raymond Poincaré.[1335] Agreeing in principle to French conditions for talks, namely the restoration to France of Alsace-Lorraine, the restoration of the independence of Belgium, and independence for Serbia, he "secretly and unofficially" gave his "assurance" that he would "support in every way and by the use of all my personal influence" these initiatives. The letter, delivered on 31 March, met with a tepid reception, until it was shown to Lloyd George by the new French Prime Minister Alexandre Ribot[1336] at a secret meeting in Folkestone on

---

1329 Lloyd George, *War Memoirs*, Vol.I, p975.

1330 See Rappaport, p274-280, on the whole issue of the King's generally discreditable involvement and the official attempts to cover it up, including the redaction of Buchanan's and Lloyd George's memoirs.

1331 Riddell, *War Diary*, p248. Richard Lloyd George quoted and approved of this "thumbnail sketch" in his *Dame Margaret*, p153-154, as being "amazingly true to life".

1332 Karl I (1887-1922), last Emperor of Austria, last King of Hungary, 21 November 1916–11 November 1918, beatified by the Roman Catholic Church on 3 October 2004 for his efforts at peace making.

1333 Zita of Bourbon-Parma (1892-1989) declared a 'Servant of God' by the Roman Catholic Church on 10 December 2009 for similar reasons to her husband, and lifelong fidelity to her faith and family.

1334 Prince Sixtus of Bourbon-Parma (1886-1934), serving as a lieutenant in the Belgian Artillery.

1335 Raymond Poincaré (1860-1934), President 1913-1920, Prime Minister 1912-1913, 1922-1924, 1926-1929.

1336 Alexandre Ribot (1842-1923), Prime Minister 1892-1893, 1895, 1914, March-September 1917.

11 April. In Paris, on 18 April, Lloyd George had a meeting with Sixtus, declaring that "We had an old feeling of friendship towards Austria. We would willingly shake hands with her even today if she would leave Germany…"[1337] Lloyd George and Ribot then sounded out the Italian Foreign Minister, Sidney Sonnino[1338], in a railway carriage, at the French Alpine resort of Saint-Jeanne-de-Maurienne on 19 April, but the meeting was abortive, foundering on Sonnino's entrenched suspicions of Austria's motives.

In Paris the next day, while returning home, Lloyd George had another meeting with Sixtus, at which the full extent of Italy's claims against Austria were revealed; being the Trentino, Dalmatia and its coastal islands, and possibly Trieste. Lloyd George described this as a '*sine qua non*', not being able to reveal–due to the clauses of the secret Treaty of London of 1915–that these had already been pledged by Britain and France. He did, however, urge Sixtus to continue his efforts and to come and see him in London if there were any new developments, which Sixtus did, visiting Lloyd George in Downing Street on 22 and 23 May–bearing a second message from Karl–and 5 June. Meanwhile, the Germans, Austria's increasingly dominant allies, were in favour of stepping up the war, putting their faith in their new submarine tactics and the prospects of Russia pulling out of the war. Ribot was also increasingly hostile to the peace initiatives. Only Lloyd George continued, in June attempting to persuade both his Cabinet colleagues and the generals that that they should mount an offensive on the southern front whilst also grasping the Austrian olive branch, potentially knocking Austria out of the war and leaving Germany isolated. The generals, however, could not be persuaded, and by the end of June the initiative was anyway dead in the water.[1339]

Meanwhile, on 6 April 1917, the United States of America finally entered the war on the Allied side. On 12 April, Lloyd George gave his expansive, hopeful address to the American Club in London, on America's entry into the war:

> I rejoice as a democrat that the advent of the United States into this war gives the final stamp and seal to the character of the conflict as a struggle against military autocracy throughout the world…
>
> … The Kaiser promises that [Prussia] will be a democracy after the war. I think he is right… Prussia was not a State–Prussia was an army. It had great industries that had been highly developed; a great educational system; it had its universities, it had developed its science.
>
> All these were subordinate to the one great predominant purpose, the purpose of all–a conquering army which was to intimidate the world. The army was the spear-point of Prussia; the rest was merely the shaft…
>
> This is the menace, this is the apprehension from which Europe has suffered for over fifty years. It paralyzed the beneficent activity of all States, which ought to be devoted to

---

1337 G. de Manteyer, Ed., *Austria's Peace Offer, 1916-1917,* 1921 London Constable, p114.

1338 Sidney Sonnino (1847-1922), Prime Minister 1906, 1909-1910, Minister of Foreign Affairs, 5 November 1914–23 June 1919. Having a Welsh mother, he was the only Protestant leader in Italy, raised as an Anglican.

1339 See Lloyd George, *War Memoirs*, Vol.II, p1175-1204; G. Egedy, *Lloyd George and the Dual Monarchy, 1917-1918*, *Central European Papers*, 2, 2, 2014 p36-50; G. Brook-Shepherd, *The Last Empress: The Life And Times Of Zita Of Austria-Hungary, 1892-1989*, 1991 London HarperCollins, p62-78.

concentrating on the well-being of their peoples. They had to think about this menace, which was there constantly as a cloud ready to burst over the land…

It was hard at first for the people of America quite to appreciate that Germany had not interfered to the same extent with their freedom, if at all. But at last they endured the same experience as Europe had been subjected to. Americans were told that they were not to be allowed to cross and re-cross the Atlantic except at their peril. American ships were sunk without warning…

There are two great facts which clinch the argument that this is a great struggle for freedom. The first is the fact that America has come in... The second is the Russian revolution…

The Russian revolution is not merely the outcome of the struggle for freedom. It is a proof of the character of the struggle for liberty, and if the Russian people realize… that national discipline is essential to the security of national freedom–they will, indeed, become a free people.

… Why did Germany, deliberately, in the third year of the war, provoke America to this declaration and to this action–deliberately, resolutely?

… [T]he answer has been afforded by Marshal von Hindenburg[1340] himself, in the very remarkable interview which appeared in the press.

He depended clearly on one of two things. First, that the submarine campaign would have destroyed international shipping to such an extent that England would have been put out of business before America was ready.

According to his computation, America cannot be ready for twelve months. He does not know America. In the alternative, that when America is ready, at the end of twelve months, with her army, she will have no ships to transport that army to the field of battle…

The road to victory… the absolute assurance of victory is to be found in one word–ships… And with that quickness of apprehension which characterizes your nation, Mr. Chairman, I see that they fully realize that, and today I observe that they have already made arrangements to build one thousand 3,000-tonners for the Atlantic…

… I rejoice… in the knowledge that America is going to win the right to be at the conference table when the terms of peace are being discussed. That conference will settle the destiny of nations…

I can see peace coming now… not a peace which will be an endless preparation for strife and bloodshed; but a real peace. The world is an old world. It has never had peace… and Europe… has always lived under the menace of the sword.

When this war began two-thirds of Europe were under autocratic rule. It is the other way about now, and democracy means peace…

The democracies sought peace; strove for peace. If Prussia had been a democracy there would have been no war. Strange things have happened in this war. There are stranger things to come, and they are coming rapidly.

---

1340 Paul von Hindenburg (1847-1934), *Generalfeldmarschall*, Chief of the General Staff, 29 August 1916–3 July 1919, President of the Reich from 12 May 1925 to his death on 2 August 1934.

> There are times in history when this world spins so leisurely along its destined course that it seems for centuries to be at a standstill; but there are also times when it rushes along at a giddy pace, covering the track of centuries in a year.
>
> Those are the times we are living in now. Today we wage the most devastating war earth has ever seen; tomorrow… war may be abolished forever from the category of human crimes…[1341]

At least one other Liberal politician foresaw trouble regarding the treatment of Germany following an Allied victory. Norman Birkett[1342], at the Annual Meeting of the Birmingham Liberal Association on 21 May, stated in no uncertain terms:

> There are people in this country and other countries who still cherish the idea that Germany shall be crushed, peace dictated in Berlin… I am bound to say that the policy of crushing Germany… seems to me to be a fatal policy… It seems to me that if that policy is followed, then no sooner is this war over, no sooner is this danger removed, than all the nations prepare for the next war. And of all things that is the calamity which has got to be avoided…
>
> … It is just as well for us to confess that that particular policy is not conducive to liberty, but the reverse. But you say partition her, dismember her, change her Government. The answer is that the stability of Europe is not advanced by any of these things. They have been tried elsewhere and without much success. For look at the Balkan States, look at Italy, look nearer home, look at Ireland, and then ask yourself is it a judicial policy, is it a wise policy, having regard to the issues at stake?[1343]

These would sadly prove to be prophetic words, chiming with the very policies Lloyd George would himself subsequently unsuccessfully try to get adopted at the Paris Peace Conference.

Meanwhile, he set up the War Policy Committee, requested by Milner on 7 June, consisting of himself, Milner, Curzon and the former Boer leader, Lieutenant General Jan Smuts,[1344] with Maurice Hankey as secretary, to discuss strategy, which held 16 meetings over the next six weeks. Bonar Law was kept in close touch. At the first meeting on 11 June Lloyd George proposed helping the Italians to capture Trieste[1345], explicitly telling the committee on 21 June that:

> The Italian casualties have been comparatively slight, and the Allies have not up to the present used Italian man-power to the best advantage. Is it not now the turn of the Italians to take their share of heavy fighting?" If they did the British Army "instead of exhausting its limited resources, will have time to accumulate.[1346]

---

1341 https://firstworldwar.com/source/usawar_lloydgeorge.htm. Retrieved 6 March 2019.

1342 Norman Birkett (1883-1962), barrister, Liberal MP for Nottingham East 1923-1924, 1929-1931, alternate British judge during the Nuremberg Trials of 1945-1946..

1343 H. Montgomery Hyde, *Norman Birkett: The Life Of Lord Birkett Of Ulverston*, 1965, London, Hamish Hamilton, p81-82.

1344 Jan Smuts (1870-1950), Boer commando general, 1900-1902, Minister of Defence of South Africa, 1910-1919, Prime Minister 1919-1924, 1939-1948. He had briefly practised as a barrister in England in 1895.

1345 Woodward, *Robertson*, p136-138.

1346 Lloyd George, *War Memoirs*, Vol.II, p1286.

Haig believed that a Flanders Offensive had a good chance of clearing the Belgian coast, from which German submarines and destroyers were operating–a popular goal with politicians–, and that victory at Ypres "might quite possibly lead to (German) collapse". Robertson was less optimistic, but preferred Britain to keep her focus on defeating Germany on the Western Front and had told Haig that the politicians would not "dare" overrule both generals, if they gave the same advice. On 20 June, Haig promised he had no "intention of entering into a tremendous offensive involving heavy losses", whilst three days later, Robertson stated he wanted to avoid "disproportionate loss".

On 8 June, Lloyd George moved Arthur Lee from the War Office to become the Director General of Food Production under Rowland Prothero as the President of the Board of Agriculture and Fisheries. Having then left the army, he was permitted to retain the honorary rank of colonel. As with so many of Lloyd George's appointments at this time, Lee had great energy and drive, and he "did a great deal to prevent an acute food shortage."[1347] On 17 July he moved the highly capable and energetic Christopher Addison to be the Minister of Reconstruction, charged with overseeing the task of rebuilding 'the national life on a better and more durable foundation', once the war was over. Addison was strongly in favour of the Whitley Councils, approved by the Cabinet on 9 October 1917, to include representatives of both employers and employees in the government and industrial sectors, and remaining a major feature of public sector industrial relations to this day. By early 1918, the Ministry had 87 committees working on the various aspects of reconstruction, really becoming a "laboratory of new ideas and social experiment,"[1348] and, within a few months, a post-war priorities programme was in being.

In August 1917, Lee bequeathed his Buckinghamshire home, Chequers, and its 1,200-acre estate to the nation as the official country residence of the Prime Minister. Lloyd George wrote to Lee on 29 August, stating: "Your offer in regard to the Chequers Estate is most generous and beneficent ... The gift which you are now bequeathing in advance to the nation is in its very essence an indication of the practical thoughtfulness which is characteristic of you; and the public spirit which the scheme displays is worthy of that which its originator has shown in all my dealings with him."[1349] A deed of settlement formally transferring the property to the nation was executed on 24 November, the deed incorporated in the Chequers Estate Act which received royal assent on 20 December,[1350] Lloyd George becoming the first Prime Minister to use it, enthusiastically starting his first weekend there as 'tenant-in-office' on 8 January 1921.[1351]

Returning to 1917, at this juncture, Lloyd George gave another of the great, passionately eloquent speeches of his life. Speaking at St Andrew's Hall, Glasgow on 29 June, he declared:

---

1347 Fry, p16.
1348 Morgan, *Portrait Of A Progressive*, p71.
1349 Quoted in Fry, p57.
1350 The Act was the first piece of legislation to recognise the existence of a Prime Minister, even though the head of government had been referred to unofficially as "Prime Minister" since the 1720s.
1351 See Riddell, *Diaries*, 1986, p333.

... It is a satisfaction for Britain in these terrible times that no share of the responsibility for these events rests on her... The part taken by our country in this conflict, in its origin, and in its conduct, has been as honourable and chivalrous as any part ever taken in any country in any operation...

... Before she entered the war Britain made every effort to avoid it... I remember the earnest endeavours we made to persuade Germany and Austria not to precipitate Europe into this welter of blood. We begged them to summon a European conference to consider. Had that conference met arguments against provoking such a catastrophe were so overwhelming that there would never have been a war. Germany knew that, so she rejected the conference, although Austria was prepared to accept it...

... Germany expected to find a lamb and found a lion. So much for our responsibility for war... I want us to carry on this war with a pure, clear conscience to the end...

I am steeped every day... in the perplexities and difficulties and the anxieties of this grim business, but all the same I feel confident... No doubt startling events in Russia modified the military situation this year, temporarily to our disadvantage, but permanently for the better. What has happened recently on both the Western fronts shows what could have been accomplished this year if all the Allied Forces had been ready to bring an all-round pressure to bear...

Revolution is a fever brought about by the constant and reckless disregard of the laws of health in the government of a country. Whilst it is on the strength of a country is diverted to the internal conflict... and it is naturally not so effective for external use during the period...

That is the case in Russia: although this distraction has had the effect of postponing complete victory... it has made surer than ever the quality of the victory we will gain... Russia is free, and the representatives of Russia at the Peace Congress will be representatives of a free people...

I ventured in August, 1915, to launch into the realms of prophecy... I referred to the great Russian defeat by the German forces... "... The enemy in their victorious march know not what they are doing. Let them beware, for they are unshackling Russia. With their immense artillery they are shattering the rusty bars, the fetters, from the strength of the people of Russia. You can hear them... preparing for the conflict with a new spirit. They are hammering a sword that will destroy them, and freeing a great nation which will wield it with a more potent stroke and mightier sweep than it ever yet commanded."

... That was the beginning of the end for autocracy... Russia is now unfettered; and when the distractions are passed away... Russia will be more formidable than ever, because in Russia in future the whole of her power will be cast on the side of liberty and democracy, and not of autocracy.

Meanwhile, France, Italy, and ourselves have to bear the greatest share of the burden, and I should like to say to those who hailed the Russian revolution with delight, as well as condemning and doing their best to thwart the military efforts of their own country, that but for these military efforts the Russian revolution would have had no chance to fructify. What would have happened if we had not been ready...? ... Germany would have concentrated one desperate effort to overwhelm free democracy in France whilst Russia was engaged in the troubles of her revolution, and whilst the new democracy was arising in the East the old democracy in the West, the great old democracy of France, would have been strangled. How long do you think the new democracy, the new democracy of the East, would have survived it? Not long. And you would have had one great outstanding military autocracy in Europe governing from the East to the West, and only these little islands standing between the world and disaster.

I would counsel those who criticise the measures we have taken to mobilise the strength of this country–strong measures, ruthless measures, if you will; interfering measures, if you will, but measures which will accomplish their purpose–I would counsel those who criticise, therefore, the action we have taken in mobilising the strength of this country to dwell upon the catastrophe… that would have befallen the free democracies throughout the world if we had not done so. It was Britain, the strength of Britain flung into the breach, that has once more saved Europe and human liberties… Now Russia is gaining strength every day. It has got a capable, strong Government of able, patriotic men guiding its destinies… and her armies will fight henceforth with that power which is inspired by freedom.

And America… is beginning to send her valiant sons to the battlefields of Europe to fight around the standards of liberty. That is why I say that although victory may have been postponed by the events of the last few months in Russia, victory is more complete, victory on higher lines than ever we could have hoped.

It is assured under two conditions. The first is, the submarine attacks must be defeated, or kept within reasonable bounds. They may, and probably will, drive us to further restrictions in some trades, perhaps to hardships, but all depends on the nation, for after carefully reckoning the chances, the probabilities, the Government have come to the conclusion, on the best advice that we can see, that submarines can neither starve us at home nor drive our armies out of the field abroad.

… Our losses in May and June were heavy, but… [w]e are beginning to get them. The arrangements that have been made for frustrating them and for destroying them are improving, and I have no hesitation in saying that if we all do our part the German submarine will be almost as great a failure as the German Zeppelin. You might be driven to eat less wheat and more barley and oats… If we do not waste we shall not starve. We have succeeded in increasing the production of the food of this country even during the present year… We are engaged in a great shipbuilding programme… for fighting as well as for carrying, but here the Clyde comes in… This is the Battle of the Clyde. If employers and workmen pull together and pull with all their might, between them they will pull us through.

What is the next condition? The moral of the nation must be kept up. That is essential… Our Army is great, and the Army now is the people. There is hardly a household which has not contributed to the Army… take care that the spirit of the people behind them is as good as that of the Army. If not, it affects the Army…

… There are people asking when are you going to bring this war to an end, how are you going to bring it to an end, and when you have brought it to an end what end do you want for it?… In my judgment this war will come to an end when the Allied Powers have reached the aims which they set out to attain when they accepted the challenge thrown down by Germany to civilisation.

These aims were set out recently by President Wilson... As soon as these objectives are reached, and guaranteed, this war ought to come to an end. But if it comes to an end a single hour before it will be the greatest disaster that has ever befallen mankind. I hear there are people going about the country saying, "Germany is prepared to give you peace now. An honourable peace, and a satisfactory peace." ... No doubt you can have peace... Germany will give us peace now, at a price. Germany wants peace... they say, "Yield a little territory here and a little land there, and just a few privileges in the other direction, and we will clear out."

Well, you can have peace at that price, but do you know what it would be? The old policy of buying out the Goth, who eventually destroyed the Roman Empire and threw Europe into the ages of barbarous cruelties... If they had bravely and wisely faced their responsibilities... as Britain did in 1914... Rome would have been grander and nobler than ever, its rule would have been more beneficent, and the world would have been spared centuries of cruelties and chaos. You can have peace today, but it would be on a basis that history has demonstrated to be fatal to the lives of any great Commonwealth that purchased tranquillity upon it.

I am told that if you are prepared to make peace now Germany, for instance, would restore the independence of Belgium... No German statesman has ever said they would restore the independence of Belgium. The German Chancellor came very near it, but the Junkers forthwith fell upon him... and he has never repeated the offence. He said, "We will restore Belgium to its people, but it must form part of the economic system of Germany, of the military and naval defence of Germany. We must have some control over its ports." ... That is not independence; that is vassalage.

Then there comes the doctrine of the status quo, no annexation, no indemnities. No German speeches are explicit on that, but what does indemnity mean?... Indemnity is an essential part of the mechanism of civilisation in every land and clime. Otherwise what guarantee have you against a repetition...? ... We are fighting for the essential principles of civilisation, and unless we insist upon it we shall not have vindicated what is the basis of right in every land.

The same thing applies to Serbia. But they say "That is not what you are after. You are after our colonies, and Mesopotamia, and perhaps Palestine." ... If we engaged in the gigantic enterprise it was not for German colonies... "But," they say, "... What is going to happen to Mesopotamia?" Well... Mesopotamia is not Turkish, never has been Turkish. The Turk is as much an alien in Mesopotamia as the German is, and everyone knows how he ruled it...

What will happen to Mesopotamia must be left to the Peace Congress when it meets... It will never be restored to the blasting tyranny of the Turk. At best he was the trustee of this far-famed land on behalf of civilisation... He has been false to his trust, and the trusteeship must be given over to more competent and more equitable hands, chosen by the Congress which will settle the affairs of the world. That same observation applies to Armenia, a land soaked with the blood of innocents massacred by the people who were their guardians, and who were bound to protect them[1352]... When you come to settle who shall be the future trustees of these uncivilised lands you must take into account the sentiments of the people themselves... The wishes, the desires, and the interests of the people of these countries themselves must be the dominant factor in settling their future government. That is the principle upon which we are proceeding.

Is there any trace of any desire on the part of Germany, any indication of a desire on the part of Germany, to settle upon these essential terms?... the Austrian Premier emphatically repudiated the principle that nations must have their destinies controlled according to their desires. Where is the common ground for peace there? Unless both principles are accepted not merely will there be no peace, but if you had a peace there would be no guarantee of its continuance, and it is important that we should never have this happen again. What will have to be guaranteed first of all by the conditions of peace that they shall be framed upon so equitable a basis that nations will not wish to disturb them? They must be guaranteed by the destruction of the Prussian military power, that the confidence of the German people shall be in the equity of their cause and not in the might of their arms. May I say that a better guarantee than either would have been the democratisation of the German Government. One of the outstanding features of the war has been the reluctance with which democratic countries entered it, and the historian will conclude... that if all the belligerent nations had been ruled by Governments directly responsible to their peoples there would have been no war, and if the German Government's constitution becomes as democratic as the French, Italian, American, Russian, or British Governments' constitutions are, that in itself would constitute the best guarantee for peace in Europe and the world that we can hope to secure.

No one wishes to dictate to the German people the form of government under which they choose to live. That is a matter entirely for themselves, but it is right we should say we could enter into negotiations with a free Government in Germany with a different attitude of mind, a different temper, a different spirit, with less suspicion, with more confidence than we could with a Government whom we knew to be dominated by the aggressive and arrogant spirit of Prussian militarism. And the Allied Governments would, in my judgment, be acting wisely if they drew that distinction in their general attitude in a discussion of the terms of peace...

... In pursuing this conflict we must think not merely of the present but of the future of the world. We are settling questions which will affect the lives of people not merely in this generation, but for countless generations to come...

This war involves issues upon which will depend the lives of our children and our children's children. Sometimes in the course of human events challenges are hurled from the unknown amongst the sons and daughters of men. Upon the answer which is given to these challenges, and upon the heroism with which the answer is sustained, depends the question whether the world would be better or whether the world would be worse for ages to come...

Now we are faced with the greatest and grimmest struggle of all–liberty, equality, fraternity, not amongst men but amongst nations; great, yea small; powerful, yea weak; exalted, yea

[1352] The Armenian Genocide, 1915-1917, the systematic destruction of the Armenian people and identity under the Ottomans, involving the deaths of between 800,000–1.5 million people.

> humblest; Germany, yea Belgium; Austria, yea Serbia–equality, fraternity, amongst peoples as well as amongst men. That is the challenge which has been thrown to us.
>
> Europe is again drenched with the blood of its bravest and best, but do not forget these are the great successions of hallowed causes. They are the stations of the cross on the road to the emancipation of mankind… Every birth is an agony, and the new world is born out of the agony of the old world. My appeal to the people of this country, and, if my appeal can reach, beyond it is this–that we should continue to fight for the great goal of international right and international justice, so that never again shall brute force sit on the throne of justice, nor barbaric strength wield the sceptre of right.[1353]

By this stage, deep into the war, Glasgow was in considerable industrial discontent and political ferment, and there were large demonstrations against Lloyd George's visit to receive the Freedom of the City, requiring him to be escorted by a heavy police and military presence.[1354] Nevertheless, the *Daily Telegraph* approvingly reported the next day "Mr. Lloyd George has broken a long silence with one of those resounding calls to the spirit, the sense, and the patriotic instinct of the nation of which he has the secret… the Prime Minister speaks for us all in making it clear that the war will be carried on until the sure foundations of liberty and reparation are laid for an enduring peace."

During the war, anti-German sentiment amongst the people of Britain had risen from derision at its start to an almost hysterical hatred of all things Teutonic or perceived to be connected with Germany. King George V's reluctance to sever all ties with Kaiser Wilhelm II and his extended family did his public image harm. To him, such pre-war links "were part of history and should be left undisturbed", but to the public, whipped up as so often by a venal, right-wing press, "they seemed to indicate the survival of a royal trade union that cut across national loyalties."[1355] It reached to the upper echelons of the political establishment, including Asquith. Charles Masterman, summoned to see the King on 27 January 1915, remarked to Frances Stevenson two days before: "I wonder what my little German friend has got to say to me!"[1356]

Hatred and suspicion reached a peak from 25 May 1917, when Gotha G.IV heavy bombers belonging to *Kagohl 3* of the *Luftstreitkräfte* (Imperial German Air Service) began bombing England as part of *Operation Türkenkreuz*, thus becoming a household name. Thwarted from reaching London by cloud, most of the 23 bombers unloaded their bombs on Folkestone instead, killing 95 people. King George V was a member of the German ducal House of Saxe-Coburg and Gotha, and resentment began to grow against the Royal Family. When H. G. Wells had written to *The Times* on 21 April of Britain's need to rid itself of "the ancient trappings of throne and sceptre", and referring to "an alien and uninspiring Court", George had famously retorted to a visitor at Buckingham Palace: "I may be

---

1353 *When Will The War End, Mr. Lloyd George's Speech At Glasgow 29 June 1917*, 1917, London, Alabaster, Passmore & Sons, Ltd. See https://catalog.hathitrust.org/Record/000440177. Retrieved 25 February 2019.

1354 MacAskill, p134-137.

1355 Rose, p173.

1356 Stevenson, *Diary*, p25. This remark is *still* routinely and *erroneously* attributed to Lloyd George himself, for instance by Ridley, p225, who uses Stevenson as a source yet makes no mention of Masterman.

uninspiring, but I'm damned if I'm alien."[1357]

The King's private secretary, Stamfordham, was inspired to call the dynasty 'the House of Windsor' on 13 June, while he was working in Windsor Castle, the very day of another air raid on London, the first in daylight, in which 14 bombers killed 162 people and wounded 432, among the dead being 18 children in Upper North Street Primary School in Poplar, hit by a 110-pound bomb. £125,000 [£11.08m in 2025] worth of damage was caused.[1358] Of the 92 British planes sent up to intercept the raiders, not one got close enough to inflict any damage on them. On 17 July, King George V issued "A Proclamation Declaring that the Name of Windsor is to be Borne by His Royal House and Family and Relinquishing the Use of all German Titles and Dignities".[1359] Thus, after three years of war, did the British ruling family seek to disassociate themselves from their heritage and lineage for the sake of power and popularity, attempting to shrug-off centuries of Hanover, Saxony, Saxe-Coburg and Gotha and other German titled blood connections, in an unseemly attempt to divert the discontent of millions of ordinary, suffering citizens by adopting a quintessentially English-sounding name. Reality was covered up to satisfy xenophobia. Kaiser Wilhelm II, George's cousin, recognised the politic move for what it was. Upon hearing that his cousin had changed the name of the British royal house to Windsor, and in reference to Shakespeare's *The Merry Wives of Windsor*, Wilhelm, in a rare flash of grim humour, remarked that he planned to see "The Merry Wives of Saxe-Coburg-Gotha".[1360]

The German bomber raids had another effect as well. RFC and RNAS[1361] aircraft continued to be able to mount little effective resistance: a further raid on London on 7 July by 22 planes had killed another 57 people and wounded 193 more, for the loss of only one Gotha. One bomber squadron, "BG3, alone dropped more than 186,000 lb [84,368 kg] of bombs on British soil in 22 raids."[1362] Fighters were hastily recalled from France to help defend the capital, but it was only with the introduction of faster climbing fighters, like the Sopwith Camel and SE5a, that the Gotha's began to encounter any real opposition. The *Daily Mail* thundered that "since the Dutch burned Chatham [sic] 250 years ago, making mock of the miserable system of passive defence which the feeble English government of that age had organised with Stewart [sic] slovenliness, there has not been a more discreditable event in our military history than Saturday's raid."[1363] Felixstowe and Harwich were bombed on 22 July and Southend and Shoeburyness on 12 August, with the loss of one Gotha, four others crashing on landing back at base.

Lloyd George knew he must act. In June, he had co-opted Jan Smuts to the War Cabinet, having introduced him on 20 March as "one of the most brilliant generals in this war."[1364] Smuts quickly came

---

1357 Nicolson, p308.

1358 This air raid was the deadliest of the war, the Germans losing no planes. In 1938, Air Commodore Lionel Charlton highlighted the raid as "the beginning of a new epoch in the history of warfare."

1359 https://www.thegazette.co.uk/London/issue/30186/data.pdf. Retrieved 3 March 2019. Kaiser Wilhelm had long relinquished his honorary titles of British Field Marshal and Admiral of the Fleet to the British Embassy in Berlin, on 5 August 1914; C. Ponting, *Thirteen Days*, p315; De Courcy, p185.

1360 M. Carter, *George, Nicholas and Wilhelm: Three Royal Cousins and the Road to World War I*, 2010, London, Random House, pxxiii.

1361 Royal Flying Corps and Royal Naval Air Service.

1362 K. Munson, *Aircraft of World War I*, 1967, London, Ian Allan, p57.[*Gotha G.II to G.V*].

1363 *Daily Mail*, 9 July 1917, p5.

1364 Quoted in Smuts, p181.

to hold Lloyd George in high regard too, stating; "Lloyd George is more than fascinating. He has genius. His mind is brilliant, energetic, resourceful, and courageous without limit… History will show him the biggest Englishman (*sic*) of them all."[1365] Now, on 11 July, Lloyd George appointed Smuts to head the Prime Minister's Committee on Air Organisation and Home Defence Against Air Raids. Smuts agreed at once. Ably supported by Lieutenant General David Henderson[1366], the Director General of Military Aeronautics, he circulated a first report on 19 July, and after a month, on 17 August, he submitted his second report to the War Cabinet, recommending:

> We must create the new directing organization–the new Ministry and Air Staff which could properly handle this new instrument of offence, and equip it with the best brains at our disposal for the purpose. The task of planning the new Air Service organization [amalgamating the RFC and RNAS] and thinking out and preparing for schemes of aerial operations next summer must tax our Air experts to the utmost.

The report met with a mixed response. The RFC and RNAS did not want to lose the connection with their respective services. Lloyd George began to have second thoughts, and, his spirits low with the news from France of the faltering Passchendaele Offensive, went on holiday in early September. The press, not knowing of the Smuts report but hearing rumours of dissension in government and among senior officers, again began pressing for action, not least when the Germans mounted further attacks on London and the east coast over six nights between 24 September–1 October, 'the week of the harvest moon,' when the Gothas were joined by six gigantic Zeppelin-Staaken R.VI 'Riesen' (*Giant*) multi-engined bombers of *Rfa501*, causing fewer casualties than before–47 deaths and 226 injuries–but considerable psychological trauma.[1367]

A fortnight later, the War Cabinet received a paper showing that German aircraft production was increasing alarmingly, and on 15 October, during continued questions in Parliament, Bonar Law, sensing serious disquiet, hinted at the formation of a separate service. It was confirmed in an official announcement the following day, and to Lloyd George's considerable relief, in November the Air Force (Constitution) Act passed through Parliament with little opposition, receiving royal assent on 29 November. Nevertheless, most senior army and navy commanders thought it a grave mistake, including Major General Hugh Trenchard[1368], who believed that it would dilute the air support required by the ground forces in France. Trenchard at this time also opposed the concept of an independent strategic bombing force, and who came to believe that it was Henderson who deserved the accolade 'Father of the Royal Air Force', not himself. The Air Ministry was duly formed on 2 January 1918, with the unlikely choice of Lord Rothermere being appointed as first–and short-lived–minister, largely because he was Lord Northcliffe's younger brother. When the Royal Air Force formally came into

1365 Ibid., p187.
1366 Lieutenant General David Henderson (1862-1921), Director General, 22 February 1916–18 October 1917.
1367 Overy, p36.
1368 Major-General Hugh Trenchard (1873-1956).

being on 1 April, wags said the initials "RAF" stood for "Royal April Foolers".[1369]

To back-track to the summer of 1917, at 3.10 am on 7 June, at Messines Ridge, for the first time in an attack, the detonation of nineteen huge mines was used by gunners as the signal for the opening of a British barrage. Within a few seconds, more than 2,000 guns opened fire; the noise of the barrage–not the mines, as often stated–was heard by Lloyd George at Walton Heath, 140 miles away.[1370] Soon, the Flanders Offensive was reluctantly sanctioned by the War Policy Committee on 18 July and the War Cabinet two days later, on condition it did not degenerate into a lengthy battle of attrition like the Somme. The War Cabinet promised to monitor progress and casualties and, if necessary call a halt, although in fact they did little to monitor progress until September. Frustrated at his inability to get his way, Lloyd George talked of resigning and taking his case to the public.[1371]

The Battle of Passchendaele began on 31 July[1372], but soon became bogged down in unseasonably wet weather, which turned much of the battlefield into a hellish morass in which men and horses often drowned, whilst the mud and rain severely reduced the accuracy and effectiveness of artillery, and grounded observation flights. Lloyd George tried to enlist support from the King for diverting efforts against Austria-Hungary, telling Stamfordham on 14 August that the King and Prime Minister were "joint trustees of the nation" who had to avoid waste of manpower. A new Italian offensive began on 18 August, but Robertson advised that it was "false strategy" to call off Passchendaele to send reinforcements to Italy, and despite being summoned to George Riddell's home in Sussex, agreed only reluctantly. The Anglo-French leadership agreed in early September to send 100 heavy guns to Italy, 50 of them French, rather than the 300 which Lloyd George wanted–Lloyd George talked of ordering a halt to Passchendaele, but in Hankey's words "funked it" on 4 September.[1373] Had he not done so his government might have fallen, for as soon as the guns reached Italy, Cadorna called off his offensive on 21 September.

At a meeting at Boulogne on 25 September, Lloyd George broached with Prime Minister Paul Painlevé[1374] the setting up of an Allied Supreme War Council and making Foch 'generalissimo'. Bonar Law had written to Lloyd George that ministers must soon decide whether or not the offensive was to continue. On 26 September, Lloyd George and Robertson met Haig in France to discuss the recent peace 'feelers' emanating from German Foreign Secretary Richard von Kühlmann[1375]–which were ultimately publicly repudiated by Chancellor Georg Michaelis[1376]–and the progress of the offensive.

---

[1369] A. Mallinson, *Fight To The Finish: The First World War–Month By Month*, 2018, London, Bantam Press, p276-277.

[1370] https://simonjoneshistorian.com/2017/04/19/the-big-bang-heard-in-downing-street/. Retrieved 15 May 2024.

[1371] Woodward, *Robertson*, p139-142.

[1372] Hedd Wyn (Ellis Humphrey Evans, 1887-1917), Welsh-language poet from Trawsfynydd in North Wales, was killed at 11 am on this day, fighting with 15th Battalion Royal Welch Fusiliers at Pilckem Ridge. He was posthumously awarded the bard's chair for his poem *Yr Arwr* ('The Hero') at the National Eisteddfod on 6 September at Birkenhead Park, in the presence of Lloyd George, his empty chair draped in black. That year's event is referred to as *'Eisteddfod y Gadair Ddu'* ('Eisteddfod of the Black Chair'). The Archdruid summed up the general feeling, saying "the festival in tears and the poet in his grave". Lloyd George, on stage, wept too.

[1373] Hankey diary, 4 September 1917; Quoted in S.W. Roskill, *Hankey: Man Of Secrets - Volume I, 1877-1918*, 1970, London, William Collins, p433.

[1374] Paul Painlevé (1863-1933), Prime Minister, 12 September–13 November 1917.

[1375] Richard von Kühlmann (1873-1948), Secretary of State for Foreign Affairs, 6 August 1917 - 9 July 1918. See D. R. Woodward, *David Lloyd George, A Negotiated Peace…*, p75-93.

[1376] Georg Michaelis (1857-1936), Chancellor, 14 July–1 November 1917.

Haig preferred to continue, encouraged by General Herbert Plumer's recent successful attacks in dry weather at Menin Road on 20-25 September and at Polygon Wood on 26 September–3 October, stating that the Germans "were very worn out and had some very poor material in the fighting line". In October, the wet weather returned for the final attack towards Passchendaele. At the final meeting of the War Policy Committee on 11 October 1917, Lloyd George authorised the offensive to continue, but warning of failure in three weeks' time. In his diary for 21 October, Hankey claimed that Lloyd George had deliberately allowed Passchendaele to continue in order to discredit Haig and Robertson and make it easier for him to forbid similar offensives the following year.

In the ever-shifting fortunes of war, from 24 October–19 November, the Italians suffered a disastrous defeat at the Battle of Caporetto, their front line breaking, and being routed along the line of the Isonzo, retreating 150 km back to the Piave River. The Austro-Hungarians were reinforced by six German divisions, and the battle was one of the first to demonstrate the effectiveness of the use of stormtroopers and infiltration tactics partly developed by General Oskar von Hutier, with poison gas and flamethrowers also being employed by the Germans. It was one of the worst defeats in Italian military history, with casualties of 308,000 (13,000 dead, 30,000 wounded and 265,000 captured, 3,152 artillery pieces lost), plus a further 300,000 desertions, compared to combined Austro-Hungarian and German losses of 70,000. The British sent five and the French sent six divisions as reinforcements, but by then the situation had been saved by the exhausted Central Powers troops outstripping their supply lines, allowing the Italians to regroup and counter-attack during the so-called *battaglia d'arresto* on the Piave from 13–26 November.

Lloyd George said he "wanted to take advantage of Caporetto to gain 'control of the War'".[1377] In response to this, the Rapallo Conference of 5-7 November, and Peschiera Conference of 8 November, saw the Allied political and military leaders agree upon the formation of a Supreme War Council intended to co-ordinate military action across each of the Allied armies. The Allies rapidly agreed upon the establishment of the council, which was to be based at Versailles. Its initial members were to be Lieutenant General Henry Wilson for Britain, General Maxime Weygand for France, General Luigi Cadorna for Italy, and Major General Tasker Bliss for the USA. On 2 November, Lloyd George, presumably recognizing in him a fellow maverick, had said to Wilson "The whole future of the war rests on your shoulders, you must get us out of the awful rut we are in. I don't like your politics, but I do like and admire you as a man and a soldier."[1378]

On 28 October, Cadorna, the Italian Chief of Staff, had posted War Bulletin No. 887 in which he unfairly placed all responsibility for the collapse of the front on his men, followed on 3 November by a letter to new Premier Vittorio Orlando[1379] stating that the situation was "critical", that his forces might prove "unequal" to the crisis and hinting that the nation might be forced to sue for peace. Lloyd George, Foch, Wilson and Robertson were consequently of the view that the 'defeatist' Cadorna must

---

1377 Woodward, *Robertson*, p191.

1378 C. E. Callwell, *Field Marshal Sir Henry Wilson: His Life and Diaries*, 1927 London Cassell, Vol.II, p20.

1379 Vittorio Orlando (1860-1952), Liberal Prime Minister, 30 October 1917 - 23 June 1919. As President of the Chamber of Deputies, 15 July 1944–25 June 1946, he was still in office at the time of Lloyd George's death!

be replaced; King Vittorio Emanuele III and Orlando concurred, Cadorna being dismissed on 9 November, replaced by the much more effective General Armando Diaz.

En route home, Lloyd George gave a controversial speech at Paris on 12 November at a luncheon hosted by Painlevé in the tapestry-hung banqueting hall of the War Ministry in the rue Saint-Dominique, in which he criticised the high casualties of recent Allied "victories", a word which he used with some sarcasm. Many senators and deputies were present, as was Churchill. It was a carefully honed speech, that he had worked on almost until the last moment, with a fighting spirit designed to appeal directly to the British public at home. It was also one of heartfelt honesty. Lloyd George stated:

> I placed before the distinguished assembly of French politicians and publicists a candid survey of the military position as it appeared to me. I pointed out that we had failed up to that date to make the best of the advantages we possessed by sea and land, that the fault had not been with the armies: it had been entirely due to the absence of real unity in the war direction of the Allied countries. From there I proceeded:-
>
> "... Conferences have been annually held to concert united action for the campaign of the coming year. Great Generals came from many lands to Paris with carefully and skilfully prepared plans for their own fronts. In the absence of a genuine Inter-Allied Council of men responsible as much for one part of the battlefield as for another... there had to be an appearance of a strategic whole, so they all sat at the same table and metaphorically... sewed these plans together... and it was solemnly proclaimed... that the unity of the Allies was complete.
>
> That unity, in so far as strategy went, was pure make-believe... It was a collection of completely independent schemes pieced together. *Stitching is not strategy*. So it came to pass that when these plans were worked out in the terrible realities of war, the stitches came out and disintegration was complete.
>
> I know the answer that is given to an appeal for unity of control. It is that Germany and Austria are acting on interior lines, whereas we are on external lines. That is no answer. That fact simply affords an additional argument for unification of effort in order to overcome the natural advantages possessed by the foe..."
>
> I then summarised the successes which Germany had achieved owing entirely to the fact that we had not realised the importance of treating the whole front as one and indivisible. As to the Italian disaster, I said it was no use minimising its extent. If we did, then we would never take adequate steps to repair it...
>
> I told them that I believed we had at last learnt the lesson of the essential unity of all the Allied fronts. If I was right in my conjecture, the new Supreme Council would be given real power and the efforts of the Allies would be co-ordinated and victory would await valour...
>
> I said that national and professional traditions, prestige and susceptibilities had hitherto all conspired to render nugatory our best resolutions, but now we had set up this Council our business was to see that "the unity it represents is a fact and not a fraud." I apologised for having spoken with perhaps brutal frankness at the risk of much misconception here and elsewhere, and risk perhaps of giving temporary encouragement to the foe.

> We shall win, but I want to win as soon as possible. I want to win with as little sacrifice as possible. I want as many as possible of that splendid young manhood which has helped to win victory to live through to enjoy its fruits.
>
> Unity–not sham unity, but real unity–is the only sure pathway to victory. The magnitude of the sacrifices made by the people of all the Allied countries ought to impel us to suppress all minor appeals in order to attain the common purpose of all this sacrifice. All personal, all sectional, considerations should be relentlessly suppressed…[1380]

When Lloyd George sat down, Painlevé thanked him as the man who, "by his energy, eloquence and ever-fruitful imagination supported, developed and untiringly stimulated the splendid effort of Great Britain and the Dominions."[1381] The next day the *Daily Telegraph* reported on the "fearless, outspoken, useful, and stimulating address" delivered by Lloyd George. For once the use of the superlative–"one of the most remarkable speeches the nations at war have yet heard is not hyperbole, as the Prime Minister is remarkably critical of the governance of the war to date in front of his Allies whilst explaining why at this juncture the new war council has been set up, especially as he had been part of this governance overseeing "disasters and blunders." Harold Spender called it "perhaps the frankest utterance of the war."[1382]

Questioned in the Commons on his return on 14 November on the details of the arrangements made at Rapallo, Lloyd George read out the actual terms of the agreement between the Governments for the creation of a Supreme War Council:

> 1. With a view to the better co-ordination of military action on the Western Front, a Supreme War Council is created, composed of the Prime Minister and a Member of the Government of each of the Great Powers whose Armies are fighting on that front. The extension of the scope of the Council to other fronts is reserved for discussion with the other Great Powers.
>
> 2. The Supreme War Council has for its mission to watch over the general conduct of the War. It prepares recommendations for the decision of the Governments, and keeps itself informed of their execution, and reports thereon to the respective Governments.
>
> 3. The General Staffs and Military Commands of the Armies of each Power charged with the conduct of military operations remain responsible to their respective Governments.
>
> 4. The general War plans drawn up by the competent military authorities are submitted to the Supreme War Council, which, under the high authority of the Governments, ensures their concordance, and submits, if need be, any necessary changes…

---

1380 Lloyd George, *War Memoirs*, Vol.II, p1442-1444. The original speech is contained in an undated typescript with Lloyd George's amendments, Lloyd George Papers, F/234.

1381 *The Times*, 13 November 1917. See also Grigg, *War Leader*, p287-289.

1382 Spender, *Prime Minister*, p273.

> 8. The Supreme War Council meets normally at Versailles, where the permanent Military Representatives and their Staffs are established... The meetings… will take place at least once a month.
>
> From the foregoing it will be clear that the Council will have no executive power, and that the final decisions in matters of strategy and as to the distribution and movements of the various Armies in the field will rest with the several Governments of the Allies… The object of the Allies has been to set up a central body charged with the duty of continuously surveying the field of operations as a whole and… of co-ordinating the plans prepared by the different General Staffs, and, if necessary, of making proposals of their own for the better conduct of the War.[1383]

This led to an angry Commons debate on 19 November, which fortunately Lloyd George survived. One not prepared to put aside "all personal, all sectional, considerations" was Asquith, and he challenged Lloyd George hostilely "Whether it is proposed that the Council is, if so advised by its Staff, to have power to interfere with or override the opinion on matters of strategy of the General Staff at home, and of the Commanders-in-Chief in the field." In his withering response, after elucidating the practical arrangements that had been made, Lloyd George moved on to the controversy caused by the value judgements he had made in his Paris speech:

> He [Asquith] has challenged some things I have said in Paris. Let me say at once about that speech that I considered it carefully… and I did it for a deliberate purpose. I have seen resolutions for unity and for co-ordination… You might as well throw them straight away into the waste-paper basket. Lord Kitchener tried it on the 28th of January, 1915. I have seen other schemes by Monsieur Briand and my right hon. Friend. Somehow or other they all came to nought, because naturally you got the disinclination of independent bodies to merge their individualities in a sort of common organisation. It is inevitable, and I was afraid that this would end in the same sort of way.
>
> We went to Rapallo with a document most carefully prepared, and… it was submitted to the Cabinet before I left. The document which was passed was hardly different–of course we had to discuss things with our Allies–but in substance it was a document prepared here… But I was afraid… [that again nothing would happen]… I made up my mind to take risks, and I took them to arouse public sentiment, not here merely, but in France, in Italy, and in America–to get public sentiment behind, to see that this document became an Act.
>
> It is not easy to rouse public opinion… I do know something of political strategy, and to get public opinion interested in a proposal, and to convince the public of the desirability of it is an essential part of political strategy… I set out to deliver a disagreeable speech, that would force everybody to talk about this scheme. They have talked about it… and the result is America is in, Italy is in, France is in, and Britain is in, and public opinion is in…

[1383]https://api.parliament.uk/historic-hansard/commons/1917/nov/14/statement-by-prime-minister#S5CV0099P0_19171114_HOC_279. Retrieved 1 May 2019.

... [I]t was absolutely necessary. Otherwise you would not have got them to think about it... They would not have discussed the Rapallo agreement... I wanted this thing to be a reality... All this talk about "Easterners" and "Westerners" is balderdash. The field is north, south, east and west, and our business is to bring pressure upon the enemy from every point of the compass... That... is why we want a Central Council which will examine the whole field of operations... We need every brain; we need all the experience... We want victory as soon as we can get it, but I do not want the whole burden to fall upon Britain; and I therefore want an Inter-Allied Council that will so order the whole field of battle that the whole resources of the Allies shall be thrown into the conflict...

My right hon. Friend has challenged my history. Well, that will be decided one day. I am not afraid of it. Serbia! If the troops that we sent out had been there six weeks earlier, we would not have had the Balkan tragedy... Really, when I see in certain quarters, "Hands off the Army!" it makes me feel as if I were crossing the Channel in a torpedo-boat destroyer on a choppy sea. I will lay down two propositions, and I defy any man to challenge them. The first is this: No soldiers in any war have had their strategical dispositions less interfered with by politicians... The whole campaign of the year has been the result of the advice of soldiers. Never in the whole history of war in this country have soldiers got more consistent and more substantial backing from politicians than they have had this year... I do not mean "backing" in speeches. I mean backing in guns, backing in ammunition, backing in transport, shipping, railways, supplies, and men...

I have only twice during this War acted against the advice of soldiers. The first occasion was with the gun programme. I laid down a programme which was in advance of the advice of soldiers and against it. They thought that I was manufacturing too many and was extravagant... I took a different view, and there is not a soldier to-day who will not say that I was right... The second case... was in the appointment of a civilian to re-organise the railways behind the lines... (Sir E. Geddes)... There is not a soldier now who will not say that he is grateful that I pressed my advice, in spite of the attacks in the Press that I was "interfering with soldiers." ... Apart from the great and matchless valour of our troops... what are the two most conspicuous features in the great attacks in Flanders? The first is the overwhelming mass of artillery and ammunition. The second is the fact that the whole of the supplies are running right into the firing line by the arrangements made by [Geddes]...

... [T]here is a vast sphere in war which is partly political and partly military. Supplies, transport, shipping, distribution of manpower, diplomacy–surely a vital part of your war considerations–the morale of the people–all these things are political even more than they are military, and to sort of divide people into politicians and soldiers in war is unscientific... It shows a lack of knowledge of what war really means. What you want is the co-operation of both... We have got to go on, and that is one reason why I am looking forward to co-operation not merely between civilians and soldiers, but between Allies and Allies.

... I have striven to get not merely co-operation between Allies, but something more–friendship, goodwill, comradeship... That is the secret of our success... If we act together, I have no fear of what will happen. I saw anxieties on the horizon, and I never concealed them,

> because it is better to tell the people what is going on… I support every scheme that brings unity, every scheme that will help unity. It is the only road to victory, real victory, lasting victory–a victory that will bring peace, and that will bring healing to a world bleeding and grief-laden.[1384]

In reply to Robertson's 19 November memo, 'Future Military Policy', which rightly warned that the Germans would use the opportunity of Russia's departure from the war to attack in 1918, before the American Expeditionary Force was present in strength, Lloyd George wrongly wrote that the Germans would not attack and would fail if they did. On 23 November he told Hankey that he "had decided to risk his whole political reputation, if necessary, in order to stop these bloody attacks of the Somme-Flanders type."[1385]

On 29 November 1917, former Foreign Secretary Lord Lansdowne published the 'Lansdowne Letter' in *The Daily Telegraph–The Times* having refused to print it–calling for a negotiated peace with Germany, an idea that he had first put in a nine-page memorandum dated 6 November and discussed with some colleagues, including Foreign Secretary Arthur Balfour and Permanent Under-Secretary at the Foreign Office, Lord Hardinge. Unknown to the public at the time, he had already circulated a previous memorandum dated 13 November 1916 at a secret session of the Cabinet in the dying days of Asquith's administration in which he was the Minister without Portfolio, arguing that the war would destroy civilisation and that therefore peace should be negotiated on the basis of the *status quo ante bellum*. Headed 'Coordination of the Allies' War Aims', and opening with the claim that "those who look forward to the prolongation of the war… [differ] only in the degree from that of the criminals who provoked it", now Lansdowne's published letter continued: "We are not going to lose this war, but its prolongation will spell ruin for the civilised world, and an infinite addition to the load of human suffering which already weighs upon it… We do not desire the annihilation of Germany as a great power… We do not seek to impose upon her people any form of government other than that of their own choice… We have no desire to deny Germany her place among the great commercial communities of the world."[1386]

Most of the British press were critical of Lansdowne's proposals; he became a pariah, while military leaders dismissed his arguments. Many ordinary readers wrote to him in support: "I have been snowed under with letters… The prevailing note is: you have had the courage to say what we have been

---

1384 https://api.parliament.uk/historic-hansard/commons/1917/nov/19/prime-ministers-statement#S5CV0099P0_19171119_HOC_264. Retrieved 1 May 2019.

1385 Woodward, *Robertson*, p173-174, 178; Roskill, *Hankey*, Volume I, p463.

1386 *Daily Telegraph*, 29 November 1917, p5-6. See M. V. B. Cash, *Lord Lansdowne's peace letter and the controversy it caused*, (1999). Master's Theses. 627.
https://scholarship.richmond.edu/masters-theses/627. Retrieved 2 April 2020. The letter is reproduced as Appendix A, p120-129. See also D. Newton, *The Lansdowne "Peace Letter" of 1917 and the Prospect of Peace by Negotiation with Germany*, *Australian Journal of Politics & History* 48, 1 December 2002 p16-39. Peace was in the air - Pope Benedict XV had issued his seven-point peace plan on 1 August to the 'Rulers of the Belligerent Peoples', who generally ignored it, each side affecting to believe that it favoured the enemy, the British Government making no formal reply to the Pope's proposals - see Lloyd George, *War Memoirs*, Vol.II, p1215-1222. The Stockholm Conference, the third and final anti-war socialist conference, had also just been held from 5-12 September. Lloyd George vetoed Arthur Henderson's attendance, leading to his resignation from the Cabinet on 11 August; See H. Meynell, *The Stockholm Conference Of 1917*, *International Review of Social History* 5, 2 1960 p202-225, especially p214-216. Lenin's 'Decree on Peace' was passed by the Second All-Russian Congress of Soviets of Workers' and Soldiers' Deputies on 8 November 1917.

thinking for so long'", he wrote in December to his daughter Evie Devonshire. The criticism of him was misplaced, as some experts had predicted the war could last until 1920. The letter and the momentum it acquired alarmed Lloyd George. On the morning of the letter's publication, Lloyd George was in Paris for the Inter-Allied Conference at Versailles; he told Lord Islington that Lansdowne's letter nearly broke up the conference. The British government immediately issued a wholly inaccurate statement about Lansdowne's intervention: "Lord Lansdowne, in his letter, spoke only for himself. Before writing it, he did not consult, nor indeed, has he been in communication with any member of the government, His Majesty's Ministers reading it with as much surprise as did everybody else."[1387]

On 3 December Lloyd George told Riddell: "The letter was ill-advised and inopportune… Lord Lansdowne advocates making a treaty with a nation whom we are fighting because they have broken a treaty. He advocates that the treaty should be enforced by a League of Nations consisting of the nations who are now engaged in attempting to enforce the treaty already in existence. The letter is really a pacifist letter… A step of that sort (Lansdowne's) should not be sanctioned or countenanced without the approval of the War Cabinet. It is a serious matter…" He did, however, feel that *The Times'* personal attack on Lansdowne was "in bad taste", carried out "too brutally."[1388]

Lloyd George gave an address to Benchers at Gray's Inn in London on 14 December in which he publicly refuted Lansdowne's proposal, rather scathingly declaring there was "no halfway house between victory and defeat" and caricaturing it as "a farce in the setting of a tragedy".[1389] On hearing of this speech, new German Chancellor Georg von Hertling in turn said talks with Lloyd George would be hopeless and that his behaviour reminded him of 'slander in the style of Homeric heroes'.[1390] Lansdowne's reputation never recovered, as he loyally kept silence on others' involvement, but two years after his death in 1927, Colonel House admitted that the letter had been the inspiration for President Wilson's 'Fourteen Points'.[1391] On 28 December, and despite his rejection of Lansdowne's 'initiative', Lloyd George remarked to C. P. Scott that:

> 'I warn you that I am in a very pacifist temper.' I listened last night, at a dinner given to Philip Gibbs[1392] on his return from the front, to the most impressive and moving description from him of what the war in the West really means that I have heard. Even an audience of hardened politicians and journalists were strongly affected. The thing is horrible and beyond human nature to bear and 'I feel I can't go on with this bloody business: I would rather resign.'[1393]

The long, gruelling war of attrition was increasingly biting on the Home Front too, especially since Germany's resumption of unrestricted submarine warfare on 1 February 1917 to try to starve Britain

---

1387 *The Times*, *Repudiation by Government*, 1 December 1917, p9.
1388 Riddell, *Diaries*, 1986, p208.
1389 Lloyd George, *Great Crusade*, p233, 234.
1390 Afflerbach, p337. Count Georg von Hertling (1843-1919), Catholic Centre Party Chancellor, 1 November 1917–30 September 1918.
1391 https://www.spectator.co.uk/article/the-great-lost-peace. Retrieved 11 February 2022.
1392 Philip Gibbs (1877-1962), journalist who served as one of five official British reporters during the War.
1393 Scott, p324.

into submission. Coal rationing had already been introduced in October 1916, and on 10 December that year a food controller, Lord Devonport[1394], had been appointed by Lloyd George as part of the newly created Ministry of Food Control: to meet this new threat, voluntary rationing was introduced in February. Fortunately, the wheat and potato harvests were exceptionally good in 1917, aided by the hard work of the Women's Land Army (WLA). Bread was subsidised from September that year; prompted by local authorities taking matters into their own hands, compulsory rationing was introduced in stages between December 1917 and February 1918 as Britain's supply of wheat decreased to just six weeks' consumption. To help the process, ration books were introduced on 15 July 1918 for sugar, butter, margarine, meat of all kinds, cheese and lard. Tea was also restricted and soon jam and marmalade were rationed too.

Lloyd George subsequently wrote:

> So far as the vast bulk of the population was concerned, this rationing system, troublesome though in some respects it was to them, ensured a regular and sufficient food supply; and it made it possible for those in charge to calculate with some precision how best they could make the stocks of available food-stuffs go round equitably… The steady improvement in our national health figures during and after the War, as compared with pre-War returns, shows that compulsory temperance in eating was in general more beneficial than harmful in its effects. Although there was a degree of scarcity, we were never faced with famine or actual privation. Credit is due to our people for the loyal manner in which they submitted themselves to these strange and unwelcome restrictions. Without general goodwill it would have been impossible to make the regulations effective…[1395]

A manpower committee was set up on 6 December 1917, consisting of the Prime Minister, Curzon, Carson, Barnes and Smuts with Hankey as secretary, and with Auckland Geddes[1396], Director General of National Service, in charge of Army recruitment, in regular attendance. The first meeting was held on 10 December, and it met twice the next day and again on 15 December. Lloyd George questioned Generals Nevil Macready (Adjutant-General) and George Macdonogh (Chief of Military Intelligence), who advised that the Allied superiority of numbers on the Western Front would not survive the transfer of German reinforcements from the East, now that Russia was leaving the war. Deeply concerned about the publicity attracted by the recent Lansdowne letter's mention of casualties, he suggested removing Haig and Robertson from office at this time, but this was met by a threat of resignation from Lord Derby. At this stage Lloyd George opposed extending conscription to Ireland, Carson advising that extending conscription to Ulster alone would be impractical.

Hankey's report reflected Lloyd George's intentions: it gave top priority to shipbuilding and

---

1394 Replaced by the more effective Lord Rhondda on 19 June 1917.

1395 Lloyd George, *War Memoirs*, Vol.II, p795. Some rationing continued into 1920.

1396 Auckland Geddes (1879-1954), younger brother of Eric. Director General of National Service, 17 August 1917–19 December 1919, succeeding Neville Chamberlain, Director General from 19 December 1916 who resigned on 8 August 1917 feeling he lacked support from Lloyd George, ramping up their existing antipathy.

merchant shipping–partly to transport US troops to Europe–and placed army manpower below both weapons production and civilian industry. The size of the Army in Britain was to be reduced from eight divisions to four, freeing about 40,000 men for service in France. In the Commons on 20 December, Lloyd George also argued that the collapse of Russia and defeat of Italy required further "combing-out" of men from industry, in breach of pledges given to the trade unions in 1916. Auckland Geddes was given increased powers to direct labour, the Military Service Act becoming law, over the opposition of the Amalgamated Society of Engineers, on 6 February 1918.

On 5 January 1918, Lloyd George spoke to a receptive conference of the Trades Union Congress at Caxton Hall, Westminster. His speech, the most significant wartime statement of British war objectives, represented an earnest attempt on his part to moderate those aims, to give them a more liberal orientation. He told delegates:

> When the Government invite organized labour in this country to assist them to maintain the might of their armies in the field, its representatives are entitled to ask that any misgivings and doubts which any of them may have about the purpose to which this precious strength is to be applied should be definitely cleared, and what is true of organized labour is equally true of all citizens in this country…
>
> When men by the million are being called upon to suffer and die, and vast populations are being subjected to the sufferings and privations of war on a scale unprecedented in the history of the world, they are entitled to know for what cause or causes they are making the sacrifice. It is only the clearest, greatest and justest of causes that can justify the continuance even for one day of this unspeakable agony of the lands, and we ought to be able to state clearly and definitely, not only the principles for which we are fighting, but also their definite and concrete application to the war map of the world.
>
> We have arrived at the most critical hour in this terrible conflict, and before any government takes the fateful decision as to the conditions under which it ought either to terminate or continue the struggle, it ought to be satisfied that the conscience of the nation is behind these conditions, for nothing else can sustain the effort which is necessary to achieve a righteous end to this war. I have, therefore… taken special pains to ascertain the view and the attitude of representative men of all sections of thought and opinion in the country… [and]… of the great dominions overseas.
>
> I am glad to be able to say… that… there is national agreement as to the character and purpose of our war aims and peace conditions, and… I can venture to claim that I am speaking, not merely the mind of the Government, but of the nation and of the empire as a whole.
>
> … We are not fighting a war of aggression against the German people… The destruction or disruption of Germany or the German people has never been a war aim with us… In defence of the violated public law of Europe, and in vindication of the most solemn treaty obligation on which the public system of Europe rested, and on which Germany had ruthlessly trampled in her invasion of Belgium, we had to join in the struggle or stand aside and see Europe go under and brute force triumph over public right and international justice. It was only the realization of that dreadful alternative that forced the British people into the war… Germany has occupied a

great position in the world. It is not our wish or intention to question or destroy that position for the future, but rather to turn her aside from hopes and schemes of military domination, and to see her devote all her strength to the great beneficent tasks of the world. Nor are we fighting to destroy Austria-Hungary or to deprive Turkey of its capital, or of the rich and renowned lands of Asia Minor and Thrace…

Nor did we enter this war merely to alter or destroy the imperial constitution of Germany, much as we consider that military, autocratic constitution a dangerous anachronism in the Twentieth Century. Our point of view is that the adoption of a really democratic constitution by Germany would be the most convincing evidence that in her the old spirit of military domination had indeed died in this war, and would make it much easier for us to conclude a broad democratic peace with her. But, after all, that is a question for the German people to decide.

It is now more than a year since the President of the United States, then neutral, addressed to the belligerents a suggestion that each side should state clearly the aims for which they were fighting. We and our allies responded by the Note of January 10, 1917.

To the President's appeal the Central Empires made no reply…

On December 25 last, however, Count Czernin[1397], speaking on behalf of Austria-Hungary and her Allies, did make a pronouncement of a kind. It is, indeed, deplorably vague. We are told that it is not the intention of the Central Powers to appropriate forcibly any occupied territories or to rob of its independence any nation which has lost its political independence during the war. It is obvious that almost any scheme of conquest and annexation could be perpetrated within the literal interpretation of such a pledge.

Does it mean that Belgium, and Serbia, Montenegro and Romania will be as independent and as free to direct their own destinies as the German or any other nation? Or does it mean that all manner of interferences and restrictions, political and economic, incompatible with the status and dignity of a free and self-respecting people, are to be imposed? If this is the intention then there will be one kind of independence for a great nation and an inferior kind of independence for a small nation. We must know what is meant for equality of right among nations, small as well as great, is one of the fundamental issues this country and her Allies are fighting to establish in this war. Reparation for the wanton damage inflicted on Belgian towns and villages and their inhabitants is emphatically repudiated.

The rest of the so-called 'offer' of the Central Powers is almost entirely a refusal of all concessions. All suggestions about the autonomy of subject nationalities are ruled out of the peace terms altogether… A pious wish for the protection of minorities 'in so far as it is practically realizable' is the nearest approach to liberty which the Central statesmen venture to make.

On one point only are they perfectly clear and definite. Under no circumstances will the 'German demand' for the restoration of the whole of Germany's colonies be departed from. All principles of self-determination or, as our earlier phrase goes, government by consent of the governed, here vanish into thin air.

---

[1397] Ottokar Graf Czernin (1872-1932), Foreign Minister, 23 December 1916–14 April 1918.

It is impossible to believe that any edifice of permanent peace could be erected on such a foundation as this… Before any negotiations can even be begun, the Central Powers must realize the essential facts of the situation.

The days of the Treaty of Vienna are long past. We can no longer submit the future of European civilization to the arbitrary decisions of a few negotiators striving to secure by chicanery or persuasion the interests of this or that dynasty or nation. The settlement of the new Europe must be based on such grounds of reason and justice as will give some promise of stability. Therefore, it is that we feel that government with the consent of the governed must be the basis of any territorial settlement in this war. For that reason also, unless treaties be upheld, unless every nation is prepared at whatever sacrifice to honour the national signature, it is obvious that no treaty of peace can be worth the paper on which it is written.

The first requirement, therefore, always put forward by the British Government and their Allies, has been the complete restoration, political, territorial and economic, of the independence of Belgium, and such reparation as can be made for the devastation of its towns and provinces. This is no demand for war indemnity, such as that imposed on France by Germany in 1871… It is no more and no less than an insistence that, before there can be any hope for a stable peace, this great breach of the public law of Europe must be repudiated and, so far as possible, repaired. Reparation means recognition. Unless international right is recognized by insistence on payment for injury done in defiance of its canons it can never be a reality. Next comes the restoration of Serbia, Montenegro and the occupied parts of France, Italy and Romania. The complete withdrawal of the alien armies and the reparation for injustice done is a fundamental condition of permanent peace.

We mean to stand by the French Democracy to the death in the demand they make for a reconsideration of the great wrong of 1871, when, without any regard to the wishes of the population, two French provinces were torn from the side of France and incorporated in the German Empire. This sore has poisoned the peace of Europe for half a century and, until it is cured, healthy conditions will not have been restored. There can be no better illustration of the folly and wickedness of using a transient military success to violate national right.

I will not attempt to deal with the question of the Russian territories now in German occupation. The Russian policy since the revolution has passed so rapidly through so many phases that it is difficult to speak without some suspension of judgment as to what the situation will be when the final terms of European peace come to be discussed…

The present rulers of Russia are now engaged without any reference to the countries whom Russia brought into the war, in separate negotiations with their common enemy. I am indulging in no reproaches; I am merely stating facts with a view to making it clear why Britain cannot be held accountable for decisions taken in her absence and concerning which she has not been consulted or had her aid invoked… The democracy of this country means to stand to the last by the democracies of France and Italy and all our other Allies. We shall be proud to fight to the end side by side with the new democracy of Russia, so will America and so will France and Italy. But if the present rulers of Russia take action which is independent of their Allies we have no means of intervening to arrest the catastrophe which is assuredly befalling their country. Russia can only be saved by her own people.

We believe, however, that an independent Poland comprising all those genuinely Polish elements who desire to form part of it, is an urgent necessity for the stability of Western Europe.

Similarly, though we agree with President Wilson that the break-up of Austria-Hungary is no part of our war aims, we feel that unless genuine self-government on true democratic principles is granted to those Austro-Hungarian nationalities who have long desired it, it is impossible to hope for the removal of those causes of unrest in that part of Europe which have so long threatened its general peace.

On the same grounds we regard as vital the satisfaction of the legitimate claims of the Italians for union with those of their own race and tongue. We also mean to press that justice be done to men of Romanian blood and speech in their legitimate aspirations. If these conditions are fulfilled Austria-Hungary would become a power whose strength would conduce to the permanent peace and freedom of Europe…

Outside Europe, we believe that the same principles should be applied. While we do not challenge the maintenance of the Turkish Empire in the homelands of the Turkish race with its capital at Constantinople, the passage between the Mediterranean and the Black Sea being internationalized and neutralized, Arabia, Armenia, Mesopotamia, Syria and Palestine are in our judgment entitled to a recognition of their separate national conditions…

With regard to the German colonies, I have repeatedly declared that they are held at the disposal of a conference whose decision must have primary regard to the wishes and interests of the native inhabitants of such colonies. None of those territories are inhabited by Europeans. The governing consideration, therefore, in all these cases must be that the inhabitants should be placed under the control of an administration, acceptable to themselves, one of whose main purposes will be to prevent their exploitation for the benefit of European capitalists or governments. The natives live in their various tribal organizations under chiefs and councils who are competent to consult and speak for their tribes and members and thus to represent their wishes and interests in regard to their disposal. The general principle of national self-determination is, therefore, as applicable in their cases as in those of occupied European territories…

Finally, there must be reparation for injuries done in violation of international law. The Peace Conference must not forget our seamen and the services they have rendered to, and the outrages they have suffered for the common cause of freedom.

… It is desirable and, indeed, essential, that the settlement after this war shall be one which does not in itself bear the seed of future war. But that is not enough. However wisely and well we may make territorial and other arrangements, there will still be many subjects of international controversy…

The economic conditions at the end of the war will be in the highest degree difficult. Owing to the diversion of human effort to warlike pursuits, there must follow a world-shortage of raw materials, which will increase the longer the war lasts, and it is inevitable that those countries which have control of the raw materials will desire to help themselves and their friends first.

> Apart from this, whatever settlement is made will be suitable only to the circumstances under which it is made and, as those circumstances change, changes in the settlement will be called for.
>
> So long as the possibility of dispute between nations continues–that is to say, so long as men and women are dominated by passion and ambition, and war is the only means of settling a dispute–all nations must live under the burden, not only of having from time to time to engage in it, but of being compelled to prepare for its possible outbreak. The crushing weight of modern armaments, the increasing evil of compulsory military service, the vast waste of wealth and effort involved in warlike preparation, these are blots on our civilization of which every thinking individual must be ashamed.
>
> For these and other similar reasons, we are confident that a great attempt must be made to establish by some international organization an alternative to war as a means of settling international disputes. After all, war is a relic of barbarism and, just as law has succeeded violence as the means of settling disputes between individuals, so we believe that it is destined ultimately to take the place of war in the settlement of controversies between nations.
>
> If, then, we are asked what we are fighting for, we reply…: we are fighting for a just and lasting peace, and we believe that before permanent peace can be hoped for three conditions must be fulfilled.
>
> First, the sanctity of treaties must be established; secondly, a territorial settlement must be secured, based on the right of self-determination or the consent of the governed, and, lastly, we must seek by the creation of some international organization to limit the burden of armaments and diminish the probability of war.
>
> On these conditions the British Empire would welcome peace; to secure these conditions its peoples are prepared to make even greater sacrifices than those they have yet endured.[1398]

The unions were placated by this statement, a masterpiece of focused, detailed, yet concise, thought. Its thrust was really threefold: to appeal to the British public concerning the reasonableness of their nation's cause, to urge them on in supporting the war effort; to reassure the governments of Britain's allies of her continued support; and to demonstrate directly to the people of the Central Powers that it was only their governments who stood in the way of a quick conclusion of a peace process that would safeguard the continuance of their national life. He also hinted at reparations, though suggesting that these would not be on the scale imposed on France after 1871, and a new international order. Certainly, the speech greatly increased his support amongst trade unions and the Labour Party.

Such were the power of Lloyd George's words, that President Wilson at first considered abandoning his own speech to a joint session of Congress on 8 January outlining US war aims, the famous 'Fourteen Points', many of which were similar to the aims outlined by Lloyd George. However, he was persuaded by his adviser 'Colonel' Edward House to deliver it[1399], duly stating:

---

[1398] Lloyd George, *Great Crusade*, p251-266.

[1399] Grigg, *War Leader*, p383. Edward House (1858-1938), diplomat, adviser to President Wilson.

> What we demand in this war… is that the world be made fit and safe to live in; and particularly that it be made safe for every peace-loving nation which, like our own, wishes to live its own life, determine its own institutions, be assured of justice and fair dealing by the other peoples of the world as against force and selfish aggression. All the peoples of the world are in effect partners in this interest, and for our own part we see very clearly that unless justice be done to others it will not be done to us. The programme of the world's peace, therefore, is our programme…

He then delineated his Fourteen Points, proposing "open covenants of peace, openly arrived at", "absolute freedom of navigation upon the seas", "the removal, so far as possible, of all economic barriers and the establishment of an equality of trade conditions among all the nations", "adequate guarantees given and taken that national armaments will be reduced to the lowest point consistent with domestic safety", and that "a general association of nations must be formed under specific covenants for the purpose of affording mutual guarantees of political independence and territorial integrity to great and small states alike." He concluded: "For such arrangements and covenants we are willing to fight and to continue to fight until they are achieved; but only because we wish the right to prevail and desire a just and stable peace such as can be secured only by removing the chief provocations to war."[1400]

In the event, Wilson's speech overshadowed Lloyd George's, and it was both commentated upon more at the time and is better remembered by posterity. And in time, it would be Wilson who was awarded the 1919 Nobel Peace Prize for his peace-making efforts, and as "the leading architect behind the League of Nations", which, ironically, the USA never joined!

Lloyd George had told General Edmund Allenby[1401], who was appointed the new commander in Egypt in June, that his objective was "Jerusalem before Christmas" and that "he was to ask for such reinforcements and supplies as he found necessary"[1402], although the exact nature of his offensives was still undecided when he was appointed. Amidst months of argument throughout the autumn of 1917, Robertson was able to block Lloyd George's plan to focus on Palestine as the main theatre of operations by having Allenby make the impossible demand that 13 extra divisions be sent to him. Nonetheless, Allenby entered Jerusalem at noon on 11 December 1917, famously entering on foot through the Jaffa Gate, out of respect for the Holy City.

In the winter of 1917-18, Lloyd George secured the resignations of both the service chiefs. Removing the First Sea Lord Admiral Jellicoe earlier in 1917, as Lloyd George wanted, would have been politically impossible given Tory anger at the return of Churchill–still blamed for the Dardanelles disaster–to office as the Minister of Munitions in July, and Lloyd George's preoccupations with Passchendaele, Caporetto and the Supreme War Council from July onward. By December, it was clear that Lloyd George would have to either sack Jellicoe or lose Eric Geddes, First Lord of the Admiralty,

---

1400 http://avalon.law.yale.edu/20th_century/wilson14.asp. Retrieved 30 April 2019.

1401 Edmund Allenby (1861-1936), Commander of Egyptian Expeditionary Force, 1917-1919, High Commissioner in Egypt, 1919-1925, Egypt attaining limited independence on 28 February 1922.

1402 Lloyd George, *War Memoirs*, Vol.II, p1089-1090.

who wanted to return to his previous job in charge of military transport in France. The Christmas holiday, when Parliament was not sitting, provided a good opportunity. Before Jellicoe left for leave on Christmas Eve, he received a letter from Geddes demanding his resignation, and left office on 10 January 1918. The other Sea Lords talked of resigning but did not do so, whilst Jellicoe's ally Carson remained a member of the War Cabinet until he resigned on 20 January over Irish Home Rule. Relations with General Robertson had worsened further over the creation of the Supreme War Council at Versailles and he was eventually forced out on 19 February 1918 over his insistence that the British delegate there be subordinate to himself, as CIGS, in London. He was replaced by General Henry Wilson.

The War Cabinet was a very successful innovation. It met almost daily, with Maurice Hankey as secretary, and made all major political, military, economic and diplomatic decisions. The compulsory rationing system, imposed in stages between December 1917–February 1918, worked smoothly. The Corn Production Act 1917, most of the provisions of which came into effect on 21 August, bestowed upon the Board of Agriculture the power to ensure that all land was properly cultivated, appointed a wages board to operate a new minimum wage in agriculture, and guaranteed minimum prices for wheat and oats. However, from 1914 to 1918, trade union membership grew from 4.14 million to 6.53 million. Work stoppages and strikes became frequent in 1917-18 as the unions expressed grievances regarding prices, alcohol control, pay disputes, dilution of labour, fatigue from overtime and from Sunday work, and inadequate housing.

Soon after Lloyd George's Caxton Hall speech of 5 January, the British Ambassador at Berne received a message that Count Czernin wished to meet Lloyd George in neutral Switzerland. The Ambassador, Sir Horace Rumbold[1403], had indirectly received a communication from Count Skrzynski[1404], Counsellor of the Austrian embassy in Berne, who had made the visit to Switzerland in order to convey the message to him. Skrzynski stated that, if Lloyd George were willing to have an interview with Count Czernin, the latter would come to Switzerland to meet him. This was a tremendous proposal, but, as Lloyd George himself recorded in his *War Memoirs*:

> The Cabinet was doubtful as to the wisdom of my accepting the invitation. A meeting of two Prime Ministers from the opposing Powers to discuss Peace was necessarily a more formal occasion and would attract much more attention than private conversations between a Minister and an ex-Ambassador. Besides, Czernin had not answered the question put to Mensdorff[1405] as to whether Austria was prepared to negotiate a separate peace. Personally I was strongly in favour of keeping up these communications with Austria. If they came to anything we should have one foe the less to fight… So I urged the Cabinet that we should take advantage of every overture which might lead to a separate peace with Austria…

1403 Sir Horace Rumbold (1869-1941), Ambassador to Switzerland, 1916-1919, High Commissioner at Constantinople, 1920-1923, later Ambassador to Germany, 1928-1933, warning of Hitler's ambitions.

1404 Aleksander Skrzyński (1882-1931), Polish diplomat, later 13th Prime Minister of Poland, 1925-1926.

1405 Albert Graf von Mensdorff-Pouilly-Dietrichstein (1861-1945), Austro-Hungarian Ambassador to London, 1904-1914, entrusted with several diplomatic missions directed towards the restoration of peace.

> It was decided that the opportunity for any serious request for peace *pourparlers* ought not to be ignored, and it was resolved to send a member of the War Cabinet to meet Count Czemin. Messages passed to and fro for weeks, but no meeting could be arranged until late in February ... Czernin was tricky, and our Foreign Office very sticky. The reluctance of the latter to press matters to a conclusion was due to their suspicions of the genuineness of Czernin. They thought he was playing a deep game for Germany... The truth of the matter probably was that the Austrian Government were pulled in both directions and that they were thoroughly distracted. On the one hand, there was the dread of approaching doom from which they wanted to escape; on the other hand, there was the fear of a powerful Germany which enchained them with infrangible steel. It was finally agreed that General Smuts should once more go on his errand of peace and proceed to Switzerland to ascertain the exact meaning and scope of these overtures...
>
> General Smuts again took with him Mr. Philip Kerr, and they reached Berne on 9th March. At first it appeared as if there had been a complete change in the Austrian attitude and that at last they were prepared to confine the discussions strictly to the problems of an Austro-Hungarian peace. It seemed as if this time the Austrians meant to get out of the War with or without their allies. They were convinced that the War was being prolonged owing to Prussian annexationist ambitions, and they were prepared, once they had negotiated a separate peace, to leave the orbit of Prussian influence, and remodel their institutions on federal lines. Mr. Kerr, being of a naturally hopeful disposition... at first look a sanguine view of the proposals and in a telegram to me... said:-
>
> "... I think that... very great results might follow from a conversation between Czernin and a British negotiator as to a possible settlement between Austria-Hungary and the Entente, provided that it were absolutely clear that we were not prepared to discuss terms with Germany at all... It therefore seems to me essential that if the Czernin meeting is to take place we should discuss basis of a separate Austro-Hungarian peace with our Allies including Serbia as soon as possible..."
>
> General Smuts was instructed that he could go ahead on these lines. He had a long conversation with M. de Skrzynski in the course of which the Austrian emissary expressed the fear on Czernin's part that the Entente were simply endeavouring to detach Austria-Hungary in order to isolate and defeat Germany. General Smuts assured him that what the Entente were after was a settlement on terms which would bring about a just and lasting peace everywhere, with a prospect of general disarmament. He added that unfortunately the treaties of Brest-Litovsk and with Roumania were not, in the eyes of the Entente, in keeping with these principles.[1406]

As so often, delicate talks were overtaken by other events. Lloyd George himself concluded about this great 'might have been':

> It may be of some interest, not untinged with regret to conjecture what might have been the effect on the settlement of Europe if peace had been concluded with Austria in the spring of

[1406] Lloyd George, *War Memoirs*, Vol.II, p1499-1501.

> 1918. The Austrian Empire would have remained; instead of breaking up into a number of independent states… there would have been perhaps a dozen autonomous dominions all owing allegiance to the Austrian Crown and working harmoniously together for their common interests.[1407]

As it was, there followed a series of military and political crises. The Germans, having moved 48 divisions from the Eastern front and retrained them in new 'infiltration tactics' as *Sturmtruppen*, now had more soldiers on the Western Front than the Allies, in some places having a local advantage of four-to-one. They launched their full-scale Spring Offensive, Operation *Michael*, starting at 4.40 am on 21 March with the biggest artillery barrage of the whole war against 60 km of the British and French lines, hoping for victory before American troops arrived in strength. Trench mortars, mustard gas, chlorine gas, tear gas and smoke canisters were concentrated on the forward trenches, while heavy artillery bombarded rear areas to destroy Allied artillery and supply lines. Over 3,500,000 shells were fired in five hours, hitting targets over an area of 400 km². The Allied armies fell back towards Amiens in confusion, ceding some 3,100 km² of French territory. Facing defeat, Lloyd George's Cabinet realised it needed more troops to fight a mobile war. Lloyd George asked President Wilson for immediate help and agreed to the appointment at the Doullens Conference of French General Ferdinand Foch as Commander-in-Chief of the Allied Armies with the title of *Généralissime* on 26 March. He briefly considered resuming the role of Secretary of State for War himself, but was dissuaded by the King, appointing Lord Milner, who had played the decisive role at Doullens, on 18 April.

Crucially, the Military Service Act was amended again, 'Military Service (No.2) Act, 1918' receiving royal assent on 18 April, its most notable provision being the extension of age eligibility so that men aged from 17 to 51 could be called up, reaching previously untapped sources of manpower. In this way, Lloyd George found 500,000 fresh soldiers and rushed them over to France–but all at a terrible domestic price. Conscription put into uniform nearly every physically fit man, six million out of ten million eligible. Of these, about 750,000 lost their lives and 1,700,000 were wounded. Most deaths were of young, unmarried men; however, 160,000 wives lost their husbands, and 300,000 children lost their fathers.

Further, despite strong warnings even from the military authorities that it was a dangerous idea, the War Cabinet decided to impose conscription on Ireland, believing that this could raise a further 150,000 men. From the Irish perspective, the most important aspect was Clause 2, which stipulated that the government "may by Order in Council extend this Act to Ireland." In other words, the British government could introduce conscription in Ireland by the 'back door', without the necessity of introducing further legislation. The main reason for the inclusion of this clause was that trade unions in Britain demanded it as the price for cutting back on conscription exemptions for certain workers. Labour wanted the principle established that no one was exempt, but it did not demand that

[1407] Ibid., p1502. For this episode and its background in detail, see G. Egedy, *Lloyd George and the Dual Monarchy, 1917-1918*, *Central European Papers*, 2, 2, 2014, p36-50.

conscription take place in Ireland. The proposal was enacted but never enforced. The Catholic bishops, for the first time, entered the dispute and called for open resistance to conscription. Many Irish Catholics and nationalists joined Sinn Féin, a decisive moment marking the dominance of Irish politics by a party committed to leaving the United Kingdom altogether.

Lloyd George had fatally connected the new conscription legislation to a new Home Rule Bill, which had the effect of alienating both nationalists and unionists in Ireland. Although large numbers of Irishmen had willingly joined Irish regiments in Kitchener's 'New Army' at the outbreak of war, the likelihood of enforced conscription created a huge backlash. The linking of conscription and Home Rule outraged the Irish nationalist parties at Westminster, including the Irish Parliamentary Party, All-for-Ireland League and others, who walked out in protest when the bill was introduced into the Commons on 10 April, and returned to Ireland to organise opposition.[1408] On 18 April, acting on a resolution of the Dublin Corporation, Laurence O'Neill, the Lord Mayor of Dublin, held a conference at the Mansion House. The Irish Anti-Conscription Committee was convened to devise plans to resist conscription, and represented different, sometimes antipathetic sections of nationalist opinion: John Dillon and Joseph Devlin for the Irish Parliamentary Party, Éamon de Valera and Arthur Griffith for Sinn Féin, William O'Brien and Timothy Healy for the All-for-Ireland League and Michael Egan, Thomas Johnson and William O'Brien[1409] representing Labour and the trade union movement.

The same day, the Roman Catholic hierarchy held a special meeting at Maynooth College, presided over by Cardinal Michael Logue[1410], issuing an uncompromising declaration: "An attempt is being made to force conscription upon Ireland against the will of the Irish nation, and in defiance of the protests of its leaders. We consider that conscription forced in this way upon Ireland is an oppressive and inhuman law, which the Irish shall have a right to resist by all the means that are consonant with the law of God."[1411] The Anti-Conscription Committee and bishops proposed an pledge, drafted by de Valera, that was to be taken at the church door of every Roman Catholic parish the next Sunday, 21 April, which read: "Denying the right of the British government to enforce compulsory service in this country, *we pledge ourselves solemnly to one another to resist conscription* by the most effective means at our disposal." On 23 April, there was a one-day general strike across industry and commerce in Ireland, even in government munitions factories.

By June, it had become apparent to most observers both in Britain and in Ireland that, following the United States entry into the war, the tide had changed in favour of the Allied armies in Europe, and by 20 June, the government had dropped its conscription and home rule plans, given the lack of agreement of the Irish Convention. However the legacy of the crisis remained. Completely ineffectual as a means to bolster troop numbers in France, the events surrounding the Conscription Crisis were

---

1408 This subsequently proved to be something of a tactical mistake on the part of the IPP, as it appeared to legitimise the original Sinn Féin policy of abstention.

1409 William O'Brien (1881-1968), trade unionist, co-founder of Labour Party of Ireland in 1912.

1410 Michael Logue (1840-1924), Archbishop of Armagh and Primate of All Ireland from 1887 until his death.

1411 https://www.irishexaminer.com/breakingnews/views/analysis/revolution-of-the-bishops-conscription-crisis-of-1918-impacted-irish-history-more-than-the-easter-rising-835050.html. Retrieved 30 October 2019.

disastrous for the Dublin Castle authorities, and for the more moderate nationalist parties in Ireland. The delay in finding a resolution to the home rule issue, partly caused by the war, and exaggerated by the Conscription Crisis in Ireland, all increased support for Sinn Féin.

Meanwhile, on 9 April 1918, Lloyd George, in introducing the National Service Bill, unknowingly misled the House of Commons in claiming that Haig's forces were stronger at the start of 1918 than they had been a year earlier–in fact the increase was in the number of labourers, most of them Chinese, Indians and black South Africans, and Haig had fewer infantry units, holding a longer stretch of front. The Prime Minister had used incorrect information furnished by the War Department office, headed by Major-General Sir Frederick Maurice.[1412] Maurice then made the spectacular public allegation that the War Cabinet had deliberately held soldiers back from the Western Front, and both Lloyd George and Bonar Law had lied to Parliament about it. Instead of going to the Prime Minister about the problem, Maurice had waited and then broken King's regulations by making a public attack, sending a letter that was published in *The Times,* the *Morning Post,* the *Daily Chronicle* and the *Daily News* on 7 May. The letter stated:

> My attention has been called to answers given in the House of Commons on 23rd April by Mr. Bonar Law to questions put by Mr. G. Lambert and Mr. Pringle as to the extension of the British Front in France. These answers contain certain misstatements which in sum give a totally misleading impression of what occurred…
>
> … this letter is not the result of a military conspiracy. It has been seen by no soldier[1413]… My reasons for taking the very grave step of writing this letter are that the statements quoted above are known to a large number of soldiers to be incorrect, and this knowledge is breeding such distrust of the Government as can only end in impairing the splendid morale of our troops at a time when everything possible should be done to raise it.
>
> I have therefore decided… that my duty as a citizen must override my duty as a soldier, and I ask you to publish this letter in the hope that Parliament may see fit to order an investigation into the statements I have made…[1414]

Asquith, the Liberal leader in the House, took up the allegations and attacked Lloyd George, which further tore the Liberal Party asunder. While Asquith's presentation was poorly done, Lloyd George vigorously defended his position, treating the debate on 9 May as a vote of confidence. As such, it was one of the most crucial debates in his Parliamentary career. He stated:

> … [T]his is the first time, as far as I can discover, that it has ever been suggested… that a Select Committee of the House of Commons should examine the question whether a Minister has made a correct statement or not in the course of a speech … A… distinguished general, who… has ceased to hold an office which he has occupied for two years challenges, after he has left

1412 Major General Frederick Maurice (1871-1951), Director of Military Operations, early 1915–20 April 1918.

1413 Patently untrue, given Maurice's closeness to William Robertson.

1414 Quoted in full in Blake, p369-370.

office, statements made by two Ministers during the time he was in that office. During the time he was in such office he never challenged those statements, when he had not merely access to official information, but when he had access to the Ministers themselves.

General Maurice was in office for weeks after I delivered that speech in the House... He never called attention to it; he never asked me to correct it... We were constantly discussing these questions of figures, because, as the Director of Military Operations, he was the authority...

I say that I have been treated unfairly... I thought that probably General Maurice had not talked to me about it, because he thought that it was his business to talk to his immediate Chief first of all... but until he left office... he never made any representations to his Chief on the subject. And this is on a question which is so important that you must set up a Select Committee to inquire into it!

Lloyd George then almost forensically went through Maurice's allegations, their foundation and their implications step by step, disproving them at each stage. This included the extension of the Western Front and:

On the comparison which I made of the British Forces in France on 1st January, 1918, and on 1st January, 1917. The other is the comparison which I drew between enemy and Allied Forces on the Western Front–both of vast importance, and both practically part of the same question... The figures that I gave were taken from the official records of the War Office... If they were incorrect, General Maurice was as responsible as anyone else. But they were not inaccurate... There is absolutely no doubt that there was a very considerable addition to the manpower of the Army in France at the beginning of 1918 as compared with the manpower at the beginning of 1917.[1415]

He now came to the issue of the extension of the Western Front and whether it was discussed at the Versailles War Council, held on 29 November–3 December 1917, stating:

As a matter of fact, the extension of the front of General Gough's Army–... the extension which is supposed to be responsible by some people for the disaster, though I do not accept that–was never discussed at that Council at all. There was a demand for a further extension. That particular extension... had taken place before the Council ever met. It had been agreed to between Field-Marshal Haig and General Pétain, and the extension was an accomplished fact before the Council ever met, and was reported... by the Field-Marshal to the Council.

Lloyd George rightly emphasized the pressure that had been exerted by the French Government and the French Army:

[1415] Total British strength in France had risen by 324,785 men, though the effective fighting strength had fallen by around 7% in the period under consideration.

> There was considerable ferment in France during the summer of last year on the subject of the length of line held by the French Army, as compared with that of our Army. The French losses had been enormous… They held a front of 326 miles. We held a line of 100 miles. That is not the whole statement, because the Germans were massed much more densely in front of our lines. Not only that, as part of the line which we held was much more vulnerable… Still, there was the fact…
>
> The French were pressing us, in order to withdraw men from the Army for the purposes of agriculture, because… the agricultural output in France had fallen enormously, owing to the fact that they had withdrawn such a very large proportion of the men from the cultivation of the fields…
>
> … We accepted in principle that there must be an extension, that the time and extent must be left to the two Commanders-in-Chief to settle together, that no extension was possible until the offensive was over, and that the line to be taken over must depend upon the military policy for 1918, and upon the role assigned to each Army…

Lloyd George then spoke in detail about the Boulogne Conference, held on 25 September 1917, originally summoned to discuss "a rather important Foreign Office question", not the extension of the Western Front. This was first raised by the French Prime Minister, Painlevé. Lloyd George asserted: "I was not in the least prepared for it, and I told Sir William Robertson that it was a matter with which he would have to deal, and the whole discussion was conducted by him. He then laid down these principles, of which I certainly heartily approved, and so did the whole of the Government…"

He continued by quoting the detailed subsequent correspondence between Robertson and Haig, before proceeding with the War Cabinet discussion of the issue on 24 October 1917:

> The War Cabinet approved the suggestion of the Chief of the Imperial Staff that he should reply to Field-Marshal Haig in the following sense–We are supposed to have overruled the Chief of the Staff…–1. The War Cabinet are of opinion that, in deciding to what extent British troops can take over line from the French, regard must be had to the necessity for giving them reasonable opportunity for leave, rest and training during the winter months, and to the plan of operations for next year; and, further, that while the present offensive continues, it would not be possible to commence taking over more line. 2. The general military policy for next year is now under consideration, and will subsequently form the subject of conference with Allied Governments. In these circumstances the War Cabinet fear that until this policy is settled, it will be premature to decide finally whether the British Front can be extended by four divisions or to a greater or less extent than this. That Resolution was communicated to Sir Douglas Haig by Sir William Robertson, and we never departed from it.

He then dealt with Cambrai, Caporetto and the arrival of Clemenceau as French Prime Minister, and the changes in circumstances these events brought about:

The military representatives at Versailles suggested a compromise between the French and the British view about extension, but they coupled it with recommendations as to the steps which ought to be taken by the French Army to assist the British if it were attacked, and by the British to assist the French if they were attacked… That recommendation was to come up for discussion at the meeting of the Supreme Council at Versailles[1416] on the 1st February. Before that meeting, Field-Marshal Haig and General Pétain met. They entered into an agreement as to the extension of the front to Barisis. Field-Marshal Haig reported that to the Versailles Council, and when the discussion took place there, no further extension of the line was made at all as a result of that discussion…

… [I]n the action which Sir Douglas Haig took for the extension of the line, he had the full approval of the British Cabinet…

… I am dealing with… the sort of pernicious rumour… that we, in spite of the remonstrances of Sir Douglas Haig and Sir William Robertson, forced them to take a risk which they ought never to have taken. Does anyone imagine that if that had been Sir Douglas Haig's view, he would have accepted the responsibility for one minute? Therefore I am sorry… that this opportunity has been given to read out the actual conclusions of the War Cabinet, in order to dispose once and for all of these pestiferous rumours, which have been circulated for purposes of their own by men who… do not like the present Chief of the Imperial Staff, or, perhaps, the present Chief of the British Ministry.

The real lesson of the controversy… is the one of the importance of unity of command. That question of the extension of the line would never have arisen had you had that unity… I am glad we have got that at last…

… I should like to say something about the effect of such action as General Maurice's on the discipline of the Army. It was a flagrant breach of discipline. The right hon. Gentleman [Asquith] admitted it. I wish he had deprecated it… He has been responsible for the conduct of this War for two years. If this Motion be carried, he will again be responsible for the conduct of the War… This is a Vote of Censure upon the Government…

I think… it is essential, having regard to his great position, that he should deprecate action like General Maurice's… The Army [in France] is 2,000,000 of men… and it is vitally important that discipline should be maintained…

… These controversies are distracting, they are paralysing, they are rending, and I beg that they should come to an end… The national unity is threatened–the Army unity is threatened… I really beg and implore, for our common country, the fate of which is in the balance now and in the next few weeks, that there should be an end of this sniping.[1417]

Lloyd George won over the House by 293 votes to 106 with his powerful refutation of Maurice's allegations, in a 'tour de force' performance. Maurice himself was put on half-pay on 11 May and was soon "retired" from the Army. More importantly, Asquith's highly dubious 'sniping' had made the rift in the Liberal Party much more visible, and therefore harder to heal. In fact, the split became glaringly

---

1416 Held 29 January–2 February 1918.

1417 https://api.parliament.uk/historic-hansard/commons/1918/may/09/prime-ministers-reply. Retrieved 18 April 2019.

evident, with 98 supporting Asquith, 70 supporting Lloyd George, and 93 abstaining or absent; as usual by this time, Lloyd George got most of his support from the Conservatives. What's more, it began to become more formalised, as the beginnings of separate 'Lloyd Georgeite' Liberal constituency organisations began to appear.[1418]

The morning of the debate, Lloyd George was walking to the House accompanied by Stanley Baldwin, Tory MP for Bewdley and Financial Secretary to the Treasury. Baldwin said:

> You know, PM [sic], that for ten years we have been trying to catch you deviating by an inch from the strict path of veracity and pin you down. We never succeeded. But now others think they have got you and they will find out this afternoon that they have caught you speaking the truth. They will have the shock of their lives." Lloyd George enjoyed the joke, laughing aloud and telling the Cabinet that "he had been caught telling the truth.[1419]

To Baldwin, he said "Poor old Bonar, he felt it very much. He doesn't like being called a liar. I don't mind. I've been called a liar all my life."[1420] This was amusing, but Baldwin was a 'snake in the grass', bidding his time: in five years, he would be Tory Prime Minister himself, and the Liberal Party would be shattered.

In August, the National Eisteddfod was held in Neath, Glamorgan, South Wales. Due 'to important matters of state', Lloyd George could not be present to preside on his usual Thursday, arriving that evening. This was no mere excuse:

> At 4:20am a short artillery barrage launched an assault by Canadian, Australian, British and French troops against German lines in what was later called the Battle of Amiens. By the time that Lloyd George reached Paddington station at 3:00pm, Parliament was being told that 7,000 prisoners had been taken and over 100 guns captured. Boarding his train, he was quoted as telling railway staff– "we are smashing through". The Prime Minister, briefed by telegram at Cardiff station, addressed large crowds from the railway carriage door telling them that the Allies had won a great victory that morning.[1421] The newspapers estimated that thousands of people had gathered at the Neath station yard from where the Prime Minister would travel by car over to Maesygwernen, Morriston… the home of T. J. Williams, the Liberal MP for Swansea District which, at the time, included Neath Borough…[1422]

---

1418 For more on this unsavoury episode, see J. Gooch *The Maurice Debate 1918, Journal of Contemporary History* 3, 4, October 1968, pp211-228; also Winter, p328-331, who believes that Maurice did not act alone, that "a ragbag of titled grandees, disgruntled politicians and disgraced soldiers had been involved in plotting the downfall of Lloyd George," including Asquith: p329. The present author strongly concurs.

1419 K. Middlemas and J. Barnes, *Baldwin*, 1969, London, Weidenfeld and Nicolson, p68.

1420 R.J.Q. Adams, *Bonar Law*, 1999, London, John Murray, p268.

1421 It was true: At the Battle of Amiens, Allied forces, ably led by Australian Lieutenant General John Monash and Canadian Lieutenant. General Arthur Currie, advanced over 11 km, one of the greatest advances of the war, Erich Ludendorff describing 8 August 1918 as "the black day of the German Army". The momentum of the war shifted as the Allied 'Hundred Days Offensive' began and German morale collapsed.

1422 D. Michael, *Neath & Lloyd George In 1918: A Civic Ceremony In Context*, July 2018, at http://www.spanglefish.com/neathantiquariansociety/index.asp?pageid=688641. Retrieved 23 October 2019.

Here the fascinating character of Winifred Coombe Tennant[1423] entered Lloyd George's life. That evening, Winifred attended a dinner in Lloyd George's honour at Maesygwernen, seated next to Philip Kerr, the Premier's Private Secretary; she "didn't like him". The previous day she had spoken at the Cymmrodorion Society on "rural reconstruction in relation to the rural working-class woman"[1424], and earlier, on the day of the dinner, she had been initiated into the Gorsedd of Bards as *'Mam o Nedd'* ('Mother from Neath'). Now, after dinner, she was introduced by Sir E. Vincent Evans to Lloyd George, who said at once "I hear you have been making a great speech."[1425] This became the basis for her entrée into mainstream politics. Demonstrating a shrewd political mind, she rapidly cemented herself as a–not always uncritical–close political ally and valued advisor of the Prime Minister, becoming a frequent guest at 10 Downing Street, then at Chequers, Cheyne Walk and his new home at Churt.[1426] A Suffragist, on 22 May 1918 she had been elected as one of the 20 members of the executive–including three women–of the Welsh National Liberal Council and of the Committee for Self-Government for Wales[1427], and was a leading campaigner for the Coalition Liberals at the general election later that year.

The Prime Minister stayed throughout the next day, 9 August, officially receiving the 'Freedom of the Borough of Neath' at Gwyn Hall. After the presentation, he spoke to the selected, but enthusiastic, emotional crowd. Following this, specially invited guests dined at the Castle Hotel. After dinner, the Prime Minister spoke again before going to the afternoon session of the Eisteddfod led by a guard of honour of women munitions workers. There, the Presidential Address was given by Thomas J. Williams[1428], Liberal MP for Swansea East, who made glowing comments about him:

> The Neath Eisteddfod… had the honour of offering welcome to one whom he considered the greatest man in the world–Mr. Lloyd George… As a nation they… took the greater joy in the knowledge that when the liberty of the world was assailed, a man truly endowed with all that is worthier in the character of the ancient Briton, was called as it were by some inspired, by happy decree of fate, to offer leadership. They had found the Prime Minister to be not only a man of words, but of deeds.

---

1423 Winifred Coombe Tennant (1874-1956), Suffragist, Liberal politician, philanthropist. She lived at Cadoxton Lodge, Neath, 1895-1931. Appointed as the first female Magistrate in Glamorganshire, 20 July 1920.

1424 W. Coombe Tennant, *Rural Reconstruction in Relation to the Rural Working-Class Woman*, *Transactions of the Honourable Society of Cymmrodorion*, 1918, p239-243.

1425 Coombe Tennant, p257. Diary entry for 8 August 1918.

1426 Winifred was a guest at Chequers on 23-24 July 1921 and 28-30 January 1922, and at No.10 on 23-24 January 1922. She visited the site of Bron-y-de on 29 January 1922, before it was even built, and visited on 9-11 December 1922, 17-19 February and 16-18 June 1923; she also signed the Visitors Book there on 10 May 1924 and 31 January 1925. Lloyd George and Margaret visited Cadoxton Lodge on 8-10 September 1923.

1427 Coombe Tennant, p253; G. Cummins, *Swan On A Black Sea: A Study In Automatic Writing: The Cummins-Willett Scripts*, 1965, London, Routledge and Kegan Paul, pxvi.

1428 Thomas Williams (1872-1919), barrister, Liberal MP for Swansea East, February 1915 until his early death.

> … He had been the great idealist, he had been the practical man, the man who translates thought into action. His words had sustained them, and his strenuous work had saved us and civilisation ... Let them remember his message: "Hold fast, and sing."[1429]

Certainly, Lloyd George had saved the National Eisteddfod for the future: that year the surplus was £2,400, by far the biggest recorded in its history up until that time.[1430]

On 22 August, the Congress of Allied Women on War Service (*Congrès des Femmes alliées au service des œuvres de guerre*), a mass meeting of 2,000 French, British, Italian, Belgian, Polish, Romanian, Serbian, Montenegrin and American women, was held in the Théâtre des Champs-Élysées in Paris. Lloyd George was to have addressed them, but events prevented this, so in the evening a message from the Prime Minister was read to the assembly by Lord Derby to enthusiastic applause, revealing as it did just how much Lloyd George valued their vital efforts:

> I extremely regret that it is impossible for me to fulfil my undertaking to address the great gathering of women war workers in Paris. I regret it all the more because I was very anxious to bear testimony to the tremendous part which women have played in this vital epoch in human history. They have not only borne their burden of sorrow and separation with unflinching fortitude and patience; they have assumed an enormous share of the burdens necessary to the practical conduct of the war.
>
> If it had not been for the splendid manner in which the women came forward to work in hospitals, in munition factories, on the land, in administrative offices of all kinds, and in war work behind the lines, often in daily danger of their lives, Great Britain and, as I believe, all the Allies would have been unable to withstand the enemy attacks during the past few months. For this service to our common cause humanity owes them unbounded gratitude.
>
> In the past I have heard it said that women were not fit for the vote because they would be weak when it came to understanding the issues and bearing the strains of a great war. My recent experience in South Wales confirmed me in the conviction that the women there understand perfectly what is at stake in this war.
>
> I believe that they recognise as clearly as any that there can be no peace, no progress, no happiness in the world so long as the monster of militarism is able to stalk unbridled and unashamed among the weaker peoples. To them this war is a crusade for righteousness and gentleness, and they do not mean to make peace until the Allies have made it impossible for another carnival of violence to befall mankind. I am certain that this resolution of the women of South Wales is but typical of the spirit of the women in the rest of Great Britain.
>
> This war was begun in order that force and brutality might crush out freedom among men. Its authors cannot have foreseen that one of its main effects would be to give to women a commanding position and influence in the public affairs of the world. To their ennobling

[1429] *The Herald Of Wales*, 10 August 1918, p4. https://newspapers.library.wales/view/4115940/4115944.
[1430] Griffiths, p194.

influence we look not only for strength to win the war but for inspiration during the great work of reconstruction which we shall have to undertake after victory is won.

The women who have flocked to France to work for the Allies are among the foremost leaders of this great movement of regeneration. My message to their representatives gathered together in Paris is this: 'Well done; carry on. You are helping to create a new earth for yourselves and for your children.'[1431]

Continued progressive Liberal reform at home had not been forgotten either, despite the maelstrom of events, as on 8 August the Education Act 1918 received royal assent. It was often called the 'Fisher Act', due to its being drawn up by the distinguished historian H. A. L. Fisher, adroitly appointed by Lloyd George to join the coalition government in December 1916 as the President of the Board of Education[1432] because "the country would take more educational reform from an educationalist than from a politician."[1433] Fisher had initially been sceptical, but Lloyd George made good on his offer:

'Would there', I asked, 'be money for educational reforms and improvements?' I saw that this was essential. Ll.G. assured me that money would be forthcoming and that he would give me his personal support. And so… I telephoned my acceptance… The Prime Minister was as good as his word. To a Cabinet so largely conservative my educational proposals must have seemed most extravagant, but the Prime Minister's strong and constant support, for which I can never be too grateful, ensured the acceptance of every plan which I placed before my colleagues.[1434]

Herbert Lewis, Lloyd George's long-time close Welsh ally, and the Parliamentary Secretary to the Board of Education from 1915 to 1922, was also instrumental in the creation of this important step forward, and energetic in piloting it through Parliament, as Fisher himself acknowledged.[1435] As Kenneth Morgan states:

Fisher's educational policies had brought tangible and measurable benefits to Wales: the 'Fisher formula' would give Wales an additional £100,000, while the Education Act of 1918 would give new educational opportunities to 20,000 boys and girls… For his part, H. A. L. Fisher clearly regarded Lewis… as his most reliable sounding-board on Welsh education. It was a constructive time of change. Education, after all, was a foremost element in the government's proclaimed intention of a brave new world of social reform after the election.[1436]

---

1431 https://www.theguardian.com/theguardian/2013/aug/22/women-first-world-war-lloyd-george. Retrieved 24 March 2021. This important Congress–and Lloyd George's message to it–is routinely neglected.

1432 Fisher was also responsible for the important School Teachers (Superannuation) Act 1918, which obtained royal assent on 21 November and provided pension provision for all teachers. The Burnham Committee considered pay scales, which finally brought teachers in line with other professions in 1919.

1433 H. A. L. Fisher, *An Unfinished Autobiography*, 1940, London, OUP, p91.

1434 Ibid., p92.

1435 Ibid., p101-102.

1436 Morgan, *Lloyd George's Flintshire Loyalist*, p27.

The Act made attendance at school compulsory for children up to the age of 14 in England and Wales, Scotland having its own separate Act. Other features of the Act included the abolition of all fees in state elementary schools, and the provision of ancillary services, such as medical inspection, nursery schools, centres for pupils with special needs, and so on. Provision was made for school leavers between the ages of 14 and 18 to attend day continuation schools for vocational training.

Fisher had the broad support of the Established Church, the Labour Party and the union movement, although there was opposition from some employers, like the Lancashire cotton manufacturers, who feared the Act would reduce available child labour. Further, some of these forward-looking measures were curtailed in the economically distressed decades that followed Lloyd George's premiership, and it took the Butler Act of 1944 to really bring its principles to full realisation. Writing towards the very end of his life, Fisher was still upbeat regarding the value of 'his' Act:

> I believe that, when the history of our English education comes to be written, no single step will be found to have contributed more effectively to the spread of the university idea through England than the decision of the Government in 1918 to allot eight millions to enable ex-Service men to enjoy the privileges of university education. Twenty-seven thousand students went to the universities with the aid of these state grants… I am in a position to affirm that this large body of students was drawn almost exclusively from families to whom the notion of a university career for one of their numbers would have seemed up to that time foreign, if not fantastic.[1437]

Soon after this, Lloyd George faced trouble from an unexpected source, the police! In September 1913, a trade union for police officers had been formed, the National Union of Police and Prison Officers (NUPPO). Commissioner of the Police of the Metropolis, Sir Edward Henry, responded that December by issuing an official police order banning the union and threatening instant dismissal to anyone found to be associated with it. But the new union appealed to the demoralised 'rank and file', who, even after 20 years' service, often earned less than unskilled labourers, coping with large amounts of unpaid overtime and almost all leave cancelled, and membership rapidly increased. By August 1918, NUPPO claimed a membership of 10,000 and soon 12,000 out of an overall strength of 20,000 in the Metropolitan Police. Police Constable (PC) Tommy Thiel, a prominent member of the force and a NUPPO organiser, was dismissed on 25 August for "grave breach of discipline in taking part in the management and being a member of an unauthorised association", and that was the catalyst for a strike.

The executive of NUPPO demanded a pay increase, improved war bonuses, extension of pension rights to include policemen's widows, a shortening of the pension entitlement period, and an allowance for school-aged children. The most significant issue was that NUPPO be officially recognised as the representative of the police workers. NUPPO informed the authorities that, unless their demands were met by midnight on the 29 August, they would call a strike. The swiftness of the strike and the solidarity of the men shocked the government, catching it off guard. By the next day, 30 August, up

---

[1437] Fisher, p114.

to 12,000 men were on strike, over half the entire complement of men in the Metropolitan Police. The government deployed troops at key points across the capital in response and its priority was to end the strike. Lloyd George, who had been in France when the strike started, called a meeting at noon on 31 August with the executive of NUPPO, and the strike was settled that same day. In a statement, Home Secretary George Cave[1438] said:

> In regard to the Police Union, the Prime Minister said to the deputation of Policemen who saw him that he could not in war time sanction recognition of a Police Union. He pointed out that the trouble in Russia had to a great extent risen from the existence of a union or a committee among the soldiers. He thought the police were a semi-military force, and that to a great extent the same conditions applied to them, and he would not have a repetition in this country of what had happened in Russia.[1439]

Just before 2.00 pm the meeting concluded, and at 5.00 pm the terms of the settlement were put to a mass meeting of members. These were enthusiastically accepted, and at 6.00 pm the executive committee returned to Downing Street to tell the Prime Minister of its acceptance. The terms of the settlement included an increase for all ranks of 13 shillings [65p] per week in pensionable pay, raising the minimum to 43 shillings [£2.15]. The right to a pension was reduced from 30 years' service to 26 years' service, and widows were awarded a pension of ten shillings [50p]. A war bonus of 12 shillings [60p] per week was granted, and a grant of two shillings and sixpence [12 ½p] for each child of school age was given.

PC Thiel was reinstated the same evening, while Sir Edward Henry resigned, feeling let down both by his men and by the government. The strike was over, and Lloyd George was given the credit he deserved for this, the Police review stating: "The strike has been settled with promptitude and a decision which are in the sharpest contrast with the dilatoriness and procrastination out of which it directly arose. For that the police have to thank the Prime Minister."[1440] Sylvia Pankhurst was moved to write in the 7 September issue of her Marxist paper *Workers' Dreadnought*: "Spirit of Petrograd! The London police on strike!… After that, anything may happen! Not the army, but the police force is the power which quells political and industrial uprisings and maintains the established fabric of British society."

By October, several other police forces around the country had been granted pay increases. An immediate consequence of the strike was the increase in union membership, which jumped from 10,000 in August to a claimed, but probably exaggerated, figure of 50,000 by November 1918. As far as union recognition was concerned, Lloyd George had stated that he "could not in war time sanction recognition of a Police Union", but the mere fact that he had met, and settled the dispute, with the union leaders was viewed by them as *de facto* recognition of the union. This ensured that trouble

[1438] George Cave (1856-1928), Tory Home Secretary, 11 December 1916–14 January 1919.

[1439] https://www.policeoracle.com/news/1918-strikes-I-rang-Scotland-Yard-and-told-them-there-is-likely-to-be-trouble_96966.html. Retrieved 7 February 2020.

[1440] Ibid.

brewed.

Having been caught off guard by the first strike, the government used the breathing space created by the settlement to prepare for the next round. On 3 September, General Nevil Macready was appointed Commissioner of Police of the Metropolis and he used the ensuing months to get ready. He immediately began reorganising the command structure of the police. As far as Macready was concerned, the days of the NUPPO were numbered. Militants were isolated, moderates won over, and a number of partial reforms introduced. Macready did nothing to encourage talks with the union. He refused to recognise both James Marston, the president of NUPPO, and Jack Hayes, the general secretary. As far as Macready was concerned, the police had had a grievance that was now settled, and NUPPO remained an unofficial body; therefore, they were not to be dealt with. He created a police council, the Metropolitan Federation Board, which held its first meeting on 17 October 1918. This representative body consisted of a committee of one inspector, five sergeants and 26 constables, which meant that one delegate was being appointed by secret ballot for each division irrespective of ranks. In addition, there were *ex officio* members of NUPPO.

A committee under the chairmanship of Lord Desborough[1441] was also convened to look at pay and conditions of all forces throughout England and Wales. One of the things the committee highlighted was the inconsistency in police pay, there being no uniform pay structure. The Desborough Committee cited a dozen examples that showed the police were paid less than menial labour occupations, six of which paid higher than the Metropolitan Police. Lord Desborough was, therefore, quite sympathetic to the plight of the ordinary constable regarding pay and, consequently, recommended comparatively generous increases. The government announced substantial pay increases on 30 May 1919.

By the end of 1918, and into 1919, it seemed that all the unions, large and small, were active in disputes throughout Britain. The government could not afford the possibility of the police aligning themselves with another union, or the TUC. It thus interpreted labour discontent, including the police, as a sign of disloyalty and was determined that it would not be caught out again. On 1 April 1919, PC William Spackman[1442] of the Metropolitan Police was brought before the Disciplinary Committee for "gross insubordination" and effectively sacked for putting up a notice, proclaiming 'All Out', in a police station, urging officers to boycott elections to the Representative Board and attempting to provoke strike action. On 4 May, a mass meeting was held in Trafalgar Square to protest against the "barbarous punishment meted out to Constable Spackman." Senior officers and members of the government had been looking to crush the renewed militancy from the start, and this was the excuse they had been seeking.

The introduction in July of the bill for the Police Act of 1919 signalled the death knell of NUPPO. Under the bill, NUPPO was outlawed as a representative body for the police and forbade police officers from belonging to a trade union. NUPPO had no option but to fight or fold, and it chose to

1441 William H. Grenfell, Baron Desborough (1855-1945).

1442 William John Spackman, Warrant No. 96376. Joined on 30 November 1908, dismissed on 4 April 1919. Last posted to X Division as a PC, died in 1926. Not known to be a relative of the author.

fight. This time, however, it was they who misread the mood of the men when it called for another strike. The second strike started on 31 July in London, spreading to other English and Welsh provincial forces, particularly Liverpool, Birkenhead and Birmingham, lasting until 3 August. It was a disaster. Out of a force of 18,200 men in the Metropolitan Police, only 1,156 participated in the strike, together with 58 City of London men, all of whom were instantly dismissed. The strike was crushed, and with it the NUPPO. The sacked men were never reinstated. The Police Act, receiving royal assent on 15 August 1919, made it illegal for police and prison officers to belong to a trade union as well as forbidding them from taking industrial action, the Police Federation being established to deal with employment grievances and provide representation to police officers.

To return to September 1918, that month Lloyd George faced a crisis of a different, more personal kind. On 11 September, he travelled to Manchester, accompanied by Margaret, Olwen and Megan. The plan was that he was to make a speech in the city, setting the tone for a possible autumn election, then go on a short tour of the North West. Fate was to decree otherwise. On arrival at London Road train station, he was greeted by the Lord Mayor, Sir Alexander Porter, and driven in an open carriage from there to the neo-gothic Town Hall on Albert Square. Lloyd George was riding high on the news of recent Allied military successes, and along Piccadilly and Deansgate the crowds of cheering female munitions workers and soldiers home on furlough had been three deep and the 'turmoil in the streets' so great that it had taken Lloyd George nearly an hour–in the rain–to reach Albert Square.[1443] At the Town Hall, he received addresses of welcome from the leaders of the Syrian, Armenian and Jewish communities, to each of whom he responded with an appropriate reply.

The next morning, he was driven, again through densely packed, cheering, 'hero-worshipping' crowds, to the Hippodrome on Oxford Street, where he was to receive the freedom of his native city in the presence of 3,000 people, including many local MPs and other dignitaries. He responded with a 90-minute speech, which he began by referencing his own personal link with the city: "It is over half a century ago that I became a citizen of Manchester. I subsequently lost that privilege, through circumstances over which I had no control, but I am deeply grateful–I am proud–that the lord mayor and corporation of Manchester, in the name of the citizens of Manchester, have restored to me my lost citizenship in no mean city…"[1444]

After this he attended a civic luncheon in the Midland Hotel, facing St Peter's Square, where he made a shorter speech, then tea at the Constitutional Club, a recognition that he was leading a coalition Government, then a meeting with the local Welsh community in Albert Hall, the large Methodist assembly room close to the Town Hall, to whom he spoke in Welsh. He was due that evening to attend a dinner at the Reform Club, but shortly beforehand he felt ill, collapsed and had to take to his bed at the Town Hall. His illness was diagnosed as influenza, which must have been developing throughout the day. He spent the next nine days confined to a sickbed in the Town Hall, too ill to

---

1443 *Manchester Guardian*, 12 September 1918; Quoted in M. Honigsbaum, *Living with Enza: The Forgotten Story of Britain and the Great Flu Pandemic of 1918*, 2009, London, Palgrave Macmillan, p65. Manchester London Road train station was renamed Manchester Piccadilly in 1960.

1444 Quoted in Grigg, *War Leader*, p591.

move and with a respirator to aid his breathing. His doctor was the eminent ENT specialist and local Liberal, Sir William Milligan:

> He [Lloyd George] would not see a doctor, but as Sir William Milligan was attending a member of the Prime Minister's family for an influenzal "throat," he was introduced into the sick room to report, and, being there, the invalid was persuaded to submit to treatment by him for a similar ailment. Subsequently the physician accompanied his patient to London, and, at a later date, to international conferences at Spa and Paris.[1445]

Margaret stayed on, with their daughters, though they both became ill with 'colds'. Bulletins issued to the press considerably downplayed the severity of the Prime Minister's condition for fear of alarming the British public and presenting the Germans with a propaganda coup. But Hankey, whom Lloyd George had sent on leave on 5 September, noted afterwards that he had been "very seriously ill" and that his valet, George Newnham, had said it was "touch and go".[1446] Lloyd George's room was at the front of the Town Hall, from where he could just make out the tops of the plane trees lining Albert Square and, below them, the statue of John Bright dripping with constant rain. To allow his patient complete rest, Milligan ordered that barriers be erected in the Square and that traffic be diverted in order to avoid the stricken man being disturbed by the clanking of the trams. Only on the sixth day was Lloyd George able to sit up in bed and receive visitors, including his friend, C. P. Scott. He finally left Manchester around noon on 21 September, still wearing a respirator, and with Milligan in attendance, travelling in a private saloon car attached to the front of the London Express. Megan accompanied him, while Margaret returned to Criccieth with Olwen.

On Lloyd George's arrival at Euston, the *Manchester Guardian*'s London correspondent spotted him on the platform, catching a brief glimpse of "the familiar figure in the unfamiliar garb of a greatcoat, a large white muffler, and a soft hat turned down over the face."[1447] From the station, his official car took him to Downing Street, but he did not preside over any meetings, instead quickly departing for a working convalescence at Danny House, an impressive Elizabethan red brick mansion near Hurstpierpoint in West Sussex, set in eight acres of gardens at the foot of the South Downs within an historic parkland of 400 acres. This was rented to him by his friend George Riddell. From there, he wrote to Margaret on 27 September: "I am crawling upward but have not yet recovered strength. Unfortunately–or fortunately–things are moving so rapidly I cannot keep off affairs of State. Someone here every day."[1448]

What he did not know was that Margaret had also succumbed to illness and was confined to bed in Bryn Awelon. Characteristically, "she hid her illness from her husband so that he would not affect his own recovery by worrying about her, and he was distressed when he learned about it later in a

---

1445 Sir William Milligan (1864-1929). Obituary in *British Medical Journal*, 1(3600), 4 January 1930, p48; https://www.ncbi.nlm.nih.gov/pmc/articles/PMC2313066/?page=2. Retrieved 22 October 2019.

1446 Letter of Hankey to Lady Hankey, 22 September 1918: Quoted in Roskill, *Hankey*, Volume I, p604. George Newnham (1865-1954).

1447 *Manchester Guardian*, 23 September 1918; Quoted in Honigsbaum, p69.

1448 Quoted in Grigg, *War Leader*, p594.

newspaper report."[1449] Fortunately, she too made a full recovery in time. Lloyd George still, however, continued to cancel some public appointments 'under medical advice', and when he travelled to Paris on 4 October Milligan accompanied him. Early that morning he wrote to Margaret:

> I am off by the 8 train from Charing X. Sir William Milligan insists on accompanying me. My temperature is still very low & my pulse too feeble…
>
> I had my first Cabinet yesterday & it tired me out so that I am not yet fit for much work. It is a pity that the Paris journey could not be put off until next week… I propose staying at Versailles… more reposeful than a Paris hotel.[1450]

Lloyd George, then aged 55, survived, but millions of others were not so lucky. In John Griggs's cogent analysis:

> Lloyd George combined enormous vitality with a strong streak of hypochondria, for which allowance must always be made. He hated illness, in himself and others, and was never one to make light of it. All the same, the evidence leaves little room for doubt that his medical experience in the latter half of September 1918 was one of the worst of his life. He seems to have been very acutely, perhaps critically, ill at a time of mounting crisis in the world, when he needed to be in full vigour to tackle a situation that took him by surprise.[1451]

At 6.00 pm on 5 October, something unprecedented took place: "the control of a modern popular newspaper passed from private ownership into the hands of the prime minister of the day."[1452] This involved Lloyd George, his eyes on the looming general election, purchasing the *Daily Chronicle*, which had a circulation of some 800,000 by 1915, a level it maintained for the duration of the war. As early as 27 April 1917, in a speech at the Guildhall on being admitted to the Freedom of the City of London, Lloyd George had stated that he hoped that when "the war is over and reconstruction begins, I hope and trust and pray that we are not going to dive into the pigeon-holes of any party for dust-laden precedents and programmes."[1453] However, on 7 October the same year, George Riddell had warned Lloyd George that that was exactly what was being contemplated, that the Liberals and Tories were already jockeying for position:

> When one party or the other would be able to seize the reins of power. Also that *they reckoned on the fact that he had no party*. I said 'They hope to see you suspended between earth and heaven like

[1449] Hague, p336.
[1450] Quoted in Grigg, *War Leader*, p594.
[1451] Ibid., p595.
[1452] McEwen, *Acquisition*, p127.
[1453] Lloyd George, *Great Crusade*, p135.

> Mahomet's coffin.' LG [sic] agreed, but added, 'They will find that I am not in my coffin yet. They will have to reckon with me when the time comes.'[1454]

Owned by Frank Lloyd, the *Daily Chronicle* had steered a middle course politically, though generally favourable to Lloyd George. The editor, Robert Donald, had however become increasingly critical of the government through 1918–especially since the 'Maurice Affair' in May–the same period in which Lloyd George had shown an increasing interest in acquiring the paper. Henry Dalziel again aided Lloyd George in the negotiations. On 1 October, Riddell recorded: "The *Daily Chronicle* purchase has been completed. LG [sic] is to have full control of the editorial policy through Sir H. Dalziel, who will in effect be his agent. The experiment will be interesting."[1455] Donald departed immediately, complaining that Lloyd George was trying to "corner public opinion", Ernest Perris, the existing news editor, replacing him. The paper came at a cost: £1.60m [£116.19m in 2025], three-quarters to be paid in cash, with the remainder in debentures held by the Lloyd family.[1456]

Meanwhile, the German offensive had stalled. By the end of May, the American Expeditionary Force under General John Pershing had 650,000 troops in France, with 10,000 more arriving each day. Although by September its troops still stood on French and Belgian soil, the German Army had used up its last reserves, was in retreat and steadily shrinking in numbers, further weakening its resolve. On 29 September, the day the Hindenburg Line was finally breached at the St Quentin Canal, the situation had improved for the Allies to such an extent that George Riddell could record: "A very cheerful day, notwithstanding the horrible weather. News of advance in the West arriving all day. The P.M. [sic] full of glee. On the arrival of the message he began to dance a hornpipe."[1457] The news must indeed have cheered the still weak Lloyd George, aiding his recovery.

On the same day, the German Supreme Army Command informed Kaiser Wilhelm and the Chancellor, Georg von Hertling, at Imperial Army Headquarters at Spa in still occupied Belgium, that the military situation facing Germany was hopeless. Quartermaster General Erich Ludendorff, fearing an imminent Allied breakthrough, stated that he could not guarantee that the front would hold for another two hours and demanded a request be sent to the Entente Powers for an immediate ceasefire. In addition, he recommended the acceptance of the main demands of President Wilson's 'Fourteen Points', including putting the Imperial Government on a democratic footing in the hope of obtaining more favourable peace terms. This enabled him to save the face of the Imperial German Army and put the responsibility for the capitulation and its consequences squarely into the hands of the democratic parties and the parliament.[1458] He expressed his view to his staff officers on 1 October: "They now must lie on the bed that they've made for us."

---

1454 Riddell, *Diaries*, 1986, p201. Emphasis added. The medieval fable of the Prophet's coffin being suspended by lodestones between heaven and earth, is a European invention, seemingly unknown to Islamic writers.

1455 Riddell, *Diaries*, 1986, p240.

1456 McEwen, *Acquisition*, p142. Lloyd George bought out Dalziel's interest in 1922.

1457 Riddell, *War Diary*, p363.

1458 See W. Deist, Trans. E.J. Feuchtwanger, *The Military Collapse of the German Empire: The Reality Behind the Stab-in-the-Back Myth*, *War in History,* 3, 2, April 1996, p186-207.

On 3 October, the liberal Prince Maximilian of Baden[1459] was appointed as Chancellor, replacing Georg von Hertling in order to negotiate an armistice. After long conversations with the Kaiser, and evaluations of the political and military situations in the Reich, the same evening, the new German government sent a message to President Wilson to negotiate terms on the basis of a recent speech of his and the earlier declared 'Fourteen Points'. In his subsequent three diplomatic notes between 8-23 October, Wilson's allusions "failed to convey the idea that the Kaiser's abdication was an essential condition for peace. The leading statesmen of the Reich were not yet ready to contemplate such a monstrous possibility."[1460]

On 5 October, a conference was held in Paris between Lloyd George, Clemenceau and Orlando. They agreed that an armistice with Germany could only be concluded if eight points were fulfilled: this included the total evacuation of Belgium, France and Alsace-Lorraine, the retreat of the German Armies behind the Rhine, and the cessation of submarine warfare. They reacted to the news of the German communiqué to Wilson with suspicion. Having not been consulted, they had entirely justifiable fears that the Americans would try to dictate peace terms without taking the other Allies sacrifices and concerns into full account. For now, however, Wilson maintained solidarity with his Allies, replying that no arrangements would be entered into unless they could guarantee the "present military supremacy" of the Allied Armies in the field, and that no armistice would be considered "as long as the armed forces of Germany continue the illegal and inhumane processes which they still persist in."[1461]

As Lloyd George wrote later, by 9 October:

> It was clear that the end was now in sight. It was no less clear that we must move with the utmost care at this critical juncture, making sure of our footing at every stride, lest by a false step we should imperil the full harvest of our long effort. We wanted to make a clean finish to the War, in such a manner that its lesson would be driven home and there would be no danger of it breaking out afresh.[1462]

In Britain, regular meetings of the Cabinet were held in the Great Hall of Danny House, and it was here, on 13 October 1918, that the terms of the armistice to be offered to Germany were decided, and authority given to President Wilson to negotiate the armistice. It was during the night of 12 October, after Lloyd George had gone to bed, Riddell recorded:

> The German reply to President Wilson's Note came over the telephone from Downing Street. It was written down and taken to LG [sic] by [Philip] Kerr, who soon returned saying, "There

---

[1459] Maximilian von Baden (1867-1929), Chancellor of Germany, 3 October–9 November 1918.

[1460] F. Czernin, *Versailles, 1919: The Forces, Events, And Personalities That Shaped The Treaty*, 1964, New York, G.P. Putnam, p7.

[1461] Quoted in Lloyd, p217.

[1462] Lloyd George, *War Memoirs*, Vol.II, p1959.

> is awful language going on upstairs, I can tell you! He thinks that the Allies are now in a devil of a mess. Wilson has promised them an armistice."[1463]

The news angered and unsettled the Prime Minister:

> The next morning he was still 'declaiming against Wilson's action' while climbing 'the hill' [Wolstonbury Hill] with Riddell and Lord Reading. Nonetheless, after lunch, a 'conference' was held in the Great Hall, which a plaque still commemorates: 'In this room a meeting of the Imperial War Cabinet was held on the 13th October 1918 at which the following were present:- Mr. Lloyd George, Mr. Bonar Law, Mr. A. J. Balfour, Viscount Milner, The Earl of Reading, Mr. W. S. Churchill, Admiral Sir R. Wemyss, General Sir Henry Wilson, Lt.-Col. Sir M. P. A. Hankey, Mr. Philip Kerr. A cable was sent to President Wilson authorising him to proceed with negotiations for an Armistice with Germany.' In actual fact the Imperial War Cabinet had disbanded in August, nor was the 'conference' a formal meeting of the War Cabinet, of which only L.G. and Bonar Law were members–indeed, absent members later complained that vital decisions were taken there without them.[1464]

That is as may be, but this meeting of these ten men was one of those hinges upon which history turns, and tragically it was Lloyd George's assessment of the future that was the correct one:

> [T]he conference in the Great Hall was momentous. Crucially, his colleagues rejected the P.M.'s fears that unless the German Fatherland was invaded, and German towns bombarded, there would be no lasting 'humiliation' of Prussian Militarism, such as Rome inflicted on Carthage after the second Punic War–*delenda est Carthago.* and without that, L.G. argued, 'In a short time the Germans would say that these miserable democrats had taken charge [the Kaiser having fled] and had become panic-stricken, and the military party would get into power again', as indeed it did in 1932, in fruitful alliance with Herr Hitler and his National Socialists.[1465]

Crucially, the other members present seemed to believe in the 'impossibility' of a future resumption of hostilities, a piece of wishful thinking, perhaps understandable after four years of gruelling warfare, that would cost Europe and the wider world dearly only two decades later:

> But the P.M.'s colleagues argued that Wilson's Fourteen Points would require Germany to evacuate all occupied territory, surrender its colonies, cede Alsace-Lorraine to France and German Poland to 'an independent Polish state'. Moreover, the peoples of the Austro-Hungarian Empire would enjoy 'self-determination' and the Turkish Empire be dissolved. So the 'War Cabinet' sent President Wilson a cable merely requiring that, before any armistice, Germany must accept Peace terms that 'in the opinion of experts', naval as well as Military,

1463 Riddell, *Diaries*, 1986, p241.
1464 C. and J. Brent, *Danny House: A Sussex Mansion Through Seven Centuries*, 2013, Andover, Phillimore, p127.
1465 Ibid., p127.

> 'would make the resumption of hostilities by the Central Powers impossible'. The cable also sought clarification of Point Two–'absolute freedom of navigation upon the seas... alike in peace and in war'–conceivably a threat to Britain's maritime supremacy. So ended the fateful conference...[1466]

As a precondition for negotiations, on 23 October, Wilson demanded the retreat of Germany from all occupied territories, the cessation of submarine activities and the Kaiser's abdication. On 26 October, Ludendorff was replaced by General Wilhelm Groener. On 5 November, the Allies agreed to enter into negotiations for a truce, now also demanding reparation payments. The latest note from Wilson was received in Berlin on 6 November. That same day, the delegation led by Matthias Erzberger[1467] departed for France. At noon on 9 November 1918[1468], with Germany fast descending into chaos and revolution, the abdication of Kaiser Wilhelm was belatedly announced, and the next morning he went into exile in the neutral Netherlands, later settling at Doorn, where he remained for the rest of his life.[1469] The same day, Max von Baden unconstitutionally handed over the office of Chancellor to Friedrich Ebert[1470], a Social Democrat. Ebert's SPD and Erzberger's Catholic Centre Party had enjoyed an uneasy relationship with the Imperial government since Bismarck's era. They were well represented in the Reichstag, which had little power over the government, and had been calling for a negotiated peace since 1917. Their prominence in the forthcoming peace negotiations would cause the new Weimar Republic to lack legitimacy in right-wing and militarist eyes.

Two days later, the Armistice was signed at 5.12 am in railway carriage No. 2419D in a siding in the forest of Compiègne[1471], famously coming into effect on 'the eleventh hour of the eleventh day of the eleventh month'. This now-iconic formula was not what was originally intended, as related by Anglican historian Robert Beaken:

> Lloyd George had instructed Admiral Sir Rosslyn Wemyss, the British representative at the Armistice negotiations at Compiègne, to arrange that the Armistice should commence at 2.30 p.m., in order that he might announce it in the House of Commons between 2.45 p.m. and 3 p.m., and, presumably, make political capital of the news.

---

1466 Ibid., p127-128.

1467 Matthias Erzberger (1875-1921), Catholic Centre Party MP, Minister without Portfolio, November 1918–June 1919, Reich Minister of Finance, June 1919–March 1920, Vice-Chancellor, June–October 1919.

1468 This date resonated through the rest of 20th Century German history: Hitler's failed coup known as the 'Beer Hall Putsch' in Munich, 1923; *Kristallnacht* ('Crystal Night') the pogrom against Jews throughout Nazi Germany, 1938; the fall of the Berlin Wall, 1989, all took place on this date.

1469 Plans to extradite him as a war criminal–*Clemenceau's initiative, not Lloyd George's*–failed due to the Dutch Government's refusal of such a request on 23 January 1920. Lloyd George thought that fair proceedings in which the rights of the defence would be sufficiently guaranteed would help in further developing international criminal law, suggesting inviting the new German Republic to participate in the tribunal that would be formed, adding: "I have no doubt she will send men, in her present state, who will judge the ex-Kaiser very impartially." Lloyd George, *The Truth About The Peace Treaties*, Vol.I, p100. P. Mevis and J. M. Reijntjes, *Hang the Kaiser! But for What, and Would It Be Justice?*, *Erasmus Law Review*, 2, 2014, p98-107.

1470 Friedrich Ebert (1871-1925), SPD Leader, 1913-1919, Chancellor of Germany, 9 November 1918–13 February 1919, first President, 11 February 1919 until his death on 28 February 1925.

1471 See Colonel Codevelle, *Armistice 1918: The Signing of the Armistice in the Forest Glade of Compiègne*, c.1959, Compiègne, Friends of the Armistice of Compiègne.

> Wemyss exceeded his orders: he felt that more lives might be lost if the war dragged on for even a few hours longer than was absolutely necessary; and the poetry of hostilities coming to a close at the 11th hour of the 11th day of the 11th month appealed strongly to him.
>
> The French and the Germans agreed to Wemyss's suggestion of 11 a.m., and the Armistice was signed at 5.10 a.m. The French agreed to transmit the news to the Allied front line.
>
> Wemyss hurried back to Paris, and, fearing Lloyd George's reaction to his initiative, he bypassed the Prime Minister and managed to telephone King George V at Buckingham Palace. The King and his staff spent the next few hours telephoning the news of the Armistice to the government and military and naval authorities.[1472]

After the signing, Marshal Foch travelled to Paris to personally present Clemenceau with the papers. On meeting, he said to the Prime Minister prophetically: "My work is finished. Your work begins."[1473] The slaughter was finally over, though men continued to be uselessly killed right up to–and in some cases, after–the very last minute: there were 10,944 casualties, of whom 2,738 men died, on the last day of the war. But finally the incessant, raging noise of the guns ceased: universally, men were stunned by the contrasting silence that fell over the ravaged battlefields, that and the fact that they could at last stand upright, their heads above the parapet, without fear of snipers. Overall, it had been the deadliest conflict in history until that time, with some 9,750,000 combatants and around 7,740,000 civilians dead as a direct result of the war. At least 3,000,000 more subsequently died of malnutrition, disease and in genocides. The British Empire alone lost 1,104,890 combatants killed in action: little wonder the people spoke of a 'lost generation'.

In London, around 10.30 am, a crowd started forming at Downing Street, as newspapers and newsboys began spreading the word. Lloyd George appeared outside No. 10 about five minutes before the Armistice was due to begin, and the crowd sang 'For He's a Jolly Good Fellow'. On his announcement that "At 11 o'clock this morning the war will be over," wild cheering ensued, and hats were thrown in the air and into the garden of 10 Downing Street.[1474] It was probably the high point of his life. Interestingly, despite all the excitement, he kept a prearranged 1.30pm lunch appointment at No. 10 with Dr Chaim Weizmann, the Zionist leader, who recorded: "I found the Prime Minister reading the Psalms; he was moved to the depths of his soul and was, indeed, near to tears…"[1475] Later that day, after being borne on the shoulders of the crowd, he announced the terms in the House of Commons, concluding: "Those are the conditions of the Armistice. *Thus at eleven o'clock this morning came to an end the cruellest and most terrible War that has ever scourged mankind. I hope we may say that thus, this*

---

1472 https://www.churchtimes.co.uk/articles/2015/6-november/features/features/lest-we-forget. Retrieved 30 November 2023. Unjustly, Lloyd George was most displeased with Wemyss; see Lady W. Wemyss, *The Life And Letters Of Lord Wester Wemyss*, 1935, London, Eyre and Spottiswoode, p396-397.

1473 Sir G. Aston, *The Biography Of The Late Marshal Foch*, 1932, London, Hutchinson, p279.

1474 At noon at Shrewsbury, one of the most famous and tragic moments of Armistice Day occurred, when as the church bells were ringing in celebration, a telegram arrived to tell poet Wilfred Owen's parents that their son had been killed in action at the Oise-Sambre Canal in Northern France on 4 November, aged 25.

1475 Chaim Weizmann (1874-1952), Russian-born biochemist, President of the World Zionist Organization, 1920-1931 and 1935-1946, first President of Israel, 1949-1952. C. Weizmann, *Trial And Error*, 1949, London, Hamish Hamilton, p298.

*fateful morning, came to an end all wars.*"[1476]

In an echo of his surprise at the start of the war–along with that of virtually everyone–Lloyd George was surprised by the suddenness of its end. On 12 November, the day after the signing of the Armistice, Paul Cambon, the French ambassador in London, had an interview with Lloyd George: "The Prime Minister said that he had never hoped for such a rapid solution nor envisaged such a complete collapse of German power."[1477] However, there was one fatal flaw in the Armistice terms which, though it did not become apparent until years later, ticked away in the heart of Europe like a time-bomb. As Margaret MacMillan perceptively notes:

> The great majority of Germans never experienced their country's defeat at first hand. Except in the Rhineland, they did not see occupying troops. The Allies did not march in triumph into Berlin, as the Germans had done in Paris in 1871. In 1918 German soldiers marched home in good order, with crowds cheering their way; in Berlin, Friedrich Ebert, the new president, greeted them with 'no enemy has conquered you!'[1478]

The real news about what was happening at the Western Front having been hidden from most Germans, the sudden collapse and surrender had been traumatic. The myth quickly grew that the Fatherland had betrayed the Imperial German Army still bravely fighting on the foreign soil of Belgium and France, that the Socialists, Marxists, Jews and Slavs back home had 'stabbed them in the back.' It was false, but pernicious, fanned by ultra-conservative elements. In a military hospital at Pasewalk, in Pomerania to the northeast of Berlin, a 29-year-old *Gefreiter* (Lance Corporal) of the Bavarian 'List Regiment' recovering from temporary blindness sustained in a British mustard gas attack on the night of 13-14 October south of Ypres, heard the devastating news from a pastor on 10 November: Adolf Hitler would soon call what had happened "the greatest villainy of the century" and henceforth dedicate himself to "liberating" Germany and righting the "betrayal" of 1918.[1479]

On 5 November, six days before the Armistice but when the outcome was assured, Lloyd George demanded of the King that an early general election be held. On 6 and 12 November, meetings were held in the House of Lloyd George's Liberal supporters, and the Coalition Government manifesto was carried with acclamation, Lloyd George pledging to secure "habitations fit for the heroes who have won the war", which became known as the 'homes fit for heroes' speech. On 14 November, at a meeting of the party whips, at which Christopher Addison represented the Liberal ministers and Laming Worthington-Evans[1480] the Unionists, it was agreed to issue a statement two days later expressing confidence in the Prime Minister and the Coalition Government. On the same day, 14 November, it was duly announced that Parliament, sitting since 1910 and extended by emergency

---

1476 https://hansard.parliament.uk/commons/1918-11-11/debates/767d1ab4-9229-411b-a1cf-cdc109465a15/ArmisticeWithGermany. Retrieved 9 March 2020. Emphasis added.
1477 Quoted in MacMillan, *Peacemakers*, p168.
1478 MacMillan, *Peacemakers*, p168.
1479 A. Hitler, *Mein Kampf*, (1925) 1989, London, Trans. R. Manheim, Hutchinson, p183.
1480 Sir Laming Worthington-Evans (1868-1931), Tory MP for Colchester, 1910-1929, Minister of Blockade, 18 July 1918–10 July 1919.

wartime action, would be dissolved on 25 November, with elections due on Saturday 14 December, the first general election to include on a single day all eligible UK voters, although the vote count was delayed until 28 December so that the ballots cast by soldiers serving overseas could be included.

This 'Khaki Election' had a unique background. Following confidential negotiations over the previous summer, it had been agreed that certain candidates were to be offered the support of the Prime Minister and the Tory leader Bonar Law at the next general election. To these 545, candidate's letters–dated 20 November–were sent, indicating the government's endorsement of their candidacy. 159 Liberal, 364 Conservative, 20 National Democratic and Labour, and two Coalition Labour candidates received such letters. 229 Liberal candidates were denied them. Asquith disparagingly termed the letters 'coupons', using the jargon of rationing with which people were familiar in the context of wartime shortages, leading to it being called the 'Coupon Election'.

Primarily, the election was not fought over what peace terms should be reached to with Germany, although naturally this played some role. More important was the voters' evaluation of Lloyd George in terms of what he had accomplished so far and what he promised for the future. On 24 November, he launched his electoral campaign by giving a rousing speech in the Grand Theatre, Lichfield Street, Wolverhampton. The recent Armistice meant he was 'the man who won the war', a national hero. On his arrival at 2 pm the previous day at Low Level Station, accompanied by his wife Margaret and his private secretary, hundreds of people had gathered at the entrance to cheer him on, while others pushed their way onto the platform to get as close as possible to their hero. The following morning at 11.00 am, Lloyd George rose in front of a packed Grand Theatre to set out his debt of gratitude to those who had aided the war effort, as well as his vision for Britain's future, in one of the greatest speeches in British political history:

> [W]e have just emerged from a great peril, we have emerged triumphantly. The greatness of the peril we can hardly conceive, and it will take time for me to fully appreciate its vastness. The greatness of the triumph we cannot estimate now…
>
> As to our sailors nothing so great in the record of the British Navy has ever before been attained. Never has its men and its leaders shown greater skills, greater resources, greater daring, greater efficiency and higher qualifications of seamanship…
>
> Today the freedom of the world owes everything to the daring, to the tenacity and to the valour of the men of the British Navy.
>
> And as to our soldiers it is difficult to talk about them. The dauntless courage which they have displayed during the last four and half years, the human courage, the human endurance. Never in the history of the world has there been such a trial of continuous tests, and the heroism of the British soldiers stood it to the very last hour…
>
> To this triumph all classes of the people have contributed. There has been no distinction of rank, no difference of creed or faith, of state or condition of life. All opinions, all ranks, all creeds, all faiths have contributed to this memorable sacrifice to save the world. It with this knowledge, that we must approach the next problem…

The stateliest homes on earth today are often the most desolate at this hour. On the other hand, the country realises in a way that it never did before, how much it owes to the citizens who dwell in the humblest of homes.

We sent millions of them thronging to the flag… Make no mistake about it… had it not been for those millions of men that came forward from humble homes to lay their lives on the altar of their country, the British Empire might have been swept away, and at this moment we might have been cowering at the foot of the most tyrannical masters that ever bullied the world.

This knowledge, of a common sacrifice, of a common patriotism, of common brotherhood, of suffering and of effort is sinking deep into the minds of the people of this country; and it is in this knowledge that we approach the next great field in front of us.

We all feel that these heroic men have made a new world possible, and they are entitled to full share of its gladness.

There is, as has never been witnessed before, a new comradeship of classes. I am glad of it, and I am glad that we are approaching the new problem in the spirit of comradeship… *Our work is not over yet–the work of the nation, the work of the people, the work of those who sacrificed. Let us work together first. This the appeal that I am making today. What is our task? To make Britain a fit country for heroes to live in.*

*I am not using the word heroes in the spirit of boastfulness, but in the humble recognition of facts. I cannot think what these men have gone through. I cannot think of it. I have been there at the door of the furnace and that is nothing. I have seen them march into the furnace. Thank God there are millions who have come back.*

*We want England to be fit for such men to live in. There is no time to waste. I want us to take advantage of this new spirit. [Don't let us waste this victory merely in ringing joybells.]*

The Great War has been like a gigantic star shell, illuminating all over the land, illuminating all the dark places, and we have places in the light that we have never seen before, and we mean to put these things right. There is another thing the great war has shown. The appalling waste of human material in this country… There is hardly one material placed by Providence in this country which is as much wasted as human life and human strength and human intellect–the most irreparable material of all.

Those in charge of the recruiting offices came to the conclusion that if the people of this country had lived under proper conditions–that is properly fed, properly housed, lived in healthy conditions that sustained life in its full vigour, then there would have been a million more men available who were fit to put in the army. There are millions that are below par.

You cannot bring up children in these conditions. There have been lives lost in this war, millions of men have been maimed, but believe me there are more lives being lost and maimed through the atrocious social conditions that prevail, than through the terrors of this war. Trade, commerce and industry all suffer through the absence of a vigorous community.

Let us deal with one point affecting housing conditions. Slums were not, and are not, intended for the men who have won this great war. They are not fit nurseries for the children…

The problem has got to be undertaken in a way that has never been undertaken before, as a great national charge and duty. It is too much to leave it to the municipality. Some of them are crippled by the restricted income which is placed at their disposal… the housing of the people must be a national concern, and must be undertaken as such.

What is the next point revealed by the great war? The enormous waste of the resources of our land. Britain is a very rich country as far as its soil is concerned, and yet we have been importing hundreds of millions of our supplies from abroad. I don't say you can grow here all that you require, but you can grow a larger proportion than you have grown in past years. We want a more intelligent agricultural policy. The land must be cultivated to its full capacity. That ought to be an essential feature of the new Britain.

During the last two years we made a special effort to increase the cultivation of the land… Under great difficulty, because thousands of our best agricultural labourers had gone to the front… and we had to increase cultivation of land with reduced labour. But in spite of this we increased the area of agriculture by four million acres. How was that done? By a great combined effort. Broad minded men, farmers and labourers, everybody concerned with the cultivation of the land–we got them to work together for that purpose, and in two years with reduced labour we brought the cultivation of England to where it was forty or fifty years ago. If we could do that with reduced labour, what could we do with the men back on the land. If we bring the population back to the land it relieves the pressures on the labour market, but still more it sustains the labour market…

A systematic effort must be made to bring the people back to the land. It is it a place to grow strong men. The touch of the soil invigorates and reinforces the people… It is an inspiring occupation. But it must be done systematically, intelligently. The principles of farming are better understood, and science has come into the farming industry like any other, and to increase capacity you must do it on scientific principles. You must have proper supplies of fertilisers which I contend the Government should be responsible for.

… There must be a scheme for re-settling returned soldiers and sailors… I do not say all soldiers will get back on to the land. The vast majority will prefer to return to their usual occupations… For those who desire to go on the land small-holdings should be provided for them, and they ought to be trained for them… There should be a special grant for the equipment of the holding… Whatever the size the grant may be for this purpose, it will be small compared to the cost of the war. For these heroic men the cost of the scheme must be provided. That is the least we can do to reward them.

I now come to the question which undoubtedly the war has demonstrated clearly as being of great importance. That is improved transportation is as essential as all other details. Your housing schemes have to be outside of the towns, as your only chance to get land is there. Otherwise you will develop another set of slums. We do not want that…

… You must pay good wages, this is essential in order to enable people to keep up their strength and to bring up their children. You must improve the conditions of the people. You cannot pay the enormous debt of this war unless you increase production all round.

For the last four or five years there has been no manufacturing in the world. It has been burned in the furnace of war, but the world is determined that these arrears shall be made up. There are new countries to be developed…

In spite of the enormous losses of the war, there is a natural increase in the numbers who are capable of productive purpose in this country. The first reason for this is there has been a complete arrest of emigration, and the second and more important reason is that you have a large number of women who for the first time have come into active productive work in our industries, and very excellent work they have done.

I believe it is possible to provide remuneration work for all. But it will take time to work out some of these plans I have laid down. There will necessarily be some dislocation of the labour market. What we have to take care of during the period of dislocation there is no privation.

That is why we want a new parliament at once to begin our plans. The difficulties of carrying it through are enormous. You cannot put it through without real support…

So you need a parliament that will take no heed of the criticism, either inside the House or in the press. You need to have a parliament that is determined to see the thing through…

The time has come when we must act courageously. The whole nation will join the in the prosperity. A prosperity in which only one class partakes is no prosperity at all.

The war has been won by the unity of all classes, by the sacrifices of every rank, in every condition of life. Patriotism is the common inheritance and virtue of all. So let us in these coming years show that Britain is not yet exhausted of it patriotism, and then you will see the affection for the old country well-up from the depth of our nature to fructify and enrich the land with the love of her children…[1481]

Following his speech–greeted by rapturous applause from the room of mainly Liberal supporters–he was given a reception at the Town Hall in North Street, where the Freedom of the Borough was bestowed on him, before he left Wolverhampton for London that evening.

In the event, Lloyd George's success during the war secured the premiership for him, as he won a massive majority in the election, winning 92.7% of the vote in Carnarvon Boroughs against an Independent candidate, Austin Harrison[1482], the disgruntled Liberal editor of the *English Review*, who campaigned on a pro-League of Nations, anti-conscription platform. Lloyd George did not even visit the constituency during the election period, while Harrison spoke at Llandudno, Conwy and Bangor. When, at Bangor, Harrison praised Lloyd George as "the greatest statesman we have", he was unsurprisingly challenged: "Then why do you oppose him?"[1483]

When Lloyd George had become the Prime Minister in December 1916, the Carnarvon Boroughs had become the first ever Welsh constituency to be represented by a serving Prime Minister. While all the other contributory districts of boroughs constituencies were abolished in the sweeping redistribution of 1918, the Carnarvon Boroughs, the seat of the Prime Minister, was allowed to continue in existence, and in fact remained until 1950. The constituency was, however, redefined, so

1481 https://www.expressandstar.com/news/politics/2018/11/23/a-fit-country-for-heroes-100-years-since-lloyd-georges-legendary-wolverhampton-speech/. Retrieved 4 February 2019. Emphasis added.

1482 Austin Harrison (1873-1928). A. Harrison, *My Contest With Mr. Lloyd George*, *English Review*, 28, January 1919, pp67-71. Lloyd George gained 13,993 votes to Harrison's 1,095, on a relatively low turnout of 63.4%.

1483 M. S. Vogeler, *Austin Harrison And The English Review*, 2008, Columbia, Mo., University of Missouri Press, p229; *North Wales Weekly News*, 19 December 1918.

that it included the then local government areas of the Municipal Boroughs of Bangor, Caernarvon, Conway, and Pwllheli; the Urban Districts of Criccieth, Llandudno, Llanfairfechan, and Penmaenmawr as well as the Lleyn Rural District.[1484]

Lloyd George's reputation now stood at its absolute zenith. Bonar Law, who was from a similarly modest provincial background, said "He can be Prime Minister for life if he likes."[1485] He told Sir Archibald Salvidge at the time of the Armistice: "Salvidge, I tell you we must never let the little man go. His way and ours lie side by side in the future. I want you to remember what I am saying now and act upon it, not only in this election but afterwards, when all the shouting has died away."[1486] Alas, he was not heeded. In a perhaps more nuanced analysis, the Earl of Crawford[1487], the Lord Privy Seal, wrote in his diary for 28 December 1918:

> The electoral process has been significant. Lloyd George's original campaign fell rather flat. He pulled himself together on realising he was being left high and dry on the shore. He revised his programme, or rather enlarged it by adding items about indemnities, aliens, punishment of the Kaiser, and pledges to end conscription. Then he got on to the wave again, and with an advancing tide has been borne to victory.[1488]

The Coalition won the election with a landslide victory, taking 525 of the 707 seats contested, but crucially–and ultimately, fatally–it was the Tories who were by far the biggest winners, with 382 seats, hugely outnumbering Lloyd George's pro-Coalition Liberals with 127 seats. Virtually all the Liberal MPs without coupons were defeated, party leader Asquith losing the seat he had held since 1886, though he returned to Parliament in the Paisley by-election of 12 February 1920. While most of the pro-Coalition Liberals were re-elected, Asquith's faction was reduced to just 36 seats and lost all their leaders from Parliament. Nine of these MPs subsequently joined the Coalition Liberal group. The remainder became bitter enemies of Lloyd George.

Indicative of the corrosive split in the Liberal Party was a letter written by Henry Gladstone, third son of the former Prime Minister, to his younger brother Herbert–himself a former Liberal Home Secretary–in which he complained that Lloyd George "has now given the wrong tone financially and morally to all his Government and underlings, and it is now impossible for him to change, so I agree with you that almost any man would be better as Prime Minister than he."[1489] The Gladstone's were scions of Flintshire: if this was the picture in North Wales, there was trouble ahead for the Liberals in general, and for Lloyd George in particular in the UK as a whole.

In the new Government, eight Liberals were given Cabinet rank. Christopher Addison had been concerned–rightly, as it turned out–that the administration should not be swamped by reactionary

---

1484 Jones, *Lloyd George And The Carnarvon Boroughs*, p36.
1485 Beaverbrook, *Men And Power*, p325.
1486 Quoted in S. Salvidge, *Salvidge Of Liverpool: Behind The Political Scene, 1890-1928*, 1934, London, Hodder & Stoughton, p166-167. Sir Archibald Salvidge (1863-1928), prominent Liverpool Tory.
1487 David Lindsay, 27th Earl of Crawford (1871-1940), Tory Lord Privy Seal, 1916-1919.
1488 J. Vincent, Ed. *The Crawford Papers: The Journals Of David Lindsay, 1892 to 1940*, 1984, Manchester, Manchester University Press, p399.
1489 St Deiniol's Library, Hawarden, Glynne-Gladstone MS 964, H. N. Gladstone to H. J. Gladstone, 30 August 1919.

Unionists. He warned Lloyd George with crystal clarity on 30 December that the people wanted reforms: "They are set on having them done and unless they are done there will be trouble."[1490] He had also noted Labour's performance at the election, seeing in this a guarantee that social reform would indeed be pursued. Labour had greatly increased its vote share, surpassing the total votes of either Liberal faction, becoming the Official Opposition for the first time. However, they only slightly increased their number of seats, to 57, and lost some of their earlier leaders like Ramsay MacDonald and Arthur Henderson. Labour won the most seats in Wales, previously a Liberal stronghold, for the first time, a feat it has continued to the present time.

Being the first general election to be held after the enactment of the Representation of the People Act 1918, enacted on 6 February 1918, it was thus the first election in which women over the age of 30[1491], and all men over the age of 21, could vote. Also, for this election only, servicemen between the age of 18 and the normal qualifying age of 21 could also vote. These measures greatly expanded the electorate, from 7.7 million to 21.4 million voters, including 8.4 million women, this huge rise making the 1918 Act the greatest of all the Reform Acts in terms of electorate addition. At the same time, it extended the local government franchise to include women aged 21 and over on the same terms as men. All these new voters had been viewed by all parties as being rather unpredictable, but in the event the newly enfranchised women in particular showed enormous 'patriotism', mostly supporting the Coalition candidates.

There was a dramatic result in Ireland, which showed clear disapproval of government policy. The Irish Parliamentary Party were reduced to a paltry seven seats by the Irish republicans of Sinn Féin ("[We] Ourselves"), who vowed in their manifesto to establish an independent Irish Republic. They refused to take their 73 seats in Westminster, instead forming a breakaway government sitting in the Dáil Éireann and declaring Irish independence.[1492] The Irish War of Independence–*Cogadh na Saoirse*– began soon after the election, on 21 January 1919, lasting until the ceasefire or truce of 11 July 1921. There was even a 'Limerick Soviet' declared from 15-27 April 1919, though it was more Republican in nature than Bolshevik, and was in any case quickly terminated by British troops.[1493]

Trouble also simmered in Scotland over wages and working conditions. In Glasgow in January 1919 an agreement negotiated on behalf of engineers and shipbuilders between the trade unions and employers for a 47-hour working week was rejected by the Clyde Workers' Committee (CWC) on the grounds that a 40-hour week was preferable because more people, particularly discharged servicemen, would be needed for jobs. Accustomed to the 'red' reputation of the Clyde, the employers and government did not take much notice of the strike called by the CWC on 27 January.

After four days, however, 40,000 men had downed tools, joined by Glasgow's electrical workers

---

1490 Addison, *Four And A Half Years*, Vol.II, p603. Entry for 3 January 1919.

1491 On 28 March 1917, the Commons had voted 341-62 that women over the age of 30 who were householders, the wives of householders, occupiers of property with an annual rent of £5 or graduates of British universities would be enfranchised. Lloyd George, of course, voted in favour. https://api.parliament.uk/historic-hansard/commons/1917/mar/28/franchise-and-electoral-reform-1. Retrieved 25 March 2021.

1492 Constance Markievicz (née Gore-Booth; 1868-1927), became the first woman elected to Parliament, as Sinn Féin member for Dublin St Patrick's, but like the other Sinn Féin MPs she did not take her seat.

1493 Gerwarth, p154.

and by 36,000 Scottish miners. Ex-servicemen were used as pickets, naturally engaging public sympathy, and on 31 January, 'Bloody Friday', up to 25,000 people–men, women and children–demonstrated peacefully in George Square, in the centre of Glasgow, while a delegation led by David Kirkwood[1494] and Manny Shinwell[1495] was granted an audience with the Lord Provost, Sir James Stewart, at the adjoining City Chambers. Many had come to listen to Willie Gallacher[1496] of the Shop Stewards' Movement, as he stood on the plinth of Gladstone's statue. An ill-considered attempt to disperse the crowd by a police baton charge led to a pitched battle in the square and in other parts of the city. Alastair Mackenzie, the Sheriff of Lanarkshire, attempted to read the Riot Act, but it was ripped from his hands. In the ensuing melee, 34 workers and 19 police were injured, one officer, PC William McGregor, subsequently dying on 1 June. Mackenzie requested that evening some 10,000 troops–from four Scottish Regiments and two English–be despatched to Glasgow, along with three Medium Mark C and three Mark V tanks. By the time they arrived, peace was restored and on 12 February the strike was called off, its aims largely unrealised.[1497]

Not in the country at the time, Lloyd George needed to show his forceful leadership on foreign policy as the Paris Peace talks began. Indeed, his moment of supreme statesmanship on the world stage came with the end of the war, taking a central role in the subsequent negotiations, culminating in the Treaty of Versailles, signed five years to the day of the assassination of Archduke Franz Ferdinand. One matter did not bode well. Woodrow Wilson visited Britain from 26-31 December 1918 before moving on to Paris, the first time a US President had visited the country. At a state banquet given in his honour at Buckingham Palace, he made a poor impression. In replying to a toast to his health, Lloyd George noted that Wilson showed "no glow of friendship or of gladness at meeting men who had been partners in a common enterprise and had so narrowly escaped a common danger," making no reference to Britain's part in "the tremendous struggle just brought to a triumphant close and to the appalling sacrifices which had been sustained by the youth of that Empire in the cause of international right… not a word of appreciation, let alone gratitude, came from his lips."[1498] The King was equally unimpressed, writing to a friend: "I could not bear him, an entirely cold academical professor–an odious man."[1499]

The Peace Conference opened in Paris on Saturday, 18 January 1919, with 27 Allied Powers represented by 70 delegates. The date was symbolic, as it was the anniversary of the proclamation of Wilhelm I as German Kaiser in 1871, in the Hall of Mirrors at the Palace of Versailles, shortly before the end of the Siege of Paris–a day itself imbued with significance in its turn in Germany as the

---

1494 David Kirkwood (1872-1955), trade unionist and socialist activist from the East End of Glasgow, a leading figure of the Red Clydeside era, Labour MP for Dumbarton Burghs, 1922-1951.

1495 Emanuel 'Manny' Shinwell (1884-1986), trade unionist and Labour politician.

1496 William Gallacher (1881-1965), a founding member of the Communist Party of Great Britain in 1920, Communist MP for West Fife, 1935-1950, the last Communist MP to date.

1497 G. Barclay, *'Duties in Aid of the Civil Power': The Deployment of the Army to Glasgow, 31 January to 17 February 1919*, *Journal of Scottish Historical Studies* 38, 2, 2018, p261-293. Demolishes previous myths.

1498 Lloyd George, *The Truth About The Peace Treaties*, Vol.I, p181-182. In Paris, Wilson made a similarly bad impression on the French and Italians: See [Stevenson], *Makers*, p55-58.

1499 Quoted in Rose, p232.

anniversary of the establishment of the Kingdom of Prussia under Frederick I in 1701. It was an object lesson in how historical dates become imbued with deep psychological importance for political or propaganda purposes.

Lloyd George faced an immensely difficult juggling act at the conference: primarily, he needed to tread the delicate middle path between the competing ideas of France and the United States. He had campaigned in the recent election promising to make Germany pay, wanting to stop German threats to the British Empire, and wanting to protect British manufacturing. Germany's navy and oversees colonies were seen as just such a threat. However, Lloyd George believed that the treaty should not punish Germany so harshly so as to provoke another war. Also, before 1914, Germany had been Britain's biggest trading partner, and he did not want British workers to lose their jobs if Germany was financially crippled. On the other hand, any leniency towards Germany might be received badly at home, as the majority of the British public at this stage, many newly enfranchised, wanted to punish Germany harshly. The problem which worried the government was how to 'wipe out the past', that is, to 'dissipate the surviving atmosphere of war', so as 'to create a new temper in Europe' and restore peace and economic stability. The key issue was how Germany should be treated, and whether or not it could, and should, be reintegrated into the international community of nations. Essentially, Lloyd George's aim was a "just peace" that would balance the will of the voters with the economic need to continue trade with a viable German state.

On the first day, Lloyd George gave his opening address seconding Wilson's nomination of Georges Clemenceau as Conference President, opining:

> I believe that in the debates of this Conference there will at first inevitably be delays, but I guarantee from my knowledge of M. Clemenceau that there will be no time wasted. That is indispensable. The world is thirsting for peace. Millions of men are waiting to return to their normal life, and they will not forgive us too long delays.
>
> … M. Clemenceau… knows that the finest eloquence is that which gets things done and that the worst is that which delays them.[1500]

Lloyd George's reference to "delays" would prove all too prescient as proceedings got underway. And, later, he would comment on the difficulty of working with Clemenceau, '*Le Tigre*', finding him personally sympathetic, but unapproachable:

> I have a difficulty in dealing with Clemenceau. He never goes out to lunch or dinner, so that I must always make a formal appointment with him. That has its disadvantages. If you meet for social purposes, you can raise a point. If you find you are progressing satisfactorily, you can proceed, otherwise you can drop it. Much business can be done in that manner. Clemenceau

[1500] https://www.firstworldwar.com/source/parispeaceconf_lloydgeorge.htm. Retrieved 4 April 2020.

> has no associate with whom I can talk. He treats Pichon as if he were his clerk or manager. Pichon is frightened to death of the old boy, who is certainly a terrifying figure.[1501]

In this age of profound social, political, psychological and artistic disruption and upheaval, there was an interesting footnote to the Conference, taking place the day after its opening. In Switzerland, Vaslav Nijinsky, 29-years-old and arguably the greatest, most innovative male dancer in the history of ballet, was warming up for a recital that would prove to be the fulcrum of his life story. Nijinsky would give "proof both of his genius and his madness. Never, perhaps, in history had an artist demonstrated so clearly how close the two are to each other."[1502] The location was the Suvretta House Hotel, on the outskirts of St Moritz, with the Alps forming a stunning backdrop. In one of the big salons that evening, the two hundred or so invited guests taking their seats were unaware they were about to witness a bizarre curtain call for a brief yet extraordinary career.

> When the lights went down Vaslav Nijinsky… emerged from the wings carrying a chair. He placed it at the centre of the stage, sat down and stared at the audience. Minutes passed. His wife Romola would say afterwards that Nijinsky sat there for a full half hour, motionless, wordless, as if trying to read the thoughts of each audience member. Eventually he stood up, removed the chair, unrolled a spool of black velvet across the stage, crossed it with a roll of white and announced, *"Now I will dance you the war, with its suffering, with its destruction, with its death. The war which you did not prevent and so are all responsible for".*
>
> As his accompanist struck up the melancholy chord progression of Chopin's Prelude no.20 In C Minor Nijinsky began to fling himself around the stage in a succession of jerky, apparently freestyle movements with a wild look in his eyes that combined fear and anger.
>
> Six weeks later he was in a Zurich mental institution, diagnosed as a schizophrenic by the man who had invented the term. He would never dance again.[1503]

Nijinsky, in the last stages of the illness that would see him committed to psychiatric hospitals and sanatoria for the last 31 years of his life, began to keep a diary. He yearned to involve himself in the Peace Conference, to advise the 'Big Four', although these "were grandiose fantasies, inflated by Nijinsky's sense of self-importance."[1504] He wrote feverishly:

> Lloyd George is a simple man, but he has a great brain. But his brain destroys feeling and therefore he has no wisdom in politics. Lloyd George is a difficult man… I know that Lloyd George does not like people who are in his way… Lloyd George does not know that he will be found out, and therefore holds his head very high. I want to lower his head. I like him, but I must write the truth. I know that if he reads these notes, he will understand me…[1505]

---

1501 Quoted in J. H. Jackson, p202. Stephen Pichon (1857-1933), Minister of Foreign Affairs, 1917-1920.

1502 R. Buckle, *Nijinsky*, 1971, London, Weidenfeld & Nicolson, p406.

1503 https://www.pressreader.com/uk/the-new-european/20180329/282553018790630. Retrieved 12 March 2020. Emphasis added.

1504 P. Ostwald, *Vaslav Nijinsky: A Leap Into Madness*, 1991, London, Robson Books, p189.

1505 Nijinsky, V. and R., *The Diary Of Vaslav Nijinsky*, 1936, New York, Simon and Schuster, p16, 27.

In a sense, Paris became the "capital of the world. The Peace Conference was the world's most important business, the peacemakers the world's most powerful people... Paris was at once the world's government, its court of appeal and parliament, the focus of its fears and hopes."[1506] The problems the peacemakers faced were literally global in their scale and complexity. As Margaret MacMillan puts it "The expectations of the Peace Conference were enormous; the risk of disappointment correspondingly great."[1507] Clemenceau would soon complain "It is much easier to make war than peace."[1508] Lloyd George later, in a similar context, wrote "where you are working with allies, it is just as difficult to negotiate an honourable peace as to wage successful war."[1509] It might have been wiser not to have held the Conference in Paris at all, but in a calmer, more detached and less belligerent location. Certainly, Lloyd George thought so, and favoured "some neutral city like Geneva"[1510], but faced Clemenceau's unwavering opposition. Later, annoyed, he exclaimed "I never wanted to hold the Conference in his bloody capital. Both [Edward] House and I thought it would be better to hold it in a neutral place, but the old man wept and protested so much that we gave way."[1511]

The scale and the scope of the whole enterprise was unprecedented. In the decades after, the Conference received much criticism for its failures–both real and imagined–but what the people involved faced was a responsibility of a complexity and magnitude as to be nearly unimaginable in human terms. Europe was as a gigantic termite nest into which a madman had vigorously and malevolently poked a big stick, with resultant turmoil for the disturbed occupants milling about in the ruined interior. It is in fact astonishing that the statesmen achieved so much, given the almost impossible balancing act they were required to perfect in a relatively short period of time and under such pressure. As one historian observed:

> The statesmen were feeling their way in Paris, trying at once to pay attention to their voters, stay true to their principles, and work out a deal they could all accept. Given the monumental task facing them, it is perhaps not surprising that they spent much time on the early days on a relatively simple but highly symbolic issue: the fate of the Kaiser.[1512]

Lloyd George had been keen to try the Kaiser, stating to the Imperial War Cabinet on 20 November 1918 "Kings have been tried and executed for offences which are not comparable." On 25 January 1919, the Allies set up a 'Commission on the Responsibility of the Authors of the War and the Enforcement of Penalties', chaired by US Secretary of State Robert Lansing[1513], which submitted its report on 29 March. To Lloyd George's regret, the idea of charging the Kaiser with starting an 'unjust

---

1506 MacMillan, *Peacemakers*, p1.
1507 Ibid., *Peacemakers*, p6.
1508 A. Ribot, *Journal d'Alexandre Ribot Et Correspondances Ineédites, 1914-1922*, 1936, Paris, Librairie Plon, p255.
1509 Lloyd George, *War Memoirs*, Vol.II, p1175.
1510 Lloyd George, *Truth About The Peace Treaties*, Vol.I, p147.
1511 Quoted in MacMillan, *Peacemakers*, p35.
1512 MacMillan, *Peacemakers*, p172.
1513 Robert Lansing (1864-1928), Barrister, Secretary of State, 24 June 1915–13 February 1920, he and Wilson rarely saw eye-to-eye at the Conference.

war' or a 'war of aggression' was dismissed, leading him to remark "In my view, if important personalities who unleash such calamities could be rendered responsible for this, the greatest of all crimes, there would be less danger of war in the future." Ultimately, the initiative ran out of steam, largely due to Wilson's opposition. Perhaps it was as well, as it avoided turning the Kaiser into a possible 'martyr'.[1514]

Talks began in the Salle de l'Horloge at the French Foreign Ministry on the Quai d'Orsay. Lloyd George–accompanied for the first few weeks, until she returned home, by his wife Margaret, and by his youngest daughter, Megan, now 16–moved into plush apartments at 23, Rue Nitot–now called Rue de l'Amiral d'Estaing–on 11 January, along with his secretary Philip Kerr, with the rest of the British Empire delegation staff being accommodated in the Hôtel Majestic and using the adjoining Hôtel Astoria as offices in the Avenue Kléber. At its peak, the staff alone comprised over 1,000 civil servants, expert advisers, secretaries and other support staff from Lloyd George's own office, the Foreign Office, the War Office, the Colonial Office and the Treasury–a huge increase over the 14 advisers that Viscount Castlereagh and then the Duke of Wellington had taken with them to the Congress of Vienna in September 1814–June 1815 at the end of the 23-year-long French Revolutionary and Napoleonic Wars.[1515]

The Conference had not long been underway, when an event occurred that nearly altered its whole course. At 8.40 am on 19 February, as Clemenceau was leaving his apartment in the Rue Benjamin-Franklin, self-styled anarchist Émile Cottin fired nine shots at his car. Clemenceau later told Lloyd George that the incident seemed to last "such a long time".[1516] One bullet hit him between the ribs, just missing his vital organs. Too dangerous to remove, the bullet remained lodged near his heart for the remaining ten years of his life. Carried back to his house, Clemenceau's assistant Mordacq found him pale but conscious. "They shot me in the back," Clemenceau told him. "They didn't even dare to attack me from the front."[1517]

The same day, Lloyd George cabled his private secretary, Philip Kerr, expressing his shock and revealing the unsettled nature of the times:

> If the attempt is a Bolshevist one it shows what lunatics these anarchists are for nothing would do them as much harm as a successful attempt on Clemenceau's life and even a failure will exasperate opinion in France and make it quite impossible to have any dealings with them... They will assume that the attack was organised by Lenin and Trotsky, though probably they had nothing to do with it for they are not fools.[1518]

Remarkably, the tough Clemenceau was walking in his garden the day after the attack, and well nursed

---

1514 See Reynolds, p290-292. The Americans would hold very different views after World War Two!

1515 Though a Tory, Castlereagh's approach was similar to that of Lloyd George a century later: he saw that a harsh treaty based on vengeance and retaliation would fail, and that bringing France back into the diplomatic balance was essential for long-term peace in Europe.

1516 Stevenson, *Diary*, p172. Entry for 15 March 1919. Also [Stevenson], *Makers*, p43.

1517 Mordacq, *Le Ministière Clemenceau*, Vol.3, p133-135.

1518 Lloyd George, *Truth About The Peace Treaties*, Vol.I, p375-376.

by a nun, Sister Théoneste, on 27 February, he returned to the meeting of the Council of Ten.[1519] However, his powers of concentration were never quite the same again. On 19 March, Lloyd George's friend Riddell observed "Clemenceau looks much shaken. He seems to be growing older every day." Lloyd George responded "Yes, unfortunately. That is one of the difficulties of the situation. The old boy has lost his power of coming to decisions. He is not the Clemenceau of six months ago. He is overcome by the torrent of Wilson's eloquence. It seems to paralyse him."[1520] Three weeks later, Lloyd George again remarked to Riddell: "I am sorry Clemenceau is failing. It is very marked. Now he so often asks for twenty-four hours in which to make up his mind. Before, he made it up in twenty-four seconds…"[1521]

Frances Stevenson arrived in Paris on 5 March[1522]–after Margaret's departure–to act as Lloyd George's secretary, staying at the Majestic. She spoke very good French, and so was employed during the negotiations to translate from French to English. The French were thwarted, as they had hoped to have a Frenchman appointed, a potential source of information from inside the English camp. Sadly, Bengy Carey-Evans believed that Lloyd George being away in Paris so much accelerated the growing divide between Lloyd George and Margaret.[1523] Ominously, on the same day she arrived in Paris, Frances also recorded the first storm-warnings of the fatal, factional Tory unrest to come:

> The Tories–at least the more difficult of them, such as Long & Curzon–have got their tails up as a result of their success at the Election. '[Lloyd] George thinks he won the election', said Walter Long to his neighbour at a dinner the other night. 'Well he didn't. It was the Tories that won the election, *and he will soon begin to find that out.*'[1524]

Crucially, Russia was excluded from the proceedings in Paris due to her new Bolshevik rulers signing a separate peace, the Treaty of Brest-Litovsk, with Germany on 3 March 1918, and her consequent withdrawal from the war.[1525] Lloyd George would rather have had representatives from Russia present, and he had argued his case cogently on 2-3 December 1918 at the Inter-Allied Conference in London:

> Mr. Lloyd George… felt that we could not proceed as if there were no Russia… it must be recognised that, great as had been the sufferings of the other Allies, Russia had probably lost more lives than any. Their troops had fought without arms or munitions; they had been outrageously betrayed by their Government, and it was little to be wondered at if, in their bitterness, the Russian people had rebelled against the Alliance. He doubted whether any other

---

1519 Watson, p86-87.
1520 Riddell, *Intimate Diary*, p36. Entry for 19 March 1919.
1521 Ibid., p51. Entry for 11 April 1919.
1522 Stevenson, *Diary*, p169.
1523 Unsurprisingly, he was not an admirer of Frances, stating that on one occasion Lloyd George gave the wrong figures in a Parliamentary debate; he took the blame, in fact Frances had given him the wrong papers.
1524 Stevenson, *Diary*, p169.
1525 Of interest in context with the reparations soon to be demanded of Germany, at Brest-Litovsk the Germans harshly demanded an indemnity from Russia of 300 million gold marks, which the Bolsheviks did in fact start to pay, plus an enormous amount of territory, amounting to 34% of its population, 54% of its industrial land, 89% of its coalfields, and 26% of its railways.

> country would have borne as much as Russia and remained in the war so long. Russia, after all, represented something like two-thirds of Europe and a large part of Asia. It was a problem that must be faced. Could it be faced without giving the Russian people a right to present their case? The affairs of nearly two hundred million people could not be settled without hearing them. It was not possible to say that the Tartars, the Finns, the Letts, should come to the Peace Conference and not the Bolsheviks, who stood for two-thirds of the whole population. The Bolsheviks, whatever might be thought of them, appeared to have a hold over the majority of the population. This was a fact, a sinister one no doubt, but facts could not be neglected because they were unpalatable. He reminded the meeting that 120 years ago similar feelings had been experienced, and similar views had been expressed… in regard to the French revolutionaries… He therefore strongly deprecated the adoption of any fixed attitude towards Central Russia.[1526]

Sidney Sonnino, the Italian Minister of Foreign Affairs, gave him unexpected support, closely backing up his points. On 16 January Lloyd George tried again, at a meeting of the Supreme Council, but to no avail.[1527] And on 21 January he and Wilson tried a compromise: if the Bolsheviks could or would not come to Paris, perhaps a mid-way point might be acceptable to all, namely Prinkipo, the largest of the Princes' Islands in the Sea of Marmara near Constantinople, the discussions to take place by 15 February. This proposal also foundered on mutual suspicion and lack of determination.[1528] Throughout the Conference, Allied policy towards Russia always remained unclear, yet containing just enough hostility to convince its Bolshevik Government that the Western Powers were implacable enemies, which would have dire consequences for the future.

Apart from Russia, the other highly significant absentee from the Conference was Germany, the defeated enemy. By Spring 1919, a number of different views as to what should be done regarding the Germans were publicly emerging, a circumstance of which German observers were well aware. The original Allied intention had been "to hold a preliminary peace conference to agree the terms to be offered and then have a full one with both sides negotiating as they had done at Vienna. It took so long to get agreement on the Allied terms with so many disagreements that the Allied leaders decided they could not go ahead as planned."[1529] This would prove absolutely fatal in the long term.

Of all the pressing issues–disarmament, territory, colonies, war crimes–it was that of reparations that was the touchstone where Germany was concerned, naturally a source of much inter-Allied wrangling, and even dispute within delegations themselves. As late as 2 June, Lloyd George wrote to George Barnes, the Coalition Labour Minister without Portfolio, stating:

> There is no doubt it would be better to fix a sum if we could agree on the figure. The difficulty is first of all to ascertain it; the next is to secure agreement amongst the Allies as the amount, and in the third place to secure an arrangement as to the proportions in which it is to be

---

1526 Lloyd George, *Truth About The Peace Treaties*, Vol.I, p321-322.

1527 MacMillan, *Peacemakers*, p77-78.

1528 Ibid., p82-85.

1529 Personal communication to the author by Professor Margaret MacMillan, 7 June 2020.

> distributed. If you have any plan that will meet these three difficulties you will have solved the most baffling problem in the Peace Treaty.[1530]

No suggestions were forthcoming from Barnes. Expectations varied wildly–House noted in his diary on 21 February that the British wanted £24 billion, the French £44 billion, and the Americans £4.4 billion.[1531] It was all largely academic anyway. Economist John Maynard Keynes argued that Germany could pay at most £2 billion: "Anything more would drive it to despair, and probably revolution, with dangerous consequences for Europe."[1532]

Having been the President of the Board of Trade, then the Chancellor of the Exchequer, Lloyd George understood the workings of finance and trade very well, and clearly understood that eventually Britain would want–and need–to trade with Germany and its population of 62 million again. As early as 26 February 1916, he had told Riddell: "For my part I still say we must beat the Germans, and when they are beaten I would endeavour to make the peace real and lasting. A great nation like Germany must live."[1533] He was consistent in this view–he never wanted to destroy Germany[1534], as did quite a number of the new Tory intake in his Coalition from the recent election, a "lot of hard-faced men who look as if they had done very well out of the war", in the famous words of Stanley Baldwin. By the end of February 1919, the British had reduced their demand down to £9.4 billion, whilst the French came down to £8 billion. In the event, no agreement was reached by the end of March, so a special commission was appointed to look into the matter.

Finally, the London Schedule of Payments of 5 May 1921 established "the full liability of all the Central Powers combined, not just Germany alone," at 132 billion gold marks–£6.5 billion for Germany. This sum was a compromise promoted by Belgium–against higher figures demanded by the French and Italians and the lower figure the British supported–that "represented an assessment of the lowest amount that public opinion… would tolerate". Taking into account the sum already paid between 1919 and 1921, Germany's immediate obligation was 41 billion gold marks. Absolute figures are impossible to determine, but ultimately, Germany probably paid around 21 billion gold marks (£1.1 billion), during the period 1919-1931, when reparations were suspended for a year, and 1932, when during the Lausanne Conference they were cancelled altogether. That figure was probably slightly less–around 2.5%–than the amount paid by France, with a considerably smaller national economy, to Germany after the Franco-Prussian War of 1870-71.

Regarding the relevant Articles in the Treaty (Articles 231 and 232), the dismayed Germans came to loathe them, but the Allies themselves were generally happy with their formulation. Lloyd George declared:

---

1530 Quoted in Rowland, *Lloyd George*, p494.

1531 MacMillan, *Peacemakers*, p195.

1532 Ibid., p193-194.

1533 Riddell, *War Diary*, p157.

1534 MacMillan, *Peacemakers*, p200, from a conversation between Lloyd George and Briand, 18 March 1919.

> The English public, like the French public, thinks the Germans must above all acknowledge their obligation to compensate us for all the consequences of their aggression. When this is done we will come to the question of Germany's capacity to pay; we all think she will be unable to pay more than this document requires of her.[1535]

In the event, hyperinflation grossly affected the German paper mark (or *Papiermark)*, the currency of the Weimar Republic, between 1921 and 1923, especially in the latter year. It caused considerable internal political instability in the country. In January 1914, the exchange rate was 4.2 marks to one US dollar, by late 1919 the rate was 48 paper marks to the dollar. Afterwards, the German currency was relatively stable at about 90 marks per dollar during the first half of 1921. Thereafter matters began to spiral out of control. In Berlin, a loaf of bread that cost around 160 Marks at the end of 1922, cost 200,000,000,000 Marks by late 1923. By November 1923, the US dollar was worth 4,210,500,000,000 German marks. Famously, employees would collect their wages in baskets or even wheelbarrows, immediately buying food or paying bills as the banknotes literally lost value hour by hour. On 16 November 1923, the new *Rentenmark* was introduced to replace the worthless paper marks issued by the Reichsbank. 12 zeros were cut from prices, and the prices quoted in the new currency remained stable. From September 1924, London and New York bankers, under the Dawes Plan, helped to fund the new German *Reichsmark* and restructure reparations at a lower level.

One significant problem the Conference always faced was that of time. The public and press in each nation were highly impatient for progress and solutions; by mid-April, a sour joke ran around Paris that the Conference was preparing a "just and lasting war".[1536] Not only that, but actual events themselves were in danger of fast overtaking proceedings in Paris. Time was against the Allies: in November 1918 they had 198 divisions available, by June 1919, as demobilization accelerated, only 39 remained, and the chances of potentially coercing the Germans into accepting Allied demands, should the eventuality arise, were correspondingly shrinking. Also, as Margaret MacMillan points out:

> By the time the Supreme Council first met on 12 January Poland had been re-created, Finland and the Baltic States were well on their way to independence and Czechoslovakia had been pieced together. In the Balkans, Serbia had joined with the Austria-Hungary's South Slav territories of Croatia and Slovenia. The new entity did not yet have a name but some people were talking of a Yugoslav state.[1537]

Lloyd George later stated that the Great Powers had been "confronted with accomplished and unreversible facts… The task of the Parisian Treaty-makers was not to decide what in fairness should be given to the liberated nationalities, but what in common honesty should be freed from their clutches

---

[1535] Mantoux, Vol.I, p147. Session of 5 April 1919.

[1536] MacMillan, *Peacemakers*, p281.

[1537] Ibid., p66. The Polish Republic had been revived on 11 November 1918; Finland had declared independence from Russia on 6 December 1917; of the Baltic States, Lithuania had declared its independence on 16 February 1918, Estonia on 24 February 1918, Latvia on 18 November 1918; Czechoslovakia was formed on 28 October 1918; and the Serbian-led Kingdom of Serbs, Croats and Slovenes had been proclaimed on 1 December 1918.

when they had overstepped the bounds of self-determination."[1538]

After the signing of the Treaty of Versailles, German political stability was always likely to be a fragile thing. Over 440 Articles, the Allies demanded, virtually without negotiation, 20 billion gold marks of provisional compensation[1539], the surrender of territories totalling 65,000 $km^2$ along with their seven million inhabitants, and the Allied occupation of the left bank of the Rhine for up to 15 years. Soon, Lloyd George was to comment: "We shall have to do the whole thing over again in twenty-five years at three times the cost."[1540] With the view of trying to prevent wars happening again, and to prevent the root causes of them, one of the Conference's principal aims, on 25 January a Commission on the League of Nations was formally established. Wilson insisted on chairing the commission, as for him the League was the essential bedrock for his proposed peace settlements. Contrary to frequent popular supposition, the notion of peaceful inter-governmental co-operation in maintaining and improving international relations did not originate with him, but ran forward along a powerful thread of European thought from Immanuel Kant's *Perpetual Peace: A Philosophical Sketch* (1795), through the post-Napoleonic concept of the Concert of Europe and on through the Geneva Convention of 1864, the foundation of the Inter-Parliamentary Union (IPU) in 1889, and the Hague Conventions of 1899 and 1907.

Lloyd George broadly shared Wilson's aims but was never a prime-mover in promoting the League, perhaps, it has been suggested, because he doubted that it could ever be truly effective in achieving its stated aims.[1541] Jan Smuts, the South African Foreign Minister, was in favour of reconciliation with Germany and limited reparations, and was correspondingly in favour of a strong League of Nations. He wrote *The League Of Nations: A Practical Suggestion*–a position-paper–on the subject. Lloyd George was clearly impressed, as Cabinet minutes noted that the Prime Minister called the paper "one of the ablest state papers he had ever read", and it was immediately published in December 1918.[1542] Wilson was impressed too, as when he came to write down his own ideas, after seeing the copy Lloyd George gave him, the result, which he showed the British on 19 January, was seen to borrow many of Smuts' ideas.[1543]

Due to all this prior thought and effort, the first meeting of the commission was held on 3 February, and by 14 February a comprehensive draft was completed, a concise document composed of 26 articles. Neither Lloyd George nor Clemenceau took part in the proceedings, Lloyd George employing

---

1538 Lloyd George, *Truth About The Peace Treaties*, Vol.I, p91.

1539 Under the Treaty of Paris of 20 November 1815 France had been forced to pay the Coalition a 700 million franc war indemnity, also having its borders reduced to their 1790 level and paying the costs of Coalition occupation forces and defensive fortifications to be built in neighbouring Coalition countries. Under the Treaty of Frankfurt of 10 May 1871 France had been forced to agree to pay Prussia a 5 billion franc (£200 million) war indemnity in gold. This was proportioned, according to population, to be the exact equivalent to the indemnity imposed by Napoleon on Prussia by the Treaty of Tilsit on 9 July 1807. France had also lost its provinces of Alsace and Lorraine. Thus did the 'vendetta' span the generations.

1540 Quoted in Watt, p11. Marshal Foch, on hearing of the signing of the treaty, would observe with uncanny accuracy: "This is not Peace. It is an Armistice for twenty years." Quoted in W. Churchill, *The Second World War: Volume 1, The Gathering Storm*, 1948, London, Cassell, p6.

1541 MacMillan, *Peacemakers*, p95.

1542 Ibid., p98.

1543 Ibid., p99.

his old tactic of appointing trusted men–in this case Jan Smuts and Robert Cecil–granting them full authority and leaving them to do the job. After a little more wrangling, centring on the United States' wishing to maintain the 'Monroe Doctrine', subsequently embodied in Article 22, on the 28 April a plenary session of the Conference approved the Covenant, the League's foundational constitution, with 44 states signing, becoming effective on 10 January 1920.

In a letter of 17 March, Lloyd George conveyed his sense of urgency in driving the business of the Conference forward at a more vigorous pace:

> We have started a series of private conversations between Clemenceau, Wilson and myself for the discussion and determination of these very baffling problems, and unless we reach an agreement peace will be definitely postponed. What is still worse for all practical purposes, the alliance will cease to exist. I am hopeful of reaching complete agreement and we are getting appreciably nearer.[1544]

On 24 March, the 'Council of Ten'–comprising two delegates each from Britain, France, the United States, Italy, and Japan–was replaced by a 'Council of Four', or 'Big Four', specifically Georges Clemenceau, Woodrow Wilson, Lloyd George and Vittorio Orlando of Italy, joining the other three for the first time. Lloyd George, in particular, was concerned and annoyed by the leaks of confidential information[1545] from the Supreme Council and about the time the peacemaking process was taking. Wilson and Clemenceau agreed, Wilson also viewing the Council of Four as being more efficient and likely to expedite matters considerably. From then on, the four men met in some 148 closed sessions, usually twice a day in Wilson's study, to make all the major decisions, which were later ratified by the entire assembly. The minor powers attended the weekly 'Plenary Conferences' that discussed issues in a general forum but made no decisions. These members were included on the 52 commissions that made various recommendations, many of which were incorporated into the final text of the treaty.

Each of the 'Big Four' had his own style. Wilson was stiff and professorial, Clemenceau more taciturn, though passionate when he did speak, while Orlando was preoccupied with Italian concerns and sometimes got lost when the other three spoke English quickly together. Lloyd George "his knee clasped in his hands, dashed at his subject, sometimes angry, sometimes full of good humour, 'wrapped in the utmost indifference to technical arguments, irresistibly attracted to unlooked-for solutions, but dazzling with eloquence and wit.'"[1546] Of the four, Lloyd George personally coped the best. Having guided Britain through the war to great acclaim, he now enjoyed triumphantly negotiating the peace. On the day he left Paris, he later told Riddell:

---

1544 Quoted in Sharp, p79.
1545 Lansing, *Big Four*, p92.
1546 MacMillan, *Peacemakers*, p282.

> I felt I was closing a book that would never be reopened–a book of intense interest. It was an anxious time, but a pleasant time. I enjoyed it. I doubt if I shall ever spend such another. It was all so vivid.[1547]

Robert Lansing, the US Secretary of State, recorded his impressions of the 'Big Four', drawing a lively and mostly balanced pen-portrait of Lloyd George, whom he placed third in prominence:

> … if he had a prepared programme… he did not follow it persistently. His course was erratic, and he so often shifted his ground that one felt that he had abandoned his plan, or at least that he did not care to follow it rigidly, preferring to depend on his own sagacity to take advantage of a situation. As questions arose, particularly those affected by changing political and military conditions, he decided the British attitude with characteristic quickness of judgment and with a positiveness which impressed one with the alertness rather than the depth of his mind, and with the confidence which he felt in his own ability to grasp a subject and decide it in the most expedient way, even though he had not given it the study and thought which other men felt were necessary for a wise decision.
>
> Ready as Mr. Lloyd George was to declare a position on any subject, he seemed to be equally ready to change that position on obtaining further information… He did this with an avowal that he had not previously been in possession of the facts or else with an explanation intended to show that his new attitude was not contradictory of the former one. His explanations were always clever and well presented, but they were not always convincing. The British Premier thus put aside that which had gone before and proceeded to handle the question under discussion as if nothing had occurred to change the course of the debate. Inconsistency never seemed to disturb him or to cause him to hesitate. If he took the trouble to explain a change of attitude, it was out of no sense of obligation to justify himself, but rather in deference to the opinion of others and to prevent complaint …
>
> … Mr. Lloyd George had a pleasing personality and a hearty manner of address, which won him friends even among those who were disposed to charge him with vacillation. Of him it may be said that he possessed personal magnetism ... His eyes were keen and twinkling, and when he smiled the wrinkles at the corners were very marked. He would enter the council chamber at the Ministry of Foreign Affairs, generally late, with a quick step, which on account of its length made it a bit swaggering, and greet his colleagues with a genial smile and a bluff heartiness which were attractive.
>
> … His manner conveyed the impression of a man who was satisfied that he had obtained all the information that he needed to deal with the several subjects to be discussed by the Council. One could not but admire the complacency which he showed as to his own ability. In the conferences of the Council, Mr. Lloyd George disclosed that his training was that of a parliamentarian rather than that of a diplomat. He did not speak in the calm, deliberate, and precise manner in which President Wilson spoke, nor in the analytical and closely reasoned style of Signor Orlando when arguing a point. The British statesman was very much of a rough-and-

---

1547 Quoted in Riddell, *Intimate Diary*, p168-169.

tumble debater, quick to seize upon the weak points of an opponent and to attack them vigorously, sometimes with sarcasm and ridicule, and often with flat denials of fact… Nothing daunted him. No antagonist was too strongly entrenched to discourage him. His quick wit, his ready tongue, and his self-confidence made him what he was, a great parliamentary leader.

… Yet nobody could come into intimate association with Mr. Lloyd George without falling under the spell of his personal charm. One might dislike his methods as those of a politician; one might even feel a measure of contemptuous surprise that he dared to discuss a question of territory without knowing exactly where the territory was; and there might be a feeling of irritation that he changed his mind whenever it seemed to him expedient; but with it all one liked the man; it was simply impossible not to like him. His cheeriness, his vivacity, his never-failing good nature, and his delightful humor were assets which counted greatly in his favor…

… More than once, while the negotiations were in progress at Paris, Mr. Lloyd George returned to London and appeared in the House of Commons for the purpose of leading the Government in repelling an attack by the Opposition. On those occasions he so adroitly explained the Government's policies and so brilliantly pictured the satisfactory progress of the work of the Peace Conference that the attempted criticisms which followed were feeble and futile. Aggressive, sanguine, and cheerfully willing to face his opponents, he successfully combated their criticisms. Having routed his antagonists at home, he returned to Paris unquestionably stronger in his own eyes, as well as in the eyes of others, because of his evident mastery of the parliamentary situation.

While opinions may differ as to whether Mr. Lloyd George is a great statesman, no one can truthfully deny that he is a great politician who shows a remarkable insight into human nature and a skill in the manipulation of political forces which have enabled him to hold his place in the most difficult circumstances. Through the critical periods of the war he maintained his ascendancy by his ability to play off faction against faction, and by his agility in keeping his equilibrium on a very flimsy structure built up of discordant and even of hostile elements. Often his position was extremely precarious, but his wit and readiness as a speaker always saved him from defeat in the House of Commons… Though his keenness of mind was fully appreciated, the way in which it was used aroused doubt as to his sincerity, and nothing can be more detrimental to a negotiator than to be credited with insincerity. The consequence was that every position taken and every suggestion offered by the British leader was suspected and a hidden purpose was frequently presumed when doubtless there was none.

… Mr. Lloyd George possessed a wonderfully alert mind which fairly bubbled over with restless energy. He made decisions rapidly and with little regard for details or fundamental principles. If he fell into error through incomplete knowledge or wrong deductions, he picked himself up with a laugh or a witticism and went ahead as if nothing had happened. In debate he was vigorous and often impetuous… He, in my opinion, had the quickest mind of the Big Four, but it seemed to lack stability…

Vivacious, good-tempered, and possessing a strong sense of humor, Mr. Lloyd George was socially an attractive person, while in debate his cleverness in finding the weak spots in an opponent's armor and his utter indifference to his own errors made him a dangerous antagonist.

> He attacked with vigor and he defended by attacking. But this unusual man possessed none of the arts of diplomacy. He was not by nature a negotiator. His successes at Paris–and they were not a few–were largely due to the excellent advice which was given him, and which he wisely received.[1548]

The 'unsung hero' at the Council of Four was the official interpreter, Professor Paul Mantoux.[1549] Remarkably, no official records were initially kept of these discussions, causing increasing problems as the days went by. Fortunately Mantoux, a historian, dictated his recollections of the previous day's meetings each morning in a confidential minute for Clemenceau, keeping a copy for himself. Mantoux was present at all the meetings, and his direct, detailed transcripts of these conversations are the only record existing for the first 37 meetings, when the great controversies raised by French claims and the crucial discussion of German reparations occurred. Thus, his work is vital in revealing both the personalities and issues involved in these debates. Only then did Hankey begin keeping the official record, which each of the 'Big Four' received.

It was Mantoux who recorded the key comment of Lloyd George on 29 March regarding the necessity, "from the point of view of British domestic politics… [of]… not abandoning our claim to the totality of war costs while admitting the obligation imposed upon us by the practical necessity to limit ourselves to a more modest demand."[1550] Lloyd George knew all too well that the negotiators walked a tightrope, needing to uphold the right to reparations, without actually exercising that right.[1551] On 5 April he reiterated his own, moderate position, stating "I have fought against those who go on repeating that Germany can pay all that the war cost", whilst also making it clear that she should pay "the extreme limit of the possible."[1552]

Curiously, of the 'Big Four' themselves, three had legal training. Lloyd George was a solicitor; Wilson was a lawyer, having been admitted to the Georgia bar in 1882 and briefly establishing a legal practice in Atlanta; Orlando was a Professor of Law at the University of Palermo in his native Sicily and an eminent jurist with over a hundred articles on legal and judicial matters to his name. Only Clemenceau broke the mould, graduating as a Doctor of Medicine in Paris in 1865, though he never practiced. In theory, this preponderance of legal training should have added some clarity and precision both to the negotiations and to the eventual Treaty itself, but in practice the overwhelming pressure of conflicting intentions, interests and personalities unfortunately blunted this possibility. Lansing noted "They were unable to think in terms of international law or to model their procedure to conform to the custom and usage of nations."[1553]

Orlando was not present the whole time. Perfectly reasonably, during negotiations he had demanded the fulfilment of the terms of Article 4 of the secret Treaty of London of 26 April 1915.

1548 Lansing, *Big Four*, p77-102.
1549 Paul Mantoux (1877-1956), first director of the Political Section of the League of Nations, 1919-1927.
1550 Quoted in Mantoux, Vol.I, p77.
1551 Crosby, *Unknown*, p259.
1552 Quoted in Mantoux, Vol.I, p152-153.
1553 Lansing, *Big Four*, p98.

By this article, the Triple Entente had promised Italy ample territorial compensation, including "the Trentino, Cisalpine Tyrol with its geographical and natural frontier (the Brenner frontier), as well as Trieste, the counties of Gorizia and Gradisca, all Istria as far as the Quarnero and including Volosca and the Istrian islands of Cherso and Lussin, [the northern part of the province of Dalmatia]"[1554] for its entry into the war on the Allied side, breaking away from its 33-year-old adherence to the Triple Alliance with Germany and Austria-Hungary. Under Article 14, Britain had also promised to extend, on "equitable terms", a loan of at least £50 million towards the Italian war effort. Italy consequently declared war on Austria-Hungary on 23 May 1915, the Ottoman Empire on 20 August 1915, and Germany on 28 August 1916. Many provisions of the Treaty were intended to be kept secret for the duration of the war, but they were published by the Bolsheviks on their coming to power in Russia in their journal *Izvestia* on 1 December 1917.

However, Wilson strongly opposed Orlando's demands as it was against his stated principles of national self-determination, meaning that Orlando failed to secure either British or French support. Matters were made worse by the personality clash between Wilson and the Italian Minister of Foreign Affairs, Sidney Sonnino. Orlando had hoped to avoid confrontation, but Wilson was unmovable. Orlando was proud of his country, had been a supporter of Italy's entry into the war, and had held the nation together when it had faced defeat after the disastrous losses at Caporetto. Leading a patriotic national front government, the *Unione Sacra*, and reorganizing the army, Orlando had proved popular, rebuilding national morale and becoming called the "Premier of Victory". Nonetheless, Italy had lost around 500,000 military personnel and some 590,000 civilians, with maybe another 900,000 wounded, and the war had been a great strain on the relatively new nation's meagre, and only slowly developing, resources. By 1919 the nation was hugely in debt to the Allies, with inflation rampant and social cohesion being sorely tested.

Unfortunately for Orlando, the Liberals and moderate Socialists withdrew their support from the government, and he had to increasingly rely on the Nationalist right. His options narrowed, and in coming up with the formula 'the Treaty of London plus Fiume' he merely gave undue stimulus to the nationalist element of his support whilst antagonising the other Allies, especially Wilson. Sonnino stood behind the Treaty of London that he had helped to negotiate but had little interest in the port of Fiume. Lloyd George opined that "He was apprehensive lest Italy should sacrifice bigger things in the frenzy for this trivial claim."[1555] Lloyd George preferred Orlando, saying that "he had an attractive and amiable personality which made him an extremely pleasant man to do business with."[1556] Orlando reciprocated this feeling, writing admiringly of Lloyd George "His Celtic blood made him like us Mediterraneans in cleverness."[1557]

Lloyd George and Clemenceau believed the promises made in the Treaty of London were predicated on the continued existence of Austro-Hungarian Empire after the war. Circumstances had

---

1554 *Agreement Between France, Russia, Great Britain And Italy. Signed At London, April 26, 1915*, 1920, London, HMSO, Cmd.671, Misc. No.7, p3.

1555 Lloyd George, *Truth About The Peace Treaties*, Vol.II, p819.

1556 Quoted in MacMillan, *Peacemakers*, p290.

1557 Orlando, p356.

changed. It had made sense to deprive a defeated enemy of its ports and naval bases, but that no longer held true with what were now new, friendly nations. Wilson felt that Italy, when she had signed armistices with the Central Powers on the basis of the Fourteen Points, had implicitly accepted that these superseded the Treaty of London. Point 9 had unambiguously stated "A readjustment of the frontiers of Italy should be effected along clearly recognizable lines of nationality." However, Orlando was not in a position to back down, due to his political support narrowing rightwards and the pressure of public opinion. Overall, the Italian delegates rarely spoke unless an issue of Italian interest was under discussion, and then they were vociferous and inflexible, earning them few friends. On the streets of Italy, there was rapidly escalating tension between the radicalised Socialist Party and the new *fasci di combattimenti* of Benito Mussolini.

Fiume, the small port of some 60,000 people which, before the war, had been Hungary's outlet to the Adriatic, became the key bone of contention between Italian nationalism on one side, and Wilson on the other. Italians were only just in the majority there, and only in 1918 did reunification with Italy become a possibility. The Italians had occupied the port as part of the armistice agreements and were now determined to stay put. Then the poet, war hero and proto-fascist Gabriele D'Annunzio[1558] made Fiume his cause, castigating the government. On 3 April Lloyd George, in a meeting of the 'Big Four', asked of Orlando "to know immediately the point of view of the Italian government on the question of the Adriatic." Orlando responded employing his by-now familiar arguments. Lloyd George asked him directly "What would happen if Fiume was a free city under the control of the League of Nations?" To which Orlando replied: "I would accept that solution for the port, but not for the city. If we look at it simply from the economic point of view, what reason could one invoke if not distrust of Italy? To make Fiume a free city is to prepare for the absorption of the Italian element by the Croats who surround the city."[1559] Private talks between the Italians and their allies in the days following were not productive, with rumours already circulating that Orlando was thinking of walking out of the Conference.[1560]

On 13 April, as the 'Big Four' met to decide when to summon the German delegates to Paris, Orlando demanded that the Italian questions be settled first, stating: "The impression would be disastrous in Italy if I told my compatriots that, five months after the conclusion of the Armistice, all the French questions are settled, whilst there is not even an agreement in principle on the Italian questions… The Italian government would then be in a very perilous situation… the consequences of a disappointment of this kind would be very grave."[1561] The other three were sympathetic, but unmoved, Lloyd George responding "I am convinced that it is in the general interest to summon the German delegates straightaway and thus to prepare ourselves to negotiate with the only enemy state still standing… There is also the matter of allowing world trade to revive; as long as we have no treaty with Germany, the economic life of the entire world will remain at standstill."[1562] Wilson's suggestion,

---

1558 Gabriele D'Annunzio (1863-1938).
1559 Quoted in Mantoux, Vol.I, p125, 127.
1560 MacMillan, *Peacemakers*, p305.
1561 Quoted in Mantoux, Vol.I, p238, 240, 244.
1562 Ibid., p243, 245.

to put off summoning the Germans until 25 April whilst meanwhile discussing the Italians issues, was agreed to, reluctantly, by Orlando.

During the 'very stormy' meeting the next day, Wilson presented the Italians with a memorandum stating that, as he had signed the armistice with the Germans on the basis of the Fourteen Points, he could not now do differently regarding the Austrians. Orlando told his own delegation that this left no room for discussion. On 19 April, six days of intense discussions began. The Italians had reached the end of their tether, and Orlando threatened to leave the Conference, no matter what the consequences, stating "I understand the tragic solemnity of this moment. Italy will suffer from this decision. For her, it is only a question of choosing between two deaths."[1563] Lloyd George responded anxiously "On account of Fiume? On account of a city where there are 24,000 Italians and where, if you count the population of the suburbs, the Italian majority is very doubtful?"[1564] He begged the Italians to think of the wider repercussions: "I do not know how Europe can get back on its feet if the United States does not stay with us and help us to oil the machinery."[1565]

Now it was the Italians turn to be unmoved. On 21 April Sonnino expressed his regret that he had been a part of negotiating the Treaty of London that had seen Italy enter the war on the Allied side: "For my part, I see my death in all of this–I mean my moral death. I have ruined my country whilst believing that I was doing my duty. Moreover, I don't want to insist any longer on something personal to me."[1566] Orlando warned of the danger of provoking "an uprising of the population… a revolution in Italy", which would be "a serious disservice to the entire world."[1567] The statement was not an unfounded one, as increasing reports came in of strikes, marches, riots, and deaths in violent clashes between left and right. Messages came from Italy exhorting Orlando to stay firm.[1568]

All attempts at compromise failed, and with the German delegates soon due to arrive, Wilson, Lloyd George and Clemenceau were anxious to present a united front, as not only the Italians, but also the Japanese and Belgians, were unhappy at how the Conference was proceeding. In what was "a capital error of judgement"[1569], Wilson sent his memorandum to the newspapers on the afternoon of 23 April. Unsurprisingly, when a special edition of *Les Temps* was delivered to the Italian delegation, there was great indignation. The Italians had known of Wilson's statement for a couple of days and had contemplated leaving even before that.[1570] The publication of the statement caused Orlando to dramatically leave the Peace Conference the next morning, 24 April, Sonnino following a couple of days later. Lloyd George commented:

> Well, the fat is in the fire at last! It is a pity that Wilson sent out the statement so hurriedly. On Sunday he produced it and read it to Clemenceau and me. Meanwhile I have been trying to bring

---

1563 Ibid., p287.
1564 Ibid., p288.
1565 L. Aldrovandi Marescotti, *Guerra Diplomatica: Ricordi E Frammenti Di Diario*, 1936, Milan, Mondadori, p247-248.
1566 Quoted in Mantoux, Vol.I, p295.
1567 Ibid., p301.
1568 For these complex negotiations, see R. Albrecht-Carrié, *Italy at the Paris Peace Conference*, 1938, New York, Columbia University Press.
1569 Di Scala, p155.
1570 MacMillan, *Peacemakers*, p308.

> about a settlement. If I had had more time, I think I might have done so. Now it is impossible to say what will happen. The Italians have acted badly.[1571]

Orlando returned to Rome to cheering crowds, asking "Have I properly interpreted the will of the Italian people?" The Senate responded with a unanimous vote of confidence in his government, followed by a huge vote of approval of 382 to 40 in the Chamber of Deputies. Nationalists, with fascists prominently involved, held mass meetings throughout Italy. The writing was on the wall, but Wilson was unheeding, and various delegations began to hold emergency meetings as it became clear that the very continuation of the Peace Conference itself was under threat. The remaining members of the Italian delegation in Paris informed Orlando that Italy's position was deteriorating rapidly, while the Americans, as so often, attempted a form of financial blackmail by holding up an urgently needed credit of $25 million.[1572] Britain and France tagged along, by stating that Orlando's withdrawal freed them from their adherence to the Treaty of London.

On 5 May, Orlando and Sonnino returned to Paris. Mutual trust had largely been eroded by the long process of attrition, with Italian resentment focusing on Wilson as the main opponent to their claims. Orlando later wrote that he had become convinced that "Wilson had his own personal engagement with the Yugoslavs; what it was I don't know but there it was."[1573] The stakes were high, given the growing crisis back home, Orlando telling Lloyd George "I must have a solution. Otherwise I will have a crisis in parliament or in the streets of Italy." Lloyd George asked "And if not, who do you see taking your place?" Orlando replied "Perhaps D'Annunzio."[1574] In the event, no satisfactory solution was found, and Orlando duly resigned as premier on 23 June, just days before the signing of the Treaty, Sonnino becoming the chief Italian signatory. The fact he was not a signatory became a point of pride for Orlando later in his life, arguing that Wilson had effectively excluded him from the Conference by appealing over his head to the people of Italy.[1575] The so-called 'Mutilated Victory' (*vittoria mutilata*)–a term coined by D'Annunzio–was much used as propaganda in the rise of Mussolini, in much the same way as the 'Stab-in-the-Back' myth was exploited by Hitler.[1576]

Lloyd George had become convinced that the terms being negotiated in Paris of what would later become the Treaty of Versailles were unduly harsh on a defeated Germany. More than once Jan Smuts, the South African premier, warned Lloyd George and Wilson that such a treaty would result in another war in a generation, writing: "We cannot destroy Germany without destroying Europe… we cannot save Europe without the co-operation of Germany… My fear is that the Paris Conference may prove one of the historic failures of the world… in the end, if she [Germany] feels that she has been unjustly

1571 Riddell, *Intimate Diary*, p56. Entry for 23 April 1919.
1572 MacMillan, *Peacemakers*, p309.
1573 Orlando, p484.
1574 Quoted in MacMillan, *Peacemakers*, p311. Orlando was wrong regarding his successor, but correct in essence, as D'Annunzio occupied Fiume, September 1919–December 1920, and Mussolini became Prime Minister on 31 October 1922.
1575 MacMillan, *Peacemakers*, p311; Orlando, p482-483.
1576 On 24 October 1918, the first anniversary of Caporetto, D'Annunzio's poem *Vittoria nostra, non-sarai mutilata* appeared in the Milan edition of *Corriere della Sera*, Anno 43, No.297, p3.

treated in the peace of 1919 she will find means of exacting retribution from her conquerors."[1577]

On Friday 21 March Lloyd George, highly concerned at the lack of progress, had told Riddell:

> I am going to Fontainebleau for the weekend and mean to put in the hardest forty-eight hours' thinking I have ever done. The Conference is not going well, and I must try to pull things together. The indemnity question is very difficult. It is impossible to get the French to come to an agreement, and the financial experts differ widely in their views as to the Germans' capacity to pay.[1578]

On Saturday Lloyd George retired with his advisers–Jan Smuts[1579], Henry Wilson, Maurice Hankey and Philip Kerr, joined later by Lord Sumner[1580] and Lord Cunliffe, his two key advisors on reparations–to the Hôtel de France et d'Angleterre at Fontainebleau in an attempt to 'brainstorm' some fresh perspectives and find acceptable solutions. In doing this, he came up with a rather novel and creative idea, the first afternoon getting each advisor to 'role-play' a different nation, to see what was spontaneously thrown up. Hankey played an Englishman, while Wilson enthusiastically played a German officer, then a French woman, before Lloyd George summed up. Kerr, as secretary, had the task of making sense of the discussions and writing it all up.[1581] The outcome was a trenchant, psychologically acute memorandum which appears pregnant with possibility in the light of what later transpired:

> Some Considerations for the Peace Conference before They Finally Draft Their Terms
>
> When nations are exhausted by wars in which they have put forth all their strength and which leave them tired, bleeding, and broken, it is not difficult to patch up a peace what may last until the generation which experienced the horrors of the war has passed away. Pictures of heroism and triumph only tempt those who know nothing of the sufferings and terrors of war. It is therefore comparative easy to patch up a peace which will last for 30 years.
>
> What is difficult, however, is to draw up a peace which will not provoke a fresh struggle when those who have had practical experience of what war means have passed away. History has proved that a peace which has been hailed by a victorious nation as a triumph of diplomatic skill and statesmanship, even of moderation, in the long run has proved itself to be short-sighted and charged with danger to the victor. The peace of 1871 was believed by Germany to insure not only her security but her permanent supremacy. The facts have shown exactly the contrary, France itself has demonstrated that those who say you can make Germany so feeble that she will never be able to hit back are utterly wrong... You may strip Germany of her colonies,

---

1577 Smuts, p227.

1578 Riddell, *Intimate Diary*, p36.

1579 Doubt has been raised whether it was Jan Smuts who accompanied Lloyd George, but rather Edwin Montagu. See Rowland, *Lloyd George*, Ft.4, p484.

1580 John Hamilton, Viscount Sumner (1859-1934), a Law Lord. The pair were named the 'Heavenly Twins', due to the "astronomically" large sums they thought should be extracted from Germany, the "beatific smile" they would adopt on giving a judgement, and the fact they were generally inseparable at Versailles.

1581 Rowland, *Lloyd George*, p484-485; MacMillan, *Peacemakers*, p207.

reduce her armaments to a mere police force and her navy to that of a fifth rate power; all the same in the end if she feels that she has been unjustly treated in the peace of 1919 she will find means of exacting retribution from her conquerors. The impression, the deep impression, made upon the human heart by four years of unexampled slaughter will disappear with the hearts upon which it has been marked by the terrible sword of the great war. The maintenance of peace will then depend upon there being no causes of exasperation constantly stirring up the spirit of patriotism, of justice or of fair play to achieve redress. Our terms may be severe, they may be stern and even ruthless but at the same time they can be so just that the country on which they are imposed will feel in its heart that it has no right to complain. But injustice, arrogance, displayed in the hour of triumph will never be forgotten or forgiven.

For these reasons I am, therefore, strongly adverse to transferring more Germans from German rule to the rule of some other nation than can possibly be helped. I cannot conceive of any greater cause of future war than that the German people, who have certainly proved themselves one of the most vigorous and powerful races in the world should be surrounded by a number of small states, many of them consisting of people who have never previously set up a stable government for themselves, but each of them containing large masses of Germans clamouring for reunion with their native land. The proposal of the Polish Commission that we should place 2,100,000 Germans under the control of a people which is of a different religion and which has never proved its capacity for stable self-government throughout its history must, in my judgement, lead sooner or later to a new war in the East of Europe. What I have said about the Germans is equally true of the Magyars… I would therefore take as a guiding principle of the peace that as far as is humanly possible the different races should be allocated to their motherland, and that this human criterion should have precedence over considerations of strategy or economics or communications which can usually be adjusted by their means. Secondly, I would say that the duration for the payments of reparations ought to disappear if possible with the generation which made the war.

But there is a consideration in favour of a long-sighted peace which influences me even more than the desire to leave no causes justifying a fresh outbreak 30 years hence. There is one element in the present condition of nations which differentiates it from the situation as it was in 1815. In the Napoleonic wars the countries were equally exhausted but the revolutionary spirit had spent its force in the country of its birth… The situation is very different now. The revolution is still in its infancy. The extreme figures of the Terror are still in command in Russia. The whole of Europe is filled with the spirit of revolution. There is a deep sense not only of discontent, but of anger and revolt amongst the workmen against pre-war conditions. The whole existing order in its political, social, and economic aspects is questioned by the masses of the population from one end of Europe to the other. In some countries, like Germany and Russia, the unrest takes the form of open rebellion, in others like France, Great Britain and Italy it takes the shape of strikes and of general disinclination to settle down to work, symptoms which are just as much concerned with the desire for political and social change as with wage demands.

Much of this unrest is healthy. We shall never make lasting peace by attempting to restore the conditions of 1914. But there is a danger that we may throw the masses of the population through- out Europe into the arms of the extremists whose only idea for regenerating mankind is to descry utterly the whole existing fabric of society. These men have triumphed in Russia. They have done so at terrible price. Hundreds and thousands of the populations have perished. The railroads, the roads, the towns, the whole structural organization of Russia has been almost destroyed, but… they seem to have managed to keep their hold upon the masses of the Russian people, and… have succeeded in creating a large army which is apparently well directed and well disciplined, and is, as to a great part of it prepared to die for its ideals. In another year Russia inspired by a new enthusiasm may have recovered from her passion for peace and have at her command the only army eager to fight, because it is the only army that believes that it has any cause to fight for.

The greatest danger that I see in the present situation is that Germany may throw in her lot with Bolshevism and place her resources, her brains, her vast organizing power at the disposal of the revolutionary fanatics whose dream is to conquer the world for Bolshevism by force of arms… The present government in Germany is weak; it has no prestige; its authority is challenged; it lingers merely because there is no alternative but the Spartacists[1582], and Germany is not ready for Spartacism, as yet. But the argument which the Spartacists are using with great effect at this very time is that they alone can save Germany from the intolerable conditions which have been bequeathed her by the war. They offer to free the German people from indebtedness to the Allies and indebtedness to their own richer classes. They offer them complete control of their own affairs and the prospect of a new heaven and earth. It is true that the price will be heavy. There will be two or three years of anarchy, perhaps of bloodshed, but at the end the land will remain, the people will remain… and Germany, having thrown off her burdens, will be able to make a fresh start.

If Germany goes over to the Spartacists it is inevitable that she should throw her lot with the Russian Bolshevists. Once that happens all Eastern Europe will be swept into the orbit of the Bolshevik revolution and within a year we may witness the spectacle of nearly three hundred million organized into a vast red army under German instructors and German generals equipped with German cannon and German machine-guns and prepared for a renewal of the attack on Western Europe. This is a prospect which no one can face with equanimity. Yet the news which came from Hungary yesterday shows only too clearly that this danger is no fantasy. And what are the reasons alleged for this decision? They are mainly the belief that large numbers of Magyars are to be handed over to the control of others. If we are wise, we shall offer to Germany a peace, which, while just, will be preferable for all sensible men to the alternative of Bolshevism. I would, therefore, put in the forefront of the peace that once she accepts our terms, especially reparation, we will open to her the raw materials and markets of the world on equal terms with ourselves, and will do everything possible to enable the German people to get upon their legs again. We cannot both cripple her and expect her to pay.

[1582] During the November Revolution of 1918, the Spartacus League established itself as a non-party group aiming to create a soviet republic. After the failed Spartacist Uprising of 5-12 January 1919 in Berlin, the remnants merged with the newly created Communist Party of Germany (KPD).

Finally, we must offer terms which a responsible Government in Germany can expect to be able to carry out. If we present terms to Germany which are unjust, or excessively onerous, no responsible Government will sign them… Yet if we can find nobody in Germany who will put his hand to a peace treaty, what will be the position? A large army of occupation for an indefinite period is out of the question… Neither the British Empire nor America would agree to occupy Germany. France by itself could not bear the burden of occupation. We should therefore be driven back on the policy of blockading the country… As a matter of fact… I very much doubt if public opinion would tolerate the deliberate condemnation of millions of women and children to death by starvation…

From every point of view, therefore, it seems to me that we ought to endeavour to draw up a peace settlement as if we were impartial arbiters, forgetful of the passions of the war. This settlement ought to have three ends in view. First of all it must do justice to the Allies, by taking into account Germany's responsibility for the origin of the war, and for the way in which it was fought. Secondly, it must be a settlement which a responsible German Government can sign in the belief that it can fulfil the obligations in incurs. Thirdly, it must be a settlement which will constitute an alternative to Bolshevism, because it will commend itself to all reasonable opinion as a fair settlement of the European problem.

It is not, however, enough to draw up a just and far-sighted peace with Germany. If we are to offer Europe an alternative to Bolshevism we must make the League of Nations into something which will be both a safeguard to those nations who are prepared for fair dealing with their neighbours, and a menace to those who would trespass on the rights of their neighbours, whether they are imperialist empires or imperialist Bolsheviks. An essential element, therefore, is in the peace settlement in the constitution of the League of Nations as the effective guardian of international right and international liberty throughout the world. If this is to happen the first thing to do is that the leading members of the League of Nations should arrive at an understanding between themselves in regard to armaments. To my mind it is idle to endeavour to impose a permanent limitation of armaments upon Germany unless we are prepared similarly to impose a limitation upon ourselves. I recognize that until Germany has settled down and given practical proof that she has abandoned her imperialist ambitions, and until Russia has also given proof that she does not intend to embark upon a military crusade against her neighbours, it is essential that the leading members of the League of Nations should maintain considerable forces both by land and sea in order to preserve liberty in the world. But if they are to preserve a united front to the forces both of reaction and revolution, they must arrive at such an agreement in regard to armaments among as themselves as would make it impossible for suspicion to arise between members of the League of Nations in regard to their intentions towards one another. If the League is to do its work for the world it will only be because the members of the League trust it themselves and because there are no rivalries and jealousies in the matter of armaments between them. The first condition of success for the League of Nations is, therefore, a firm understanding between the British Empire and the United States of America and France and Italy that there will be no more competitive building up of fleets or armies between them… [then the League] will be able to ensure as an essential condition of peace that

> not only Germany, but all the smaller states of Europe undertake to limit their armaments and abolish conscription. If the small nations are permitted to organize and maintain conscript armies running each to hundreds of thousands, boundary wars will be inevitable and all Europe will be drawn in. Unless we secure this universal limitation we shall achieve neither lasting peace, nor the permanent observance of the limitation of German Armaments which we now seek to impose.
>
> I should like to ask why Germany, if she accepts the terms we consider just and fair, should not be admitted to the League of Nations, at any rate as soon as she has established a stable and democratic Government. Would it not be an inducement to her both to sign the terms and to resist Bolshevism? Might it not be safer that she should be inside the League than that she should be outside it?
>
> Finally, I believe that until the authority and effectiveness of the League of Nations has been demonstrated, the British Empire and the United States ought to give France a guarantee against the possibility of a new German aggression. France has special reason for asking for such a decree… If, however, the peace conference is really to secure peace and prove to the world a complete plan of settlement which all reasonable men will recognize as an alternative preferable to anarchy, it must deal with the Russian situation. Bolshevik Imperialism does not merely menace the states on Russia's borders. It threatens the whole of Asia and is as near to America as it is to France. It is idle to think that the Peace Conference can separate, however sound a peace it may have arranged with Germany, if it leaves Russia as it is today… Paris, March 25, 1919.[1583]

Wilson, Clemenceau and Orlando were presented with copies of the memorandum. The President was broadly sympathetic to Lloyd George's views, but Clemenceau was furious and predictably against any lessening of pressure on Germany. Unfortunately, the memorandum was leaked. On 8 April, a menacingly uncompromising telegram inspired by Lord Northcliffe and William Kennedy Jones[1584], and signed by 233 Coalition MPs, was sent to Lloyd George in Paris. It read:

> The greatest anxiety exists throughout the country at the persistent reports from Paris that the British delegates instead of formulating the complete financial claim of the Empire are merely considering what amount can be exacted from the enemy…
>
> Our constituents have always expected–and still expect–that the first action of the Peace Delegates would be, as you repeatedly stated in your election speeches, to present the Bill in full, to make Germany acknowledge the debt and then to discuss ways and means of obtaining payment.

---

1583 Lloyd George, *Some Considerations For The Peace Conference Before They Finally Draft Their Terms*, Cmd.1614. Emphasis added. Those who later criticised Lloyd George's attitude of so-called 'appeasement' towards Germany in the 1930s would have done well to heed his recommendations and warnings in 1919.

1584 William Kennedy Jones (1865-1921), part-owner and content editor on Northcliffe's *Daily Mail* and *The Times*, 1896-1912, Tory MP for Hornsey, 1916 until his death.

> Although we have the utmost confidence in your intention to fulfil your pledges to the country, may we… have your assurance that you have in no way departed from your original intention.[1585]

The telegram was published in full the next day in *The Times*, then owned by Northcliffe. It showed the Opposition had no more understanding of the dire situation, and no more forward-thinking vision, than a grocer presenting an inflated shop bill to a complete bankrupt. Northcliffe was a poorly educated, arrogant and embittered man, who believed himself to be 'Napoleon' reborn and who revelled in 'gutter press' populist virulence, hostile to women's suffrage, trade unionism, pensions, Germans, Jews and much else. He also exercised huge power without responsibility–by 1914, he controlled 40% of Britain's morning newspaper circulation, 45% of the evening circulation, and 15% of the Sunday circulation. Lloyd George had apparently–accounts differ–offered Northcliffe a Cabinet post as the Minster for Air on 15 November 1917, but he had very publicly declined, on the grounds that it would reduce his "independence" to criticise the government[1586], eventually becoming the Director for Propaganda in Enemy Countries on 13 February 1918, until he resigned the day after the Armistice was signed.[1587] Now he felt himself slighted by not being credited with winning the war or being given a post in the Peace Delegation.

In Germany itself, people were starving, an estimated 100,000 dying between the Armistice and the eventual lifting of the naval blockade on the country on 11 July 1919.[1588] As early as 8 March, Lloyd George, with a blend of humanitarianism and political acumen, had stated at a meeting of the Supreme War Council that:

> He wished to urge with all his might that steps should at once be taken to revictual Germany. The honour of the Allies was involved. Under the terms of the armistice the Allies did imply that they meant to let food into Germany. The Germans had accepted our armistice conditions… and they had complied with the majority of those conditions. But so far, not a single ton of food had been sent into Germany… The Allies were now on top, but the memories of starvation might one day turn against them. The Germans were being allowed to starve whilst at the same time hundreds of thousands of tons of food were lying at Rotterdam, waiting to be taken… into Germany:… The Allies were sowing hatred for the future: they were piling up agony, not for the Germans, but for themselves. The British troops were indignant about our refusal to revictual Germany. General Plumer had said that he could not be responsible for his troops if children were allowed to wander about the streets, half starving. The British soldiers would not stand that, they were beginning to make complaints, and the most urgent demands were being received from them… As long as the people were starving they would listen to the argument of the Spartacists, and the Allies by their action were simply encouraging elements of

1585 Reproduced in Lloyd George, *Truth About The Peace Treaties*, Vol.I, p563.
1586 Thompson, *Northcliffe*, p292. Northcliffe published his refusal in *The Times*, 16 November 1917.
1587 Ibid., p297, 313.
1588 S. L. Bane and R. H. Lutz, Eds., *The Blockade Of Germany After The Armistice, 1918-1919*, 1942, Stanford, Stanford University Press, p791. Another 763,000 had already died of starvation and disease prior to this.

> disruption and anarchism… As long as order was maintained in Germany, a breakwater would exist between the countries of the Allies and the waters of Revolution beyond. But once the breakwater was swept away, he could not speak for France, but trembled for his own country. The situation was particularly serious in Munich. Bavaria, which once had been thought to represent the most solid and conservative part of Germany, had already gone[1589]… Meanwhile the Conference continued to haggle. Six weeks ago the same arguments about gold and foreign securities had been raised, and it had then been decided that Germany should be given food. He begged the Conference to re-affirm that decision in the most unequivocal terms… if as a result of a process of starvation enforced by the Allies, the people of Germany were allowed to run riot, a state of revolution among the working classes of all countries would ensue with which it would be impossible to cope.[1590]

Northcliffe, who had been:

> Disgusted to learn that he [Lloyd George] had actually made a passionate appeal at a session of the Council of Ten for food to be sent into Germany, was now waging another of his virulent campaigns. A new slogan appeared on the front page of the Daily Mail–"The Junkers will cheat you yet"–and a strident series of leading articles held forth about the snivelling Hun and recalled, in lingering detail, the various atrocities that needed to be avenged. Edith Cavell was shot at dawn yet again; the *Lusitania* went down for a second time; Belgian nuns were raped several times over for good measure.[1591]

Northcliffe's culpability for later events is colossal.

Faced by this onslaught, culminating in the telegram, Lloyd George had to back down, with unfathomably tragic consequences for Europe in the coming decades, involving yet greater misery and loss of 'life, limb and property'.[1592] He was determined to have his say, however. From 14-17 April Lloyd George was forced to break off negotiations and return to London to give his version of events, to try to rally support and face down his political enemies in the House and 'armchair experts' in the Press, and to give an impression of the very real difficulties faced by the statesmen involved in the complex negotiations. As he wrote later:

> I felt that if the uneasiness amongst our supporters represented a real distrust of the Peace delegation, it would be better to resign my position and hand over the seals to someone who

---

1589 The Bavarian Soviet Republic, 6 April–3 May 1919, established after a period of anarchy caused by the assassination of socialist Minister, President Kurt Eisner, in Munich on 21 February.

1590 https://history.state.gov/historicaldocuments/frus1919Parisv04/d15. Retrieved 24 February 2021.

1591 Rowland, *Lloyd George*, p489.

1592 In later years Philip Kerr believed that Lloyd George, in backing down on his moderate reparations policy, had compromised his future as a Liberal leader, and that his weakness in the face of this challenge had been the turning point of his career. Butler, p83, quoting a Letter to Col. House, 13 February 1933.

represented more truly the attitude of Parliament. *I could not conscientiously become the instrument of forcing upon Germany a peace conceived in the spirit of the Kennedy Jones message.*[1593]

The last sentence says it all about the antipathetical ethos prevailing, and the true nature of Lloyd George's political and philosophical position. On 16 April he made a statement on the situation in the Commons:

> I am fully aware that there is a good deal of impatience in the world for peace–some of it very natural impatience, and some of it, perhaps, calculated impatience. I propose to address myself to the really sincere, honest impatience which is felt throughout all lands.
>
> The task with which the Peace Delegates have been confronted has indeed been a gigantic one. No Conference that has ever assembled in the history of the world has been confronted with problems of such variety, of such complexity, of such magnitude, and of such gravity. The Congress of Vienna was the nearest approach to it. You had then to settle the affairs of Europe. It took eleven months. But the problems at the Congress of Vienna… sink into insignificance compared with those which we have had to attempt to settle at the Paris Conference… With very few exceptions, every country… [has been involved]… in this great world struggle. There has never been in the whole history of this globe anything to compare to it. Ten new States have sprung into existence, some of them independent, some of them semi-independent, some of them may be Protectorates, and, at any rate, although you may not define their boundaries, you must give indications of them. The boundaries of fourteen countries have to be re-cast.
>
> That will give some idea of the difficulties, purely of a territorial character, that have engaged our attention. But there are problems, equally great and equally important, not of a territorial character, but all affecting the peace of the world, all affecting the well-being of men, all affecting the destiny of the human race, and every one of them of a character where, if you make blunders, humanity may have to pay. Armaments, economic questions, which are the life of commerce and trade, questions of international waterways and railways, the question of indemnities–not an easy one, and not going to be settled by telegram–and international arrangements for labour practically never attempted before! Thanks very largely to the skill and real statesmanship displayed by my right hon. Friend the Member for the Gorbals Division of Glasgow (Mr. Barnes), and thanks also to the assistance which he has had from some hon. and right hon. Gentlemen opposite, and from others who are in the Trade Union movement, a great world scheme has been adopted. And there is that great organisation–a great experiment, but an experiment upon which the whole future of the globe for peace hangs–the Society of Nations.
>
> All, and each of them separately, would occupy months. A blunder might precipitate universal war–it may be near, it may be distant. And all nations, almost every nation on earth, engaged in the consideration of all these problems! We were justified in taking some time. In fact, I do not mind saying that it would have been imperative in some respects that we should have taken more time but for one fact, and that is that we are setting up a machinery which is

[1593] Lloyd George, *Truth About The Peace Treaties*, Vol.I, p564. Emphasis added.

capable of readjusting and correcting possible mistakes. That is why the League of Nations, instead of wasting time, has saved the time of the Conference. We had to shorten our labours and work crowded hours, long and late, because, whilst we were trying to build, we saw in many lands the foundations of society crumbling into dust, and we had to make haste. I venture to say that no body of men ever worked harder, and that no body of men have ever worked in better harmony. I am doubtful whether any body of men with a difficult task have worked under greater difficulties… and when enormous issues are depending upon it, you require calm deliberation. I ask it for the rest of the journey. The journey is not at an end. It is full of perils, perils for this country, perils for all lands, perils for the people throughout the world. I beg, at any rate, that the men who are doing their best should be left in peace to do it, or that other men should be sent there.

Those are merely artificial difficulties. They are difficulties that are more trying to the temper than to the judgment. But there are intrinsic difficulties of an extraordinary character. You are dealing with a multitude of nations, most of them with a problem of its own, each and every one of them with a different point of view, even where the problems are common, looking from a different angle at questions–sometimes, perhaps, with different interests; and it requires all the tact, all the patience, and all the skill that we can command to prevent different interests from developing into conflicting interests. I want the House and the country to bear that in mind. I believe that we have surmounted those difficulties, but it has not been easy. There were questions one never heard of which have almost imperilled the peace of Europe while we were sitting there.

… How many Members have heard of Teschen?[1594]… I had never heard of it, but Teschen very nearly produced an angry conflict between two Allied States, and we had to interrupt the proceedings to try and settle the affairs at Teschen. There are many questions of that kind where commissions have had to be sent, and where we have had to smooth difficulties, in order to enable us to get on with the bigger problems of the War. And those questions are important. They are questions of small States. It was the quarrel for small States that made the great War. The difficulties of the Balkans–I believe they disturbed Europe, they created the atmosphere of unrest which began the trouble, they aroused the military temper, and I am not at all sure they did not excite the blood lust in Europe. One of the features of the present situation is that, owing to the break-up of great Empires, Central Europe is being broken into small States, and the greatest care must be taken that no cause of future unrest shall be created by the settlements which we make…[1595]

Later in that day's debates, Lloyd George turned specifically to the matter of the telegram, launching a stinging and unanswerable attack on Northcliffe, whom he did not actually name:

1594 Cieszyn Silesia, or the Duchy of Teschen, was a small area in south-eastern Silesia. Czechoslovak and Polish forces clashed here from 23-31 January 1919.

1595 https://api.parliament.uk/historic-hansard/commons/1919/apr/16/prime-ministers-statement. Retrieved 29 April 2019.

> I did not object to that telegram… but… I object to the information on which it was based. I saw the telegram, and you must remember that these things, when they are sent abroad, become international questions. France sees it, America, Italy, and Germany. I am told that it was sent because of information which came from "a reliable source".

Noting a discrepancy in the alleged source between the statements of William Kennedy Jones and Claude Lowther, Tory MP for Lonsdale, he quipped "Really they ought to have compared notes! I blame their solicitor", before continuing:

> I know the "reliable source," and I will tell the House something about it. There were peace terms published in November as a model for us to proceed upon. In those peace terms there was not a word about indemnities, not a word about the cost of the War. Reparation–yes, in the strictest and narrowest sense of the term, but no reparation for lost lives, no reparation for damaged houses, not even at Broadstairs… We were not at that time to try anybody responsible for the War. We were to try those who had been guilty of offences against the law, but the tribunals must be German. That is the "reliable source"! Now we must have everything–the cost of the War, damage to all sorts of property–hanging everybody all round, especially members of the Government! In December there were hundreds of thousands of newspapers circulated freely, at somebody's expense, among the soldiers in France, asking them to return candidates. If those candidates had been returned, the two peace delegates in Paris now would certainly not have been the Foreign Secretary (Mr. Balfour) and myself, but perhaps Mr. Ramsay Macdonald and Mr. Philip Snowden. Who issued that appeal? The "reliable source"…
>
> … At the beginning of the Conference there were appeals to everybody all round to support President Wilson and his great ideals. Where did these come from? From the same "reliable source" that is now hysterically attacking all those great ideals… Reliable! That is the last adjective I would use. It is here to-day, jumping there to-morrow, and there the next day. I would as soon rely on a grasshopper.
>
> Still, I am prepared to make some allowance–even great newspapers will forgive me for saying so–and when a man is labouring under a keen sense of disappointment, however unjustified and however ridiculous the expectations may have been, he is always apt to think the world is badly run. When a man has deluded himself, and all the people whom he ever permits to go near to him help him into the belief that he is the only man who can win the War, and he is waiting for the clamour of the multitude that is going to demand his presence there to direct the destinies of the world, and there is not a whisper, not a sound, it is rather disappointing; it is unnerving; it is upsetting.
>
> Then the War is won without him. There must be something wrong. Of course it must be the Government! Then, at any rate, he is the only man to make peace… So he publishes the Peace Terms, and he waits for the "call." It does not come … [W]hen that kind of diseased vanity is carried to the point of sowing dissension between great Allies, whose unity is essential to the peace and happiness of the world, and when an attempt is made to make France distrust Britain, to make France hate America, and America to dislike France, and Italy to quarrel with

> everybody, then I say that not even that kind of disease is a justification for so black a crime against humanity.
>
> ... I have been in France for weeks. Here nobody takes notice of this thing–everybody knows it. But it is not the case in France. They still believe in France that the "Times" is a serious organ. They do not know that it is merely a threepenny edition of the "Daily Mail." On the Continent of Europe they really have an idea that it is a semi-official organ of the Government. That shows how long these traditions take to die out. I want them to know what all this means. I am doing this in the interests of good will. That is my only apology for taking notice of that kind of trash, with which some of these papers have been filled during the last few weeks.[1596]

It was a devastating critique of irresponsible, unelected press baronage, still deeply relevant today. Notably, neither Kennedy Jones nor any of his co-signatories to the telegram made any attempt to justify their misgivings.

Regarding the military occupation of the Rhineland, Lloyd George did not want a lengthy occupation, partly because of the drain this would be on British resources, but also because he correctly foresaw that this would cause great resentment in Germany. Unfortunately, during his absence in London, Clemenceau persuaded Wilson to accept a 15-year occupation, with one third of the occupied territory being evacuated every five years, in exchange for France agreeing to the rest of the other Rhineland conditions. The French saw the situation as a unique opportunity to establish a secure frontier on the Rhine. Throughout the conference, the politicians and generals of the right conducted a vigorous campaign to achieve France's 'natural frontier.' The separation of the Rhineland from Germany would have three clear advantages for France. It would diminish Germany's superiority in population; it would establish a buffer zone between the two nations, and it would render impossible a German troop concentration west of the Rhine itself. Such a *'paix française'*, however, would have been contrary to one of the main considerations of the Conference, the creation of a lasting European peace that satisfied the conflicting foreign policies of the major allies. To preserve the alliance, Clemenceau was forced to abandon the proposed separation and to accept a compromise. On his return to Paris, Lloyd George was presented with a *fait accompli*, which he most reluctantly had to accept. Clemenceau was pleased, stating "I have the fifteen years. I now consider that the peace is made."[1597] He would, of course, prove to be profoundly wrong, though he would not live to see the resumption of European war.

Two days after Lloyd George's parliamentary speech, on 18 April, the German representatives were summoned to Versailles and shown the draft Treaty for the first time.[1598] The delegation–180 diplomats, experts, secretaries and journalists–travelled on special trains, that the French ominously ensured were slowed down as they passed through areas devastated by the war. On arrival in Paris,

---

1596 https://api.parliament.uk/historic-hansard/commons/1919/apr/16/information-from-a-reliable-source#S5CV0114P0_19190416_HOC_207. Retrieved 23 April 2020.

1597 Quoted in Sharp, p124. The last Allied troops left the Rhineland four years early, on 30 June 1930, and the territory was remilitarized by Hitler on 7 March 1936.

1598 Lloyd George's own, signed and annotated copy of the draft Treaty is in the Lloyd George Museum.

they were deposited in the cold Hôtel des Réservoirs, the same hotel where the French leaders had stayed while they negotiated with Bismarck in 1871. It was stockaded, 'for their protection'. On 4 May, the 'Big Four' ordered that the draft Treaty should be sent to the printers. Two days later a plenary session was called to vote on the terms. As no final version was as yet available, the delegates listened to a long summary read in French. Sir Henry Wilson noted in his diary: "So, we are going to hand out terms to the Boches without reading them ourselves first. I don't think in all history this can be matched."[1599] The next day, 7 May[1600], the Germans were summoned to see the terms at the Trianon Palace Hotel, where, as Lloyd George later wrote, "the Allied Supreme Council had held its anxious meetings less than a year ago to the continuous sound of the throb and thud of the German guns at Chateau Thierry."[1601]

Clemenceau addressed the German Foreign Minister, Ulrich von Brockdorff-Rantzau, coldly, outlining the main headings of the treaty, stating portentously "The hour has struck for the weighty settlement of our account. You asked us for peace. We are disposed to grant it to you."[1602] Brockdorff-Rantzau unfortunately had to make his long reply whilst remaining seated, as he "was so nervous he was physically incapable of standing up", a fact unknown at the time.[1603] This, and his harsh voice, coupled with the ineptitude of his translators, created a very poor impression. Clemenceau went red with anger, while Lloyd George moved uneasily in his seat and snapped an ivory paperknife in two[1604], telling Frances Stevenson it "made him more angry than any incident of the war… [and that] for the first time he has felt the same hatred for them that the French feel."[1605]

On reading and analysing the terms afterwards, the Germans were deeply shocked and outraged. At a historical remove, this may seem surprising, as their own Foreign Office had anticipated many of the terms beforehand. A likely explanation for their reaction is given by Margaret MacMillan, quoting an American observer who said in April:

> 'The Germans have little left but Hope. But having only that I think they have clung to it–the Hope that the Americans would do something, the Hope that the final terms would not be so severe as the Armistice indicated and so on. Subconsciously, I think the Germans have been more optimistic than they realized.' And, he added prophetically, 'when they see the terms in cold print, there will be intense bitterness, hate and desperation.'[1606]

On 18 May, Lloyd George made a visit to the great Somme battlefields to see where his son had fought with the 38th (Welsh) Division and met with the Headquarters Staff at Villers-Bretonneux. The terms

---

1599 Quoted in MacMillan, *Peacemakers*, p469.
1600 This was the fourth anniversary of the sinking of the RMS *Lusitania* by the German U-boat *U-20*, 18 km off the southern coast of Ireland, inside the declared war zone, with the loss of 1,198 passengers and crew.
1601 Lloyd George, *Truth About The Peace Treaties*, Vol.I, p675.
1602 Quoted in MacMillan, *Peacemakers*, p474.
1603 Lloyd George, *Truth About The Peace Treaties*, Vol.I, p676.
1604 Riddell, *Diaries*, 1986, p274-275.
1605 Stevenson, *Diary*, p183.
1606 Quoted in MacMillan, *Peacemakers*, p475-476.

of the treaty were as yet still undecided, as Lloyd George spoke in determined fashion to the soon-to-be demobilized Welshmen for the last time:

> I see you now at the end of the struggle, and we have presented our peace terms. These terms are written in the blood of fallen heroes…
>
> The Germans say they will not sign… We say, "Gentlemen, you must sign. If you don't do so in Versailles, you shall do so in Berlin."
>
> But it is useless for four of us to go "on our own" to Berlin to say "You must sign." If we four go we must have the Army behind us. We are not going to give way.
>
> The future of the world is dependent on this peace being imposed on Germany. If it is necessary for you to march to Berlin, if your leave is cancelled or your departure for England delayed, you will know that I alone am responsible… See that the seal is put on the document which you have helped to write, and we shall have peace reigning throughout the whole world.[1607]

Jan Smuts foresaw trouble, on 22 May addressing a memorandum, 'Procedure for Alterations', to Lloyd George against turning the Treaty into a *Diktat*, stating:

> For the sake of the future, they [the Germans] should not merely be made to sign at the point of the bayonet… The Treaty should not be capable of moral repudiation by the German people hereafter… [The Allies] should as far as possible carry the German delegates with us and we should listen to what they have to say.

He highlighted the biggest flaw in the Conference and in the Treaty, recommending nominating three minor delegates to discuss matters with the Germans, but he was ignored, two days Lord Cecil noting that Lloyd George "seemed averse to any such plan, saying that it would be very dangerous".[1608]

By 29 May the German delegation in Paris had prepared and delivered its memorandum in response to the conditions, in the form of 443 pages of closely reasoned objections and counter-proposals. Their general tenor was that the terms were not the equitable ones promised by the Allies. They resisted the fact that territory was being taken from Germany, that Germans were being denied self-determination, were being enslaved by reparations, and that Germany alone was being disarmed. Concerned about the nature of the Treaty, and as to whether the Germans would sign it, Lloyd George summoned his key Cabinet colleagues to Paris for a series of joint meetings with the British delegation from 30 May to 1 June. By the final day, at his apartment, all present were in agreement that some concessions needed to be made, with Smuts again arguing most vehemently in this regard. In his summing up that evening, Lloyd George praised his colleagues' magnanimity:

---

1607 https://www.southwalesargus.co.uk/news/17675795.scrap-in-the-baltic-100-years-ago/. Retrieved 4 April 2020.

1608 Quoted in A. Lentin, *General Smuts*, 2010, London, Haus, pp88-89.

The members of the Delegation represented a great victorious Power with a most formidable enemy at their mercy after long and cruel fighting. The whole discussion had taken the form of an earnest and sometimes a passionate plea for justice for the fallen enemy. He thought that they erred rather on the side of consideration for the enemy.

There was no note of vengeance. He thought it an extraordinary tribute to the temper of the British Empire that in such circumstances there could be a discussion in such a spirit…

They had presented their demands and now they heard the criticism. The question had been asked that morning why it was only at this late stage that mistakes were discovered. The answer was that they now had fresh information from the Germans, and that on the whole they found that it required investigation. He had no fear of changing his view if he was shown that the information on which he had acted in the first instance was proved afterwards not to be in accordance with the actual conditions.

The first thing was to have an absolutely just Peace, and that standard must be applied to the whole Peace.

They must have no hesitation in admitting that they were wrong, if they were wrong, and in modifying the terms accordingly. But they must also see that the terms imposed were expedient as well as just.

Justice was a question which the Germans were at liberty to raise, but expediency was a matter for the Allies to consider and not the Germans. The Allies were entitled to go to the limit of justice so far as Germany was concerned.

He thought that the Allies had gone too far in two or three directions.

First, regarding the Eastern frontiers, he thought that the Allies had gone too far and that the matter should be put right. Regarding the Army of Occupation, that was rather a question of expediency than of justice. There were several points on which he would like to make suggestions for a departure from the original terms and for an attempt to meet the Germans…

… He said that he had talked a good deal with the Germans at Versailles and found that they were most concerned about the two questions of Silesia and the League of Nations.

They were very sensitive on the latter subject, because they felt they were being driven out of the community of nations. They attached even more importance to that than to Silesia…

Some months ago, he (Mr. Lloyd George) had circulated his views about the Terms of Peace, and had proposed that the Germans should join the League of Nations at once. Now, however, he had modified those views. He did not think that the Germans could be admitted until the Allies had settled their own differences…

… He thought that the Germans would be satisfied if they were brought in within two years. If making such a concession to them would induce them to sign, it would be well worth while…

He had found the subject of compensation the most baffling and perplexing of all…

The Germans had inflicted on the Allies a loss which, in cash, amounted to something like £30,000,000,000. If loss of trade were included as well as war debts, he doubted whether that sum would cover the Allied loss. By every principle of justice, by the principles of justice which were recognised as applicable between individuals, the Germans were liable for the whole of the damages and the cost of recovering them. The Allies were not doing anything which was unjust in their demand for reparation. They had not presented a bill for the whole sum, which might amount to £10,000,000,000 or £11,000,000,000...

It was resolved that the Prime Minister, in his negotiations at the Council of the Allied and Associated Powers, should press for concessions to be made to the enemy in the Treaty of Peace in the following respects:-

(a) A modification of the clauses dealing with the Eastern frontiers in the direction of-

(i) Leaving to Germany the districts where the population was predominantly German in cases where there was no overwhelming reason for transferring such districts to Poland, and (ii) Providing for plebiscites being held in doubtful cases.

(b) The extension to Germany of some promise that she should enter the League of Nations at an earlier date than at present arranged in the Treaty, subject to the condition that Germany was making a real effort to perform her obligations.

(c) A modification of the clauses dealing with the Army of Occupation in the direction of-

(i) Reducing the numerical strength, having regard to the reductions made and about to be made in the German forces, and (ii) Making the period of occupation as short as possible.

(d) A modification of the Reparation Clauses in the direction of fixing the liability of the Germans to the Allies at a definite amount, by one or other of the following methods:-

(i) The Germans to undertake the whole task of restoration and, in addition, to pay at as early a date as possible a fixed sum to be divided between the Allies in proportions to be agreed upon between them. (ii) The Germans to sign the Reparation Clauses as they stand, but, within three months, to make an offer of a fixed sum... in discharge of their total liabilities for reparations; in the event of the Germans making no satisfactory offer the present Reparation Clauses to stand.

The Delegation authorised the Prime Minister, in the event of any resistance on the part of any of his colleagues on the Council, to use the full weight of the entire British Empire even to the point of refusing:-

1. The services of the British Army to advance into Germany.

2. The services of the British Navy to enforce the Blockade of Germany.[1609]

Unfortunately, Lloyd George made only limited headway against the other leaders. Strangely, Clemenceau and Wilson seem to have concluded that Lloyd George had personally lost his nerve, despite him fully informing them that it was the mandate of the whole British Cabinet and delegation, supported by British public opinion, that he negotiate this way[1610], and two weeks of acrimony followed. With much difficulty, he persuaded Wilson to agree to a plebiscite in Upper Silesia, got the 'Big Four' to agree to an anodyne formula offering Germany the prospect of joining the League after a probationary period, and won minor concessions on the costs, but not the length, of the military occupation of Germany. Regarding reparations, he resisted Wilson's attempt to name a fixed sum,

[1609] Lloyd George, *Truth About The Peace Treaties*, Vol.I, p700-720.
[1610] Mantoux, Vol.II, p268-272.

merely, with Clemenceau's aid, authorizing the Germans to make their own proposal within four months of the signature of the Treaty. These minor modifications did not add up to what he had deemed necessary to obtain Germany's agreement to the terms.[1611]

On 16 June, Germany was threatened with military action, unless she accepted the Treaty within five days. Brockdorff-Rantzau and his chief advisers departed the same night for Weimar, an angry crowd jeering as their cars departed for the railway station, a secretary, Greta Dorlblush, sustaining permanent injury to her head by a rock being thrown.[1612] Before leaving, Brockdorff-Rantzau, backed by his whole delegation, sent telegrams to his government urging rejection of the treaty, and he resigned on 20 June. The Allies deadline was subsequently extended until 7.00 pm on 23 June. At the 'Big Four' meeting on the afternoon of 16 June, the mood was dark. Clemenceau said determinedly, "If Germany refuses, I favour a vigorous and unremitting military blow that will force the signing." Wilson, Lloyd George and Sonnino immediately fully agreed with him.[1613]

On 21 June, two days before the deadline expired, an incident took place that further hardened the Allied position against the Germans. At the signing of the Armistice, it had been agreed that the German High Seas Fleet should be interned at Scapa Flow, the Royal Navy's base in the Orkney Islands, whilst negotiations took place over the fate of the ships. Not knowing the deadline had been extended and fearing that all of the ships would be seized and divided amongst the Allies, Rear Admiral Ludwig von Reuter, decided to scuttle the fleet, which began around 11.30 am on the fateful day, all ships hoisting the Imperial German Ensign at their mainmasts. The last ship sank by 5.00 pm. Of the 74 German ships at Scapa Flow, 15 of the 16 capital ships, five of the eight cruisers, and 32 of the 50 destroyers were sunk, 490,200 tons of valuable shipping in all, the biggest loss of shipping in a single day in history.[1614] Nine Germans were shot and killed, and some 16 wounded, in fights with British seamen trying to prevent the scuttling, the last casualties of the war.

Wilson was justifiably annoyed at this act of defiance, stating the next day "It must be said that it is a violation of the Armistice Agreement." Lloyd George agreed, adding "And a violation of their given word."[1615] Privately, some, including Admiral Wemyss, who had suggested the internment in the first place, considered it a relief, writing to Admiral Hope: "I look upon the sinking of the German Fleet as a real blessing. It disposes once for all the thorny question of the distribution of these ships and eases us of an enormous amount of difficulties."[1616] As far as the Royal Navy was concerned, incorporating German ships in its own fleet would have been problematic, whilst distribution to other navies–particularly the French or American–would have challenged its own position as the world's premier sea power.

Germany really had no choice over signing the Treaty: the government headed by Social Democrat,

---

1611 Sharp, p88.
1612 MacMillan, *Peacemakers*, p481.
1613 Mantoux, Vol.II, p462.
1614 Many of the ships were salvaged between 1922-1939. In an act of supreme irony, from 1935 some of the salvage was bought by Krupps of Essen for a re-arming Nazi Germany, much of the steel being used in making U-boats, thus serving Germany at sea again in the Second World War.
1615 Mantoux, Vol.II, p513.
1616 Wemyss, p432.

Philipp Scheidemann[1617] was unable to agree on a common position, and Scheidemann himself resigned rather than sign. In a passionate speech before the National Assembly on 12 May, he had called the Treaty a "murderous plan" and exclaimed, "Which hand, trying to put us in chains like these, would not wither? The treaty is unacceptable." After his resignation, the Weimar Assembly voted 237 to 138 to approve the Treaty of Versailles, with certain provisos. Gustav Bauer[1618], another Social Democrat and the head of the new government, duly sent a telegram stating his intention to sign the Treaty if certain articles were withdrawn. These included Articles 227, concerning the arraignment of "William II of Hohenzollern, formerly German Emperor, for a supreme offence against international morality and the sanctity of treaties"; 230, concerning the German Government undertaking "to furnish all documents and information of every kind, the production of which may be considered necessary to ensure the full knowledge of the incriminating acts, the discovery of offenders and the just appreciation of responsibility"; and 231, concerning Germany accepting "the responsibility of Germany and her allies for causing all the loss and damage to which the Allied and Associated Governments and their nationals have been subjected as a consequence of the war imposed upon them by the aggression of Germany and her allies."

In response, the Allies issued an ultimatum stating that "The German government must accept or refuse, without any possible equivocation, to sign the treaty within the fixed period of time."[1619] Refusal would mean Germany facing an invasion of Allied forces across the Rhine within 24 hours. On 23 June, Bauer capitulated and sent a second telegram with a confirmation that a German delegation would arrive shortly to sign the treaty. The note arrived just in time, Paul Dutasta, the Secretary-General of the Conference, presenting it to the relieved Council of Four at 5.40 pm. A French officer translated the German note, the statesmen crowding around him. Lloyd George smiled, Wilson grinned, and Clemenceau sent orders to Marshal Foch to halt his advance and to the military in Paris to fire their guns. No more work was done at the Conference that day.[1620]

Diplomatic tradition held that signatures on treaties were accompanied by a personal seal, leading many of the plenipotentiaries to scour antique shops looking for suitable stamps. Lloyd George thought he might use a gold pound coin. Clemenceau quipped "Then leave it for me." Lloyd George replied "I don't have any more. They've all gone to America."[1621] In the event he used an ornate silver seal bearing a 'DLG' monogram. On 27 June, a secretary carefully dripped red wax through a funnel as the statesmen wielded their stamps on the treaty preparatory to the next day's signing. There was also a scramble for guest tickets. Novelist Elinor Glyn had been in France working as a war correspondent. She became one of only two women to witness the signing of the Treaty at Versailles, gaining her entry to the ceremony by persuading Lloyd George to allocate her a ticket.[1622]

Saturday 28 June dawned as a beautiful summer day. On that day the vindictive Treaty, inflicted on

---

1617 Philipp Scheidemann (1865-1939), *Ministerpräsident*, 13 February–20 June 1919.

1618 Gustav Bauer (1870-1944), *Reichskanzler*, 21 June 1919–26 March 1920.

1619 Mantoux, Vol.II, p513.

1620 MacMillan, *Peacemakers*, p484, from Aldrovandi Marescotti, *Nuovi Ricordi*, p83-84.

1621 Ibid., p484, from Aldrovandi Marescotti, *Nuovi Ricordi*, p96.

1622 Ibid., p485. The other woman was Elizabeth Frazer, of the *Saturday Evening Post*.

Germany virtually, in Smuts words, at the "point of the bayonet", was signed in the Hall of Mirrors (*Galerie des Glaces*). Naturally, the Germans had trouble in finding ministers willing to accept the odious responsibility of signing. In the end, Foreign Minister Hermann Müller[1623] and Minister of Colonial Affairs Johannes Bell[1624] were delegated, arriving at 3.00 am on 26 June.

What is little remembered, is that on the morning of 28 June, at President Wilson's apartment in the Place des Etats Unis, a meeting took place between him, Lloyd George and Clemenceau. Yet the occasion was of considerable significance, for there were signed the Anglo-French and Franco-American treaties of assistance, or guarantee treaties, secondary in importance only to the Treaty of Versailles itself. These two collateral treaties supplemented, strengthened and indeed made possible the Treaty of Versailles, representing the prime goal of Clemenceau's policy. Of the two treaties, that with Britain was by far the more important. It was the personal initiative of Lloyd George, proposed to Wilson and then to Clemenceau on 14 March in conditions of total secrecy, with no officials or secretaries present, and so with no notes being taken.[1625] For the French, it was an integral part, if not the pivot, of the Versailles settlement, "the keystone of European peace", according to Clemenceau.[1626] Versailles would never have come about in the form it did–Clemenceau would not have agreed to sign it–had not Lloyd George first signed this treaty with France stipulating that "Great Britain agrees to come immediately to her assistance in the event of any unprovoked movement of aggression against her being made by Germany."[1627] Ratification followed quickly, Lloyd George steering it unopposed through the Commons as the 'Anglo-French Treaty (Defence of France) Act 1919' on 21 July. Clemenceau secured overwhelming approval in the National Assembly, André Tardieu informing the Chamber of Deputies, on Lloyd George's assurance, that "in a few months' time" the two countries would also be linked by a Channel tunnel.[1628] Formalities between London and Paris were exchanged in November.

However, the mechanism was flawed. Britain was not at all keen to become embroiled in another future European conflict unless absolutely necessary. On the day before the signing, Lloyd George added one word–*only*–to the text of the treaty.[1629] Article 2 stated: "The present Treaty, in similar terms with the Treaty of even date for the same purpose concluded between the French Republic and the United States of America, will only come into force when the latter is ratified."[1630] In the event, on 19 November 1919 the US Senate refused to ratify both it and the Versailles Treaty, thus nullifying the British assent.

The formal signing of the Treaty of Versailles was the first time that a major ceremony was filmed.

---

1623 Hermann Müller (1876-1931), Social Democrat, Foreign Minister, 21 June 1919–26 March 1920, twice Chancellor, 1920, 1928-1930, in the Weimar Republic.

1624 Johannes Bell (1868-1949), Centre Party politician, Minister of Colonial Affairs, February-June 1919.

1625 A. Lentin in Loades, p117.

1626 G. Clemenceau, *Grandeurs Et Misères D'Une Victoire*, 1930, Paris, Librairie Plon, p210.

1627 Lentin, p48.

1628 Lloyd George had mentioned the Channel tunnel to both Colonel House and Clemenceau on 12 March and repeated his undertaking to Foch on 31 March. He also included it as a corollary to the guarantee to France in a policy statement on 23 March (LGP, F/147/3/2/2).

1629 Sharp, p125.

1630 https://history.state.gov/historicaldocuments/frus1919Parisv13/ch27. Retrieved 14 April 2020.

Frances Stevenson was present. She commented on the already growing media intrusion into public affairs, noting: "Almost half the room was taken up with representatives of the Press. The Press is reducing everything that is noblest and impressive in modern life into terms of Press photographs and Press interviews... the people who are speaking *know* that they are taking notes. One or two reporters, for the sake of preserving a record, would not be so bad. But they have to be dealt with in armies nowadays... They are as unscrupulous as they are vulgar."[1631]

At 3.00 pm the packed assembly was called to order, and the two German delegates were shortly ushered in behind an Allied guard. Many felt sorry for them, Harold Nicolson recording: "They are deathly pale. They do not appear as representatives of a brutal militarism."[1632] Clemenceau was seated almost immediately under the ceiling decoration that bore the legend "*Le roi gouverne par lui-meme*", almost on the exact spot where Wilhelm I of Prussia stood when he was proclaimed German Emperor in 1871. At 3.15 pm he rose and announced briefly that the session was opened, before asking the German plenipotentiaries to approach to affix their signatures to the treaty. The German delegates stepped forward to sign, using their own fountain pens, signing with trembling hands but otherwise showing little outward signs of emotion. There was to be only one official treaty of peace, to be placed in the archives of the Ministry of Foreign Affairs of France, and a copy given to all the governments concerned in its signing. After the Germans, the representatives of the Allied and Associated Powers added their signatures, starting with Wilson, then Lloyd George, Clemenceau and Sonnino,[1633] before then signing two further agreements, a protocol on the administration of the Rhineland, and a treaty with Poland.

The audience were initially respectfully quiet, but as time went on conversation began, and some delegates moved around in order to get programmes autographed. Finally, Clemenceau declared "Messieurs, all the signatures have been given. The signature of the conditions of peace between the Allied and Associated powers and the German Republic is an accomplished fact. The session is adjourned"[1634], and the Germans were escorted out. The whole unceremonious process had lasted a mere fifty minutes. Müller had promised himself that he would be business-like: "I wanted our ex-enemies to see nothing of the deep pain of the German people, whose representative I was at this tragic moment." Returning to the hotel, he collapsed, a physical reaction to the huge psychological strain he had been under. He and the rest of the delegation insisted on returning to Germany by a 9.00 pm train that same night.[1635] Before departing, they gave a statement to the United Press:

> We have signed the treaty without any mental reservation. What we have signed we will carry out. The German people will compel those in power to hold to and conform to the clauses. But

---

[1631] Stevenson, *Diary*, p187.

[1632] H. Nicolson, *Peacemaking 1919*, 1965, London, Grosset & Dunlap, p368.

[1633] The leaders of 32 nations signed the Treaty, representing some 75% of the world's 1.8 billion population.

[1634] Quoted in H. Hansen, *The Adventures Of Fourteen Points: Vivid and Dramatic Episodes of the Peace Conference from its Opening at Paris to the Signing of the Treaty of Versailles*, 1919, New York, Century Co., p357. The official protocol verifies the fact that Clemenceau used the word "republic" in his final statement.

[1635] Quoted in MacMillan, *Peacemakers*, p487.

> we believe that the Entente in its own interest will consider it necessary to modify some articles when it becomes aware that the execution of these articles is impossible…
>
> The central government has not aided any attack against Poland. Germany will make every effort to prove that she is worthy of entering the League of Nations.[1636]

That there was already a mention of the modification of terms, and of the "impossibility" of meeting them, on the day of the great signing should have given some pause for thought, but in the general atmosphere of relief and joy it passed without much notice. On the completion of the signing, the battery of guns outside near the *Orangerie* fired a salute, and "the great fountains of the park were turned on, and the water marvels of Lenotre began to play in the mellow sunshine throughout one of the most impressive playgrounds of the world."[1637] The three jubilant peacemakers–Clemenceau, Lloyd George and Wilson–walked arm-in-arm down to the terrace above the fountain of Latona that overlooks the great formal gardens leading to the canals and woods beyond, while an immense and enthusiastic crowd surged around them. The moment almost descended into farce, as Wilson was nearly pushed into a fountain. Lloyd George was rescued, somewhat dishevelled, by a protective guard of soldiers. Annoyed, he told an Italian diplomat "A similar thing would never have happened in England. And if it had happened, someone would have had to pay."[1638] He was further irritated to be made to write a letter to the King formally announcing that the peace had been concluded.[1639] After tea in the salon of the old senate, where they met Sidney Sonnino, Wilson immediately left for Le Havre to sail back to the United States, the British held a celebratory dinner in the Hôtel Majestic. In Paris itself, the streets filled with crowds, singing and dancing, the wartime *"le calme et la dignite"* being finally thrown aside. The Grands Boulevards blazed with lights, and cars towed the captured German guns around, which it took the authorities some days to retrieve.

Naturally, the atmosphere in Germany was utterly different, funereal, as flags flew at half-mast. The Treaty was formally ratified by the Weimar National Assembly on 9 July by a vote of 209 to 116. Among many, talk was of "a peace of shame". The intense national disgrace and humiliation was used by the Nationalists, blaming the alleged traitors at home who had stabbed Germany in the back, and the Coalition government that had signed the detested treaty. For a while there was some panic that, having signed the Treaty, Germany would not actually ratify it! By 14 October 1919 Britain, its Dominions, France and Italy had all ratified the Treaty, and could thus bring it into effect. However, this did not happen, for various reasons. Firstly, the Germans were refusing to evacuate the Baltic provinces, Baltic German barons having briefly set up the United Baltic Duchy on 9 November 1918, and *Freikorps* units were battling against both the Communists and the newly independent democracies of Estonia and Latvia.[1640] Secondly, they were refusing to surrender alleged war criminals like

---

1636 Quoted in Hansen, p358.
1637 Hansen, p357.
1638 Quoted in MacMillan, *Peacemakers*, p487.
1639 Rowland, *Lloyd George*, p495.
1640 In the event the Germans evacuated the provinces in December 1919 and January 1920.

Bethmann-Hollweg and Hindenburg[1641], or to pay any compensation for the scuttling of the High Seas Fleet.

The Allies could not decide what action to take to resolve this without taking sanctions. On 6 December 1919, Clemenceau drafted a note threatening "to place Germany in face of a rupture of armistice with all consequences which would follow there from"[1642] unless the Germans agreed to the conditions for final ratification. Lloyd George dispatched his private secretary Philip Kerr to Paris to negotiate an amended draft. He was against the high numbers of alleged war criminals sought, stating that had matters been reversed, and the Germans sought 800 officers, "he did not believe they would ever comply with it. No British or French Government could do so." His advice was that "we should confine our demands to surrender of the most important and notorious offenders and let the rest go."[1643] The Germans backed down, avoiding a resumption of hostilities. The Treaty duly came into force on 10 January 1920, and, on 21 January, a year and three days after it had opened, the Paris Peace Conference formally came to a close.

The Weimar Republic would never develop robustly enough to surmount this poisoned burden of alleged 'war guilt' on the one hand, and 'betrayal' on the other. Especially after the onset of the Great Depression during October 1929, economic unrest destabilized the already vulnerable government. Many saw the reparations issue as "the continuation of the war by other means." The Nationalists endlessly stigmatized the parties and individuals that had been in favour of the Treaty–often only so as to prevent renewed hostilities–for their alleged lack of patriotism. One such was Matthias Erzberger, the German signatory to the Armistice. The denunciations of the Nationalist press went far beyond the normal limits of party polemics: the *Tägliche Rundschau* observed, in allusion to Erzberger's personal appearance, "he may be as round as a bullet, but he is not bullet-proof." The climax of these attacks was that Erzberger was murdered on 26 August 1921 whilst on holiday in Bad Griesbach, by two members of the ultra-nationalist death squad *Organisation Consul.* Another leading Nationalist paper then opined: "The man whose spirit unhappily still prevails in many of our government offices and laws, has at last secured the punishment suitable for a traitor."[1644] Without this pervasive, hate and revenge-filled Nationalist culture of the 'stab-in-the-back myth' (*Dolchstoßlegende*) against the so-called 'November Criminals' (*Novemberverbrecher*) who had signed the hated 'dictated treaty' (*Diktat*), it is virtually certain that Hitler would never have gained sufficient leverage to attain power in 1933, meaning that the very particular set of conditions that sparked the outbreak of the Second World War would never have existed either.

Lloyd George had clashed with Clemenceau, Wilson, and Orlando. Unlike Clemenceau and Orlando, Lloyd George on the whole stood on the side of generosity and moderation. He did not

1641 The earliest Allied demands amounted to over 3,000 names, but these were reduced to 853 men–and one woman, Elsa Scheiner, a prison guard of Frenchwomen at Valenciennes–by the Allied conference in Paris on 20 January 1920. Ultimately, only 17 were tried, by the *Reichsgericht* in Leipzig in 1921-1922; See https://encyclopedia.1914-1918-online.net/article/leipzig_war_crimes_trials. Retrieved 16 April 2020.

1642 Quoted in Sharp, p172.

1643 Ibid., p187.

1644 Quoted in MacMillan, *Peacemakers*, p488.

want to destroy the German economy and political system–as some in the French camp, like Marshal Foch, demanded–with massive reparations. Privately, Lloyd George opposed revenge and attempted to compromise between Clemenceau's demands and Wilson's Fourteen Points, knowing Europe would eventually have to reconcile with Germany. He wanted terms of reparation that would not cripple the German economy, so that Germany would remain a viable economic power and trading partner. By arguing that British war pensions and widows' allowances should be included in the German reparation sum, he ensured that a large amount would go to the British Empire.

Lloyd George was also largely responsible for the pro-German shift in the peace conditions regarding the borders of Poland. In this regard, Lloyd George was haunted by a scene he had witnessed in the Place de la Concorde when he first visited Paris. After the Franco-Prussian War, and the consequent loss of Alsace-Lorraine, the statue in the square representing the city of Strasbourg had been draped in black mourning crepe on state occasions. Lloyd George recalled: "the strongest impression made upon me by my first visit to Paris was the statue of Strasbourg veiled in mourning. Do not let us make it possible for Germany to erect a similar statue."[1645] This vivid, highly symbolic image recurred to him whenever the danger of an avoidable national grievance arose, particularly so during the debates on the proposed Polish-German frontiers.

Poland's re-emergence after 123 years of partition by the Austro-Hungarian, German and Russian Empires was one of the biggest stories played out in Paris–and after–but it was also one of the most contentious: the committee charged with determining its borders had more meetings than any other at the conference.[1646] The Commission on Polish Affairs was appointed on 12 February, chaired by the former French ambassador to Germany, Jules Cambon.[1647] It faced a monumental task. Few countries were as fragmented as Poland was in 1919, ethnically, bureaucratically, legislatively, economically, all in a land completely broken and picked-clean by warfare, German economic requisitioning, and just plain looting.[1648] Esmé Howard[1649], who visited Posen (Poznań) in early March 1919, wrote: "Certainly after 150 years of oppression the Poles show wonderful moderation. All German monuments are respected, only the statue of Bismarck was one morning found with an old hat on his 'pickelhaube' and a fourth class ticket to Berlin in his hand!"[1650] Meanwhile, the complexity and acrimoniousness of the wrangling engendered quickly brought forth black humour amongst the exasperated attendees assembling at Paris: "People joked that when an Englishman wrote a book on the elephant, he dealt with its habitat and how to hunt it; a German wrote a treatise on its biology; but the Pole started with 'The elephant is a Polish question.'"[1651]

In all seriousness, the Poles had high hopes from the Conference. The British agreed that Poland

---

[1645] Quoted in Sharp, p118.

[1646] MacMillan, *Peacemakers*, p217.

[1647] Jules-Martin Cambon (1845-1935), younger brother of Paul Cambon. Ambassador to Germany, 1907-1914, where he had worked hard to secure a friendly détente.

[1648] The author thanks Angelika M. Dewar, student of twentieth century Polish history, for her valuable insights into the significance of the Paris Peace Conference *from a Polish point of view*.

[1649] Sir Esmé Howard (1863-1939), British Civil Delegate on the International Commission to Poland.

[1650] Howard, *Diary*, 6 March 1919; Quoted in Sharp, p130.

[1651] MacMillan, *Peacemakers*, p224-225.

should be independent but were not prepared to invest too heavily in protecting its future, as they had little national interest at stake and did not care to be its guarantors if Poland was attacked in future by a resurgent Germany or Bolshevik Russia. Margaret MacMillan found some justification for the British position, noting:

> The British… feared, with some reason, that Poland could become a liability. Who would defend it if its neighbours, Germany and Russia in particular, attacked? Moreover, the British did not particularly care for either Polish faction. Piłsudski[1652] had fought against them and was a dangerous radical. Dmowski[1653] and the Polish National Committee were too right-wing. 'In fact the prevailing opinion,' said a British diplomat in Warsaw, 'which to a great extent influenced me at the time seemed to be that to do anything the Polish Committee asked for would be to fasten upon Poland a regime of wicked landlords who spent most of their time in riotous living, and establish there a Chauvinist Government whose object was to acquire territories inhabited by non-Polish populations.[1654]

Lloyd George was cautious, stating with classic, ironical understatement: "Action undertaken without further knowledge might lead to a mess."[1655] This was certainly true in the case of Poland and its kaleidoscopic affairs. With Poland hundreds of miles to the east, the Allies had no way of accurately assessing the specifics of any given situation on the ground, though they did try sending fact-finding missions. When the Supreme Council considered the Commission on Polish Affairs report on 19 March, Lloyd George questioned the proposed inclusion of the so-called 'Polish Corridor' to the Baltic Sea, a predominantly German area. This could be the seed of a future 'Alsace-Lorraine' situation, a future cause for war. The Commission was told to reconsider its report.

Instead of handing over Upper Silesia, with a population of 2,073,000 people, and the southern part of East Prussia, with 720,000 people, to Poland as was initially planned, after German protests, a plebiscite was held–in the first instance, on 20 March 1921, resulting in 59.6% for Germany, and in the second, on 11 July 1920, resulting, despite allegations of falsification, in votes of 97.89% and 92.36% in favour of East Prussia. In a compromise worked on by James Headlam-Morley[1656], the important port of Danzig, with its population of 366,000, of whom 95% were ethnically German, was to be organised as a free city, as it had been in 1807-1814. The 'Big Four' accepted this proposal on 1 April, and this was what duly took place on 15 November 1920. Poland and Germany signed a separate treaty guaranteeing that Poland would have all the facilities it needed to carry on its trade.

From the time of the small British Military Mission to Poland after November 1918–in support of the larger French Military Mission–the Poles were initially grateful that Lloyd George had helped save that country from the Bolsheviks, but soon his position came to be regarded negatively:

---

1652 Józef Piłsudski (1867-1935), Chief of State, 1918-22, First Marshal of Poland from 1920.

1653 Roman Dmowski (1864-1939), co-founder and chief ideologue of the National Democracy movement.

1654 MacMillan, *Peacemakers*, p221-222.

1655 Quoted in MacMillan, *Peacemakers*, p225.

1656 James Headlam-Morley (1863-1929), influential Assistant Director of the Political Intelligence Department of the Foreign Office, 1918-20, Historical Adviser to the Foreign Office, 1920 until his death.

> His actions at the Peace Conference were deplored; his supposed opinions about the Poles being 'children who gave trouble,' his confession that he had never heard of Cieszyn, the *lèse-majesté* of his remarks about Paderewski[1657], were widely reported in Poland, where, it is no exaggeration to say, Lloyd George was in 1919-20 usually regarded as a public enemy. A number of his advisers held the country in no high regard, and talk among British ministers on the subject of Poland was often antipathetic.[1658]

One such adviser was Lewis Namier[1659], who worked for the Political Intelligence Department of the Foreign Office from March 1918 to April 1920. Namier was born Ludwik Bernstein Niemirowski, near Lublin in south-eastern Poland, into a family of secular-minded Polish-Jewish gentry, emigrating to Britain in 1907. Unfortunately, he "devoted much time and effort to creating an unfavourable atmosphere towards Poland in British public opinion and governing circles. He did so both through a cascade of memoranda and analyses written for… the Foreign Office, and through his wide ranging activities as a publicist."[1660] Namier's baleful hostility to the Poles had been engendered by the anti-Semitism he encountered in Galicia. Though his bias was noted by colleagues and supervisors, he possessed extensive contacts in British government circles, including Lloyd George, by proxy of his personal secretary, Philip Kerr.

Lloyd George was held to be the 'tool' of sinister capitalist forces opposed to a strong Poland. In fact, like most liberals, he strongly sympathized with the undoubted sufferings of the Poles. However, he felt that *some* of their demands were unreasonable, and this was dangerous, as it would create enemies and be the root of future trouble. In particular, both the Germans and Russians would have to recognise the justice of Polish claims. It was for this reason that he had warned against placing over two million Germans under Polish rule. On 27 March he had told the Council of Four: "My conclusion is that we must not create a Poland alienated from the time of its birth by an unforgettable quarrel from its most civilized neighbour."[1661] His reasoning was to leave, as far as possible, Poles in Poland, and Germans in Germany. As was to be expected, it was Clemenceau who strongly demurred, as he wanted a strong Poland as a barrier separating Germany and Russia.

On the north-eastern border of Poland, rekindled Polish national pride came up against that of the Lithuanians, equally determined to have a secure national homeland after sublimation in the Russian Empire from 1795 and a rapacious German occupation since 1915. The two peoples had been co-joined in the Polish-Lithuanian Commonwealth from 1569-1795, and in *de facto* personal union between the ruling families before that, dating from 1386, so there was significant history between them. Due to numerical imbalance, the Poles had always dominated. Now many Poles wished to do so again. On 5 June, on being informed by Paderewski that the Lithuanians were "a small people of

---

[1657] Ignacy Paderewski (1860-1941), pianist, composer, a spokesman for Polish independence, and from January-December 1919 the new nation's Prime Minister and Foreign Minister.

[1658] N. Davies, *Lloyd George and Poland*, p132.

[1659] Lewis Namier (1888-1960). For more on his influence, see Nowak, p130-150.

[1660] B. Rusin, *Lewis Namier, the Curzon Line, and the Shaping of Poland's Eastern Frontier after World War I*, *Studies into the History of Russia and Central-Eastern Europe*, XLVIII, 1, 2014, p95-116. Quote: p12, PDF.

[1661] Quoted in MacMillan, *Peacemakers*, p228. The Lithuanian population was 2.32 million in 1919.

two million inhabitants", Lloyd George speculated "It is as if independence were given to Wales."[1662] The very fact this thought occurred to him must have led him to re-think his position, and by later in the summer of 1919 he had warmed to the idea. Meanwhile the Poles had seized Vilna (Vilnius) on 19 April, and soon annexed the region, to the great resentment of the Lithuanians, who did not regain their historic capital city until 10 October 1939–the process of transferring administration back to the city still ongoing when the Soviets took over on 15 June 1940. Nonetheless, in 1919, at last both nations had finally achieved their long desired–and deserved–statehood.[1663]

The Polish-Soviet War (14 February 1919–18 October 1920) raged between the new Polish Republic and Soviet Russia over an area that is now eastern Poland and western Ukraine and Belarus. On 21 July 1920, Lloyd George launched the Interallied Mission to Poland, a diplomatic mission, at the height of the war, weeks before the decisive Battle of Warsaw of 12-25 August, the 'Miracle on the Vistula' which saw the Russians repulsed. The purpose of this mission was to send a high level delegation from Britain and France to Poland in an attempt to influence Polish policy, possibly through effecting a change in government. The mission included the French diplomat, Jean Jules Jusserand[1664] with General Maxime Weygand[1665] and for the British, diplomat Lord D'Abernon[1666] and Major General Percy Radcliffe[1667], working alongside Brigadier General Adrian Carton de Wiart, who commanded the British Military Mission to Poland.[1668]

Also attached to the mission for ten days, ostensibly as 'Secretary', was Maurice Hankey, who in effect acted as Lloyd George's personal observer in Poland.[1669] On 21 July, Lloyd George sent a warning to the Soviets from the floor of the Commons. Whilst stating that the Polish offensive against Russia was both "foolish and reckless", he nonetheless insisted that such a "mistake" did "not justify a nation being wiped out." An independent Poland was "essential to the whole fabric of peace."[1670] Hankey's 'Personal Report', presented to Cabinet on 9 August, was valueless and ill-informed, against helping the Poles, whom he felt were bound to be defeated almost immediately. On 10 August, Lloyd George again told the Commons:

> The independence of Poland and its existence as an independent nation is an essential part of the structure of European peace, and its extinction could not be regarded with indifference by any of the nations who are interested in preserving the peace of Europe. The re-partition of

---

1662 Quoted in Mantoux, Vol.II, p309. The Polish population was 23.8 million in 1919.

1663 The author thanks the late Jolanta Maceviciene for her valuable insights into Lithuanian history and culture. Vilnius had been the capital of the Grand Duchy of Lithuania from 1323-1795. See Č. Laurinavičius, *The Lithuanian Buffer Problem of 1920*, *Lithuanian Historical Studies*, 23, 2019, p59-83.

1664 Jean Jules Jusserand (1855-1932), Ambassador to the USA, 1903-1924.

1665 General Maxime Weygand (1867-1965), chief of staff to Marshal Foch.

1666 Edgar Vincent, Lord D'Abernon (1857-1941), Ambassador to Germany, 1920-1925.

1667 Maj. General Percy Radcliffe (1874-1934), Director of Military Operations, 1918-1922.

1668 Brig. General Adrian Carton de Wiart (1880-1963).

1669 See N. Davies, *Sir Maurice Hankey and the Inter-Allied Mission to Poland, July-August 1920*, *Historical Journal*, 15, 3, September 1972, p553-561.

1670 Ullman, Vol.3, p176.

> Poland would not merely be a crime, it would be a peril, and we have to consider both those contingencies as the basis of our policy. That is why we intervened at Spa.[1671]

The crucial battle of Warsaw was won soon after by the sheer tenacity of the Poles, before the mission could achieve anything of significance.

Lloyd George also intended to maintain a European balance of power to thwart a French attempt to establish itself as the dominant European power. A revived Germany would be a counterweight to France and a deterrent to Bolshevik Russia. Lloyd George also wanted to neutralize the German Navy to keep the Royal Navy as the greatest naval power in the world; dismantle the German colonial empire with several of its territorial possessions ceded to Britain and others being established as League of Nations mandates, a position opposed by some of the Dominions.

Of the many provisions in the Treaty, which came into force on 10 January 1920[1672], one of the most important and controversial required "Germany [to] accept the responsibility of Germany and her allies for causing all the loss and damage" during the war–the other members of the Central Powers signed treaties containing similar articles. This, Article 231, later became known as the 'War Guilt' [*'Kriegsschuldfrage'*] clause. The Treaty forced Germany to disarm, make substantial territorial concessions, and pay reparations to certain countries that had formed the Entente powers. On 27 April 1921, the total cost of these reparations was assessed at 132 billion marks, then £6.6 billion [£412.88 billion in 2025]. Germany was to lose 13% of its territory and 10% of its population.

As Ulrich von Brockdorff-Rantzau[1673], Germany's foreign minister, put it: "This fat volume was quite unnecessary. They could have expressed the whole thing more simply in one clause–Germany renounces its existence." Despite much debate among the Allies, and over strenuous German protests, Article 231 remained in the Treaty. Brockdorff-Rantzau wrote to Clemenceau as Conference President on 13 May about the peace terms:

> We came to Versailles in the expectation of receiving a peace proposal based on the agreed principles. We were firmly resolved to do everything in our power with a view of fulfilling the grave obligations which we had undertaken. We hoped for the peace of justice which had been promised to us.
>
> We were aghast when we read in documents the demands made upon us, the victorious violence of our enemies. The more deeply we penetrate into the spirit of this treaty, the more convinced we become of the impossibility of carrying it out. The exactions of this treaty are more than the German people can bear.

---

1671 https://api.parliament.uk/historic-hansard/commons/1920/aug/10/statement-by-prime-minister#S5CV0133P0_19200810_HOC_363. Retrieved 13 October 2020.

1672 Considering the degree of input that Wilson, a Democrat, had had in shaping the Treaty, on 19 November 1919 the Republican-led US Senate refused to ratify it by a vote of 39-55, well short of the required two-thirds, based primarily on objections to the League of Nations. On 2 October 1919 the exhausted Wilson had a serious stroke and so was unable to 'fight his corner.'

1673 Ulrich von Brockdorff-Rantzau (1869-1928), Foreign Minister, 13 February–20 June 1919. During the war he had been critical of German policies and had urged a compromise peace.

He proceeded to list what he regarded as the iniquities of the Allied position, including the loss of "indisputably German territory", the occupation of the Rhineland, the demand that Germany "bear all the war expenses of her enemies, which would exceed many times over the total amount of German State and private assets" and which would render "economic life… impossible", the loss of colonies, and the renunciation of "the realization of all our aims in the spheres of politics, economics, and ideas." He concluded: "Thus must a whole people sign the decree for its proscription, nay, its own death sentence", adding "Germany knows that she must make sacrifices in order to attain peace. Germany knows that she has, by agreement, undertaken to make these sacrifices, and will go in this matter to the utmost limits of her capacity." Finally, Brockdorff-Rantzau made largely constructive counter-proposals:

> 1. Germany offers to proceed with her own disarmament in advance of all other peoples, in order to show that she will help to usher in the new era of the peace of justice… She stipulates… that she shall be admitted forthwith as a State with equal rights into the League of Nations. She stipulates that a genuine League of Nations shall come into being, embracing all peoples of goodwill…
>
> 2. In territorial questions Germany takes up her position unreservedly on the ground of the Wilson program. She renounces her sovereign right in Alsace-Lorraine, but wishes a free plebiscite to take place there. She gives up the greater part of the province of Posen, the district incontestably Polish in population, together with the capital. She is prepared to grant to Poland, under international guarantees, free and secure access to the sea by ceding free ports at Danzig, Konigsberg, and Memel, by an agreement regulating the navigation of the Vistula and by special railway conventions… The preponderantly Danish districts of Schleswig will be given up to Denmark on the basis of a plebiscite. Germany demands that the right of self-determination shall also be respected where the interests of the Germans in Austria and Bohemia are concerned. She is ready to subject all her colonies to administration by the community of the League of Nations, if she is recognized as its mandatory.
>
> 3. Germany is prepared to make payments incumbent on her in accordance with the agreed program of peace up to a maximum sum of 100,000,000,000 gold marks… Germany presumes in this connection that… she will recover her freedom of economic movement at home and abroad.
>
> 4. Germany is prepared to devote her entire economic strength to the service of the reconstruction. She wishes to cooperate effectively in the reconstruction of the devastated regions of Belgium and Northern France… Germany will facilitate further deliveries of coal to France, Belgium, Italy, and Luxemburg. Germany is, moreover, prepared to make considerable deliveries of benzol, coal tar, and sulphate of ammonia, as well as dyestuffs and medicines.
>
> 5… 6… 7… 8…

9. The German delegation again makes its demand for a neutral inquiry into the responsibility for the war and culpable acts in conduct. An impartial commission should have the right to investigate on its own responsibility the archives of all the belligerent countries and all the persons who took an important part in the war. Nothing short of confidence that the question of guilt will be examined dispassionately can leave the peoples lately at war with each other in the proper frame of mind for the formation of the League of Nations…

The feeling of the peoples who have made such immense sacrifices makes them demand that their fate should be decided by an open, unreserved exchange of ideas on the principle: "Quite open covenants of peace openly arrived at, after which there shall be no private international understandings of any kind, but diplomacy shall proceed always frankly in the public view."…

Treaties of peace signed by the great powers have… again and again proclaimed the right of the stronger. But each of these treaties of peace has been a factor in originating and prolonging the world war. Whenever in this war the victor has spoken to the vanquished, at Brest-Litovsk and Bucharest, his words were but the seeds of future discord.

The lofty aims which our adversaries first set before themselves in their conduct of the war, the new era of an assured peace of justice, demand a treaty instinct with a different spirit.

Only the cooperation of all nations, a cooperation of hands and spirits, can build up a durable peace. We are under no delusions regarding the strength of the hatred and bitterness which this war has engendered, and yet the forces which are at work for a union of mankind are stronger now than ever they were before.

The historic task of the Peace Conference of Versailles is to bring about this union…[1674]

Lloyd George's reaction was typical of many of the leading Allied statesman. He later wrote:

As to its challenge of the war guilt of Germany, I could not accept the German point of view without giving away the whole of our case for entering into the War. I considered the Guilt issue reasons addressed by the German Note utterly inadequate to shake conviction on the issue which had carried Britain reluctantly into a war that had cost her so much. But once more I reviewed the considerations which had impelled us to throw in our lot with Belgium, Serbia, France and Russia and I had not one wavering doubt as to the culpability of the Central Powers. I am still of the same opinion.

I also considered the claim made by the German delegation that the fact of the repudiation by the German people themselves of the rulers who had the supreme responsibility for making war absolved them from liability for the actions of these rulers. Should this consideration weigh with the Allies to the extent of inducing them to effect any changes in the Treaty in the direction of greater leniency? It had no bearing on the readjustment of boundaries. Those changes were justifiable, apart from any question of war guilt, on the grounds of national liberty and independence. They constituted a restoration of freedom to the nations that had been deprived of it by force. But when one came to the questions of reparations, the Colonies and German disarmament, one could not forget that the German people were not in a position to repudiate

[1674] https://www.firstworldwar.com/source/parispeaceconf_germanprotest1.htm. Retrieved 5 November 2018.

> responsibility for the War and its consequences, for they had without distinction of class or party enthusiastically applauded the action of their rulers in declaring war and in the invasion of Belgium, and given them whole-hearted support in their most aggressive and indefensible actions during the War. And had they won, they would have acclaimed the victory and all the demands for annexation of foreign territory in the East and the West which would have inevitably followed.[1675]

Others were unsure and uneasy. Robert Lansing, the largely side-lined US Secretary of State, wrote of the Treaty in a memorandum on 8 May: "The impression made by it is one of disappointment, of regret, and of depression. The terms of peace appear immeasurably harsh and humiliating, while many of them seem to me impossible of performance."[1676] In the British delegation, Harold Nicolson was more specific in the source of his dismay: "We came to Paris confident that the new order was about to be established; we left it convinced that the new order had merely fouled the old. We arrived as fervent apprentices in the school of President Wilson; we left as renegades."[1677] The Archbishop of Canterbury, Randall Davidson, no pacifist, sent a private letter to Lloyd George in Paris on 24 May, expressing his disquiet and declaring that:

> I have thought that… I should tell you how many communications are reaching me from people who to a large degree eschew ordinary politics… to the effect that they are anxious and disquieted about the terms of Peace… What my friends to whom I refer keep saying is, that while presumably each item may be plausibly justified, the cumulative effect is to ask impossibilities. It is perfectly certain that this view is entertained with almost trembling earnestness by a great many people…
>
> … we trust you… to succeed in securing a Peace which shall correspond with our purposes in entering the War… and which shall be of the kind that will be lasting and not the beginning of new strife… I am thinking of, and indirectly voicing, a great central body which is ordinarily silent and which has no adequate representation in the ordinary channels of the Press.[1678]

Lloyd George had shown his three colleagues in the 'Big Four' the letter, then responded on 30 May:

> We shall certainly give the fullest and most impartial consideration to the German reply. We have given them an extension of time, in order to make sure that they had time in which to marshal their case. If they can establish a just case for modification, I am sure modifications will be made. We shall not be influenced by public clamour if we think that we ought to make concessions to meet the German point of view.
>
> At the same time, I am certain that what is most important is that we should not weaken the fundamental principles which underlie the peace. It is always difficult in human affairs to adjust

[1675] Lloyd George, *Truth About The Peace Treaties*, Vol.I, p684-685.
[1676] Lansing, *Peace Negotiations*, p272.
[1677] Nicolson, *Peacemaking 1919*, p187.
[1678] Quoted in G. K. A. Bell, *Randall Davidson, Archbishop Of Canterbury*, 1935, Oxford, Oxford University Press, Vol.II, p946-947.

> mercy and justice, and, if it is important that we should remember mercy, it is not less important that we should remember justice. No nation has ever committed such a crime against its neighbours as have the German people, under the instigation of Prussian Kultur. It will not make for lasting peace, for early appeasement, nor even for the future well-being of the German people themselves and their future position in the world, should we refrain from imposing on their country the conditions which justice demands.[1679]

Meanwhile, former German Chancellor Bethmann-Hollweg added a bitter foreword to his memoirs that same month:

> The conditions of peace have been published while this work is in the press. The world has never yet seen so appalling an apparatus for the oppression of a vanquished nation. This peace is the crowning of the work that began with the creation of the Entente. The Paris findings have more than abundantly confirmed the views advanced in the following pages...[1680]

As Germany had been humiliated, with dire consequences for the future, so now was Austria. On 2 June, the Austrian delegates were presented with their peace terms in the great hall of the Chateau of St Germain-en-Laye on the western outskirts of Paris. The walls of the hall were decorated with pictures of extinct Stone Age animals: Clemenceau's aide, General Henri Mordacq, wrote "Several among us could not help but notice that."[1681] The future economic and political viability of Austria, or of Hungary, was little regarded, and neither country was allocated its own commission to work on its behalf. Vienna had gone from being the capital city of a sprawling empire of some 52 million people, to that of a small republic of some 6.5 million. In January 1919 Austria was dangerously near to social collapse. Fearing that she might go the way of Russia or Hungary–which had its own Communist Revolution, existing as the Hungarian Soviet Republic from 21 March to 1 August 1919–from the end of March, the Allies lifted their blockade and supplied credits to the Austrian government. They also began shipping in essential food and clothing, Austria becoming the fourth largest beneficiary of Allied aid after Germany, Poland and Belgium.

Karl Renner[1682] had become the first Chancellor of that newly established German-speaking republic, which refused to be considered the heir of the Habsburg monarchy and wished to be known as the Republic of German-Austria (*Republik Deutsch-Österreich*). This name, however, was prohibited by the Allies. They also vetoed a resolution of the Constituent National Assembly in Vienna passed on 12 November 1918 that "German-Austria" was to be part of the German Weimar Republic. Even before the collapse of the Austro-Hungarian monarchy, Renner had proposed a future union of the

---

1679 Ibid., Vol.II, p947-948.

1680 T. von Bethmann-Hollweg, *Reflections On The World War*, 1920 London Trans. Young, G. Thornton Butterworth, pv. His work only covers 1909-1914, as he died before he could complete it.

1681 Quoted in MacMillan, *Peacemakers*, p254.

1682 Karl Renner (1870-1950), Socialist, 'Father of the Republic', leading the first government of German-Austria and the First Austrian Republic, 30 October 1919–7 July 1920, also being decisive in establishing the Second Republic, becoming its first President after the Second World War on 20 December 1945 until his death.

German parts of Austria with Germany, using the word "*Anschluss*"–a word irrevocably linked with the annexation of Austria into Nazi Germany carried out by Hitler on 12 March 1938. The Allies were a little easier on Austria than Germany: regarding war guilt, it would be one thing to punish the Kaiser, but as Lloyd George pointed out to President Wilson on 8 May, Emperor Karl I "wasn't there when war was declared, and his responsibility is nil."[1683] After deliberating for two years, the Reparations Commission admitted that Austria need not pay anything at all.[1684]

Renner was the leader of the delegation that represented this new German-Austria in the negotiations of St. Germain where the "Republic of Austria" was acknowledged but was declared to be the responsible successor to Imperial Austria. By the Treaty of St Germain-en-Laye, signed on 10 September and to come into effect on 16 July 1920, Renner had to accept that his new Austria was prohibited from having any political association with Germany, had to accept the loss of German-speaking South Tyrol to Italy, and the loss of German-speaking parts of Bohemia and Moravia, where he was born, to Czechoslovakia. Further, conscription was abolished and the Austrian Army was limited to a force of 30,000 volunteers. Lloyd George was not present at the signing; the British delegation being headed by Balfour as Foreign Secretary.

Regarding Hungary, Lloyd George's reaction to the news of events there was interesting, and both typical and consistent of him. On 27 March he ended a Council of Four session by stating:

> There has been talk of suppressing the revolution in Hungary. I don't see why we should do that: there are few countries so much in need of a revolution. This very day, I had a conversation with someone who has visited Hungary and who knows it well; he tells me that this country has the worst system of landholding in Europe. The peasants there are as oppressed as they were in the Middle Ages, and manorial law still exists there.[1685]

Two days later, he proposed that they "enter into conversation" with the Hungarians, going on to say "Let's take a decision; let's not deal with Hungary as with Russia. One Russia is enough for us."[1686] He recommended sending Jan Smuts, who was dispatched to Budapest on a special train on the evening of 1 April, arriving on the morning of 4 April. The ostensible reason for the mission was to arbitrate an armistice line between the Hungarians and the Romanians, but its real purpose was to see if leader Béla Kun, who was in radio communication with Lenin, would be a useful conduit between the Allies and Moscow. Smuts was singularly unimpressed by the "unscrupulous" Kun[1687] and his "brigand clique". After barely two days of inconclusive negotiations he left, deciding "that Kun really had no authority and was of no use to them", and concluding, rightly as it happened, that the regime would not last long.[1688] When the Romanians and the Czechs subsequently attacked the crumbling regime,

---

1683 Quoted in Mantoux, Vol.II, p6.
1684 MacMillan, *Peacemakers*, p261.
1685 Quoted in Mantoux, Vol.I, p49.
1686 Ibid., p75.
1687 Béla Kun (1886-1938), *de facto* dictator of the Hungarian Soviet Republic, 12 March–1 August 1919. On its collapse, Kun fled to Russia, where he was executed in the Great Purge of the late 1930s.
1688 Smuts, p225-226.

on 9 June an exasperated Lloyd George exclaimed "They are all little brigand peoples who only want to steal territories."[1689]

The Treaty of Trianon was finally signed with Hungary at the Grand Trianon Palace in Versailles on 4 June 1920, the signatory for Britain being the Earl of Derby, Ambassador to France. The treaty regulated the status of the Hungarian state and defined its borders. Unfortunately, it left Hungary as a landlocked state that covered only 28% of what had constituted the pre-war kingdom. Its population was a mere 7.6 million, only 36% of the pre-war nation. Hungary's Army was limited to 35,000 men, and her navy ceased to exist. The Hungarian delegates signed under protest and, as with Germany, the vindictiveness of the terms imposed meant that it became an almost universal aim amongst Hungarians to reverse its terms. War hero Admiral Horthy[1690], acting as Regent, later reluctantly drew diplomatically closer to the other revisionist powers, Nazi Germany and Fascist Italy, pursuing an irredentist foreign policy.

"Poor little Belgium", the invasion of which had been the cause of drawing Britain and France into the war in the first place, fared poorly at the Conference, being sadly overlooked by the overloaded peacemakers. Belgium had been almost entirely occupied by the Germans for the duration of the war, and they had ruthlessly and systematically stripped the small country bare of resources, machinery, spare parts, railway stock, even factories, and millions of livestock. In 1919, around 80% of the workforce was unemployed and, if the Allies had not provided relief, many Belgians would have starved in the harsh winter of 1918-1919. To his discredit, Lloyd George had an angry scene with the Belgian Prime Minister, Léon Delacroix, over Belgium's 'preposterous' demands, being oddly unsympathetic to the prostrated nation's predicament, and fuming "I had to tell him quite plainly that the Belgians lost comparatively few men in the war, and that, when all was said, Belgium had not made greater sacrifices than Great Britain."[1691] Ultimately, the Commission on Belgian Affairs recommended that Belgium receive the small area of Eupen-Malmedy and the miniscule neutral territory of Moresnet, both on its eastern borders with Germany. Belgium also got far less than it hoped for in reparations, a deal finally being agreed after the British withdrew their objections on 29 April. Belgium would get a total payment of three billion German gold marks ($500 million) as soon as Germany made its reparation payments, and it took until 1925 for Belgium to get its priority payment in full.

One nation's concerns that interested Lloyd George at Paris would later play into his eventual downfall in 1922. That nation was Greece, newly resurgent after the Balkan Wars of 1912-1913 and its participation in the Great War on the Allied side from 29 June 1917. Lloyd George was a supporter of Greece, and, in particular, its popular Prime Minister, Eleftherios Venizelos[1692], to a very considerable degree, Venizelos being in his opinion "the greatest statesman that Greece had thrown up since the days of Pericles."[1693] Lloyd George firmly believed that a strong Greece would be a

---

1689 Quoted in Mantoux, Vol.II, p352.

1690 Admiral Miklós Horthy de Nagybánya (1868-1957), Regent of Hungary, 1 March 1920–15 October 1944.

1691 Quoted in MacMillan, *Peacemakers*, p285. Belgium lost 40,425 military personnel and 85,700 civilians.

1692 Eleftherios Venizelos (1864-1936), prominent leader of the Greek national liberation movement, Liberal Party Leader, eight times Prime Minister, serving from 1910-1920 and from 1928-1933.

1693 Lloyd George, *Truth About The Peace Treaties*, Vol.II, p1204.

valuable Mediterranean ally, and so he backed Venizelos and his territorial claims against the collapsing Ottoman Turks, writing later: "He was essentially a liberal and a democrat, and all the reactionary elements hated and feared his ideals, his legislation and his personality."[1694] As Margaret MacMillan points out, in some ways Venizelos was in the same mould as Lloyd George: "the fighter, orator, iconoclast, the man who held out, as Lloyd George had done in the Boer War, against an unjust policy and his own government."[1695] The two men had first met on 12 December 1912 in London, and they had established a friendship that lasted for the rest of Venizelos' life. To Venizelos, Lloyd George was like an Old Testament prophet, with "splendid capacities and clear insight of people and events", while to Lloyd George, Venizelos was "a big man, a very big man."[1696] The pair kept in close contact during the war, Lloyd George being encouraging about Greek claims, without committing himself.

When it came to presenting his case to the Supreme Council, Venizelos was sure that he had received a sympathetic hearing from all parties, except for the Italians, who had their own eyes set on Albania and Asia Minor, and who hoped to keep the Dodecanese Islands, despite their population being overwhelmingly Greek. As the Commission on Greek and Albanian Affairs held meetings through February and March, Venizelos kept up the pressure most eloquently, though Italian opposition gradually increased. The Greek position worsened, again due to American intransigence. On 5 September 1919, Venizelos informed Lloyd George that his position at home would be very dangerous unless he could show some solid gains.[1697] On 27 November 1919 the Treaty of Neuilly-sur-Seine required Bulgaria–one of the former Central Powers–to cede Western Thrace to the Entente, which awarded it to Greece at the San Remo Conference. This did not resolve Greek claims in Asia Minor, the issue continuing to fester for several years.

There was further trouble, this time between Greece and the Turks. On 6 May, Lloyd George pressed for a decision on Smyrna, a port city on the Aegean coast of Anatolia with a majority Greek population. With the Italian delegation temporarily absent, he saw an opportunity to break the impasse over Smyrna and suggested that Greek troops could be landed there to protect the Greek and other Christian minorities. For this reason, and to limit increasing Italian action in Anatolia, Clemenceau and Wilson supported a Greek military occupation of Smyrna. Although Smyrna would be occupied by Greek troops, authorized by the Allies, the Allies did not sanction Greece to take sovereignty over the territory until further negotiations settled the matter. The next day, the returned Italian delegation acquiesced.

Clemenceau was as enthusiastic about Venizelos as Lloyd George was at this time, stating: "Ulysses is only a small man beside him. He is a diplomat of the first rank, very sensible, very well prepared, very shrewd, always knowing what he wants."[1698] The afternoon after the decision was taken, Lloyd George asked Venizelos for a meeting before the Council of Four met, giving him the go-ahead.[1699]

---

1694 Ibid., Vol.II, p1216.

1695 MacMillan, *Peacemakers*, p364-365.

1696 Quoted in MacMillan, *Peacemakers*, p365.

1697 MacMillan, *Peacemakers*, p375.

1698 Quoted in MacMillan, *Peacemakers*, p443.

1699 Ibid., p443.

Greek troops duly occupied the city on 15 May. Unfortunately, after initial celebration amongst the Greek population, inter-ethnic rioting and looting broke out, with some 300-400 Turks and 100 Greeks dead by the end of that same evening, the disorder spreading into surrounding areas over the next few days. It was a disaster for the Greek cause, as it instantly sparked consternation, anger, resentment and protest throughout Turkey. One who was roused to anger and action was Kemal Atatürk. Assigned as the inspector of the Ninth Army Troops Inspectorate, on 19 May he reached the Black Sea port of Samsun, aiming to establish an organized national movement against the occupying forces. Allied policy in Turkey was confused and chaotic, and he took advantage of this, travelling ceaselessly to raise nationalist opposition. Lloyd George later wrote that "no information had been received as to his activities in Asia Minor in reorganising the shattered and depleted armies of Turkey. Our military intelligence had never been more thoroughly unintelligent."[1700]

On 22 June, Atatürk issued the Amasya Circular, declaring that the independence of the country was in danger, resigning from the Ottoman Army on 8 July. The 'reality gap' between what was being discussed hypothetically in Paris and what was actually happening in Turkey widened. All the time, the Allies forces grew weaker, while those of the Turks grew stronger. Balfour was appalled by the 'Big Four's' suggestions for partitioning Turkey, and sent Lloyd George a strongly-worded memorandum outlining the danger this would cause.[1701] Lloyd George's military advisors were almost unanimously opposed, as were Churchill and Montagu, who travelled to Paris from London to warn again that dismembering Turkey would mean 'eternal' war with the Muslim world, including that in India. Suggestions and counter-suggestions were made as opinions shifted, the main players often seemed to be increasingly trailing events rather than shaping them, culminating in a ludicrous situation on 21 May with a violent argument between Clemenceau and Lloyd George, in which the former reputedly offered the Welshman a choice of pistols or swords.[1702] On 17 June, three Ottoman Government representatives, headed by Grand Vizier Damat Ferid[1703], spoke before Lloyd George, Clemenceau, Wilson and their Foreign Ministers. Ferid blamed Turkey's entry into the war and its massacre and expulsion of between 700,000 to 1.5 million Armenian Christians on his predecessors, assured his listeners that his country wished to become a useful member of the League of Nations, and begged them to leave the Ottoman Empire intact.

None of the peacemakers were impressed by his arguments. At a meeting on 25 June, Lloyd George stated that they were "the best proof of the complete political incapacity of the Turks." Again, though, the peacemakers could not decide on a common plan of action, and the desultory discussion concluded with Lloyd George wishfully exclaiming "If we could only make peace summarily and finish with it." Clemenceau replied, more realistically, "I fear that is not possible."[1704] Curzon, in London in charge of the Foreign Office in Balfour's absence until he became Foreign Secretary himself on 23

[1700] Lloyd George, *Truth About The Peace Treaties*, Vol.II, p1285.
[1701] MacMillan, *Peacemakers*, p446.
[1702] Ibid., p447.
[1703] Damat Ferid Pasha (1853-1923), liberal statesman, twice Grand Vizier, the *de facto* prime minister, during the reign of the last Ottoman Sultan Mehmed VI, 4 March–2 October 1919 and 5 April–21 October 1920.
[1704] Quoted in Mantoux, Vol.II, p556.

October, sent a constant stream of communications warning of the dangers inherent in delaying a comprehensive settlement, but unfortunately Lloyd George, largely because of his antipathy to Curzon and what he represented, paid him little attention. A few years previously he had explained to Frances Stevenson "how he loathed the Curzon set, and all that they stood for–loathed their mannerisms, their ideals, their customs, their mode of life."[1705] In time he came to grudgingly respect Curzon's knowledge and ability, but by then it was too late, as it was Curzon who ultimately brought him down only three years later.

Curzon would later call the landing at Smyrna "the greatest mistake that had been made in Paris."[1706] His warnings went unheeded. Lloyd George remained firm in his determination that Greece should occupy Smyrna. Meanwhile, nationalist Turkish power continued to grow in Turkey, Atatürk controlling more than a quarter of the interior by the end of 1919 and establishing a rival capital at Ankara. The British, followed by the reluctant French and Italians, took over full control in Constantinople on 16 March 1920 to 'establish law and order'. Atatürk responded by calling his own nationalist parliament, opened on 23 April. Curzon came to believe that it would be best to allow Turkey to come into existence, with Atatürk as its leader, but Lloyd George was not to be persuaded.

At the San Remo Conference, held on 19-26 April 1920 at Villa Devachan in San Remo on the north-western Ligurian coast of Italy, the four Principal Allied Powers were represented by Francesco Nitti[1707] as Chairman, Lloyd George, Alexandre Millerand[1708], and by Ambassador Keishirō Matsui for Japan. The Americans were by now merely present as observers. A draft treaty was stitched together and presented to representatives of the government in Constantinople. Importantly, the decisions of the San Remo Conference confirmed the mandate allocations of the Conference of London.

The San Remo resolution, adopted on 25 April, incorporated the Balfour Declaration of 1917, it and Article 22, Paragraph 4 of the Covenant of the League of Nations becoming the basic documents upon which the British Mandate for Palestine was constructed. Under the Balfour Declaration, the British government had undertaken to favour the establishment of a national home for the Jewish people in Palestine without prejudice to the civil and religious rights of existing non-Jewish communities in Palestine or the rights and political status enjoyed by Jews in any other country. Lloyd George said to Chaim Weizmann "You have got your start. It all depends on you."[1709] Weizmann would have another meeting at 4, Carlton Gardens, Balfour's London home, with Lloyd George, Balfour and Churchill on 22 July 1921, at which he was assured of the Prime Minister's "support and high regard,"[1710] and after a number of redrafts, Britain formally received the Mandate for Palestine on 22 July 1922, as well as Iraq on 10 October 1922; France received the Mandate for Syria, including present-day Lebanon, on 29 September 1923. The boundaries of the territories were "to be determined [at a later date] by the Principal Allied Powers", leaving the status of the outlying areas of Zor and

---

1705 Stevenson, *Diary*, p76. Entry for 22 November 1915.
1706 Quoted in Macmillan, *Peacemakers*, p451.
1707 Francesco Nitti (1868-1953), Radical, Prime Minister, after Vittorio Orlando, 23 June 1919 - 15 June 1920.
1708 Alexandre Millerand (1859-1943), Prime Minister, 20 January–23 September 1920, President, 23 September 1920–11 June 1924.
1709 T. Segev, *One Palestine, Complete: Jews And Arabs Under The British Mandate*, 2000, London, Little, Brown, p144.
1710 Ibid., p194-195.

Transjordan temporarily undefined.

Following the secret, verbal Clemenceau–Lloyd George agreement made at the French Embassy in London on 1 December 1918, Britain and France also signed the San Remo Oil Agreement on 24 April, whereby Britain granted France a 25% share of the oil production from Mosul, with the remainder going to Britain, and France undertook to deliver oil to the Mediterranean. The draft peace agreement with Turkey signed at the conference became the basis for the 1920 Treaty of Sèvres. Germany was called upon to carry out its military and reparation obligations under the Versailles Treaty, and a resolution was adopted in favour of restoring trade with Soviet Russia.

British troops were also being sent to parts of the Caucasus, Baku and its great oilfields, the port of Batum in Georgia, and elsewhere. On 12 May, Henry Wilson, Chief of the Imperial General Staff, and on the verge of promotion to Field Marshal, told Lloyd George "The sooner we get out of the Caucasus the better."[1711] In June, the Cabinet finally took the decision to withdraw all British troops from the region by the end of the year. Kurdistan was even more problematic, as Atatürk's forces and those of the Russian Bolshevik's to the north started to forge tentative links through their common opposition to the British, both pressing on the territory. British forces in the Ottoman Empire shrank to 320,000 men by the summer of 1919 and continued to decline.

At San Remo, Lloyd George admitted:

> He himself had tried to find out what the feelings of the Kurds were. After inquiries in Constantinople, Baghdad and elsewhere, he found it impossible to discover any representative Kurd. No Kurd appeared to represent anything more than his own particular clan… On the other hand, it would seem that the Kurds felt they could not maintain their existence without the backing of a great Power… But if neither France nor Great Britain undertook the task–and he hoped neither would–they appeared to think it might be better to leave them under the protection of the Turks. The country had grown accustomed to Turkish rule, and it was difficult to separate it from Turkey unless some alternative protector could be discovered.[1712]

In the peace terms presented to the Turks the status of Kurdistan remained vague, possibly autonomy within Turkey, a mandate under a power or complete independence. In Ankara, the nationalist parliament rejected both these terms and the sultan's government. Increasing numbers of nationalists left Constantinople to join Atatürk's forces. The Allied high commissioners sent strong warnings that Turkish opinion, already inflamed, would not accept the loss of Smyrna, where the Greeks were digging in. Curzon had feared this and passed on the warnings to Lloyd George.

In June 1920, Greek troops then pushed inland from Smyrna, while in Thrace another Greek army pushed back the weak Turkish forces there. On 10 August, the Allies and Damat Ferid, representing the sultan's government, signed a peace treaty in an exhibition room at the Sèvres porcelain factory in the south-western suburbs of Paris. Allied military advisers warned that it would take at least 27

---

1711 Quoted in MacMillan, *Peacemakers*, p454.
1712 Ibid., p458.

divisions to enforce the terms, divisions they did not have. In Turkey, a national day of mourning was declared. Atatürk continued his fight, by now controlling most of the nationalist forces in Turkey, and in the north he and the Bolsheviks were crushing the nascent Caucasian republics. On 4 December Armenia fell under Soviet control, with the People's Commissar for Nationalities, Joseph Stalin, being active in bringing this about.

Kurdistan was finished as a realistic idea too. By March 1921, the Allies had backed away from the vague promises in the Treaty of Sèvres. As far as Kurdistan was concerned, they were ready to modify the treaty in "a sense of conformity with the existing facts of the situation". The 'existing facts' were that Atatürk had denounced the whole treaty; he had successfully kept part of the Armenian territories within Turkey; and he was about to sign a treaty giving the rest to the Soviet Union. Kurdish nationalists protested, but the Allies no longer had any interest in an independent Kurdish state. Stability on his northern and eastern fronts enabled Atatürk to deal with the Greek invasion in the west. Events began to run in his favour. On 14 November 1920, in Greece, Venizelos was unexpectedly defeated in an election, which ended the remnants of the Allied policy in Turkey. Italy and France argued that they were no longer under any obligation to support Greece and that the Treaty of Sèvres must be revised. The Italians hinted that they would be willing to work with Atatürk to modify its terms. On 20 October 1921, France signed the Treaty of Ankara with Atatürk's government which provided for the withdrawal of all French forces from Cilicia in the south.

On 26 August 1922, the Turkish counterattack finally neared Smyrna. The orders were simple: "Soldiers, your goal is the Mediterranean." The Greek forces were shattered and, on 10 September, Atatürk rode in triumph into Smyrna. The city was packed with many refugees who had fled from Greek villages inland. In the back streets and alleys, the looting, raping and killing began. The conquering soldiers and the Turks of Smyrna had many scores to settle. The remaining Greeks were now abandoned to their fate. Most notably, Chrysostomos[1713], the Orthodox Metropolitan Bishop, was brutally lynched by a mob of Turkish citizens. As–shamefully–Allied troops watched from no fewer than 21 warships anchored offshore, from 13-22 September, the Greek and Armenian quarters of the city were systematically torched, destroying them utterly and killing many, estimates ranging from 10,000 to 100,000, a true atrocity.

The collapse of the over-stretched Greek army left the small Allied occupation forces in Constantinople and guarding the straits suddenly exposed. As Atatürk's armies advanced northwards toward the Sea of Marmara and Constantinople, the British government decided that it must stand firm at Chanak and Ismid on the Asiatic side. The Italians declared themselves neutral, while the French ordered their troops out of Chanak. Lloyd George was for war, but cooler heads, including Curzon's and those of the military on the spot, finally prevailed. Atatürk was now ready for negotiations. The Armistice of Mudanya, signed with the Grand National Assembly of Turkey on 11 October, provided for the Turks to take over Eastern Thrace from the Greeks. In return, Atatürk promised not to move troops into Constantinople, Gallipoli or Ismid until a peace conference could

---

1713 Chrysostomos Kalafatis (1867-1922), Saint Chrysostomos of Smyrna, declared a martyr and saint of the Eastern Orthodox Church on 4 November 1992.

decide their fate. All over Asia Minor and then Thrace, over a million Greeks were displaced, moving into a Greece that was ill-equipped to receive them all.

The calamitous Greco-Turkish War in Asia Minor had already brought down Venizelos; now it also brought down his great patron, Lloyd George. The Chanak crisis was too much for the increasingly fragile coalition government. Curzon discreetly abandoned his old colleagues. When a new Tory government under Bonar Law took office on 23 October 1922, Curzon was reappointed as Foreign Secretary. He left almost immediately for the Conference of Lausanne in Switzerland from 21 November 1922 to 24 February 1923 and from 23 April to 24 July 1923, leading to the Treaty of Lausanne, where peace with Turkey peace was at last concluded. Few of those there had been at the Paris Peace Conference–Curzon, acting as co-ordinator, Poincaré, a subdued Venizelos, who had been invited by the new government to represent Greece, Prime Minister Aleksandar Stamboliyski of Bulgaria with his glamorous interpreter, Nadejda Stancioff, the only woman at the conference. Some faces were missing, like that of Lloyd George of course. There were some new ones, among them Benito Mussolini, who had only recently become Prime Minister of Italy on 31 October 1922 after his 'March on Rome', ill at ease at his first major international conference.

After lengthy horse-trading, and Curzon refusing to return to the Conference when it reconvened on 23 April–a futile measure designed to pressurize the Turks–a peace agreement was finally worked out and signed on 24 July 1923. The Treaty of Lausanne was unlike Versailles, Trianon, St. Germain, Neuilly and Sèvres, products of the Paris Peace Conference. The political axis of the world had already started to tilt. Curzon reflected: "Hitherto we have dictated our peace treaties. Now we are negotiating one with the enemy who has an army in being while we have none, an unheard-of position."[1714] Almost nothing remained of the terms agreed at Sèvres with the Ottoman government. There was no provision for an independent Armenia or Kurdistan, and the Turks refused to guarantee protection to minorities on the grounds of sovereignty. Turkey's borders now included virtually all the Turkish-speaking territories, from Eastern Thrace down to Syria. The straits remained Turkish, but with an international agreement on their use. On 4 October 1923, the last Allied troops left Constantinople, which was renamed Istanbul on 28 March 1930.

At Paris, Britain and France came to have significant differences in another part of the now dissolved Ottoman Empire, namely the Middle East. This was despite the Sykes-Picot Agreement, a secret treaty between the Britain and France, with assent from the Russian Empire and Italy, to define their mutually agreed spheres of influence and control in an eventual partition of the Ottoman Empire. The principal negotiations occurred between 23 November 1915 and 3 January 1916, on which date the British and French diplomats, Sir Mark Sykes[1715] and François Georges-Picot[1716], initialled an agreed memorandum, duly ratified by their respective governments on 9 and 16 May 1916. The Agreement effectively divided the Ottoman provinces outside the Arabian Peninsula into areas of British and French control and influence. The British- and French-controlled countries were divided

---

[1714] Quoted in MacMillan, *Peacemakers*, p464.
[1715] Colonel Mark Sykes (1879-1919), died in Paris on 16 February 1919, a victim of the Spanish flu pandemic.
[1716] François Georges-Picot (1870-1951), diplomat and lawyer.

by the Sykes-Picot line. The agreement allocated to Britain control of what is today southern Israel and Palestine, Jordan and southern Iraq, and an additional small area that included the ports of Haifa and Acre to allow access to the Mediterranean. France gained control of south-eastern Turkey, northern Iraq, Syria and Lebanon. The agreement was publicly exposed by the Bolsheviks in Moscow on 23 November 1917.

Neither party had taken sufficient note of the rise of Arab nationalism, useful in the fight against the Turks, harnessed by T. E. Lawrence[1717]–Lawrence of Arabia–, during the Arab Revolt from June 1916, but potentially inconvenient now. Lawrence accompanied Emir Faisal[1718], the leader of the Arab Delegation, to Paris, dramatically appearing before the Council of Ten on 6 February[1719], and Lloyd George later recorded his impressions of "that strange man of genius":

> He was a man who possessed military flair and daring to an exceptional degree… As one who saw a great deal of Lawrence during the Peace Conference, I felt he was a most elusive and unassessable personality. The mystery that has always surrounded him has added cubits to his stature as a guerrilla chief… but that he rendered effective service, both as a fighter and as a counsellor, cannot be questioned. His literary productions [*The Seven Pillars Of Wisdom*] still remain and there can be no doubt about their rare quality…
>
> In the military operations on the Palestine front, the Arab cavalry and camelry rendered invaluable service… Lawrence took part in cutting the railway upon which the Turks relied for their supplies at over 80 different points. In the final advance, after the British had broken through the Turkish defences, the Arab cavalry swept round the retreating Turks and occupied Damascus. The Arabs were entitled to claim that they rendered undoubted aid to the British armies that defeated the Turks and finally drove them out of the Arab regions of the Turkish Empire.[1720]

Lawrence also recorded his impressions of Lloyd George, writing to Churchill on 18 March 1929 on the publication of the latter's *The World Crisis*:

> I particularly like your fairness toward Lloyd George. The future is going to flay our generation for its unfairness to him. He's ever so much bigger than the statesmen of the Napoleonic times. He's said magnificent things, & his own performances, with that team, were marvellous… LG [sic] has been a very grand figure. He was a big man in Paris…[1721]

On 21 May 1919, major disagreements took place between Lloyd George and Clemenceau on the whole issue of the former Ottoman Empire, especially regarding Mesopotamia, which corresponded

---

1717 Colonel T. E. Lawrence (1888-1935). Born in Tremadog, Caernarfonshire, renowned for his role in the Arab Revolt and the Sinai and Palestine Campaign against the Ottoman Empire.

1718 Faisal I bin Hussein bin Ali al-Hashemi (1885-1933), King of Syria, 1920, and King of Iraq, 1921-1933.

1719 M. Korda *Hero: The Life And Legend Of Lawrence Of Arabia*, 2010, London, JR Books, p473-474.

1720 Lloyd George, *Truth About The Peace Treaties*, Vol.II, p1028-1029.

1721 Quoted in Lloyd George, *David & Winston*, p201.

to the old Ottoman provinces of Mosul, Baghdad and Basra. It was at this time that it became clear that oil was the fuel of the future, and the wrangling between the wary allies did not end until December. Palestine was another problem area, with the growing claims of Chaim Weizmann and the Zionists for the establishment of a national homeland for the Jewish people there. During the war, Weizmann had cultivated Balfour, and, even more importantly, Lloyd George also became a supporter. Lloyd George was delighted when General Allenby entered Jerusalem on 11 December 1917 at the head of British, French and Italian detachments, enthusing that this was "something which generations of the chivalry of Europe failed to attain."[1722] Because of his strong Nonconformist upbringing, Lloyd George knew his Bible well and had an interest in Palestine. He was very familiar with the geography of the Holy Land and understood its importance to the Jews. On 25 May 1925 he said:

> I was brought up in a school where I was taught far more about the history of the Jews than about the history of my own land. I could tell you all the kings of Israel. But I doubt whether I could have named half a dozen of the kings of England, and not more of the kings of Wales.[1723]

Lloyd George had considerable sympathy with the plight of the Jews. At a dinner given in his honour by the British Zionist Federation at the Savoy Hotel, London on 12 April 1931, looking back at the Balfour Declaration, Lloyd George said:

> The first duty of a Government is to protect the lives and property of all its citizens without respect of race or creed. If it fails in that elementary duty it has no right to occupy the seat of Government. The Jew at Tel Aviv has as much right to protection as the Mohammedan in Cawnpore. The honour of the British flag is involved in guaranteeing protection to both.[1724]

In *Is It Peace?* he wrote, in words that stand the test of time:

> Of all the bigotries that savage the human temper there is none so stupid as the anti-Semitic. It has no basis in reason; it is not rooted in faith; it aspires to no ideal; it is just one of those dank and unwholesome weeds that grow in the morass of racial hatred. How utterly devoid of reason it is may be gathered from the fact that it is almost entirely confined to nations who worship Jewish prophets and apostles, revere the national literature of the Hebrews as the only inspired message delivered by the deity to mankind, and whose only hope of salvation rests on the precepts and promises of the great teachers of Judah. Yet in the sight of these fanatics the Jews of to-day can do nothing right.[1725]

---

1722 Rowland, *Lloyd George*, p424.
1723 Guedalla, *Napoleon And Palestine*, p48.
1724 https://www.jta.org/archive/mr-lloyd-george-explains-jewish-national-home-policy-i-was-prime-minister-when-balfour-declaration. Retrieved 5 October 2022.
1725 Lloyd George, *Is It Peace?*, p312.

There was a further connection between Lloyd George and Weizmann in the form of a 'debt of honour'. During Lloyd George's time as the Minister of Munitions, Britain had been running critically short of acetone, an essential ingredient in the production of cordite, used to propel bullets and shells. Weizmann, an industrial chemist, had just perfected the 'Weizmann Process' for producing it on a large scale, and he magnanimously made it available to the British for the duration of the war without payment. When Lloyd George asked him to accept an honour from the King, Weizmann replied "There is nothing I want for myself." Pressed further, he asked for support for the Zionist cause.[1726] Lloyd George claimed later "That was the fount and origin of the famous declaration about the National Home for the Jews in Palestine."[1727] This was, however, not correct, as Weizmann had engaged the interest of Balfour in the subject in Manchester in January 1906, in London on 12 December 1914 and at Manchester again in March 1915, long before the industrial use of his new process had eased the acetone issue.[1728] Indeed, Lloyd George had himself already expressed great sympathy with the subject in Cabinet on 9 November 1914, to Weizmann himself, in the company of C. P. Scott[1729] and Herbert Samuel, on 15 January 1915[1730] and again to Lord Reading in early February 1915.[1731]

Palestine had been promised to the French under the Sykes-Picot Agreement, but from 7 February 1917, with Lloyd George's encouragement, Sykes met privately with Weizmann and other Zionists. By the end of October that year, the Cabinet had agreed a formula, and on 2 November Balfour sent a sympathetic letter to Walter Rothschild[1732], a leader of the British Jewish community, and active Zionist, who had been involved in the complex drafting process, for forwarding to the Zionist Federation of Great Britain and Ireland. The text of the 'Balfour Declaration' was published in the press on 9 November:

> His Majesty's Government view with favour the establishment in Palestine of a national home for the Jewish people, and will use their best endeavours to facilitate the achievement of this object, it being clearly understood that nothing shall be done which may prejudice the civil and religious rights of existing non-Jewish communities in Palestine, or the rights and political status enjoyed by Jews in any other country.

Weizmann and three notable Zionists presented their case before the Supreme Council–including Balfour and Milner–in Paris on 27 February 1919. However, as increasingly at the Conference, nothing

---

1726 According to Lord Nathan, Weizmann had said simply "A country for my people.": Hyde, p245.
1727 Lloyd George, *War Memoirs*, Vol.II, p586. See also Guedalla, p50.
1728 Stein, pp153-155; Samuel, p144, 147. Samuel wrote *The Future of Palestine* Memorandum, circulated in Cabinet in January and–revised–March 1915.
1729 Charles Prestwich Scott (1846-1932), editor of the *Manchester Guardian*, 1872-1929, its owner from 1907 until his death. Liberal MP for Leigh, 1895-1906, he pursued a progressive liberal agenda in the paper.
1730 Weizmann, *Trial And Error*, p192;
https://ipsonet.org/wp-content/uploads/2021/12/Proceedings-No.-24-Full-Issue.pdf. Retrieved 29 February 2024; Stein, p140.
1731 Wasserstein, p206; Samuel, p143.
1732 Walter Rothschild, 2nd Baron Rothschild, (1868-1937), Liberal Unionist MP for Aylesbury, 1899-1910, Zionist leader and friend of Weizmann, President of the Board of Deputies of British Jews, 1925-1926.

was decided at that meeting, and the subject was subsequently barely raised. It was not 'settled' until the San Remo Conference in April 1920, when Britain got the Palestinian Mandate. However, gradually organized Palestinian Arab nationalism grew in response to Zionism, generating both petitions and political protest as well as violence against Jews.

Lloyd George came out of all this with a mixed reputation, known in his lifetime as 'The Man Who Won the War' and sometimes as the man who lost the peace. As Prime Minister, he had brought new vigour and determination to the prosecution of the war and to strengthening Britain's relations with its Allies and its Empire. With the coming of peace, he had led the British Empire delegation to the Paris Peace Conference and played a key role in shaping the peace treaties and bridging the differences between the Americans and the French. Although his detractors accused him of a lack of knowledge and experience in foreign relations, he was quick to grasp the complex issues before him and generally showed good judgement and common sense. Lloyd George originally commented that he did "not do badly" at the Peace Conference, "considering I was seated between Jesus Christ and Napoleon," a reference to the idealism of Wilson on the one hand and the stark realism of Clemenceau on the other.

Liberal economist John Maynard Keynes[1733], present in a relatively junior capacity as an advisor to the Treasury–particularly on the issue of Inter-Allied Debt–until his resignation on 7 June, had been impressed by Lloyd George at the Conference, writing:

> [He had an] unerring, almost medium-like sensibility to everyone around him… watching the company, with six or seven senses not available to ordinary men, judging character, motive, and subconscious impulse, perceiving what each [man] was thinking and even what each was going to say next, and compounding with telepathic instinct the argument or appeal that best suited the vanity, weakness, or self-interest of his auditor…[1734]

However, this did not prevent him from writing to Lloyd George on 5 June:

> I am slipping away from the scene of nightmare. I can do no more good here. I've gone on hoping even through these last dreadful weeks that you'd find some way to make of the Treaty a just and expedient document. But now it's apparently too late. The battle is lost…[1735]

It also did not hold him back from making a more colourful, damning, if faintly ridiculous, judgement on Lloyd George published much later. The Germans, he wrote acerbically, could not possibly pay what the victors were demanding. Calling Clemenceau a xenophobe with "one illusion–France; and one disillusion–mankind, including Frenchmen, and his colleagues not least"[1736], and Wilson a "blind and deaf Don Quixote"[1737], he finally unleashed the purple prose he had reserved for Lloyd George:

---

1733 John Maynard Keynes (1883-1946).

1734 Keynes, *Economic Consequences*, p37. While the influential, polemical book has never been out of print since 8 December 1919, Keynes later came to realise that what he had then proposed, arguing from a narrowly economic perspective, had not been possible.

1735 Quoted in R. Skidelsky, *John Maynard Keynes: Hopes Betrayed 1883-1920*, 1983, London, Viking, p375.

1736 Keynes, *Economic Consequences*, p29.

1737 Ibid., p38.

> How can I convey… any just impression of this extraordinary figure of our time, this syren, this goat-footed bard, this half-human visitor to our age from the hag-ridden magic and enchanted woods of Celtic antiquity? One catches in his company that flavour of final purposelessness, inner irresponsibility, existence outside or away from our Saxon good and evil, mixed with cunning, remorselessness, love of power, that lend fascination, enthralment and terror to the fair-seeming magician of North European folklore… Lloyd George is rooted in nothing; he is void and without content; he lives and feeds on his immediate surroundings; he is an instrument and a player at the same time which plays on the company and is played on by them too; he is a prism, as I have heard him described, which collects light and distorts it and is most brilliant if the light comes from many quarters at once; a vampire and medium in one.[1738]

An outraged Keynes prophesied that the reparations would keep Germany impoverished and ultimately threaten all Europe. He concluded:

> No wonder that in the eventual settlement the real victor was Clemenceau… These were the personalities of Paris… Clemenceau, aesthetically the noblest; the President, morally the most admirable; Lloyd George intellectually the subtlest. Out of their disparities and weaknesses the Treaty was born, child of the least worthy attributes of his parents, without nobility, without morality, without intellect.[1739]

Against what he derided as Clemenceau's "Carthaginian Peace"[1740], he made a grim prophecy:

> If we aim at the impoverishment of Central Europe, vengeance, I dare predict, will not limp. Nothing can then delay for very long that final civil war between the forces of Reaction and the despairing convulsions of Revolution, before which the horrors of the late German war will fade into nothing, and which will destroy, whoever is victor, the civilisation and the progress of our generation.[1741]

The bestselling book subsequently became popular with discontented Germans as ammunition for their arguments against the Versailles settlement, undermining the Allied statesmen.

Much later, historian Antony Lentin evaluated Lloyd George's role in Paris as a major success:

> Unrivalled as a negotiator, he had powerful combative instincts and indomitable determinism, and succeeded through charm, insight, resourcefulness, and simple pugnacity. Although sympathetic to France's desires to keep Germany under control, he did much to prevent the French from gaining power, attempted to extract Britain from the Anglo-French entente,

---

1738 Keynes, *Essays In Biography*, pp36-37. This sketch was intended for inclusion in 'Economic Consequences' but excised and published separately in *Essays* in 1933. It caused a rupture in relations between the two men.

1739 Ibid., p40-41.

1740 Keynes, *Economic Consequences*, p56.

1741 Ibid., p268.

> inserted the war-guilt clause, and maintained a liberal and realist view of the postwar world. By doing so, he managed to consolidate power over the House, secured his power base, expanded the empire, and sought a European balance of power.[1742]

Many now wanted to recognise the extraordinary services that Lloyd George had rendered to the nation. On 29 June 1919, after months of strenuous negotiations, Lloyd George returned from Paris, arriving in London at Victoria Station just after 6.30 pm. Breaking protocol, King George V came with the Prince of Wales to greet him at the station. En route back to Buckingham Palace, the assembled crowds threw flowers into the carriage, and a laurel wreath fell onto the King's lap. "This is for you" he said and handed it to the feted peacemaker.[1743] Winifred Coombe Tennant was in Downing Street, when soon after 7.00 pm there was:

> A roar of cheering and I saw the flash of scarlet coming through the roadway from the Horse Guards. It was the scarlet livery of a royal carriage and sitting in it, bare headed and bowing to the crowd was Lloyd George–the little Welsh peasant! Such [a] welcome he was given, people swarming up the carriage to touch him, and when he had gone into No.10 they roared until he appeared several times at the window. Can this man of the people fail the people? I hope against hope he is true to full democratic truth–God grant it! How much he might do to make this country 'fit for heroes'. It was wonderful to see him there today… the idol of the populace. If he only be true to his race and upbringing! Wales is fond of him. 'God bless you', I cried, though he was far beyond earshot.[1744]

On 5 July, Lloyd George travelled back home to Criccieth, where he was met by hundreds of locals and visitors, the town adorned with flowers and banners. Addressing the crowd, he struck a personal note, telling them: "My dear neighbours, thank you for this warm welcome. I have been doing the most important job that I have ever had to do. War is over and a beautiful peaceful rainbow is in the sky."[1745] On 5 August, King George showed further appreciation of his Prime Minister by awarding him the Order of Merit, his letter stating:

> Honours and rewards to officers of the army, navy and air force having been submitted to Parliament, I feel that my people will share with me with regret that it is not possible to express the nation's grateful recognition of the persistent services rendered by the Prime Minister, both in carrying the war to a victorious end and in securing an honourable peace. To rectify somewhat this omission and personally to mark my high appreciation of these services, it gives me great pleasure to confer upon you the Order of Merit.[1746]

---

[1742] A. Lentin, *Several Types of Ambiguity: Lloyd George at the Paris Peace Conference, Diplomacy and Statecraft*, 6.1, 1995, p223-251.

[1743] Stevenson, *Diary*, p187. The wreath is in the Lloyd George Museum.

[1744] Coombe Tennant, p274. Diary entry for 29 June 1919.

[1745] *Y Dydd*, 11 July 1919, p3 (*Translated from the Welsh*).

[1746]https://timesmachine.nytimes.com/timesmachine/1919/08/07/118153638.pdf. Retrieved 16 February 2019.

Churchill, Secretary of State for War, campaigned for Lloyd George to be awarded the three war medals issued to all members of the Armed Services with the requisite service. On 16 October he wrote persuasively to the King:

> As the Prime Minister must have made 30 or 40 journeys to France and was on several occasions in zones where shells were falling, and as all these journeys were made in strict performance of necessary duty of the highest possible consequence, Mr. Churchill considers that the grant of the War Medals in these circumstances will be in every respect appropriate.[1747]

Churchill wrote again on 7 December, acknowledging that Lloyd George had been consulted and had expressed great pleasure, saying "I would rather have these than an Earldom". On 8 January 1920, the newspapers announced: "At 10 Downing Street, last night, Mr. Winston Churchill and the members of the Army Council waited upon the Prime Minister to present him with the special award of the 1914-15 Star, the British War Medal and the Victory Medal, approved by the King."[1748]

Lloyd George's services were also recognised across Europe. He was made Knight of Grace, Order of Saint John; Chancellor of the Welsh Priory from 1918 and Prior of Wales from 1943. France awarded him the Grand-Croix, Ordre national de la Légion d'honneur, in 1920. Belgium awarded him the Grand Cordon of the Order of Leopold, and Italy the Order of St. Maurice and St. Lazarus. On 29 April 1925, Estonia presented him with the Cross of Liberty, (3rd class 1st rank) for civilian service. Academia followed suit. The University of Wales had already made him LLD in 1908, with Oxford University making him DCL the same year and a Fellow of Jesus College in 1910. Glasgow University had made him LLD in 1917, and University of Edinburgh LLD in 1918 and Rector in 1920 (until 1923). Now Durham University made him DCL (1919), Sheffield University DLitt (1919), Cambridge University LLD (1920), Birmingham University LLD (1921), and Leeds University LLD (1922).[1749]

Civic society was also in the mood to extend recognition. Lloyd George had already been made an Honorary Freeman of Pwllheli in 1903, of Caernarfon and Cardiff in 1908, and of the City of London, Glasgow and Dundee in 1917. Now the same honour was conferred on him by Blackpool, Llandovery, Manchester, Neath, Newcastle-Upon-Tyne, Salford, Southampton and Wolverhampton in 1918; Criccieth, Portsmouth and Wakefield (1919); Barnsley, Birmingham and York (1921); Aberystwyth and Leeds (1922); Montreal, Canada; Brecon, Bristol, Carmarthen, Conway, Inverness, Kidwelly, Llanelli, Swansea and Wrexham (1923); Banff and Kingston-Upon-Hull (1925); Cowbridge and Tenby (1930); Port Talbot (1932)[1750]. On 10 October 1935, he was made a Liveryman of the Worshipful Company of Curriers in a ceremony at Cordwainers Hall, 7 Cannon Street, London, on the motion of

---

1747 Quoted in Rose, p260.

1748 Beaverbrook, *Men And Power*, p326.

1749 *Burke's Peerage*, 1949, [99th Edition] London, Burke's Peerage Ltd., p1241 [*Lloyd-George of Dwyfor*]. LLD is Doctor of Laws, DCL is Doctor of Civil Law.

1750 The list is not exhaustive. Dates shown here are those of the award, not the actual presentation.

his associate Sir Gordon Hewart, Lord Chief Justice of England.[1751]

Recognition was also rightly due to the Prime Minister's tireless but self-effacing wife, Margaret. Apart from all else, she had often stood in for him at political and civic rallies and meetings, not shying away from contentious issues. She had long campaigned for her husband in his own constituency: from the war's cessation she had become "the first, and perhaps the only wife of a British Prime Minister to campaign on the political hustings around the country…[who]… seized the opportunities and avoided the minefields with great skill."[1752] Grandson Bengy particularly emphasised her core role in Lloyd George's life and work, and more recently came to light in this regard, as the Welsh Political Archive at the National Library of Wales revealed new acquisitions: "Most [important] is a collection of twenty-two speeches made by Dame Margaret Lloyd George at various events including political meetings, charity functions, the opening of schools, exhibitions, bazaars, an unveiling of a war memorial, and the presentation of awards. Six of the speeches are in Margaret Lloyd George's own hand, the rest by her private secretary… the Rev. J.T. Rhys."[1753]

Three instances show Margaret's unique role. The first is from 17 June 1919, when she visited Lampeter to give a speech at the Cardiganshire Liberal Association's Annual Meeting. By this period there were tensions within Welsh Liberalism, caused by both the rise of Welsh Labour and by the strain in relations between Lloyd George's supporters and Asquith's. The sitting Liberal MP, Matthew Vaughan-Davies[1754], was a supporter of Lloyd George, but he was expected by this time to be elevated to the Lords, although in the event this did not occur until 1921. Margaret's visit to Lampeter was part of a speaking campaign as she made her way from Criccieth to London, and there were some unfounded rumours circulating that Lloyd George might call an autumn election. Her campaign was aimed at three things: "(1) to sustain support for her husband's Coalition–noting he held fewer seats than his Tory partners; (2) to sustain support for Lloyd George; and, (3) to sustain support for his policies, whether in concluding the Peace agreement… or in pursuing further social reforms in the country."[1755]

After a "great ovation", Margaret gave her speech in the packed Victoria Hall, with 585 delegates present, a third of whom were women, and a large gathering of the public. Appealing for continued support for the Government, she said:

> The soldiers and sailors could not have won the war without having statesmanship behind them and the Government had done all that was humanly possible to aid them… The Peace

---

[1751] E. Mayer and D. Adamson, *The Curriers' Company: A Modern History*, 2000, London, Worshipful Company of Curriers, pp208, 330. Gordon Hewart (1870-1943), Liberal MP for Leicester 1913-1918, Leicester East 1918-1922, Lord Chief Justice 1922-1940. Cordwainers Hall was destroyed in the Blitz on 10 May 1941. The author thanks Company historians Dr Donald Adamson and Dr Ian Stone for this reference.

[1752] O'Brien, *Campaigns*, p15.

[1753] Reverend John T. Rhys, known as J. T. (1867-1938), Margaret's private secretary, 1917-1922. Author of *Wales and Its Drink Problem*, 1912, Aberystwyth, Welsh Gazette: dedicated to David Lloyd George. Quote https://lloydgeorgesociety.org.uk/en/article/2019/1333069/new-collections-at-the-welsh-political-archive. Retrieved 8 January 2020.

[1754] Matthew Vaughan-Davies (1840-1935), Liberal MP for Cardiganshire, 1895-1921. Created Baron Ystwyth in New Year Honours, 1921.

[1755] O'Brien, *Lampeter*, p8.

> Conference had to reconcile hostile interests and conflicting ideas… *There could be no greater dishonour to the brave soldiers and no greater disservice to the present and future generations than to have a peace which would not stand the test of time…* In addition to increased pensions and allowances… the Government had a good record of domestic legislation… When peace was declared and the Prime Minister returned home he would be only too glad to start on those reforms and to fulfil his election pledges.[1756]

The second instance is from 30 June 1919, the day after Lloyd George returned to London having signed the Versailles Treaty, when the *Liverpool Courier* carried an article from his wife, its message being reported widely in the press. On the Saturday she had presided over the massive London women's Victory Loan demonstration in Trafalgar Square. Ahead were the Peace Day celebrations due for 19 July. As author Richard Rhys O'Brien rightly states:

> Dame Margaret is greatly under-appreciated, not only for tirelessly canvassing support for Liberalism, for her husband and for his Coalition government but also for the gentle, subtle and energetic ways in which she promoted her own causes. Perhaps most consistently she was a champion for opportunities for women in a man's world. The article is written in her familiar style, with the simple opening: "Women have at least two substantial reasons for rejoicing in the establishment of peace on earth".
>
> "War is absolutely alien to woman's nature and does violence to everything that she cherishes in life. Woman's thoughts are thoughts of peace, and to her war is an unspeakable torture, an indescribable agony. Woman is so constituted that peace is essential to her wellbeing and the return of peace she therefore hails with joy unfeigned.
>
> "She can rejoice, too, because she has contributed so magnificently by her endeavours and by her endurance to the great victory which has made peace possible. Though she loves peace and loathes war, yet she laboured with unexampled devotion to end the war. Without women's help we… could not have seen the war end in victory for us–victory which crowns the efforts of our valiant men on land, on sea, and in the air… In every sphere the women of Britain have undertaken work uncongenial, arduous and often very perilous…"
>
> "Nor must we forget the women whose part in the tragic struggle was to suffer in silence, and today are longing for 'the touch of the vanished hand' and for 'the sound of the voice that is still'. 'They also serve who stand and wait'. They have mourned; they have never murmured…"
>
> "If we can for the purpose of peace retain that spirit of unity, the Peace day will mark not only the end of the war, but the end of one and the beginning of another era in the history of Britain, an era brighter and better than Britain has ever known in her long history; and the inauguration of that era will be the richest compensation for all the sacrifices of the war. We have an unexampled opportunity and responsibility".[1757]

---

1756 *Cambrian News*, 20 June 1919, quoted in O'Brien, *Lampeter*, p15. Emphasis added.

1757 https://richardrhysobriencomblogs.wordpress.com/2019/06/24/women-in-war-and-peace-1919/. Retrieved 9 January 2020.

The third example is from 14 November 1919, the eve of by-election day in Plymouth, when Margaret travelled down to the West Country to support the Coalition Tory candidate Nancy Astor. The opposing Independent Liberal was not a Lloyd George/Coalition Liberal. But for Margaret this was not primarily about coalition politics but support for a woman running for Parliament–who would, as it turned out, become the first woman to take her seat in the Commons.[1758] On 7 November, Lloyd George had himself already written an open letter of support to Nancy Astor, stressing that:

> Now that women have been enfranchised I think it important that there should be a certain number of women in Parliament in order to represent the woman's point of view. There are a good many questions in regard to housing, child welfare, food, drink, and prices in which it would be an immense advantage both to the nation and to the House of Commons to have a woman' s view presented by a woman.[1759]

This was just the occasion for Margaret to address the crowds at the Guildhall, to enthuse the women, to support her husband's Coalition and furthermore support her fellow Temperance campaigner.

> It is a classic Margaret Lloyd George speech: the arguments simply put and well-structured, and would undoubtedly have been embellished as she would warm to her audience, in this case the women of Plymouth. Press reports relate the meetings were packed to overflowing…
>
> She begins with the reminder that that women have won the right to vote, the more passive word "obtain" being crossed out. In other speeches she would make the point that women had earned the right to vote, not just been granted the right. She emphasises that the next task is to exercise that right and then gain direct representation in parliament by electing a woman. In reality the women's turnout was good, but it was important that the hard-won vote was not squandered. It would not have been forgotten that in the recent 1918 election, 16 of the 17 women candidates failed to be elected, the exception being Sinn Féin's Countess Markiewicz.
>
> *I am very delighted to see so large a gathering at this meeting. For very many years women worked hard to* ~~obtain~~ *win the right to vote at Parliamentary Elections. Your presence here this afternoon shows you appreciate the responsibility & mean to show yourselves worthy of the franchise. This is altogether satisfactory and very hopeful for the future of the country…*
>
> She goes on to stress why it was important for everyone that there were more women in the House of Commons, a theme she would pursue on many other occasions–as one might say, it was not just about equal representation but better representation...
>
> *… I think Parliament will be far more serviceable to the country if there are a few women among the members. As you all know… modern legislation deals very much with… the life of the home. We have now laws to deal with Housing, with Health, with the education & development of children. We shall probably have still more*

[1758] Nancy Astor, Viscountess Astor (1879-1964), American-born Tory, the second female MP, the first to take her seat, serving Plymouth Sutton, 28 November 1919–5 July 1945.

[1759] https://richardrhysobriencomblogs.wordpress.com/2019/11/05/dame-margaret-lloyd-george-and-nancy-astor-on-election-eve-14th-november-1919/. Retrieved 15 May 2021.

> *laws that will affect our home life still more closely. That being so it is of the utmost importance that women, who have most of the care of the home, should have a direct voice in shaping the laws....*
>
> *... I think the ideal woman for Parliament must be a wife, a mother and a politician. Lady Astor has the three essential qualifications...*
>
> *Though she may be a little unconventional in her electioneering methods, I assure you from my own intimate knowledge of her that she is a woman of strong conviction. In season and out of season she has toiled to help all sorts & conditions of men & women. She will be listened to with respect in Parliament because of her great reputation as a social worker...*
>
> *I therefore appeal to you very earnestly to vote for her return & to work for her return. Give her such a majority that will encourage other women of her position and experience to champion our cause & to fight our battles.*

The *Exeter and Plymouth Gazette* of 15 November 1919 reported:

> Mrs. Lloyd George said her husband and herself had been taunted because they supported Lady Astor against a member of their own Party. But this was not time for Party strife, it was time for unity. She based her appeal for support to the Coalition candidate on one simple fact, and that was the record of the present Government. There was not a single measure by this Government which was not in keeping with Liberal principles...[1760]

In the event, Astor won the seat–which had a slim majority of female voters, 17,175 women to 16,986 men–handsomely with 51.9% of the vote, well ahead of the Labour candidate on 33.3% and the Independent Liberal on 14.8%.

With the war and its immediate aftermath now over, Margaret began to energetically take on public roles in her own right. On 24 December 1919, the day after the Sex Disqualification (Removal) Act 1919 received royal assent, Margaret was one of the first seven women to be appointed as a magistrate, being the first Welsh woman to hold this office.[1761] While she had no desire to enter into a formal political career herself–turning down, according to son Richard, at least ten invitations to enter Parliament during the period 1910 to 1920[1762]–she was very willing to enter public service in her home area. At the end of March 1919, she stood for election to Criccieth Urban District Council, coming co-equal third in the poll, being re-elected annually until her death. From 1931-34 she chaired the Council, also being appointed to five other Committees.[1763] Further, Margaret became the first female Justice of the Peace in Caernarfonshire and was president of the Women's Liberal Federation of North and South Wales.[1764]

---

1760 https://richardrhysobriencomblogs.wordpress.com/2019/11/05/dame-margaret-lloyd-george-and-nancy-astor-on-election-eve-14th-november-1919/. Retrieved 9 January 2020.

1761 https://www.magistrates-association.org.uk/About-Magistrates/History-of-the-magistracy/100-Years-of-Women-Magistrates. Retrieved 7 January 2020.

1762 Lloyd George, *Dame Margaret*, p161.

1763 Hague, p375.

1764 Lloyd George, *Dame Margaret*, p200.

Lloyd George recognised his wife's work on his behalf, and was grateful, in May 1919 writing her one of his most appreciative letters: "I have watched with gratitude, appreciation & admiration the way you have filled my place in my absence. I am proud of it. You are doing it with unostentatious dignity & efficiency."[1765] This appreciation led him to seek for official recognition for her the following year. On 18 August 1920 she was duly made Dame Grand Cross of the Order of the British Empire (GBE) for her wartime fundraising of some £250,000 [£18.15m in 2025] for 'charities, hospitals and other public-spirited movements'. Lloyd George wrote to his wife: "I signed, yes, today, your D.B.E. This is the greatest & the highest of all. You wear on State occasions a gorgeous sash across your chest."[1766] Such was the respect that Dame Margaret commanded that her title was universally recognised.

Margaret also played a significant role in the Cardiganshire by-election held on 18 February 1921. The election was important for the bitterness of the contest between the Coalition and Independent factions within the Liberal Party and the deepening of this division within the party as a factor in the long-term decline of Liberalism in Wales. The by-election was caused by Lloyd George's desire to find a Parliamentary seat for his private secretary Captain Ernest Evans.[1767] Lloyd George persuaded the sitting Coalition Liberal MP, Matthew Vaughan-Davies, who had represented the constituency for more than 25 years, to accept a peerage so creating an opportunity for Evans to enter Parliament. The Coalition Liberals duly chose Evans as their candidate, also being supported by Lloyd George's Unionist partners in the Coalition.

In the event, at a rowdy selection meeting at Lampeter, Cardiganshire Liberals voted by 206 to 127 to adopt W. Llewelyn Williams as an Independent Liberal in opposition to Evans. In an unexpectedly heavy turnout of 80.1%, Evans won the seat for the Coalition by a majority of 3,590 votes. Riddell recorded in his diary on 19 February:

> To Chequers. Long talk with L.G [sic].. Much excited as to the Cardigan election… Mrs. LG has been working like a Trojan in the constituency, delivering fifty-eight speeches in a fortnight. While LG and I were walking in the park, Mrs LG came running out breathless, to tell him that Evans had won by a majority of 3,500. He was delighted and said that if the result had been the other way it would have been a serious personal set-back. He warmly embraced Mrs LG, bestowing several hearty kisses upon her and telling her that she had won the election[1768]… He said that Mrs. L.G. had displayed remarkable skill, and had said some very shrewd things, particularly on the drink question. She is no doubt very popular. Her simple, direct ways appeal to the people.[1769]

To return to Lloyd George's own life and doings, he was instrumental in the final form of the

---

1765 Quoted in Hague, p375.

1766 Ibid., p375. Margaret was invested GBE on 8 November by the King; O'Brien, *Campaigns*, p131.

1767 Ernest Evans (1885-1965), lawyer, private secretary to Lloyd George, November 1918–December 1920.

1768 Riddell, *Diaries*, 1986, p337-338.

1769 Riddell, *Intimate Diary*, p279.

Cenotaph in Whitehall, the great national monument to the fallen. After the signing of the Versailles Treaty, the government planned to hold a Victory Parade–alternatively and less plausibly referred to as Peace Day–in London on 19 July 1919, which would involve nearly 15,000 soldiers marching down Whitehall. The initial design for what would become the Cenotaph was one of a number of temporary structures erected for this parade. A similar parade was planned to be held in Paris on 14 July, and Lloyd George learnt that it was to include a saluting point for the marching troops and was keen to replicate the idea for the British one.

How architect Sir Edwin Lutyens became involved in the project is unclear, but he was close friends with Sir Alfred Mond and Sir Lionel Earle–respectively government minister and senior civil servant at the Office of Works, responsible for public building projects–so it is likely that one or both men discussed the idea with him. Lloyd George summoned Lutyens in early July and asked him to design a "catafalque", which would serve as "a point of homage" for the British parade. Lloyd George emphasised that the structure was to be non-denominational: the monument having no cross, it was to represent those of all faiths and of no faith. On 11 November 1919, Lloyd George walked from Downing Street to place a wreath, the police having to clear space for him to do so in the midst of the crowd estimated at some 6,000 clustered around the memorial. The original monument was constructed in wood and plaster, but by Armistice Day the following year it had been replaced by a near-identical one, 36 feet high and constructed from Portland stone. The Cenotaph quickly captured the public imagination. Exhumation and repatriation of the dead had been forbidden since April 1915, so the Cenotaph–'*an empty tomb*'–came to represent the absent dead and served as a substitute for a tomb. Beginning almost immediately after the Victory Parade and continuing for days afterwards, members of the public began laying flowers and wreaths around the base. Within a week, an estimated 1.2 million people had paid their respects to the dead there.

Lloyd George also facilitated the placing of the coffin in the Tomb of the Unknown Warrior in the west end of the nave of Westminster Abbey on 11 November 1920. The inspiration for this came from Padre David Railton, who had contacted the Dean of Westminster, Bishop Herbert Ryle in August. As late as 7 October, King George V was sceptical about the idea, but the enthusiasm of his Prime Minister won him round, and by 15 October the Government had accepted the proposition. However, a few days before the interment it was found that the metal handles on the coffin prevented it being lowered into place. Lloyd George ordered the Ministry of Works to send a telegram to an art metal worker from Caernarfon who he had known since the National Eisteddfod of 1909, David J. Williams, urgently requesting his presence in London. Williams took the next train, and on his arrival:

> … in London was commissioned to create the handles for the coffin, the iron banding that would bind the coffin and to antique hammer the plaque that was to be placed on top of the coffin. The plaque was to carry the inscription:

## A BRITISH WARRIOR WHO FELL IN THE GREAT WAR 1914-1918 FOR KING AND COUNTRY[1770]

Williams worked for two days and nights to complete his task on time, and, at 11.45 am on Thursday 11 November, the coffin was ceremoniously buried in the presence of King George V, Queen Mary, Lloyd George and other dignitaries, though the real guests of honour were a group of some one hundred women, chosen because they had each lost their husband and all their sons in the war. The guard of honour was composed of 100 holders of decorations of special valour, including 74 holders of the Victoria Cross, from all three services.[1771] The ceremony helped to bring about a catharsis for collective mourning on a scale not previously known. Afterwards, Lloyd George wrote to Lutyens, that "the memorial (the Cenotaph)… has become a national shrine not only to the British Isles but also for the whole empire; the Cenotaph, it may be said, is the token of our mourning as a nation; the grave of the unknown warrior is the token of our mourning as individuals."[1772]

On 28 July 1920, in pouring rain, Lloyd George had unveiled another monument in Parliament Square, a dignified statue of his hero, Abraham Lincoln, the gift of the American people. He gave a noble address on the late President's qualities, celebrating Lincoln, not so much as an American but as an international hero, saying: "In his life he was a great American, but he is no longer so. He is one of those giant figures, of whom there are very few in history, who lose their nationality in death." Lloyd George seized on the opportunity to call for Americans to resist the isolationist mood that had set in after the Great War. Diplomatically, he pronounced that the good judgment to choose leaders such as Lincoln and Robert E. Lee was a reflection of the type of people "needed now more than ever in the settlement of the world." In closing, he declared, "This torn and bleeding earth is calling today for the help of the America of Abraham Lincoln."[1773]

Apart from his leadership of the war effort, and his primary role in the negotiations to find peace afterwards, as Prime Minister, Lloyd George continued to oversee a major, wide-ranging programme of social reform in the last months of the war, and in the post-war years. The Workmen's Compensation (Silicosis) Act 1918, introduced a year later, empowered the Secretary of State to make schemes "for the payment of compensation by the employers of workmen in any specified industry… involving exposure to silica dust, who are certified to have suffered death or total disablement from silicosis…, or who, though not totally disabled, are found on medical examination to be suffering from silicosis… to such a degree as to make it dangerous to continue work in the industry and are for that reason suspended from employment…"

In pursuance of the Act a scheme, the Refractories Industries (Silicosis) Scheme, 1919, was made and came into force on 1 February 1919. The Scheme did not include any definition of silicosis, but

---

1770 http://brunswickironworks.co.uk/downloads/lloyd_george.pdf. Retrieved 9 March 2019. The author thanks Bengy Carey-Evans for first bringing this story to his notice.

1771See
https://www.youtube.com/watch?v=giJlKBKzy-8 http://www.victoriacross.org.uk/aaunksol.htm . Retrieved 11 November 2020.

1772 N. Hanson *The Unknown Soldier*, 2005, London, Corgi, p462.

1773https://quod.lib.umich.edu/j/jala/2629860.0040.103/--dedication-of-the-living-augustus-saint-gaudenss-abraham?rgn=main;view=fulltext#N33-ptr1. Retrieved 11 May 2020.

in view of the antecedent discussions it obviously was intended to signify fibroid phthisis associated with work in certain industries and processes. The refractories industries were defined as "the following processes carried on at mines, quarries, factories and workshops at which refractory material containing not less than 80% of silica (Si02) is got or manipulated with a view to manufacture or sale."[1774] Dr Robert D. Evans[1775] of Blaenau Ffestiniog supported the quarrymen in the inquiry into silicosis but was simply credited as 'Mr Evans'.

The Education Act 1918, and the Representation of the People Act, 1918, have already been examined. On 3 June 1919, the Ministry of Health Act received royal assent, with Dr Christopher Addison[1776] being appointed as first Minister of Health on 24 June. This was a vitally important and overdue piece of legislation, bringing rationalization out of chaos, Section 2 stating that:

> It shall be the duty of the Minister… to take all such steps as may be desirable to secure the preparation, effective carrying out and co-ordination of measures conducive to the health of the people, including measures for the prevention and cure of diseases, the avoidance of fraud in connection with alleged remedies therefor, the treatment of physical and mental defects, the treatment and care of the blind, the initiation and direction of research, the collection, preparation, publication, and dissemination of information and statistics relating thereto, and the training of persons for health services.[1777]

Whilst in post, Addison reviewed and increased the provisions of the National Insurance system and introduced programmes to improve healthcare and training. Provision for infant welfare and expectant mothers saw a dramatic improvement, the Ministry's approach being preventative and educative rather than merely curative.[1778]

Given Lloyd George's interest in the land and in agriculture, another measure enacted at this period was significant. By the end of the war, Britain's timber supply was vastly depleted. Her forests had been in decline since the relaxation of the Forestry Laws in the 13th and 14th Centuries, and the additional strain of the war–especially trench warfare–had left the nation's woodlands in a dire state. From a countryside that was once largely forest, just 5% of tree cover remained, an all-time low, and urgent action was required. In 1918, the Acland[1779] Committee reported to Lloyd George that an organisation with state backing would be the most effective way of restoring and restocking the nation's forests. On 1 September 1919, the Forestry Act came into force, establishing the Forestry Commission and granting it responsibility to look after woods across the UK. On 8 December, the first trees were planted at Eggesford Forest, Devon, paving the way for the future of forestry in Britain;

---

1774 https://oem.bmj.com/content/oemed/11/3/198.full.pdf. Retrieved 16 February 2019.

1775 Robert D. Evans (1871-1920), father of Thomas Carey-Evans, who married Olwen.

1776 Addison was Minister of Reconstruction until 10 January 1919, then President of the Local Government Board until 24 June 1919, then, when the Board was abolished and its duties transferred to the new ministry, first Minister of Health until 1 April 1921, lastly Minister without Portfolio until his resignation on 14 July 1921.

1777 https://www.legislation.gov.uk/ukpga/Geo5/9-10/21/enacted. Retrieved 16 July 2020.

1778 Morgan, *Portrait Of A Progressive*, p103-104.

1779 Sir Francis Dyke Acland (1874-1939), Liberal MP, 1906-1924, 1932-1939.

by 1939 the Forestry Commission was the largest landowner in the country.

On 19 August 1919, three important, parallel acts obtained royal assent. The Acquisition of Land (Assessment of Compensation) Act ensured that local authorities compulsorily purchased land on fair terms, while the Land Settlement (Facilities) Act 1919, very much in line with Lloyd George's stated ideals, empowered county councils to purchase and lease land for the provision of smallholdings with government providing financial support, also eliminating the need for the recipient to have experience or training in farming. For example, Surrey County Council bought and leased 2,162 acres between 1919-1926 to provide smallholdings for 257 ex-servicemen.

Meanwhile, the Profiteering Act gave the Board of Trade the power to prosecute people who made excessive profits from articles in common use. The latter Act was a wide-ranging but temporary measure designed by the Government to meet peculiar circumstances. It was a measure "to check profiteering" and accordingly was framed to avoid, so far as possible, any interference with legitimate commercial enterprise. The main powers conferred upon the Board of Trade by the Act was, firstly, to investigate prices, costs and profits at all stages; secondly, to receive and investigate complaints regarding the making of excessive profits on the sale of any article to which the Act was applied by the Board, and after giving the parties an opportunity of being heard either to dismiss the complaint or to declare the reasonable price for such articles, and to order the seller to refund to the buyer any amount paid in excess of such reasonable price. The Board also had power to take proceedings against the seller in a court of summary jurisdiction.

The Act was applied by the Board of Trade by a series of orders to practically every article of ordinary everyday use, including all articles of wearing apparel, household utensils and requisites, articles for mending and knitting, furniture, building materials, drugs and medicinal preparations, medical and surgical appliances and dressings, mineral waters, all articles used for fuel and lighting, tools, weights, measures, weighing and measuring instruments, motor spirit, stationery, and, in agreement with the Ministry of Food, to practically all articles of food the price of which was not otherwise controlled, including milk, bread, fish, tea, coffee, cacao, margarine and meat.

The Electricity (Supply) Act, which obtained royal assent on 23 December 1919, ensured the complete reorganisation of the supply of electric power throughout the country. It established a statutory body, the Electricity Commissioners, "to promote, regulate and supervise the supply of electricity" under the direction of the Board of Trade. It provided for the formation of electricity districts and, where necessary, the establishment of joint electricity authorities, "to provide or secure the provision of a cheap and abundant supply of electricity." The Sex Disqualification (Removal) Act 1919, enacted the same day, provided that "A person shall not be disqualified by sex or marriage from the exercise of any public function, or from being appointed to or holding any civil or judicial office or post, or from entering or assuming or carrying on any civil profession or vocation, or for admission to any incorporated society…"

Also on the same day, the Government of India Act 1919 received royal assent, passed specifically to expand the participation of Indians in the government of their nation. The Act embodied the reforms recommended in the report of the Edwin Montagu, Secretary of State for India, and Lord

Chelmsford, the Viceroy. The Act covered ten years, from 1919 to 1929, representing the end of benevolent despotism and the genesis of responsible government in the sub-continent. George V, as King-Emperor, issued a proclamation stating the intent of the Act, concluding: "The Act which has now become law entrusts the elected representative of the people with a definite share in the Government and points the way to full responsible Government hereafter."[1780] Unfortunately, the Act came on the back of the appalling massacre at Amritsar, Punjab, on 13 April, when Brigadier General Reginald Dyer ordered his troops to open fire on massed but peaceful demonstrators hemmed into a tight square, resulting in the deaths of at least 400 and the injury of some 1,500 more. The subsequent ineffective Hunter Commission inquiry fuelled great anger against the British among the Indian populace, leading to the Non-cooperation Movement of 1920-22. For Indian nationalists, who had expected much more from the British after the country's major contribution to the Imperial war effort, the concessions in the Act simply did not go nearly far enough.

Back at home, the Housing and Town Planning Act 1919 received royal assent on 31 July, becoming known as the Addison Act after Minister of Health, Christopher Addison, who had determinedly steered it through Parliament. The Act provided subsidies for house building by local authorities, aiming to build 500,000 new homes within three years. Addison had estimated that 800,000 would be needed. In some ways, the Act was ahead of its time, Section 1(3) specifying:

> Provided that local authorities in preparing, and the Local Government Board in approving, any scheme shall take into account, and so far as possible preserve, existing erections of architectural, historic, or artistic interest, and shall have regard to the natural amenities of the locality, and, in order to secure that the houses proposed to be built under the scheme shall be of a suitable architecture and that the natural amenities of the locality shall not be unnecessarily injured, the Local Government Board may, in any case where it appears to them that the character of the locality renders such a course expedient, require as a condition of their approval the employment by the local authority of an architect to be selected from a panel of architects.

Due to increasingly hostile Tory opposition, not all of the funding was ultimately made available, Addison fighting an increasingly uphill battle from the spring of 1920, and only 213,800 homes were built under the 1919 Act scheme. Along with the opposition of the 'anti-waste' campaigners, after the immediate post-war speculative bubble had burst, there were also the issues of "the high and increasing cost of building materials, the reluctance of the building trade unions to admit semi- and unskilled labour into their ranks, the inadequacies of the local authorities and the financial problems they faced, and the disorganization of the private enterprise building industry…"[1781] All these things led to the failure to build the number of houses planned. Not all of these factors were the government's fault, but it was the government, and increasingly Addison in particular, who took the popular blame. Nonetheless, it was a landmark measure, firmly establishing "the principle that housing was a social

---

[1780] C. P. Ilbert, *The Government of India*, 1922, Oxford, Clarendon Press, p125.
[1781] Morgan, *Portrait Of A Progressive*, p122-123.

service".

The National Health Insurance Act (1920) received royal assent on 20 May, and came into force on 5 July, greatly overhauling the previous system. It included in the compulsory insurance two groups of people: first, all persons, men and women, 16 years of age and over, under any contract of employment for which remuneration… was paid and whose employment was manual in character; second, a similar group whose employment was non-manual in character, if their total income was less than £250 annually. Persons 70 years of age or over were not required to insure and insured persons on attaining 70 would not receive pecuniary benefits, as the national old-age pension system benefits began at that age. The means limit for pensions was raised by about two-thirds, aliens and their wives were allowed to receive pensions after living in Britain for ten years, and the imprisonment and "failure to work" disqualifications for receiving pensions were abolished. In addition, pensions were introduced for blind persons aged 50 and above. Old age pensions were doubled, efforts were made to help returning soldiers find employment, and the Whitley Councils were established to arbitrate between employees and employers.

Naturally, the after-effects of the Great War and Versailles were still hugely important in both the national psyche and economy, and from 12 February–10 April 1920 Lloyd George headed the Conference of London, at which he, French Prime Minister Alexandre Millerand and Prime Italian Minister Francesco Nitti, met to discuss the partitioning of the Ottoman Empire and the negotiation of agreements that would become the Treaty of Sèvres. The Allies reached agreements that would form the basis of their arguments at the subsequent San Remo Conference, already detailed.

From 5-16 July 1920 Lloyd George attended the Spa Conference, a meeting between the Supreme War Council and the government of the Weimar Republic at Villa Freineuse in Spa, Belgium. The Spa Conference was different from its predecessors in that it was the first post-war conference to include German representatives, the main topics being German disarmament, coal shipments to the Allies and war reparations. The Allies rightly considered that, if there were violations of the peace treaty and issues concerning reparations, it would be better to discuss the problems face-to-face than through an exchange of notes. The conference was high-powered, attended by heads of state, heads of government and foreign secretaries. Alongside Lloyd George was German Chancellor Constantin Fehrenbach.[1782] The British and French ambassadors to Germany, Lord D'Abernon and Charles François Laurent, were also present, tasked with supervision of reparation payments and control of the Berlin-based Reparation Commission.

The German Foreign Minister, Walter Simons[1783], outlined the German position on reparations on 10 July, mostly following a proposal endorsed by the German Cabinet beforehand, and he avoided naming any hard numbers or dates. On 12 July, the German delegation handed over a number of proposals, once again without definite sums, calling for a total of 30 annual payments. On 13 July

[1782] Constantin Fehrenbach (1852-1926), a leader of the Catholic Centre Party or *Zentrum*. President of the Reichstag in 1918, President of the Weimar National Assembly, 1919-1920. Chancellor, 25 June 1920–4 May 1921, resigned over the issue of war reparation payments.

[1783] Walter Simons (1861-1937), Foreign Minister, 25 June 1920–4 May 1921.

these proposals were discussed by a sub-committee of the Conference, but the concurrent coal discussions had escalated to such a degree that debate on this issue was stopped. The topic was only revisited a few weeks later at a conference in Geneva. Ultimately, there was no settlement of the total sum of German reparations, but the shares of the recipients were fixed: France 52%, UK 22%, Italy 10%, Belgium 8% with the remaining 8% to be distributed among the other Allied nations.

The discussions of disarmament focused on the strength of the German army and the treatment of the *Sicherheitspolizei,* paramilitary police units. The German side arrived with the negotiation goal of a 200,000-man army and the intent to keep the police units, with the possibility of making concessions concerning their equipment. However, on this issue also the Allied side was unwilling to move. By the second day the Allies threatened to break off the talks and to implement sanctions unless the German delegation abandoned the 200,000-target. The German counterproposal agreed to 100,000 men but asked for a longer period of implementation. This was rejected by the Allies and on 8 July they handed over a note that specified their position and demanded its signature by the Germans by the next day. Fehrenbach contacted Berlin and on the morning of 9 July his cabinet agreed but instructed the delegation not to sign the sanction threat the protocol contained. The protocol signed by Fehrenbach and Simons called for *Sicherheitspolizei* and militias to be disarmed immediately and for laws to be passed to disarm the general population. The regular German army was scheduled to be reduced to 100,000 men by 1 January 1921–less than six months away, but later than initially demanded by the Allies–conscription was to be abolished and replaced by a professional army and substantial materiel was to be handed over to the Allies. This was backed up by an Allied threat to occupy additional German territory in case of violations. However, the Germans introduced a proviso clause that they did not accede to this last point.

On 18 August, Lloyd George left for a holiday on the continent, as later detailed by son Richard–although, of course, a 'holiday' for Lloyd George was rarely just that:

> According to my mother, one of the most anxious times she ever lived through… was when my father went to Switzerland… to meet Giolitti[1784], the Italian Prime Minister. In London there had been rumours of a planned attempt to assassinate my father if he visited the Continent, and naturally this worried my mother… But my father declared he must have a holiday… Off they went–my mother, Megan, Gwilym, Sir Maurice and Lady Hankey and their son, J. T. Davies, Miss Cazalet[1785], and Miss Evans, a Welsh singer… The fact that three detectives never let my father out of their sight proved how seriously Scotland Yard considered the danger was…
>
> The King of the Belgians had given my father the use of the Villa Hasilhorn in Lucerne as headquarters… but my mother's enjoyment was definitely marred by her discovery that the place was surrounded day and night by the Swiss police. After the arrival of Giolitti my mother learned that six men had been arrested as suspects, but the Lucerne police seemed not to be sure whether the prisoners had designs on my father or on the Italian Prime Minister. In

1784 Giovanni Giolitti (1842-1928), Prime Minister five times between 1892-1921, a leader of the Historical Left and the Liberal Union, second-longest serving Prime Minister in Italian history, after Benito Mussolini.

1785 Thelma Cazalet-Keir (née Cazalet; 1899-1989), friend of Megan, feminist, Tory MP, 1931-1945.

> describing this tall, stately old man (he was then seventy-eight) my mother told me he was as smart as a fox, with cunning in his eyes. She made me laugh with her word-picture of the two Premiers–the one very tall and walking with a stately tread, with my father almost trotting by his side![1786]

Of the serious business Lloyd George discussed with Giolitti, on 23 August he informed the Italian Premier that, unless the British and Italian Governments joined the French in supporting the Poles over the issue of Danzig, it would appear that they were not upholding the Treaty of Versailles when Poland was clearly in the right. In this he had been influenced by Hankey, and telegrams were duly sent to the British and Italian Embassies in Paris giving this joint support.[1787] News of this caused a threatened strike by Danzig dockworkers and railwaymen to collapse, and they resumed handling all cargoes to and from Poland.[1788]

Back home, Lloyd George's government continued to push ahead with progressive legislation. The landmark Blind Persons Act, enacted on 16 August 1920, coming into effect on 10 September, provided a pension allowance for blind persons aged between 50 and 70–when they became eligible for the old age pension–directed local authorities to "promote the welfare of blind persons" and regulated relevant charities. Passed in response to pressure from the National League of the Blind (NLB) who rightly stated many of their members were living in poverty, and whose leader, Ben Purse, led a deputation to meet Lloyd George at No. 10 on 30 April, the Act was the first disability-specific legislation to be passed anywhere in the world.[1789]

The Unemployment Insurance Act 1920, passed on 9 August, extended national insurance to 11.75 million additional workers. This was considered to be a revolutionary measure, in that it extended unemployment insurance to almost the entire labour force–except domestic service, farm workers, railway workers, and civil servants–whereas only certain categories of workers had been covered before. As a result of this legislation, roughly three-quarters of the British workforce were now covered by unemployment insurance. Funded in part by weekly contributions from both employers and employed, it created the dole system of weekly cash payments of 15s for unemployed men, 12s for unemployed women, and half these rates for insured contributors under the age of 18.

The Agriculture Act (1920), receiving royal assent on 23 December, provided for farm labourers to receive a minimum wage while the state continued to guarantee the prices of farm produce until 1921. It also provided tenant farmers with greater protection by granting them better security of tenure. Designed to support price guarantees for agricultural products, and to maintain minimum wages for farm labourers, it sadly proved ineffective, and the guarantees were abandoned in July 1921. With the relevant parts of the Act repealed, the price of wheat crashed from 84s 7d a quarter to 44s

---

[1786] Lloyd George, *Dame Margaret*, p188-189.

[1787] https://history.state.gov/historicaldocuments/frus1920v03/d461. Retrieved 16 December 2023.

[1788] J.R. Ullman, *Anglo-Soviet Relations, 1917-1921, Volume 3: The Anglo-Soviet Accord*, 1973, Princeton NJ, Princeton University Press, p251-252.

[1789] C.K. Lysons, *The Development of Social Legislation for Blind or Deaf Persons in England 1834-1939*, 1973, D.Phil. Thesis, Brunel Law School; p195-204.

7d within one year, a fall of 48%. The Act had established wage committees to fix minimum agricultural pay, but these, too, were soon abandoned. A replacement system of "conciliation committees" was set up to mediate between employers and labourers, but these had no legal powers, and the average weekly wage fell from 46s at the beginning of 1921 to 36s by the end of the year, and to 28s a week within eighteen months of the repeal. The Act had been ahead of its time, and unable to cope with the depressed conditions existing: the next attempt to fix agricultural wages would be Labour's Agricultural Wages (Regulation) Act 1924.

The Employment of Women, Young Persons and Children Act (1920), passed on 23 December, prohibited the employment of children below the limit of compulsory school age in railways and transport undertakings, building and engineering construction works, factories, and mines. The legislation also prohibited the employment of children in ships at sea, except in certain circumstances, such as in respect of family members employed on the same vessel. From 12 May the following year the Public Health (Tuberculosis) Act 1921 increased the obligation of local authorities to treat and prevent TB, by obliging county and county borough councils to provide sanatoria, care and after-care services for tuberculosis patients. Councils were also required to remove infectious patients to hospital. This law was later included in the provisions of the Public Health Act of 1936. The Unemployed Workers' Dependants (Temporary Provisions) Act 1921 of 8 November provided payments for the wives and dependent children of unemployed workers, introduced as 'winter relief', made permanent the following 12 April by the Unemployment Insurance Act 1922.

On 28 July 1921, the landmark Dentists Act (1921) was enacted, coming into force on 30 November 1922, regulating the hugely unsatisfactory situation left by the 1878 Act which had failed to prevent unqualified and unregistered persons practicing dentistry. A committee had been set up in July 1917, chaired by Francis Dyke Acland, to "Investigate the extent and gravity of the evils connected with the practice of dentistry and dental surgery by persons not qualified under the Dentists Act". Its conclusions, published in 1919 after comprehensive investigation, were damning:

> Unregistered dental practice constitutes a menace alike to the public health, the registered dental profession and the more reputable unregistered practitioners... Dental practice is carried on by the unregistered persons of widely varying grades of social standing, education and training ranging from few fully trained and qualified to... the butcher and blacksmith.

Radically, it concluded:

> The state cannot afford to allow the health of the workers of the nation to be continuously undermined by dental neglect. Steps should be taken without delay to recognise dentistry as one of the chief means for preventing ill health, and all possible means should be employed for enlightening the public as to the need for conservative treatment of diseased teeth. The dental profession should be treated as one of the outposts of preventive medicine, and as such encouraged and assisted by the state. Treatment should be rendered available for all needing it.

To ensure compliance, under the Act a Dental Board was set up, chaired by Acland, in effect a subcommittee of the General Medical Council. The Board's recommendations were all subject to approval by the Council which retained control of dental education, training and examinations and the Dentists Register.[1790]

Back on 18 May 1917, Lloyd George had proposed an Irish Convention in an attempt to settle the Home Rule for Ireland issue, highly contentious for half a century. This assembly had sat in Regent House, Trinity College, Dublin–with a few sessions in Belfast and Cork–from 25 July 1917 to 5 April 1918, with Sir Horace Plunkett[1791] as the unanimously elected Chairman, and Francis Hopwood, created Baron Southborough on 1 November 1917, as the Secretary. The 101 members were comprised of Nationalists, Ulster Unionists, Southern Unionists, Labour representatives and the Catholic hierarchy–Sinn Fein boycotted the process, as the Convention's terms of reference provided that Ireland must be "within the Empire". On 19 January 1918, Plunkett reported to Lloyd George that "the situation… had reached a very critical stage." On 6, 7, 13 and 14 February, Lloyd George had detailed talks with Convention members, but it became apparent that the time for a negotiated settlement had passed. On 25 February, he wrote to Plunkett with a pledge of action. On receiving the Convention's report, the Government would "proceed with the least possible delay to submit legislative proposals to Parliament". He then outlined his ideas for a compromise, interim settlement, but the Ulster Unionists opposition to an All-Ireland parliament remained implacable, the other main area of contention being Customs.[1792]

The Convention's final report recommended that an 'Irish Parliament for an undivided Ireland', with a Senate of 64 members and a Commons of 200, be instituted. However, less than half the Convention–44 out of 89–supported this, well short of a 'substantial agreement,' while the largest of two minority reports, signed by 22 nationalists, called for full Dominion Home Rule, with full powers over taxation. Five 'notes' were also appended. The number who voted for self-government in one form or another was 66. Significantly, on 14 March the Convention had also voted 54-17 that conscription could not be applied to Ireland without the consent and cooperation of an Irish parliament.

On 12 September 1919, the British authorities declared Dail Eireann to be illegal, after which it met in secret. On 15 January 1920, Ireland held elections for Borough and Urban District Councils. The overriding issue was whether or not a republic should be established. Of the 206 Councils elected, 172 declared for a republic. The Unionists only managed to hold the City of Belfast and just four of the counties of Ulster, majorities in the Ulster counties of Fermanagh and Tyrone voting for Sinn Fein. On 12 June, Sinn Féin took control of 338 out of 393 local government bodies, county councils, boards of guardians and rural district councils across the whole land. Their success extended even to

---

[1790] https://bda.org/museum/exhibitions-and-events/The-Dentists-Act-1921/Pages/A-turning-point.aspx ; https://bda.org/museum/exhibitions-and-events/The-Dentists-Act-1921/Pages/The-Magna-Carta-of-the-dentists-profession.aspx. Retrieved 17 August 2023.

[1791] Sir Horace Plunkett (1854-1932), Anglo-Irish agricultural reformer, supporter of Home Rule.

[1792] R. B. McDowell, *The Irish Convention, 1917-18*, 1970, London, Routledge and Kegan Paul, p157-168; *Report Of The Proceedings Of The Irish Convention*, Cmd.9019, 1918, Dublin, HMSO.

Ulster, the party winning control of 36 of Ulster's 55 rural districts. For those who had eyes to see, the writing was clearly on the wall for British control in Ireland.

On 13 August 1920, the Restoration of Order in Ireland Act 1920 received royal assent, passed to address the collapse of British civil administration in Ireland. In effect a special extension of the Defence of the Realm Acts, it aimed to increase convictions of nationalist rebels while averting the need to declare martial law. Trial by jury was to be replaced by courts-martial in those areas where IRA activity was prevalent and a further extension of the jurisdiction of courts-martial was to include capital offences. In addition, military courts of enquiry were to be substituted for coroners' inquests, and disaffected local governments could be punished by withholding grants of money. In response, the IRA altered their guerrilla tactics, organising into small, mobile flying columns or active service units, more suited to ambushes of British patrols and convoys. Next, the rather ineptly-named Better Government of Ireland Act, enacted on 23 December 1920, partitioned Ireland into Southern and Northern Ireland, effective from 3 May 1921. It already lagged far behind reality, as the Irish War of Independence became increasingly vicious. Speaking at the Lord Mayor's Banquet at the Guildhall on 9 November 1920, Lloyd George had denounced the insurgency as "organized assassination, of the most cowardly character" but assured his audience, that "at last, unless I am mistaken, by the steps we have taken we have murder by the throat."[1793] He was indeed mistaken, and soon began the necessary negotiations with IRA leaders–'yielding to circumstances' as C. P. Scott[1794] put it–to recognise their authority and to end the bloody conflict. Sadly, although Scott was an old friend and admirer of Lloyd George, the issue caused an estrangement between them.

Early in 1921, Lloyd George had another potential close brush with death, or at least kidnap. The IRA had intelligence officers in London, trailing the movements of Cabinet members. Frank Thornton, then Deputy Assistant Director of Intelligence, recorded later:

> One day when Seán Flood [Director of Operations, Britain] and I were going out to Acton on a routine check-up… we ran into Westminster Station to find the lift gates just closing. Seán… said, "I'll race you to the bottom down the runway". It was a long winding passage with about three bends on it. Seán raced off in front and disappeared around the second last bend… I heard a terrific crash and on coming around the corner I fell over two men on the ground, one of whom was Seán Flood. We picked ourselves up and both assisted in helping to his feet the man whom Seán Flood had knocked down. To our amazement two other men who were with him ordered us to put our hands up. We more or less ignored them and started to brush down the man and apologise to him when to our amazement we discovered that the man we had knocked down was Lloyd George… The first act of Lloyd George was to tell his two guards to put their guns away, which they were very reluctant to do, pointing out that from our speech we were evidently Irishmen–Lloyd George's answer to this was, "Well, Irishmen or no Irishmen, if they were out to shoot me I was shot long ago". Little he knew the people he was dealing

[1793] Owen, p570. He had made a similar speech at Caernarfon on 9 October, condoning reprisals in Ireland.

[1794] J. L. Hammond, *C. P. Scott of the Manchester Guardian*, 1934, London, Bell, p271.

> with on that particular occasion but after a few muttered apologies on our part we went on our way.[1795]

Protest spread across the UK through 1921, led by the Labour Party and Trades Union Congress, which Asquith and the Liberal opposition did not fail to join. On 31 March, even Winifred Coombe Tennant wrote to Lloyd George, warning of the growing Liberal disaffection and opposition to the government and its policies, within the Liberal Associations of Wales, the Nonconformist ministry and amongst university staff and students. She told him: "The staffs of the Welsh Colleges almost to a man where [sic] opposed to you and at least 80% of the students… *Ireland* is being run for all it is worth against you."[1796]

In an attempt to reach some accord, Sinn Féin leader Éamon de Valera[1797] and Ulster Unionist leader James Craig[1798] had already had a secret meeting at 8 Howth Road, Dublin on 5 May, organised from Dublin Castle with the blessing of Lloyd George. Despite the meeting being outwardly unproductive, the fact the two had come together, "if only for half an hour," was described by the *Irish Times* as "a political event of the first importance". "It is," the paper editorialised, "the most hopeful news that a despondent and almost despairing country has heard for a long time." Lloyd George also expressed optimism. Delivering a speech to Unionists in Maidstone, he made a pointed reference to Irish affairs. "I am delighted to see that the two national leaders… have met to discuss questions bearing upon the future of that country… it is a good sign that they are discussing things together."[1799] Lloyd George was often directly involved in what Mark Sturgis, Assistant to the Joint Under-Secretaries at Dublin Castle from July 1920 to February 1922, called 'peace balloons'. These included many secret initiatives and interviews with a wide variety of important players in Ireland, including businessmen, local politicians, imperial statesmen and even members of the Dáil, which Sturgis then believed to be "an enormous step towards peace."[1800] Assistant Under-Secretary Alfred Cope was a key player here, as Lloyd George "set great store by his opinion."[1801]

One such initiative was the meeting, in the Commons on 1 December 1920, of Archbishop Patrick Clune with Lloyd George. Lloyd George asked Clune to go to Dublin to mediate "a temporary truce in order to prepare an atmosphere for negotiations." On 4 December Clune met Arthur Griffith[1802] in Mountjoy Prison, then Michael Collins three days later. Unfortunately, murders and reprisals

---

[1795] https://www.militaryarchives.ie/collections/online-collections/bureau-of-military-history-1913-1921/reels/bmh/BMH.WS0615.pdf. Retrieved 20 January 2024.

[1796] Morgan, *Rebirth Of A Nation*, p189, quoting Lloyd George Papers, F/96/1/15.

[1797] Éamon de Valera (1882-1975), born in New York, USA, President of Sinn Féin, 1917-1926, President of Dáil Éireann, 1 April 1919–26 August 1921, President of the Irish Republic, 26 August 1921–9 January 1922.

[1798] James Craig (1871-1940), stockbroker, Leader of the Ulster Unionist Party from 4 February 1921, first Prime Minister of Northern Ireland, 7 June 1921 until his death on 24 November 1940.

[1799] https://www.rte.ie/centuryireland/index.php/articles/craig-and-de-valera-hold-historic-meeting-but-ulster-will-offer-no-more-con. Retrieved 28 May 2021.

[1800] M. Hopkinson, Ed., *The Last Days of Dublin Castle: The Mark Sturgis Diaries*, 1999, Dublin, Irish Academic Press, p89. See also G. Sloan, *Hide Seek and Negotiate: Alfred Cope and Counter Intelligence in Ireland 1919-1921*, *Intelligence and National Security* 33, 2, 2018, p176-195.

[1801] G. Shakespeare, p74. Sir Alfred Cope (1877-1954), knighted in the 1922 Dissolution Honours for his role.

[1802] Arthur Griffith (1871-1922), founder of Sinn Féin in 1905. Minister for Foreign Affairs, 26 August 1921–9 January 1922, President of Dáil Éireann, 10 January 1922 until his death on 12 August.

continued on both sides, sowing distrust. Although negotiations continued until Christmas Eve, ultimately Clune's diligent efforts were thwarted by hardliners in the British Cabinet, Dublin Castle and the military, who insisted on the surrender of all IRA arms–a capitulation, not a truce. The time was not yet ripe.[1803]

On 22 June 1921, King George V gave a well-received speech at the opening of the new Parliament of Northern Ireland in City Hall, Belfast, appealing "to all Irishmen to pause, to stretch out the hand of forbearance and conciliation, to forgive and to forget, and to join in making for the land which they love a new era of peace, contentment, and goodwill."[1804] Lloyd George was initially reluctant to engage in the process, given his unstable coalition with the majority pro-unionist Tories, saying privately "This country was united in its desire to defeat Germany, it has never been united on Ireland. My government is a shaky coalition which I barely hold together."[1805] Nonetheless, capitalising on the King's speech, on 24 June he wrote to de Valera, the succeeding correspondence showing just how far both parties had to travel to reach the ensuing uneasy agreement: "The British Government are deeply anxious that… the King's appeal for reconciliation in Ireland shall not have been made in vain… [so] they felt it incumbent upon them to make a final appeal… for a conference between themselves and the representatives of Southern and Northern Ireland." He thus sent invitations to de Valera and James Craig "That you should attend a conference here in London… to explore to the utmost the possibility of a settlement… We make this invitation with a fervent desire to end the ruinous conflict which has for centuries divided Ireland and embittered the relations of the peoples of these two islands, who ought to live in neighbourly harmony with each other."[1806]

Realising that Lloyd George had, to some extent, recognised his status, on 28 June de Valera replied: "We most earnestly desire to help in bringing about a lasting peace between the peoples of these two islands, but see no avenue by which it can be reached if you deny Ireland's essential unity and set aside the principle of national self-determination."[1807] On 8 July he wrote again: "The desire you express on the part of the British Government to end the centuries of conflict… is the genuine desire of the people of Ireland… I am ready to meet and discuss with you on what bases such a Conference… can reasonably hope to achieve the object desired."[1808] A truce was declared, to start from noon on 11 July. On 9 July Lloyd George telegraphed: "I… shall be happy to see you… at Downing Street any day this week."[1809] Four meetings duly took place between the two men at No. 10 on 14, 15, 18 and 21 July. The first lasted some three hours. Frances Stevenson noted that she had:

---

1803 Patrick Clune (1864-1935), RC Archbishop of Perth, Australia, 1913-1935. See *Activities of Archbishop Clune as mediator between Lloyd George and Michael Collins 1920. Witness Rev J.T. McMahon, Secretary to Most Rev. Dr. Clune, Irish Military Archives (1913–1921)*, https://bmh.militaryarchives.ie/reels/bmh/BMH.WS0362.pdf. Retrieved 24 May 2025. Quote on p3.

1804 The speech was drafted by Edward Grigg (1879-1955), one of Lloyd George's private secretaries, May 1921-October 1922, on recommendations from Jan Smuts, PM of South Africa, then in London for the Imperial Conference. Father of John Grigg, one of Lloyd George's biographers.

1805 https://www.irishexaminer.com/news/spotlight/arid-40328531.html. Retrieved 14 January 2024.

1806 *Official Correspondence relating to the Peace Negotiations June-September, 1921*, Dublin, Dáil Éireann, October 1921. https://celt.ucc.ie//published/E900003-007/index.html, Ed. Orla McDonald. Retrieved 6 October 2019.

1807 Ibid.

1808 Ibid.

1809 Ibid.

> Never seen D. [sic] so excited as he was before de Valera arrived… I could see he was working out the best way of dealing with DeV [sic]… He had a big map of the British Empire hung up on the wall in the Cabinet room, with its great blotches of red all over it… In fact, D. says that the aim of these talks is to impress upon DeV the greatness of the B.E [sic]…. D. said to DeV.: "The B.E. is a sisterhood of nations–the greatest in the world. Look at this table: There sits Africa–English & Boer; there sits Canada–French, Scotch & English; there sits Australia, representing many races…; there sits India; here sit the representatives of England, Scotland & Wales; all we ask you to do is to take your place in this sisterhood of free nations. It is an invitation, Mr De Valera: we invite you here."[1810]

Lloyd George said that it had been "very difficult to keep to the point" as de Valera had "kept on going off at a tangent, & talking in formulas and refusing to face facts", adding that whenever de Valera "appeared to be warming, he suddenly drew back as if frightened and timid." Lloyd George also characterised him as "the man with the most limited vocabulary that he has ever met!" He made some threats which angered de Valera, saying: "I shall be sorry if this conference fails: terrible as events have been in Ireland, it is nothing to what they will be if we fail to come to an agreement… I hesitate to think of the horror if war breaks out again in Ireland." At this, de Valera got "very excited", complaining that this was "a threat of force–of coercion." Lloyd George responded that he was "simply forecasting what will inevitably happen if these conversations fail, & if you refuse our invitation to join us."[1811] Geoffrey Shakespeare noted that after the meeting Lloyd George was "white and exhausted." Asked how he had got on with de Valera, he replied: "I made no impression. I listened to a long lecture on the wrongs done to Ireland starting with Cromwell, and when I tried to bring him to the present day back he went to Cromwell again. It reminded me of a circus roundabout when I was a boy. I used to sit on a rocking horse that raced round and round after the horse in front, and when the roundabout came to rest I was still the same distance from the horse in front as when I started. That's how I ended with de Valera."[1812]

The pair met again the next day. Stevenson wrote that Lloyd George's impression was that de Valera "had evidently been afraid he had gone too far the previous day, & was bent on impressing on D. the idea that he had proposed nothing and consented to nothing." She noted that de Valera had "insisted that what the people of Ireland wanted was a republic, & asked D. if the *name* of republic could not be conceded at any rate." Lloyd George replied that that "was just what they could *not* have–that the people of this country would not tolerate it after all that had happened."[1813]

Lloyd George had already drafted a summary of terms which he proposed sending to de Valera on 20 July. Stevenson noted that he had delayed giving the draft to de Valera "as he thought the time was not ripe." Smuts had seen de Valera "& impressed upon him the great difficulty with Ulster" but was

[1810] Stevenson, *Diary*, p227-228.
[1811] Ibid., p228.
[1812] G. Shakespeare, p.76. Sir Geoffrey Shakespeare (1893-1980), Liberal MP for Wellingborough, 1922-1923, Norwich, 1929-1945. Private Secretary to Lloyd George, March 1921–December 1923.
[1813] Stevenson, *Diary*, p228.

not optimistic as de Valera did not really appreciate that Ulster provided the Lloyd George government with any "real difficulty", believing that they were "just using Ulster to frighten him." Lloyd George had seen James Craig, finding him "quite obstinate", as was his cabinet who, for their part, believed that Lloyd George was "trying to use Sinn Féin to persuade them to concede something." Stevenson summarised: "So the position is tightening a little, & it looks very much as though Ulster would again prove a stumbling block in the settlement." Lloyd George remained "a little worried about it", but she thought that "in his heart of hearts he is bent on settling it." She also pointed up the increasingly fragile nature of the Coalition government, noting that there were "lots of people who don't want a settlement and who would be very glad to see him fail."[1814]

The two leaders were to have their final meeting on 21 July. On the eve of that meeting she recorded that matters were "more hopeful." The previous night they had "looked black" with de Valera taking exception to a statement made by Craig in which he had presumed himself to be Northern Ireland's spokesman with de Valera being confined to representing Ireland south of the new border. De Valera warned that if Lloyd George shared that view "it was not worthwhile continuing the conversations." Lloyd George replied "saying that he was no more responsible for Craig's views than he was for the statement de Valera had made to which Craig's statement was a reply. De Valera did not answer, but did not publish the letters, and Smuts saw him this morning and reports that he is in a better state of mind and not nearly so obstinate." Stevenson noted that Lloyd George would forward the terms that evening, meet de Valera on the following "critical day" and that he was "getting very excited about it", saying "if he settles Ireland, he is prepared to go out of office… he can go no higher."[1815]

At 11.00 pm on 20 July, the day preceding the last of these conversations, the surprisingly broad 'Proposals of the British Government for an Irish Settlement,' were presented to the President, staying at the Grosvenor Hotel:

> [T]he British Government… propose that Ireland shall assume forthwith the status of a Dominion… [and] enjoy complete autonomy in taxation and finance; that she shall maintain her own courts of law and judges; that she shall maintain her own military forces for home defence, her own constabulary and her own police; that she shall take over the Irish postal services and all matters relating thereto; education, land, agriculture, mines and minerals, forestry, housing, labour, unemployment, transport, trade, public health, health insurance and the liquor traffic… subject only to the considerations set out in the ensuing paragraphs…
>
> 1. The common concern of Great Britain and Ireland in the defence of their interests by land and sea shall be mutually recognised. Great Britain lives by sea-borne food; her communications depend upon the freedom of the great sea routes. Ireland lies at Britain's side across the sea ways… In recognition of this fact… it is essential that the Royal Navy alone should control the

1814 Ibid., p229.
1815 Ibid., p230.

seas around Ireland and Great Britain, and that such rights and liberties should be accorded to it by the Irish State as are essential for naval purposes…

2. In order that the movement towards the limitation of armaments which is now making progress in the world should in no way be hampered, it is stipulated that the Irish Territorial force shall within reasonable limits conform in respect of numbers to the military establishments of the other parts of these islands.

3. The position of Ireland is also of great importance for the Air Services, both military and civil. The Royal Air Force will need facilities for all purposes that it serves; and Ireland will form an essential link in the development of Air routes between the British Isles and the North American Continent. It is therefore stipulated that Great Britain shall have all necessary facilities for the development of defence and of communications by Air.

4. Great Britain hopes that Ireland will in due course and of her own free will contribute in proportion to her wealth to the regular Naval, Military and Air forces of the Empire. It is further assumed that voluntary recruitment for these forces will be permitted throughout Ireland…

5. While the Irish people shall enjoy complete autonomy in taxation and finance, it is essential to prevent a recurrence of ancient differences between the two islands, and in particular to avert the possibility of ruinous trade wars. With this object in view, the British and Irish Governments shall agree to impose no protective duties or other restrictions upon the flow of transport, trade and commerce between all parts of these islands.

6. The Irish people shall agree to assume responsibility for a share of the present debt of the United Kingdom and of the liability of pensions arising out of the Great War…

In accordance with these principles, the British Government propose that the conditions of settlement between Great Britain and Ireland shall be embodied in the form of a Treaty…

The form in which the settlement is to take effect will depend upon Ireland herself. It must allow for full recognition of the existing powers and privileges of the Parliament of Northern Ireland, which cannot be abrogated except by their own consent. For their part, the British Government entertain an earnest hope that the necessity of harmonious co-operation amongst Irishmen of all classes and creeds will be recognised throughout Ireland… But no such common action can be secured by force… It will come in Ireland by no other way than consent…

The British Government will therefore leave Irishmen themselves to determine by negotiations between themselves whether the new powers which the Pact defines shall be taken over by Ireland as a whole and administered by a single Irish body, or be taken over separately by Southern and Northern Ireland, with or without a joint authority to harmonise their common interests…

> By these proposals the British Government sincerely believe that they will have shattered the foundations of that ancient hatred and distrust which have disfigured our common history for centuries past.[1816]

The two leaders met for the final time on 21 July which Stevenson recorded as "a not too satisfactory interview". "D. was very depressed." After de Valera had read the terms, he told Lloyd George he could not advise his people to accept them. "Very well, Mr. DeV.", was Lloyd George's answer, "then there is only one thing more left for us to discuss." And when de Valera asked what that was, Lloyd George replied: "The time for the truce to come to an end." At this de Valera had gone "perfectly white" but said that he would put the terms "before his people" and report back. Although Lloyd George thought the meeting "pretty hopeless", Stevenson was "perfectly convinced DeV. was only bluffing… it is evident that the bulk of Irish opinion wants peace." Lloyd George stated that were Sinn Féin to reject the terms there was "only one thing to be done–to reconquer Ireland." Balfour allegedly "squirmed at the Cabinet when the terms were discussed preliminary to sending them to DeV." But Stevenson concluded that he had given in "gracefully" and that Lloyd George had succeeded in having "a unanimous Cabinet, which was a great achievement."[1817]

Following the ill-tempered meeting[1818], de Valera returned to Dublin. After consultation, he sent a letter confirming Dáil Eireann's rejection to the Prime Minister, presented at No. 10 on 11 August, the first of 15 items of correspondence before the two sides would talk face-to-face again:

> The outline given in the draft is self-contradictory, and 'the principle of the pact' not easy to determine. To the extent that it implies a recognition of Ireland's separate nationhood and her right to self-determination, we appreciate and accept it. But in the stipulations and express conditions concerning the matters that are vital the principle is strangely set aside and a claim advanced by your Government to an interference in our affairs, and to a control which we cannot admit.
>
> Ireland's right to choose for herself the path she shall take to realise her own destiny must be accepted as indefeasible… The Irish people's belief is that the national destiny can best be realised in political detachment, free from Imperialistic entanglements… Like the small states of Europe, they are prepared to hazard their independence on the basis of moral right… [I]t is our deep conviction that true friendship with England… can be obtained most readily now through amicable but absolute separation… 'Dominion' status for Ireland everyone who understands the conditions knows to be illusory…
>
> It should be obvious that we could not urge the acceptance of such proposals upon our people. A certain treaty of free association with the British Commonwealth group… we would have been ready to recommend, and as a Government to negotiate and take responsibility for, had we an assurance that the entry of the nation as a whole into such association would secure

1816 McDonald, Op.cit.
1817 Stevenson, *Diary*, p230-231.
1818 Coogan, p236-237.

> for it the allegiance of the present dissenting minority, to meet whose sentiment alone this step could be contemplated.
>
> Treaties dealing with the proposals for free inter-trade and mutual limitation of armaments we are ready at any time to negotiate. Mutual agreement for facilitating air communications, as well as railway and other communications, can, we feel certain, also be effected. No obstacle of any kind will be placed by us in the way of that smooth commercial intercourse which is essential in the life of both islands, each the best customer and the best market of the other...
>
> The question of Ireland's liability 'for a share of the present debt of the United Kingdom' we are prepared to leave to be determined by a board of arbitrators...
>
> As regards the question at issue between the political minority and the great majority of the Irish people, that must remain a question for the Irish people themselves to settle. We cannot admit the right of the British Government to mutilate our country, either in its own interest or at the call of any section of our population... We agree with you 'that no common action can be secured by force.' Our regret is that this wise and true principle which your Government prescribes to us for the settlement of our local problem it seems unwilling to apply consistently to the fundamental problem of the relations between our island and yours...
>
> Thus we are ready to meet you in all that is reasonable and just... We have no conditions to impose, no claims to advance but the one, that we be freed from aggression... The road to peace and understanding lies open.[1819]

On 13 August Lloyd George replied in the negative, clearly 'hamstrung' by British political conditions over which he had no control whatsoever:

> [W]e must direct your attention to... the claim that we should acknowledge the right of Ireland to secede from her allegiance to the King. No such right can ever be acknowledged by us. The geographical propinquity of Ireland to the British Isles is a fundamental fact. The history of the two islands for many centuries... is sufficient proof that their destinies are indissolubly linked...
>
> When you, as the chosen representative of Irish National ideals, came to speak with me, I made one condition only, of which our proposals plainly stated the effect–that Ireland should recognise the force of geographical and historical facts. It is those facts which govern the problem of British and Irish relations. If they did not exist, there would be no problem to discuss...
>
> We are profoundly glad to have your agreement that Northern Ireland cannot be coerced... We gladly give you the assurance that we will concur in any settlement which Southern and Northern Ireland may make for Irish unity within the six conditions already laid down... but we cannot agree to refer the question of your relations with Northern Ireland to foreign arbitration.[1820]

On 24 August de Valera replied confirming Dáil Eireann's unanimous rejection of the proposals:

---

1819 McDonald, Op. cit.

1820 Ibid.

> From your letter of August 13th it was clear that the principle we were asked to accept was that the 'geographical propinquity' of Ireland to Britain imposed the condition of the subordination of Ireland's right to Britain's strategic interests as she conceives them, and that the very length and persistence of the efforts made in the past to compel Ireland's acquiescence in a foreign domination imposed the condition of acceptance of that domination now.
>
> We cannot believe that your Government intend to commit itself to a principle of sheer militarism destructive of international morality and fatal to the world's peace. If a small nation's right to independence is forfeit when a more powerful neighbour covets its territory… there is an end to liberty. No longer can any small nation claim a right to a separate sovereign existence… If nations that have been forcibly annexed to empires lose thereby their title to independence, there can be for them no rebirth to freedom. In Ireland's case, to speak of her seceding from a partnership she has not accepted, or from an allegiance which she has not undertaken to render, is fundamentally false, just as the claim to subordinate her independence to British strategy is fundamentally unjust. To neither can we, as the representatives of the Nation, lend countenance…
>
> On the basis of the broad guiding principle of government by the consent of the governed, peace can be secured–a peace that will be just and honourable to all, and fruitful of concord and enduring amity. To negotiate such a peace, Dáil Eireann is ready to appoint its representatives, and, if your Government accepts the principle proposed, to invest them with plenary powers to meet and arrange with you for its application in detail.[1821]

After working on his draft with Tom Jones, on 26 August Lloyd George responded:

> [W]hen I asked you to meet me six weeks ago, I made no preliminary conditions of any sort… The proposals which I made to you after those meetings were based upon full and sympathetic consideration of the views which you expressed… *[M]y colleagues and I went to the very limit of our powers* in endeavouring to reconcile British and Irish interests. *Our proposals have gone far beyond all precedent*, and have been approved as liberal by the whole civilised world… Your letter shows no recognition of this…
>
> … Under the settlement which we have outlined Ireland would control every nerve and fibre of her national existence… And our proposals go even further, for they invite Ireland to take her place as a partner in the great commonwealth of free nations united by allegiance to the King.
>
> We consider that these proposals completely fulfil your wish that the principle of 'government by consent of the governed' should be the broad guiding principle of the settlement which your plenipotentiaries are to negotiate. That principle was first developed in England, and is the mainspring of the representative institutions which she was the first to create…
>
> The British Government… [is] met only by an unqualified demand that we should recognise Ireland as a foreign power. It is playing with phrases to suggest that the principle of government

[1821] Ibid.

> by consent of the governed compels a recognition of that demand on our part… We do not believe that the permanent reconciliation of Great Britain and Ireland can ever be attained without a recognition of their physical and historical inter-dependence, which makes complete political and economic separation impracticable for both.[1822]

Picking up the pace, de Valera fired back a tightly argued reply on 30 August:

> The present is the reality with which we have to deal. The conditions today are the resultant of the past… giving in simplest form the essential data of the problem. These data are
>
> 1. The people of Ireland, acknowledging no voluntary union with Great Britain and claiming as a fundamental natural right to choose freely for themselves the path they shall take to realise their national destiny, have by an overwhelming majority declared for independence, set up a Republic, and more than once confirmed their choice.
> 2. Great Britain, on the other hand, acts as though Ireland were bound to her by a contract of union that forbade separation. The circumstances of the supposed contract are notorious, yet on the theory of its validity the British Government and Parliament claim to rule and legislate for Ireland, even to the point of partitioning Irish territory against the will of the Irish people, and killing or casting into prison every Irish citizen who refuses allegiance.
>
> The proposals of your Government submitted in the draft of July 20th are based fundamentally on the latter premises. We have rejected these proposals and our rejection is irrevocable…
>
> The main historical and geographical facts are not in dispute, but your Government insists on viewing them from your standpoint. We must be allowed to view them from ours… You refuse and threaten to give effect to your view by force. Our reply must be that if you adopt that course we can only resist, as the generations before us have resisted.
>
> Force will not solve the problem… If you again resort to force, and if victory be not on the side of justice, the problem that confronts us will confront our successors. The fact that for 750 years this problem has resisted a solution by force is evidence and warning sufficient… Threats of force must be set aside… We have proposed the principle of government by consent of the governed… On this basis, and this only, we see a hope of reconciling 'the considerations which must govern the attitude' of Britain's representatives with the considerations that must govern the attitude of Ireland's representatives, and on this basis we are ready at once to appoint plenipotentiaries.[1823]

By this time both the King and Lloyd George were on holiday in the Scottish Highlands, the latter staying at Flowerdale House, Gairloch in Wester Ross. The pair met at Moy Hall, Inverness, where the King was grouse shooting with the head of the Mackintosh Clan. With de Valera appearing to be deliberately obstructing progress by this time, the King exercised a moderating influence on the near

[1822] Ibid. Emphasis added.
[1823] Ibid.

ultimatum which Lloyd George initially drafted in response. Perceivable threats or contentious phrases were removed, and the Cabinet, after emergency session at 11.00 am at the Town House in Inverness, its first ever meeting outside of Downing Street or Chequers, replied on 7 September with the so-called 'Inverness Formula':

> The principle of government by consent of the governed is the foundation of British constitutional development, but we cannot accept as a basis of practical conference an interpretation of that principle which would commit us to any demands which you might present–even to the extent of setting up a republic and repudiating the Crown…
>
> … His Majesty's Government must therefore ask for a definite reply as to whether you are prepared to enter a Conference to ascertain how the association of Ireland with the community of nations known as the British Empire can best be reconciled with Irish national aspirations.[1824]

On 12 September, de Valera replied, declaring his side's willingness to enter such a conference.[1825] Lloyd George must have had trouble concentrating at this point: on 14 September he had such a severe tooth abscess that a dentist had to come from Inverness to treat him. Further, terse communication ensued, until on 19 September de Valera responded in more conciliatory tones:

> We have had no thought at any time of asking you to accept any conditions precedent to a Conference. We would have thought it as unreasonable to expect you, as a preliminary, to recognise the Irish Republic formally, or informally, as that you should expect us formally, or informally, to surrender our national position. *It is precisely because neither side accepts the position of the other that there is a dispute at all, and that a Conference is necessary to search for and to discuss such adjustments as might compose it.*
>
> … We request you, therefore, to state whether your letter of September 7th is intended to be a demand for a surrender on our part, or an invitation to a Conference free on both sides and without prejudice should agreement not be reached. If the latter, we readily confirm our acceptance of the invitation.[1826]

Lloyd George took ten days to respond, before telegraphing on 29 September:

> My colleagues and I remain… keenly anxious to make in co-operation with your delegates another determined effort to explore every possibility of settlement by personal discussion… We, therefore, send you herewith a fresh invitation to a conference in London on October 11th, where we can meet your delegates as spokesmen of the people whom you represent with a view to ascertaining how the association of Ireland with the community of nations known as the British Empire may best be reconciled with Irish national aspirations.[1827]

1824 Ibid.
1825 Ibid.
1826 Ibid. Emphasis added.
1827 Ibid.

At last, on 30 September de Valera telegraphed accepting the invitation, and on 11 October, the essential negotiations opened between Lloyd George and the Irish Republican delegation. Why de Valera did not head the delegation himself has always been a moot point, but it is probable that he foresaw trouble ahead and wished to avoid personal opprobrium. At any rate, it "was against the will of the majority of the Cabinet."[1828] The delegation–headed by Arthur Griffith as Chairman, with Michael Collins–distrustful of de Valera's motives in remaining, Robert Barton[1829], Eamonn Duggan[1830] and George Gavan Duffy[1831]–set up headquarters at 22 Hans Place, Knightsbridge, except for Collins, who set up at 15 Cadogan Gardens, Chelsea. After a fortnight's exploratory discussions, Lloyd George began to think that Griffith and Collins might be more amenable to freer discussion of the issues without the presence of the other delegates, and so a private session was arranged with Lloyd George and Austen Chamberlain on one side, Griffith and Collins on the other. Thus began a series of such sessions after the daily plenary conferences. This conformed to Lloyd George's usual preference for direct dealing with individuals, and the sessions quickly began to yield fruitful results.[1832] After one such session on 30 October, when the conciliatory Lord Birkenhead[1833] had been his co-negotiator, Lloyd George remarked to Geoffrey Shakespeare: "We have really made progress tonight, for the first time… I really feel there is a chance of pulling something off."[1834]

The next day, Lloyd George faced a vote of censure from Tory diehards in the Commons but the mood for a solution prevailed, and the vote was defeated by 439 to 43.[1835] On 5 and 6 November he had talks with James Craig, pressing him to accept an All-Ireland Parliament, but this initiative was rejected outright. On 11 November, Craig wrote to Lloyd George that "Such a Parliament is precisely what Ulster has for many years resisted by all the means at her disposal."[1836] On 12 November, Lloyd George met Griffith alone at Philip Sassoon's house at 25 Park Lane, explaining that he intended to offer Ulster two alternatives, an All-Ireland Parliament, which had already been refused, or a boundary commission to adjust the Ulster boundary as closely as possible in accordance with the wishes of the population. If both were refused, he would proceed with the commission. Lloyd George said he needed an assurance that "he [Griffith] would not let Lloyd George down" before the Unionists' Conference in Liverpool on 17 November.

Next day, Tom Jones, Secretary of the British Delegation, showed Griffith a record of what he had agreed to, and he simply gave his assurance that he would not repudiate publicly the outline proposal on a boundary commission, acknowledging the existing fact of partition but not its principle, just as de Valera had already done in the Dáil. The document read:

---

1828 Coogan, p247.
1829 Robert C. Barton (1881-1975), Protestant, Minister for Economic Affairs, 26 August 1921–9 January 1922.
1830 Eamonn S. Duggan (1874-1936), solicitor from County Armagh.
1831 George Gavan Duffy (1882-1951), solicitor who defended Sir Roger Casement, 26-29 June 1916.
1832 G. Shakespeare, p82.
1833 Frederick Smith, Earl of Birkenhead (1872-1930), Tory Lord Chancellor, 10 January 1919–19 October 1922.
1834 Ibid., p83.
1835https://researchbriefings.files.parliament.uk/documents/CBP-9260/CBP-9260.pdf. Retrieved 30 December 2023.
1836 *Correspondence Between His Majesty's Government And The Prime Minister Of Northern Ireland Relating To The Proposals For An Irish Settlement*, Cmd.1561, 1921, London, HMSO, p5.

> If Ulster did not see her way to accept immediately the principle of a Parliament of All-Ireland–coupled with the retention by the Parliament of Northern Ireland of the powers conferred upon it by the Act of 1920 and such other safeguards…–we should then propose to create such Parliament for All-Ireland but to allow Ulster the right… to elect to remain subject to the Imperial Parliament for all the reserved services. In this case she would continue to exercise through her own Parliament all her present rights; she would continue to be represented in the British Parliament ... In this case however it would be necessary to revise the boundary of Northern Ireland. This might be done by a Boundary Commission which would be directed to adjust the line both by inclusion and exclusion so as to make the Boundary conform as closely as possible to the wishes of the population.[1837]

On 5 December final talks took place from 3.00 pm to 8.00 pm, and again from 11.15 pm until 2.20 am on 6 December, the fifth anniversary of Lloyd George becoming Premier, when the Republican delegation decided during heated discussions to recommend the negotiated agreement to the Dáil Éireann and signed the Anglo-Irish Treaty, though Barton and Gavan Duffy did so reluctantly, and Collins because he saw the British would concede no more. Only Griffith was certain he was doing the right thing, and Duggan sided with him and Collins.[1838]

The exact details of this momentous day have remained contentious, but the general consensus is that it appears Griffith thought that on 12 November he had merely assented to a tactical manoeuvre to help Lloyd George in "fighting the Ulster crowd". However, at the start of talks on 5 December, Barton noted that Lloyd George stated:

> That he must know once and for all exactly where we stood as regards the Ulster proposals. He said that the Ulster proposals in the document now before us were exactly those to which Arthur Griffith had agreed and on which he had undertaken not to let him (Lloyd George) down.
> Arthur Griffith replied that he had not let him down and did not intend to do so, but that before he gave a decision on the earlier articles in the document he must have a reply from Craig either accepting or refusing the unity of Ireland.[1839]

Griffith replied that he personally would dispense with a reply from Craig but that his colleagues had not been involved in the 12 November discussion with Lloyd George, and that 'it was not fair to demand acceptance or refusal from them before Craig replied.' Michael Collins afterwards claimed that at the last-minute Lloyd George threatened the Irish delegates with a renewal of "terrible and immediate war" if the treaty was not signed at once.[1840] This was not mentioned as a threat in the Irish

---

[1837] https://www.theirishstory.com/2022/08/12/betrayal-or-breakthrough-arthur-griffith-the-boundary-commission-and-an-unsigned-memorandum/#_ftn15. Retrieved 7 January 2024. The Counties of Fermanagh and Tyrone had slight nationalist majorities. See P. Murray, *Partition And The Irish Boundary Commission: A Northern Nationalist Perspective*, *Clogher Record*, 18 February 2004, p181-217; especially p182-183. The Boundary Commission's establishment was provided for in Article 12 of the Treaty, it duly sitting in 1924-1925.

[1838] Younger, p3-4.

[1839] https://www.difp.ie/volume-0/0/1921/213/#section-documentpage. Retrieved 9 January 2024.

[1840] M. Collins, *The Path to Freedom: Notes by General Michael Collins*, 1922, Dublin, Talbot Press, p34.

memorandum about the close of negotiations, but as a personal remark made by Lloyd George to Robert Barton, and merely a reflection of the reality of any military truce. Barton noted:

> Lloyd George stated that he had always taken it that Arthur Griffith spoke for the Delegation, that we were all plenipotentiaries and that it was now a matter of peace or war and we must each of us make up our minds. He required that every delegate should sign the document and recommend it, or there was no agreement. He said that they as a body had hazarded their political future and we must do likewise and take the same risks. At one time he particularly addressed himself to me and said very solemnly that those who were not for peace must take full responsibility for the war that would immediately follow refusal by any Delegate to sign the Articles of Agreement.[1841]

Collins clearly foresaw trouble ahead, from his own side, writing to a friend later that day:

> When you have sweated, toiled, had mad dreams, hopeless nightmares, you find yourself in London's streets, cold and dank in the night air... Think–what have I got for Ireland? Something which she has wanted these past seven hundred years. Will anyone be satisfied at the bargain?... I tell you this–early this morning I signed my death warrant. I thought at the time how odd, how ridiculous–a bullet may just as well have done the job five years ago... These signatures are the first real step for Ireland. If people will only remember that.[1842]

One historian neatly summed all this up:

> In that period of Truce, the twilight of one war and the dawn of another, signs of a crack appeared, signs reflected in the bitter argument among the Irish plenipotentiaries at their London headquarters in Hans Place before, having won a great deal but not quite enough, they finally capitulated to Lloyd George's consummate mixture of cajolery, statesmanlike generosity, sincere but insufficiently grounded promises, plain trickery and the ultimate theatrical threat of "immediate and terrible war."[1843]

On the day of signing, King George V wrote in his diary: "It is mostly due to the P.M.'s patience and conciliatory spirit, and is a great feather in his cap. I trust that now after seven centuries there may be peace in Ireland."[1844] This trust proved to be illusory.

Éamon de Valera called a cabinet meeting to discuss the treaty on 8 December, where he came out

---

1841 Notes by Robert Barton of two sub-conferences held on December 5/6, 1921 at 10 Downing St: https://www.difp.ie/docs/Volume1/1921/213.htm. Retrieved 7 October 2019.

1842 Quoted in R. Taylor, *Michael Collins: The Big Fellow*, 1958, London, Hutchinson, p189. On Collins death, Lloyd George sent a message of sympathy to William Cosgrave, acting Chairman of the Provisional Government of the Irish Free State, saying "His engaging personality won friendships even amongst those who first met him as foes, and to all who met him the news of his death comes as a personal sorrow."

1843 Younger, p4.

1844 Quoted in Rose, p242.

against the treaty as signed. The Cabinet decided by four–Griffith, Collins, Barton, Cosgrave[1845]–votes to three–de Valera, Brugha[1846] and Stack[1847]–to recommend the treaty to the Dáil on 14 December. This was then ratified in triplicate, firstly, narrowly by Dáil Éireann on 7 January 1922, by 64 votes to 57, so giving it legitimacy under the governmental system of the Irish Republic, de Valera resigning as President two days later and being replaced by Arthur Griffith. Secondly, by the House of Commons of Southern Ireland–involving 64 pro-Treaty Sinn Féin TDs and four Unionist MPs from the University of Dublin–on 14 January 1922, so giving it constitutional legitimacy according to British theory of who was the legal government in Ireland. Thirdly, it was ratified by both Houses of the British parliament, the Commons approving the treaty on 16 December 1921 by a vote of 401 to 58, the House of Lords also voting in favour by 166 to 47 on the same day. Under the terms of the treaty, Southern Ireland, representing 22.4% of the United Kingdom's territory, seceded exactly one year later on 6 December 1922 to form the Irish Free State.

Of course, this was not the end of the matter, as the Irish Civil War raged from 28 June 1922 to 24 May 1923 between the pro-Treaty Provisional Government and the anti-Treaty IRA, before the ultimate victory of the former. The anti-Treaty opposition saw it as a betrayal of the Irish Republic which had been proclaimed so boldly during the Easter Rising. The war was a tragic one between brothers, as many of those who fought on both sides in the conflict had been members of the Irish Republican Army (Old IRA) during the War of Independence. Ultimately the Free State forces won, benefiting as they did from substantial quantities of weapons supplied by the British Government. The conflict probably claimed some 2,000 lives, more than the War of Independence that preceded it, and left Irish society divided and embittered for generations. Today, two of the main political parties in the Republic of Ireland, *Fianna Fáil* and *Fine Gael*, are direct descendants of the opposing anti- and pro-Treaty sides of the war.

An interesting sidelight on Michael Collins view of Lloyd George was originally told by Lloyd George's son Richard. Hayden Talbot, Collins official biographer, told him "Collins had a very high opinion of your father's political skill," adding that there was one tale he had not incorporated in his biography:

> I'd been chiding Mick for being a bachelor, telling him if ever a man stood in need of a good wife he was that man…
>
> "Don't think I don't know how much a good wife means to a man," he said. "Sure, I've seen with my own eyes what a good wife can do for her husband. Cunning as a fox they say the Welsh Wizard is. Clever and artful and full of guile. But I'll let you into a secret. He'll never live to see the day when he'll outsmart that quiet little wife of his. She's a jump ahead of him all the time and has all the wisdom of Eve in keeping that fact very much to herself. A lucky man is the Welsh Wizard! God knows what I'd give to have a wife like that."[1848]

---

[1845] Minister for Local Government, 2 April 1919–22 August 1922.

[1846] Cathal Brugha (1874-1922), Minister for Defence, 1 April 1919–9 January 1922.

[1847] Austin Stack (1879-1929), Minister for Home Affairs, 22 August 1921–9 January 1922.

[1848] Lloyd George, *Dame Margaret*, p182-183.

Lloyd George took, and continues to take, opprobrium for the violent actions of the infamous 'Black and Tans', officially the Royal Irish Constabulary Special Reserve, in Ireland. Although, as Prime Minister, Lloyd George must take ultimate responsibility, the force was largely the initiative of Winston Churchill, firstly as Secretary of State for War (10 January 1919–13 February 1921), subsequently as Secretary of State for the Colonies (13 February 1921–19 October 1922).[1849] As such, "the future of Ireland was Churchill's responsibility."[1850]

This most important fact was backed up *at the time* by no less an authority than Michael Collins himself, when he told his biographer:

> "I want to take this opportunity of correcting a misapprehension that exists widely regarding the part Lloyd George was playing in Irish affairs at that time. It is generally supposed that the English Premier was responsible for instituting the Black and Tan reign of terror, as well as the provocative acts of terrorisation which preceded the coming of the Black and Tans. This is untrue.
>
> In those days Lloyd George did not have time for Ireland his whole attention being absorbed by the world war. The British Government's Irish policy, so far as military operations were concerned, was conceived and executed by Cabinet Ministers to whom Lloyd George had given a free hand.
>
> Unhappily, during the years that followed the Armistice he could not take the time to attempt to find a solution of the Irish question, counting it of less importance to England than a settlement of the European problem. For what happened then, in the period 1918 to 1921, Lloyd George had only nominal responsibility. I emphasise this fact because it seems to me high time that we who know the truth should disseminate it, and by so doing help to remove the causes of hatred and bitterness which are largely based on ignorance."
>
> Collins made this statement to me at the outset of one of our last meetings in Dublin again evidencing what had come to be his greatest driving ambition ending fratricidal strife by ending venomous and deliberate distortion of the truth.[1851]

*This truth still needs to be firmly established, over a century later.* It was Churchill who, on 25 March 1920, made the fateful decision to deploy the irregular, paramilitary 'Black and Tans' in Ireland, having also been responsible for their recruitment from January that year, and thereby driving Irish opposition to British rule to new heights.[1852] Brought into a Cabinet committee that was charged with the 'suppression of crime and disorder' in Ireland in mid-June 1920 by Lloyd George, by 1 July Churchill was already advocating draconian measures, suggesting to his advisers at the War Office that, if a large number of Sinn Feiners were drilling, with or without arms, and could be located and identified from the air: "I see no objection from a military point of view, and subject of course to the discretion of

---

[1849] See Jordan, A. J., *Churchill, A Founder of Modern Ireland*, 1995, Dublin, Westport Books, p70-75. By November 1924 Churchill had re-joined the Tories, "re-rating" in his own words.

[1850] N. Knight, *Churchill: The Greatest Briton Unmasked*, 2008, Newton Abbot, David & Charles, p45. See also Reynolds, p31.

[1851] H. Talbot, *Michael Collins' Own Story*, 1923 London Hutchinson; quote on p73-74.

[1852] Wynn, p46.

the Irish (Free State) government and of the authorities on the spot, to airplanes being dispatched with definite orders in each particular case to disperse them by machine-gun fire or bombs, using of course no more force than is necessary to scatter and stampede them."[1853]

On 15 May, Churchill's old friend Hugh Tudor[1854] had been appointed 'Police Adviser' to the Dublin Castle administration in Ireland and promoted to Lieutenant-General. As already noted, after the Restoration of Order in Ireland Act in August, Dublin Castle was given the power to govern by regulation. Accordingly, Tudor assumed control of Ireland's police forces, by November styling himself 'Chief of Police'. Under his administration, the police were militarised: indeed, at a Cabinet conference on 23 July 1920, Tudor contested that, as a police force, "within a few months" the Royal Irish Constabulary (RIC) "would cease to function; but as a military body he thought they might have great effect."[1855] Like his patron, Churchill, Tudor gave police posts to his military colleagues. With the regular army stretched to the limit, from January 1920 the beleaguered RIC was reinforced with a 'special reserve' of 7,684 British ex-servicemen–the notorious 'Black and Tans', many brutalized and traumatized by their recent wartime experiences. In July 1920, Tudor created the Auxiliary Division, the 'Auxies', a temporary but heavily armed gendarmerie which recruited 2,263 ex-commissioned officers, also recruiting 2,189 'temporary constables' from that September.[1856]

At a Cabinet meeting on 11 May 1920, Churchill proposed a force of 8,000 ex-soldiers be raised to reinforce the RIC[1857], but Field Marshal Sir Henry Wilson, Chief of the Imperial General Staff, thought this force of "scallywags"–the Auxiliary Division as it became–would be ill-trained and poorly led, fears which in the event proved to be fully justified. Lloyd George was unenthusiastic, saying in Cabinet on 31 May "I read the appeals and I do not think you would make any young fellow drop his tools and go over to Ireland."[1858] On 12 July, Wilson noted in his diary that Churchill "evidently had some lingering hope of our rough handling of the Sinn Feins."[1859] On 30 August, Wilson discussed the 'Black and Tans' with Churchill, noting in his diary: "Black & Tans carrying out wild reprisals & deprecating their policy. I told Winston that I thought this a scandal & Winston was very angry. He said these Black & Tans were honourable & gallant officers, etc. etc. & talked much nonsense."[1860] The following month, Wilson argued that Churchill should stop the 'Black and Tans' operations, but he refused. On 2 November, Wilson yet again noted in his diary: "I had a long talk with Winston and for the 100th time I urged him to take over the Govt of Ireland and not leave it to the Black & Tans

1853 Gilbert, *Churchill*, p422. Also Secretary of State for Air (10 January 1919 - 13 February 1921), Churchill personally authorised the same tactics during the Iraqi Revolt of May-October 1920, during which the RAF "flew missions totalling 4,008 hours, dropped 97 tons of bombs and fired 183,861 rounds": See https://www.theguardian.com/world/2003/apr/19/iraq.arts. Retrieved 5 February 2025.
1854 Hugh Tudor (1871-1965), a friend of Churchill's since their meeting in Bangalore, India, in 1895.
1855 Quoted in D.M. Leeson, *Black and Tans: British Police and Auxiliaries in the Irish War of Independence, 1920-1921*, 2011, Oxford, Oxford University Press, p33.
1856 J. Herlihy, *The Black & Tans, 1920-1921: A Complete Alphabetical List, Short History And Genealogical Guide*, 2021, Dublin, Four Courts Press, p1.
1857 Leeson, p31.
1858 Ibid.
1859 Gilbert, *Churchill*, p423.
1860 Quoted in Knight, *Churchill*, p45.

& the soldiers."[1861] However, such was Churchill's commitment to the organisation that, the next day, he wrote to Lloyd George "I am prepared to support and defend in Parliament a policy of reprisals… [by the Black and Tans and the soldiers]."[1862]

In one biographer's words: "Ironically, Churchill was much more responsible for the heavy-handedness of the 'Black and Tans' in the south and the 'B Specials' in the north than Henry Wilson, who was a critic of both forces. It was, however, Wilson who was blamed most and who was, indeed, to lose his life on this account."[1863] Another author concludes: "In any other circumstances some of the actions carried out by the Black and Tans and the Auxiliaries would have undoubtedly been deemed to have constituted war crimes and dealt with accordingly. How far up the chain of command that would have gone is debateable, but it could have resulted in *certain politicians* facing *criminal charges*."[1864] In the aftermath of the Anglo-Irish Treaty, the 'Black and Tans' and the 'Auxies' were disbanded between January-April 1922, but, understandably, they left a legacy of hatred.

Long close to Lloyd George's radical, Nonconformist heart, and with his instrumental support, the Welsh Church Act had received royal assent on 18 September 1914, separating Anglicanism in Wales from the Church of England. On 21 June 1906, a Royal Commission 'To enquire into the nature, origin, amount and application of the temporalities, endowments and other properties of the Church of England in Wales and Monmouthshire' had been appointed. Its work was marked by acrimony and dragged on until November 1910. The Bill itself, moved by Asquith on 21 April 1909–before the Commission had even issued its report–resembled in its proposals those made in 1895. Lloyd George recognised that "fifteen years have now gone by, and a new nation and new questions have come to the surface. The nation does not look at disestablishment now as it did then. All is now social questions."[1865] Nonetheless, the Bill was fiercely resisted by the Tories and blocked in the Lords, but a revised Established Church (Wales) Bill was introduced on 21 April 1912.

On 16 May Lloyd George defended the Bill in the Commons in powerfully graphic terms:

> The Duke of Devonshire issues a circular applying for subscriptions to oppose this Bill, and he charges us with the robbery of God. Why, does he not know–of course he knows–that the very foundations of his fortune are laid deep in sacrilege, fortunes built out of desecrated shrines and pillaged altars… I say that charges of this kind brought against a whole people… ought not to be brought by those whose family trees are laden with the fruits of sacrilege. I am not complaining that ancestors of theirs did it, but they are still in the enjoyment of the same property, and they are subscribing out of that property to leaflets which attack us and call us thieves. What is their story? Look at the whole story of the pillage of the Reformation. They robbed the Catholic Church, they robbed the monasteries, they robbed the altars, they robbed the almshouses, they robbed the poor, and they robbed the dead. Then they come here when

---

1861 Ibid.

1862 Ibid.

1863 P. Bew, *Churchill And Ireland*, 2016, Oxford, Oxford University Press, p97.

1864 Wynn, p56. Emphasis added.

1865 Gilbert, *Architect of Change*, p313.

> we are trying to seek, at any rate to recover some part of this pillaged property for the poor for whom it was originally given, and they venture, with hands dripping with the fat of sacrilege, to accuse us of robbery of God.[1866]

On 28 May, Lloyd George spoke on the issue again to a crowd estimated at 30-40,000 at Victoria Park, Swansea, rebutting any suggestion of generosity to the Church: "If the property belongs to the nation, or if it was given for the benefit of the Welsh people, it is theirs, and we cannot give away the property of a nation in order to obtain a meretricious credit for generosity… For Heaven's sake let us apply our principles fearlessly."[1867] When the Act was eventually passed in 1914, it was the first under the provisions of the Parliament Act 1911. However, because of the war, a suspensory Act was passed at the same time, meaning that it did not come into effect until 31 March 1920. When it did, it was hugely popular, as it meant tithes could no longer be collected from mostly Methodist tenants, removing the right of the four–soon six–Welsh Bishops in the new Church in Wales to apply *ex officio* to sit in the House of Lords and removing (disendowing) certain pre-1662 property rights. Lloyd George was criticised by some for his conciliatory gesture of taking communion with the newly elected Archbishop of Wales, A. G. Edwards, at his enthronement at St Asaph Cathedral on 1 June 1920 and for allegedly settling on too generous terms the disendowment aspect of the new organisation of the Church.[1868]

A curious footnote to this history exists at the Parish Church of St Mary, in Mold, Flintshire. As the disestablishment legislation was being hotly debated in Parliament in 1911, this old church was undergoing restoration, including the reconstruction of its south porch in the perpendicular style. One of the pinnacles on the western corner of its roof was given "a small but unmistakeable likeness of Lloyd George's head"[1869], presumably to show the workmen's approval of his actions.

One of the few failures of Lloyd George's reform programme was the lost opportunity to deal with the terrible conditions still existing in the mining industry. On 12-13 January 1919, at a special conference in Southport, the Miners' Federation drew up a charter proposing a six-hour working day, a 30% increase in total earnings and the nationalisation of all mines and minerals. The government's reply being unsatisfactory, the miners balloted on national strike action. The result was a resounding 615,164 to 105,082 in favour. Lloyd George asked the miners to postpone the strike and participate in a commission to investigate the coal industry, which they agreed to do.[1870] On 26 February, the Coal Industry Commission was set up, headed by High Court Judge Sir John Sankey, joined by 12 members representing owners, miners, industrial experts and Labour. They began work on 3 March and on 20 March produced no fewer than three interim reports. The six miners' representatives recommended

---

1866 https://api.parliament.uk/historic-hansard/commons/1912/may/16/second-reading-fourth-days-debate#S5CV0038P0_19120516_HOC_350. Retrieved 9 November 2022.

1867 *Disestablishment Demonstration. Mr. Lloyd George's Pledge to Wales*, *The Times*, 29 May 1912, p6. See N. Evans, *'A Nation in a Nutshell': The Swansea Disestablishment Demonstration of 1912 and the Political Culture of Edwardian Wales*, in R. R. Davies and Geraint Jenkins, Eds., *From Medieval to Modern Wales. Historical Essays in Honour of Kenneth O. Morgan and Ralph A. Griffiths*, 2004, Cardiff, University of Wales Press. The author thanks Dr Evans for bringing this event to his notice.

1868 See K. O. Morgan, *Freedom Or Sacrilege? A History Of The Campaign For Welsh Disestablishment*, 1966, Penarth, Church In Wales.

1869 M. Fraser, *West Of Offa's Dyke: North Wales*, 1959, London, Robert Hale, p37.

1870 Mowat, *Britain Between The Wars*, p31.

that the miners claims be met in full. The three owners' representatives recommended an increase of 1s 1d per day in the wages of adult workers and a seven-hour working day. Sir John and the three industrialists steered midway between these positions, recommending a seven-hour day, to be reduced to six hours in July 1921, if the economic condition of the industry justified it, a wage increase of 2s per day for adults, and a levy of 1d per ton to improve the housing and amenities of mining districts, many houses being, it was said, "a reproach to our civilization" for which "no judicial language is sufficiently strong or sufficiently severe to apply to their condemnation." Regarding nationalisation, recommendation IX of Sankey's report clearly stated: "Even upon the evidence already given, the present system of ownership and working in the coal industry stands condemned, and some other system must be substituted for it, either nationalisation or a method of unification by national purchase and/or joint control."[1871]

This lack of overall consensus gave Lloyd George a chance to stall the miners with promised concessions on working conditions. However, on the same day that the interim reports were produced, Bonar Law, Leader of the House, stated: "In regard to this whole Report we have had it discussed at the Cabinet this afternoon, and I say now on behalf of the Government that we are prepared to adopt the Report in the spirit as well as in the letter, and to take out all the necessary steps to carry out its recommendations without delay."[1872] A major victory for the Labour movement seemed in prospect so the miners' union continued to postpone strike action, accepting Sankey's report in a national ballot held on 15 April, voting standing at 693,684 to 76,992 in favour.[1873]

On 20 June, the Sankey Commission revealed its final findings, this time producing four reports! All recommended nationalisation of royalties–the money that mining companies paid the owners of the land beneath which the coal was mined–improved distribution of coal, and the creation of a ministry of mines. Sankey himself went further and recommended complete state-ownership, on the grounds that the existing system, with 3,000 pits owned by 1,500 concerns, was inefficient and created "distrust and recrimination" between owners and men. The six miners' representatives endorsed Sankey's views but went further in urging workers' control. The owners and industrialists, naturally, rejected nationalisation and recommended no change in the system of private ownership. Their only conciliatory gesture was to agree to the miners' claim for pit committees, district councils and a national council representing owners and men. The owners agreed that these should be established to discuss questions relating to the industry, but not conditions of employment in mining–a restriction that would have rendered the councils pointless. Finally, a fourth report, by the industrial engineer, Sir Arthur Duckham, attempted to reach a compromise between outright nationalisation and unreconstructed private ownership: in each area, all collieries should be acquired by district coal boards and operated by them with a limit on profits.

There was thus no majority report. Even so, a narrow majority of commissioners did back some form of nationalisation, Sir John's report and that of the six miners' representatives making it 7 out of

---

[1871] Quoted in Mowat, *Britain Between The Wars*, p33.

[1872] https://api.parliament.uk/historic-hansard/commons/1919/mar/20/government-decision. Retrieved 8 June 2021.

[1873] Davies, *A History Of Wales*, p531.

13 in favour. The government, though, was not enthusiastic, and made no official statement. In mid-July, 305 MPs, mostly Conservative supporters of the Coalition, signed a memo from an organization of coal owner MPs called the Parliamentary Coal Committee, which was duly presented to Lloyd George, which called for steps to be taken "to protect our great industries against the organised, revolutionary, and predatory forces of direct action, and against the nationalisation of the mines."[1874] This obviously put great pressure on the Prime Minister. In a Cabinet vote on 7 August on nationalisation of the mines, only five voted in favour–Addison, Montagu, Milner, and Labour members George Barnes and George Roberts.[1875] Most of the rest, including Lloyd George and Bonar Law, were strongly against.[1876] Finally, on 18 August Lloyd George broke silence, stating that as "the course that we proposed did not commend itself to either miners or owners, the action that we have taken has been confined to giving effect, by means of the Mining Industry Act, 1920, to certain proposals on which there was a substantial measure of agreement among the members of the Commission, as, for instance, the establishment of a Department of Mines, statutory provision for setting up joint committees of owners and men, and the creation of a fund for the improvement of social conditions in mining districts."[1877]

The Coal Mines Act of 1919, which received royal assent on 15 August, did enact the seven-hour working day, but it was all nothing like nationalisation, and wages remained unchanged. After all the hope for a new model of nationalised industry, Lloyd George and his Conservative allies had made it clear that they had no intention of changing anything. Lloyd George was against nationalisation–one reason he was not especially popular in South Wales, then heavily influenced by the coal miners–as, according to Bengy Carey-Evans, he said it is "like the sands of the desert, it gets into everything", in other words, it clogged the machinery, was inefficient. Historian Charles Mowat opined: "The bitterness and the troubles in the coal-mines for the next seven–or for that matter twenty-seven–years derived in great part from the feeling of both miners and owners that they had been betrayed."[1878] What the Act did do, was to set in place a mandatory requirement to provide social welfare opportunities to mining communities. The Miners' Welfare Fund was set up under the provisions of Section 20 of the Act. It was to be used for purposes approved by the Board of Trade and administered by a miners' welfare committee in the interests of "the social well-being, recreation and conditions of living of workers in or about coalmines and with mining education and research."[1879] The committee was appointed by the Board of Trade in January 1921, including representatives of the Mining Association of Great Britain and the Miners' Federation. The fund was raised from a levy, initially a levy of 1d per ton of coal produced.

A sign of the troubled times was the passing of the Firearms Act, 'An Act to amend the Law

---

1874 *The Times*, 14 July 1919.

1875 George Roberts (1868-1928), Labour MP for Norwich, 1906-1923, Minister for Labour, 1917-1919, Minister of Food Control, 1919-1920.

1876 Morgan, *Portrait Of A Progressive*, p114.

1877 https://api.parliament.uk/historic-hansard/commons/1921/may/24/sankey-commission-report. Retrieved 21 August 2019.

1878 Mowat, *Britain Between The Wars*, p34.

1879 http://www.legislation.gov.uk/ukpga/Geo5/10-11/50/enacted. Retrieved 16 July 2020.

relating to Firearms and other Weapons and Ammunition, and to amend the Unlawful Drilling Act, 1819', receiving royal assent on 16 August 1920. This was innovatory legislation, for the very first time creating a national system of gun licensing and control. Its principal aim was to enable the government to control the overseas arms trade and so fulfil its commitment to the Arms Traffic Convention, signed at St. Germain-en-Laye on 10 September 1919, known as the Convention of St. Germain. The Act made the right to bear arms conditional upon the approval of the Home Secretary and local police chief constables.

In the international sphere, on 16 March 1921, the ground-breaking Anglo-Soviet Trade Agreement was signed by the President of the Board of Trade–and soon-to-be Chancellor of the Exchequer–Robert Horne, and the Commissar of Foreign Trade, Leonid Krasin.[1880] This was in tandem with Lenin's 'New Economic Policy', promulgated on 21 March 1921, after the closing of the 10th Congress of the All-Russian Communist Party, intended as a 'temporary expedient' which downplayed socialism and emphasized doing business with capitalist nations in an effort to restart the depressed Russian economy. Britain, under Lloyd George's premiership, was the first nation to accept Lenin's offer of such an arrangement. The Agreement was very much Lloyd George's own pragmatic initiative, as it was he who first raised the proposal to drop the blockade on Soviet Russia, following the October Revolution at a meeting of the Allied Supreme Council, held on 14 January 1920, only four days after the ratification of the Treaty of Versailles.[1881] Originally trade was to be restricted to being with the "Russian people", through Centrosoyuz, the All-Russian Union of Consumer Co-operative Societies. On 10 February 1920, Lloyd George had justified trading with Russia to the Commons in clear-eyed terms:

> With regard to the whole question of our Russian policy… When you come to decide a policy it is essential that you should recognise facts, whether they are palatable or not… The first… is that you cannot restore Europe without putting into circulation the resources of Russia…
>
> The horrors of Bolshevism have revolted the consciences of mankind… There was deep resentment in the Allied countries at the betrayal of Brest-Litovsk. There is the fact that Bolshevism is not democracy… It is rule by a privileged minority… It is perfectly clear now to every unprejudiced observer that you cannot crush Bolshevism by force of arms. I was of that opinion, quite frankly, a year ago, and I never hesitated to express it. I then tendered advice based on that assumption to the warring factions in Russia. Unfortunately that advice was declined, I think by all sections…
>
> There is a suggestion made from another quarter–"Make peace with the Bolsheviks."… We have failed to restore Russia to sanity by force. I believe we can save her by trade. Commerce has a sobering influence in its operations… The Russian with his head in the clouds finds he is cold, and discovers that he is not clad and that he is hungry. He has no machinery for his land…

---

[1880] Leonid Krasin (1870-1926). For the terms of the treaty, see https://wwi.lib.byu.edu/index.php/Anglo-Soviet_Trade_Agreement. Retrieved 6 May 2019.

[1881] *Documents on British Foreign Policy, 1919-1939*, First Series (DBFP), II, No.71/3, p867-875.

> He is short of locomotives, wagons and lorries for his business, and the whole of Europe is short of what he can give in return…
>
> Trade, in my opinion, will bring an end to the ferocity, the rapine, and the crudities of Bolshevism surer than any other method. Europe needs what Russia can give… the withdrawal of Russia from the supplying markets is contributing to high prices, high cost of living, and to scarcity and hunger. Russia supplied before the War one-fourth of the whole export wheat of the world–4,000,000 tons. Four-fifths of the flax… grown in the world was produced in Russia… The grain and flour of Russia of all kinds, maize, barley, oats, &c. came to nearly 9,000,000 tons… The world needs this supply.
>
> … It is not a question of recognising the Government; it is a question of dealing with the people who have got commodities to sell and to exchange for what we can give them. When people are hungry, you cannot refuse to buy corn in Egypt because there is a Pharaoh on the throne. The conditions in Europe are serious… [H]igh prices. They have been used to stir up strife, suspicion and jealously of existing institutions throughout the land. The dangers are not in Russia, they are here at home. I speak with knowledge, with apprehension, and with responsibility, and I warn the House, in the face of things that may happen, that we must take every legitimate weapon to contend against these things. There is but one way–we must fight anarchy with abundance.[1882]

Two days later, Britain and the Soviets signed an agreement in Copenhagen for an exchange of prisoners, the first formal agreement between them. The prime mover behind this, "in the face of strong opposition in his own government and influential political circles", was Lloyd George himself.[1883] On 31 May, Leonid Krasin had arrived to meet the Prime Minister at No. 10, and the terms of the proposed trading agreement had shifted. Also, although originally an Allied proposal, the French declined to participate, the Italians merely sending a *chargé d'affaires* to one session. Meanwhile, the Bolsheviks, on learning of the Supreme Council's intention of lifting of the blockade and developing trade with the Co-operatives, took Centrosoyuz over, Krasin and his fellow delegates being nominally co-opted on to the board, keeping the fiction that negotiations were being carried out with the Co-operatives Union.[1884] Lenin gave an interview declaring "If peace is a corollary of trade with us, the Allies cannot avoid it much longer… But Churchill is still strong in England, and Lloyd George, who probably wants to do business with us, dare not risk an open rupture with the political and financial interests supporting the Churchill policy."[1885] Privately, on 12 June he cabled, warning Krasin: "That swine Lloyd George has no scruples or shame in the way he deceives. Don't believe a word he says and gull him three times as much."[1886] Lenin was right about Lloyd George wanting to do

---

1882 https://api.parliament.uk/historic-hansard/commons/1920/feb/10/debate-on-the-address#S5CV0125P0_19200210_HOC_83. Retrieved 6 May 2019.

1883 N. H. Gaworek, *From Blockade To Trade: Allied Economic Warfare Against Soviet Russia, June 1919 to January 1920*, *Jahrbücher für Geschichte Osteuropas*, Neue Folge, Bd.23, H.1 (1975), pp39-69; quote on p59.

1884 M. V. Glenny, *The Anglo-Soviet Trade Agreement, March 1921*, *Journal of Contemporary History*, 5, 2, April 1970, p63-82.

1885 V. I. Lenin, *Selected Works*, 3, 1964 (1977), Moscow, Progress Publishers, pp267-268. Interview with Lincoln Eyre of the US newspaper *The World*, *Allies Playing "Chess Game"*, 21 February 1920, No. 21368.

1886 C. Andrew, *The Defence of the Realm: The Authorized History of M15*, 2009, London, Allen Lane, p144.

'business', quite wrong about his lack of 'daring' and 'scruples'.

Krasin was accompanied by Viktor Nogin to London to engage in the negotiations. The Cabinet discussed the proposed agreement at No. 10 on 28 May. Curzon had previously briefed the meeting:

> We know… that the Russian Government is threatened with complete economic disaster, and that it is ready to pay almost any price for the assistance which we–more than anyone else–are in a position to give. We can hardly contemplate coming to its rescue without exacting our price for it, and it seems to me that price can far better be paid in a cessation of Bolshevik hostility in parts of the world important to us, than the ostensible exchange of commodities, the existence of which on any considerable scale in Russia there is grave reason to doubt.[1887]

Four meetings were held, on 31 May, 7, 16 and 29 June. The first two were more formal, but the third meeting consisted only of Lloyd George, Krasin, Robert Horne, Philip Kerr and Fridtjof Nansen.[1888] The last meeting was to prove crucial, Krasin and Lloyd George agreeing that there were two principal issues: hostile propaganda and subversion, and pre-1917 debts to British creditors. Faced with an impending meeting with Britain's allies, Lloyd George drew up a four-point plan: an armistice and end to hostile propaganda; the exchange of prisoners; mutual recognition of outstanding debts for goods and services; exchange of trade missions. Krasin was given seven days in which to reply and provided passage on a destroyer to Réval [Tallinn]. People's Commissar for Foreign Affairs Georgy Chicherin replied on 7 July agreeing to the terms in principle.

The negotiations proved to be protracted. Lenin remarked at the 8th All Russian Congress of Soviets on 21 December 1920:

> The treaty, the trade agreement with Britain is not signed yet. At this very moment Krasin is conducting urgent talks on it in London… but it is still obvious that the British government is dragging its feet over the agreement because the reactionary war party is still hard at work there; it has had the upper hand so far and is hindering the conclusion of a trade agreement. It is in our direct interest… to give all our support to whatever can help to fortify those parties and groupings who are striving for the signature of this treaty with us.[1889]

Ivan Maisky highlighted the importance of the eventual agreement thus:

> This diplomatic document, though modest in scope, is of truly historic significance. The Anglo-Soviet Trade Agreement was not an ordinary trade treaty with the mere object of regulating commercial operations between two countries; it was an agreement of politico-commercial character: it gave the RSFSR defacto recognition by the most powerful capitalist power in

[1887] Cabinet Paper: *Negotiations with M. Krasin–Note by Lord Curzon*. C.P.1350, 27 May 1920. CAB.241106.

[1888] Fridtjof Nansen (1861-1930), Norwegian explorer, diplomat and humanitarian. President of Norwegian League of Nations Society, active in prisoner repatriation and, as head of the Nansen Mission, in attempts to mitigate starvation in Russia and Ukraine, 1920-1922.

[1889] V. I. Lenin, *Polnoe Sobranie Sochinenii*, XLII, 1963, 5th Ed., Moscow, Izdatel'stvo Politicheskoĭ Literatury, p97-98.

> Europe, a power which in those days still successfully contended with the USA for the role of the foremost capitalist country in the world.[1890]

The Russians recognised the innovative and productive significance of Lloyd George's initiative, which opened a period of extensive trade, but it is not certain that the British did, as it is little remarked upon in Lloyd George literature. One fallout of the Anglo-Soviet Trade Agreement was that other European countries, anxious not to be excluded from any trade opportunities, lest they be left behind by other powers, also entered into similar agreements with Russia.[1891]

Another domestic measure that was not as far-reaching or lastingly successful as it might have been was the Railways Act 1921, also known as the Grouping Act, intended to stem the losses being made by many of the country's 120 railway companies, move the railways away from internal competition and retain some of the benefits which the country had derived from a government-controlled system during and after the Great War. The provisions of the Act, which received royal assent on 19 August 1921, took effect from 1 January 1923, ushering in "The Big Four of the New Railway Era", just after Lloyd George's fall from power. Complete nationalisation had been considered, and the 1921 Act is sometimes considered as a precursor to that, but, as with mining, the concept was rejected, for the same reasons. It was, however, a significant step in the right direction of rationalisation. Like other legislation initiated under Lloyd George's leadership, nationalisation of the railways was subsequently carried out by the Attlee Government, under the Transport Act 1947.

The form of the 1921 Act was developed by Eric Geddes, the former railway executive, now the Minister of Transport. Geddes favoured privately-owned regional monopolies through amalgamations and suggested increased worker participation from pre-war levels. Geddes viewed the pre-war competition as wasteful but was opposed to nationalisation on the grounds that it led to poor management, as well as a mutually corrupting influence between railway and political interests. In his 9 March 1920 Cabinet paper 'Future Transport Policy', he proposed five English groups (Southern, Western, North Western, Eastern and North Eastern), a London passenger group, and separate single groupings for Scotland and Ireland. Geddes' proposals became the 1920 white paper 'Outline of Proposals as to the Future Organisation of Transport Undertakings in Great Britain and their Relation to the State'. This suggested the formation of six or seven regional companies: additionally, it suggested worker participation on the board of directors of the company. The white paper was opposed by the Railway Companies' Association and MPs representing railway companies' interests. The move to greater worker participation was strongly opposed by the Association but supported by the Labour Party. Worker-directors were not included in the final Act, being replaced by agreed negotiating mechanisms.

Unfortunately, soon afterwards, the rest of Lloyd George's reform programme was also substantially curtailed by the so-called 'Geddes Axe' in the last year of his premiership. During and after the Great War, government expenditure and taxation had naturally considerably increased.

---

1890 I. Maisky, *Anglo-sovetskoe torgovoe soglashenie 1921 goda*, *Voprosy Istorii*, 5, 1957, p76-77.

1891 On 26 May 1927 Baldwin predictably severed diplomatic ties with Moscow and cancelled the Agreement.

Taxation per head per annum was £18 in 1919; £22 in 1920; and £24 in 1921. In 1913-14 the Civil Services and Revenue Departments cost £81.3 million; in 1920-21 they cost £523.3 million; and in 1921-22 they cost £590.7 million. The Armed Forces cost around £77 million in the year before the war and approaching £190 million in 1921-22. Similarly, the National Debt and other Consolidated Fund Services increased over the same time from £37.3 million to £359.8 million.[1892] In January 1921, the Anti-Waste League had been formed by Lord Rothermere, younger brother of Lord Northcliffe, to campaign against what they considered wasteful government expenditure, and three of its candidates won by-elections from government supporters between February and June 1921. In May 1921 HM Treasury sent all government departments a circular citing that in 1921-22 the cost of supply services would be £603 million and that this should be reduced in the next financial year to £490 million–economies totalling £113 million. Instead, the response was a plan to reduce this expenditure by £75 million.

Lloyd George appointed Eric Geddes as Chairman of the Committee on National Expenditure on 15 August 1921 to establish where economies could be found in various government departments for 1922-23. Other appointees were also businessmen; Lord Inchcape, a senior partner in the trading firm, Mackinnon, Mackenzie & Co., had sat on numerous government committees and had organised the post-war disposal of captured enemy shipping; Lord Faringdon, chairman of Great Central Railway, had sat on a number of government committees on commercial questions; Sir Guy Granet, formerly general manager of Midland Railway Company, served in the war as director general of Military Railways and Sir Joseph Maclay, a shipping magnate, the Minister of Shipping, 1916-21. The committee's terms of reference were: "To make recommendations… for effecting forthwith all possible reductions in the National Expenditure on Supply Services, having regard especially to the present and prospective position of the Revenue. Insofar as questions of policy are involved in the expenditure under discussion… it will be open to the Committee to review the expenditure and to indicate the economies which might be effected if particular policies were either adopted, abandoned or modified."

The committee first met in early September 1921 and sat at the Treasury for three or four days a week until its final report was ready in February 1922.[1893] Sometime after its appointment the Chancellor Sir Robert Horne[1894] requested that the committee find where expenditure could be reduced by £175 million, which meant total expenditure down to £428 million. The committee's reports were shown to the Cabinet in December 1921 and January 1922, where Cabinet committees reviewed and modified them before publication in February. Three reports were published, which advocated economies totalling £87 million; the Cabinet decided on savings amounting to £52 million. Total defence expenditure fell to £111 million in 1922-23 from £189.5 million in 1921-22; total social spending–education, health, housing, pensions, unemployment–fell from £205.8 million in 1920-21 to £182.1 million in 1922-23.

---

[1892] H. Higgs, *The Geddes Reports and the Budget*, *Economic Journal*, 32, 126, June 1922, p251-264.

[1893] Geddes, p245.

[1894] Robert Horne (1871-1940), Unionist MP for Glasgow Hillhead, 1918-1937.

Christopher Addison had been responsible for a great deal of social legislation, including the first Housing and Town Planning Act, under which the state built low-rent homes–'council houses'–for the working-class. He had also reviewed and increased the provisions of the National Insurance system and introduced programmes to improve healthcare and training. Moved from the Ministry of Health on 1 April 1921, he reluctantly became the Minister Without Portfolio. However, as Addison later recorded in his tellingly entitled book *The Betrayal of the Slums*:

> On Saturday, July 2nd, I received, marked "for information," the findings of a Finance Committee presided over by the Prime Minister, which had decided to arrest the scheme. I at once challenged the findings of this body, and in the discussion that subsequently ensued received substantial and influential support. So much so that the subject was referred to a specially appointed Committee… on Wednesday, the 13th… the Committee was informed by certain of its members that they had been instructed that morning by the Prime Minister that the findings of the Finance Committee must still be adhered to. In this way deliberations on the merits of the case were brought at an end. I declined to accept an autocratic ruling of this kind on so grave an issue of domestic policy, and resigned my office the next day.[1895]

On Addison's departure from the Ministry of Health, the medical members of parliament had passed a resolution expressing their appreciation of his services, noting their "admiration of his zeal and devotion to duty and untiring work in the interests of public health."[1896] The major medical press was also sympathetic of his efforts, in contrast to feeling within some Coalition circles. In his biographers' words, "Addison was merely a convenient scapegoat for right-wing reaction,"[1897] and he became collateral damage in the unfortunate retreat from social reform that took place in the last year of Lloyd George's premiership.

On 13 June Riddell, himself no longer quite as intimate with Lloyd George as he had been since the previous July, was at Chequers and noted in his Diary: "Saw LG [sic]. He said, speaking at large, 'I cannot get into touch with Addison. He is under the impression that he is a popular hero, whereas in fact he is nothing of the sort.' From this observation I gathered that Dr Addison is going to be thrown to the wolves."[1898] On 21 June Frances Stevenson recorded in her Diary:

> D. [sic] having trouble with Addison. The former says he cannot possibly persist in retaining him, especially as Addison has not been too loyal & is intriguing with Winston on Ireland… McCurdy[1899] says Addison has no conception of the real position–says that the whole conspiracy

1895 Addison, *Betrayal Of The Slums*, p29-30.
1896 Quoted in Morgan, *Portrait Of A Progressive*, p133.
1897 Morgan, *Portrait Of A Progressive*, p138.
1898 Riddell, *Diaries*, 1986, p344.
1899 Charles McCurdy (1870-1941), Liberal MP for Northampton, 1910-1923, Minister of Food Control, 1920-1921, Chief Whip of the Coalition Liberals, 1921-1922.

> is against him as a Liberal & progressive, & to separate D. from his Liberal colleagues. Addison has no idea how unpopular he himself is.[1900]

Stevenson was wrong: sadly, Addison was all too aware of what was afoot, even if he did not *want* to believe it. Lord Beaverbrook opined that: "In the Addison affair Lloyd George, intending to shelter his Government from the stormy blast of criticism over the failure of his housing programme, succeeded only in damaging himself… For the first time in the years of his downfall Lloyd George had made a fatal mistake,"[1901] dating the eventual fall of Lloyd George's government to this time.

Having been a great Lloyd George loyalist since before the war, he subsequently became a strong critic of the government concerning its reneging on its pledges on housing and education, its general rightward drift, joining the Labour Party in November 1923.[1902] This was another sign that the Liberals were losing the cutting edge of social reforms. Despite the housing scheme's cancellation under Tory pressure, however, Addison could still proudly claim that 213,800 high-quality houses had been built for working people, and that an important new social principle of housing as a social service had been enacted. In fine tribute to his work, some 92 streets are named after Addison across Britain, all in areas of social housing.[1903]

Calculatingly jettisoning Addison in a desperate attempt to conciliate his already unhappy Tory coalitionists was probably one of the worst political–and personal–mistakes Lloyd George ever made. In Addison's biographer, R. J. Minney's words:

> By this sacrifice of a friend to placate his enemies, as it was described by many at that time, Lloyd George was able to live on borrowed time for a span of only a few more months. His administration was already doomed. By discarding Addison and throwing him to the wolves, Lloyd George, politically, drove the spear into his own heart. Addison came back. Lloyd George never did.[1904]

As his later biographers, Kenneth and Jane Morgan, perceptively note:

> Addison is highly significant in being the only leading Coalition Liberal to move into the Labour Party. Most of the others who remained in politics, men like Winston Churchill, Hamar Greenwood[1905], Freddie Guest, Edward Grigg, Hilton Young[1906], and Alfred Mond, were to

1900 Stevenson, *Diary*, p223. Addison advocated the offer of a truce to Sinn Fein and the IRA, the very position that Lloyd George himself embarked on in his negotiations with de Valera in August.

1901 Beaverbrook, *Decline And Fall*, p77, 78.

1902 Kinnear, p11; *Liverpool Evening Express*, 21 November 1923; c.203/29, Addison Papers.

1903 https://municipaldreams.wordpress.com/2019/07/16/addison-streets-a-celebration-of-the-1919-housing-act/. Retrieved 12 July 2020.

1904 Minney, p190.

1905 (Thomas) Hamar Greenwood (1870-1948), Canadian-born lawyer, Liberal MP for Sunderland 1910-1922, last Chief Secretary for Ireland, 1920-1922.

1906 (Edward) Hilton Young (1879-1960), Liberal Financial Secretary to the Treasury 1921-1922, defected to the Tories in 1926, Minister of Health, 1931-1935.

> move to the right… The Coalition, especially in its latter period, had adopted a strongly anti-socialist and anti-labour stance that made its supporters natural recruits for the Conservatives after 1922… Such Liberal recruits as there had been to the Labour party–and they were numerous in the immediate aftermath of the war–were almost wholly from the anti-Coalition section of the party… But Addison, almost uniquely for a Coalitionist, retained his commitment to radical reform and to collectivist policies throughout the wartime and post-war periods; indeed, he regarded the 'war socialism' of 1914-18 as a major justification for them in practical terms.[1907]

Good though the housing programme was, it was not enough to counteract the impression created by the climbing unemployment levels; by the time of the November 1922 general election the level had reached nearly 2.5 million, with close to 15% of the labour force being unemployed.[1908] Lloyd George, still largely focused on international diplomacy, was starting to lose his pre-war status of being the worker's champion. The worst cuts were in education, including teachers' wages, and the abolition of the Agricultural Wages Board. Civil Service numbers were cut by 35%–mostly female staff hired during the war. However, this was largely forced on Lloyd George by his Tory Coalition allies who had become disillusioned with him, and in no way undermines his personal record. After 1922-23 defence spending increased to £114.7 million in 1924-25, and social spending–after dipping to £175.5 million in 1923-24–increased to £177.4 million in 1924-25, but all this was after Lloyd George had fallen from power. When enacted, the public expenditure cuts depressed the economy further. Geddes resigned as the Minister of Transport on 7 November 1921 and as MP for Cambridge on 23 February 1922.

Lloyd George recognised the brewing trouble in the Coalition, with himself as its focus, seeing that many Tory MPs would continue with it, but only under a Tory Prime Minister. Accordingly, on 27 February he wrote to Austen Chamberlain, offering to resign, though G. H. Bennett sees it as "a politically astute move which Chamberlain's sense of morality and loyalty would not allow him to accept."[1909] Judging by his comments when he did resign just under eight months later, it seems more likely that Lloyd George did really want a way to be relieved of the burden of office under the existing, ever-tightening restraints imposed by backbench Tory dissent and unrest. Recognising that the troublous times called for "unity and concentration" to overcome them, he wrote:

> I have been driven to the conclusion that I cannot any longer render useful service to my country by retaining office under existing conditions. I am conscious of the tremendous difficulties with which Governments are confronted at this hour. Were it not for that fact I should have insisted on resigning long ago, but I was anxious not to rest under the imputation of running away from trouble. I never sought my present position ; as you are aware, I was ready to serve either under Mr. Balfour or Mr. Bonar Law during the crisis of the war. In fact, I urged that one or other of

---

1907 Morgan, *Portrait Of A Progressive*, p157-158.
1908https://www.nationalarchives.gov.uk/cabinetpapers/themes/lloyd-Georges-coalition.htm. Retrieved 4 May 2020.
1909 Bennett, p25. See also Rowland, *Lloyd George*, p562.

> them should form a National Government. They decided otherwise, and I undertook to form a Government under pressure from them.
>
> I have always felt the anomaly of holding the first position in a Government the majority of whose supporters belong to another Party, although I must at once say that I have never been thwarted in my action through any lack of support on the part of the Unionist supporters of the Government ... I have… felt for some time that it would have been wiser for the Unionists to form their own Administration and for my supporters and myself to give them independent support in the carrying out of the policy upon which we were agreed. I have repeatedly offered Mr. Bonar Law, and I renewed the offer to you when you succeeded him, to go out and give independent and loyal support to a government formed by either of you to carry out the policy upon which I knew we were in complete agreement. I suggest in all sincerity to you that the time has come for you to accept that offer.
>
> No man can hope successfully to assist in handling such a baffling world situation as that which we witness unless the support on which he relies is confident and continuous. Recent debates have shaken that confidence…
>
> … I urge you to agree to my freedom so that you may be in a position to form a homogeneous Government. I shall, of course, continue to sustain to the best of my ability those causes for which we have worked in common…[1910]

On receiving this, Chamberlain immediately called on Lloyd George. He urged him not to resign and said that it was "the unanimous opinion of all whom he had consulted that Mr. Lloyd George should remain as Prime Minister, and that his resignation would be a disaster. It was, indeed, not without difficulty that he gained his point, and it is at least an interesting speculation what the history of the ensuing decade might have been had Austen become Prime Minister at this time."[1911]

Meanwhile, Lloyd George's government had one last success, namely the signing of the Washington Naval Treaty, signed between the major nations that had won the Great War, Great Britain, the USA, France, Italy, and Japan, aiming to prevent another arms race by limiting naval construction. It was negotiated at the Washington Naval Conference, held in Washington, D.C. from 12 November 1921 to 3 February 1922, with the signing taking place on 6 February.[1912] Arthur Balfour was the Britain's chief negotiator, along with Admiral of the Fleet Earl Beatty, Lord Lee of Fareham, and Rear-Admiral Ernle Chatfield, keeping in touch with Lloyd George, who stayed in London due to the Irish negotiations, by telegraph. Despite the new concept of 'open diplomacy' that was supposed to be in operation, the American 'Black Chamber'–the Cypher Bureau, the US intelligence service's cryptanalytic organization–was spying on the delegations' communications with their home capitals, particularly the Japanese, but also the British.[1913]

---

1910 Quoted in Sir C. Petrie, *The Life And Letters Of The Right Hon. Sir Austen Chamberlain K.G., P.C., M.P.*, Vol.II, 1940, London, Cassell, p174-178.

1911 Petrie, p178-179. An interesting speculation indeed!

1912 Ratifications were exchanged in Washington on 17 August 1923, and it was registered in the League of Nations Treaty Series on 16 April 1924, after the fall of Lloyd George's Coalition.

1913 See H. O. Yardley, *The American Black Chamber*, 1931, Indianapolis, Bobbs-Merrill; Ch.XVI *The Washington Armament Conference*, p283-317.

Lloyd George gained from the Conference:

> Although not a firm adherent of disarmament, the nimble Welshman had been able to hold his coalition Cabinet together by giving the chief British delegate in Washington, Arthur Balfour, leeway in forming a position. Lloyd George had bolstered his own position while reducing government expenditure (a necessary move if his long-cherished welfare reforms were to come), all the while repairing Anglo-American relations. The treaty had left Britain the strongest sea power, though weakened in the Far East.[1914]

The Treaty limited the construction of battleships, battlecruisers and aircraft carriers by the signatories. The contracting powers would limit their naval strength in capital ships to the following amounts: USA–525,850 tons; Great Britain–558,950 tons; France–221,170 tons; Italy–182,000 tons; Japan–301,320 tons.[1915] The numbers of other categories of warships, including cruisers, destroyers and submarines–the latter at French insistence[1916]–were not limited by the Treaty, but those ships were limited to 10,000 tons displacement each. As with Versailles, it was only as good as the compliance of the signatories: between 1929 and 1936 Italy and Japan violated then formally renounced the Treaty. Nonetheless, it stands as an honourable landmark in the history of peace negotiations.

On 19 March, Lloyd George's old ally, Edwin Montagu, resigned as Secretary of State for India, criticising his personal style of leadership:

> We have been governed by a great genius–a dictator who has called together from time to time conferences of Ministers, men who had access to him day and night, leaving all those who, like myself, found it impossible to get him for days together. He has come to epoch-making decisions, over and over again. It is notorious that members of the Cabinet had no knowledge of those decisions.[1917]

Still not everyone saw the storm coming. In an essay entitled 'The New Party' published in October 1922–the very month the Coalition finally dissolved–Lord Birkenhead, in a section entitled 'The True Position of the Coalition', wrote:

> I myself have no doubt that if a plebiscite were taken at this moment, of the British nation, in order to determine who should become Prime Minister of the country for the next five years, the choice would fall upon Mr. Lloyd George…

[1914] R. W. Fanning, *Peace And Disarmament: Naval Rivalry and Arms Control, Peace And Disarmament: Naval Rivalry and Arms Control, 1922-1933*, 1994, Lexington, University of Kentucky Press, pp9-10. Lloyd George wrote that Balfour's "conduct… affords indubitable proof of his capacity to decide when he was confronted with a dilemma which he also had the authority to solve."; *War Memoirs*, Vol.I, p606.

[1915] https://www.peacepalacelibrary.nl/2017/11/the-washington-naval-treaty-averting-the-allied-arms-race/. Retrieved 3 May 2020.

[1916] https://www.nytimes.com/1977/10/02/archives/the-1921-salt-talksand-you-are-there-disarmament.html. Retrieved 3 May 2020.

[1917] Quoted in Rowland, *Lloyd George*, p568.

> I am satisfied that the community, as a whole, has formed a view of the resource, the courage, the resiliency, and, above all, the patriotism of the present Prime Minister, which is the greatest asset of the Coalition.[1918]

The Lord Chancellor's summary of Lloyd George's sterling qualities and value to the country was accurate, but his political assessment of the nation's mood was considerably awry! That Lloyd George was personally still a highly popular and high-profile figure is evidenced by the fact that the popular impersonator and character actor-manager Bransby Williams[1919] did well-received impersonations of him. Journalist John Roberts, a personal friend, recorded that on Warriors Day, 31 March 1921, Williams performed at the London Hippodrome[1920], presenting 12 'tableaux' as advertised… until the point where the audience had a surprise:

> Bransby is a veritable wizard in his impersonation of Mr. Lloyd George… he deceived H.R.H. the Prince of Wales and led him to believe that the great Welshman was actually in the theatre…
>
> "Lloyd George" addressed the audience which included the Prince and many other notable men and women, from a Stage Box and later from the stage, where he made a speech, and not until Bransby removed his make-up that the Prince and the audience realised how well they had been deceived.
>
> Bransby has the mannerisms characteristic of Mr. Lloyd George weighed up to a wonderful degree.
>
> "Bransby Williams as 'Lloyd George'" says a report in the North Wales press, "will stand out as one of his best in his departure from characters from Dickens, in which delineations he has no compeer."
>
> And they should know!"[1921] Prince Edward–later King Edward VIII–must have been impressed too, as he "solemnly bowed to the bogus 'Prime Minister'".[1922]

The last time that Lloyd George appeared on the international stage was at the Genoa Economic and Financial Conference, a formal gathering of 34 nations held in Genoa from 10 April to 19 May 1922. Like the Anglo-Soviet Trade Agreement, this was an initiative of Lloyd George's, planned by him to resolve the major economic and political issues facing Europe, and to deal with the pariah nations of Germany and Russia, both of which had been excluded from the Paris Peace Conference. The conference was particularly concerned with developing a strategy to rebuild Germany, as well as Central and Eastern Europe, and to negotiate a relationship between European capitalist economies and the Bolshevik regime in Soviet Russia. However, Russia and Germany signed a separate agreement

---

1918 Viscount Birkenhead, *Points of View*, 1922, London, 2 Vols. Hodder and Stoughton; Quote, Vol.II, p204.

1919 Bransby Williams (1870-1961).

1920 J. E. Roberts, *The Life Of A Strolling Player: Bransby Williams–The Man And His Work*, p109 (Unpublished Manuscript). The event was part of Earl Haig's Appeal to raise funds for ex-servicemen.

1921 Ibid., p190.

1922 Ibid., p110.

at Rapallo and so Genoa was a noble failure with few positive results.[1923]

The idea for such a conference of European nations had roots in the 6-13 January 1922 session of the Supreme War Council held in Cannes. With Europe facing an economic catastrophe brought about by more than four years of grossly destructive war, Lloyd George sought an authoritative international gathering to set Europe's political and financial house in order, and to firmly establish his leadership at home. The formal proposal was made on 6 January, presented by Lloyd George and approved unanimously the same day. On 3 April he rose in the Commons to move "That this House approves the Resolutions passed by the Supreme Council at Cannes as the basis of the Genoa Conference, and will support His Majesty's Government in endeavouring to give effect to them", treating the Motion as a vote of confidence in his Government. He continued:

> The Conference has been called to consider the problem of the reconstruction of economic Europe, devastated and broken into fragments by the devastating agency of war. Europe, the richest of all continents, the continent which possesses the largest amount of accumulated wealth and certainly the greatest machinery for the production of wealth, the largest aggregate of human beings with highly civilised needs and with highly civilised means of supplying those needs, and therefore Europe, the best customer in the world and of the world, has been impoverished by the greatest destruction of capital that the world has ever witnessed... International trade has been disorganised through and through. The recognised medium of commerce, exchange based upon currency, has become almost worthless and unworkable; vast areas, upon which Europe has hitherto depended for a large proportion of its food supplies and its raw material, completely destroyed for all purposes of commerce. Nations, instead of cooperating to restore, are broken up by suspicions and creating difficulties and new artificial restrictions. Great armies are ready to march, and nations already over-burdened with taxation have to bear the additional taxation which the maintenance of these huge armaments to avoid suspected dangers render necessary. Genoa has been summoned to examine the best method of restoring order out of this welter and recovering prosperity... The first condition, which is of prime importance in the reconstruction of Europe, is to establish the relations of all the countries on the basis of a stable and enduring peace. Then... [there are]... the financial measures that are necessary to meet the abnormal financial conditions in Europe...
>
> ... There must be patience, persistence, continuity...
>
> ... I would earnestly appeal to all those who are rather disposed to criticise conferences to hesitate before they tie their hands in advance. This Government will not last for ever. I have been assured that we are a dying Coalition... I do not know who will succeed us... But... I entreat those who look forward to partaking of the responsibility... not to condemn themselves in advance to impotence, when they come to deal with the state of Europe and the world, by condemning the only rational process, short of force, of bringing the world gradually back to something like normal conditions, and from normal conditions to something which is better.

---

1923 See Mills, *Genoa Conference*; Fink, *Genoa Conference*; and D. Bakić, *Great Britain, The Little Entente And The Genoa Conference Of 1922*, 2011, University of Leeds at http://istorija20veka.rs/wp-content/uploads/2017/11/2011_3_07_Bakic.pdf. Retrieved 7 May 2019.

... Because Europe, as a result of the War, from the Atlantic to the Urals, is a devastated area... there is no country... which is not suffering from the consequence of that great War. What is the first problem...? It is to restore the machinery of international trade... It was working well before the War, but it is exactly as if a bomb had been thrown into that machine and shattered it...

... Last year the quantity of our export trade was only about 50 per cent of what it was before the War... That necessarily affects the home market. We are a country depending more, probably, on international trade than any other country in the world. Thirty per cent of the output of this country... was exported, before the War. Last year 24 per cent of the output was exported. In addition to that, we had invisible exports reduced very considerably last year. That depresses the home market, because the population have not the same means of purchasing goods if they are deprived of that great trade on which they are depending by buying, selling and carrying abroad. Therefore, this is a problem of the most vital importance to the population of this country.

... We are often asked a question: "If you lost your trade in Europe, could you not make it up by trading with the Dominions, trading with the Colonies and with other parts of the world?" The world is one trade unit. Our customers depend on their sales in European countries to pay for goods that we sell them... Therefore, the trade of Europe is of the greatest importance to us, not merely directly, but indirectly, and unless you restore the trade of Europe as a whole, our purchasers will not be in a position to pay for the commodities which they get from us...

Therefore, the fact that international trade has broken down is one which is affecting this country very specially, and it is not merely because Europe is impoverished; it is because the machinery of exchange has also been shattered... I am told that in Vienna a housewife has always to consider in the morning whether she will pay her bill before noon or in the afternoon... And that applies to other capitals now. Between the date that an order is given and delivery is effected the exchange may change by 20, 100 or 200 per cent. It is almost impossible for anyone to do business under those conditions... Currency has gone adrift... and one of the first things to be attended to at the Genoa Conference is the question of restoring the exchanges. You must have a sound basis to proceed upon. In this country wonders have been achieved in this respect...

But before trade can be fully restored... one of the first considerations is to induce the nations to balance their budgets... That is a matter where pressure can be exercised at a great international conference of the leading Ministers of the various nations. But, above all, it is essential that there should be a real peace between the nations. Until that is established the trader, the financier and the merchant are unnerved by the present conditions of things...

... perhaps the most controversial part of the issue which will come before the Genoa Conference... is the question of peace in Russia and peace with Russia... a subject where perhaps legitimate prejudices cloud reason. The doctrine, the demeanour, and the actions of the Bolshevists have undoubtedly been of a character which has excited wrath and just anger, and made it exceedingly difficult for us to exercise judgment when we come to deal with the problem of our relations with that country...

Lloyd George gave two apposite quotations from William Pitt the Younger when trying to deal with the French revolutionary government in the 1790s, illustrating that if peace could be honourably attained, and security maintained, then "peace is desirable, peace is then anxiously to be sought", continuing:

> We are not at peace; I am not sure that present conditions are very much better than war, except for the actual fact that war is no longer in progress. But we have the effects of war in many ways, and one is the closing down of Russia. There is no intercourse with that country, and... there will not be until peace is established...
>
> *I do not believe you are going to restore trade, business, and employment until you appease the whole of Europe. Until you establish peace over the whole of Europe there will be a standing element of disturbance, and trade will not go on.* The nerves of commerce will be shaken while there are constant rumours of great armies being built up... There are... rumours of such an intention by the revolutionaries to reduce the countries of Europe to the terrible condition of famine, pestilence, and desolation in which Russia is. Naturally there is great apprehension...
>
> What difference would this make? First of all, once the trader is admitted there, we should get to know the facts. In the second place, if trade were introduced there, it would be to the interests of the country itself to retain it, and it will not retain it while these rumours are afloat... The effect of those great revolutionary armies is to provide an excuse, if not a real justification, for huge armies in other countries... *These armaments are absorbing the strength of the nations, but they will never be reduced until there is peace in Europe.* Another reason is that Europe needs what Russia can supply... It has labour, it needs capital, and it will not get capital without security, confidence and peace, internal as well as external... Germany cannot pay the full demand of reparation until Russia is restored.
>
> Now what are the conditions of peace laid down at Cannes?... [I]n substance they mean that Russia must recognise all the conditions imposed and accepted by civilised communities as the test of fitness for entering into the comity of nations. She must recognise her national obligations... They could not pay immediately. Nobody expects that...
>
> Where the property of our nationals has been confiscated, it must... be restored or compensation paid. Impartial tribunals must be established... There must be a complete cessation of attacks upon the institutions of other countries. There must be an undertaking that there will be no aggressive action against the frontiers of their neighbours. In fact, the Pact which is embodied in the League of Nations will have to be extended in principle to Russia... The only difference would be... that I do not think we could undertake the responsibility as a country which we have incurred under Article 10 of the League of Nations to defend any frontiers which are attacked in that quarter of the globe.
>
> Is Russia prepared to accept these conditions?... The famine has been a great eye-opener to Russia... The new Decrees recognise private property, set up courts, and acknowledge responsibilities... [T]his new policy was propounded... on 1st November, 1921... in a speech by Lenin. It was an admission of the complete failure of the Communist system, and in that respect it is a singularly courageous speech... He points out that the result of Communism has

> been completely to destroy the very proletariat upon whom they were depending… It is a very remarkable admission to make… [a]… very remarkable condemnation and exposure of the doctrines of Karl Marx by… its greatest exponent, the only man who has ever tried honestly to put these doctrines into operation …
>
> … If this represents the real determination of Russia in its dealings with the world…–respect for private property, respect for the rights of individuals, fair play to those who make investments there, acknowledgment of honourable debts incurred by people who put the savings… into Russian investments–then there is a real basis upon which we can treat..
>
> … [W]hat recognition of Russia would this involve?… It is… felt that the character and extent of the diplomatic representation accorded depends not merely on the conditions which Russia is prepared to accept, but upon the actual proof which she gives of her bona fides. Let me say quite frankly that the way in which some of the more important of the Clauses of the Trade Agreement have been violated has not been encouraging. Propaganda, interference in our country, and in other countries in which we are interested, has not ceased as completely as we had a right to expect…
>
> If the agreement is ratified… Russia would be represented here by a chargé d'affaires, and we should be represented in Russia by a corresponding official, until such time as we felt that it was desirable to establish full ceremonial diplomatic relations... That would present a period of probation… Those will be the conditions which we propose that the British delegates shall submit to the Genoa Conference.
>
> … [I]t would open out, undoubtedly, a new outlook for trade, and the effect from the psychological point of view would be great… It is our duty to see it is the establishment of a complete peace throughout the whole of Europe, with a view to dealing with the serious problems of trade and unemployment which are confronting us at home at this moment. Do my hon. Friends imagine that the workmen of this country are prepared to wait, with all this unemployment, while half Europe is practically closed down, if there is a real prospect of making peace? I am convinced they are not…
>
> We are proposing, I consider, a moderate course… Believe me, unless peace is made–if we fail because there are men who will not go as far, either here or elsewhere–the movement will not be in their direction; it will be away from them. Let them be wise in time. We propound these measures, in all consciousness feeling that the people of England demand them; Europe needs them; the world is crying out for them.[1924]

The Prime Minister was persuasive: when the House finally divided, the Ayes were 372, Noes 94. Lloyd George controversially sought the inclusion of Germany and Russia to the conference as equals, meeting strong opposition from the French, who sought to neutralize and isolate the two pariah nations by relegating them to an inferior status. The apparent softening the economic terms of the peace at Cannes had led to the resignation of Republican-Socialist Prime Minister Aristide Briand[1925]

---

[1924]https://api.parliament.uk/historic-hansard/commons/1922/apr/03/vote-of-confidence. Retrieved 7 May 2019. Emphasis added.

[1925] Briand, a Breton, was a Celt like Lloyd George, and the pair, who had a good working relationship, could converse in Breton and on 12 January, and left his successor, conservative Raymond Poincaré, with little appetite for participation, which threatened the Conference. Only through a dedicated diplomatic offensive by Lloyd George towards the French government during February was its participation, under terms previously agreed to by Briand, won. Although antagonism between France and Britain had developed in the immediate post-war months, France found herself having to submit to Britain on the matter of an economic conference, as without its support, she would have little chance of collecting reparations from Germany or entering into any potential strategic military alliance. The second potential hurdle to holding the Conference surrounded participation of the Bolshevik government of Russia, as most European nations did not maintain formal diplomatic relations with the regime and held economic claims against it. This situation had been resolved by the Supreme Council, which on 10 January invited Soviet participation.

The opening ceremony of the Genoa Conference took place on 10 April at the Palazzo di San Giorgio, where once Marco Polo had been imprisoned. Lloyd George was met with "a great ovation"[1926] in the hall as he took his seat to the left of the chairman. As chief architect of the gathering, he would effectively dominate its public sessions, "by virtue of his personal character, by the sense and sanity of his judgements, and, perhaps above all, by that humour and good-humour of his."[1927] Great hopes were held for the conference: on 22 April, King Vittorio Emanuele III entertained all the delegations on the battleship *Dante Alighieri*, on 7 and 29 April, newly elected Pope Pius XI offered prayers for the conference's success, and the Fascists and Communists agreed on a six-week truce for its duration. After Italian Premier Luigi Facta's[1928] opening address, Lloyd George rose to speak. John Saxon Mills, a witness, pictured the scene:

> Mr. Facta had read his address in a formal manner, but with the British Prime Minister we were at once in a different atmosphere. There was now no lack of that *actio* which Cicero regarded as so essential to the art of oratory. Mr. Lloyd George was in his best platform mood. He had a complete command of himself, and in a few moments had complete command of his audience. He spoke with great energy, turning to right and left, now emphasizing a point with clenched fist, now shaking an admonitory finger, and with every modulation, through the whole gamut from tears to laughter, of his wonderful instrument of a voice. To the greater part of his audience English must have been an unknown or imperfectly-known language. Yet the whole assembly was held by the orator's musical tones, by his eloquent gestures and the impression of sincerity and good faith the entire speech conveyed. It was interesting to notice… that the thirty-four nations all seemed to appreciate in common Mr. Lloyd George's recurring strokes of humour. No one seemed to miss the sly reference to Christopher Columbus and the absence of the Americans from the Conference.[1929]

---

Welsh respectively when confidentiality was required. Briand referred to Lloyd George and himself as "Les deux Bretons": [Stevenson], *Makers*, p38.

1926 Mills, *Genoa Conference*, p46.

1927 Ibid., p46-47.

1928 Luigi Facta (1861-1930), Liberal, last Prime Minister, 26 February-31 October 1922, before Mussolini.

1929 Mills, *Genoa Conference*, p53. John Saxon Mills (1863-1929), barrister and journalist.

In his finely nuanced, politically attuned and far-sighted speech, which could almost be read as a blueprint of the *raison d'être* of the later European Union, Lloyd George told the assembly:

> This is the greatest gathering of European nations which has ever been assembled in this continent, and having regard to the magnitude of the assembly, the character of its representation, the importance of the topics we are here to discuss, the results of the Conference will be far-reaching in their effects either for better or for worse upon the destiny, not merely of Europe, but of the whole world.
>
> We meet on equal terms, provided we accept equal conditions... We are assembled as the representatives of all the nations and peoples of Europe to seek out in common the best methods for restoring the shattered prosperity of this continent. We may each build up in his own land, each in his own way, a better condition of things for the people than the world has yet enjoyed. But if we meet on terms of equality it must be because we accept equal conditions.
>
> These conditions... apply to all alike; they are the conditions which heretofore have been accepted by all civilized communities as the basis of international good faith. *They in themselves are honourable; they are essential to any intercourse between nations; they do not derogate the complete sovereignty of the States.* We fully accept them ourselves; they are the only conditions on which we can consent to deal with others...
>
> The first is that when a country enters into contractual obligations with another country or its nationals for value received, that contract cannot be repudiated whenever a country changes its Government without returning the value.
>
> The second is that no country can wage war on the institutions of another.
>
> The third is that one nation shall not engage in aggressive operations against the territory of another.
>
> The fourth is that the nationals of one country shall be entitled to impartial justice in the courts of another.
>
> If any people reject these elementary conditions of civilized intercourse between nations, they cannot be expected to be received into the comity of nations. These conditions... were incorporated in the invitation to this Conference. They are the fundamental basis of its proceedings...
>
> ... Europe undoubtedly needs a common effort to restore the devastation wrought by the most destructive war ever waged in this world... Europe, exhausted with its fury, with the loss of blood and treasure which it involved, is staggering under the colossal burdens of debt and reparation which it entailed... legitimate trade, commerce and industry are everywhere disorganized and depressed. There is unemployment in the West, there are famine and pestilence in the East... and unless some common effort of all the nations of Europe is... made immediately, to restore European efficiency I can see symptoms not merely that the suffering will continue, but that it may even deepen into despair.
>
> *What is the first need of Europe? Peace–a real peace.* We propose to study the currency... to examine the question of exchanges... to discuss transportation and credit... *But unless peace is established and good will among nations, all these discussions will be of no avail...* But is there no peace in Europe?

It is true that actual fighting has ceased, but the snarling goes on, and as there are many dogs in every country who imagine that the louder they bark the deeper impression they make of their ferocity and determination, Europe is deafened by this canine clamour. It is undignified; it is distressing; it destroys confidence; it has rattled the nerves of a nerve-ruined continent, and we shall only make a real contribution to the restoration of Europe if at this conference we can stop the snarling.

*Europe needs rest, quiet, tranquillity–that is, she needs peace.* If we act together in that same spirit we shall succeed, not in the spirit of a greedy vigilance over selfish interests, but with a common desire to do the best to restore the world to its normal condition of health and vigour. We shall do so if we measure the success of the Conference by the good we achieve and not by the good we prevent… Let us think more of what we can accomplish than of what we can restrict.

We have all of us one common restriction in the public opinion of our own countries. The public opinion of one country is concentrated, perhaps, more upon one aspect of affairs and the public opinion of another upon a different object. That undoubtedly creates difficulties… but public opinion… is amenable to guidance, to direction, and to the appeal of reason and of conscience… *It can be taught that the good of another country is not necessarily an evil for its own; on the contrary, that what benefits all lands must necessarily be the best for its own.*

*The world is one economic unit.* Economically it is not even two hemispheres; it is one round unbroken sphere. For that reason I regret that the great American Republic is not represented here… A distinguished citizen of this city once upon a time discovered America, and as Genoa in the past discovered America to Europe I am hopeful that Genoa once more will render another immortal service to humanity by rediscovering Europe to America.

There are thirty-four nations represented at this table, and the interest taken in the Conference by the world is by no means exhausted by that representation. The Press of practically the world is represented. They would not be here if the great publics… were not deeply concerned in our proceedings and anxious as to the results… Europe is the cradle of a great civilization, which during the last five hundred years has spread across the globe; that civilization has been menaced with destruction by the horrors of the last few years, but if we do our duty manfully and fearlessly we shall prove that this Conference, meeting as it does in the sacred week of that civilization, is capable of achieving its exalted purpose by establishing on a firm basis peace and good will amongst men.[1930]

An interesting personal footnote to events was provided by A. J. Sylvester:

At the Genoa Conference Signor [Francesco] Giannini, one of the representatives of the Italian Government, asked T. J. [Tom Jones, Secretary to Lloyd George] if he would arrange for Signor Mussolini, then a reporter at the conference, to have an interview with the Prime Minister Lloyd George. T. J. refused, and the two men never met. The Prime Minister knew nothing of it at the time.

---

[1930] Ibid., p53-57. Emphasis added.

> Many years later T. J. casually mentioned the request he had had to L.G. He was very disappointed and showed his displeasure. In a flash he said: You were far too busy thinking of the dead (Mazzini) of years ago to have any thought of the living, and Mussolini marched an army on Rome, took it without force, and became the Dictator of Italy.[1931]

Among the propositions formulated at the Conference was the proposal that central banks make a partial return to the gold standard, which had been dropped to print money to pay for the war. Central banks wanted a return to a gold-based economy to ease international trade and facilitate economic stability, but they wanted a gold standard that "conserved" gold stocks, with the gold remaining in the vaults and day-to-day transactions being conducted with representative paper notes. The partial return to the gold standard was done by permitting central banks to keep part of their reserves in currencies, which were themselves directly exchangeable for gold coins. However, citizens would not receive gold coins in exchange for their notes, unlike the pre-war gold standard.

On 16 April 1922, on the side-lines of Genoa, the Russian Soviet Federative Socialist Republic (RSFSR) and Germany signed the Treaty of Rapallo. It did not include military clauses and, contrary to contemporary rumour, it did not contain a secret additional protocol on military cooperation. This was negotiated in advance. Thus, the economic cooperation agreed at Rapallo mainly concerned activities that *de facto* circumvented military restrictions imposed at Versailles. Extensive secret military cooperation began immediately.[1932] With Rapallo removing the focus on Russia and Germany, the Conference stalled. Initially, the major powers agreed on a contingency package of financial aid to Russia, but the Allies could not agree on the final plan and no offer was made. The issue of German reparations stalled after Poincaré threatened to unilaterally invade Germany if she defaulted on her next payments. Lloyd George was increasingly undermined by heavy attacks in the London press, especially *The Times* on 8 May.[1933] Nevertheless, he offered a series of linked proposals, which would reduce Germany's liabilities for reparations, increase the French share of payments, and float an international loan to finance German payments, with the money from the loan going directly to France. But by the Conference's conclusion on 19 May, nothing was approved. Germany was expelled, France and Belgium withdrew, and the final draft communiqué to Russia was signed only by Britain, Italy, Japan, Poland, Romania, Switzerland, and Sweden, leaving out the key world powers except Britain. Russia rejected this document. The last decision was to set up another conference at The Hague to take up the same issues. Kenneth Morgan concluded: "Genoa was a watershed in international diplomacy… Never again would such a large, rambling assembly, on the lines of Paris in 1919, be convened, until San Francisco in 1945… There was too little detailed preparation, too much

---

1931 A. J. Silvester, *Rough Notes On Professor Thomas Jones, C.H., LL.D.*, January 1975: https://www.library.wales/fileadmin/fileadmin/docs_gwefan/amdanom_ni/cylchgrawn_llgc/cgr_erth_XXXVrh1_2010_3.pdf. Retrieved 28 May 2020. Mussolini was writing for his paper '*Il Popolo d'Italia*'.

1932 See I. O. Johnson, *Faustian Bargain: The Soviet-German Partnership and the Origins of the Second World War*, 2021, Oxford, Oxford University Press.

1933 Mills, *Genoa Conference*, p133. The editor, Wickham Steed, also in Genoa, detested Lloyd George.

generalized optimism, too many disparate issues muddled up with one another."[1934]

Back home, on 3 June, Lloyd George was in Criccieth to lay the foundation stone for the new Memorial Hall, accompanied by Margaret, in the presence of a large, enthusiastic gathering. The names of the 37 (actually 44) men of Criccieth who lost their lives were to be inscribed on panels in the inner Hall of Memory. A silver trowel was presented to Lloyd George who, in laying the stone, deposited a bottle containing a copy of the first subscription list, newspapers, a coin and a letter written by himself which read: "These young men died that the Dominion of Right and Reason should be more firmly established in the government of men." Having laid the stone Lloyd George said:

> I felt it my duty to come here to pay my tribute of respect to these fine young men for they did it in order to achieve justice for countries they knew not, for a people whose language they did not speak, for men of a race which were not their own kith and kin… They did it, for the cause of right and fair play, even for other lands… they will have died in vain if the nations do not acknowledge that right is supreme.[1935]

Now Winifred Coombe Tennant reappeared in Lloyd George's life. Through her close friendship with him, on 14 August 1922[1936] she was invited to act as a substitute delegate to the Third Assembly of the League of Nations, to be held between 4-30 September, making her the first woman to ever represent Britain at this organisation, and was tasked with being Lloyd George's 'eyes and ears' in Geneva. On 28 August she wrote sending Lloyd George a copy of her pamphlet *'The Mines and The Miners'* that Liberal Party H.Q. had just printed 25,000 copies of, and suggesting that he himself should "go to the Assembly at Geneva whilst it is in session."[1937]

From the moment she arrived at the League, she actively sought to publicise a conception of international affairs, founded on maternalistic principles similar to those espoused by Margaret Lloyd George, which held the involvement of mothers in the League to be vital to its success. She wrote in her 'League Journal' on her first day: "It is strange for me to imagine how we women endured to be shut out from all this, where the threads of our destiny are spun–and where our lives and those of our children have been sometimes bartered for a song."[1938] As historian Rob Laker notes, her connection to Lloyd George "was of as much interest to the French delegation, who took the opportunity… to vie for her influence, particularly as the Chanak crisis worsened. On 18 September, her diary entry notes with satisfaction her long discussion on international politics with 'a clever Frenchman' in the ILO (Albert Thomas) who, deploring the emerging rift between Britain and France, expressed his 'vehement admiration' for Lloyd George. Pleased to have finally found a Frenchman to whom she

---

1934 Morgan, *Consensus and Disunity*, p314-315. The United Nations Conference on International Organization (UNCIO), the 'San Francisco Conference', a convention of 50 Allied nations that took place 25 April–26 June 1945, resulting in the creation of the UN Charter.

1935 *The Times*, 5 June 1922, p15; R. D. Cadwalader, *Criccieth Memorial Hall 1922-2022*, 2022, Criccieth, p5.

1936 Coombe Tennant, p367. Diary entry for 14 August 1922.

1937 https://discovery.nationalarchives.gov.uk/details/r/6365d416-9f85-4d42-9a6a-fc6c7ff894f3. Retrieved 7 October 2021. Coombe Tennant, p369. Diary entry for 28 August 1922.

1938 Quoted in Laker, p21, from West Glamorgan Archive, Coombe Tennant Diary, D/DT 3978, p9.

could relate, she recalls that the two spent much of the night talking of Lloyd George, to whom she revealed herself to be a close ally."[1939]

Sadly, in late October, Coombe Tennant returned home to Neath–pausing only to call at No. 10 on Lloyd George's last day there–and faded into political obscurity. She stood as National Liberal candidate for the Forest of Dean in the November election but trailed third to the sitting Labour MP and a last-minute Independent Tory, despite a warm endorsement from Lloyd George on her election posters praising her "single-minded enthusiasm for all that is good and progressive".[1940] Winifred recorded the next day that it had been "a great experience".

After the disappointment of Genoa, and the attendant press criticism, what finally, and rather suddenly and irrevocably, brought Lloyd George down, was a 'scandal' over the awarding of honours. As Kenneth Rose noted: "The sale of honours to replenish party funds or their bestowal in return for political support is as old as parliamentary government itself."[1941] In practice there was no substantial difference between the awarding of honours and any other governmental act: ministers made proposals, the sovereign duly giving his consent. However, as honours were conferred in his name and usually bestowed by him in person, King George exercised his prerogative in this field to the limit, studying each proposal painstakingly. Even some of Asquith's nominations had been resisted by His Majesty, on grounds of 'incompetency' or nepotism.

The war, however, had seen a new class of faceless industrialists and financiers arise whose services, as Curzon put it in a memorandum of 1 April 1917, had "not been wholly untinged by the expectation of social preferment to come."[1942] Indeed, some of these 'new men' had been accommodated by Asquith's Liberal and Coalition administrations, but it was not until Lloyd George became Prime Minister that their aspirations were fully realised, at a cost. Kenneth Rose again:

> Between 1917 and 1922 there were four aspects of the distribution of honours which increasingly disturbed the King. They were the failure of the Prime Minister to consult him before promising titles to certain political or financial supporters; the number of honours recommended by the Prime Minister; the character of the recipients; and the use of go-betweens to sell the royal prerogative in the market-place.[1943]

The scandal erupted on 3 June 1922 when the list of new peers to mark the King's birthday was published: Sir Robert Borwick, Sir Joseph Robinson, Sir William Vestey, Sir Samuel Waring and Sir Archibald Williamson. Only Borwick–nominated by Austen Chamberlain–escaped the ensuing hostile public criticism and derision. In fact, Borwick "had made a number of large payments to *Unionist funds*."[1944] A "substantial cheque had passed to the managers of the Union Party Fund in respect to

---

[1939] Laker, p59-60, and quoting Coombe Tennant Diary, D/DT 3978, p35.
[1940] Coombe Tennant, p377-378.
[1941] Rose, p245.
[1942] Quoted in Rose, p247.
[1943] Rose, p247.
[1944] Cook, p330. Emphasis added.

Waring's peerage", while Vestey's "cheque was destined for the Liberal Coalition Whip's office".[1945] On 23 June, Robinson–a South African gold magnate convicted in 1921 as a war profiteer and fined £500,000–was belatedly persuaded to decline the honour.[1946] As Andrew Cook points out:

> It is no coincidence that the majority of sold peerages occurred during 1922. Both Lloyd George and Chamberlain knew that a general election in the later part of that year was more than likely and both therefore strove to accumulate as much money as possible for their campaign coffers.[1947]

But now King, Parliament and public opinion united in condemnation of tainted honours.

The King resented Lloyd George's "manipulation of the royal prerogative to secure the political support of the Press. In four years, nearly fifty proprietors and editors had become Privy Counsellors, peers, baronets and knights."[1948] In the world of industry and finance, 26 peerages, 130 baronetcies and 481 knighthoods were conferred, though of these some would naturally have been bestowed for "more conventional public service or by giving their money to genuine charities."[1949] Of course, during the Coalition, the Honours List was actually drawn up jointly by Lloyd George and the Tory Leader. Statistically:

> Of the eighty-two new peerages created between 1917 and 1922, no more than fourteen involved any monetary consideration. Of these fourteen, eight were actually nominated by Andrew Bonar Law and Austen Chamberlain, not by Lloyd George.[1950]

Nonetheless, the system was judged by its excesses, and in the ensuing public 'scandal' and in the popular imagination lasting until the present day, it was Lloyd George who was held in bad odour. Bowing to the near-universal outrage, on 17 July he rose in the Commons to defend his position and to appoint a Royal Commission:

> Are men to be ruled out because of such contributions? If you do not rule men out because they have contributed, you will always be liable to the retort that that has influenced you… If the system of party political honours is to be terminated, let the House deliberately make up its mind on that subject…
>
> … There is nothing dishonourable in rewarding an honourable act of service… whether a man be of the best or of the worst, an encouragement, a stimulus, a reward for him to do his duty always helps him along. If you abolish this system, there are two alternatives… I speak

1945 Ibid., p329-330. Vestey, a meat importer, was a wartime tax-evader; Waring, a war profiteer through government contracts; Williamson, an oil magnate, was accused of trading with the enemy during the war.
1946 Cullen, p116.
1947 Cook, p329.
1948 Rose, p249.
1949 Ibid., p250.
1950 Cook, p278.

> now as a fairly old politician… who believes in representative institutions, believes in the House of Commons, believes it is the finest Assembly of its kind in the whole world, and I want the House carefully to consider… what is the alternative to the system… The danger is that political organisation will collapse, and the alternative to political organisation is political chaos…
>
> The responsibilities of the Chief Minister must, in our judgment, remain. You cannot transfer that responsibility to anyone else. He is the man who is responsible to the Sovereign, he is the man who is responsible to public opinion, and he is the man who must be responsible to the House of Commons. He is the man who can be arraigned, and who should be arraigned. Therefore no Committee which you set up can relieve the Chief Minister of the Crown of the main, and as far as the House of Commons is concerned, the sole responsibility for the advice given to the Sovereign. The whole question is whether there is any method by which you can strengthen his hands, and help him to discharge a difficult, delicate and invidious task… That is obviously a question that ought to be considered calmly… by men who are quite independent.
>
> As it would deal with the prerogative of the Crown, it must be a Royal Commission, and *the Government is prepared to assent to the appointment of a Royal Commission, to consider and advise on the procedure to be adopted in future to assist the Prime Minister in making recommendations to His Majesty of the names of persons deserving of special honour…*[1951]

Even Asquith, while still 'digging' at Lloyd George in his opening remarks, defended the principle and practice of rewarding contributors to party funds with honours, emphasizing: "You will never obtain your purpose… unless the members of a great political organisation realise that it is not only their right, but their duty to put their hand into their pocket and contribute to party funds… You cannot carry on political life, you cannot organise political warfare, except by these means."[1952]

Chaired by Lord Dunedin, the Commission recommended, first, that a committee of three Privy Councillors should be formed to scrutinize the records of all candidates for honours before their names were submitted to the sovereign; second, that an Act be passed imposing penalties on those who promised to secure honours in return for payment and vice versa. Arthur Henderson, a member of the Commission, "regretted that his colleagues had declined to inquire into previous transactions and to expose the names of both touts and customers in that unsavoury trade. He also urged that never again should an honour be conferred for political services alone."[1953] He was ignored, but he stuck to his principles his whole life. A major attack on Lloyd George's alleged corruption in the Lords followed, resulting in the Honours (Prevention of Abuses) Act 1925. Although what Lloyd George had done was not illegal, under his tenure the practice had become more systematic and brazen: it became known that he had awarded honours and titles to businessmen in return for cash–£10,000 for a knighthood, £30,000 for a baronetcy, £50,000 and upwards for a peerage–through 'political fixer'

[1951]https://api.parliament.uk/historic-hansard/commons/1922/jul/17/prime-ministers-statement#S5CV0156P0_19220717_HOC_303. Retrieved 23 April 2020. Emphasis added.
[1952]https://api.parliament.uk/historic-hansard/commons/1922/jul/17/prime-ministers-statement#S5CV0156P0_19220717_HOC_310. Retrieved 9 October 2019.
[1953] Rose, p252.

John Maundy Gregory[1954], having hired him as a broker to obtain funds for the United Constitutional Party he was planning to form in May-June 1920.[1955]

Long after resigning as Prime Minister, on 3 May 1928, Lloyd George privately commented on the sale of honours to Tory fundraiser J. C. C. Davidson:

> You and I know perfectly well it is a far cleaner method of filling the Party chest than the methods used in the United States or the Socialist Party… Here a man gives £40,000 to the Party and gets a baronetcy. If he comes to the Leader of the Party and says I subscribe largely to the Party funds, you must do this or that, we can tell him to go to the devil. The attachment of the brewers to the Conservative Party was the closest approach to political corruption in this country. The worst of it is you cannot defend it in public, but it keeps politics far cleaner than any other method of raising funds.[1956]

This view, if expressed seriously, naturally does not conform even to modern-day less-than-perfect standards, but by the standards of the day it was not exceptional. As Rose observes: "the Conservatives at that time had been no less active than their Liberal partners in the sale of honours, merely less successful in disposing of their wares and retaining the proceeds."[1957] It was a tawdry business all round. Both three-time Tory premier Baldwin and Ramsay MacDonald–figurehead premier of the National Government of 1931-1935, consisting of a majority of Tories–had 'dirty hands' in this regard: "Lloyd George was not the only Prime Minister of King George V to muddy the Fountain of Honour."[1958]

Lloyd George's problem stemmed back as far as November 1917 and was an obvious one. With the end of the war and elections impending, he clearly foresaw the split that would occur among 'The Liberals' and the inevitable challenges to his leadership that would take place. The Liberal Party machinery was in Asquith's hands and that of the Tory's in Bonar Law's. Having no significant capital, unlike most other landed, moneyed, aristocratic politicians of both major parties at that time, Lloyd George would have to devise his own. With Freddie Guest:

> … as his chief administrative lieutenant, therefore, he slowly and quietly began to build up a political fund which would enable him to operate as an independent force. His wealthier supporters contributed to this fund, but the really lucrative source of revenue would come from

1954 Rowland, *Lloyd George*, p448. Maundy Gregory (1877-1941), later worked for the Tories; Cullen, p193. On 21 February 1933, after intervention from senior Tory John Davidson, he pleaded 'guilty' and was convicted of selling honours under the 1925 Act, receiving the lightest possible sentence of a £50 fine and two months in jail. Davidson later admitted: "He (Gregory) was met at the prison gates by a friend of mine who drove him in a motor car to Dover, took him to France, ensconced him in previously arranged accommodation, gave him a sum of money and promised him a quarterly pension, on condition that he never disclosed his identity or made any reference to his past."; R. Rhodes James, *Memoirs Of A Conservative: J. C. C. Davidson's Memoirs And Papers, 1910-37*, 1969, London, Weidenfeld & Nicolson, p288.

1955 Cook, pp87-88. This was one of nine names considered, plans foundering over control of funding.

1956 Quoted in Rhodes James, p279, Campbell, *Lloyd George*, p174-175.

1957 Rose, p253.

1958 Ibid., p255.

> those people–newspaper proprietors, rich industrialists, profiteers and landowners–who wanted titles for themselves and their descendants. There was nothing novel in such an arrangement... but Lloyd George was in a hurry and could not be bothered to work it as discreetly as his predecessors had done. If there were really people about who were foolish enough to want to pay for the privilege of featuring in the annual Honours List, then he saw no reason why their cheques should not be made out to the Lloyd George Political Fund and their money put to some useful purpose.[1959]

This was so very much in Lloyd George's psychological make-up: having no interest in such useless worldly trappings himself, he clearly saw those who did as having more money than sense.[1960] There is no suggestion that he ever took money for personal aggrandisement or luxury, or for reasons of vanity, it was through sheer political need, but that cut no ice in the politically, socially and economically depressed mood of the time. By autumn 1922 Lloyd George's position, leading the fractured and minority Liberals in coalition with the increasingly restless majority Tories, who made partisan political capital by attacking him as lacking any executive accountability as Prime Minister, claiming that he rarely appeared at Cabinet, became untenable.

The final straw was the Chanak Crisis[1961], a war scare that arose in September 1922 between Britain and the Grand National Assembly of Turkey, who had come to power with the collapse of the Ottoman Empire. The crisis, in the offing throughout 1921 and the first eight months of 1922, was caused by Turkish efforts to resist Greek attempts to control the western provinces of Turkey and to restore Turkish rule in the Allied occupied territories, primarily in Constantinople and Eastern Thrace. On 26 August, Turkish troops launched a major attack on the Greeks and began driving them back to Smyrna on the Aegean, and also to Chanak on the Dardanelles where British, French and Italian troops were positioned in the Dardanelles Neutral Zone.

The last day the Commons sat before recess was 4 August, and neither Lloyd George nor anybody else could know that it would be the last time he addressed the House as Prime Minister. He spoke on the Near East, stating: "it is desirable above all things that peace should be established in that portion of the world. The Government have no other desire. There is, however, one very important consideration, and it is that the peace must be a just and fair peace, and one which is likely to be enduring."[1962] He nonetheless made it abundantly clear that he supported the Greek position.

In Cabinet on 7 September Foreign Secretary Lord Curzon proposed that Britain should retain the Gallipoli Peninsula, which it had occupied since December 1918. Churchill supported him, stating "If the Turks take Gallipoli and Constantinople we should have lost the whole fruits of our victory."[1963] Lloyd George agreed. On 9 September, the Turks took Smyrna, ending Greek presence in Asia Minor.

---

1959 Rowland, *Lloyd George*, p447-448.

1960 His own acceptance of an earldom at the very end of his long life was for very different reasons.

1961 Chanak refers to Çanakkale, a city on the Anatolian side of the Dardanelles Strait. For a thorough overview of events, see D. Walder, *The Chanak Affair*, 1969, London, Hutchinson.

1962 https://api.parliament.uk/historic-hansard/commons/1922/aug/04/near-east#S5CV0157P0_19220804_HOC_127. Retrieved 14 October 2022.

1963 Gilbert, *Churchill*, p450.

The local British commander in Chanak, Brigadier Digby Shuttleworth, decided not to withdraw his 1,000 troops, but to remain. Lloyd George supported him, telling the Cabinet on 15 September of his determination to keep the Turks out of Europe, by force if necessary. Ministers were now unanimous that the Neutral Zone on both sides of the Straits must be held, and that to prevent the Turks crossing to the European shore two towns on the Asiatic side must be defended, namely Chanak, and Ismid on the Constantinople-Baghdad railway. In Curzon's absence, Churchill drafted a telegram stating: "[We] should be glad to know whether the Dominion Governments wish to associate themselves with the action we are taking, and whether they will desire to be represented by a contingent?" The telegram was sent with Lloyd George's approval, and in his name.[1964]

On 16 September Lloyd George and Churchill also drafted a press communiqué urging that: "Adequate force must be available to guard the freedom of the Straits and defend the deep-water line between Europe and Asia against a violent and hostile Turkish aggression." Fatally, this was published in British and Dominion newspapers the following morning before Lloyd George's explanatory telegram to the Dominion Prime Ministers had been decoded in the respective capitals. The Australian and Canadian Governments were naturally angry both at not being consulted before the peremptory, public call to arms, and at the appeal itself. Australian Prime Minister Billy Hughes telegraphed "In a good cause we are prepared to venture our all, in a bad one, not a single man." Canadian PM Mackenzie King replied that Canada would not automatically support Britain if it came to war. South African PM Jan Smuts made no official reply at all. Only New Zealand PM William Massey and Newfoundland PM Richard Squires agreed to support 'the Mother Country'.[1965]

Lloyd George and Churchill remained convinced that a show of force would deter the Turks from attempting to cross the Dardanelles. In Cabinet they continued to seek means of reinforcing the Chanak garrison, and they were supported by the Chancellor of the Exchequer, Robert Horne, and the First Lord of the Admiralty, Lord Lee. However, on 18 September the French and Italians withdrew their troops from Chanak and Ismid, leaving Britain to stand alone. On 20 September Churchill now sounded a note of caution in Cabinet, stating "All our misfortunes had arisen in the past from trying to do that for which we had not the strength." The Cabinet then decided that Chanak alone should be held, but the next day the *Daily Mail* reflected growing public concern in its banner headline "Get out of Chanak." Resolving not to bow to press pressure, on 22 September Lloyd George appointed Churchill as chairman of a Committee of Ministers to take overall control of the transfer of troops, ships and aircraft to Chanak. The next day 1,100 Turkish cavalry entered the Neutral Zone south of Chanak and advanced to within sight of the British fortified positions. Fortunately, no shots were fired.

Churchill had been right; Britain did not have the strength to resist. By 27 September, the 3,500 British troops were faced by 23,000 Turkish soldiers. Churchill suggested evacuating the British forces

---

1964 Ibid.

1965 https://paperspast.natlib.govt.nz/newspapers/CHP19220920.2.43?end_date=31-12-1923&items_per_page=10&query=chanak+telegram&snippet=true&sort_by=byDA&start_date=01-01-1922. Retrieved 24 January 2024; Gaw, p313; *The Times*, 19 September 1922, p10.

to the European shore, but Lloyd George was insistent that "The evacuation of Chanak, having regard to all that had happened, would be the greatest loss of prestige which could possibly be inflicted on the British Empire." Churchill replied that defeat would be even more disastrous. Lloyd George seems to have been in an unusually bellicose mood, on 29 September instructing the War Office to order the senior officer at Constantinople, Lieutenant General Charles Harington, to inform the Turks that, unless they withdrew by a time to be settled by him, all British forces would open fire. Fortunately, Harington decided to delay in sending the ultimatum, counting on negotiations leading to a settlement. The next day Marshal Mustafa Kemal Atatürk initiated the opening of armistice talks, telling the British that he had ordered his troops to avoid any incident at Chanak, offering to withdraw from the Chanak area if the British would withdraw to the European shore, and nominating Mudanya as the venue for peace negotiations. The Turks were not prepared to try to drive the British into the sea. The parties met there on 3 October and agreed to the terms of the Armistice of Mudanya on 11 October, two hours before British forces were due to attack.

The same day, the highly experienced British High Commissioner, Sir Horace Rumbold, reported; "Factors which probably determined the Turks to sign were our display of force, and their knowledge that we would use it in the last resort."[1966] However, public opinion in Britain had now been so excited, that it could no longer be calmed by the facts that war had been averted and British policy–*Lloyd George's policy*–had largely been successful. For a time, war between Britain and Turkey had seemed possible. The pro-Turk Tories in the coalition government refused to follow Lloyd George, who with Churchill and Lord Birkenhead, was pro-Greek. Furthermore, the public had been alarmed by the Chanak episode and the possibility of going to war again. It further undermined Lloyd George that he had not fully consulted the Dominion prime ministers.

Lloyd George's mishandling of the crisis contributed to his downfall via the Carlton Club meeting. The crisis raised the issue of who decided on war for the British Empire and was Canada's first assertion of diplomatic independence from London. The Chanak incident led to Balfour's definition of Britain and the dominions as "autonomous Communities within the British Empire, equal in status, in no way subordinate one to another in any aspect of the domestic or internal affairs, though united by a common allegiance to the Crown, and freely associated as members of the British Commonwealth of Nations."[1967] British and French forces were ultimately withdrawn from the Neutral Zone, following the ratification of the Treaty of Lausanne on 24 July 1923. On 11 December 1931, Balfour's formula was enacted into law through the Statute of Westminster 1931, which explicitly declared that the Dominions had the power to declare war.

On 7 October 1922, Bonar Law had a letter published by *The Times*, outlining his views on future British policy in the Near East, which differed from that of the Coalition, stating that "We cannot alone act as the policeman of the world. The financial and social condition of this country makes that impossible."[1968] Lloyd George made a vigorous defence of himself and the Coalition's policy at the

---

[1966] Quoted in Gilbert, *Churchill*, p453.
[1967] Balfour Declaration of 15 November issued by the 1926 Imperial Conference of British Empire leaders in London.
[1968] *The Near East Pronouncement by Mr Bonar Law*, Correspondence, *The Times*, 7 October 1922, p11.

Manchester Reform Club on 14 October, telling his 300 listeners "It is always a mistake to threaten unless you mean it, and it is because not merely we threatened, but we meant it, and the Turks knew that we meant it, that you have peace now."[1969] It was, however, too late, the damage was too great. On 18 October, a by-election, occasioned by the sudden death of the Liberal incumbent, was held in Newport, widely seen as a crucial litmus test of the viability of the continuance of the Coalition at the forthcoming elections. The Liberal candidate ran simply as a 'Liberal', declining to run as either a Lloyd George or an Asquith supporter, instead using the slogan "reunited Liberalism" implying opposition to the Coalition. Thus, there was no official Coalition candidate standing. The result was an upset. The Tory won handsomely, with Labour second and the Liberal trailing a poor third. Many interpreted the result as a rejection of the Coalition, even though locally it appeared more a rejection of Labour and a vote for the Tories.

Tory leader Austen Chamberlain, facing a growing rebellion amongst Tory MPs over the Party's continued support for the Coalition, had called a three-line whip meeting of MPs at the Carlton Club–then at Pall Mall–to decide the issue.[1970] Expecting a Labour victory in Newport, it was scheduled for 11.00 am on 19 October in the hope that the result would persuade many Tories of the merits of remaining in alliance with the Liberals as the only way to keep Labour out of power. 286 of the 335 MPs heeded the call. Chamberlain, Balfour and most Tory leaders supported Lloyd George. Chamberlain was, however, out of touch with rank-and-file opinion, and they rejected the Coalition. Another factor was the attitude of Lord Birkenhead, again displaying his lack of political acumen, his hectoring of the junior ministers and backbenchers playing a part in their withdrawal of support.[1971] The main attack, however, came from Stanley Baldwin, then President of the Board of Trade, who spoke of Lloyd George as:

> A dynamic force, and it is from that very fact that our troubles, in our opinion, arise. A dynamic force is a very terrible thing; it may crush you, but it is not necessarily right.
>
> It is owing to that dynamic force, and that remarkable personality, that the Liberal Party, to which he formerly belonged, has been smashed to pieces; and it is my firm conviction that, in time, the same will happen to our party.[1972]

He was reluctantly supported by Bonar Law. They sealed Lloyd George's fate with a vote of 187-86, with at least 12 abstentions, in favour of the motion moved by Ernest Pretyman "That this meeting… declares its opinion that the Conservative Party, whilst willing to cooperate with Coalition Liberals, fights the election as an independent party, with its own leader and its own programme."[1973] Chamberlain immediately resigned the party leadership rather than act against what he believed to be

---

[1969] *The Times*, 16 October 1922, p17.

[1970] Bennett, p10.

[1971] Beaverbrook, *Decline And Fall*, p200-203.

[1972] Young, p41.

[1973] The exact figures have been a matter of lasting confusion and debate. See Kinnear, p124-134, 221-242; Bennett, p7. Ernest Pretyman (1860-1931), Tory MP for Chelmsford, 1908-1923.

his duty. On 23 October he was succeeded by Bonar Law, whose views and intentions he had predicted the evening before the unanimous vote at a private meeting.

At No. 10, Lloyd George accepted his fate with remarkably good grace. He told his close Welsh confidant, the Deputy Cabinet Secretary, Tom Jones, that "the moment he had learned the result of the Newport election and heard definitely that Bonar was going to the meeting, he had told Stamfordham [the King's Private Secretary] that he would be resigning in the course of the day." Lloyd George duly drove to Buckingham Palace the same afternoon and at 4.15 pm submitted his resignation to King George V, who accepted it with regret, recording in his diary: "I am sorry he is going, but some day he will be Prime Minister again."[1974] On meeting him at No. 10 immediately after the vote, Maurice Hankey reported that Lloyd George was "jaunty and cheerful, and showed no sign of regret at leaving office."[1975] George Riddell said to him on his return from Buckingham Palace "Well, the die is cast!", the now former Prime Minister replying "Yes, and I am glad of it. One could not go on under the circumstances."[1976] The next day, "he was in good fettle, and not in the least cast down"[1977], and on taking his formal leave of his staff on 23 October was "full of fun"[1978] and "absolutely hilarious"[1979], at 4.00 pm motoring away with his son Gwilym to Churt. His primary personal reaction, after seventeen years in extremely stressful high office, seems to have been one of relief. To Winifred Coombe Tennant, he said "I've not been so happy for months. I was getting worried–bothered–now I'm a free man. It's going to be a great fight."[1980] His first word to Tom Jones was '*Rhyddid*'–'Freedom'[1981]–and on leaving London for Leeds on 20 October to receive the freedom of that city, he told reporters "I come as a free man, I have shaken the burden from my shoulders."[1982]

Bonar Law became both leader of the Conservative Party and Prime Minister on 23 October 1922.[1983] A general election was called for on 15 November, Bonar Law appealing for "tranquillity and stability both at home and abroad". Asquith's daughter, Violet Bonham-Carter, told an audience at Paisley "We have to choose between one man suffering from St Vitus's Dance [Lloyd George] and another from Sleeping Sickness [Bonar Law]."[1984] There were around 29 seats where Liberals stood against one another, which may have cost them at least 14 seats, ten of them to Labour, so in theory a reunited Liberal Party would have been much closer to, possibly even leading, Labour in terms of seats. However, in reality the two factions were on poor terms.

---

1974 Quoted in Nicolson, p481. See also Rowland, *Lloyd George*, p584; Rose, p264.

1975 Roskill, *Hankey Volume II, 1919-1931*, 1972, London, William Collins, p296-297.

1976 Riddell, *Diaries*, 1986, p378-379.

1977 Ibid., p297.

1978 Jones, *Whitehall Diary*, Vol.I, p216.

1979 Roskill, *Hankey* Volume II, p299-300. Lloyd George was the first Prime Minister to be filmed leaving office: see 'End of an era for the "Welsh Wizard"' at: http://www.youtube.com/watch?v=GYeLTdW2b4c.

1980 Quoted in Coombe Tennant, p375. Diary entry for 23 October 1923. Like many, Winifred thought Lloyd George would be back, adding "He will yet play a big part in the history of this country, I feel certain."

1981 Jones, *Whitehall Diary*, Vol.I, p212.

1982 *The Times*, 21 October 1922.

1983 Bonar Law was dying of terminal throat cancer, resigning on 20 May 1923, the shortest-serving PM of the 20th century. He died on 30 October. After his funeral in Westminster Abbey, Asquith reputedly commented unkindly "It is fitting that we should have buried the Unknown Prime Minister by the side of the Unknown Soldier." Blake, p531.

1984 Jenkins, *Asquith*, p495.

At the election, the Tories won comfortably, taking 344 seats to Labour's 142, with the Liberals taking 115, divided between 62 Asquithian Liberals and 53 coalitionist National Liberals. It was an election fought largely on "atmosphere, personalities, and party image."[1985] Churchill was one of the most conspicuous of the defeated supporters of the former Prime Minister as, uniquely, standing as a National Liberal in Dundee with no Tory opposition, he lost his seat to a Scottish Prohibitionist. Significantly, the results made it the first election in which Labour surpassed the combined strength of both Liberal parties in votes and seats. It had been the only major party to present any clear policies, offering a reformist manifesto–*'Labour's Call to the People'*–of nationalisation for the mines and railways, the imposition of a levy on financial capital, land taxation, Indian self-government, and the revision of the peace treaties, with a reduction of German reparations. It promised a higher standard of living for workers, higher wages, and better housing. Some of this was clearly an attempt to steal Lloyd George's clothes.

Towards the end of the election campaign, Lloyd George moved closer to Labour, bidding for working-class support by contrasting his own political record with that of Socialism. At Llanelli on 11 November he stated, with some justification: "There is no British minister who has ever devoted so much energy, made more liberal provision for the misfortunes of the wage-earning classes than I have done."[1986] In his own seat of Caernarfon Boroughs, he was re-elected unopposed for the only time in his long career. On leaving office, Lloyd George did not seem dissatisfied with his record, his own assessment being remarkably modest, not even mentioning his pre-premiership achievements, telling C. P. Scott on 6 December 1922:

> I cannot accept the part often proposed to me of a traitor to Liberalism who can only be taken back as a penitent. As a matter of fact the record of Liberal measures passed by the Coalition Government is a fine one–the greatest measure of Irish self-government ever proposed or thought of, a very great measure of franchise extension, a remarkable temperance measure, a not insignificant measure of land reform which accepts my land valuation survey as its basis, an important international agreement as to disarmament.[1987]

What nobody, including Lloyd George himself, could or would have predicted, was that this great leader of the nation and champion of the people would never hold public office again. Megan's perspective on her father's downfall was shown in a letter to her sister Olwen on 25 October 1922:

> Tada had wonderful receptions both at Manchester & Leeds & made wonderful speeches in both places. The people are absolutely with him, altho' very tired of the government, more

---

[1985] Campbell, *Lloyd George*, p34.
[1986] Quoted in Campbell, *Lloyd George*, p35.
[1987] C. P. Scott Papers, BM Add. MSS 50,906 (FF.206-7), Quoted in Rowland, *Lloyd George*, p585.

particularly because of its being a coalition than anything else. Whatever happens Tada will be in power. He will be tremendous in opposition–& Bonar [Law] knows it.[1988]

[1988] Morgan, *Family Letters*, p197.

# 6

## 'THE WIZARD IN THE WINGS', 1922-1945

Lloyd George was only 59 when he resigned the premiership. He never again held executive power, and the effective waste of the rest of his active life and fertile mind stands as a rebuke to the whole British nation as it underwent a long period of traumatic change. Throughout the 1920s Lloyd George remained prominent in politics, with predictions of his imminent return being common. He still controlled a large fund–estimated at between £1m and £3m [£72.62m-£217.85m in 2025] from his investments in newspaper ownership and from his sale of titles.

A week after the election, on 22 November 1922, Lloyd George published the first of many articles he wrote after leaving office, for a considerable fee, for the Hearst Press of America. Syndicated around the world and published in Britain, first in the *Daily Chronicle* and *Daily Telegraph*, later in the *Sunday News* and various local papers, they were often forthright and critical of the government of the day, often in turn earning their author criticism for allegedly attacking his country in the foreign press. Lloyd George always retorted that writing was now his only source of income. On his death on 11 August 1919, Dunfermline-born billionaire philanthropist Andrew Carnegie left Lloyd George a bequest of £2,000 per annum for his war services to the nation.[1989]

Lloyd George's first article was entitled *The Moral of the Election. Tragic Lesson for Liberalism. The Future of Parties.* If the divided Liberals did not reunite, he held out another prospect:

> Progressive minds are by no means confined to the Liberal Party. I have met and worked with them in the Conservative Party, and the election will have taught many men and women in the Labour Party that violent and extravagant proposals impede progress. If the limits are not too narrowly drawn, this Parliament will witness the effective association of men of many parties who are genuinely concerned in the advancement of mankind along the paths of peace and progress for the attainment of their common ideals.[1990]

Lloyd George continued by attacking the workings of the electoral system itself. He pointed out that Bonar Law had won a parliamentary majority with a minority of votes cast.[1991] This discredited and thereby threatened democracy–this same anomaly might work to the advantage of Labour next time,

---

1989 Rowland, *Lloyd George*, p514.

1990 Quoted in Campbell, *Lloyd George*, p42-43.

1991 The Tories won 38.5% of the popular vote, Labour 29.7%, Asquith's Liberals 18.9%, Lloyd George's Liberals 9.9%. Despite this, the Tories took 55.9% of the seats.

and it would mean that a minority could always attain power. The moral that Lloyd George drew from this "was not so much the need for electoral reform–already a Liberal demand–but rather that no party on its own could guarantee stable Government, and that the majority of moderate men of all parties should therefore stand together."[1992]

On 8 March 1923, two Independent Liberal MPs, James Hogge and Cyril Entwistle, in consultation with Lloyd George, with fellow MP Alexander Shaw acting as principal 'go-between', published a memorandum signed by 73 members calling for Liberal reunion[1993], backed by the 'Lloyd Georgeite' *Daily Chronicle* and the 'Asquithian' *Liberal Magazine*. The parliamentary parties duly held two joint meetings on 12 and 20 March, the second voting by 41-12 in favour of a resolution that "a consultative committee consisting of Mr. Asquith, Sir John Simon, Mr. Lloyd George, and Sir Alfred Mond should be formed to discuss policy in the House and make such arrangements for a common programme as they deemed advisable."[1994] Asquith, true to form, had no intention of participating in such essential activity, the next evening dismissing it, pouring:

> … scorn on the proposal of the deputation. Suppose, he said, he and Mr. Lloyd George were to meet, what were they to discuss? Every day he was receiving messages from the constituencies urging them not to compromise or in any way depart from their great Liberal tradition. Mr. Asquith found the meeting fully in sympathy with him, and a resolution was carried with one dissentient to the effect that "regular and continuous co-operation in the division lobby and the constituencies should be a condition precedent to the setting up of any formal machinery for Liberal reunion."[1995]

On 22 March Lloyd George prophetically said "If we do not reunite, Liberalism is done as a national driving force. For that reason, I have welcomed every proposal for reunion put forward by Liberals of both sections, and I do not see what more I can do."[1996]

However, reunion was opposed by senior Asquith supporters like John Simon, Viscount Gladstone and Charles Masterman. By July, Asquith was superficially friendly to Lloyd George and consulted him, but pointedly did not include him in the Shadow Cabinet. Asquith wanted Lloyd George to initiate matters, but although the latter put out feelers to senior Asquith supporters he insisted that he was "neither a suppliant nor a penitent".[1997] Asquith felt that with Lloyd George's faction declining in strength he had everything to gain by waiting, while too quick an approach would antagonise the Labour leaders who hated Lloyd George and whose support he might need for a future Lib-Lab coalition. Asquith's "gloating" over the defeat of Coalition Liberals in 1922 is unpleasant evidence that "the most important factor influencing Asquith against quick reunion was his personal dislike of

---

1992 Campbell, *Lloyd George*, p43.
1993 Scott, p.437; Campbell, *Lloyd George*, p62.
1994 *Annual Register: 1923*, Vol.165, 1924, London, Ed. M. Epstein, Longmans, Green, p27.
1995 Ibid., p27.
1996 *Lloyd George Liberal Magazine*, April 1923, p528.
1997 Spender and Asquith, Vol.II, p341.

Lloyd George and his desire for vengeance."[1998]

At this time Lloyd George got a pivotal new staff member from the Cabinet Secretariat. Introduced to him by Hankey, Albert Sylvester served as the indefatigable, dedicated Principal Private Secretary–a title he asked for–to Lloyd George from summer 1923 until the latter's death. Grandson Bengy related that Lloyd George picked him when he heard Sylvester was the fastest Pitman shorthand recorder on record. Aged 21, he had won a competition to find the fastest typist in Britain[1999] , attaining champion speeds of 210 words a minute in shorthand and 80 in typing.[2000]

The political situation was transformed when Stanley Baldwin, Prime Minister since May, came out in favour of protection at Plymouth on 22 October 1923. As a declared free trader himself, Lloyd George was obliged, at least formally, to submit to Asquith's leadership. Parliament was dissolved on 16 November, and the election was set for 6 December. Baldwin feared and despised Lloyd George, and one of his principal aims was to keep him out of power. He later claimed that he had adopted tariffs, which cost the Tories their majority, out of concern that Lloyd George was about to do so on his return from his 5 October-6 November tour of North America. Although there was press speculation that Lloyd George would do so, or–according to the *Observer* and *Spectator*–adopt US-style prohibition to appeal to newly enfranchised women voters, there is no evidence that this was his intent, although clearly Baldwin believed it to be so.[2001]

Lloyd George had been invited to the US by former Ambassador to the UK, John W. Davis[2002] nearly a year before, and the purpose of his tour to the USA and Canada was to personally thank both countries for their aid during the Great War. Margaret, Megan, and secretary A. J. Sylvester accompanied him. The party arrived on RMS *Mauretania* to a ticker-tape reception in New York on 5 October where Lloyd George delivered a speech, then travelled to Montreal, Canada. Other Canadian cities on the tour included Ottawa, Toronto, Niagara Falls, Hamilton, and Winnipeg. After this, he travelled back to the US to St. Paul and Minneapolis on 16 October, continuing on to Chicago, Springfield, St. Louis, Louisville, Indianapolis, Pittsburgh, and Washington DC. The tour–largely arranged by the Welsh-American '*Gorsedd*', notably through a newspaper, '*The Druid*', in Pittsburgh–was a personal triumph for Lloyd George, being acclaimed wherever he went.[2003] He covered some 6,000 miles in a special train and made over 80 speeches. In the Mount Royal Arena, Montreal, on 8 October, he became the first British politician to use a microphone before the 15,000 people packed inside and thousands more outside. At an outdoor venue in Cleveland, Ohio, on 23 October, he addressed a record-breaking crowd estimated at 100,000.[2004]

Many of his addresses were cabled to newspapers around the globe, and in them he made no secret of his sympathy for Germany and his belief in the importance of taking a lenient attitude toward her

---

1998 Kinnear, p213; also p37-44 for other references to Asquith's "personal revenge" and "vendetta", despite Lloyd George's attempts at reconciliation. As Roy Jenkins put it "The anti-Pope was almost as strong as the Pope"; *Asquith*, 1978, p496.

1999 *Albert James Sylvester*, *The Times*, 28 October 1989, p12; (24 November 1889–27 October 1989).

2000 Sylvester, *Life*, p11.

2001 See Campbell, *Lloyd George*, p47-48.

2002 John W. Davis (1873-1955), US Solicitor General, 1913-1918, Ambassador to the UK, 1918-1921.

2003 Rowland, *Lloyd George*, p599.

2004 *Cleveland Plain Dealer*, 24 October 1923, p1.

for the sake of future peace. His statements reached into upper echelons of American political power, with some influential Americans now starting to express a wish to re-engage with Europe and its reconstruction.[2005] In Washington he met former President Wilson, but more importantly, the new President Calvin Coolidge[2006] and Secretary of State Charles Evans Hughes.[2007] In a speech in Ottawa on 9 October, Lloyd George had revived a proposal made by Hughes at New Haven, Connecticut in 29 December 1922 to appoint an International Commission of economic experts to set the amount of Germany's indemnity and the method of payment. The British Government had ignored it–as had the French–a fact of which Lloyd George opined "It is one of the blunders of history that this should have been overlooked, one of the blunders which lead to catastrophies."[2008] In the ensuing press sensation, the same day Coolidge repeated Hughes proposal, with the proviso "it is for any foreign Government that is interested in it to take it up of their own consideration."[2009] "The British note of acceptance was sent on 13 October, the American reply on the 15th, and on the 26th both notes were made public."[2010] The French were thus pressured into agreement.

On 25 October, at a dinner in Washington, a message was read from Coolidge: "I am certain that Mr Lloyd George's visit to America has been a piece of good fortune both for his country and our own, and for the cause of international accord… It has been a fine thing for our people to become better acquainted with this eminent leader in civilisation's struggle to maintain itself, and I hope he will feel… that his effort in bringing his message to us has not been entirely a vain one."[2011] *The Times*, when publishing the message, acknowledged that this was firm evidence that Lloyd George had "stimulated, somewhat, the laggard American sense of the peculiar and joint responsibility of English-speaking peoples everywhere."[2012] A few days later the paper grudgingly acknowledged his part in rousing public opinion, stating "He probably contributed to its crystallisation in the sense of intervention."[2013] Hughes duly selected Charles Dawes[2014], former Director of the US Bureau of the Budget, to head a committee to assess Germany's capacity to pay reparations and to produce a revised payment plan, starting its work in Paris on 14 January 1924, reporting on 9 April, the Allies and Germany accepting the plan on 16 August.

Lloyd George retained his interest in the American Civil War, and his trip included a tour of the battlefield of Gettysburg, Pennsylvania, the war's turning point, the great battle being fought on 1-3 July 1863, the year of his birth. Local papers enthused:

---

2005 Rudman, p143-146.

2006 Calvin 'Silent Cal' Coolidge (1872-1933), lawyer, President, 1923-1928.

2007 Charles Evans Hughes Sr. (1862-1948), son of a Welshman, jurist, Secretary of State, 1921-1925.

2008 https://trove.nla.gov.au/newspaper/article/31193200/2762752. Retrieved 29 November 2024.

2009 https://coolidgefoundation.org/resources/press-conference-october-9-1923/. Retrieved 29 November 2024.

2010 Thomas Jones, *Lloyd George*, p206.

2011 Sylvester, *Real Lloyd George*, p138. Lloyd George's visit was long remembered in the US and later recalled by President's Franklin D. Roosevelt and John F. Kennedy.

2012 *The Times*, 26 October 1923, p11.

2013 *The Times*, 5 November 1923, Quoted in Thomas Jones, *Lloyd George*, p206.

2014 Charles Dawes (1865-1951), banker, general, diplomat, Vice President, 1925-1929, co-recipient of the Nobel Peace Prize in 1925 for his work on the Dawes Plan.

> On October 27, 1923, David Lloyd George… drove from Washington DC to Gettysburg with Secretary of War John W. Weeks… [who] acted as the official battlefield guide… The former prime minister spent considerable time at the Bloody Angle and in the spot in the National Cemetery where Abraham Lincoln delivered his Gettysburg address… [He]… later travelled to Richmond to visit the Fredericksburg and Wilderness battlefields. After Richmond, Lloyd George and his party travelled to Philadelphia and Scranton, the latter so he could observe Welsh mining communities in the United States.[2015]

At Richmond, Lloyd George met some Confederate veterans, and on 28 October he visited Guinea's Station, near Chancellorsville, where General 'Stonewall' Jackson died of his wounds on 10 May 1863. He remarked: "That old house witnessed the downfall of the Southern Confederacy. No doubt the history of America would have to be rewritten had 'Stonewall' Jackson lived." In Minneapolis, he was inducted into the Sioux tribe by Chief Brave Eagle as '*Wambli Napa*'–'Chief Two Eagles–Eagle in Peace and Eagle in War'. In the same city, Jewish citizens, through Dr. Maurice Lefkovit, presented him with a parchment testimonial in recognition of his services in the attempt to establish in the Holy Land a national home for the Jews.

The personal focus of his tour was his hero, Abraham Lincoln. At Manchester, Vermont, on 6 October, he briefly met Lincoln's 80-year-old son Robert, who had been Minister to the UK from 1889 to 1893. He was greatly moved by discussing his father's qualities with Robert, to whom he observed how a civil war was "immeasurably harder" than even his own wartime experiences.[2016] On 18 October, he visited Lincoln's home in Springfield, Illinois, and saw his tomb at Oak Ridge Cemetery, laying a wreath bearing the inscription 'A humble and reverent homage to one of the world's greatest men.' At Springfield, Lloyd George spoke movingly on Lincoln's ageless qualities: "He was one of those rare men whom you do not associate with any particular creed, or party… not even with any country, for he belongs to mankind in every race, in every clime and in every age." His "lofty soul could see over and beyond party walls the unlimited terrain beyond." He was "misrepresented, misunderstood, maligned, derided", but triumphed in the end. He was "the finest product in the realm of statesmanship of Christian civilisation, and the wise counsel he gave his own people in their day of their triumph he gives today to the people of Europe in the hour of their victory over the forces that menace their liberties." In Lloyd George's opinion, Lincoln had a clear message for his own times, standing for two great principles. The first was "clemency in the hour of triumph", Lincoln's doctrine being to "reconcile the vanquished." The second was to "trust the common people"–he believed in their sincerity, their common sense, their inherent belief in justice. Thus, the two great conclusions that Lloyd George drew from the Great War he linked to Lincoln's ideas–the need for reconciliation and reconstruction of a shattered continent, and for faith in democracy. A time would come "when the principles of Abraham Lincoln will have to be fought for again." In this was the implication that

---

[2015] https://gettysburgcompiler.org/2013/02/21/the-welsh-wizard-at-gettysburg/. Retrieved 18 April 2020.

[2016] K. O. Morgan, *Revolution To Devolution: Reflections On Welsh Democracy*, 2014, Cardiff, University of Wales Press, p67-68.

the US should modify its isolationist stance towards Europe to help give them effect.[2017] On 21 October, he visited Lincoln's birthplace at Sinking Spring Farm, just south of Hodgenville, Kentucky, shown around by Mary Edwards Brown, great-grandniece of Mrs Mary Lincoln, walking around the log cabin several times, being photographed at its doorway and kneeling to drink at a nearby stream. He declared that it was "a glorious day".

Sailing from New York on 6 November, Lloyd George reached Southampton three days later, his reputation as an international statesman greatly enhanced, calling Baldwin's protectionist tariff policy "an unutterable, unintelligible folly" as soon as he disembarked. He and Asquith quickly reached agreement on 13 November and issued a joint free trade manifesto, followed by a more general one. Lloyd George, together with Charles McCurdy, was largely responsible for the former, which condemned the government's failure to prevent the French occupation of the Ruhr and claimed that the maintenance of a long-term peace settlement was dependent upon Europe's economic recovery. They also advocated the admittance of all countries to the League of Nations and pledged to re-open diplomatic relations with Soviet Russia. In addition, the programme contained the first traces of the radical industrial policy put forward by the Liberals in 1929, including plans for schemes of afforestation and a reference, at Lloyd George's insistence, "to use National Credit in times of depression for the purpose of creating means for production which should be used in better times, and to employ people in creating these means."[2018] Winifred Coombe Tennant had a close relationship with both Lloyd George and McCurdy, and, in Peter Lord's estimation, "the manifesto that emerged was consistent with her views on many issues, notably in its condemnation of the government for its failure to prevent the occupation of the Ruhr, its opposition to the imposition of trade tariffs, its proposal to open the League of Nations to all countries, and in the suggestions it contained of a move towards radical industrial policies."[2019]

Lloyd George travelled to Asquith's constituency of Paisley to speak in his support on 24 November.[2020] Characteristically, Asquith was ungrateful, stating "the rites of Liberal Reunion were celebrated at an enthusiastic meeting in the Town Hall… I have rarely felt less exhilaration than when we got to the platform amid wild plaudits and a flash-light film was taken, 'featuring' me and Ll.G [sic] separated only by the chairman."[2021] Lloyd George agreed to contribute £100,000 towards campaign funds. In the event he claimed to have contributed £160,000 [£12.36m in 2025] including help given to individual candidates; Liberal HQ put the amount at £90,000. Lloyd George fought a vigorous campaign. The day after visiting Paisley, the *Observer* opined:

> Mr. Lloyd George is a miracle of flamboyant energy, and has easily thrown all the other Liberal leaders into the shade. His optimism is quite evidently enthusiastic, and his whirlwind tour in

---

2017 Ibid., p68.
2018 Quoted in Campbell, *Lloyd George*, p73-74.
2019 Lord in Coombe Tennant, p404-405.
2020 Koss, p261-263.
2021 Asquith, *Letters Of The Earl of Oxford And Asquith To A Friend, Second Series*, 1934, London, Geoffrey Bles, p84-85.

> the next twelve days means a prodigious effort. If the Liberals gain largely it will be his victory, so far as the party is concerned.[2022]

Fresh from his trip to the USA, he ridiculed the idea that tariffs could cure unemployment, citing that country as proof.

In the event, the Tories won 258 seats, but Labour, with 191, led by Ramsay MacDonald, and the reunited Liberals, with 158, gained enough seats–albeit with some fragile majorities–to produce a hung parliament. Asquith scraped in only because of a split Labour vote in Paisley. The result in the country threw many Tories into a panic at the prospect of a possible socialist government, brought about by Baldwin's foolhardiness in calling the election. Lloyd George wryly commented "The Western skies are already black with the flight of capital seeking safety beyond the Atlantic. The fright is real. There has been nothing like it since horror filled the streets of Rome at the approach of Attila."[2023] Of personal note, Goronwy Owen[2024] was elected as Liberal MP for Caernarvonshire, taking the seat from Labour. Owen would become distantly related to Lloyd George by marriage; his wife Gladwyn, whom he married in 1925, was the sister of Edna, the wife of Gwilym Lloyd George. During the later Liberal splits Owen would therefore become part of Lloyd George's so-called 'family group' of four Independent Liberal MPs, which also comprised Lloyd George, Megan and Gwilym.

MacDonald formed the first ever Labour Government on 22 January 1924 with tacit support from the Liberals: Asquith's decision to support a minority Labour administration was seconded by Lloyd George and approved by a party meeting on 18 December 1923.[2025] Asquith's motivation for permitting Labour to enter power, rather than trying to bring the Liberals back into government, was that he hoped they would prove to be incompetent and quickly lose support. He thought the new Labour Government "a beggarly array", believing that MacDonald would soon be discredited both in the eyes of the country and of his own more left-wing supporters, and the Liberal revival would continue.[2026] He was right on the first score, but totally wrong on the second. Asquith's decision only hastened his party's destruction, the Tory Austen Chamberlain writing to his colleague Sir Samuel Hoare: "We have got (unexpectedly and by our own blunders and Asquith's greater folly) a second chance. Have we got the wit to take it?"[2027] Asquith's spite, his blind self-denial that he had been out of his depth ever since 1916, his putting self before party, was most certainly the cause of the death of traditional British Liberalism. Of course, Lloyd George was also keen on his own political position and reputation, but he stuck to promoting progressive Liberal principles, almost alone, as the 1920s wore on into the 1930s. If he wanted personal power for himself, it was for the same reason as in 1916, namely that he thought that the nation was suffering under weak, indecisive leadership, and that he could give it the energetic direction that it needed.

---

2022 *Observer*, 25 November 1923.
2023 *Daily Chronicle*, 5 January 1924.
2024 Goronwy Owen (1881-1963), Liberal MP for Caernarvonshire, 1923-1945.
2025 Jenkins, *Asquith*, [1964], p500.
2026 Ibid., p501; Koss, p265.
2027 J. Ramsden, *A History of the Conservative Party–The Age of Balfour and Baldwin: 1902-1940*, 1978, London, Longmans, p183.

Constructively, on 12 July, Lloyd George published '*Coal and Power*', the fruit of his independent policy committee which had been working since March, an attempt to tackle the continuing crisis in the coal mines, one of falling markets and rising costs, causing lower profits, high unemployment and declining wages. Lloyd George's proposed solution rejected 'Socialization' (nationalisation) but aimed at increased colliery efficiency by the unified ownership and control of the mineral resources of the nation; judicious amalgamation or grouping of the mines; altering the status of the miner in the industry; concentration on better mines and the progressive development of new mines for old; better housing and the reconstruction of mining village conditions; the conversion of coal into electricity. All this was close to the Sankey Commission's recommendations in 1919; probably nobody regretted that they had largely been ignored more than Lloyd George himself. In the Introduction, signed on 8 July, he wrote:

> Nothing could do more damage both to miners and mine-owners and to the nation than that the industry which produces its primary raw material should now become the centre of a prolonged and bitter political struggle. It would aggravate the unrest in the mines. It would delay the development of new mines and that reorganisation which is the real road to better wages and better times. It would postpone that electrification of the national industries which is essential if Great Britain is to maintain its economic standing in the world. To-day of all times, when what is needed most is work and reconstruction to make good the losses of the war and to equip the nation for that more intense competition which is inevitable in international trade, it would be almost fatal to start a struggle over the coal-mining industry which would divide the nation and involve years of turmoil and strife.[2028]

Being a minority, MacDonald's government barely lasted ten months, finally losing a motion of no confidence called by Liberal John Simon on 8 October. This led to another general election, held on 29 October 1924. Lloyd George, realising that Liberal defeat was inevitable and keen to take control of the party himself, spent only £60,000. Influencing the election was the lurid publication by the *Daily Mail*, on 25 October, of the forged 'Zinoviev Letter', purporting to be a directive from Grigory Zinoviev, Chairman of the Communist International (Comintern) in Moscow, to the Communist Party of Great Britain, ordering it to engage in seditious activities.[2029] This development would have constituted significant interference in British politics, and as a result it antagonised many uneasy voters, turning them against both Labour and particularly their Liberal allies, thereby aiding, as intended, the Tories.

Baldwin won a landslide victory, taking 412 seats, with leading coalitionists such as Austen Chamberlain, Lord Birkenhead and former Liberal Winston Churchill agreeing to serve under him and thus ruling out any restoration of the Coalition. Labour only won 151 seats, with the Liberals being reduced to 40, Asquith losing his seat to Labour. Once again, Lloyd George himself bucked the

---

2028 Lloyd George, *Coal And Power*, pviii. Less than two years later the miners' strike led to the General Strike.
2029 *Daily Mail*, *Civil War Plot By Socialists' Masters*, 25 October 1924, p9.

trend. Standing for the first time against a Labour candidate, Alfred Zimmern[2030], he held Caernarvon Boroughs with a 19.4% swing in his favour. Nationally, the dire result left the Liberals as a weak and fatally disunited third party in British politics. Although Asquith, who was created Earl of Oxford and Asquith on 10 February 1925, remained Liberal leader, Lloyd George was elected chairman of the Liberal MPs–by 26 votes to 7–on 2 December 1924. John Simon and his followers were still loyal to Asquith: after 1931 Simon would lead a breakaway National Liberal Party, which eventually merged with the Tories, whilst Walter Runciman led a separate 'Radical Group' of nine anti-Lloyd George MPs within the Parliamentary Party.

Lloyd George was now mainly interested in the reform of land ownership, a life-long, passionate interest and concern of his, but had only been permitted to put a brief paragraph about it in the hastily drafted 1924 Liberal manifesto. In the autumn of 1925, despite the hostility of Charles Hobhouse, Walter Runciman and Alfred Mond, who defected to the Tories the next January, he began an independent campaign. Addressing a crowd exceeding 25,000, who stood listening in the rain for 90 minutes at Killerton Park, Devon, on 17 September, Lloyd George made an impassioned speech in which he described the system of landlordism as inherently obsolete and inefficient and insisted that the state needed to 'resume' possession of the land. It was said that he did not lose one member of his audience. Stopping studiously short of advocating the wholesale 'nationalization' of agricultural land in Britain, he advocated state ownership "for the purpose of giving the necessary security to the cultivator of the soil that, if and so long as he cultivates it, he and his children shall reap the full harvest of their own labour and enterprise."[2031]

On 9 October 1925, *The Land and the Nation*, the 'Green Book', the first of a series of policy pamphlets produced by Lloyd George in the late 1920s, was published. The result of a detailed study begun in 1923, largely written by Waldo McG Eager[2032], this was a substantial publication of 570 pages, crucially stating "The State shall be deemed to have resumed possession of all land in the United Kingdom which at that date is used for or capable of use for the production of foodstuffs, timber or other natural products".[2033] Charles Masterman said, with grudging appreciation, "I've fought him as hard as anyone, but I have to confess, when Lloyd George came back to the party, ideas came back to the party."[2034]

The report's core recommendation was the implementation of a novel system of 'cultivating tenure' whereby each farmer should become the tenant of a new County Agricultural Authority, thus enjoying complete security on condition that he continued to farm his land efficiently. Rentals were to be fixed and the supervision strict. It was claimed the farmer would consequently enjoy 'the legitimate rights of ownership without its risks, and the advantages of yearly tenancy without its insecurity'. This proposal amounted to the virtual nationalisation of agricultural land. Compensation would be paid to the landlords, while the farmer would enjoy relative security of tenure on condition that he farmed

---

2030 Alfred Zimmern (1879-1957), political scientist, originator of the phrase 'welfare state' in 1934.

2031 Quoted in Jones, *The 'Land And The Nation' And Wales*, p28-29.

2032 Waldo McG Eager (1884-1966), sociologist. See G. Shakespeare, p46-47.

2033 *The Land and the Nation: Rural Report of the Liberal Land Committee*, 1923-25, 1925, London, Hodder and Stoughton, p299.

2034 L. Masterman, *C. F. G. Masterman*, p345-346.

properly, as judged by the new agricultural committees which would assume responsibility for the allocation of allotments, larger gardens, smallholdings and very small farms of new creation. Full compensation would be paid to a farmer who lost some or all of his land to the new holdings.[2035] Lloyd George set up the 'Land and Nation League' the same month, with himself as President, to campaign for 'Cultivating Tenure' across the country, utilising 13 publicity vans. Over the next couple of years, he appears to have ploughed some £240,000 into the League.[2036]

On 24 November, *Towns and the Land*, the 'Brown Book', followed, less radical and more acceptable to the Party as a whole, devoted to town planning on regional lines, embodying the principles of site value taxation and reform of the leasehold system, though still calling for local authorities to be given greater powers of compulsory purchase.

On 25 November, Asquith rebuked Lloyd George, warning him:

> … that the recent setting up of 'a new organisation' had immediately led to 'much concern' and was thus likely to impede the 'full and free discussion' now sorely required on the proposed reforms. Asquith drew Lloyd George's attention to the 'frequent, almost daily communications from stalwart and hard-working members' of the Liberal Party voicing 'their own doubts and difficulties and deprecating at this stage anything in the nature of propaganda, either on the one side or the other'. He insisted that it would be 'a very curious matter' if there should be 'any conflict, or appearance of conflict, between the National Liberal Federation and the new organisation proposed for promoting the views of the Land Enquiry Committee'.[2037]

Lloyd George essentially ignored him, and they reached an agreement in principle on 2 December, together presenting Lloyd George's revised 'Green Book' and the original 'Brown Book' proposals to the National Liberal Federation on 26 February 1926. They were adopted as party policy.

Soon after this, between 3 to 12 May, a nine-day general strike took place, called by the General Council of the Trades Union Congress (TUC) in an unsuccessful attempt to force the government to act to prevent wage reduction and worsening conditions for 1.2 million locked-out coal miners. Some 1.7 million workers struck, especially in transport and heavy industry. However, the government had been preparing for such an eventuality for nine months, and they enlisted middle class, right-wing volunteers from subsidised groups like the 'Organisation for the Maintenance of Supplies' to maintain essential services. In the Commons, Lloyd George "stood practically alone in advocating, on May 5 and again on May 9, a negotiated peace."[2038] There was little violence and the TUC gave up in defeat, acknowledging that 'the government could hold out longer than the workers', while at the time the strike was perceived as a 'brilliant failure'. The miners continued their resistance until the end of November, when, due to sheer poverty, most were back at work. However, many remained unemployed for years, and those still in work were forced to accept longer hours, lower wages and

2035 Jones, *The 'Land And The Nation' And Wales*, p29.
2036 Campbell, *Lloyd George*, p124.
2037 Jones, *The 'Land And The Nation' And Wales*, p30.
2038 D. H. Robertson, *A Narrative Of The General Strike Of 1926*, *Economic Journal* 36, 143 September 1926 p375-393; Quote, p388.

district wage agreements.

The Liberal Shadow Cabinet, including Lloyd George, unequivocally backed Baldwin's handling of the General Strike on 3 May, but the following day Lloyd George condemned the Government more than he did the strike, and wrote a syndicated article for the US press–still a regular commitment of his–sympathetic to the strikers, pessimistic about the Government's ability to win. He did not attend the Shadow Cabinet on 10 May, sending a letter dated the previous day to the Chief Whip, Godfrey Collins, announcing his intention of absenting himself, expressly stating that his reason for doing so was that he dissented from the line taken by "the leader of the party and others wielding great authority in the party," and that he thought the Government's action "precipitate, unwarrantable, and mischievous."[2039] He added, pointedly: "I prefer the Liberal policy of trusting to conciliation rather than to force."[2040]

Asquith reflected, then sent him a portentous public letter on 20 May:

> I should not be doing my duty as Leader of the Liberal Party if I did not now convey to you my regret of the course which you have pursued in the greatest domestic crisis which the country has had to confront in your time or mine…
>
> I summoned another meeting of the Shadow Cabinet on Monday, May 10th. All my colleagues attended with the notable exception of yourself. The reasons for your absence, as set out in a letter dated the same morning, seem to me to be wholly inadequate.
>
> The main ground alleged was that declarations have been made… by the Leader of the Party (i.e. myself) and other Liberals of authority from which you felt obliged to dissent. You added that you could not see your way "to join in declarations which condemned the General Strike, while refraining from criticism of the Government, who are equally, if not more responsible."…
>
> I regard this as a very grave matter. We had reached the most critical moment of the Strike. It was, in my judgement, the primary duty of all who were responsible for Liberal policy, and certainly not least of the Chairman of the Parliamentary Party in the House of Commons, at such a time to meet together for free and full discussion, and to contribute their counsels to the common stock. Your refusal to do so I find impossible to reconcile with my conception of the obligations of political comradeship.[2041]

Lloyd George's letter of 10 May had not been published, making it appear that Asquith had fired the first shot, and Lloyd George sent a public reply, moderate in tone–journalist C. P. Scott helping him to considerably tone down his initial, acerbic draft–on 25 May. In the words of Asquith's biographers:

> He passed lightly over the fact that he had definitely declared his dissent from the action of his colleagues, and represented his absence from the Shadow Cabinet as an endeavour not to make but avoid differences. Wherein, he asked, had he done wrong? He had said nothing in public

[2039] Spender and Asquith, Vol.II, p361.
[2040] Quoted in Campbell, *Lloyd George*, p139.
[2041] Quoted in Spender and Asquith, Vol.II, p362-363.

> which clashed with the decision of the Shadow Cabinet; his offence, if any, was only that he had urged a Liberal policy of conciliation, and supported the appeal of the Archbishop of Canterbury for a resumption of negotiations on the basis of calling off the General Strike.[2042]

In late May, the executive of the National Liberal Federation convened to plan the agenda for the following month's conference. 16 were pro-Asquith and eight pro-Lloyd George; they planned a motion expressing confidence in Asquith, but another option was also proposed to seek Asquith's opinion first, and also general feeling of regret at having been forced to choose between Asquith and Lloyd George. Asquith then wrote another public letter on 1 June, stating that in his view no other inference could be drawn than that Lloyd George intended to withdraw from the party councils and take a line of his own on the General Strike:

> I have sat in many Cabinets under various Prime Ministers, and I have not known one of them who would not have treated such a communication from a colleague, sent at such a time, as equivalent to a resignation. I certainly so regarded it. Nor was the difference of attitude and policy which is announced one that in my judgment could be smoothed away, as a trivial matter of transient importance. It was clear and clean cut. If the leaders of the Liberal Party as a body had adopted Mr. Lloyd George's view, we should have been doing our best to weaken the authority of the Government, which was for the moment the embodiment and organ of the national self-defence against the gravest domestic danger which has threatened the country in our time…[2043]

On 2 June, 12 leading Liberals wrote in Asquith's support to *The Times*, although only three–Grey, Simon and Runciman–were MPs. However, Lloyd George had more support in the wider party than among the grandees: on 3 June, the London Liberal Candidates' Association defied its officers and expressed its dismay at the split, effectively supporting Lloyd George, and on 8 June the Liberal MPs voted 20-10, passing a resolution "deprecating the publicity given to the differences between the Liberal leaders," and expressing the "earnest hope that these leaders will use their best endeavours to restore unity in the ranks of the party."[2044] Asquith planned to launch a fightback at the National Liberal Federation Conference in Weston-Super-Mare, but on 12 June, five days before, he suffered a stroke which put him out of action for three months. Lloyd George was given a rapturous welcome. On 17 June, the conference passed a resolution pointedly demanding unity upon "a vigorous and constructive policy of social and industrial reform."[2045] Asquith's legitimacy as party leader was broken, and he resigned on 15 October. Even now he could not go gracefully. On 5 October he sent a 'secret' memorandum to his supporters, decrying all talk of unity and announcing his resignation in self-justifying terms. He made his decision public on 14 October, and the next day gave an emotional

---

[2042] Ibid., p365.
[2043] Ibid., p366.
[2044] Ibid., p368.
[2045] Wilson, *Downfall Of The Liberal Party*, p332.

farewell address at Greenock, in which he again implicitly criticised Lloyd George.[2046] A deeply embittered man, he suffered two further strokes during 1927 and died aged 75 on 15 February 1928.

Lloyd George immediately issued a gracious statement:

> I hear with the deepest regret of the death of Lord Oxford. I worked in the closest association with him for a great number of very eventful years. I served with him in a Campbell-Bannerman administration and under him in the administration of which he was the head, and I could wish for no better colleague or chief. On a solemn occasion like this I prefer to recall the days of our pleasant and… fruitful association when we were working together for great causes. He was undoubtedly one of the greatest Parliamentarians of all time.[2047]

This marked the end of the greatest feud in British politics since that of Gladstone and Disraeli–except that had been the open and natural rivalry of the leaders of two opposing parties, rather than the internecine warfare of two leaders nominally on the same side.

On 16 February 1927, another 'ghost' from the Victorian age raised his head, Lord Rosebery, almost 80 and out of politics since soon after his resignation as Prime Minister in 1895. What–or who–prompted him to write to the *Times* about Lloyd George's Political Fund is unclear, but it was clearly intended to force disclosure as to its origin:

> [W]hat is this sum, how was it obtained, and what is its source? It surely cannot be the sale of Royal Honours? If that were so, there would be nothing in the worst times of Charles II or Sir Robert Walpole to equal it… An authoritative statement should be furnished as to the source of this Fund.[2048]

On 28 February a second letter appeared, Rosebery calling for a commission to investigate the issue: "The sight of some 90 peers explaining to a Commission the origins of their nobility would be something worth making a sacrifice for."[2049]

Lloyd George's office swiftly responded by issuing a brief statement that "the Fund which Mr. Lloyd George controls was raised in a way which does not differ from that followed by the Conservative Party or by the Liberal Party in the days before the Coalition, and… all along it has been devoted to legitimate party purposes."[2050] On 3 December, Lloyd George issued a longer statement, reiterating that his fund–the National Liberal Fund–had been collected in the same way as every other, and particularly in the same way as the Tory fund during the Coalition. He and Bonar Law, and later Austen Chamberlain, had drawn up the Honours Lists together, without regard to financial

---

2046 Campbell, *Lloyd George*, p155-156.

2047 *The Times,* 16 February 1928; Clarke, p33. Even after her husband's death, Margot Asquith kept up a stream of vituperative attacks on Lloyd George to all and sundry; see Wasserstein, p300, 306.

2048 *The Times*, 16 February 1927, p15.

2049 *The Times,* 28 February 1927, p13. On his death in May 1929, Rosebery's estate was probated at £1,500,122 3s. 6d., [£121.79m in 2025] making him the richest PM ever until Tory Rishi Sunak in 2022.

2050 *The Times*, 17 February 1927, p14.

contributions. The present size of the fund left in his hands after the break-up of the Coalition was mainly due to the success of the newspapers–principally the *Daily Chronicle*–in which he had invested it. He denied having spent a penny of it for his personal use, listed the political objects to which he had devoted it, and named the Board of Trustees who actually administered it.[2051]

On 12 May 1927, the premises of the Soviet Trade Delegation and ARCOS–the All-Russian Cooperative Society–at Soviet House, 49 Moorgate, London, was raided by the Metropolitan Police and Special Branch, on the pretext of looking for a missing War Office document–a Signals training pamphlet! Despite a four-day search, nothing incriminating was found, but the ramifications were huge. In intelligence terms, it was a disaster. To justify the raid to Parliament, the government was forced to publish telegrams from Moscow discovered at the premises. The source was obvious, leading the Soviets to abandon their encryption system in favour of an unreadable One Time Pad system. Thereafter no high-level Soviet diplomatic messages could be read. On 26 May, Lloyd George rose in the Commons to add his voice to united Labour and Liberal opposition to the government on their breaking off diplomatic relations with Russia and cancelling the Anglo-Soviet Trade Agreement, negotiated by him in 1921. His criticism, though it had no effect, was the weightiest offered, excoriating in its analysis, and held by the *Manchester Guardian* to be "by common consent the best speech that he had made for years":[2052]

> There are three questions which the House of Commons and the country have to consider. I am afraid the Cabinet did not consider them… The first is, whether there is sufficient evidence to justify a break if it is desirable; the second is, whether it is desirable at this stage that strong action should be taken; and the third is, whether the Government have not gone too far, even if that were conceded. With regard to the question of whether there is sufficient evidence to warrant a break, if it were desirable to have a rupture between two of the greatest nations in the world, I say at once I think the evidence is sufficient… [L]ooking over the last five or six years… I must frankly admit that the Soviet Government have not kept faith…
>
> … Personally, I am in favour, and so is the Foreign Secretary, of making considerable allowances for the difficulties of a revolutionary Government… [which] does not govern under the same conditions as old-established Governments… In making allowances for all that, and still I say the Russians have not kept faith with us.
>
> … In regard to the Trade Agreement, the conduct of the Soviet Government has too often looked like a clumsy attempt to reconcile a genuine desire to have every advantage of peace with the greatest Empire in the world, with an equally genuine desire to have the satisfaction of witnessing its overthrow…

He referred to the evidence of the raid published by the government as "an extravaganza of incredible nonsense," continuing:

2051 Campbell, *Lloyd George*, p173; *The Times*, 3 December 1927.
2052 *Manchester Guardian*, 27 May 1927.

> I think the raid forced the hands of the Government... The Government have not considered the action which they have taken under those conditions of calm which are necessary before committing themselves to a policy of such far-reaching importance as the present one. I think the Foreign Secretary has had his hands forced in regard to this breach of relations... I do not think the Foreign Secretary came to the conclusion before the Home Secretary acted that the time had arrived to have a rupture with Soviet Russia... I think he was right, and I do not think the time was well chosen.
>
> ... I am perfectly certain... that the right hon. Gentleman would not have chosen this particular moment if his hand had not been forced by his more hot-headed colleague, the Home Secretary. It is very unfortunate that the foreign policy of this country should have been dictated by the Home Office, and not by the Foreign Office, in the most important diplomatic act since the War...
>
> ... I think it is one of the gravest things that have been done in this country, short of embarking upon war, to rupture diplomatic relations with a Power with a population of 100,000,000... and coming in contact with us at so many points. I think it was one of the riskiest and most hazardous decisions ever taken by a Government...

He pointedly asked what the government's purpose in rupturing relations was:

> Is the object to diminish propaganda? You have doubled and intensified it... Is your object to prevent action by Soviet agents which embarrasses us in Asia?... It will make it worse than ever... Is your object to promote trade in a country that has a million unemployed?... I am certain it will be less...
>
> ... Have we gained nothing by diplomatic relations? I say emphatically "Yes!" Can we derive any advantage from a rupture. I say emphatically "No!" I listened to the Foreign Secretary with great care. He did not point out a single advantage which would be gained to this country by rupture. The question of trade has been rather scoffed at. The Anglo-Russian Chamber of Commerce, in which you have about 300 British firms enrolled, gave the trade we have done with Russia during the last five or six years... [as] about £180,000,000...
>
> ... There is no doubt at all that it would be an increasing trade. Russia is the greatest undeveloped country in the world and, whatever may be said about the Soviet Government, they are undoubtedly concentrating upon economic development. They are giving orders for machinery for production and for textiles. That would have increased. They have increased year by year their production until they have very nearly come to the level of pre-War, and we have quarrelled with that Government at a moment when we were negotiating an order of £10,000,000 and an arrangement had been made for credit... That transaction has gone. How many traders will carry on when there is a quarrel?... The answer is... [t]here is a great difference between breaking relations after you have begun them and never having started them. You have turned out the Soviet representative, charging him with falsehood. You charge the Foreign Secretary with falsehood. There is a quarrel. There is a rupture. Does anyone imagine that trade with Great Britain will be considered in the same light as trade with America after that?...

> … I am honestly concerned for the interests of this country, and I say it is a serious mess.
>
> … Breaking diplomatic relations… is a serious business. You cannot treat is as if everything were going on exactly as it did before. It will not. In my judgment, the thing you are thinking about would be infinitely worse. There were 24 Powers that had recognised Russia, following, undoubtedly, our lead–24 Powers, friends of ours, allies of ours… We shall be completely isolated in this respect in a Europe which is full of trouble. Nobody knows that better than the Foreign Secretary, and he has been doing his very best to try to secure a pacific Europe.
>
> What is the trouble in Europe today? Immediately after the War the danger was Communism. The danger today is an aggressive nationalism. It is the trouble which you get in Italy and South-Eastern Europe. It is the trouble which you get in the Balkans. It is the trouble which you have got on the Eastern Frontier of Germany, where there is a much more powerful party than the Communist party in favour of aggressive action. That is the trouble today, and into this troubled Europe… you throw this stone, this bone of contention. It is a leap in the dark and a leap into a whirlpool.[2053]

On 11 July, Lloyd George sold his controlling interest in the *Daily Chronicle*, for £2.9m [£232.82m in 2025], to the Daily Chronicle Investment Group, a joint venture of Liberal interests. A covenant in the sales document restricted the owners to running the paper "in accordance with the policy of Progressive Liberalism" to further social and industrial reform, free trade, and "other programmes of Liberal and Radical measures adopted by the Liberal party."[2054] His fighting funds thus greatly enlarged, the same year Lloyd George gave £300,000 plus an annual grant of between £30,000 and £40,000 for the operations of the Liberal headquarters. He also gave £2,000 per annum to the parliamentary party until 1931.

In December 1927, Lloyd George visited Brazil with Margaret and Megan, a rare trip for a European statesman before the era of transatlantic flights. At a speech given at the Reception to the British Community of Rio de Janeiro held at the Copacabana Palace Hotel on 7 January 1928, literally delivered on a hastily improvised soapbox, Lloyd George congratulated Brazil on its economic progress and reminisced:

> You represent a great Country and you are living in a country of vast possibilities. I was here 31 years ago. I would not have believed it was the same city had it not been for the eternal beauty of those hills…
>
> But the change which has taken place in Rio is the change which has taken place in your country, Your Excellency [Dr. Fernando de Melo Viana, Vice-President of the Republic]. It has grown and its possibilities are infinite. I doubt whether there is a country on earth where the

[2053]https://api.parliament.uk/historic-hansard/commons/1927/may/26/russo-british-relations#S5CV0206P0_19270526_HOC_345. Retrieved 14 May 2020.

[2054]http://www.fundinguniverse.com/company-histories/united-business-media-plc-history/. Retrieved 13 May 2020. See also http://www.edwardlloyd.org/united-newspapers.pdf.

> possibilities are so great, but the surface has not been explored let alone the hidden treasures underneath…[2055]

In another speech delivered at the Banquet offered by Dr Otávio Mangabeira, Minister of Foreign Affairs, on the same day, Lloyd George made an important appeal:

> I am… grateful for the eloquent tribute paid by your Excellency to the part my country has taken as the pioneer of free institutions and the champion of liberty and justice in the world. We can never forget that the British Empire and the Republic of Brazil fought together side by side in a colossal struggle for these exalted ideals.
>
> I had the honour of being the Prime Minister of Great Britain when Brazil threw in its lot with the Allies in that conflict. You did not launch your boat on the tide of victory, but whilst the tempest was still raging and the event was still in doubt[2056]… There are moments in the history of mankind when nations spring to the defence of some great principle which matters more to the progress of humanity than even millions of lives. Equal rights for all individuals or nations, whether they be great or small, strong or weak, is an eternal principle of the faith of Christendom… That principle was challenged and your great people and ours were amongst those who ranged ourselves under its banners.
>
> The work of appeasement has now begun, and the line taken by you in these fateful years matters greatly to the future of humanity. You are at the beginning of your greatness… You will forgive me… expressing a hope that this great country will remain in that Council of the Nations which can do so much to fashion the destiny of mankind. Your presence and influence are needed there. The nations of the future are the guardians of the future. It is for them to guide humanity along the path that ascends towards the dawn. If you are there to help the old continents of the world to solve their troubles, you will be rendering a service to mankind by helping to accelerate the divine promise of peace on earth and goodwill amongst men.[2057]

Back home, as Liberal Leader at last, Lloyd George used his fund to finance candidates and put forward innovative ideas for public works to reduce unemployment, as detailed in pamphlets such as *Britain's Industrial Future*, popularly known as the 'Yellow Book', published on 2 February 1928, and *We Can Conquer Unemployment*, the 'Orange Book', launched on 1 March 1929. Lloyd George was helped by a 'brains trust' of key economists and theorists such as John Maynard Keynes, Seebohm Rowntree, E. D. Simon, Walter Layton, Ramsay Muir, Herbert Samuel and Philip Kerr to write these. Kerr and Muir identified the key problem as the conflict between capital and labour. Lloyd George and Keynes thought the real problem of industry was unemployment, Lloyd George wanting to attack it directly.

---

2055 *Wileman's Brazilian Review*, 19, 2, 12 January 1928, p42. http://memoria.bn.br/pdf/183741/per183741_1928_00002.pdf. Retrieved 20 April 2020.

2056 Brazil declared war on the Central Powers on 26 October 1917, the only Latin American country to do so.

2057 *Wileman's Brazilian Review*, 12 January 1928, p42-43. Brazil, a founder member of the League of Nations, withdrew on 14 June 1926. In the event, she did not re-join.

Large-scale unemployment had begun during his post-war premiership, when he had been beset by so many huge issues, but unlike most commentators he did not foresee an early revival in trade, forcefully stating in the Commons as early as 16 July 1923: "I fear that the period of depression is going to be prolonged. I am honestly apprehensive about it–I ventured in this place, in November, to predict that we should hardly find our unemployed below 1,000,000 at the end of this year… I was attacked then for being unduly alarmist… I do not say there will not be fluctuations, spurts… but I do say that we are in for a long period of depression such as we have not seen in our lifetime."[2058]

On 12 April 1924, Lloyd George had written to the Liberal weekly, the *Nation and Athenæum*, a signal letter on unemployment entitled *The Statesman's Task*:

> A far-seeing manufacturer utilizes periods of slackness to repair his machinery, to re-equip his workshop, and generally to put his factory in order, so that when prosperity comes he will be in as good a position as his keenest competitor to take advantage of the boom. I suggest that the nation ought to follow that wise example, and that this is the time to do so. Let us overhaul our national equipment in all directions–men and material–so as to be ready, when the moment arrives, to meet any rival on equal or better terms in the markets of the world. No man who has examined the use now being made of our national resources can believe that we are making the best use of them. In power–in our transport arrangements–in the use we make of our soil and of the minerals underneath it–in the organization of our industries–in the use of our capital–in the possibilities of development at home or in the Empire across the seas, and, above all, in the use we make of our fine manhood, we are not taking full advantage of the assets at our command. Capital and labour are alike strangled by vested prejudices and traditions. Both are capable of producing infinitely more wealth for the benefit of the community than they are now creating… The best means of achieving production seems to be the most urgent task of our industrial and political leaders at this hour.[2059]

This was non-ideological common-sense. The idea of public works was not a new one, but the scale that Lloyd George proposed was unprecedented, as was the idea that the work itself would add to public prosperity. Beveridge[2060] and others had written in support. In 1926, Lloyd George duly provided Simon and Muir with £10,000 from his political fund 'to finance a thorough enquiry', with no conditions, never being one to avoid exploring unconventional economic policies to solve unemployment. The Chairman of the resulting Liberal Industrial Inquiry was Walter Layton, with five principal sub-committees, Lloyd George chairing the one on unemployment. The whole of 1927 was taken up with research, discussion and drafting.

Lloyd George often entertained the committee members at Churt for working weekends, where he delighted in feeding them entirely on home-grown produce and refreshing them with cider, buttermilk

---

[2058]https://api.parliament.uk/historic-hansard/commons/1923/jul/16/capitalist-system. Retrieved 16 May 2020.

[2059] Lloyd George, *Statesman's Task*, p40.

[2060] *The Outlook For Great Britain*, *Nation and Athenæum*, XXXV, 3, 19 April 1924, p74-75. William Beveridge (1879-1963), economist, Liberal politician, progressive social reformer.

and mead. Simon recorded: "He was a perfect host. He gave us the benefit of his vast experience; he never made the least attempt to use his position to influence his report, except by contributing to the discussion on an equality with all other members."[2061] Seebohm Rowntree later wrote an account for Thomas Jones on how his host conducted these investigations, which throw interesting light on his working methods:

> He was a hard taskmaster. During the many years I spent at his home with different committees between 1926 and 1935 he worked us without mercy. We would work from breakfast to lunch. Then he would ask us to work at some problem in the afternoon and he would meet us at tea time and then discuss what we had done. He, of course, rested in the afternoon. After tea he would be all fresh and ready to discuss the work we had done and he would work on till dinner time, which was usually at 8 o'clock. After dinner he would meet with us again for a short time and then just before ten o'clock he would discuss the programme for the following day and the subject we would discuss. He would suggest that we might do some preliminary work on a particular problem and leave any documents we had prepared outside his bedroom door, which he would get when he woke at six o'clock in the morning and read in bed, so as to be prepared to discuss them with us at breakfast next morning.[2062]

When *Britain's Industrial Future* appeared, it ran to 503 pages of detailed analysis and recommendations, divided into five sections. Its brief introduction advanced the Liberal belief that the opposition of individualism and Socialism was anachronistic and harmful in modern conditions, where there was already large-scale public ownership and where private industry was also increasingly large and impersonal.

Book I, 'The Condition of British Industry', analysed Britain's industrial problems and observed that unemployment was primarily caused by the loss of export markets since the war. It warned–correctly–that the old exporting industries such as coal, cotton, iron and steel might never recover, concluding that "industrial revival may require a migration of labour from the threatened industries and the diversion to home development of capital normally devoted to foreign investment."[2063]

Book II 'The Organisation of Business', primarily the work of Keynes, recommended that a powerful Board of National Investment should replace the "stream of national investment which is at present chaotically controlled by a multiplicity of public authorities and private interests".[2064] It also contained proposals for controlling public and private enterprises; the latter would be required to publish full and accurate balance-sheets to aid investment and their directors would be answerable to employees and a supervisory council of shareholders. In underlining the unsatisfactory nature of directorships, and the urgent need for reform, the report called them "the 'pocket boroughs' of the

---

2061 Simon in S. Hodgson, Ed., *Ramsay Muir: An Autobiography And Some Essays*, 1943, London, Lund Humphries, p183.

2062 Rowntree to Jones, 24 May 1945, quoted in A. Briggs, *Social Thought And Social Action: A Study Of The Work Of Seebohm Rowntree 1871-1954*, 1961, London, Longmans, p199.

2063 *Britain's Industrial Future*, p3.

2064 Ibid, p61.

present day."[2065] Private monopolies would be put under more state control, and it recommended that an economic general staff should be set up to advise the government. There should be a standing Cabinet Committee on economic policy and–crucially for the accurate analysis of data–a continuous census of production co-ordinating and publishing all essential economic information.

Book III, 'Industrial Relations', stemming from Muir's work, envisaged a council of industry and a ministry of industry working closely together to ensure industrial cooperation, coupled with family allowances and minimum wages for each industry. As an alternative to nationalization, it recommended profit sharing as a way of encouraging the "popular ownership of industry". Workers would also become shareholders in their firms and progressive taxation, together with the spread of banking and investment amongst all classes, would constitute a "real advance towards that goal of Liberalism in which everybody will be a capitalist, and everybody a worker, as everybody is a citizen".[2066]

Book IV, 'National Development', drew its inspiration from the ideas of Lloyd George, including the revival of agriculture and the reorganisation of the coal industry. It also dealt with the expansion of education. Primarily, it argued that a large programme of public works would be necessary to deal with unemployment; this would include road-building, house-building, slum clearance, electrification, afforestation, drainage and the renovation of canals and docks. This would be financed by the Board of National Investment, utilising unused savings, and by the Committee of National Development, drawing on site-value taxation, responsible to the Prime Minister. This was the most striking and controversial section of the whole report, "affirming Lloyd George's passionate belief in the power of political will in language that is surely his own"[2067]: "We cannot acquit the timid, unimaginative, unenterprising policy of the present Government of a major responsibility for damming up in the stagnant pool of unemployment so much of the available forces of willing labour, which might be employed–if only the stimulus, the encouragement, the central direction, were there to give it the lead–to make the soil more fruitful, the roads more serviceable, the housing more sufficient, and the environment of life ampler and more decent."`[2068]

Book V, 'National Finance', which again owed much to Keynes, argued that the "control of our credit system… should be exercised more deliberately and systemically than hitherto, with a view to the maintenance of steady trade conditions".[2069] It also recommended greater public control over the Bank of England and economy in armaments expenditure. Cuts in social spending were ruled out as it was considered essential for the redistribution of wealth. Industry should be relieved by reforming the rating system so that the National Exchequer shouldered much of the burden.

Writing in 1977, biographer John Campbell astutely argued that *Britain's Industrial Future*, though disregarded in its day, "over the generation following its publication its philosophy so thoroughly permeated British political attitudes that most of its recommendations have come to seem

2065 Ibid., p90.
2066 Ibid., p261.
2067 Campbell, *Lloyd George*, p199.
2068 *Britain's Industrial Future*, p281.
2069 Ibid., p414.

commonplace, and it stands out today as the most far-sighted policy document produced by any party between the wars… [it was] a prophetic vision of post-war society… [and] the harbinger of a typically quiet British revolution."[2070]

The 'Yellow Book' did indeed prove to be the forerunner or inspiration for a decade of so-called 'Middle Opinion' manifestos proposing varying degrees of government intervention in economic management. In January 1930, Oswald Mosley submitted his famous *Memorandum* to the Labour Cabinet, calling for high tariffs to protect British industries from international finance, for state nationalization of main industries, and for a programme of public works to solve unemployment. When it was rejected, he left both the Party and democratic politics. In early 1931, a group headed by Basil Blackett, an expert on international finance, and including several industrialists, economist Arthur Salter, and the zoologist Julian Huxley, established Political and Economic Planning (PEP), a policy 'think tank' which published periodic pamphlets advocating this. In July 1935 Blackett, Salter and Huxley were involved with Harold Macmillan, Walter Layton, Seebohm Rowntree and others in producing *The Next Five Years: An Essay In Political Agreement*, a form of British five-year plan. On 21 August 1935, Macmillan even travelled to visit Lloyd George at Churt to discuss ideas with him.[2071] In 1938 Macmillan further published *The Middle Way: A Study of the Problems of Economic and Social Progress in a Free and Democratic Society*, a proposal for Tory collectivism he had been working on since 1927 with other young Tories, such as Robert Boothby.

Lloyd George made a major speech on unemployment in the Commons, on 9 November 1928, stating:

> I thought it was a grave blunder on the part of the Treasury to return to the gold standard in the very precipitate manner… [as] they did [in April 1925]…
>
> … These are extraordinary times and conditions, and you must have extraordinary measures to deal with them…
>
> … Unemployment ought not to be treated merely as a misfortune to be regretted, but as an opportunity to be taken advantage of. There are 1,300,000 people out of work. That is a misfortune. It is also an opportunity. Every big concern run at high pressure demands occasional overhauling. The machinery needs repair and renovation. Some of it needs to be scrapped, and new machinery substituted. The organisation ought to be reconsidered, revitalised, re-energised. The structure very often needs extensions, alterations, improvements, and the best time to take these in hand in any business is during the slack time. When the demand is great, it is as much as you can do to produce the output by turning every machine on… The time to overhaul and to put things right is during the slack time, and every rich concern has the necessary reserves of credit for the purpose of doing it even in times of depression. When prosperity returns, what happens? That concern will then be equipped to meet the increased demands without danger of a breakdown.

---

[2070] Campbell, *Lloyd George*, p201. In the same year Campbell wrote, a second impression of *Britain's Industrial Future* was published, with a foreword by Liberal Leader, David Steel.

[2071] D. R. Thorpe, *Supermac: The Life Of Harold Macmillan*, 2010, London, Chatto & Windus, p104.

The same thing applies to a great nation as to a great business. We have been working for over 50 years in this country at very high pressure; we have had the extra pressure during the War. There is no doubt at all that the social and economic machine needs overhauling thoroughly in many respects, and this is the time to do it, a time of slackness, a time when you have labour at your disposal… although we are moving very, very slowly… in that direction, the stream is flowing in the direction of prosperity… When prosperity comes, we shall be too busy, too pre-occupied, and the real danger then is that you get an inevitable breakdown in the middle of prosperity, and anybody who looks at some of the symptoms–political symptoms if you like–must realise that we are getting very much nearer the point of the breakdown.

What is it that I mean by the things that could be put right, that ought to be put right, and that this is the time for putting them right? I will give two or three illustrations, because they all go straight to the problem of finding work for the workless! The housing problem in town and country… the traffic problem, the transport problem, and the very urgent problem… of the decay of the countryside. It is a feature which, in my judgment, you do not find in any other country in the world. It is due really to our exceptional prosperity, to the enormous riches which we were able to accumulate through the special opportunities which we have had in this country of making money out of other industries. We neglected the countryside, and we have a problem in the countryside which they have not in any other country, not merely in agriculture but in the complete departure of rural industries.

Then there is the reorganisation of our industries, which is known by the word "rationalisation."… Before you can deal with that, the Treasury must really revise their ideas about expenditure. They must adopt the business view of expenditure that all unproductive expenditure is wasteful, and that productive expenditure ought to be encouraged, within the means at the command of the concern, whether it be national or private, that it enriches a concern; it develops it, it strengthens it, it makes it more powerful to meet the future, it adds to the profits of the concern. We have restored our credit at very great expense, and there is no country which has taxed itself like this country. I think that the Chancellor of the Exchequer has paid too high a price for restoring our credit, but having got it, having paid for it at enormous expense, why should we not use it? It is our greatest asset. It should not be there like the talent buried in the ground, merely to be dug up whenever we want a conversion scheme. Does the right hon. Gentleman remember the fate that befell the man who used his talent in that way? He was cast out, and the talent was taken from him. That parable is the greatest lesson in political economy ever taught.

Having got credit for this country, use it. There never was a moment when this country stood more in need of it. There never was a moment when you could make more fruitful and profitable use of it, and yet it is down there in the foundations of the Treasury… Let us use our credit in improvements and developments that will make us a better equipped nation, a nation equipped for prosperity, which we are not now… To spend money on work which is not required is folly… but not to spend money on work which is seriously needed by the nation, and which the nation will sooner or later have to do in order to be an efficient nation, work which is

> productive–not to spend money on that now, when by its means you can provide employment, is not merely a folly, it is a crime.
>
> … You cannot deal with this gigantic problem of unemployment until you have men who are capable of handling big problems of that kind. Once you do it and face it boldly you will be able to go a long way towards solving what is the darkest and most menacing problem of our day.[2072]

Then *We Can Conquer Unemployment*[2073] came out on 1 March 1929, the cover portraying Lloyd George–at Rowntree's suggestion–with his arms dramatically outstretched, the busy munitions factories of 1915 on one side, the dole queues of 1928 on the other. As might be expected, the document was essentially the 'National Development' section from the 'Yellow Book', presented in a more popular and challenging form. By the scheme of costed public works, it was calculated that 600,000 men could be directly employed for two years at a cost of £250m, the stimulus given to the economy providing permanent work for many more. The money would be raised by a special loan which the work itself would largely repay in a few years; for the rest, existing taxation would yield increased returns, great savings would be made in unemployment benefit, and some economies would be made in armaments.[2074]

With the General Election of 30 May 1929 looming, Lloyd George embarked upon a round of public meetings, including a key gathering, on 26 March, at the Royal Albert Hall, his speech carried across London to an overflow meeting in the Kingsway Hall, and broadcast around the country to audiences totalling 50,000 in 12 other towns. He gave a long, detailed and lively exposition of Liberal plans, which was generally very well received. The *New Statesman* opined:

> At last, after five years of political stagnation, somebody has said something; and once more Mr. Lloyd George has become the biggest figure in English politics. It is a position, of course, which naturally belongs to him, and as he probably has before him another twenty years of active political life, it is not easy to set a limit to what he may achieve… Is there any other politician in Britain who can really set the heather on fire?… If we had no Lloyd George, we might presently, out of sheer boredom with Baldwin and the rest, be looking round for an English Mussolini.[2075]

The schemes for national development contained detailed plans for house building, road construction and the extension of the telephone system, all of which would stimulate the economy by providing jobs for the unemployed. The manifesto included a breakdown of the levels of employment that would be generated by each scheme and identified the total cost and financing arrangements for each programme. 350,000 men would be put to work constructing roads and bridges alone, and the Liberals claimed that the cumulative effect of all schemes would generate an annual saving of £30,000,000 to

---

2072 https://api.parliament.uk/historic-hansard/commons/1928/nov/09/debate-on-the-address#S5CV0222P0_19281109_HOC_81. Retrieved 17 May 2020.

2073 Lloyd George apparently preferred the more cautious title *The Problem Of Unemployment*: Campbell, *Lloyd George*, p225.

2074 The 'Yellow Book' had devoted several pages to the desirability of reducing defence expenditure; *Britain's Industrial Future*, p426-428.

2075 *New Statesman*, XXXII, 831, 30 March 1929, p781.

the Unemployment Fund. Lloyd George's deputy, Herbert Samuel, was highly active and undertook a 23-day speaking tour that took him to all parts of the country.

Oddly, Lloyd George did not do as much as he might have to capitalise on this and promote the document, the fruit of so much labour, though he did make another major speech at Manchester Free Trade Hall on 12 April, this being relayed to 28 other towns. Noting Labour's main election pamphlet–G. D. H. Cole's *How To Conquer Unemployment: Labour's Reply To Lloyd George*–Lloyd George pointed out that "The Labour Party could not make up its mind whether to treat the Liberal plan as a freak or to claim its paternity."[2076] Bengy Carey-Evans believed that Frances Stevenson did not want him to campaign at this time, but wanted him to stay at home, possibly for a very personal reason. According to Ruth Longford: "In the late 1920s Lloyd George became temporarily discouraged about his political future, so he thought he would allow [Frances] to have the baby she longed for. She was 40 in 1928, and in previous years she had had two abortions to protect him from scandal," in February 1915 and May 1922. Jennifer Mary Stevenson (later Longford) was born in London on 4 October 1929. As she wrote in 2007: "My mother spent much of her pregnancy in France, where she had relatives, but returned to England for the birth, as things did not go very well, and Lloyd George trusted English doctors more than French ones… As they had agreed, neither of them ever claimed that I was Lloyd George's child."[2077]

However, the situation surrounding the birth was complex. Frances had also been having an affair with Thomas Tweed[2078], a novelist and political advisor to Lloyd George from 1927, originator and organiser of the Liberal summer schools. Frances naturally encouraged Lloyd George to believe that the girl was his, but no DNA test was ever carried out on Jennifer before her death in 2012, and biographers are divided on the issue. The father's name was not entered on the birth certificate. While Frances, entered as 'a woman of private means', was named as mother, she formally adopted her natural daughter, a common practice among single parents at the time. Aged 12–after Tweed's death but before Lloyd George's–Jennifer was told that Frances was her natural mother, Tweed her father. Nonetheless, Lloyd George treated her with fatherly affection, and she called him '*Taid*' (Grandfather). However, he never acknowledged her as his daughter and, whereas Tweed bequeathed her £500 [£35,769 in 2025][2079], Lloyd George left her nothing in his will.

Lloyd George was also in dispute over his 'Political Fund' that had been created for fighting elections. The Liberal Party claimed that the £765,000 in the fund belonged to them, but Lloyd George disagreed:

> The usual Party Fund represents an accumulation of gifts made through the Party Whip for Party purposes. My Fund does not represent gifts made to any Party. It started with donations

---

2076 Lloyd George certainly captured the centre of the debate; the Communist pamphlet, by J. R. Campbell, was entitled *Only Communism Can Conquer Unemployment: A Reply To Lloyd George And Others.*

2077 https://www.telegraph.co.uk/news/obituaries/politics-obituaries/9194393/Jennifer-Longford.html. Retrieved 25 October 2018.

2078 Lieutenant Colonel Thomas Tweed MC (11 May 1890–30 April 1940), aged 26 named the youngest lieutenant colonel in the British Army at the time, Secretary of the Manchester Liberal Federation, 1918-1926.

2079 Longford, p143. Tweed also left Frances £2,000.

> made through my Whip to me when I was a non-Party Premier (1916-1922) to be used for such political purposes as I thought desirable to spend them upon.[2080]

However, he faced another uphill struggle, one of an invidious nature and symptomatic of much that was wrong with inter-war British society and politics. This was demonstrated by an incident related by 'Cato'[2081] in the book *Guilty Men*, first published on 5 July 1940, which attacked 15 public figures for their failure to re-arm and their appeasement of Nazi Germany in the 1930s. Lloyd George was *not* one of them, and what 'Cato' had to say was instructive:

> One sunny May morning in… [1929] two trains stood for a few minutes close to one another in Crewe railway junction. The first train bore Prime Minister Stanley Baldwin to the North. The second one bore Socialist Leader Ramsay MacDonald from the North.
>
> Both these politicians were electioneering, for a few weeks earlier Mr. Baldwin had decided to "go to the country". He was now on his way to speak in the great northern city where Mr. MacDonald had performed the previous evening. Such are the amenities of British politics that the rival protagonists hastened to greet one another and exchange opinions…
>
> There was a third contestant in the electoral field of 1929. This was Lloyd George who had "won the War" by his galvanising leadership plus a prodigal expenditure of public money. Now, backed by a number of expansionist business men and inflationist economists, he proposed an energetic and grandiose programme of public works to "conquer unemployment".
>
> Neither Mr. Baldwin nor Mr. MacDonald viewed Mr. Lloyd George with favour. The re-eruption of this incalculable figure into their orderly arena might well upset their implicit understanding of taking turn and turnabout in office. Also, the fellow wanted to do something.
>
> This was decisive. It was not that Lloyd George was, in the belief of either of them, about to do harm or even do good. His offence was supremely that he wanted to do something. Both Mr. Baldwin and Mr. MacDonald had already fallen once from the premiership by reason of doing a foolish thing; henceforth they were resolved to sit fast and do absolutely nothing.
>
> Thus it came about that this May morning the Tory Premier and the Leader of the Socialist Opposition chatted on Crewe Station. What did they say? I cannot remember the small talk, but this I will never forget. As they parted Mr. MacDonald remarked, "Well, whatever happens we shall keep out the Welshman.[2082]

This fear and hatred was visceral, based on both ingrained racism and a real, if inverted, regard for Lloyd George's political abilities. Both MacDonald and Baldwin, who alternated as prime minister from 1923 to 1937, had an intense dislike for Lloyd George: when MacDonald had stayed at Chequers in 1924, he had consigned Lloyd George's picture to a drawer because "it makes me see red"[2083], while

2080 Lloyd George, letter to Rufus Isaacs, Marquis of Reading, 14 August 1929.

2081 'Cato' was the pseudonym of three journalists: Michael Foot (future Labour Leader), Frank Owen (former Liberal MP for Hereford, 1929-1931, future biographer of Lloyd George), and Peter Howard (Tory).

2082 'Cato', *Guilty Men*, 1940, London, Victor Gollancz, p17-19.

2083 Jones, *Whitehall Diary*, Vol.I, p181. See also L. MacNeill Weir, *The Tragedy Of Ramsay MacDonald: A Political Biography*, 1938, London, Secker and Warburg, p323-326.

Baldwin had childishly defaced a photograph of Lloyd George as Chancellor of the Exchequer in his album.[2084] The animosity was evident to all, right across the political spectrum. Political chameleon Oswald Mosley insightfully noted: "All the dull people combined to get Lloyd George down. They succeeded–but they got the country further down: the epitaph of an epoch."[2085]

Biographer John Campbell summed up this bizarre and dubious phenomenon. Pointing out that Lloyd George was not on the sidelines of politics during the 1920s, but rather at the centre of a spectrum of parties in flux, he states that Lloyd George:

> … was also at the centre in a deeper sense. For we know that Lloyd George was constantly in the minds of his opponents and at the hearts of all their political calculations, to a degree far beyond the normal run of personal and party rivalry. We know that Baldwin and MacDonald were both obsessed by fear of 'the Goat' and his possible influence; that the timing and content of their speeches were 'largely determined in relation to the movements of Ll.G. known or guessed';[2086] that Lloyd George's spectre haunted the Cabinet Room of his successors like Banquo's ghost; that the Chairman of the Conservative Party from 1926 to 1930 was appointed on the basis of his supposed knowledge of Lloyd George, and that Davidson and Baldwin, supported by the leading section of their party, conceived it as the primary mission of Conservatism from 1922 onwards to exorcize the spirit of Lloyd Georgism from British politics. It is not too much to say that the whole inter-war period was a conscious reaction against Lloyd George.[2087]

This is a seriously damning and shameful indictment of the majority of the political establishment of the day.

Even with Lloyd George's injection of money into the campaign the results at the election–often referred to as the 'Flapper Election', because it was the first in which women aged 21-29 were allowed to vote, under the provisions of the Representation of the People Act 1928–were disappointing for the Liberals.[2088] Lloyd George had set the agenda of the election, but he spoke little outside of North Wales during the actual campaign, and the notion that the government could reduce unemployment by creating work, and promote prosperity by spending money, was still too radical for most of the electorate to accept. Though they fielded 513 candidates and polled 5,104,638 votes, 23.54% of the total, the Liberals only increased their support to 59 seats, largely in agricultural districts, a paltry 9.59% of the seats available, while Labour became the largest party for the first time, with 287 seats, ahead of the Tories with 260. Again, the Liberals ended up supporting a minority Labour government.[2089]

---

2084 Sharp, p197; Jones, *Whitehall Diary*, Vol.I, pp243, 255-256. Jones, in an entry for November 1923, noted "How they do hate him."

2085 O. Mosley, *My Life*, 1968, London, Thomas Nelson, p276.

2086 Jones, *Whitehall Diary*, Vol.I, p190.

2087 Campbell, *Lloyd George*, p3.

2088 The new involvement of young women was reflected in a curious Liberal Campaign twopenny novelette in 1929 entitled *Her Decision*. Belle England, a typist, the heroine of the tale, is a new woman voter who rejects her Tory and Labour wooers for the Liberal candidate, John Strong. See West, p77-81.

2089 Having lost his Liberal seat in 1922, at this election Christopher Addison returned to Parliament as the Labour MP for Swindon,

In Caernarvon Boroughs, Lloyd George increased his personal vote, against, for the first time, both a Tory, John Bowen Davies, and a Labour candidate, blind war veteran Tomos Ap Rhys[2090], coming in 9,133 votes ahead of Davies, with 58.0% of the vote on a constituency turnout of 81.8%. One of the Liberal seats won was Anglesey, taken by Megan Lloyd George with 13,181 votes, 49.4% of the total, who at the age of just 27 became the first female MP to be elected in Wales.[2091] On 31 May her father became 'Father of the House', the longest-serving member of the Commons, a purely honorific position. Megan's maiden speech, delivered on 7 April 1930, was a strongly worded peroration in support of the Labour government's Rural Housing Bill, a sign of things to come.

Stanley Baldwin resigned on 4 June, and the next day Ramsay MacDonald formed another minority Labour government, at first with Lloyd George's cordial support. Lloyd George expressed great hopes of Arthur Henderson as Foreign Secretary in the field of peace and disarmament, and of Jimmy Thomas, as Lord Privy Seal, in combatting unemployment. This 'honeymoon' period did not last long. On 4 November, with unemployment continuing to rise, Lloyd George attacked Thomas in the Commons for his "timid, pusillanimous and unintelligent" proposals.[2092] The Wall Street Crash of 24-29 October 1929 had heralded the global Great Depression and Britain was hit badly, though not as badly as many other industrialized nations. The Labour government had been trying to achieve several different, contradictory objectives: to maintain Britain's economic position by maintaining the pound on the gold standard, balancing the budget, and providing assistance and relief to tackle unemployment. The gold standard meant that British prices were higher than its competitors, so the all-important export industries suffered.

It was now that Lloyd George employed Gareth Jones[2093], recently graduated from Cambridge, fluent in French, German and Russian, as Foreign Policy Adviser. Introduced to him by Thomas Jones, a family friend, on 21 October 1929, Gareth commenced work on 1 January 1930. Sir Bernard Pares, eminent Professor of Russian Language, Literature and History at the University of London, a personal friend, wrote to him enthusiastically: "Very hearty congratulations. You have thrown in your lot with a very great Welshman, with one of the most brilliant minds of Europe, and the work is bound to be very fascinating."[2094] Jones enjoyed working for his boyhood idol, despite the heavy demands that Lloyd George made of him, having to read seven French, one Swiss, two Italian, three German, four Russian papers and the *Chicago Tribune*, and write a weekly report on the Foreign and Welsh

---

holding the seat until 1931, and again, 1934-1935. In the absence of a Liberal candidate at the October 1934 by election, Lloyd George spoke on his behalf.

2090 In 1931, Ap Rhys became one of the first four men in the UK to work with a guide dog, 'Folly'.

2091 Megan held the seat until 1951. She became Deputy Liberal Leader, 1949-1950. In 1955 she joined Labour, winning Carmarthen in a by-election in 1957, holding the seat until her death. On 14 April 1938 A. J. Sylvester noted: "LG. thinks that Gwilym will go to the right and Megan to the left, eventually. He wants his money spent on the left."; Sylvester, *Life*, p206-207. Lloyd George obviously knew his children well, proving to be correct.

2092 https://api.parliament.uk/historic-hansard/commons/1929/nov/04/privy-seal-office. Retrieved 18 May 2020.

2093 Gareth Jones (1905-1935), Welsh journalist who first reported in the West, under his own name, the existence of the Soviet famine of 1932-33, including the Holodomor.

2094 NLW, Gareth Vaughan Jones Papers, File 20/13: Sir Bernard Pares to G.V.J., 30 October 1929. Sir Bernard Pares (1867-1949), historian and diplomat linked with the War Propaganda Bureau during the Great War.

Press.[2095] Once Lloyd George, who Jones called 'The Chief', asked for "an account of Proportional Representation and of the electoral system of Germany. It was to be ready by 1.15 that day. "I want you to get" he said, "an account of the electoral system in Germany, Belgium, France and any other country where there is either a second ballot, or the alternative vote or P.R. Get it done by tomorrow.""'[2096] Lloyd George drove himself and others hard, but frequently inspired good work. With Jones, he got more than the average scholar, as Jones also had the perspective of the 'common man', unusually, for the time, taking "great interest in the affairs of ordinary people."[2097]

On 6 January, a Syro-Palestinian Delegation had written a letter to Lloyd George drawing attention to the pledges made to the Arabs during the war and stating that the Balfour Declaration was in total opposition to these. It pointed out that: "the Mandate was in opposition to Article 22 of the Covenant. The enquiry Commission suggested in Balfour, Lloyd George and Smuts' letter to *The Times* could merely aggravate the position. Why were pledges to the Jews honoured and those to Arabs disregarded?" Sylvester wished him to study the letter in *The Times*.[2098] In their joint letter of 22 December 1929, the trio, viewing the deteriorating situation with anxiety, had declared:

> As members of the war cabinet which was responsible for the Balfour Declaration… we view with deep anxiety the present situation in Palestine. On the events of last August which are now the subject of an inquiry by a special commission we forbear comment. But it seems clear that whatever the finding of the commission may be on the responsibility for the August outbreak, the work to which Britain set her hand at the close of the war is not proceeding satisfactorily.
>
> The Balfour declaration pledged us to a policy; the Palestine mandate entrusted us with vital administrative duties; but causes which are still obscure have impeded the task of administration and consequently the full carrying out of the policy.
>
> In these circumstances we would urge on the government the appointment of an authoritative commission to investigate the whole working of the mandate. The commission at present in Palestine was appointed with limited terms of reference to inquire into specific matters. This commission, in our view, must, as soon as it has reported, be supplemented by a searching inquiry into major questions of policy and administration. Our pledge is unequivocal, but in order to fulfil it in letter and spirit, a considerable readjustment of the administrative machine may be desirable.
>
> Such a commission would be an advertisement to the world that Britain has not weakened in a task to which her honour is pledged and at the same time an assurance to Jews and Arabs alike that any proven defects in the present system of government will be made good.[2099]

---

2095 Colley, p52.

2096 https://www.garethjones.org/margaret_siriol_colley/lloyd%20george/lloyd%20George%20complete%20lecture.htm. Retrieved 24 June 2020. There are 44 documents from Jones to Lloyd George in the Parliamentary Archives alone, dated 7 February 1930–20 February 1933, covering a wide range of topics: See https://archives.parliament.uk/collections/getrecord/GB61_LG_G_26_1#. Retrieved 19 January 2021.

2097 Personal communication to the author by Philip Colley, 23 November 2020.

2098 Colley, p52, citing Gareth Vaughan Jones Papers, NLW Correspondence Series B6/2. 7 March 1930.

2099 https://www.jta.org/1929/12/22/archive/lord-balfour-lloyd-george-and-smuts-in-joint-statement-ask-new-commission-for-searching-probe-of-a. Retrieved 19 July 2020.

Gareth Jones set to work to study the question, and by 30 April he had prepared a detailed brief for Lloyd George on 'The Situation In Palestine'. Along with providing statistics on the relative sizes of the Jewish, Moslem and Christian populations, on Jewish immigration and on imports and exports, Jones stated that the current problem was mainly economic, centring on the questions of immigration and land purchase. There followed a summary of Chaim Weizmann's and Zionist views on these issues, interesting in the light of what would soon happen with the rise of Nazism in Germany and the subsequent issues surrounding the foundation of the State of Israel in 1948.

Concerning immigration, it was felt that there was "room for another 50,000 families if modern scientific methods are adopted", the proof that this could be absorbed being that "there is no unemployment there". It was felt, however, that the "Administration is unsatisfactory… What is required is a first class High Commissioner with a first class Chief Secretary." More controversially, it was stated that "No case of injustice to the Arabs is quoted in the report," and that the "Arab accusation that the Jews seize the best land is not true. We make it the best land." Jones' summary continued:

> The Commission however has vindicated the Government. The Administration is placed in a difficult position by the tendency of Arabs and Jews to accuse the Government of favouring the other side, because it does not favour their own side… The competition between the Arabs and the Jews is mainly the competition, not between two religions and races, but between old-fashioned methods and science. The efficient are ousting the inefficient as everywhere in the world. The leaders play upon religious feeling, but at the bottom of it all is the fear that the Arabs will be deprived of their livelihood.

Concerning land settlement, it was reported:

> The British Administration's Land Ordinance provides that long notice to quit must be given and that the tenant must be fully compensated for improvements effected by him. The report of the High Commissioner on the Administration of Palestine for 1920-25 states "The price paid for these purchases (i.e. land) is usually some two or three times the pre-war value of the land. Large as is the demand the quantity of land which is offered for sale is far in excess of the possibility of purchase."
>
> The Commission differs profoundly from Dr. Weizmann on the problem of land settlement. The report states: "There is no alternative land to which persons evicted can remove. In consequence a landless and discontented class is being created."
>
> The main conclusion is that after the Government has clearly stated its policy with regard to the rights of non-Jewish communities and to Immigration and land-purchase, drastic measures must be taken to increase the productiveness of Palestine.[2100]

On 17 November 1930, in the Commons Lloyd George would powerfully attack the Government's

[2100]https://www.garethjones.org/margaret_siriol_colley/lloyd%20george/Palestine%20brief.htm. Retrieved 19 July 2020.

Passfield[2101] White Paper on Palestine, issued on 20 October, undoubtedly basing some of his points on information provided by Jones. The paper was anti-Zionist in tone, and limited official Jewish immigration to a much greater degree. Contrary to Zionist claims, it stated that the development of a Jewish National Home in Palestine was not considered central to the Mandate, whilst claiming that the British did intend to fulfil their obligations to both Arabs and Jews and would resolve any conflicts that might arise as a result of their respective needs.[2102] In the House, Lloyd George stated:

> It is a very difficult problem to discuss, because you have here two races involved, with both of whom we have the most friendly relations… Our firm conviction is that justice should be done to both, but that the White Paper which has been issued by the Government is really unjust to both…
>
> … the Balfour Declaration was truly national in the sense that it represented the views of the three parties in the State. It was a Declaration which was issued for reasons regarded by the Allies as paramount in that great conflict, and it gave an undertaking that if Palestine were conquered, a home, a national home, for the Jewish people would be established in that country. Before the Declaration was made, it received the sanction of all the great Allied Powers… Two years after the War, the representatives of the Allied Powers met at San Remo, and they considered how that Declaration should be incorporated in the Mandate which was given to our country for the government of Palestine.
>
> It is rather important to consider the words of that Mandate. They were settled by all the Allied Powers and they are the words under which we are responsible for the Government of Palestine… Here is the preamble, and, oddly enough, it is not merely omitted from the White Paper, but any allusion to it is excluded: "Whereas the principal Allied Powers have also agreed that the mandatory should be responsible for putting into effect the Declaration… adopted by the said Powers, in favour of the establishment in Palestine of a national home for the Jewish people, it being clearly understood that nothing should be done which might prejudice the civil and religious rights… of existing non-Jewish communities in Palestine or rights and political status enjoyed by the Jews in any other country; … recognition… has thereby been given to the historical connection of the Jewish people with Palestine and to the grounds for reconstituting their national home in that country…" The reason why I think that those words are important and control the whole of the policy is this: It means that the idea was not to establish a Jewish colony in Palestine… the dominant idea was that there should be a national home for the Jews in Palestine… and the conferring upon them of special rights and interests in that country. It was an opportunity for recreating a Hebrew culture which has already rendered such eternal service to mankind, so that the contribution of the Jews to civilisation should… once more… be the contribution of a people dwelling in a home of their own. That is not colonisation; that is not settlement; that is a national home. That is what this country accepted at a critical moment in its fate for reasons which had to do with that crisis, and its successful emergence out of it. That is why the Allies accepted and endorsed it, and it is a pledge of honour… which we are called upon to honour. The White Paper is almost universally regarded as a revocation of that Mandate… The leaders of the Opposition have expressed their opinions; I as one of those

---

2101 Sidney Webb, Baron Passfield (1859-1947), Secretary of State for the Colonies, 1929-1931.

2102 https://www.jewishvirtuallibrary.org/the-passfield-white-paper. Retrieved 20 July 2020.

responsible for the Mandate, have expressed my opinion… Not merely the Jews, but the Arabs take this view. The Jews regret, the Arabs rejoice. In their hearts, they believe that this means an end of the establishment of the national home for the Jews in Palestine… It is vital that an opportunity should be given in this House, if there be any misunderstanding, to clear it up in such a way that no nation on earth, and certainly not the parties that are most directly concerned, should be under any misapprehension as to the meaning.

This document was issued without anyone being consulted… The League of Nations were not consulted, the Mandatory Commission of the League of Nations were not consulted; the Allied Powers… were not consulted… It is a State document which, in our judgment, altered the whole Mandate. We were never consulted about the terms of that document…

… This is not a British colony. We are mandatory, and Palestine is in a different situation from almost any other country on earth. It is more international in its interest; it is of interest to three of the greatest creeds on earth… It is a mandate for a country which has international interests and international susceptibilities, and where you cannot do anything without running the risk of offending some susceptibility or another… Therefore, it was essential that we should have kept here in touch with the League of Nations and the Mandatory Commission. What has happened? Before this White Paper was ever issued, the Mandatory Commission had issued the report which… was full of the most severe criticism of their administration. It is the first time that the Mandatory Commission has rebuked a Power to whom a mandate has been issued. What was the answer of the Government?… Their answer was practically to tear up the mandate… You cannot tear it up; it is an international document. It is a Treaty which has been signed, and if we say that this mandate is so difficult and so delicate that we cannot carry it out in the sense of the words incorporated in it, there is only one thing for us to do, and that is to hand the mandate back to the League of Nations…

This White Paper… is biased. Its whole drift is hostile to the spirit of the mandate. It breathes distrust and even antagonism of the Jewish activities…

… I am bound to remind this House of our obligations… I see from one of the members of the Mandatory Commission that they contemplate the possibility of, at any rate, 3,000,000 ultimately occupying that land. When we took it over, there were about 700,000 or 800,000, and, perhaps, another 300,000 in Transjordania. Since we took it over, the Jews have increased by 100,000 and so have the Arabs... So far, taking the last 25 centuries, the Jews are the only people who have made a success of this rather stony land…

It is a great experiment… which will leave its mark on history. The Jews left their mark on history when they lived in that land. They have still got the same gifts, and by cultivating them under conditions which will intensify their gifts through a spirit of patriotism for their native land, they are capable again of rendering service to humanity as a whole. We thought that that opportunity ought to be afforded them… If the Government of this country say they cannot carry it out… let us give an opportunity to somebody else that can do it… It needs judgment, it needs courage, it needs perseverance… If we fail in Palestine our failure will be visible to the nations of the earth. If we succeed it will restore confidence in the gift of Britain to govern an empire.[2103]

Lloyd George was not alone in his criticism of the White Paper. Zionist organizations worldwide

[2103]https://api.parliament.uk/historic-hansard/commons/1930/nov/17/palestine. Retrieved 20 July 2020.

mounted a vigorous campaign against it. It led to Ramsay MacDonald's clarification of the paper in the Commons on 11 February 1931, in which he stated that he was "very unwilling to give [the letter] the same status as the dominating document." The letter he referred to, which became known as the MacDonald Letter, dated 13 February, was sent to Chaim Weizmann and aimed to placate the Zionists while disturbing the Arabs as little as possible. When many Zionists took the letter as a withdrawal of the White Paper, it became known as the 'Black Letter' by Arabs. The letter itself also stated that it aimed to provide justice to "non-Jewish sections of the community". By confirming that the policy of the Palestine Mandate was to continue to support Jewish immigration, the letter in effect negated some of the implications of the White Paper and facilitated increasing immigration during the growth of anti-Semitism in Europe in the 1930s.[2104]

Gareth Jones worked for Lloyd George until April 1931, and again from late May 1932 to 31 March 1933, and the relationship would prove to be an important one. Jones acted as his 'eyes and ears' in key areas, making his first trip to Soviet Russia from 6-26 August 1930, spending significant time in Ukraine. On his return, on 5 September he was called to Churt, where Seebohm Rowntree, Lord Lothian and Wallace Stewart[2105] were also present. In his diary Jones noted the conversation:

> 'Poor devils,' said Lloyd George when I told him about Donetz. Tell us what would they do with us if we had a Soviet Government here?' I replied, 'You would be shot Sir.'… We went to the fine, large sitting room where they made me talk for hours, from about 8.30 until 10.45. Lloyd George went to bed at about 10.15… After Lloyd George had gone to bed, Wallace said, "I've never heard Lloyd George listen like that. Usually it's we who listen to him all the time.[2106]

On 12 June 1930, during a ceremony at Caernarfon to mark his 40 years in Parliament, Lloyd George voiced his frustration and concern over what he called "the old inadequate windmill set up by Simon de Montfort"[2107], the slow processes of normal government, urging that they should be temporarily suspended in favour of an emergency programme. During the same month, he worked with Seebohm Rowntree, who had probably studied unemployment more than anyone in the country, and Philip Kerr–newly created 11th Marquess of Lothian on 16 March–along with other experts like Sir Arthur Salter, to work on a memorandum to present to the government on the issue. It was a pressing one, as unemployment climbed past two million. The memorandum, which Lloyd George delivered to No. 10 in August, and which largely followed Kerr's proposals for both public works and longer term modernization of industry with assistance from the banks, on the continental model, stated:

---

[2104]See
https://unispal.un.org/UNISPAL.NSF/0/BBAA033C46A9AA8B8525712C0070B943 for the text of the MacDonald Letter. Retrieved 20 July 2020.

[2105] Charles Wallace Stewart (1885-1950), Canadian Progressive Party politician and farmer.

[2106] Colley, p76.

[2107] Quoted in Campbell, *Lloyd George*, p274.

> It must pay the community better… to have its citizens engaged on useful work in regenerating agriculture and in equipping the nation to maintain its competitive industrial position in the world, than to have them deteriorating in idleness; the expenditure which will bring this about is wise investment, and wise investment is true economy. There is nothing inconsistent in cutting down unnecessary and unproductive costs and simultaneously spending freely in new equipment. It is the practice of all successful enterprise.

It thus recommended: "That an emergency session of Parliament shall be declared, and emergency methods adopted for its conduct, whereby there may be pressed through with the utmost despatch a special body of extraordinary legislation that will give the Government the necessary powers to meet the urgent call for action which comes from the extraordinary growth of unemployment and industrial depression."[2108]

Sadly, these constructive proposals made no traction with MacDonald's ineffectual administration, which had no grasp of the situation and no sense of urgency. The same occurred on 18 September when Lloyd George and Kerr held a three-hour meeting with MacDonald and Philip Snowden, Chancellor of the Exchequer, at No. 10 to discuss electoral reform. After fruitless discussion on unemployment and agriculture, as later recorded by Snowden:

> When we had finished our talk on these matters, Mr. Lloyd George raised the question of the future of the Parliamentary relations between the Government and the Liberal Party. He said that the Liberals could not promise to continue to support the Government in Parliament unless they could get something in return for their support. The co-operation of the Liberals in the coming session would be dependent upon a definite understanding that the Government would introduce and pass legislation for Electoral Reform… They attached supreme importance to a reform of the electoral system which would give the Liberals the representation in Parliament to which they were entitled by their voting strength in the country.
>
> He indicated that the Tories were open to bargain with him… Mr. Lloyd George did not want to enter into any alliance with the Tories, and would prefer to continue co-operation with the Labour Government provided we would pass such a measure of Electoral Reform. He thought it likely that the House of Lords would reject a Reform Bill, and in that case it would have to be passed under the provisions of the Parliament Act. In that case the Labour Government must be kept in office for the two years necessary to overcome the obstruction of the House of Lords. If the Labour Government would agree to his terms, the Liberals in Parliament would support the Government until Electoral Reform had been secured. He did not think that there ought to be much difficulty in coming to an understanding of this sort. It was not likely that the Labour Government would introduce legislation which the Liberals would oppose.[2109]

---

2108 *Memorandum on the Liberal Proposals on Unemployment and Agriculture*, Summer 1930, Lloyd George Papers, G/13/3/1; Quoted in Campbell, *Lloyd George*, p271, 274.

2109 Snowden, *An Autobiography: Volume Two, 1919-1934*, p884-885.

Lloyd George already clearly foresaw what proved to be the eternal trap of third-party status in the traditional British 'first past the post' electoral system, and the lost opportunity–the issue again foundered on MacDonald's opposition and indecisiveness–has been a profound tragedy for progressive British politics and society ever since.

One measure Lloyd George approved of was the Agricultural Land (Utilisation) Bill, introduced by the new Minister for Agriculture, Christopher Addison, his former Liberal colleague, on 5 November, "to promote the better utilisation of agricultural land in Great Britain and the settlement of unemployed persons thereon, to amend the law relating to small holdings and allotments, and for purposes connected with the matters aforesaid." At the Second Reading on 18 November Lloyd George stated:

> This is a Measure… after my own heart. I have taken an interest in agriculture and agricultural reform ever since I entered public life, and I was looking forward to someone who would bring in a Bill of this kind. I am glad the right hon. Gentleman has had the boldness, courage and enterprise, to introduce it, and, as far as I am concerned and my Friend's also, I will give him whole-hearted support in any measures he takes for the purpose of carrying it through… I feel confident… that [he] will do his best. I know that he is as enthusiastic about it as anyone…[2110]

In general, though, Lloyd George did not let up on the floundering government, and on 12 February 1931 he launched a stinging attack on both them and the 'money-barons' of the City during a Commons debate on unemployment:

> Since the War the City of London has been invariably wrong in advising the Government, not merely in the advice which it gave us, and the advice which it gave to the late Government, but in the advice it is giving now…
>
> Take the cause of depression throughout the world at the present moment… a very large part of it is due to the mishandling of monetary questions on the advice of the money barons. What is the result? This depression is not due to the fact that there is a lack of things in the world. It is due to the mishandling of gold and silver very largely… These men who have mishandled this monetary question not merely advise us what to do, but establish a veto upon every proposal which is made for national development. We got rid of the veto of the Lords. Take care that you do not establish a more sordid one.
>
> If you go to the City of London, what is their only remedy for depression? Their only remedy is by placing artificial barriers to prevent plenty from reaching want… As Chancellor of the Exchequer… you must make allowances for the political bias of the City. They have always been against a progressive Government–always. They have always been tolerant of the faults of a reactionary Government…
>
> I beg the Government not to be too nervy and jumpy when the City of London threatens… do not let the Government run away the moment a few volleys are fired from the City of

[2110] https://api.parliament.uk/historic-hansard/commons/1930/nov/18/agricultural-land-utilisation-bill. Retrieved 19 May 2020. The Act received royal assent on 31 July 1931.

> London. It may save them trouble for a short time but no progressive Government can survive long under the protection of the white flag. I ask the Prime Minister to go on; that is what this Motion means…[2111]

This demonstrable return of the old Lloyd George rhetorical fire caused a stir. The Tory *Morning Post* hysterically proclaimed that "The leadership of the extreme left has passed to Mr. Lloyd George."[2112] More importantly, George Lansbury, First Commissioner of Works, a figure of great stature in Socialist circles, one dedicated to the Labour cause and never a personal or political friend of Lloyd George's, was sufficiently moved to write directly to him the next day with a remarkable offer. Recognising Lloyd George as "the most powerful and purposeful figure on the British Left"[2113], he appealed for his aid in the growing crisis by asking him to join the Labour Party, offering him the prospect of the deputy premiership and three or four Cabinet seats for his colleagues! In a most extraordinarily forthright manner, he wrote:

> I have thought of writing to you, many times, during the past few years. Your speech last night has finished my thinking, so here goes.
>
> Why won't you join the Labour Party? 'Labour and the Nation' is only Socialism reduced to everyday expedients. You are willing as an outsider to help us to put these expedients into operation. Your help would be invaluable, *as one of us*. As matters now stand we gibe, humour, abuse, coax each other to the bewilderment of all who read or hear us…
>
> People have said you are an opportunist, and will take any line that suits you. At times I have thought and said so. But these past months' experience and your observations last night compel me to believe you are as sincere as any of your critics… I can't believe of you anything worse than of myself and because this is so I want you in the best place for doing good work, and that I am sure is in the Labour Party. All your people in the House would not come with you, but those who count, the young in mind, those who have faith in our common stock, they will come and in any case your coming would crown a progressive life with the knowledge that as the world of thought and action moved on, you never closed your mind, and when the hour came and you were needed, you flung aside all thought of self and came over to the new groupings of true Liberalism and progressive thought, taking your place once more as a pioneer among pioneers.[2114]

Lloyd George quickly and candidly responded to this heartfelt personal approach in revealing terms:

> I was very gratified to receive your frank and cordial letter. It indicates that there is some prospect of clearing up the atmosphere of suspicion which has hitherto confined and hindered

[2111] https://api.parliament.uk/historic-hansard/commons/1931/feb/12/unemployment-1. Retrieved 19 May 2020.
[2112] *Morning Post*, 13 February 1931.
[2113] Campbell, *Lloyd George*, p282
[2114] Lansbury to Lloyd George, 13 February 1931; Quoted in Campbell, *Lloyd George*, p282-283. George Lansbury (1859-1940), Labour MP for Bow and Bromley, 1910-1912, 1922-1940, First Commissioner of Works, 7 June 1929–24 August 1931, Labour Leader, 25 October 1932–8 October 1935, campaigner for world peace.

co-operation between progressive minds in both our parties. I propose to reply to you in the same spirit of good will and complete candour.

The great majority of our party are in accord with yours on the general line of advance for the next ten years. The differences are not vital and can easily be adjusted. It will be time enough to determine the programme for the following decade when we come within sight of completing our present tasks. I am for the moment leaving out of account the possibility that economic developments throughout the world may drive us all to revise our ideas. The outlook is alarming.

I quite agree with you that attacks and counter-attacks which a lack of understanding between us inevitably provokes weakens and imperils the chances of fulfilling our economic policy. Anything which removes these misconceptions would be of advantage to us both. I have given a parliamentary undertaking on behalf of myself and my colleagues that we will give real support to the Government in any effective plans they put forward and press through to carry out the unemployment proposals sketched out in *Labour and the Nation*. So far we have been given no chance of implementing our pledge. The one exception is Addison's Bill. You know the problems of the town workers better than any living man. I have been brought up amongst the country workers. That is why Addison's Bill gave me real joy. By the way A. and I had passed through a real bad quarrel. That did not prevent my hailing his first Bill with delight.

As to the best method of ensuring co-operation I should like to speak freely. 'Coming over' is not the best way to help. It would antagonize millions of Liberals with hereditary party loyalties who otherwise would gladly support any Government from another party provided it carried through a bold programme for the reconditioning of Britain. I am sure I can render more effective assistance to a government of energetic action by remaining where I am. If the Government go ahead fearlessly with measures for the redemption of their electoral promises on unemployment they will not be turned out by our party, so far as I can foresee events. And when the Dissolution comes then through the agency of the Alternative Vote there will be such co-operation at the polls as will ensure a fresh opportunity for a progressive Government to complete the great programme upon which we are agreed.

Personally I have had enough of office. Seventeen years is just as much as anyone can put up with. Like yourself I am now merely concerned with spending the remainder of my life and strength in advancing ideas and causes which I was brought up to believe in. Despite the 'opportunism' which is one of the temptations and necessities of office and now and again deflects every man from his course, I have always sincerely striven to do my best for the class from which I sprang. As an Independent Member I am confident I can now be more helpful to that class. I can and will give effective assistance to the Government–if they mean business.

At present I am genuinely perplexed and disappointed by the stickiness of some of your colleagues. They are always finding reasons for not doing things. They are too easily scared by obstacles and interests. Unless you can inoculate them with some of your faith and courage your Party and ours will be landed in an overwhelming catastrophe.[2115]

It is interesting to speculate on the path British politics might have taken had Lansbury written sooner, and had Lloyd George responded affirmatively, but it was not to be. For the reasons Lloyd George gave, the overture was sadly stillborn, but it forms a rare insight into the political times. His focus was

---

2115 Lloyd George to Lansbury, 16 February 1931; Quoted in Campbell, *Lloyd George*, p283-285.

far more rural than the mostly urban trade unionists and Socialist intellectuals of the Labour Party, and he was too much of a Liberal individualist to submit to the far stricter Labour constitution.

There was still some political co-operation. On 16 April the Tories moved a vote of 'no confidence' in the government "having failed to carry out their election pledges with regard to unemployment, and having ceased even to attempt any remedial measures". Lloyd George led 30 Liberals into the government lobby, and so Labour survived by 305-251 votes, against five Liberals, including John Simon, Robert Hutchison and Ernest Brown, who voted with the Tories. But divisions were becoming more tightly drawn. On 26 June Simon, Hutchison, Brown and 25 other right-wing Liberal MPs finally relinquished the Liberal Whip. On 3 July Simon unwisely claimed in the Commons that he was the one 'keeping the faith', which Lloyd George and the Liberals had abandoned. Lloyd George responded with a speech like a surgeon's scalpel, taking apart Simon and his assertions, using some colourful imagery derived from his Welsh upbringing along the way:

> It is the old method of those who are transferring their allegiance always to say that those who are behind are departing from principle and that they alone are sound…
>
> It is very difficult for… Members on either side of the House to realise the peculiar position which the right hon. and learned Member has always held in our party, and what a shock it is to see the line taken by him now. There used to be in the Calvinistic Churches in Scotland and in Wales one man who made it his business to see that there was no departure by the preacher or anyone else from the strict lines and dogmas of the doctrine. He was called in our parts the "Guardian of the Doctrine." The right hon. and learned Member in our party was the guardian of the doctrine… and anybody departing from them had to reckon with [him]. I was never thought to be a joy to the orthodox, and [he] was always held up to me as an example… They said "on doctrine you cannot always trust Lloyd George; but" the elect said, "there is always Simon"…
>
> To all those who have been strictly orthodox there is a satisfaction in seeing the mighty fallen… However, there is one comfort. Although the right hon. and learned Gentleman has left us we have always his great utterances in the past to cheer us on and to keep us straight–on land values most enthusiastic and encouraging; on Protection there never was such an exposure of the fallacies to which his new friends are committing themselves. We, his late lamented friends as he called us shall always think of them with a great sense of satisfaction…
>
> … I do not object in the least to the right hon. and learned Gentleman changing his opinions. Every man, in the course of his lifetime, is entitled to do that… But I do object to his treating it as if he were the only man who was obeying conscience and principle. I do object to this intolerant self-righteousness… Greater men… have done it in the past, but in doing so they have not taunted those who have not agreed with them, and who have still adhered to the underlying principles, which they have pursued through their lives. They never taunted them with lack of principle, with being mere maneuverers and tacticians. They, at any rate, did not leave behind the slime of hypocrisy in passing from one side to another. It is a thing that I protest against most strongly.[2116]

[2116]https://api.parliament.uk/historic-hansard/commons/1931/jul/03/finance-bill. Retrieved 19 May 2020.

In July 1931, Lloyd George was closer to regaining office than at any time since 1922. He appeared to be in fine form, attacking the Tory leadership in the Commons on 20 July. In the words of Scottish Labour MP, Lauchlan MacNeill Weir:

> There was a startling awakening when Lloyd George took the floor. To him it was a gala day and he was as happy as a winner at a flower show. Members crowded in to hear him, attracted like filings to a magnet. No wonder, for the most distinguished Member of the British Parliament, the world famous orator, was addressing the House. No one willingly misses a speech by Lloyd George, even Tory leaders being soundly trounced. From him they take their correction mildly and kiss the rod.
>
> He dominated the debate. Standing right in the centre of the House, the only place visible from both the Press Gallery and the Members' Gallery, the best illumined point, he stood clear as if a spotlight had singled him out against the red of the carpet and the dark green of the benches. He was a picturesque figure that filled the eye. He was a man full of vigour and thrilled with animation and energy. He knew the old adage that the best form of defence is to attack, and he was attacking as only he could do.
>
> 'Two hundred rank and file,' he cried in gleeful banter, 'and not a single leader! I understand that not a single leader of the Party means to speak, unless Lord Wolmer has a claim to that rank. This is a charge of the Light Brigade, but it is not war, and it is not magnificent.'
>
> This was a most devastating attack on the Conservative leaders for not stating their policy. Rarely had the Commons heard such a display of the lighter side of oratory.
>
> Seated on the Front Opposition Bench, not three yards from the Liberal orator was Mr. Baldwin, Mr. Neville Chamberlain, and Sir Thomas Inskip. They sat 'domes of silence,' motionless as the Trafalgar Square lions, as harmless, as imposing, and as mute. Their presence there that day was merely formal *Cum tacent clamant*...[2117]

The evidence regarding the possibilities of Lloyd George being interested in joining a MacDonald Government is somewhat conflicting and shadowy.[2118] One piece in favour, a memorandum dictated by Lloyd George to Frances Stevenson after a meeting with MacDonald in 'the last days of July 1931', was partially quoted by Frank Owen in 1954, before the original document went missing:

> Generally speaking, Labour would like an alliance. They would be willing to drop certain of their present Ministers...
>
> Ramsay would be Prime Minister. Lloyd George would be Leader [of the House] at the Foreign Office or the Treasury. Ramsay thinks he can adjourn early in August and resume late in the autumn, and then continue till the next Budget. No fear of immediate Election. It might be contemplated that the Army, Air and Navy join up under one Ministry...[2119]

What might have happened remains, however fascinating, in the realm of speculation, another 'What

2117 MacNeill Weir, p331. Lauchlan MacNeill Weir (1877-1939), PPS to Ramsay MacDonald, 1929-1931.

2118 See Campbell, *Lloyd George*, p293-296.

2119 Owen, p717. See also Marquand, p602; no record exists in MacDonald's diary or papers of such decisions.

if?' in his life story, as on 26 July Lloyd George was struck by what was described as haematuria–essentially, the presence of blood in the urine–and was confined to his bed at 2 Addison Road, Kensington. His surgeon son-in-law, Sir Thomas Carey-Evans, ascertained his heart, kidneys and other organs were sound, and advised one big, single operation, rather than two separate, smaller ones, saving the patient stress. Three days later, at 9.45 am, Lloyd George underwent a prostate operation, a difficult procedure in those days, at home at the hands of Royal Physician Lord Dawson and leading prostate expert Dr John Swift Joly, with Sir Francis Shipway performing the anaesthesia, and Dr Howard Humphries, an X-Ray specialist, in attendance.[2120] Aged 68, hitherto Lloyd George had enjoyed generally robust, rude good health, and so it was particularly hard that he was incapacitated at the very time while the financial and economic crisis precipitated the political crisis he had tried to stave off for the preceding two years.[2121]

At this juncture Gareth Jones called on Lloyd George. En route from Ukraine to the USA, on 30 September he visited 'the Chief' at Churt:

> We… were taken… into a large room where Lloyd George was reclining on a sofa… I told him that everywhere in America, Russia, Germany, France I heard people asking about him. He said. 'Well, I've turned the corner.' He looked bright, well and his eyes flashed as much as ever… His colour was good and he looked much better and much less tired than he did the day I went to see him from Cambridge two years ago.

Lloyd George asked about the situations in Germany, Russia and the USA.

> Just then Miss [Winifred] Russell, the typist came in with the news she had received over the phone. She read out that MacDonald made no decision about the General Election. Lloyd George's facial expression changed immediately and there was a look of tremendous impatience and anger. 'He's a poor thing!' with absolute scorn. 'He's betrayed his own party and now he's going to betray ours.' Then he almost snarled 'neurotic.'…
>
> … we heard a car arriving and in came… Sir Herbert Samuel (Home Secretary), Sir Donald Maclean (Minister for Education)… and Sir Archie Sinclair[2122] (Secretary for Scotland)… Sylvester and I went to the library drawing room and had tea. The historic interview between Lloyd George and the Liberal Ministers in the National Government took place in the next room and then I could hear raised voices. Lloyd George seemed to be putting vim into them. They had been wavering. Lloyd George was saying: "If there is an election the pound will go down, down, down." You could hear the word 'tariff' being repeated often. Lloyd George is as firm against tariffs as ever…
>
> At 6.45pm however Lloyd George came out, and told me… 'I want you, Gareth, to keep on

2120 Sylvester, *Life*, p32-34. Bertrand Dawson, Viscount Dawson of Penn (1864-1945), first met Lloyd George professionally in France during the war. In December 1916 he had written warmly to Lloyd George welcoming the latter's becoming Premier: quoted in Watson, *Dawson Of Penn*, p142-143.

2121 His illness meant that 1931 was one of only two years between 1890 and his death that Lloyd George missed the National Eisteddfod, that year held in Bangor, Megan delivering his message on his behalf. The other was 1901, the event being held at Merthyr Tydfil.

2122 Archibald Sinclair (1890-1970), Liberal Leader, 26 November 1935–26 July 1945.

> informing me as to what is 'happening'...'[2123]

Lloyd George clearly knew that he was receiving valuable, top-quality information from Jones.

On a personal level, the progress of his recuperation caused a minor family issue. The famous cartoonist David Low[2124] had done many depictions of Lloyd George. Low once happened to sit next to Bengy's father, Dr Carey-Evans, at a dinner. Sir Thomas said to him:

> You are causing a lot of trouble with my father-in-law. 'Oh', said Low, 'what have I done wrong there?' 'Well', said [Sir Thomas], 'every time that my son meets his grandfather, he rushes up to him and gives him a heavy punch in the tummy!' And the reason is, Lloyd George is my father-in-law, and my son considers his grandfather to be a comedian, like Charlie Chaplin, because he always sees these cartoons of him, sitting cross-legged, in your paintings of him, and its causing a lot of trouble!" And the next morning, a taxi drove up, there was this large cartoon of myself and my grandfather, sitting next to him, saying 'What's the policy Taid?'[2125]

At the time of his operation, Carey-Evans told Lloyd George he had 15 years to live, and he did indeed die just short of 15 years later in 1945.

On a political level, hindsight shows that this period was catastrophic for Lloyd George. During 1931 the economic situation deteriorated and there was much fear that the budget was unbalanced. This was borne out by the majority report of the Committee on National Expenditure, headed by Sir George May, on 31 July, which revealed a huge and unexpected deficit on the budget of £120 million–an underestimate–and recommended cuts in Government spending, particularly in unemployment benefits, along with increased taxation, to correct this. This triggered a confidence crisis and a run on the Bank of England in which foreign investors were withdrawing £2.5 million a day in gold.

Daily reports on Lloyd George's health were given in the *Times*: by 2 August he was reported 'comfortable', two days later he was said to be free from pain and sleeping well; by another two days his pulse and temperature were normal and there were no complications; by 12 August he had made 'an exceptionally good recovery.'[2126] During this time Herbert Samuel and Donald Maclean, who had proposed the May Committee, kept him abreast of their consultations with the government.[2127] Unfortunately for Lloyd George, these few weeks were crucial. The government agreed in principle to make changes in taxation and to cut expenditure to balance the budget and restore confidence. However, the Cabinet could not agree on the two options available: either introduce tariffs–taxes on imports–or make 20% cuts in unemployment benefit. In the end, MacDonald and his Chancellor Snowden drafted a proposal that would cut benefits by 10%. Even this was rejected by the Trade Unions. When a final vote was taken, the Cabinet was split 11-9 with a minority, including important

---

2123 Colley, p128-129. Jones was taken to Churt by A. J. Sylvester, who oddly makes no mention of him in his own diary: Sylvester, *Life*, p39-40.

2124 Sir David A. C. Low (1891-1963), working for the *Evening Standard*, 1927-1950.

2125 Taped interview with author, Beaumaris, 11 October 2018. The cartoon in question remains with the family.

2126 *The Times*, 29 July-12 August 1931; Quoted in Campbell, *Lloyd George*, p297.

2127 Samuel, p205.

leaders such as Arthur Henderson and George Lansbury, threatening to resign rather than agree. The divide was unbridgeable, and the government resigned on 24 August, the very day that Lloyd George was first allowed out of doors for a short drive.

The financial crisis grew worse and decisive government action was needed as the leaders of both the Tory and Liberal Parties met with King George V, and MacDonald, at first to discuss support for the measures to be taken but later to discuss the shape of the next government. MacDonald had originally wished to resign but was told to re-consider by the King on the grounds that the majority of opposition MPs and the country at large supported the cuts proposed by the May Report, even if Labour and the Trade Unions led by Ernest Bevin did not. MacDonald duly changed his mind during the night and met with the Tory and Liberal MPs the following morning. On 24 August, MacDonald agreed and formed the National Government. The new Cabinet had four Labourites–now called 'National Labour'–who stood with MacDonald, plus four Tories led by Baldwin and Chamberlain, and two Liberals, Herbert Samuel as Home Secretary and Lord Reading (Rufus Isaacs) as Foreign Secretary and Leader of the House of Lords.

Although officially party leader, crucially Lloyd George had been absent from the negotiations which led up to the formation of the National Government due to having undergone his operation from which he was recuperating, although he had been consulted daily.[2128] Samuel Hoare, Tory Treasurer and one of his party's chief negotiators with MacDonald, well-knew that Lloyd George, had he been fit and well, would have strenuously opposed to the direction now being taken.[2129] On 23 August–the day *before* the government resigned–he wrote to Neville Chamberlain: "As we have said several times in the last few days, we have had some great good luck in the absence of Winston and LG [sic]."[2130] On 26 August Hoare was appointed Secretary of State for India. Acting Liberal Leader Samuel had endorsed the government on 13 August, accepting office as Home Secretary on 26 August. Further, party grandee Lord Reading, who became Foreign Secretary on 25 August, stated at public meetings that Lloyd George was "in full accord" with what the party had done.[2131] On 20 September Lloyd George was well enough to issue a statement which declared that the nation would pull through, and that "a faction fight among ourselves at this juncture would be unpatriotic lunacy".[2132]

Within a few days, events caused Lloyd George to dramatically change his attitude. The immediate cause was the prospect of an early general election, to which Lloyd George was totally opposed: he believed that the government would put forward the Tory policy of tariffs, countering the Liberal's firm commitment to free trade. The Liberal Party also opposed an early election when the prospect was raised towards the end of September, but the Liberal 'shadow Cabinet' under Samuel approved a memorandum which allowed an investigation of a special tariff.[2133] Leading Liberals visited Lloyd George at home at Churt to try to come to an agreement but found that he became more

---

2128 H. Berkeley, *The Myth That Will Not Die: The Formation Of The National Government 1931*, 1978, London, Croom Helm.

2129 MacDonald also knew it; see MacNeill Weir, p371.

2130 Quoted in Gilbert, p502. Churchill was at Juan-les-Pins, on the French Riviera, on a painting holiday.

2131 *Economy*, *The Times*, 29 August 1931, p10; Samuel, pp205-206, Wasserstein, ft.21, p317.

2132 *Mr Lloyd George's Message*, *The Times*, 21 September 1931, p12.

2133 *The Liberal Dilemma*, *The Times*, 1 October 1931, p12.

confrontational. On 4 October, Samuel noted:

> I had a very long conversation with Lloyd George. In the course of it he expressed himself very strongly against any lasting alliance between the Liberal Party and the Conservatives. He said that he himself would not contemplate it, and he added, with some emotion, "If I am to die, I would rather die fighting on the Left."[2134]

On 5 October, Ramsay MacDonald himself visited Churt: to him, Lloyd George said that if an election were held, he would fight as a supporter of free trade and demand a definite statement of the Government's policy on the issue. Faced with Lloyd George's intractability, the Cabinet decided to call an election anyway; there would be no specific statement on tariffs, but the manifesto would appeal for a 'Doctor's mandate' to do whatever was necessary to repair the economy. Liberal ministers accepted this decision.[2135] When the election was announced, Lloyd George did as he had indicated and issued a semi-official statement through the Press Association which denounced the Liberal ministers who had "commit[ted] themselves to the consideration of a tariff policy" as having engaged in "a gross betrayal alike of the interest of the country and of the party to which they profess allegiance". Ominously the statement concluded by encouraging all candidates who were elected in support of free trade to "provide… the nucleus of a new progressive party".[2136] Lloyd George still controlled a political fund which he had set up while the party was divided between him and Asquith, and declined to release it to support Liberal candidates who endorsed the National Government. Three Liberal MPs allied to Lloyd George who opposed the election–his son Gwilym, Goronwy Owen and Frank Owen–resigned from the Government on 8 October.[2137] At the election, six Liberal candidates formally declared their opposition to the National Government. Five had sat in the previous parliament, with the addition of journalist and novelist Edgar Wallace making his first and last appearance as a political candidate.

Labour unions were strongly opposed and the Labour Party officially repudiated the new National Government. It expelled MacDonald and made Henderson Leader, leading it into the election on 27 October against the three-party National coalition. It was a disaster for Labour, which was reduced to a rump. MacDonald won the largest landslide in British political history, his National Government winning a total of 554 seats and a Parliamentary majority of 493. The Tories won 470 seats, Simon's Liberal Nationals 35 and National Labour 13. Samuel's Liberals, those who wished to associate with the National Government, won 32 seats, while Lloyd George's Liberals, bitterly opposed, won a mere four. Labour was decimated by what they saw as MacDonald's treachery, being reduced to 52 seats, losing a staggering 235. Lloyd George himself was out of action, so Margaret loyally fought his seat for him, with the aid of gramophone records of his voice, and the efforts of stalwarts like Ernest Evans. Sylvester noted on 25 October, "Dame Margaret has been working very hard both in the

---

2134 Samuel, p211.

2135 *The Cabinet Decides*, *The Times*, 6 October 1931, p12.

2136 *Dissolution*, *The Times*, 7 October 1931, p14.

2137 *Parties And The Election*, *The Times*, 9 October 1931, p12; Jones, *David Lloyd George*, p353.

Boroughs and for Megan in Anglesey. Here she is loved, admired and is the uncrowned queen."[2138] In the event, Lloyd George's personal vote slightly increased against Tory candidate, stockbroker Captain F. Page Gourlay, to 59.3% of the vote. The next day a relieved Lloyd George telegraphed from Churt to his agent in Caernarfon, Caradog Evans "Thankful the peaks of Snowdonia remain above the deluge."[2139]

The government was initially applauded by most, but the Labour Party were left in a state of confusion with the loss of several of their most prominent figures, and MacDonald, Philip Snowden and J. H. Thomas did little to explain themselves, with the result that Labour soon swung fully against the government. This was in part because of the Trade Unions' decision to oppose all forms of cuts proposed by MacDonald and Snowden in response to the May Report. The Trade Unions that represented a large proportion of Labour's base refused to support any cuts to benefits or wages except to "the salaries of Ministers".

On 3 July–in a speech already noted–Lloyd George intervened in the Third Reading of Snowden's Finance Bill to reaffirm his commitment to Land Value Taxation, whilst admitting that in his own Bill of 1909 he had made "far too many deductions". He stated that:

> In undeveloped land there is, undoubtedly, a very considerable source of revenue, and it is an increasing source of revenue… The Government have a programme of national development. I am one of those who criticise them on the ground that the programme is not bold enough, but even as it is it is a programme that involves the expenditure of scores of millions of public money in roads and in development. There is not one of those enterprises that does not double the value of land in particular districts, not merely double it but quadruple it, and even far more. In the aggregate they raise the value of land by scores of millions of pounds… By this Bill he will bring the whole of that land into contribution to the extent of one penny in the pound… That is what I call a just principle, and that just principle is embodied in this Bill.[2140]

The Bill passed by 274–222 votes but was soon revoked by the succeeding National Government.

Efforts to bring public expenditure cuts produced further problems, including a mutiny in the Royal Navy over pay cuts, the Invergordon Mutiny, an industrial action by some 1,000 sailors in the Atlantic Fleet that took place on 15-16 September 1931. For two days, ships there were in open mutiny, in one of the few military strikes in British history. The result was panic on the London Stock Exchange as the pound came under renewed pressure, and the government was forced to take the radical step of taking it off the Gold Standard altogether on 21 September. Debate then broke out about further steps to tackle the economic problems. On 28 September, the Labour Party expelled all members who supported the National Government, including MacDonald. Increasingly, the majority of the Cabinet came to believe that a protective tariff was necessary to support British industry and provide revenue and that a general election should be fought to secure a mandate, but this was

2138 Sylvester, *Life*, p44.
2139 Ibid., p45. Megan also increased her personal vote.
2140 https://api.parliament.uk/historic-hansard/commons/1931/jul/03/finance-bill /. Retrieved 20 June 2025.

anathema to the Liberal Party. Their acting leader and Home Secretary, Herbert Samuel, fought in Cabinet against an election but found the Liberals dividing in several directions over the course of action. One group, under John Simon, emerged as the Liberal Nationals, was prepared to accept the tariff and expressed willingness to take the place of the main Liberals in the government.

It was eventually agreed that the government as a whole would seek a "Doctor's Mandate" to take a free hand and that each party would issue its own manifesto. Supporters of MacDonald formed the National Labour Organisation and the parties agreed to allow their local organisations to agree whether or not to oppose each other. The government was opposed by the Labour Party, Lloyd George and his Liberals and the New Party of Oswald Mosley.[2141] Within the parties there was particular conflict between the Tories and Liberals. The campaign for the 1931 general election run by the National Government was based mainly on fear of a repeat of events, which had occurred in Germany during the start of Great Depression, in Britain. At Shotton on 19 October MacDonald waved a German 50,000,000 Reichsmarks note, nominally worth £250,000, but which during the German financial collapse could be bought for 2d, to emphasise the point.[2142]

In the new Parliament, the group of Independent Liberal MPs rejected attempts to reunify all the Liberals, including the pro-tariff Liberal National Party, under a single party whip and consistently opposed the National Government. On 3 November Lloyd George officially stepped down as Liberal Leader and was succeeded by Herbert Samuel. He wrote to Samuel: "As you are aware, I am completely at variance with the disastrous course into which the party has recently been guided. It may, therefore, ease matters and, at any rate, save embarrassment to my friends, if I write to tell you that I am not a candidate for election to any office in the group."[2143] In the Commons Lloyd George, now no more than a backbencher, sat on the Opposition–that is, Labour–front bench in the corner seat next to the gangway, rather than with the rest of the Independent Liberals, continuing to occupy this seat until the end of his Commons career.

On 18 November 1931, a recuperating Lloyd George entertained Mahatma Gandhi to tea at his home in Churt for three-and-half-hours.[2144] Gandhi was in England as the representative of the Indian National Congress for the second Round Table Conference with the British Government to discuss Indian constitutional reforms, also famously touring the East End of London and visiting the Lancashire cotton mills. Although the servants at Churt were used to distinguished visitors, they paid Gandhi the unique honour of all coming out to see the Holy Man. Lloyd George would later relate a story concerning a black cat. This cat, someone's collared pet, had first come to the house a day or two before Gandhi's visit. On the evening in question, she entered through a window of the drawing room and went straight to Gandhi as he squatted on a sofa by the fireplace, settling in his lap until he

---

2141 Oswald Mosley (1896-1980). The New Party became the British Union of Fascists, BUF, on 1 October 1932.
2142 Marquand, p669.
2143 HLRO, Samuel Papers A/84/6, Lloyd George to Samuel, 3 November 1931.
2144 *The Collected Works of Mahatma Gandhi*, Vol.54, p336. The signature of 'M K Gandhi' is clearly written in the visitors book from Churt: the author thanks the late Lord Tenby for this reference.

got up to leave. She was gone the next morning, and Lloyd George never saw her again.[2145] Concerning Gandhi himself, Lloyd George told Sylvester that he was:

> A most remarkable man, and they had a most interesting discussion… Gandhi had insisted on shaking hands with all the domestic staff. L.G. thought he showed a good deal of dignity, even though he wore few clothes, and that he was the cleverest of all the Indians he had seen. Although he might be called a mystic, he knew precisely what he wanted and was fighting stubbornly for it. L.G. said he spoke to Gandhi as one politician to another. Gandhi wanted the best of both worlds: that was why he was such a good politician.[2146]

Many other famous people visited Lloyd George, including Greek premier Eleftherios Venizelos–spelling his name 'Venisolo'–in July 1931 and August 1934, and women's rights campaigner Marie Stopes in November 1932. Others included Churchill, Smuts, Chaim Weizmann, David Ben-Gurion, H. G. Wells, novelist Francis Brett Young (frequently), J. M. Barrie, composer Walford Davies, newspaper publisher William Randolph Hearst and Lord Beaverbrook.

On 20 November 1931, Lloyd George left with Margaret, Megan, Gwilym and his wife Edna, and A. J. Sylvester, on a cruise to India and Ceylon (now Sri Lanka). He passed some of his time by reading Churchill's war memoirs. They arrived at Bombay (now Mumbai) on 4 December, and Colombo on 7 December. As a holiday, the trip was not a great success, being generally plagued by bad weather, and Lloyd George was doubtless glad to be back at Churt by 7 January 1932.[2147] More interesting were his reflections whilst away from home. On 15 December his old friend Herbert Lewis wrote to him from his Flintshire home at Plas Penucha, Caerwys, "greatly concerned" about his illness, and offering frank advice:

> I wish it were possible for you to cut yourself loose from party moorings and to free yourself from the heavy and engrossing labour of building up a new party with the inevitable manoeuvres, compromises and political management and tactics which it involves, to emancipate yourself from even National considerations and interests… and to devote yourself entirely to those wider issues which have emerged from the rapidly growing inter-dependence of all countries, and to opposition to that selfish perversion of true Nationalism which infects the policy of all countries and threatens to plunge the world into ruin and chaos.
>
> In brief, I suggest that you adopt the role of a World Statesman, using the House of Commons and the Press as a platform from which you can counsel the world for its own good and thereby help to save it from the frightful cataclysm of a World War to which the present policy of the nations is inevitably tending…
>
> The world crisis calls for such a man and you are now the only man living with the experience, the prestige and the driving power that are necessary to lead the world out of the material and

---

2145 M. Behn [M. Slade], *The Spirit's Pilgrimage*, 1960, London, Longmans, Green, p185; L. Fischer, *The Life of Mahatma Gandhi*, 1951, London, Jonathan Cape, p307; Carey Evans, p110.
2146 Sylvester, *Life*, p47.
2147 Jones, *Radical Life*, p95.

> moral quagmire which threatens to engulf it. This is the greatest and noblest task to which you could devote the closing years of your life...[2148]

This was a very fair summation of Lloyd George's standing and abilities at this juncture–as well as being highly prescient about the trend to war–however difficult it would have been to practically apply his skills to the world's problems. Lloyd George replied from on board the P&O Liner SS *Rajputana*, on 31 December, showing both his appreciation of his old friend's advice and his knowledge of his own personal limitations:

> I am very grateful to you for your frank and friendly letter... When I return to Britain I have a very difficult decision to take, and no one seems to realise that more thoroughly than you do. For the present I am very impressed with your argument, and my inclination is towards the acceptance of your penetrating advice.
>
> As you know, I have always found it very difficult to keep out of a 'scrap', more particularly so when I find causes in which I am interested being so inadequately and ineptly defended. Those who were responsible for Liberal direction after I was placed *hors de combat* surrendered all the passes to the enemy. The heights are now in the command of the Protectionists: we are entirely at their mercy. The poor abject mob of Liberals are there cowering down in the swamps. They have ceased entirely to count. No one talks now of the extermination of the Liberal Party; for all practical purpose it is annihilated.
>
> Please keep writing to me with your reflections on the position. I need counsel very badly. Liberal leaders have all gone, and anyhow they are a miserable lot. When I was stricken down in the late summer we had complete control of the Parliamentary situation, and the Labour Government was getting more and more into our hands. We had over 5,000,000 of electors. Where are they now? I have never seen a case of more complete disaster following so promptly on fatuous and pusillanimous leadership.[2149]

Lewis did indeed write again, on 5 January 1932, reiterating his previous comments:

> I can fully realise how difficult it would be for you... to divorce yourself from party politics and confine yourself to the role of a great international statesman whose aim is to conciliate and persuade... I cannot bear the idea of a man with your personality, position and achievements frittering away his strength in party turmoil and bickering. You are the doyen of the elder statesmen of the world–a unique man for a unique opportunity in its history...[2150]

By this time, Lloyd George's position on the Treaty of Versailles had subtly changed. In his *The Truth About Reparations and War-Debts*, published on 14 April 1932–originally intended to be a long memorandum for submission to the international conference on reparations at Lausanne–he pleaded for the complete abolition of reparations and inter-Allied debts, and demanded in addition the

[2148] Lewis to Lloyd George, 15 December 1931, Lloyd George Papers, G/12/1/19. Emphasis added.
[2149] Lloyd George to Lewis, 31 December 1931, Lloyd George Papers, G/12/1/20.
[2150] NLW, Sir John Herbert Lewis Papers D30/109, Lewis to Lloyd George, 5 January 1932.

downward revision of high tariffs and thoroughgoing disarmament. His words were very little heeded, and Hitler came to power as Chancellor in Germany on 30 January 1933.

In May 1932 Gareth Jones, back from the USA, resumed working for Lloyd George. Jones had been a spectator to the Depression in that great capitalist nation. In two letters to Lloyd George, he had written an account of the conditions in America and how the Depression was affecting the wealthy country. Lloyd George quoted the January letter in his book the *Truth about Reparations and War Debts* as one from 'a friend in the States', Jones describing the feeling in America as one of "*disillusionment*".[2151] No sooner was he in London than Lloyd George invited him to Criccieth for the weekend and on 22 May he wrote his Sunday letter to his family from the Lion Hotel, describing his visit to Brynawelon with Sylvester:

> … L.G [sic]…. Megan and I went for a walk and he asked me questions about personalities in America, which I was able to answer well. L.G. has a fine gift of getting the very best of your knowledge out of you. He is a perfect questioner and gives one complete confidence…
>
> We then returned… to the house… L.G. was in great form, bright, witty, and looking well…
>
> Lloyd George spoke highly of Stalin: "Stalin is trying an experiment. Of course, he fails but he recognises his failure. He's man enough. I take off my hat to Stalin and to Mussolini. And when Stalin recognises failure or tries a new method they say, 'I told you so.' Every scientist fails time and time again before he makes a great discovery. People in America are finding that the great business leaders are alright when the car is going along a smooth road, but they are helpless now that the car has broken down."
>
> He thinks that the international situation is desperate. The Lausanne Conference will lead to nothing.[2152]

Jones was not back in Britain for long. On 27 June, Lloyd George informed Jones that he wanted him to go to Italy immediately. From Le Grand Hotel in Rome Gareth reported to his parents that:

> Mussolini is building roads, bridges, canals, and viaducts in many parts of Italy. He aims at a rebuilding of his native country, and it is remarkable that his programme follows the lines laid down by the Liberal party in Great Britain and almost identical with Lloyd George's Liberal Plans! What irony that the enemy of Democracy should be carrying out the policy advocated by British Liberals…
>
> I thought Italy was wonderful, and I got masses of things to tell L.G. Mussolini is carrying out a program which is almost identical with L.G.'s Liberal Plans!…[2153]

Amongst others, he met Professor Arrigo Serpieri, Mussolini's Head of Land Reclamation, and duly reported back on the ongoing draining of the Pontine Marshes.[2154]

---

2151 Lloyd George, *Truth About Reparations*, p126-128.

2152 Colley, p165-167.

2153 Ibid., p172.

2154 For a well-illustrated overview, see Ruth Sterling Frost, *The Reclamation Of The Pontine Marshes*, *Geographical Review*, 24, 4, October 1934, p584-595.

From 2 September, Jones spent a week at Churt with Lloyd George, helping to prepare information for the latter's Memoirs.[2155] During the last months of 1932 he spent many weekends at Churt, "researching some of the most 'vital and confidential' government wartime documents for Lloyd George's *War Memoirs*", including shipping, food production, and the 'American attitude towards the War in 1916.'[2156] However, tragedy was beginning to unfold, both personal and international. In autumn 1932 rumours began to circulate in London of the terrible famine occurring under Stalin's regime in the Soviet Union and particularly Ukraine[2157], and Jones made plans to visit the country. The importance of his connections and the potential influence of his reporting was considerable by this time, as evidenced by a letter of 25 January 1933 from Soviet Ambassador Ivan Maisky to A. F. Nieman, a deputy in the Foreign Press Department: "I urge you to take Jones under your special care… and put him in touch with those people and institutions whose assistance he will need. The impressions Jones forms will to a significant degree determine Lloyd George's attitude toward the USSR."[2158] Nieman replied on 4 February, stating that every attempt would be made to fulfil Maisky's recommendations, acknowledging Jones connection with Lloyd George and his journalistic influence, but, significantly, also noting that his most recent articles "makes us be on guard that his sympathies have changed [from 1930]. It is, of course, our job to persuade him otherwise, but I know Jones a little and am afraid that his impressions will not generally yield to our influence."[2159]

But dramatic events were also occurring in Germany. So in late January–early February 1933 the intrepid traveller visited firstly a country he knew extremely well, having visited Germany every year since 1923. On 27 January, en route to Germany on the SS *Bremen*, Jones wrote to Lloyd George:

> The next month, I shall spend investigating the situation in Germany… During March, I shall be in Russia visiting Moscow and the Ukraine. I shall send you reports on what I see. In the future… I hope I may be of some service to you.
>
> Yesterday I saw the Soviet Ambassador [Maisky], who has been remarkably kind in obtaining material for you in Moscow.[2160]
>
> He added: "The Captain's woman-secretary comes from Danzig. 'We Danzigers bless Lloyd George,' she said. 'It was touch or go whether we should belong to Poland or not, and he saved us.'"[2161]

Jones was present in Leipzig the day Hitler was made Chancellor, and on 23 February flew with him in his famous Junkers Ju52/3m (D-2202 'Richthofen') from Berlin to Frankfurt am Main. His article about this flight classically began: "If this aeroplane should crash the whole history of Europe would be changed. For a few feet away sits Adolf Hitler, Chancellor of Germany and leader of the most

---

2155 Colley, p175.
2156 Ibid., p177-178.
2157 Ibid., p180. The exact death toll is impossible to determine, but at a median estimate, some 3.9 million died in the Ukrainian Holodomor alone, with some 4.5 million in the rest of the Soviet Union.
2158 Quoted in Gamache, *Eyewitness*, p122.
2159 Ibid., p123.
2160 Colley, p187.
2161 https://www.garethjones.org/overview/llg1.htm. Retrieved 3 October 2020.

volcanic nationalist awakening which the world has seen."[2162] The import of his hypothetical speculation grew in significance as history unfolded over the following years. Meanwhile, Jones got a dark glimpse of the future, seated on the dais near Hitler as the latter launched into his vitriolic rally speech before 25,000 fervent supporters. He reported that it was "primitive, mass worship… The people are drunk with nationalism. It is hysteria." As for Hitler, Jones made an unusual comparison with his own employer, one he felt Welsh readers of the *Western Mail* would understand:

> It is the emotion of the National Eisteddfod exaggerated multifold. Imagine the Welsh national feeling responding to Mr. Lloyd George and add to bitterness of defeat, the depth of humiliation which, Germany has gone through; the painful poverty of the middle class, the sufferings through inflation, the rankling injustice of the War Guilt Clause and savage political hatred, and a picture of the Hitler crowd is there.
>
> Imagine a speech of Mr. Lloyd George. Take away the wit, take away the intellectual play, the gift of colour, the literary and Biblical allusions of the Welsh statesman. Add a louder voice, less varied in tone, a more unbroken stretch of emotional appeal, more demagogy, and you have Hitler. Hitler has less light and shade than Mr. Lloyd George. He has less variety of gesture. Hitler's main motion is to point out his right hand, which trembles. He is without the smile and the sharp glance of Mr. Lloyd George, without his hush and sudden drop of the voice.
>
> Mr. Lloyd George is more of an artist and knows that life is not all emotion or all tragedy. He lightens a grave speech with humour… Hitler is pure tragedy or heightened melodrama... His only comic relief is bitter irony. Mr. Lloyd George has a wider scale and… makes lighter mood follow or precede a tragic part. Hitler is… a master in repeating the leitmotiv in many varied forms, and the leitmotiv is "The Republican régime in Germany has betrayed you. Our day of retribution has come." … [H]e thunders out his resounding blows against Bolshevism and against democracy …
>
> Whereas Mr. Lloyd George is more complex and more subtle and a speech of his is kaleidoscopic, changing in tone and colour from one moment to another, Hitler is more uniform, and his oratory is in colour; one blazing red which makes the people mad.[2163]

After the rally, Jones also spent several hours as the dinner guest of soon-to-be Reichsminister of Public Enlightenment and Propaganda, Dr Joseph Goebbels. He noted Goebbels emphasis on the return of German militarism and his statement: "We'll stick to power. Nothing will get us out. From now on there'll only be Nazi Ministers."[2164] Goebbels, in his turn, noted the meeting with Jones in his diary: "Long conversation with Lloyd George's Secretary. Is in Germany for study purposes. An intelligent young man. Tells me terrible things about Soviet Union."[2165]

It was in the next month, March 1933, that Jones made his third and final visit to Russia and Ukraine to investigate the reports that had filtered through of the terrible starvation. In Moscow, on 6 March he met Malcolm Muggeridge and they discussed the famine in Ukraine. Soon after this,

---

2162 Gareth Jones, *With Hitler Across Germany*, *Western Mail*, 28 February 1933, p6; Colley, p200-201.

2163 Gareth Jones, *Primitive Worship Of Hitler*, *Western Mail*, 2 March 1933, p13.

2164 Four days later the Reichstag fire took place in Berlin.

2165 Quoted in Gamache, *On Assignment*, p64.

Muggeridge's articles were published in the *Manchester Guardian* on 25, 27 and 28 March, though according to Muggeridge these had been drastically edited by the left-leaning paper. Jones then made his own trip to Kharkov in Ukraine. He left his train early, to witness events first-hand, without 'supervision', and saw the horror of what was taking place in the Black Earth District and Kharkov itself. On his return to Moscow, he used his credentials as private secretary to Lloyd George to obtain a comprehensive, wide-ranging personal interview with Maxim Litvinov[2166], the Commissar for Foreign Affairs, on 23 March. During this, Litvinov made a point of stating:

> Respects & regards to Mr L[loyd] G[eorge]. Always enjoyed being with him. Always admired. Followed with great interest LGs activities when in London as [an[ émigré. Remember writing article with gr[ea]t enthusiasm about the Insurance Scheme [of] 1909. Always studied his speeches, admired his boldness.[2167]

Careful about what he wrote in his letters home from the Soviet Union, on his return to Berlin, Jones immediately gave his famous press release on the 29 March 1933, printed in many US and British newspapers including the *New York Evening Post*–under the title 'Famine Grips Russia, Millions Dying'– and the *Manchester Guardian*–the next day, entitled 'Famine In Russia'.[2168] He appears to have offended Lloyd George in a letter he wrote immediately he arrived in Berlin on 27 March, giving him "first-class information", stating that:

> I have just arrived from Russia where I found the situation disastrous. The Five-Year Plan has been a complete disaster in that it has destroyed the Russian peasantry and brought famine to every part of the country. I tramped alone for several days through a part of the Ukraine... I spoke with a large number of workers, among whom unemployment is rapidly growing...
>
> *The situation is so grave, so much worse than in 1921 that I am amazed at your admiration for Stalin...* Therefore I have much material on which you may want to question me... Should you wish me to come to Churt at any time... I should be delighted to come and report.[2169]

This letter, however, and the fact that Jones had exploited his connection with Lloyd George to gain access to Litvinov, meant that their previously close relationship cooled considerably from this point, and Jones got no call from Lloyd George.

A. J. Sylvester was called to the Soviet Embassy on 8 April by Ambassador Maisky.[2170] Maisky was friendly with Lloyd George, so he lodged the Soviets complaint through this more personal channel. Sylvester duly replied on behalf of Lloyd George, stating that the latter was "extremely annoyed" that

---

2166 Maxim Litvinov (1876-1951), Commissar for Foreign Affairs, 21 July 1930–3 May 1939.

2167 Colley, p210.

2168 George Orwell's *Animal Farm* was inspired by Jones's articles on the Great Famine of 1932-1933.

2169 https://www.garethjones.org/soviet_articles/Gareth_Jones_1933_correspondence.pdf. Retrieved 7 July 2020. Emphasis added.

2170 Sylvester, *Life*, p94. Sylvester merely states that Maisky was "very helpful about the Russian edition of L.G.'s book' - presumably the first volume of his *War Memoirs*.

Jones had made it seem that he "was visiting Russia for and on behalf of Mr. Lloyd George."[2171] On 16 April a telegram, marked 'Secret', was sent to the Soviet Embassy by an angry Litvinov, which accused Jones of being "an imposter."[2172] Jones was placed on the blacklist of the O.G.P.U., the Soviet Secret Police, indicting many crimes to his name, including that of espionage, and banned from entering the Soviet Union. After this, for his honest reporting, Jones was repudiated by the foreign press corps in Russia and ostracized by the British establishment.[2173]

Lloyd George could now obviously wield little influence in the Commons, but this did not stop him from forthrightly speaking his mind, acting as the nation's conscience. At the end of a wide-ranging survey of the calamitous political situation on 12 July 1932, he exclaimed:

> This Government is the most abject picture I have ever seen of statesmanship in a funk! To cut down research at this moment, when agriculture is fighting for its life, is a lunatic policy… But let us meanwhile do something for our country, and not always be looking forward to something happening just round the corner. Do not let this country be like that Pompeian slave just discovered in Italy who was found among the ruins clutching the leather bag of his savings. Utilise them! The land of this country was reclaimed in the Middle Ages by people who were consecrated to service. Let us revive the ages of faith, and instead of Britain standing for ever at the doors of Employment Exchanges, Foreign Offices and conferences expecting something to happen, let it exert its great strength in the spirit of faith. And if we do it boldly, fearlessly, in these trying days, then when the trouble is over you will have a country which has not been dilapidated and deteriorated by these years of crisis, but is a stronger, mightier, richer and more contented land.[2174]

From 12 June to 27 July 1933, representatives of 66 nations met for the London Economic Conference, held at the Geological Museum. Its purpose was to win agreement on measures to fight the Great Depression, revive international trade, and stabilize currency exchange rates. On 15 June, Lloyd George addressed the Conference, Gareth Jones reporting for the *Western Mail*:

> Speaking of the World Conference, he said he had listened to the Prime Minister in the House of Commons, and there had been a good deal of complaint that he had said nothing. He, (Mr. Lloyd George) saw a reason why. There were lots of people behind him watching every word he said lest he should commit himself in a way such as would interfere with some protected industry…
>
> Had the Government any plans for unemployment? He had been looking for any indication that anybody in authority was thinking out the problem of national planning. Could they tell him from a study of the Prime Minister's speeches what his plans were?

2171 Quoted in Gamache, *Eyewitness*, p135.
2172 Gamache, *Eyewitness*, p136.
2173 Colley, p226; Gamache, *Eyewitness*, p152.
2174 https://api.parliament.uk/historic-hansard/commons/1932/jul/12/consolidated-fund-appropriation-bill-1. Retrieved 21 May 2020.

"Tariffs," said Mr. Lloyd George, "were not a plan. We were undertaking the leadership of the world conference." He proceeded, when, he supposed, the questions of war debts, tariffs, restrictions, and quotas would be dealt with. He presumed the question of the effect of mechanisation upon labour would also be a vital issue.

Had anyone heard what were the plans or proposals the Government were going to submit on those vital issues upon which the future of the world might depend, not merely for ten years, but for generations? What were they?

"No, there are no plans; I regret it" said Mr. Lloyd George.[2175]

The Conference itself collapsed in disarray after President Roosevelt revoked US participation on 3 July.

Shortly after Hitler became Chancellor, but while Hindenburg was still President of Germany, Lloyd George went to Barmouth on 22 September 1933 to officially open the new sea defence works. At the ceremony, relayed over the BBC Radio Western Region from the Pavilion, his old friend Reverend Gwynoro Davies[2176] gave a speech of welcome. In replying, he voiced a concern that was on many people's minds in those economically troubled times, namely the rise of militant communism in Europe. He said:

All the trouble that had arisen in Europe had come from a flagrant breach of the undertaking to disarm by all the victors except one… He knew that there had been horrible atrocities in Germany, and they all deplored and condemned them, but a country passing through a revolution was always liable to ghastly episodes owing to the administration of justice being seized here and there by an infuriated rebel. He was neither a Nazi nor a Fascist nor a Communist. If the Powers succeeded in overthrowing Nazism in Germany, what would follow? Not a Conservative, Socialist or Liberal régime, but extreme Communism. Surely that could not be their objective. A Communist Germany would be infinitely more formidable than a Communist Russia.[2177]

He also had more personal comments to add. Nearly forty years before, in 1894-1895, he had been Clerk to Barmouth Urban District Council, and his brother William, who was present, still held that office. He "spoke with gratitude of those old days of small things, and publicly gave thanks to his brother who had done so much to smooth for him the path to fame."[2178]

Writing to jeweller Morris Wartski[2179] shortly after, on 3 October, Lloyd George struck exactly the same note as he had in Barmouth, in a letter which is important for two reasons. First, that even so early on he both knew about and condemned the Nazi treatment of the Jews. Second, that he blamed the current worsening European political situation on the flaws of Versailles and the subsequent bad

---

2175 https://www.garethjones.org/unemployment/unemployment_11.htm. Retrieved 7 July 2020.

2176 John Gwynoro Davies (1855-1935), Calvinistic Methodist minister of Capel Caersalem, Barmouth, from 1887 until his death, also Chairman of Barmouth Urban District Council, 1894-1903.

2177 *The Times*, 23 September 1933, p7.

2178 W. W. Davies, p59.

2179 Morris Wartski (1855-1946), Polish-Jewish émigré who first set up business in Bangor, Lloyd George having been the firm's lawyer.

faith of the victors. He professed himself "profoundly shocked at the outrages" perpetrated especially against the Jews. He also claimed that there would have been no Hitler nor Nazi Party if the powers had not "constantly broken faith" with Germany and had unfairly treated that country since the Great War. He concluded "Injustice breeds injustice."[2180]

This period saw the start of one of Lloyd George's last great projects, the writing of his *War Memoirs*, his *apologia*, which naturally went on to become a best seller. After his illness in 1931, that November he had gone on extended vacation to India and Ceylon with Margaret and Megan. Lloyd George refreshed his memories of the war years by reading the accounts of Churchill and Liddell Hart, convinced that the time was now ripe for his work to commence. With him he had "a huge trunk of every book that had ever been written on the War by anyone of importance. These he read, marked and annotated."[2181] On his return, Bron-y-de became a vast, chaotic document centre, managed with some difficulty by A. J. Sylvester and Frances Stevenson, expert advisers such as Captain Basil Liddell Hart[2182] and Malcolm Thomson[2183] also being recruited. The first two volumes of the original six-volume edition of the work came out in September-October 1933, the next two in September-October 1934, the final two in September-October 1936.

The news that he was engaged in this enterprise was not universally welcomed. The King detested works which, in his opinion, refought the war's battles, and through the Cabinet Secretary, Hankey, he tried to dissuade Lloyd George from proceeding. This royal intervention was, unsurprisingly, not well received, the former premier justifiably 'flaring up': "Why should the King be against my book? Was he against Arthur's book on Kitchener[2184], or against the book on Haig?[2185] No, he was not. He raised no objection to what was said about me, yet when I am about to defend myself he does not like it. He can go to Hell. I owe him nothing; he owes his throne to me."[2186]

Nevertheless, Lloyd George duly submitted his draft of his chapter on the King to the palace, and it was returned with only one tiny correction, which Lloyd George happily accepted. However, he became angry again a year later after submitting his draft chapter on labour unrest to the palace, when the suggestion was returned that perhaps he could be more magnanimous towards men like MacDonald and Snowden who, though the parts they had played in the war were not very creditable, had later gone on to achieve high office. It was hoped that the reference to them could be deleted. This time it was Sir Clive Wigram[2187] who was tasked with carrying the unpalatable suggestion to A. J. Sylvester at Lloyd George's London office at Thames House. Sylvester "talked to L.G.[sic] on the telephone immediately afterwards. He said he would not alter it."[2188] It was virtually a replay of what

---

2180 Quoted in Crosby, *Unknown*, p504, Ft.31, quoting Parliamentary Archives LG/G/34/2/27. Wartski wrote to Lloyd George from Llandudno on the persecution of the Jews in Europe on 13 May 1938; See Parliamentary Archives LG/G/40/3/79.

2181 Jones, *The Lloyd George War Memoirs*, p100.

2182 Captain Basil H. Liddell Hart (1895-1970), soldier, military historian and theorist.

2183 Malcolm Thomson (1885-1984), research assistant to Lloyd George, 1925-1940, later official biographer.

2184 G. Arthur, *The Life Of Lord Kitchener*, 1920, 3 Vols., London, Macmillan & Co.

2185 Presumably, J. Charteris, *Field-Marshal Earl Haig*, 1929, London, Cassell.

2186 Quoted in Sylvester, *Life*, p94. Entry for 4 April 1933. As Cabinet Secretary, Hankey was involved in Lloyd George's use of Government documents.

2187 Clive Wigram (1873-1960), Private Secretary to the Sovereign, 1931-1936, after Stamfordham's death.

2188 Sylvester, *Life*, p108. Entry for 25 April 1934.

had transpired the day before. On that day, Frances Stevenson had recorded in her diary Lloyd George's response and reasoning in more detail:

> Today we had back from the King the chapter D[avid] had submitted to him containing the references to H.M. The latter very gratified with what D. says about him, but requesting that certain derogatory references to Ramsay MacDonald should be deleted. D. furious & says he certainly will not do this, & that H.M. has no right to make the request.
>
> The only effect of the King's interference is to make D. rewrite the passage on Ramsay MacDonald in the chapter on Labour Unrest, and strengthen the case against Ramsay in doing so–make it more hostile & more vehement. He says that he has not refrained in his book from attacking certain people, e.g. Asquith & Kitchener, who were doing their very best according to their own lights to *help* during the war. He is therefore not going to spare one who, like Ramsay, did his best to thwart and hinder every effort to prosecute the war vigorously.[2189]

Thus, when the (original) fourth volume of the *War Memoirs* appeared, it reproduced MacDonald's letter of 23 May 1917 summoning a joint Convention of the Independent Labour Party and the British Socialist Party to be held in Leeds on 3 June 1917, in which it was stated that the Convention would "begin a new era of democratic power in Great Britain. *It will begin to do for this country what the Russian Revolution has accomplished in Russia.*"[2190]

Grandson Bengy remembered Lloyd George writing his *War Memoirs* in the library at 'Bron-y-de':

> … sat in a high, Windsor chair, with a table to his right, and what did surprise me, was that he had no papers out, no great, open documents, checking everything, it all seemed to be flowing from his memory, and he had these notebooks, with a little stubby pencil, and I would go in, and obviously disturb the whole thing, so he would give me a notebook and tell me to go to the office and type it out for him, and he would pay me a sum of money for the completion… and I've often wondered whether that was either to get rid of me, or to show me the value of good business [laughs]… I would type this thing out, painfully, with one finger, and produce the typewritten sheet of paper for him… but it was such a calm atmosphere, that he was in this big, lovely room he had at Churt, writing away, stuff just pouring out of him, without any reference to anything. He would ask for the odd document, just to have a glance at it, or remind him of something, I suppose, but on the whole, it just flowed out of his memory, quite remarkable.[2191]

Most of the time, it took two secretaries to keep up with Lloyd George's huge productivity.

A. J. Sylvester commented on Lloyd George's method of writing whilst staying at Churt with his wife Evelyn in 1940:

---

2189 Stevenson, *Diary*, p269. Entry for 24 April 1934.

2190 Lloyd George, *War Memoirs*, Vol.II, p1153. This referred to the first revolution of March 1917.

2191 Taped interview with author, Beaumaris, 11 October 2018.

> On this small table there is also a notebook, beside which is a big yellow pencil, about a foot long and as far round as my big fingernail. He uses these enormous pencils… because he cannot so easily lose them, and because they are easier to hold, especially with his terribly shaky hand. Whenever L.G. has a brain-wave, he immediately flies to his notebook and writes it down. Sometimes this is on the international situation, sometimes about the farm, sometimes about an individual with whom he is on bad terms…[2192]

Bengy's older brother Robin also had revealing memories of these years, from the clear-eyed, uncomplicated point-of-view of a child:

> I was born in 1923… and my earliest recollection of him are the occasions my brother and I went to have breakfast with him at his Surrey home Bron-y-de. At that time we lived nearby at Green Farm. We would walk there across the fields and go up to his bedroom where we had our breakfast. He was always an exciting person for a child to be with because he immediately involved you in a host of questions usually about what sort of egg we would like, how cooked and all sorts of things we had never ever had to think about. At Easter he had two chocolate eggs we had to choose. One was very large and the other normal size. I remember him saying now Bengy is the youngest, so I am going ask him to choose first. Well of course Bengy did not hesitate to point to the large egg. He roared with laughter obviously enjoying Bengy's no hesitation choice.
>
> I remember lunching at his home from time to time. There were usually distinguished guests, but he always made sure we were involved by asking us a question about our school or something similar… He insisted on good manners, but it was always done kindly and without embarrassment. His conversation with other guests was fascinating. We might not understand the meaning of what was being discussed, it was just fascinating to watch Taid. His personality was spellbinding and when he reminisced he might mimic someone's voice hilariously. He was a very good mimic, but he sometimes laughed so much he could not finish.
>
> I stayed with him for a week on one occasion in about 1935 and I remember the house was a fever of activity with secretaries everywhere. I think he must have been writing his war memoirs. Nonetheless he found time to take me for a walk in the afternoon down to his orchards at Churt. He seemed to know every tree and in front of one apple tree loaded with what seemed like thousands of apples he said to me now count the apples on that tree. I said Taid I can't begin to do that. He immediately replied there is no such word as can't. So I started counting and to my astonishment was able to come to an acceptable figure. He was very pleased and put me to a further task by multiplying that figure with the number of trees of that apple to reach a useful estimate of the crops output. He was very thorough and kept a watchful eye on his estate. He took me to Farnham to see a Wild West film… He enjoyed it as much as I did. He was exciting company.
>
> I heard him speak publicly on only one occasion. It was the Caernarvon National Eisteddfod in 1935. He was magnificent. He had the whole assembly completely captivated hanging on

[2192] Sylvester, *Life*, p272. Diary Entry for 6 July 1940.

every word and gesture. I have never heard anyone else master an audience like that.[2193]

As for Lloyd George's actual voice, grandson Bill remembered it as "warm, Welsh, melodic," one that drew a listener in, while grandson Bengy remembered it as "a high-pitched tenor".[2194] Geoffrey Shakespeare remembered it as having "a unique quality. It was soft, rich and musical, and flexible in its range. If he had been a singer he would have been a tenor."[2195] It is notoriously hard to judge vocal quality from audio recordings of the 1920s and 30s, which tend to render most voices as rather 'reedy', but it is clear that, when at the height of his powers and coupled with his magnetic presence and dynamic style of oratory, his speeches were captivating. On 19 October 1933 Lloyd George went to the World's News Theatre in Shaftesbury Avenue, London, to see the film he had made the day before on the international situation caused by Germany's withdrawal from the League of Nations: "Afterwards he said: 'Surely that is not my voice.' He had heard his voice on the talkies for the first time."[2196]

Bengy and Robin's elder sister Eluned, who lived to be 94, retained vivid memories of her grandfather: "She took walks with him, listened to his stories and found him charming because he treated her as an equal. She also had fond memories of gardening with her grandmother in northern Wales."[2197] Her own eldest daughter, Margaret MacMillan, relates: "I do remember my mother saying that he was always good at listening, even when she was a child."[2198] Bengy himself related that Lloyd George did not really talk about his own childhood, but indulged in a lot of good-natured play-acting with his grandson when out on walks with him, going to a driveway of a house, saying whether it was a friendly place to visit–or not! Bengy felt the quality of Lloyd George's oratory declined in his final years, his speeches no longer had their previous deftness and power, perhaps he longer made so much effort, was simply tired, or thought people would just listen whatever he said. He was still very interested in life and in people, however, and continued to travel, visiting Brazil in December 1927, and making trips to Europe in 1929. In January of that year, he sailed by cruiser along the coast from Cannes to Naples and also motored through Belgium and France to the Italian Lakes with Margaret, Megan, Gwilym and his wife Edna. He made a trip to Morocco in December 1935–January 1936, where he met with Winston Churchill in Marrakesh on 30 December.

On 28 November 1934, in replying to Churchill in the Commons on the issue of German rearmament, specifically regarding comparative strengths of the nations' air forces, Lloyd George picked up on the thread he had pursued in Barmouth in September the previous year, stating that it was important "to organise a defence which is adequate to our reasonable needs and to practical probabilities–not things which you can imagine merely, but things which are likely to happen." However, he believed that the Germans currently only had defensive capability, adding:

2193 Personal communication to the author by Davina Carey-Evans, 16 November 2018.
2194 Interviews with author at Crondall, 18 June 2019, and Beaumaris, 29 May 2019 respectively.
2195 G. Shakespeare, p39.
2196 Sylvester, *Life*, p101; *Lloyd George on Germany*, British Paramount News Issue No. 276, 19 October 1933.
2197 https://www.theglobeandmail.com/news/national/conservationist-lyn-macmillan-led-effort-to-save-niagara-escarpment/article26266503/. Retrieved on 12 February 2019.
2198 Personal communication to the author by Margaret MacMillan, 11 February 2019.

> [T]he German Government have for the last 18 months been doing their best to work up a bad Press against themselves. It has offended every kind of sentiment–Jew and Gentile, Protestant and Catholic, Communist, Socialist, trade unionist, the Constitutionalists who believe in constitutional government and in law and order, and those with Liberal sympathies. There is no sentiment which they do not seem to have set themselves to exasperate and outrage. The right hon. Gentleman used the word "revolution" in reference to what has happened in Germany. I think it is the right word. It is a revolutionary temper, and a revolutionary temper is the temper of a fever, and a fever-stricken person is not an easy neighbour. He is not normal for the time being. But a revolutionary country is a very dangerous country to treat as a pariah…
>
> You want time for them to calm down, and meanwhile, let us make it clear to them that we mean to give fair, impartial and judicial consideration to their grievance. What is it? It is that they were promised solemnly by the signatories of the Treaty of Versailles that if they disarmed the rest would follow suit. That was the promise. For 14 years they waited for a redemption… They entreated the great Powers to begin redeeming their bond. They were mocked by a succession of pacts and pacts outlawing war, and meanwhile every country except Britain increased its armaments… and money was lent to Germany's neighbours to build up formidable armies right on her frontier. Can you wonder that at last they were driven into… this revolt against what they regarded… as this chronic deception of the great countries? You must put that right. You will never get disarmament in Europe until you do it.[2199]

This was not 'appeasement', as Lloyd George has sometimes been charged with, but a wholly rational analysis of the actual situation, coupled with a reasoned, calm assessment of how to best attempt to tackle that situation with the information then available.

On 17 January 1935, his 72nd birthday, Lloyd George launched his last great campaign at a meeting in the Drill Hall, Bangor. He was heard by 7,000 people packed inside and another 5,000 listening by loudspeakers outside. Speaking for an hour and 55 minutes, he exclaimed "In 1914 the God of War sent the world reeling through the gates of hell. The God of Money has since been completing the tragedy."[2200] Nearly 70 press representatives were present, including those from Germany, France, Poland and the USA. His proposed programme was called "Lloyd George's New Deal" after the American New Deal. To tackle social and economic problems he proposed the establishment of a national development council with representatives from industry, commerce, finance, workers and economic thinkers. Composed of a maximum of five members, it would be responsible for planning bold schemes in the field of housing, roads, land and in the reconstruction of depressed industries. Lloyd George submitted a 107-page memorandum to the Cabinet on 14 March, and six meetings were held with him between 18 April and 15 May[2201], but unfortunately, his plans had no influence on the policies of the National Government; though MacDonald was initially half-attracted to considering Lloyd George entering his National administration[2202], two-thirds of Tory MPs were against it, and

---

2199 https://api.parliament.uk/historic-hansard/commons/1934/nov/28/debate-on-the-address. Retrieved 24 August 2021.
2200 Quoted in Sylvester, *Life*, p114.
2201 Dutton, p58.
2202 Marquand, p764-765.

some Cabinet members, including Neville Chamberlain, would have resigned if he had joined.[2203] On 16 July Lloyd George duly published the memorandum as *Organizing Prosperity: A Scheme of National Reconstruction.*

Just after his Bangor speech, on 1 February, the *Daily Express* published a popularity poll by columnist 'William Hickey'. Readers had been invited to write in naming the public personalities they most liked reading about: 'Public Favourite No.1' was Lloyd George who beat, amongst others, Winston Churchill, Gracie Fields, Franklin D. Roosevelt, Mussolini, Rudyard Kipling, Greta Garbo and the Aga Khan! The paper mused:

> What is it they all possess which attracts this searchlight of interest? Is it the ability they have in the jobs they perform? No, I don't think so. I think it is because besides doing whatever they choose to do well, they do it slightly differently from the others. There is a bit of colour about them and the way they do things.[2204]

Indeed, in the later 1920s and the 1930s, Lloyd George's popularity meant he had 'the largest postbag of any British politician', though, unsurprisingly, he apparently read little of it, that duty generally falling to A. J. Sylvester.[2205]

Despite by now spending much of his time in Churt, Lloyd George's heart was still never far away from North Wales. Thus, he wrote a warm–and mildly self-revealing–foreword to Wyn Griffith's autobiographical 'Spring of Youth'[2206]:

> The soul of a people is to be sought in its villages. It is there you find that pedigree of national culture which gives to a folk its distinctive character and merit. It is in the village that a lad achieves his natural growth, with roots deep in the ancestral soil of the traditions, folklore, habits and social outlook of the race from which he springs.
>
> And therefore it gives me special pleasure to commend to the reading public this delicately drawn study of his own village boyhood by my young fellow-countryman, Wyn Griffith. Whoever is willing to understand the forces that shape the Welsh peasant, the environment which fosters in him that blend of moral puritanism with keen poetic and artistic sensibility by which the Welsh are distinguished, will find them here graphically portrayed.
>
> … Note, for example, his account of the awe inspired by the mountains in the children of a mountain-dwelling folk: "In mist and rain and snow the mountains lived their lives above us, remote and dimly menacing, present always, seen or unseen: they held the wind in their teeth in the winter gales, and thrust the swirling mist into the very doors of the houses…" Hill and farmstead, cottage home, school desk, slate quarry and the socially dominant chapel are all depicted with touches and incidents photographic in their vividness.[2207]

---

2203 Jones, p238-239; Crosby, *Unknown*, p358.

2204 Quoted in H. Montgomery Hyde, *Norman Birkett*, p419.

2205 Lentin, p91; Jones, *Real Lloyd George*, p5.

2206 Llewelyn Wyn Griffith (1890-1977), Captain in the 15th Battalion, Royal Welch Fusiliers, part of the 38th (Welsh) Division. *Spring of Youth* (1935) was his follow up to *Up to Mametz* (1931).

2207 Lloyd George, Foreword to *Spring of Youth*, 1935, London, Constable, pvii-viii.

On 9 May Lloyd George had an audience with the ailing King George V, and they spoke of the international situation and the possibility of war: "D[avid] said he hoped His Majesty would not listen to the warmongers like Mussolini. H.M. fired up and broke out vehemently, 'And I *will* not have another war. I *will not.* The last war was none of my doing, & if there is another one & we are threatened with being brought into it, I will go to Trafalgar Square and wave a red flag myself sooner than allow this country to be brought in. D. says it was a most extraordinary outburst."[2208] Interestingly, in the build up to the Abyssinian War, Mussolini was seen as a greater threat to international peace than Hitler. Yet only 15 months before, Lloyd George had spoken of Mussolini as one of the main "bulwarks against trouble".[2209] On 4 August he entertained H. A. L. Fisher and his family to dinner, and talk turned to the Abyssinian situation:

> Fisher asked D[avid] what *he* would do if he were in power now. D. replied that first of all, he did not think that he would have allowed things to drift into their present impossible position, i.e. he would have insisted on the League [of Nations] taking a stronger line with Japan, in the first place. The moment they abandoned their authority in that question it was practically impossible for them to deal with any other dispute.[2210] However, things being as they are, he would see that an enormous amount of equipment & ammunition were supplied to the Abyssinians, which would enable them to put up a good fight. He says he feels sure that that is what Palmerston would have done.[2211]

On 27 September Lloyd George was "very pleased" with an interview he had over lunch in London with Dino Grandi[2212], the Italian Ambassador. Frances Stevenson recorded:

> They talked first of all on art, about which D[avid] confessed he knew nothing save whether he liked a thing or not. Grandi said after all this was the ultimate test… Then they talked about the war, and finally about the present crisis. Grandi said that Mussolini was a great admirer of D., and had had every utterance of D.'s sent to him during the last 3 years. "And now that you have turned against him", said Grandi, "he still wants to be kept informed as to what you are saying. He says you are the only person who understands him."
>
> It was agreed that it would be extremely difficult for Mussolini now to turn back. D. said that if he had had authority he would have suggested giving Italy some of the German Colonies and bringing the Germans themselves into the deal. "You could have your whack and they could have theirs", said D. Grandi said that if the Italians thought they could have got that, they would

---

2208 Stevenson, *Diary*, p309. Entry for 10 May 1935.

2209 Ibid., p254. Entry for 18 February 1934.

2210 Japan's Kwantung Army had invaded Manchuria on 18 September 1931, after the Mukden Incident, establishing the puppet state of Manchukuo, which lasted until 17 August 1945. Historians have agreed with Lloyd George: the Manchurian Crisis had a significant negative effect on the moral influence of the League. As critics had predicted, it was powerless to intervene against strong, aggressive nations.

2211 Stevenson, *Diary*, p314. Entry for 4 August 1935. Maybe, but the world had changed since the days of Palmerston's 'gunboat diplomacy'. Lloyd George was surely speculating on an 'ideal scenario', as at a time when the British Government was starving its own Armed Forces of finances, it was unlikely to sanction "enormous" amounts for distant Abyssinia.

2212 Dino Grandi (1895-1988), Ambassador to the UK, 3 August 1932–13 October 1939, recalled to Italy after attempting a pact between his country and Britain to prevent Italy from entering the Second World War.

> not have proceeded in their war preparations. And he thought that such a possibility might influence them even now. "But in any case", advised D., "don't go on once you have reached Addis Ababa. And don't bomb villages, & women & children."
>
> Grandi said that as early as January last Mussolini had made his intentions known to Laval[2213], who must have, & did in fact pass them on to Simon.[2214] More-over, Mussolini had 'made his arrangements' with the French. Grandi hinted that this meant some agreement by which the French had been able to remove garrisons from the Italian frontier…
>
> D. assured Grandi constantly that the British were sympathetic to Italy's claim for expansion.[2215]

On 12 June 1935, Lloyd George had launched a political campaign with the publication of a manifesto, signed mainly by Nonconformist church leaders, attacking the government for the failure of its domestic and foreign policies. It announced that a non-party 'Council of Action for Peace and Reconstruction' was to be established by a convention at Caxton Hall, Westminster on 1-2 July 1935. In all, 2,680 delegates, including 82 MPs and 445 ministers of various denominations, accepted invitations; among attendees were George Lansbury, Herbert Samuel, Lord Cecil of Chelwood[2216], Lord Lothian, Isaac Foot[2217] and Harold Macmillan. Lloyd George spoke on the second day, making an eloquent attack on armaments expenditure, stating that the money should be devoted to social purposes. The Council was apparently inspired by Roosevelt's New Deal, but its focus on the Nonconformist Churches, already a declining force, proved to be an inherent weakness.

There followed an initial statement, soon withdrawn, that the Council of Action would stand up to 350 candidates at the next general election. Lloyd George's plan seems to have been to frighten Stanley Baldwin–who had replaced the ailing Ramsay MacDonald as Prime Minister on 7 June–with the prospect of Labour wins in many constituencies as a result of the intervention of Council candidates, where supported by the local Liberal parties and to get his National Government to make policy concessions in areas favoured by Lloyd George.[2218] It also seems to have been a convenient device for Lloyd George to get out of political commitments which he did not wish to enter. A. J. Sylvester recorded that he often used his association with the Council, as a non-political body, to avoid meetings based on party politics.[2219]

Victor Finney[2220] was a strong supporter of this campaign and its objectives. He went on to become the organising secretary of the Council of Action at its headquarters in Abbey Street, Westminster and later at Horseferry House, Horseferry Road just behind Lloyd George's own offices in Thames House. He often accompanied Lloyd George to meetings in Britain and abroad and was a regular visitor to

---

2213 Pierre Laval (1883-1945), Foreign Minister, October 1934–January 1936.
2214 Sir John Simon, Foreign Secretary, November 1931–June 1935, then Home Secretary until May 1937.
2215 Stevenson, *Diary*, p318. Entry for 27 September 1935. Of course, Stevenson was not present herself.
2216 As an architect and defender of the League of Nations, Cecil was awarded the Nobel Peace Prize in 1937.
2217 Isaac Foot (1880-1960), Liberal MP for Bodmin, 1922-1924, 1929-1935, father of Michael Foot.
2218 Rowland, *Lloyd George*, p717; Toye, p310.
2219 Sylvester, *Real Lloyd George*, p250-251.
2220 Victor Finney (1897-1970), Liberal MP for Hexham 1923-1924.

north Wales.[2221] By the time of the election however, the Council was finding it hard to make a real impact. It published a booklet on 'Peace and Reconstruction: Action!' and sent a questionnaire to all candidates but Lloyd George did not campaign nationally as its figurehead, though he reportedly spent a staggering £400,000 [£36.35m in 2025] from his Political Fund in its support. On 14 November, the National Government was re-elected with a reduced majority, and although 67 out of 362 candidates endorsed by the Council won seats in Parliament–11 Tories, 21 Liberals, 34 Labour and one Independent–they never tried to behave as a group.[2222] Finney recognised that the Council of Action could only be a success if Lloyd George committed to it more actively and permanently, but he was not able to persuade him, so while the Council was kept going until 1940, it was unable to exercise much political influence.[2223]

On 20 August 1935, Lloyd George was called to the Foreign Office to discuss Italy's increasingly threatening attitude towards Abyssinia with Foreign Secretary Samuel Hoare and the Minister for League of Nations Affairs, Anthony Eden. Interestingly, while Churchill was neutral, or even pro-Italian in his stance, Lloyd George supported the Abyssinian side. Lloyd George:

> Asked if they intended to raise the embargo on munitions and was informed that this would be lifted. He told them that if, as seemed certain, Mussolini was going to fight we ought to see that Abyssinia was supplied with munitions. He told them not to be frightened by our fighting services. They would be sure to say that they had not a sufficient force and that there was a shortage of ships. He had had all that in the Great War… He said that Mussolini ought to be told what would be the consequence of war. It was no use waiting to tell him this when the Council of the League met…[2224]

This was some six weeks before the Italians invaded Abyssinia–without a prior declaration of war–on 3 October.

Now the life of Gareth Jones touched that of Lloyd George once more. Still using his former position as Foreign Affairs Secretary to Lloyd George as leverage to give him entrée to important people, Jones travelled to Manchuria, then a crucible of conflict between various Chinese factions, the Japanese and, more covertly, the Russians. In mysterious, but undoubtedly politically motivated circumstances, Jones was murdered on 12 August 1935, the day before his 30th birthday, 16 days after being captured for ransom by Chinese bandits, a brilliant life cut short. Gareth's parents, as soon as they heard of his capture contacted Lloyd George, and A. J. Sylvester tirelessly acted as an intermediary on their behalf only to be thwarted by intransigent Foreign Office mandarins. Gareth's mother wrote: *"If it were not for Lloyd George's secretary, who has been wonderful, nothing would have been done. Little do they care! So much for our Foreign Office!"…*

On behalf of Lloyd George, on 29 July Sylvester informed the Foreign Office that a press telegram

[2221] Sylvester, *Real Lloyd George*, p235, 238, 241.
[2222] Toye, p313; Dutton, p59.
[2223] Rowland, *Lloyd George*, p723-724, 778.
[2224] Sylvester, *Life*, p128.

had reported that Gareth had been captured by bandits in Inner Mongolia. It was news to them, and they promised to make enquiries. On 3 September, Sylvester wrote to C. W. Orde at the Foreign Office on Gareth's parents behalf: "Mr Lloyd George would like a full enquiry to be made into the tragic affair of Gareth's death if the Foreign Office had not already done so in order to establish just how the whole tragedy had happened, and precisely who gave advice to Gareth Jones and what that advice was."[2225] On 7 September, Sylvester again wrote to Orde: "I had passed on to you the suspicion that is in the minds of some of his [Gareth's] friends that he may have been the victim of a plot to get him out of the way because of some knowledge he may have happened on that neither the Japanese nor the Germans would want to have published."[2226] Correspondence continued but, as more information was uncovered, the Foreign Office became less forthcoming, leading Orde to note on 16 September to a Whitehall colleague, Mr Kitson:

> We can give Lloyd George, as a former employer of Mr Gareth Jones, a great deal of information, which is of legitimate interest in the case. The basis that there is a German-Japanese conspiracy is far-fetched. I cannot help imagining that Mr Lloyd George is trying to make political capital out of this. We could tell Mr Sylvester that we are trying to get hold of [Dr Herbert] Müller and take his story.[2227]

On 23 September, A. W. G. Randall of the Foreign Office stated that there was no foundation whatever to substantiate a German-Japanese Pact. However, he noted: "But I am afraid that if we were to send Mr Sylvester the enclosures to this despatch it would be difficult to get either him or Mr Lloyd George to agree with Peking's conclusion, and Mr Lloyd George would probably be provided with some useful ammunition for awkward questions in the next Parliament."[2228] He duly annotated the document: "I have now read this report and annexes, and agree that it is premature to disclose any of it to Mr Lloyd George."[2229] Siriol Colley, Gareth's niece, concluded:

> The Foreign Office acted in line with the policy which later became known as 'appeasement'. If, in so doing, their aim was to thwart Lloyd George from discovering the truth about a possible German-Japanese alliance, then they were clearly successful. However in so doing they also prevented Sylvester and the Jones family from finding out the truth about Gareth Jones' murder *for fear of Lloyd George embarrassing His Majesty's Government.*[2230]

The Anti-Comintern Pact between Nazi Germany and the Empire of Japan was concluded a little over

---

[2225] Quoted in Colley, *Gareth Jones*, p203.
[2226] Ibid., p203.
[2227] Ibid., p207. Müller, at one point accompanying Jones, had Soviet NKVD connections.
[2228] https://www.garethjones.org/margaret_siriol_colley/lloyd%20george/lloyd%20George%20complete%20lecture.htm. Retrieved 10 October 2020.
[2229] Colley, *Gareth Jones*, p211.
[2230] https://www.garethjones.org/margaret_siriol_colley/lloyd%20george/lloyd%20George%20complete%20lecture.htm. Retrieved 10 October 2020. Italicized portion not in the statement in Colley, *Gareth Jones*, p211.

a year later, on 25 November 1936.

On 16 August 1935, Lloyd George was quoted by the London *Evening Standard* as saying:

> That part of the world is a cauldron of conflicting intrigue and one or other interests concerned probably knew that Mr Gareth Jones knew too much of what was going on… He had a passion for finding out what was happening in foreign lands wherever there was trouble, and in pursuit of his investigations he shrank from no risk. Doubtless he had notes in his possession that would have been of great interest to me or to many other foreign powers interested in Mongolia… He had the almost unfailing knack of getting at things that mattered.[2231]

At the General Election of 14 November 1935 Lloyd George contested his Caernarvon Boroughs seat for the 14th and final time as, owing to the outbreak of war in 1939, there would not be another election until 1945, just after his death. He told Sylvester on 4 October that it would be "the last fight he would make".[2232] The Liberals continued their slow collapse, dropping from 33 to 21 seats, with their leader, Herbert Samuel, losing his seat. Lloyd George, however, again bucked the trend, increasing his majority by 7.3% to win 66.6% of the vote against 23-year-old Tory barrister, Arthur R. P. Du Cros.

Lloyd George could still very much capture individuals with his voice. Bengy Carey-Evans remembered being at a meal with his grandfather at the Savoy Hotel, London, about this time. Lloyd George was meeting with two Germans, who had come to ask his opinions on such issues as solving unemployment. The Germans did not touch their sumptuous meals, as they were too busy making notes in their notebooks to eat their food.

On 18 June 1936 he rose in the Commons to denounce Government policy, and its agreement in the League of Nations dropping all sanctions against Fascist Italy after its capture of the Ethiopian capital Addis Ababa on 5 May. In answer to Foreign Secretary Anthony Eden, he stated:

> I was one of those who was primarily responsible, as Prime Minister… in committing Britain and her Empire to the League, its Covenant, its obligations, its risks, its sanctions…
>
> If… the Government… are going to Geneva to say, "We are beaten, the League has failed, we do not propose any further sanctions, we propose to abandon our position altogether," believe me, there is, an end of the authority of the League of Nations… there will be international anarchy the moment it is known and recognised. It is no use saying, as the Foreign Secretary did, that he is going to reconstitute and reform the League… The League is sufficiently loose in its constitution to adapt itself to every contingency… You can pursue any policy you like under the conditions of the Covenant. What is needed is that, once you have undertaken a line of action, you should stand by it.
>
> The fundamentals are not that you should have a League of Nations which meets there like a debating society… We have had that for years over disarmament. You must have some sort

2231 Quoted in Colley, *Gareth Jones*, p177.
2232 Sylvester, *Life*, p133.

of authority there and the nations must stand by it… Which of the nations have failed to stand by sanctions?… Not one… The… Foreign Secretary… was hailed everywhere as the champion of the League… I am sorry that I am one of those who were taken in… But the right hon. Gentleman, with all the authority he has acquired… is going to Geneva to smash the League. If you go there and go back upon the challenge you made to an aggressor… and say you cannot bring him to heel, there is an end of the authority of the League of Nations.

… *I have never before heard a British Minister, one holding the most important position in the Government next to the Prime Minister… come down to the House of Commons and say that Britain was beaten… and that we must abandon an enterprise we had taken in hand…* I cannot understand it of an Empire that faced one of the greatest emergencies that any Empire was ever confronted with… and for four and a-half years fought her way through. That is not the Empire which I thought would ever say, through its spokesmen in the House of Commons, after six months, with no loss of life, with only £7,000,000 of trade loss, "We are beaten, we cannot go on."… Why have we done it?… There is no intolerable burden of sacrifice…

Why? "The danger of war" said the right hon. Gentleman. The danger of war is less than when we entered into these sanctions. I know the kind of thing that was then being said: that our Navy was unprepared, that it had insufficient ammunition, that it was ill-equipped under this patriotic Government. It was broadly said that this great Navy of Britain could not face the Italian Navy… Now the Navy is fully equipped, well equipped, perfectly ready for any emergency, and there is less danger of war. What more? There has been a complete change, of the most vital importance, in the attitude of the two greatest Mediterranean Powers. Not a word was said about that. The Laval administration was hostile… It was only dragged unwillingly into sanctions because it was afraid to quarrel with Britain… Now there is a Government of a totally different character… The Cabinet and M. Blum, the Prime Minister, have informed the British Foreign Office… more than once that France would be ready to back Britain in every step she was prepared to take to enforce the League Covenant … Is not that a very vital fact…?[2233]

Lloyd George now faced a series of interjections, but he was far from done:

"… Does anyone mean to tell me that he believes in his heart that the attitude of the French Government to-day is the same as the attitude of the French Government before the elections?… They take a totally different point of view… Spain has altered its Government and its attitude is different. So that from the point of view of war you have got the Mediterranean Pact, which you have had since sanctions. You have Spain and France infinitely more favourable than they were then. You have the whole of the Mediterranean Powers except Italy prepared to support you. And yet you are running away. Why?

The German menace?… As a matter of fact, when sanctions were imposed Germany had already challenged Europe. She had carried conscription, she was doubling her Air Force, she was building a new Navy–the present Government came to terms with her to sanction it–including submarines. There, at any rate, was something you might say was the menace of impending war–the building of a great new army and air force which were going to be equal to the greatest Power in Europe. But we knew that when we undertook sanctions… Three months

[2233]https://api.parliament.uk/historic-hansard/commons/1936/jun/18/foreign-office. Retrieved 4 November 2019. Emphasis added.

ago there was the Rhineland occupation… and there was a good deal of apprehension in Europe. Nobody believes now that the French Government are going to war over the occupation of the Rhineland. I am not minimising the peril of war in Europe. All I say is that the dangers are less now than when you undertook sanctions.

I am trying to find out your reasons for changing your mind… I am just telling you what my conviction is about the feeling of the country, and there is not one of you can deny it. [HON. MEMBERS: "Abyssinia."] Yes, but you have accepted sanctions for Abyssinia…

… I am dealing now with an action of this Government, in which it has taken the lead, in which it has condemned the aggressor and has organised the world behind it to enforce sanctions against the aggressor. The Government say, "We have failed," and therefore they have funked… Where is the failure? You imposed economic sanctions. We, on this side of the House, said that they were inadequate; what was the answer of the Foreign Secretary? He said, "They will take time."… Oil sanctions would have been immediate, but economic sanctions, he said, would probably take time. We have not given them time. The foreign trade of Italy has dwindled to more than half. Why do you say sanctions have failed? You say: "Addis Ababa has been reached. Abyssinia is conquered. What is the good of going on?"… Abyssinia has not been conquered… Addis Ababa is not even traditionally the centre of Abyssinia. It is not, even now, the nerve centre of Abyssinia…

… Why are we giving up now, merely because Addis Ababa has been conquered? You say, "What is the motive?" The motive is, the strain on Italy would increase… and if you kept it up for another year you would find that you would be able to make terms with Mussolini. You may say: "You will never restore the thing as it was." Probably not, but you would restore freedom and independence, and the form of some better organisation, which would be an infinitely better thing for both Italy and Abyssinia. It is a fatal error to deprive yourselves of the means of bringing the necessary pressure, which would enable you in the end to establish a very much better peace than you could do now by running away.

But there you are; Italy knows… I am asking the Prime Minister what our attitude is going to be, with the withdrawal of sanctions, towards those men who are still in possession of two-thirds of Abyssinia and are organising the… guerrilla fighting. What is our attitude going to be? Are we going to close our frontiers? We surround the country on two sides out of three. Are we going to prevent their getting arms through our territory? I am told that the one advantage of private enterprise in arms is that arms can go through without the Government accepting the responsibility. Are we going to try it down there? You imposed an embargo on Abyssinia. You absolutely forbade her to sell concessions of property which were her own when she wanted to raise money to buy arms. You accepted the responsibility of defending her by those two acts. Now I ask:… Are you going to stop the whole trade in arms with Abyssinia by closing the frontiers?…

Mr. EDEN… [W]e have, of course, done our best to get in touch with the situation in Western Abyssinia… That is the area where the Italians are not in occupation. Our information… is that the independent Gallo tribes there are strongly hostile to the Emperor's administration…

Mr. LLOYD GEORGE The right hon. Gentleman has not answered my question. If the Abyssinians take a different view with regard to that, and they are of opinion that they can get arms through, provided they get them to the frontier, are the Government going to put an embargo upon them? I understand that they are not. That is definite.

Mr. EDEN… My point is that there is no Abyssinian authority, in Western Abyssinia–none.

Mr. LLOYD GEORGE I again ask: If those who are organising guerrilla warfare… in two-thirds of Abyssinia, are able to buy arms and to get them to the frontier, are the British Government going to impose an embargo on their passage?…

Mr. EDEN… If such an occasion should arise, of course, we would consider the demand…

Mr. LLOYD GEORGE That means that the Government have not really considered it. The fact of the matter is… that there is no evidence that the Government ever meant business over sanctions… During the Election they never suggested any doubts at all. We have heard some very striking questions this afternoon, but I think the most striking quotation of all is not merely the Government manifesto, in which it was stated: In the present unhappy dispute between Italy and Abyssinia, there will be no wavering in the policy we have hitherto pursued, but most important in that document are the signatures. Their names were the guarantee that there could be no wavering: Stanley Baldwin, J. Ramsay MacDonald, John Simon. Who could doubt that we should have unflinching adherence to the policy which the Government had adopted?

… A book came into my hands a short time ago, known as "This Torch of Freedom." It contains the speeches of the Prime Minister… They are the speeches delivered by him before the Election. In one, he is talking about the difficulties of Abyssinia, and he says it is essential that this country stand like a rock in the waves, however rough they may be. The rock has turned out to be mere driftwood… He said, in a great message to the Peace Society, talking about this dispute: Let your aim be resolute and your footsteps firm and certain. Here is the resolute aim; here is the certain footstep–running away. He states that this speech, which was delivered on the eve of the Election, was delivered to assure the world that we stand by our pledges. Only a few weeks after the Election was over, they were negotiating treachery to their pledges. Fifty nations ranged themselves behind that torch…

They said, "Here is the British Prime Minister, with the greatest Empire in the world marching; we will range ourselves behind him." The Abyssinians believed it; the vast majority of the people of this country believed it. The Government had not been in for more than a few weeks before that torch was dimmed. To-night it is quenched–with a hiss; a hiss that will be re-echoed throughout the whole world…

… There have never been so many vacillations in the course of a few months in the conduct of foreign policy. The right hon. Gentleman has boasted to-day… that we led the nations. That increased our responsibility. We led in the imposition of sanctions; we led also in the denunciation of the aggressor. We led, too, in proposing, I think, oil sanctions in principle; and we also led in selling oil in practice.

What were we doing? We were leading! We dawdled for weeks before taking any action at all... We put an embargo on arms for Abyssinia when we knew she was going to be attacked, and when the Italians were massing armies and piling up arms… We put on an embargo. What were we doing? We were leading the nations in the way of showing how an aggressor–a well-equipped aggressor–could be effectively dealt with! We tried to compound a felony. We said: "This is a crime–the robbing of a nation of its liberty. It is a crime; we condemn it." And then we entered into negotiations to give the burglar half the goods. What were the Government doing? They were just leading the nations, they were just leading civilisation in the right way to deal with crime!

They were driven back by an outraged opinion. They were afraid of Mussolini. They dared not retreat very much further, so they skulked for three months in the communication trenches.

> What were they doing? They were showing the National Government's ideas as to leadership! And now they are running away, brandishing their swords–still leading! The right hon. Gentleman said so. "I am going to Geneva," he said, "to lead." They are running away on the battlefield…
>
> Fifty nations trusted us… They will not when they see the British Empire saying they cannot go on. They will never trust this crowd. I began my politics when you had very great names–Disraeli, Gladstone, Balfour, Joseph Chamberlain… they were men of dauntless courage. They pursued their policies without flinching and without fear. Now in their successors you have this exhibition of poltroonery. The speech of the Chancellor of the Exchequer has been quoted… [He] is heir to the throne and recently he has been trying the crown on to see how it fits... which is just the sort of thing that heirs do when there are weak monarchs. *The right hon. Gentleman said at the last election: The choice before us is whether we shall make a last effort at Geneva for peace and security or whether by a cowardly surrender we shall break all the promises we have made and hold ourselves up to the shame of our children and their children's children. To-night we have had the cowardly surrender, and there are the cowards.*[2234]

With a sweeping gesture at the Government front bench, he sat down an hour after launching this devastating salvo. A visibly shaken Baldwin had to acknowledge "that extraordinarily brilliant speech… which showed me that he has not lost the least atom of the vigour which I remember in this House nearly 30 years ago and I congratulate him. It was a very remarkable performance."[2235] Frances Stevenson, admittedly not a neutral witness, recorded: "D[avid] had smashing success in House on Thursday, a real resurrection of his old fighting days… The Front Bench literally cowed before his onslaught, & Baldwin's reply was pitiable. There was consternation on the faces of the Tory back benchers. After the speech a young Tory back bencher went up to Winston & said he had never heard anything like it in the House. "'Young man', replied W., 'you have been listening to one of the greatest parliamentary performances of all time.'"[2236]

On 30 July Lloyd George was back in North Wales to address the crowds, with Margaret, at novelist Daniel Owen's centenary celebrations at Mold, Flintshire.[2237] Owen was brought up in near poverty and worked as a tailor. Little known outside Wales, his fame rests particularly on his novel *Rhys Lewis* (1885) and its sequel *Enoc Huws* (1891), his work was influenced by Charles Dickens but is firmly grounded in Welsh-language culture and his own Calvinistic Methodist background. He once said "I did not write for the wise and knowledgeable, but for the ordinary man". Loudspeakers had been affixed to the platform that Lloyd George spoke from, to carry his words to the crowd of thousands gathered in the town's Bromley Park.

Now completing his *War Memoirs*, Lloyd George very much wanted to visit Germany, and he accepted

---

[2234]https://api.parliament.uk/historic-hansard/commons/1936/jun/18/foreign-office. Retrieved 4 November 2019. Emphasis added.
[2235]https://api.parliament.uk/historic-hansard/commons/1936/jun/18/foreign-office#S5CV0313P0_19360618_HOC_408. Retrieved 21 May 2020.
[2236] Stevenson, *Diary*, p324. Entry for 20 June 1936. Churchill had, in his time, been a great admirer of Mussolini, as late as 17 February 1933 calling him "the greatest lawgiver among living men" and "one of the most wonderful men of our time".
[2237] Daniel Owen (1836-1895), generally regarded as the foremost Welsh-language novelist of the era.

the invitation made by German Ambassador Joachim von Ribbentrop on 27 April.[2238] This proved controversial, then and after, but it was very much in line with his 1908 visit.[2239] He told A. J. Sylvester:

> I want to see the great roads, the development around the towns which has provided work for all the unemployed; to see the reconditioning and reclamation of the land and the great agricultural enterprises. I am not interested in the armament work the Germans are supposed to be doing. I would like to talk to the German workers, to visit the factories and find out how the ordinary man is represented in the new Germany; to see how their needs and grievances are met.[2240]

Given little or no attention in most biographies on Lloyd George is the fact that von Ribbentrop's invitation was *first* extended to Prime Minister Stanley Baldwin, the German hope being that Baldwin could be persuaded to hold a summit meeting with Hitler that circumvented British diplomats and Foreign Office officials believed to be pro-French.[2241] Through Dr Thomas Jones, former Deputy Secretary of the Cabinet, a member of the Unemployment Assistance Board (UAB) and a close confidant of Baldwin, von Ribbentrop attempted to invite Baldwin during April and May 1936. However, Baldwin had already turned down previous invitations in late 1933 and early 1934, believing that such diplomacy was best left to Foreign Secretaries and their staff.[2242]

On 26 March 1935 a lunch was organised in the British Embassy in Berlin, concluding two days of talks at the Führer's Chancellery. Hitler was invited and he met the Foreign Secretary, John Simon, and Simon's soon to be successor, Anthony Eden, who at the time was 'Minister without Portfolio for League of Nations Affairs'. It was a highly successful event, Hitler and Eden discussing the Battle of Ypres in which they had both taken part, in fact roughly opposite each other in their respective trenches. Both men felt that they could work together after their preliminary talks and Hitler was pleased when Eden was made Foreign Secretary the following December. Meanwhile, Philip Conwell-

---

2238 Joachim von Ribbentrop (1893-1946), Ambassador to London, 1936-1938, Reichsminister of Foreign Affairs, 1938-1945. See W. R. P. George, *88 Not Out*, p186.

2239 George Lansbury visited Hitler in Berlin on 19 April 1937, then Mussolini in Rome on 9-10 July, recording largely positive impressions, describing the latter as "a mixture of Lloyd George, Stanley Baldwin and Winston Churchill". Though criticized at the time, he was nominated for the Nobel Peace Prize in 1940, receiving little of the subsequent censure that Lloyd George attracted. Indeed, he has been unjustly almost forgotten.

2240 Sylvester, *Real Lloyd George*, p192.

2241 Pride, p13. W. Emrys Pride (1904-1989). A member of the Home Office, he accompanied Lloyd George's party as an advisor on industrial and economic matters, along with Ben Bowen Thomas (1899-1977), a member of the Executive Committee of the Welsh League of Nations Union. Pride and Thomas were the only members of the party to attend the Nuremburg Rally on 8 September.

2242 See C. Spicer, *'Ambulant Amateurs': The Rise and Fade of the Anglo-German Fellowship*, 2018, Unpublished D.Phil. Thesis, Institute of Historical Research, University of London. https://sas-space.sas.ac.uk/9193/1/FINAL_Ambulant%20Amateurs%20Charles%20Spicer%20IHR%20Ph%20D%20thesis%20August%202018.pdf. Retrieved 10 January 2021. 'Lloyd George', p107-118; Lloyd George was never a member of the Fellowship, but his son Gwilym was; Spicer, p278.

Evans[2243] and Ernest Tennant[2244], Secretaries of the Anglo-German Fellowship, had been writing to Lloyd George, pressing him to meet Hitler 'at home'.[2245] Conwell-Evans, a graduate of Oxford and the London School of Economics, fluent in German, formerly a lecturer at Konigsberg University who knew both von Ribbentrop and Hitler, had been recommended to him by Philip Kerr. Through 1935, Lloyd George several times considered a visit to Germany, principally because of his great interest in solving unemployment. He himself advocated a public works programme, the building of roads, modernizing ports and railways. Hitler was seen to be doing this, and Lloyd George wanted to see how these policies were working in practice, as was always his way. Margaret was adamant that Lloyd George should not go to Germany and firmly refused to accompany him.[2246]

He also wanted to meet Hitler himself, and to discuss the Great War with General Ludendorff. His chosen intermediary was Conwell-Evans, and it was arranged that with Gwilym, Megan, A. J. Sylvester[2247], and Conwell-Evans, Lloyd George should leave London for Munich on 2 September[2248], dine with von Ribbentrop and his wife Anna in Berchtesgaden on the 3rd, and that he should meet Hitler alone next day. Lord Dawson and Tom Jones would independently join the party at Munich on the 3rd, Jones in fact keeping Baldwin regularly posted with a short account of the party's progress and the people they met.[2249]

Before he departed, Lloyd George lunched with Ivan Maisky[2250], the Soviet Ambassador, with whom he was on friendly terms. Maisky heard the news of his proposed visit with dismay. Moscow, he declared, was convinced that Nazi Germany was going to build a great *Mittel-Europa* State, that she would attack Czechoslovakia, overrun the Polish corridor, annex the Baltic States, and then attack the Soviet Union, in itself a very clear appreciation of Hitler's 'grand design'. Lloyd George was not to be deterred. He believed that France and Germany could come to terms, and in this he was certainly not alone–even two years later there were many leading statesmen in Europe who still believed it, after Lloyd George had seen the light.

He found von Ribbentrop tiresome, though von Ribbentrop was clearly impressed by him,

---

2243 Philip Conwell-Evans (1892-1968), Welsh-born Visiting Lecturer in English History, University of Konigsberg, 1932-1934, (Joint) Secretary of Anglo-German Fellowship, September 1935-September 1939, Lloyd George's interpreter during his visit, author of *None So Blind: A Study of the Crisis Years, 1930-1939, Based on the Private Papers of Group-Captain M. G. Christie*, 1947, London, Harrison.

2244 Ernest Tennant (1887-1962), merchant banker, industrialist, cousin of Margot Asquith, friend of von Ribbentrop from 1932, author of *True Account*, 1957, London, Max Parrish.

2245 Pride, p16.

2246 Information from Bengy Carey-Evans, who went to Germany with his father the year before, retaining a clear impression of travelling on the autobahn from Heidelberg to Munich, being much impressed as a boy.

2247 Sylvester shot a 16 minute, 16mm colour, silent film *Visit of the Rt. Hon. D. Lloyd George, OM, MP to Germany, September 2nd-16th, 1936*. See https://player.bfi.org.uk/free/film/watch-visit-of-the-rt-hon-d-lloyd-george-om-mp-to-germany-september-2nd-26th-1936-1936. Retrieved 21 May 2019.

2248 As far as the author can ascertain Lloyd George - unlike, say, Chamberlain on his mission to Munich in 1938–never flew in an aeroplane, preferring the greater comfort and safety offered by ships and cars at the time. Watson, *Dawson Of Penn*, p291, states that on 10 September the party were flown from Stuttgart to Nuremberg "in Ribbentrop's own aeroplane to be present at the Labour Rally", but that was only Dawson and Jones, Lloyd George staying to listen to the speeches on the radio: Sylvester, *Real Lloyd George*, p224.

2249 Pride, p24.

2250 Ivan Maisky (1884-1975), Ambassador, 8 November 1932–12 August 1943. Maisky, often with his wife, Agniya (1895-1987), is recorded in the Churt Visitors Book and his own Diary* as visiting Lloyd George in 1933, July 1937*, August and October 1938*, September and December 1939*, February, March, May, June and December 1940*, March, May and August 1941*, and June 1942*, and finally on 27 May 1943*.

boasting that "the Germans have in Hitler their Lloyd George".[2251] But at 3.45 pm the next day he met Hitler at his newly refurbished and much enlarged retreat, the *Berghof*, situated at an elevation of 921m, above Berchtesgaden, with a large terrace and huge picture window which could be lowered into the wall to give a panoramic, open air view of the snow-capped Obersalzberg mountains in Hitler's native Austria. On arrival, his host descended the stone steps from the *Berghof* to the Alpine Road, smiling and firmly shaking his guest's hand. Lloyd George was taken by Hitler's sheer magnetism, "his gestures, his eyes, his voice, his talk". "Fuhrer is the proper name for him," he said enthusiastically of him when he got back to his hotel. "He is a great and wonderful leader. He is a man who can not only plan, but can put his plans into execution. He is the Saviour of Germany."

Lloyd George added that he had found Hitler "not in favour of rearmament or conscription"! Building roads and developing agriculture, the Führer declared, interested him far more. He insisted that the future of civilization depended on "complete co-operation" between England and Germany, and said that the recently signed Anglo-German Naval Agreement[2252] was ample proof of German willingness in this regard "and proof also that Germany was not unmindful of the interests of the British Empire".[2253] Lloyd George replied that both countries must do their utmost to ensure the real success of the forthcoming Locarno Conference. England, Germany, France, Italy and Belgium (which, though not a Great Power, held a key frontier position) must meet and talk there on terms of complete equality. The issue of Spain–whose fearful civil war had just broken out on 17 July–set the Führer off on Bolshevism, as did mention of Czechoslovakia. Russian Communism he compared with the great historical migrations, or the Mohammedan invasion of Europe. Lloyd George, though taken with Hitler, did not lose all critical faculties as Churchill and others have alleged. Mindful of his meeting with Maisky, "he warned Hitler that 'his emphasis upon the Bolshevik danger might be regarded by some people as an obsession'. He raised concerns about Nationalist atrocities in Spain, such as the massacre at Badajoz, damning Hitler's ally, Franco[2254], as 'no statesman… [with] little or no experience of war' leading 'a purely reactionary and military party.'[2255]

When they talked about the new German autobahn, concluding that the optimum speed for them was 80kph, Hitler told Lloyd George that Germany was short of both petrol and rubber, and he spoke of the need of Germany recovering her lost colonies and her access to vital raw materials. The German interpreter Paul Schmidt diplomatically left this out of his translation to the visitor. The two statesmen moved to other political matters:

> "Alliances are always dangerous," said Lloyd George. "In the last war they extended the hostilities like a prairie fire. But for them the conflict might have been localised." Consciously or unconsciously, he had exactly expressed Hitler's opinion on collective security. One of

2251 Conwell-Evans, *None So Blind*, p162.

2252 The Anglo-German Naval Agreement of 18 June 1935, fixing a ratio whereby the total tonnage of the *Kriegsmarine* was to be 35% of that of the Royal Navy on a permanent basis.

2253 Sylvester, *Real Lloyd George*, p205.

2254 General Francisco Franco (1892-1975), Nationalist leader, *Caudillo*, 1 April 1939–20 November 1975.

2255 Conwell-Evans, *Notes of a Conversation between Lloyd George and Hitler at Berchtesgaden, 4 September 1936*, in M. Gilbert, *The Roots Of Appeasement*, 1966, London, Weidenfeld and Nicolson, Appendix 2, pp197-211; quote on p203.

> Hitler's favourite mottoes was: "No multilateral undertakings, but only mutual non-aggression pacts between neighbours." Hitler elaborated this theme as though he had only been waiting for a cue, expounding the peace plan which I had translated in the plane to London in March, and which had since somewhat sunk into oblivion. Lloyd George took this opportunity of expressing himself very definitely, if in quite general terms, about the German peace efforts, "which," he said, "have unfortunately been frustrated by the staff talks." Intentionally or not, he had again touched upon a favourite theme of Hitler's.[2256]

One thing disappointed and irritated the Führer, and that was his guest's refusal of his invitation to attend the forthcoming Nuremberg Rally, Lloyd George declined, saying: "I have not come to Germany for matters of politics; I wanted to study your social institutions and above all your solution to the unemployment problem, which is threatening us in England also. If I went to Nuremberg, England would be offended."[2257] After the three-hour meeting Lloyd George returned to his party at their quarters in the Grand Hotel convinced that Hitler wanted peace, based fundamentally on a better understanding with Britain. Hitler had certainly done his best to indicate that he was much impressed with Lloyd George, too.[2258] Restating what he had written in *Mein Kampf*, he had told Lloyd George: "The Allies won the war… rather, that great victory was due to one statesman, a great statesman, yourself, Mr Lloyd George."[2259] Hitler was "quite enchanted by his visitor, not only on that afternoon but long afterwards whenever he referred to his talk 'with the great British statesman, Lloyd George.'"[2260]

Next day, Lloyd George and his party all went to take tea with the Führer at his home again. With Hitler were Chief of the Presidential Chancellery Otto Meissner, Joachim and Anna von Ribbentrop, her brother Stefan Henkell (a DEG founder member)[2261], Baron Geyr and Schmidt. Taking his guest by the arm, Hitler showed him his paintings, tapestries and a bust of Wagner. But it was the view through that huge window which entranced Lloyd George. Witnesses recorded: "Suddenly we all found ourselves listening to a talk between Mr Lloyd George and Hitler. It is difficult to describe the atmosphere. It seemed to become all of a sudden almost solemn… Everybody listened intensely and it was a moving experience."[2262] "[We strained] to miss no word of the dialogue of two men whose word had settled the fate of two nations and whose power for good and evil was not yet spent."[2263]

After tea, Hitler presented Lloyd George, "the Man Who Won the War", with a signed half-length silver print portrait of himself in a silver frame. It was inscribed in German to *"Mister Lloyd George, zur freundlichen Erinnerung an seinen Beitrag in meinen Deutschland in umsichtiger Vorahnung, Adolf Hitler, Berchtesgaden den 4 / Sept. 1936."* ["Mister Lloyd George, in kind remembrance of his contribution to

2256 P. Schmidt, *Hitler's Interpreter*, 1951, London, William Heinemann, p57.

2257 Quoted in Jones, p246. See also Schmidt, p58.

2258 Owen, p734-735.

2259 Quoted in Pride, p5.

2260 Schmidt, p58.

2261 The Deutsch-Englische Gesellschaft, the German equivalent to the Anglo-German Fellowship.

2262 Conwell-Evans, *Notes*, 5 September 1936, p208. Conwell-Evans later wrote that had Hitler listened to Lloyd George, he might "not have met such a horrible end.": Quoted in Spicer, *Coffee With Hitler*, p321.

2263 Thomas Jones, *Diary*, 5 September 1936.

my Germany with circumspect presentiment, Adolf Hitler, Berchtesgaden, 4 September 1936."][2264] Much moved, Lloyd George jumped up from his easy chair and grasped his hand while he thanked him for this gift from "the greatest living German".

"Would you mind," he asked, "if I placed it on my desk beside those of the great War leaders, Clemenceau, Marshal Foch, and President Wilson?"

"I should raise no objection to that," replied Hitler, "but I should object very much if you put it beside such men as Erzberger and Bauer!"

This caused general laughter, but it also launched the Führer off on a vehement and obviously favourite onslaught on the politicians whom, he claimed, had let Germany down at the end of the war and in the peace which followed. He and Lloyd George then exchanged further compliments on the great parts which each had played in his own country, and the tea-party ended with Lloyd George telling Hitler that he should visit England:

> "Tell him," said L.G.[sic] "that he would be welcomed by the British people."
>
> Conwell-Evans translated the words, and Hitler threw up his hands in a gesture, at the same time pursing his lips. He said nothing.
>
> "Ah well," L.G. smiled "The time will come, and possibly quite soon."
>
> "Possibly," Hitler returned.[2265]
>
> Hitler escorted his departing guest to his car, afterwards saying to his long-time official photographer, Heinrich Hoffmann, "For me it has been a great honour to make the acquaintance of this renowned British statesman."[2266]

A glimpse behind the façade of this meeting is provided by Bill Tenby's recollections of subsequent family evaluation of their day with the Fuhrer:

> The purpose of the visit to Germany was to see the steps they were taking to alleviate people who were out of work, the unemployment situation, which they did by building autobahns and things like that, and it was the thing in which my grandfather was passionately interested, and so they thought it was a good idea to go out there. It should be remembered that in those days, at that time, very few people had any idea of the horrors that were going on in Germany, and so it was quite normal to expect to go there, and equally normal, in view of his status as an international statesman, for him to be entertained, at least once, by the top brass, as it were. And also in the party was his secretary, a splendid Englishman called A. J. Sylvester,… very dogged, and very determined, and L.G. [sic] had just been given, or bought, a cine camera, which were quite novel in those days, and A. J., as he was known, was busy assiduously taking photographs, shots of all the party, major elements in the trip, and my father remembered particularly going to Berchtesgaden, where the Fuhrer had his hideaway, in the Bavarian Alps, and being greeted

---

[2264] https://www.wiltsglosstandard.co.uk/news/15640559.signed-photo-of-hitler-to-go-under-the-hammer-in-cirencester/. Retrieved 20 April 2020. The photo, Lot 907, sold at auction for £13,500 on 9 November 2017.

[2265] Sylvester, *Real Lloyd George*, p214-215.

[2266] H. Hoffmann, *Hitler Was My Friend: The Memoirs Of Hitler's Photographer*, 1955, London, Burke.

> by all the Nazi notables, being shown the view and everything, and A. J. wishing to take photographs, films, was pushing them all round, saying 'Not over there, Mr. Hitler, come and stand over here please, wouldn't you listen, would you listen to me please?', and the family found it absolutely hilarious that all these jackbooted people were scuttling around like rabbits.[2267]

On 6 September, Lloyd George had tea with Deputy-Führer Rudolf Hess and his wife Ilse, who spoke good English, at his house near Munich, and questioned him closely about the functions of the local Gauleiters and their part in helping to frame Nazi Party policy, and also about German rearmament and military service. The next day, at Munich, Lloyd George, accompanied by von Ribbentrop, laid a wreath on the War Memorial, inscribed: "A respectful and sincere tribute to the memory of the very brave men who fell fighting for their Fatherland in the Great War. D. Lloyd George." [2268] From Munich, the party drove through Augsburg to Stuttgart. There followed a busy tour of factories, including camera works, a milk process factory, a spectacles works, and a worsted mill. Next came agricultural undertakings–which were more to Lloyd George's taste–, land reclamation centres and settlements for industrial workers in Württemberg. The party also visited a labour camp which was formerly a disused mill. On 12 September at Heidelberg, Lloyd George talked with experts from the Ministry of Agriculture who had come to see him from Berlin. He failed to see Ludendorff, but did meet General Georg Wetzell, his former Chief of Staff, on 13 September. One of his last engagements was to meet Baron Friedrich von der Ropp and Rev. Friedrich W. Simoleit, two of Germany's leading Baptists, both favourable to Hitler. Finally, on 15 September, Lloyd George inspected Emsland, near the Dutch frontier, where around 400,000 acres of marshland were being reclaimed by some 4,800 political prisoners in 32 labour camps.[2269] Here he impressed experts with his comments on the growing of potatoes.[2270]

Lloyd George himself was initially highly impressed with both Hitler and the new Germany that he had seen, as he recorded for the *Daily Express* in an article entitled 'I Talked To HITLER', published the day after he returned to England on 16 September:

> I have now seen the famous German Leader and also something of the great change he has effected. Whatever one may think of his methods–and they are certainly not those of a parliamentary country–there can be no doubt that he has achieved a marvellous transformation in the spirit of the people, in their attitude towards each other, and in their social and economic outlook. He rightly claimed at Nuremberg that in four years his movement has made a new Germany.
>
> It is not the Germany of the first decade that followed the war–broken, dejected, and bowed

---

2267 Taped interview with author, Crondall, 18 June 2019.

2268 Lloyd George had first written "*the* Fatherland", changing it to "*their* Fatherland" at Dawson's suggestion. Watson, *Dawson of Penn*, p291. Dawson also tried to persuade Lloyd George to be less effusive about Hitler in his articles for the British press, but to no avail: Watson, *Dawson Of Penn*, p289.

2269 Typed account by Dawson of a *Visit to Labour Camp in Emsland Westphalia*. [15 September 1936.] https://richardfordmanuscripts.co.uk/catalogue/%EF%BB%BF24578. Retrieved 5 December 2024.

2270 Much of this paragraph is based on Sylvester, *Real Lloyd George*, p221-226.

down with a sense of apprehension and impotence. It is now full of hope and confidence, and of a renewed sense of determination to lead its own life without interference from any influence outside its own frontiers. There is for the first time since the war a general sense of security. The people are more cheerful... It is a happier Germany. I saw it everywhere, and Englishmen I met during my trip and who knew Germany well were very impressed with the change. One man has accomplished this miracle. He is a born leader of men. A magnetic, dynamic personality with a single-minded purpose, a resolute will and a dauntless heart. He is not merely in name but in fact the national Leader. He has made them safe against potential enemies by whom they were surrounded. He is also securing them against that constant dread of starvation, which is one of the poignant memories of the last years of the War and the first years of the Peace. Over 700,000 died of sheer hunger in those dark years. You can still see the effect in the physique of those who were born into that bleak world. The fact that Hitler has rescued his country from the fear of a repetition of that period of despair, penury and humiliation has given him unchallenged authority in modern Germany. As to his popularity, especially among the youth of Germany, there can be no manner of doubt. The old trust him; the young idolize him. It is not the admiration accorded to a popular Leader. It is the worship of a national hero who has saved his country from utter despondency and degradation.

It is true that public criticism of the Government is forbidden in every form. That does not mean that criticism is absent. I have heard the speeches of prominent Nazi orators freely condemned. But not a word of criticism or of disapproval have I heard of Hitler... He is the George Washington of Germany–the man who won for his country independence from all her oppressors. To those who have not actually seen and sensed the way Hitler reigns over the heart and mind of Germany this description may appear extravagant. All the same, it is the bare truth. This great people will work better, sacrifice more, and, if necessary, fight with greater resolution because Hitler asks them to do so. Those who do not comprehend this central fact cannot judge the present possibilities of modem Germany.

On the other hand, those who imagine that Germany has swung back to its old Imperialist temper cannot have any understanding of the character of the change. The idea of a Germany intimidating Europe with a threat that its irresistible army might march across frontiers forms no part of the new vision. What Hitler said at Nuremberg is true. The Germans will resist to the death every invader of their own country, but they have no longer the desire themselves to invade any other land. The leaders of modern Germany know too well that Europe is too formidable a proposition to be overrun and trampled down by any single nation, however powerful may be its armaments. They have learned that lesson in the war. Hitler fought in the ranks throughout the war, and knows from personal experience what war means. He also knows too well that the odds are even heavier today against an aggressor than they were at that time. What was then Austria would now be in the main hostile to the ideals of 1914. The Germans are under no illusions about Italy. They also are aware that the Russian Army is in every respect far more efficient than it was in 1914. The establishment of a German hegemony in Europe which was the aim and dream of the old pre-war militarism, is not even on the horizon of Nazism.

As to German re-armament there can be no question of its existence. All the victors of the great war except Britain having overlooked the obligation of their own treaty as to disarmament, the Führer has deliberately smashed the remnant which bound his own country. He has followed the example of the nations responsible for the Versailles Treaty. It is now an avowed part of the Hitler policy to build up an army which will be strong enough to resist every invader from whatever quarter the attack may come. I believe he has already achieved that measure of immunity… Three years of feverish preparation have so strengthened the defences of Germany as to make them impenetrable to attack except at a sacrifice of life which would be more appalling than that inflicted in the great war… Germany has constructed strong defensive positions and has, I have no doubt, a sufficient number of trained or rather half-trained men with enough machine-guns and artillery to hold these positions against attack. She has also a very efficient and powerful air fleet.

There is no attempt to conceal these facts. Re-armament proceeds quite openly, and they want it. It accounts for the outburst of defiance hurled against Russia. They feel safe now. But it will take Germany at least ten years to build up an army strong enough to face the armies of Russia or France on any soil except her own. There she can fight successfully, because she can choose battlefields which she has carefully prepared and fortified… But her conscript army is very young–there is a gap of years to fill up in the reserves and particularly in officers… But any attempt to repeat Poincare's antics in the Rühr would now be met with a fanatical resistance from myriads of brave men who count death for the Fatherland not a sacrifice but a glory. This is the new temper of the German youth. There is almost a religious fervour about their faith in the movement and its Leader.

That impressed me more than anything I witnessed during my short visit to the new Germany. There was a revivalist atmosphere. It has had an extraordinary effect in unifying the nation. Catholic and Protestant, Prussian and Bavarian, employer and workman, rich and poor, have been consolidated into one people. Religious, provincial and class origins no longer divide the nation. There is a passion for unity born of dire necessity. The divisions which followed the collapse of 1918 made Germany impotent to face her problems, internal and external. That is why the clash of rival passions is not only deprecated, but temporarily suppressed. Public condemnation of the Government is censored as ruthlessly as it is in a state of war. To a Briton accustomed to generations of free speech and a free Press this restraint on liberty is repellent, but in Germany, where such freedom is not as deeply rooted as it is here, the nation acquiesces not because it is afraid to protest, but because it has suffered so much from dissension that the vast majority think it must be temporarily called off at all costs. Freedom of criticism, is therefore for the time being in suspense. German unity is the ideal and the idol of the moment, and not liberty.

I found everywhere a fierce and uncompromising hostility to Russian Bolshevism, coupled with a genuine admiration for the British people with a profound desire for a better and friendlier understanding with them. The Germans have definitely made up their minds never to quarrel with us again. Nor have they any vindictive feelings towards the French. They have altogether put out of their minds any desire for the restoration of Alsace-Lorraine. But there is a real hatred and fear of Russian Bolshevism, and unfortunately it is growing in intensity. It constitutes the driving force of their international and military policy. Their private and public talk is full of it… Their eyes are concentrated on the East as if they were watching intently for the breaking of the day of wrath. Against this they are preparing with German thoroughness.

This fear is not put on. High and low they are convinced there is every reason for apprehension. They have a dread of the great army which has been built up in Russia in recent years. An exceptionally violent anti-German campaign of abuse printed in the Russian official Press and propelled by the official Moscow radio has revived the suspicion in Germany that the

Soviet Government are contemplating mischief against the Fatherland. Unfortunately the German leaders set this down to the influence of prominent Russian Jews, and thus the anti-Jewish sentiment is being once more stirred up just as it was fading into turpitude. The German temperament takes no more delight in persecution than does the Briton, and the native good humor of the German people soon relapses into tolerance after a display of ill-temper. Every well-wisher of Germany–and I count myself among them–earnestly pray that Goebbels's ranting speeches will not provoke another anti-Jewish manifestation. It would do much to wither the verdant blades of good will which were growing so healthily in the scorched battleground which once separated great civilized nations.[2271]

But we should do wisely not to attach extravagant importance to recent outbursts against Russia. The fact of the matter is, the German Government in its relations with Russia is now in the stage from which we ourselves have only just emerged. We can all recall the time when Moscow… made atrocious personal attacks on individual British Ministers… and denounced our political and economic system as organized slavery… This has been the common form of diplomatic relationship between Communist Russia and the rest of the world on both sides. We must not forget that even when we had a Russian Minister here we actually sent the police to raid one of the official buildings of the Russian Embassy to rummage for treason… No one imagined that was intended as a preliminary or a provocation to war on either side. The slinging of scurrilities between Germany and Russia is only the usual language of diplomacy to which all countries have been accustomed during the last 20 years where Communist Russia is concerned.

It is important we should realize for the sake of our peace of mind that a repetition of this unseemly slanging match does not in the least portend war. Germany is no more ready to invade Russia than she is for a military expedition to the moon. What then did the Führer mean when he contrasted the rich but under-cultivated lands of the Ukraine and Siberia and the inexhaustible mineral resources of the Urals with the poverty of German soil? It was simply a Nazi retort to the accusation hurled by the Soviets as to the miseries of the peasantry and workers of Germany under Nazi rule. Hitler replied by taunting the Soviets with the wretched use they were making of the enormous resources of their own country. In comparison with the Nazi achievement in the land whose natural wealth was relatively poor…

I have no space in which to give a catalogue of the schemes which are being carried through to develop the resources of Germany and to improve the conditions of life for her people. They are immense and they are successful. I would only wish to say here that I am more convinced than ever, that the free country to which I have returned is capable of achieving greater things in that direction if its rulers would only pluck up courage and set their minds boldly to the task.[2272]

On 21 September, the Liberal-leaning *News Chronicle* published an interview with Lloyd George conducted by the political editor A. J. Cummings. At the outset Lloyd George firmly established that he had gone to Germany as a Liberal and come back as a Liberal. The interview proper then

---

[2271] On 18 February 1947, Frances Lloyd George, responding to what she felt to be omissions in A. J. Sylvester's forthcoming *The Real Lloyd George*, published a letter in the *Sunday Dispatch*, stating: "on his return my husband [to-be] gave me a very full account of what took place… [he] took Hitler to task for his treatment of the Jews and attempted to influence him on that matter… [and] did not conceal from Hitler his opinion of Germany's action in breaking the naval clauses of the Treaty of Versailles." Quoted in Longford, p172.
[2272] *Daily Express*, 17 September 1936, p12, 17; Quoted in Pride, p32-37.

proceeded:

A. J. C.: I gather that you do not regard Germany as a menace to the peace of Europe?

L.G.: That depends on the way Germany is treated. If she is attacked and her territories invaded as they were by Poincaré in 1923 then she will no longer crouch peaceably under the lash. You may call this new attitude of self-defence and self-respect a menace to peace."

A. J. C.: Has not Hitler set up a military dictatorship?

L.G.: A dictatorship, yes, but no more militarist than any other ruler who relies on his army to defend his frontiers. Blum, the Socialist premier [of France], has millions of fully trained and equipped soldiers behind him…

A. J. C.: What do you regard as the facts about German militarism?

L.G.: My answer is that Germany has no desire to attack any country in Europe and that Hitler is arming for defence and not attack. My conviction is that for at least ten years war between Russia and Germany is impracticable. Even if Germany desired war, which she certainly does not unless other better-equipped nations butt in to attack her. The German army is not ready and could not be ready in that time. It is not in a position to attack anybody. Though a formidable army for defence, it has neither the weapons nor the trained men for any such enterprise …

A. J. C.: Doesn't he want to fight Russia?

L.G.: No. He has a fanatical hatred of Bolshevism… [ but] he scoffs at the suggestion that he means to march to Moscow or that he covets the Ukraine… [Although he] naturally wants Memel and Danzig, which are as German as Hull is English, and much more so than Cardiff is Welsh, he has no desire to absorb millions of Slavs, whom he despises and would regard as an offence to the doctrine of racial purity…

A. J. C.: What do you think of Germany under the dictatorship?

L.G.: Hitler has done great things for his country. He is unquestionably a great leader… the workers and particularly the younger generation are absolutely devoted to him. He has effected a remarkable improvement in the working conditions of both men and women… And they appreciate it… Though they criticise things said and done by Goering and Goebbels or other subordinates they will never say a word against Hitler. He is a dynamic personality. It is a grave misfortune that great leaders are not being thrown up by the European democracies… The dictators are acting whilst the democratic leaders are fumbling. That is the real menace…

A. J. C.: Did you see any of the concentration camps while you were in Germany?

L.G.: No… But I accept the description of their condition… I need hardly say that I am no advocate of the immuring of political opponents in concentration camps. But unfortunately once you establish an authoritarian state it is the only alternative to the wholesale massacres which disgraced the first years of the Russian Revolution… The suppression of liberty in Germany as in all countries under a dictatorship is a terrible thing to an old Liberal like myself. But you must remember that the German democracy, like the Italian democracy, was very young. It was not deepened as in our country. Political and personal liberty does not yet mean to Germany what it means to us…

A. J. C.: The persecution of the Jews: when will that end?

L.G.: Ah, that is a grave and deplorable thing in the new Germany which, as I pointed out in an article I wrote the other day, must continue to alienate Liberals all the world over. A renewal of the anti-Jew manifestations would wither incipient goodwill in other lands.

A. J. C.:… If, as you believe, Germany is no menace to the peace of Europe or to Britain, what is the menace against which all Europe is rearming, what is the menace against which Britain is rearming, with the endorsement, apparently, of all parties in the State?

L.G.: (throwing up his arms in a gesture of despair) It is madness! We can come to terms with Germany which will not be dishonourable to us but which will establish not only peace between Germany and France but the peace of the world. If we do not establish peace democracy is doomed, for democracy will never survive another world war. I want peace in Europe. We will not get it if we insist on foreign countries adapting their forms of government to our conceptions before we come to any arrangements with them. They must be allowed to fight out their own internal problems in their own way. Cobden[2273] and Gladstone insisted on that view of our foreign policy in their attitude towards Napoleon III. That is why I advocated a good understanding with him even after his sanguinary coup d'état.[2274] In foreign affairs I am still a Gladstonian.[2275]

On 23 September, *The Post* published an interview with Lloyd George entitled *Nazi Regime–Lloyd George's Visit–Hitler's Hold On People–Desire For Peace*, in which he naturally reiterated many of the same points he had already made in his previous two articles. He did, however, re-emphasise:

I have always thought, and still think, that the persecution of Jews in Germany has been a great misfortune. But Germany is not the only country that has persecuted Jews. We must not forget the pogroms in Russia and in other European countries…

One of the foremost impressions which I derived from my visit was the universal desire to remain on terms of closest friendship with Great Britain. I found that among everyone I met, from Hitler down to the working men with whom I spoke. Everywhere Britain is held in deepest respect, and there is a profound desire that the tragic circumstances of 1914 should never be repeated…

We hear a great deal… of the efforts that Germany is making in the direction of re-armament, but little is said of the colossal schemes that are being pushed through for the development of the internal resources of the country, and the improvement of the conditions of the working population.

I saw a good deal of the latter, and I was enormously impressed by the boldness and beneficence of the German plans. The Germans are reclaiming over 4,000,000 acres of land which was either completely waste or barely cultivated at all. They are building millions of houses for their working population, and everywhere they are constructing settlements for their town workers outside the city boundaries, with gardens attached to each house.

The new roads which they are constructing are magnificent. By these and similar means they have reduced unemployment from 6,000,000 to 1,000,000 in three and a half years. Whatever we may think of Hitler and the present regime, that in itself is a very great achievement.[2276]

---

2273 Richard Cobden (1804-1865), manufacturer, Radical and Liberal MP.

2274 The so-called 'Night of the Long Knives', 30 June–2 July 1934, in which Hitler purged up to a thousand opponents, many in the SA, to consolidate his own power within the Nazi Party and in Germany.

2275 *News Chronicle*, 21 September 1936; Rowland, *Lloyd George*, p735-737.

2276 https://thegreateststorynevertold.tv/lloyd-georges-impressions-adolf-hitler/ . Retrieved 21 May 2019.

Commenting on Lloyd George's *Daily Express* article, biographer Kenneth Morgan rightly stressed that:

> Despite this wild eulogy, which added to the suspicions widely entertained about the ageing statesman's judgement, it would be wrong to see him as just an uncritical advocate of appeasement of Germany. On the contrary, more than any other figure in British public life, he had unrivalled knowledge of the aggressive aspects of German nationalism, and its urge to acquire territory in the east. He urged, therefore, simultaneously with efforts to reach diplomatic agreement with Germany, a steady build-up of British armed strength, especially the air force, so that Britain could confront the dictators from a position of strength.[2277]

As Paul Addison noted, Lloyd George:

> Cared very little indeed for the Nazi system and admired only one man in Germany. The British ambassador [Sir Eric Phipps[2278]] wrote home privately to report that Lloyd George had simply refused to see Goering or Goebbels. Never before had anyone flouted their invitations in this way. 'Lloyd George', he wrote, 'must have been a sore trial to his hosts. Except at the interviews with the Führer he rode the high horse, and flatly refused to keep to the programme or play up to the local bigwigs'.[2279]

At the time, Lloyd George did not believe that the persecution of the Jews was as bad as it was being portrayed, and this was for a most unfortunate reason. He had known the wild exaggerations and false imputations made against the Germans during the Great War, when the British press had accused them of eating babies, raping Belgian nuns and much else. Thus, he doubted the new atrocity stories.[2280] It was a tragic case of the insidious, often evil effects of 'Crying Wolf'. On 21 October Conwell-Evans wrote to Sylvester that 'the effect of the visit in Germany has been tremendous' explaining how Lloyd George was especially popular with the German youth who admire 'his energy, youthfulness and *great broadness of mind*,' and that '*his sense of fair play for Germany* [was] the talk of the country'.[2281]

Balancing the perceived tone of his article, and given much less publicity both then and now, was a speech Lloyd George gave to a Council of Action rally at the Manchester Free Trade Hall on 23 October before 3,000 people. Before his speech he received an address of welcome from the Manchester Jewish community. In his own speech, he addressed international affairs and attacked the British rearmament programme. He said that as far as Hitler, Mussolini and Franco were concerned he was "against dictatorships out and out, root and branch, lock, stock and barrel", and that it was not rearmament that was wanted but the consolidation of the power of the League of Nations, collective

2277 Morgan, *Lloyd George*, p189.
2278 Sir Eric Phipps (1875-1945), Ambassador to Germany, 1933-1937, France, 1937-1939.
2279 Addison in Taylor, *Lloyd George: Twelve Essays*, p.65, quoting Phipps to Anthony Eden, 21 October 1936.
2280 Longford, p126.
2281 Quoted in Spicer, p117. Emphasis added.

security and all-round disarmament.[2282]

By the start of 1937, therefore, Lloyd George's attitude had altered, as neatly summed up by author Antony Lentin:

> While he never ceased to regard Hitler as a genius and to regret that a unique opportunity had been missed, he soon came to appreciate the threat to peace posed by Hitler's Germany. Hitler's blatant intervention on Franco's side in the Spanish Civil War despite his adhesion to the Non-Intervention Pact, in Lloyd George's eyes put a question mark over his good faith… A deal with Hitler must wait until such time as Hitler had been taught a lesson, links with France strengthened and overtures made to Russia.[2283]

Neville Chamberlain, however, who became Prime Minister on 28 May 1937, had the opposite approach:

> An accord with Germany, by which he meant concessions to Germany, would make Hitler more reasonable and warlike alignments with other states unnecessary. Hitler would learn that he could satisfy his territorial grievances through peaceful accommodation with Britain. Chamberlain wanted nothing to do with Russia and favoured Germany as a bastion against communism.[2284]

It was Chamberlain who would be the standard-bearer of appeasement. A profoundly obstinate man, he "was blinkered, complacent, and in the pursuit of his foreign policy impervious to any view other than his own. Since he lacked all insight into Hitler's character and his policy was based on a complete misreading of that character, his predictions were consistently wrong and his policy invariably failed. Chamberlain never established the slightest credibility with Hitler, who held him in contempt; yet he prided himself that he had won an ascendancy over him."[2285]

Worth noting too is the little-known fact that Hitler had already long before written about Lloyd George in his infamous *Mein Kampf*, dictated whilst he was imprisoned in Landsberg in 1924. In particular, the passage dealt with Lloyd George's oratorical skills, naturally a matter of deep personal interest to the future German dictator:

> [An article] came into my hands during the War. It dealt with the speeches of Lloyd George, who was then Minister of Munitions, and examined them in a painstaking way under the microscope of criticism. The writer made the brilliant statement that these speeches showed inferior intelligence and learning and that, moreover, they were banal and commonplace productions. I myself procured some of these speeches, published in pamphlet form, and had

2282 Sylvester, *Life*, p158: Rowland, *Lloyd George*, p737-738.
2283 Lentin, p108.
2284 Ibid., p108.
2285 Ibid., p109.

> to laugh at the fact that a normal German quill-driver did not in the least understand these psychological masterpieces in the art of influencing the masses. This man criticized these speeches exclusively according to the impression they made on his own blasé mind, whereas the great British Demagogue had produced an immense effect on his audience through them, and in the widest sense on the whole of the British populace. Looked at from this point of view, that Englishman's speeches were most wonderful achievements, precisely because they showed an astounding knowledge of the soul of the broad masses of the people. For that reason their effect was really penetrating. Compare with them the futile stammering's of a Bethmann-Hollweg… Nevertheless, to the average stupid brain of the German writer, who is, of course, endowed with a lot of scientific learning, it came quite naturally to judge the speeches of the English Minister–which were made for the purpose of influencing the masses–by the impression which they made on his own mind, fossilized in its abstract learning… That the genius of Lloyd George was not only equal but a thousandfold superior to that of a Bethmann-Hollweg is proved by the fact that he found for his speeches that form and expression which opened the hearts of his people to him and made these people carry out his will absolutely. The primitive quality itself of those speeches, the originality of his expressions, his choice of clear and simple illustration, are examples which prove the superior political capacity of this Englishman. For one must never judge the speech of a statesman to his people by the impression which it leaves on the mind of a university professor but by the effect it produces on the people. And this is the sole criterion of the orator's genius.[2286]

What Lloyd George himself may have thought of this is unknown. At dinner with von Ribbentrop in Munich he had declared "Ah, Mein Kampf is a Magna Charta."[2287] It may fairly be assumed that by this that he meant it was a document of national significance, not that he approved of all its contents. Lloyd George had read the book in its English translation, but crucially only an abridged version which had been published in English in October 1933.[2288] Lloyd George had said to the Soviet Ambassador, Ivan Maisky, whom he knew well: "'I don't know why you tell me all these things are in Mein Kampf–I've read it and they aren't.' It turned out that what Lloyd George had read was [the] abridged version, which was only about a third of the length, and which had been controlled to a certain extent by the Nazis. Some of the worst things were taken out of it."[2289]

One last insight into this episode in Lloyd George's life is offered by Hitler's later table talk, noted on the evening of 27 January 1942. The Fuhrer remarked that:

---

2286 Adolf Hitler, *Mein Kampf*, Vol.II, Chapter VI: *The Struggle Of The Early Period–The Significance Of The Spoken Word.* Hitler's error concerning Lloyd George's race is peculiar. Interestingly, as late as 1939 a book on the *Intonation and Phonetics in the Speech of Lloyd George* was published by Herbert Rohmann in Berlin, based on his study of gramophone record Columbia 5344 (A 8825/26), a recording of a 1929 election speech.

2287 Sylvester, *Life*, p151. Entry for 6 September 1936.

2288 *My Struggle*, translated by E. T. S. Dugdale, published in London in 1933 by Hurst and Blackett as No.II in the 'Paternoster Library'. The comments concerning Lloyd George are on p190-191.

2289 https://www.bbc.co.uk/news/magazine-30697262. Retrieved 19 April 2019. Interview with John Murphy, grandson of Dr James Murphy, original translator of full text of *Mein Kampf* into English in March 1939.

> The man who, without any doubt, will find himself justified by history is Lloyd George. In a memorandum drafted at the time, Lloyd George declared that, if peace were made in the conditions foreseen, it would help to start a new war. "The Germans fought so heroically," he wrote, "that this proud nation will never be content with such a peace." If Lloyd George had had the necessary power, he would certainly have been the architect of a German-English understanding.[2290]

Too much has been made of this; this was pure speculation on Hitler's part, years afterwards, virtually delivering a monologue to a private, uncritical, captive audience of followers. He did not specify what the terms of this hypothetical understanding might have been. Lloyd George was sympathetic to Germany's economic plight for a long time after the Great War, but whatever his passing interest in the phenomenon of Hitler in 1936, his condemnation of the Munich Agreement of 1938 shows that he would not have settled for any one-sided deal with Hitler. Like Churchill, increasingly alarmed by growing German ambitions, Lloyd George looked for an alliance with the Soviet Union, but neither had the power to act.

Meanwhile, Welsh nationalism was ignited in 1936 when the Government decided to establish an RAF training camp and aerodrome on the site at Penyberth, a 16th Century house on the Llŷn Peninsula not far from Criccieth, and which had been the home to generations of patrons of poets, and also a waystation for pilgrims to Bardsey Island. The events surrounding the protest, known as *Tân yn Llŷn* ("Fire in Llŷn"), helped define Plaid Genedlaethol Cymru. In June, Prime Minister Baldwin refused a request to meet a Welsh national deputation representing 500,000 protesters. On 8 September, while Lloyd George was in Germany, three Plaid Cymru members, dramatist and lecturer Saunders Lewis, poet and preacher Lewis Valentine and novelist D. J. Williams[2291], set fire to the bombing school and then gave themselves up at Pwllheli police station, in accordance with Gandhian principles. The trial at Caernarfon, on 13 October, failed to agree on a verdict and the case was sent to the Old Bailey. At the trial on 19 January 1937, the "Three" were sentenced to nine months imprisonment in Wormwood Scrubs, and on their release on 27 August they were greeted as heroes by 15,000 supporters at Caernarfon pavilion. Many Welsh people were angered by the judge's scornful treatment of the Welsh language, by the decision to move the trial to London, and by the decision of University College, Swansea, to dismiss Lewis from his post before he had been found guilty. Dafydd Glyn Jones wrote of the fire that it was "the first time in five centuries that Wales struck back at England with a measure of violence… To the Welsh people, who had long ceased to believe that they had it in them, it was a profound shock."[2292] As for the station, RAF Penrhos was opened on 1 February 1937, remaining operational until 21 October 1946.

Many wrongly assumed–both then and now–that Lloyd George had lost interest in Welsh Home Rule since his *Cymru Fydd* days in the 1890s. However, during the London trial of the "Three", whilst

---

[2290] H. R. Trevor-Roper, Ed., *Hitler's Table Talk 1941-1944: Secret Conversations*, 1953, London, Trans. N. Cameron & R. H. Stevens, Weidenfeld & Nicolson, p197-198.

[2291] Saunders Lewis (1893-1985); Lewis Valentine (1893-1986); David J. Williams (1885-1970).

[2292] Davies, *A History of Wales*, p593.

he was over 'wintering' in Jamaica working on his memoirs from November 1936-February 1937, he wrote a letter to Megan on 1 December full of anger and indignation:

> I think it an unutterable piece of insolence, but very characteristic of this Government. They crumple up when tackled by Mussolini and Hitler, but they take it out on the smallest country in the realm which they are misgoverning. It is the way cowards try to show they are strong by bullying. They run away from anyone powerful enough to stand up to them and they take it out on the weak… I wish I were there, and I certainly wish I were 40 years younger. I should be prepared to risk a protest which would be a defiance. If I were Saunders Lewis I would not surrender at the Old Bailey; I would insist on their arresting me, and I am not sure that I would not make it difficult for them to do that. The Government will take no heed of protests which do not menace it. I hope the Welsh Members will make a scene, and an effective one in the House.[2293]

Action was required on another issue too, and here Lloyd George did get involved. The Palestine Royal Commission, headed by Lord William Peel, had sat in Jerusalem for some six weeks from 12 November 1936 to investigate the causes of unrest in Palestine, still a British Mandate, following a six-month-long Arab general strike. In all, 62 witnesses gave public testimony, while 61 gave testimony in secret session. The penultimate witness, heard in secret in April 1937 after the commissioners return to London, was Lloyd George.[2294] His testimony revolved around the motives for the Balfour Declaration:

> Balfour did not envision the immediate creation of a Jewish state regardless of the wishes of Palestine's majority, he said. 'On the other hand, it was contemplated that when the time arrived for according representative institutions to Palestine, if the Jews had meanwhile responded to the opportunity afforded them by the idea of a National Home and had become a definite majority of the inhabitants, then Palestine would thus become a Jewish Commonwealth.' Any notion of artificially restricting that growth 'never entered into the heads of anyone' engaged in the policy and would have been regarded as a 'fraud' upon those whom the Declaration addressed…
>
> 'We could not get in touch with the Palestinian Arabs as they were fighting against us. The Arab leaders did not offer any objections, so long as the rights of the Arabs were respected,' Lloyd George explained. 'There was a twofold undertaking given to them, that the establishment of a Jewish National Home would not in any way, firstly, affect the civil or religious rights of the general population of Palestine; secondly, would not diminish the general prosperity of that population. Those were the only pledges we gave to the Arabs.'
>
> The ex-premier challenged any critic of Britain's Palestine policy to point to an instance in which non-Jewish civil or religious rights had been compromised, and he marshalled statistics

2293 NLW, MS.20,475C, no.3151, DLG to Megan LG, 1 December 1936.

2294 https://fathomjournal.org/mandate100-a-dangerous-people-to-quarrel-with-lloyd-georges-secret-testimony-to-the-peel-commission-revealed/. Retrieved 25 February 2024. The texts–*Palestine Royal Commission: Minutes of Evidence Heard at Secret Sessions*, FO 492/19, National Archives–were not released until 2017.

on revenue, exports, wages, land prices, public health and a half-dozen other indicators of the land's newfound prosperity. 'There can be no doubt that the Arab population of Palestine has profited enormously by the Zionist enterprise.'

Chairman Peel asked if Balfour's proclamation meant the Jews could 'come in pretty nearly as they like,' regardless of any negative effects on the Arabs.

'Yes,' said Lloyd George. 'There is no doubt about that, from the words used by Lord Balfour, that it was contemplated by him that, in the course of political evolution, the Jews would have a majority.' He said President Wilson, who had given his assent to the Declaration and made similar comments about a future 'Jewish Commonwealth,' felt likewise.

A possible recourse, one commissioner offered, was 'to try the idea of division…'

'That is surrender,' Lloyd George interjected. 'That is going back on our declaration.'

The British Empire seemed to be losing its nerve, he complained. He was the only Welshman ever elected premier, and 'as an old Briton, who belongs to the most ancient race in the islands, I do not like it.'

On 7 July 1937, the Commission published its 404 page report that, in its final 16 pages, for the first time stated that the League of Nations Mandate had become unworkable, recommending partition and briefly outlining borders and other arrangements for carrying it out. The Cabinet endorsed the Partition plan in principle but requested more information.[2295]

Most mainstream Zionist leaders, led by Weizmann and Ben-Gurion, were thrilled by the prospect of a Jewish state, even as they strategically feigned disappointment, both viewing the scheme as an opening to sovereignty, not a last word on borders. But for Lloyd George, the report was a complete betrayal. On 18 July he published an article, *A Scandalous Report*, in the *Sunday Express*, stating:

'The Palestine Report is a deplorable ending to one of the most imaginative and promising experiments which the Great War made possible'… The national home 'is to be mutilated and left to shamble along, a disfigured and shapeless cripple.'

The Jews, he wrote, not only fulfilled their end of the bargain, but seem to have done it too well: 'Trouble has arisen entirely from the magnitude of their success.' They have drained swamps, he said, birthed industries, and multiplied the country's revenue and trade. 'They have built Tel Aviv, a modern city of 150,000 inhabitants …'

What will sixteen and a half million Jews, dispersed over the globe, think of this proposal to break a solemn pledge, he wondered. They were being offered a 'mutilated Canaan, without Zion, Bethlehem or Judea… a Jewish home without Judea–Zionism without Zion. They will return to their promised land to find a promise broken by those who gave it.'[2296]

Of course, Lloyd George did not live to see the creation of the State of Israel in 1948, and, as the world knows, the anguishing fate of the Holy Land and its peoples has continued to tragically play out, with no mutually satisfactory, peaceful end in sight.

Meanwhile in Europe, war clouds continued to darken. On 25 June 1937, in his first foreign affairs speech as Prime Minister, Neville Chamberlain spoke airily of the need "to try to keep cool heads and

---

2295 *Report of the Palestine Royal Commission*, Cmd.5479, 1937, London, HMSO; https://fathomjournal.org/mandate100-a-clean-cut-for-palestine-the-peel-commission-reexamined/. Retrieved 25 February 2024.

2296https://fathomjournal.org/mandate100-a-dangerous-people-to-quarrel-with-lloyd-georges-secret-testimony-to-the-peel-commission-revealed/. Retrieved 25 February 2024.

neither say nor do anything to precipitate a disaster which everybody really wishes to avoid."[2297] Lloyd George responded:

> When the Prime Minister says that we want to keep out of war… we are all in complete accord. When he says that we must keep cool heads, yes, but we must not only have cool heads but stout hearts… our great failure has been, during the last four or five years, that our hearts have failed us. That is why I always deplore, from the point of view of our influence, when we embark upon a particular policy, the constant taunt of hon. Members opposite, "Would you go to war?" If that is taken as an indication of our attitude, as far as the majority of the House is concerned, a foreign Power can safely defy us in any policy which we may take up. Whether we will go to war or not is a matter which we must keep to ourselves and judge for ourselves; but beforehand, to proclaim to the world that whatever other nations do, at any rate as far as the majority of the House is concerned, they would not countenance war, is a great diplomatic weakness. Keep to yourself whether you will go to war or not; stand by your policy, and then judge…
>
> … Germany and Italy have withdrawn from control. What does that mean? Is the agreement not to supply any war material or reinforcements to one or other of the belligerents in operation, and does Germany mean at last to keep it? We are entitled to know that. We have not had any sort of assurance with regard to it. Has any assurance been asked? We have heard a good deal about the outrage on the "Deutschland."[2298] I agree with everything that was said, but I should have liked to hear a little more about the 200 aeroplanes that devastated the Basque Provinces and the heavy artillery which crashed its way into Bilbao–German artillery, Italian artillery, manned by Italians, led by Italians, sent by the Italian and German Governments, with congratulations on their success… They are breaking faith with this country and with France… Is that to go on? I would like to know exactly where we stand in that matter. The Prime Minister said that we must preserve an attitude of complete impartiality. Impartiality in a judge does not mean that you give complete latitude to counsel on one side because they are troublesome, whereas you always repress counsel on the other side. What happened at Bilbao is that Germany had latitude, Italy had latitude; they sent enough troops and guns and aeroplanes there to force their way through, and the Bilbaons had practically nothing. Is that impartiality?…
>
> Let us see what the position is. *During the peace and after the peace, when I was Prime Minister, and afterwards when I was a private Member of this House, I always pleaded for fair treatment for Germany. I never attended a conference where I did not stand out against excessive demands upon Germany. I always stood out… for fair treatment for Germany. I have done so in this House. I have been subjected to criticism in this country and to a great deal of criticism in France for that reason. I would like to have seen an arrangement come to with Germany for a Western European Pact.* I think it was a mistake when Herr Hitler proposed it a year ago that we did not proceed immediately and take him at his word. But I am bound to say that the difficulties, which used to come from France, in the way of any scheme which appeared to promise appeasement, which gave justice and fair treatment to Germany–those difficulties now

---

[2297] Neville Chamberlain (1869-1940), Prime Minister, 28 May 1937–10 May 1940, Tory Leader, 27 May 1937–9 October 1940. He died on 9 November 1940.

[2298] On 29 May 1937, two Soviet bombers attached to the Republican Air Force raided Nationalist air bases and the port of Ibiza. The German cruiser *Deutschland*, part of the International Non-Intervention Committee patrol, was anchored off Ibiza and misidentified as the Nationalist cruiser *Canarias* by the bombers' crew, who dropped bombs on her, killing 31 sailors. In retaliation, on 31 May, the German cruiser *Admiral Scheer* shelled the Republican held city of Almería, killing 19. On 23 June, Germany and Italy left the Committee.

are made by Germany herself.

... No one knows it better than the Foreign Secretary. Many a time I have heard the late Sir Austen Chamberlain... say, "What is the good of making any pact with Germany? She will only keep it as long as it suits her. The moment she has a good excuse for breaking it, and it suits her to do so, she will break it."... I am sorry to say that during the last few months Germany has done her best to justify that criticism. Now that, I think, is the most serious thing in the whole situation–that international faith in treaties, in compacts, in arrangements between countries is vanishing. Here is a pact revised twice... broken flagrantly by Germany, and Germany is on the point of sending her Ambassador over here to arrange another pact of nonaggression, signed by the same hand that signed the Treaty of Non-Intervention which has been trampled upon, disregarded, despised, and spurned by Germany for nine months... before we can come to any arrangement which would create confidence in this country, Germany has got to make it clear that the arrangement she made... with regard to Spain, is to be kept in the letter and in the spirit.

... *There is a lack of straightforwardness in the whole business which is to me perplexing, and which I frankly say I would not have expected from the present head of the German Government. It was not the impression, at any rate, which he created upon my mind*... First of all there was an effort made by the right hon. Gentleman... to secure an arrangement whereby none of the Powers should permit war materials to be supplied to either of the belligerents in Spain... I never thought it would work, but there it is. It was a defensible policy, and if it had been kept it would have been a success.

What happened? First of all they delayed... Negotiations were prolonged... Germany at last accepted it, but Italy did not. She had to be persuaded upon other trivial details... The British Government felt themselves bound by the fact that they had made the proposal not to send any stuff. We had discouraged anything being sent, and we were in the position of being responsible for initiating the policy. The French Government as a Government did the same thing. These other Powers said, "Let us take advantage of this delay to pour in aeroplanes, guns, ammunition, technical details."...

... At that time almost everybody on both sides was convinced that Franco had an easy job... He had a trained army, with officers. He had about the best fighting troops in Spain on his side. On the other side you had nothing but an ill-organised and wrangling mob of sectaries who had never been trained to fight... I met a Spaniard then who... said... that Franco would be in by October. Everybody thought so, but it just miscarried... But by that time the Pact had been signed.

What happened then? Germany was bound by her signature and Italy was bound by her signature. Franco then said, "Unless I get more material, I can never get in." Without hesitation they brushed it on one side, and they poured in men and material... The men who were sent were on their pay roll... The material came out of their arsenals. It was a Government transaction as much as the invasion of Abyssinia was. What did we do? We held meetings of the Non-Intervention Committee... while they were pouring in ammunition in defiance of treaty obligations–one of them the country which is coming to us to sign another pact of non-aggression in Europe.

Then the right hon. Gentleman said, "This has got to be amended, we must stop volunteers." They were not volunteers; they were units in the Italian army, complete units, and so were the aeroplanes and the guns sent by Germany. However, they said, "We will stop volunteers." How did they get round that? By sending conscripts... Who can doubt that Signor Mussolini sent these men there?…

What we want to know is this: Is this cruel imposture going on any longer?… Bilbao was not a Red Republic, but I had rather be charged with being a red than with being green [Nationalist]… Here is a little Province that, at any rate, was very friendly to us at a critical moment. I have been talking to… Englishmen who were there, and they said to me, "There were about 200 aeroplanes, German"–sent by the country that signed the Pact with the right hon. Gentleman not to send any war material into Spain. What had the Basques against that? One obsolete, little anti-aircraft gun. That is how we left our friends when they were being attacked, the people who only a few years ago had helped us to protect our ships against enemy submarines in the Bay of Biscay. There was one man who had been in the Great War and who told me that… he had never witnessed a greater concentration of artillery bombardment on any front–all German guns, German ammunition, followed by Italian troops, sent by the men who signed the Pact of Non-Intervention.

What had the Basques against the artillery? They had practically no ammunition, with very inadequate artillery. Why was it stopped? Ha! the Pact of Non-Intervention. This was not one of the gaps. The gaps happened to be always at the wrong point from the Government's point of view. It will be said… that material has been sent there from Russia. I believe that is so. Once the thing began, I wish they had been able to send more. But… [i]t is no use pretending that the thing has worked impartially… The French Government have sent nothing…

… They are right on the Frontier, and they had every facility. They could easily have sent, but they did not. The Russians… sent some material there, but look at it from the point of view of impartiality and the working of the pact of non-intervention. You have nearly 100,000 Germans and Italians there. You have 12,000 of every other nationality, including Russians, and Russians are in a minority… As far as aeroplanes are concerned, the overwhelming majority have been supplied by the others. If you are to have a pact of non-intervention with gaps, why should the gaps be so arranged that it tells eight to one in favour of Franco's forces as against those of the Government? If the gaps are to be filled, let them be filled on both sides.

There are only two or three courses that the Government can take. The first is to enforce the pact of non-intervention. If the powers do not carry it out, I agree that it cannot be enforced. The second is to have an agreement with regard to volunteers. That, again, depends on the Powers carrying it out. These two courses are dependent on your coming to an agreement with people who have not kept a single agreement they have ever entered into. The third course is to cry "Hands off," and to wind up this fraudulent pact, and let them on both sides buy their material where they can get it. You are talking as if this had never happened before. In every war which has been engaged in… neutral countries by international law have been entitled to supply war materials to the belligerents, and they do it… we were very glad that that rule was applicable in the Great War, because America sold materials to us, France, Italy and Russia…

Asked whether he would recognize both sides as belligerents, Lloyd George continued:

On the whole, I should personally have taken the attitude which this country took in regard to the Civil War in America, when we recognised the Government… I should take the same attitude here. I should only recognise the Government and would not recognise the rebels until they became the Government de facto for the whole of Spain.

> … It is a very deplorable alternative, but it is better than the present system. Under the present system the machinery of war is being sent by foreigners in the proportion of eight to one to one side. You are not stopping equipment, you are not stopping the war, you are not stopping bloodshed. All you are doing is to give the overwhelming advantage to one side. It would be far better to have an honest return to the old principles of neutrality. Then nobody could complain what happened.
>
> After all… Spain is not the only country that has settled the issue of good government by reference to the sword. The Spanish people of both sides have decided that it is to be settled in that way. That is why I do not think they would accept the intervention of the League of Nations… If they were to return to the ordinary machinery for the expression of public opinion, that is, of course, the proper way of settling these issues. But Spain is not the only country that has refused to do that. The very existence of Parliament and the liberties of this country have been settled by these means. What is happening in Spain shows that we have not yet got out of that obsession of the human mind. It is for the Spaniards in Spain to decide.
>
> If the landed aristocracy in Spain have the loyalty of their peasants and their workers… if the hierarchy of Spain have the devotion of their flock… if the great financiers of Spain are so respected by the workmen that they would support them, the battle is won by Franco… An hon. Gentleman… said "Franco occupies the greater part of Spain." If the black troops [from Morocco] were withdrawn and their Aryan confederates from Germany and from Italy were withdrawn, he would occupy but a very ragged small area… I beg the Government to make up their minds, that whatever happens they are not going to have a continuation of this deception, this evasion of a treaty which is not a treaty, this pact which is not honoured. It is a peril to Europe; it is a humiliation to them.
>
> *The whole trouble… is that we have retreated from one position after another for the last five years until these dictators have come to the conclusion that we will stand at no point.* If the great Powers France and Russia– that are acting with us, and ourselves talked quite frankly… these three great Powers together have such a force that there is no one in Europe could stand up against them. But what has happened? *These dictators are very clever men, very daring men, very astute men, in fact very exceptional men. They have taken advantage of the weakness of the government in France and here… They are taking at the present moment rather a low view of the intelligence and the courage of our Government–very low. I wish to God I could say it was too low.* I can only judge the right hon. Gentleman from his speeches. I think his intentions are sound and his aims are high. Let him make up his mind to stand up to these people who have driven the British Government from one position to another of retreat, and then you would find the peace of Europe would be established.[2299]

This was unequivocal–Lloyd George openly stated his past defence of the German viewpoint; his initial estimation of Hitler; his error regarding his trustworthiness and his own subsequent change of mind; his view of the facts and what needed, in his estimation, to be done, and the consequences of not so doing. It was something of an understated masterpiece and should stand higher in the annals of anti-appeasement than it does.

From 2 to 7 August 1937, the National Eisteddfod was held at Machynlleth, and Lloyd George

[2299]https://api.parliament.uk/historic-hansard/commons/1937/jun/25/foreign-office#S5CV0325P0_19370625_HOC_62. Retrieved 28 May 2020. Emphasis added.

made his usual Thursday address on 5 August, which the BBC broadcast. Machynlleth saw the final amalgamation of the Gorsedd of Bards and the National Eisteddfod Association, which, with the local committees, had until then exercised divided control over the Eisteddfod. Lloyd George was appointed President of the new Council, and he treasured the title of bard, *Sior o Ddwyfor*, more than any other honour bestowed upon him.[2300] The advantages of the new scheme were considerable, as lack of continuity in the Eisteddfod from year to year had been a serious weakness. Importantly, Lloyd George played a big role in securing the 'All Welsh Rule', though it was only fully adopted at Caerphilly in 1950.[2301]

Grandson Bengy related that Herbert Morrison[2302]–a close friend of Megan–visited Lloyd George at Bryn Awelon in Criccieth in the summer of 1937 or 1938 to try to persuade him to accept, as a Liberal, the coalitional leadership of the Labour Party. Clement Attlee[2303] had been elected Labour leader on 3 December 1935, defeating Morrison and Arthur Greenwood[2304] in the process, but none of these men could stand each other or work easily together. Morrison presumably had in mind to use Lloyd George's arbitration and conciliation skills, but nothing came of the move, Lloyd George turning him down flat, considering himself past such active leadership, not being a 'post-seeker'.

Increasingly, through the Thirties, Lloyd George spent the majority of the year at Churt, in Surrey, near the Hampshire border. Frances Stevenson bought the 60-acre farm on Lloyd George's behalf from Roland Cubitt, Baron Ashcombe, as part of the sale of Ashcombe's 2,000 acre Churt estate in 1921; at the time of Lloyd George's death, it had grown to over 600 acres. Lloyd George had wanted his new house, designed by architect Philip Tilden, to be built facing the sun… when he arrived, he found if faced North-West! He laughed and said, "We shall call it Bron-y-de" (breast–or slope–of the south). With Lloyd George's occupation of Bron-y-de, Tilden wrote that the 'centre of the political universe was moved from London'. Frances Stevenson lived nearby in 'Avalon', a timber bungalow overlooking the orchards of Bron-y-de.

Bron-y-de was the subject of the main article of the 4 November 1922 issue of *Country Life*. The architect and engineer Owen Williams installed a large panoramic window at Lloyd George's behest following the latter's visit to Hitler's Berghof in the Bavarian Alps which featured a similar window. The study or library, forming the west wing, was the largest room in the house at 36 ft long and 27 ft wide, with a high curved ceiling and a mural on one wall by John Churchill–Churchill's nephew–of The Gulf of Tigullio, with his first wife in the left foreground holding up a copy of the 1922 Treaty of Rapallo. Next to the large, wide, red brick fireplace was Lloyd George's favourite high-backed chair, in which he sat to write much of his *War Memoirs*.[2305] The oak bookshelves held "many valuable and interesting books", including a set of over a hundred volumes on British statesman, bound in red calf

---

2300 Lloyd George, *Dame Margaret*, p171-172; Price, 2006, p205.

2301 Ibid.

2302 Herbert Morrison (1888-1965), MP for Hackney South, 1935-1945, Home Secretary, 1940-1945. Bengy, aged 12 or 13, was at Criccieth for the summer holidays. In his *An Autobiography*, 1960, London, Odhams Press, Morrison makes no mention of this episode.

2303 Clement Attlee (1883-1967), MP for Limehouse, 1922-1950, Prime Minister, 1945-1951.

2304 Arthur Greenwood (1880-1954), MP for Nelson and Colne, 1922-1931, Wakefield, 1932-1954.

2305 Sylvester, *Life*, p271. He gives a full description of this room, p271-275, Diary entry for 6 July 1940.

with gold embossed titles, lined with green silk, the gift of Sir Henry Fildes in 1922.[2306]

Despite the local scrubland being unsuitable for agriculture, in time the estate became an innovative farm, the honey from the apiary being sold to Harrods and Fortnum & Masons under the direction of his Welsh secretary, Ann Parry, and winning a national award for its high quality in 1936.[2307] Lloyd George was often enormously successful, using sometimes rather unconventional methods. In May 1938, he asked Mrs Mary Wyllie, a water diviner from Blairgowrie, Perthshire, to use hazel sticks to find water, and had a well, 230 ft deep, dug where she indicated. Members of his staff were sceptical, but Lloyd George had seen the process at work in Wales and trusted her. Sure enough, 80 ft down there was water exactly where the hazel sticks had said it would be, and he was able to build an irrigation system for his soft fruit. Surplus produce was sold from a stall opposite the 'Pride of the Valley' hotel in the centre of Churt. A five-minute cine film shot in October-November 1938 demonstrates the use of a rototiller and caterpillar tractor on the farmland. He also kept poultry and established a model pig farm. Later, residents who had worked for Lloyd George said that "he always paid above the minimum agricultural wage."[2308]

Asked about his grandfather's interest in, and love of, nature, Bill Tenby replied that:

> It was a very important part of his life. I mean, I suppose, coming as he did, from agrarian roots both in Pembrokeshire and in North Wales, he was really passionately interested in it. Of course, he had this farm in Churt, as well as his lovely house, and the purpose of the farm was to show that you could actually make infertile soil produce lots of quality goods. In his case it was a fruit farm, in which they produced lots of apples and, in due season, raspberries and all that sort of thing, and he would always go round, every day, on long walks round his farm, cloak flapping, hair flapping, surrounded by dogs and various people connected with the farm, always passionately interested, not only in the farm itself, but in all the fauna and everything that was around him, the animals, the flowers, anything to do with nature. And I think that was a very important part of his life, actually.[2309]

Lloyd George's son, Gwilym, sold the house in 1946, soon after his father's death.[2310] The new owner soon sold, and the next occupant was keen on point-to-point. In 1968 he left a bale of hay in the house, it caught fire and the house burned down.[2311]

Bengy related that Lloyd George was very fond of singing, though he never heard him sing himself. He used to have Welsh choirs come to Churt on Sunday evenings. Hywel Davies[2312] was compere for the choirs, and Lloyd George complimented him on his use of language. On Saturdays, he used to

---

2306 Sylvester, *Life*, p273-274.
2307 https://lloydgeorgearchive.co.uk/lloyd-george-farm. Retrieved 24 July 2020.
2308 Cotton, p78.
2309 Taped interview with author, Crondall, 18 June 2019.
2310 Jones, *David Lloyd George*, p553.
2311 My thanks to the late Emrys Williams for his initial outlining of Lloyd George's life at Churt.
2312 Hywel Gethin Davies (1919-1965), from 1958 BBC Head of Programmes in Wales.

have films shown on a projector, operated by his chauffeur, George Dyer.[2313] One such was the 1940 classic *Proud Valley*, starring Paul Robeson, authentically portraying the dangers faced by South Wales coal miners.[2314]

As 1938 dawned, Lloyd George and Dame Margaret celebrated their golden wedding anniversary with a holiday at the luxury Cap d'Antibes Hotel on the Côte d'Azur between Cannes and Nice. On their return, at a gathering of friends at the Capitol Theatre in Cardiff on 1 March, Lloyd George made a speech in response to his guests, his son Richard recording his father's wit:

> 'We have lived together in perfect harmony for fifty years,' he said. Then he went on to sum up their characters in one of those humorous inversions dear to the Welsh mind. 'One of us is contentious, combative, and stormy. That is my wife. Then there is the other partner, placid, calm, peaceful and patient. That is me.'
>
> To this day I can hear the peals of laughter with which my mother met that ridiculous statement. It was unquestionably his ability to make her laugh that so endeared my father to my mother.[2315]

At this period there was ill-informed speculation in some quarters that Lloyd George might return to high office, perhaps even as Chancellor of the Exchequer, with a future Labour government. Unimpressed with such idle gossip, Lloyd George told Colonel Tweed at Liberal Party headquarters that:

> 'He would never take office again. Fancy having to be in town every day, running a department, or in the House [of Commons]–it would kill me'. Sylvester noted stoically that this was the first occasion that his employer had 'made an admission of that kind'. Lloyd George was, however, always ready to assist in an advisory role–'They could always come to see me at Churt!'[2316]

Lloyd George may have lost the desire for high office, but he had not lost his passion for negotiation. On 17 March 1938, he returned to France, this time to Paris, staying in the same room at the Crillon Hotel where he had stayed during his visits during the Great War.[2317] He was accompanied by A. J. Sylvester, Frances, and her nine-year-old daughter Jennifer. Interviewed on his departure, he commented acerbically:

> Since I have been in political life I have never seen such a mess in foreign affairs. There is no clear direction and no leadership except in the Dictator States. Our policy seems to be one of

---

2313 George Dyer (1889-1962), Lloyd George's chauffeur and general factotum from c.1921-1945.

2314 https://lloydgeorgesociety.org.uk/en/article/2007/0130322/memories-of-david-lloyd-george-by-jennifer-longford. Retrieved 24 October 2021.

2315 R. Lloyd George, *Dame Margaret*, p.224.

See https://www.youtube.com/watch?v=6uv82yo3DjQ for British Pathé footage; Retrieved 4 November 2019. There is a twinkle in Lloyd George's eye as he speaks.

2316 Sylvester, Diary Entry for 14 March 1938, quoted in Jones, *Lloyd George At Paris, 1938*, p88.

2317 Jones, *Lloyd George At Paris, 1938*, p88.

> stubborn muddle. Napoleon knew the strategic advantage of securing Spain in a struggle with Britain, but luckily, the British Ministry of the day realised the dangers in time, but our Ministry seems to be as blind as bats.[2318]

On the morning of 18 March, Lloyd George laid a huge wreath of lilies and carnations at the tomb of Marshal Foch, who had died in 1929, at Les Invalides. Next he visited Napoleon's great sarcophagus of red porphyry, taking Jennifer by the hand as they surveyed Napoleon's bronze death mask. An animated Lloyd George commented that it was "a kindly face though the head had shrunken from the size it was in life". They also saw one of Napoleon's famous bicorne hats, his sword from Austerlitz, and the Grand Cordon of the Légion d'Honneur. Lloyd George told Jennifer that tradition held that Napoleon's sword was to be for the man who saved the French nation. After the Great War it had consequently been presented to Marshal Foch, who had proudly worn it at the Armistice ceremonies, but it had then been returned to this, its place of honour. Jennifer remembered this visit all her life, saying Lloyd George "was a great admirer of Napoleon, the foreign upstart who had risen to the top of his world."[2319] After this they visited the former home of Clemenceau at 8, Rue Benjamin Franklin, where he had lived from 1895 until his death in 1929, and which had largely been preserved as he left it on the day he died. The caretaker there gave Lloyd George and Jennifer a private tour of the property, which they clearly enjoyed.

Now Lloyd George got down to serious business, conducting a series of meetings with several prominent French government ministers. The first, at 11.30 am at the Quai d'Orsay, was with Foreign Secretary Joseph Paul-Boncour, viewed as one of the prominent moderate French Socialists. Acting as interpreter for Lloyd George was an old friend, Paul Mantoux, who had acted in that capacity for Clemenceau at the Paris Peace Conference. Their discussion lasted some 50 minutes, taking in the urgent situation developing in Spain, and the Russian proposal for a meeting of the powers excluding the totalitarian states:

> You won't get the British Govt saying to you 'open your frontiers'; but if you were to open your frontiers, and pour your stuff in there, nothing would be said. The British Govt would not intervene at all. They would allow it to be done. The British Govt is a government of the Right. Several of the more intelligent members of the Party like Winston Churchill were pro-Franco at first; now he begins to see the danger and is anti-Mussolini now. In my opinion, they would be rather glad if it were done by France without her saying a word. All the intelligent men on the Govt side are coming round to that way of thinking.[2320]

After lunch, Lloyd George met with Pierre Cot, the Minister of Commerce. At 6.00 pm he was visited

---

2318 Quoted in *Western Mail*, 19 March 1938.

2319 Jones, *Lloyd George At Paris, 1938*, p89; https://lloydgeorgesociety.org.uk/en/article/2007/0130322/memories-of-david-lloyd-george-by-jennifer-longford. Retrieved 26 April 2020. On 23 June 1940, the day after France signed an armistice, Hitler–another 'foreign upstart'–also visited Napoleon's tomb during his only visit to Paris. On leaving he said "That was the greatest and finest moment of my life."

2320 A. J. Sylvester, Diary Entry for 18 March 1938, quoted in Jones, *Lloyd George At Paris, 1938*, p90.

by the Spanish Ambassador to London, Pablo de Azcárate. He was anxious, "but said that the Spanish Govt forces had stopped the advance of Franco's forces." Just before dinner, Lloyd George showed some elaborate maps to André Géraud, the prominent journalist who wrote under the pseudonym 'Pertinax':

> 'Make no mistake about it, if the French take the plunge, England and especially the workmen will be behind France. During the War South Wales was more Socialist than any other part, yet they sent more men to the war on a voluntary basis than any other part of the country. But don't wait for the British to take the initiative.' L.G. said he was anxious to influence those on the Right. Now was the time; 10 days hence may be too late.[2321]

The next morning, Lloyd George, accompanied by Frances and Jennifer, visited the Palace of Versailles, his first visit there since he had been a signatory to the Peace Treaty nineteen years before. The party viewed the Hall of Mirrors with evident excitement. Afterwards, with Mantoux, Lloyd George visited the Trianon Palace Hotel, where the German delegation had been presented with the peace terms in June 1919. Turning his thumb down, Lloyd George exclaimed "Think now, that here we had them like this!"[2322] They also visited the chateau of Marie Antoinette and King Louis XIV at Versailles. Just after midday, Lloyd George met with Prime Minister Léon Blum at Hotel Matignon, again taking with him the three, large-scale maps of Europe. Blum had only just taken office on 13 March. In the event, he was unable to establish a stable ministry and on 10 April his Socialist government fell. However, his premiership lasted long enough to ship heavy artillery and other much needed military equipment to the Spanish Republicans.

There followed a packed day. After the meeting with Blum, Lloyd George and Sylvester proceeded to the Restaurant Laperouse to meet the Deputies of the Right, led by Paul Reynaud, later to become Prime Minister of France himself in March 1940. A sumptuous feast preceded the meeting, potentially 'a very vital talk on the Spanish situation between L.G. and men who did not agree with him for they were on the Right.' At 3.00 pm he met Édouard Herriot, the President of the French Chamber of Deputies. At 5.15 pm he met Léon Jouhaux, Leader of the French Trades Unionists (who won the Nobel Prize for Peace in 1951). At 6.00 pm he laid another wreath at *'La tombe du soldat inconnu'* at the Arc de Triomphe. It was "a moving, impressive act of personal homage for which several thousands of people had assembled. L.G. was received by one of the senior generals in the French army, representatives of the British Legion and of the Societé de Flame whose responsibility it was to keep constantly alive the flame which flickered at the side of the grave. Lloyd George paid solemn homage to the French dead."[2323]

He had also met a number of prominent academics, writers and journalists, including antifascist physicist Professor Paul Langevin; Ellen Wilkinson, Labour MP for Jarrow and author, who came to

---

[2321] Ibid., p91.

[2322] Jones, *Lloyd George*, p250; Rowland, *Lloyd George*, p750.

[2323] Jones, *Lloyd George At Paris, 1938*, p92. It was the first eternal flame lit in Europe since the Vestal Virgins' Sacred Flame was extinguished in Rome in 394.

breakfast one morning with M. Simon, the personal representative of Juan Negrin, the socialist Spanish Prime Minister; and Geneviève Tabouis, the historian and journalist. At one private luncheon Lloyd George produced some maps showing the locations of Allied shipping sunk in the Mediterranean, urging "Now think of a war to be waged with Germany and Italy, all the Spanish ports being at their disposal as well as all the Italian bases."[2324]

Lloyd George left Paris at 7.30 pm that evening. His main purpose in holding these interviews was to persuade the French government to assist the Republican Government in Spain against the rebellious and increasingly successful Nationalist and fascistic Falangist forces led by General Franco, still vigorously supported by Hitler and Mussolini.[2325] Though brief, these meetings mark another important and neglected point in Lloyd George's growing opposition to the rise of the Right in Europe as the Thirties drew towards a close. His opinions had changed greatly from those he had held in 1936, but although he was given a warm welcome and respectful hearing by the senior figures he saw, it is impossible to tell how much his views influenced French policy; probably little. Of note is the fact that Halifax, the new Foreign Secretary, ordered Sir Eric Phipps, the British Ambassador to France, "to keep a close eye on him and after his return deprecate his influence to those French politicians the ex-Premier had met."[2326] On leaving Paris, Sylvester asked Lloyd George for his impressions of his mission. Lloyd George replied at once that:

> 'He was not very pleased and thought he ought to have done it before, but he thought he had stiffened the French in their resolve.' He had been totally nonplussed that M. Herriot, as president of the French chamber, should have politely agreed with L.G.'s viewpoints, and then used the noun 'prudence'–'Well, when a man uses a word of that kind in the middle of a crisis, I know he does not mean to do anything.'[2327]

By the autumn of 1938, all that Lloyd George had feared for so long, another war, loomed ever more darkly on the lowering horizon. On 26 September, Hitler–before 15,000 fervid supporters in the Berlin Sportspalast–declared: "The Sudetenland is the last territorial demand I have to make in Europe, but it is a claim from which I will not swerve, and which I will satisfy, God willing." Lloyd George made his views plain to the South Wales Liberal Federation: "We can hardly abandon the Czechs, who acted upon our counsel–not without dishonour to ourselves… If war is to be avoided, what is required is a clear statement by the British Government that the Czechs have, in their opinion, gone to the limit of reasonable concession… and that if there is any attempt to crush the Czech Republic by force the British Government would side with France and other countries to resist aggression."[2328]

The British and French governments felt differently. In response to Hitler's demands concerning the Sudetenland, which had a majority of ethnic Germans in its population,–some 3.2 million, around

---

2324 Jones, *Lloyd George*, p250; Rowland, *Lloyd George*, p750.
2325 Sylvester, *Real Lloyd George*, p233.
2326 Roberts, p132. Churchill was also under similar surveillance, a measure of Chamberlain's nervousness.
2327 A. J. Sylvester, Diary Entry for 19 March 1938, quoted in Jones, *Lloyd George At Paris, 1938*, p92.
2328 *The Times*, *Mr Lloyd George on the Crisis*, 28 September 1938, p7.

23.4% of the total population of Czechoslovakia–a deal was reached on 29 September, and at about 1.30 am the next morning, 30 September, Hitler, Chamberlain, Mussolini and Daladier[2329] signed the 'Munich Agreement' at the Führerbau. Czechoslovakia was informed by Britain and France that it could either resist Germany alone or submit to the prescribed annexations. The Czechoslovak government, realizing the hopelessness of fighting the Nazis alone, reluctantly capitulated and agreed to abide by the agreement. The settlement gave Germany the Sudetenland starting 10 October, and de facto control over the rest of Czechoslovakia as long as Hitler promised to go no further. Later that morning, Chamberlain persuaded Hitler to sign the Anglo-German Declaration of Peace, before heading home.

Chamberlain's aeroplane landed at Heston Aerodrome at around 5.40 pm, and he immediately spoke to the assembled crowd, famously waving a document aloft:

> The settlement of the Czechoslovakian problem, which has now been achieved is, in my view, only the prelude to a larger settlement in which all Europe may find peace. This morning I had another talk with the German Chancellor, Herr Hitler, and here is the paper which bears his name upon it as well as mine… I would just like to read it to you: "We regard the agreement signed last night and the Anglo-German Naval Agreement as symbolic of the desire of our two peoples never to go to war with one another again." At 7.30pm that evening he stood outside 10 Downing Street and again read from the document and concluded: "My good friends, for the second time in our history, a British Prime Minister has returned from Germany bringing peace with honour. I believe it is peace for our time. We thank you from the bottom of our hearts. Go home and get a nice quiet sleep.[2330]

It was only the well-intentioned, but deluded, Chamberlain who slept. Labour's foreign policy spokesman Hugh Dalton, a bitter enemy of Chamberlain's appeasement policy, suggested that the piece of paper which Chamberlain was waving was "torn from the pages of Mein Kampf".[2331] Lloyd George, speaking at a meeting of the London Free Church Federation Ministers' Club at the City Temple on 26 October, deplored Hitler's "wiping out… that small democratic state." He blamed the Chamberlain government for its abandonment of Czechoslovakia as only the latest victim of fascist aggression, peace having been achieved at "the price of conscience and honour." Britain had begun to descend "a ladder of dishonour rung by rung."[2332]

The same month, Lloyd George published his two-volume memoir titled *The Truth About the Peace Treaties*, really a continuation of his *War Memoirs*, in which he defended the treaties against their subsequent abuse:

---

2329 Édouard Daladier (1884-1970), Radical-Socialist Prime Minister, 10 April 1938–21 March 1940.

2330 The phrase echoed Benjamin Disraeli, who, upon returning from the Congress of Berlin on 16 July 1878, stated, "I have returned from Germany with peace for our time".

2331 F. McDonough, *Neville Chamberlain, Appeasement and the British Road to War*, 1998, Manchester, Manchester University Press, p106.

2332 Quoted in Crosby, *Unknown*, p371. At the height of the Munich Crisis, Bob Boothby asked Lloyd George "what he felt about Mr. Chamberlain's repeated journeying's to see Hitler, and their results. He gave a hard stare, and then said abruptly, 'In my time, they came to see *me*.'" Boothby, *At Home*, p57.

> Let the critics of the Treaties take the highest standard of right attained in any civilised community or between one civilised nation and another, and then measure the Peace settlement by that canon. As one of the authors of that settlement I protest against its being judged on the subsequent abuse of its provisions and powers by some of the nations who dictated its terms. The merits of a law cannot be determined by a fraudulent interpretation of its clauses by those who are in a position temporarily to abuse legal rights and to evade honourable obligations. It is not the Treaties that should be blamed. The fault lies with those who repudiated their own solemn contracts and pledges by taking a discreditable advantage of their temporary superiority to deny justice to those who, for the time being, were helpless to exact it. It is not fair to charge the authors of the Treaties with these abuses or their consequences.[2333]

On 19 December, Lloyd George spoke powerfully in the Commons in support of Hugh Dalton's motion "That this House has no confidence in the Foreign Policy of His Majesty's Government." His message was essentially that the longer the Government took to make a stand against Hitler, the stronger and more ambitious he would become. He further believed that, if thus challenged, Hitler would draw back from the brink of war, at least for some time. Despite the motion being lost by 340-143, Lloyd George had at least laid down another clear anti-appeasement marker.[2334] Indeed, he now seemed to have accepted that war was inevitable. To a packed and receptive crowd of 3,000 at the Pier Pavilion, Llandudno, on 19 January 1939 he angrily laid the blame at the feet of the government:

> The outlook had become still more threatening since the Pact of Munich. So far from that notorious surrender purchasing appeasement, it had encouraged the dictators to a greater display of insolence… Three years ago we discovered that our armaments in essentials for our defence had fallen far behind those of Germany, Italy, and Japan. It was a piece of criminal negligence… During the past two years the dictators had, through our lack of foresight, through the gross stupidity of our national leaders, cleverly but relentlessly succeeded in placing the British Empire and France in the most dangerous strategical position which they had ever been situated… I still look forward to an awakening in the national spirit of Britain and France which will rouse and inspire democracy throughout the world to a great combined effort to save liberty from utter overthrow in our generation.[2335]

On 31 March 1939, in response to Germany's defiance of the Munich Agreement and occupation of Czechoslovakia on 15 March, Chamberlain pledged the support of Britain:

> In the event of any action which clearly threatened Polish independence, and which the Polish Government accordingly considered it vital to resist with their national forces, His Majesty's

---

2333 Lloyd George, *Truth About The Peace Treaties*, Vol.I, p6.

2334 https://hansard.parliament.uk/Commons/1938-12-19/debates/e729e0ea-8e68-4f07-b276-9a7a9f521602/ForeignPolicy. Retrieved 6 December 2021.

2335 *The Times*, 20 January 1939, p14.

> Government would feel themselves bound at once to lend the Polish Government all support in their power. They have given the Polish Government an assurance to this effect.
>
> I may add that the French Government have authorised me to make it plain that they stand in the same position in this matter as do His Majesty's Government.[2336]

This sudden pledge of Chamberlain's in support of Polish independence "left Lloyd George incredulous and appalled at an act of supreme folly. Unsupported by any understanding with Russia, it was a terrible failure of judgement and comprehension, misconceived in every particular. Without Russian backing, it was bound to seem a bluff, and one which Hitler was likely to call. It immeasurably increased the risk of war."[2337] Interviewed that day by Sylvester on Lloyd George's behalf, Ambassador Maisky said "We were not consulted about it and have not been informed. I heard something about it, but not officially."[2338] Lloyd George was amazed.

The same day, immediately after announcing the guarantee to Poland in the Commons, Chamberlain asked Lloyd George to come and see him. He wished to find out how Lloyd George would react in the coming debate. Had he not now done what his critics called for? He had sent Hitler a clear warning. He had drawn a line beyond which Hitler would not venture. Germany, he told Lloyd George, would not fight on two fronts. "What is there on the other front?" Lloyd George asked. "The Polish army", replied Chamberlain. Lloyd George dismissed this. Poland's poorly equipped army was no match for Hitler's Wehrmacht, and Poland had no air-force. Could the Prime Minister still not see that the key to the whole situation was Russia? Chamberlain expressed the view that "Russia would come in ultimately." Lloyd George warned that "this was a very reckless gamble". Chamberlain repeated his belief that "Hitler would recoil when he realised that he was being confronted with a war on two fronts."[2339]

At the Nefyn Agricultural Show on Easter Monday, 10 April 1939, Lloyd George suggested that the British armed forces must be strengthened immediately. He also stressed the important role which local agriculture would play in providing food for the nation in the event of war. He said "We are in greater danger than we have been since 1918… Whatever happens, I ask people of all parties to stand firm for the old country."[2340]

On 27 April, Chamberlain announced in the Commons that the government would introduce the first ever peacetime conscription in Britain, the legislation empowering it to call up men of 20 and 21 for six months' full-time military training before transfer to the reserve. There was to be provision for conscientious objectors. On 8 May, Lloyd George tore into the Government during the bill's second reading. He said he would support the measure, but that he regarded it as being "grossly inadequate to the emergency". He continued:

---

[2336] https://api.parliament.uk/historic-hansard/commons/1939/mar/31/european-situation-1. Retrieved 28 May 2020.
[2337] Lentin, p110.
[2338] Sylvester, *Life*, p225.
[2339] Lentin, p110.
[2340] *Caernarfon and Denbigh Herald*, 14 April 1939, p11.

> You have to defend freedom, which has been challenged–the freedom of the world. We all accepted that statement, and we were very glad to hear it made; it was an acknowledgment and confirmation of the position we had taken up. But you cannot defend the freedom of the world to the limit of the Super-tax and then let it drop. You cannot even do it to the limit of those who are willing, unless you are going to abandon the part which a great country like this is bound to play in the civilisation of mankind. We have not voted against rearmament. From the moment that we accepted the position that it was essential, not merely for the security of this country but for the safety of civilisation, from the moment that we accepted the position that it was necessary for us to embark on the greatest programme of rearmament that this country has ever contemplated–from that moment we accepted also the necessity for taking measures to secure a sufficient number of men to handle those armaments. Voluntary effort could not do it; it certainly could not do it in time… It is only when a country is frightened that you can get a flow of volunteers to the flag, but it is too late then to train them.

He pointed out that, three years before the war in 1914, there had been detailed preparations, with the respective roles of the British, French and Russians worked out. But now, no plans were in place:

> What is the position now?… Russia is out. The Prime Minister and his Government have guaranteed to go to the aid of Poland, Rumania and Greece. If Herr Hitler were to strike to-morrow, what would be the forces ranged on both sides? I ask the House in all gravity to consider that situation. We should have France ready, with a very great Army, highly trained, well equipped, brilliantly led. Then there would be Poland. I do not want to disparage the Poles, but nobody will say that theirs is as good an army, even in quality, as the French… Ourselves, I doubt whether we could send to the Continent the same force as we did in 1914: certainly not more… What have you got on the other side? You have got the immense army of Germany. You have got the Army of Italy which, according to all accounts–and I have asked French officers who have seen it–is twice as powerful an army as it was in 1915. It is more numerous, better disciplined, better trained, more experienced …
>
> … I do hope that the Government have taken these facts into account. Germany and Italy have not merely completed a military alliance: they have announced it. It is a challenge. Their staffs have been meeting… They have got their plans made. Then there is Spain… Take the first two nations. They have concluded a military alliance. The number of men at their disposal is twice that which France and Poland and ourselves could put into the field. If Spain does not come in actively, is there a French Minister that would dare treat her as if she were a friendly or even a reliable neutral? Is there a French general who would not… have to take into account that there was a potential enemy on the Pyrenees…? France would have to defend herself on the Italian frontier and get considerable forces to protect her on her southern flank, and she would only have 150,000 men to support her attack on Germany to relieve Poland.
>
> And Russia is out. I ventured a short time ago… to say that without Russia that was an impossible guarantee. Without Russia those three guarantees to Poland, to Rumania and to Greece are the most reckless commitments that any country has ever entered into… They are demented pledges that cannot be redeemed with this enormous deficiency, this great gap

between the forces arrayed on the other side and the forces which at the present moment we could put in. What do we offer? To build more armaments, and to provide 200,000 conscripts in leisurely instalments of 50,000. It is madness…

We are not at the end of the things that we have to consider… We leave out the East as if it will not count in the least in our computations. Japan has said, "We are not concerned with Europe. We are not going to send forces to help the Axis. All we are interested in is the East." This was hailed with great glee by people who never gave a thought to what it meant… Let them follow through the Japanese march from the north, pointing like a spearhead down towards our frontiers. They have marched, since the present Government came into power… nearly 2,000 miles towards the frontier of India… They are not so far away.

Their only interest is in the East… They are one of the dictator countries… who are out for dominance, and they mean to dominate the East. The last time we were at war we had the reinforcement of one million from India. We were practically able to leave to them the defence of our interests in Egypt, in Palestine, and in Mesopotamia. As to the French, the Japanese are within a few square miles of their frontier. Nobody is taking much notice. The French last time had half a million men from their Indo-China Empire helping them. How are you going to fill these gaps? Russia out, and Japan out, an enemy marching straight down in that direction. It is the greatest menace we have ever had to our Empire in the East. How are we going to fill that gap? By a conscript army of 200,000 men which you will start calling up in a short time in packets of 50,000. I beg of the Government… to remember that in a great war it is a question of arraying on your side as many forces as you possibly can from every quarter of the globe…

You need Russia, but you do not want Russia. Without her, there are two alternatives. If you are called upon to redeem these pledges, maybe in a few days or perhaps in a few weeks, you have two alternatives–to face certain disaster or to skulk from your pledge as you did before. [HON. MEMBERS: "When?"] The pledge to guarantee the frontiers of Czechoslovakia. Have you already forgotten Munich, which was said to be a great triumph for the Government? Why all this tarry when the hour may arrive immediately?… Why do we chatter as if we were in a bazaar, when the need is so urgent?…

… [The Government] dawdled over the rebuilding of our Air Fleet and over armaments. They dawdled with the Ministry of Supply, which everybody realises is an essential part of any great scheme of rearmament. They dawdled for three years before they accepted it. They are dawdling now over Russia, and yet they could not spare one day to consult men who had been supporting them loyally in their programme of rearmament. My hon. Friends below the Gangway at any rate represent 1,750,000 voters. The Government had no time. They broke the pledge without even discussing the matter, when it was important to get real national unity and to secure behind them those powerful interests which I know from experience could in the last War have wrecked our efforts if they had legitimate ground for disgruntlement. The Prime Minister could not spend a day on that. But he flew to Berchtesgaden. He flew to Munich, but he had no time even to consult Czecho-Slovakia whether she would like to be exterminated. To adapt a phrase used about a Prime Minister of the eighteenth century he is "Often in a hurry, always late, and entirely inadequate."…

I cannot see any sign at the present time that the Government have worked out this problem. Who is with them? What force can they put into the field? How can they get them there?… On the other side… Hitler and Mussolini… know all these facts. I ask the Government now whether they will complete the only combination which would give us a chance of triumph,

> which would give us a chance of carrying out the engagements the Government have entered into; a combination which would secure a triumph if it were affected wholeheartedly…
>
> … The time came for the abandonment of appeasement; but there are signs of a resurrection and not a glorious one… Had we not better carry through our engagements and take the necessary measures to do so effectively? The Prime Minister is very angry when questions are put… He has no right to object… I am a little personally offensive myself at times, and I am the last one to complain of the right hon. Gentleman; but he reminded me that it is a very long time since I held office, and suggested that that may have affected my views. Well, the public memory is notoriously short, and the Prime Minister has good reason to congratulate himself that there has been enough time to forget our respective contributions in the last great emergency.
>
> I can assure the Prime Minister that when my… Friends behind me ask questions, they represent a good deal more than their own party. They represent a very deep anxiety in the country… There is not quite the same confidence in the Prime Minister as a man who gets things done, as there was before. He has no diplomatic triumph in his record but he has several very bad failures, and when we ask questions on behalf of millions of very anxious people in this country let him remember that this country is ours as well as his.[2341]

Lloyd George's speech had been well prepared, and it hit home. The Act was passed on 26 May, but events rapidly outstripped this laggardly measure.[2342] On 23 August, Germany and the Soviet Union concluded their infamous Treaty of Non-Aggression in Moscow, which included a secret protocol, which did not become known until the Nuremberg trial, dividing Poland, Romania, Lithuania, Latvia, Estonia and Finland into German and Soviet 'spheres of influence'. This was a bombshell to the British and French governments and made a German attack on Poland virtually inevitable. The next day Sylvester found Lloyd George "exceedingly apprehensive lest Neville Chamberlain had not landed us in a trap. I have not seen L.G. [sic] so pessimistic, ever."[2343] The day following he said pointedly to a reporter: "The country ought to be informed of the course of the Russian negotiations and why they fell through. The whole story is a revelation of almost criminal incompetence."[2344]

On 25 August, two days after the Molotov-Ribbentrop Pact, the Agreement of Mutual Assistance between Britain and Poland was signed in London. The agreement contained promises of mutual military assistance between the nations if either was attacked by "a European Power", Britain vainly seeking to discourage German aggression by this show of solidarity. In another secret protocol, Britain specifically offered assistance in the case of an attack on Poland by Germany, but in the case of attack by other countries, the parties were required only to "consult together on measures to be taken in common." On 22 August, Chamberlain had sent a forthright letter to Hitler warning that "No greater mistake could be made" than to doubt that "intervention by Great Britain on behalf of Poland is no longer a contingency that need be reckoned with." Hitler delayed his invasion by six days, but the die

---

2341 https://api.parliament.uk/historic-hansard/commons/1939/may/08/military-training-bill. Retrieved 29 June 2020.

2342 The Military Training Act 1939 was superseded by the National Service (Armed Forces) Act 1939, enacted on 3 September, enforcing full conscription on all males between 18 and 41 who were UK residents.

2343 Sylvester, *Life*, p234.

2344 *Manchester Guardian*, 26 August 1939, Quoted in Bilainkin, p278.

was cast.[2345] Chamberlain's well-intentioned, but deluded, phrase about 'peace for our time' is now mostly remembered for its cruel irony: less than a year after the agreement, and after mounting pressure for return of the Polish corridor by Hitler, Germany finally invaded Poland just before 5.00 am on 1 September. The next day Labour's deputy leader Arthur Greenwood–encouraged by Leo Amery's famous cry "Speak for England, Arthur!"–accused the Prime Minister of vacillating when "Britain and all that Britain stands for, and human civilization, are in peril." This was followed by declarations of war on Germany by the United Kingdom and France at 11.00 am and 5.00 pm respectively on 3 September. In the Commons at 12.39 pm Lloyd George rose to state, supportively:

> I am one of those who… have from time to time challenged the handling of foreign affairs by the Government, but this is a different matter. The Government are now confronted with the latest, but I am afraid not the last, of a series of acts of brigandage by a very formidable military Power, which if they are left unchallenged will undermine the whole foundations of civilisation throughout the world. The Government could do no other than what they have done. I… will back any Government that is in power in fighting this struggle through… I have been through this before… One thing that struck me then was that it was in moments of disaster, and in some of the worst disasters with which we were confronted in the War, that I found the greatest union among all classes… The nation closed its ranks then. By that means we went through right to the end, and after 4½ years, terrible years, we won a victory for right. We will do it again.[2346]

In a discussion in the Strangers' dining room in the House afterwards, Lloyd George said that Chamberlain was not the man to wage a war. Asking "Who else is there?", he answered his own question by quickly adding "Well, there is always the pale young curate", by which he meant Halifax.[2347] In fact, he had no regard for Halifax: referring to his orchard of plum trees at Churt, he remarked to his friend Ivan Maisky: "The short ones yield a lot of fruit. The very tall ones devour a ton of fertilizers but bear no fruit at all. They're absolutely barren… The same with Halifax: he is tall and good-looking, but barren as a fig tree."[2348] By contrast, Maisky found Lloyd George himself to have "an exceptional brain: a sort of clot of high-voltage intellectual energy. He catches your meaning at once and responds with a cascade of brilliant thoughts and comparisons… [He is] a man of the highest calibre, a cut above all around him… an astonishing person."[2349] On 10 September, Lloyd George published an article in the *Sunday Express*, still castigating the government over Russia: "The tragic story of the rejection of Voroshiloff's[2350] plan has yet to be told, and responsibility for the stupidities that lost us Russia's powerful support justly affixed, and sternly dealt with."[2351]

There followed a relatively quiet period in western Europe, soon dubbed by journalists the 'Phoney

---

2345 See Self, p375-376.

2346 https://api.parliament.uk/historic-hansard/commons/1939/sep/03/prime-ministers-announcement. Retrieved 29 June 2020.

2347 Sylvester, *Life*, p235.

2348 Quoted in Maisky, *Complete Diaries*, Vol.2, p759. Entry for 16 March 1940.

2349 Maisky, *Complete Diaries*, Vol.2, pp743-744. Entry for 11 February 1940.

2350 Marshal Kliment Voroshilov (1881-1969), People's Commissar for Defence, 6 November 1925–7 May 1940.

2351 *Sunday Express*, 10 September 1939, Quoted in Bilainkin, p283.

War'. Matters were not so in Eastern Europe, where the German forces 'steam-rolled' through Poland. Lloyd George wrote in the *Sunday Pictorial* on 10 September: "Germany is again the aggressor. Once more it is a fight for international right–the recognition of the equal right of nations, weak as well as strong, to lead their own independent lives so long as they do not interfere with the rights of their neighbours… Russian non-intervention is… worrying for the Allies."[2352] Poland was attacked from the east by the Soviets on 17 September. On 27 September, the Warsaw garrison surrendered to the Germans, and two days later the country was partitioned between the invaders.[2353]

In the car on his way to the House on 3 October, Lloyd George said to Sylvester, "I want to stop this war, otherwise it will mean the break-up of the Empire."[2354] Of course, he was right, if not quite in the manner he meant. Intervening in the debate itself, he declared:

> [T]he Prime Minister said that his difficulty with regard to even considering any proposals of peace which come from Herr Hitler himself is that he has very good reason for doubting his good faith. I quite sympathise with him in that respect; there is certainly every reason, and no one has greater reason than the Prime Minister himself. If the whole situation with regard to the question of peace were dependent upon the word of Herr Hitler I am afraid that we should have no alternative but to proceed until we got some other and better and more assured guarantee… It is clear that the statement issued last week, the combined statement of the Russian and German Governments with regard to the agreement they had arrived at, was only a provisional one. They were not putting forward any terms of peace. It was a proposal which we certainly should not contemplate. It was that we should accept as an accomplished fact the conquest of Poland and the absorption or assimilation of Poland and that we should base any terms of peace upon that assumption. We do not agree with that.
>
> But it is quite clear… that there has been a discussion between the parties concerned, I mean Russia and Germany and Italy, of more detailed terms of peace. There is a good deal that we do not know. We do not know, for instance, what is proposed to be done with Poland, and that is a very vital matter. I was very glad that the First Lord of the Admiralty [Churchill] in his powerful broadcast on Sunday night did draw a distinction between the attitude of the Russian Government and that of the German Government. I could give many reasons… for treating even the partition of Poland, in so far as the Russian part is concerned, in a totally different spirit from that part which appertains to Herr Hitler and the German Government. Whether the parts of Poland which they have annexed are truly Russian is a matter for discussion. Since the announcement that it was proposed that peace terms should be proffered there has been detailed discussion in Moscow between the German Government and Mr. Stalin. What happened we do not know. There have been discussions at the invitation of Herr Hitler with the Italian Government, and let me say that I do not think the Italian Government have shown any hostility towards this country during the last few days; on the whole they have shown a friendly disposition.

---

2352 Quoted in Lloyd George, *David & Winston*, p220.

2353 Despite its military defeat, Poland never surrendered; instead, it formed the Polish government-in-exile and the clandestine 'Underground State' apparatus which remained in occupied Poland.

2354 Sylvester, *Life*, p238.

We do not know, therefore, what has really passed, but it is quite clear that somebody is going to submit… detailed terms for the consideration of the Government… It needs very careful consideration. I agree with the Prime Minister entirely that if it depended on the statement of Herr Hitler that we should accept the conquest of Poland as an accomplished fact and enter into peace on those terms we should be dishonoured, but it is quite clear that you are going to get something which goes far beyond that… There are other questions which will have to be considered–not merely Poland. There is the question of Czecho-Slovakia, which in many ways is, I think, a better case… Not a word has been said about that by Herr Hitler or any other Government…

… I would ask the House and the Government to pause, not to hurry to come to a conclusion if, for instance, there is a document which comes from the Italian Government or the Russian Government, which as far as we are concerned are both neutral. I hope that the Government are treating them purely as neutrals; the First Lord did so on Sunday night, and it is vital that we should. We do not want to multiply our enemies…

… We are entering upon something which involves the… whole future of our people. What I want to ask the Prime Minister is this: Suppose we get a document of that kind, it makes a difference in two respects. In the first place, it comes from neutral Governments, and, in the second place, they will be just as involved as we are in seeing that whatever terms are come to are implemented; they will not be dependent merely on the word of one Government. You will have the signatures of at least two more. The third question is that of disarmament, because no peace would be a permanent peace unless it involved some agreement with regard to disarmament.

… [E]conomic questions would have to be discussed. The question of disarmament might involve bringing in the Far East, for the simple reason that you could not have disarmament as long as there were great armies in the Far East attacking a friendly nation. Then there would be the question of whether the United States of America should be brought in. In my judgment, if you had a conference… it would be a first-class mistake, to enter into it unless you invited not merely Russia and Italy, but also the United States of America. There you have one great Power the interests of which are not European interests, and which has not been involved in any of these European disputes and quarrels. I should like to ask the Prime Minister whether he does not think it desirable, when he gets a more detailed proposal… that we should have a discussion on it in the House? The House of Commons ought to be consulted. In my judgment, there have been too many hasty decisions… with regard to the whole of this war ... We have nothing to lose–perhaps everything to gain…–by taking time. If we had a broken enemy and we were pursuing him, and we were giving him time to reorganise his forces, it would be another matter; but we are only just beginning, and neither of us in that position…

I would also urge upon the Prime Minister, quite earnestly, the suggestion… that our discussion should be in secret Session. After all, here you have the representatives of the people… We had three secret Sessions during the Great War… I never heard of a single word going out from those secret Sessions… I was Prime Minister… and it enabled us to go on with greater confidence…

There is one additional reason why I urge that the Government and the House should take seriously into consideration any proposals for peace which were specific, detailed, broad, which excluded nothing, but reviewed all the subjects that have been the cause of all the troubles of the last few years. It would be of no use doing this unless you put an end to them. A mere

> patched-up peace would not be of the slightest use, because you would have to begin again. Therefore, you have to settle all the problems that are menacing the peace of the world, including the claims of Italy… My reason is this. The fate of this war may depend not upon Britain and France and Germany, but upon neutrals… Italy has proclaimed herself neutral. Russia has proclaimed herself neutral. Do not rule that out in too great a hurry. The United States of America are neutral. The fate of this war may depend upon the attitude of those three Powers. There are three things which they can do. One is to take sides–and we should have a real peril if we had to face three great Powers, or two great Powers, instead of one. But without taking sides, they can be either friendly or unfriendly neutrals… We know that of the United States of America; the United States of America know it. They can help us as neutrals. When you come to Russia and Italy, within the limits of neutrality they can make all the difference in the world between being helpful and friendly neutrals and hostile neutrals.
>
> My two questions to the Prime Minister are these. First… if there are detailed declarations in the course of the next few days… will he give the House an opportunity to discuss them?… The second question is whether the Prime Minister does not think it desirable that we should have a secret Session where all those who feel that they have a real contribution to make will be able to do so without feeling… they are saying something that may be distorted into something which is encouraging to the enemy.[2355]

Chamberlain's reply was bland and added nothing material to the debate. Lloyd George had conveyed an impression far beyond the words he had used, hinting at the prospect of an immediate peace conference involving Germany. He soon dropped the idea, but in the uncertain early days of the war he was very far from being alone in considering such matters as reasonable, desirable and realistic.[2356] In Stockholm, during 18-19 October, King Gustaf V of Sweden, King Haakon VII of Norway, King Christian X of Denmark, President Kyösti Kallio of Finland, and their respective foreign ministers, met in conference, issuing a statement affirming their neutrality and offering mediation. On 20 October, Pope Pius XII issued his first encyclical *Summi Pontificatus*, subtitled 'On the Unity of Human Society', which critiqued major errors at the time, such as the ideologies of racism, cultural superiority and the totalitarian state, and lamented the destruction of Poland, denounced the Molotov-Ribbentrop Pact, and called for the restoration of an independent Polish state.

In Caernarfon Pavilion, on 21 October, Lloyd George spoke before an audience of between 6,000-9,000 people. Sylvester watched in awe as played the disparate sections of his massed listeners with consummate skill:

> It was superb. One moment he was playing up to the blue-blooded Tories–and many were present–talking about our superb air force and about the greatest navy in the world; you could feel them puff with pride. Next he was playing up to the peacemongers, by advocating a conference and peace. Next he was giving a recital of intimate facts, not before stated, regarding

[2355]https://api.parliament.uk/historic-hansard/commons/1939/oct/03/war-situation. Retrieved 21 April 2020. No contemporary analyst predicted Italy entering the war on the Axis side on 10 June 1940, Soviet Russia entering on the Allied side on being attacked by Germany on 22 June 1941, and the USA entering on the Allied side on 7 December 1941 on being attacked by Japan.
[2356] Sharp, p201.

> our relations with Russia. The burden of his speech was really to influence the Government to bring in Russia on our side, and to send a highly placed minister to see Stalin. Thus he carried everybody off their feet, and there was not even a single heckle or question. He had them so that he could make them laugh or cry at his will and pleasure.[2357]

Son Richard later recorded that his mother Margaret "was present at a great meeting in Caernarvon early in the course of the war when my father made what history must eventually acclaim as one of the great prophecies of all time. On that occasion she heard him tell the vast gathering that this war would be won–*in Russia*!"[2358] This would not be the last time that Lloyd George would emphasise the importance of Russia in determining the outcome of the war.

On 7 November, Queen Wilhelmina of the Netherlands and King Leopold III of Belgium issued a joint statement announcing their willingness to take the initiative on behalf of peace. Addressed to Hitler, French President Albert Lebrun and King George VI, the message requested that the Heads of State accept the neutral monarchs' "good offices" as a "first step towards the establishment of a durable peace."[2359] Although rejected by Hitler on 14 November, in the immediate aftermath No. 10 received some 14,000 letters of support from George Lansbury, Lloyd George, George Bernard Shaw, the Independent Labour Party, some senior Church figures, Basil Liddell Hart, the still considerable pacifist movement and a number of prominent City and business leaders, all manifesting their desire for an early negotiated peace.[2360] Lloyd George was clearly much more in tune with a wider pacifist mood that many critics, both at the time and subsequently, were willing to acknowledge.

At 10.30 am on 13 March 1940, Lloyd George was called upon by President Roosevelt's special envoy, Under Secretary of State Sumner Welles, accompanied by the US Ambassador, Joseph P. Kennedy. Welles had previously visited the Holy See, Italy, Germany and France to discuss German peace making proposals. His seeking out of Lloyd George was remarkable, seeing as he was neither in office nor the leader of a major party. According to Ambassador Maisky, the Foreign Office 'forgot' to put Lloyd George on the list of individuals it advised Welles to see, a 'mistake' which Welles corrected himself, saying privately afterwards that compared with all the other conversations he had in London, that with Lloyd George was "a breath of fresh air."[2361] Scheduled to be of half an hour's duration, the interview ran to nearly two hours, totally disrupting the official schedule. Welles reported that Lloyd George was "alert, mentally very keen, and minutely familiar with every detail of both British domestic affairs and British Foreign Relations."[2362] Consistently, Lloyd George laid the blame for the war on Germany's treatment after Versailles, the hardline attitude of the French and the general bad faith of the Allies.

The 'Phoney War' phase was short-lived, as the war escalated rapidly with the coming of spring.

---

2357 Sylvester, *Life*, p242.
2358 Lloyd George, *Dame Margaret*, p199.
2359 M. F. Palo, *Neutrality As A Policy Choice For Small / Weak Democracies: Learning From The Belgian Experience*, 2019, Leiden and Boston, Brill, p160.
2360 Roberts, p243.
2361 Maisky, Complete Diaries, Vol.2, p763. Entry for 18 March 1940.
2362 https://history.state.gov/historicaldocuments/frus1940v01/d28. Retrieved 1 March 2025.

On 9 April, Germany invaded Denmark and Norway to protect shipments of iron ore from Sweden, which the Allies were attempting to cut off. Denmark capitulated after less than six hours, and Norway was conquered within two months, despite Allied support. Domestic discontent over the Tory-dominated National Government's mishandling of the botched Norwegian campaign was considerable. On 8 May, Neville Chamberlain made a weak defence of his government's direction of it, then pathetically asked for "my friends in this House" to stand by him in the division, appearing to reduce a matter of national crisis and unity to a matter of personal or 'whipped' loyalty. Lloyd George had been reluctant to take part in the 'Norway Debate', having already written a *Sunday Pictorial* article lambasting the government on their "faulty… feeble and foolish" conduct of the war on 5 May[2363], but daughter Megan and others, including Herbert Morrison, Clement Davies and Percy Harris, urgently convinced him.[2364] At 5.37 pm, Lloyd George, rose to make his crucial intervention, a devastating critique that was instrumental in Chamberlain's resignation:

> I have heard most of the speech of… the Secretary of State for Air[2365], and I should think that the facts which he gave us justify the criticism against the Government and are no defence of the Government. He said that we had practically no chance of making good in our Norwegian expedition unless we were able to have air bases there which would enable us to put our fighters into the air in order to counteract the very destructive effect of the German aeroplanes…
>
> The right hon. Gentleman admits… that the Government knew beforehand that there were no air bases unless they were captured from the enemy. He even intimates that the object of the Trondheim expedition was to capture an air base. In that case we ought to have had picked men, and not a kind of a scratch team… We ought also to have had combined action between the Army and the Navy. We had neither. We gambled on the chance of getting air bases… This vital expedition, which would have made a vast difference to this country's strategical position, and an infinite difference to her prestige in the world, was made dependent upon this half-prepared, half-baked expeditionary force, without any combination at all between the Army and the Navy. There could not have been a more serious condemnation of the whole action of the Government in respect of Norway. They knew perfectly well that the Germans were preparing for a raid on some adjoining country… and it is a severe condemnation of them that they should have gambled in this way…
>
> Now, the situation is a grave one… and it would be a fatal error on our part not to acknowledge it. In such experience as I have had of war direction I have never tried to minimise the extent of a disaster… because unless you really face the facts you cannot overcome the difficulties and restore the position. There is no case, in my judgment, for panic. I say that deliberately, after a good deal of reflection, but there is a grave case for pulling ourselves together. We cannot do that unless we tell the country the facts. They must realise the magnitude of our jeopardy. We have two immense Empires federated in the struggle for liberty, the two greatest Empires in the world, the British Empire and the French Empire, with almost

2363 Rowland, *Lloyd George*, p769-770; Rintala, *Lloyd George And Churchill*, p130; N. Shakespeare, p177.

2364 Lippiatt, p3. "By the end of this parade of supplicants, Lloyd George's office must have resembled the Marx Brothers' state room in 'A Night at the Opera'. If only to escape the crush, the old man came down to the Chamber to speak."

2365 Samuel Hoare, briefly Secretary of State for Air, 3 April–11 May 1940.

inexhaustible resources but not easily mobilised, not easily roused, especially ours.

You are not going to rouse the British Empire… to put forth the whole of its strength unless and until you tell it the facts and realities of the peril that confronts it. At the cost of unpleasantness, I am going to do that, not with a view to terrifying them or spreading dismay and consternation, but with a view to rousing real action and not sham action such as we have had…

First of all, we are strategically in a very much worse position than we were before… The greatest triumph of this extraordinary man Hitler has been that he has succeeded in putting his country into an infinitely better strategical position to wage war than his predecessors did in 1914, and by what he has done now he has increased his own advantages and he has put us into greater jeopardy. Let us face it like men of British blood… Czecho-Slovakia, that spear-head, aimed at the heart of Germany, broken. A million of the finest troops in Europe of a very well-educated race of free men, all gone. Such advantage as there is in Czecho-Slovakia, with its great lines of fortifications and its Skoda works… are in the hands of Hitler. That is one strategic advantage which we have handed over to the enemy.

… The second is that you had a Franco-Russian Alliance, negotiated by an old friend of mine, M. Barthou[2366], by which Russia was to come to the aid of Czecho-Slovakia if France did. There would have been a two-front war for Germany. She knows what that means, because she had it before. That door is closed. We sent a third-class clerk[2367] to negotiate with the Prime Minister of the greatest country in the world, while Germany sent her Foreign Secretary with a resplendent retinue. That door is closed. Oil in Russian ships is now coming across the Black Sea for the aeroplanes of Germany. Strategically, that was an immense victory for the Nazi Government.

The third–Rumania. We have tried to form one big syndicate, but Germany has been there starting, not one syndicate, but little syndicates here and there to develop the land, to increase production of work and to give her all sorts of machinery. She has practically got Rumania in her hands; and if she did not have it in her hands a month ago, by this failure in Norway you have handed over Rumania… Now you have Scandinavia and Norway, which were one of the great strategic possibilities of the war, and they are in German hands. It is no use criticising Sweden. Sweden is now between… Germany in Norway and Germany on the Baltic. What right have we to criticise the little Powers? We promised to rescue them. We promised to protect them. We never sent an aeroplane to Poland. We were too late in Norway, although we had the warning of ships in the Baltic and barges crammed with troops… They do not want German troops on their soil, and they are definitely frightened, and for good reasons. Just see what it means strategically. It deprives us of a possible opening in that direction. That has gone. It brings the German aeroplanes and submarines 200 miles nearer our coast. It does more than that. There is the opening-up of the Baltic. I venture to say that that will be considered, in regard to the protection of our trade and commerce. It is a grave menace. Strategically, we are infinitely worse off.

With regard to our prestige, can you doubt that that has been impaired? You have only to read the friendly American papers to find out, highly friendly papers that were backing us up

---

2366 Louis Barthou (1862-1934), Foreign Minister in 1934, the primary figure behind the Franco-Soviet Treaty of Mutual Assistance of 1935, though it was signed by his successor, Pierre Laval.

2367 William Strang (1893-1978), Head of the Foreign Office's Central Department, also a member of the Anglo-German Fellowship.

through thick and thin, in a country which was pro-Ally… [W]hat has happened was a hammer blow to Americans… Before that, they were convinced that victory was going to be won by the Allies, and they had never any doubt about it. This is the first doubt that has entered their minds, and they said, "It will be up to us to defend Democracy."

Then there are the neutral countries. We promised Poland; we promised Czecho-Slovakia. We said: "We will defend your frontiers if you will revise them." There was a promise to Poland, to Norway, and to Finland. Our promissory notes are now rubbish on the market… Tell me one country at the present moment, one neutral country, that would be prepared to stand up and finance us on a mere promise from us?…

… That is the situation with regard to our strategical position… We have to restore that prestige in the world if we are to win this war. There is also the fact that the state of our preparations is known to the world. We started these preparations five years ago, in 1935. In 1935 a promise of rearmament was made; in 1936 active proposals were submitted to this House and were passed without a Division. The Government said they would commit us to £1,500,000,000. If they had asked for more and had said that it was necessary, there was no party in this House which would have challenged it… If any party had challenged it, you had your majority. What has been done?… Everybody knows that whatever was done was done half-heartedly, ineffectively, without drive and unintelligently. For three or four years I thought to myself that the facts with regard to Germany were exaggerated by the First Lord, because the then Prime Minister… said that they were not true. The First Lord was right about it. Then came the war. The tempo was hardly speeded up… Will anybody tell me that he is satisfied with what we have done about aeroplanes, tanks, guns, especially anti-aircraft guns? Is anyone here satisfied with the steps we took to train an Army to use them? Nobody is satisfied. The whole world knows that. And here we are in the worst strategic position in which this country has ever been placed.

Sir Patrick Hannon (Birmingham, Moseley): We have our sea power…

Mr. Lloyd George: I wish we had used it in some parts of Norway. I do not think that the First Lord was entirely responsible for all the things that happened there.

Mr. Churchill: I take complete responsibility for everything that has been done by the Admiralty, and I take my full share of the burden.

Mr. Lloyd George: *The right hon. Gentleman must not allow himself to be converted into an air-raid shelter to keep the splinters from hitting his colleagues.*[2368]

His witty metaphor produced raucous laughter in the House, except on the government front bench where, with one exception, all the faces were stony. A spectator in the gallery, Baba Metcalfe, recorded that the exception was "Winston, like a fat baby swinging his legs on the front bench, trying not to laugh."[2369] When order was restored, Lloyd George resumed, turning his fire onto Chamberlain personally:

---

2368 Grandson Bengy Carey-Evans, then aged 14, was present in the gallery, and he retained a clear memory of Lloyd George, in his morning coat, standing to say this, and of his being disappointed in his grandfather for defending Churchill. Interview with author, Beaumaris, 30 May 2019.

2369 Lippiatt, p4. Lady Alexandra Metcalfe (née Curzon; 1904-1995), third daughter of Lord Curzon, was watching events 'on behalf' of Lord Halifax.

> But that is the position, and we must face it. I agree with the Prime Minister that we must face it as a people and not as a party, nor as a personal issue. The Prime Minister is not in a position to make his personality in this respect inseparable from the interests of the country.
>
> The Prime Minister:... On the contrary, I took pains to say that personalities ought to have no place in these matters.
>
> Mr. Lloyd George: I was not here when the right hon. Gentleman made the observation, but he definitely appealed on a question which is a great national, Imperial and world issue. He said, "I have got my friends." It is not a question of who are the Prime Minister's friends. It is a far bigger issue. The Prime Minister must remember that he has met this formidable foe of ours in peace and in war. He has always been worsted. He is not in a position to appeal on the ground of friendship. He has appealed for sacrifice. The nation is prepared for every sacrifice so long as it has leadership, so long as the Government show clearly what they are aiming at and so long as the nation is confident that those who are leading it are doing their best. *I say solemnly that the Prime Minister should give an example of sacrifice, because there is nothing which can contribute more to victory in this war than that he should sacrifice the seals of office.*[2370]

At 6.10 pm Lloyd George resumed his seat to a strained silence and one observer said that all the frustrations of the past eight months had been released. Violet Bonham Carter, Asquith's unforgiving daughter was, almost despite herself, deeply impressed at "the most dramatic debate I have almost ever heard in my whole Parliamentary memory" and Lloyd George's remarks: "He made the best & most deadly speech I have ever heard from him–voice–gesture–everything was brought into play to drive home his indictment. Material was not lacking. The House was profoundly shaken."[2371] His old colleague Addison was sitting in the Peers' Gallery, and he immediately wrote Lloyd George a supportive note: "I have been listening to you. It did my heart good. Nothing truer can be said than your last sentence. Get rid of the P.M. and a real coalition could become possible."[2372]

Chamberlain was perturbed and, two days later, told Princess Olga of Yugoslavia that "Lloyd George's personal attack on him surpassed anything he had ever heard in Parliament." Churchill was overheard saying to Kingsley Wood[2373] "This is all making it damned difficult for me tonight."[2374] He managed, however, to conclude the debate with a vigorous speech in support of the government. When the division took place that evening, the government, which had a notional majority of 213, prevailed by only 81 votes–281 to 200–with 33 Tories and eight of their allies who normally supported the government voting with the opposition and 60 other Tories deliberately abstaining. Lloyd George himself rated the debate "the most momentous in the history of Parliament."[2375]

Chamberlain spent much of 9 May in meetings with his Cabinet colleagues. Many Tory MPs, even

---

2370 https://api.parliament.uk/historic-hansard/commons/1940/may/08/conduct-of-the-war. Retrieved 20 February 2019. Italics added.

2371 Pottle, *Champion Redoubtable*, 14 May 1940, p210.

2372 N. Shakespeare, p289-290. He had been created Baron Addison on 11 June 1937.

2373 Howard Kingsley Wood (1881-1943), Lord Privy Seal, then Chancellor of the Exchequer until his death.

2374 N. Shakespeare, p290.

2375 Ibid., p7. Boothby wrote to Lloyd George and congratulated him on his speech, noting the "fox is dragging his brush": Letter dated 10 May 1940, Lloyd George Papers.

those who had voted against the government, indicated they did not wish Chamberlain to depart but rather would seek to reconstruct his government. Chamberlain decided he would resign unless Labour were willing to join his government, and so he met with Attlee later that day. Attlee was unwilling but agreed to consult his National Executive then meeting in Bournemouth. Chamberlain favoured the Foreign Secretary, Halifax[2376] as next Prime Minister, as did Labour, the Liberals, the Lords and the King, but Halifax proved reluctant to press his own claims, writing in his diary for 9 May:

> I had no doubt at all in my own mind that for me to succeed him [Chamberlain] would create a quite impossible situation. Apart altogether from Churchill's qualities as compared with my own at this particular juncture, what would in fact be my position? Churchill would be running Defence, and in this connexion one could not but remember the relationship between Asquith and Lloyd George had broken down in the first war… I should speedily become a more or less honorary Prime Minister, living in a kind of twilight just outside the things that really mattered.[2377]

Churchill duly emerged as the choice. The same day, 9 May, provoked during a discussion on the conduct of the war to respond to remarks by Beverley Baxter[2378] that some of his earlier comments had at certain times encouraged Hitler, Lloyd George stated forcefully in the Commons:

> The Treaty of Versailles was not carried out by those who dictated it. A good deal of the trouble was due to that fact. We were dealing with Governments in Germany which were democratic Governments, based on a democratic franchise, with democratic statesmen, and it is because we did not carry out the undertakings we had given to those democratic Governments that Hitler came into power. There was a good deal that was done to Germany, more particularly with regard to disarmament. The solid promise that we gave, not merely in the Treaty itself, but in a document which I took part in drafting, which was signed by M. Clemenceau on our behalf, that if Germany disarmed, we should immediately follow her example, was not carried out, and there is no Government that is more responsible for that than the present National Government which came into power in 1931. They had their opportunity. America was ready, Germany was ready–it was a time when Herr Bruening[2379] was in charge–but we refused to carry out the terms after Germany had been completely disarmed…
>
> The same thing applies to minorities. I repeatedly called attention to it. Mr. Benes[2380], in the conference in Paris… was responsible, first of all, for giving a direct pledge to the conference that if Sudeten Germany were to become part of Czechoslovakia–the same thing applied to the

---

2376 Edward Wood, Earl of Halifax (1881-1959), Secretary of State for Foreign Affairs, 21 February 1938–22 December 1940, a leading Tory proponent of appeasement from 1936-1938 and again in May-June 1940, although he modified his opinion considerably after the Munich Crisis.

2377 Quoted in Roberts, p277.

2378 Arthur Beverley Baxter (1891-1964), Canadian-born Tory MP for Wood Green, himself strongly associated with support for appeasement in the late 1930s, a staunch supporter of Chamberlain.

2379 Heinrich Brüning (1885-1970), Centre Party politician, Chancellor, 30 March 1930–30 May 1932.

2380 Edvard Beneš (1884-1948), Minister of Foreign Affairs, 1918-1935, Prime Minister, 1921-1922, President 1935-1938, 1939-1948 (1939-1945 in exile in London).

> Hungarians and to the Slovakians–the same autonomy would be given to them as in the Swiss Confederation of men of different races under the same flag and forming part of the same federal constitution. It was not carried out. The last conference I attended as Prime Minister was at Genoa in 1922, three years after the signature of the Treaty of Versailles. I begged that the promises which had then been given to the minorities, to the Hungarians and to the Germans–the same thing applies to Poland and to the Ukrainians–should be carried out. It was not my fault that they were not carried out.
>
> … ever since the signature of the treaty I did my very best, as Prime Minister, and I did not alter my policy in the least when I became an independent Member of the Opposition or when I was Leader of the Liberal party… I urged the conquering powers who were then all powerful to exert their authority to compel these countries to carry out the pledges which they had given. I pointed out over and over again that if they did not do so, it would end in a great European war and that there would be trouble. My predictions, unfortunately, have turned out to be true, and… most of this trouble has originated in the fact that the victors in the late war did not carry out solemn pledges which they gave in a Treaty which they themselves dictated. They had the opportunity. Germany was prostrate. The creation of this terrible power in Germany, the spirit which is behind it, and what makes it so formidable at the present moment is due to the fact that we did not carry out our pledges. What is the result? Democracy has been swept away in Germany; democracy has been attacked by Germany. That spirit in Germany was created by the fact that the dominating democracies in Europe did not keep faith. We are now confronted with the most terrible answer that has ever been given to those who have broken faith and broken covenants.[2381]

At dawn the following day, 10 May, Germany invaded the Low Countries and Chamberlain hoped to remain in office. However, towards 5.00 pm Attlee confirmed that Labour would not serve under him, though they were willing to serve under someone else. Accordingly, at 6.00 pm Chamberlain went to Buckingham Palace to tender his resignation, advising King George VI to send for Churchill. In his resignation speech broadcast at 9.00 pm that evening, Chamberlain told the nation: "the hour has now come when we are to be put to the test… And you and I must rally behind our new leader, and with our united strength, and with unshakable courage fight." Churchill wrote later: "At last I had the authority to give directions over the whole scene. I felt as if I were walking with destiny, and that all my past life had been but a preparation for this hour and for this trial… and I was sure I should not fail."[2382]

Lloyd George's intervention proved to be his last major speech in the Commons, as age and events overtook him. At least three times in those crisis months of May-June 1940, Churchill broached the subject of bringing Lloyd George into his government. Each time, Chamberlain indicated that, due to their long-time antipathy, he would immediately retire if Lloyd George were appointed a minister–crucially, Churchill was still insecure concerning his standing amongst suspicious and resentful Tory backbenchers, and felt that he needed Chamberlain in his administration, serving as Lord President of the Council. On 31 May Chamberlain noted disingenuously in his diary:

---

2381 https://api.parliament.uk/historic-hansard/commons/1940/may/09/conduct-of-the-war. Retrieved 8 April 2019.
2382 Churchill, *The Second World War: The Gathering Storm*, 1948, London, Cassell, p532.

> When W.C. [sic] was forming his Govt he did ask me about Ll.G [sic]. I said I would not work with him. W.C. then asked whether I should object to his being M/Agriculture. I said it might be that that would not bring us into association but I knew we couldn't work together. At that he dropped the subject only saying... that he didn't trust him not to be a defeatist. I was therefore never asked to agree to his being M/Agriculture & therefore the question of my agreement did not arise.[2383]

On 13 May Churchill made his first speech in the Commons as Prime Minister, famously stating: "I have nothing to offer but blood, toil, tears and sweat." Responding, Lloyd George was moved to say:

> May I, as one of the oldest friends of the Prime Minister in this House... congratulate him personally upon his succession to the Premiership... I congratulate the country upon his elevation to the Premiership at this very, very critical and terrible moment... He is exercising his supreme responsibility at a graver moment and in times of greater jeopardy than have ever confronted a British Minister... The friends of freedom and of human right throughout the world will wish him God speed; their hopes are centred in him now because it will depend upon him more than on any of his associates... because the man who has got the supreme direction is the man upon whom most of the responsibility depends. May I say that their prayers will be for him and that, in my judgment, the sacrifices of Britain and her Empire will be at his disposal.[2384]

Churchill was moved by this sincere testimony, A. J. Sylvester noting: "Winston's eyes filled with tears; he buried his face quickly in his left hand and wiped his face. He admitted afterwards that L.G.'s words had caused him to break down."[2385] However, Lloyd George's lifelong political acumen enabled him to see behind the scenes, Sylvester also noting: "L.G. told Winston privately in the lobby that if he could not fight Neville Chamberlain how could he hope successfully to tackle Hitler?"[2386]

Lloyd George knew by now that he would not be a member of the War Cabinet. Pride now mixing with his acumen, he told Sylvester "Neville would have infinitely more authority than I would have, and he would oppose everything I proposed."[2387] In this he was probably correct, but he was wrong in believing Churchill would not approach him again. On 28 May, immediately after making a statement in the Commons concerning the surrender of Belgium, Churchill sent for Lloyd George. According to Sylvester "The P.M. then offered him a position in the War Cabinet, subject to the approval of Neville Chamberlain."[2388] Lloyd George consulted Gwilym and Megan, and both "agreed that he should not accept under such conditions."[2389] The next day, Lloyd George wrote to Churchill:

---

2383 Quoted in Toye, p353-354.

2384 https://api.parliament.uk/historic-hansard/commons/1940/may/13/his-majestys-government-1. Retrieved 8 April 2019.

2385 Sylvester, *Life*, p261-262.Entry for 13 May.

2386 Ibid., p262. Entry for 13 May.

2387 Quoted in Toye, p355.

2388 Sylvester, *Life*, p263. Entry for 28 May. During this time, 26 May–4 June, the Dunkirk evacuation of 338,226 soldiers was taking place.

2389 Ibid., p263.

> You were good enough yesterday to ask me if I would be prepared to enter the War Cabinet if you secured the adhesion of Mr Chamberlain to the proposal. It is the first time you have approached me personally on the subject, and I can well understand the reason for your hesitancy, for, in the course of our interview, you made it quite clear that if Chamberlain interposed his veto on the ground of personal resentment over past differences you could not proceed with the offer. This is not a firm offer. Until it is definite I cannot consider it.
>
> … I am no office seeker. I am genuinely anxious to help to extricate my country from the most terrible disaster into which it has ever been plunged by the ineptitude of her rulers. Several of the architects of this catastrophe are still leading members of your Government, and two of them [Chamberlain and Halifax] are in the Cabinet which directs this war.[2390]

Churchill then sounded out Chamberlain, who was strongly opposed to the idea, saying that the Prime Minister would have to choose between them. Churchill immediately replied that Chamberlain was of more use to him and wrote accordingly to Lloyd George on 30 May. Still, he tried again. Pressure from the press and the Labour Party had been growing for Chamberlain, Halifax and other pre-war appeasers to be removed from office. This gave Churchill a little leverage. On 4 June he wrote to Chamberlain again concerning Lloyd George: "I am sure he would bring added strength to the Government, and that otherwise, being treated as an outcast, he will become the focus for regathering discontents." This time Chamberlain wrote back that he would agree, but only on condition that Churchill should obtain from Lloyd George "his personal assurance that on coming into the War Cabinet he will drop his personal feud and prejudice against me."

The same day, Churchill invited Lloyd George to No.10, and the two had a meeting that evening that lasted for an hour and a quarter. Afterwards, Lloyd George told Sylvester that Churchill "had made him a firm offer this time to go in," but that he "had told Winston that he must give him time to think it over. L.G. said: "I told Winston if you cannot stand up to Neville Chamberlain and Margesson[2391] how can you stand up to Hitler?""[2392] What further thinking Lloyd George felt that he needed to do at this stage is unfathomable. If he thought that Churchill would fire Chamberlain, he was much mistaken: Chamberlain was still the influential Leader of the Tory Party with the continued support of many MPs. Meanwhile the pace of the war rapidly accelerated. On 10 June, Italy declared war on Britain and France. On 14 June, the Germans entered Paris and on 22 June the new French Premier, Marshal Philippe Pétain[2393], signed an armistice with the Nazis. The longer Lloyd George failed to commit himself, the more Churchill's mistrust grew. The answer never came, and the time passed.

On 7 October, in writing to A. J. Sylvester from Criccieth, Lloyd George vigorously–though privately, and despite his earlier expressed opinion–condemned the holding of secret sessions of Parliament which Churchill had initiated, which he said were designed "to repress all criticism". He

---

2390 Quoted in Sylvester, *Life*, p264-265. The letter was re-drafted several times.

2391 David Margesson (1890-1965), Tory MP, disciplinarian Government Chief Whip, 1931-1940.

2392 Sylvester, *Life*, p267.

2393 Pétain was Chief of the French State, 1 July 1940–20 August 1944 at Vichy. Tried as a collaborationist and convicted for treason, he died in prison aged 95.

declared that "I am not going to take part in that pernicious sham–all the more hypocritical because it takes place during a War 'to restore liberty to Europe.'"[2394] On 14 October, he gave his last public speech at Caernarfon, when he urged greater food production for the successful prosecution of the war.

There was one last possibility of a return to office. During the night of 11-12 December, Philip Kerr, Lord Lothian, Ambassador to the still neutral United States, died quite suddenly in Washington aged 58. On hearing the news, Lloyd George was shocked, as he had only dined with Kerr on 5 November in London. In the Commons, on 19 December, Lloyd George recalled Kerr's cheerfulness at the worst moments of the first war and his "deep spiritual placidity": "He was intensely religious but never flaunted it; he was intensely religious without bigotry, without intolerance, and without any of the hatreds that too often mar an ardent faith." Owing to his understanding of the American people and his affection for them, of which they were aware, he could "talk to them in a language which no other man of British birth could dare."[2395]

Churchill had a reputation for using foreign vacancies as a means of side-lining politicians who might prove troublesome to him at home. He soon thought of Lloyd George, still somewhat lukewarm regarding the prosecution of the war, feeling that this attitude could be problematic, if the tide of war turned further against Britain. On the plus side, he felt that Lloyd George's record, dynamism, Liberalism and magnetic personality would play well with the Americans. Indeed, President Roosevelt "immediately approved the mooted appointment."[2396] He would also be given a largely honorary seat in the War Cabinet as a form of personal compensation for having to serve under Halifax. Halifax himself had no objections to Lloyd George when he and Churchill met the next day but did also advance his own suggestions.

By 15 December, with advances in North Africa also following on from the Fleet Air Arm's disabling of the Italian fleet at Taranto on 11-12 November, Churchill felt in a politically stronger position. It was probably that evening, in conversation with Anthony Eden, Secretary of State for War, that the decision was made that, should Lloyd George refuse the offer, then Churchill would appoint Halifax, also a potential rival in times of trouble. At lunch at No. 10 the next day, 16 December, Lloyd George formally turned the offer down, ostensibly on the advice of his doctor, Dawson, who sagely wrote privately to his patient: "Neither the P.M's genius nor your genius carries with it the special aptitude of an ambassador. Listening patiently to much talk, and sometimes from people who 'go deeply into the surface of things', would ill fit you and therefore strain you unduly."[2397] On receiving Lloyd George's answer, Churchill reverted to his plan of appointing the reluctant Halifax, who became Ambassador on 23 December, being replaced as Foreign Secretary by Eden.[2398]

Tragedy broke in on Lloyd George's personally settled way of life early in 1941. On the afternoon

---

2394 NLW, A. J. Sylvester Papers E3, DLG to AJS, 7 October 1940.

2395 Quoted in Butler, p313. Brought up a Roman Catholic, Kerr later became a Christian Scientist.

2396 Lloyd George, *David & Winston*, p235.

2397 Watson, *Dawson Of Penn*, p306.

2398 Roberts, p366-368. Possibly Lloyd George had Margaret's health in mind as well as his own. Churchill referred to the aristocratic, church-going, fox-hunting Halifax as the 'Holy Fox' for his political guile, but he was ultimately outfoxed by Churchill himself.

of 26 November 1940, Dame Margaret was visiting her sister-in-law, Anita George, at her home at Garth Celyn, Criccieth.[2399] The two had attended a Women's Institute meeting in the Memorial Hall, and Anita was pouring tea, when the telephone rang in the next room. Margaret said "You sit down, Anita, I'll answer the telephone," and walked out of the room to do so.[2400] Here, she slipped on a rug and fell heavily on a highly polished parquet floor. Her son Richard later recorded: "As bad luck would have it, my mother's physician was off in the country somewhere, attending a patient, and my mother insisted on being taken to Portmadoc to have her hip X-rayed. For whatever reason, there was no ambulance available, but my mother gritted her teeth and insisted on making the four-mile journey in her own car."[2401]

The X-ray at Madoc Memorial Hospital showed that Margaret had fractured her hip.

> Eventually, back in Brynawelon, she was put to bed. As quickly as they could get to her, Olwen and Megan came down from London. Naturally we all realized that such an accident, considering her age, was serious, but I am sure none of us had the faintest suspicion that the result of it would be fatal. Everything that could be done by way of nursing and medical attendance was done, of course, but as the days lengthened into weeks and she was still bedridden it began to be evident that she would never recover. On the other hand, her unflagging high spirits and the absence of any alarming symptoms deceived us into thinking she might be spared to us for a long time.[2402]

Complications set in, aggravated by an unsuspected heart condition. On 15 January, her doctor telephoned Sylvester in Churt that he was concerned. Three days later news came that Margaret's condition was much worse. The redoubtable lady retained her wit and dignity to the last, Richard recording that, having:

> Been warned of the imminence of death, [daughters Olwen and Megan] did their best to hide their grief as they fussed over the still cheery, animated sufferer. The last night, when together they took more than usual pains in brushing her hair and making her comfortable, she eyed them with a roguish look.
>
> "Whatever are you two girls up to?" she demanded, in Welsh. "Anyone would think I was going to die." And she laughed at her own macabre jest!"[2403]

That day, 19 January, Lloyd George set out early in the morning with his secretary, Ann Parry, in his Rolls-Royce Phantom III. Driving westwards across England, the weather gradually worsened, with snow falling heavily. At Bridgnorth, towards the end of the day, they ran into a snowdrift and had to be dug out. They drove north-westwards to Shrewsbury and then into Wales, along the A5 road. At

---

2399 Sylvester, *Life*, p281.

2400 George, *My Brother And I*, p104.

2401 R. Lloyd George, *Dame Margaret*, p207.

2402 Ibid., p207.

2403 Ibid., p210.

Cerrig-y-Druidion, and with the light already fading, they ran into another deep snowdrift, the car completely buried, and they had to be dug out by the local garage proprietor and a gang of volunteers. They could obviously not continue; Lloyd George was shaken by the incident and so they stayed in the local village inn, The White Lion–*Y Llew Gwyn*–for the night.

Early the next day, Monday, 20 January, forty men turned out to try to enable him to continue his journey westwards, but the atrocious weather defeated them. Shortly before 11 o'clock, Lord Dawson phoned through from Bangor to the inn, and after a minute or two Lloyd George was informed of the sad news "Your wife died at twenty minutes past ten this morning." Lloyd George's response was that he had been prepared for it. He then asked to speak to Sylvester, who recorded:

> It was most pathetic. L.G. [sic] was broken and he sobbed at the other end of the telephone. I expressed my deep grief for him: he sobbed: 'She was a great old pal.'
>
> I said: 'You are very brave,' but he said: 'No I am not.' He then said: 'Don't take any risks but come through to me here as soon as you can, I want your companionship'.[2404]

It was a sad finale to a good life, and a pathetic end to 55 years of marriage.

The next morning, a vast army of men managed to clear the road to the south-east of the village, and Lloyd George drove back nine miles the way he had come as far as Corwen, where Sylvester and Carey Evans met him, Sylvester noting that "I have never seen anybody looking so like death. His face was an awful colour. For the first time in my life I saw him wearing a woollen scarf."[2405] Lloyd George was "deeply touched" by the fact that in the gang of volunteers "there were all classes of men... including the Wesleyan Minister, the schoolmaster, the local garage proprietor named Bob Roberts and many of the Home Guard. Five of the latter had come to Corwen in Bob's car with spades in case of accident... L.G. [sic] said that although Cerrig-y-Druidion was only a very small place, no place he could imagine could have shown him more kindness and assistance."[2406]

They took a private room at the 'Owain Glyndwr' Hotel, and after an hour or so in front of a roaring fire, drinking hot milk to which Carey Evans had added a tonic, Lloyd George revived somewhat.[2407] A few hours later the London train arrived bringing Richard and Gwilym and their wives, Winifred and Edna. Lloyd George, sobbing violently, collapsed into the arms of his eldest son. Richard, who had been determined to upbraid him for his treatment of Margaret, was stopped dead in his tracks: "this little old man, weeping so copiously, bore no resemblance whatsoever to the arch-philanderer on whom he had intended to vent his wrath."[2408] Supported on the arms of his family, Lloyd George boarded the train and went to sleep. Son Dick noted his father's great "ability to throw off his worries... He never took his worries to bed with him–nothing could upset his sleep. His power

---

2404 Sylvester, *The Real Lloyd George*, p284.

2405 Ibid., p285.

2406 Ibid.

2407 The author visited the cosy private resident's parlour of the old coaching inn, in which Lloyd George was most likely given hospitality, on the 78th anniversary of his visit.

2408 Rowland, *Lloyd George*, p783.

of willing sleep to come almost at any hour undoubtedly gave him reserves of strength which carried him through many a dark period."[2409] After his sleep, he said he was hungry and "had a very good meal of cold goose, some cold beef, cheese and hot milk and whiskey" which had been prepared by the Hotel, after which he "seemed considerably cheered". Sylvester added: "Outside Canada and America, I have never seen such snow. The Great Western Railway had been very enterprising and had had snow ploughs at work."[2410]

The day before the funeral a touching and very telling incident took place whilst the little, elderly gravedigger was hacking away the ice beneath the snow that covered the family vault in the cemetery. A passer-by asked him what he considered would be a fitting epitaph for Dame Margaret: "For a space the grave-digger pondered the matter. Then, reverently and simply, he made answer, 'She bore her troubles like a great lady.'"[2411] The funeral itself took place on 23 January, a *cynhebrwng bach*–a little or private funeral–held at Bryn Awelon at 2.00 pm, the service being conducted by Reverend J. W. Jones and Reverend J. Lloyd Jones. Sylvester recorded:

> The coffin was borne on a lorry and pulled by 65 Home Guardsmen each carrying a wreath. For the only time during these sad days the sun came out in all its glory. The fields on the mountainside showed green patches around which there were deep snowdrifts. I walked alongside the lorry. L.G. was in a car immediately behind.
>
> I watched the coffin lowered into the vault, L.G., standing between Dick and Gwilym, trembled and sobbed, but he bore his grief bravely. I have been to many important funerals, but none was so impressive as this. The funeral procession through the little town past the village green, the profusion of flowers and the reverence of the people was most impressive.[2412]

Thousands of wreaths of flowers had been sent from the locality and from all over Britain, a very remarkable tribute in wartime and harsh winter conditions. Telegrams and cables also came from all over the world, including ones from the King and Queen, the Duke of Windsor, Churchill, General Smuts and President Roosevelt. Sir Alfred T. Davies paid a gentle, insightful tribute to "this gracious lady," thought worth quoting by her son Richard in his own book on his mother:

> The niche–and that no small one–which she afterwards came to occupy in the hearts of her fellow-countrymen was of her own carving… Her natural sphere, it is true, was in her home. But she could–and did–hold her own with the great ones of the land, with whom in later years she was destined to be brought into close and even intimate contact.
>
> Best known in her native county of Caernarvonshire, to which (and especially to her beloved Criccieth) she remained loyal to the last day of her life, Dame Margaret Lloyd George

2409 Lloyd George, *Dame Margaret*, p155. His private secretary, Geoffrey Shakespeare, noted the same trait: G. Shakespeare, p39, as did A. J. Sylvester, *Real Lloyd George*, p204, and Liberal Acting Director of Propaganda in 1928-1929, Gordon West, p26.

2410 Sylvester, *Life*, p286. Entry for 21 January 1941. He slightly mis-names the Hotel.

2411 R. Lloyd George, *Dame Margaret*, p4.

2412 Sylvester, *Life*, p286. He mourned Dame Margaret's passing as that of a "real friend" and "staunch supporter." There were no female mourners present at the interment, as was usual at the time.

deliberately eschewed the lure of the city and even also the attractions of her husband's adopted countryside in heather-clad Surrey. This she did in order that she might the better serve her day and generation in 'her own place.'[2413]

And from Clement Davies:[2414]

We in Wales knew David Lloyd George as the combative, stormy eagle of Snowdonia, and Dame Margaret the calm, patient, but withal strong and powerful personality worthy in every way of her mighty mate. She was more than the wife of a great man; she had a distinctive quality of her own–unobtrusive, never forcing its way to the forefront, but nevertheless there–sure, certain, reliable. It has been my good fortune to know them for over forty years–a period during which they passed through and knew every variety of public opinion from the execration of the Jingo mob of the Boer War to the adulation of the masses whom he led to victory in a greater war, a period which counted in it years of unremitting care, when the value of every penny had to be carefully weighed and assessed. Whatever were the changes, Dame Margaret never changed. Her friends of comparative obscurity were her friends in the hours of power and of triumph. Wales knew this, and Wales never changed in its affection, loyalty and devotion to her. She was the friend of all, and all were friends to her… Dame Margaret was a great lady… She was the embodiment of the best in Welsh culture.[2415]

Bengy Carey-Evans remembered visiting from nearby Hindhead for Sunday lunch at Churt when the news broke that Hitler had invaded Soviet Russia, 22 June 1941:

We were very lucky to be having Sunday lunch with him. Before we went into lunch, Gwilym… and Megan wanted to find out what their father thought of events, but they knew that if they plunged in, and asked him too abruptly, he'd clam up, they wanted to try to introduce the subject gently, halfway through the meal, as if it was an aside. And this happened, we got halfway through the meal, and Gwilym said 'Well, what do you think, now, is going to be the consequence of the invasion of Russia by Hitler?' I remember, he stopped eating, he put his knife and fork down, and he just waited a moment before he'd speak, 'Well', he said, 'it all depends on who gets to Berlin first!' And I remember thinking to myself, well, what a silly answer, [Laughs], it didn't mean anything to me at all, but looking back on it now, he realised that nobody has ever invaded Russia and got away with it, it's far too big a country, and he knew that this was the beginning of the end for Hitler, and the future of Europe would depend on who got to Berlin first… as indeed it did![2416]

Lloyd George was clearly thinking three steps ahead, already believing such folly would cost Germany

2413 Quoted in R. Lloyd George, *Dame Margaret*, p122.
2414 Clement Davies (1884-1962), Liberal MP for Montgomeryshire from 1929 until his death, Liberal Leader, 1945-1956.
2415 Quoted in R. Lloyd George, *Dame Margaret*, p227.
2416 Taped interview with author, Beaumaris, 11 October 2018.

the war, the exact outcome all depending on which of the Allies occupied the German capital first.

Cousin William, who became 3rd Viscount Tenby in 1983, also had clear memories of his grandfather during wartime:

> I am the youngest of the Grandsons and was still at school during the War. Dad was a junior member of Churchill's Wartime Coalition (amongst other things, the first Minister of Fuel & Power)[2417] and frequently spent weekends at Bron-y-De, Taid's attractive house in Churt… This was not only his home but was the centre also of the fruit farm he established there. It was a remarkable enterprise being largely based on poor soil, a deliberate decision on his part to show that crops could be produced on the most unproductive land (he even produced the Lloyd George Raspberry, which was unusual in fruiting in the early Autumn!).[2418]
>
> I was away at school during the War, but in the holidays when we were not in our permanent Tenby home, I would join my parents in Churt, so I saw him on occasion. He had great charm and one of his biggest assets was his interest in people generally, no matter their status. Most politicians affect a similar interest, but it's part of the make-up. With Taid it was absolutely genuine. He seemed to follow a daily routine. Walks round the farm estate, always accompanied by dogs (Chows) and whoever was staying or passing through. Meals were punctual, tasty and full of local produce (many vegetables!) and wine was available for guests, though he drank sparingly himself, confining his input to a weak Irish Whiskey with much water. At night he would retire early and at that time he would read for entertainment only (Zane Grey Westerns for example)[2419] but during the day he would read extensively from the Classics to Current Affairs and he was undoubtedly one of the best read people I have ever met. He was by no means a heavy smoker but would perhaps enjoy a cigar with guests, and I seem to recall him with a pipe in his mouth once or twice. On Sundays he would invariably listen to whatever religious service was being broadcast from Wales. He would follow the hymns with his own Welsh Hymn Book and listen intently to the sermon, usually in Welsh.[2420]
>
> I was not present, so far as I can recall, when Taid entertained important visitors. Important and worldly matters were discussed "*en famille*," but my memories were very much of topics like the farm and how it was performing, local matters, and nature generally. Despite his international fame, he was still a countryman at heart with a keen interest in country-side affairs, nature and, above all, animals. It's an obvious point to make, but he was intensely Welsh to his very core and this relationship to the country of his birth and his background separated him, I would suggest, from most other politicians of his generation, or indeed later, with the possible exception of someone like, say, Nye Bevan.[2421]

Among other interesting facets of Lloyd George's life at Churt during wartime, was his habit of

---

[2417] Gwilym Lloyd George, 1st Viscount Tenby, Liberal MP for Pembrokeshire, highly regarded Minister of Fuel & Power, 3 June 1942–26 July 1945, National Liberal Home Secretary, 19 October 1954–14 January 1957.

[2418] Long thought to have disappeared, genuine stock has recently been re-cultivated: the medium sized madder-rose berries are claimed to be "moderately firm and exceedingly flavourful."
https://www.chrisbowers.co.uk/product/lloyd-george-raspberry-canes/. Retrieved 19 June 2019.

[2419] Pearl Zane Grey (1872-1939), known for his popular adventure stories idealizing the Wild West.

[2420] Personal communication with the author, 16 December 2018.

[2421] Ibid., 17 January 2019.

listening to 'Lord Haw Haw' on the radio, as well as to the BBC broadcasts, such was his interest in hearing all points of view.[2422] For the safety of himself and his household, Lloyd George, at the cost of £6,000 [£429,231 in 2025], had by mid-September 1940 constructed a four-room, air conditioned air-raid shelter 60 ft underground at Churt, containing non-flammable furniture, which A. J. Sylvester likened to "a Piccadilly underground station."[2423] This was not altogether an extravagance, as raids in that year were quite frequent[2424], although ultimately the only actual casualties on the estate were two pigs in their sty on the farm, and a damaged medieval fish pond.[2425]

On 7 May 1941 something of a final breach between Lloyd George and Churchill occurred, when Lloyd George made a speech that was called 'defeatist', but which in fact was relevantly critical of some aspects of the government's handling of the war effort, and not unreasonably a little pessimistic of the task ahead in crushing the dominant Axis position in mainland Europe at that time. He stated:

> I would like to say one word about the speech of the Foreign Secretary[2426]… I was frankly very disappointed. I really expected from him… a full and a frank statement of the foreign policy of the Government… There has never been a war in which diplomacy has counted for so much as in this war. In fact, our worst defeats have been diplomatic defeats. Our greatest triumph has been a diplomatic triumph–that is, the work of the late Lord Lothian in the United States of America. Therefore, *diplomacy has a great bearing upon the conduct of the war, and, surely, we are not at the end of it yet–at least, I hope not. I can see no real triumph until the work of diplomacy has been exhausted in this war.* I think that we might have heard more about our relations with Turkey; we might have heard something about Spain; we might have heard a good deal about Vichy, which counts a great deal; we might have heard how we are getting on with Russia.

Churchill bristled at the perceived personal criticism, lashing back:

> I must, however, say that I did not think the speech of my right hon. Friend was particularly helpful at a period of what he himself called discouragement and disheartenment. It was not the sort of speech which one would have expected from the great war leader of former days, who was accustomed to brush aside despondency and alarm, and push on irresistibly towards the final goal. *It was the sort of speech with which, I imagine, the illustrious and venerable Marshal Pétain might well have enlivened the closing days of M. Reynaud's Cabinet.* But in one respect I am grateful to my right hon. Friend for the note which he struck, because if anything could make it clearer that we

---

2422 Morgan, *Lloyd George*, p192; Wilkinson, *Lloyd George*, p219. William B. Joyce (1906-1946), nicknamed Lord Haw-Haw, British Nazi propaganda broadcaster to Britain during the Second World War. Taking German citizenship in 1940, he was the last person executed for treason in Britain on 3 January 1946. In 1940, at the peak of his influence, Joyce had an estimated six million regular and 18 million occasional listeners in Britain.

2423 Sylvester, *Life*, p278, 281, Entries for 17 September and 10 November 1940. See also Longford, p141.

2424 These included a daytime raid on 12 September 1940, with two casualties recorded, http://www.warstateandsociety.com/Content/wtss.ho203/000004/001/336; a night raid on 23/24 November 1940, http://www.warstateandsociety.com/Content/wtss.ho203/000005/001/527. Retrieved 7 October 2021.

2425 Longford, p144.

2426 Anthony Eden (1897-1977), Foreign Secretary, 22 December 1940–26 July 1945.

> ought to close our Debate by a Vote of Confidence, it is the kind of speech which he delivered.[2427]

"Coming from his oldest political associate, indeed friend, these words were meant to hurt Lloyd George; almost certainly they did."[2428] The vote of confidence in the government was carried by 447-3: Lloyd George abstained. Sadly, he miscalculated: "His pessimism was in many ways justified. He did not foresee, and few could have confidently predicted, events such as the Nazi invasion of the Soviet Union [22 June 1941] and the Japanese attack on Pearl Harbour [7 December 1941], which transformed Britain's strategic outlook."[2429]

There was still interest in some influential quarters in getting Lloyd George into Churchill's Cabinet. Prompted by proprietor Beaverbrook–in between government posts as Minister of Aircraft Production and Minister of Supply–Michael Foot, on the staff of the *Evening Standard*, had written an editorial "comparing a Lloyd George return to the House of Commons with that of Chatham in 1761." So, with Frank Owen, the editor, he "went on a mission to Churt." Lloyd George was "still in command of his incomparable faculties" but feeling defeatist about how Churchill could lead the nation to victory, still deeply offended by Churchill's comment a few weeks before. When Foot and Owen spoke of the reason for their visit, therefore, Lloyd George "brushed the inquiry aside with the suggestion 'What, me? Old Papa Pétain?'"[2430]

On 11 June 1942, Lloyd George made his last speech in the Commons, this time briefly expressing his approval of the address of Foreign Secretary Anthony Eden, on his informing the House "that His Majesty's Government have concluded a Treaty with the Union of Soviet and Socialist Republics which confirms our Alliance with that country during the war against Germany and her associates in Europe". Eden also noted "the valuable contribution to Anglo-Russian understanding made by Mr. Maisky over a long period of years." In reply Lloyd George stated pointedly, but without rancour, turning his head towards his friend the Soviet Ambassador in the Diplomatic Gallery: "As one who has laboured for over 20 years to establish a good understanding between Soviet Russia and this country, I felicitate the Prime Minister and the Foreign Secretary and the Government upon the accomplishment of this Treaty. Had it been a fact some years ago many grave blunders in foreign policy would have been avoided. Not only that: this war could never have occurred."[2431]

On 14 July, Lloyd George had lunch with Churchill, before the pair inspected the old chamber of the Commons[2432], the scene of so many triumphs and clashes over half a century, destroyed by incendiary bombs on the night of 10-11 May the previous year.

---

2427 https://api.parliament.uk/historic-hansard/commons/1941/may/07/war-situation#S5CV0371P0_19410507_HOC_243 . Retrieved 19 – 5 – 2019. Emphasis added. See Sylvester, *Life*, p290-291.

2428 Dutton, p61.

2429 Ibid., p62.

2430 M. Foot, *Loyalists And Loners*, 1986, London, William Collins; *David Lloyd George*, p141-158, quotes on p157-158. The present author thanks Duncan Hill for this reference.

2431 https://api.parliament.uk/historic-hansard/commons/1942/jun/11/great-britain-and-soviet-russia-treaty. Retrieved 20 February 2019; Bilainkin, p373. The Anglo-Soviet Treaty, signed on 26 May 1942, established a military and political alliance between Britain and the USSR during the Second World War, and for 20 years after it.

2432 Sylvester, *Life*, p304. Churchill had the Chamber restored exactly as it was.

On 21 October, Field Marshal Smuts, Prime Minister of South Africa, spoke in the Royal Gallery at the Palace of Westminster at the invitation of Churchill, the first time that a Dominion statesman had addressed both Houses of Parliament. As Father of the House, Lloyd George acted as Chairman and briefly introduced him, though now looking somewhat frail in his simple navy-blue suit. Speaking with deep emotion, Lloyd George told the thousand-member audience; "Smuts is one of the foremost statesmen of my generation… No one in calmness or discernment exceeds him in this age."[2433] Smuts replied warmly: "I am very proud to be honoured by the presence here today of my old leader, Mr. Lloyd George, but for whom who knows what might have happened in the mortal crisis of 25 years ago. Today, in this greater crisis, we gratefully remember his imperishable service and thank God for the gift and saving grace of his great historic leadership. He stands out as the supreme architect of victory in the last war."[2434] The speech was broadcast by the BBC, to an estimated audience of some 15 million in Britain alone.

On 3 August 1938, during the National Eisteddfod in Cardiff, William George had drafted a national petition on the legal status of the Welsh language. His brother David had been the most generous of the subscribers supporting the petition, giving £25 [£2,150 in 2025] and, by January 1939, pledging his "sympathy and support", had agreed to become one of the campaign's honorary presidents in both Caernarfonshire and West Denbighshire. In July 1941, the petition forms containing 394,864 signatures were delivered to Westminster, where Lloyd George and Megan were two of the four MPs to receive them. After due debate, some lobbying from Lloyd George of Home Secretary Herbert Morrison, and supported by 30 of the 36 Welsh MPs, the outcome was the Welsh Courts Act, which received royal assent on 22 October 1942. Imperfect, it was at least a step in the right direction, Section 1 repealing Section 17 of the 1536 Act of Union, declaring: "it is hereby enacted that the Welsh language may be used in any court in Wales by any party or witness who considers that he would otherwise be at any disadvantage by reason of his natural language of communication being Welsh."[2435]

Lloyd George reached his eightieth birthday on 17 January 1943, and two days later Anthony Eden, the Tory Leader of the House, paid him a warm tribute:

> To-day we salute him not only as the dominant statesman of his generation, not only as the man who led this country through a period of storm and stress like unto that through which we now strive, but, more than all these things, we salute him as a great House of Commons man. For over half-a-century he has been a champion in our midst. Neither his courage nor his resilience has ever failed him. He has needed both, because he has given hard blows and taken them. To-day we regard him with pride and with affection…

---

2433 R. Kraus, *Old Master: The Life Of Jan Christian Smuts*, 1944, New York, E.P. Dutton, p432; Smuts, p423. On 24 October, Smuts visited Lloyd George at Churt where they talked about fruit growing and prize bulls.

2434 http://www.ibiblio.org/pha/policy/1942/421021a.html. Retrieved 19 October 2020.

2435 J. Graham Jones, *The National Petition On The Legal Status Of The Welsh Language, 1938-1942*, *Welsh History Review*, 18, 1, 1996, p92-124.

In responding, Lloyd George said "Among all my recollections of the last 80 years there is none of which I am prouder than the fact that I have for 53 years been a Member of this honoured and this great Assembly."[2436]

On 2 December 1942, Liberal economist Sir William Beveridge had published his 299-page report, entitled *Social Insurance and Allied Services*, proposing widespread reforms to the system of social welfare to address what he identified as "five giants on the road of reconstruction": "Want… Disease, Ignorance, Squalor and Idleness."[2437] The *Daily Telegraph* correctly noted that it was a consummation of the revolution begun by Lloyd George in 1911, the *Manchester Guardian* opining how "time has vindicated" him. On 16 February 1943, a three-day debate began in the Commons. Lloyd George duly cast his last vote in the Commons on 18 February on Arthur Greenwood's motion that "That this House welcomes the Report of Sir William Beveridge on Social Insurance and Allied Services as a comprehensive review of the present provisions in this sphere and as a valuable aid in determining the lines on which developments and legislation should be pursued as part of the Government's policy of post-war reconstruction."

The government won the vote with "Ayes, 335; Noes, 119," but, in what constituted the biggest parliamentary revolt of the war[2438], Lloyd George was one of the 119 MPs–97 Labour, 11 Independents, nine Liberals, three Independent Labour and one Communist–condemning the government for its failure to back the Beveridge Report.[2439] The Labour Party eventually adopted Beveridge's recommendations, and after their landslide victory in the 5 July 1945 general election–which Lloyd George only just failed to witness–they proceeded to implement many social policies, which became known as the Welfare State. These included the Family Allowances Act 1945, National Insurance (Industrial Injuries) Act 1946, National Insurance Act 1946, National Health Service Act 1946, Pensions (Increase) Act 1947, Landlord and Tenant (Rent Control) Act 1949, National Insurance (Industrial Injuries) Act 1948, National Insurance Act 1949. Fittingly, therefore, Lloyd George's final vote was in defence of the welfare state, which he had so greatly helped to create.

On 23 October 1943, Lloyd George married Frances Stevenson at Artington House, Guildford's Registrar's office, a very quiet affair with only two witnesses, A. J. Sylvester and Frances's younger sister Muriel, the Registrar being Mr G. W. Catt.[2440] The press was excluded. The little party then drove back to Bron-y-de via the Punch Bowl, Lloyd George looking "immensely happy". "The autumn tints of brown and red on the trees in the great bowl and beyond, and the rolling hills up to the Hogs Back looked wonderful. And the sun shone through a rather angry sky. It was a picture representative of L.G's life."[2441]

On 24 May 1944, Lloyd George went to the Commons to hear Churchill speak on Foreign Affairs,

---

[2436] http://www.ukpol.co.uk/anthony-eden-1943-speech-on-david-lloyds-george-80th-birthday/. Retrieved 20 October 2020.

[2437] W. H. Beveridge, *Social Insurance and Allied Services*, Cmd.6404, 1942, London, HMSO, p6.

[2438] Renwick, p234.

[2439] https://api.parliament.uk/historic-hansard/commons/1943/feb/18/social-insurance-and-allied-services. Retrieved 20 February 2019.

[2440] Sylvester, *Real Lloyd George*, pp291-292; *North Wales Weekly News*, 28 October 1943, p8.

[2441] Sylvester, *Life*, p318. Entry for 23 October 1943.

and then, on 6 June, D-Day, he visited the Commons for the last time, around noon, hearing Churchill momentously announce "that during the night and the early hours of this morning the first of the series of landings in force upon the European Continent has taken place. In this case the liberating assault fell upon the coast of France."[2442] Afterwards, he spoke a few words of congratulation to Churchill.[2443]

Virtually Lloyd George's last literary act was to pen a brief foreword to *A History Of Anglo-Soviet Relations* by William and Zelda Coates, significantly still angling on how war might have been avoided:

> When on that memorable day, June 11, 1942, the Foreign Secretary, Mr. Eden, announced in the House of Commons the conclusion of a Treaty of Alliance with the U.S.S.R., I immediately commented: "As one who has laboured for over 20 years to establish a good understanding between Soviet Russia and this country, I felicitate the Prime Minister and the Foreign Secretary and the Government upon the accomplishment of this Treaty. Had it been a fact some years ago many grave blunders in foreign policy would have been avoided. Not only that, this war could never have occurred. There was no exaggeration in these words; I meant every one of them. I might have added that the Covenant of the League would have become an established and irresistible factor in the affairs of nations; the era of disarmament would have begun in earnest, and the age of "peace on earth and good-will amongst men" would have been well on the way.
>
> … I trust that this volume… will help us to realise our past errors in dealing with Soviet Russia and assist in establishing Anglo-Soviet friendship on an unshakable foundation.[2444]

Lloyd George left Churt for Ty Newydd, Llanystumdwy, for the last time on 20 September 1944. It was meant to be another brief visit, but he never returned south.[2445] He was suffering from bowel cancer–suspected by Lord Dawson since January 1941–though he was not in pain and not informed of the diagnosis.[2446] Bengy visited his grandfather there, when home on leave, saying it was very important for Lloyd George to come back to Wales for his final months. He remembered going for a walk with him, Lloyd George meeting an old childhood acquaintance on the road… Lloyd George had a very good memory, he remembered the old man very well, saying to Bengy afterwards "He was a very naughty boy." Lloyd George liked to walk in a very direct manner, crossing straight over hedges or walls[2447], but would sometimes get a little lost in the process.

On 13 October, Lloyd George attended a children's concert organised in his honour in the village

---

[2442] Toye, p388; https://api.parliament.uk/historic-hansard/commons/1944/jun/06/liberation-of-rome-landings-in-france#S5CV0400P0_19440606_HOC_230. Retrieved 19 October 2020.

[2443] Taylor, *My Darling Pussy*, p250.

[2444] Lloyd George in Coates, pV. William and Zelda Coates were members of the Communist Party (CPGB) and founders of the Anglo-Russian Parliamentary Committee in 1924.

[2445] The last signature in the Bron-y-de guestbook, in the possession of Lord Tenby, is dated 29 August 1944. It starts in September 1923, forming a veritable 'Who's Who' of British political, literary and 'high society' circles.

[2446] Jones, *Radical Life*, p164.

[2447] Waldo McG Eager also related, in *The Countryman*, that Lloyd George had "a lovely technique for getting over a hedge without leaving a trace of passage": G. Shakespeare, p51.

hall. In his speech of thanks, he said:

> I mean to make my home at Llanystumdwy, which is always dear to me. I came here after sixty-five years. I could not find much change, because you had the river, the same old river, the same old floods… The river makes the village. It gives character to it. It gives its meaning to it, and I am delighted to come to its sound once more.[2448]

On 9 November, Lloyd George, Frances and Goronwy Owen were entertained at a luncheon in the Royal Hotel, Caernarvon hosted by the newly re-elected mayor, Councillor H. R. Phillips, and Lloyd George made a short speech in response to the toast of "The Visitors". However, Frances recorded that he was now "noticeably failing, and it was pathetic to see him making a brave effort to be his old self."[2449] In this, his last public statement, which deserves to be much better known, and encompassing the broad sweep of the historical past, present and future, he said:

> Heaven knows what is going to happen. It is dark. It is the fog of war. You cannot peer through it. Occasionally, it looks as if you had a gleam of light, then it retreats again. You ask how it is going to end. There are predictions. It is going to end before Christmas. It will end in the spring anyway. I hope so. I watch the times… and I try to find a way out. What is going to happen? I would not like to say. Victory, yes–but victory when? Victory how? Victory, and what will happen afterwards? What will happen in Europe? I do not know. There is Poland–what has happened to Poland? Poland is not going to be the Poland it was when the war started, that we know. Then what is it going to be? Are we going to leave behind another Alsace-Lorraine which might break out into another war in five or ten years, in forty or fifty years? Let us hope that wisdom prevails.
>
> *There are great men at the reins, but great men lose their heads sometimes. Let us hope that this time they will maintain them and that when victory is assured that these great men will sit down and reckon what the future is going to be. What is the best method of arranging the future, not merely for their own country but for other lands as well. There are many lands in Europe; there are many nations in Europe, including our little nation. All I can say is… let us hope that the best will be loved.*[2450]

On 29 September, A. J. Sylvester had been approached by E. P. Evans, the chairman of the executive committee of the Caernarfon Boroughs Liberal Association as to Lloyd George's intentions regarding the next general election. The character of the constituency had changed a lot since the last election in 1935, with at least 10,000 mostly English civil servants and other evacuees still being present, due to stay another eighteen months after the end of the war, and of whom very few were Liberal supporters. Many of Lloyd George's old stalwarts had died over the years, and the outcome of a contest was clearly uncertain. Lloyd George himself was under no illusions. When Sylvester talked to

---

2448 Quoted in Sylvester, *Life*, p331.
2449 F. Lloyd George, *Years That Are Past*, p273.
2450 Quoted in Rowland, *Lloyd George*, p794-795. Emphasis added.

him of trying to arrange a 'walkover', he replied "You can tell them it will not be for very long."[2451] The Caernarfon Conservative and Labour Associations steadfastly refused to guarantee the ailing statesman this favour. It was only after these attempts failed that, on 17 November, Sylvester approached Sir Archibald Sinclair, Liberal Leader and the Secretary of State for Air, a close friend of Churchill, to sound the Prime Minister out on securing an earldom for Lloyd George. Sinclair was sympathetic, couching his approach in terms of Lloyd George's health.[2452] So it was at Ty Newydd that, on the evening of 18 December 1944, a Royal Marine courier, Marine Davidson, arrived with a message from Churchill, conveying his hope to recommend Lloyd George for an earldom in the New Year Honour's List. It read:

> My dear David,
>
> Some of your friends have been to me expressing the desire to spare you the labours of a contested election at Criccieth. It has occurred to me that perhaps you might be willing to allow me to submit your name to the King for an Earldom. I have reason to believe that this would be agreeable to His Majesty, and I am sure it would give the greatest pleasure to all those who worked with you and under you in the old days, and to none more than to
>
> Your old friend,
>
> Winston S. Churchill.[2453]

Lloyd George, fighting all his radical Liberal principles, decided to sleep on the matter. In the morning, he accepted the honour, Ann Parry taking his note to the post office to be sent as a telegram to London that was a masterpiece of brevity: "Gratefully accept." He told his brother William–who felt that he should preserve his position as a 'Great Commoner'–on that morning, 19 December, that "he had never found it so difficult to come to a decision as he had on this occasion", but that his reason for accepting was that "I feel I cannot face another election, but there is something on my mind about Peace which I want to say, and if I accept this offer I could say it in the House of Lords."[2454]

The wording is interesting: "about Peace", not "about the peace". What great philosophical insight, based on his vast and unique experience at Paris in 1919, and all the years afterwards, trying to prevent another world war, did Lloyd George want to set forth? Unless some overlooked scrap of paper containing his handwriting comes to light, a most unlikely occurrence, we will never know, but it would be a fair assumption that it would reiterate his belief, expressed a quarter of a century before, that true, lasting peace would have to involve compromise with a defeated enemy so as not to trigger

---

2451 NLW, A. J. Sylvester Papers A57, diary entry for 15 October 1944. At a meeting on 27 December 1944, Evans called Lloyd George "one of the immortals." In 14 successive elections–only one unopposed–Lloyd George had secured a grand total of 113,849 votes cast for him, against 59,314 for his opponents, a record unique in modern British politics. See Jones, *David Lloyd George*, p462.

2452 Jones, *David Lloyd George*, p461.

2453 Quoted in Toye, p389. Churchill was the only person outside the family to call him 'David'; Sylvester, *Real Lloyd George*, p287; Sylvester, *Life*, p288; Frances Lloyd George, *Introduction* to Thomson, p17.

2454 George, *My Brother and I*, p297, 298.

future reasons for renewed enmity. Years later, Sylvester wrote in defence of his old chief; "He felt he had a contribution to make in settling the peace terms, based on his unique experience, and he needed a platform from which to do this. Lloyd George's respect for the hereditary peerage, as such, was nil. It was a platform Lloyd George wanted, not a title."[2455]

From thoughts of large, worldly events, virtually his last action in the public sphere was on a very small, local, human scale, but none the less important for that. This concerned the Children's Meeting held annually at Berea Chapel in Criccieth on New Year's Day, an event that Lloyd George had always taken a lively interest in, never failing to send his greetings for its success, together with a basketful of oranges for distribution to the children–a 'bigger deal' in those hard-pressed times than might appear evident today. His brother William poignantly recorded that on 1 January 1945:

> Dafydd himself, rather unexpectedly, turned up and partook of a cup of tea with the children, after which he got up to address them.
>
> For a while he seemed unable to get his words out, but with an effort, he managed to say how pleased he was that the children looked so happy. He began another sentence which I thought was an expression of his wish that they should always remain so, but he failed to round it off and sat down again… it was with difficulty that I was able to control my feelings as it came home to me so forcibly that the man who, in the hey-day of his strength was able to play on the feelings of his audiences as a maestro plays his violin, was now hardly able to say a few words to the little children in front of him.[2456]

From then on, Lloyd George's health declined rapidly, and he spent his time re-reading Dickens, gazing out of the windows overlooking Cardigan Bay, or sleeping peacefully.[2457] On 12 February 1945, he duly became 1st Earl Lloyd-George of Dwyfor[2458] and 1st Viscount Gwynedd of Dwyfor in the County of Caernarvon, taking as his motto the Welsh proverb *Y Gwir Yn Erbyn Y Byd* (The Truth Against The World), but his health was visibly fast ebbing and he was destined never to take up his seat in the Lords. His friend and neighbour Lord Nathan[2459] commented on this development:

> A good many people feel an affectionate regret that he has not remained to the end the Great Commoner… I do not quite know what the factors were which influenced Mr Lloyd George's mind, but he must have been affected by the fact that this was something which he could do for his wife… they came to see me at Churt when I was convalescing. It was obvious from what he said to me at the time that he had the possibility of taking an Earldom in his mind… 'Lord Lloyd George' does not sound very euphonious to me and I am quite certain that he will go

2455 *Observer*, 19 February 1984; Quoted in Jones, *David Lloyd George*, p465.
2456 George, *My Brother and I*, p293.
2457 Rowland, *Lloyd George*, p797.
2458 https://www.thegazette.co.uk/London/issue/36938/page/883. Retrieved 30 December 2019. His name appeared thus as the Garter King At Arms refused to accept the name in unhyphenated form.
2459 Harry Nathan (1889-1963), Liberal MP for Bethnal Green North East, 1929-1934, Labour MP for Wandsworth Central, 1937-1940, created Baron Nathan of Churt in 1940. On his defection to Labour in 1934, Lloyd George allegedly told Nathan: "If I were a young man, I should join the Labour Party myself. But I'm too old now. I was born a Liberal and a Liberal I shall die." Quoted in Hyde, p113.

down to history–for go down to history he certainly will as one of the greatest of our Prime Ministers–just as 'Mr Lloyd George.'[2460]

Bengy said Lloyd George was "first and foremost a family man", always very concerned about all his grandchildren's welfare. Bengy's brother, Robin, was the last person to really talk with Lloyd George. He was on leave, staying at Bryn Awelon at Criccieth, when a phone-call came saying that his grandfather wished to see him at Ty Newydd. Once there, Lloyd George asked him if he was going to go back to university after the war, saying that it was most important to get qualifications. Robin assured him that he was. As Robin himself put it simply: "In 1945 I had been on leave from the RAF and went down to see him at Ty Newydd… to say good bye. He was lying in bed very weak, but he raised his head and took my hand and was just able to wish me a safe return to my squadron. He died that night."[2461]

According to subsequent report at Ty Newydd, the great orator's last words were "The cows are coming in…"[2462], his mind presumably drifting back to a scene from his youth. Faithful witness Albert Sylvester set the scene that then unfolded in the barrel-vaulted Library, which had been converted into a bedroom so that Lloyd George could see the beautiful view out towards the sea through the semi-circular panoramic window: "After hours of patient watching, with the Countess holding his left hand and Megan his right, in the presence of Dr. Prytherch, Nurse Thomas, Lady Carey-Evans, Ann Parry, Jennifer, Mrs. Bennett, Sarah Jones and myself at 8.35pm on Monday, March 26th, 1945, he drew his last breath."[2463] Rather poetically, Harold Macmillan later described Lloyd George's death as being "like the crashing of a great oak in the forest."[2464]

The funeral was set for 2.30 pm on Friday, 30 March–Good Friday–which being a public holiday meant that thousands of ordinary people could attend if they wished. "At day-break… the summits of the Snowdon range were veiled in cloud and Criccieth was only faintly visible… The day kept grey throughout, with a keen cold wind blowing. In the late afternoon the sea was shrouded in mist."[2465] Photographs, and footage shot by British Pathé[2466], show many boys and youths up in the elm trees above the throng of mourners and well-wishers, watching events, as the great man's coffin of polished panelled elm, covered in flowers, was carried the short distance from Ty Newydd by a horse-drawn farm wagon–the same one which had borne Margaret's body just over four years before–upon which rode Lloyd George's childhood friend, 78-year-old Robert Evans. "The local newspaper said there were five thousand people there, others said seven. They covered the hillside where the grave was to be and massed in the fields on the other side of the river. They sang magnificent Welsh hymns,

---

2460 Quoted in Hyde, p164.

2461 Personal communication to the author from Davina Carey-Evans, 16 November 2018. Robin was a Flight Lieutenant in the Royal Air Force Volunteer Reserve, winning a DFC [Cited 13 April 1945] flying Halifax Mk.III/IV heavy bombers with No. 640 Squadron, Bomber Command, based at RAF Leconfield, Yorkshire.

2462 Personal communication with professional storyteller Fiona Collins, 6 July 2023.

2463 Sylvester, *Real Lloyd George*, p310.

2464 H. Macmillan, *The Past Masters: Politics And Politicians, 1906-1939*, 1975, London, Macmillan, p78.

2465 T. Jones, p260-261.

2466 British Pathé, *Funeral of Lloyd George*, Film ID 1149.2, Issue Date 5 April 1945, B&W, 2:47 minutes. See https://www.britishpathe.com/video/funeral-of-lloyd-george. Retrieved 23 January 2020.

thundering above the sound of the river."[2467] The burial service was conducted by the Anglican Rector and Baptist Minister. Movingly, Ann Parry noticed "a line of Italian prisoners of war standing bareheaded on the lower bank of the river."[2468]

Grandson Bengy was in a convoy from Grimsby to London, and he vividly remembered what happened next:

> I was on a convoy [on the light cruiser HMS *Enterprise* (D52)] in the North Sea when the signalman got a signal from the First Lord of the Admiralty, which he thought was a hoax. He took it up to the Captain who said no, it isn't a hoax. The message said proceed immediately to the nearest port and disembark Midshipman Carey-Evans. So, that's what happened, we left the convoy, fled into Harwich, swept into the harbour, I was jumped ashore, and the ship turned around and went straight out again… I was then driven off to take the train back to Criccieth. The funeral was a remarkable occasion, because I never realised that so many people could turn up to a funeral… And when you think that it was in the days of strict petrol rationing, where they got the ability to get there, I don't know, they must have come on horseback, bicycle… the whole of the road down to where he was to be buried was lined with people, all singing… the field the other side of the river was packed with people.[2469]

Grandson Owen (28 April 1924–29 July 2010), the son of Lloyd George's eldest son Richard, was a Lieutenant fighting with the 3rd Battalion, Welsh Guards, at Porto San Giorgio, on the Adriatic coast of Italy. He later remembered:

> Winston Churchill, in the midst of conducting a great war, had been inspired to think that it would be a fine thing for the four grandsons of his old friend and political ally to be at his graveside, and he accordingly issued the necessary instruction. I was the farthest afield…
>
> Early… [on] Good Friday, I was out at Northolt and climbed into a Hurricane for the final leg to North Wales. The pilot was a Pole… Somewhere over Cheshire he decided we would not have enough fuel to do the easy route over Liverpool Bay and thus to Anglesey and so made a sharp left turn towards the mountains. Visibility was poor and the next twenty minutes were hair-raising as we threaded our way through the Berwyns and peaks of Snowdonia before we finally touched down at Valley airfield.
>
> I arrived at Ty Newydd only an hour before the funeral…
>
> There was a short service in the library, just the family standing around the coffin, and then, when it had been taken down and placed on a farm wagon drawn by a single shire horse, we went slowly down the drive and to the spinney above the river… A last-minute hitch had nearly wrecked the arrangements as no one had thought of consecrating the site, but this had been done early that morning by one of the clergy.
>
> As David, Robin, Bengy and I walked beside to the coffin to the graveside we were met by

[2467] Longford, p161. The *Caernarvon and Denbigh Herald*, 6 April 1945, said 10,000.

[2468] Parry, *Thirty Thousand Yesterdays*, p76. Neither Bengy Carey-Evans nor Bill Tenby had any recollection of this, being personally preoccupied, but it was noted by the *Caernarvon and Denbigh Herald*, 6 April 1945.

[2469] Taped interview with author, Beaumaris, 11 October 2018.

> an amazing and very moving spectacle. There were literally thousands of men, women and children thronging the lane and on the steep hillside around the grave, with thousands more in the meadows just across the river. The singing started as the cortège approached; many of Taid's favourite Welsh hymns–'Llef', 'Tyddyn Llwyn' (Cottage in the Spinney) and of course 'Cwm Rhondda'–all sung with immense fervour… it was just the right send-off for one who had done so much for his own people and who had chosen to be buried among them.[2470]

Grandson William, then 17, recalled:

> I was at school when Taid died, at Eastbourne College, which in the War was evacuated to… Radley [College, in Oxfordshire]. I was the youngest Grandson, whilst my brother, David[2471], was the eldest, [a Captain in the Royal Artillery]… I recall my brother, who was in an observation post overlooking The Rhine, telling me how he had a fit on being told that his CO wanted to see him at HQ immediately![2472]
>
> The four Service Grandsons were at each corner of the coffin in the funeral cortege. I followed immediately behind with my father, Gwilym.[2473]

The grave itself is unique, beautiful. Lloyd George told his family in 1944 "I have no wish to be buried in Westminster Abbey. I want to be buried where people can see my grave." He wished to be buried "high on the banks of his beloved River Dwyfor–on his own land–in sight of the old bridge, his old school and above all within hearing of the never ending sound of the rushing waters of the River Dwyfor."[2474] He had chosen his last resting place with care; it was his favourite spot, the glade where as a boy he used to sit above the river. He pointed the site out to his brother William, saying "That is where I want to be buried. That is the stone which I sit on to admire the view of the river. I want no inscription on my grave, only that boulder."[2475]

After the funeral, the renowned architect Clough Williams-Ellis, creator of the famous Italianate village of Portmeirion and a long-standing friend who had also helped to remodel the rather run-down Ty Newydd from 1942 after its purchase along with 37 acres of farmland in August 1939 from the Broom Hall Estate, was commissioned to erect an enclosure around the grave. In 1946, on the first anniversary of Lloyd George's death, during the dedication service led by the Rector of Llanystumdwy, soil from the Acropolis sent by the Pan-Hellenic Union of Reserve Officers and other ranks was scattered on the grave.[2476] The beautiful iron gates to the little enclosure and the monogram above them were created by David J. Williams–the same man who had worked on the coffin of the Unknown Warrior a quarter of a century before! The wall also bears an *englyn* (strict-metre stanza) engraved on

---

2470 Owen Lloyd George, p103-104, 105-106.

2471 David Lloyd George, 2nd Viscount Tenby (4 November 1922–14 July 1983).

2472 Personal communication to the author from the late Lord Tenby, 17 January 2019.

2473 Ibid., 1 February 2019.

2474 E. Williams, p28. He had first indicated the spot to Thomas Jones, Deputy Secretary to the Cabinet, in 1922; Jones, *Whitehall Diary*, Vol.I, p206-207.

2475 E. Williams, p30. The view is not as clear as it was in 1945, many trees having grown along the riverbank. The official memorial service was held in Westminster Abbey on 10 April.

2476 Ibid., p31.

slate in his memory composed by his nephew W. R. P. George. It reads:

> The Grave of David Lloyd George (Earl Dwyfor)
>
> The rough stone, stone of his crown, is the grave / of a man who was a hero to his people; / a beauteous watercolour is the merry Dwyfor, / t'will ever caress his grave.[2477]

Clough Williams-Ellis himself retained clear memories of Lloyd George, writing later:

> Asked to renovate for Lloyd George the old Welsh House to which he retired and in which he later died, I fell immediately under the spell of his most subtly exercised charm…
>
> At breakfast… [at Churt] I happened to quote some odds and ends from *1066 And All That*[2478] that had delighted me, as I found they also did him. He had never even heard of the book–a shocking gap in his political education as I told him–a gap that I subsequently repaired by sending him a copy. Anyway, we were having such fun over cock-eyed history generally, that when his barber was announced, he insisted that I should come into his study with him and sit in on his overdue haircutting, the barber patiently poising his scissors whilst Lloyd George laughed…
>
> When the end came I was asked to pin-point the exact spot for his burial within the wood on the banks of the hardby river Dwyfor that he had known and loved from boyhood and where he had always wished to lie. The setting seemed itself to dictate the form that the grave should take–a simple oval enclosure of rugged masonry with an arched entry and a surrounding stepped pavement following the natural fall of the ground–the great boulder on which he used to sit at the centre of the enclosed lawn marking the grave itself.[2479]

Many representations of Lloyd George exist. One of the first was an excellent bronze bust produced by D. Arthur Thomas in 1902, now in the Lloyd George Museum, full of forward-looking vision. On 6 August 1921, a 2.7m high bronze statue of Lloyd George by W. Goscombe John was unveiled in Castle Square, Caernarfon by W. M. 'Billy' Hughes, Prime Minister of Australia–Hughes' father came from North Wales–in the presence of Dame Margaret. High relief bronze panels to the sides portray the village school at Llanystumdwy and the Paris Peace Conference of 1919. The gift of Owen Jones of Glanbeuno, Mayor of Caernarfon 1919-1921, the statue was the first to be erected to a Prime Minister during their lifetime.[2480] On the same day in Llanystumdwy, a bronze bust of him by Kathleen Scott was unveiled by Herbert Lewis. It is now situated in front of the Lloyd George Museum, also designed by Clough Williams-Ellis, unveiled in its new location at the opening of the Museum at Llanystumdwy on 30 May 1960.

On 7 July 1960, a 2.4m bronze statue of Lloyd George by Michael Rizzello was unveiled by Prime

---

[2477] In the original Welsh: *"Y maen garw, a maen ei goron, - yw bed / Gŵr i'w bobl fu'n wron; / Dyfrliw hardd yw Dwyfor lon, / Anwesa'r bedd yn gyson."*

[2478] W.C. Sellar and R.J. Yeatman, *1066 And All That*, 1930, London, Methuen.

[2479] C. Williams-Ellis, *Architect Errant*, 1971, London, Constable, p146-147. Williams-Ellis had first seen Lloyd George at the Caernarfon Investiture in 1911. The structure is Grade II* Listed.

[2480] https://www.britishpathe.com/video/VLVA3QS0WKV7WA9USJJKEFEP3LC05-NEWS/query/David. Retrieved 22 March 2019.

Minister Harold Macmillan in the Gorsedd Gardens, Cathays Park, Cardiff, opposite the main entrance to the National Museum of Wales.[2481] On 18 December 1963, a larger-than-life-size bronze statue of Lloyd George by Julius 'Uli' Nimptsch was unveiled by Prime Minister Alec Douglas-Home in the Members' Lobby of the Commons, on the right-hand side of the Churchill Arch. It stands opposite the statue of Winston Churchill, added in 1969, both statues featuring a worn foot as it was the custom–now rather discouraged–for MPs to rub the foot for good luck as they enter or leave the Chamber.[2482] On 25 October 2007, a 2.4m high bronze sculpture of Lloyd George by Professor Glynn Williams was unveiled by HRH Prince Charles in Parliament Square, London. On 2 September 2018 a slightly larger-than-life-size bronze statue of Lloyd George, by Philip Jackson, was unveiled in the grounds of Danny House, Hurstpierpoint, West Sussex, portraying him delightedly dancing the jig at receiving the news of the impending victory on the Western Front on 29 September 1918, and was unveiled by Colin Prickett, aged 98, who as a youth had met Hitler in Munich in 1937 and the exiled Kaiser in Doorn in 1938![2483]

On his death, under the terms of his will dated 12 November 1943, with two codicils dated 2 and 19 September 1944, Lloyd George left an estate with a gross value for 1946 Probate of £139,855 [£7,485,229 in 2025].[2484] The family home, Bryn Awelon in Criccieth, had been willed to Megan in its entirety by Dame Margaret in 1941. On Megan's tragically early death from cancer on 14 May 1966 aged 64, in 1969 her nephew Robin sold the property, which passed through several hands until it became a nursing home in 1988. Sadly, in the mid-1950s, it was proposed to pull Lloyd George's birthplace down. The local council could not decide, neither could Manchester City Council. It went all the way to the Home Secretary, who was his son Gwilym![2485] He said pull it down, as his father would never have wanted to stand in the way of an improvement in housing for the poor! Tŷ Newydd, Lloyd George's last home, in which he died, was sold by Frances in 1948, and given Grade II* listed building status in 1971, becoming the National Writing Centre for Wales in April 1990.

---

2481 https://www.britishpathe.com/video/ll-g-remembered. Retrieved 22 March 2019.

2482 Susan Elan Jones, Labour MP for Clwyd South, 2010-2019, touched Lloyd George's foot during the passage of what became the Wales Act 2017, devolving further powers on the Senedd. Personal communication with the author, 1 June 2022.

2483 https://www.msn.com/en-gb/news/world/revealed-the-obscure-country-bolthole-where-lloyd-george-plotted-the-end-of-ww1/ar-BBPyzgD?li=BBoPWjQ&ocid=mailsignout. Retrieved 23 October 2019.

2484 McCormick, p302; Ivatt, p119.

2485 The house was demolished in June 1957, a photograph having been taken on 31 May 1956 to record it before redevelopment. L. S. Lowry painted *David Lloyd George's Birthplace, Manchester*, in 1958. A council house–34 Wadeson Road–now stands on the site.

# 7

## LEGACY: 'HIS NAME WILL NOT ONLY LIVE BUT SHINE…'

On the day of his death on 2 August 1792, former Tory Prime Minister Lord North spoke to the assembled family at his bedside of his "considerable anxiety on the subject of his character and fame–that he should have wished to know how he stood and would stand with the world."[2486] He owned that this "might be a weakness, but he could not help it," whilst claiming that it gave him satisfaction that he could look back on his political career without regret. Most eminent people in public life would share his concern, and the always controversial David Lloyd George must surely have reflected similarly during his own last days, so a view of society's verdict is appropriate.

Lloyd George died on 26 March 1945, just weeks before the end of the Second World War–in the European theatre of operations at least-a war that he had so uncannily predicted back in 1919. His success laying the foundations for radical social reform and in winning the Great War were, in a sense, both double-edged swords for him. The rise of the Labour Party stole his thunder on the back of the appetite he had whetted for a more egalitarian society, whilst the old Liberal Party was split over the war between his supporters and those of Asquith. This meant that the country was deprived of his undoubted talents and leadership as he spent his last 23 years in political exile during the dark years of the Depression.

Two days later, on 28 March, the Commons devoted an entire sitting to 'EARL LLOYD-GEORGE OF DWYFOR, O.M.', the record of which forms an impressionistic, encapsulated biography in its own right, drawing out contemporaries' pithiest opinions. The range and breadth of appreciation was extraordinary, a great honour from across the spectrum of politics, from both sexes. In his address, Lloyd George's old friend, and political rival, Prime Minister Winston Churchill said of him:

> It was Lloyd George who launched the Liberal and Radical forces of this country effectively into the broad stream of social betterment and social security along which all modern parties now steer. *There was no man so gifted, so eloquent, so forceful, who knew the life of the people so well.* His warm heart was stirred by the many perils which beset the cottage homes, the health of the bread winner, the fate of his widow, the nourishment and upbringing of his children, the meagre and haphazard provision of medical treatment and sanatoria, and the lack of any organised accessible medical service of a kind worthy of the age from which the mass of the wage earners

---

2486 Bickley, F., Ed., *The Diaries of Sylvester Douglas (Lord Glenbervie)*, 1928, London, Constable, Vol.I, p61.

and the poor suffered. All this excited his wrath. Pity and compassion lent their powerful wings. He knew the terror with which old age threatened the toiler–that after a life of exertion he could be no more than a burden at the fireside and in the family of a struggling son. When I first became Lloyd George's friend and active associate, now more than 40 years ago, this deep love of the people, the profound knowledge of their lives and of the undue and needless pressures under which they lived, impressed itself indelibly upon my mind.

Then there was his dauntless courage, his untiring energy, his oratory, persuasive, provocative, now grave now gay. His swift, penetrating, comprehensive mind was always grasping at the root, or what he thought to be the root, of any question. His eye ranged ahead of the obvious. He was always hunting in the field beyond. I have often heard people come to him with a plan, and he would say "That is all right, but what happens when we get over the bridge? What do we do then?"

In his prime, Sir, his power, his influence, his initiative were unequalled in the land. He was the champion of the weak and the poor. These were great days. Nearly two generations have passed. *Most people are unconscious of how much their lives have been shaped by the laws for which Lloyd George was responsible.* Health insurance and old age pensions were the first large-scale State-conscious efforts to set a balustrade along the crowded causeway of the people's life and, without pulling down the structures of society, to fasten a lid over the abyss into which vast numbers used to fall, generation after generation, uncared for and indeed unnoticed. Now we move forward confidently into larger and more far-reaching applications of these ideas… I have lived to see long strides taken, and being taken, and going to be taken, on this path of insurance by which the vultures of utter ruin are driven from the dwellings of the nations. The stamps we lick, the roads we travel, the system of progressive taxation, the principal remedies that have yet been used against unemployment–all these to a very great extent were part not only of the mission but of the actual achievement of Lloyd George; and *I am sure that as time passes his name will not only live but shine on account of the great, laborious, constructive work he did for the social and domestic life of our country.*

When the calm, complacent, self-satisfied tranquillities of the Victorian era had exploded into the world convulsions and wars of the terrible Twentieth Century, Lloyd George had another part to play on which his fame will stand with equal or even greater firmness. Although unacquainted with the military arts, although by public repute a pugnacious pacifist, when the life of our country was in peril he rallied to the war effort and cast aside all other thoughts or aims…

I have already… recorded two characteristics of him which seemed to me invaluable in those days: first, his power to live in the present yet without taking short views; and, secondly, his power of drawing from misfortune itself the means of future success…

Thus the statesman and guide whose gentle passing in the fullness of his years we mourn to-day served our country, our island and our age both faithfully and well in peace and in war. His long life was, from almost the beginning to almost the end, spent in political strife and controversy. He aroused intense and sometimes needless antagonisms. He had fierce and bitter quarrels at various times with all the parties. He faced undismayed the storms of criticism and hostility. In spite of all obstacles, including those he raised himself, he achieved his main purposes. As a man of action, resource and creative energy he stood, when at his zenith, without a rival. His name is a household word throughout our Commonwealth of Nations. *He was the*

> *greatest Welshman which that unconquerable race has produced since the age of the Tudors.* Much of his work abides, some of it will grow greatly in the future, and those who come after us will find the pillars of his life's toil upstanding, massive and indestructible; and we ourselves, gathered here to-day, may indeed be thankful that he voyaged with us through storm and tumult with so much help and guidance to bestow.[2487]

Every word Churchill spoke in his eulogy was pregnant with generous and informed, personal insight, and he spoke truly. Churchill's wife, Clementine, writing to her husband from Cairo, en route to Moscow for a tour to promote Anglo-Soviet relations, let her mind go back, "not to the difficult and sometimes embittered moments in the First World War, but to those glorious, crusading days of radical reform, which had left such an undying impression on her mind: 'I loved your speech about Ll.G [sic].. It recalled forgotten blessings which he showered upon the meek & lowly.'"[2488]

Leader of the Opposition Arthur Greenwood responded nobly to the Prime Minister's sentiments:

> We mourn the passing of a great Parliamentarian, and I am certain my right hon. Friend has expressed, irrespective of party, the views held by the House about the great Mr. Lloyd George, as I still prefer to call him. He was a man of dynamic personality, a great and generous friend and a very bitter foe, a man who had a gift of repartee unknown in this House for a long time… he was a doughty debater, a man fearless in pursuit of all the causes in which he was interested… He was the friend of the oppressed. He was born with that Welsh Radical Nonconformist tradition which meant a good deal to him. Always his mind came back to the things that mattered to the life of the common people. I believe he will go down in history for two things… He will go down in history as a great war leader… in the days of the last great war it is undoubtedly true that but for Mr. Lloyd George's vivid personality, his strength of character, his foresight, his understanding of the issues that were at stake, Britain might have fallen upon more evil days than we fell on in May, 1940. That is a great thing. This is not a question of party. It is not a question of politics. It is a question of paying a tribute to a great man who played a great part in our national life.
>
> … in that Parliament of 1906 the powerful character of the late Mr. Lloyd George did much to make that Government the success that it was in inaugurating and establishing the great system of social and industrial legislation on which we now build. I would pay my late right hon. Friend that tribute, that… at a time when we were beginning to learn that poverty was not due to the vices of the poor, Mr. Lloyd George was an inspiring force in that Liberal Government, and much we owe to him, and much the working people of the country owe to him. I should like, speaking for the organised working people of this country, to read to the House a tribute paid yesterday morning by the National Council of Labour, for whom I speak to-day, the most representative body of people in the country: The Council places on record its appreciation of the contribution to social and industrial legislation made by Earl Lloyd-George in the course of his long Parliamentary career and his achievements of British statesmanship at critical times in

---

[2487] https://api.parliament.uk/historic-hansard/commons/1945/mar/28/earl-lloyd-george-of-dwyfor-om#S5CV0409P0_19450328_HOC_303. Retrieved 17 August 2018. Emphasis added.

[2488] M. Soames, *Clementine Churchill*, 1979, London, Cassell, p367.

the history of the British people.[2489]

Sir Percy Harris, Deputy Liberal Leader, said:

> Lloyd George was a great Liberal… He entered the House of Commons half a century ago, when the dominant political figure was Mr. Gladstone. As "L.G." himself told some of us at a private gathering, in those days the issues were mainly political issues, like Home Rule, the extension of the franchise and the status of the House of Lords. The Prime Minister reminded us how, in the 20th century, the problems before Parliament changed, but that was largely due to the dynamic force and personality of character of Lloyd George himself. He took up the cause of the common man. He laid the foundation of our social legislation, which now in this Parliament we hope to complete. His success was due to his understanding of social and economic problems and his ability to make them live when he brought them before the public. He stimulated controversy, but yet his energy and personality managed to translate his ideas into legislation… It must have been some satisfaction to him to see his ideas taken over by the Government and embodied in their White Paper.[2490]

Sir Geoffrey Shakespeare, speaking on behalf of the Liberal Nationals, and a former private secretary to Lloyd George from 1921-1923, said:

> Those were the days of a Coalition which had to face all the difficult problems of the transition from war to peace… What impressed me most in Mr. Lloyd George was his infinite resourcefulness, his resiliency of mind and his complete and utter absorption in the tasks that lay to hand. If he found the frontal attack on a problem blocked, to use a military metaphor, he would send his armour round the flank searching for a weak spot. He was an empiricist. He was never afraid to make an experiment.
>
> May I tell one story which will illustrate his mistrust of dogma and rigid belief? He told me that once in the village where he lived there were two sects of one denomination and the members of either sect would not speak to the other. One believed in baptism in the name of the Father, and the other believed in baptism into the name of the Father. Mr. Lloyd George added: "I believed passionately in one and I would have given my life to the cause, but for the moment I forget which sect it was." It was this resourcefulness and fertility of mind that enabled him to see the fundamentals of our economic and, political problems… With the passing of Earl Lloyd-George there is the passing of an era, and we shall never see his like again.[2491]

In response, another great Welshman, Aneurin Bevan–chairman of the Welsh Parliamentary Party, and soon to be the Labour Government's Minister of Health, ushering in the National Health Service in 1948, built on Lloyd George's foundations–said unequivocally:

---

2489 https://api.parliament.uk/historic-hansard/commons/1945/mar/28/earl-lloyd-george-of-dwyfor-om. Retrieved on 17 August 2018.

2490 Op. cit. Sir Percy Harris, (1876-1952), MP for Bethnal Green South West, 1922-1945.

2491 Op. cit.

> We have lost our most distinguished member and Wales her greatest son. I knew him, of course, merely towards the end, but I knew him intimately, and I was the recipient of his advice and of his encouragement on many occasions. I also… had some exchanges with him, and he was… a most formidable and even terrifying debater, but he possessed… the generosity of greatness. Despite the sharp exchanges, his spirit was sufficiently urbane to enable him to forgive everything afterwards and to be good friends. His name and the name of Wales are inextricably associated in men's minds, and neither has lost by the association. What the nation fathered in him the man brought to fulfilment in his career. The qualities that Lloyd George possessed we like to behove are the qualities of Wales–quick imagination, eager and ardent spirit and an insatiable curiosity. He never seemed, no matter where he was, to be tired of learning new things and meeting new people, and I believe that it was this insatiable curiosity, this ability to see things freshly, which was mainly responsible for some of his success.
>
> … Lloyd George was a very democratically-minded man. He was first and last a democrat. He was at home in the village as well as in the central councils of the State. It was because of this universality of his that his speeches were always informed and enlivened by concrete metaphors. He always hated the tired phrase or the abstract noun, and if anyone wishes to learn the art of persuasive oratory he could not do better than read his speeches, because, although they may lack the classic form, every metaphor comes with an impact on the mind. At the same time, David Lloyd George was a patriot. His love of Wales was deep and passionate, but it was also associated with a cosmopolitan quality. The larger embraced the smaller. His patriotism was not exclusive. It functioned at the level of universal tolerance, and that, I think, was one of his most charming characteristics. He was able to give a universal significance to the local and the immediate because his preoccupation was as great in the smaller as in the larger. We ourselves in the Welsh Parliamentary Party mourn his passing. We have lost in his death the most iridescent figure that ever illumined the British political scene.[2492]

Next Nancy Astor, Tory and first woman to sit as an MP at Westminster, stated fulsomely:

> First I want to say how grateful the women of my generation were to him [Lloyd George] because, even in their darkest hour when they were fighting for the suffrage, Mr. Lloyd George backed them and thought they were worthy of citizenship. Well do I remember Mr. Lloyd George and Mr. Arthur James Balfour, both champions of the women's cause, leading the first woman up the aisle of the old House of Commons. This woman could not help feeling that though they had wanted women to enter the race, they were slightly embarrassed at having to lead in the winner.[2493] After I had been in the House some time I understood and respected their shyness…
>
> … Of all men I have ever known he was freer than any from personal vanity. I shall never forget the night after the armistice, when a few of us dined with him in Downing Street. As we

[2492] Op. cit. Aneurin "Nye" Bevan (1897-1960), Labour MP for Ebbw Vale, 1929-1960.

[2493] This took place shortly before 4.00 pm on 1 December 1919. The actual cause of Lloyd George and Balfour's embarrassment was the fact that Lady Astor talked the whole time, and it was against the rules to talk on the floor of the House. The occasion was commemorated in Charles Sims excellent painting, *Introduction of the First Woman Member, December 1, 1919* (1924). See Riddell, *Diaries*, 1986, p296; M. Collis, *Nancy Astor: An Informal Biography*, 1960, London, Faber and Faber, p72-74.

came out of the dining room I looked at an appalling oil painting of him, and I asked him why on earth he did not get John Sargent to do a good one of him. He replied quite simply: "I would like to have asked him to paint me, but I am told he is tired of painting portraits, so I never asked him." It never entered his head, even at that supreme moment of his life, that he would be asking Sargent to paint the world's foremost figure. There was no vanity there.

Secondly... He was more free from "side" and snobbishness than any man I have ever met in public life. He was far too great a gentleman in the real sense of the word either to be a snob or to be class conscious. We know how he hated and fought inherited privileges… Yet he never hated the privileged. He was far too great either to hate or to fear ... He might have so easily in these bitter fights carried a little hate in his heart, but I never saw it. I should not have called Mr. Lloyd George a spiritually-minded man, but yet he loved and respected goodness, and he certainly recognised it. He always seemed to me to be a man who had walked with men who had walked with God. He was a great Nonconformist, and he never conformed to the shams and shibboleths of this wicked world.

We all know his passionate love of mankind, and that made him hate war with all his heart…

Lastly, Mr. Lloyd George was, above all public men I have ever known… the most simple, the most natural and the easiest to talk to. The limelight never blinded his vision. He will ever live as a symbol of British democracy. He wanted freedom and a better world for all mankind, and the whole world is better for his fight for the things he thought right.

It is curious that we sometimes hear him spoken of as a common man. He was a most uncommon man…

… It is hard to speak of Mr. Lloyd George without great emotion… but I, like other people, feel that if democracy is on a sound footing in this country at this time, that has as much to do with Mr. Lloyd George as with any single British man who has ever lived, and I am proud of my friendship with him and am grateful for all that he did for the causes which he loved so well.[2494]

William Brown, Independent, spoke movingly on a great stain on British politics:

At any time in the last 20 years, Lloyd George might have appropriated the title, which was once applied to Cromwell, "the great Independent." The tributes that have been paid so far have laid emphasis on the successes of that astonishing career. When he was at the zenith of his power I never knew him, except as a name and an inspiration. When I came into this House in 1929, he had already passed, by some six years, the peak point of his career and he was, till the end of his life, in *the political wilderness. Of all fates to impose upon a great man, none could be so harsh or so melancholy as that he should be condemned to watch the things that he has fought for successfully in his time, dissipated and squandered, while he is in the wilderness, and facing advancing age.* That fate England, in my lifetime, has put upon its two greatest sons. In the years between the great wars, the period that I describe as the ignoble years and the period that history will surely characterise as the locust years, that fate was imposed both on the present Prime Minister and upon Mr. Lloyd George. When this war came, the Prime Minister was young enough and strong enough to set about the business

[2494] Op. cit.

> of redeeming the years which the locusts had eaten, but about the head of Mr. Lloyd George there were already gathering the shadows of oncoming death.[2495]

George Lambert, a long-serving National Liberal, added with some emotion:

> Mr. Lloyd George came to a commanding position. He owed nothing to birth and to wealth, but achieved everything by his native ability and his perseverance... During his stormy, turbulent career... I remember the great Budget days... During the time of buffets and blows, Mr. Lloyd George was always able to return to a sheltering home and to a welcome by an appreciative and loving comrade. *I cannot help thinking that he owed much of his success to Dame Margaret Lloyd George, that maternal female, proud of her husband and proud still more that she lived to see her son and her daughter leaving their mark upon the House of Commons.* Wales has lost its most distinguished citizen, Parliament a great Parliamentarian and the Empire a devoted public servant.[2496]

Next, family friend and Tory MP, Thelma Cazalet-Keir, gave close insight into the personal nature of the man:

> Having been privileged to know "L.G." in the intimacy of his family life for the last 26 years, I should like to pay my tribute to him as a wonderful friend, because that is what he always was to me. Apart from the greatness and glory of his unique life, those who were fortunate enough to be numbered among his personal friends will always remember his simplicity and naturalness. He never needed to turn on his charm, brilliance and kindness for a special person or occasion, because they were an integral part of the man himself. No matter who you were, important or quite insignificant, "L.G." was always the same. I shall never forget the advice he gave to... (Lady Megan Lloyd George) and myself when we decided on a political career. "Never, never," he said, "allow yourselves to grow bitter and never jog backwards." Although "L.G." could, on suitable occasions, bite with his oratory, he had absolutely no bitterness in his nature.[2497]

Finally, to underline the near universal regard in which Lloyd George was held, William Gallacher, Communist MP for West Fife, stated movingly:

> It is a little over 40 years ago in the great days of which the Prime Minister spoke, that I first heard Lloyd George speak, and even now I can recall the throb and the thrill of that great meeting. Courage–it was there in abundance; eloquence–his tongue was like a silver trumpet or a flashing sword. This is not the time to recall old controversies, but it may be permissible to say that when others were not so kindly disposed towards him Glasgow opened its heart to him and gave him a welcome. Thirty years ago, I met him under different circumstances in Glasgow. But no matter how bitter and deep the dispute might be, the hon. Member for Dumbarton

[2495] Op. cit. Emphasis added. William Brown (1894-1960), trade unionist, MP for Rugby, 1942-1950.
[2496] Op. cit. Emphasis added. George Lambert (1866-1958), MP for South Molton, 1891-1924, 1929-1945.
[2497] Op. cit.

Burghs (Mr. Kirkwood) will join with me in saying that in the conversations we had he was always courteous, understanding and considerate.

In 1920 I met Lenin… Lenin advised me… to study David Lloyd George. He held the opinion that David Lloyd George was the greatest political leader this country had known. Much has been said about the part he played in the first world war. It is true that his name is interwoven with every gigantic effort of that time, but we should also remember the effort he made in trying to preserve peace, and prevent this present terrible war from coming upon Europe and the world. Eagerly, anxiously, he sought for understanding and alliance with the Soviet Union. He recognised what a mighty combination that would be in maintaining peace… In the strange drama of life he played many parts, great parts, always with the fervour and intensity of a son of the people, for it was the common people that bore him. It was the suffering of the common people that called him forth to battle against poverty and neglect.[2498]

Lord Nathan gave a tribute on behalf of Labour in the Lords, but gave a more personal and highly perceptive one in a letter to his son:

For almost the whole of the twenty years we were neighbours, I was the recipient to a quite exceptional degree of his friendship, and confidence… I knew him really well. To be in his presence was to know that you were in the presence of greatness–greatness without trappings. There was nothing about him of pomposity or pomp. He lived… quite simply. In his home there was nothing marking out very particularly that it was the home of a most remarkable world figure…

He had the peculiar quality of making those with him feel better, more confident men than they probably were in fact. He admired above all courage, vision, drive and resourcefulness, and he himself was the exemplar of all these qualities… People have often spoken of his 'magnetism'; there was magnetism and, consciously or unconsciously, he could exercise it with equal ease over the public or the individual. I have seen him sway great audiences at will: I have seen him turn hostility in private persons into devotion.

His crucial error was not to have resigned after the last War ... He often told me–though perhaps it was not the whole of the truth–that he had wanted to resign, but those around him said: 'Prime Minister, you can't resign; the country needs you more now than ever; you have got the country through the perils of war–only you can now pull her through the perils of peace. It's your duty to carry on.' And then he would go on to say: 'But they weren't really thinking of the country–they weren't really thinking of me–they were thinking of *themselves*; for if *I* went *they* went.' But he allowed himself to be deceived at the time and it was his undoing …

When I first knew him, he had fairly recently ceased to be Prime Minister–his mind was on the preparation of new policies for Britain and the reintegration of the Liberal Party. But the chasm was too deep–try as he would, the old enmities persisted, not so much arising out of differences in policy as out of personal hostility, on the part of those displaced in 1916–they never forgave.

Yet the country owes much to L.G. for his work after the War, which led to the Liberal Yellow Book (in which I had a part, albeit a small part) and the pamphlet, *We Can Conquer*

[2498] https://api.parliament.uk/historic-hansard/commons/1945/mar/28/earl-lloyd-george-of-dwyfor-om. Retrieved 17 August 2018.

*Unemployment*, with which, again, I was concerned, and which was the central feature of the 1929 General Election. It is noteworthy that now, years later, the policies for which L.G. was then responsible, and for putting forward he incurred every kind of contumely, are the politics which the Conservatives (a little less) and the Labour Party (a little more) are putting forward for the coming General Election[2499]...

It is difficult for my generation to think of L.G. as dead... It is difficult to appraise him. That he was one of the world's great men History will no doubt declare. Indeed one of the greatest... I think myself that the true measure of his greatness may be found in a comparison with Churchill. Churchill is without doubt a very great man; he is an outstanding leader of men. But with Churchill war–this War and the last War–is his life. Take away these two Wars and what have you? With L.G., who dominated the world as Churchill never has, who was in the last War all, and more than all, that Roosevelt or Stalin (or the two together) have been in this, the War was but an episode. Men will long argue whether his true greatness arose because of his leadership of the People in War or his earlier leadership of the People in Peace: either would have gained him the accolade of greatness; together they are incomparable.[2500]

Diplomat Harold Nicolson gave a vivid, perceptive summation of Lloyd George in his biography of King George V. Speaking of Lloyd George at the time he became Chancellor of the Exchequer in 1908, he wrote:

Imaginative, resourceful, impetuous, endowed with unusual demagogic powers and compelling personal charm, Mr Lloyd George was not encumbered by the vestigial affections which his colleagues still cherished for the ancient monuments of English tradition... The very fact that he was closer to the people than were his classic colleagues enabled him to realise more clearly than they that the old Gladstonian formulas were losing their glamour and their potency; and that if Liberalism were to become outmoded or overwhelmed by the rising tide of Socialism, some more stimulating doctrine must be devised. He determined to preach Social Democracy and to lead the attack on privilege–a cause and a battle which were to him supremely congenial.[2501]

One who knew him intimately, Lord Lothian, wrote perceptively in June 1930 of the reason why Lloyd George had an "enduring place... in the affections of the plain people":

To all in authority Mr. Lloyd George is a constant provocation and offence. He is a respecter neither of position, of money nor lineage. He is a merciless challenge to every orthodoxy, a persistent enemy to every tradition and every institution which seems to him to stand in the way of getting progressive things done, a ruthless and resourceful fighter who welcomes battle for its own sake with all others in the political arena, whether they be friend or foe.[2502]

---

2499 In the General Election of 5 July 1945 Churchill was spectacularly swept out of office, Labour winning 393 seats to the Tories 197, Liberals 12, National Liberals 11, Communists 2.

2500 Quoted in Hyde, p165-167.

2501 Nicolson, *King George V*, p149-150.

2502 Lord Lothian in Edwards, 1913, Vol.I, pxii.

The Marxist historian A. J. P. Taylor, who did so much to prompt the ongoing reassessment of Lloyd George from the 1960s, rated Lloyd George highly, writing:

> Despite his achievements he was always distrusted by many–a fact that grows increasingly incomprehensible with the passage of time… the only true son of the people who has risen to the highest post… Though always calling himself a Liberal he never put party before country as so many did… Count up all his faults, set them against what he achieved, and it is difficult to resist the feeling that Lloyd George was the greatest ruler of England since Oliver Cromwell.[2503]

Lifelong Lloyd George scholar Kenneth Morgan opined of him:

> Lloyd George was, from first to last, a politician. He breathed politics every moment of the day. He believed that it was ultimately through political work that his world, with all its injustices and cruelties, could be transformed and made more bearable for ordinary people.[2504]

American biographer Bentley Gilbert concluded in similar vein:

> The real Lloyd George exists in the structures of British state machinery that he invented. These, far more than his love of letters, reflect the man, his impatience with convention, his need for action–call it a desire for power and his preoccupation with ends rather than means. With the war as the crucible he hammered out the framework for the modern British executive. For better or worse he designed twentieth century British politics.[2505]

In relation to his beloved homeland of Wales, it has been fairly said "he did more than perhaps any other to give it a new political status as a nation and to make it something of a political reality, so that he may be regarded as a leading representative of the modern sense of Welsh identity."[2506] Emyr Price argued for a continuity between the *Cymru Fydd* movement led by Lloyd George and the creation of the National Assembly for Wales in 1999. Price rightly called Lloyd George "the first architect of Welsh devolution and its most famous advocate" and "the pioneering advocate of a powerful parliament for the Welsh people."[2507] Wales was always important to Lloyd George, both for emotional reasons and as something of a measure of just how far he had come in life. It literally formed his grounding, his bedrock.

As early as 1906, Lloyd George had expressed his views on 'the vitality of the Welsh Nation and the Welsh language' at a St David's Festival Dinner, held under the auspices of the Cardiff Cymmrodorion Society on 10 March at Andrews Hall in Cardiff. Talking of his constituency 'home' of Caernarfon, he said:

---

2503 Taylor, Introduction to Morgan, *Lloyd George*, (1974), p7-8.
2504 Morgan, *Lloyd George*, (1981), Preface [p7].
2505 Gilbert, *Lloyd George And The Historians*, p85-86.
2506 M. Stephens, *Lloyd George, David* in *The New Companion to the Literature of Wales*, 1998, Cardiff, University of Wales Press, p454.
2507 Price, 2006, pxi, 208.

> Carnarvon was founded 2,000 years ago as the outpost of a great Empire–the greatest Empire the world had seen. It was the Bulawayo of the Roman Empire, the very extreme of barbarism and savagery, just a fortified camp. The ruins are still there and little children go to a school close by. They learn a language in that school, a dead language; it is the language of the great Empire. They go out and play amongst the ruins, and they talk a language, a living one; it is the language of the conquered and the savages. Let no man despise Wales, her language or her literature; she has survived many storms; she has survived many Empires. Her time will come. When the last truckload of coal reaches Cardiff, when the last black diamond is dug out of the earth of Glamorgan, there will be men then digging gems of pure brilliants from the inexhaustible mines of the literature and the language of Wales.[2508]

Meanwhile, Lloyd George's widow, Frances, had been married for less than eighteen months. As the Dowager Countess Lloyd-George of Dwyfor, Frances lived in her house at Churt for the remainder of her life, devoting her time to her family, charitable activities, perpetuating the memory of Lloyd George and writing. Her memoir *The Years That Are Past* was published in 1967, and her diary of her life with Lloyd George was published in 1971. She died soon afterwards, on 5 December 1972, at the age of 84. She had wanted to be buried in Churt under a cherry tree, but in the event she was cremated.[2509] Her funeral was a quiet affair, at Guildford Crematorium, attended only by her immediate family and Lloyd George's old political friend Lord Boothby.

In estimating Lloyd George's character and legacy in our own times it can fairly be said that his deepest, lifelong and most fundamental impulse–stemming from his own childhood roots in North Wales–was to try to improve the basic lot of humanity, especially that of the poor and those on the margins of society. Perhaps the most important 'What if?' question regarding him is that concerning how European history would very probably been quite different had Lloyd George's more tolerant, more realistic view of Germany–and the severe crises it faced–prevailed at the Paris Peace Conference in 1919! The rise of Hitler and the Nazis would almost certainly never have taken place, and subsequently neither would the Second World War, with its well over 60 million list of the dead.

In a speech he gave at Queen's Hall in London on 4 August 1917, the third anniversary of the declaration of war, and whilst it still raged at its height, Lloyd George had declared in no uncertain terms:

> *War is a ghastly thing, but not as grim as a bad peace.* There is an end to the most horrible war, but a bad peace goes on and on staggering from one war to another. What do they mean? Do they mean peace when they talk? The truth is… the Prussian war lords have not yet abandoned their ambitions. They are not discussing that. They are only discussing the postponement of the realisation of these ambitions. There is a feeling among them… that this time the plot has miscarried. They are perfectly honest about that, and they blame this country with its Fleet and its factories, and they say, "Had it not been for Britain all would have been well." Next time

---

2508 *Cardiff Times*, 10 March 1906, p5. Lloyd George was referring to the Roman fort of Segontium.
2509 Personal communication to the author from Ruth Nixon, 18 December 2019.

> they mean to make sure. There must be no "make sure."… They say, "Well, there are many things we ought to have foreseen. We ought to have had plenty of food stored in Germany. Next time we will see to that. We ought to have had plenty of cotton. Then, we have made a mistake about submarines. Instead of having two or three hundred, we ought to have had at least two or three thousand." *Next time! There must be no "next time"! Far better, in spite of all the cost, all the sorrow, and all the tragedy of it–let us have done with it! Do not let us repeat this horror! Let us be the generation that manfully, courageously, resolutely eliminated war from among the tragedies of human life. Let us, at any rate, make victory so complete that national liberty, whether for great nations or for small nations, can never be challenged.* That is the ordinary law. The small man, the poor man, has the same protection as the powerful man. So the little nation must be as well guarded and protected as the big nation.[2510]

A few months later, on 14 December, in a speech at Gray's Inn in London, Lloyd George had rounded out these principles with their practical corollary:

> The danger is not the extreme pacifist. I am not afraid of him. But I warn the nation to watch the man who thinks that there is a halfway house between victory and defeat. *There is no halfway house between victory and defeat.* These are the men who think that you can end the war now by some sort of what they call pact of peace, by the setting up of a League of Nations with conditions as to arbitration in the event of disputes, with provision for disarmament, and with a solemn covenant on the part of all nations to sign a treaty on those lines, and not merely to abide by it themselves, but to help to enforce it against any nation that dares to break it.
>
> *That is the right policy after victory.* Without victory it would be a farce. Why, we are engaged in a war because an equally solemn treaty was treated as a scrap of paper. Who would sign the new treaty? I presume, among others, the people who have so far successfully broken the last. Who would enforce the new treaty? I presume that they would be the nations that have so far not quite succeeded in enforcing the last. To end the war entered on, to enforce a treaty without reparation for the infringement of that treaty, merely by entering into a new, a more sweeping and a more comprehensive treaty, would be, indeed, a farce in the setting of a tragedy. We must take care not to be misled by mere words–"league of nations," "disarmament," "arbitration," "security." *They are all great and blessed phrases, but without the vitalising force of victory they are nothing but words. You cannot wage war with words. You cannot secure peace with words. You cannot long cover defeat with words. Unless there are deeds behind them, they are but dead leaves which the first storm will scatter and reveal your strangled and abandoned purpose to the world.*
>
> We ought never to have started unless we meant, at all hazards, to complete our task. There is nothing so fatal to character as half-finished tasks.[2511]

Between 1919 and 1922, Lloyd George personally attended thirty-three special conferences as the world tried to re-fashion itself more equitably after the terrible war.[2512] The Paris Peace process alone,

2510 Lloyd George, *Great Crusade*, p182-183. Emphasis added.
2511 Ibid., p233-234. Emphasis added.
2512 MacMillan, *Peacemakers*, p495.

culminating in the Treaty of Versailles, should have stood as a fine and lasting memorial to Lloyd George's standing as a statesman of international repute. By the time he left office, Germany no longer posed any military threat to European peace. The fact that the Treaty ultimately failed to maintain peace was a shame both in this regard and, of course, far more so for the millions who lost their lives in the subsequent Second World War. That the process was fatally flawed and compromised owed something to Woodrow Wilson's personal dominance. For all his high-minded principles, he was as fallible as any other statesman present, as he was just as prone to bend in the direction of perceived American interests as other national leaders were to theirs, and was also personally inflexible. This became patently obvious during the course of the Conference, leaving both it and its corollary treaties and creations tinged with the taint of hypocrisy, distrust, disappointment and–fatally–resentment. Wilson was an autocrat, almost single-handedly trying to drive through what he thought was right. But ultimately he could not even persuade his own Senate to vote its approval of the League of Nations, leaving it fatally flawed and weakened.

Lord Lexden, official historian of the Conservative Party since 2009 and thus having no obvious political axe to grind, has written in no uncertain terms concerning Lloyd George's record over the Versailles Treaty:

> At the peace conference, Lloyd George was the most zealous advocate of moderation on the central issues relating to Germany, with which the peacemakers had to deal. At the final meetings of the ill-assorted triumvirate in June 1919, he strove hard, though admittedly with results that often disappointed him, to revise and soften the terms to be offered to Germany. His underlying aim never deviated: Germany's political system must be rebuilt along new democratic lines and the country given the central place it deserved in European and wider international affairs…
>
> Throughout he was an advocate of leniency. He argued that the statesmanlike course would be to try to build up the economies of the new nations of central and eastern Europe, victors and vanquished alike, so that trade and economic prosperity could be restored…
>
> Everything would have utterly different if Lloyd George had been heeded at an early stage…
>
> But in the quest for a new European order, Lloyd George was often wiser and more far-sighted than his colleagues. He deserved his laurels.[2513]

In some important senses the war did not actually end on 11 November 1918. Of course, the guns ceased firing on the Western Front on that memorable date. But in 2016 historian Robert Gerwarth urged a fundamental re-think concerning the true legacy of the war. He argued cogently that, though terrible, it was not the fighting on the Western Front which proved so ruinous to Europe's future, but rather the way in which the war ended and the devastating aftermath, as countries on both sides of the original conflict were wrecked by revolutions, civil wars, pogroms, mass expulsions and further major military clashes which continued for some five years after the traditional date for the coming of

---

[2513] Lexden, *Lloyd George And The Versailles Treaty*, p21, 22, 23.

peace. The war was the "unintentional enabler"[2514] of the strife that followed: it would have required the Treaty of Versailles, and the other 'subsidiary' treaties, to have been more robust and more equitable, as argued for by Lloyd George, to have at least partly ameliorated this dire situation. The perhaps almost inevitable collective failure to resolve the conflicting mass of issues in a manner acceptable to all parties often led to feelings of "perceived national humiliation to be redeemed through yet another war" establishing "subsequent cycles of violence that often extended beyond 1939."[2515]

William George remembered his brother resting at Criccieth before leaving for the Paris Conference, "seeing him pondering over a map and, in casting it aside, muttering, 'It can't be done.' Well, it wasn't done, as we all know very well by this time–though I believe Dafydd did his best to make the treaty one of peace rather than punishment."[2516] In his memoirs, retired diplomat Charles Hardinge recorded that in 1923:

> I happened to sit next to Lloyd George at a public dinner. During the course of conversation he referred to the Treaty of Versailles and I allowed free rein to my pent-up feelings on the subject of this particular Treaty and told him frankly my opinion of it and his own heavy responsibility for some of its most regrettable features. He angrily asked me to what parts of the Treaty I referred, I at once gave him several examples of the unpractical nature of the Treaty. He said nothing for about ten minutes and then remarked in a friendly way, "If I had to go to Paris again I would conclude quite a different treaty."[2517]

How that might have been must remain a matter for speculation.

Lloyd George himself was sanguine about the true nature of the First World War and its import in the following years. In concluding his *War Memoirs* in October 1936, he noted that "No other Minister in any of the belligerent countries held an official position from the 1st of August, 1914, to the 11th of November, 1918", before reflecting:

> If Germany had been led by Bismarck and Moltke[2518] instead of by von Bethmann-Hollweg and Falkenhayn[2519], the event of the great struggle between a military autocracy and democracy would in all human probability have been different. The blunders of Germany saved us from the consequences of our own. But let all who trust justice to the arbitrament of war bear in mind that the issue may depend less on the righteousness of the cause than on the cunning and craft of the contestants. It is the teaching of history, and this war enforces the lesson. And the cost is prohibitive. It cripples all the litigants. The death of ten millions and the mutilation of another

---

2514 Gerwarth, p12.

2515 Ibid., p266. Charles Emmerson agrees that peace, albeit temporary, did not truly return to Europe until 1924, a decade after the Great War began; Emmerson, pxi.

2516 George, *My Brother And I*, p246.

2517 C. Hardinge, *Old Diplomacy*, 1947, London, John Murray, p240.

2518 Graf Helmuth von Moltke (1800-1891), Prussian Field Marshal, Chief of Staff for 30 years and leading military strategist.

2519 General Erich von Falkenhayn (1861-1922), Chief of the German General Staff, 1914-1916.

> twenty millions amongst the best young men of a generation is a terrible bill of costs to pay in a suit for determining the responsibility and penalty for the murder of two persons, however exalted their rank. When you add to that £50,000,000,000 expended in slaughter and devastation, the complete dislocation of the international trade of the world, unemployment on a scale unparalleled in history, the overthrow of free institutions over the greater part of Europe, and the exasperation and perpetuation of international feuds which threaten to plunge the world into an even greater catastrophe, *one must come to the conclusion that war is much too costly and barbarous a method of settling quarrels amongst the nations of earth.*[2520]

Some of the same factors already referred to are important when considering why Lloyd George does not have an equivalent reputation to Churchill as a great war leader. Firstly, there is the nature of the two respective world wars. The first is seen as a war of great waste, of needless European imperialist devastation and loss, that signally failed to be the 'war to end all wars'[2521], while the second is still viewed as something of a noble global 'crusade' against totalitarian aggression and genocide, causes that can still be clearly identified with by most. Of course, in many ways it is ironic that Lloyd George even has to be regarded as a war leader, as for most of his earlier life he was passionately against war at all–the Second Anglo-Afghan War (1878-1880), the Anglo-Egyptian War (1882) and especially the Second Boer War (1899-1902) all garnered him severe censure and opposition, at some personal risk to himself. This was a matter of genuine principle with him, not opportunism, and he has received insufficient recognition in this regard.

His desire for peace with Germany after the First World War comes under the same umbrella. In 1922 Lloyd George wrote a preface to John Saxon Mills book on *The Genoa Conference*, the first post-Great War conference that Germany attended as an equal, and also the last international conference that Lloyd George attended. In it he made a clarion call that, sadly, was ignored by the majority of politicians who came to power in Britain and across Europe after his fall the same year:

> The new world… believes in nationalism no less firmly than the old, for nationalism is the individual force, the genius, the salt in every varied impulse which makes up Western Civilization as a whole. But it also believes with its whole heart that in the welter of passion, and in the economic chaos to which the world has been reduced by war, the welfare of every nation depends upon peace, co-operation, a helping hand from the strong to the weak, a regard for the welfare of all.
>
> The British Empire Delegation stood for that faith at Genoa, and had behind it, as I believe, the goodwill and the deep desire of a majority of all true democracies throughout the world. *The campaign for peace is only beginning. We have won positions from which we must press forward again. We are bivouacked on the field. We must not rest till we have won.*"[2522]

---

2520 Lloyd George, *War Memoirs*, Vol.II, Preface, pv, ix-x. Emphasis added.

2521 Even during the war itself, the phrase, originated by novelist H. G. Wells, met with a degree of scepticism, Lloyd George himself being reputed to have said, "This war, like the next war, is a war to end war."

2522 Lloyd George in Mills, Preface, no page number. Emphasis added.

Secondly, the First World War is at a greater historical remove, with much less vivid and extensive footage to bring the horrors alive to succeeding generations. Lloyd George, the great orator, did not even have access to the radio as Prime Minister: the British Broadcasting Company (BBC)[2523] was not formed until 18 October 1922, first broadcasting from London station 2LO on 14 November, Lloyd George having resigned on 19 October. The technology was largely lacking, and we have no recordings that can be replayed to reinforce the impression of his words and voice in our minds, and consequently none of his stirring war speeches have entered the popular memory. Lloyd George spoke more immediately, to his audience, whereas Churchill often spoke with one eye on the historical record.

Thirdly, there is the nature of the two men themselves: Lloyd George spent many years in the political wilderness after his wartime and immediate postwar premiership, leaving office aged 59, a member of the once proud Liberal Party that subsequently dwindled away to almost nothing before losing its name altogether, whilst Churchill returned to office after his war years at the head of a Tory Party still very much active–though radically altered–today, leaving office aged 80.

Regarding the implosion of the Liberal Party, its future was blighted by Herbert Asquith, who never had the grace to retire from the leadership scene, to make way for a more vigorous man, one more able and suited to the new, more complex, more precarious times. It was an unnecessary and unedifying spectacle of great sadness. Asquith put self before Party interest, sniping from the side-lines as both he and the divided Liberals drifted into irrelevance with Labour increasingly filling their parliamentary and council seats and often re-inventing their policies. A. J. P. Taylor wrote in 1965 concerning Asquith's role in 1916: "Asquith in fact, not Lloyd George, pursued a personal vendetta. He split the Liberal Party and riveted on his adherents, however unwillingly, the appearance of opposing a government that was fighting the war."[2524] Writing in 1958, the admittedly not unbiased William George had come to the same conclusion, opining:

> Unfortunately Asquith took his fall very badly, and far from being loyal to Dafydd, as Dafydd had been to him for so many years, he took an active part with disgruntled military leaders in making things difficult for my brother, when the war was at a critical stage, particularly in 1918. In my view, Asquith nursed his personal grievance and was not a big enough man to bury his disappointment and to accept without bitterness the changed situation. His injured personal vanity must be regarded as one of the factors which led to the break-up of the Liberal Party, for his personal antagonism towards my brother practically ruled out any hope of co-operation between them in leading the Liberal Party in the post-war era.[2525]

In any case, it ill-became Asquith to complain of being levered out of office, as in early September 1905 he had himself, with other Liberal Imperialists Edward Grey and Richard Haldane, planned to kick prospective Prime Minister Campbell-Bannerman upstairs to the House of Lords and render him at best "a dummy prime minister", while Asquith himself would wield the real power as Leader in the

---

[2523] The Company became the British Broadcasting Corporation on 1 January 1927.

[2524] Taylor, *English History*, p70.

[2525] George, *My Brother And I*, p256.

Commons and Chancellor of the Exchequer, with Grey as the Foreign Secretary and Haldane as the Lord Chancellor. This was the infamous 'Relugas Compact', named after the fishing village in Moray where the 'plotters' met. Fortunately, 'C. B.' stood firm in his resolve to stay in the Commons, and by 13 November the would-be 'triumvirate' had caved in.

In the 1920s, Lloyd George had the drive for revival, reinvigoration and renewal, full of ideas. He was, as he himself alluded to in a debate on the Coal Mines Bill on 19 December 1929, a man "genuinely seeking work."[2526] By the mid-1930s, he was immersed in fighting the battles of the past, writing his voluminous memoirs, and both his time and that of the Liberals was past. Added to Asquith's attitude, was the extraordinary, vindictive and colluding nature of Baldwin and MacDonald's determination to exclude Lloyd George from the political scene in the 1920s and 1930s.

Fourthly, the subject of Lloyd George's other great battle against inequality and injustice, that of the rights of Nonconformists against the Established Church, has equally dwindled into virtual irrelevance in an age when few citizens are formally Christian believers and who care still less about the niceties of theological hair-splitting between different Christian denominations. Lastly, once again, the fact must be mentioned of his Welsh nationality, its minority status within the United Kingdom as a whole, and the almost in-built suspicion attaching to it.[2527]

It must also be borne in mind that Churchill had Lloyd George's experience to build upon, as noted by Walter Layton, who had been a Ministry of Munitions official during the First World War: "Lloyd George was finding his way through an untried field. Winston Churchill was applying the lessons of the first war and adapting a highly developed apparatus of government."[2528] Writing to Frances, shortly after Lloyd George's death, on 20 April 1945, Leo Amery observed: "How he [Lloyd George} will compare in history with Churchill is indeed an interesting speculation. He had not the same knowledge of war in the narrower sense, but a much wider grasp of all the many other factors which come into the picture of war on the modern scale. In other ways it would be difficult to imagine two more wholly dissimilar types of mind and character."[2529]

Charles Mowat, historian of the inter-war years and biographer of Lloyd George, wrote about the fall of the Coalition in 1922: "And thus ended the reign of the great ones, the giants of the Edwardian era and of the war; and the rule of the pygmies, of the 'second-class brains' began, to continue until 1940. Lloyd George remained in public life, admired, distrusted, unused, and stonily watched the country sink in the hopeless morass of depression and unemployment, while lesser men frittered away Britain's power in the world."[2530] This summation, first written in 1955, remains a sadly true but still generally unrecognised fact.

Lloyd George's policies to tackle the great problem of the age, mass unemployment, as set out in his 'Yellow Book', were totally ignored in the corridors of power. Governments–Labour, Tory and

---

[2526] Quoted in Rowland, *Lloyd George*, p657.
[2527] See Campbell, *Lloyd George*, p4.
[2528] *Commemoration of the Centenary of the Birth of David Lloyd George, 17th January, 1863: Prichard-Jones Hall, University College of North Wales, Bangor, Saturday, 30th March, 1963*, p3. Also quoted in Toye, p405. John Ehrman reached the same conclusion; Ehrman, p107.
[2529] Quoted in Jones, *David Lloyd George*, p450. Leopold Amery (1873-1955), Tory MP for Birmingham Sparkbrook.
[2530] Mowat, *Britain Between The Wars*, p142.

'National'–preferred to just passively 'sit it out', follow failed orthodoxies, and let prosperity return 'naturally'. Where governments abroad did pursue active, interventionist policies of large-scale public works, these were shown to be demonstrably practical and effective. Lloyd George's ideas where both an emergency programme and a new political philosophy of co-operation and partnership aimed at bridging the gap between irresponsible, unfettered Capitalism and the inflexibility of doctrinaire Socialism. Politics was polarizing towards Communism and Fascism, and Lloyd George offered a way forward.

Only the Second World War broke these orthodoxies and created something of a sense of national social obligation and common purpose, with the post-war Labour Government embracing 'managed capitalism'–some nationalization in the public service sector; the regulation of monopolies; some direction of investment; government involvement in industrial relations through a Ministry of Labour; Government responsibility for town and country planning – all objectives explicitly or explicitly prefigured in the 'Yellow Book'. Lloyd George would have been gratified but no doubt rather amazed. As John Campbell rightly wrote: "The success of the post-war Labour Government in laying the foundations of the 'affluent society' owed more… to twenties Liberalism than to pre-war Labour thinking. For twenty-five years after 1945, indeed, both governing parties lived on the inheritance of 'new' Liberalism."[2531]

Only with the subsequent onset of the rigidly doctrinaire, narrow, hard-line Toryism–nationalist, populist, monetarist, deregulatory, privatization-based–under the iron grip of Prime Minister Margaret Thatcher from 1979 to 1990, was the broad consensus in British life and politics really smashed, with the dire, divisive consequences still being played out and bearing sour fruit under her successors. In this regard, what John Campbell wrote nearly half-a-century ago is *still* true–in its recommendations for industrial democracy and co-ownership the 'Yellow Book' has still proved to be too radical to find acceptance. What seemed too idealistic to be practicable in 1928 is still proving elusive nearly a century later!

Lloyd George was not always the originator of ideas, but it was he who often had the personal drive and political will to push ideas forward, to enthuse and marshal people to a common purpose. "He was a great believer, in office and out, in picking the brains of the best-qualified and least orthodox experts on any subject."[2532] In 1919 Keynes had likened Lloyd George to "a prism, as I have heard him described, which collects light and distorts it and is most brilliant if the light comes from many quarters at once."[2533] This image highlights his entrepreneurial qualities in organizing and promoting such collaborative works as the 'Yellow Book', works which also help to demonstrate "his exceptional openness to new ideas and his remarkable modernity of outlook."[2534]

Lloyd George was not an intellectual, but his thought remained fresh, flexible, adaptable, open to new input until very late in his life. To a remarkable degree, and in stark contrast to virtually all other

---

2531 Campbell, *Lloyd George*, p203.

2532 Ibid., p204.

2533 Keynes, *Essays In Biography*, p37.

2534 Campbell, *Lloyd George*, p204.

leading politicians of the day, he continued to look to the future, to make positive and constructive plans for it, and to keep his lifelong radicalism sharpened and updated. Perhaps Christopher Addison, in the fields of agriculture and health, and George Lansbury, regarding world disarmament, peace and women's rights–both originally radical Liberals before moving to Labour–rivalled him in passion and commitment, but neither were so well-rounded, so experienced, such leaders of men, or so popular and famous as Lloyd George. In a sea of stagnation and complacency, Lloyd George stood ready as a national leader who could have led the nation through its crisis of economic decline and ebbing confidence, and the waste of his talent and the loss to the nation is a matter of lasting regret.

Lloyd George himself had a psychologically interesting view on the uneasy relationship between the law and politics. His nephew William R. P. George related:

> When I was a law student in 1933 and staying with him at Churt I remember asking him his views on the relationship between the law as a profession and politics. He replied that the law tended to inhibit the politician from ever developing into a statesman and reaching the heights. I asked him to explain, and he then instanced men like F. E. Smith (Lord Birkenhead), Lord Reading and John Simon, all of them men of the most brilliant intellect and persuasive speakers, but none of them memorable as statesmen. 'The truth is', he said, 'that a lawyer is taught from the beginning to speak on behalf of someone else–a solicitor is bound by his instructions and a barrister by his brief. To succeed as a politician you must say what you yourself think.'[2535]

In the light of this statement, it is worth noting that, although 16 Prime Ministers have been barristers, to date Lloyd George is the only solicitor to have held the office.

On a personal level, much of the erroneous view of Lloyd George as promiscuous came from his own embittered eldest son, Richard, who wrote a warm, affectionate and appreciative book, *Dame Margaret: The Life Story Of His Mother*, which came out in 1947, and another, much more critical and abrasive, *Lloyd George*, in 1960. Bengy Carey-Evans related that the second book was virtually ghost-written by two journalists who only paid Richard, sadly by this time a shell-shocked alcoholic who had been declared bankrupt on 4 July 1947[2536], £50 [£1,472 in 2025]. Richard formerly owned Glyn House from 1919, opposite Capel Curig Training Camp in Snowdonia: it was probably not a coincidence that a subsequent owner, who ran a B&B, had a guest book in which it stated, totally falsely, that it was where Lloyd George entertained his mistresses in a log cabin in the grounds.[2537]

From 4 March to 29 April 1981, BBC TV screened its *The Life and Times of David Lloyd George* historical drama series, with fine Welsh actor Philip Madoc giving a strong, intelligent performance in the leading role, and Welsh actress Lisabeth Miles giving a sensitive, luminous performance as Margaret. The historical consultant was historian A. J. P. Taylor. The series was generally accurate

---

[2535] George, *Making Of Lloyd George*, p134. William R. P. George qualified as a solicitor in November 1934, joining his father's firm, William George & Son, in Porthmadog, practising with them until his death aged 94.

[2536]http://bankruptcyandinsolvency.blogspot.com/2010/05/peerage-and-mp-ledger-richard-2nd-earl.html. Retrieved 17 November 2021. See also Longford, p189-192.

[2537] Private information; https://www.dailypost.co.uk/news/prime-ministers-snowdonia-love-nest-13216192. Retrieved 17 November 2021.

concerning Lloyd George's Welsh context and the political developments and was well-received at the time. Unfortunately, however, it did determinedly perpetuate the view of Lloyd George as being a life-long, promiscuous philanderer. Sadly, the drama was a missed opportunity for the Welsh scriptwriter and director to set the record straight before a UK-wide audience, and consequently it has dated badly in this respect.

The present author finds there to be a lot of poignant truth in the 'Tribute To Their Grandfather' by Robin and Bengy Carey-Evans:

> Although David Lloyd George is now largely remembered for his role in the First World War, he was not like Winston Churchill, battle experienced and inspired by warfare. He was a man of peace whose interest was not so much in foreign affairs but in building a fairer society at home. He had opposed the nation's involvement in the Boer War as a result of which he and his family had been cruelly vilified as traitors. He had reluctantly agreed to Britain's involvement in the First World War after the shocking reports of German cruelty and destruction as their army marched through Belgium. He became convinced that Germany must be prevented from dominating Europe.
>
> He became Prime Minister at a critical time when political leadership was clearly lacking, causing the progress of the war to suffer. History has confirmed that his energy and organising abilities brought the country into a much-needed state of total war, which ultimately led to its successful conclusion. It was a time of great stress, the main cause of which was the ever-increasing slaughter of precious lives on the Western Front. He had no confidence in the military command and attempted to persuade an obstinate War Office to change the leadership and to agree a joint command of both the British and French armies to unite their operation and effectiveness. This strategy was finally achieved by the appointment of General Foch in the closing stages of the war. Lloyd George also insisted on convoys for merchant shipping over the reluctance of the Naval Authorities, which when finally implemented resulted in a dramatic reduction of losses. Victory for him was always blemished by the dreadful loss of life which could have been reduced, in his view, by better military naval judgment.
>
> If one were able to ask him now what he would like to be remembered for, it would I believe be the "other war" he waged from 1909 to 1912, the war against poverty and social injustice. This was a war he clearly won without any loss of life: in fact, it gave life to millions of workers by awarding them for the first time a Government sponsored pension and ultimately a National Health Insurance scheme. This war was fought against a reluctant and at that time privileged and socially indifferent House of Lords. This helped to prevent violent class conflict in Britain and made it a more stable and united society in the succeeding decades.[2538]

A key impression that struck the present author forcibly on reading through Lloyd George's writings and speeches, is the astonishing modernity, freshness and continuing relevance of so many of his ideas and observations, across a wide range of issues. Lloyd George very definitely had a deep, clear and lasting vision of human life, its essentials, its problems and potential methods of bettering it. He was

[2538] Personal communication to the author by Davina Carey-Evans, 16 November 2018.

a profound humanitarian who remained consistently fired by this guiding principle throughout his life, through all his personal and political vicissitudes. So much of his recorded thought can still be read with benefit to this day, sometimes a little dated in phrasing, but still applicable in meaning. Many of the social, political and economic battles he fought still remain to be carried through, and he can still serve as something of an inspiration–no mean feat for a man whose peak of influence was a century ago, a century of such revolutionary change in so many ways.

Grandson Bengy firmly believed that, on probably the most important issue of contemporary times, Lloyd George would have voted 'Remain' in the UK Referendum on EU Membership on 23 June 2016. The present author fully agrees, believing that the elder statesman would be aghast at the renewed rise of populist and overtly racist rhetoric in the nation's government of the day and sections of the national press, just as he was at the time of the Boer War. When considering how clearly Lloyd George spoke to the 34 nations[2539] represented at the Genoa Conference, the whole tenor of his advocacy of 'the common effort of the nations of Europe being needed to restore European efficiency', of 'Europe needing peace', about 'acting together in the same spirit', 'the common statesmanship of Europe', and of 'the world being one economic unit', without the loss of 'national sovereignties', it is frankly impossible to believe otherwise.

The present author is also convinced that, weighed in the balance, Lloyd George left the world a materially better place than he found it. In his memoirs, Bob Boothby singled this out, writing: "The two things I remember most vividly about Lloyd George, apart from his inexhaustible vitality and good humour, were his genuine concern for the poor, the old, and for the sick; and his burning zeal for disarmament … For my part, I shall believe until the end of my life that the fall of Lloyd George and his subsequent exclusion from office for twenty years when at the height of his powers was one of the greatest disasters that has ever befallen the British people, and indeed the world."[2540] Earlier, in 1940, he had written "A hundred years hence the historians will write that the greatest man produced by this country in our time was unquestionably David Lloyd George… [as] the dominating political figure not only in Europe but in the world."[2541]

The chief charge levelled against Lloyd George, marring his memory, is the often unsourced one of philandering. As detailed previously, Lloyd George was highly attracted by articulate, intelligent, influential and beautiful women all his life. The interesting point to the present author is that particular opprobrium attaches itself so especially to him. The cases of Charles Dilke, Charles Stewart Parnell, and Asquith and Venetia Stanley have already been mentioned. Venetia Stanley herself went on to have an affair with Lord Beaverbrook. Gerald Balfour, younger brother of the former Prime Minister, himself Chief Secretary for Ireland from 1895 to 1900 and President of the Board of Trade from 1900 to 1905, married to Elizabeth since 1887, from January 1912 had an extra-marital affair with Lloyd George's soon-to-be friend Winifred Coombe Tennant, their union producing a son, (Augustus) Henry, in April 1913. Both being interested, in the grand Victorian-Edwardian manner, in

[2539] At the time of writing–December 2025–the European Union (EU) has 27 Member States.

[2540] R. Boothby, *Boothby: Recollections Of A Rebel*, 1978, London, Hutchinson, p162-163.

[2541] Boothby, *At Home*, p19-20.

parapsychology–Winifred practising as a medium under the name 'Mrs Willett'–they had a 'Plan' and were hopeful that Henry would be the "New Messiah".[2542]

There was also the case of Foreign Secretary, Edward Grey, who had an affair with Pamela Tennant whilst he was married to Dorothy, before the latter's death on 4 February 1906. The relationship lasted for years before they married on 4 June 1922, Grey having very probably already fathered her fourth child in 1902.[2543] Further, Grey also had two illegitimate children–in 1890 and 1894–as a result of two other extra-marital affairs[2544], with the strong possibility of a third in 1912.[2545] Indeed, over time Lloyd George and Grey came to dislike each other, and it would seem that Lloyd George himself had some knowledge of Grey's complex love life; little wonder that in October 1932 Lloyd George came to refer to Grey's "sham honesty".[2546] As so often, class and connections covered some people's 'sins' more than those of others. Many other politicians, from before Lloyd George's time to the present day, and from many nations, could also be cited.[2547]

This, of course, does not necessarily make Lloyd George's conduct right, particularly regarding his long-suffering yet loyal wife Margaret. However, it does raise the question as to why–concerning a man who did so much right by his ordinary fellow citizens in the United Kingdom–should be singled out in this area? Lloyd George was always the 'Great Outsider'–racially, class-wise, educationally, religiously, professionally, politically–, and the present author suspects lack of genuine knowledge about him, plus an unspoken, unconscious anti-Welsh racism amongst majority English-speakers, has at least something to do with it. To 'put him down' is to 'put down' his political achievements without having to come up with closely-argued alternatives. The present work was written in large measure as an attempt at correcting popular opinion in this regard.

In a very real sense, present-day Welsh Liberal Democrats, Nationalists, Labour and Greens all owe Lloyd George some debt of gratitude, one that is not sufficiently acknowledged, for significantly advancing the cause of Wales, its identity, its political, social and material progress, even to some extent, through his lifelong support of the National Eisteddfod, its cultural reawakening. Meanwhile, the English majority in the United Kingdom should recognise, along with their fellow Welsh citizens, the great political, social and economic advancement that Lloyd George gifted to them through his progressive reforms, pushed through in the face of intense, steely opposition from their very own 'ruling classes'.

Another facet of Lloyd George's life not sufficiently considered by biographers, regarding the potential psychological effects on him, is the fact that, in various ways, Lloyd George came close to death at least seven times during his life. Firstly, when his life was "despaired of" whilst ill with croup around February 1864; secondly, when he was bludgeoned on his head in Bangor in April 1900; thirdly,

---

2542 J. Gray, *The Immortalization Commission: Science And The Strange Quest To Cheat Death*, 2011, New York, Farrar, Straus and Giroux, pp80-83. Henry (1913-1989), did not become the 'Messiah', but did become a Benedictine monk, Dom Joseph, at Downside Abbey, Somerset, in 1961. See B. Lewis, *Wales' Unknown Hero - Soldier, Spy, Monk: The Life of Henry Coombe-Tennant, MC, of Neath,* 2021, Talybont, Y Lolfa.

2543 Waterhouse, p94-95.

2544 Ibid., p43-48.

2545 Ibid., p256-257.

2546 Ibid., p44.

2547 See Popplewell, p89-90.

when he was nearly lynched during the serious rioting in Birmingham in December 1901; fourthly, when he suffered a severe throat haemorrhage in October 1905; fifthly, in August 1910 near Treviso in Italy, when the car in which he was travelling hit a peasant's cart at 60mph, the only casualty being the horse[2548]; sixthly, when he narrowly missed being on HMS *Hampshire* with Lord Kitchener when it was sunk by a mine in June 1916; and finally, when it was "touch and go" whether he lived or died in the Spanish Flu epidemic during September 1918. Allowing for the fact that life was often more precarious and physically dangerous in the late nineteenth-early twentieth centuries than many Westerners are now used to, this is still a lot of incidents in one lifetime and may have subconsciously at least led to some degree of his feeling invincible or somehow 'marked out' to survive and succeed.

Let the last word be from the present generation, from the great statesman's great-granddaughter Davina, born long after his death, on how she feels about his memory and his legacy:

> I'm proud of what my Great Grandfather achieved, my Grandmother (his daughter), Lady Olwen Carey-Evans… often spoke warmly of her parents and siblings. Her father was a family man and Margaret his wife stood lovingly and respectably by him… for 52 years until her death…
>
> The family films and photographs of family life ending with a cine of my very elderly Great Grandparents going around their garden smelling the roses, something I believe they never forgot to do. I believe he needed a match in life who could cater for his love of knowledge and conversation…
>
> My Grandmother told me so many stories, how her father was a great storyteller, how his energy would fill the home, his love of the Countryside, the tragic death of her sister Mair, aged 17, which deeply affected them all. When living at No. 10, all the staff were Welsh speaking, the main housekeeper was with the family for 50 years. Visitors would often bring them gifts from all over the World, one of these gifts was a jewelled beetle which had to be buried in the back garden because the housekeeper believed that Beetles bought bad luck. How the likes of Churchill, Asquith would come for all meals including breakfast.[2549]

---

[2548] Grigg, *People's Champion*, p265.

[2549] Personal communication to the author by Davina Carey-Evans, 1 October 2019.

# SIMPLIFIED FAMILY TREE

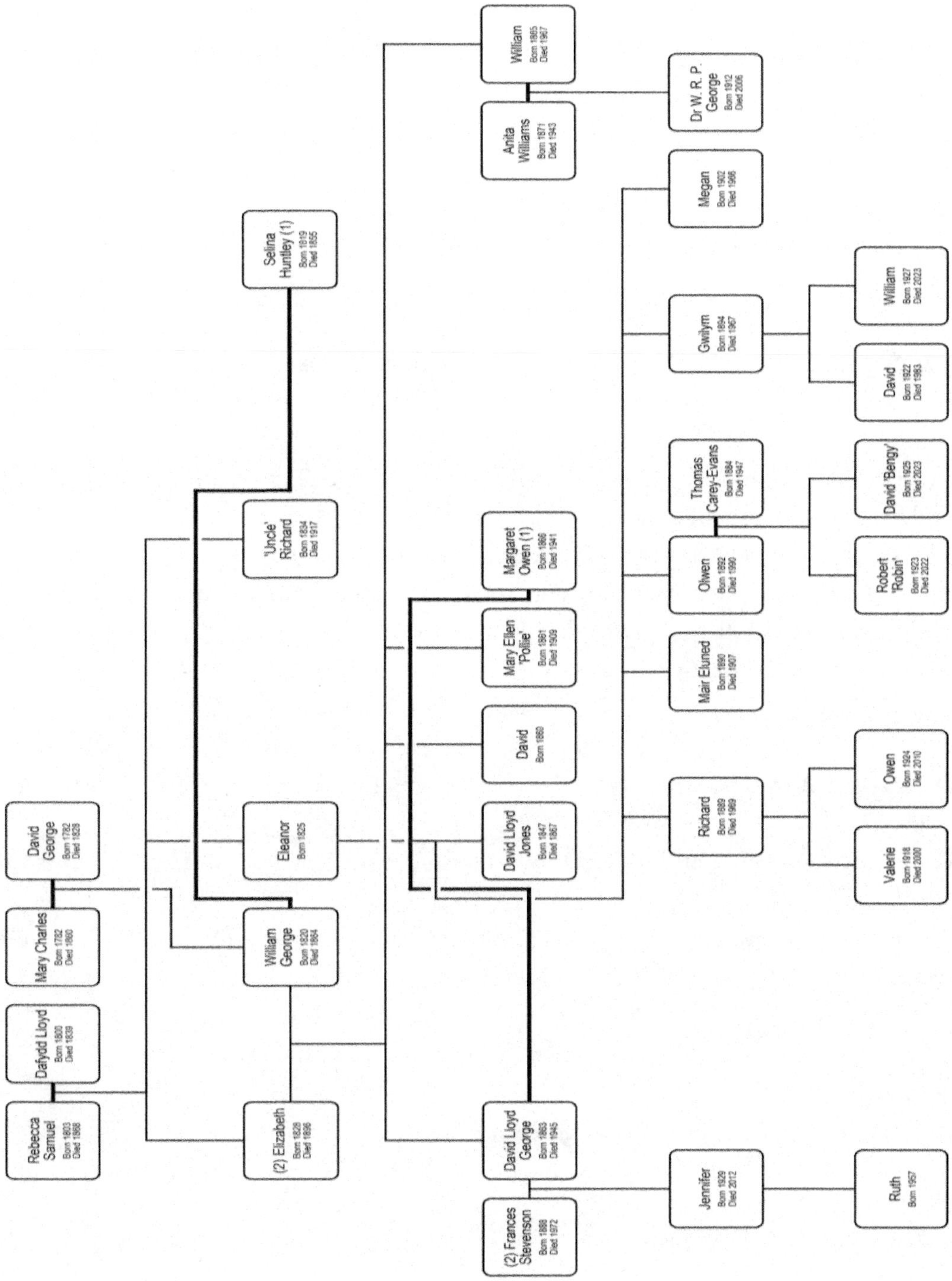

# BIBLIOGRAPHY


Adams, R. David Lloyd George: The Formative Years, 1863-1890 1990 Rhyl WEA

- David Lloyd George: A Political Genius, 1863-1945 2005 Rhyl WEA

- David Lloyd George 1916-18: The Man Who Won The War 2008 Rhyl WEA

- Commemorating And Celebrating The Centenary Of David Lloyd George Becoming Prime Minister 7th December 1916 2016 Rhyl WEA

- Lloyd George And Wales, Wales And Lloyd George 2018 Rhyl WEA

Adams, R. J. Q. Arms And The Wizard: Lloyd George And The Ministry of Munitions, 1915-1916 1978 London Cassell

Adams, W. S. Lloyd George And The Labour Movement *Past & Present* 3, 1 February 1953 p55-64

"An Independent Liberal" Lloyd George And The War: A Personal History Of His Part In Armageddon 1918 London Hutchinson

Anon. [Alfred G. Gardiner] The Life Of David Lloyd George: The Man, The Statesman, The Orator 1912 London Daily News and Leader

Anon. The Lloyd George Millions 1928 London Morning Post

Beaverbrook, Lord Politicians And The War 1914–1916 1960 London William Collins

- Men And Power 1917-1918 1956 London Hutchinson

- The Decline And Fall Of Lloyd George 1963 London William Collins

Begbie, H. Mr. Lloyd George And The Humanity Of Liberalism 1911 Brecon Radnor Express

Benedictus, D. Lloyd George 1981 London Weidenfeld and Nicolson / Sphere [Novel]

Berry, D., and Horrocks, S., Eds. David Lloyd George: The Movie Mystery 1998 Cardiff University of Wales Press

Blake, R. An Incongruous Partnership: Lloyd George And Bonar Law 1992 Aberystwyth National Library of Wales

Blaxill, L., and Saleh, T. Lloyd George And The Electoral Decline Of The British Liberal Party In The 1920s *Historical Journal* 64, 3, June 2021 p696-726

Bliss, B. The Lloyd George Fund *New Outlook* 59, November 1966 p34-37

Bloom, C. A Conspiracy Of Silence? Lloyd George And Basil Zaharoff *Journal of Liberal History* 86 Spring 2015 p22-29

Boothby, R. At Home With Lloyd George *Picture Post* 7, 3, 20 April 1940 p19-25, 55, 57

Borsa, M. Un Colloquio Con Lloyd George. Perché Egli Ha Fede Nella Vittoria *Il Secolo* 29 Gennaio 1916 p1

- Lloyd George Ed I Suoi Colleghi (Ricordi Di Uno Che Li Ha Visti Ed Avvicinati) *Il Secolo* 12 Dicembre 1916 p1-2

Boyd, N. D. The Emergence Of The Welsh Bounder: David Lloyd George's Oratorical Attacks During The Anglo-Boer War *Communication Monographs* 52, March 1985 p78-91

Boyle, T. New Light On Lloyd George's Mansion House Speech *Historical Journal* 23, 2, June 1980 p431-433

Braithwaite, W. J. Lloyd George's Ambulance Wagon 1957 London Ed. Bunbury, H. N. Methuen

Burbidge, W. F. The Wizard Of Wales: A Biographical Sketch Of The Rt. Hon. David Lloyd George 1943 London John Crowther

Campbell, J. Lloyd George, The Goat In The Wilderness, 1922-1931 1977 London Jonathan Cape

- If Love Were All…: The Story Of Frances Stevenson And David Lloyd George 2006 London Jonathan Cape

Carey Evans, O., with Garner, M. Lloyd George Was My Father 1985 Llandysul Gomer Press

Cassar, G. H. Lloyd George At War, 1916-1918 2009 London Anthem Press

'Centurion' [John Hartman Morgan] The Man Who Didn't Win the War: An Exposure Of Lloyd Georgism 1923 London National Review Office

Chirol, V. Four Years of Lloyd Georgian Foreign Policy *Edinburgh Review* 237, 483 January 1923 p1-20

Clarke, P. 'We Can Conquer Unemployment': Lloyd George And Keynes *Journal of Liberal History* 77 Winter 2012-2013pp46-49

- Lloyd George, Empire And The Making Of Modern Ireland *Welsh Political Archive Annual Lecture*, Neuadd Senedd Cymru, Cardiff Bay, 2 November 2021, p1-18

Clarke, T. My Lloyd George Diary 1939 London Methuen

Cliffe, S. Churchill, Kitchener And Lloyd George: First World Warlords 2014 [Stroud] Fonthill

Collins, D. Rivals In The Storm: How Lloyd George Seized Power, Won The War And Lost His Government 2024 London Bloomsbury Continuum

Constantine, S. Lloyd George 1992 London Routledge

Conybeare, J. The Crisis Of 1911-1913: Lloyd George And The Doctors *Lancet* 269, 6977, 18 May 1957, p1,032-1,035

Cosgrove, R. A. A Note On Lloyd George's Speech At The Mansion House, 21 July 1911 *Historical Journal* 12, 4, December 1969 p698-701

Costigan. G. Makers Of Modern England: The Force Of Individual Genius In History 1967 London Collier-Macmillan [VII. David Lloyd George (1863-1945), p197-242]

Cott, N. "Liberal Unity Frustrated": The Asquith-Lloyd George Split In The Liberal Party *Journal of Liberal Democrat History* 32 Autumn 2001 p6-11

Cregier, D. M. Bounder From Wales: Lloyd George's Career Before The First World War 1976 Columbia University of Missouri Press

Crosby, T. L. The Unknown Lloyd George: A Statesman In Conflict 2014 London I. B. Tauris

Curran, J. M. Lloyd George And The Irish Settlement, 1921-2 *Éire-Ireland* 7/2 1972 p14-46

Davies, A. T. The Lloyd George I Knew: Some Side-Lights On A Great Career 1948 London H. E. Walter

Davies, N. Lloyd George And Poland, 1919-20 *Journal of Contemporary History* 6, 3 1971 p132-154
Davies, W. W. Lloyd George 1863-1914 1939 London Constable
Debo, R. K. Lloyd George And The Copenhagen Conference Of 1919-1920: The Initiation of Anglo-Soviet Negotiations *Historical Journal* 24, 2, June 1981 p429-441
Derry, J. W. The Radical Tradition: Tom Paine To Lloyd George 1967 London Macmillan
Desmarias, R. Lloyd George And The Development Of The British Government's Strikebreaking Organization *International Review of Social History* 20, 1 1975 p1-15
Dilnot, F. Lloyd George: The Man And His Story 1917; 2nd Edition 1923 London Harper & Brothers
Douglas, R. Lloyd George And The Partition Of Ireland *Journal of Liberal Democrat History* 33 Winter 2001-2002 p23-28
- The Lloyd George Land Taxes *Journal of Liberal History* 73 Winter 2011-12 p3-13
Du Parcq, H. The Life Of David Lloyd George 1912-1913 4 Vols London Caxton
- David Lloyd George 1915 London George Newnes [Condensed and Revised]
Dutton, D. The Wonderful Wizard As Was: Lloyd George, 1931-1945 *Journal of Liberal History* 77 Winter 2012-13 pp54-63
- The Odd Couple: Lloyd George, Austen Chamberlain And The Post-War Coalition, 1918-22 *Journal of Liberal History* 119 Summer 2023 p38-51, 61
Edwards, J. H. From Village Green To Downing Street. The Life Of The Rt. Hon. D. Lloyd George MP 1908 London George Newnes
- The Life Of David Lloyd George; With A Short History Of The Welsh People 1913-1919 London 4 Vols Waverley Book Co.
- David Lloyd George, The Man And The Statesman 1930 London Introduction by Marquess of Lothian 2 Vols Waverley Book Co.
Egerton, G. W. The Lloyd George Government And The Creation Of The League Of Nations *American Historical Review* 79, 2 April 1974 p419-444
- The Lloyd George War Memoirs: A Study In The Politics Of Memory *Journal of Modern History* 60 March 1988 p55-94
Ehrman, J. Lloyd George And Churchill As War Ministers *Transactions of the Royal Historical Society* 11, 1961, p101-115
Evans, B. G. The Life Romance Of David Lloyd George 1915 London Everyman
- Mr. Lloyd George As Minister Of Democracy, *Fortnightly Review*, 104, November 1915, p884-896
French, D. The Strategy Of The Lloyd George Coalition, 1916-1918 1995 Oxford Clarendon Press
Fry, M. G. Lloyd George And Foreign Policy: The Education Of A Statesman: 1890-1916 1977 Montreal McGill-Queen's University Press
- Political Change In Britain, August 1914 To December 1916: Lloyd George Replaces Asquith: The Issues Underlying The Drama *Historical Journal* 31, 3, September 1988 p609-627
- And Fortune Fled: David Lloyd George, The First Democratic Statesman, 1916-1922 2011 London Peter Lang
Gaw, J. L. David Lloyd George: The Politics Of Religious Conviction 2023 Knoxville University of

Tennessee Press
George, W. Richard Lloyd, Cricieth 1934 Caerdydd Western Mail A'r Echo [*Welsh Language*]
- Cymru Fydd: Hanes Y Mudiad Cenedlaethol Cyntaf 1945 Liverpool Gwasg y Brython {*Welsh Language*]
- Atgof A Myfyr 1948 Wrecsam Hughes [*Welsh Language*]
- My Brother And I 1958 London Eyre & Spottiswoode
George, W. R. P. The Making Of Lloyd George 1976 London Faber and Faber
- Lloyd George: Backbencher 1983 Llandysul Gomer Press
- 88 Not Out: An Autobiography 2001 Caernarfon Gwasg Dwyfor
George, W. R. P., et al., David Lloyd George–The Llanystumdwy Lectures 1990-1996 1997 Caernarfon Gwynedd Council
Gilbert, B. B. Lloyd George And The Historians *Albion* 11, 1, Spring 1979 p74-86
- Pacifist To Interventionist: David Lloyd George In 1911 And 1914. Was Belgium An Issue? *Historical Journal* 28, 4 December 1985 p863-885
- David Lloyd George: A Political Life / Vol.1 The Architect Of Change 1863-1912 1987 London B. T. Batsford / Vol. 2 Organizer Of Victory 1912-16 1992 London B. T. Batsford
- David Lloyd George And The Great Marconi Scandal *Historical Research* 62, 149 October 1989 p295-317
Gilbert, M., Ed. Lloyd George 1968 Englewood Cliffs, N. J. Prentice-Hall [Great Lives Observed]
Gollin, A. M. A Tearful Scene: Lloyd George On The Ladder In March 1915 Historical Reflections / Réflexions Historiques 5, 2 Winter/Hiver 1978 p161-176
Greenhaigh, E. David Lloyd George, Georges Clemenceau, And The 1918 Manpower Crisis *Historical Journal* 50, 2 June 2007 p397-421
Gresham, C. A. Highgate And The Lloyds Of Llanystumdwy *Transactions of the Caernarfonshire Historical Society* 51, 1990 p135-151
Grieves, K. Improvising The British War Effort: Eric Geddes And Lloyd George, 1915-18 *War & Society* 7, 2 1989 p40-55
- Sir Eric Geddes, Lloyd George And The Transport Problem, 1918-21 *Journal of Transport History* 13, 1 1992 p23-42.
Grigg, J. The Young Lloyd George 1973 London Eyre Methuen / Lloyd George: The People's Champion 1902-1911 1978 London Eyre Methuen / Lloyd George: From Peace To War 1912-1916 1985 London Eyre Methuen / Lloyd George: War Leader 1916-1918 2002 London Allen Lane
- Lloyd George And Wales 1988 Aberystwyth National Library of Wales
- Lloyd George: The Last Best Hope Of The British Empire 1999 Caernarfon Gwynedd Council
Hague, F. The Pain And The Privilege: The Women In Lloyd George's Life 2008 London HarperPress
Hall III, H. Lloyd George, Briand And The Failure Of The Anglo-French Entente *Journal of Modern History* 50, 2, On Demand Supplement June 1978 pD1121-D1138
Harrison, H. W. Lloyd George Family History: A Short Account Of The George family Of Tresynwen, Pantecoch And Trecoed, Pembrokeshire, And The Lloyd Family Of Llanystumdwy,

Caernarfonshire, And Their Descendants 1999 St Albans H. W. Harrison
Hattersley, R. David Lloyd George: The Great Outsider 2010 London Little, Brown
Henderson-Livesey, A. H. David Lloyd George: The Liberal Leader 1929 London Social Services Ltd.
Hill, L. B. David Lloyd George As Minister Of Munitions: A Study Of His Speaking Tour Of Industrial Centers *Southern Speech Journal* 36, 4 June 1971 p312-323
Hughes Jones, W. Wales Drops The Pilots 1937 London Foyle's Welsh Co.
Humphreys, E. M. David Lloyd George 1943 Llyfrau'r Dryw, Llandebie, Sir Gaerfyrddin [*Welsh Language*]
Hussey, C. Bron-Y-Dê, Churt, Surrey, The Property Of The RT. Hon. D. Lloyd George *Country Life* VII, 1348, 4 November 1922 p578-584
'Independent Liberal' Lloyd George And The War: A Personal History Of His Part In Armageddon 1917 London Hutchinson
Ivatt, I. Frances Stevenson, Lloyd George And The Surrey–Sussex Dimension *Journal Of Liberal History* 46 Spring 2005 p24-27
- The Financial Affairs Of David Lloyd George 2019 Aberystwyth Welsh Academic Press
- Lloyd George's Presidency Of The Board Of Trade *Journal Of Liberal History* 103 Summer 2019 p22-29
Jackson, J. Losing The Plot: Lloyd George, F. E. Smith And The Trial Of Alice Wheeldon *History Today* 57, 5 May 2007 p42-49
Johnson, M. Lloyd George, The Liberal Crisis, And The Unionist Party During The First World War *Journal of Liberal History* 119 Summer 2023 p18-29
Jones, J. Lloyd George's Favourite Recipes 1996 Ruthin John Jones Publishing [First published as The Criccieth Women's Institute Cookery Book; Including Recipes For The Favourite Dishes Of The Prime Minister (The Right Hon. D. Lloyd George, M.P.), 1919]
Jones, Jack The Man David: An Imaginative Presentation, Based On Fact, Of The Life Of David Lloyd George From 1880 To 1914 1944 London Hamish Hamilton [Novel]
Jones Sr., J. Mr. D. Lloyd George, M.P., As The Apostle Of Welsh Nationalism *Young Wales* 2, 20 1896 p196-199
Jones, J. Graham Framing 'The People's Budget': A New Perspective *Transactions of the Honourable Society of Cymmrodorion* 1991, p285-298
- Lloyd George, Cymru Fydd And The Newport Meeting Of January 1896 *National Library of Wales Journal* 29, 4, Winter 1996 p435-453
- Michael Davitt, David Lloyd George And T. E. Ellis: The Welsh Experience, 1886 *Welsh History Review* 18, 3, June 1997 p450-482
- Lloyd George, Caernarfon Boroughs and Manchester East' *Transactions Of The Caernarfonshire Historical Society* 59, 1998 p117-134
- Lloyd George, W. Llewelyn Williams M.P. And The 1916 Conscription Bill *National Library of Wales Journal* 31, 2 Winter 1999 p173-187
- Lloyd George Papers At The National Library Of Wales And Other Repositories 2001 Aberystwyth

National Library of Wales
- Lloyd George And The Suffragettes *National Library Of Wales Journal* 33, 1, Summer 2003 p1-33
- The Last Months of David Lloyd George, September 1944–March 1945 *Transactions Of The Caernarfonshire Historical Society* 66, 2005 p168-190
- Honiton, Dumfriesshire And The Lloyd George Fund *Journal of Liberal History* 49 Winter 2005-06 p4-11
- The Reminiscences Of Dame Margaret Lloyd George *National Library Of Wales Journal* 34, 1 2006 p101-128
- The Real Lloyd George *Journal of Liberal History* 51 Summer 2006 p4-12
- David Lloyd George And Thomas Edward Ellis *National Library Of Wales Journal* 34, 2 2007 p253-291
- Life With Lloyd George *Journal of Liberal History* 55 Summer 2007 p28-36
- The Lloyd George War Memoirs *Transactions of the Honourable Society of Cymmrodorion* 14, 2008 p127-43 (Reprinted in *Cercles* 21 2011 p95-111)
- David And Maggie *Journal of Liberal History* 63 Summer 2009 p18-31
- The Golden Wedding Of Lloyd George And Dame Margaret *Transactions of the Caernarvonshire Historical Society* 71 2010 p132-148
- David Lloyd George And Welsh Liberalism 2010 Aberystwyth National Library of Wales
- Lloyd George At Eighty *Transactions of the Honourable Society of Cymmrodorion* 16, 2010 p61-81
- Lloyd George At Paris, 1938 *Transactions of the Honourable Society of Cymmrodorion* 17, 2011 p86-96
- David And Frances *Journal of Liberal History* 74 Spring 2012 p30-39
- The 'Land And The Nation' And Wales *Journal of Liberal History* 81 Winter 2013-14 p26-36
- Lloyd George And The Carnarvon Boroughs, 1890-95 *Journal of Liberal History* 82 Spring 2014 p26-37
- David Lloyd George And The Second World War *Transactions of the Honourable Society of Cymmrodorion* 26, 2020 p74-94
Jones, M. A Radical Life: Biography Of Megan Lloyd George, 1902-66 1991 London Hutchinson
Jones, T. Lloyd George 1951 London Oxford University Press
- 'Lloyd George, David' Dictionary of National Biography, 1941-1950 1959 London Oxford UP p515-529
Kashine, T. Lloyd George And The Social Reform Before The First World War *Keio Economic Studies* 14, 1, 1977 p67-81
Kernek, S. J. Distractions Of Peace During War: The Lloyd George Government's Reactions To Woodrow Wilson, December, 1916-November, 1918 *Transactions of the American Philosophical Society* 65, 2 1975 p1-117
Kiernan, R. H. Lloyd George 1940 London George G. Harrap
Kinnear, M. The Fall Of Lloyd George: The Political Crisis Of 1922 1973 London Macmillan
Koss, S. E. Lloyd George And Nonconformity: The Last Rally *English Historical Review* 89 January 1974 p77-108

Lentin, A. Lloyd George And The Lost Peace: From Versailles To Hitler 1919-1940 2001 Basingstoke Palgrave (*Previously published as* Guilt At Versailles: Lloyd George And The Pre-History Of Appeasement 1985 London Methuen)
Lexden, A. Lloyd George And An Anglo-Irish Centenary *Journal of Liberal History* 107 Summer 2020 p23-25
- Lloyd George And The Versailles Treaty *Journal of Liberal History* 113 Winter 2021-22 p18-23
- A Prime Minister Of The Left In Coalition With The Right: Lloyd George And The Unionists, 1918-22 *Journal of Liberal History* 119 Summer 2023 p30-37
- Lloyd George And The 1922 Committee *Journal of Liberal History* 119 Summer 2023 p62-64
Lloyd George, D. The Issues Of The Budget *The Nation* 6, 5 30 October 1909 p180-182
- Better Times: Speeches By The Right Hon. D. Lloyd George, M.P., Chancellor Of The Exchequer 1910 London Hodder & Stoughton
- Lloyd George's Supper Party, By The Member For Britain 1912 London Simpkin, Marshall
- Through Terror To Triumph: Speeches And Pronouncements Of The Right Hon. David Lloyd George, M.P., Since The Beginning Of The War 1915 London Hodder & Stoughton
- Why The Allies Will Win: An Interview By the Editor of *Secolo* of Milan 1916 London Daily Chronicle
- Wit And Wisdom Of Lloyd George 1917 London Ed. D. Rider Grant Richards
- The Great Crusade: Extracts From Speeches Delivered During The War 1918 New York George H. Doran
- Some Considerations For The Peace Conference Before They Finally Draft Their Terms [Cmd.1614] "Fontainebleau Memorandum" 25 March 1919
- Is It Peace? 1923 London Hodder and Stoughton
- Zionism And Anti-Semitism 1923 New York American Jewish Congress
- The Statesman's Task *The Nation and Athenæum* XXXV, 2 12 April 1924 p39-40
- Liberalism And Liberty 1924 London Liberal Publication Department
- Coal And Power 1924 London Hodder and Stoughton
- Slings And Arrows: Sayings Chosen From The Speeches Of The Rt. Hon. David Lloyd George 1929 London Ed. Guedalla, P. Cassell & Company
- The Truth About Reparations And War-Debts 1932 London William Heinemann
- War Memoirs 1933-1936 6 Vols London Ivor Nicholson & Watson, 1938 2 Vols London Odhams Press
- Organizing Prosperity: A Scheme Of National Reconstruction 1935 London Ivor Nicholson & Watson
- The Truth About The Peace Treaties 1938 2 Vols London Victor Gollancz
Lloyd George, D., Rees, W. J., and Llewelyn Williams, W. Prominent Welshmen On The Resources Of Western Canada [Report Of Visit To Canada In 1899] 1900 Swansea Daily Post Printing Works
Lloyd George, F. The Years That Are Past 1967 London Hutchinson
Lloyd George, O. A Tale Of Two Grandfathers 1999 London Bellew
Lloyd George, Richard Dame Margaret–The Life Story Of His Mother 1947 London George Allen

& Unwin Ltd.
- Lloyd George 1960 London Frederick Muller
Lloyd George, Robert David And Winston: How A Friendship Changed History 2005 London John Murray
Loades, J., Ed. The Life And Times of David Lloyd George 1991 Bangor Headstart History
Locker, W. A. Lloyd George By Mr. Punch 1922 London Cassell & Company
Longford, R. Frances, Countess Lloyd George: More Than A Mistress 1996 Leominster Gracewing
Low, D. Lloyd George And Co. 1921 London G. Allen & Unwin
Ludwig, E. Leaders Of Europe 1934 London Ivor Nicholson and Watson ['Lloyd George: The British Odysseus', p.213-256]
Lynch, M. Lloyd George And The Liberal Dilemma 1993 London Hodder & Stoughton
Lytton, N. Some Episodes In The Life Of David Lloyd George *Blackwood's Magazine* 258, 1557 July 1945 p69-72
MacArthur-Seal, D-J. Intelligence And Lloyd George's Secret Diplomacy In The Near East, 1920-1922 *Historical Journal* 56, 3 September 2013 p707-728
Machin, I. David Lloyd George: Nonconformity And Radicalism, c.1890-1906 *Journal of Liberal History* 77 Winter 2012-13 p12-17, 74
Mallet, C. Mr Lloyd George: A Study 1930 London Ernest Benn
Masterman, L. Recollections Of David Lloyd George *History Today* Vol. 9 Issues 3 & 4 March & April 1959 p160-169 & 274-281
McCearney, J. David Lloyd George (1863-1945) 2019 Paris P-G de Roux [*French Language*]
McCormick, D. The Mask Of Merlin: A Critical Biography Of David Lloyd George 1963 London MacDonald
McEwen, J. M. The Struggle For Mastery In Britain: Lloyd George Versus Asquith, December 1916 *Journal of British Studies* 18, 1, Autumn 1978 p131-156
- Lloyd George's Liberal Supporters In December 1916: A Note *Bulletin of the Institute of Historical Research* 53, 128, November 1980 pp265-272
- Northcliffe And Lloyd George at War, 1914-1918 *Historical Journal*, 24, 3, September 1981, p651-672
- Lloyd George And The Acquisition Of The *Daily Chronicle* In 1918 *Journal of British Studies* 22, 1, Autumn 1982 p127-144
McGill, B. Lloyd George's Timing Of The 1918 Election *Journal of British Studies* 14, 1, November 1974 pp109-124
Millman, B. The Lloyd George War Government, 1917-18 *Totalitarian Movements and Political Religions* 3, 3 Winter 2002 p99-127
Mills, J. S. David Lloyd George: War Minister 1924 London Cassell
Morgan, K. O. David Lloyd George: Welsh Radical As World Statesman 1963 Cardiff University of Wales Press
- Twilight Of Welsh Liberalism: Lloyd George And The 'Wee Frees', 1918-35 *Bulletin of the Board of Celtic Studies*, XXII May 1968, p389-391

- Lloyd George's Premiership: A Study In 'Prime Ministerial Government' *Historical Journal*, 13, 1, March 1970 p130-157
- Lloyd George And The Historians *Transactions of the Honourable Society of Cymmrodorion* Pt.1 1971 p65-85
- The Age Of Lloyd George: The Liberal Party And British Politics, 1890-1929 1971, 2nd Ed. 1978 London Allen & Unwin
- Ed. Lloyd George: Family Letters, 1885-1936 1973 London Oxford University Press
- Lloyd George 1974 London Weidenfeld and Nicolson [British Prime Ministers Series]
- Consensus And Disunity: The Lloyd George Coalition Government, 1918-22 1979 London Clarendon Press
- David Lloyd George, 1863-1945 1981 Cardiff University of Wales Press
- 'Lloyd George And The Irish', in *Ireland after the Union*, 1989, Ed. Blake, R., Oxford, Oxford University Press, p83-103
- Lloyd George And Germany *Historical Journal*, 39, 3, September 1996 p755-766
- Lloyd George, Keir Hardie And The Importance Of The 'Pro-Boers' *South African Historical Journal*, 41, 1, November 1999 p290-311
- 'Rare And Refreshing Fruit': Lloyd George's People's Budget *Public Policy Research*, 16, 1, March-May 2009 p28-33
- Lloyd George And Leadership: The Influences Of Gladstone And Abraham Lincoln *Journal of Liberal History* 77 Winter 2012-13 p6-11, 74
- David Lloyd George, 1863-2013 2013 Cardiff University Press
- 7 December 1916: Asquith, Lloyd George And The Crisis Of Liberalism, The History of Parliament Annual Lecture, 2016, *Parliamentary History* 36, 3, 2017 p361-371
- Lloyd George's French Connection *Journal of Liberal History* 117 Winter 2022-23 p34-40
- Lloyd George And The Hard-Faced Men, 1918-22 *Journal of Liberal History* 119 Summer 2023 p4-17, 29
- David Lloyd George And America *Welsh History Review* 32, 4 December 2025 pp673-682

Mowat, C. L. Lloyd George 1964 London Oxford University Press [Clarendon Biographies]

Mumford, A. David Lloyd George: A Biography In Cartoons 2014 Leicester Matador
- Churchill And Lloyd George: Liberal Authors On The First World War? *Journal of Liberal History* 94 Spring 2017 p20-31

Murray, B. L.G. 1932 London Sampson Low, Marston

Murray, B. K. The People's Budget, 1909-1910: Lloyd George And Liberal Politics 1980 London Oxford University Press
- "Battered and Shattered": Lloyd George And The 1914 Budget Fiasco *Albion* 23, 3, Autumn 1991 p483-507
- The 'People's Budget' A Century On *Journal of Liberal History* 64, Autumn 2009 p4-13

Neuberger, J. Lloyd George's Disestablishment Legacy: Reaching For Egalitarianism 2000 Caernarfon Gwynedd Council

Nevinson, H. W. Lloyd George: The Leader Of British Liberals *Foreign Affairs* 9, 3, April 1931 p457-468

'Northumbrian' Mr Lloyd George's Future: The Liberal Party's Great Peril; Reconciliation And Resurrection [1919] London Wm. Cate

Nowak, A. The Forgotten Appeasement Of 1920: Lloyd George, Lenin And Poland 2023 London Routledge

O'Brien, R. R. Mrs Lloyd George Goes To Lampeter 17th June 1919 2019 Lampeter Lampeter Museum

- The Campaigns Of Margaret Lloyd George: The Wife Of The Prime Minister 1916-1922 2022 Talybont Y Lolfa

O'Leary, P. Lloyd George, Empire And The Making of Modern Ireland, Welsh Political Archive Annual Lecture, Neuadd Senedd Cymru, Cardiff Bay, 2 November 2021

Owen, F. Tempestuous Journey: Lloyd George, His Life And Times 1954 London Hutchinson

Packer, I. Lloyd George 1998 Basingstoke Palgrave Macmillan

- Lloyd George, Liberalism And The Land: The Land Issue And Party Politics In England, 1906-1914 2001 London Royal Historical Society/Boydell Press

- Lloyd George And Land Reform: The Welsh Context *Transactions of the Honourable Society of Cymmrodorion* 15, 2009 p127-145

Parry, A. Thirty Thousand Yesterdays 1977 Staines Temple Press

Parry, B., Price, E., and Price, G. David Lloyd George 1981 [Caernarfon] Gwynedd Archives Service

Parry, C. David Lloyd George 1984 Denbigh Gwasg Gee [*Welsh Language*]

Price, E. The Pre-Parliamentary Political Career Of Lloyd George 1974 University of Wales [Unpublished MA Thesis]

- Lloyd George And Merioneth Politics, 1885, 1886–A Failure To Effect A Breakthrough *Journal of the Merioneth Historical and Record Society* VII, 3, 1975 p292-307

- Lloyd George And The By-Election In The Caernarfon Boroughs 1890 *Transactions of the Caernarfonshire Historical Society* 36, 1975 p140-142

- Lloyd George A 'Rhyfel Y Degwm' Yn Llyn Ac Eifionydd, 1886-8 *Transactions of the Caernarfonshire Historical Society* 39, 1978 p150-169 [*Welsh Language*]

- Prentisiaeth Wleidyddol Lloyd George A Pwllheli 1979 Pwllheli Glwb y Bont [*Welsh Language*]

- Megan Lloyd George 1983 Caernarfon Gwynedd Archives Service

- Y Port A Lloyd George 1878-1890: Prentisiaeth Y Dewin 1995 Porthmadog Cyngor Sir Gwynedd [*Welsh Language*]

- Lloyd George Y Cenedlaetholwr Cymreig: Arwr Ynteu Bradwr? 1999 Llandysul Gwasg Gomer [*Welsh Language*]

- Lloyd George A'r Eisteddfod Genedlaethol A Phrifwyliau Bangor A Chaernarfon 2005 Caernarfon Gwasg y Bwthyn [*Welsh Language*]

- David Lloyd George 2006 Cardiff University of Wales Press

Pride, E. Why Lloyd George Met Hitler 1981 Newport, Gwent Starling Press

Pugh, M. Lloyd George 1988 London Longman
- Lloyd George's Coalition Proposal Of 1910 And Pre-War Liberalism *Journal of Liberal History* 77 Winter 2012-13 p18-23, 74
Purcell, H. Lloyd George 2006 Oxford Oxford University Press
Rageot, G. Lloyd George: Conférence Donnée à l'Institut Thiers, Le 18 Octobre 1918 1919 Paris Bloud et Gay [*French Language*}
Raine, G. E. The Real Lloyd George 1913 London George Allen
- Lloyd George And The Land: An Exposure And An Appeal 1914 London Allen
Rast, M. C. The Ulster Unionists "On Velvet": Home Rule And Partition In The Lloyd George Proposals, 1916 *American Journal of Irish Studies* 14 2017 p113-138
Raymond, E. T. [E. R. Thompson] Mr Lloyd George 1922 London Collins
Ridgwell, S. The 'Mangold's Champion': Lloyd George, The Game Laws And The Campaign For Rural Land Reform In Edwardian England *Journal of Liberal History* 105 Winter 2019-20 p18-29
Rintala, M. Renamed Roses: Lloyd George, Churchill, And The House Of Lords *Biography* 8, 3, Summer 1985 p248-264
- Made In Birmingham: Lloyd George, Chamberlain, And The Boer War *Biography* 11, 2 Spring 1988 p124-139
- Lloyd George and Churchill: How Friendship Changed Politics 1990 Lanham, MD Madison Books
Rippon, N. The Plot To Kill Lloyd George: The Story Of Alice Wheeldon And The Pear Tree Conspiracy 2009 Barnsley Wharncliffe Books
Robertson, J. M. Mr Lloyd George And Liberalism 1923 London Chapman & Dodd
Roch, W. Mr Lloyd George And The War 1920 London Chatto & Windus
Rohmann, H. Intonation Und Lautgebung In Der Sprache Von Lloyd George 1939 Berlin Walter de Gruyter [*German Language*]
Rothe, A. Lloyd George Of Dwyfor, David Lloyd George, 1st Earl *Current Biography* 5 1944 p419-423
Rowland, P. Lloyd George 1975 London Barrie & Jenkins
- Lloyd George's Tada 2014 London and Cardiff Publish Nation
Rudman, S. Lloyd George And The Appeasement Of Germany, 1919-1945 2011 Newcastle upon Tyne Cambridge Scholars
Savage, D. W. "The Parnell Of Wales Has Become The Chamberlain Of England" Lloyd George And The Irish Question *Journal of British Studies* 12, 1, November 1972 p86-108
Scally, R. J. The Origins Of The Lloyd George Coalition: The Politics Of Social-Imperialism, 1900-1918 1975 London Princeton University Press
Sharp, A. David Lloyd George 2009 London Haus
- 'If I Had To Go To Paris Again…': David Lloyd George And The Revision Of The Treaty Of Versailles' *Journal of Liberal History* 77 Winter 2012-13 p30-37
Smith, R. W. David Lloyd George's Limehouse Address *Central States Speech Journal* 18, 3 August 1967 p169-176
Snow, C. P. Lloyd George: Britain's Great Radical *Atlantic* 219 February 1967 p68-79

Snowden, P. Mr Lloyd George's New Deal 1935 London Ivor Nicholson & Watson
Spender, H. The Prime Minister 1920 London Hodder & Stoughton
Spender, S. The Character Of Lloyd George *Twentieth Century* 150 1951 p511-20
Stevenson, F. Lloyd George: A Diary 1971 Ed. Taylor, A. J. P. London Harper & Row
Storey, H. The Case Against The Lloyd George Coalition 1920 London George Allen & Unwin
Suttie, A. Rewriting the First World War: Lloyd George, Politics & Strategy, 1914-1918 2005 Basingstoke Palgrave Macmillan
Sylvester, A. J. The Real Lloyd George 1947 London Cassell
- Life With Lloyd George: The Diary of A. J. Sylvester 1975 London Ed. C. Cross Macmillan
Taylor, A. J. P. Lloyd George: Rise And Fall 1961 London Cambridge University Press
- Ed. Lloyd George: Twelve Essays 1971 London Hamish Hamilton
- My Darling Pussy: The Letters Of Lloyd George And Frances Stevenson 1913-41 1975 London Weidenfeld & Nicolson
Terraine, J. Lloyd George's Dilemma *History Today* 11, 5, May 1961 p350-359
- Lloyd George's Expedients *History Today* 13, 4 & 5, April & May 1963 p219-229, 321-330
Thomson, M. David Lloyd George: The Official Biography 1948 London Hutchinson
Toye, R. Lloyd George And Churchill: Rivals For Greatness 2007 London Macmillan
- Lloyd George's War Rhetoric, 1914-1918 *Journal of Liberal History* 77 Winter 2012-13 p24-29
Turner, J. Lloyd George's Secretariat 1980 Cambridge Cambridge University Press
Walters, E. W. The 'New' Lloyd George And The 'Old' 1916 London Joseph Johnson
Ward, A. J. Lloyd George And The 1918 Irish Conscription Crisis *Historical Journal* 17, 1 March 1974 p107-129
West, G. Lloyd George's Last Fight 1930 London Alston Rivers
Wilkinson, R. Lloyd George: Statesman Or Scoundrel 2018 London IB Tauris
Williams, C. J. Gladstone, Lloyd George And The Gladstone Rock, *Caernarvonshire Historical Society Transactions*, 60, 1999 p55-75
Williams, E. Amgueddfa Lloyd George Museum [1993] [Caernarfon] Gwynedd Culture & Leisure
Williamson, D. Lloyd George: A Man Of The People 1917 New York George H. Doran
Wilson, H. A Prime Minister On Prime Ministers 1977 London Michael Joseph / Weidenfeld and Nicolson [Chapter 6, 'David Lloyd George', p137-163]
Wilson, P. W. Lloyd George Resurgent *Current History (1916-1940)*, 42, 1, April 1935 p25-30
Winnett, R. David Lloyd George: The Religious Factor *Epworth Review* 14 September 1987 p83-91
Woodward, D. R. David Lloyd George, A Negotiated Peace With Germany, And The Kühlmann Peace Kite Of September 1917 *Canadian Journal Of History* 6, 1, March 1971 p75-93
- The Origins And Intent Of David Lloyd George's January 5 War Aims Speech *The Historian* 34, 1 November 1971 p22-39
- Lloyd George And The Generals 1983 Newark University of Delaware Press
- Did Lloyd George Starve The British Army Of Men Prior To The German Offensive of 21 March 1918? *Historical Journal* 27, 1, 1984 p241-52

Wrigley, C. J. David Lloyd George And The British Labour Movement: Peace And War 1976 Hassocks Harvester Press
- Lloyd George And The Challenge Of Labour: The Post-War Coalition, 1918-1922 1990 Hemel Hempstead Harvester Wheatsheaf
- Lloyd George 1992 Oxford Basil Blackwell
- Lloyd George And Gladstone *The Historian* 85, Spring 2005 p8-17
- The Beaverbrook Library, A. J. P. Taylor And The Rise Of Lloyd George Studies *Journal of Liberal History* 77 Winter 2012-13 p64-68
- The Nonconformist Mind Of David Lloyd George *Journal of Liberal History* 96 Autumn 2017 p18-24
- The Lloyd George Coalition Governments: Labour And Industrial Relations *Journal of Liberal History* 119 Summer 2023 p52-61

**Other Works**

Addison, C. The Betrayal Of The Slums 1922 London Herbert Jenkins
- Politics From Within, 1911-1918 1924 London 2 Vols. Herbert Jenkins
- Four And A Half Years: A Personal Diary From June 1914 To January 1919 1934 London Hutchinson
Adelman, P. The Decline Of The Liberal Party, 1910-1931 2014 2nd Ed. Abingdon Routledge
Afflerbach, H. On A Knife Edge: How Germany Lost The First World War 2022 Cambridge Cambridge University Press
Anon. The Tithe War 1978 Hawarden Clwyd Record Office
Asquith, C. The Diaries Of Cynthia Asquith 1915-1918 1968 London Hutchinson
Asquith, H. H. Memories And Reflections 1928 London 2 Vols. Cassell & Co.
Asquith, M. Margot Asquith's Great War Diary 1914-1916: The View from Downing Street 2014 Eds. Oxford E. and M. Brock OUP
Bennett, G. H. The 1922 General Election Reconsidered: High Politics And The Birth Of The Modern British Election 2025 London University Of London Press
Bentley, M. The Liberal Mind 1914-1919 1977 Cambridge Cambridge University Press
Best, G. Churchill: A Study In Greatness 2001 London Hambledon & London
Bethmann-Hollweg, T. von Seven War Speeches By The German Chancellor 1914-1916 1916 Zurich Orell Füssli
Bilkainkin, G. Maisky: Ten Years Ambassador 1944 London George Allen & Unwin
Blake, R. The Unknown Prime Minister: The Life And Times Of Andrew Bonar Law 1858-1923 1955 London Eyre & Spottiswoode
Blewett, N. The Peers, The Politics And The People: The General Elections of 1910 1972 London Macmillan
Bogdanor, V. The Strange Survival Of Liberal Britain: Politics And Power Before the First World War 2022 London Biteback

Bonham Carter, M., and Pottle, M., Eds. Lantern Slides: The Diaries And Letters Of Violet Bonham Carter 1904-1914 1996 London Weidenfeld and Nicolson
Bouverie, T. Appeasing Hitler: Chamberlain, Churchill And The Road To War 2019 London Bodley Head
Butler, J. R. M. Lord Lothian (Philip Kerr) 1882-1940 1960 London Macmillan
Campbell, J. F. E. Smith, First Earl Of Birkenhead 1983 London Jonathan Cape
Campbell, J.. with McLauchlan, R. Haldane: The Forgotten Statesman Who Shaped Modern Britain 2020 London C. Hurst
Cassar, G. H. Kitchener: Architect Of Victory 1977 London William Kimber
- Asquith As War Leader 1994 London Hambledon Continuum
Churchill, W. S. The World Crisis 1923-1931 5 Vols London Thornton Butterworth
Clark, C. The Sleepwalkers: How Europe Went To War In 1914 2012 London Allen Lane
Close, D. Conservatives And Coalition After The First World War *Journal Of Modern History* 45, 2, June 1973 p240-260
Coates, W. P. and Z. K. A History Of Anglo-Soviet Relations 1944 London Lawrence & Wishart [Foreword by David Lloyd George]
Colley, M. S. Gareth Jones: A Manchukuo Incident 2001 Newark Nigel L. Colley
- More Than A Grain Of Truth: The Official Biography Of Gareth Jones 2005. 2020 2nd Edition London Ed. N.L. Colley Lume Books
Coogan, T. P. De Valera: Long Fellow, Long Shadow 1993 London Hutchinson
Cook, A. Cash For Honours: The Story Of Maundy Gregory 2008 Stroud History Press
Coombe Tennant, W. Between Two Worlds: The Diary Of Winifred Coombe Tennant 1909-1924 2011 Aberystwyth Ed. P. Lord National Library of Wales
Cosens, M. Lloyd George's Munition Girls 1916 London Hutchinson
Cotton, O. Churt Remembered 2002, Revised 2021 Churt O.M. Cotton
Cregier, D. Chiefs Without Indians: Asquith, Lloyd George And The Liberal Remnant, 1916-1935 1982 Washington, DC University Press of America
Crosby, T. L. Joseph Chamberlain: A Most Radical Imperialist 2011 London I.B. Tauris
Cross, C. The Liberals In Power (1905-1914) 1963 London Barrie & Rockliff
Cullen, T. Maundy Gregory: Purveyor Of Honours 1974 London Bodley Head
Dangerfield, G. The Strange Death Of Liberal England 1936 London Constable
David, E., Ed. Inside Asquith's Cabinet: From The Diaries Of Charles Hobhouse 1977 London John Murray
Davies, Sir J. The Prime Minister's Secretariat 1916-1920 1951 Newport, Mon. R. H. Johns
Davies, J. A History Of Wales 1993 London Allen Lane. 2007 Rev. Ed. London Penguin
De Courcy, A. Margot At War: Love And Betrayal In Downing Street 1912-16 2014 London Weidenfeld & Nicolson
DeGroot, G. J. Blighty: British Society In The Era Of The Great War 1996 London Longmans
Di Scala, S. M. Vittorio Orlando 2010 London Haus

Dockrill, M., and Fisher, J., Eds. The Paris Peace Conference, 1919: Peace Without Victory? 2001 London Palgrave
Donaldson, F. The Marconi Scandal 1962 London Rupert Hart-Davis.
Downing, T., Ed. The Troubles 1980 London Thames / Futura
Ebenezer, L. Fron-Goch Camp 1916–And the Birth of the IRA 2012 Rev. Ed. Llanrwst Gwasg Carreg Gwalch
Ellis, T. E. Speeches And Addresses By The Late Thomas E. Ellis, M.P. 1912 Wrexham Hughes and Son
Emmerson, C. Crucible: The Long End Of The Great War And The Birth Of A New World, 1917-1924 2019 London Bodley Head
Evans, D. Bywyd Bob Owen 1977 Nant Peris, Caernarfon Gwasg Gwynedd [*Welsh Language*]
Fair, J. D. Politicians, Historians, And The War: A Reassessment Of The Political Crisis Of December 1916 *Journal of Modern History* 49, 3, On Demand Supplement September 1977 pD1329-D1343
Farr, M. Reginald McKenna 1863-1916: Financier Among Statesmen 2007 London Routledge
Farwell, B. The Great Boer War 1976 New York Harper & Row, 1977 London Allen Lane
Fest, W. B. British War Aims And German Peace Feelers During The First World War (December 1916-November 1918) *Historical Journal* 15, 2, June 1972 pp285-308
Fink, C. The Genoa Conference: European Diplomacy 1921-1922 1984. 1994 2nd Edition New York Syracuse University Press
Finnan, J. P. John Redmond And Irish Unity, 1912-1918 2004 New York Syracuse University Press
FitzGibbon, C. Out Of The Lion's Paw: Ireland Wins Her Freedom 1969 London Macdonald
Fraser, P. British War Policy And The Crisis Of Liberalism In May 1915 *Journal of Modern History* 54, 1, March 1982, p1-26
Fry, P. S. Chequers: The Country Home Of Britain's Prime Ministers 1977 London HMSO
Gamache, R. Gareth Jones: Eyewitness To The *Holodomor* 2013. 2018 2nd Edition Cardiff Welsh Academic Press
- Gareth Jones: On Assignment In Nazi Germany 1933-34 2021 Cardiff Welsh Academic Press
Gardner, B. The Big Push: A Portrait Of The Battle Of The Somme 1961 London Cassell
Geddes, Baron The Forging Of A Family 1952 London Faber and Faber
Gerwarth, R. The Vanquished: Why the First World War Failed To End, 1917-1923 2016 London Allen Lane
Gibbon, J. M. Weighed In The Balance: The Case For Welsh Disestablishment 1910 London National Council of Evangelical Free Churches [Foreword by David Lloyd George]
Gilbert, M. Churchill: A Life 1991 London William Heinemann
- First World War 1994 London Weidenfeld and Nicolson
Gleasure, J. and E. Criccieth: A Heritage Walk 2012 3rd Ed. Porthmadog Eifionydd History Society
Goldstein, E. Winning The Peace: British Diplomatic Strategy, Peace Planning, And The Paris Peace Conference, 1916-1920 1991 Oxford Clarendon Press
Gollin, A. M. Proconsul In Politics: A Study Of Lord Milner In Opposition And In Power 1964

London Anthony Blond
Goodman, D. No Thanks To Lloyd George: How the Pension Was Won–The Forgotten Story 1998 2nd Ed. London Third Age Press
Grayson, R. S. Liberals, International Relations And Appeasement: The Liberal Party, 1919-1939 2001 Abingdon Routledge
Griffiths, R. H. Welsh Soldiers, Civilians And Eisteddfodau in WWI 2015 Llanwrst Gwasg Carreg Gwalch
Guedalla, P. Napoleon And Palestine 1925 London George Allen & Unwin [Afterword by David Lloyd George]
Hamilton, M. A. Arthur Henderson: A Biography 1938 London William Heinemann
Harrison, G. Sir John T Davies And Lloyd George 2020 Cheltenham South Books
- Sir John T Davies: PPS To Lloyd George 2020 Cheltenham South Books
Harmsworth, C. Parliament And Politics In The Age Of Asquith And Lloyd George: The Diaries Of Cecil Harmsworth, MP, 1909-1922 2016 Eds. Thorpe, A., and Toye, R. London Cambridge University Press
Hastings, M. Catastrophe: Europe Goes To War 1914 2013 London William Collins
Hay, J. R. The Origins Of The Liberal Welfare Reforms 1906-1914 1983 London Palgrave
Hazlehurst, C. Asquith As Prime Minister, 1908-1916, *English Historical Review* 85, 336 July 1970 p502-531
- Politicians At War, July 1914 To May 1915: Prologue To The Triumph Of Lloyd George 1971 London Jonathan Cape
Henig, R. The Peace That Never Was: A History Of The League Of Nations 2019 London Haus
Hyde, H. Montgomery Lord Reading: The Life Of Rufus Isaacs, First Marquess of Reading 1967 London Heinemann
- Strong For Service: The Life Of Lord Nathan Of Churt 1968 London W. H. Allen
Jackson, J. H. Clemenceau And The Third Republic 1946 London Hodder & Stoughton
Jenkins, R. Mr Balfour's Poodle: An Account Of The Struggle Between The House Of Lords And The Government Of Mr. Asquith 1954 London William Heinemann
- Asquith 1964, 1986 3rd Ed. London HarperCollins
John, S. Welsh At War: From Mons To Loos And The Gallipoli Tragedy / The Grinding War: The Somme And Arras / Through Mud To Victory: Third Ypres And The 1918 Offensives 2017-2018 3 Vols. Barnsley Pen and Sword Military
Johnson, P. B. Land Fit For Heroes: The Planning Of British Reconstruction, 1916-1919 1968 Chicago Chicago University Press
Jones, H. For King And Country: The British Monarchy And The First World War 2021 Cambridge Cambridge University Press
Jones, J. Graham Gareth Vaughan Jones (1905-35) *National Library Of Wales Journal* XXVI, 4, 1990, pp457-463; A Further Note *National Library Of Wales Journal* XXVII, 4, 1992, p453-465
Jones, T., and Middlemas, K. (Ed.) Whitehall Diary–Volume I: 1916-1925, 1969; Volume II: 1926-

1930, 1969; Volume III: Ireland 1918-1925, 1971 London Oxford University Press
Jones, W. Thomas Edward Ellis 1859-1899 1986 Cardiff University of Wales
Judd, D. Lord Reading: Rufus Isaacs, First Marquess Of Reading, Lord Chief Justice And Viceroy Of India, 1860-1935 1982 London Weidenfeld & Nicolson
Keegan, J. The First World War 1998 London Hutchinson
Kerry, S. Lansdowne: The Last Great Whig 2017 London Unicorn
Kershaw, I. Hitler 1889-1936: Hubris; Hitler 1936-1945: Nemesis 1998-2000 London Allen Lane
Keynes, J. M. The Economic Consequences Of The Peace 1919 London Macmillan
- Mr. Lloyd George's General Election 1920 London Liberal Publication Department
- Essays In Biography 1933 London Macmillan
Keynes, J. M., and Henderson, H. D. Can Lloyd George Do It? An Examination Of The Liberal Pledge 1929 London The Nation and Athenaeum
King, C. T. The Asquith Parliament (1906-1909): A Popular History Of Its Men And Its Measures 1910 London Hutchinson
Koss, S. E. Asquith 1976 London Viking
Kruger, R. Good-bye Dolly Gray: The Story Of The Boer War 1959 London Cassell
Laker, R. Geneva In Motion: Winifred Coombe Tennant's Experiences At The Third Assembly Of The League Of Nations 2020 Unpublished MA Thesis Swansea University
Lansing, R. The Big Four And Others Of The Peace Conference 1921 New York Houghton Mifflin
- The Peace Negotiations: A Personal Narrative 1921 New York Houghton Mifflin
Liddell Hart, B. H. History Of The First World War 1934. 1970 London Cassell
Lindsay, J. The Great Strike: A History Of The Penrhyn Quarry Dispute Of 1900-1903 1987 Newton Abbot David & Charles
Lippiatt, G. The Liberal Party And The Fall Of The Chamberlain Government *Liberal Democrat History Group Newsletter* 13 December 1996 p2-4
Lord, P. Winifred Coombe Tennant: A Life Through Art 2007 Aberystwyth National Library Of Wales
MacGregor Dawson, R. The Cabinet Minister And Administration: Asquith, Lloyd George, Curzon *Political Science Quarterly* 55, 3 September 1940 p348-377
MacMillan, G. Honours For Sale: The Strange Story Of Maundy Gregory 1954 London Richards Press
MacMillan, M. Peacemakers: The Paris Peace Conference Of 1919 And Its Attempt To End War 2002 London John Murray
- The War That Ended Peace: The Road To 1914 2013 London Profile Books
Magnus, P. Kitchener: Portrait Of An Imperialist 1958 London John Murray
Maisky, I. The Complete Maisky Diaries 2017 3 Vols. London Ed. G. Gorodetsky, Trans. T. Sorokina and O. Ready Yale University Press
Mantoux, P. The Deliberations Of The Council Of Four 1992 2 Vols. Ed. and Trans. A.S. Link Oxford Princeton University Press

Marcuzzi, S. Britain And Italy In The Era Of The Great War: Defending And Forging Empires 2020 Cambridge Cambridge University Press
Marquand, D. Ramsay MacDonald 1977 London Jonathan Cape
Masterman, N. The Forerunner: The Dilemmas Of Tom Ellis, 1859-1899 1972 Swansea Christopher Davies
Mills, J. S. The Genoa Conference 1922 London Hutchinson [Preface by D. Lloyd George]
Minney, R. J. Viscount Addison: Leader Of The Lords 1958 London Odhams
Mitchell, A. C. The Unionist Press And The Politics Of The Great War 1999 D.Phil. Thesis University of York
Morgan, J. Vyrnwy Welsh Political And Educational Leaders In The Victorian Era 1908 London James Nisbet
Morgan. K. O. Wales In British Politics, 1868-1922 1963, 1991 4th Ed. Cardiff University of Wales Press
- Rebirth Of A Nation: Wales 1880-1980 1981 Oxford Clarendon Press
- Lloyd George's Flintshire Loyalist: The Political Achievement Of John Herbert Lewis *Journal of Liberal History* 57 Winter 2007-08 p18-30
Morgan, K. O., and Morgan, J. Portrait Of A Progressive: The Political Career Of Christopher, Viscount Addison 1980 Oxford Clarendon Press
Morris, M. Porthmadog: Yesterday's Tide 1991 Caernarfon Gwynedd Archives and Museums Service
Morton, B. Woodrow Wilson 2008 London Haus
Mowat, C. L. Britain Between The Wars 1918-1940 1955, 1956 Revised Ed. London Methuen
Murphy, R. Walter Long, The Unionist Ministers, And The Formation Of Lloyd George's Government In December 1916 *Historical Journal* 29, 3 1986 p735-745
Newman, V. Suffragism And The Great War 2018 Barnsley Pen & Sword Military
Nicolson, H. King George The Fifth: His Life And Reign 1952 London Constable and Co
Nicolson, J. The Perfect Summer: England 1911, Just Before The Storm 2006 London John Murray
O'Brien, T. H. Milner: Viscount Milner Of St James's And Cape Town 1854-1925 1979 London Constable
O'Connor, T. P. Sir Henry Campbell-Bannerman 1908 London Hodder & Stoughton
O'Mahony, S. Frongoch: University Of Revolution 1987 Killiney, Co. Dublin FDR Teoranta
Orlando, V. E. Memorie (1915-1919) 1960 Milan Ed. R. Mosca Rizzoli
Overy, R. The Birth Of The RAF, 1918: The World's First Air Force 2018 London Allen Lane
Pakenham, T. The Boer War 1979 London Weidenfeld & Nicolson
Pike, E. R. Human Documents Of The Lloyd George Era 1972 London George Allen & Unwin
Popplewell, O. The Prime Minister And His Mistress 2014 Raleigh, NC Lulu Publishing [Asquith]
Pottle, M., Ed. Champion Redoubtable: The Diaries And Letters Of Violet Bonham Carter, 1914-1945 1998 London Weidenfeld & Nicolson
Pottle, M., and Ledingham, J. G. G., Eds. We Hope To Get Word Tomorrow: The Garvin Family Letters, 1914-1916 2009 London Frontline Books

Pretty, D. A. Farmer, Soldier And Politician: The Life Of Brigadier-General Sir Owen Thomas, MP Father of the 'Welsh Army Corps' 2011 Wrexham Bridge Books
Renwick, C. Bread For All: The Origins Of The Welfare State 2017 London Allen Lane
Reynolds, D. The Long Shadow: The Great War And The Twentieth Century 2013 London Simon & Schuster
- Did The Versailles Peace Trigger Another War? *BBC History Magazine*, January 2019, p31-36
Riddell, Lord Lord Riddell's Intimate Diary Of The Peace Conference And After, 1918-1923 1933 London Victor Gollancz
- More Pages From My Diary 1908-1914 1934 London Country Life
- War Diary 1914-1918 1933 London Nicholson & Watson
- The Riddell Diaries, 1908-1923 [Ed. with Introduction by J.M. McEwen; Foreword by J. Grigg] 1986 London Athlone Press [A Revised Selection]
Ridley, J. George V: Never A Dull Moment 2021 London Chatto & Windus
Riley, J. Ghosts Of Old Companions: Lloyd George's Welsh Army, The Kaiser's Reichsheer And The Battle For Mametz Wood, 1914-1916 2019 Warwick Helion
Roberts, A. The Holy Fox: The Life Of Lord Halifax 1991 London Weidenfeld & Nicolson. 2014 London Head of Zeus
- The Chief: The Life Of Lord Northcliffe 2022 London Simon & Schuster UK
Rose, K. King George V 1983 London Weidenfeld & Nicolson
Rowland, P. The Last Liberal Governments: The Promised Land, 1905-1910 1968 London Barrie & Rockliff (The Cresset Press)
- The Last Liberal Governments: Unfinished Business, 1911-1914 1971 London Barrie & Jenkins
Russell, A. K. Liberal Landslide: The General Election Of 1906 1973 Newton Abbot David & Charles
Samuel, Viscount Memoirs 1945 London Cresset Press
Scott, C. P. The Political Diaries Of C. P. Scott 1911-1928 1970 London Ed. Wilson, T. William Collins
Searle, G. R. The Quest For National Efficiency: A Study In British Politics And Political Thought, 1899-1914 1971 Oxford Basil Blackwell
- The Liberal Party: Triumph And Disintegration, 1886-1929 1992 Basingstoke Macmillan
- A. J. Balfour's Secret Coalition Talks Memorandum, 1910 *Historical Research* 66, 160, June 1993 p222-229
Self, R. Neville Chamberlain: A Biography 2006 Aldershot Ashgate
Sforza, Count C. Makers Of Modern Europe: Portraits And Personal Impressions And Recollections 1930 London Elkin Mathews & Marrot [Chapter XV 'Lloyd George', p173-182]
Shakespeare, Sir Geoffrey Let Candles Be Brought In 1949 London Macdonald
Shakespeare, N. Six Minutes In May: How Churchill Unexpectedly Became Prime Minister 2017 London Vintage
Sharp, A. Aspects Of British Policy And The Treaty of Versailles: Of War And Peace 2020 London Ed. B.J.C. McKercher and E. Goldstein Routledge

Shipton, M. Mr Jones–The Man Who Knew Too Much: The Life And Death Of Gareth Jones 2022 Cardiff Welsh Academic Press
Smuts, J. C. Jan Christian Smuts 1952 Cape Town Heinemann & Cassell [South African Edition]
Spender, J. A. The Life Of The Right Hon. Sir Henry Campbell-Bannerman, G.C.B. 1923 London 2 Vols. Hodder & Stoughton
Spender, J. A., and Asquith, C. The Life Of Herbert Henry Asquith, Lord Oxford And Asquith 1932 London 2 Vols. Hutchinson
Spicer, C. Coffee With Hitler: The British Amateurs Who Tried To Civilise The Nazis 2022 London Oneworld
Stanley, L. The Rebel Chief Whip: The Role Of Leslie Wilson In The Fall Of The Lloyd George Coalition, 1922 *Parliamentary History* 38, 2, June 2019 p224-243
Stein, L. The Balfour Declaration 1961 London Vallentine, Mitchell
Stevenson, F. ['One Who Knows Them'] Makers Of The New World 1921 London Cassell
Steyn, R. Milner: Last Of The Empire Builders 2022 London Jonathan Ball
Sutherland, W. 1916-1920: The Lloyd George Coalition In War And Peace 1921 London L. J. Gooding
Tampke, J. A Perfidious Distortion Of History: The Versailles Peace Treaty And The Success Of The Nazis 2017 London Scribe
Taylor, A. J. P. Politics In The First World War 1959 London Oxford University Press
- English History 1914-1945 1965, 1976 Revised Ed. Oxford Oxford University Press
Thompson, J. Lee Northcliffe: Press Baron In Politics, 1865-1922 2000 London John Murray
Walker, J. 'The Blue Beast': Power & Passion In The Great War 2012 Stroud History Press
Wasserstein, B. Herbert Samuel: A Political Life 1992 Oxford Clarendon Press
Waterhouse, M. Edwardian Requiem: A Life Of Sir Edward Grey 2013 London Biteback
Watson, D. R. Georges Clemenceau 2009 London Haus
Watson, F. Dawson Of Penn 1950 London Chatto & Windus
Watt, R. M. The Kings Depart: The Tragedy Of Germany: Versailles And The German Revolution 1968 New York Simon and Schuster
Wilks, J. and E. The British Army In Italy, 1917-18 1998 Barnsley Leo Cooper
Williams, E. W. Liberalism In Wales And The Politics Of Welsh Home Rule 1886-1911 *Bulletin of the Board of Celtic Studies* 37, 1990 p191-207
Wilson, J. C. B.: A Life Of Sir Henry Campbell-Bannerman 1973 London Constable
Wilson, T. The Downfall Of The Liberal Party 1914-1935 1966 London William Collins
Woodward, D. R. Field Marshal Sir William Robertson: Chief Of The Imperial General Staff In The Great War 1998 Westport, Connecticut Praeger
Wynn, S. Churchill's Flawed Decisions: Errors In Office Of The Greatest Briton 2020 Barnsley Pen & Sword Military
Younger, C. Ireland's Civil War 1968 London Frederick Muller
Zelikow, P. The Road Less Traveled: The Secret Battle To End The Great War, 1916-1917 2021 New

York Public Affairs

## Visual Media

'The Life Story Of David Lloyd George' 1918 (2009 DVD) Ideal Film Co. 152 minutes B&W Written by Sidney Low, Directed by Maurice Elvey [Silent Biopic, Starring Norman Page]
'At Home: The Family Home Of David Lloyd George at Brynawelon Criccieth' 1963 BBC TV 34 minutes B&W Introduced by Hywel Davies, Produced by Selwyn Roderick [Family Interviews]

## Internet

https://archives.parliament.uk/collections/getrecord/GB61_LG
http://lloydgeorge.net/
http://wbo.llgc.org.uk/en/s2-LLOY-DAV-1863.html
https://api.parliament.uk/historic-hansard/people/mr-david-lloyd-george/index.html
https://lloydgeorgearchive.co.uk/
https://lloydgeorgesociety.org.uk/en/
https://www.library.wales/fileadmin/fileadmin/docs_gwefan/arddangosfeydd_digidol/david_lloyd_george/llythyron_dllg/William%20George%20Schedule.pdf
https://www.in2013dollars.com/UK-inflation [Used to calculate all 2025 inflation equivalents]

# INDEX

# ABOUT THE AUTHOR

Paul is a graduate of King Alfred's College, Winchester (now University of Winchester). His first book, *God's Candidate*, is a life of Pope John Paul I (Albino Luciani), a much-expanded edition of which is being published in Italy as '*Il Candidato di Dio'*. Living in North Wales for over 30 years, he became inspired to write this present biography of David Lloyd George, the United Kingdom's last Liberal and only Welsh Prime Minister to date.

David Lloyd George was, in his lifetime, a controversial figure, and he remains so today. The present author contends that this is largely due to oft-repeated misunderstandings and misconceptions of the true nature of the man and of his policies.

A century after the end of the Great War (1918), the 'Spanish Flu' Pandemic (1918-1920) that nearly killed Lloyd George–and which strikes such resonance in the era of the COVID-19 Pandemic–, the signing of the Treaty of Versailles (1919) and the end of Lloyd George's premiership (1922), it is a good time to reassess the legacy of this Great Statesman in the life of the United Kingdom, indeed of Europe and the wider World.

Paul Spackman has spent seven years researching the extraordinarily broad, original and far-reaching nature of Lloyd George's early 'labourite' views and of his social reforms, that laid the bedrock of much of the 1945-51 Attlee Labour Government's Welfare State legislation; the crucial importance of Lloyd George taking over the helm of government from the foundering Asquith at the height of the Great War; Lloyd George's approach to the treatment of defeated, devastated Germany at the Versailles negotiations, how his more merciful and tolerant approach, if adopted, might have changed the course of history for the better; his role in Irish affairs between 1916-22, pointing out those actually largely responsible for much of the undoubted tragedy and its long-drawn out aftermath; and showing that the period after his resignation as premier were not, from an 'ideas' point of view, the oft-quoted 'wilderness years', but rather a fertile period of creative, practical plans to solve the immense issues of the 1920s and 1930s, unfortunately neglected by the nation.

What emerges is a vibrant but often disregarded story, here retold as a human tale, not just another purely political biography–Paul's researches, combined with a reappraisal of early works and study of recent investigations by others, now enables a 'truer', more holistic picture of Lloyd George the man to finally emerge.

Printed in Dunstable, United Kingdom

82150762R10413